CW01083903

THE BRITISH YEAR BOOK OF INTERNATIONAL LAW

THE
BRITISH YEAR BOOK OF INTERNATIONAL LAW

2003

SEVENTY-FOURTH YEAR OF ISSUE

OXFORD
AT THE CLARENDON PRESS

This book has been printed digitally and produced in a standard specification in order to ensure its continuing availability

OXFORD
UNIVERSITY PRESS

Great Clarendon Street, Oxford OX2 6DP

Oxford University Press is a department of the University of Oxford.
It furthers the University's objective of excellence in research, scholarship, and education by publishing worldwide in

Oxford New York

Auckland Cape Town Dar es Salaam Hong Kong Karachi
Kuala Lumpur Madrid Melbourne Mexico City Nairobi
New Delhi Shanghai Taipei Toronto

With offices in

Argentina Austria Brazil Chile Czech Republic France Greece
Guatemala Hungary Italy Japan South Korea Poland Portugal
Singapore Switzerland Thailand Turkey Ukraine Vietnam

Oxford is a registered trade mark of Oxford University Press
in the UK and in certain other countries

Published in the United States
by Oxford University Press Inc., New York

Reprinted 2007

ISBN 978-0-19-926785-9

Printed and bound by CPI Antony Rowe, Eastbourne

Editorial Communications should be addressed as follows:

Articles and Notes:

PROFESSOR JAMES CRAWFORD
Lauterpacht Research Centre for International Law,
5 Cranmer Road, Cambridge, CB3 9BL.
JRC1000@hermes.cam.ac.uk

Books for Review:

PROFESSOR J. G. MERRILLS
University of Sheffield Faculty of Law,
Crookesmoor Building, Conduit Road,
Sheffield, S10 1FL.
J. G. Merrills@Sheffield.ac.uk

The British Year Book of International Law is indexed in *Current Law Index*, published by Information Access Company, and in *Legal Journals Index*, published by Legal Information Resources Limited.

CONTENTS

LIST OF ABBREVIATIONS

A&T	Administrative and Technical [Staff]
ACOPS	Advisory Committee on the Protection of the Sea
AFLEG	African Forest Law Enforcement and Governance
ATA	Afghan Transitional Administration
ATCS Act	[UK] Anti-terrorism, Crime and Security Act 2001
BMD MoU	Ballistic Missile Defence Memorandum of Understanding
BOT	British Overseas Territory
BWC	Biological Weapons Convention
CARICOM	Caribbean Common Market
CAT	[UN] Convention against Torture
CCJ	Caribbean Court of Justice
CCJ	Child Concessionary Journey
CEN-SAD	Committee of Sahel and Sahara States
CFE	Conventional Armed Forces in Europe Treaty
CFSP	[EU] Common Foreign and Security Policy
CITES	Convention on International Trade in Endangered Species
COHA	Cessation of Hostilities Agreement
CPA	[Iraq] Coalition Provisional Authority
CRC	[Iraq] Constitutional Preparatory Commission
CTBT	Comprehensive Test Ban Treaty
CW	Chemical Weapons
CWC	Chemical Weapons Convention
DCMS	[UK] Department for Culture, Media and Sport
DEFRA	[UK] Department for Environment, Food and Rural Affairs
DPKO	[UN] Department of Peacekeeping Operations
DPRK	Democratic People's Republic of Korea
DRC	Democratic Republic of Congo
DTI	[UK] Department of Trade and Industry
DU	Depleted Uranium
EC	European Communities
ECE	Economic Commission of Europe
ECGD	[UK] Export Credits Guarantee Department
ECHR	European Convention on Human Rights
ECJ	European Court of Justice
ECOWAS	Economic Organisation of West African States
EEA	European Economic Association
EEZ	Exclusive Economic Zone
EM	Explanatory Memorandum
ESDP	European Security and Defence Policy
ETV	Emergency Towing Vehicle
EU	European Union
EUMC	European Union Military Committee
FAC	[UK] Foreign Affairs Committee

FAM	Free Aceh Movement
FATF	Financial Action Task Force
FCO	[UK] Foreign & Commonwealth Office
FEPOW	Far East Prisoners of War
FGM	Female Genital Mutilation
FTAA	Free Trade Area of the Americas
GA	[UN] General Assembly
GAERC	[EU] General Affairs and External Relations Council
GAM	Free Aceh Movement
GC	[Iraq] Governing Council
GCPP	Global Conflict Prevention Pool
GLA	General Lighthouse Authority
GMOs	Genetically Modified Organisms
GSP	Generalised System of Preferences
HDC	Centre for Humanitarian Dialogue
HIPC	Highly Indebted Poor Countries
HKSAR	Hong Kong Special Administrative Region
HMG	Her Majesty's Government [UK]
HOSG	Heads of State and Governments
IAEA	International Atomic Energy Agency
IAT	Immigration Appeal Tribunal
ICAO	International Civil Aviation Organisation
ICC	International Criminal Court
ICRC	International Committee of the Red Cross
ICTY	International Criminal Tribunal for the Former Yugoslavia
IDA	International Development Assistance
IDF	Israel Defence Force
IGC	Inter-governmental Conference
ILO	International Labour Organisation
IMF	International Monetary Fund
IPU	Inter-Parliamentary Union
ISAF	[Afghanistan] International Security Assistance Force
ISG	Iraq Survey Group
ISI	[Pakistan] Directorate for Inter-Services Intelligence
JCCC	[EU] Joint Customs Consultative Committee
JHA	[EU] Justice and Home Affairs
KFOR	Kosovo Force
LCD	[UK] Lord Chancellor's Department
LURD	Liberians for Reconciliation and Development
MARPOL 73/78	Maritime Pollution Conventions
MEHRA	Marine Environmental High Risk Areas
MEK	[Iran] Mujaheddin-e-Khalq
MINSURO	United Nations Mission for the Referendum on Western Sahara
MLA	Mutual Legal Assistance

MLAC	Mutual Legal Assistance Convention
MMR	Minimum Military Requirements
MoD	[UK] Ministry of Defence
MRCC	Maritime Rescue Co-ordination Centre
NAC	North Atlantic Council
NATO	North Atlantic Treaty Organisation
NBC	Nuclear, Biological, Chemical
NCIS	National Criminal Intelligence Service
NCP	National Contact Point
NCS	National Crime Squad
NePAD	New Partnership for African Development
NGO/ngo	Non-governmental organisation
NPT	(Nuclear) Non-Proliferation Treaty
NRF	NATO Response Force
NWS	Nuclear Weapons State
OAS	Organisation of American States
OECD	Organisation for Economic Co-operation and Development
OECS	Organisation of East Caribbean States
OFF	Oil for Food Programme
OGD	Other Government Department
OHQ	Operational Headquarters
OIEL	Open Individual Export Licence
OPCAT	Optional Protocol, [UN] Convention against Torture
OPCW	Organisation for the Prohibition of Chemical Weapons
OPLAN	Operating Plan
ORHA	Office for Reconstruction and Humanitarian Affairs
OSCE	Organisation for Security and Co-operation in Europe
OTs	Occupied Territories
PCC	[NATO] Prague Capabilities Committee
PE	(UNSG's) Personal Envoy
PLO	Palestine Liberation Organisation
PoA	Programme of Action
PP	Personnel Policy
PSI	Proliferation Security Initiative
PSC	[EU] Political and Security Committee
RCAs	Riot Control Agents
RAF	Royal Air Force
RIPA	[UK] Regulation of Investigatory Powers Act 2000
RN	Royal Navy
RNEP	Robust Nuclear Earth Penetrator [Weapon]
ROK	Republic of Korea
RUF	Revolutionary United Front
SADC	Southern African Development Community
SALW	Small Arms and Light Weapons
SaM	Serbia and Montenegro

SBA	[UK] Sovereign Base Areas [on Cyprus]
SDPRP	Sustainable Development and Poverty Reduction Programme
SGSSI	South Georgia and South Sandwich Islands
SIAC	Special Immigration Appeal Commission
SIEL	Standard Individual Export Licence
SFOR	Stabilisation Force [in Bosnia-Herzegovina]
SOAT	Sudanese Organisation against Torture
SOFA	Status of Forces Agreement
SOLAS	Safety of Life at Sea [Convention]
SOSREP	Secretary of State's Representative for Maritime Salvage and Intervention
SSHD	Secretary of State for the Home Department
TPA	Tripartite Agreement
TWT	Travelling Wave Tube
UK	United Kingdom
UN	United Nations
UNAMI	United Nations Assistance Mission in Iraq
UNCC	United Nations Claims Commission
UNCLOS	United Nations Convention on the Law of the Sea
UNESCO	United Nations Education, Scientific and Cultural Organisation
UNGA	United Nations General Assembly
UNHCR	United Nations High Commissioner for Refugees
UNICEF	United Nations Children's Fund
UNIFEM	United Nations Development Fund for Women
UNITA	Unino Nacional para Independencia Total de Angola
UNMAS	United Nations Mine Action Service
UNMIK	United Nations Interim Administration Mission in Kosovo
UNMOVIC	United Nations Monitoring Verification and Inspection Committee
UNRWA	United Nations Relief and Works Agency
UNSCOM	United Nations Special Commission
UNSCR	United Nations Security Council Resolution
UNSECOORD	United Nations Security Co-ordinator
UNSG	United Nations Secretary-General
US	United States [of America]
USAID	United States Agency for Development
USVF	United States Visiting Forces
VCDRs	Vienna Convention on Diplomatic Relations
WEU	Western European Union
WHO	World Health Organisation
WMD	Weapons of Mass Destruction
WTO	World Trade Organisation

Richard Orme Wilberforce
(1907–2003)

Richard Orme Wilberforce 1907–2003

Richard Wilberforce was one of a number of the judicial figures of the last century who combined intellectual distinction of a high order with a long career of public service. Even late in his life he was active in the House of Lords working on Bills, and he retired as Chairman of the Executive Council of the International Law Association not far short of his eightieth year.

His intellectual foundations were laid at Winchester and New College, Oxford. At Oxford he read classics and got a first in mods and Greats. He won the Craven, Hertford, and Ireland Scholarships and became a Prize Fellow of All Souls in 1932. He practised at the Chancery Bar from 1933 onward before going on the Bench in 1961. After a short period in the Chancery Division, he became a Law Lord (and a Life Peer) in 1964, retiring in 1982 at the mandatory age of seventy-five.

The characteristics which stand out include versatility. He was essentially a lawyer, not a specialist, but one who could tackle a great variety of problems with the weapons of careful analysis and common sense. His practical experience ranged from his important work during the war in the Army Legal staff and subsequently, in the Supreme Headquarters Allied Expeditionary Forces and the Control Commission in Berlin, to the framing of awards in high profile industrial disputes. Another characteristic which stood him in good stead was his habit of combining geniality with seriousness of purpose. Furthermore, he had a well-developed facility for understanding other people, including complex colleagues, and this is vividly illustrated in his Memorial Address, delivered in the University Church in Oxford in 1992, on John Sparrow, the former Warden of All Souls, scholar of the Renaissance, collector, and controversialist.

In the course of his career Richard Wilberforce was directly involved with public international law in several practical contexts. In the first place, having resumed his practice at the Chancery Bar after the war, he was instructed by the Government in two high profile cases in the International Court in which the United Kingdom was the Claimant State. The first of these was the *Corfu Channel* case,[1] involving the mining of two British warships in the North Corfu Strait with great loss of life and serious damage to the vessels. The mining took place in the territorial sea of Albania in circumstances in which the Albanian authorities either knew, or should have known, of the presence of the mines. In response the British Government carried out a unilateral mine-sweeping

[1] [1948] ICJ Rep 15 (Preliminary Objection); ibid., 1949, p. 4 (Merits); ibid., p. 241 (Assessment of Compensation).

exercise with naval support. The proceedings were based upon a Special Agreement which raised significant questions of law concerning the right of innocent passage in straits, the criteria of lawful self-help, and the law of State responsibility. Richard Wilberforce was Counsel in the British delegation under the leadership of Sir Eric Beckett, in the *Preliminary Objection* and *Merits* phases of the case. Years later he participated, with evident enjoyment, in a well-organised seminar based upon the case in the Foreign and Commonwealth Office.

He also appeared in another team under Beckett's leadership in the *Anglo-Norwegian Fisheries* case.[2] Whilst the facts were in some ways very distinctive, involving the fjord coast of Norway and a fringe of islands, the case was in its day, and still remains, a major precedent. There were no preliminary objections, and no compensation phase, because the British request, as modified during the oral hearings, was simply for a declaration. Richard addressed the Court, in the first round, on the merits of the Norwegian argument concerning the economic interests of the coastal State, interests which, in the British contention, were entirely irrelevant to the legal issues before the Court.

It was natural for Richard Wilberforce to take an interest in the practical articulation of municipal law and public international law and he took an active interest in the legal aspects of post-war aviation.[3] He was a member of the British delegation which negotiated the Warsaw Convention on International Carriage by Air. In recognition of this work he was appointed CMG in 1956. In *Fothergill v Monarch Airlines*[4] the House of Lords, including Lord Wilberforce, had the task of interpreting the Warsaw Convention, of which the English and French texts were scheduled to the pertinent legislation. In deciding that it was appropriate to refer to the *travaux préparatoires*, Lord Wilberforce stated that, in the interest of uniformity of application, it was desirable to have regard to the general practice applied in the Courts of other contracting States.[5]

During his tenure as a Law Lord and as a member of the Judicial Committee of the Privy Council, Richard dealt with hundreds of cases. Most were not concerned with public international law, but a significant minority involved the important and difficult borderland known loosely as foreign relations law.[6] These cases called for the careful articulation of elements of public international law, English public policy, and the principles of conflict of laws.

Of this group of cases four stand out. The first, in chronological order, was the *Carl Zeiss* case,[7] decided in 1966. The general outline is familiar. The House of Lords construed the Foreign Secretary's letter in such

[2] *International Court of Justice: Pleadings, Oral Arguments, Documents; Fisheries Case*, Vol. IV, pp. 153–61 (1 October 1951).

[3] See the Grotius Society, *Transactions*, Vol. 35 (1940), 73–89: 'Some Recent Developments in the International Law of Aviation'.

[4] [1981] AC 251.

[5] Ibid., pp. 276–7.

[6] See Olmstead, *Liber Amicorum* (ed. Bos and Brownlie), Oxford, 1987, 77–89.

[7] [1967] 1 AC 853.

a way as to treat the USSR as the *de jure* governing authority of the Eastern Zone of Germany and the territory of the unrecognised German Democratic Republic as a subordinate body of the USSR. This approach eliminated the problem of non-recognition and treated the German Democratic Republic, in conflict of law terms, as a law district. In consequence the relevant East German legislation was applicable. The five Law Lords were agreed but Lord Wilberforce carried the analysis one step further. In his opinion:[8]

> It was said by the respondents that to recognize the Law setting up the Council of Gera of 23 July 1952 would in effect be to recognize the Government of East Germany and to create a conflict with the views of the Executive. The principle is well established that the courts of Her Majesty do not speak with a different voice from that of Her Majesty's Executive Government (it was stated as early as *Taylor v. Barclay* and has been accepted ever since) but we are not here under the risk of committing the courts to action of this kind. Merely because in the class of case of which *Aksionairnoye Obschestvo A.M. Luther v James Sagor & Co.*, is an example, non-recognition of a 'Government' entails non-recognition of its laws, or some of them, it does not follow that in a different situation this is so, nor that recognition of a law entails recognition of the law-maker as a Government with sovereign power. The primary effect and intention of non-recognition by the Executive is that the non-recognized 'Government' has no standing to represent the State concerned whether in public or private matters. Whether this entails non-recognition of its so-called laws, or acts, is a matter for the courts to pronounce on, having due regard to the situation as regards sovereignty in the territory where the 'laws' are enacted and, no doubt, to any relevant consideration of public policy. I can see no inconsistency in (a) accepting the view of the Executive that there is no recognized (that is, independent) Government in the Eastern Zone apart from the *de jure* governing authority of the U.S.S.R. and *(b)* attributing legal validity, if no other legal obstacle exists, to a 'law' or act of that 'Government' as a subordinate or dependent body.

This is a good example of law-making by means of the drawing of distinctions and the isolation of the unnecessary element in the assessment. In the result the judiciary, in face of the politics of recognition, may have more options.

Another case in the group is *Attorney-General v Nissan*[9] decided in 1969. This involved difficult questions as to the legal status of national contingents forming part of United Nations peacekeeping forces. The proceedings were confined to certain preliminary issues of law. The plaintiff was seeking damages against the Crown for alleged damage done to his hotel in Cyprus by British troops. The Crown raised various defences in law based principally upon the argument that the acts alleged were acts of State or otherwise acts of a United Nations Force and not cognisable. Lord Wilberforce contributed a full, but carefully qualified, analysis of the different rules of which the 'act of State' concept is made up.[10] In general the speeches of the Law Lords presage a growing disenchantment with the concept.

[8] Ibid., 961. [9] [1970] AC 179. [10] Ibid., pp. 229–36.

The last two cases in the group involving 'foreign relations law' were decided in 1981 when Richard was the senior Law Lord. The first of these was *1° Congreso del Partido*.[11] The Law Lords held, unanimously, that the restrictive theory of sovereign immunity had become part of general international law and had been incorporated into English Law by the decisions of the Privy Council in *Philippine Admiral*[12] and of the Court of Appeal in *Trendtex Trading Corporation Ltd. v Central Bank of Nigeria*.[13] The contribution which the decision makes lies in the careful examination of the complex facts in order to decide which acts were done *iure imperii* and which not. In respect of the Marble Islands Lord Wilberforce dissented together with Lord Edmund Davies. The decision well illustrates the fact that there remains a frontier between immunity and non-immunity the determination of which calls for cautious analysis.

The last case in this series is *Buttes Gas and Oil Company v Hammer*.[14] In this unanimous decision the House of Lords accepted the principle that a municipal court cannot adjudicate upon inter-State issues governed by international law. This emerges as a principle of non-justiciability by the English courts of a certain class of sovereign acts. In addition, in his speech Wilberforce emphasised that the principle was to be considered 'not as a variety of "act of state" but one for judicial restraint or abstention'.[15]

In this instance the reasoning points to 'restraint' on grounds of policy, and the absence of 'judicial or manageable standards by which to judge these issues . . .'.[16] However, the reasoning is in this respect too extensive, suggesting that English courts should not examine the legality of acts of other states. It is not surprising that the House of Lords have found a need to clarify the criteria stated in *Buttes Gas*. Thus in the *Kuwait Airways Corporation* case,[17] Lord Nichols stated the position in this way:[18]

'24 On behalf of IAC Mr Donaldson submitted that the public policy exception to the recognition of provisions of foreign law is limited to infringements of human rights. The allegation in the present action is breach of international law by Iraq. But breach of international law by a state is not, and should not be, a ground for refusing to recognise a foreign decree. An English court will not sit in judgment on the sovereign acts of a foreign Government or state. It will not adjudicate upon the legality, validity or acceptability of such acts, either under domestic law or international law. For a court to do so would offend against the principle that the courts will not adjudicate upon the transactions of foreign sovereign states. This principle is not discretionary. It is inherent in the very nature of the judicial process: see *Buttes Gas and Oil Co v Hammer* (No 3) [1982] AC 888, 932. KAC's argument, this submission by IAC continued, invites the court to determine whether the invasion of Kuwait by Iraq, followed by the removal of the ten aircraft from Kuwait to Iraq and their transfer to IAC, was unlawful under international law. The courts below were wrong to accede to this invitation.

[11] [1983] AC 244. [12] [1977] AC 373. [13] [1977] QB 529. [14] [1982] AC 888.
[15] Ibid., p. 931. [16] Ibid., pp. 937–8. [17] [2002] 2 AC 883. [18] Pp. 1080–1.

25 My Lords, this submission seeks to press the non-justiciability principle too far. Undoubtedly there may be cases, of which the *Buttes* case is an illustration, where the issues are such that the court has, in the words of Lord Wilberforce, at p 938, "no judicial or manageable standards by which to judge [the] issues":

> "the court would be asked to review transactions in which four sovereign states were involved, which they had brought to a precarious settlement, after diplomacy and the use of force, and to say that at least part of these were 'unlawful' under international law."

This was Lord Wilberforce's conclusion regarding the important inter-State and other issues arising in that case: see his summary, at p. 937.

26 This is not to say an English court is disabled from ever taking cognisance of international law or from ever considering whether a violation of international law has occurred. In appropriate circumstances it is legitimate for an English court to have regard to the content of international law in deciding whether to recognise a foreign law. Lord Wilberforce himself accepted this in the *Buttes* case, at p 931D. Nor does the "non-justiciable" principle mean that the judiciary must shut their eyes to a breach of an established principle of international law committed by one state against another when the breach is plain and, indeed, acknowledged. In such a case the adjudication problem confronting the English court in the *Buttes* litigation do not arise. The standard being applied by the court is clear and manageable, and the outcome not in doubt. That is the present case.

Richard Wilberforce was, it has already been pointed out, not a specialist but, what is no less important, a good generalist. None of the appreciations published by other judges and contemporaries seek to apply a label: see the *Liber Amicorum* published in 1987. It follows that it would be inappropriate to describe Richard as a public international lawyer, but no one familiar with his life and work would think that this could matter.

He was, for a high proportion of his life, a benevolent agent of influence in relation to international law. He was a member of the editorial committee of this *Year Book* from 1960 until his death. He played an active role as the Chairman of the Executive Council of the International Law Association for twenty-two years. The Executive Council is involved in the organisation of the biennial conferences and the maintenance of the general health of the Association. Professor Olmstead, his successor as Chairman, has described his contribution. In his words:[19]

> His dedicated service to our Association has given it greater prominence in the field of international law. Always ready to respond to the needs of the International Law Association, his tenure as Chairman has produced a number of innovations and improvements in the functioning of our work including establishment of the office of Director of Studies, a broadening of the work of the international committees, celebration of the ILA Centenary in 1973, publication of the Centenary Volume, the index to Conference Reports, and the

[19] International Law Association, *Report of the Sixty-Second Conference at Seoul*, 1986, p.v.

extension of conferences to all areas of the world. His judicious manner of dealing with difficult issues is a model for all of us.

Writing in 1987, Sir Robert Jennings, then a Judge of the International Court (and subsequently President of the Court), recorded that 'he has, in his leadership of the International Law Association, made an important contribution to the progress and development of international law.'[20]

IAN BROWNLIE[*]

[20] *Liber Amicorum*, Oxford, 1987, p. 39.

[*] Chairman of the Editorial Committee, British Year Book of International Law.

THE LAW AND PROCEDURE OF THE INTERNATIONAL COURT OF JUSTICE 1960–1989

PART THIRTEEN

By HUGH THIRLWAY

V. QUESTIONS OF PROCEDURE (*continued*)

Introductory note: The title of this series of articles incorporates two dates, indicating the chronological period covered. The initial date, the *terminus a quo*, has had to be modified for some of the articles, to take account of the fact that the series of articles by Sir Gerald Fitzmaurice, covering the period up to 1968, was never completed, so that for a number of subjects it was necessary to examine decisions between 1954 and 1968. The second date, the *terminus ad quem*, has become more and more artificial, as the period originally intended to be covered has retreated into the past, and more recent decisions of the Court have demanded to be treated if the series was not to give a misleading impression. In the present article, mention has had to be made of a decision on revision of judgments given as recently as December 2003! It is hoped that this discrepancy between the title and the content will not cause too much inconvenience to librarians or scholars.

A second development which may be mentioned is that the author has, from March 2003, resumed his former post as Principal Legal Secretary of the Court. It may therefore be appropriate to repeat the essence of the *caveat* given in the very first article,[1] that the views expressed are solely those of the author, and in no way represent those of the Court or the Registry; and that the articles are based solely on published material, and not on any confidential information which might have been available to the author as a result of his functions.

5. *Jurisdiction and its exercise in incidental proceedings*

(1) *Merits jurisdiction and incidental jurisdiction*

The jurisdiction of the Court to admit an intervention, to entertain an application for interpretation or for revision, and to interpret or revise a judgment on the basis of such an application, derives directly from the Statute of the Court, in the same way as does the jurisdiction to indicate provisional measures. In the case of that latter jurisdiction, as we have seen, the existence, or the likelihood of existence, of jurisdiction over the merits is a consideration affecting the exercise of the statutory jurisdiction under Article 41 of the Statute. In the case of an application by a State to intervene under Article 62 of the Statute, the question of jurisdiction over the merits, or more precisely the question of the relevance of possible merits jurisdiction as between the State seeking to intervene and the original parties, has been the source of much controversy. The question has however also been raised[2] whether similarly there is any relationship between, in particular, the statutory jurisdiction to interpret and revise a judgment and the merits jurisdiction underlying the judgment to be revised or interpreted.

A jurisdiction derived directly from the Statute of the Court is nonetheless a consensual jurisdiction, the consent being given by accession to the Statute.[3] As the Chamber dealing with the application of Nicaragua to intervene in the *Land, Island and Maritime Frontier Dispute* observed,

> The competence of the Court in this matter of intervention is not, like its competence to hear and determine the dispute referred to it, derived from the consent of the parties to the case, but from the consent given by them, in becoming parties to the Court's Statute, to the Court's exercise of its powers conferred by the Statute. There is no need to interpret the reference in Article 36, paragraph 1, of the Statute to 'treaties in force' to include the Statute itself; acceptance of the Statute entails acceptance of the competence conferred on the Court by Article 62.[4]

[1] [1989] *BYBIL*, p. 7.

[2] Espaliú Berdud, *Desarrollos jurisprudenciales y práctica reciente en la jurisdicción de la CIJ*, p. 326.

[3] It is therefore inappropriate to refer to it as 'compulsory jurisdiction' (cf. Fernández Sánchez, 'The interpretation of international judgments in the framework of the ICJ', *Thesaurus Acroasium*, Vol. XVIII, 1991, p. 527, cited in Espaliú Berdud, op. cit., p. 326, who rightly prefers the term 'statutory jurisdiction').

[4] [1990] ICJ Rep 133, para. 96. The source of the theory as to Article 36, paragraph 1, of the Statute, here refuted, is not indicated.

It follows that such statutory jurisdiction cannot be exercised in relation to a State not a party to the Statute. If a State party to proceedings which have culminated in a judgment ceases at some moment thereafter to be a party to the Statute (e.g. by withdrawal from the United Nations), could the Court, on the application of the other party, exercise its jurisdiction to interpret or revise the judgment? The simplest answer would be that this is not possible;[5] but it is perhaps not inconceivable that the doctrine of the *Nottebohm* decision might be regarded as applicable. Certainly if a request were made by one party for interpretation or revision while the other party was still a party to the Statute, the subsequent withdrawal from the Statute would, on the *Nottebohm* precedent, not deprive the Court of jurisdiction.

However, the point may be pressed further. If a judgment is interpreted by the Court, it continues to be binding on the original parties to it, as so interpreted; and at the moment when the original judgment was given, the Court possessed both jurisdiction to give it (*ex hypothesi*) and jurisdiction to interpret it on the request of a party. Withdrawal from the Statute does not deprive the judgment of its binding force; does it render it thereafter incapable of being interpreted? Similarly, if a judgment is revised by the Court, although the revision is effected by a judgment, it is (*semble*) the original judgment, though as revised, that continues to bind. Does the withdrawal of one party from the Statute after the original judgment has been given mean that revision becomes impossible, so that both parties would continue to be bound by a decision which, on the contention of one of them, ought never to have been given, or not to have been given to that effect?

The problem has not arisen in practice; and it is only tentatively that it is suggested that, on the withdrawal of a State from participation in the Statute, the jurisdiction to interpret or revise a judgment to which that State has been party continues to exist. It could be said that the seising of the Court in respect of the original dispute entitles and requires the Court to 'exercise its powers, as defined in the Statute' for the purpose of 'the administration of justice'.[6] Withdrawal from participation in the Statute is 'an event which is unrelated to the exercise of the powers conferred on the Court by the Statute, which the Court must exercise whenever it has been regularly seised';[7] once it has given judgment on the merits it becomes *functus officio* as regards merits jurisdiction, but need not be treated so in relation to its statutory, post-judgment, jurisdiction.

Interventions, like counter-claims, are necessarily integrated into an existing case before the Court.[8] Interpretation or revision is sought when an existing case is, or appears to be at an end. The proceedings on the

[5] For Espaliú Berdud, this solution is in fact 'obvious': op. cit., p. 327.

[6] Cf. *Nottebohm* [1953] ICJ Rep 122. [7] Ibid.

[8] 'Every intervention is incidental to the proceedings in a case': *Haya de la Torre* [1951] ICJ Rep 76, quoted in *Land, Island and Maritime Frontier Dispute* [1990] ICJ Rep 4.

application itself, whether for interpretation or for revision, are treated as constituting a new case separate from the original proceedings, with a new number on the Court's General List;[9] this reflects the fact that no question of the original merits jurisdiction arises directly in that context.

There are, it seems, two ways in which the question of merits jurisdiction in the original case might arise. First, if an application is made for the interpretation or revision of a judgment given on the basis of a title of jurisdiction which has subsequently expired, or been withdrawn, does that circumstance affect the matter? It would seem that it does not.[10] That view could be based either on the view that statutory jurisdiction is sufficient unto itself; or by an extension of the *Nottebohm* doctrine similar to, but less extreme than, its application above to the case of withdrawal from the Statute. The second way in which the relevance of merits jurisdiction might arise is in the form of the question whether it is possible to apply for interpretation or revision of a judgment by which the Court found that it had no jurisdiction in the case before it. A request for interpretation of such a judgment would seem to be of no evident practical utility,[11] except perhaps if the Court had ruled, in obscure terms requiring interpretation, on the application of a compromissory clause which might be invoked in other disputes.[12] That cannot however be said of a request for revision, which might be directed to achieving a judgment upholding jurisdiction, just as, in the case concerning *Application of the Genocide Convention*, it was sought to transform a judgment upholding jurisdiction into a judgment rejecting it. There would seem to be no reason of principle why such a request could not be entertained; as indicated below, the Court has taken the view that it has jurisdiction to entertain requests for interpretation of any judgment given by it,[13] and the same would seem to be true of an application for revision.

Fitzmaurice took the view that in such a case there would be a relationship between merits jurisdiction and statutory jurisdiction:

> the jurisdiction [the Court] exercises in respect of the request for revision or interpretation is not independent of, but consequential upon, a determination (even a negative determination) of the question of substantive jurisdiction.[14]

A negative determination of substantive jurisdiction is an exercise of jurisdiction, not however of the substantive jurisdiction, but rather of the

[9] As the Permanent Court observed as early as 1927: see PCIJ Rep Series E No. 4, 289, cited in Guyomar, *Commentaire du Règlement de la CIJ*, p. 632.

[10] In this sense, Zimmermann, *Interpretation of judgments of the International Court of Justice under Article 60 of the Statute*, 1989, p. 79; Espaliú Berdud, op. cit., p. 327.

[11] In the case of the *Land and Maritime Boundary between Cameroon and Nigeria*, Nigeria applied for the interpretation of the Court's judgment on its preliminary objections; but since those objections had not been upheld, and the case was continuing, it was arguable that an interpretation could serve a useful purpose. In fact the Court found Nigeria's request inadmissible: see further below.

[12] It might however in such circumstances be difficult to show a 'dispute as to the meaning or scope *of the judgment*' for purposes of Art. 60 of the Statute: see Section 7(3) below.

[13] *Request for Interpretation, Land and Maritime Frontier between Cameroon and Nigeria*, [1999-I] ICJ Rep 35 para. 10.

[14] [1958] *BYBIL* p. 108; *Collected Edition*, Vol. II, p. 535.

compétence de la compétence; so the relationship is perhaps more between two sorts of statutory competence.[15] In any event, this amounts to little more than saying that, for there to be a request for revision or interpretation, there must first be a judgment to be revised or interpreted. *Pace* Fitzmaurice, the existence or otherwise of merits jurisdiction in the dispute which led to the giving of the original judgment is wholly independent of, and has no effect on, the statutory jurisdiction to revise or to interpret.

However, in view of the principle of the consensual nature of international judicial jurisdiction, it may also be asked whether the consent of the parties to the case is of any relevance to the exercise of this statutory jurisdiction. The consent of the parties (or, to be precise, of the party other than the applicant in revision or interpretation) is not *required* for the exercise of such jurisdiction. The question remains whether such consent might for example render the exercise of a statutory jurisdiction possible even though one of the normal conditions for its exercise was not met. This could amount to a waiver by the consenting party of a right under the Statute, a possibility referred to, and not totally ruled out, in relation to interpretation, in the judgment on Tunisia's application for interpretation in the *Continental Shelf (Tunisia/Libya)* case (see further Section 7(1) below).

As regards intervention, in one recent case, that concerning the *Land and Maritime Boundary between Cameroon and Nigeria*, a third State (Equatorial Guinea) applied to intervene as a non-party to the proceedings—an option which, as we shall see, was held by the Chamber in the *Land, Island and Maritime Boundary Dispute* to be available under Article 62 of the Statute. The parties to the case, Cameroon and Nigeria, made no objection to the intervention, and the Court decided to admit the intervention, without holding any hearings, and embodying its decision in the form of an Order rather than a judgment.[16] In that Order the Court referred to the fact that the parties did not object to the intervention, and then found that Equatorial Guinea had sufficiently established that it had an interest of a legal nature which could be affected by any judgment that the Court might give in the case, the condition required by Article 62. The Court then stated that

> *in view of the position of the Parties* and the conclusions which the Court itself has reached, the Court considers that there is nothing to prevent the Application by Equatorial Guinea for permission to intervene from being granted.[17]

The Court therefore presumably did regard the attitude of the Parties as relevant, but does not appear to have regarded consent of the parties as a substitute for compliance with the condition laid down in Article 62. Since however compliance with that condition is generally held to confer a right to be permitted to intervene, or—to put it another way—the

[15] This is not to say that the *compétence de la compétence* is purely statutory: see a previous article in this series, [1999] *BYBIL*, pp. 2–7.
[16] *Order of 21 October 1999*, [1999-II] ICJ Rep 1029.
[17] Ibid., p. 1035, para. 16.

Court is obliged to permit intervention once the condition has been complied with,[18] it is not clear what significance the consent of the parties might have other than to justify intervention without compliance with the condition of Article 62.

In the case of revision, a recent decision has contained a specific finding on the question of the lack of relevance of the consent of a party. In its decision on a request by El Salvador for revision of the 1992 judgment in the case of the *Land, Island and Maritime Frontier Dispute*, the Chamber seised of that request referred to an argument by El Salvador that Honduras had recognized the admissibility of its request, by asking the Chamber to require previous compliance with the judgment before admitting proceedings in revision, as contemplated by Article 61 of the Statute. That argument is not very substantial, and the Chamber found that in fact Honduras had not made any such request, but merely alluded to it as a possibility. Nevertheless, the Chamber went on to make the following finding of principle:

> the Chamber notes that, regardless of the parties' views on the admissibility of an application for revision, it is in any event for the Court, when seised of such an application, to ascertain whether the admissibility requirements laid down in Article 61 of the Statute have been met. Revision is not available simply by consent of the parties, but solely when the conditions of Article 61 are met.[19]

As regards interpretation, the only condition laid down by Article 60 of the Statute for the admission of a request for interpretation is that there is a 'dispute as to the meaning or scope of the judgment'. It is difficult to imagine circumstances in which one party would consent to an application for interpretation by the other party while at the same time maintaining that there was no such dispute. The question of the possible role of consent in this field is therefore probably academic, not to say unrealistic.

The question has also arisen whether the procedure of a request for interpretation can be made subordinate, by agreement of the parties, to an extra-statutory procedure for 'clarification'; this will be discussed below (Section 7(1)).

(2) *Exercise of incidental jurisdiction: the Court and Chambers*

The problems that may arise when an application is made to intervene in a case pending before a Chamber of the Court have already been examined in a previous article.[20] As was there seen, the principle applied is that it is for the organ dealing with the main case to deal with such subsidiary matters as intervention. When statutory competences over such subsidiary matters fall to be exercised during the pendency of the main case, there is at least no problem in determining what body is dealing with that main case. Applications for interpretation and revision are however made after the case is (apparently) closed, so that further questions of this kind may arise.

[18] See below, Section 6(1). [19] [2003] ICJ Rep 400, para. 22. [20] [2001] *BYBIL*, pp. 52 ff.

The general principle is, as regards interpretation, *eius est interpretare cujus est condere*: it is for the body that gave the judgment to deal with its interpretation, as being the body that is best placed to know what it meant by its decision.[21] This is also valid for revision, particularly in view of the requirement that revision has to be based on the discovery of a 'fact of such a nature as to be a decisive factor'—the tribunal that gave the judgment being, again, best placed to judge whether a particular fact could have had this impact. The principle finds expression in Article 100, paragraph 1, of the 1978 Rules of Court:

> If the judgment to be revised or interpreted was given by the Court, the request for its revision or interpretation shall be dealt with by the Court. If the judgment was given by a Chamber, the request for its revision or interpretation shall be dealt with by that Chamber.

The principle is not applied so literally, however, that the composition of the Court for the interpretation or revision must be identical with its composition when the original judgment was given;[22] 'the Court' is seen as an unchanging entity, whatever its current membership.[23]

What, however, of the expression 'that Chamber' in the second part of the sentence? Clearly it excludes interpretation or revision by the Court of a decision of a Chamber; and if there is more than one Chamber of the Court in existence, it avoids any suggestion that one Chamber might interpret or revise the decision of another (though the words 'the Chamber' might have been sufficient for this). When a Chamber is formed to deal with a specific case, under Article 26, paragraph 2, of the Statute, it is normally treated as having ceased to exist once it has completed its task by giving judgment on the merits.[24] The words 'that Chamber' seem to contemplate that a request for interpretation or

[21] But note the apparent denial by the Permanent Court, in the *Jaworzina* case, of any general principle whereby an arbitrator possesses implied powers to interpret his award: PCIJ Rep Series B No 8, 38 Rosenne, *The Law and Practice of the International Court, 1920–1996*, Vol. III, pp. 1669–70.

[22] Compare, for example, the composition of the Court for the decision in the *Continental Shelf (Tunisia/Libya)* case, [1982] ICJ Rep 18, with that for the decision on Tunisia's application for interpretation and revision, [1985] ICJ Rep 192.

[23] Article 66 of the 1922 Rules of the Permanent Court, after providing that interpretation or revision of a judgment given by a Chamber should be given by 'the same Chamber', and interpretation or revision of a judgment of the Court should be given by the Court, continued: 'The provisions of Article 13 of the Statute shall apply in all cases.' The reference can only have been to what is now para. 3 of Art. 13 (the paragraphs of the articles of the PCIJ Statute were originally not numbered separately), which provides that 'The Members of the Court shall continue to discharge their duties until their places have been filled. Though replaced, they shall finish any cases which they may have begun.' The Court decided in 1927 that there was no need, on a request for interpretation, to reassemble the same bench, from among the sitting judges and deputy-judges, as that which had given the original decision, since Art. 13 of the Statute referred only to judges who had ceased to belong to the Court or to one of its Chambers: Hudson, *The Permanent Court of International Justice*, pp. 298–9, and Guyomar, *Commentaire du Règlement de la CIJ*, pp. 632–3, both citing PCIJ Rep Series E No 4, 295.

[24] But note the Order, dated 9 April 1987, of the Chamber formed to deal with the *Frontier Dispute* between Burkina Faso and Mali, appointing experts to assist in the implementation of the judgment of 22 December 1986; this was consequent upon a provision in the Special Agreement conferring jurisdiction, and the Chamber had referred to the matter in its judgment.

revision has the effect of reviving the Chamber to deal with the request. Obviously in some cases this would be impossible, if some of its members had died in the meantime; but if all members were still alive, and still Members of the Court, presumably the Chamber could not be re-formed with a different composition. On the other hand, if some members of the Chamber were still living but had retired from the Court, would they be recalled from retirement to re-constitute the Chamber?

In the only case in which the question has arisen, the Court's handling of the matter does not permit of any firm conclusions being drawn. The judgment of 11 September 1992 in the case of the *Land, Island and Maritime Frontier Dispute* was given by a Chamber composed of Judges Sette-Camara, Jennings, and Oda, and Judges *ad hoc* Valticos and Torres Bernárdez. When, nearly ten years later, El Salvador requested a revision of part of the judgment, Judge Sette-Camara and Judge Valticos were dead, and Judge Jennings had ceased to be a Member of the Court. Was Judge Jennings to be recalled to the colours, and another Member of the Court elected to replace Judge Sette-Camara? Was Judge Oda obliged, or at least entitled, to sit? Was Honduras obliged to reappoint Torres Bernárdez as judge *ad hoc*?[25]

El Salvador, in view of this situation, took the initiative of asking for the formation of a new Chamber to deal with the request for revision, and Honduras made no objection to this, and nominated Torres Bernárdez as judge *ad hoc*. By an Order of 27 November 2002, the Court accepted this request and formed a Chamber which included Judge Torres Bernárdez as judge *ad hoc* appointed by Honduras, but did not include Judge Oda. It made no comment at all on the possibility of re-forming the original Chamber so far as possible, i.e. by including both Judge Oda and Judge Torres Bernárdez.

A Chamber so formed would in fact have had very little more claim to be 'that Chamber', as referred to in Article 100 of the Rules, than the Chamber actually formed. It remains uncertain however to what extent—if, indeed, at all—that expression binds the Court to entrust the interpretation or revision to something approximating to the original Chamber. As already observed, if a request were made for an interpretation or a revision shortly after the original decision, at a time when all the original members of the Chamber (other than judges *ad hoc*) were still Members of the Court, it would be difficult to suppose that the Court could form a wholly new Chamber for the interpretation or revision, including perhaps none of the original members. Does the death, or even the retirement, of a single one of the original judges on the Chamber mean that the original Chamber is beyond resuscitation, and if so does the Court have a free hand in selecting members for a new Chamber?

[25] Fortunately the request asked for revision only of a part of the judgment concerning the land boundary, in respect of which Nicaragua, intervener in the original case, had not been authorized to intervene, thus simplifying the situation.

As regards the effect of the retirement of original members of the Chamber, Article 13, paragraph 3, of the Statute provides that retiring judges are to 'finish any cases which they may have begun'.[26] Proceedings on a request for interpretation or revision are however treated as a new case; and it is difficult to suppose that this provision could have been invoked to call back, for example, Sir Robert Jennings from retirement, nearly ten years after the decision of which revision was sought, and seven years after his term of office had come to an end.[27]

All that can be deduced from the Court's Order on the request for revision of the decision in the *Land, Island and Maritime Frontier Dispute* is that the Court did not consider that the presence of one surviving regular judge, and the availability of one of the judges *ad hoc*, from the original Chamber, prevented it from forming a new Chamber (which would nonetheless be 'that Chamber' for the purposes of Article 100 of the Rules), and selecting freely the judges to constitute the Chamber.

A further complication which may be mentioned in passing is that the procedure of revision of a judgment begins with a judgment on the admissibility of the request, and if that judgment is favourable there then follow proceedings on the merits.[28] It is therefore quite possible that, in a case dealt with by a chamber, a change in the composition of the Chamber might result from the death or illness of one of its members after the decision on admissibility, so that the original judgment, the judgment on admissibility of revision, and the judgment effecting revision would each be given by a different group of judges. On the other hand, the expiry of the term of office as Member of the Court of one of the members of the chamber, between the judgment on admissibility and the proceedings on the merits of the revision, might justify invocation of Article 13, paragraph 3, of the Statute, coupled with Article 17, paragraph 4, of the Rules of Court.

(3) *'Revived' jurisdiction: the* Request for an Examination of the Situation *filed by New Zealand in 1995*

When in 1995 New Zealand endeavoured to reopen the proceedings it had brought in 1973 against France in the *Nuclear Tests* case by filing with the Court a 'Request for an Examination of the Situation', referring to paragraph 63 of the 1974 judgment in that case, it stated explicitly that it

[26] On the interpretation of this text in the Rules of Court, see a previous article in this series, [2000] *BYBIL*, pp. 159–62.

[27] As noted above (n. 23), Art. 66 of the 1922 Rules of the Permanent Court, after providing for interpretation or revision of a Chamber judgment by the Chamber, and interpretation or revision of a Court judgment by the Court, continued: 'The provisions of Article 13 of the Statute shall apply in all cases'. This reference to Art. 13 was maintained in the 1931 Rules of the PCIJ, but was omitted from the corresponding article (Art. 80) of the 1936 Rules, on the proposal of the Co-ordination Commission, which suggested that it could lead to complications or even impossibilities if the request for interpretation was submitted years after the judgment (Guyomar, *Commentaire du Règlement de la CIJ*, p. 633, citing PCIJ Rep Series D No 2, *addendum*, 334–5). No corresponding provision has ever been included in the Rules of the post-war Court.

[28] Rules, Art. 99, para. 4.

was 'not seeking an interpretation of the 1974 judgment under Article 60 of the Statute, nor a revision of that judgment under Article 61'.[29] The Court further found that paragraph 63, while it authorised the Applicant, in the circumstances there contemplated, to request an examination of the situation 'in accordance with the provisions of the Statute', had not been intended 'to limit the Applicant's access to legal procedures such as . . . a request for interpretation (Statute, Art. 60) or a request for revision (Statute, Art. 61) which would have been open to it in any event'.[30] The procedure contemplated by paragraph 63 was *sui generis*: as Judge Weeramantry observed,

> The Court [in 1974], well aware of the provisions in its established procedure relating to interpretation and revision, was not indulging in an exercise in tautology. It was devising an unprecedented procedure to meet an unprecedented situation.[31]

Not merely was the situation unprecedented; it is practically certain never to be repeated, since the 1995 proceedings have demonstrated the unwisdom of the inclusion of paragraph 63 in the 1974 judgment. Nevertheless, some commentary on the case is justified; and despite the contrast between the unprecedented procedure and the procedures of revision and interpretation, that commentary is perhaps as well placed in the present section of these articles as anywhere else.[32]

The 1974 judgment in the case, and in the parallel case brought by Australia, was already of an unusual, if not unprecedented, nature. The two applicant States had brought proceedings against France on the jurisdictional basis of the 1928 General Act for the Pacific Settlement of International Disputes, and on the basis of the acceptance by France of jurisdiction under the optional clause of Article 36 of the Statute, claiming that France was internationally responsible for damage to the Applicants by fall-out from the French atmospheric nuclear tests at Mururoa Atoll. Apart from the substantive question whether nuclear tests were wrongful under international law as it stood at that date, the Applicants faced formidable jurisdictional obstacles: it was contended by France that the 1928 General Act had lapsed, or fallen into desuetude,[33] and could no longer be invoked, and that the reservation to the optional clause declaration concerning matters of French national defence excluded jurisdiction in relation to the tests. The Court opened a phase

[29] *Request for an Examination of the Situation in accordance with paragraph 63 of the Court's judgment of 20 December 1974 in the* Nuclear Tests (New Zealand *v* France) *case*, [1995] ICJ Rep 303, para. 50. Some aspects of the case have already been examined in an earlier article in this series: [1998] *BYBIL*, pp. 45–6.

[30] Ibid., para. 52. The expression 'limit . . . access' is ambiguous: the apparent meaning would be better expressed as 'confine . . . access'.

[31] Dissenting opinion, [1995] ICJ Rep 321.

[32] It might perhaps have formed part of the discussions of jurisdiction in [1998] and [1999] *BYBIL*; but as indicated at the outset of this series, the structure of the series might involve afterthoughts (see [1989] *BYBIL*, p. 6).

[33] On this aspect see a previous article in this series, [1992] *BYBIL*, pp. 94–6.

of the proceedings devoted to questions of jurisdiction and admissibility; but its decision left these aspects entirely open, being based simply on a finding that France had unilaterally undertaken to cease atmospheric nuclear testing (but not underground testing), and that therefore, the Applicants having obtained what they were seeking, the case had become 'without object'. The jurisdiction to make this finding was stated to be

> an inherent jurisdiction enabling it to take such action as may be required, on the one hand to ensure that the exercise of its jurisdiction over the merits, if and when established, shall not be frustrated, and on the other, to provide for the orderly settlement of all matters in dispute, to ensure the observance of the 'inherent limitations on the exercise of the judicial function' of the Court, and to 'maintain its judicial character' (*Northern Cameroons, Judgment*, [1963] ICJ Rep 29).[34]

This jurisdiction was thus result-oriented: the Court had jurisdiction to declare a case to be 'moot' or 'without object', and in order to do so had jurisdiction to make the factual/legal finding that France had unilaterally undertaken a binding legal obligation.[35] It was therefore able to leave aside the question of jurisdiction under the General Act and the optional clause; but it was aware that France had terminated its acceptances of jurisdiction under these instruments. In application of the *Nottebohm* principle, such termination would not have deprived the Court of any jurisdiction it possessed on the basis of these texts to deal with the case brought by New Zealand; but it would not have any jurisdiction at a later date to deal with any fresh proceedings that New Zealand might bring against France.

What then would be the situation if France went back on its undertaking to cease atmospheric nuclear tests, or denied that it had ever been meant to be legally binding? New Zealand would not have the benefit of a ruling of the Court on the substance of its claim, that the fall-out from the French tests amounted to an internationally wrongful act; and it would no longer be able to invoke the jurisdictional titles it had relied on in 1973 to ask for such a ruling. In the circumstances, the Court evidently decided to depart from the principle that it does not envisage the possibility of non-compliance with its decisions.[36] Paragraph 63 of the 1974 judgment, invoked by New Zealand 20 years later, provided as follows:

> Once the Court has found that a State has entered into a commitment concerning its future conduct it is not the Court's function to contemplate that it will not comply with it. However, the Court observes that if the basis of this judgment were to be affected, the Applicant could request an examination of the situation in accordance with the provisions of the Statute; the denunciation by France, by

34 [1974] ICJ Rep 463, para. 23.

35 On this aspect see two previous articles in this series, [1989] *BYBIL*, pp. 8–17, and [1998] *BYBIL*, pp. 42–6.

36 See *S.S. Wimbledon*, PCIJ Rep Series A No 1, 32; *Factory at Chorzów (Indemnity)*, PCIJ Rep Series A No 17, pp. 62–3.

letter dated 2 January 1974, of the General Act for the Pacific Settlement of International Disputes, which is relied on as a basis of jurisdiction in the present case, cannot constitute by itself an obstacle to the presentation of such a request.[37]

In 1995 France announced its intention to carry out eight nuclear weapons tests in the South Pacific starting in September 1995; these were not to be atmospheric tests, but in New Zealand's view they would, in the light of up-to-date scientific information, cause the same injury to New Zealand's interests as the atmospheric tests of 1973. It therefore brought to the Court its 'Request for an Examination of the Situation', and asked the Court to adjudge and declare that the conduct of the tests would violate New Zealand's rights under international law, and that such conduct would be unlawful unless an Environmental Impact Assessment showed that there would be no radioactive contamination of the marine environment.

The procedural complications resulting from this request were considerable. Did the request, which corresponded to nothing in the Statute and Rules of Court, have any legal effect at all? Could it be entered on the General List? Could any effect be given to the accompanying request for the indication of provisional measures?[38] Could any effect be given to the purported resignation of the judge *ad hoc* appointed by New Zealand in 1973, and the nomination of a replacement?

The Court adopted the sensible course of holding public hearings on the matter, and permitting the judge *ad hoc* appointed by New Zealand to sit for this purpose, while expressly indicating that these arrangements 'shall in no way prejudice any decision which the Court will subsequently take regarding the existence or not of a case before it'.[39] The question of entry in the General List was also left open, but in the Order which the Court issued on 22 September 1995, after the hearings, the Court indicated that even if it was disputed whether the New Zealand request fulfilled the conditions of paragraph 63 of the 1974 judgment, that request

must nonetheless be the object of entry in the General List of the Court for the sole purpose of enabling the latter to determine whether those conditions are fulfilled,[40]

and that accordingly the Registrar was directed to enter the case in the General List.[41]

In its Order, the Court identified two problems: first, what procedure the Court had envisaged as open to New Zealand under paragraph 63 of the 1974 judgment; and secondly whether the 'basis' of that judgment

[37] [1974] ICJ Rep 477, para. 63.

[38] Which in turn was accompanied by a request that the President exercise his powers under Art. 66, para. 3, of the 1972 Rules of Court, these being the Rules in force when the original proceedings had been instituted.

[39] [1995] ICJ Rep 296, para. 27.

[40] Ibid., p. 302, para. 44.

[41] Later in the same Order, the Court directed him to remove it again: ibid., p. 306, para. 66.

had been 'affected' within the meaning of that paragraph.[42] It treated these questions in the order stated, although, as Judge Ranjeva pointed out, since it gave a negative answer to the second question, it might better have taken the questions in the reverse order, the discussion of the first question being 'without object'.[43] This suggests that the majority of the Court considered it desirable to make a finding on the procedural consequences of paragraph 63, even though they were unable to find in favour of New Zealand's contentions—and this even though, as already noted, the case promised to be a *unicum*, never to be repeated.

Nevertheless, the Court's treatment of the procedural issue is disappointingly brief: it merely found that, by inserting the words 'the Applicant could request an examination of the situation in accordance with the provisions of the Statute',

> the Court did not exclude a special procedure, in the event that the circumstances defined in that paragraph [63] were to arise, in other words, circumstances which 'affected' the 'basis' of the Judgment.[44]

It observed that 'such a procedure appears to be indissociably linked . . . to the existence of those circumstances', and then turned to an examination whether the circumstances envisaged in fact existed.

Despite the curiously negative formula 'the Court did not exclude a special procedure', this seems to be a finding that the Court could legally provide for a power to reopen the case long after judgment was given. What is less clear is whether the Court was making any finding on the efficacity of the implementation of the power. Judge Shahabuddeen, in a separate opinion, pointed out that

> New Zealand is not simply asking the Court to reconsider the matters complained of in its 1973 Application in the light of the new situation; it is asking for substantive reliefs in respect of the new situation in like manner as it would if, instead of its request, it had brought a new case. Its request for an examination of the situation is asking for declarations as to the legality of the underground tests; its request for an indication of provisional measures is seeking measures restraining France from conducting the tests. The acts complained of are new acts.[45]

Judge Shahabuddeen did not read paragraph 63 as having been intended to make this possible. But if that was not the intention it is not apparent what use paragraph 63 would have been to the Applicant. If after the 1974 judgment had been given France had announced a new series of atmospheric tests, this would have 'affected the basis' of the Judgment, but the new tests (and the announcement of them) would equally have been 'new acts'. Judge Shahabuddeen's emphasis was however on the fact that, in his view, paragraph 63 *could not* have had the effect that New Zealand was claiming.

42 Ibid., p. 302, para. 47.
43 Declaration of Judge Ranjeva, ibid., p. 311.
44 Ibid., pp. 303–4, para. 53.
45 Ibid., p. 315.

Where the Court has jurisdiction at the time when the Application is brought, the *Nottebohm* principle entitles it to continue to exercise that jurisdiction in relation to the dispute presented in the Application notwithstanding that the jurisdiction was terminated during the course of the proceedings. The last sentence of paragraph 63 of the 1974 Judgment sought to treat a request made pursuant to that paragraph as falling within the application of that principle, in the same way that the principle would have applied to the original case had it continued; the sentence could not be construed as an attempt by the Court, by force of its own decision, to vest itself with jurisdiction not otherwise available to it. I have not been able to find any principle of law which entitles the Court to exercise a terminated jurisdiction over fresh acts occurring after the termination, in this case some 21 years after the jurisdiction (if it existed) was terminated.[46]

Other Members of the Court who attached opinions took a different view. For Judge Weeramantry, the Court had 'expressly empower[ed] New Zealand to return to the Court on the basis of the original case if New Zealand was able to show that the basis of the judgment was affected';[47] Judge Koroma found it a 'plausible' argument that

the Court decided, *using its inherent powers*, and in the interest of the administration of justice, that the jurisdictional link which it found to exist when New Zealand filed its Application in 1973 must be preserved and serve as the jurisdictional link for a possible request for an examination of the situation, were the basis of the Judgment to be affected.[48]

A similar view was taken by Judge *ad hoc* Palmer.

None of these judges however countered Judge Shahabuddeen's point that the Court had no power to keep alive, or revive, the original jurisdiction to extend to facts occurring long after the relevant instruments had been denounced. In support of that view, it may be recalled that the jurisdiction of the Court is based on the consent of States. France had accepted jurisdiction under the General Act and under the optional clause on the basis, or with the implied proviso, that it could withdraw those acceptances in accordance with their terms, and with the General Act itself and the Court's Statute, and that the Court could not be seised of proceedings relating to acts occurring after such withdrawal. Any exception to this system could only be created by the consent of France. Such consent might have been given as one of the terms of a settlement negotiated between France and New Zealand; but it cannot be read into the unilateral announcement of an intention to stop the tests complained of.

Why, one may ask, did the Court include paragraph 63 at all? If it had found in 1974 that it had jurisdiction, and had then upheld

[46] Ibid. [47] Ibid., p. 338.

[48] Ibid., p. 375. It might be objected that the Court in 1973/1974 did not in fact find the existence of a jurisdictional link, though it did find that there was sufficient *prima facie* jurisdiction to justify the indication of provisional measures. Judge Koroma however did not think that the Court could immediately give New Zealand satisfaction, but merely that the Court could proceed to a full examination of the case, including examination of objections by France to jurisdiction, which it might well uphold.

New Zealand's claim on the merits, and if thereafter France had conducted fresh atmospheric tests, no return to the Court would have been possible in view of the denunciation of the jurisdictional instruments. Would something analogous to paragraph 63 still have been included, or was that text related to the finding of 'mootness'?

An ingenious answer, though one that can be only speculative,[49] was offered by Judge *ad hoc* Palmer. In his dissenting opinion he drew attention to a passage in the 1974 joint dissent of Judges Onyeama, Dillard, Jiménez de Aréchaga and Waldock. The dissenters regarded the claim of New Zealand as requesting a declaration of illegality of the French nuclear tests, not merely a cessation of those tests; the decision of the majority was, in their view, based upon an alteration of New Zealand's submissions. They then argued that

> A radical alteration of an applicant's submission under the guise of interpretation has serious consequences because it constitutes a frustration of a party's legitimate expectations that the case which it has put before the Court will be examined and decided. In this instance the serious consequences have an irrevocable character because the Applicant is now prevented from resubmitting its Application and seising the Court again by reason of France's denunciation of the instruments on which it is sought to base the Court's jurisdiction in the present dispute.[50]

Judge Palmer noted the close match between the language of this text and that of paragraph 63, and made the following suggestion:

> In my opinion a possible explanation of paragraph 63 is that it was adopted by the Court, after having seen the dissent circulated in draft, in order to blunt [the] power of the central point made by the dissenters and to ensure it did not come to pass. In that way the majority may have attempted to secure more support within the Court for the Judgment and may in fact have done so.[51]

If this were the explanation, there was a misunderstanding by the draftsmen of the majority judgment of the point being made by the dissenters. Their point surely was, not that New Zealand would be prevented from coming back to the Court if France went back on its undertaking; it was that New Zealand would be prevented from coming back to the Court to ask (perhaps immediately) for the *declaratory judgment* that, according to the dissenters, it had been seeking all along. Such a return to the Court would not necessarily be prompted by a resumption of atmospheric tests, though that would have made such a return more likely. On this basis, paragraph 63 afforded New Zealand absolutely no consolation.

The general legal conclusion that may perhaps be drawn from this unhappy episode is that the Court has recognized that it can provide in

[49] The present writer, who was Secretary of the Drafting Committee that prepared the 1974 judgment, is coincidentally now the only person still living who participated in its preparation. No revelations should however be expected: the principle of secrecy of the deliberations does not lose force with the passage of time (though memory, alas, does).

[50] Joint dissenting opinion, [1974] ICJ Rep 499, para. 12, quoted in [1995] ICJ Rep 395, para. 42.

[51] [1995] ICJ Rep 396, para. 43.

advance for something that might be called a reopening of a case concluded with a judgment; but that the argument of Judge Shahabuddeen is convincing, that by doing so it cannot preserve a jurisdiction that has in the meantime been terminated by the State so as to extend to acts and events subsequent to that termination; at most, it may still be exercised, according to the *Nottebohm* principle, in respect of elements of the original claim. Reopenings of this kind must in any event remain highly exceptional, and there would be no need to provide for them in the Statute and Rules of Court, which—it appears—are in this respect not exhaustive.

6. *Intervention*

(1) *Introduction*

In previous articles, and indeed at the beginning of this one, the time that has proved necessary to complete the series has been deplored inasmuch as it has meant that the limitation, stated in the title, to the period prior to 1990 has become more and more artificial, and more and more decisions have demanded to be commented upon. Turning to intervention, however, in particular under Article 62 of the Statute, the writer finds that his task, though still daunting, has in some respects been made easier by the delay. In 1990, as a result of the confusing and inconsistent decisions on intervention in the two *Continental Shelf* cases—the attempted intervention of Malta in the case between Tunisia and Libya, and that of Italy in the case between Malta and Libya—the law on intervention was obscure. The subsequent decisions of the Chamber in the *Land, Island and Maritime Frontier Dispute*, and of the Court in *Land and Maritime Frontier between Cameroon and Nigeria* and *Sovereignty over Pulau Ligitan and Pulau Sipadan* constitute a jurisprudence which has much clarified the position.

Two Articles of the Statute provide for intervention by third States in proceedings before the Court: Articles 62 and 63. The first of these contemplates the situation in which a State considers that 'it has an interest of a legal nature which may be affected by the decision in the case'; it is for the State concerned to take the initiative, on the basis initially of such details of the case as may be found in the application instituting proceedings, circulated to all States entitled to appear before the Court under Article 40, paragraph 3, of the Statute.[52] The second Article contemplates the situation in which 'the construction of a convention to which other States than those concerned in the case are parties in question', and in such a case the initiative is with the Registrar to notify all such States 'forthwith'.

[52] This para. of the Art. merely requires the Registrar to 'notify' those States, whereas under para. 2 he is to 'communicate the application to all concerned', i.e. the other party or parties. In practice, however, a printed bilingual copy of the application or special agreement is sent to all States entitled to appear.

In both cases, the Statute confers upon the State a right to intervene in the proceedings. This aspect is however obscured by the fact that, while Article 63 speaks unequivocally of a 'right' to intervene,[53] Article 62 provides for a 'request to the Court to be permitted to intervene', and states that 'It shall be for the Court to decide upon this request.' However in its decision on the attempted intervention of Malta in the case of the *Continental Shelf (Libya/Tunisia)*, the Court emphasized

> that it does not consider paragraph 2 [of Article 62] to confer upon it any general discretion to accept or reject a request for permission to intervene for reasons simply of policy. On the contrary, in the view of the Court the task entrusted to it by that paragraph is to determine the admissibility or otherwise of the request by reference to the relevant provisions of the Statute.[54]

As Judge Ago however observed, commenting on this passage, in his dissenting opinion in a subsequent case, 'That, however, is not to say that the relevant provisions of the Statute speak for themselves; rather they leave room for a substantial margin of appreciation, as has been demonstrated by intermittent discussion in the Court for some 60 years.'[55]

From a historical standpoint, the form of intervention contemplated by Article 63 was the first to be developed,[56] and it will be discussed first.

(2) *Intervention under Article 63 of the Statute*

(a) Notification and procedure

The distinction just noted, between the procedure of Articles 62 and 63 of the Statute, is clearly based on the idea that the fact that the construction of a multilateral or plurilateral convention in question is something capable of objective determination; whereas it will usually only be the State itself that can say whether or not it has an interest of a legal nature likely to be affected by the decision in the case. It would hardly be possible for the Registrar to make an assessment of this kind, and issue a notification; whereas he can be expected to determine the presence of a question of

[53] It has however suggested that the decision on the application of El Salvador in the *Military Activities* case (*infra*, Section 2(B)), implies the existence of a discretion to deny intervention: Iwasawa, 'Third Parties before International Tribunals', *Liber Amicorum Judge Oda*, Vol. II, p. 887.

[54] *ICJ Reports*, 1981, p. 12, para. 17. On the importance in practice of this finding, see the declaration of Judge Kooijmans in *Sovereignty over Pulau Ligitan and Pulau Sipadan*, [2001] ICJ Rep. Judge Oda however considers that Article 62 confers a 'discretionary power' on the Court: separate opinion, [1981] ICJ Rep 24, para. 23; 'The ICJ viewed from the Bench', 244 *Recueil des cours* (1993-VII), p. 84, para. 123.

[55] *Continental Shelf (Libya/Malta)*, [1984] ICJ Rep 136, para. 14. Rosenne observes that this dictum 'merely indicates that, although the Court has a wide discretion in the matter, it is not a "general discretion" but is one to be exercised within the limits laid down by the law. The difficulty is that the law on the central question of what those limits are is far from certain.' (*The Law and Practice of the International Court, 1920–1996*, Vol. III, p. 1495, para. III.358).

[56] A comparable provision appeared in the 1899 Hague Convention in relation to arbitral proceedings; and in 1920 the first draft prepared by the Drafting Committee of the Advisory Committee of Jurists provided for intervention on the lines of Art. 63: see Torres Bernárdez, 'L'intervention dans la procédure de la CIJ', 256 *Recueil des cours* (1995), p. 242.

interpretation of a convention. In practice, of course, this is not always as easy as it looks: States sometimes cite a multilateral convention in argument without necessarily advancing an interpretation of it (except perhaps by implication).[57] The present practice is apparently to err on the generous side, and to notify in respect of any convention that is referred to by way of more than a passing mention in the pleadings of a party.[58]

One result of the distinction is this: a State will in principle only be able to rely on the application instituting proceedings in order to determine whether it has a legal interest that might be affected, and that question therefore normally only arises at that stage. If the State has reason to suspect that such an interest might be disclosed by the pleadings in the case, it can however apply to have sight of these under Article 53, paragraph 1, of the Rules.[59] On the other hand, if a multilateral convention, not mentioned in the application instituting proceedings, is subsequently relied on in argument in the pleadings, so that its construction appears to be in issue, the Registrar will at that point be called upon to notify the other States' parties.[60]

According to the text of Article 63, paragraph 2, of the Statute, 'Every State so notified has the right to intervene in the proceedings . . .'; the implication is that if one State party is overlooked, or the Registrar fails to carry out the notification at all, then the forgotten State, or all the other States parties, cannot intervene. In practice however it is the status of party that carries the right to intervene, and Article 82, paragraph 3, of the Rules recognizes that a State that has not received the notification may still file a declaration of intervention. The reverse case is less clear: if the Registrar notifies a State that is *not* a party to the convention in question, may that State insist on intervening? The text just quoted suggests that this is so; but Article 84 provides that 'The Court shall decide whether . . . an intervention under Article 63 of the Statute is admissible . . .', and an evident ground of non-admissibility would seem to be that the applicant State was not in fact a party to the convention in question.[61] Fortunately

[57] The 1899 Hague Convention (Art. 56) laid the duty of notifying third States' parties to a multilateral convention on the parties to the case themselves. The problem was the subject of discussion by the Permanent Court at the time of the 1926 revision of the Rules, when the view was taken that the right of intervention (and consequently the notification under Art. 63) should be limited to those conventions in respect of which the Court had an essential and principal jurisdiction to interpret (PCIJ Rep Series D No 2, *addendum*, p. 252).

[58] Nor is it always crystal clear which States are in fact parties to a given convention: cf. the attitude of Yugoslavia to the Genocide Convention in the cases of *Application and Interpretation of the Genocide Convention and Legality of the Use of Force*.

[59] That is not to say that it will necessarily succeed, particularly if the parties to the case object: see the cases of Malta in the *Continental Shelf (Tunisia/Libya)* case and the Philippines in the *Pulau Ligitan* case, below.

[60] Hence an intervention under Art. 63 may be made very late in the course of the proceedings: see Art. 82, para. 1, of the 1978 Rules, and cf. PCIJ Rep Series D No 2, 216.

[61] Under the 1946 Rules, the responsibility for the notification was that of the Registrar, but the 1978 Rules added a provision (Art. 43) that 'Whenever the construction of a convention to which States other than those concerned in the case are parties is in question, within the meaning of Article 63, paragraph 1, of the Statute, the Court shall consider what directions shall be given to the

the hypothesis is somewhat academic: if a State is not a party to the Convention, it would not usually have any reason to desire to argue about its interpretation.

The meaning of the expression 'a convention to which States other than those concerned in the case *are parties*' is not as clear as might be wished, particularly since the French text uses a quite different expression: 'une convention à laquelle ont participé d'autres États que les parties en litige'.[62] It is obviously directed, primarily if not exclusively, to the case of a multilateral convention to which the parties to the case and the State seeking to intervene have become parties, by ratification, accession, or whatever other means. A bilateral treaty between the parties to the case, or between one of the parties and the intending intervener, is excluded,[63] even if (for example) it is a bilateral treaty of a standard type, the interpretation of which might be taken to be significant for the interpretation of another treaty of that type, concluded with a different partner.[64] Also excluded is any treaty, whether bilateral or plurilateral, to which neither the parties to the case nor the intending intervener were parties, but which constitutes (for example) an element in a chain of title relied on both by a party to the case and by the intending intervener, but in respect of different territories. This was the situation when the Philippines sought to intervene in the case of *Sovereignty over Pulau Ligitan and Pulau Sipadan*; that intervention could, in the circumstances, only be based on Article 62 (and failed, for reasons examined below).

Article 63 clearly includes the case when the Convention has come into force, and both the parties to the case and one or more other States have signed and ratified it (or otherwise become bound by it); but is that the whole extent of the provision? What if the parties to the case and certain other States have signed and ratified a convention, but it has not yet received a sufficient number of ratifications to come into force? Rosenne suggests a distinction: citing Article 24, paragraph 4, of the Vienna

Registrar in the matter.' An error in notification thus becomes an error of the Court, more embarrassing to correct later. Furthermore, the standard letter which the Registrar sends out when so instructed is worded so as to constitute the notification under Art. 63, but with a proviso that it is without prejudice to any later decision of the Court; in effect, the Court, having interfered in the functions of the Registrar, then has to cover its tracks by a contradictory form of notification. In this respect the 1978 Rules, and practice based thereon, cannot be said to have effected an improvement. Cf. Rosenne, *The Law and Practice*, Vol. III, p. 1496, who regards the text as 'a divergence from the Statute'.

[62] See Rosenne, *The Law and Practice of the International Court, 1920–1996*, Vol. III, pp. 1489 ff.

[63] Chinkin (*Third Parties in International Law*, p. 187), writing before the decision in the *East Timor* case, suggests that in that case Indonesia should have been notified under Art. 63, since 'the negotiation of the Timor Gap Treaty [between that State and Australia] is the activity complained of by Portugal'; she concedes that 'it is arguable that the construction of the Timor Gap Treaty will not be in issue before the Court', but suggests that 'this seems an excessively formalistic argument'. Presumably she would also regard as formalistic the argument that this was not a treaty 'to which States other than those concerned in the case are parties'; but either or both of these arguments justify, in the view of the present writer, the non-notification to Indonesia.

[64] But note the observations in an earlier article in this series on the question whether treaties containing identical wording are necessarily to be given identical interpretation: [1991] *BYBIL*, pp. 66 ff.

Convention on the Law of Treaties, he suggests that States in this situation can be regarded as 'parties' for the purpose of Article 63, and all signatory States as 'parties' to the final clauses of the treaty.[65]

The modern trend towards use of multilateral conventions for codifying purposes has added one complication. A case may involve a dispute over whether a particular article in a multilateral convention does or does not represent a rule of customary international law, and at the same time a dispute over the exact scope or meaning of the alleged rule. For example, in the *Gabcikovo/Nagymaros Project* case, Slovakia relied on both Article 12 and Article 34 of the 1978 Vienna Convention on the Succession of States in respect of Treaties in order to contend that it was a party by succession to the 1977 Treaty between Hungary and Czechoslovakia which was the basis of the case. Since Hungary was not a party to the 1978 Convention, the Convention *as such* was not applicable between the parties. Was their dispute nevertheless one about the construction of a convention to which other States than those concerned in the case were parties? From one point of view, it would seem difficult to deny that such was the case, since the Court expressly found that the 1977 Treaty was one 'establishing a territorial regime *within the meaning of Article 12 of the Vienna Convention*'.[66] On the other hand, according to the terms of Article 63, if any third State party to the Convention had intervened, the construction given by the Court could only have been binding upon it 'equally' with the parties to the case; and that interpretation of the Vienna Convention was not binding on the parties as a matter of treaty law. No notification was in fact issued to States' parties to the 1978 Vienna Convention, and it is submitted that this was correct.[67]

The Convention which may be the subject of interpretation must then, it seems, be in force for both the parties to the case. An obvious difficulty arises where one party alleges that the Convention is in force, and the other party denies it. This occurred in the *Nuclear Tests* cases, where the Applicants relied, *inter alia*, on the 1928 General Act for the Pacific Settlement of International Disputes as a basis of jurisdiction, and France contended that that Convention had ceased to bind through desuetude.[68] Any notification by the Registrar might seem to imply recognition of the continued existence of the Convention; but a failure to notify might seem to imply taking the opposite position. In those cases, the Registrar did in fact notify the other parties to the General Act, without any qualifying language:[69] it is submitted that it is correct, and

[65] Op.cit., p. 1493. The latter would thus only be notified if the dispute related to the interpretation of one of the final clauses. Cf. the PCIJ ruling in the *Free Zones* case (text and n. 70 below).

[66] [1997] ICJ Rep 72, para. 123.

[67] There is of course a textual problem in that Art. 63 refers to States 'other than those concerned in the case' being parties, with the implication (or perhaps the assumption) that it is not applicable unless the parties to the case are also both parties to the Convention.

[68] See a previous article in this series: [1992] *BYBIL*, pp. 94 ff.

[69] *Pleadings*, Vol. II, p. 384, No. 99; and cf. the criticisms of Judge Petrén, [1973] ICJ Rep 125 and 160. In subsequent cases, a new form of notification has been adopted (for examples see *Border and*

does not involve any prejudgment, to make the notification on the basis of an assertion by one party that the interpretation of a multilateral convention is in question.[70]

In modern multilateral conventions it is rare to find provisions that are applicable only to one State, or to certain specified States, but this was the case of the 1919 Treaty of Versailles; and the Permanent Court appears to have interpreted Article 63 as inapplicable when the dispute was related such a provision, which could be regarded as of no concern to other States.[71]

(b) The jurisprudence

In the *Haya de la Torre* case, an intervention by Cuba was admitted under Article 63; the case was commented on briefly by Fitzmaurice in his series of articles in this *Year Book*.[72] During the period under review, however, the only further recourse that has been had to this Article was the attempt by El Salvador to intervene on that basis in the *Military and Paramilitary Activities* case, which was rejected by the Court as being addressed to questions whose treatment would be premature in the stage of the proceedings devoted to jurisdiction; and the intervention was not renewed at the merits stage.[73]

This intervention, if it had been examined by the Court, would have raised the question whether it is possible to rely on Article 63 in order to intervene in a preliminary phase of the proceedings, and in particular a phase devoted to questions of jurisdiction and admissibility. [74] If for example a case is brought on the basis of the compromissory clause in a multilateral convention, the interpretation of that clause may be of interest to all the other States parties (or at least those of them who have not made a reservation to the clause).[75] It would therefore seem that

Transborder Armed Actions, Pleadings, Oral Arguments, Documents, Vol. II, pp. 233–4, No. 14), which informs the addressee State of the situation and then goes on to deny that it constitutes a notification under Article 63 (like Byron's lady who 'swearing she would ne'er consent—consented').

[70] In some cases, the question whether the convention was in force, or was in force for the parties to the case, might itself depend on a question of the interpretation of the convention, though this was not so in the *Nuclear Tests* cases, where the alleged cause of invalidity was *ab extra*.

[71] See the *Free Zones* case, PCIJ Rep Series A/B No 46, 100, and Rosenne, *The Law and Practice of the International Court, 1920–1996*, Vol. III, p. 1490.

[72] [1958] *BYBIL*, pp. 126–8; *Collected Edition*, Vol. I, pp. 553–5.

[73] [1984] ICJ Rep 215. For comment see the article of Rogers, Beat and Wolf, 'Application of El Salvador to Intervene in the Jurisdiction and Admissibility Phase of Nicaragua *v.* United States' in *AJIL*, 1984, p. 929, and that of Sztucki, 'Intervention under Article 63 of the ICJ Statute in the Phase of Preliminary Proceedings', ibid., p. 1005.

[74] This question was not clearly decided in the *Military and Paramilitary Activities* case, though that decision has been read as rejecting in principle an intervention at the stage of jurisdiction: e.g. Günther, 'Zulässigkeit und Grenzen der Intervention bei Streitigkeiten vor dem IGH', 34 *German Yearbook of International Law*, 1991, p. 290.

[75] For example, the effect of Article IX of the Genocide Convention was in question in the case brought by Bosnia and Herzegovina against Yugoslavia (Serbia and Montenegro). The Court interpreted that clause as permitting one State to seise the Court of a dispute alleging the responsibility of another State for a breach of the Convention. However, an alternative interpretation which is eminently arguable was that advanced by Judge Oda in his declaration in the case, that a failure to

there is no reason why intervention under Article 63 should not be possible to argue a question of jurisdiction or admissibility, if that question involves the interpretation of a multilateral treaty.[76] Sir Hersch Lauterpacht would have favoured intervention under Article 63 of States parties to the Statute itself, when the question arose, in the *Norwegian Loans* case, of the effect of an optional-clause declaration subject to an invalid condition.[77] The practice of the Court has been to make the notification required by Article 63, paragraph 1, to the parties to a multilateral convention where such a convention is invoked as a basis for the jurisdiction of the Court (but not simply where questions of interpretation of the Statute may arise).

The decision on the intervention of El Salvador is not inconsistent with this practice; the intervention was not rejected on the basis of any general finding that intervention at a jurisdictional phase is premature, though the handling of the matter by the Court was less than adroit, and thus lent it itself to misunderstanding on the point.

Notwithstanding the paucity of the jurisprudence, examination of intervention under Article 63 may be of interest for such light as that provision may throw on the interpretation of Article 62.[78]

(c) The effect of an intervention under Article 63

Article 63, paragraph 2, of the Statute provides that if a State exercises its right to intervene as a party to a convention the interpretation of which is in question, 'the construction given by the judgment will be equally binding upon it'. The word 'equally' implies 'on the same footing as the parties', thus it is assumed that the judgment will in fact give an authoritative interpretation of the convention. If the eventual judgment is upon some other basis, so that there is no authoritative interpretation of the convention, then the intervening State is not bound in any way.

A question of at least theoretical interest—but perhaps only of theoretical interest—is whether a State intervening under Article 63 is to be regarded as a party to the case. For some commentators, a confrontation of Article 63, paragraph 2, of the Statute with Article 59 necessarily leads to the conclusion that the intervening State is a party.[79] It is however also possible to read Article 63 as an implied exception to Article 59; or

comply with the Convention could not be raised as a matter of State responsibility and brought before the Court under Art. IX ([1996-II] ICJ Rep 626 ff.). Theoretically, other states might have wished to argue for this interpretation; politically, however, this would have carried unwelcome implications.

[76] In this sense, Rosenne, *Interpretation in the International Court of Justice*, p. 89; Espaliù Berdud, *Desarrollos jurisprudenciales y práctica reciente en la jurisdicción de la CIJ*, p. 289.

[77] Separate opinion, *Certain Norwegian Loans, ICJ Reports*, 1957, p. 64.

[78] Cf. on this, for example, Jennings in [1984] ICJ Rep 156–7.

[79] In this sense, for example, the authors cited in Cellamare, *Le forme di intervento nel processo dinanzi alla Corte internazionale di giustizia*, pp. 214–15. The opposite view is taken by, for example, Günther, 'Zulässigkeit und Grenzen der Intervention bei Streitigkeiten vor dem IGH', 34 *German Yearbook of International Law*, 1991, p. 288, and the authors cited by Cellamare, op.cit., pp. 216–22.

to concentrate on the distinction between the binding effect of the *judgment* (Article 59) and that of the *construction of the convention* contained in the judgment (Article 63). Since it is clear that it is no more than the construction of the convention that is binding, it is not apparent what practical difference it makes whether the intervening State is or is not classified as a 'party' to the case; the *res judicata*, in relation to the intervener must be limited to the interpretation given to the convention. On the theoretical level, arguments from Article 63 have however been used to support interpretations of Article 62, on the question of the status of 'party' of a State intervening under Article 62, but the value of such arguments is not evident.

A State party to the convention that does not choose to intervene can point to Article 59 of the Statute, and argue *a contrario* from Article 63, so as to claim that the interpretation given by the Court is not binding upon it.[80] The difficulty for a State in this position is that, as Judge Oda has pointed out, regardless of this legal postulate,

> there is little doubt that, in a case where the interpretation of a particular convention is in dispute, the interpretation placed upon it by the Court in a previous case will tend to prevail. In this sense there will not be much difference between those States which have intervened in a case and those States which have not intervened, as far as the practical effect of the Court's interpretation of an international convention is concerned.[81]

This creates something of a dilemma for a State which is relying on a particular convention in a case before the Court, when the same convention is also being invoked in other current cases, which may come to trial first. Should it intervene in such cases, in order to assert the interpretation on which it will be relying in its own case?[82]

(3) *Intervention under Article 62 of the Statute*

(a) Introduction

At the time Fitzmaurice was writing, no intervention had been made under Article 62 of the Statute,[83] and his comments on that procedure, based simply on an examination of the text of the Article,[84] were by way of prevision of the problems that were likely to arise. In recent years

[80] This was expressly stated to be so in the Report of the Advisory Committee of Jurists adopted by the Council of the League on 27 October 1920 (see Stauffenberg, *Statut et Règlement de la CPJI: éléments d'interprétation*, p. 443).

[81] 'The International Court of Justice viewed from the Bench (1976–1993)', 244 *Recueil des cours*, 1993-VII, p. 79.

[82] An evident current example is the Genocide Convention, relied on by Bosnia and Herzegovina in *Application of the Genocide Convention*, by Serbia and Montenegro in the *Legality of the Use of Force* cases, and by the Democratic Republic of the Congo in the cases of *Armed Actions on the Territory of the Congo*, brought by it against Uganda and Rwanda.

[83] Fitzmaurice discusses Art. 62 of the Statute from the standpoint of jurisdiction: [1988] *BYBIL*, pp. 23–8; *Collected Edition*, Vol. II, pp. 550–5.

[84] For a brief survey of the drafting of Art. 62, see the decision on the request of Malta to intervene in the *Continental Shelf (Tunisia/Libya)* case, [1981] ICJ Rep 13–14, para. 22.

a number of applications have been made under that Article, and the Court has had to tackle a number of difficult questions, some of which were among those that Fitzmaurice had foreseen.

Article 62 provides as follows, in the two official languages:

1. Should a State consider that it has an interest of a legal nature which may be affected by the decision in the case, it may submit a request to the Court to be permitted to intervene [as a third party].
2. It shall be for the Court to decide upon the request.

1. Lorsqu'un État estime que, dans un differend, un intérêt d'ordre juridique est en cause, il peut adresser à la Cour une requête, à fin d'intervention.
2. La Cour décide.

In the English text the words in brackets, which were included in the 1922 text,[85] were deleted from the text adopted in 1946; it was stated by the Committee of Jurists that drafted the post-war Statute that this deletion was not intended to change the sense of the text,[86] but it was doubtful at the time, and subsequently, what *was* the sense of the text. The French text adopted in 1946 is identical with that drawn up for the Permanent Court; as will be apparent, it contained nothing to correspond to the words 'as a third party'; yet the Court in 1981 suggested that at the time of the establishment and revision of the Rules of the Permanent Court, 'it seems to have been assumed that a State permitted to intervene under Article 62 would become a "party" to the case'.[87]

It is evident that the text is by way of a blank cheque, to be filled in by the Court as and when applications might be made to it for permission to intervene: the draftsmen of the Statute did no more than indicate that there might be circumstances in which a State might desire to intervene, and the Court might consider it appropriate to allow this; but the conditions, modalities, and effects of such an intervention were not specified, and it is probable that the draftsmen had no very clear idea of what they should be.[88] Among the unanswered questions prompted by the text, one might mention the following: What sort of 'interest of a legal nature' would have to be shown, and in what way could the Court's decision affect it? Does the Court enjoy a wholly independent jurisdiction to admit and pass upon an intervention, or must the intervening State be able to show that the Court would have had jurisdiction over a claim made by it directly against one or both of the parties? What procedural or other rights would the third State acquire by being permitted to intervene? Or, in other words, what difference would it make to the legal situation, and to the Court's powers of decision, if an intervention were sought and

[85] Though not in the original draft: see [1981] ICJ Rep 14, para. 22.

[86] Report of the Committee of Jurists, cited in [1981] ICJ Rep 15, para. 25.

[87] [1981] ICJ Rep 14, para. 24; *contra*, Judge Oda, ibid., p. 24.

[88] The number of drafts of a text on intervention submitted during the work of the 1920 Commission of Jurists demonstrated the varying views as to the nature and function of intervention: see Torres Bernárdez, 'L'intervention dans la procédure de la CIJ', 256 *Recueil des cours* (1995), p. 243.

admitted, as compared with the situation if the third State took no action? Would the intervening State become a party to the case, or be otherwise bound by the decision?[89]

The Rules of Court relating to intervention, adopted first by the Permanent Court and subsequently by the post-war Court, did not purport to regulate any of these questions, but merely laid down an orderly procedure for the making of applications for permission to intervene, and their handling by the Court. This was the result of a conscious decision by the members of the Permanent Court, in face of controversy over the proper interpretation of the Statute. The procedure laid down was, naturally enough, to be *contradictoire*, and the possibility was recognized that one or both of the parties might oppose the intervention; this fact was therefore presumably regarded as a material factor for the Court, but there is no implication that the consent of the original parties would be required, or might be determinative. The 1946 Rules of Court[90] followed those of the Permanent Court; but when the Rules were revised in 1978, the new texts,[91] while in principle still limited to practical procedural issues, contained one innovation. A State applying for permission to intervene was henceforth to indicate in its application, *inter alia*, 'any basis of jurisdiction which is claimed to exist as between the State applying to intervene and the parties to the case'. The significance of this addition will be examined below.

It will be convenient to enumerate at this point the applications for permission to intervene under Article 62 submitted since 1973:

(i) In 1973 Fiji sought to intervene in the *Nuclear Tests* proceedings brought by Australia and New Zealand against France, seeking a cessation of atmospheric nuclear testing at Mururoa, on the grounds of injury to their populations from fall-out from the tests. When the claims of the Applicants were found to be moot, the application of Fiji to intervene also ceased to have any object.[92]

(ii) In 1980 Malta sought to intervene in the proceedings in the case of the *Continental Shelf (Tunisia/Libya)*, whereby those two States asked the Court to determine the international legal principles and rules applicable to the delimitation of their continental shelves; Malta's application was rejected.[93]

(iii) In 1984 Italy sought to intervene in the case of the *Continental Shelf (Libya/Malta)*, a further case concerning the law applicable to continental shelf delimitation; Italy's application was rejected.[94]

(iv) In 1989 Nicaragua sought to intervene in the *Land, Island and Maritime Frontier Dispute* between El Salvador and Honduras; the

[89] A further unforeseen problem, though of rather a different nature, was that of the procedure on an application to intervene in a case being heard by a Chamber of the Court; this problem has already been examined in a previous article in this series: [2001] *BYBIL*, pp. 52–5.

[90] 1946 Rules of Court, Art. 64–5.

[91] 1978 Rules of Court, Arts. 81, 83–5.

[92] *Orders of 20 December 1974*, [1974] ICJ Rep 530 and 535.

[93] *Judgment of 14 April 1981*, [1981] ICJ Rep 3.

[94] *Judgment of 21 March 1984*, [1984] ICJ Rep 3.

Court decided that the application should be dealt with by the Chamber that had been formed to deal with the case,[95] and that Chamber accepted the intervention so far as it related to the dispute over the 'legal situation of the maritime spaces' within and without the Gulf of Fonseca, but rejected it so far as concerned delimitation of those spaces.[96]

(v) When New Zealand endeavoured to reopen the *Nuclear Tests* cases by bringing in 1995 its *Request for an Examination of the Situation*, a number of Pacific island States applied to intervene in the proceedings (see Section 5(3) above). The dismissal of that request entailed the dismissal of the applications to intervene.[97]

(vi) In 1999 Equatorial Guinea sought to intervene in the case concerning the *Land and Maritime Boundary between Cameroon and Nigeria*, a further maritime delimitation case. The parties did not object, and the Court, by an Order, admitted the intervention.[98]

(vii) In 2001 the Philippines sought to intervene in the case concerning *Sovereignty over Pulau Ligitan and Pulau Sipadan* between Indonesia and Malaysia; the dispute was as to sovereignty over two small islands. The interest of the Philippines was somewhat indirect, being to safeguard its historical and legal rights in respect of sovereignty over North Borneo, which it apparently thought might be affected if the Court were to decide in a particular way on a certain treaty. The application was rejected.[99]

Some at least of the questions left open by the text of Article 62 have now been answered, both by the decisions admitting applications to intervene, and by those refusing such applications. In the two cases in which interventions have been admitted, the decisions on the merits are significant as demonstrating the impact of an intervention on the proceedings. These various decisions, particularly those rejecting an intervention, are however lengthy, not always consistent, and accompanied by extensive separate and dissenting opinions. The subject still remains a controversial one, as witness the immense amount of scholarly writing that has been devoted to it.[100] The present writer is therefore faced again with the problem that full treatment of an issue of procedural law would have to be so extensive as to unbalance

[95] *Order of 28 February 1990*, [1990] ICJ Rep 3; see a previous article in this series, [2001] *BYBIL*, pp. 53–5.

[96] *Judgment of 13 September 1990*, [1990] ICJ Rep 92.

[97] *Order of 22 September 1995*, [1995] ICJ Rep 306–7. The applications were 'dismissed', whereas in the *Nuclear* Tests cases the applications of Fiji were found to 'lapse' (see the Orders cited in n. 92 above).

[98] *Order of 21 October 1999*, [1999] ICJ Rep 1029.

[99] *Order of 23 October 2001*, [2001] ICJ Rep 575.

[100] Some of this has become obsolete as a result of the decision of a Chamber of the Court in 1990, in the *Land, Island and Maritime Frontier Dispute*, to admit an intervention for the first time; literature since that date however includes Cellamare, *Le forme di intervento nel processo dinanzi alla Corte Internazionale di Giustizia*, 1991; the monograph of Rosenne, *Intervention in the International Court of Justice* (Nijhoff, 1993); the Hague Academy course of Torres Bernárdez, 'L'intervention dans la procédure de la Cour internationale de justice', 256 *Recueil des cours*, 1995, p. 193; and numerous articles: Oellers-Frahm, 'Überlegungen anlässlich der Zulassung der Intervention

this series of studies.[101] A further difficulty in analysing the subject results from the fact that several of the questions enumerated above (and, indeed, others not yet mentioned) turn out to be intimately linked. Furthermore, the decision in the *Land, Island and Maritime Frontier Dispute* has introduced what from one point of view is a complication (though from another, it is a simplification): the finding that there are, apparently, in fact two kinds of intervention possible under Article 62: intervention as a party, and intervention as a non-party, the conditions for each, and the effects, being thus different. Nevertheless, the attempt will here be made to treat the various questions *seriatim*, and if it is not possible to pursue every hare that has been started (particularly in judges' opinions), it is hoped that all the main issues will have been expounded.

(b) What is intervention?

When the Permanent Court at its initial session came to consider the drafting of Rules of Court applying to intervention, it became apparent that there was no clear and established view as to what intervention actually was—or rather would be, since it was an innovation in international procedure, being hardly possible except before a standing tribunal.[102] There were, broadly speaking, two approaches. One saw intervention as a means for a State to bring before the Court issues in dispute between itself and one or other of the parties, issues which were the same as, or linked with, those already raised by the original proceedings;[103] the result of a successful application to intervene, and a successful intervention,

Nicaraguas im Streit zwischen El Salvador und Honduras', 50 *Zeitschrift für ausländisches öffentliches Recht und Völkerrecht*, 1990, p. 795; Kohen, 'La requête à fin d'intervention du Nicaragua dans l'affaire du différend frontalier, terrestre et maritime', 36 *Annuaire français de droit international*, 1990, p. 341; Günther, 'Zulässigkeit und Grenzen der Intervention bei Streitigkeiten vor dem IGH', 34 *German Yearbook of International Law*, 1991, p. 254; de Hoogh, 'Intervention under Article 62 of the Statute and the Quest for Incidental Jurisdiction without the Consent of the Parties', 6 *Leiden Journal of International Law*, 1993, p. 17; Macdonald and Hughes, 'Intervention before the International Court of Justice', 5 *African Journal of International and Comparative Law*, 1993, p. 1; Riquelme Cortado, 'Las claves de la limitada autorización de intervención de Nicaragua en la controversia insular y maritima entre Honduras y El Salvador', 44 *Revista española de derecho internacional*, 1992, p. 25; Ruda, 'Intervention before the International Court of Justice', in Lowe and Fitzmaurice (eds.), *Fifty years of the International Court of Justice, (Mélanges Jennings)*, 1996, p. 541. For an earlier bibliography, see the dissenting opinion of Judge Ago appended to the judgment of 21 March 1984 rejecting Italy's application in the *Continental Shelf (Libya/Malta)* case: [1984] ICJ Rep 115–16, n. 1.

[101] See the introduction to the part of this series devoted to procedure, [2000] *BYBIL*, pp. 158–9.

[102] The draft Règlement for arbitral procedure prepared by the *Institut de droit international* in 1875 recognized the possibility of 'intervention spontanée d'un tiers' with the consent of the original parties. Intervention of the kind contemplated by Art. 63, where a multilateral convention falls to be interpreted in the case, was foreseen in the context of arbitration by the 1899 Hague Convention, Art. 56. A practical problem is however the lack of publicity of arbitration proceedings: even before the ICJ, it may be difficult for a third State to ascertain exactly what is going to be litigated, as was the experience of the Philippines in *Sovereignty over Pulau Ligitan and Pulau Sipadan*.

[103] This was from the outset the sole type of intervention recognized by the Statute of the Court of Justice of the European Communities, under Art. 34 of the Statute of ECSC and Art. 37 of the Statute of the EEC. See now Art. 40 of the Statute of the European Court of Justice. The Statute of ITLOS (Art. 31) uses the same wording as Art. 62 of the ICJ Statute: see the comments of Judge Sette-Camara, dissenting opinion in *Continental Shelf (Libya/Malta)*, [1984] ICJ Rep 88–9.

would be a decision of the Court which was in some sense in favour of the intervening State. The other approach saw the role of the intervening State as limited to the expression of its opinion on the legal issues raised in the original proceedings, insofar as these were relevant also to the position of the intervening State; the eventual decision of the Court might prove to have been influenced by the contentions of the intervener, but would not in terms give that State any direct satisfaction of a claim.

These approaches could each find support in the provisions for intervention in municipal legal systems, which the members of the Commission of Jurists no doubt had in mind. They did not have available a comparative-law study of such provisions; but when in the *Continental Shelf (Tunisia/Libya)* case Malta, in support of its application to intervene, commissioned such a study, its author concluded that municipal law showed the existence of two kinds of intervention, *intervention accessoire* and *intervention principale*, corresponding closely to the two schools of thought revealed in the discussions of 1920.[104]

The first view found expression in the Report of the 1920 Commission of Jurists, which introduced the text on the 'right of intervention', which was to become Article 62,[105] as follows:

> There are three possibilities: a party may wish to take sides with the plaintiff or the defendant; a party may claim certain exclusive rights; or a party may request that one of the two contesting States should withdraw on the ground that it is not the real *dominus* of the right which it claims.[106]

The second view was however not absent from the discussions of 1920 and, as we shall see, is in effect the view that has prevailed in the jurisprudence. Attention may however be drawn here to the repeated use, in the passage just quoted, of the word 'party': one influence of municipal law thinking has been to lead some commentators to start from the premise that intervention of its nature involves becoming a party to the proceedings in which intervention is made.[107] A merit of the 1990 decision of the Chamber in the *Land, Island and Maritime Frontier Dispute*, to be examined below, was to sever this unjustified link, and recognize the possibility of intervention as a non-party, with a purpose other than that of pressing an individual claim against one or both parties.

[104] See the study of Prof. Habscheid, *Continental Shelf (Tunisia/Libya), Pleadings, Vol. III*, pp. 479–80.

[105] Curiously enough, the actual text proposed for the article on intervention was omitted from the Report, but this seems to have been a simple oversight, and it is reasonably clear to what text the Report was referring: see Rosenne, *Intervention in the International Court of Justice*, p. 23.

[106] *Report of the Commission of Jurists*, p. 745. On the second possibility, cf. Jennings in [1984] ICJ Rep 149. Cf. the categories of intervention *ad adjuvandum and ad excludendum* cited by Judge Jiménez de Aréchaga from Italian civil procedure, in his opinion in the *Libya/Malta* case: [1984] ICJ Rep 67–8, para. 34.

[107] Thus Cellamare (*Le forme di intervento nel processo dinanzi alla Corte internazionale di giustizia*, pp. 214 ff.) argues that an intervener under Art. 63 must, as a matter of principle, be a party to the proceedings, and rejects the view of the Chamber in the *Land, Island and Maritime Frontier* case that Nicaragua's intervention did not make it a party, essentially on the same ground of principle (op. cit., pp. 71 ff., section 7).

Whichever view was adopted, according to the terms of Article 62 of the Statute, the State seeking to intervene would have to show the existence of some 'interest of a legal nature' of its own; and that that interest would be somehow be *en cause*, or affected by the decision. This latter consideration took shape in the jurisprudence as a quest for identification of the 'object of the intervention'. Furthermore, the institution of intervention had to be understood in a sense consistent with Article 59 of the Statute, according to which 'The decision of the Court has no binding force except between the parties and in respect of that particular case'.[108] If decisions of the Court were always to be *res inter alios acta* in relation to third States, why should third States need a means of interfering in the litigation? Or, to put it another way, how could a decision whose legal effects were strictly limited to the parties to the case 'affect' in any way the 'legal interest' of another State?[109] This is a question to be examined further in Section C below.

The need for a coherent system of intervention has been increased by the development of the law of maritime delimitation, and the practice (initiated in the *North Sea Continental Shelf* case) of asking the Court to declare the applicable rules and principles of law, or even to draw the actual delimitation line. If two States request the Court to determine the course of the delimitation between their respective continental shelves (or other maritime zones), a third State fronting on the same or a nearby area of sea may well fear that the Court, hearing only the contentions of the two States' parties, may extend the line into areas claimed by the third State; or draw it in such a way as otherwise to prejudice any future delimitation to be negotiated between the third State and one or both of the parties; or make findings of law prejudicial to the pretensions of the third State. As we shall see, this was the motivation of the applications to intervene made by Malta in the case of the *Continental Shelf (Tunisia/Libya)*, by Italy in the case of the *Continental Shelf (Libya/Malta)*, by Nicaragua in the *Land, Island and Maritime Frontier Dispute* between El Salvador and Honduras, and by Equatorial Guinea in the case of the *Land and Maritime Boundary between Cameroon and Nigeria*. At first sight, the third State appears again to be protected by Article 59 of the Statute: but the situation was less clear,[110] and it is no occasion for surprise that States preferred to take a step that seemed to promise some protection.

[108] In fact, in the drafting process, the text that became Art. 59 was included at a later stage than the text that became Art. 62, on the initiative of the Council of the League; it is however clear from the *travaux préparatoires* that the relationship between the two Arts. was not overlooked—indeed, the need for Art. 59 was seen as flowing from, *inter alia*, the inclusion of Art. 62. See Rosenne, *Intervention in the International Court of Justice*, pp. 27–8, citing the 1921 Bourgeois Report to the League Council.

[109] Cf. the problem that arises on requests for provisional measures, in the light of the dictum in the *South-Eastern Greenland* case that action taken *pendente lite* cannot affect the legal situation, so that theoretically no measures for the preservation of rights would ever be necessary; see the discussion in the previous article in this series, [2001] *BYBIL*, pp. 91–2.

[110] Cf. the distinction that was to be made in the *Frontier Dispute* case between the status of a judicial finding as to the position of a land boundary as *res inter alios acta* for third States, and the more complex situation as regards a maritime boundary: [1986] ICJ Rep 578, para. 47.

(i) First approach: intervention to press a claim: the jurisdictional problem

The simplest example—at first sight—of an intervention as understood on the basis of the first approach would be that in which the third State seeks to invoke the same wrongful act as that relied on by the Applicant in the original proceedings, and to complain that the consequences of that act are felt in the same way by the intending intervener. This is exemplified by the case of Fiji in the *Nuclear Tests* cases, where it was claimed that the fall-out from the French atmospheric tests at Mururoa had the same impact on Fiji and its population as it did on Australia and New Zealand.[111] Since the case was brought to a premature end by the finding that the Applicants' claims no longer had any object, the application by Fiji to intervene fell by the wayside, and the Court did not rule upon it. In effect, Fiji was not merely claiming that it had an interest that would be affected by the decision; it was claiming that it had a legal right that was being infringed by the acts of France complained of. But how would that right or interest be *en cause* in the case, let alone affected *by the decision*? The cases as such concerned solely the rights of the two Applicants, Australia and New Zealand. If the decision went in favour of the Applicants, Fiji would be politically in a strong position (despite the terms of Article 59 of the Statute) to assert France's responsibility toward Fiji; contrariwise, if the decision went in favour of France, on the merits, Fiji could hardly continue to press an independent claim against France. The implication of Article 62 is however that being permitted to intervene will make a difference to the *legal* situation. So far as Fiji is concerned, a decision taken in its absence will have no *legal* impact; and as regards the States originally parties to the case, it is to be presumed that the Court's decision on the claims of the Applicant will be correct, whether or not the third State is involved in the proceedings.

However, another problem with the first approach to intervention is that it appears to conflict with the basic principle of consent as the basis of the Court's jurisdiction. If a State could take advantage of the fact that proceedings had been brought, on the basis of a jurisdictional title valid between applicant and respondent but no further, to graft on to those proceedings a claim of its own, and in effect obtain judgment upon it, it would have done so despite the absence of any consent of the respondent creative of jurisdiction between itself and the intervening State.[112] All States parties to the Statute have consented to the exercise by the Court of its incidental jurisdiction: the *compétence de la compétence* under Article 36,

[111] When New Zealand attempted to reopen the case in 1995, there was a rush of applications to intervene: from Australia, the Solomon Islands, the Marshall Islands, and Micronesia, but not (oddly enough) from Fiji: see [1995] ICJ Rep 292.

[112] The problem of the 'jurisdictional link' is most evident where the intervener wishes to become a co-plaintiff, but it could also arise where it sought to be a co-defendant. As Judge Gros did not fail to point out in his dissenting opinion in the *Nuclear Tests* cases ([1974] ICJ Rep 280–1), at one time the UK Government had carried out nuclear tests on Australian territory, with the consent of Australia: if Fiji (for example) had brought proceedings against Australia, on the basis of a jurisdictional title unique to Fiji and Australia, could the UK have intervened to defend its actions?

paragraph 6, and the jurisdiction to indicate provisional measures under Article 41; but can Article 62 be read as creating an incidental jurisdiction so wide as to take the place of merits jurisdiction in any case in which, fortuitously, proceedings on a related matter have been brought by another State?

One way round the difficulty is to suppose that intervention—or at least intervention of that kind—is only possible if the intervening State could have brought independent proceedings against the respondent State, on the basis of a jurisdictional instrument binding on the two of them (and possibly on the applicant State also). This would suppose the existence of a condition precedent to intervention, not mentioned in the Statute. In the *Nuclear Tests* cases, the Orders of the Court finding that Fiji's application lapsed with the termination of the main proceedings were accompanied by declarations by six of the judges (Gros, Onyeama, Dillard, Waldock, Jiménez de Aréchaga, and Judge *ad hoc* Barwick); Judge Gros merely stated that Fiji's application 'could not in any way be regarded as a request to intervene, within the meaning of Article 62', but the other judges made it quite clear that, at the least, if the case had continued 'the issue of Fiji's intervention would have required examination in order to determine whether or not there existed a sufficient jurisdictional link between Fiji and France to justify the former's intervention under Article 62'.[113]

This supposition however prompts the question: if the intention underlying Article 62 is that an intervener must, if it is to ask for direct relief, be able to rely on an existing title of jurisdiction vis-à-vis the parties, what is the point of intervention? It may bring about some procedural economy, from the point of view of the Court, but does not offer the would-be intervener any very noticeable advantage, and is likely to be regarded as, at the very least, a nuisance by the original parties. Such an interpretation of Article 62 would mean that intervention is only legally possible when it is not necessary.

Furthermore, if such had been the intention of the Statute, it would have been to be expected that the existence of such a 'jurisdictional link', as it came to be called, would have been indicated in Article 62 as a condition of intervention.[114] This was the reason why in 1922 the President of

[113] Declaration of Judges Dillard and Waldock, [1974] ICJ Rep 532. The other judges went further, indicating that they would have rejected Fiji's application on the ground that there was no such link: ibid., pp. 532–3.

[114] One theory why no such condition was included was that, since the original plan for the Permanent Court of International Justice had involved universal compulsory jurisdiction over disputes between parties to the Statute, such a qualification of Art. 62 would have been unnecessary; and that when the intended compulsory jurisdiction was replaced by the system of the optional clause, the need to make provision in Art. 62 for jurisdiction was simply overlooked. Unfortunately this theory does not survive close examination of the process of drafting of the PCIJ Statute: see Jiménez de Aréchaga, separate opinion, *Continental Shelf (Libya/Malta)*, [1984] ICJ Rep 55, paras. 2–3; Oda, dissenting opinion, ibid., p. 96, para.13; Rosenne, *The Law and Practice of the International Court of Justice*, Vol. III, pp. 1485–6. For a fuller survey, see the Annex, 'La thèse de l'existence d'une "condition juridictionnelle implicite" dans l'article 62 ne trouve aucun fondement dans les travaux

the Permanent Court (Loder) declined even to put to the vote a proposal by Judge Anzilotti that the rules should contain such a condition on intervention, because he considered that the Court could not, in the Rules, cut down a right given to States by the Statute.[115]

This consideration also explains the existence, and the limited scope, of the modification, referred to above, made in the revised Rules of Court of 1978, Article 81, paragraph 2(*c*), with its requirement that an intending intervener indicate 'any basis of jurisdiction which is claimed to exist'; it is reasonable to suppose that it was the case of Fiji that had focused attention on the problem, and led the Court to lay down some requirement related to jurisdiction.[116] There remained however the problem raised by Judge Loder in 1922: could the right of intervention be limited, in the Rules, by a condition not provided for in the Statute? This consideration probably explains why the Rules do not state in terms that an intervention which cannot point to an existing title of jurisdiction can, for that reason alone, be rejected; and the Chamber in the *Land, Island and Maritime Frontier Dispute* rejected an objection based on that argument.[117]

The Court later explained the motivation of the new rule as follows: it had introduced the new text

> in order to ensure that, when the question did arise in a concrete case, it would be in possession of all the elements which might be necessary for its decision. At the same time the Court left any question with which it might in future be confronted in regard to intervention to be decided on the basis of the Statute and in the light of the particular circumstances of each case.[118]

The explanation does not however satisfy: if the Court was leaving open any question relating to intervention, why modify the existing rules on the subject? It was also to be supposed that if a State applying to intervene could show a jurisdictional title, it would not fail to mention it: the judges' declarations in the *Nuclear Tests* cases had already sufficed to draw the attention of practitioners to the point.

One may suspect another explanation: that the Court was divided, just as the Permanent Court had been in 1922, between those who wished to see a jurisdictional link made a condition of intervention, and those who feared that to do so would be incompatible with the Statute. On that basis, paragraph 2(*c*) looks like a compromise, and an unhappy one. Furthermore, while it was probably wise both in 1922 and 1978 not to try to regulate intervention without the experience of one or more actual

de 1920 sur le Statut', to the course of Torres Bernárdez, 'L'intervention dans la procédure de la CIJ', 256 *Recueil des cours*, 1995, p. 443.

[115] *PCIJ Series D, No. 2*, p. 96.

[116] In this sense Ago, dissenting opinion in *Continental Shelf (Libya/Malta)* [1984] ICJ Rep 116–17, para. 5.

[117] [1990] ICJ Rep 111, para. 44. Cf. also the dissenting opinion of Judge Weeramantry on the request of the Philippines to intervene in *Sovereignty over Pulau Ligitan and Pulau Sipadan* [2001] ICJ Rep 646–7, para. 28.

[118] *Continental Shelf (Tunisia/Libya), Application of Malta to Intervene* [1981] ICJ Rep 16, para. 27.

cases, it is impossible to evade the hard truth that a question of consistency with the Statute is one of principle, one that does not depend on 'the particular circumstances of each case', though those circumstances might assist in making the issue of principle more clear-cut. To say that the existence of a jurisdictional link '*might* be necessary' for the Court's decision, and therefore the Court should arrange to be informed on the point, is loose thinking: if the Loder view was correct, the existence of a jurisdictional link would always be irrelevant.

The text of Article 81, paragraph 2(*c*), of the Rules of Court, and the declarations and opinions in the *Nuclear Tests* cases, did however suggest that a jurisdictional link might be required in certain circumstances, or for a certain kind of intervention, but the position otherwise remained obscure.

(ii) Second approach: intervention to inform the Court

After the *Nuclear Tests* cases, no further attempt was made to intervene in a case in order openly to press a claim parallel to that of the Applicant. The next occasion on which an application was made to intervene was the application made by Malta in the case concerning the *Continental Shelf (Tunisia/Libya)*. The purpose of this intervention was more difficult to characterise, and the relevance (if any) of a jurisdictional link less clear-cut.

Malta's request was at first sight an excellent example of the non-contentious sort of intervention that, according to the second approach, was what Article 62 was designed for. Tunisia and Libya had, by special agreement, asked the Court to indicate 'the principles and rules of international law which may be applied for the delimitation' of their respective areas of continental shelf in the Mediterranean.[119] Malta had claims to areas of continental shelf in the same region, and had not concluded any delimitation agreement with either Tunisia or Libya. It applied for permission to intervene in the case in order to protect its position; but in what way did that position need protection, taking into account Article 59 of the Statute?

The Court noted as, apparently, a defect in Malta's application for permission to intervene that it

> seeks permission to enter into the proceedings in the case but to do so without assuming the obligations of a party to the case within the meaning of the Statute, and in particular Article 59 under which the decision in the case would hereafter be binding upon Malta in its relations with Libya and Tunisia.[120]

The Court did not however examine the question whether, in such a case, there might be no need for a 'jurisdictional link'; it rejected the application for other reasons, and then added that it found it 'unnecessary' to decide 'whether the existence of a valid link of jurisdiction with the parties to the case is an essential condition for the granting of permission

[119] Special Agreement, Art. 1, set out in [1982] ICJ Rep 21.

[120] [1981] ICJ Rep 18, para. 32.

to intervene under Article 62 of the Statute'.[121] While this may be no more than an instance of judicial caution, it does suggest that the prevailing view was that even for 'non-party' intervention, the jurisdictional link would be required.[122]

The Court rejected Malta's application, for reasons to be examined, but then took care to emphasize that its eventual findings and reasoning on the merits in the *Tunisia/Libya* case would apply only to that case, and 'no conclusion or inferences may legitimately be drawn from those findings or that reasoning with respect to rights or claims of other States not parties to the case'.[123] In doing so, it focused attention on the fact that while this might be legally correct, in practice the opposite was the case: any finding by the Court on the still developing law of continental shelf delimitation would be seized on and exploited by States whose claims would be favoured by the more general application of such a finding.

The rejection of Malta's request was a unanimous decision, and the judgment makes use of a number of arguments; the relation between them is not always clear, which makes it difficult to extract a simple *ratio decidendi*. One reason seems to be that Malta had leant over too far backward to avoid presenting a claim of its own:

> Malta . . . seeks permission to submit its views with respect to the applicable principles and rules of international law, not merely from the point of view of their operation as between Libya and Tunisia but also of their operation as between those States and Malta itself. Yet Malta attaches to its request an express reservation that its intervention is not to have the effect of putting in issue its own claims with regard to those same matters vis-à-vis Libya and Tunisia. This being so, the very character of the intervention for which Malta seeks permission shows . . . that the interest of a legal nature invoked by Malta cannot be considered to be one 'which may be affected by the decision in the case' within the meaning of Article 62 of the Statute.[124]

Had Malta sought to assert a claim of its own, this would, as the Court noted, have raised the issue of the jurisdictional link,[125] on the basis that Malta would then have been 'seeking permission to submit its own legal interest in the subject-matter of the case for decision by the Court, and to become a party to the case'.[126]

The next decision of the Court, in chronological sequence, on an application for permission to intervene was that of Italy in the case

[121] Ibid., p. 20, para. 36.

[122] This was the view stated in the separate opinion of Judge Morozov ([1981] ICJ Rep 22); Judge Schwebel expressly stated the opposite view in a separate opinion, with an air of being conscious of being in a minority (ibid., p. 40). Judge Oda set out in his separate opinion the view that was ultimately to be adopted (with his participation) by the Chamber in the *Land, Island and Maritime Frontier Dispute*, that intervention as a non-party is possible without a jurisdictional link.

[123] [1981] ICJ Rep 20, para. 35.

[124] [1981] ICJ Rep 19, para. 33.

[125] No pre-existing title of jurisdiction was relied on, but Malta had deposited a curiously worded acceptance of optional-clause jurisdiction which was apparently designed to create bilateral jurisdiction by a unilateral act: on this see a previous article in this series, [1999] *BYBIL*, pp. 36–39.

[126] [1982] ICJ Rep 18, para. 32.

concerning the *Continental Shelf (Libya/Malta)*. Some aspects of this decision will be commented on below (Section D(ii)); but for purposes of the analysis of the nature of intervention, the decision is unhelpful, and even perhaps self-contradictory. What may be observed was that the problem of the so-called 'jurisdictional link' continued to plague the discussion of intervention.

In this case the Court adopted the curious procedure of setting out two parallel arguments as to the significance of the jurisdictional link requirement in the case before it, and then indicating that it saw no need to choose between them, since in either event they led to the dismissal of Italy's application.[127] These were described as 'two approaches to the interpretation of Article 62 of the Statute';[128] both of them took as starting point that the Court had found that 'Italy is requesting it to decide on the rights which it has claimed',[129] thus in effect asking for the status of a party. The first approach was the familiar one based on the 'fundamental principles underlying [the Court's] jurisdiction: primarily the principle of consent, but also the principles of reciprocity and equality of States'. The court concluded that

> the view could be taken that Article 62 does not permit an intervention of the kind referred to except when the third State desiring to intervene can rely on a basis of jurisdiction making it possible for the Court to take a decision on the dispute or disputes submitted to it by the third State.[130]

The second approach was to find that an intervention which in effect sought a judgment on the intervener's rights 'would not be a genuine intervention within the meaning of Article 62';[131] the intervener ought to have brought its own 'mainline' proceedings against one or both parties, and perhaps asked for a joinder of the proceedings. On this interpretation,

> Article 62 would not derogate from the consensualism which underlies the jurisdiction of the Court, since the only cases of intervention afforded by that Article would be those in which the intervener was seeking only the preservation of its rights, without attempting to have them recognized . . .'[132]

The difference between the two approaches appears to be that the second leaves no room for a dual system, of party and non-party intervention, whereas the first does. Judge Mbaye, who voted for the decision, expressly found that these two different sorts of intervention existed,[133] and that Italy's intervention was a proper 'non-party' intervention.[134] His rejection of the Italian application was based on the view that Italy had not proved the existence of a legal interest likely to be affected.[135] Judge

[127] It is legitimate to suspect that, as on the occasion of the inclusion of para. 2(*c*) of Art. 81 of the 1978 Rules, the text was drafted to paper over the cracks between two irreconcilable groups within the Court.

[128] [1984] ICJ Rep 22, para. 34.

[129] [1984] ICJ Rep 22, para. 35.

[130] Ibid., p. 23, para. 36.

[131] Ibid., para. 36.

[132] Ibid.

[133] Separate opinion, [1984] ICJ Rep 43, 45.

[134] Ibid., p. 54.

[135] Ibid., p. 35.

Jiménez de Aréchaga, however, drew attention to the fact that the case had been brought by special agreement, in terms carefully defined by the Parties, and to the principles of reciprocity and equality (mentioned in the passage from the judgment quoted above), which in his view led to the result that Italy should not be permitted to intervene in any event. He rejected the view expressed by Judge Oda in his opinion in the case of the Maltese intervention, that no jurisdictional link would be required for a non-party intervention.[136]

(iii) Two kinds of Article 62 intervention?

In the *Land, Island and Maritime Frontier Dispute* the Chamber formed to deal with the case made what may be called a breakthrough in the analysis of the problem; though in doing so it took up an idea which had, as we have seen, already been adumbrated in the earlier cases of intervention. It reserved to a late stage in its judgment the question of the possible requirement of a jurisdictional link, having first established that Nicaragua's application was otherwise admissible. It then tackled the jurisdictional problem by approaching it from the standpoint of the nature of intervention, and the status, as a party or otherwise, of a State permitted to intervene.

It first stated the consensual principle of international jurisdiction, and concluded that only the applicant and respondent States

> are the 'parties' to the proceedings, and are bound by the Court's eventual decision because they have agreed to confer jurisdiction on the Court to decide the case, the decision of the Court having binding force as provided for in Article 59 of the Statute. Normally, therefore, no other State may involve itself in the proceedings without the consent of the original parties.[137]

Nevertheless, the Statute does provide for intervention: and the competence of the Court to admit an intervention in a case is not derived from the consent of the parties that creates the jurisdiction to hear that case. Consequently, intervention must be intended to do something other than permit the intervener to join in the case to enforce its claims as a party.

> Intervention under Article 62 of the Statute is for the purpose of protecting the State's 'interest of a legal nature' that might be affected by a decision in an existing case already established between other States, namely the parties to the case. It is not intended to enable a third State to tack on a new case, to become a new party, and so have its own claims adjudicated by the Court.[138]

The Chamber thus rejected the first approach to intervention; but it did so only insofar as the intention of the intervening State was to become a party to the case. In this it was taking up an implication in the 1982 judgment on the intervention of Malta in the case between Tunisia and Libya: as noted

[136] Ibid., p. 68, para. 36, referring to [1981] ICJ Rep 27.
[137] [1990] ICJ Rep 133, para. 95.
[138] [1990] ICJ Rep 133–4, para. 97.

above, the Court there referred to the question of the jurisdictional link as arising on the hypothesis that Malta was 'seeking permission to submit its own legal interest in the subject-matter of the case for decision by the Court, and to become a party to the case',[139] with the clear implication that an attempted intervention as a non-party would not raise a question of a jurisdictional link.

Assuming that the objective of Fiji in the *Nuclear Tests* cases, for example, was to enforce against France a claim for injury suffered from nuclear fall-out, then Fiji needed to be recognized as a party to the case, capable of enforcing the hoped-for judgment against France. If however the objectives of Malta and Italy in the two *Continental Shelf* cases had been merely to protect an 'interest of a legal nature', then they could have been permitted to intervene as non-parties. Whether the decision of the Chamber in the *Land, Island and Maritime Frontier* case amounts to a *revirement de jurisprudence*, a dissent *ex post facto* from the decisions in those cases, is a question we may leave aside.

The link between the nature of the intervention and the status of party is evident, in one direction: if a State were to be permitted, in the role of intervener, to 'have its own claims' against one or both parties 'adjudicated by the Court', then it would necessarily have to have the status of a party; only a party to a case can rely on the decision as a matter of *res judicata*, as is specifically laid down in Article 59 of the Statute.[140] But does the link operate in the reverse direction? Does it follow that a State which is permitted to intervene merely to protect its 'interest of a legal nature' is necessarily not a party, something less than a party? The answer must depend on the nature of the protection given to the 'interest of a legal nature'; if such protection entails a need to rely on the decision against the States parties to the case, then one would suppose that the intervener might need to enjoy the status of party to the proceedings.

In this connection, the Chamber gave in its judgment 'some indications of the procedural rights acquired by the intervening State as a result of [the] permission granted to it to intervene'.[141]

In the first place, . . . the intervening State does not become party to the proceedings, and does not acquire the rights, or become subject to the obligations, which attach to the status of party, under the Statute and Rules of Court, or the general principles of procedural law.[142]

One of those rights is, we may suppose, the right to assert the judgment as *res judicata* against the other (original) parties; and similarly one of those obligations is that of being bound by the judgment vis-à-vis those

139 [1982] ICJ Rep 18, para. 32.

140 See Section G(ii) below on the effect of the judgment for the intervening State.

141 In parenthesis, it may be noted that the rights result, not merely from the grant of the permission, but from the act of intervention pursuant to the permission; a State that has been granted permission to intervene may presumably think better of it, and take no further part in the case.

142 [1990] ICJ Rep 135–6, para. 102.

parties, and as we shall see, this was a relevant consideration at a later stage, when the question arose of the effect of the judgment on Nicaragua.[143]

The Chamber therefore was acting to protect the 'interest of a legal nature' of Nicaragua in some way that did not involve putting Nicaragua in a position to assert the binding force of the judgment against the original parties.[144] Whatever that protection might be (and it is not entirely clear what it was) the Chamber was categorical on the link between the two concepts, that of the status of party and the question of a link of jurisdiction:

> It is therefore clear that a State which is allowed to intervene in a case, does not, by reason only of being an intervener, become also a party to the case. It is true, conversely, that provided that there be the necessary consent by the parties to the case, the intervener is not prevented by reason of that status from itself becoming a party to the case . . . [T]he competence given to the Court in Article 62 of the Statute is not extendable to making an intervener a party to the case unless the parties to the case have consented to the change . . .[145]
>
> It thus follows from the juridical nature and from the purposes of intervention that the existence of a valid link of jurisdiction between the would-be intervener and the parties is not a requirement for the success of the application. On the contrary, the procedure of intervention is to ensure that a State with possibly affected interests may be permitted to intervene even though there is no jurisdictional link and it therefore cannot become a party.[146]

The Chamber thus did not assert that intervention can never be as a party, or that the concept of intervention was inconsistent with the status of a party. While a little earlier in its decision the Chamber stated that

> A case with a new party, and new issues to be decided, would be a new case. The difference between intervention under Article 62, and the joining of a new party to a case, is not only a difference in degree; it is a difference in kind.[147]

Nevertheless it recognized, in the passage just quoted, that, where there is consent, 'the intervener is not prevented by reason of that status from itself becoming a party to the case'. The Chamber was therefore recognizing that there are two kinds of intervention possible: intervention as a non-party, which does not require the existence of any jurisdictional link other than the Statute itself; and intervention as a party, with the consent of the existing parties to the case.

A number of questions remain, however. First, what is the relationship between the consent of the parties and the jurisdictional link; are these cumulative requirements for an intervener to be admitted as a party, or

[143] See below, Section G(ii).

[144] This implies that the parties would have been free to vary the Chamber's decision by agreement in any way they wished, without having to consult Nicaragua.

[145] [1990] ICJ Rep 134–5, para. 99.

[146] Ibid., p. 135, para. 100.

[147] [1990] ICJ Rep 134, para. 97; the Chamber went on to quote the decision on Italy's application in *Continental Shelf (Libya/Malta)* [1984] ICJ Rep 23, para. 37.

alternatives?[148] The last sentence of the passage just quoted appears to require, for the intervener to become a party, a jurisdictional link in all cases; the previous passage appears to require for that purpose the *ad hoc* consent of the parties in all cases. Once again, the question is whether a link is unidirectional or bidirectional. The mere existence of a separate title of jurisdiction, under which the intervener could have brought its own proceedings, would not appear in itself to justify the admission of the intervener as a party if the existing parties oppose this. But, applying the principle of *forum prorogatum*, one would suppose that if the parties to the case agree that the third State may intervene as a party, to press its own claims, the existence *vel non* of such a separate title of jurisdiction would be irrelevant.[149]

Secondly, one may speculate as to the legal nature, in the Chamber's thinking, of a consensual intervention as a party. Is this an alternative application of Article 62: in other words, is Article 62 to be read as authorising two sorts of intervention: party and non-party? Or is intervention under Article 62 strictly on a non-party basis,[150] and intervention as a party merely a procedure not specifically provided for in the Statute, but justified on the basis of the agreement of the parties? The language of the passages quoted above is ambiguous or inconsistent: generally however it points rather in the direction of an interpretation of Article 62 as contemplating only non-party intervention, to protect an interest of a legal nature.[151] Furthermore, interpretation of a single text as permitting two separate and inconsistent meanings is a technique of dubious validity, as we have seen in relation to the Court's interpretation of Article 13, paragraph 3, of the Statute.[152] If however, intervention as a party is a procedure needing, and possessing, no authority in the Statute, it may be contended that it escapes the control of the Court. While intervention under Article 62 is, as noted above, a right, the Court has the power and the discretion (though a fettered discretion, a *compétence liée*) to decide on the admissibility of an intervention. If however the parties inform the Court that they are agreed that a new party shall join in the

[148] When the Philippines sought to intervene in *Sovereignty over Pulau Ligitan and Pulau Sipadan*, Malaysia contended that the jurisdictional link was 'twice lacking', because there was no jurisdictional title and because both parties opposed the request: [2001] ICJ Rep 588, para. 32. Since however the request was to intervene as a non-party, the Court put aside the question of a jurisdictional link: ibid., para. 36.

[149] In this sense (apparently) Ruda, 'Intervention before the ICJ', *in* Lowe and Fitzmaurice (eds.), *Fifty Years of the International Court of Justice*, p. 501.

[150] In this sense Günther, 'Zulässigkeit und Grenzen der Intervention bei Streitigkeiten vor dem IGH', 34 *German Yearbook of International Law* (1991), pp. 283–4, 292.

[151] On the other hand, attention is drawn to the statement that 'the competence given to the Court *in Article 62 of the Statute* is not extendable to making an intervener a party to the case *unless the parties to the case have consented* . . . '; and the Chamber did refer to the position of 'a State permitted to intervene under Article 62 of the Statute, but which does not acquire the status of party to the case', with the implication that a State might be permitted to intervene *under that Article* but with the status of party: [1990] ICJ Rep 609, para. 423.

[152] See a previous article in this series: [2000] *BYBIL*, pp. 160–2.

proceedings as intervener (and agreed also, if necessary, that there exists also a jurisdictional link), has the Court any power to reject the intervention?[153]

The settlement of the question of the jurisdictional link, by a Chamber of the Court, was endorsed by the full Court in the case concerning *Sovereignty over Pulau Sipadan and Pulau Ligitan* between Indonesia and Malaysia. The Philippines requested permission to intervene in that case, over the objections of both parties to it. The object of the intervention was slightly obscure, but the Philippines made it perfectly clear that it did not seek to intervene as a party. The Court cited with approval the decision of the Chamber in the *Land, Island and Maritime Frontier* case that 'a jurisdictional link between the intervening State and the parties to the case is required only if the State seeking to intervene is desirous of "itself becoming a party to the case" ',[154] and concluded that since the Philippines was seeking to intervene as a non-party, 'the absence of a jurisdictional link between the Philippines and the Parties to the main proceedings does not present a bar to the Philippine intervention'.[155]

To complete this initial enumeration of the jurisprudence on the question of the two kinds of intervention, mention should be made of the admission of the intervention of Equatorial Guinea in the case concerning the *Land and Maritime Boundary between Cameroon and Nigeria*.[156] The decision in this case does no more than confirm the existence of a system of non-party intervention, without any requirement for a jurisdictional link. It was however the first case in which neither of the original parties objected to the intervention, and thus raises the question of the relevance of this circumstance as a matter of law—a point to be considered below.

Since no application to intervene as a party has yet been upheld, any further commentary would have to be essentially speculative. Two implications of the status of an intervener as a party may however here be noted. First, the status of party implies subjection to the *res judicata* effect of the judgment on the merits; as will be seen, the Chamber in the *Land, Island and Maritime Frontier Dispute* in effect held *a contrario* that this was so, by finding that Nicaragua as a non-party was not so subject. Secondly, the status of party normally carries the right to choose a judge *ad hoc* (this right was asserted by Nicaragua, but not upheld in the circumstances of the case).[157]

153 The statement of the Chamber that 'no other State may involve itself in the proceedings without the consent of the parties' ([1990] ICJ Rep 133, para. 95) leads itself to an a *contrario* interpretation.

154 [1990] ICJ Rep 135, para. 99.

155 [2001] ICJ Rep 589, para. 36.

156 *Order of 21 October 1999* [1999-II] ICJ Rep 1029.

157 If the intervention as a party is in effect in support of one party, or to assert a parallel right, as was the case of Fiji in the *Nuclear Tests* cases, the intervening party will probably be 'in the same interest' as that party for the purposes of Art. 31, para. 5, of the Statute, so that only one judge *ad hoc* may be appointed.

(c) The relationship between Article 59 and Article 62 of the Statute

Article 59 of the Statute is one of the ways in which expression is given to the fundamental principle that international judicial jurisdiction depends on the consent of the parties. If it is only by the consent of two or more States that the Court can pronounce on their legal rights, it necessarily follows that the rights of States who have not given such consent cannot be affected by such a pronouncement, that the decision of the Court remains for them *res inter alios acta*. It would seem also to follow that intervention under Article 62 of the Statute must be purely facultative—a right, but not an obligation—in the sense that a State that chooses not to intervene may simply rely on the protection of Article 59, with confidence that its legal situation cannot be adversely affected by its choice not to intervene.

On this basis, however, and even setting aside the actual terms of Article 62, the question evidently arises, what purpose is to be served by an intervention? As we have seen, one evident answer is that by intervening a State might press its own claim against one or both parties, in the framework of existing proceedings, rather than commencing its own 'mainline' proceedings (as the Court has termed them[158]), thus ensuring some procedural economy of means. This however is only possible, it appears, by intervention as a party, and Article 62 is intended to provide, either solely or principally, for non-party intervention. What then is the point of non-party intervention? In terms of the actual text of Article 62, how can a 'legal interest' of a State be 'affected' by a decision of the Court in view of the restriction on the effect of such a decision imposed by Article 59?

In its judgment on the merits in the case concerning *Land and Maritime Boundary between Cameroon and Nigeria (Cameroon v Nigeria: Equatorial Guinea intervening)*, the Court considered the significance for its decision of the presence of Equatorial Guinea as a non-party intervener, and of the implications for the rights and interests of that State and of Sao Tome and Principe as States bordering on the maritime delimitation area. The Court first observed that

> The jurisdiction of the Court is founded on the consent of the parties. The Court cannot therefore decide upon legal rights of third States not parties to the proceedings. In the present case there are States other than the parties to these proceedings whose rights might be affected, namely Equatorial Guinea and Sao Tome and Principe. Those rights cannot be determined by decision of the Court unless Equatorial Guinea and Sao Tome and Principe have become parties to the proceedings. Equatorial Guinea has indeed requested—and has been granted—permission to intervene, but as a non-party intervener only. Sao Tome and Principe has chosen not to intervene on any basis.[159]

It will be observed that the Court speaks here of the 'legal rights' of third States as being affected, not merely their interests of a legal nature. The

[158] E.g., *Continental Shelf (Libyan Arab Jamahiriya/Malta)* [1984] ICJ Rep 13, para. 18.
[159] [2002] ICJ Rep 421, para. 238.

Court continued:

The Court considers that, in particular in the case of maritime delimitations where the maritime areas of several States are involved, the protection afforded by Article 59 of the Statute may not always be sufficient. In the present case, Article 59 may not sufficiently protect Equatorial Guinea or Sao Tome and Principe from the effects—even if only indirect—of a judgment affecting their legal rights.[160]

The first sentence of this passage is at first sight puzzling. Article 59 was included in the Statute to put beyond doubt the application to judicial decisions of the established principle *res inter alios acta nec nocet nec prodest*.[161] A State not party to proceedings before the Court could maintain without contradiction that the judgment in those proceedings had no binding effect upon it, and that if the Court purported to regulate its rights or obligations, the decision in that respect was without effect.[162] How then could the protection of Article 59 be insufficient in the special case of maritime delimitations?

A possible interpretation of the dictum is however to understand it as saying, not that the third State could not rely on Article 59 to protect its rights (and its legal interests), but that in maritime delimitation cases it is not sufficient for the *Court* to rely on Article 59, and recklessly indicate a maritime delimitation between the parties before it which might extend too far, so as to encroach on areas appertaining to a third State. Such a delimitation, so far as it so encroached, would not be binding on that third State, and neither of the parties could rely upon it against that third State; but that consideration should not excuse the Court from having gone beyond its mandate. Such an interpretation of the decision in the *Cameroon/Nigeria* case would be consistent with the decision in the *Continental Shelf (Libya/Malta)* case, in which the Court found itself obliged to restrict the delimitation of the respective areas of continental shelf appertaining to the parties, in order not to encroach on the possible rights of Italy.

Thus when the Court continued its judgment in the *Cameroon/Nigeria* case by concluding that 'it cannot rule on Cameroon's claims so far as they might affect rights of Equatorial Guinea and Sao Tome and Principe',[163] it was not asserting that such a ruling *would* affect those rights, and therefore must not be given; it was indicating that the Court

[160] Ibid.

[161] Its insertion was in fact prompted by the inclusion of Article 63, with its implication *a contrario* of the limited effect of a judgment as *res judicata*: see Stauffenberg, *Statut et règlement de la CPJI, Éléments d'interprétation*, pp. 4201.

[162] In the case of the *Arrest Warrant of 11 April 2000*, the Congo asked the Court to declare that the illegality of the warrant precluded 'any State, including Belgium, from executing it' ([2002] ICJ Rep 8). The Court responded that it could not, 'in a judgment ruling on a dispute between the Congo and Belgium, indicate what the judgment's implications might be for third States' (ibid., p. 32, para. 77). Despite the cautious language ('might be'/'implications éventuelles'), this carries some suggestion that the judgment would have some implications for third States.

[163] [2002] ICJ Rep 421, para. 238.

should refrain from giving a ruling that, on the face of it, would affect those rights, even though—as a result of the principle stated in Article 59—the rights would not in fact be affected in any way.

How then would such an obligation of restraint on the part of the Court relate to the obligation, declared in the *Monetary Gold* case, to refrain from giving a decision where to do so would involve pronouncing on the rights of a third State, not party to the proceedings, where such rights would form 'the very subject-matter of the decision'?[164] In the *Land, Island and Maritime Frontier Dispute*, Nicaragua cited this case and claimed, as an argument in support of its intervention,

> that its interests are so much part of the subject-matter of the case that the Chamber could not properly exercise its jurisdiction without the participation of Nicaragua.[165]

The Chamber interpreted the *Monetary Gold* decision as being a finding that

> While the presence in the Statute of Article 62 might impliedly authorize continuance of the proceedings in the absence of a State whose 'interests of a legal nature' might be 'affected', this did not justify continuance of the proceedings in the absence of a State whose international responsibility would be 'the very subject-matter of the decision'.[166]

The Chamber noted that if Nicaragua could show that its interests would be the very subject-matter of the decision, it could certainly intervene, inasmuch as Article 62 'lays down a less stringent criterion'; it questioned however whether, in such a case, the Chamber would be able to give a decision even with the presence of Nicaragua as an intervener.[167] After examining the legal interests asserted by Nicaragua it concluded that, while these were, to some extent, likely to be 'affected' by the decision in the case, so as to justify an intervention, they would not constitute 'the very subject-matter of the decision'. It therefore concluded that

> the question whether the Chamber would have power to take a decision on these questions [of Nicaragua's interests], without the participation of Nicaragua in the proceedings, does not arise . . .[168]

It would seem therefore that the duty of restraint adverted to in the *Cameroon/Nigeria* case, is an attenuated form of the duty resulting from

[164] [1954] ICJ Rep 32. The application in subsequent cases of the *Monetary Gold* doctrine was examined in a previous article in this series: [1998] *BYBIL*, 69, pp. 34 ff.

[165] [1990] ICJ Rep 114, para. 52.

[166] Ibid., pp. 115–16, para. 55.

[167] Ibid., p. 116, para. 56. At this stage of its decision, the Chamber had not yet examined the nature of intervention in relation with question whether a jurisdictional link was required, but it was presumably looking ahead to its findings, referred to above, that Art. 62 contemplated intervention as a non-party, without the need for a jurisdictional link, and had also in mind that Nicaragua had not shown the existence of any such link. It would seem that if a State whose interests would form 'the very-subject-matter of the decision' were to intervene *as a party* on the basis of such a link or of consent, the *Monetary Gold* principle would not debar the Court from deciding the case.

[168] Ibid., p. 122, para. 73.

the *Monetary Gold* principle. When the interests of the third State would 'form the very subject-matter' of the decision, no decision at all can be given, unless that State intervenes as a party on the basis of a jurisdictional link, or of consent. When those interests are merely such as to be 'affected' by the decision, the Court may proceed with the case, but must limit its decision so as not to 'affect' those interests. In the first type of case, the effect of an intervention is to enable the Court to give a wider decision than it would be able to give in the absence of the intervention; but in the second type of case, the function of the intervention is to equip the Court better to judge how it can and should proceed in order not to encroach on the third State's interests.

In neither situation is there any derogation from Article 59, in the sense that a third State that chooses not to intervene remains protected. If Equatorial Guinea had not intervened in the *Cameroon/Nigeria* case, and the Court in its judgment had ruled in such a way as, prima facie, to encroach on the interest of Equatorial Guinea, that State could still have asserted that the decision was *res inter alios acta*, with no binding or other effect.[169] It must however also follow that if in the *Monetary Gold* case the Court had rejected the objections of Italy, and had given judgment on the dispute contemplated by the Washington Agreement, that judgment would also have had no legal impact whatever on Albania, even though the result would have affected the gold claimed by Albania.

A more difficult question, but one which fortunately has so far remained academic, is the effect of a judgment given (perhaps *per incuriam*) in circumstances in which the legal situation of a third State could be said to be the 'very subject-matter of the decision'. The dividing line between such a case and a case in which 'legal interests' are merely 'affected' may not always be so clear as it was in the *Monetary Gold* and *East Timor* cases. If a third State which had not intervened were to assert that a decision of the Court had purported to determine its rights, directly and indirectly, it could invoke Article 59 of the Statute to deny that decision any force of *res judicata* in relation to itself, whether it alleged that its 'interests' had been 'affected' or that its rights had been the 'very subject-matter of the decision'.

This suggests the perhaps unexpected conclusion that the *Monetary Gold* principle has nothing to do with the binding force of judgments as *res judicata*. The Court in that case, and in the *East Timor* case, considered that it *should* not 'decide' on the rights or legal situation of a third State (Albania, Indonesia) without its consent; but it *could* not in any event 'decide' any such rights or situation with the force of *res judicata*. It was not deterred from deciding on the competing claims to the gold by the prospect of thereby giving a decision on the legal position of Albania which would be *res judicata* for that State,—which would indeed require

[169] Cf. the ruling in the *Frontier Dispute case* as to the lack of effect on Niger, as third State, of the boundary delimitation between Burkina Faso and Mali effected by the Chamber: [1986] ICJ Rep 577–80, paras. 46–50.

the consent of Albania—since to do so would have been legally impossible in the absence of Albania. It could have given a decision which would have had the force of *res judicata* for the parties to the case, but was deterred by the fact that its decision would have a *de facto* impact on Albania's interests, in that the gold, to which Albania had made a claim, would pass either to the United Kingdom or to Italy.

However that may be, in practical terms it may be concluded that a State whose neighbours have brought, for example, a maritime delimitation dispute before the Court is not obliged to have recourse to intervention to protect its interests: it may simply sit back and watch the proceedings, relying on Article 59 of the Statute for substantive legal protection, and on the Court's self-declared duty of restraint for protection against any overly extensive judgment. It may however choose to intervene, not because it has fears for its substantive rights, since (despite the apparent statement to the contrary in the *Cameroon/Nigeria* case) those are fully protected by Article 59, but in order to explain to the Court what should be the limits of its decision, to avoid the inconvenience of having subsequently to convince the parties to the case that the judgment they have obtained extends too far, into the areas appertaining to the third State.

This interpretation also explains another apparent paradox: that in the judgment in the *Cameroon/Nigeria* case, the Court took care to protect the interests, not only of Equatorial Guinea, as intervening State, but of Sao Tome and Principe, which had chosen to remain passive. At first sight this suggests that intervention is unnecessary and ineffective.[170] The true position is however, it is submitted, that intervening States and non-intervening States share the protection both of Article 59, as to the substance, and of the Court's duty to avoid excessive judgments; but the intervening State enjoys the advantage, under the latter head, of ensuring that the Court is fully aware of the point at which a judgment would become excessive. Thus intervention does have advantages, even if they are less substantial than might appear; and the *Continental Shelf (Libya/Malta)* decision appears to indicate that the advantages attach to the fact of application to intervene, regardless—as we shall see—of whether or not the intervention is admitted. In its decision on the merits, it is not at first sight clear why the Court in the *Cameroon/Nigeria* case referred to the protection of the legal *rights* of third States rather than their 'interests of a legal nature', the terminology of Article 62. Taking account of the distinction suggested above, a possible interpretation of the texts would be the following. Article 59 of the Statute, or to be precise, the principle reflected in that Article, ensures that the legal rights of third States are in no way affected by a judgment of the Court. Such a judgment may however, if the Court is incautious or misguided, be so worded as to *appear* to affect the

[170] The judgment on the merits did not in fact affect the rights or interests of either Equatorial Guinea or Sao Tome and Principe.

rights of a third State; and while those rights are not in fact affected, the legal *interests* of the third State are involved, since it will have to assert the principle of *res inter alios acta* in negotiation with the parties in order to protect its rights.

In this connection, another distinction may be recalled: that made in the *Frontier Dispute* case, in connection with the legal situation of States not party to the proceedings, between cases of terrestrial frontier delimitation, and delimitation of maritime areas. The Chamber took the view that its frontier delimitation between Burkina Faso and Mali would be *res inter alios acta* for the neighbouring State of Niger, which would be protected by Article 59 of the Statute, and therefore there was no need to limit the delimitation to the areas in which it was certain that there was no claim by Niger. The previous year had however seen the decision in the *Continental Shelf (Libya/Malta)* case, in which the Court had restricted the scope of its decision to areas of shelf in which Italy made no claims. The Chamber explained the difference of approach by making a distinction between the process of land frontier determination and the process of maritime delimitation as follows:

> The legal considerations which have to be taken into account in determining the location of the land boundary between parties are in no way dependent on the position of the boundary between the territory of either of those parties and the territory of a third State . . . On the other hand, in continental shelf delimitations, an agreement between the parties which is perfectly valid and binding on the treaty level, may, when the relations between the parties and a third State are taken into consideration, prove to be contrary to the rules of international law governing the continental shelf (see *North Sea Continental Shelf* [1969] ICJ Rep 20, para. 14; 27–8, paras. 35–6).[171]

Whatever the merits of the distinction thus drawn, the practice of the Court has not so far contradicted it, since it is only in the context of maritime delimitations that the Court has found, in effect, that Article 59 of the Statute is not a sufficient protection. On the other hand, neither in the *Continental Shelf (Libya/Malta)* case nor in the *Cameroon/Nigeria* case has the language of the judgment suggested that the Court would have acted otherwise if a land frontier had been the subject of the decision. In the latter case, the Court held that, in the circumstances, a third State could not be affected by a decision as to the boundary in the waters of Lake Chad: see Section F below.

(d) The 'interest of a legal nature' and the object of an intervention

The reasoning of the Chamber in the *Land, Island and Maritime Frontier Dispute*, endorsed by the Court in *Sovereignty over Pulau Ligitan and Pulau Sipadan*, is based on the idea that the 'juridical nature' of intervention—that is, non-party intervention under Article 62—is something different from participation in the case as a party, and thus the object of such an

[171] [1986] ICJ Rep 578, para. 47.

intervention must not be to act, in effect, as a party. The intervention of Fiji in the *Nuclear Tests* cases would thus have been doomed to failure; and the approach to intervention which saw it as a way of pressing a parallel claim has proved to be incorrect, at least so far as the type of intervention possible under Article 62 is concerned. This leaves unsettled the question of what is the proper object of an intervention, and indeed complicates that question, by excluding the simplest hypothesis: the object of an intervention to press a parallel claim is evident, even if the way on which it can be said to be inspired by the possibility of an 'interest of a legal nature' being 'affected' remains obscure. What then is the situation in which the Statute envisages a need for intervention, and what is the purpose of an intervention under Article 62?

It might be thought that if an interest were to be affected by the decision of the Court in a case, it would be the likely content of the operative part of the future decision that would have to be looked to in order to judge of its potential effect on the legal interest asserted. The French text of the Statute is however much less specific: it refers to assertion by the intending intervener of 'un intérêt d'ordre juridique [qui] est pour lui en cause'; and the *travaux préparatoires* of the PCIJ Statute suggest that this was the original wording, the English text being an attempt to convey the idea of 'en cause'. The Court accordingly, in the case of *Sovereignty over Pulau Sipadan and Pulau Ligitan*, interpreted the word 'decision' in the English text in a broad sense, as not limited to the operative part of the future decision.

> [T]he interest of a legal nature to be shown by a State seeking to intervene under Article 62 is not limited to the *dispositif* alone of a judgment. It may also relate to the reasons which constitute the necessary steps to the *dispositif*.[172]

In one sense, this makes the task of the would-be intervener easier, since it can point to, for example, the likelihood of the Court making a ruling of principle in the reasoning of its decision that would be relevant to the legal situation of the intervener, even if the *dispositif* is limited, as it would necessarily be, to the resolution of the specific dispute between the parties. On the other hand, it is less evident how a legal interest would be *affected* by the decision if there is no more than some relationship between the content of the reasoning of the decision and that legal interest. The Court did not go so far as to give the expression 'en cause' in the French text a wide interpretation, independent of the English text: it remains a requirement that the decision, taken as a whole, 'affects', i.e. has some impact on, the legal interest asserted.[173]

(i) Malta's application to intervene (Continental Shelf (Tunisia/Libya))

The attempted intervention of Malta in the *Tunisia/Libya* case has already been considered above (Section 3(B)(ii)). In that case, the Court deduced

[172] Ibid., p. 596, para. 47.

[173] In this sense, Torres Bernárdez, 'L'intervention dans la procédure de la CIJ', *Recueil des cours*, 256 (1995), p. 293.

the nature of the legal interest invoked by Malta from 'the character of the intervention for which Malta seeks permission'.[174] Among the reasons (for there seem to be several) for the rejection of Malta's application to intervene was one already considered above, but which it is now convenient to set out again:

Malta now requests permission to intervene on the assumption that it has an interest of a legal nature that is in issue in the proceedings in [the] case. It seeks permission to submit its views with respect to the applicable principles and rules of international law, not merely from the point of view of their operation as between Libya and Tunisia but also of their operation as between those States and Malta itself. Yet Malta attaches to its request an express reservation that its intervention is not to have the effect of putting in issue its own claims with regard to those same matters vis-à-vis Libya and Tunisia. That being so, the very character of the intervention for which Malta seeks permission shows, in the view of the Court, that the interest of a legal nature invoked by Malta cannot be considered to be one 'which may be affected by the decision in the case' within the meaning of Article 62 of the Statute.[175]

The argument is not of the clearest,[176] but seems to mean that if Malta *had* 'put in issue' its own claims—i.e. empowered the Court to rule on them in the same judgment, which would require the existence of a jurisdictional link—then those claims would have been 'affected' by the decision; but the claims would not be 'affected' merely if the Court were to rule in its decision between Libya and Tunisia that, for example, the equidistance method was required by a rule of international law, even though the result would be that Malta would find it difficult to resist the application of that method when negotiating its delimitations with other States (particularly Tunisia and Libya).[177] In short, to be able to rely on a legal interest likely to be affected, an intending intervener must 'put in issue' that interest; but, unless it can show a jurisdictional link, it must at the same time not ask to be made a party. This interpretation of Article 62 leaves little room for manoeuvre.

A further element of the Court's reasoning in this case is noteworthy. It stated that

What Malta in effect seeks to secure by its application is the opportunity to argue in the present case in favour of a decision in which the Court would refrain from adopting and applying particular criteria that it might otherwise consider appropriate for the delimitation of the continental shelf of Libya and Tunisia. In short it seeks an opportunity to submit arguments to the Court with possibly prejudicial

[174] [1981] ICJ Rep 19, para. 33. [175] [1981] ICJ Rep 19, para. 33.

[176] In the case of *Sovereignty over Pulau Sipadan and Pulau Ligitan*, the Court interpreted the rejection of the Maltese application as being 'because the Court felt it was in effect being asked to prejudge the merits of Malta's claim against Tunisia in a different dispute, which Malta had nonetheless put before the Court': [2001] ICJ Rep 599, para. 53.

[177] This is confirmed by the emphasis with which the Court asserted that 'no conclusions or inferences may legitimately be drawn from' its decision, taken in the absence of Malta, 'with respect to rights or claims of other States not parties to the case': ibid., p. 20, para. 35.

effects on the interests either of Libya or of Tunisia in their mutual relations with one another.[178]

The implications of this are curious. It is surely to be supposed that the Court would in any event apply to the dispute between Libya and Tunisia what it held to be the correct rules and principles of international law, and the correct criteria for delimitation indicated by those principles and rules. Those rules and principles of law would, on the basis of *jura novit curia*, be what they would be, whoever argued the case, from whatever standpoint.

It seems a remarkable tribute to the eloquence of counsel for Malta to suppose that the Court could be led to apply something other than the correct principles and rules; and it is difficult to see why the principles and rules applied after hearing Malta might not have a better claim to be the correct ones than those which might have been applied without the benefit of Maltese argument. It is of course true that in the particular field of maritime delimitation, the extent to which a judicial delimitation follows, as it were automatically, from the application of the law has always been somewhat uncertain; for example are the methods of delimitation part of the applicable law, or factual aspects merely invoked by a rule of law?[179] Nevertheless, it is difficult to see how hearing counsel for Malta could, as a matter of law, have 'prejudicial effects' on the interests of the parties to the case.

(ii) Italy's application to intervene (Continental Shelf (Libya/Malta)) The Court's handling of the attempted intervention of Italy in the *Continental Shelf* case between Libya and Malta was not such as to elucidate the various problems surrounding the concept of intervention. Italy had evidently studied the decision on the application of Malta to intervene in the *Tunisia/Libya* case, and endeavoured to avoid the pitfalls that the decision in that case had illustrated. Yet Italy's application was not more successful than that of Malta; and speaking very broadly, one may say that Malta failed because it did not go far enough, and Italy failed because it went too far. Furthermore, Italy's application inevitably caused the vexed question of the jurisdictional link to be raised, which proved to be an obstacle to admission of the application; as we have seen (Section 3(B)(ii) above), two possible interpretations were offered in the judgment on Italy's application, but the Court did not indicate which of them was right.

It will be recalled that in the *Tunisia/Libya* case, because Malta wished 'to submit its views with respect to the applicable principles and rules of international law, not merely from the point of view of their operation between Libya and Tunisia but also of their operation as between those States and Malta itself', and yet was 'not putting in issue its own claims

[178] [1981] ICJ Rep 19–20, para. 34.

[179] See a previous article in this series: [1993] *BYBIL*, pp. 30 ff.

with regard to those same matters vis-à-vis Libya and Tunisia', therefore the legal interest invoked was not one which might be affected by the decision in the case.[180]

In its application to intervene in the Libya/Malta case, Italy was careful to indicate that it

> seeks to participate in the proceedings to the full extent necessary to enable it to defend the rights which it claims over some of the areas claimed by the Parties . . . so that the Court may be as fully informed as possible as to the nature and scope of the rights of Italy in the areas of continental shelf concerned by the delimitation, and may thus be in a position to take due account of those rights in its decision.[181]

The Court however considered that

> While formally Italy requests the Court to safeguard its rights, it appears to the Court that the unavoidable practical effect of its request is that the Court will be called upon to recognize those rights, and hence, for the purpose of being able to do so, to make a finding, at least in part, in disputes between Italy and one or both of the Parties.[182]
>
> Whether the relations between Italy and the Parties in the matter of continental shelf delimitation be regarded as three disputes, or one dispute, the fact remains that the Court cannot adjudicate on the legal relations between Italy and Libya without the consent of Libya, or on those between Italy and Malta without the consent of Malta.[183]

The rejection of Italy's application was therefore essentially on the ground that Italy had gone so far as to invite the Court to decide on its claims against each of the two Parties, neither of whom consented to such judicial settlement. It was therefore difficult, following this decision, to see how an application for permission to intervene could be framed so as to escape both the Scylla of the too-detached approach of Malta in the *Tunisia/Libya* case, and the Charybdis of the too-involved approach of Italy in the *Libya/Malta* case.

(iii) Nicaragua's application to intervene (Land, Island and Maritime Frontier Dispute)

As Torres Bernárdez has well observed, the two judgments in the *Continental Shelf* cases, that on the application of Malta, and that on the application of Italy, 'se complètent donc pour nous dire ce qui n'est pas une véritable intervention au sens de l'article 62'.[184] In that negative sense, but only in that negative sense, they help to define what *is* a true intervention. It is hardly surprising that the Agent of Nicaragua, addressing the Chamber on that State's application for permission to intervene, appealed to the Chamber to adjust that application to fit the bed of

180 Ibid. 181 Italian Application, quoted in [1984] ICJ Rep 12, para. 17.

182 Ibid., p. 19, para. 29. 183 Ibid., p. 20, para. 31.

184 Torres Bernárdez, 'L'intervention dans la procédure de la CIJ', *Recueil des cours*, 256 (1995), p. 384.

Procrustes: 'if the Chamber should feel that the Application of Nicaragua goes too far or remains too limited, Nicaragua would be willing to adjust to any procedure indicated by the Chamber'.[185] The Chamber did not expressly respond to this appeal, but found that Nicaragua's application could only be upheld in part.

Nicaragua was found to have a legal interest which might be affected by the decision insofar as El Salvador and Honduras were asserting, respectively, that the waters of the Gulf of Fonseca were subject to a condominium of the three States, and that those waters were subject to a community of interests of the three States. It appeared to the Chamber that both the alleged condominium and the alleged community of interests would 'embrace Nicaragua as one of the three riparian States, and Nicaragua must therefore be interested' in the question whether that was the legal situation.[186] There is in this language a toning-down of the requirements of Article 62: is it the same thing to say that a State is 'interested' in the settlement of a question as to say that the settlement of that question 'may affect' its legal interest?

In general, it is to be presumed that the intention of the Statute was that intervention would confer a benefit on the intervening State, that an intervention would be capable of modifying the situation that would result if no intervention had taken place. There may here however be an effect of the confusion, at the time of the preparation of the PCIJ Statute, between the two kinds of intervention discussed above. The advantage to be gained by the author of a 'Fiji-type' intervention, as a party and to enforce a separate claim, is perfectly evident; but this type of intervention proves not to be that intended by Article 62. Nothing in the *travaux préparatoires* indicates that the draftsmen had a clear idea of the advantage to be gained by an intervention of the non-party kind; the parallel with Article 63 suggests that what was contemplated may have been no more than the opportunity to influence the Court in its interpretation of a rule of law involved in the case. Presumably the benefit of this would be that, as a result of the intervention, the 'legal interest' of the third State would not be 'affected', as it would otherwise have been; or would be affected differently, or to a lesser extent. In the case of the Nicaraguan intervention concerning the condominium/community, Nicaragua would be able to argue as intervener in favour of, or against, these analyses, and thus to influence the Court's decision.[187]

This was the least difficult aspect of the matter: more complex was the question whether Nicaragua had a legal interest which might be affected by the delimitation which the Court was asked to effect within the Gulf of Fonseca and (according to one of the parties) outside the Gulf. The Chamber asserted roundly that it did not consider

[185] C4/CR 90/1, p. 27. [186] [1990] ICJ Rep 121, para. 72.

[187] As a practical matter, that is: we have already noted that, in the light of the principle of *jura novit curia*, additional argument from a third State ought in theory to make no difference.

that an interest of a third State in the general legal rules and principles likely to be applied by the decision can justify an intervention.[188]

Judge Oda, in a separate opinion, questioned whether

a legal interest of a more concrete nature is required than a simple interest in the interpretation of the rules of international law, whether general or special, which are applicable to the case in hand,[189]

but preferred not to enlarge on the point in the context of that case. In his Hague Academy lectures in 1993, he argued persuasively against the Chamber's ruling:

If an interpretation of a multilateral convention given by the Court is necessarily of concern to a State which is a party to that instrument, though not a party to the case, there seems no convincing reason why the Court's interpretation of the principles and rules of international law should be of less concern to a State. If, therefore, the interpretation of an international convention can attract the intervention of third States under Article 63 of the Statute, it may be asked why the interpretation of the principles and rules of international law should exclude a third State from intervening in a case [under Article 62].[190]

This approach is also consistent with the history of the matter, whereby intervention of the type contemplated by Article 62 seems to have developed from the prior recognition of intervention in relation to the interpretation of a convention. However, one reply to Judge Oda's question was given in 1958 by Fitzmaurice:

it would clearly be depriving Article 62 of all limiting elements . . . if an interest of a legal nature could be postulated simply on the basis that all States have an interest in the law, and in the condition of the law; for in that case, . . . there could never be a case in which a third State (whatever its identity) would not possess a potential legal interest in the result.[191]

To which one might riposte: why must it be supposed that such was not the intention of the draftsmen of the Statute? At all events, the generally negative and restrictive approach of the Court to intervention, characterised by the *Continental Shelf* cases, and itself attributable to the confusion over the significance of intervention, may perhaps be blamed for the rejection of the eminently reasonable interpretation espoused by Judge Oda.

By 'interest' must presumably be understood something more than an academic interest: the third State must in any event be concerned, as Nicaragua was, because the law 'likely to be applied by the decision' could then be asserted against that State in another, perhaps related, context. According to the Chamber, this is however still not enough.

188 [1990] ICJ Rep 124, para. 76.

189 [1990] ICJ Rep 138. Judge Oda also favoured a parallelism between Article 63 and Article 62 as regards the effect of the judgment on the intervening state, a point on which he dissented from the final judgment in the *Land, Island and Maritime Frontier case*: see [1992] ICJ Rep 620, and 'The International Court of Justice viewed from the Bench', 244 *Recueil des cours*, 1993-VII, p. 85.

190 Ibid.

191 [1958], *BYBIL*, p. 25; *Collected Edition*, Vol. II, p. 552.

Nicaragua urged further that in the Gulf of Fonseca 'it would be impossible to carry out a delimitation which took into account only the coasts in the Gulf of two of the three riparian States'.[192] The Chamber observed that 'the taking into account of all the coasts and coastal relationships within the Gulf' would not itself necessarily affect the legal interest of Nicaragua; and that Nicaragua had failed to demonstrate that it would.[193] The possibility that, in some circumstances, it could be demonstrated that the legal interest of a third riparian State might be affected was thus left open. Similarly, the decision to refuse Nicaragua permission to intervene in the case so far as it related to delimitation outside the Gulf was essentially based on Nicaragua's failure to indicate how any specific delimitation, in particular a suggested depiction by Honduras of the 'relevant maritime area' might affect a Nicaraguan interest of a legal nature.

(iv) Equatorial Guinea's application to intervene (Land and Maritime Boundary between Cameroon and Nigeria)

On the application of Equatorial Guinea to intervene in the case of the *Land and Maritime Boundary between Cameroon and Nigeria*, the Order of the Court observed laconically that 'in the opinion of the Court Equatorial Guinea has sufficiently established that it has an interest of a legal nature which could be affected' by any decision on the disputed maritime boundary. One is thus thrown back on the description, in the Order, of the arguments advanced by Equatorial Guinea. A special aspect of the case was however that one of the parties (Nigeria) had already suggested, in a preliminary objection, that the delimitation asked for by the other party would affect the interests of third States to such an extent that the Court would in fact not be able to decide in the absence of those States; and the Court, in ruling on the objection, had left this possibility open.[194] However, Equatorial Guinea had been very clear in its application as to the geographical aspects of the legal interest it asserted. It explained that it claimed rights up to the median lines between itself and each of the parties, so that in respect of any Cameroon/Nigeria delimitation line that crossed those lines, its 'rights and interests would be prejudiced'.[195] It also explained the object of its intervention as being 'to protect [its] legal rights . . . by all legal means available', and 'to inform the Court of the nature of the legal rights and interests of Equatorial Guinea that could be affected by the Court's decision in the light of the maritime boundary claims' of the two parties.[196]

It should be recalled also that in this case, neither party had any objection to the intervention of Equatorial Guinea. Had it sought to intervene as a party, this would apparently have resolved any question of

[192] Nicaraguan Application, para. 2(*f*), quoted in [1990] ICJ Rep 124, para. 77.

[193] [1990] ICJ Rep 124–5, para. 77.

[194] *Land and Maritime Boundary between Cameroon and Nigeria, Preliminary Objections, ICJ Reports*, 1998, 324, quoted in [1990-II] ICJ Rep 1030–1, para. 2.

[195] Quoted in [1999-II] ICJ Rep 1031–2, para. 3.

[196] Ibid., p. 1032, para. 4.

the 'jurisdictional link'. But does the consent (or, as the case may be, lack of opposition) of the parties have a further impact? Such consent could be regarded as a recognition by the parties that, at least in their view, the would-be intervener has an interest of a legal nature that may require protection. If so, the question arises whether the Court's discretion remains unaffected, or whether it is bound to accept the parties' assessment, and admit the intervention without more. An intervention as a party, with consent or a jurisdictional link, may be equated with a situation in which the three States together, or the applicant and the intervener, bring the proceedings as a joint exercise; it would therefore seem inappropriate to single out one State and refuse to admit its interest in the matter. Should non-party intervention require a higher standard of demonstration of the existence of a legal interest to be protected?

In the *Continental Shelf (Libya/Malta)* case, the Court had commented on the fact that both parties had opposed the intervention, and made the following general statement:

> While the Court attaches great importance to the element of the will of States, expressed in a special agreement or other instrument creative of jurisdiction, to define the extent of a dispute before the Court, it is worth recalling that under paragraph 2 of Article 62, 'it shall be for the Court to decide' upon a request for permission to intervene, and the opposition of the parties to the case is, though very important, no more than one element to be taken into account by the Court.[197]

This is a clear indication that the Court considers itself empowered to permit an intervention over the objection of both parties, as the Chamber in effect did in the *Land, Island and Maritime Frontier Dispute*; presumably the contrary is also implied, that the Court may refuse an intervention, even if both parties agree to it. This may however only apply in the case of a non-party, informative, intervention, in which there is no question of the enlargement of the 'extent of a dispute', a matter to a considerable extent governed by the 'will of the parties'. Such refusal would however have to be motivated by the non-compliance with the conditions of Article 62—the absence of a legal interest that might be affected—rather than a mere discretionary refusal.[198]

(v) The Philippines' application to intervene (Sovereignty over Pulau Ligitan and Pulau Sipadan)

As the case-title indicates, the dispute between Malaysia and Indonesia was over sovereignty over the two islands of Pulau Ligitan and Pulau Sipadan. The Philippines had made it clear to those States, even before applying to intervene in the case, that it made no claim of sovereignty whatever in respect of those islands, and it was perfectly happy to see the Court award sovereignty to either of the Parties. The Philippines was however concerned to protect its claim to the territory of Sabah (North Borneo),

[197] [1984] ICJ Rep 28, para. 46. [198] See Section 6(1) above.

which it claimed under a title deriving from the Sultanate of Sulu. It argued that

> Evidently, the chain of title which Malaysia asserts to defend its territorial claim to Sipadan and Ligitan, based as it is on its own interpretations of, and representations on, specific treaties, agreements and other documents, is linked to the chain of title which the Philippines relies on to defend its territorial claim to North Borneo.[199]

The question which had to be resolved was stated by the Court in the following terms:

> whether a third State may intervene under Article 62 of the Statute in a dispute brought to the Court under a special agreement, when the State seeking to intervene has no interest in the subject-matter of that dispute as such, but rather asserts an interest of a legal nature in such findings and reasonings that the Court might make on certain specific treaties that the State seeking to intervene claims to be in issue in a different dispute between itself and one of the two Parties to the pending case before the Court.[200]

The Court first considered whether the 'interest of a legal nature' that has to be shown may be 'in anything other than the operative decision of the Court in the existing case'.[201] This is a curious choice of words: the English text of the Statute does not refer to the interest as being 'in' any part of the decision, but rather as being capable of being 'affected by the decision'; the question would appear to be whether the interest asserted can be 'affected' by some part of the reasoning of the decision, as distinct from the operative clause. Clearly an operative clause simply finding that the disputed islands were under the sovereignty of the one Party or the other would not affect any interest of the Philippines; what it was anxious to avert was anything being said in the reasoning that might cast doubt on its title to North Borneo. At all events, the Court, basing itself in particular on the broad terms of the French text of the Statute ('un intérêt . . . est pour lui en cause'), decided that

> the interest of a legal nature to be shown by a State seeking to intervene under Article 62 is not limited to the *dispositif* alone of a judgment. It may also relate to the reasons which constitute the necessary steps to the *dispositif*.[202]

The Court referred to its decision on the application of Malta in the case of the *Continental Shelf (Tunisia/Libya)*: in that case, Malta had in effect sought to intervene in order to avert, if possible, any findings in the reasoning of the decision that might prejudice Malta's position in negotiations for the delimitation of its own areas of continental shelf. However the Court in the later case interpreted its rejection of Malta's request as follows:

> Malta's Application was rejected, but not on the grounds that its expressed intention did not fall within the scope of the dispute as defined in the Special

[199] Quoted in [2001] ICJ Rep 591, para. 41. [200] Ibid., pp. 595–6, para. 46.
[201] Ibid., p. 596, para. 47. [202] Ibid.

Agreement. Malta's Application to intervene was not granted because the Court felt it was in effect being asked to prejudge the merits of Malta's claim against Tunisia in a different dispute, which Malta had nonetheless not put before the Court.[203]

and the Court found that

The situation is different in the present case. Indeed, the Court considers that the request of the Philippines to intervene does not require the Court to prejudge the merits of any dispute that may exist between the Philippines and Malaysia, and which is not before the Court.[204]

The Court then embarked on a lengthy examination of the claims of the Philippines, so far as it had been made aware of them, in relation to the claims of the parties to the case. Its conclusion was not that the type of interest alleged by the Philippines was inappropriate, but rather that the Philippines had failed to prove its case.

Some of the instruments which the Philippines has invoked, and the submissions it has made as to them, may indeed have shown a certain interest in legal considerations before the Court in the dispute between Indonesia and Malaysia; but as regards none of them has the Philippines been able to discharge its burden of demonstrating that it has an interest of a legal nature that may be affected, within the sense of Article 62. The Philippines has shown in these instruments no legal interest on its part that might be affected by reasoning or interpretations of the Court in the main proceedings, either because they form no part of the arguments of Indonesia and Malaysia or because their respective reliance on them does not bear on the issue of retention of sovereignty by the Sultanate of Sulu as described by the Philippines in respect of its claim in North Borneo.[205]

The Court also noted that, with the exception of one particular instrument (the 'Sulu-Overbeck Grant'), the various instruments referred to by the Philippines were

said to be confirmatory of title, or treaties in respect of which the Philippines wishes to advance interpretations that preclude them being read as entailing a loss of any previous title that may have existed in the Sultan of Sulu. Not only are they not, for the most part, at the centre of the Court's attention in the case between Indonesia and Malaysia, but they are not themselves sources of title for the Philippines.

The Court observed in this respect that

the wish of a State to forestall interpretations by the Court that might be inconsistent with responses it might wish to make, in another claim, to instruments that are not themselves sources of the title it claims, is simply too remote for purposes of Article 62.[206]

If an *a contrario* interpretation is justified, the Court would appear to recognize that an interest in the interpretation of an instrument constituting a source of title common to one of the parties and to the

[203] Ibid., p. 597, para. 53. [204] Ibid., para. 54. [205] Ibid., p. 603, para. 82.
[206] Ibid., p. 604, para. 83.

State seeking to intervene is a legal interest that may be affected by the decision in the case.

The conclusion reached by the Court would appear to be sufficient to justify a rejection of the request of the Philippines: but the Court nonetheless then turned to an examination of the question of 'the precise object of the intervention', required to be stated by the intending intervener by Article 81, paragraph 2(*b*) of the Rules of Court. It took note of the three objects indicated by the Philippines, which were:

a) First, to preserve and safeguard the historical and legal rights of the Government of the Republic of the Philippines arising from its claim to dominion and sovereignty over the territory of North Borneo, to the extent that these rights are affected, or may be affected, by a determination of the Court of the question of sovereignty over Pulau Ligitan and Pulau Sipadan.
b) Second, to intervene in the proceedings in order to inform the Honourable Court of the nature and extent of the historical and legal rights of the Republic of the Philippines which may be affected by the Court's decision.
c) Third, to appreciate more fully the indispensable role of the Honourable Court in comprehensive conflict prevention and not merely for the resolution of legal disputes.[207]

The first of these, the Court found, corresponded to similar formulations employed in previous applications to intervene, which 'have not been found by the Court to present a legal obstacle to intervention':[208] the cases referred to were the application of Italy in the *Continental Shelf (Libya/Malta)* case, the application of Nicaragua in the *Land, Island and Maritime Frontier Dispute*, and the application of Equatorial Guinea in the case of the *Land and Maritime Boundary between Cameroon and Nigeria*. In connection with the second stated object, the Court recalled the dictum of the Chamber in the *Land, Island and Maritime Frontier Dispute*, approved by the full Court in the *Cameroon/Nigeria* case, that

> [s]o far as the object of [a State's] intervention is 'to inform the Court of the nature of the legal rights [of that State] which are in issue in the dispute', it cannot be said that this object is not a proper one: it seems indeed to accord with the function of intervention.[209]

Thus far the Court therefore did no more than confirm its previous jurisprudence, which, it may be noted, is expressed in curiously grudging terms ('have not been found . . . to constitute a legal obstacle'; 'it cannot be said that this object is not a proper one').

The third object is in obscure terms, and was virtually abandoned by the Philippines during oral argument: the Court rejected its 'relevance under the Statute and Rules'.[210]

The purpose served by this part of the judgment is not clear: if the Court, while not satisfied that the Philippines had 'demonstrated an

[207] Quoted in [2001] ICJ Rep 591, para. 84.
[208] Ibid., p. 606, para. 87.
[209] [1990] ICJ Rep 130, para. 90, quoted in [1999] ICJ Rep 1034, para. 14; requoted in [2001] ICJ Rep 606, para. 88.
[210] [2001] ICJ Rep 606, para. 90.

entitlement to intervene in the pending case',[211] had thought it useful to develop its jurisprudence on the question of a proper object of an intervention, the excursus on the subject would have been understandable; but as we have seen, the Court added nothing to previous decisions.

(e) How is the 'interest of a legal nature'[212] to be 'affected'?

The first sentence of Article 62 begins 'Should a State consider that it has an interest of a legal nature . . .' (and in French, 'Lorsqu'un État estime que . . .'); it was suggested by the Philippines in the case of *Sovereignty over Pulau Sipadan and Pulau Ligitan* that 'the threshold for the invocation of Article 62 is . . . a *subjective* standard: the State requesting permission to intervene must "consider" that it has an interest'.[213] It was not however suggested that this would be sufficient, that the Court would merely have to ascertain the existence of this subjective belief in order to admit the intervention.[214] In fact the Chamber had ruled in the *Land, Island and Maritime Boundary* case that

> it is for a State seeking to intervene to demonstrate convincingly what it asserts, and thus to bear the burden of proof; and . . . it has only to show that its interest 'may' be affected, not that it will or must be affected.[215]

The English text of Article 62 refers to a legal interest that 'may' be affected, not to one that 'will' or 'must' be affected;[216] the French text does not permit of this distinction, but the expression 'est pour lui en cause' does not appear to contradict the interpretation suggested by the word 'may'. It may in many cases be impossible at the stage of a request for permission to intervene to say whether or not the legal interest will or will not be affected;[217] this might, for example, depend on whether the Court upheld the contentions of the applicant or those of the respondent. Thus in the *Land, Island and Maritime Frontier Dispute*, the Chamber pointed out that

> The present case raises a further problem, namely that the Parties to the case are in dispute about the very provision of the Special Agreement—paragraph 2 of

[211] Ibid., p. 607, para. 94.

[212] Mention has been made in Section 3(C) above of the *Cameroon/Nigeria* case, in connection with the question of the relationship between Arts 59 and 62 of the Statute. As was then noted, the Court spoke consistently of the impact of a decision of the Court on the legal *rights* of a third State, rather than the 'interest of a legal nature' that might be shown to be affected. For the reasons explained above, it is nonetheless the *interest* of the third State that may require protection.

[213] [2001] ICJ Rep 590, para. 40. Cf. also Sette Camara, dissenting opinion, *Continental Shelf (Libya/Malta)* [1984] ICJ Rep 86, para. 77

[214] The sense of Art. 62 is in fact 'If it is shown that a third State has an interest of a legal nature, then an intervention may be admitted', but intervention being a voluntary act (cf. Torres Bernárdez, *Cours*, p. 288), it was necessary to begin by indicating the circumstances in which a State might seek to intervene: hence the wording chosen.

[215] [1990] ICJ Rep 117, para. 61.

[216] See the decision of the Chamber in the *Land, Island and Maritime Boundary* case cited below (text and n. 217).

[217] In this sense, Torres Bernárdez, 'L'intervention dans la procédure de la CIJ', *Recueil des cours*, 256 (1995), p. 293.

> Article 2—which is invoked in Nicaragua's Application [to intervene]. This means that the legal interests of Nicaragua have to be assessed, in relation to the legal issues in the case, under two different possible situations: an eventual finding by the Chamber in favour of El Salvador's view of the meaning of Article paragraph 2; or an eventual finding in favour of the view of Honduras.[218]

As the Chamber added, this was a difficulty not only for the Chamber, but also for Nicaragua in framing its Application.

In the case of the *Land and Maritime Boundary Between Cameroon and Nigeria*, the Court stated that the legal interest of Equatorial Guinea 'could be affected by *any* judgment which the Court might hand down', but it does not appear that this would be essential (and the phrase '*could* be affected' preserves the aspect of unpredictability). In the *Land, Island and Maritime Frontier* case, Nicaragua contended that it had a legal interest which would be affected by a delimitation of the waters of the Gulf of Fonseca; the Chamber observed that it 'does not . . . have to consider the possible effect on Nicaragua's interests of every possible delimitation which might be arrived at; it is for the State seeking to intervene to show that its interests might be affected by a particular delimitation, or by delimitation in general'.[219]

Does this then signify that, if a would-be intervener shows the existence of a 'legal interest', an intervention may be refused only if that interest *cannot* be affected by the future judgment? Once again, it would be difficult to assert with confidence that this must be the case when the content of the future decision has not been identified. In the case of the *Land and Maritime Boundary between Cameroon and Nigeria*, the curious situation arose that the Court determined, in advance and without any initiative of the third State, that its interests could not be affected. The question was the impact, if any, of the future decision on the Cameroon/Nigeria boundary on the Cameroon/Chad/Nigeria tripoint in Lake Chad: Nigeria contended, by way of preliminary objection, that the Court could not determine the boundary up to that tripoint without encroaching on the interests of Chad. Cameroon and Chad had already agreed a boundary in the Lake; and the Court ruled that its decision on the Cameroon/Nigeria boundary, if it affected the tripoint at all, could only result in moving it along the Chad/Cameroon boundary, and that the interests of Chad thus did not constitute the very subject-matter of the case.[220] Judge Parra-Aranguren objected to this decision, since he interpreted it as 'precluding any possible intervention by the Republic of Chad at a later stage of the present case', in his view 'a quite astonishing decision, in particular because the Court

[218] [1990] ICJ Rep 118, para. 62.

[219] [1990] ICJ Rep 123, para. 74. The meaning of the last phrase is not entirely clear: the French text has 'ou par toute délimitation en général', i.e. *any* delimitation, which seems to contradict the beginning of the sentence.

[220] [1998] ICJ Rep 311–12, paras. 77–9. The situation was very similar to that in the Burkina Faso/Mali *Frontier Dispute*, save that in that case a land frontier was in issue: see Section C above.

does not have the slightest idea as to what is the viewpoint of the Republic of Chad on the matter'.[221]

A parallel may be seen between the situation at the time of an application to intervene, when it cannot yet be known with certainty whether or not the asserted legal interest will or will not be affected, and the situation on a request for the indication of provisional measures. As the *Anglo-Iranian Oil Co.* case shows, measures may be indicated on the *summaria cognitio* on the basis of probabilities—among others, the probability of the existence of jurisdiction over the merits—and if ultimately it is shown that there was no such jurisdiction, the measures indicated do not become retrospectively unlawful or invalid.[222] As in the case of provisional measures, the Court is called upon to balance the interests of the States concerned: the possibility that refusal of intervention will cause the legal interests of the would-be intervener to be prejudiced, against the inconvenience, or more, caused to the parties by the admission of the intervention. For this reason, the attitude of the original parties must be an important factor: if they both raise no objection to the intervention, a decision to admit the intervention rather than refuse it becomes a more compelling prospect, even though the Court must conserve a discretion to refuse an inappropriate intervention. In the *Continental Shelf (Libya/Malta)* case the Court emphasized its power of decision, and referred to the *opposition* of the parties as being, 'though very important, no more than one element to be taken into account by the Court'.[223] The *agreement* of the parties should however, it is suggested, only be set aside in exceptional circumstances. It is striking that the decision to admit the intervention of Equatorial Guinea in the case of the *Land and Maritime Boundary between Cameroon and Nigeria*, where the intervention was unopposed, could be made by the comparatively routine method of an Order rather than a judgment.[224]

A significant indication of the meaning of the requirement that the legal interest be 'affected' by the decision is of course to be found in those judgments by which the Court (or a Chamber) has admitted an intervention: the *Land, Island and Maritime Frontier Dispute*, and the case of the *Land and Maritime Boundary between Cameroon and Nigeria*. In the latter case, the decision to admit the intervention of Equatorial Guinea was unanimous, and made by an Order; the Court, in its decision on the preliminary objections in the case, had in fact come near to inviting an intervention.[225] The part of the Order devoted to the Court's satisfaction that the conditions of Article 62 were met was somewhat brief, in effect referring back to

[221] Ibid., p. 352, para. 10. The Court had in fact only ruled that the interest of Chad was not the *subject-matter* of the case, not that it could not be *affected* by the decision: for the distinction, cf. *Military and Paramilitary Activities in and against Nicaragua* [1984] ICJ Rep 431, para. 88.

[222] See a previous article in this series: [2001] *BYBIL*, (72), p. 79; see also ibid., p. 124.

[223] [1984] ICJ Rep 28, para. 46.

[224] *Order of 21 October 1999* [1999-II] ICJ Rep 1029.

[225] See the passage in [1998] ICJ Rep 324, para. 116, quoted in the application of Equatorial Guinea to intervene, and in the Court's Order on the application, [1999] ICJ Rep 1031–2, para. 3

the contentions of Equatorial Guinea set out earlier in the Order, and citing a dictum from the *Land, Island and Maritime Boundary* case.

(f) Intervention at an interlocutory stage

The question of the nature of the legal interest to be shown by the would-be intervener, and how it can be 'affected' by the decision in the case, is relevant to the problem of the possibility of intervention at a stage of a case other than that of the merits. It was observed above, in connection with intervention under Article 63 of the Statute, that there would seem to be no reason why a State party to a multilateral convention containing a clause conferring jurisdiction on the Court could not intervene in a case between two other States parties to that convention on the basis of that clause.[226] The interpretation of the clause would be likely to be in question, and intervention should thus be possible as in relation to any other provision of the convention. What of the possibility of intervention under Article 62 during a phase of proceedings devoted to questions of jurisdiction and admissibility, in particular a phase devoted to the examination of preliminary objections?

One objection might be that, *ex hypothesi*, at the moment of the application to intervene, the Court would not have established its jurisdiction over the merits of the case: could it admit an intervention in a case over which, as it might later turn out, it had no jurisdiction whatever? On this basis, the Court would, it has been suggested,[227] have to resolve the preliminary objections before it turned to the intervention; but, assuming that the intervener could have shown a legal interest that might be affected *by the decision on the objections*, this would defeat the whole purpose of intervention. It is of course true that it is not easy to imagine a scenario in which such an interest could be shown:[228] if the problem were a question of interpretation of a multilateral compromissory clause, then intervention under Article 63 would be the appropriate course. However, if the Court were seised on the basis of an optional-clause declaration containing a reservation common to a number of such declarations (as, for example, the Connally reservation), another State having entered such a reservation might well have an interest in the Court's decision upon it; as noted above (Section 6(2)(B)), Lauterpacht thought that such a State would be entitled to receive a notification under Article 63, but an alternative would be intervention under Article 62.

If it be recognized that a mere interest in the principles and rules of international law to be applied is sufficient, then one might offer the hypothesis of an objection to admissibility based on non-exhaustion of local remedies in a specific class of case:[229] a State which intended to

[226] See above, Section 6(2)(B).

[227] See Cellamare, *Le forme di intervento nel processo dinanzi alla Corte internazionale di Giustizia*, 1991, p. 127

[228] In this sense Espaliù Berdud, op. cit., p. 287.

[229] Cf. the objection of Italy in the *Electronica Sicula* case of non-exhaustion of local remedies, and the counter-argument of the United States that the rule does not apply to treaty-based claims: [1989] ICJ Rep 42, para. 50.

bring proceedings (perhaps against the same respondent) in a case of that class would be just as interested in the treatment by the Court of that contention as would a coastal State in the Court's handling of maritime delimitation law. As we have seen, however, the decision of the Chamber in the *Land, Island and Maritime Frontier Dispute* suggests that an interest of this kind is not enough, despite the powerful arguments to the contrary of Judge Oda in his Hague Academy course.[230]

A further procedural aspect is that special agreements and applications instituting proceedings are notified to all States entitled to appear before the Court,[231] and the purpose of this is to enable them to assess whether or not they should seek to intervene in the case.[232] No such transmission of preliminary objections is now effected; until 1952, preliminary objections were regarded as a new case (with a new entry in the General List), and therefore the objections were circulated to States. The abandonment of this practice, and later of the subsequent practice of notifying States of the filing of the objections,[233] has had the (presumably unappreciated) effect of making it more difficult for a State to become aware that an objection is such that the decision on it might affect that State's legal interest.

(g) The effect of intervention

(i) Participation in the proceedings

When admitting the intervention of Nicaragua in the *Land, Island and Maritime Frontier Dispute*, the Chamber seised of that case observed that it was 'the first case in the history of the two Courts in which a State will have been accorded permission to intervene under Article 62 of the Statute'.[234] It therefore thought it appropriate

> to give some indication of the extent of the procedural rights acquired by the intervening State as a result of that permission. This is particularly desirable since the intervention permitted relates only to certain issues of the many submitted to the Chamber.[235]

The first obvious limitation was that Nicaragua's intervention was on a non-party basis, and therefore it 'does not become party to the proceedings, and does not acquire the rights, or become subject to the obligations, which attach to the status of a party, under the Statute and Rules of Court, or the general principles of procedural law'. This was to prove important, as we shall see, in relation to the question of the effect of the

[230] See page 59 above. [231] Statute, Art. 40, para. 3.

[232] See the case of the *Société Commerciale de Belgique*, PCIJ Rep Series A/B No 78, 173.

[233] See Rosenne, *The Law and Practice of the International Court*, 2nd rev.ed., 1985, pp. 529–30.

[234] [1990] ICJ Rep 135, para. 102.

[235] Ibid. Rosenne has suggested that this is the first time that the Court (or a Chamber) has alluded to such 'general principles'.

judgment for the intervening State. The Chamber continued:

Nicaragua, as an intervener, has of course a right to be heard by the Chamber. That right is regulated by Article 85 of the Rules of Court, which provides for submission of a written statement, and participation in the hearings.[236]

Since Nicaragua had only been permitted to intervene in respect of certain aspects of the case (not, for example, in relation to the dispute over the land frontier), its right to be heard was limited to those aspects.[237] Similarly in the *Cameroon/Nigeria* case, Equatorial Guinea was only concerned in that part of the case relating to maritime delimitation: since it had made clear in its application that that was all it was asking, the Court was able to define the extent of its participation simply by reference to that application.[238]

The right to be heard is normally a corollary of the status of a party, but clearly the status of non-party intervener would be meaningless without it. Apart from the limitation on the scope of Nicaragua's participation, what rights did it not enjoy that would have been enjoyed by a party? One, as it turned out, was the right to assert the force of *res judicata* of the judgment against the parties; the only other would seem to be the right to appoint a judge *ad hoc*.[239] At the time of its application to intervene, Nicaragua had not asserted such a right, but had claimed that the admission of its intervention would have, as a practical consequence, 'the reformation of the Chamber as presently constituted',[240] i.e. at least the appointment of a judge *ad hoc*, if not participation in the process of formation of the Chamber. Any request for a judge *ad hoc* at that stage would, it seems, have been rejected, on the ground that a State which has submitted a request for permission to intervene on which a decision has not yet been taken 'has yet to establish any status in relation to the case'.[241]

(ii) The effect of the judgment on the merits for the intervener State

Whatever the stated object of an intervention, if admitted it has the effect of enabling the intervening State to inform the Court of its concern lest an interest of a legal nature be affected by the decision in the case. As we shall see, the same result may however be achieved even if the intervention is rejected, as the argument on the admissibility of the intervention will offer a similar opportunity to the would-be intervener to make its position clear, and the Court has expressly indicated that it takes account of such position when preparing its judgment on the merits.

The benefits, in comparison with this, of an admitted intervention, are not as evident as one might expect. In the case of the *Land and Maritime Boundary between Cameroon and Nigeria*, the Court explained, as noted

236 [1990] ICJ Rep 136, para. 102.
237 [1990] ICJ Rep 136, paras. 103–4.
238 [1999-II] ICJ Rep 1035, para. 18(1).
239 See below, sub-s (ii).
240 [1990] ICJ Rep 5, citing Nicaragua's Application.
241 *Continental Shelf (Tunisia/Libya)* [1981] ICJ Rep 6, para. 8, quoted in [1990] ICJ Rep 5.

above, in relation to the admitted intervention of Equatorial Guinea, that particularly in maritime delimitation cases, 'the protection afforded by Article 59 of the Statute may not always be sufficient',[242] with the implication that intervention gives better protection. However, a striking aspect of this finding is that it is not apparent in what way the position of Equatorial Guinea differed from that of Sao Tome and Principe; at first sight, therefore, the admission of the intervention of Equatorial Guinea would not seem to have achieved anything. As explained in Section 3(C) above, the advantage gained would seem to be, at most, that Equatorial Guinea had the opportunity of indicating how the Court could avoid prejudicing its interests, whereas as regards Sao Tome and Principe, the Court would have to ascertain for itself what interests might be prejudiced, and in what way.

The effect of Article 59 of the Statute when a third State has legal interests that may in some way be affected by the decision in a case before the Court, has been examined in Section 3(C) above: there is, it appears, a duty of the Court to avoid affecting such interests, but its decision cannot in any event affect the third State's rights. Three possible situations may be envisaged (and have been observed): the third State may succeed in intervening, and explaining the nature of its fears (Equatorial Guinea); or it may apply to intervene, fail to obtain permission, but have the opportunity of explaining its fears in the course of the proceedings on its application (Malta and, in particular, Italy in the *Continental Shelf* cases); or it may take no action, and rely on the Court's duty, as expressed in the *Cameroon/Nigeria* decision, to avoid encroachment on its interests (Sao Tome and Principe).

It would seem to follow from the status of an intervening State as a non-party to the proceedings that it would neither be bound by the judgment given, nor entitled to enforce it, as *res judicata*, against the original parties. This in fact was stated to be the position in the *Land, Island and Maritime Frontier Dispute*:

> The terms on which intervention was granted . . . were that Nicaragua would not, as intervening State, become a party to the proceedings. The binding force of the present Judgment for the Parties, as contemplated by Article 59 of the Statute of the Court, does not therefore extend to Nicaragua as intervener.[243]

It went on to state as a general rule that 'a State permitted to intervene under Article 62 of the Statute, but which does not acquire the status of party to the case, is not bound by the judgment given in the proceedings in which it has intervened', and recalled that when admitting Nicaragua's intervention it had stated that the intervening State did not become a party, and 'does not acquire the rights, or become subject to the obligations, which attach to the status of party'.[244] For the Chamber, the intervener acquired a right to be heard, without the obligation of being bound by the decision.

[242] [2002] ICJ Rep 421, para. 238.

[243] [1992] ICJ Rep 609, para. 421.

[244] Ibid., para. 423.

This ruling is consistent with the terms of Article 59 of the Statute (which, curiously enough, the Chamber did not cite) that 'The decision of the Court has no binding force *except between the parties* and in respect of that particular case.'

In the *Land, Island and Maritime Frontier Dispute* case however Judge Oda drew attention to the fact that some of the findings of the Chamber were as to joint entitlements of the three States, El Salvador, Honduras, and Nicaragua, inside and outside the Gulf of Fonseca, and he asked rhetorically whether Nicaragua was not bound to comply with these decisions. In his view, 'Nicaragua, as a non-party intervener, will certainly be bound by this judgment in so far as it relates to the legal situation of the maritime spaces of the Gulf'.[245] In this, Judge Oda was being consistent with his dissents in respect of the applications of Malta and Italy to intervene in the two *Continental Shelf* cases, in which he described a system of non-party intervention similar to that recognized by the Chamber in 1992, and went on to say that

> The intervening State cannot, of course, escape the binding force of the judgment, which naturally applies to it to the extent that the intervention has been allowed.[246]

This view prompts the question: if a non-party intervener is bound by the decision, how does its status differ from that of a State intervening as a party? For Judge Oda, the difference is simply that the intervener plays a reduced role in the proceedings, as compared with that of a true party: any concrete claim that it makes 'must be confined to the scope of the original Application or Special Agreement in the principal case'.[247]

Judge *ad hoc* Torres Bernárdez in the *Land, Island and Maritime Frontier* case, while agreeing with Judge Oda, drew a distinction: he agreed with the majority that the judgment was not *res judicata* for Nicaragua, but thought that it had effects other than *res judicata* for Nicaragua.[248] These he did not spell out, but apparently he considered the passages of the judgment concerning joint entitlements as binding on Nicaragua. Judge Torres Bernárdez based his view on

> the fact that I cannot, as a general proposition, conceive of rights without obligations as well as upon the general economy of the institution of intervention as embodied in Articles 62 and 63 of the Statute. Interventions under Article 63, for example, are non-party interventions and nevertheless the intervening State is under the obligations set forth in that article.[249]

[245] [1992] ICJ Rep 609, pp. 609–10, para. 423.

[246] [1981] ICJ Rep 27, para. 9; quoted in [1984] ICJ Rep 98, para. 18.

[247] Ibid.

[248] [1992] ICJ Rep 730–1, para. 208.

[249] Ibid., pp. 730–1. The distinction made here by Torres Bernárdez between *res judicata* and the binding effect of the judgment is somewhat obscure. In his Hague Academy lectures it becomes clearer that he is distinguishing between the effect of the judgment itself, as a whole, and the binding nature of the legal principles or rules enunciated in the judgment insofar as these were the subject of the intervention, thus preserving the parallelism with Art. 63: see 'L'intervention dans la procédure de la CIJ', 256 *Recueil des cours*, 1995, pp. 428–9.

The parallel thus drawn would apparently mean that, in the case of intervention under Article 62, that part of the judgment that would 'affect' the 'interest of a legal nature' of the intervening State would be binding upon it. There are obvious difficulties in ascertaining exactly which parts of the judgment would have that effect—if indeed there were any: for the object of the intervening State may be taken to have been to *prevent* the judgment from having such an effect.

In his course at the Hague Academy, Torres Bernárdez returned to the issue of the effect of the judgment for the intervener, or rather (since he continued to agree that such judgment would not have the force of *res judicata*) the effects of the intervention itself. He argued that inherent in any form of intervention is a rule that can be found expressly stated in Article 31, paragraph 3, of the Statute of the International Tribunal for the Law of the Sea:

> If a request to intervene is granted, the decision of the Tribunal in respect of the dispute shall be binding upon the intervening State Party in so far as it relates to matters in respect of which that State Party intervened.

For him, this is a matter of general principles governing intervention as a procedural institution: the rule can only be excluded by express legislative enactment.[250] He also drew attention to the anomalies resulting from the opposite view, in relation to the express provision in Article 63 for a limited binding effect.

The difficulty with this approach is it requires the silence of Article 62 on the point to prevail, in the name of a *soi-disant* general principle of law,[251] over the express statements in Articles 63 and 59, the latter amounting very nearly to the express legislative exclusion to which Torres Bernárdez refers.

A complication in the *Land, Island and Maritime Frontier Dispute* was that at one stage of the proceedings Nicaragua had announced that, if permitted to intervene, it would voluntarily subject itself to the binding effect of the judgment (though it had subsequently gone back on this undertaking). The Chamber did not consider that such a unilateral submission could be effective: it recalled the need for the consent of the parties, *ad hoc* or in the form of a jurisdictional link, and continued:

> This is essential because the force of *res judicata* does not operate in one direction only: if an intervener becomes a party, and is thus bound by the judgment, it becomes entitled equally to assert the binding force of the judgment against the other parties. A non-party to a case before the Court, whether or not admitted to intervene, cannot by its own unilateral act place itself in the

[250] 'L'intervention dans la procédure de la CIJ', 256 *Recueil des cours*, 1995, p. 430.

[251] The question whether general principles of law can prevail over express treaty provisions is not without difficulty: on the relationship of sources in general, see the first article in this series, [1989] *BYBIL*, pp. 143 ff.

position of a party, and claim to be able to rely on the judgment against the original parties.[252]

Judges Oda and Torres Bernárdez apparently did not dissent from this aspect of the decision.

(h) The effect of a failed application to intervene

It might be supposed that if an application to intervene under Article 62 were rejected, the proceedings between the original parties would continue undisturbed, and the decision of the Court on the merits would take no particular account of the contentions of the would-be intervener. In the case of *Sovereignty over Pulau Ligitan and Pulau Sipadan (Indonesia/Malaysia)*, this would appear to have been so, but the asserted 'interest of a legal nature' was so marginal in that case that it could hardly have been otherwise.

In other cases, however, relating to the delimitation of maritime areas, the Court has recognized a certain impact of a rejected application to intervene, in the form of a fetter on the Court's freedom to give judgment having the fullest scope requested by the parties. In the case between Tunisia and Libya, the Court made no mention of Malta in its judgment, but when defining the 'general area relevant for the delimitation' it noted the existence of a region to the north-east 'where conflicting claims of other States regarding the same areas have been made or may be made in the future,' and added 'The Court has no jurisdiction to deal with such problems in the present case and must not prejudge their solution in the future.'[253] The situation was made particularly clear in the case of the *Continental Shelf (Libya/Malta)*: having first found Italy's application to intervene inadmissible, the Court at a later stage of its judgment on Italy's application indicated that it would, in its subsequent judgment on the merits, 'take account, as a fact, of the existence of other States having claims in the region'.[254] It continued with a certain degree of prescience:

> If, as Italy has suggested, the decision of the Court in the present case, taken without Italy's participation, had for that reason to be more limited in scope between the Parties themselves, and subject to more caveats and restrictions in favour of third States, than it might otherwise have been had Italy been present, it is the interests of Libya and Malta which might be said to be affected, not those of Italy. It is material to recall that Libya and Malta, by objecting to the intervention of Italy, have indicated their own preferences.[255]

In the judgment, given the following year, on the merits of the case, the Court recalled this observation, and held that

[252] Ibid., p. 610, para. 424. For an attempt to acquire procedural status unilaterally, cf. the unusual declaration made by Malta under Art. 36, para. 2, of the Statute, purporting to exclude reciprocity, discussed in a previous article in this series: [1999] *BYBIL*, pp. 36 ff.

[253] [1982] ICJ Rep 42, paras. 33, 35; see also para. 75. This aspect complicated the task of the Court in applying to its delimitation the test of proportionality of areas and coastal lengths, but it was able to get round the difficulty: see ibid. p. 91, para. 130.

[254] [1984] ICJ Rep 26, para. 43.

[255] Ibid., p. 27, para. 43.

> The present decision must, as then foreshadowed, be limited in geographical scope so as to leave the claims of Italy unaffected, that is to say that the decision of the Court must be confined to the area in which, as the Court has been informed by Italy, that State has no claims to continental shelf rights.[256]

The paradoxical result was thus that while Italy, if it had been permitted to intervene, would have had to argue the legal bases of its claims in the area, as a result of the refusal of its intervention those claims were taken as an unchallengeable 'given' which had to be respected in any delimitation the Court might make.

Similarly in the case of *Sovereignty over Pulau Ligitan and Pulau Sipadan*, the Court, after rejecting the application of the Philippines to intervene, stated in its judgment on that application the following:

> The Court nevertheless observes that, notwithstanding its finding that the Philippines has not demonstrated an entitlement to intervene in the pending case between Indonesia and Malaysia, it remains cognizant of the positions stated before it by Indonesia, Malaysia and the Philippines in the present proceedings.[257]

(4) *Some conclusions on intervention under Article 62*

It is probably not possible to reconcile all the dicta in the jurisprudence of the Court on the subject of intervention under Article 62, but the following conclusions may perhaps be advanced, particularly if the early decisions in the two *Continental Shelf* cases are treated as more tentative than definitive.

(i) The type of intervention primarily authorized under Article 62 is intervention without the status of party; its purpose is to inform the Court of legal and factual contentions of the intervener in defence of an interest of a legal nature which might be affected by the decision in the case.

(ii) The legal rights of third States are protected by Article 59 of the Statute; a judgment of the Court cannot affect such rights, being *res inter alios acta*, rather than *res judicata* as far as they are concerned. A legal *interest* of a State may require protection, in the sense that a judgment may leave third-State rights unaffected, but prejudice their recognition or implementation, in which case the protection of Article 59 may not be sufficient, particularly in cases of maritime delimitation (*Cameroon/Nigeria*).

(iii) The choice by a State not to intervene does not, or should not, result in such a legal interest being affected: it is the duty of the Court so to limit its judgment as to avoid this, just as it has the duty to refrain from deciding the case at all if the rights and interests of a third State form 'the very subject-matter of the decision'.

[256] [1984] ICJ Rep 26, para. 21. [257] [2001] ICJ Rep 607, para. 94.

(iv) Third States in general have the protection both of this duty and of Article 59, which ensures that the effect of *res judicata* of the decision is limited to the parties to the case. The 'added value' of intervention is thus simply to ensure that the Court is fully informed of the interest of the intervening State when considering the limits within which it should decide.

(v) It is doubtful whether non-party intervention is possible simply to defend a particular thesis as to the law applicable to the dispute; at the least, something more than a mere hypothetical interest must be demonstrated (*Sovereignty over Pulau Ligitan and Pulau Sipadan*).

(vi) It is possible to intervene also as a party, but for this either a 'jurisdictional link' with at least one, and probably both, parties is required, or both parties must consent to the intervention. It is not clear whether such an intervention is also authorized under Article 62, or whether it follows simply from an application of the principle of consent as creative of international jurisdiction.

(vii) When a third State seeks to intervene as a non-party, the consent of the parties cannot substitute for compliance with the conditions of Article 62 (existence of a legal interest that may be affected), but the Court will probably be reluctant to refuse such an intervention in the face of implied recognition by the parties of the existence of such an interest.

(viii) In the earlier cases, the States parties to the case tended to oppose intervention because of the prevailing uncertainty as to its effects, and to some extent the Court's reluctance to permit intervention may be attributed to that uncertainty, and to the continuing controversy over the nature of intervention, and consequently the relevance of a 'jurisdictional link'. The Chamber in the *Land, Island and Maritime Frontier Dispute*, being composed of judges generally more favourable to non-party intervention, broke the deadlock, and its approach was subsequently approved by the full Court. It now appears that non-party intervention normally poses no threat to the interests of the parties, so it may be that there will be less opposition in future cases.

(5) *Information supplied by international organizations (Statute, Article 34)*

Intervention under Articles 62 and 63 of the Statute is only open to States,[258] whether or not the result of an intervention is to make them 'parties' to the case in which the intervention is made. However, the same Article of the Statute that provides that 'Only States may be parties in cases before the Court', Article 34, also provides for a procedure somewhat analogous to intervention whereby the Court may request information

[258] In 1920 there was a proposal to allow intervention by the ILO and similar institutions, but this was rejected by the Third Committee of the First Assembly of the League: see Hudson, *The Permanent Court of International Justice*, p. 209, section 211.

relevant to cases before it from international organizations, and shall receive information supplied by such organizations on their own initiative. These texts were added to Article 34 in 1945, and were in fact explained as being justified by the fact that the jurisdiction of the Court was limited to States.[259]

The parallel with the texts on intervention is pursued inasmuch as Article 34, paragraph 3, corresponds to Article 63 by providing that

> Whenever the construction of the constituent instrument of a public international organization or of an international convention adopted thereunder is in question in a case before the Court, the Registrar shall so notify the public international organization concerned and shall communicate to it copies of all the written proceedings.

One difference between this text[260] and Article 63 is however that when States are notified under the latter provision that the construction of a convention is in question, the notification is not necessarily accompanied by copies of the pleadings, which are normally confidential unless and until the Court decides to make them available to a third State, or accessible to the public, under Article 53 of the Rules of Court.

This difference was highlighted in the case of *Border and Transborder Armed Actions (Nicaragua v Honduras)*, when the Secretary General of the Organization of American States responded to a notification under Article 34 in connection with the Pact of Bogotá.[261] The Secretary General took the view that he himself had no authority to submit observations, and

> the convening of the Permanent Council of the Organization on this matter would require that each Member State be provided with copies of all the written proceedings on the case which may contravene the Rules of Court.[262]

The matter was apparently allowed to rest there, no observations being submitted, and no further comment being made by the Court.

This aspect of the matter was also emphasized by Iran when, in the case concerning the *Aerial Incident of 3 July 1988 (Islamic Republic of Iran v United States of America)*, it sought to convince the Court that no information should be sought or received from ICAO. That Organization had been notified under Article 34, paragraph 3, and had indicated an intention to submit information; when Iran was informed of this, it addressed a letter to the Court arguing that it would be inappropriate for such information

[259] UNCIO, documents, Vol. 14, p. 697. Some States had apparently gone further, and suggested that international organizations might be parties to cases (ibid.).

[260] Article 34 provides for the Registrar to send copies of the pleadings with the notification; but curiously enough Art. 69 of the 1978 Rules of Court adds the qualification 'on the instructions of the Court, or of the President if the Court is not sitting'. While the general tendency of the 1978 Rules is to restrict the independent action of the Registrar by the Court, it does not seem that the intention was that the Court might decide not to send copies of the pleadings: see Guyomar, *Commentaire du Règlement de la CIJ*, pp. 445–6.

[261] *Border and Transborder Armed Actions, Pleadings, Oral Arguments, Documents*, Vol. II, p. 240, No. 31.

[262] Ibid., p. 242, No. 36.

to be submitted.[263] Citing the precedent of the Organization of American States in the *Border and Transborder Armed Actions* case, it observed that any observations to be presented by ICAO would be submitted to the Council of the organization for comment, and that

> In the light of the confidentiality of the pleadings, however, it would obviously be inappropriate for any of the Parties' positions as set forth in their pleadings or documents to be reflected in those comments lest such confidentiality be compromised.[264]

The Court however was apparently not convinced by this argument, or the other arguments presented by Iran, and observations of ICAO under Article 34 were received,[265] though since the case was discontinued they never came to be examined by the Court.

This is in fact the only occasion on which observations have been submitted by an international organization under Article 34;[266] and there is therefore no material to indicate how they would be treated by the Court. Since an international organization cannot be a party to a case, it presumably also cannot be bound, as such, by any interpretation given by the Court of its constituent instrument 'or of an international convention adopted thereunder'. It might seem that such an interpretation by the Court would carry more weight if it were given after examination of the views of the organization; but one may ask what in fact would be meant by the expression 'the views of the organization'?[267] Does the council or governing body of an international organization have authority to interpret its constituent instrument, not for purposes of its own action, but for the guidance of the International Court? As noted above, the Secretary General of the Organization of American States did not think that it was his views that were wanted; and the observations submitted by ICAO in the *Aerial Incident* case were very carefully confined to an analysis of the facts of the handling of the matter by the Organization, leading merely to a conclusion as to the Articles of the Chicago Convention under which Iran's request to the Organization had been handled.

It is probably to be concluded that Article 34, paragraph 3, of the Statute has not proved to have any particular usefulness, and is likely to remain a dead letter.

[263] *Aerial incident of 3 July 1988, Pleadings, Oral Arguments, Documents*, p. 639, No. 3.

[264] Ibid., p. 643. [265] Ibid., pp. 617 ff.

[266] In the *South West Africa* cases, the ILO offered to supply information, but the Court did not take up the offer (*Pleadings*, pp. 543–4, Nos. 56, 57). In the *Appeal relating to the Jurisdiction of the ICAO Council*, ICAO was notified under Article 34 but did not consider it appropriate to submit observations (*Pleadings*, p. 779, No. 29).

[267] A similar problem sometimes arises in advisory proceedings: note the reticence of the Secretary General of WHO in the proceedings on the request of that Organization for an advisory opinion on *Legality of the Use by a State of Nuclear Weapons in Armed Conflict*, a request presented against the advice of the Secretary General and Legal Counsel.

7. *Interpretation of judgments*

As Judge Weeramantry observed in the case of the request of Nigeria for interpretation of the judgment concerning the *Land and Maritime Frontier between Cameroon and Nigeria*,

> A judgment, however well crafted, could well embody phraseology which, in the context of a given set of circumstances, may require some clarification. It is one of those incidents of litigation which the judicial experience of ages has shown may arise from time to time, and it is precisely for this reason that Article 60 of the Court's Statute made such clear provision for the right to interpretation.[268]

He also noted that that Article is drafted in imperative terms so as to lay a duty on the Court: it reads: 'The judgment is final and without appeal. In the event of dispute as to the meaning or scope of the judgment, the Court shall construe it upon the request of any party.'

In the same case, the Court drew out what it regarded as the implications of the fact that the reference to interpretation directly follows the assertion of the finality of judgments of the Court, in one and the same Article of the Statute.[269]

> The question of the admissibility of requests for the interpretation of the Court's judgments needs particular attention because of the need to avoid impairing the finality, and delaying the implementation, of these judgments. It is not without reason that Article 60 of the Statute lays down, in the first place, that judgments are 'final and without appeal'. Thereafter, the Article provides that in the case of a 'dispute as to the meaning or scope of the judgment', it shall be construed by the Court upon the request of any party. The language and structure of Article 60 reflect the primacy of the principle of *res judicata*. That principle must be maintained.[270]

The Court then went on to repeat what it had already stated in the *Asylum* case, that the 'real purpose of the request must be to obtain an interpretation of the judgment'.[271]

With all due respect, the logic of this passage is obscure. If there is doubt about the meaning of a judgment, about what has been decided with the force of *res judicata*, it is in no way a contradiction or qualification of the principle of *res judicata* to recognize a possibility of authoritative interpretation. The implementation of the judgment may have to wait upon the availability of the interpretation: but an obscure or unintelligible judgment is not capable of immediate implementation, and perhaps not of any implementation at all. It appears that what the Court may have intended was what was put much more simply by Judge

[268] Dissenting opinion, [1999-I] ICJ Rep 47.

[269] The text of Art. 60 was based on two separate articles of the 1907 Hague Convention, the one (dating from 1899) providing for the finality of arbitral decisions and the other (added in 1907) for interpretation of awards: see Stauffenberg, *Statut et règlement de la CPJI: Éléments d'inteprétation*, p. 424. For another possible significance of the linking in Art. 60 of the two concepts, see Subsection 2 below.

[270] [1999-I] ICJ Rep 36, para. 12.

[271] *Request for Interpretation of the judgment of 20 November 1950 in the Asylum Case* [1950] ICJ Rep 402.

Weeramantry: that the parties are not entitled, 'in any circumstances, to use a request for interpretation as a way of gaining time'; such a device is 'to be discountenanced, and the Court will in no way lend its assistance to such procedures.'[272] However, even deliberate delay in the implementation of a judgment does not necessarily amount to a contradiction of its force as *res judicata*.

Only three applications for the interpretation of a judgment have been made to the post-war Court. The first of these was in the *Asylum* case, and was briefly dealt with by Fitzmaurice in his series of articles.[273] He there drew attention to the reasons why in that case the Court declined to exercise the power of interpretation: because the real object of the request was not to obtain an interpretation of the actual judgment, but to obtain a decision on other questions not covered by the judgment; and because the dispute was not of the kind contemplated by Article 60. Of the other two applications,[274] one was found to have been properly brought under Article 60, and an interpretation was given (though not that asked for), while the second was found inadmissible; but in neither of them did the applicant for interpretation obtain from the Court what it had hoped to achieve.

(1) *The jurisdiction to interpret: effect of the will of the Parties*

The jurisdiction to interpret is of course a further example of the incidental jurisdiction of the Court, conferred by accession to the Statute, and thus not dependent on the *ad hoc* consent of the parties to a case.[275] The modalities of its exercise are therefore apparently also independent of the will of the parties, so that its exercise in a specific case cannot be excluded by, for example, a provision in the special agreement by which the case is brought. That at least appears to follow from a ruling by the Court in the proceedings brought by Tunisia for (*inter alia*) interpretation of the Court's judgment in the *Continental Shelf* case between Tunisia and Libya.

The special agreement in that case provided for the parties to agree a delimitation following the judgment of the Court, and failing such agreement within three months, the parties might jointly apply to the court for 'explanations and clarifications'. Libya contended that this provision

[272] [1999-I] ICJ Rep 43.

[273] [1952] *BYBIL* 29, pp. 45–6, and [1958] *BYBIL* 34, pp. 128–30; *Collected Edition*, Vol. I, pp. 113–14 and Vol. II, pp. 555–7.

[274] *Application for Revision and Interpretation of the judgment of 24 February 1982 in the Case concerning the Continental Shelf (Tunisia/Libyan Arab Jamahiriya), ICJ Reports, 1985, p.192; Request for interpretation of the judgment of 11 June 1998 in the case concerning the Land and Maritime Boundary between Cameroon and Nigeria (Cameroon v Nigeria), Preliminary Objections (Nigeria v Cameroon)* [1991-I] ICJ Rep 31.

[275] The Permanent Court had some doubts, when discussing the 1926 revision of the Rules of Court, whether this was an independent form of 'compulsory' jurisdiction, so as to be exercisable even where the original decision had been given in the exercise of jurisdiction conferred by a special agreement; it decided to leave the point open (Stauffenberg, op. cit (n. 165 above), p. 427). The question seems to have been tacitly settled by the subsequent jurisprudence.

entailed prior negotiations before such approach to the Court, and that since Tunisia had not endeavoured to negotiate in good faith, it could not seek an interpretation under Article 60. As the Court noted, the question thus arose of the relationship between this special procedure and the possibility of seeking an interpretation under Article 60.

The Court drew a distinction between consensual jurisdiction in respect of the merits of a case, and special jurisdiction deriving from the provisions of the Statute.

> When examining its [merits] jurisdiction under Article 36 of the Statute, the Court is accordingly bound to examine and give effect . . . to . . . any jurisdictional pre-conditions, and to any unambiguous waiver of a jurisdictional objection.[276] The jurisdiction of the Court to give an interpretation of one of its own judgments, on the other hand, is a special jurisdiction deriving from Article 60 of the Statute. Thus the Court has in any event to consider whether the conditions for the existence of that jurisdiction are fulfilled. Furthermore, the Parties to this case, in becoming parties to the Statute of the Court, have consented to that jurisdiction without pre-condition.[277]

The Court however did not go quite so far as to say that any condition that the parties might agree to attach to the exercise of statutory jurisdiction would be ineffective: it preferred to adopt a more moderate interpretation of the special agreement.

> Whether or not such an agreement could validly derogate—as between the parties thereto—from the Statute, it is not lightly to be presumed that a State would renounce or fetter its right under Article 60 of the Statute to request an interpretation unilaterally.[278]

Judge Ruda dissented on this point; in his view,

> it does not seem to be the intention of the Parties to waive their rights under the Statute, but to establish a previous procedure for coming to the Court, before they decide to ask unilaterally for an interpretation . . .
>
> It would be an interesting juridical exercise to study whether States may waive their rights under the Statute in a special agreement, but this theoretical problem is not before the Court . . .[279]

A separate question, not dealt with by the Court, is whether the arrangements contemplated in the special agreement for the Court to be asked for 'explanations and clarifications' could have been implemented. There does not seem to be any reason why not. In the *Haya de la Torre* case, the parties to the earlier *Asylum* case (and to the proceedings on the request for interpretation in that case) came back to the Court on the basis of an application filed by Colombia asking, in effect, how the *Asylum* judgment was to implemented. The Court found that the Parties had

[276] This aspect was relevant, because it was not clear whether Libya had insisted on its argument that jurisdiction under Art. 60 was, in the specific case, subject to the preconditions of the special agreement.

[277] [1985] ICJ Rep 216, para. 43.

[278] Ibid.

[279] Ibid., separate opinion of Judge Ruda, pp. 234–5, paras. 13–14.

consented to the jurisdiction of the Court (a question that, as between Tunisia and Libya, would be regulated by the special agreement), and made a finding on one of the submissions of the parties.[280] If it did not give Colombia satisfaction on the main issue it had raised, that of how the *Asylum* judgment was to be implemented, this was because the reply to that question was not one that could be based on legal considerations,[281] not because the procedure was inappropriate, or lacking jurisdiction.

A request by Tunisia or Libya for 'explanations and clarifications' would thus apparently have been receivable; and in fact the question raised by Tunisia in its request for interpretation was resolved, as the Court explained, in the course of the Court's ruling on its parallel request for revision.[282] In other words, it does not seem that the existence of the special procedure under Article 60 of the Statute excludes the submission to the Court, as a separate case, of a dispute over the meaning of a previous judgment. Such a special procedure could not, however, be invoked in priority to an application under Article 60, and so as to block or suspend it.

(2) *What decisions may be interpreted?*

Only a judgment may be the subject of an interpretation: the Statute and Rules are silent on the course open to an organ or organization that has requested an advisory opinion, and finds that there is doubt over the meaning of some passage in it. Presumably however there is no bar to that organ or organization seeking a second advisory opinion on the question.

The linking of the two sentences of Article 60—the finality of the judgment and the possibility of interpretation—does suggest that only a decision of the Court that is 'final and without appeal' is open to interpretation. Orders of the Court would therefore be excluded, even such 'substantive' orders as those indicating provisional measures, since these are by definition effective only pending the final judgment in the case. Another reason that has in the past been advanced for excluding orders indicating provisional measures from the scope of interpretation under Article 60 is that the reference to a decision that is 'final and without appeal' signifies also that the decision must be binding; that indeed is the significance of *res judicata*. While there was controversy on the point, many scholars—perhaps the majority—considered that an order indicating provisional measures was not binding;[283] and it was therefore argued that no interpretation of such an order was possible under Article 60.[284] Now that the Court has held that such orders do create binding

[280] [1951] ICJ Rep 78, 83. On this aspect of *Haya de la Torre*, see Fitzmaurice, [1958] *BYBIL*, 34, pp. 130–1; *Collected Edition*, Vol. II, pp. 555–6.

[281] Ibid., p. 79.

[282] [1985] ICJ Rep 220, para. 50.

[283] See the discussion on this point in the previous article in this series, [2001] *BYBIL*, pp. 11 ff.

[284] Zimmermann, *Interpretation of judgments of the ICJ under Article 60 of the Statute*, Max-Planck-Institut, Heidelberg, 1989, p. 67.

obligations,[285] this argument falls. Nevertheless, one may question the usefulness of a request under Article 60, given that under Article 76 of the Rules of Court a party may seek revocation or modification of 'any decision concerning provisional measures'.

There are however of course judgments of the Court other than those disposing of a case on the merits, in particular decisions on preliminary objections, which have traditionally been given in the form of a judgment, as is now provided in Article 79, paragraph 9, of the 1978/2000 Rules of Court. In the *South West Africa* case, the Court adverted to the question whether a judgment on preliminary objections has the effect of *res judicata* and can be interpreted by the Court, but left it open:

> the Court finds it unnecessary to pronounce on . . . whether a decision on a preliminary objection constitutes a *res judicata* in the proper sense of that term—whether it ranks as a 'decision' for the purposes of Article 59 of the Court's Statute, or as 'final' within the meaning of Article 60.[286]

In the case concerning the *Land and Maritime Boundary between Cameroon and Nigeria*, a request was made by Nigeria for interpretation of the judgment given on 11 June 1998 disposing of Nigeria's preliminary objections. Cameroon did not assert that interpretation was not available in respect of a judgment on preliminary objections, but expressed doubts. It suggested that, since the judgment was not on the merits, but on preliminary objections, and the questioned portion of the judgment related to an objection declared not to have 'an exclusively preliminary character', the Parties 'do not have to "apply" such a judgment; they only have to take note of it'.[287] The Court did not directly comment on this contention, but held that

> By virtue of the second sentence of Article 60, the Court has jurisdiction to entertain requests for interpretation of any judgment rendered by it. This provision makes no distinction as to the type of judgment concerned. It follows, therefore, that a judgment on preliminary objections, just as well as a judgment on the merits, can be the object of a request for interpretation.[288]

On this basis, the decision on a request for revision, or indeed on a request for interpretation, can apparently be the subject of a request for interpretation, since Article 100, paragraph 2, of the Rules of Court provides that such a decision 'shall itself be given in the form of a judgment'. The Rules do not contain a comparable provision for the decision on an intervention under Article 63 of the Statute, or an application for permission to intervene under Article 62 of the Statute (Rules, Article 84, paragraph 1), but these in practice take the form of a judgment.[289]

[285] *LaGrand*, [2001] ICJ Rep 501–6, paras. 98–109.

[286] [1966] ICJ Rep 36–7, para. 59.

[287] Quoted in the judgment, [1999-I] ICJ Rep 35, para. 9.

[288] *Request for Interpretation, judgment of 25 March 1999* [1999-I] ICJ Rep 35, para. 10.

[289] The decision whether or not the subject of a counter-claim should be joined to the original proceedings, though normally final in effect, is made by an Order: see *Application of the Genocide Convention, Order of 17 December 1997* [1997] ICJ Rep 243.

(3) *Existence of a dispute as to the meaning or scope of the judgment*

Article 60 of the Statute confers power on the Court to interpret a judgment '[i]n the event of dispute as to the meaning or scope' thereof. This might appear no more than an indication of the circumstances in which an interpretation might be required; but it has been interpreted strictly as a condition of validity of an application for interpretation. Thus in the *Asylum* case, the fact that the request for interpretation was made the very day the judgment was delivered was treated as showing that 'such a dispute could not possibly have arisen in any way whatever',[290] and that the requirements of the Statute and Rules had not been satisfied.

In the *Tunisia/Libya* case, Libya complained that Tunisia had not made it clear, before applying to the Court, what was the nature of the alleged dispute; the Court quoted from the decision of the Permanent Court on the *Interpretation of judgments Nos. 7 and 8 (Factory at Chorzów)*, and in particular the statement that

> It would no doubt be desirable that a State should not proceed to take as serious a step as summoning another State to appear before the Court without having previously, within reasonable limits, endeavoured to make it quite clear that a difference of views is in question which has not been capable of being otherwise overcome. But in view of the wording of the article, the Court considers that it cannot require that the dispute should have manifested itself in a formal way: according to the Court's view, it should be sufficient if the two Governments have in fact shown themselves as holding opposite views in regard to the meaning or scope of a judgment of the Court.[291]

A further point emphasized both in the Permanent Court decision and in the *Tunisia/Libya* case was that the difference of opinion should be one 'as to those points in the judgment in question which have been decided with binding force', including a difference of opinion 'as to whether a particular point has or has not been decided with binding force'.[292] In this respect, the judgment that had been given in the *Continental Shelf* case between Tunisia and Libya was of a special nature, since the Court had not been asked to decide on a delimitation line, but to indicate the international legal principles and rules applicable to the delimitation. It had gone further than that, however, giving indications as to the delimitation that referred to specific points and angles. Was a dispute over these eligible to be determined by a process of interpretation under Article 60?

The Court made it clear that the special nature of the task it had been asked to perform did not deprive its decision of the force of *res judicata*. As to the specific figures for the location of points or the definition of angles, the Court indicated that no general rule could be laid down.

[290] [1950] ICJ Rep 403.

[291] PCIJ Rep Series A No. 13, 10–11, quoted in [1985] ICJ Rep 218, para. 46.

[292] *PCIJ* loc. cit., pp. 11–12, quoted in *ICJ Reports*, loc. cit.

> . . . it is not possible to argue *a priori* that any specific indications as to angles, distances or co-ordinates to be found in the 1982 Judgment are necessarily . . . to be read as no more than approximations or 'guidance' . . .
>
> However, the opposite presumption would also be false: in particular it is not to be supposed that all figures used in the Judgment would have to be regarded as absolute. Each such reference must be read in its context, to establish whether the Court intended it as a precise statement, an approximation for working purposes, or a simple indication subject to variation.[293]

In the *Land and Maritime Boundary* case, the Court however indicated one limitation on the scope of the provision in the Statute for interpretation of judgments, arising in effect out of the coupling, in Article 60 of the Statute, of interpretation with the final character of the decision to be interpreted. The Court quoted the dictum of the Permanent Court in the case of *Interpretation of judgments Nos. 7 and 8 (Factory at Chorzów)*, that

> the second sentence of Article 60 was inserted in order, if necessary, to enable the Court to make quite clear the points which had been settled with binding force in a judgment, . . . a request which has not that object does not come within the terms of this provision,[294]

and concluded that

> In consequence, any request for interpretation must relate to the operative part of the judgment and cannot concern the reasons for the judgment except in so far as these are inseparable from the operative part.[295]

The Court did however appear to be ready to adopt a not over-strict interpretation of the criterion of inseparability of the reasons from the operative part.[296]

This is in fact a criterion which it is difficult to apply: one would think that all the reasoning in a judgment would be necessary to, and therefore inseparable from, the operative part. One may also wonder whether it was the same, or a different, criterion that was contemplated in the context of intervention, in the case of *Sovereignty over Pulau Ligitan and Pulau Sipadan*, where the Court considered that

> the interest of a legal nature to be shown by a State seeking to intervene under Article 62 of the Statute is not limited to the *dispositif* alone of a judgment. It may also relate to the reasons which constitute the necessary steps to the *dispositif*.[297]

For purposes of interpretation, the appropriate test might be: is clarification necessary in order for the judgment to be implemented? This however is not consistent with the decision in the *Cameroon/Nigeria* case, since, as noted above, Cameroon pointed out in that case that the judgment did not need to be implemented, but was, as it were, self-executing,

293 [1985] ICJ Rep 219, para. 49.
294 *Judgment No. 11, 1927* PCIJ Rep Series A No. 13, 1.
295 [1999] ICJ Rep 35, para. 10.
296 See para. 11 of the judgment [1999-I] ICJ Rep 35–6.
297 [2001] ICJ Rep 596, para. 47. See above, Section D. In the case of revision, there is no specific requirement that the revision relate to the operative part, but since the new fact shown must be such as to be a 'decisive factor' in the decision, it would normally relate (*inter alia*) to the operative part.

but the Court nevertheless held that Article 60 applied. The test applied by the Permanent Court was based on the view that the provision in the Statute for interpretation

> was inserted in order, if necessary, to enable the Court to make quite clear the points which had been settled with binding force in a judgment . . .[298]

and even a self-executing judgment, or a declaratory judgment, has the force of *res judicata*. In the *Continental Shelf* case between Tunisia and Libya, the Court had been asked in the special agreement only to indicate the applicable rules and principles of international law, the delimitation being left to the parties to effect by agreement. The Court explained that this fact 'in no way affects the judgment of the Court or its binding effect on the parties as a matter of *res judicata*,'[299] so that the test indicated by the Permanent Court was satisfied.

(4) *The procedure*

The procedure on a request for the interpretation of a judgment differs from that on an application to intervene or an application for revision inasmuch as it only involves a single stage of procedure. An intervention under Article 62 of the Statute involves an initial stage at which the Court considers whether to grant permission to intervene, and a second stage at which the intervener (if so permitted) presents its case. An application for revision involves first a decision on the admissibility of the application, and then a decision on whether or not to effect the revision requested.

On an application for interpretation, the Court may decide immediately to give the interpretation requested; or it may decide that the application is inadmissible, and take the matter no farther.[300] If the application goes beyond the proper scope of a request for interpretation, the Court may sever the true request from the rest, and deal with it under Article 60.[301] As will be seen below, the second of the two requests for interpretation made by Tunisia in the case of the *Continental Shelf (Tunisia/Libya)* was first found to be admissible, and then given effect by declarations of the Court as to the meaning of the questioned passages in the judgment.[302] The request by Nigeria for interpretation of the judgment on preliminary objections in the case of the *Land and Maritime Boundary between Cameroon and Nigeria* was simply declared inadmissible.[303]

The Court indicated in the *Asylum* case the 'two conditions for the admissibility of such a request', on the basis of the terms of Article 62 of the Statute: the real purpose of the request must be to obtain an

[298] *Interpretation of judgments Nos. 7 & 8*, PCIJ Rep Series A No. 13, 11.

[299] [1985] ICJ Rep 218, para. 48.

[300] For the procedure adopted on the combined request of Tunisia for interpretation and revision in the *Continental Shelf* case, see [1985] ICJ Rep 197–8, paras. 8–10.

[301] Ibid., p. 223, para. 56.

[302] [1985] ICJ Rep 229–30, para. 69(B) and (D).

[303] [1999] ICJ Rep 40, para. 19.

interpretation of the judgment (and not to obtain an answer to new questions), and there must be 'a dispute as to the meaning and scope of the judgment'.[304] This statement implies that the enumeration of the conditions is exhaustive, that if both conditions are satisfied, then the request is admissible. It is however difficult to fit the decision in the *Cameroon/Nigeria* case into this pattern. In that case, the Court found expressly that there was no need for it to examine the second condition:[305] but its rejection of the request does not seem to be based on a finding that the 'real purpose' of the request was not to obtain an interpretation, though the reasoning of the judgment is not easy to follow.

Nigeria was proposing a restrictive reading of the judgment on preliminary objections. The purpose of its sixth objection had been to exclude Cameroon's claim of Nigerian responsibility for border incidents alleged in its application instituting proceedings, on the ground that Cameroon had not supplied sufficient details of these for Nigeria to be able to respond. In its judgment on the preliminary objections, the Court had ruled that the application had been sufficiently detailed to comply with the requirements of Article 38, paragraph 2, of the Rules of Court, and that if Cameroon's presentation was inadequate, so much the worse for Cameroon: 'It is the applicant which must bear the consequences of an application that gives an inadequate rendering of the facts and grounds on which the claim is based.'[306] Nicaragua sought by its request for interpretation to exclude the presentation of alleged incidents additional to those referred to in the Application, and occurring at a later date; for this purpose expressed its request in the form of three findings that it asked the Court to make. The first of these was to the effect that 'the dispute before the Court does not include any alleged incidents other than' those specified in the Application. The Court found that it had 'already clearly dealt with and rejected' this submission in the judgment of which interpretation was requested, so that 'the Court would therefore be unable to entertain this first submission without calling into question the effect of the judgment concerned as *res judicata*'.[307]

The word 'clearly' is somewhat question-begging: Nigeria evidently had not found the original judgment so clear on the point, or it would not have asked for interpretation. Furthermore, the status of the judgment as *res judicata* would only be called in question if Nigeria was asking the Court to *alter* what it had decided; therefore, presumably Nigeria's interpretation would have this effect, and must therefore be incorrect as an interpretation.

The other two findings requested

endeavour to remove from the Court's consideration elements of law and fact which it has, in its Judgment of 11 June 1998, already authorized Cameroon to

[304] [1950] ICJ Rep 402. [305] [1999] ICJ Rep 39, para. 17.

[306] [1998] ICJ Rep 319, para. 101, citing the judgment in the case of *Military and Paramilitary Activities in and against Nicaragua* [1984] ICJ Rep 437, para. 101. [307] Ibid., p. 39, para. 16.

present, or which Cameroon has not yet put forward. In either case, the Court would be unable to entertain these submissions.[308]

Here again, what the Court is in effect saying is that it has already made findings, in the original judgment, on the points raised, and is not going to reopen them (a request for such reopening would indeed not be a real request for interpretation), or sees no need to explain them further.

On all three Nigerian submissions, the Court in fact is giving an interpretation of the kind given by Pontius Pilate: *quod scripsi, scripsi*,[309] rather than finding the Nigerian requests inadmissible. (Ironically, it turned out that in its judgment on the merits the Court would find that Cameroon had not proved the facts of the incidents complained of, nor their imputability to Nigeria, and would therefore summarily dismiss the claim of international responsibility.[310])

(5) *The interpretation*

There is not a lot of material on which one may assess what the Court might or might not do by way of interpretation; only one of the requests made to the Court for an interpretation has in fact succeeded in obtaining one. In the *Continental Shelf (Tunisia/Libya)* case, Tunisia made two requests for interpretation: the first was found by the Court to be admissible, but based on a misunderstanding of the judgment, and the Court had been able to 'clear up the misunderstanding in the course of its reasoning on the admissibility of the [simultaneous] request for revision' made by Tunisia, so that there was nothing to be added.[311] Its handling of the second request is however perhaps a textbook example of a Court explaining its meaning in a passage which the two parties interpreted differently.

The main issues (to simplify the problem slightly) were, first, what the Court had meant when it decided that the maritime delimitation line should change direction at 'the point of intersection with the parallel passing through the most westerly point of the Tunisian coastline' between certain coastal features.[312] The reason for this change of direction was that the Tunisian coastline changed direction, from a generally north-westerly direction to generally north-easterly: thus the most westerly point on the coastline could be said to correspond broadly to the point at which the coastline started to trend north-eastwards. Secondly, the Court had specified a latitude for the change of direction: was this an express finding, or merely indicative? An expert consulted by Tunisia raised two problems: he rejected what objectively was the 'most westerly point', first because he regarded it as a 'localized feature', which did not correspond to the point of change of direction of the coast; and secondly because it was the mouth of a wadi, and therefore the closing line should

[308] [1998] ICJ Rep 319, para. 101, citing the judgment in the case of *Military and Paramilitary Activities in and against Nicaragua* [1984] ICJ Rep 437, para. 101.

[309] St. John, 19, v. 22.

[310] [2002] ICJ Rep 453, paras. 323–4.

[311] Ibid., para. 50. It could be argued that this was in effect an interpretation: cf. the way in which the Court dealt with the Nigerian request for interpretation in the *Cameroon/Nigeria* case, below, text and n. 317.

[312] [1982] ICJ Rep 94, para. 133 C(2).

be employed.[313] The Court explained that by 'most westerly point' it had meant exactly what it said: it had chosen that formulation because it regarded it as impossible to determine objectively the point of change of direction of the coastline;[314] and if it had meant to refer to a closing line or a baseline, it would have said so.[315] The fact that the Court in this case had to do little more than repeat what it had already said in the original judgment does not mean that the interpretation was any less valuable, or that Tunisia had not requested it in good faith.[316]

On a request for interpretation, the Court clearly can indicate, where there is doubt, precisely what it decided with the force of *res judicata*; as the Permanent Court pointed out in the *Chorzów Factory* Interpretation decision, the dispute between the parties might be on that very question of whether particular issue had or had not been decided with binding force. What the Court cannot do is modify what was so decided. On this ground the Court in the *Cameroon/Nigeria* case refused one of the submissions of Nigeria as to the interpretation requested, inasmuch as 'The Court would . . . be unable to entertain this first submission without calling into question the effect of the judgment concerned as *res judicata*.'[317]

Nor can the Court go beyond the limits of the original judgment, determined by the original *petita*, so as to decide, under cover of interpretation, something which was not decided by the original judgment. The purpose of a request for interpretation must be to obtain an interpretation of what was decided, 'and not to obtain an answer to questions not so decided'.[318]

8. *Revision of judgments*

It is not to be expected that recourse to the procedure for seeking revision of judgments under Article 61 of the Statute would be frequent. Only three such applications have been made since 1946, and none of these has been successful, or even found admissible.

The intention underlying the inclusion in the Statute of the possibility of revision is clear enough: while in general *res judicata pro veritate habetur*, and it is undesirable to disturb the situation established by a credible judicial decision, this is on the assumption that the decision, whatever its other faults, has been taken on the basis of full and accurate information. If it is shown subsequently that the Court or tribunal was not supplied with a piece of information that would, in all probability, have led it to decide otherwise, there should, it was thought, be a mechanism whereby this could be brought to the Court's attention, and an opportunity for it to modify its decision appropriately.

[313] Ibid., pp. 223–4, para. 57. [314] Ibid., p. 225, para. 58. [315] Ibid., para. 59.

[316] Libya had in fact contended that the request was in fact a disguised request for a revision of the judgment: ibid., p. 223, para. 56.

[317] [1999-I] ICJ Rep 39, para. 16.

[318] *Asylum (Request for Interpretation)* [1950] ICJ Rep 402.

Article 61 lays down a number of conditions for the admissibility of an application for revision; if the application passes these stiff tests, then the Court recognizes that the new fact relied on 'has such a character as to lay the case open to revision'. The Statute says nothing about the subsequent procedure, but the implication is that the Court then decides whether or not to effect the revision requested; Article 99, paragraph 4, of the Rules provides for 'such further proceedings on the merits of the application' as the Court considers necessary. Since, on the one hand, the Statute lays down no further conditions for the actual revision, and on the other hand, no further proceedings would be necessary if a revision followed automatically from a finding of admissibility of the request, it is to be supposed that, once the conditions of admissibility are satisfied, the Court has some measure of discretion as to how far to revise or not to revise the earlier judgment, as it sees fit.[319]

(1) *Revision and mistake*

Revision is clearly distinguishable from the correction of a mistake. The two concepts overlap to the extent that a decision given on the basis of incorrect or incomplete information may be treated as a mistaken decision, but one which may, in appropriate circumstances, be corrected by revision. If however it is suggested that the tribunal made a mistake in its *assessment* of the material, legal or factual, before it at the time of its decision, no mechanism exists at the international level for effecting a correction.[320] In principle, parties who agree to refer settlement of a dispute to a given tribunal must accept the possibility that the tribunal may not be infallible, that a mistake of law or of fact may be made, and if it has been agreed or accepted that no appeal lies against the tribunal's decision,[321] then the decision is effective and binding notwithstanding any alleged defects in its reasoning.

This reasoning applies, however, only to errors of substance; it is well established that any tribunal has an inherent power to correct a material error.[322] In the *Continental Shelf* case between Tunisia and Libya, Tunisia sought to rely on this rule in order to persuade the Court to change the

[319] Judge *ad hoc* Bastid in the case of Tunisia's application for revision of the judgment in *Continental Shelf (Tunisia/Libya)* observed that, in the silence of the Statute, only 'an examination of the very concept of revision in the light of any existing practice of international tribunals and the, at times, conflicting practice of the various municipal judiciaries' would give an answer to such questions as the implications of reopening the merits, and the extent to which the case as a whole might be reviewed: [1985] ICJ Rep 247.

[320] In the *Continental Shelf (Tunisia/Libya)* case, Judge Oda considered that the reasoning of the Court's 1982 judgment was open to severe criticism, but recognized that 'the Statute makes no provision for reviewing a judgment of the Court on such grounds': [1985] ICJ Rep 241, para. 10.

[321] On the possibilities of appeal against decisions of arbitral or other tribunals, see a previous article in this series: [1998], *BYBIL* 69, pp. 37–72.

[322] Cf. Second Decision of the Arbitral Tribunal in the *Western Approaches* dispute, 14 May 1978, para. 112, *UNRIAA*, Vol. XVIII, pp. 295 ff.; and Article 31 of the ILC Model Rules on Arbitral Procedure, which provides for the rectification, within one month of the award, of any 'clerical, typographical or arithmetical error in the award, or any obvious error of a similar nature'.

geographical co-ordinates of a point mentioned in the operative clause of its 1982 judgment.[323] If the co-ordinates had been shown to be the result of a simple clerical error—'12' where '21' was meant, for example—this would have been perfectly admissible, though the Rules of Court in their present form do not provide any procedure for making such a request. As Tunisia pointed out in argument, the Rules of the Permanent Court had at one time contained a provision (Article 75) authorising the Court, or the President, to correct clerical errors in a decision. That provision had only remained in the Rules between 1931 and 1935, but as Tunisia observed, 'It cannot be tenably argued that the deletion of that article in 1935 has deprived the Court of a power that naturally belongs to any judicial body'.[324]

The power is exercised regularly, but unobtrusively. It is not uncommon for clerical errors of this kind to be corrected in the Court's decisions, either before delivery, by manuscript corrections authenticated by the Court's official stamp and the Registrar's initials; or less frequently, after delivery of the decision, by a separate protocol with the Court's seal, transmitted to the parties. Even the printed text in the Court's *Reports* series sometimes has to be provided with *errata* slips.

The same procedure would be applicable to evident arithmetical errors, for example in a calculation of monetary reparation. Even the correction of co-ordinates, as proposed by Tunisia, might be effected in this way if the error was arithmetical or geometrical: for example if an equidistance line were drawn as part of a maritime delimitation, but one of the turning points was misidentified as a result of a calculation error.[325]

What Tunisia was asking for was something more substantial: or to be precise, it was asking for an alteration of the co-ordinates as a purely clerical consequence of a particular interpretation of the Court's reasoning, of which the co-ordinates were the product. It was seeking a revision of the judgment, the result of which would have been, *inter alia*, the substitution of the new co-ordinates as a consequence of the revised reasoning. However, for procedural reasons, to be explained below, Tunisia could at the then current stage of the proceedings only ask the Court to declare its request for revision admissible, not to uphold it; it therefore simultaneously asked the Court to interpret the judgment in the sense it would have if revised, and then invited the Court, as a consequence of such interpretation, to treat the co-ordinates as erroneous and capable of being corrected as no more than a clerical or material error.

323 Tunisia's submission was that 'there is cause to replace the co-ordinates 33° 55' N, 12° E, mentioned in section C(2) of paragraph 133 of the judgment of 24 February 1982, with the co-ordinates 33° 50' 17" N, 11° 59' 53" E" ([1985] ICJ Rep 220, para. 51).

324 Tunisian Application for Revision and Interpretation, para. 61, *Pleadings, Oral Arguments, Documents*, p. 17, quoted in English by Libyan counsel, ibid., p. 75.

325 Cf. the Second Decision of the Arbitral Tribunal in the *Western Approaches* dispute, cited in n. 310 above.

In response to Tunisia's request for interpretation, the Court explained that it was 'founded upon a misreading of the purport of the relevant passage of the operative clause of the 1982 judgment'.[326] Consequently, the request for correction of an error, being based on a misreading of the judgment 'ha[d] thus become without object', and the Court added that 'There is therefore no need for the Court to examine the wider question of the correction of an error in a judgment'.[327] This can hardly have been intended to call in question the power of the Court to correct clerical errors *stricto sensu* in its decisions; the object was presumably to leave open the possibility that even semi-material or quasi-material errors might be corrected without the need for proceedings for revision, and indeed in cases in which such proceedings would be inappropriate inasmuch as the error did not result from incomplete or erroneous information. What more serious errors might be capable of being corrected after judgment must be a matter of speculation: presumably errors of law must be excluded, as a corollary of the maxim *jura novit curia*, but what of a demonstrable gross error of fact?

If such a factual error affected only the reasoning of the decision, and not the decision itself, if, in the terminology of Article 61 of the Statute, it was not 'of such a nature as to be a decisive factor', it might be regarded as a clerical or material error open to correction. If however correction of the factual error would involve a modification of the operative clause of the decision, it may be that the principle of acceptance by the parties of the judge's decision, right or wrong, must come into play. In the *Continental Shelf* case itself, had it been correct, as Tunisia contended, that the decision in the case was determined solely by the Court's belief that the exploration concessions granted by the two parties met precisely along a straight line,[328] and if that belief was shown to be unfounded, not by a subsequent discovery, but as immediately evident as a misreading by the Court itself of the documents placed before it, would the judgment constitute a miscarriage of justice?

(2) *The existence of a 'new fact'*

The essence of revision is re-examination of the decision given in the light of some new element; and this is defined in Article 61, paragraph 1, of the Rules as 'some fact of such a nature as to be a decisive factor'. In paragraph 2 reference is made to 'the existence of the new fact'; in this context, the adjective 'new' appears to mean 'newly-discovered', or 'new' in the sense that one says of something discovered that it is 'new to me'. It must mean something that has only been *discovered* since the decision: it would not normally be appropriate to treat it as meaning something that has only *happened* since the judgment, since that would be an element that could not have been before the Court at the time of the decision, and thus could not have influenced it.

[326] [1985] ICJ Rep 220, para. 50.
[327] [1985] ICJ Rep 221, para. 52.
[328] See a previous article in this series: [1994] *BYBIL* 65, pp. 20 ff.

In the application made by Yugoslavia (FRY) for revision of the 1996 judgment on jurisdiction in the *Genocide* case, a key factor was the admission of the 'new' Yugoslavia to the United Nations on 1 November 2002, which in Yugoslavia's contention showed that at the time of the 1996 judgment, it could not have been a party to the Court's Statute, or to the Genocide Convention. The Court observed that both paragraphs 1 and 2 of Article 61

> refer to a fact existing at the time when the judgment was given and discovered subsequently. A fact which occurs several years after a judgment has been given is not a 'new' fact within the meaning of Article 61; this remains the case irrespective of the legal consequences that such a fact may have . . .
>
> In the present case, the admission of the FRY to the United Nations occurred on 1 November 2000, well after the 1996 Judgment. The Court concludes accordingly, that that admission cannot be regarded as a new fact within the meaning of Article 61 capable of founding a request for revision of that Judgment.[329]

In the *Continental Shelf* case, this chronological aspect gave rise to no problem, since the fact which Tunisia invoked was the relationship between the areas of oil exploration concessions granted by the two parties some years before the proceedings were brought.

What is a 'fact' for the purposes of Article 61? Is a legal situation also a fact for this purpose? This problem arose in the *Genocide* case also. As the Court stated,

> In the final version of its argument, the FRY claims that its admission to the United Nations and the Legal Counsel's letter of 8 December 2000 simply 'revealed' two facts which had existed in 1996 but had been unknown at the time: that it was not then a party to the Statute of the Court and that it was not bound by the Genocide Convention. In advancing this argument, the FRY does not rely on facts that existed in 1996. In reality, it bases its Application for revision on the legal consequences which it seeks to draw from facts subsequent to the Judgment which it is asking to have revised. Those consequences, even supposing them to be established, cannot be regarded as facts within the meaning of Article 61. The FRY's argument cannot accordingly be upheld.[330]

The Court then went on, as a subsidiary argument, to rule that in 1996 the FRY had been in a *sui generis* position, so that it was incorrect to deduce that, because it had been accepted as a UN Member in 2000, it had necessarily been a non-UN Member in 1996. Prior to that finding being made, however, the argument had to proceed on the basis that the status of Member and the status of non-Member are mutually exclusive. If then the FRY only became a Member in 2000, it must have been a non-Member in 1996. It is true that, as the Court states, this is a consequence—a logical consequence—derived from a fact, an event, that occurred in 2000. But is it any less of a fact that in 1996 the FRY was a non-Member, even though it was thought to be a Member, or to have

[329] [2003] ICJ Rep 30, paras. 67–8. [330] [2003] ICJ Rep 30, para. 69.

some intermediate status, and that fact was a fact existing in 1996? Let it be supposed that an essential element in a litigated dispute was the question whether X was alive or dead on a particular date, and judgment was given on the basis that he had been dead on that day; if a death certificate were later produced showing that he had died on a later date, perhaps after the date of the judgment, it would be a consequence, a logical deduction, that he had been alive on the earlier date. But it would also be a fact that he had been alive on the earlier date.

The Court's rejection of the FRY's argument in this paragraph can therefore only be justified on the basis that the legal status of the FRY vis-à-vis the UN in 1996 was a question of law and not a question of fact: this seems to be the force of the statement that the 'legal consequences' of a fact are not themselves facts.[331] There is some force in this view, and not only because Article 61 refers specifically to 'the discovery of a fact'. If the Court based a decision on some rule that it found to exist in customary law, and it was subsequently established (though it is difficult to see how) that it had been mistaken, an application for revision would not be receivable, nor is it desirable that it should be. In the *Genocide* case, the 1996 decision was based on the belief that FRY was, at the relevant time, a party to the UN Charter and the Statute, and to the Genocide Convention, by succession; if this belief was wrong, was it an error of fact or of law? More difficult would perhaps be the hypothesis of a decision based on the view that State A was a party to a particular treaty by accession; if it were thereafter discovered that its accession to the treaty had been null and void *ab initio*, or even that it had never acceded at all,[332] would this be a 'new fact', or an error of law?

A decision of an international tribunal in international law may be influenced or determined by considerations of a particular system of national law, for example in the application of the *uti possidetis juris*. Applying the general rule that matters of domestic law are, for the Court, matters of fact, it would seem that a misconception of national law based on the material before the Court might give rise to an application for revision if it was later 'discovered' that this had been so.

[331] There seems to be some confusion also on two other points. First, about the idea of a fact that 'existed' in 1996: the suggestion seems to be that because it was not yet known whether the FRY was a UN Member or not, therefore it was not then a 'fact' that it was not a Member—nor, presumably, would it have been a 'fact' that it was, if later events had shown this to be the correct view. Secondly, because something is the *logical* consequence of something else, it does not necessarily mean that it also follows it chronologically, except as a succession of synapses in the mind of the observer; the logical consequence of the admission of the FRY to the UN in 2000 was a conclusion as to what *had been* the situation before that date. On the question of chronological/logical relations between propositions, cf. the *Certain Phosphate Lands in Nauru* case, and the present writer's comments in [1998] *BYBIL* 69, pp. 49–50.

[332] Cf. the problem of Nicaragua's 'lost' ratification of the Protocol of Signature of the PCIJ Statute, in the case of *Military and Paramilitary Activities in and against Nicaragua* [1984] ICJ Rep 399–400, paras. 15–16.

(3) *The critical date and requirements as to time*

The critical date is thus in principle 'the time when the judgment was given'; but is there always a single critical date? If the contested fact was one which affected, not the merits of the claim, but its admissibility, one might recall the ruling, recently reiterated in the *Lockerbie* cases, that 'The critical date for determining the admissibility of an application is the date on which it is filed.'[333] In that case the Court held in 1998 that the admissibility of Libya's application had to be assessed at the date of its filing: 3 March 1992, and that therefore Security Council resolutions adopted after that date did not affect the question of admissibility.[334] Had application been made for the revision of the 1998 judgment, it would not have served to point to the resolutions adopted after 3 March 1992, but before the Court's decision in 1998, and suggest that these constituted 'new facts'. The question to be resolved would have been: was the Court correctly informed in 1998 of the situation in March 1992? Only a resolution (or other event or fact) previous to March 1992, of which the Court had not been informed, would have sufficed as a 'new fact'.

To determine the admissibility of an application for revision, it is therefore necessary to compare the actual situation at the critical date, understood in this sense, as it has since been discovered to have been, with the situation that the Court (and the party seeking revision) believed then to exist.

A critical date in a different sense is enunciated by the requirement in Article 61, paragraphs 4 and 5, that the application must be made 'at latest within six months of the discovery of the new fact,' and within ten years from the date of the judgment.[335] The latter condition is capable of objective determination, but only the applicant State knows when it 'discovered' the new fact, and indeed it may not be easy to fix an exact date of the 'discovery';[336] not only may this not be an instant event as, for example, the production of an unknown document, but even on that hypothesis, at what date does the *State* effect the discovery—when the

[333] *Border and Transborder Armed Actions (Nicaragua v Honduras)* [1988] ICJ Rep 95, para. 66, cited in *Lockerbie* [1998] ICJ Rep 25, para. 43. This ruling is perhaps controversial, but convenient for our purposes as an example; note also the observations, in the context of a request for interpretation, of the Court in the *Cameroon/Nigeria* case on the distinction between 'the conditions for the admissibility of an application at the time of its introduction, and the question of the admissibility of additional facts and legal grounds': [1999-I] ICJ Rep 38.

[334] [1998] ICJ Rep 26, para. 44.

[335] When New Zealand brought its *Request for an Examination of the Situation* on the basis of para. 63 of the *Nuclear Tests* judgment, France argued (*inter alia*) that that request was really an application for revision, and was therefore out of time under Art. 61: [1995] ICJ Rep 300, para. 40. The application of El Salvador in the *Land, Island and Maritime Frontier* case was made within days of the expiry of the ten-year time limit. Honduras made some suggestion that it was therefore inadmissible as an abuse of procedure, but did not press the point, and the Chamber made no reference to it in its decision.

[336] Cf. the dispute in the *LaGrand* case over the date at which Germany became aware of the relevant facts concerning its national, in the context of the admissibility of its request for provisional measures: [2001] ICJ Rep 486–7, paras. 53–7.

researcher realises its significance, or when he reports to the relevant Minister, or when?

(4) *The discovery of the 'new fact'*

The fact relied on as justifying an application for revision must not only have been unknown to the Court but also to 'the party claiming revision'; this of course penalises any lack of frankness by that party in presenting its original case to the Court. The text of Article 61 does not require that the fact should have been unknown to *both* parties; thus an application for revision can be made if one party has kept the other in ignorance of a material fact, and the latter party discovers it subsequently. This need not necessarily imply bad faith on the part of the well-informed party: while there is probably an obligation on parties before the Court to disclose all material facts known to them, the Court sometimes bases its decision on a ground which neither party had anticipated, and in respect of which therefore neither party would necessarily have fully informed the Court. On the other hand, if the Court in the *Qatar/Bahrain* case had based its decision on the apparently forged documents that were presented to it and later withdrawn, the innocent party could undoubtedly have asked for revision if it had discovered the forgery only after judgment had been given.[337]

The idea of a 'fact' being 'unknown' to a party is apparently simple: but it may not always be so. A fact which was an element in the case as originally argued must have been known to all concerned. As the Court observed on the application of Tunisia for revision in the *Continental Shelf* case,

> So far as knowledge of the fact in question could be derived from the pleadings and material submitted to the Court in the proceedings leading up to the original judgment, anything which was known to the Court must equally have been known to the part claiming revision. The Court must be taken to be aware of every fact established by the material before it, whether or not it expressly refers to such fact in its judgment; similarly, a party cannot argue that it was unaware of a fact which was set forth in the pleadings of its opponent, or in a document annexed to those pleadings or otherwise regularly brought before the Court.[338]

However, if the case turns on a disputed question of fact, and the Court rejects the contention of a party that fact X exists, what is the position if

[337] On this very unfortunate incident, see Mendelson, 'The Curious Case of *Qatar v. Bahrain* in the International Court of Justice', [2001] *BYBIL* 72, p. 183, at pp. 197–201.

[338] [1985] ICJ Rep 203, para. 19. In the *Land, Island and Maritime Frontier Dispute*, the Chamber referred to a particular document as not having been produced; in its application for revision of the judgment, El Salvador was able to show that in fact the document had been before the Chamber, but fortunately it does not appear that this *lapsus* on the part of the Chamber has any significance for the requested revision.

subsequently it is discovered that fact X did exist? If the losing party applies for revision, can it be said that fact X had been 'unknown' to it at a time when it was arguing in favour of the existence of fact X? The fact or circumstance subsequently discovered which proves fact X to have existed was (presumably) unknown to the party, but that is not the unknown fact that has to be demonstrated. This would have been the position of the FRY in the *Genocide* case if it had argued in 1996 that it was not a UN Member nor a party to the Genocide Convention.

This question arose in the recent application by El Salvador for revision of the 1992 judgment in the *Land, Island and Maritime Frontier Dispute* but was not dealt with by the Chamber seised of that application, which rejected the application on other grounds. In the original proceedings, Honduras had argued that the *uti possidetis* boundary at the time of independence followed the river Goascorán, while El Salvador had contended that it followed a former course of the river, abandoned following an abrupt change of course in the seventeenth century, in accordance with a rule of Spanish colonial law concerning 'avulsion'. The Chamber had found in favour of Honduras on the point. El Salvador produced, in support of its application for revision of the judgment, new scientific material supporting the contention that there had indeed been an avulsion in the sixteenth century, and that the old river bed could be identified on the ground. Could the avulsion of the river be regarded as a 'fact [which] was, when the judgment was given, unknown to the Court and also to the Party claiming revision' for the purposes of Article 61? It was suggested that El Salvador was debarred from advancing this argument because in 1992 it had pleaded the existence of avulsion.

This however betrays a confusion of thought. If the Chamber had decided in 1992 that there had been no avulsion,[339] then that was the 'fact' on which the decision was based. The 'fact' that there really had been an avulsion would thus be a fact unknown to all concerned; El Salvador, the party concerned, could not be said to 'know' a fact which was judicially held not to be a fact; it could only have 'believed' it to be a fact. Hence it was open to El Salvador to present the existence, or the occurrence, of the avulsion, as a 'new fact' for the purposes of revision.

The party's ignorance of the new fact must, under Article 61, paragraph 1, not have been 'due to negligence'. This goes some way to resolve the evident delicacy of ascertaining whether at a particular past time a State did or did not know of a particular fact: if it could only have been unaware of the fact through negligence, then it cannot rely on its

[339] Or even that it had not been proved there had been avulsion, since a finding that a fact has not been proved is equivalent to a finding that the fact is not a fact: cf. the rule on witnesses: *de non apparentibus et non existentibus eadem est ratio*. The Chamber in 1992 however did not make any finding on whether or not there had been an avulsion, but held that El Salvador could not claim that the frontier followed an old river bed because it had consistently recognized the modern course of the river as the frontier: see [1992] ICJ Rep 547, para. 312.

ignorance to justify revision.[340] In the *Continental Shelf* case, Tunisia was unable to surmount this hurdle. The fact which was allegedly unknown to Tunisia was the precise situation of the boundary co-ordinates of the oil exploration concessions granted by Libya: some details, and a map of sorts, of these had been produced during the proceedings, but no list of co-ordinates. The Court examined the question

> whether the circumstances were such that means were available to Tunisia to ascertain the details of the co-ordinates of the concessions from other sources; and indeed whether it was in Tunisia's own interests to do so.[341]

The Court found that the co-ordinates could have been obtained from the Libyan National Oil Corporation, or from independent consultants in the petroleum industry; and that since Tunisia needed to know them in order to negotiate with Libya (and had in fact announced that the concessions in question encroached on the Tunisian continental shelf), it was very much in its interest to ascertain them.

An aspect of this finding that caused Judge Oda some concern, though he did not dissent from the Court's ruling, was that the importance attached in the Court's judgment to the position of the co-ordinates of the oil concessions came as something of a surprise to the parties; had they known that the Court would employ an argument based on those co-ordinates as one of the bases for its decision, they might well have been more diligent in establishing the precise details.[342]

(5) *The 'decisive effect' on the decision*

Article 61 of the Statute requires that the new fact relied on as justifying revision should be 'of such a nature as to be a decisive factor': i.e. it must be clear that if the Court had been aware of the new fact at the time of its original decision, there could be no doubt that that decision would have been a different one. In none of the applications for revision has such a fact been shown. However, the recent decision on the application of El Salvador for revision of the 1992 judgment in the case of the *Land, Island and Maritime Frontier* affords a characteristic example of the operation of this condition, as the lack of a 'decisive' character of the new fact alleged was the sole reason for the dismissal of the application.

The application for revision concerned one of the six sectors of the land boundary between El Salvador and Honduras which the Chamber

[340] Cf. the finding in the *Fisheries* case on the argument of the United Kingdom that the Norwegian system of delimitation was unknown to it, and therefore unenforceable against it on the basis of historic title:

> As a coastal State on the North Sea, greatly interested in the fisheries in this area, as a maritime Power traditionally concerned with the law of the sea and concerned particularly to defend the freedom of the sea, the United Kingdom *could not have been ignorant* of the Decree of 1869 . . . ([1951] ICJ Rep 139, emphasis added).

[341] [1985] ICJ Rep 205, para. 23.

[342] In fact Judge Oda went further, and suggested that it was the Court that had been at fault: [1985] ICJ Rep 239, para. 8.

of the Court seised of the case had been asked to determine. The agreed basis of the determination of the boundary was the principle of *uti possidetis*: and it was also agreed that during the Spanish colonial period the boundary between the administrative divisions that, with independence, became territory of Honduras and El Salvador respectively, had been the River Goascorán. As noted above, Honduras therefore argued that the international frontier followed the present-day course of the Goascorán; El Salvador however claimed that at some date unspecified, but prior to the independence of the two States, the river had undergone a violent change of course, and that according to Spanish colonial law[343] the administrative boundary continued thereafter to follow the abandoned course of the river, by virtue of a principle relating to 'avulsion'. Therefore, according to El Salvador, the application of the principle of *uti possidetis* at the time of independence in 1821 meant that the international frontier similarly followed the abandoned course of the Goascorán, which it claimed could still be identified. For reasons to be examined in a moment, the 1992 Chamber rejected El Salvador's claims, and found that the boundary followed the present course of the Goascorán, as asserted by Honduras.

The 'new fact' relied on in 2003 by El Salvador was in effect new scientific evidence confirming that the Goascorán had in fact suddenly changed its course at approximately the date claimed by El Salvador in 1992. The Chamber formed in 2003 to deal with the application for revision left aside the question whether this evidence could amount to a 'fact' within the meaning of Article 61 of the Statute, and concentrated its attention on the question whether, assuming that it could, and assuming the avulsion of the Goascorán to be established, this 'fact' would be of such a nature as to be a decisive factor. On what basis had the 1992 Chamber decided that the frontier followed the modern course of the river? If its decision had been on the basis of a finding that no avulsion had occurred, or that no such avulsion had been proved to have occurred, then evidence of the avulsion might well be decisive for purposes of revision.

This was not, however, the reasoning of the 1992 Chamber as interpreted by the 2003 Chamber. The 1992 decision on this sector of the frontier had been based on evidence of boundary negotiations between the two States, which referred to *uti possidetis* as a basis, and identified the River Goascorán as the frontier; and evidence was available (particularly in the form of a chart and report of a Spanish survey vessel dated 1794) that the River Goascorán had been flowing in its modern course at the time of independence of the two States in 1821. When in 1880 the delegates of the

[343] There was some ambiguity in El Salvador's argument as to the date of the supposed avulsion, and consequently the question whether it was Spanish colonial law or international law that applied; the Chamber interpreted the contention of El Salvador as being that the avulsion antedated independence, but took the view that the same conclusion would follow even if it was subsequent to independence: [1992] ICJ Rep 546–7, paras. 310–11.

parties agreed to recognise 'the river Goascorán' as the frontier, they must have meant the river, not a long-abandoned course of the river. The basis of the decision of the 1992 Chamber was therefore that the nineteenth-century negotiations constituted a recognition of the river as constituting the *uti possidetis* boundary, or possibly an agreement that, whether or not the river had in fact been the Spanish administrative boundary, it should be the international frontier.[344] Even assuming that there had been an avulsion of the Goascorán before 1794, and assuming that the old course of the river had continued to be the Spanish administrative boundary,[345] this would mean no more than that the nineteenth-century negotiations were based on an agreement to treat the river as boundary, rather than on a recognition that the river had been the boundary.[346]

A further element in the decision on the request for interpretation in the *Land, Island and Maritime Frontier* case indicates that, in order to show that the 'new fact' would have been a 'decisive factor', it is not sufficient that the new fact does no more than cast doubt on the evidence on which the original decision was based. El Salvador also advanced a second 'new fact' in support of its application for revision. For the purpose of determining the location of the course and mouth of the River Goascorán in 1821, the 1992 Chamber had relied (*inter alia*) on the report of the expedition of a Spanish survey vessel, the *El Actívo*, in 1794, and a map, referred to as the 'Carta Esférica', annexed to that report. After the 1992 judgment had been given, El Salvador discovered another copy of the report and the map in a library in Chicago: this copy diverged to some extent from the copy that had been before the Chamber. Furthermore, El Salvador contended that 'on all the *Actívo* charts in question geographic data appear that did not exist at the time the charts were drawn'[347] (1795 or 1796), namely volcanic islands created by a major eruption in 1835. Accordingly, El Salvador suggested that there were thus 'real doubts as to the reliability of a chart (and a report) that were crucial to the outcome of the judgment', and that 'This in itself is sufficient cause to admit the application for revision under Article 61 of the Statute of the Court.'[348]

The 2003 Chamber did not accept this contention: it observed that the various versions of the *Carta Esférica* and the report differed only in minor

[344] [1992] ICJ Rep 548, para. 312, *in fine*.

[345] Incidentally, El Salvador in 1992 offered very little evidence that Spanish colonial law attributed this legal effect to avulsion, and no evidence was produced either in 1992 or in 2003 that this particular boundary was, at the time of independence, regarded as running along a dry river-bed.

[346] The 2003 Chamber appears to have read the 1992 decision as based on an agreement between the parties to vary the strict *uti possidetis* boundary; while this is a possible reading, the terms of the 1992 decision, and of the record of the Saco negotiations in 1880 there cited ([1992] ICJ Rep 548, para. 312) seem more suggestive of a finding of joint recognition of the *uti possidetis* boundary. On either basis, however, the application for revision fails to show a fact which could have been a decisive factor.

[347] Application of El Salvador for Revision (available on the ICJ website), para. 82.

[348] Ibid., para. 83.

details, and that the mouth of the River Goascorán appeared in the same place on all copies: 'The new chart produced by El Salvador thus does not overturn the conclusions arrived at by the Chamber in 1992; it bears them out.'[349] The Chamber did not refer at all to the anachronistic inclusion of the volcanic islands; since these appeared also on the version of the chart that was before the Chamber in 1992, their presence on the chart could not be treated as a 'new fact' for the purposes of Article 61.

The Court's judgment on the application of Tunisia for revision of the judgment in the case of the *Continental Shelf (Tunisia/Libya)* also dealt with the problem of the 'decisive' effect of the alleged new fact; but the circumstances were much more complicated, and a simplified summary is all that is required for present purposes. In its judgment of 1982, the Court had indicated a delimitation line between the areas of continental shelf appertaining to the two parties which took into account (*inter alia*) the position of oil exploration concessions granted by the parties in the area. The western boundary of the various Libyan concessions added up to a straight line on a bearing of approximately 26 degrees; the eastern boundary of the Tunisian concessions made a zig-zag line, the westerly points of which, according to the information before the Court in 1982, more or less coincided with the Libyan line.

The new fact discovered by Tunisia was that the information as to the position of the Libyan concessions was inaccurate, and in fact the straight Libyan boundary crossed the Tunisian zig-zag boundary in a number of places. Tunisia understood the 1982 decision as having based the delimitation line solely on the circumstance that the two parties had in effect recognised a line at 26 degrees as equitable; and it therefore contended that, had the Court known of the overlap, it would have decided differently.

The Court in its decision on the application for revision explained that this was a misunderstanding of its 1982 judgment. In the first place, the line it had indicated was based on a combination of factors, only one of which was the meeting of the concession lines (the others being that the line chosen was more or less perpendicular to the coast and represented a prolongation of the general direction of the land boundary).[350] Secondly, when the Court referred to the 'alignment of the one set of concessions on the other set', it had not meant that 'the boundaries of the relevant concessions formed a perfect match', so that the fact that it had become apparent that the match was even less perfect than then supposed did not affect the matter.[351] Thirdly, Tunisia's contentions rested on the assumption that the line chosen by the Court had been based on an agreement between the parties not to grant concessions beyond the 26 degree line: but the Court had made it very clear that this was not so. The position of the concession boundaries merely indicated, in the view of the Court, what sort of line both parties regarded as equitable.[352]

349 [2003] ICJ Rep 410, para. 53.
350 [1985] ICJ Rep 210–11, para. 35.
351 Ibid., pp. 211–12, para. 36.
352 Ibid., pp. 212–13, para. 37.

The Court thus concluded that its 'reasoning [of 1982] is wholly unaffected by the evidence now produced as to the boundaries' of the relevant concessions. The fact adduced was, it may be said, not merely not decisive: it would not have involved any variation in the line drawn by the Court.[353]

9. *Discontinuance*[354]

A case before the International Court normally comes to an end with a decision: either a decision on the merits, or a decision upholding one or more preliminary objections. However, as the Permanent Court memorably observed, 'the judicial settlement of international disputes . . . is simply an alternative to the direct and friendly settlement of such disputes',[355] and if the withdrawal or discontinuance of a case is to favour, or a result of, such a settlement, then it is evidently a development to be welcomed, and a possibility to be provided for in the Rules of Court. The current provisions on the matter are Articles 88 and 89;[356] they correspond to Articles 68 and 69 of the 1946 Rules of Court. A discontinuance is a withdrawal of the whole of a case from the agenda of the Court; it is thus to be distinguished from the withdrawal of one particular head of claim, or of a preliminary objection,[357] or a request for the indication for

353 [1985] ICJ Rep 210–11, p. 212, para. 38.

354 The subject of discontinuance was not examined by Fitzmaurice in his series of articles (though there is a passing reference in [1958] *BYBIL* 34, p. 14; *Collected Edition*, Vol. II, p. 441). There were however a number of examples of discontinuance that occurred during the period covered by his articles: *Société Electricité de Beyrouth* (*Order of 29 July 1954* [1954] ICJ Rep 107); the two cases concerning the *Aerial Incident of 27 July 1955, Order of 3 August 1959* [1959] ICJ Rep 264, and *Order of 30 May 1960* [1960] ICJ Rep 146; *Compagnie du port, des quais et des entrepôts de Beyrouth, Order of 31 August 1960* [1960] ICJ Rep 186. None of these raised any particular legal problems; it was only the *Barcelona Traction* case which brought the subject of discontinuance to attention, and by then Fitzmaurice was a Member of the Court (and, indeed almost certainly had a hand in the drafting of the judgment).

355 *Free Zones of Upper Savoy and the District of Gex*, PCIJ Rep Series A No. 22, 13.

356 *Article 88*: 1. If at any time before the final judgment on the merits has been delivered the parties, either jointly or separately, notify the Court in writing that they have agreed to discontinue the proceedings, the Court shall make an order recording the discontinuance and directing that the case be removed from the list. 2. If the parties have agreed to discontinue the proceedings in consequence of having reached a settlement of the dispute and if they so desire, the Court may record this fact in the order for the removal of the case from the list, or indicate in, or annex to, the order, the terms of the settlement. 3. If the Court is not sitting, any order under this Article may be made by the President. *Article 89*: 1. If in the course of proceedings instituted by means of an application, the applicant informs the Court in writing that it is not going on with the proceedings, and if, at the date on which this communication is received by the Registry, the respondent has not yet taken any step in the proceedings, the Court shall make an order officially recording the discontinuance of the proceedings and directing the removal of the case from the list. A copy of this order shall be sent by the Registrar to the respondent. 2. If, at the time when the notice of discontinuance is received, the respondent has already taken some step in the proceedings, the Court shall fix a time-limit within which the respondent may state whether it opposes the discontinuance of the proceedings. If no objection is made to the discontinuance before the expiration of the time-limit, acquiescence will be presumed and the Court shall make an order officially recording the discontinuance of the proceedings and directing the removal of the case from the list. If objection is made, the proceedings shall continue. 3. If the Court is not sitting, its powers under this Article may be exercised by the President.

357 Cf. *Rights of US Nationals in Morocco, Order of 31 October 1951* [1951] ICJ Rep 111.

provisional measures.[358] Similarly the withdrawal of a counter-claim,[359] while it may raise similar problems of interpretation to those resulting from a discontinuance, leaves the main proceedings unaffected, and is thus closer to a mere withdrawal of a head or claim or a specific defence.

These texts provide for the discontinuance of proceedings to be effected either jointly, or by the applicant State alone, though in the latter case the respondent State has, if it has 'taken some step in the proceedings' the opportunity to object.[360] As regards unilateral discontinuance, the only difference between old Article 69 and new Article 89 is purely formal; but Article 88 differs substantially from the old Article 68, apparently as a result of a revision inspired by the *Barcelona Traction* case, to be examined below.

According to one view of international judicial proceedings, the idea of a joint discontinuance, except in cases brought by special agreement, is erroneous. The applicant in a case is the *dominus litis*: it is the applicant that has unilaterally decided to bring the proceedings, and he may unilaterally decide to abandon them. If the discontinuance is the result of an agreement with the other party, either that the claim be totally abandoned, or that the proceedings cease without prejudice to the legal positions of the parties, that is no more than the underlying reason for the discontinuance, not an element of the discontinuance itself. This view was advanced during the discussions in the Permanent Court on the revision of the Rules of Court in 1936; it was countered by the view that once the respondent party has *fait acte de procédure* (a concept translated as 'has taken a step in the proceedings'), both parties have an interest in seeing the matter through, and a discontinuance is no longer a matter for the applicant alone.[361] The latter view prevailed in the drafting of the Rules, and Article 89 thus confers on a respondent that has taken a step in the proceedings the right to be consulted, and to oppose the discontinuance, in which case 'the proceedings shall continue'.[362] Further confirmation of this view came with the decision in the *Barcelona Traction* case, in which the Court explained that:

> The right of objection given to a respondent State which has taken a step in the proceedings is protective, to enable it to insist on the case continuing, with a view to bringing about a situation of *res judicata;* or in other words (perhaps more pertinent for the present case), to enable it to ensure that the matter is finally disposed of for good.[363]

[358] Cf. *Military and Paramilitary Activities in and against Nicaragua, Order of 31 May 1988* [1988] ICJ Rep 9.

[359] As in the case of *Application of the Genocide Convention* discussed further below (text and n. 385).

[360] For an example of a discontinuance where the Respondent had not taken any step in the proceedings, see *Trial of Pakistani Prisoners of War, Order of 15 December 1973* [1973] ICJ Rep 347.

[361] See PCIJ Rep Series D No. 2 3rd *addendum*, pp. [318].

[362] No such objection has yet been made, and the practical consequences are unclear: see below. If a counter-claim had been presented, *quaere* whether the respondent could insist that the proceedings continue on the counter-claim alone.

[363] [1964] ICJ Rep 20.

What is 'a step in the proceedings'? Clearly the filing of a counter-memorial or preliminary objection would be such; but the Court has regarded the mere appointment of an agent as sufficient.[364] On the other hand, the appointment of a judge *ad hoc* is not a 'step in the proceedings'.[365]

The *Barcelona Traction* case concerned the effect of a discontinuance on the substantive and procedural rights of the parties: something with which the Court is not normally concerned, since, as the Court observed in the case, 'ordinarily, discontinuances have been final in fact,' (i.e. whether or not the claim had continued to be pressed outside the Court, no further approach had been made to the Court), 'whether or not they would have proved to be so in law had an attempt to bring further proceedings been made'.[366] Such an attempt had however then been made, and the Court found itself faced with the question of the effect of a discontinuance.

There are in fact three possible situations. Some systems of law distinguish between what is called, in French terminology, *désistement d'instance* and *désistement d'action*. The distinction is explained by an authoritative writer as follows:

> Le désistement d'instance traduit une renonciation à l'instance engagée. Mais le droit litigieux n'est pas atteint et le plaideur conserve la possibilité d'introduire une nouvelle instance devant le juge pour faire valoir à nouveau ce droit. Au contraire, le désistement d'action est celui qui porte sur le droit lui-même d'être entendu par le juge. Il rend impossible dans l'avenir la reprise du procès.[367]

In municipal law these two hypotheses cover, in effect, all possibilities; but in international law, where the judicial settlement of disputes is the exception rather than the rule, a third hypothesis has to be distinguished. As Judge Morelli pointed out in his dissenting opinion in the *Barcelona Traction* case, in international law

> it is easy to conceive of an abandonment of the right of action deriving from a given rule which would not in any way affect the substantive right. The abandonment which is contemplated in municipal law, on the contrary, is usually not an abandonment of the right of action as such, but rather of the substantive right.[368]

Thus a State which discontinues proceedings before the Court may be saying or implying that it reserves the right to bring fresh proceedings before the Court, or to enforce the substantive right it claims in any other way; or it may be saying that it renounces the right which it was claiming, so that it debars itself from attempting to enforce that right by any means; or that it renounces the right to bring any proceedings before the Court, but reserves

[364] See *Protection of French Nationals and Protected Persons in Egypt, Order of 29 March 1950* [1950] ICJ Rep 59.

[365] See *Trial of Pakistani Prisoners of War, Order of 15 December 1973* [1973] ICJ Rep 347.

[366] *Barcelona Traction, Light and Power Co.* [1984] ICJ Rep 18.

[367] Guillaume, 'Le désistement devant la CIJ', *Liber Amicorum Bengt Broms*, 1999, reproduced in Guillaume, *La Cour internationale de justice à l'aube du XXIe siècle: le regard d'un juge*, 2003, p. 155; page references in these notes are to the latter publication.

[368] [1964] ICJ Rep 106.

the right to assert and enforce the substantive right it claims in any other way—e.g. before some other tribunal or by lawful counter-measures, etc.[369]

Article 89 leaves all these possibilities open; but Article 88, concerning discontinuance by agreement, is more specific inasmuch as it makes it possible for the parties to have recorded in the Order of the Court the fact that the parties 'have agreed to discontinue the proceedings in consequence of having reached a settlement of the dispute'—i.e. not merely a *désistement d'action* but a settlement of the substantive underlying claim.

The proceedings which Belgium had instituted against Spain alleging responsibility for injury to Belgian nationals arising out of the bankruptcy of the Barcelona Traction, Light and Power Company had been discontinued by Belgium following contacts between the various private interests—Belgian and Spanish—involved. This was a unilateral discontinuance under Article 69 of the 1946 Rules of Court, to which Spain, consulted in accordance with that Article, had made no objection. A year or so after the discontinuance, Belgium filed a fresh application against Spain, citing the same cause of action; and Spain raised a preliminary objection to the effect that 'the discontinuance . . . of previous proceedings relative to the same events in Spain, disentitled the Applicant Government from bringing the present proceedings'.[370]

The Court took the opportunity to comment generally on the effect of a discontinuance followed by new proceedings. After observing, as noted above, that previous discontinuances had turned out to be final, it continued:

Sometimes a discontinuance, though in form unilateral, and therefore notified under Article 69 of the Rules, has been consequent on a settlement of the dispute; in other cases the claimant State has had reasons, which appeared to it to be of a final character, for not continuing to attempt to prosecute its claim before the Court; in others yet, it might well have been that, the current proceedings once discontinued, the jurisdictional basis for instituting new ones would no longer have been available.

But, in the opinion of the Court, these various considerations are essentially fortuitous in character; and the fact that past discontinuances have in practice proved 'final' cannot of itself justify the conclusion that any *a priori* element of finality inherently attaches to them. This can readily be demonstrated by reference to circumstances in which the Court considers that no question could arise as to the right to institute further proceedings following upon a discontinuance, quite irrespective of whether any reasons for it were given, or any right of further action reserved.[371]

After giving examples (local remedies not yet exhausted, questions as to the nationality of the individual diplomatically protected, etc.), the Court concluded:

The existence of these possibilities suffices in itself to show that the question of the nature of a discontinuance cannot be determined on any *a priori* basis, but

[369] Morelli enumerates these three possibilities, and adds a fourth, that in which the discontinuing State gives no indication at all of the significance it attaches to its discontinuance.

[370] Ibid., p. 16. [371] Ibid., pp. 18–19.

must be considered in close relationship with the circumstances of the particular case. In consequence, each case of discontinuance must be approached individually in order to determine its real character. There would therefore be little object in the Court's entering upon any exhaustive discussion of the theory of discontinuance as it is provided for by Articles 68 and 69 of the Court's Rules.[372]

Nevertheless, the Court proceeded to notice certain points 'by way of clarification'. In particular, it drew attention to the two distinct possibilities afforded by Articles 68 and 69, and observed that

whereas in cases coming under Article 68 the act of discontinuance is to all intents and purposes a joint act, in those coming under Article 69 it is an essentially unilateral act, whatever may underlie it, and even though acquiescence is necessary before it can actually take effect. Under Article 69, any notifications, whether of intention to discontinue, or in acceptance of discontinuance, are notifications made to the Court and not passing between the parties, so that any understandings between them (and such may certainly exist) must precede and be sought for outside the act of discontinuance itself.[373]

The implication seems to be that when there is an agreed discontinuance under Article 68, the 'understanding' between the parties is, or may be, embodied in their joint act, whereas in the case of a discontinuance notified under Article 69, the non-objection of the respondent party is neutral, and does not signify any particular understanding. This is confirmed by the next sentence of the judgment, concerning the reason for the right of objection given to a respondent State which has taken a step in the proceedings.[374]

The *Barcelona Traction* case concerned a discontinuance under Article 69, and the Court did not have to consider further what the effect of an agreed discontinuance under Article 68 would be as regards the possibility of renewing the proceedings. There seems to be a suggestion, however, that whereas an Article 69 discontinuance is neutral in this respect, an agreed discontinuance is, or would normally be, final.[375] Certainly in practical terms a joint discontinuance of proceedings is likely to be the product of a settlement of the case; but the essence of the analysis in the *Barcelona Traction* case remains valid: that a discontinuance in itself is neutral as to the possibility of renewing the claim or the proceedings. This is in fact the sense of the revision of the Rules effected in 1978.

The 1946 Rules contemplated that the parties might inform the Court that they had 'conclude[d] an agreement as to the settlement of the dispute . . . or by mutual agreement inform the Court in writing that they are not going on with the proceedings', and the Court by order would then officially record 'the conclusion of the settlement or the discontinuance of the proceedings'. This in effect took account, in the case of

[372] Ibid., p. 19. [373] Ibid., p. 20. [374] Quoted above, text and n. 338.

[375] But what is it that is 'final'? As noted above, Judge Morelli in the *Barcelona Traction* case distinguished an intention to abandon the right of action from an intention to abandon the substantive right or recognize its non-existence: [1994] ICJ Rep 105–6.

agreement, of the distinction between *désistement d'instance* and *désistement d'action*. The new Rule starts from the premise that the normal situation is that the Court is informed that the parties 'have agreed to discontinue the proceedings'. In paragraph 2 of Article 88, however, the possibility is recognized that the parties may do so 'in consequence of having reached a settlement of the dispute', and in that case they may ask the Court to record the fact.[376] The normal *désistement* is thus of the proceedings only (*d'instance*), and the recording of a *désistement d'action* is merely an option available to the parties.[377]

In a number of subsequent cases, it is clear that the lesson of the *Barcelona Traction* case has been learned: the parties have made it clear in their approach to the Court whether or not the discontinuance is to be treated as putting an end to the claim as well as to the proceedings. In the first such case, however, the President of the Court adopted a rather unexpected analysis of the significance of Article 88 of the Rules.

By the judgment in the case of *United States Diplomatic and Consular Staff in Tehran*, the question of reparation was reserved to a later phase, and the case therefore remained on the General List. After the conclusion of the Algiers Agreement between the United States and Iran, which provided (*inter alia*) that on the release of the hostages, 'the United States will promptly withdraw all claims now pending against Iran before the International Court of Justice', the United States applied to the Court for a discontinuance, referring specifically to Article 88, paragraph 1, of the Rules. In its letter it stated specifically that it reserved 'the right, however, to reinstitute such proceedings if the Government of Iran fails to live up to its commitments under' the Algiers Agreement.[378] The President of the Court wrote to the United States' Agent as follows:

> The Court desires to be informed whether, by that sentence, the United States intends that the discontinuance which it requests of the proceedings . . . is to be subject to the condition that it shall retain the right, in the circumstances indicated in the sentence, to reinstitute and pursue those proceedings, notwithstanding the present request for their discontinuance. Article 88, paragraph 1, of

[376] This was the situation in the case of *Certain Phosphate Lands in Nauru*, but whereas the joint notification from the parties mentioned that they had agreed to the discontinuance 'in consequence of having reached a settlement' (the precise words of Art. 88), the discontinuance is simply placed on record as being 'by agreement of the Parties', which is not the same thing: see the *Order of 13 September 1993* [1993] ICJ Rep 322. The same procedure was followed in *Aerial Incident of 3 July 1988*: see the *Order of 22 February 1996* [1996] ICJ Rep 9. In the case concerning *Maritime Delimitation between Guinea-Bissau and Senegal*, it was clear that the joint discontinuance was in consequence of an agreement for the delimitation and exploitation of the disputed area, but the parties did not specifically ask for this to be recorded in the Order: see *Order of 8 November 1995* [1995] ICJ Rep 423.

[377] In the case of *United States Diplomatic and Consular Staff in Tehran*, the Court accepted a notification by the United States of an agreement reached with Iran (and a copy of the authentic text of that agreement) coupled with the silence of Iran as sufficient to justify placing on record 'the discontinuance of the proceedings in the case, following upon an agreement between the Parties', despite the fact that even the United States had not asked for the inclusion of the reference to the settlement in the Order: see the *Pleadings, Oral Arguments, Documents* in the case, p. 526, No. 93; and cf. Wegen, 'Discontinuance of International proceedings: the *Hostages* case', 76 *AJIL*, 1982, p. 717.

[378] *Pleadings Oral Arguments, Documents*, p. 524, No. 89.

the Rules provides, in certain circumstances, for the discontinuance, without any condition or qualification, of proceedings in a case and the removal of the case from the Court's list also without any condition or qualification. Accordingly, if the above is the meaning to be given to the sentence in question the discontinuance requested by your Government could not be considered by the Court as falling within the terms of Article 88, paragraph 1, of the Rules.[379]

This may have come as something of a surprise to the United States: all the trouble in the *Barcelona Traction* case had arisen because the parties had not made clear what the intended effect of the discontinuance was to be; now the United States had spelled out that effect specifically, and was told that their approach did not comply with the Rules! It would, it is suggested, have been more in the spirit of the *Barcelona Traction* decision if the Court had simply recited in its Order the statement of the United States, and then placed on record the discontinuance. In that decision, the Court had stated that it was 'not called upon to enquire into the motives either of the discontinuing or the respondent party',[380] and the same is surely true for the extra-judicial effect, the effect outside the framework of the proceedings before the Court, intended by the parties.

The United States wrote in reply, quoting the *Barcelona Traction* decision, that they understood that the effect of a discontinuance is exclusively procedural, and that the controverted sentence was intended 'to reflect for the record our understanding that the request for discontinuance would neither renounce nor prejudice any further right of action with regard to these claims in the circumstances mentioned'.[381] The Court thereupon made an Order recording the discontinuance 'following upon an agreement between the Parties'.[382]

The Court is thus not concerned with the motives for a discontinuance, which will normally be to favour a negotiated settlement. There is a presumption that a discontinuance is intended merely as a withdrawal of the proceedings before the Court, with no abandonment of the original claim. This is the more compelling when there are evident reasons why the proceedings would be ineffective to enforce what may yet be, in itself, a perfectly valid claim. This was the situation in the case concerning the *Aerial Incident of 27 July 1955*: the shooting-down by Bulgaria of an El Al civilian airliner had led to three parallel sets of proceedings before the Court, brought against Bulgaria by Israel, the United Kingdom and the United States, all based on the same title of jurisdiction.[383] When the Court ruled on the Israeli claim that it had no jurisdiction to entertain it,[384] the proceedings brought by the other two States were clearly doomed to suffer the same fate, and were therefore discontinued; but just as the Court's decision in the case brought by Israel neither stated nor implied any view on the

379 Ibid., p. 525, No. 91.

380 [1964] ICJ Rep 20.

381 *Pleadings, Oral Arguments, Documents*, p. 526, No. 93.

382 [1981] ICJ Rep 45.

383 The Bulgarian declaration of acceptance of jurisdiction under Art. 36 of the Statute of the Permanent Court, dated 12 August 1921.

384 *Aerial Incident of 27 July* 1955 [1959] ICJ Rep 127.

merits of the claim, so the withdrawal of the UK and US proceedings implied no withdrawal of the substantive claims of those States, or lack of intention to pursue the matter extra-judicially.

The motives for a discontinuance may however also be a matter of political tactics: such at least was the suggestion of Costa Rica when Nicaragua discontinued the proceedings against it in the *Border and Transborder Armed Actions* case, avowedly 'with the purpose of giving Costa Rica an opportunity to comply' with the Esquipalas Peace Plan.[385] The Agent of Costa Rica, while not opposing the discontinuance, accused Nicaragua of 'inadmissible cynicism', since the President of Costa Rica was responsible for the Peace Plan, and 'In any case, Nicaragua would have lost its case, because its action is based on allegations which are supported neither by facts nor by law'.[386]

Nicaragua also discontinued its case against Honduras entitled *Border and Transborder Armed Actions*, and in this case specified in its notification that it 'had decided to renounce all further right of action based on the case and . . . did not wish to go on with the proceedings'.[387] The Court, in accordance with the procedure laid down in the Rules, merely placed on record the discontinuance. In the case concerning the *Aerial Incident of 3 July 1988*, the agreement to discontinue was expressed to be 'in full and final settlement of all disputes, differences, claims, counter-claims and matters directly or indirectly raised by, or capable of arising out of, or directly or indirectly related to or connected with, this case', a formula recommended to the collector of gems of legal prose.[388]

In the case concerning the *Vienna Convention on Consular Relations* brought by Paraguay against the United States, Paraguay indicated to the Court that it 'wished to discontinue the proceedings with prejudice', and requested a removal from the list. The United States, consulted in accordance with Article 89 of the Rules, indicated that it 'concurred in Paraguay's discontinuance of the proceedings with prejudice'.[389] The expression 'with prejudice' was not explained, but it presumably meant, by opposition to a discontinuance 'without prejudice to the Applicant's rights to recommence the proceedings', that no such right was to continue to exist. But did this mean that the underlying claim was renounced, or merely that the possibility of recommencing the proceedings in the same forum was abandoned?[390] The decision of the Court was

[385] *Pleadings, Oral Arguments, Documents*, p. 145, No. 42.

[386] Ibid., p. 147, No. 47. An interesting complication was a request, more or less simultaneous with the discontinuance, by Honduras for copies of the pleadings under Art. 53 of the Rules; since only the Memorial of Nicaragua had been filed, this would mean publicity for Nicaragua's contentions, but not for any repudiation or defence by Costa Rica. For the Court's handling of the matter, see ibid., pp. 146–52.

[387] Quoted in *Order of 27 May 1992* [1992] ICJ Rep 222.

[388] *Order of 22 February 1996* [1996] ICJ Rep 9. For more of these flowers of legal literature, see the text of the Settlement Agreement of 9 February 1996, reproduced in *Pleadings, Oral Arguments, Documents*, pp. 649–51.

[389] *Order of 10 November 1998* [1998] ICJ Rep 427.

[390] The Registry translation into French of the recital in the Order renders 'with prejudice' by the circumlocution: 'se désister de l'instance et renoncer à toute action en l'affaire', which probably preserves the ambiguity.

simply to the effect that it 'places on record the discontinuance', without reference to 'without prejudice'; the recital of the request of Paraguay and the concurrence of the United States was clearly sufficient to prevent any attempt to renege on the agreement.

Equally clear, but in the opposite sense, was the approach to the Court by the Democratic Republic of the Congo in the case concerning *Armed Activities on the Territory of the Congo (DRC v Rwanda)*, notifying the Court that 'the Government of the Democratic Republic of the Congo wished to discontinue the proceedings and stated that it "reserve[d] the right to invoke subsequently new grounds of jurisdiction of the Court"'.[391] In this case also, the Court simply placed on record the discontinuance without further comment; and the Congo did in due course commence further proceedings without objection (in this respect) from Rwanda.

On the other hand, in one more recent Order the Court has, apparently for the first time, adopted in the operative clause of its decision the distinction between *désistement d'instance* and *désistement d'action*. The cases just mentioned were cases of unilateral discontinuance under Article 89 of the Rules. However, when the two *Lockerbie* cases were discontinued, the application for discontinuance was a joint one in each case, and the relevant Orders adopted a slightly different wording. In these cases, the parties notified the Court jointly that they had 'agreed to discontinue with prejudice the proceedings instituted' by Libya; they did not specifically say that the discontinuance was 'in consequence of having reached a settlement of the dispute', as provided for in Article 88 of the Rules,[392] unless the mere words 'with prejudice' are meant to imply this. The Court in each case indicated in the operative part of its Order that it 'places on record the discontinuance, with prejudice, by agreement of the Parties, of the proceedings instituted' by Libya.[393]

Thus the words 'with prejudice' were included, not merely in the motivation of the Order, but in the operative clause. The difference may seem slight, but it does mark a departure from the philosophy of the Rules and of the *Barcelona Traction* decision. In that case the Court stated that its role was, 'there being no objection to the discontinuance, . . . simply to record it and to remove the case from the list'.[394] The main object of the provisions in the Rules, the Court observed, was 'to provide a procedural facility, or rather—since it would in any event never be practicable to compel a claimant State to continue prosecuting its case—to reduce the process of discontinuance to order'.[395] A legitimate reading of the Rules

[391] *Order of 30 January 2001* [2001] ICJ Rep 7; and the similar Order in the case brought against Burundi, ibid., 4. The DRC did in fact subsequently institute fresh proceedings against Rwanda, but not against Burundi.

[392] The reason for this was probably political, since it was a matter of public knowledge that the discontinuance was part of a package including an admission by Libya that it had been responsible for the bombing, and payment of compensation.

[393] *Orders of 10 September 2003* [2003] ICJ Rep 150, 153. The French text read 'Prend acte du désistement, par accord des parties, de l'instance introduite . . . , ainsi que de toute action en l'affaire.'

[394] [1964] ICJ Rep 20.

[395] Ibid., p. 19.

and of the Court's analysis in that case is that the discontinuance there provided for is primarily a *désistement d'instance*; in the case of a unilateral discontinuance under Article 89, this is always so. Under Article 88, it can, in effect, be exceptionally declared to be a *désistement d'action* if the parties specify that they have 'reached a settlement of the dispute', and ask for this to be 'recorded' in the Order—though even in such case, the use of the word 'record' suggests a recital rather than an operative clause. In other words, what the Court actually *does* on a discontinuance is record the bare act of discontinuance and thus remove the case from the List. Whether this puts an end to the possibility of action is still to be resolved in the light of the surrounding circumstances, but those circumstances may include the recording by the Court of the existence of a 'settlement of the dispute'.

It was noted above that Article 89 of the Rules of Court, concerning unilateral discontinuance, provides that if the other party has taken any step in the proceedings, it is given an opportunity to 'state whether it opposes the discontinuance of the proceedings'.[396] This provision was also in the corresponding 1946 Rule, and in the *Barcelona Traction* case the Court indicated what it saw as the rationale of the text, in a passage quoted above. This possibility prompts the query: what is the situation if the respondent party does oppose the discontinuance? It is evident that it can, in its relations with the applicant, seek to impose conditions: it may only consent to the discontinuance if it is made clear that this is a *désistement d'action*, or that the claim is withdrawn and 'the matter is finally disposed of for good'. If however the parties are not in agreement as to the significance of the discontinuance, and the respondent maintains its opposition, then the rule prescribes that 'the proceedings shall continue'—i.e. the Court has no discretion to over-rule the objection of the respondent. But while you may lead a litigant to the courtroom, you cannot make him plead: the applicant may presumably abandon the proceedings, by withdrawing the nomination of its agent, and failing to file any more pleadings, or to appear at the hearing.

Such a course of action would presumably bring into play Article 53 of the Statute, whereby 'Whenever *one of the parties* does not appear before the Court, or does not defend its case, the other party may call upon the Court to decide in favour of its claim'. This text, as the italicised words make clear, does not only refer to the absence of the respondent party.[397]

[396] This provision has been implemented in most cases: see (e.g.) the discontinuance of the *Passage through the Great Belt* case, *Order of 10 September 1992* [1992] ICJ Rep 348. Only in *Trial of Pakistani Prisoners of War* and *Maritime Delimitation between Guinea-Bissau and Senegal* has the respondent taken no step in the proceedings, and the latter case was a joint discontinuance. Guillaume (op.cit., n. 342 above, p. 101) suggests that the fact that the other party has taken a step in the proceedings also prevents the applicant from withdrawing a discontinuance.

[397] The words 'defend its case' might suggest otherwise, but the French text has 's'abstient de faire valoir ses moyens', which could apply to either party. On non-appearance generally, see the previous article in this series, [2001] *BYBIL* 72, pp. 157–74.

An applicant State that wishes to discontinue, but finds itself faced with the opposition of the respondent, has thus the choice of continuing what it may regard as a lost battle, or of seeing judgment given against it by default. However, a default judgment is not, as in many municipal systems, given simply on the basis that the claim is undefended: paragraph 2 of Article 53 provides that the Court, before finding in favour of the active party, must satisfy itself not only that it has jurisdiction, but also that 'the claim is well-founded in fact and law'. The 'claim' however, in the circumstances we are considering, would be likely to be the negative claim that the facts were not as the applicant alleged, or that they did not establish the responsibility asserted; and to establish a negative of this kind, in the absence of pleadings by the applicant, might prove difficult. There could thus be no guarantee that the respondent State, by opposing a discontinuance, would be able to bring about a situation of *res judicata*; nor should the possibility be overlooked that the Court might find, with the force of *res judicata*, in favour of the absent applicant! It is perhaps not surprising, therefore, that in no case up to the present has a unilateral discontinuance been opposed by the respondent party.

The right to seek a discontinuance is recognized by the Rules of Court as appertaining to the applicant party, which remains *dominus litis* to that extent. Where a counter-claim has been submitted, the right to seek to withdraw it similarly appertains to the respondent as author of the counter-claim; such withdrawal puts an end to the proceedings on the counter-claim, but not of course the proceedings on the claim. The Rules do not in terms confer on the applicant a right to state its opposition to withdrawal of a counter-claim. In the case concerning *Application and Interpretation of the Genocide Convention*, when Serbia and Montenegro withdrew its counter-claim in the proceedings brought against it by Bosnia and Herzegovina, the latter State was consulted.[398]

The right to *achieve* a discontinuance is a right of the two parties jointly, in the sense that if they are agreed, the Court has no power to refuse to bring the proceedings to an end. As was observed by Sir Cecil Hurst during the drafting of the Rules of the Permanent Court,

> if the parties were agreed to remove a case from the Court, the latter's jurisdiction ceased and there was not even anything to make an order upon, since the Court's jurisdiction was derived exclusively from the agreement between the parties,[399]

[398] See the Order of 10 September 2001, *Application of the Genocide Convention* [2001] ICJ Rep 572; when Yugoslavia informed the Court that it 'intended to withdraw' its counter-claim against Bosnia and Herzegovina, the latter State was notified and indicated that it had no objection, whereupon the President of the Court made an Order placing on record the withdrawal of the counter-claim. The Order refers to Art. 80 of the Rules, concerning counter-claims (which says nothing about withdrawal or discontinuance), but not to Art. 88 and 89.

[399] PCIJ Series D No. 2, Third Addendum, p. 318; quoted in the dissenting opinion of Judge Armand-Ugon in *Barcelona Traction* [1964] ICJ Rep 118. Judge Armand-Ugon concluded that a case could not be reinstituted after a discontinuance, a view which however rested on a confusion as to the meaning of 'jurisdiction' in this context.

though practical considerations dictate that the Court should place the situation on record in an Order.

The right to seek a discontinuance of the action is exclusively that of the applicant, in the sense that, for obvious reasons, there is no possibility for the respondent to put an end to proceedings against it, save by agreement with the applicant. There is no equivalent in the Court's procedure to 'dismissal for want of prosecution'; the Court does not have a power to remove a case from the list in the absence of a discontinuance, even if neither party appears to be still actively interested in pursuing it. In the *Monetary Gold* case, in which Italy fulfilled the requirements of the Washington Agreement by instituting proceedings against France, the United Kingdom and the United States, but then filed a 'Preliminary Question' casting doubt on the jurisdiction of the Court,[400] the United Kingdom argued (*inter alia*) that the effect of this was that the application 'has been in effect withdrawn or cancelled by Italy'. The Court did not accept this, drawing attention to Article 69 (now 89) of the Rules, and observing that 'The raising of the Preliminary Question by Italy cannot be regarded as equivalent to a discontinuance'.[401]

In the *Nuclear Tests* cases, the Court considered that it faced 'a situation in which the objective of the Applicant has in effect been accomplished',[402] and went on to find that the Applicants' claims 'no longer have any object', and the Court was not called upon to give a decision thereon.[403] In this connection, the Court observed that 'It would of course have been open to Australia, if it had considered that the case had in effect been concluded, to discontinue the proceedings in accordance with the Rules of Court', and added 'If it has not done so, this does not prevent the Court from making its own independent finding on the subject'.[404] It has been powerfully argued that in this case the Court in effect imposed an unwanted discontinuance on the parties, in breach of its own Rules.[405] There is much force in this criticism. As we have seen, discontinuance does not necessarily imply settlement of the underlying dispute: it may be effected for other reasons. Similarly, settlement of the dispute does not necessarily imply discontinuance: the parties might agree to ask for an agreed declaratory judgment, for example. Discontinuance is a faculty open to the applicant party to a case, and its exercise depends solely on the appreciation by that party of its best interests.

[400] This is a slight over-simplification, as the challenge was to the Court's jurisdiction to award the disputed gold to Italy, but Italy had by a second submission asked for a determination simply of the priority between its claim and that of the United Kingdom; see the dissent on this point of Judge Levi Carneiro [1954] ICJ Rep 37.

[401] [1954] ICJ Rep 30. As Guillaume (op. cit., n. 342 above, pp. 151–2) observes, this does not amount to a finding that a discontinuance can never be effected by implication, without express recourse to the procedure of Arts. 88 and 89.

[402] [1974] ICJ Rep 270, para. 52 (Australia); ibid., p. 475, para. 55 (New Zealand).

[403] Ibid., p. 272, para. 62 (Australia); p. 478, para. 65 (New Zealand).

[404] Ibid., p. 270, para. 54 (Australia); slightly different wording at p. 475–6, para. 57 (New Zealand).

[405] Scobbie, 'Discontinuance in the International Court: the Enigma of the *Nuclear Tests* cases', 41 *ICLQ*, p. 808.

Given that the Court cannot dismiss a case for want of prosecution on the basis of an application by the respondent party, in view of the requirements of paragraph 2 of Article 53, what is a respondent to do if the applicant State does not discontinue proceedings, but does not actually pursue them either? On the basis of the decision in the *Nuclear Tests* cases, the applicant might in some circumstances be treated as having achieved its object, so that the case would have become 'moot' or 'without object'; but it would be difficult for the respondent to establish this to the satisfaction of the Court.[406]

[406] In the pending cases concerning the *Legality of the Use of Force*, the Applicant, Serbia and Montenegro, has responded to the Respondents' preliminary objections to jurisdiction by agreeing with them that there is no jurisdiction, but has not discontinued the proceedings, nor asked for a finding of no jurisdiction. In this unprecedented situation, the Respondents have, *inter alia*, asked the Court to find that Serbia and Montenegro has in effect discontinued the proceedings (see CR 2004/6 to CR 2004/23). At the time this article went to press, the Court was deliberating on the matter.

INDIRECT EXPROPRIATION AND ITS VALUATION IN THE BIT GENERATION

By W. MICHAEL REISMAN & ROBERT D. SLOANE*

I. INTRODUCTION: THE SHIFT IN PARADIGM

The number of bilateral investment treaties (BITs) has increased dramatically in the past decade. Until the mid-1970s, a bare handful of BITs existed, and the numbers increased only at a slow or moderate pace until the early 1990s.[1] By September 1994, however, some 140 states had concluded more than 700 BITs;[2] by 1999, more than 1300 BITs had entered into force among about 160 states;[3] and by the end of 2002, 2181 BITs had been signed.[4] Particular provisions of BITs vary from state to state. But certain general features, which respond to the demands of expanding globalization and, as a consequence, the increasing interdependence of national economies, characterize virtually all BITs.[5] BITs seek to establish a stable, orderly framework for investment by creating, as the preamble to a typical United Kingdom BIT states, 'favourable conditions for greater investment by nationals and companies of one state in the territory of the other state'.[6]

* Myres S. McDougal Professor of International Law, Yale Law School; and Schell Fellow, Yale Law School, respectively. The authors acknowledge with gratitude the valuable comments and criticisms of Charles N. Brower, Stephen M. Schwebel, William W. Park, and Jan Paulsson.

[1] Kenneth J. Vandevelde, *The Political Economy of a Bilateral Investment Treaty*, (1998) 92 AJIL 621, 627–8.

[2] Rudolf Dolzer & Margrete Stevens, Bilateral Investment Treaties xii (1995); *see also id.* at 267–326 (chronological list of BITs as of 1994).

[3] Antonio R. Parra, *The Role of ICSID in the Settlement of International Investment Disputes*, 16 ICSID News, Winter 1999, at 5–8; *see also* Kenneth J. Vandevelde, *The Economics of Bilateral Investment Treaties*, (2000) 41 Harv. Int'l L.J. 469, 469 ('By the mid-1990s, [BITs] were being negotiated at the rate of one every other day.').

[4] U.N. Conference on Trade and Development, World Investment Report 2003, at 17. The numbers continue to grow, *see* Dolzer & Stevens, *supra* n. 2, at xii; ICSID, *Bilateral Investment Treaties, 1959–1996, at* <http://www.worldbank.org/icsid/treaties/intro.htm> (last visited July 17, 2003). A number of multilateral treaties, including the North American Free Trade Agreement (NAFTA), Dec. 17, 1992, Can.-Mex.-U.S., 107 Stat. 2066, 32 ILM 289 (1993), and the Energy Charter Treaty, Dec. 17, 1994, (1995) 34 ILM 360, contain substantively similar provisions on the treatment of foreign investment. *See* NAFTA, ch. 11; Energy Charter Treaty, Pt. III, art. 10.

[5] Vandevelde, *supra* n. 3, at 469–70; ICSID, *supra* n. 4 ('Modern BITs have retained broad uniformity in their provisions. In addition to determining the scope of application of the treaty, that is, the investments and investors covered by it, virtually all bilateral investment treaties cover four substantive areas: admission, treatment, expropriation and the settlement of disputes. Almost all modern BITs include provisions dealing with disputes between one of the parties and investors having the nationality of the other party.')

[6] Agreement Between the Government of the United Kingdom of Great Britain and Northern Ireland and the Government of the Republic of Panama for the Promotion and Protection of Investments, Oct. 7, 1983, U.K-Pan., pmbl., (1984) 23 ILM 708, 708 [hereafter U.K-Pan. BIT].

The two states that conclude a BIT most frequently elect to create such a regime for different, albeit interlocking and interdependent, reasons, and based on distinct, albeit interrelated, interests. For capital-exporting states, on the one hand, BITs offer their investors vital insurance against expropriation or other arbitrary treatment of investments;[7] for developing, capital-importing states, on the other, BITs 'send an important signal to the international business community to the effect that that [state] not only welcomes foreign investment but will also facilitate and protect certain foreign ventures'.[8] This latter interest distinguishes BITs in a vital but under-appreciated respect from their predecessors of an earlier generation, viz., Friendship, Commerce and Navigation treaties (FCNs).

FCNs, like BITs, were premised on the assumption that an increase in foreign investment in a developing state would benefit both parties: The foreign investor would earn a reasonable profit, and the host state's economy would experience the benefits of the multiplier effect, i.e. the investment would introduce new human resources and capital, transfer skills and technologies, create additional employment, develop new industries and markets, and so forth, the benefits of which would, in turn, multiply themselves throughout various areas key to the health and continuing growth of the developing state's economy. International law's assumption has been that the increase in direct foreign investment, especially in resource extraction, would also benefit the world community as a whole by bringing more goods onto the market and thereby lowering costs. FCNs, like BITs, are instruments to achieve these goals. But while FCNs addressed diverse matters in the areas of trade and investment, in the context of expropriations, the prototypical FCN treaty did little more than impose upon the host state an obligation not to expropriate covered foreign investments without paying compensation for them. Insofar as the host state honored that commitment, it had discharged its obligations to its treaty partner and that partner's national investors.

In this regard FCNs implicitly relied on a relatively simple theory of economic development: Merely put foreign investment into an underdeveloped economy, and, provided the host state refrains from expropriating the

For analogous language in a typical United States BIT, see, for example, Treaty Between the Government of the United States of America and the Russian Federation Concerning the Encouragement and Reciprocal Protection of Investment, U.S.-Russ., June 17, 1992, pmbl., (1992) 31 ILM 794, 799 [hereafter U.S.-Russ. BIT] (noting the parties mutual 'desir[e] to promote greater economic cooperation between them, with respect to investment by nationals and companies of one Party in the territory of the other Party').

[7] Gary B. Born, International Commercial Arbitration 192 (2001); *see generally* Theodor Meron, Investment Insurance in International Law (1976).

[8] Dolzer & Stevens, *supra* n. 2, at 12; *see also* Dale R. Weigel & Burns H. Weston, *Valuation Upon the Deprivation of Foreign Enterprise: A Policy-Oriented Approach to the Problem of Compensation Under International Law*, in 1 The Valuation of Nationalized Property in International Law 3, 4–6 (Richard B. Lillich ed. 1972); *cf. Revere Copper v Overseas Private Inv. Corp. (OPIC)*, Award of Aug. 24, 1978, (1980) 56 ILR 258, 271–2 (observing that private parties 'committing large amounts of capital over a long period of time require contractual guarantees for their security; governments of developing countries in turn are willing to provide such guarantees in order to promote much needed economic development').

investment, it will generate a reasonable profit while the host state will experience the benefits of the multiplier effect. A generation weaned on Hayek and navigating amid the detritus of hundreds of well-intentioned but disastrous multilateral and national development programs now knows better.[9] BITs reflect this knowledge, in particular, by relying on a far more sophisticated understanding of the 'favourable conditions' necessary to achieve the intersecting goals of the investor and the host state.

The economic and development theory of the BIT may be seen as part of a larger phenomenon:[10] the 'structural readjustment' movement identified with the International Monetary Fund and, latterly, the Organisation for Economic Co-operation and Development's (OECD) and private initiatives' 'transparency' programs. That movement recognizes that the profits of the foreign investor, no less than the multiplier effect in the host state's economy, depend on appropriate internal legal, administrative, and regulatory structures, all conducted through 'transparent' procedures designed to ensure that things are actually done the way they are supposed to be done. The 'favourable conditions' established by BITs consist, not merely of natural phenomena such as climate, resources, and access to the sea, nor even of an educated population in the host state receptive to and eager to participate in the benefits of foreign investment; they also contemplate, more significantly and innovatively, an effective *normative* framework: impartial courts, an efficient and legally restrained bureaucracy, and the measure of transparency in decision that has increasingly been recognized as a control mechanism over governments and as a vital component of the international standard of governance. Hence, in a BIT regime, the host state must do far more than open its doors to foreign investment and refrain from overt expropriation. It must establish and maintain an appropriate legal, administrative, and regulatory framework, the legal environment that modern investment theory has come to recognize as a *conditio sine qua non* of the success of private enterprise. This is not to say, of course, that every governmental adjustment to this normative framework that adversely affects the conditions for foreign investment will constitute an expropriatory act, but that an appropriately operational governmental framework must be in place.[11]

Given the socioeconomic revolution of which they are part, it is no surprise that the proliferation of BITs coincides with large-scale privatization policies in developing states. Privatization, the BIT generation recognizes, demands far more than selling off economically inefficient publicly-owned or -managed companies to private investors. It also requires, particularly in the utility sector, the simultaneous establishment

[9] *See generally* Friedrich A. Hayek, Law, Legislation & Liberty (3 Vols., 1973, 1976, 1979).

[10] For a thorough analysis of the economic and development theories of BITs, and their philosophical underpinnings, see generally Vandevelde, *supra* n. 3, at 488–96; Vandevelde, *supra* n. 1, at 628–33.

[11] See, in this regard, *Mondev Int'l Ltd. v United States*, ICSID Case No. ARB(AF)/99/2, Award of Oct. 11, 2002, (2003) 42 ILM 85, 110, para. 127.

of a regulatory environment (unnecessary, of course, for state-owned industries) that forms part of the indispensable normative and legal framework without which private industry, no less than the public it serves, cannot survive, let alone thrive. Privatization, that is, calls for the very 'stable and orderly framework for investment' that BITs strive to establish. In this respect BITs pursue the macrolegal side of the macroeconomic structural readjustment policies encouraged by multilateral financial institutions. BITs consciously seek to approximate in the developing, capital-importing state the minimal legal, administrative, and regulatory framework that fosters and sustains investment in industrialized capital-exporting states.

II. Indirect Expropriation in the BIT Generation

By no means, however, has this shift in regime paradigm obviated the need to deter expropriation in the BIT generation; if anything, that need has increased. To shield investors from illegal expropriation and other arbitrary or discriminatory governmental conduct that threatens to discourage foreign investment remains a vital purpose of BITs. For that reason, BITs almost invariably include provisions codifying a *lex specialis* to handle claims of expropriation.[12] Because states at times find themselves compelled to take private property for a public purpose such as development or environmental preservation,[13] the practice of eminent domain, insofar as it serves quintessential sovereign interests, will not cease. But with the eclipse of socialism, overt expropriation by formal decree has become relatively rare.

Recognizing the need to attract private foreign capital and technology,[14] many putative capital-importing states in the BIT generation, as in the FCN generation, do not wish to be perceived internationally as posing a frequent or arbitrary threat of expropriation. For this reason, those states far more frequently expropriate foreign investments indirectly. The BIT generation therefore appreciates, more than its FCN predecessor, that foreign investments may be expropriated 'indirectly through measures tantamount to expropriation or nationalization'.[15] This phrase, contained in the United States-Russia BIT and mirrored in substance in virtually all BITs, includes, not simply intentional and obvious indirect expropriations, nor only intentional creeping expropriations, a frequent form of taking in prior generations. It also captures the multiplicity of inappropriate regulatory acts, omissions, and other deleterious conduct

[12] We do not explore in this article the question whether, and at what point, BITs and associated jurisprudence may, in the aggregate, indicate the emergence of customary international law. *See* n. 158 *infra*.

[13] *E.g. Compañia del Desarrollo de Santa Elena, S.A. v Costa Rica*, ICSID Case No. ARB/96/1, Award of Feb. 17, 2000, (2000) 39 ILM 1317 (award on claim arising from a legal expropriation carried out for the avowed purpose of environmental conservation).

[14] Dolzer & Stevens, *supra* n. 2, at 11–12.

[15] U.S.-Russ. BIT, art. III(1).

that undermines the vital normative framework created and maintained by BITs—and by which governments can, in effect but not name, now be deemed to have expropriated a foreign national's investment. The major innovation of the 'tantamount' clause, found in substance in almost all BITs, therefore consists in extending the concept of indirect expropriation to an egregious failure to create or maintain the normative 'favourable conditions' in the host state.[16]

Jurists and scholars refer to indirect expropriations variously, and often interchangeably, as regulatory, constructive, consequential, disguised, de facto or creeping.[17] Some of these terms, however, connote behavior that may not have been legally cognizable under an FCN regime, but could furnish a sound basis for a claim under a BIT regime. This development, together with the proliferation of international jurisprudence on expropriation since the early 1980s—much of which emanates from the Iran-U.S. Claims Tribunal[18] and ICSID tribunals constituted pursuant to BITs or multilateral investment treaties such as NAFTA, but some of which may be found in less obvious sources, such as, for example, the case law of the European Court of Human Rights—invites inquiry into, and further refinement of, the concept of indirect expropriation and the problem of its valuation.

A. INDIRECT EXPROPRIATIONS

The general concept of indirect expropriations is not novel. In a seminal study in 1962 in the *British Yearbook of International Law*, G.C. Christie analyzed two early international decisions concerning expropriation:[19] the judgment of the Permanent Court of International Justice in *Certain German Interests in Polish Upper Silesia*,[20] and the arbitral award rendered by a tribunal established pursuant to a special agreement between Norway and the United States in the *Norwegian Shipowners Claims* case.[21] These cases, Christie concluded, establish *(i)* 'that a State may expropriate property, where it interferes with it, even though the State expressly disclaims any such intention,' and *(ii)* 'that even though a State may not purport to interfere with rights to property, it may, by its actions, render those rights so useless that it will be deemed to have expropriated

[16] As emphasized above, we do not suggest that every governmental adjustment to the normative framework for foreign investment that adversely affect the conditions for foreign investment, *ipso facto*, constitutes an expropriatory act.

[17] Burns H. Weston, *'Constructive Takings' Under International Law: A Modest and Foray into the Problem of 'Creeping Expropriation'*, (1975) 16 Va. J. Int'l L. 103, 106.

[18] George H. Aldrich, *What Constitutes a Compensable Taking of Property? The Decisions of the Iran-United States Claims Tribunal*, (1994) 88 AJIL 585, 585 n. 2 (noting that [w]hile the Algiers Declarations gave the Tribunal broad discretion in its choice of law (art. V of the Claims Settlement Declaration), international law almost invariably has been applied by the Tribunal in its decisions on takings of property).

[19] G.C. Christie, *What Constitutes a Taking Under International Law*, (1962) 38 *BYBIL* 307, 310–11.

[20] *Certain German Interests in Polish Upper Silesia (Germany v Poland)*, 1926 PCIJ Rep Series A. No. 7 (May 25).

[21] *Norwegian Shipowners Claims (Norway v U.S.)* (1922) 1 RIAA 307.

them.'[22] Subsequently, international decisions and commentary alike have incorporated these conclusions.

The Iran-U.S. Claims Tribunal, for example, has repeatedly held that '[t]he intent of the government [concerning expropriation] is less important than the effects of the measures on the owner and the form of the measures of control or interference is less important than the reality of their impact'.[23] As in *Phillips Petroleum Co. v Iran*,[24] a deprivation of property may be effected by 'a series of concrete actions rather than [by] any particular formal decree'.[25] A recent ICSID panel emphasized the 'ample authority for the proposition that property has been expropriated when the effect of the measures taken by the state has been to deprive the owner of title, possession or access to the benefit and economic use of his property.'[26] Jurisprudence emanating from the European Court of Human Rights, while technically an exercise in interpretation of a human rights treaty,[27] provides additional evidence of the authoritative consensus that international law prohibits de facto and indirect, not only de jure and direct, expropriations. In *Sporrong v Kingdom of Sweden*, for example, the Court found that while certain 'expropriation permits left intact in law the owners' right to use and dispose of their possessions, they nevertheless in practice significantly reduced the possibility of its exercise', and concluded that '[i]n the absence of a formal expropriation, that is to say a transfer of ownership, the Court . . . must look behind appearances and investigate the realities of the situation complained of [because] the Convention is intended to guarantee rights that are "practical and effective" '.[28]

Hence, in 1989, the *Restatement (Third) of Foreign Relations Law* could say, on the basis of a solid body of authority, that States 'bear responsibility,

[22] Christie, *supra* n. 19, at 311; *accord* Judge Rosalyn Higgins, *The Taking of Property by the State: Recent Developments in International Law, in* (1983) III Recueil Des Cours 259, 322–4 (analyzing the same decisions and arriving at the similar conclusion that 'these two cases certainly indicate that an expropriation of a given property may in fact—regardless of stated intention—involve a taking of closely connected ancillary rights').

[23] *Tippets v Tams-Affa Consulting Eng'rs*, (1984) 6 Iran-US CTR 219, 225–6; *accord Int'l Sys. & Control Operations v Indus. Dev. and Renovation Org.*, (1986) 12 Iran-US CTR 239, para. 97; *Payne v Iran*, (1986) 12 Iran-US CTR 3, para. 22; *Phelps Dodge Corp. v Iran*, (1986) 10 US CTR 121, para. 22; *see also* Aldrich, *supra* n. 18, at 603.

[24] *Phillips Petroleum Co. v Iran*, (1989) 21 Iran-US CTR 79.

[25] *Id.* at 115–16.

[26] *Compañia del Desarrollo de Santa Elena, S.A. v Costa Rica*, ICSID Case No. ARB/96/1 Award of Feb. 17, 2000, (2000) 439 ILM 1317, 1330, para. 77 (citing *Tippets*, 6 Iran-US CTR. at 225–6).

[27] *See* European Convention for the Protection of Human Rights and Fundamental Freedoms, Nov. 4, 1950, 213 U.N.T.S. 221, and especially the protocols thereto.

[28] *Sporrong v Kingdom of Sweden* Series A (1982) 52 EHRR paras 60, 63.; *cf. De la Grange v Italy*, (1995) 19 EHRR 368, para. 26(d) (finding no expropriation on the facts, but observing that '[w]here, following an administrative decision concerning specific property, the owner retains the ownership subject to restrictions which reduce to virtually nothing the economic value of the use or exchange of the property, this is known as "value expropriation" (*espropriazione di valore*) and it gives rise to an entitlement to compensation'); *Agrotexim v Greece* (1996) 21 EHRR 250, 270 (disclaiming jurisdiction based on considerations of standing, but noting the European Commission's conclusion that the Municipality of Athens, by 'repeated declarations of officials [threatening to] acquire the company's land and . . . the placement of signposts indicating that the area would be expropriated even though they left intact in law the company's property rights', had created a situation whereby the company could neither operate effectively nor attract potential investment).

not only for "avowed" expropriations in which the government formally takes title to property, but also [for] other actions of the government that have the effect of "taking" the property, in whole or in large part, outright or in stages'.[29] A more recent U.N. study provides: 'Indirect expropriation occurs when the country takes an action that substantially impairs the value of an investment without necessarily assuming ownership of the investment. Accordingly, indirect expropriation may occur even though the host country disavows any intent to expropriate the investment.'[30] Scholars, finally, almost without exception, concur. In her 1982 Hague Lectures, for example, Judge Rosalyn Higgins analyzed the jurisprudence on indirect expropriations in some detail, and her conclusions corroborate the general principles formulated by Christie.[31]

In short, international tribunals, jurists, and scholars have consistently appreciated that states may accomplish expropriation in ways other than by formal decree; indeed, often in ways that may seek to cloak expropriatory conduct with a veneer of legitimacy. For this reason, tribunals have increasingly accepted that expropriation must be analyzed in consequential rather than formal terms. What matters is the effect of governmental conduct—whether malfeasance, misfeasance, or nonfeasance, or some combination of the three—on foreign property rights or control over an investment,[32] not whether the state promulgates a formal decree or otherwise expressly proclaims its intent to expropriate. For purposes of state responsibility and the obligation to make adequate reparation,[33] international law does not distinguish indirect from direct expropriations.[34]

[29] Restatement (Third) of Foreign Relations Law section 712 cmt. (g) (1989).

[30] U.N. Conference on Trade and Development, Bilateral Investment Treaties in the Mid-1990s, at 66 (1998).

[31] Higgins, *supra* n. 22, at 322–4; Christie, *supra* n. 19, at 309–12; *see also* Martin Domke, *Foreign Nationalizations: Some Aspects of Contemporary International Law*, (1961) 55 AJIL 585, 588–9. For the contrary (minority) view, see, for example, M. Sornarajah, The International Law of Foreign Investment (1994).

[32] *See*, in this regard, the classic statement of the arbitral tribunal in *Revere Copper v Overseas Private Inv. Corp. (OPIC)*, Award of Aug. 24, 1978, (1980) 56 ILR 258, 271–2:

> the effects of the Jamaican Government's actions in repudiating its long term commitments to RJA ha[d] substantially the same impact on effective control over use and operation as if the properties were themselves conceded by a concession contract that was repudiated . . . OPIC argues that RJA still has all the rights and property that it had before the [expropriatory] events of 1974: it is in possession of the plant and other facilities; it has its Mining Lease; it can operate as it did before. This may be true in a formal sense but . . . we do not regard RJA's 'control' of the use and operation of its properties as any longer 'effective' in view of the destruction by Government actions of its contract rights

Id. at 292.

[33] *See generally* Articles on the Responsibility of States for Internationally Wrongful Acts, arts. 1, 31, *in* Report of the International Law Commission on the Work of its Fifty-third Session, U.N. GAOR, 56th Sess., Supp. No. 10, at 43, U.N. Doc. A/56/10 (2001), annexed to G.A. Res. 56/83 (Dec. 12, 2001) (noting the principles, respectively, that '[e]very internationally wrongful act of a State entails the international responsibility of that State' (art. 1), and that 'the responsible State is under an obligation to make full reparation for the injury caused by the internationally wrongful act' (art. 31)); *see also id.*, arts. 34–8 (setting forth the general forms of reparation available under international law, viz., restitution, compensation, satisfaction, and interest).

[34] That BITs embrace this equivalence is evident from, for example, the text of the BIT between the United States and Argentina. Article VI(1) of that BIT proscribes all expropriations, including

Within the normative legal regime created by BITs, as under customary international law, indirect expropriations—typically denominated by phrases such as 'measures tantamount to expropriation',[35] 'measures having effect equivalent to nationalisation or expropriation',[36] or by some substantively comparable language—require fact-sensitive inquiries into the practical effect of an event or events on a foreign investor's rights. In general, '[w]here the effect is similar to what might have occurred under an outright expropriation, the investor would in all likelihood be covered under most BIT provisions'.[37] Moreover, again as under customary international law, the impact of each governmental measure must be analyzed, not in isolation, but cumulatively, because, as the European Court of Human Rights wrote in this context, 'the consequences of [the state's] interference [are] undoubtedly rendered more serious by the[ir] combined use'.[38]

The concept of indirect expropriation has therefore become an established feature of customary international law on state responsibility to aliens. Within the BIT generation, however, at least two 'species' of the genre of indirect expropriations can be usefully identified and distinguished.[39] Because these distinctions may facilitate the appraisal of liability for indirect expropriations, their valuation processes, and the liquidation of the amount of compensation due for foreign property so expropriated, it is worthwhile to identify and define these species in greater detail.

B. CREEPING EXPROPRIATIONS

Not every indirect expropriation is properly described as 'creeping'. Creeping expropriations pose unique problems, both with respect to the determination of *(i)* liability, i.e. at what stage, if any, the accretion of wrongful interferences (many of which, alone, may seem innocuous) should be deemed expropriatory as a matter of law; and *(ii)* valuation, i.e. as of what date the value of property rights so expropriated should be

those accomplished 'indirectly through measures tantamount to expropriation or nationalization,' which, as the immediately following parenthetical confirms, must be deemed indistinguishable from expropriation *simpliciter*.

[35] *E.g.* Treaty Between the United States of America and the Argentine Republic Concerning the Reciprocal Encouragement and Protection of Investment, U.S.-Arg., Nov. 14, 1991, art. IV(1), (1992) 31 ILM 124 [hereafter U.S.-Arg. BIT].

[36] *E.g.* U.K.-Pan. BIT, art. V(1).

[37] Dolzer & Stevens, *supra* n. 2, at 100 (citing *Starrett Hous. Corp. v. Iran* (1984) 4 Iran-US CTR 123, 23 ILM 1090, 1115); K. Scott Gudgeon, *Valuation of Nationalized Property Under United States and Other Bilateral Investment Treaties, in* IV The Valuation of Nationalized Property in International Law 101, 102 (Richard B. Lillich ed., 1987) (noting that BITs define expropriation 'in a manner that promotes substance over form,' thereby employing the so-called 'effects test', which reaches all forms of creeping expropriation).

[38] *Sporrong v Kingdom of Sweden*, Series A 52 EHRR at 26, para. 60.

[39] Substantial overlap between the various gradations of indirect expropriation can, and frequently will, exist. It is nevertheless useful to identify and distinguish these species because, as we explain below, it helps to clarify *(i)* the existence *vel non* of an expropriation under a BIT regime; *(ii)* the moment at which that expropriation occurs; and *(iii)* the moment from which the value of an enterprise so expropriated should be valuated for purposes of respecting paramount principles of international law on reparation.

assessed. Without concurrently purporting to take title to property or to appropriate a foreign investor's commercial rights, a state might, for example, appoint an unreasonably intrusive government 'supervisor', or fix prices for a commodity indispensable to the production process at a level that destroys an enterprise's economic viability, or refuse to hold feckless administrators to account for failure to carry out their assigned tasks. A wide variety of measures—including taxation,[40] regulation, denial of due process, delay and non-performance, and other forms of governmental malfeasance, misfeasance, and nonfeasance—may be deemed expropriatory if those measures significantly reduce an investor's property rights or render them practically useless.[41] But if one or two events in that series can readily be identified as those that destroyed the investment's value, then to speak of a creeping expropriation may be misleading. Keith Highet cogently explained in a dissenting opinion that

> a 'creeping' expropriation is comprised of a number of elements, none of which can—separately—constitute the international wrong [i.e. the creeping expropriation]. These constituent elements [may] include non-payment, non-reimbursement, cancellation, denial of judicial access, actual practice to exclude, non-conforming treatment, inconsistent legal blocks, and so forth. The 'measure' at issue is the [creeping] expropriation itself; it is not merely a sub-component part of expropriation.[42]

In what one commentator described as 'the case closest to true "creeping" expropriation, the government of Somalia directed sundry acts of harassment (including occasional arrests of key employees, blocking access to the plant site, and the nationalization of an oil depot which was a portion of the activities of the project) against a foreign-owned shellfish processing facility', ultimately compelling the plant manager to terminate operations.[43] OPIC decided, upon confirmation of these facts by the U.S. State Department, 'that the actions of the Somalian government, though not openly expropriatory, were calculated to disrupt the operations of the foreign enterprise to such an extent that an inference of expropriatory intent could be drawn'; it therefore 'honored the claim'.[44]

Where, as in *Fearn International, Inc.*, the decision-maker can infer expropriatory *intent*, it tends to be simple to characterize the aggregate of events as a taking. In some, if not most other, creeping expropriations, however, that intent, though possibly present at some level of the host state's government, will be difficult, if not impossible, to discern. Discrete

[40] Tax measures alleged to be expropriatory may raise unique concerns. By its 'tax veto' provision, for example, NAFTA suggests a qualitative difference between taxation and other measures that can, alone or in combination, culminate in an apparent expropriation. NAFTA, art. 2103(6); *see* William W. Park, *Arbitration and the FISC: NAFTA's 'Tax Veto'*, 2 Chi. J. Int'l L. 231 (2001).

[41] Dolzer & Stevens, *supra* n. 2, at 100; *see also* Restatement (Third) of Foreign Relations Law section 712 cmt. (g) (1989).

[42] *Waste Mgmt., Inc. v United Mexican States* ICSID Case No. ARB(AF)/98/2, Award of June 2, 2000, (2001) 40 ILM 56, 73 (Keith Highet, dissenting).

[43] Vance R. Koven, *Expropriation and the 'Jurisprudence' of OPIC*, (1981) 22 Harv. J. Int'l L. 269, 291.

[44] *Id.*

acts, analyzed in isolation rather than in the context of the overall flow of events, may, whether legal or not in themselves, seem innocuous vis-à-vis a potential expropriation. Some may not be expropriatory in themselves. Only in retrospect will it become evident that those acts comprised part of an accretion of deleterious acts and omissions, which in the aggregate expropriated the foreign investor's property rights.[45] Indeed, the acts—malfeasance, misfeasance, and non-feasance—comprising the expropriation in creeping expropriations may be part of a series that includes many lawful ones. The *Restatement* confirms that a creeping expropriation may occur where State action 'makes it impossible for the [foreign investor] to operate at a profit,' because 'a State may seek to achieve the same result [i.e. expropriation] by taxation and regulatory measures *designed* to make continued economic operation of a project uneconomical so that it is abandoned'.[46] We emphasize 'designed' because the actual taking may not be comprised of acts that were specifically intended *to expropriate*, even though that is their natural and foreseeable consequence.

Because of the absence of a manifest intent in such cases, Judge Brower once observed that 'it is difficult to envision a de facto or "creeping" expropriation ever being lawful, for the absence of a declared intention to expropriate almost certainly implies that no contemporaneous provision for compensation has been made. Indeed, research reveals no international precedent finding such an expropriation to have been lawful'.[47] Were disclaimers of expropriatory intent sufficient to validate otherwise

[45] At the same time, one unlawful act within a series of otherwise lawful regulatory acts by the State cannot transform an innocent progression of legitimate, reasonable regulations in the public interest into a creeping expropriation. But this is simply to restate a point made earlier and throughout this article: that indirect expropriations of all kinds, but particularly creeping expropriations, require acutely fact-sensitive inquiries.

[46] Restatement (third) of Foreign Relations section 712 nn. 6–7 (1989) (emphasis added). It is noteworthy that U.S. case law on the Takings Clause of the Fifth Amendment adopts substantially the same principle in the context of utility-rate regulation. *See, e.g., Duquesne Light Co. v. Barach*, 488 US 299, 310 (1989) ('[I]t is not theory but the *impact* of the rate order which counts . . . [W]hether a particular rate is unjust or unreasonable will depend to some extent on what is a fair rate of return given the risks under a particular rate-setting system, and on the amount of capital upon which the investors are entitled to earn that return'.) (quoting *FPC v Hope Natural Gas Co.* 320 US 591, 602 (1944)) (emphasis added); *Covington & Lexington Turnpike Rd. Co. v Sandford* 164 US 578, 597 (1896) (finding a rate to be impermissibly low if it is 'so unjust as to destroy the value of [the] property for all the purposes for which it was acquired', and therefore 'to practically deprive [ ] the owner of property without due process of law'). On regulatory takings generally, see, for example, the classic statement of Justice Holmes in *Pennsylvania Coal Co. v Mahon*, 260 US 393 (1922):

> Government hardly could go on if to some extent values incident to property could not be diminished without paying for every such change in the general law. As long recognized some values are enjoyed under an implied limitation and must yield to the police power. But obviously the implied limitation must have its limits or the contract and due process clauses [of the Constitution] are gone. One fact for consideration in determining such limits is the extent of diminution. When it reaches a certain magnitude, in most if not all cases there must be . . . compensation to sustain the act . . . The general rule at least is that while property may be regulated to a certain extent, if regulation goes too far it will be recognized as a taking.

Id. at 413, 415. The Takings Clause has also created a rich jurisprudence on valuation that arguably contributes to the evolution of international standards. *See* Thomas W. Merrill, *Incomplete Compensation for Takings*, (2002) 11 N.Y.U. Envtl. L.J. 110, 115–28.

[47] *Sedco, Inc. v Nat'l Ir. Oil Co.*, 10 Iran-US CTR 180, (1986) 25 ILM 629, 649 (Brower, J., concurring).

expropriatory acts, states could avoid their obligation to make reparation simply by asserting the absence of that intent. Because of their gradual and cumulative nature, creeping expropriations also render it problematic, perhaps even arbitrary, to identify a single interference (or failure to act where a duty requires it) as the 'moment of expropriation'. Several ICSID awards illustrate these problems well.

In *Benvenuti et Bonfant v People's Republic of the Congo*,[48] the claimant, an Italian firm (B&B), entered into a joint venture with the Congo to create a company to manufacture plastic bottles of mineral water (PLASCO). The Congolese government agreed to establish a special tax regime for PLASCO, to adopt protectionist measures to obviate the threat of foreign competition, and to guarantee PLASCO's financing.[49] Almost immediately after it began operations, however, problems developed. Over the ensuing months and years, the government, *inter alia*, defaulted on its financing obligations, unilaterally fixed the prices for bottles of mineral water bottles below the level agreed upon at the initial meeting of PLASCO's Board of Directors, failed to establish the preferential tax regime contemplated by the joint venture, neglected or refused to call regular meetings of the Board, and failed to adopt protectionist measures limiting the import of mineral water.[50]

Ultimately, the Congolese military occupied PLASCO's corporate headquarters, and the government instituted criminal proceedings against one Corrado Bonfant, a principal of B&B, compelling B&B to shut down operations and quit the Congo.[51] At no time, however, did the Congolese government purport to expropriate B&B's share of PLASCO. In fact, it insisted throughout the subsequent arbitration 'that the Italian party can return and take back its share at any time.'[52] The ICSID tribunal convened to hear B&B's claim nonetheless agreed with B&B that the cumulative effect of the government's acts (e.g. price-fixing) and omissions (e.g. failure to establish a preferential tax regime or prohibit foreign imports) 'de facto expropriated [B&B's] corporate shares in the PLASCO company'.[53]

In *Liberian Eastern Timber Corp. (LETCO) v Liberia*,[54] Liberia concluded a concession contract, the 'Forest Products Utilization Contract' with LETCO, a company wholly owned by French nationals. The contract gave LETCO 'the exclusive right to harvest, process, transport and market timber and other forest products and to conduct other timbering operations in the "Exploitation Area", which covered some 350,000 to 400,000 acres of forest, for a twenty-year period'.[55] In exchange, LETCO agreed to pay specified taxes, to avoid exploiting certain species of trees, to abide by Liberian labor law, 'to give preference to competent and qualified Liberian citizens when hiring', and 'to erect and maintain an efficient sawmill plant' and other assets and infrastructure, which the contract

[48] *Benvenuti et Bonfant v People's Republic of the Congo,* ICSID Award of Aug. 8, 1980, (1982) 21 ILM 740.

[49] *Id.* at 748–9.

[50] *Id.* at 749–50, 753–7.

[51] *Id.* at 758.

[52] *Id.*

[53] *Id.*

[54] *Liber. E. Timber Corp. v Liberia*, ICSID Award of Mar. 31, 1986 (rectified May 14, 1986), (1987) 26 ILM 647.

[55] *Id.* at 658.

contemplated would be left 'in good and safe-running order' upon the expiration of the concession.[56] Subsequently, over a period of several years, Liberia withdrew portions of the Exploitation Area, demanded renegotiation of the concession contract, failed to comply with certain notification provisions of the contract,[57] and granted repossessed forest areas within the concession's scope to 'foreign companies . . . run by people who were "good friends" of the Liberian authorities'.[58]

As in *Benvenuti et Bonfant*, Liberia never expressly expropriated LETCO's property rights, directly or indirectly. Indeed, while this case involved a breach of contract, the tribunal effectively found that Liberia's act constituted expropriation even absent an avowed expropriatory intent.[59] But the tribunal found that even assuming, arguendo, that Liberia had sought to justify its actions as a legitimate act of nationalization, any such contention would fail because 'the taking of LETCO's property was not for a bona fide public purpose, was discriminatory and was not accompanied by an offer of appropriate compensation'.[60] Indeed, while Liberia ultimately defaulted, it had previously justified its actions by claiming that LETCO had breached various obligations under the concession contract—a claim rejected on the facts by the ICSID tribunal convened to hear LETCO's claim.

In *Metalclad Corp. v United Mexican States*,[61] an ICSID tribunal heard a claim brought against Mexico under Chapter 11 of NAFTA, alleging that Mexico expropriated Metalclad's purchase, construction, and development of a hazardous-waste landfill. Examining '[t]he totality of the[ ] circumstances', the tribunal found 'a lack of orderly process and timely disposition [with respect to Metalclad's application for certain perfunctory municipal permits] in relation to [a foreign] investor acting in the expectation that it would be treated fairly and justly in accordance with the NAFTA'.[62] The tribunal concluded that an accumulation of harmful acts and omissions of the Municipality of Guadalcazar, which interfered with Metalclad's reasonable expectations, 'taken together with the representations of the Mexican federal government, on which Metalclad relied, and the absence of a timely, orderly or substantive basis for the denial by the Municipality of a local construction permit, amount[ed] to an indirect expropriation'.[63] Again, the defendant government denied an intent to expropriate. And again, the tribunal found proof *vel non* of that intent to be immaterial. The tribunal's conclusion that Mexico had expropriated Metalclad's investment rested on an examination of the aggregate effects or consequences of Mexico's conduct:

[E]xpropriation under NAFTA includes not only open, deliberate and acknowledged takings of property, such as outright seizure or formal or obligatory transfer of title in favour of the host State, but also covert or incidental interference

[56] *Id.* at 659. [57] *Id.* at 660–2. [58] *Id.* at 665. [59] *Id.* [60] *Id.*

[61] *Metalclad Corp. v United Mexican States*, ICSID Case No. ARB/96/3, Award of Aug. 30, 2000, (2001) 40 ILM 36. [62] *Id.* at 50.

[63] *Id.*

with the use of property which has the effect of depriving the owner, in whole or in significant part, of the use or reasonably-to-be-expected economic benefit of property . . .[64]

In each of the above cases, the host government therefore accomplished an expropriation, not only indirectly, but furtively, through often seemingly trivial acts of sometimes nebulous legality or propriety. Considered in isolation, for example, it would be implausible to say that the Congolese government's neglect to call regular meetings of PLASCO's Board of Directors, ipso facto, effected an indirect expropriation. Conversely, however, it would be equally implausible to deny that *all* the acts preceding the Congolese military's occupation of PLASCO's corporate headquarters, appraised in terms of their cumulative impact, did *not* effect an indirect expropriation until the dramatic moment at which that occupation forced B&B's staff to flee the country and initiate arbitration.[65] In an analogous context, former Judge of the Iran-U.S. Claims Tribunal Howard M. Holtzmann, concurring in the *Starrett Housing Corp.* Interlocutory Award, wrote:

The Interlocutory Award correctly holds that [the appointment of a government manager] was an act of expropriation because it denied Claimants their right to manage and control Shah Goli and the Project. The appointment of the manager was not, however, the first or only act of expropriation; in fact, it was the last of a series of such measures. The Interlocutory Award ignores the real impact of other decisive acts which resulted in a taking of Claimant's property rights many months before. Although the Government of Iran on 30 January 1980 took the formal step of appointing a manager for the property which it had already taken, that final measure cannot logically serve to obscure the earlier acts of expropriation. In my view, a realistic assessment of the facts would have been preferable to the sterile formalism of the Interlocutory Award.[66]

By a 'steady and inexorable' progression of expropriatory acts and omissions,[67] the governments in each of these cases deprived foreign investors of their property rights or rendered those rights practically useless.

[64] *Id.* at 51. A Canadian court subsequently vacated the Metalclad award in part. *See The United Mexican States v Metalclad Corp.*, Supreme Court of British Columbia, Reasons for Judgment, 2001 BCSC 664, 119 ILR 647, (2002) 5 ICSID Rep 238. Judge Tysoe held that the NAFTA Tribunal exceeded its jurisdiction insofar as it held that the events preceding Mexico's Ecological Decree constituted an expropriation, because the Tribunal's analysis of section 1105 of NAFTA imposed a transparency obligation not found in that section, which 'infected' its section 1110 analysis to the extent that the latter involved analysis of the cumulative impact of events preceding the Decree—including failure to abide by the transparency obligation. *See id.* paras 77–80. Wholly apart from the substantive merits of Judge Tysoe's judgment, an inquiry beyond the scope of this article, we note that this judgment did not cast doubt on the definition of a creeping expropriation under customary international law; its import is limited to the treaty regime established by NAFTA. But see *id.* para. 100 (suggesting that the Tribunal employed an 'extremely broad' definition of expropriation, but finding that this is an issue to which the court must defer under the arbitration law of British Columbia).

[65] *Cf. Koven, supra* n. 43, at 278 ('Where a "creeping" expropriation manifests itself over a long period of time, the definition of expropriatory action appears to ignore the chain of events prior to the one "act" which is ultimately deemed to be the one determining the date of expropriation.').

[66] *Starrett Hous. Corp. v Iran*, 4 Iran-US CTR 123, (1984) 23 ILM 1090, 1125 (Holtzmann, J., concurring).

[67] *Id.*

A creeping expropriation therefore denotes, in the paradigmatic case, an expropriation accomplished by a cumulative series of regulatory acts or omissions over a prolonged period of time, no one of which can necessarily be identified as the decisive event that deprived the foreign national of the value of its investment. Moreover, they may be interspersed with entirely lawful state regulatory actions. By definition, then, creeping expropriations lack the vividness and transparency not only of formal expropriations, but also of many regulatory or otherwise indirect expropriations, which may be identified more closely with a few discrete events. The gradual and sometimes furtive nature of the acts and omissions that culminate in a creeping expropriation tends to obscure what tribunals ordinarily denominate the 'moment of expropriation'.

Because a creeping expropriation, by its nature, cannot be defined by reference to a single, readily identifiable, expropriatory act, whether direct or not, attempting to discern the precise moment of expropriation, the 'date on which the governmental "interference" has deprived the owner of his rights or has made those rights practically useless',[68] will often prove a daunting task for an international tribunal. Creeping expropriations, then, require in the first instance a meticulously fact-sensitive inquiry in order to determine the moment at which liability for an expropriation attaches. But that moment need not—and in many cases, we suggest below, should not—be equated with the moment at which the value of expropriated property rights properly should be appraised for compensation purposes. Consistent with customary international law and any relevant bilateral or multilateral investment treaty provisions, which in any event generally incorporate customary international law as a minimum standard for the treatment of all investments,[69] the latter moment should be established in a manner that will enable a tribunal seized with a claim based on a creeping expropriation to give full effect to the venerable compensation principles articulated in *Chorzów Factory*.

C. CONSEQUENTIAL EXPROPRIATIONS

Other 'measures tantamount to expropriation' within the purview of a BIT regime prove even more elusive than creeping expropriations because they consist of the host state's failures to create, maintain, and

[68] *Compañia del Desarrollo de Santa Elena, S.A. v Costa Rica*, ICSID Case No. ARB/96/1, Award of Feb. 17, 2000, (2000) 439 ILM 1317, 1330; *accord Starrett Hous. Corp.*, 23 ILM at 1115 ('[I]t is recognized in international law that measures taken by a state can interfere with property rights to such an extent that these rights are rendered so useless that they must be deemed to have been expropriated, even though the state does not purport to have expropriated them and the legal title to the property formally remains with the original owner.'); *see* Weston, *supra* n. 17, at 106 (noting the 'truism that judgments of this kind [i.e. about when a series of events ripens into a creeping expropriation] commonly depend on highly subjective responses to the fact patterns discerned').

[69] *E.g.* U.S.-Russ. BIT, arts. II(2)(a), III(2).

properly manage the legal, administrative, and regulatory normative framework contemplated by the relevant BIT, an indispensable feature of the 'favourable conditions' for investment. Again, this is not to say that every governmental adjustment to the normative framework of the host state that adversely affects foreign investment will constitute an expropriatory act. As the NAFTA tribunal in *Feldman v Mexico*[70] said:

> To paraphrase *Azinian*, not all government regulatory activity that makes it difficult or impossible for an investor to carry out a particular business, change in the law or change in the application of existing laws that makes it uneconomical to continue a particular business, is an expropriation under Article 1110. Governments, in their exercise of regulatory power, frequently change their laws and regulations in response to changing economic circumstances or changing political, economic or social considerations. Those changes may well make certain activities less profitable or even uneconomic to continue.[71]

Lawful regulation, that is, is not expropriation. Some self-described 'regulation', however, can and should properly be deemed expropriatory. In *Feldman*, the tribunal also aptly explained that

> the ways in which governmental authorities may force a company out of business, or significantly reduce the economic benefits of its business, are many. In the past, confiscatory taxation, denial of access to infrastructure or necessary raw materials, imposition of unreasonable regulatory regimes, among others, have been considered to be expropriatory actions. At the same time, governments must be free to act in the broader public interest through protection of the environment, new or modified tax regimes, the granting or withdrawal of government subsidies, reductions or increases in tariff levels, imposition of zoning restrictions and the like. Reasonable governmental regulation of this type cannot be achieved if any business that is adversely affected may seek compensation, and it is safe to say that customary international law recognizes this.[72]

Thus, while a host state is not, of course, precluded from regulating foreign investments, some regulations, and equally importantly, failures to regulate, may rise to the level of expropriatory action. The ultimate expropriatory effect of these failures will be painfully apparent, and at least in retrospect, the causes can be identified: for example, feckless or corrupt bureaucracies, lack of political will at the leadership level, negligence or failure to make timely decisions incumbent on the state by virtue of contracts or concession agreements, and so forth. But in consequential expropriations, while there exists, to borrow terms from criminal law, an *actus reus* and a *corpus delicti*, there may not exist a *mens rea*, an intent to expropriate. The absence of this intent within at least some echelon of the host state's government distinguishes consequential expropriations from garden-variety indirect expropriations and also from most, though not all,

[70] *Feldman v Mexico*, ICSID Case No. ARB(AF)/99/1, Award of Dec. 16, 2002, (2003) 42 ILM 625.

[71] *Id.*, para. 112, 42 ILM at 648 (paraphrasing *Azinian v United Mexican States*, ICSID Case No. ARB(AF)/97/2, Award of Nov. 1, 1999, (2000) 39 ILM 537, 549, para. 83).

[72] *Id.*, para. 103, 42 ILM at 646.

creeping expropriations—for consequential expropriation can be accomplished in the same manner as creeping expropriations.

Consequential expropriations involve deprivations of the economic value of a foreign investment, which, within the legal regime established by a BIT, must be deemed expropriatory because of their causal links to failures of the host state to fulfill its paramount obligations to establish and maintain an appropriate legal, administrative, and regulatory normative framework for foreign investment. But because consequential expropriations result from misfeasances, malfeasances, and nonfeasances of the host state, it often proves difficult to determine whether the acts and omissions of the host state *(i)* were themselves the *causa causans* of the loss of economic value or *(ii)* contributed to that loss; or by contrast, *(iii)* whether the loss should rather be ascribed chiefly to the foreign investor's misjudgments or *(iv)* to exogenous economic factors independent of the actions (or inactions) of the host state. Where the losses that are the basis of a claim should be ascribed chiefly to the latter two factors, as the Permanent Court of Justice long ago established in the *Oscar Chinn* case, the foreign investor enjoys no right to compensation.[73] In some cases, of course, the causes of the loss will fall clearly or predominantly in one of these categories; in others, where they fall will be far less clear.

But even when it is clear that the host state's acts and omissions caused, or substantially caused, a legally significant depreciation in the economic value of the investment, and would therefore qualify as expropriatory within a BIT regime, determining the moment of expropriation for purposes of valuation remains, as we noted earlier, an especially daunting task. This intellectual operation, difficult in any indirect or creeping case, becomes even more so in those cases of consequential expropriation where *some* responsibility for the decline of the economic value of the investment could be attributable to actions or judgements of the foreign investor or to exogenous market factors. In these circumstances the depreciation of the investment's value may be caused by a complex series of interactions between failures of the host state to fulfill its obligations under the BIT, on the one hand, and misjudgements of the investor or exogenous market factors, on the other.

The absence of an expropriatory decree, but the presence of an expropriatory consequence, defines a generic indirect expropriation. But also common to most past indirect expropriations was an expropriatory intent at some level of the governmental apparatus of the host state. In consequential expropriations, states do not form an express intent to expropriate; indeed, they may not have such an intent at all. Even though a state's responsibility to pay compensation for expropriation does not, in any event, 'depend on proof that the expropriation was intentional',[74] the

[73] *The Oscar Chinn Case (Belgium v UK)* 1934 PCIJ Rep Series A/B No. 63 (Dec. 12).

[74] *Phillips Petroleum Co. v Iran* (1989) 21 Iran-US CTR 79, 115; *see also Tippets v Tams-Affa Consulting Eng'rs*, (1984) 6 Iran-US CTR 219, 225–6; *Int'l Sys. & Control Operations v Indus. Dev. and Renovation Org.*, (1986) 12 Iran-US CTR 239, para. 97; *Payne v Iran* (1986) 12 Iran-US CTR 3,

manifestation of that intent at some level of the state's government generally furnishes a tribunal with a useful demarcation. It enables a decision-maker not only to confirm that an expropriation has taken place, but to set, based on relatively objective evidence, the moment of valuation—typically, a point in time before the host state's conduct occasioned the depreciation in the value of the foreign investment.

Consequential expropriations lack such demarcations. Consider a few hypothetical examples:

- the host state, privatizing a theretofore state-owned enterprise, promises to establish a regulatory apparatus, but fails to;
- alternatively, the host state creates the appropriate regulatory apparatus, but it proves to be grossly inefficient;
- alternatively, the host state creates the appropriate regulatory apparatus, but in order to avoid layoffs in the public sector, staffs it with a bloated and ineffective bureaucracy comprised principally of former employees of the state-owned enterprise;
- a government agency of the host state delays beyond the statutory deadline the grant to the foreign investor of a license required to engage in certain investment activities, even though those same activities had been authorized previously by a concession or build-operate-transfer agreement with the government;
- local courts defer interminably decisions required by the BIT and critical to the profitability of the investment; or, because of the host state's failure to establish internal legal mechanisms to accommodate a BIT regime, local courts enjoin, on the basis of that state's internal laws, investment activities previously authorized by the host state or one of its political subdivisions;
- local government officials of one federated unit within the host state, in order to curry favor with their political constituency, blame the foreign investor in a theretofore publicly-owned but now privatized utility, for economic difficulties caused principally by the inefficient bureaucracy and infrastructure that the investor inherited, and indeed, which it was the very intention of the host state to ameliorate by privatization and the attraction and investment of foreign resources.

These types of actions (or, at times, delayed actions or failures to act) would not have been cognizable as indirect expropriations under an

para. 22; *Phelps Dodge Corp. v Iran*, (1986) 10 US CTR 121, para. 22; *but see Sea-Land Service, Inc. v Iran*, (1984) 6 Iran-US CTR 149, 166 ('A finding of expropriation would require, at the very least, that the Tribunal be satisfied that there was deliberate governmental interference with the conduct of Sea-Land's operation, the effect of which was to deprive Sea-Land of the use and benefit of its investment. Nothing has been demonstrated here which might have amounted to an intentional course of conduct directed against Sea-Land. A claim founded substantially on omissions and inaction in a situation where the evidence suggests a widespread and indiscriminate deterioration in management, disrupting the functioning of the port of Bandar Abbas, can hardly justify a finding of expropriation.'). Since *Sea-Land*, however, the principle that proof of intent is a necessary component of an expropriation has 'obtained no support in subsequent Tribunal awards, which generally [have] quoted the relevant language from *Tippetts*'. Aldrich, *supra* n. 18, at 603.

FCN regime, for in that regime the foreign investor took the host state's legal, administrative, and regulatory apparatus on an 'as is' basis. Ineffective or inefficient government was often a manifest part of the 'is' and often the reason for, or a significant contributing factor to, the non-development or impeded development in the host state. But in a BIT regime, these delayed actions or inactions may represent violations of legal obligations and therefore may, if the facts warrant it, be characterized as 'acts tantamount to expropriation', for the BIT obliges the host state to create normatively 'favourable conditions' for the investment. This imports, as explained above, a variety of constitutive, judicial, administrative, and regulatory actions to be undertaken by the host state.

One of the reasons why failures to take internationally required administrative or judicial actions, characteristic of consequential expropriations, present particularly knotty problems for tribunals engaged in determining the moment of expropriation and moment of valuation is that the foreign investor often will fail to perceive certain actions or non-feasances as expropriatory at the time they occur. The management of a complex business in any environment is perforce a process of problem-solving. Managers may, at least initially, view these failures on the part of the administrative or judicial apparatus of the host state as transient problems or early points on a learning curve for a new bureaucracy or one relatively inexperienced in regulating foreign investment. Nor will there exist evidence of an expropriatory intent on the part of the administrative or judicial actors concerned. In hindsight, managers (or their critics) may come to believe that they should have seen the events in a more ominous light, as the first in a series of actions that would culminate in a consequential expropriation.

But hindsight, of course, is notoriously lucid. Only in retrospect does it become evident that, regardless of the state's intent, the cumulative impact of its interferences with property rights would inevitably culminate in an aggregate effect tantamount to expropriation. And in any event, had the foreign investor or its manager immediately sought to initiate arbitration under a BIT, a tribunal might well have thought it unrealistic or premature, if not an abuse of process. Unlike direct expropriations, consequential expropriations need not, and seldom will, be accomplished *d'un coup*, by a single act tantamount to expropriation; for example, the decree of the Mossadegh Government of Iran expelling the management of the Anglo-Iranian Oil Company from the company's premises and installing new management,[75] or the Indonesian military police's expulsion and replacement of the management of Amco Asia's hotel in Jakarta.[76] Hence, as with creeping expropriations, no obvious overt markers will exist to enable a tribunal to set the moment of valuation at some point before the investor's contemporaneous conclusion

[75] *See generally* A. Ford, The Anglo-Iranian Oil Dispute of 1951–52 (1954).

[76] *See Amco Asia Corp. v Indonesia*, ICSID Award of Nov. 21, 1984, (1985) 24 ILM 1022.

that it had been expropriated. Both creeping and consequential expropriations therefore make the tasks of discerning liability for expropriation in the BIT generation—and, subsequently, assigning an economic value to the enterprise so expropriated—far more difficult than the corresponding tasks for direct expropriations (and, for that matter, many garden-variety indirect expropriations).

III. Moment of Expropriation and Valuation

Two widely accepted propositions of international law create a peculiar problem for the arbitration tribunal seized of a consequential or creeping expropriation claim cognizable under a governing BIT. The first is that BITs, consistent with customary international law, require states to pay compensation for expropriation, whether lawful or not, based on a formula that calculates loss from the moment of expropriation. In the words of one representative BIT: 'Compensation shall be equivalent to the fair market value of the expropriated investment immediately before the expropriatory action was taken or became known, whichever is earlier.'[77] The second is the venerable principle articulated more than seventy years ago by the Permanent Court of International Justice in *Chorzów Factory*:[78] 'that reparation must, as far as possible, wipe out all the consequences of the illegal act and reestablish the situation which would, in all probability, have existed if that act had not been committed'.[79] Because creeping and consequential expropriations, by their nature, involve, respectively, either *(i)* an accretion of acts and omissions over time, the propriety of which may be contemporaneously unclear or evident only in retrospect; or *(ii)* acts or omissions the illegality of which derives from the state's failure or neglect to create and maintain an appropriate normative environment, the moment of expropriation seldom will be vividly demarcated and readily discernable by a tribunal seized with a claim for compensation based on such state conduct.[80] In the BIT generation, this epistemic difficulty raises

77 U.S.-Russ. BIT, art. III(1); *compare* U.K.-Pan. BIT, art. 5(1) ('[C]ompensation shall amount to the fair value which the investment expropriated had immediately before the expropriation became known.'); *accord* World Bank: Report to the Development Committee and Guidelines on the Treatment of Foreign Direct Investment, adopted Sept. 21, 1992, (1992) 31 ILM 1363, 1382 [hereafter World Bank Guidelines] ('Compensation will be deemed "adequate" if it is based on the fair market value of the taken asset as such value is determined immediately before the time at which the taking occurred or the decision to take the asset became publicly known.').

78 *Factory at Chorzów (Germany v Poland)*, 1928 PCIJ Rep Series A No. 13 (Sept. 13).

79 *Id.* at 47.

80 *See* Weston, *supra* n. 17, at 105–6 (noting that 'it is very hard to get agreement on whether any one or a combination of governmental acts, at once or over time, constitutes an "indirect," "de facto," "disguised," "constructive," or "creeping expropriation" giving rise to State responsibility,' partly because of 'the extremely complex facts ordinarily involved and partly [because of] the problems of proof that attend them'); Koven, *supra* n. 43, at 277. ('For "creeping" expropriation, where a slow accretion of interferences with the investor's management or control of the foreign enterprise results in the inability of the project to continue, determining the date on which "an action" created that result is an absurd exercise.')

certain practical problems with respect to, first, the determination of liability; second, assuming the tribunal finds liability, the determination of what should constitute adequate reparation; and finally, how to calculate that figure.[81]

A. THE CONDITIONS FOR A LAWFUL EXPROPRIATION

Consistent with customary international law, BITs do not prohibit expropriation per se.[82] In the exercise of their sovereignty over natural resources or police powers, states remain entitled to expropriate foreign property for a public purpose, provided it is done in a non-discriminatory manner and accompanied by payment of 'prompt, adequate, and effective' compensation.[83] 'International law', in the words of a recent ICSID award, 'permits [a state] to expropriate foreign-owned property within its territory for a public purpose and against the payment of adequate and effective compensation'.[84] This so-called 'compensation rule', which permits expropriation conditional on the payment of 'prompt, adequate, and effective' compensation,[85] has been widely, if not always unanimously, embraced by jurists and scholars throughout the twentieth century.[86]

[81] In certain cases it may also raise a jurisdictional issue, for the moment of expropriation may determine whether a tribunal has jurisdiction under the applicable conventional regime. *See, e.g.*, *Mondev Int'l Ltd. v United States*, ICSID Case No. ARB(AF)/99/2, Award of Oct. 11, 2002, (2003) 42 ILM 84, 93–9. At the same time, the moment that suffices to establish jurisdiction may operate to impede the tribunal's efforts to award compensation pursuant to the principles enunciated in *Chorzów Factory*. The authors are grateful to Judge Charles N. Brower for pointing out this issue, which, while not necessarily unique to the Algiers Accords and Iran-U.S. Claims Tribunals cases, assumed a particular significance in that context.

[82] *E.g.*, U.K.-Pan. BIT, art. 5(1) ('Investments of nationals or companies of either Contracting Party shall not be nationalised, expropriated or subjected to measures having effect equivalent to nationalisation or expropriation (hereinafter referred to as "expropriation") in the territory of the other Contracting Party except for an internal public or social purpose against prompt, adequate and effective compensation, and in conformity with the internal law.'); U.S. Arg-BIT, art. IV, section 1 ('Investments shall not be expropriated or nationalized either directly or indirectly through measures tantamount to expropriation or nationalization ("expropriation") except for a public purpose; in a non-discriminatory manner; upon payment of prompt, adequate and effective compensation; and in accordance with due process of law and the general principles of treatment provided for in Article II (2) [which specifies the treatment that each state party must afford to investments of nationals or companies of the other].'); *compare, e.g.*, *INA Corp. v Iran*, (1985) 8 Iran-US CTR 373 ('It has long been acknowledged that expropriations for a public purpose and subject to conditions provided for by law . . . are not per se unlawful.').

[83] Ian Brownlie, Principles of Public International Law 70 (5th ed. 1998); Dolzer & Stevens, *supra* n. 2, at 97; Christie, *supra* n. 19, at 307.

[84] *Compañia del Desarrollo de Santa Elena, S.A. v Costa Rica*, ICSID Case No. ARB/96/1, Award of Feb. 17, 2000, (2000) 39 ILM 1317, 1329; *accord Sedco, Inc. v Nat'l Ir. Oil Co.*, (1986) 10 Iran-US CTR 180, 25 ILM 629, 647–8 (Brower, J., concurring) ('A taking is unlawful under customary international law when it occurs in a discriminatory context, is not for a public purpose, or constitutes a breach of a specific obligation undertaken by the nationalizing State in relation to the property in question, e.g., violates the terms of an agreement between that State and an alien.'). The legitimacy of the public purpose invoked to justify expropriation does not 'alter the legal character of the taking for which adequate compensation must be paid'. *Santa Elena*, 39 ILM at 1329.

[85] *E.g.*, Brownlie, *supra* n. 83, at 535–8 (explaining the compensation rule).

[86] Brice M. Clagett, *Just Compensation in International Law: The Issues Before the Iran-United States Claims Tribunal*, *in* IV The Valuation of Nationalized Property in International Law 31, 42 (Richard B. Lillich ed., 1987); Christie, *supra* n. 19, at 307.

Conventionally known as the 'Hull formula',[87] the phrase 'prompt, adequate, and effective' provides a facially clear standard. In practice, however, 'apart from the use of force, no question of international law seems to have aroused as much debate—and often strong feelings—as the question of the standard for payment of compensation when foreign property is expropriated'.[88] Particularly in the 1960s and 1970s, developing and communist states sought to establish an alternative rule authorizing states to resort to their municipal laws to determine the appropriate standard of compensation.[89] With the demise of the Cold War and the rise of the BIT generation, however, the Hull formula has firmly reestablished itself as the preeminent standard.[90] BITs generally incorporate its traditional criteria in one form or another.[91]

Merely restating the Hull formula, however, begs a number of questions, foremost among them, the meaning of 'prompt, adequate, and effective' and comparable phrases.[92] Because *Chorzów Factory* remains, notwithstanding the passage of more than 70 years, the seminal international decision about compensation under international law, it still provides the fundamental normative framework within which to consider the propriety of particular methods employed to determine 'prompt, adequate, and effective' compensation for expropriation:[93]

The essential principle contained in the actual notion of an illegal act—a principle which seems to be established by international practice and in particular by the decisions of arbitral tribunals—is that reparation must, as far as possible, wipe out all the consequences of an illegal act and reestablish the situation which would, in all probability, have existed if that act had not been committed. Restitution in kind, or if this is not possible, payment of a sum corresponding to the value which a restitution in kind would bear; the award, if need be, of damages for loss sustained which would not be covered by restitution in kind or payment in place of it—such are the principles which should serve to

[87] Dolzer & Stevens, *supra* n. 2, at 97 & note 262. The Hull formula originated in correspondence from former U.S. Secretary of State Hull to the Mexican government in 1938, in which he asserted that 'under every rule of law and equity, no government is entitled to expropriate private property, for whatever purpose without provision for prompt, adequate and effective payment therefor.' 3 G. Hackworth, (1943) Digest of International Law 657.

[88] Gudgeon, *supra* n. 37, at 108; *see also* Oscar Schachter, Foreword, *in* IV The Valuation of Nationalized Property in International Law vii (Richard B. Lillich ed., 1987).

[89] Clagett, *supra* n. 86, at 31–2.

[90] *See* Brownlie, *supra* n. 83, at 547 ('[A] considerable number of hosts to foreign capital are willing to conclude treaties for the protection of investments which commonly contain a provision for the payment of "prompt, adequate, and effective" compensation in case of expropriation. While these are negotiated deals, the pattern of agreements surely constitutes evidence of an international standard based upon the principle of compensation.'); *see also* Haliburton Fales, *A Comparison for Nationalization of Alien Property with Standards of Compensation Under United States Domestic Law, in* IV The Valuation of Nationalized Property in International Law 173, 175–76 (Richard B. Lillich ed., 1987). [91] Dolzer & Stevens, *supra* n. 2, at 97, 109; *see also* Brownlie, *supra* n. 83, at 547.

[92] The United States favors the Hull formula of 'prompt, adequate, and effective' compensation, while other states use comparable or more general phrases 'such as "just," "full," "reasonable" or "fair and equitable" '. Dolzer & Stevens, *supra* n. 2, at 109; *see also* Gudgeon, *supra* n. 37, at 113–14.

[93] *See* Higgins, *supra* n. 22, at 315.

determine the amount of compensation due for an act contrary to international law.[94]

Countless international tribunals have cited *Chorzów Factory* as the paramount compensation principle to guide determinations of the appropriate measure of damages for expropriation.[95] Notwithstanding some suggestions to the contrary,[96] it continues to represent the *locus classicus* on compensation under international law.[97]

B. PRINCIPLES OF VALUATION

To implement *Chorzów Factory*'s imperative in the context of an expropriation has traditionally required consideration of two issues: *damnum emergens*, the value of the expropriated enterprise, including tangible property, contract rights, and intangible valuables such as business goodwill; and *lucrum cessans*, lost profits.[98] On the one hand, 'the *value* of an expropriated enterprise does not vary according to [its] lawfulness or . . . unlawfulness', because that value does not logically depend on the legal 'characterization of a fact totally foreign to the economic constituents of the undertaking, namely the conduct of the expropriating State'; on the other, considerable, but hardly unanimous, authority supports the view that international law requires states to pay a higher level of compensation for unlawful expropriations.[99] The Iran-U.S. Claims Tribunal has emphasized that the 'first principle established by the Court [in *Chorzów Factory*] is that a clear distinction must be made between lawful and unlawful expropriations, since the rules applicable to the compensation to be paid by the expropriating State differ according to the legal characterization of the taking'.[100] The Tribunal continued: 'The difference is that if the taking is lawful the value of the undertaking at the time of the dispossession is the measure and the limit of the compensation, while if

[94] *Factory at Chorzów (Germany v Poland)*, 1928 PCIJ Rep Series A No. 13, at 47 (Sept. 13). The Court confirmed the customary character of this obligation elsewhere in the judgment, remarking that '[r]eparation therefore is the indispensable complement of a failure to apply a convention and there is no necessity for this to be stated in the convention itself.' *Id.* at 21. More recently, the International Court of Justice held that the same principles applies to violations of customary international law. *Corfu Channel (U.K. v Albania)* (Merits), [1949] ICJ Rep 4, 23 (Apr. 9).

[95] *E.g., Metalclad Corp. v United Mexican States*, ICSID Case No. ARB(AF)/97/1, Award of Aug. 30, 2000, (2001) 40 ILM 36, 52; *see also Amco Asia Corp. v Indonesia*, Award of Nov. 21, 1984, (1985) 24 ILM 1022, 1037 (collecting decisions and arbitral awards applying *Chorzów Factory*).

[96] Fales, *supra* n. 90, at 175. For an overview of the challenges to the traditional rule, which concludes that its vitality nonetheless remains intact, *see* Clagett, *supra* n. 86, at 38–48.

[97] *See, e.g., Amoco Int'l Fin. Corp. v Iran*, (1987) 15 Iran-US CTR 189, (1988) 27 ILM 1314, 1360.

[98] *See id.* at 1361–2; *see also* Clagett, *supra* n. 86, at 61–2. ('International decisions rendered both before and after *Chorzów Factory* have declared as "universally accepted rules of law" that an investor cannot be fully compensated for the going-concern value of his expropriated interests unless he is awarded both the "damage that has been sustained" as a result of the taking and the reasonably ascertainable "profit that has been missed." ') (footnote and citations omitted).

[99] *See Amoco Int'l Fin. Corp.*, 27 ILM at 1363 (collecting cases and arbitral awards).

[100] *Id.* at 1360 (citing *Chorzów Factory*, 1928 PCIJ Rep Series A No. 17, at 46–7 (Sept. 13)).

it is unlawful, this value is, or may be, only part of the reparation to be paid.'[101] Ian Brownlie's treatise asserts to similar effect that

> [t]he practical distinctions between expropriation unlawful *sub modo*, i.e., only if no provision is made for compensation, and expropriation unlawful *per se* would seem to be these: the former involves a duty to pay compensation only for direct losses, i.e., the value of the property, the latter involves liability for consequential loss (*lucrum cessans*); . . .[102]

One line of authority would therefore hold that for a lawful expropriation, payment of *damnum emergens* suffices; for an unlawful expropriation, the host state also owes compensation for reasonably ascertainable lost profits.[103]

The distinction between *damnum emergens* and *lucrum cessans* provides a useful moral compass for distinguishing between lawful and unlawful expropriations. But it is economically anachronistic when applied to expropriations of foreign investments. In modern economic terms, the value of an enterprise is not the enterprise itself; it is the stream of profits it can be expected to produce over its lifetime. That forecast is what determines the price that the hypothetical willing buyer would pay the hypothetical willing seller. To say that in an unlawful expropriation, the victim must be awarded the value of the expropriated property *and* lost profits is therefore to double-count. Yet the distinction between *damnum emergens* and *lucrum cessans*, for all its anachronism, serves a useful policy purpose insofar as it permits international tribunals to penalize egregious expropriations and, hopefully, to deter them in the future. For this reason, the traditional distinction proves particularly significant in the context of creeping expropriations. By definition, they seldom, if ever, will be lawful.[104] Full compensation therefore should include *lucrum cessans* to further the goal of deterrence. Otherwise, as Judge Brower suggested, 'the host state would pocket the difference between the lower value the undertaking was shown by post-taking experience to have had and the higher

[101] *Id.* [102] Brownlie, *supra* n. 83, at 541.

[103] *See Amoco Int'l Fin. Corp.*, 27 ILM at 1369. ('To this element of *damnum emergens*, a complementary one is added where the expropriation is unlawful: the value of the revenues the owner would have earned if the expropriation had not occurred, i.e., *lucrum cessans*.')

[104] *Sedco, Inc. v Nat'l Ir. Oil Co.*, (1986) 10 Iran-US CTR 180, 25 ILM 629, 649 (Brower, J., concurring). While a government conceivably might acknowledge the expropriatory effect of its regulatory acts and omissions at some point and pay an investor compensation as required by international law, in practice, governments that expropriate an investment serially, by regulation or other cumulative acts that depreciate its value, rarely, if ever, acknowledge that such acts comprise an expropriation. Most frequently, they will claim that the acts represent a valid exercise of their police powers, a response to a contractual breach by the investor or, perhaps, that the investor 'assumed the risk' of the effect such acts would have on its investment and cannot now expect the government to pay compensation for losses incurred in the ordinary course of business. Moreover, it is difficult to see how an expropriation accomplished furtively, by a series of ostensibly valid measures that collectively deprive an investor of its property rights, could be deemed to comport with the due process requirements for a lawful expropriation under most BITs. Hence, creeping expropriations, in practice if not by definition, almost without exception prove to be unlawful.

value it objectively enjoyed at the moment of taking . . . [N]o system of law sensibly can be understood as intended to reward unlawful conduct'.[105]

To digress briefly, it is important to recognize here that Judge Brower's approach is crafted for an indirect expropriation where no express decree of expropriation exists, but credible evidence of an intent to expropriate does. A further award of *lucrum cessans* serves to deny the expropriating state any benefit from its delict. That the investor receives a reinforced value of its expropriated investment is coincidental, for as Judge Brower acknowledges, international law does not require an award of *lucrum cessans* in cases of lawful expropriation. In cases of consequential expropriation, no expropriatory intent may be found, and the result of the actions of the host state usually leave little in the way of the original investment. The investment has not been seized and transferred to the state or its designated beneficiary; it has been destroyed. Hence, an award of *lucrum cessans* does not serve to deprive the host state of the profits of the enterprise, for there are none. What is called, in this context, *lucrum cessans* is essentially additive, a fine, the amount of which is supposedly equivalent to the *lucrum cessans* of the failed enterprise. There may well be sound reasons to sanction a state that fails to fulfill its BIT obligation to create or maintain a normative environment propitious to foreign investment. But we find no basis for such a punitive award under customary international law at this time. We would therefore conclude that while an award of what is called *lucrum cessans* may be warranted for some creeping expropriations, it should not be for consequential expropriations.

BITs generally adopt the principles enunciated in *Chorzów Factory* in substance if not form.[106] A representative provision provides:

> ['[P]rompt, adequate, and effective'] [c]ompensation shall be equivalent to the *fair market value* of the expropriated investment immediately before the expropriatory action was taken or became known, whichever is earlier; be paid without delay; include interest at a commercially reasonable rate from the date of expropriation; be fully realizable; and be freely transferable at the prevailing market rate of exchange on the date of expropriation.[107]

'Fair market value' is a term of art. It is generally taken to mean the price that a willing buyer would pay a willing seller.[108] The proper method to calculate fair market value differs, however, depending on the nature of the expropriated enterprise and the circumstances attending the

[105] *Amoco Int'l Fin. Corp.*, 27 ILM at 1400 note 22 (Brower, J., concurring); *cf. Sedco, Inc. v Nat'l Ir. Oil Co.*, (1986) 10 Iran-US CTR 180, 25 ILM 629, 648 note 35 (Brower, J., concurring) (suggesting that punitive or exemplary damages might be sought for an unlawful expropriation because otherwise 'the injured party would receive nothing additional for the enhanced wrong done it and the offending state would experience no disincentive to repetition of the unlawful conduct').

[106] *See* Gudgeon, *supra* n. 37, at 113.

[107] U.S.-Arg. BIT, art. IV(1) (emphasis added); *compare* U.K.-Pan. BIT, art. 5(1) ('Such compensation shall amount to the fair value which the investment expropriated had immediately before the expropriation became known, shall include interest until the date of payment, shall be made without delay, be effectively realisable and be freely transferable.').

[108] *INA Corp. v Iran* (1985) 8 Iran-US CTR 373, section III; *see also* Restatement (Third) of Foreign Relations Law section 712 (1989).

expropriation.[109] Because the willing buyer is hypothetical, and because the expropriated investor can hardly be characterized as a willing seller, the willing-buyer-willing-seller formula, despite its redolence of economic precision, is actually quite speculative—far more of an art than a science, as anyone who has reviewed expert opinions in these matters can attest. Still, for going concerns (i.e. enterprises with a history of profitability), fair market value generally includes, in addition to the net value of the enterprise's tangible assets on the date of the expropriation, 'an estimate of future profits subject to a discounted cash flow analysis'.[110] Economists employ the 'going-concern' method subject to a discounted cash flow analysis in order to account for a potential decrease in the projected value of money over time and potential business risk.[111]

The going-concern method has been adopted by many international tribunals, for it seems to comport best with the principles established by *Chorzów Factory* and its progeny.[112] But it will not always be practicable. In *Metalclad*, for example, the tribunal observed that 'where the enterprise has not operated for a sufficiently long time to establish a performance record or where it has failed to make a profit, future profits cannot be used to determine going concern or fair market value'.[113] In these circumstances tribunals must resort to one of several common alternatives. These include *(i)* 'book value', the net value of an enterprise's assets; *(ii)* 'replacement value', an estimate of the amount 'necessary to create a similar undertaking';[114] *(iii)* 'liquidation value', the amount 'at which individual assets comprising the enterprise or the entire assets of the enterprise could be sold under conditions of liquidation to a willing buyer less any liabilities which the enterprise has to meet';[115] and *(iv)* 'actual investment', the amount in fact invested prior to the expropriation.[116]

Each method is appropriate in some circumstances but not others. In 1992, the World Bank, '[w]ithout implying the exclusive validity of a single standard for the fairness by which compensation is determined', proposed guidelines to assist decision-makers in determining the most suitable method in light of the nature of the expropriated enterprise:

(i) for a going concern with a proven record of profitability, on the basis of the discounted cash flow value;

[109] Dolzer & Stevens, *supra* n. 2, at 110; *see also* Cornelius F. Murphy, Jr., *Limitations Upon the Power of a State to Determine the Amount of Compensation Payable to an Alien Upon Nationalization, in* III The Valuation of Nationalized Property in International Law 49, 61 (Richard B. Lillich ed., 1975) ('The fairness of a compensation award depends upon a proper regard being paid to all relevant considerations that, in varying degrees, touch upon the history of a given investment and its future potential after acquisition by the nationalizing State.').

[110] *Metalclad Corp. v. United Mexican States* ICSID Case No. ARB(AF)/97/1, Award of Aug. 30, 2000, (2001) 40 ILM 36, 52. Future profits must be reasonably ascertainable, not speculative, for '[o]ne of the best settled rules of the law of international responsibility of States is that no reparation for speculative or uncertain damage can be awarded'. *Amoco Int'l Fin. Corp. v Iran* (1987) 15 Iran-US CTR 189, (1988) 27 ILM 1314, 1371.

[111] Clagett, *supra* n. 86, at 49.

[112] *See id.* at 60–7.

[113] *Metalclad Corp.*, 40 ILM at 52.

[114] *Amoco Int'l Fin. Corp.*, 27 ILM at 1369.

[115] World Bank Guidelines, *supra* n. 77, at 1383.

[116] *See Metalclad Corp.*, 40 ILM at 52.

(ii) for an enterprise which, not being a proven going concern, demonstrates lack of profitability, on the basis of the liquidation value;
(iii) for other assets, on the basis of (a) the replacement value or (b) the book value in case such value has been recently assessed or has been determined as of the date of the taking . . .[117]

Each of these methods perforce requires a tribunal to ascertain or stipulate the moment or date of expropriation. That date establishes the reference point for calculating fair market value pursuant to any of these methods. Decision-makers must therefore settle, by one mode of analysis or another, upon a 'moment of expropriation' at which to appraise fair market value. The often nebulous and convoluted factual circumstances that comprise a creeping expropriation, and *a fortiori* a consequential expropriation, tend to make the moment of expropriation elusive, assuming, that is, that one can meaningfully be identified at all in such cases.[118] At one extreme, a tribunal could elect to set the moment of expropriation at the date of the first governmental act or omission in the series of deleterious measures that, in the aggregate, constitute the expropriation; at the other, at the date of the last such measure. In the former case, adequate compensation may not be provided because investors often continue—not necessarily irrationally or irresponsibly, given the information available to them contemporaneously[119]—to invest after the initial act 'tantamount to' expropriation. In the latter, the 'fair market value' may well have depreciated substantially, making compensation on that basis, too, inadequate insofar as it evidently fails to respect *Chorzów Factory*'s imperative of *restitutio in integrum*. The proper procedure in these circumstances is not obvious.

C. ALTERNATIVES: DELINKING EXPROPRIATION AND VALUATION

In a series of awards rendered in the 1980s, the Iran-United States Claims Tribunal proposed that 'where the alleged expropriation is carried out by way of a series of interferences in the enjoyment of the property, the breach forming the cause of action is deemed to take place on the day when the interference has ripened into a more or less irreversible deprivation of the property rather than on the beginning date of the events'.[120] That date, according to the Tribunal, must be ascertained by reference to the fact-specific 'circumstances of each case'.[121] The Tribunal

[117] World Bank Guidelines, *supra* n. 77, at 1383.

[118] *Cf.* Koven, *supra* n. 43, at 277 (expressing the view that 'where a slow accretion of interferences with the investor's management or control of the foreign enterprise results in the inability of the project to continue, determining the date on which "an action" created that result is an absurd exercise').

[119] *See infra* text accompanying n. 137–40.

[120] *Malek v Iran*, Award No. 534–193–3 (1992) Iran-US CTR, para. 114 (citing *Int'l Technical Prods. Corp. v Iran* (1985) 9 Iran-US CTR 206, 240–1, and *Foremost Tehran Inc v Iran*, (1986) 10 Iran-US CTR 228, 249).

[121] *Int'l Technical Prods. Corp. v Iran*, (1985) 9 Iran-US CTR 206, 241; *see also Compañia del Desarrollo de Santa Elena, S.A. v Costa Rica*, ICSID Case No. ARB/96/1, Award of Feb. 17, 2000,

enunciated this proposition, however, in a series of decisions that, while arising from diverse factual scenarios, nonetheless shared a common political context, the 1979 Islamic Revolution in Iran. That meant, in practice, that in most cases involving indirect or creeping expropriations, the events culminating in a compensable expropriation tended to be similar; for example, the Iranian government's gradual assumption of managerial control or appointment of governmental 'supervisors' who tended over time to interfere with foreign property rights in increasingly more intrusive ways.

Jurists and scholars generally cite *Starrett Housing Corp. v Iran*[122] for the proposition 'that measures taken by a State can interfere with property rights to such an extent that these rights are rendered so useless that they must be deemed expropriated, even though the State does not purport to have expropriated them and the legal title to the property formally remains with the original owner'.[123] That proposition remains valid, and indeed, finds ample support in more recent arbitral awards.[124] But it is worth recalling that the majority award in *Starrett* adopted what Judge Holtzmann, concurring, aptly described as a 'sterile formalism', for it declined to appreciate the legal significance of the 'steady and inexorable' progression of expropriatory events that preceded the Iranian government's formal appointment of a manager for the claimant's property.[125] In consequence, the Tribunal effectively left it to an expert to determine to what extent, if any, these events should be considered in assessing the fair market value of Starrett's property rights as of the moment of expropriation.[126] While the Iran-United States Claims Tribunal added immeasurably to international jurisprudence on expropriation, including indirect expropriation, the question of the moment of expropriation therefore rarely arose. As one judge of the Tribunal acknowledged, 'the often-difficult question of when allegedly temporary interference with the rights of property owners should be considered to have ripened into compensable taking or deprivation of those rights rarely troubled the Iran-United States Claims Tribunal'.[127]

The proliferation of bilateral and multilateral investment treaties over the past decade, coupled with the tendency of governments now to

(2000) 39 ILM 1317, 1330 ('[E]xpropriated property is to be evaluated as of the date on which governmental "interference" has deprived the owner of his rights or has made those rights practically useless. This is a matter of fact for the Tribunal to assess in light of the circumstances of the case.').

122 (1983) 4 Iran-US CTR 122.

123 *Id.* section IV(1) ((Holtzmann, J., concurring).

124 *See, e.g.*, *Metalclad Corp. v United Mexican States*, ICSID Case No. ARB(AF)/97/1, Award of Aug. 30, 2000, (2001) 40 ILM 36, 50 (affirming that expropriation under the North American Free Trade Agreement include not only formal expropriations, but also 'covert or incidental interference with the use of property which has the effect of depriving the owner, in whole or in significant part, of the use or reasonably-to-be-expected economic benefit of property').

125 *Starrett Hous. Corp.*, (1983) 4 Iran-US CTR 122 section IV(2) (Holtzmann, J., concurring).

126 *Id.* section IV(3) (noting that the majority award's determination that the expropriation did not occur until January 31, 1980, 'may, as a practical matter, have little effect on whatever damages may be determined' because, *inter alia*, 'it is not yet known what method the expert will use to determine the value of the expropriated property', and '[u]nder some methods of valuation, the later date of expropriation might have relatively little monetary significance').

127 Aldrich, *supra* n. 18, at 587.

eschew formal expropriation, forces the phenomena of creeping and consequential expropriations into sharper focus. More recent arbitrations, principally conducted under the auspices of ICSID, indicate the extent to which the relevant 'moment of expropriation' in cases of creeping expropriations can prove slippery and elusive. But because '[v]irtually no BITs make reference to [the] different valuation methods in their expropriation clause', BITs deliberately invite or perhaps even require decision-makers to exercise discretion in determining the appropriate method under the circumstances, including, where necessary, to ascertain the appropriate 'moment' from which to calculate compensation pursuant to the method elected.[128]

BITs establish the moment of expropriation by reference to 'the fair market value of the expropriated investment immediately before the expropriatory action was taken or became known, whichever is earlier'.[129] The pertinent moments under the BIT therefore occur either on the date of the expropriation or when the expropriation 'bec[o]me[s] known'. In the case of a direct, formal expropriation, both of these moments will almost invariably be vivid and clearly demarcated, for example, the date on which the government promulgates an executive or legislative decree proclaiming its intent to expropriate. A creeping expropriation, by contrast, involves an accretion of acts and omissions of often nebulous legality that accrue over a longer time period, culminating in an aggregate *effect* tantamount to an outright expropriation.[130] A consequential expropriation involves a state's interference with or failure to create or maintain the normative legal, administrative, and regulatory framework contemplated by a BIT, as a consequence of which managerial control, profitability, and ultimately viability, erode. Thus, the events comprising a creeping or consequential expropriation far less frequently reveal a dramatic moment that demarcates the act of expropriation.

[128] *See* Francisco Orrego Vicuña, *The International Regulation of Valuation Standards and Processes: A Reexamination of Third World Perspectives, in* III The Valuation of Nationalized Property in International Law 131, 134 (Richard B. Lillich ed., 1975) ('In view of present international realities, it is neither possible nor desirable to try to establish a single standard or principle for the valuation of nationalized foreign property as a universal rule of international law. It is more realistic to approach the problem through the development of a plurality of well-defined standards.'); *see also* World Bank Guidelines, *supra* n. 77, at 1383; *cf.* Richard B. Lillich, *The Valuation of Nationalized Property by the Foreign Claims Settlement Commission, in* I The Valuation of Nationalized Property in International Law 95, 99 (Richard B. Lillich ed., 1972) (noting, in the context of appraising the United States Foreign Settlement Claims Commission, the desirability of submitting multiple methods of appraising the value of expropriated property into evidence because it increases the 'probability . . . that an adequate award will be made') (citation and internal quotation marks omitted).

[129] *E.g.*, U.S.-Arg. BIT, art. IV(1); *compare* Model BIT of Austria, art. IV ('[C]ompensation shall amount to the value of the investment immediately preceding the time in which the actual or impending [expropriatory] measure became public knowledge.'), *with* Model BIT of the United Kingdom, art. 5(1) ('[C]ompensation shall amount to the genuine value of the investment expropriated immediately before the expropriation or before the impending expropriation became public knowledge, whichever is earlier . . .'), *in* Dolzer & Stevens, *supra* n. 2, at 167, 169–70; 228, 232.

[130] *See* Higgins, *supra* n. 22, at 325.

In *Compañia del Desarrollo de Santa Elena, S.A. v Costa Rica*,[131] an ICSID Tribunal echoed the standard enunciated by the Iran-U.S. Claim's Tribunal's in *Malek*,[132] remarking that 'expropriated property is to be evaluated as of the date on which governmental "interference" has deprived the owner of his rights or has made those rights practically useless'.[133] But in *Santa Elena*, Costa Rica had expropriated the claimant's property directly and lawfully: by formal decree, in a non-discriminatory manner, and for a public purpose, viz., preservation of the environment. It did not contest the claimant's right to compensation. In fact, Costa Rica agreed that 'the expropriating state [owes] a duty, in both Costa Rican and international law, to pay compensation in respect of even a lawful expropriation', and 'that the compensation to be paid should be based upon the fair market value of the Property'.[134]

The sole dispute in *Santa Elena* centered on determining the date on which the claimant's property had been expropriated for purposes of assessing its fair market value.[135] Costa Rica argued that the date of its formal decree of expropriation also constituted the relevant moment of expropriation for purposes of assessing fair market value. The Tribunal agreed because '[a]s of that date, the practical and economic use of the Property by the Claimant was irretrievably lost, notwithstanding that [the Claimant] remained in possession of the Property.'[136] The Tribunal chose this formal date of expropriation, not *because* it was the formal or legal date, but because, as an economic fact, that was when the deprivation occurred. *Santa Elena* therefore seems to instruct us that the moment of expropriation for purposes of assessing the fair market value of the investment is the moment when the practical and economic use of the investment is irretrievably lost. In the circumstances of a creeping or consequential expropriation, however, where the state takes property rights indirectly and unlawfully, it becomes difficult if not impossible to discern when, precisely, the foreign investor 'irretrievably lost' the value of its investment.[137]

In the case of a direct expropriation accomplished by a formal decree, such as *Santa Elena*, the expropriating state, by definition, determines in the first instance the moment of expropriation. If the investor disputes that determination, then, as in *Santa Elena*, it will be reviewed by the jurisdiction to which the parties consented to submit their dispute. Conversely, it is the foreign investor, by its allegation, that 'determines' in the first instance the moment of expropriation where, as in the case of a creeping or consequential expropriation, the state has allegedly

[131] ICSID Case No. ARB/96/1, Award of Feb. 17, 2000, (2000) 39 ILM 1317.

[132] *See supra* n. 120–1 and accompanying text.

[133] *Id.* at 1330, para. 78 (emphasis added).

[134] *Id.* at 1328–9.

[135] *See id.* at 1329.

[136] *Id.* at 1330.

[137] The *Santa Elena* tribunal implicitly recognized that creeping expropriations may present a distinct inquiry vis-à-vis valuation. The tribunal observed, for example, that '[a] decree which heralds a process of administrative and judicial consideration of the issue [i.e. control over an investment or property rights] in a manner that effectively freezes or blights the possibility for the owner reasonably to exploit the economic potential of the property, can, if the process thus triggered is not carried out within a reasonable period of time, properly be identified as the actual act of taking.' *Id.* at 1330.

expropriated an investment through a gradual accretion of acts of malfeasance and nonfeasance or, even more elusively, by failing to establish or undermining the normative framework on which the foreign investor relied. Needless to say, that allegation, if disputed, remains subject to review by the jurisdiction to which the parties consented to submit their dispute. The point is not to enable foreign investors to obtain a windfall by identifying an unreasonably early stage as the relevant date of expropriation; it is to enable the tribunal to appreciate the effect of the investor's perception of expropriation in determining the fair market value of the expropriated investment in circumstances where the state concerned has less to contribute to the clarification of this issue. Because of the nature of creeping and consequential expropriations, that is, it will be the foreign investor's initial allegation of when the expropriation 'became known' that frames the dispute.

The paramount policy objectives of BITs support this conclusion. States conclude BITs principally to encourage reciprocal foreign investment, and, as a means to that end, to provide a stable and predictable framework for investment by each party's nationals in the territory of the other. That goal obviously would be ill-served by any policy that rewards creeping or consequential expropriations. Yet investors will often be either unaware or inclined to resist the conclusion that a host state has, by an act or acts of nebulous legality (the economic effects of which remain unknown at the time), initiated what will ultimately constitute an expropriation. Often, foreign investors will be anxious to rescue or fortify their investments in the face of discrete harmful acts or regulatory omissions. Government officials may also assure them that a single 'measure tantamount to expropriation' represents an anomaly; it will be swiftly repaired or compensated, whether directly or by some other indulgence or offset. In these circumstances investors anxious to save their investments may well be inclined to sink further capital into them in an effort to compensate for the harmful governmental interferences or other measures tantamount to expropriation. This is particularly so where an investor reasonably believes, based on knowledge of the prevailing political and economic conditions, that the host state will not provide 'prompt, adequate, and effective' compensation. Investment of further capital in such cases reflects a desperate attempt to save the investment, and under the circumstances, may be the only rational and responsible course of action. To penalize the investor for such efforts may well be, to use an American expression, 'Monday-morning-quarter-backing', unreasonably requiring clairvoyance on the part of the investor.

While the decision to invest further capital, to hang on 'stoically . . . in the face of host government interference',[138] may at times be ascribed in part to the vicissitudes of business risk (and, as such, should

[138] Koven, *supra* note 43, at 277.

not be compensable), at other times it reflects a natural reaction to prior measures tantamount to expropriation. The decision of the Iran-United States Claims Tribunal in *Foremost Tehran, Inc. v Iran*,[139] for example, indicates 'that continued efforts within a company by shareholders to protect their interests [in the face of escalating governmental acts that serially diminish the value of their property rights] could endanger [the shareholders'] ultimate prospects of success [on a claim for expropriation]'.[140] Victims of creeping or consequential expropriations therefore may recognize expropriatory conduct at a relatively early stage, but resist yielding to it for as long as possible, hoping to reverse it.

Alternatively, foreign investors may realize only in retrospect that the ineluctable consequence of various acts of governmental interference or measures already taken, being taken or—in the case of nonfeasance—not being taken, has been to effect an expropriation. Many of the constituent pieces of a creeping expropriation may be disguised as legitimate, or arguably legitimate, regulatory acts, responses to alleged contract breaches or temporary exercises of a state's police power. In *Liberian Eastern Timber Corp. (LETCO) v Liberia*,[141] it will be recalled, the Liberian government withdrew portions of LETCO's initial concession first in 1970, then in 1971, and again in 1977. It demanded renegotiation of LETCO's concession agreement in 1979. It then accused LETCO of breaching that agreement, and on that basis, withdrew still greater portions of the concession. The government ultimately claimed that LETCO could not exploit the remaining concession areas and thereby justified its decision to reassume control of them.[142] But only in November 1984, more than one year after LETCO finally elected to institute arbitration, did the government formally acknowledge its decision to nullify the concession agreement based on alleged breaches by LETCO.[143] While LETCO undoubtedly understood that the government's actions threatened its investment and had already depreciated that investment's value substantially, it chose not to institute arbitral proceedings until March 1983. This suggests that LETCO's management either failed fully to appreciate the aggregate expropriatory effect of the Liberian government's actions until that time or that it sought desperately to rescue its investment by all means before resorting to compulsory dispute resolution, for, in the interim, 'LETCO continued to petition the highest governmental bodies of the Republic of Liberia so that they might intervene on its behalf to correct the situation'.[144]

139 (1986) 10 Iran-US CTR 228.

140 Adrich, *supra* n. 15, at 591; *see also id.* at 607 (observing that 'in several cases property owners found that their claims before the Tribunal had been prejudiced by their prior efforts to retain or exercise their rights in the property after they had been substantially deprived of those rights by actions attributable to Iran').

141 Award of Mar. 31, 1986 (rectified May 14, 1986), (1987) 26 ILM 647.

142 *LETCO*, 26 ILM at 660. 143 *Id.* 144 *Id.* at 660.

All this is not to suggest, however, that investors should, or should be entitled to, cry 'expropriation' at the first sight of adverse governmental conduct. That, too, would be contrary to the objective of BITs to establish a stable, hospitable, normative framework for reciprocal foreign investment. It would be destructive of the normative goals of BITs for the law to encourage foreign investors prematurely to claim that their investments have been expropriated and to resort to compulsory dispute resolution under the relevant BIT provision. General international law has long discouraged and reprehended premature invocation of third-party dispute resolution. At the same time, for the foregoing reasons, the general rule proposed by the Iran-U.S. Claims Tribunal may not always be well-tooled for determining the moment of expropriation for purposes of assessing the fair market value of an investment subjected to a creeping or consequential expropriation. Were the critical moment of expropriation for purposes of valuation set at the date of the *last* of the series of deleterious governmental acts of malfeasance or nonfeasance that 'ripened into a more or less irreversible deprivation of the [investment]', then the fair market value of that investment may well be determined to be substantially less than were the critical moment set at the date of one of the earlier acts. The ironic, indeed perverse, result of that theory would be to reward states for accomplishing expropriation *tranche par tranche* rather than *d'un coup* and to encourage states to accomplish expropriation furtively, either by a creeping or disguised series of regulatory acts and omissions of nebulous legality (creeping expropriation) or by evasion or abdication of the often politically difficult task of establishing an appropriate normative environment for investment (consequential expropriation). Conversely, it would penalize foreign investors for attempting to avoid expropriation and sustain their investments by, *inter alia*, fortifying them with additional capital in the face of measures of nebulous legality.

These results would be calamitous. In the first place, they contravene the venerable and general legal principle, common to municipal and international law, that a delictor may not benefit from its own delict. Second, contrary to the objectives of BITs, they would encourage foreign investors promptly to resort to compulsory dispute-resolution at an early stage rather than seek to resolve matters amicably through negotiation with the host state—lest the investor risk losing potential compensation as the fair market value of its investment progressively depreciates with each subsequent measure 'tantamount to expropriation'.[145] It would be implausible to ascribe an intention to produce such results to the drafters of BITs. It would also be wholly inconsistent with the general principles of international law on compensation explained in the preceding section and for which *Chorzów Factory* remains the lodestar.[146] Hence, the

[145] *See* Koven, *supra* n. 43, at 316 (noting one example of this phenomena arising out of the Iranian revolution, whereby 'every month allowed to lapse between the closing of the [investor's] plant and the [formal] date of expropriation reduced the value of the net investment').

[146] *Factory at Chorzów (Germany v Poland)*, 1928 PCIJ Rep Series A No. 13, at 47 (Sept. 13).

Iran-U.S. Claim's Tribunal's proposition—that 'where the alleged expropriation is carried out by way of a series of interferences in the enjoyment of the property', the moment of expropriation is 'the day when the interference has ripened into a more or less irreversible deprivation of the property rather than on the beginning date of the events'[147]—may threaten to work a manifest injustice in circumstances of creeping or consequential expropriations: It conflates the 'moment of expropriation' with what might be denominated the 'moment of valuation', the date on which the fair market value of an investment so expropriated should be assessed for purposes of determining the 'prompt, adequate, and effective' compensation required by customary international law and codified in BITs. There is no reason why the results of these two analyses should be temporally congruent.

Some methods of calculating fair market value may mitigate or even obviate the problem.[148] If, for example, the host state accomplishes a creeping expropriation before a foreign enterprise begins operating or even before the entire investment has been made, then it may be legally sufficient to award the foreign investor the sum total of its actual investment. The ICSID tribunal in *Metalclad Corp. v United Mexican States* reached that conclusion, for example, and cited precedents reaching the same result under comparable circumstances.[149] But to calculate fair market value on the date of the *last* 'measure tantamount to expropriation' that 'ripened' into a manifest expropriation would be, according to most other methods of valuation (e.g., book value, liquidation value, and replacement value), to assess an investment's value at the very 'moment' when the accretion of unlawful acts of the host state has *so dramatically devalued* the investment as to render it de facto expropriated—its 'practical and economic use' having been, by that time, 'irretrievably lost'.[150] That theory of valuation could encourage states to accomplish expropriations furtively and indirectly, by regulatory malfeasance, misfeasance, or non-feasance, or by a 'creeping' progression of deleterious actions or inactions, no one of which, however, may be readily identified by an objective decision-maker as the critical 'moment'.

[147] *Malek v Iran*, Award 534–193–3, para. 114 (1992) (citing *Int'l Technical Prods. Corp. v Iran*, (1985) 9 Iran-US CTR 206, 240–1).

[148] *Cf. Starrett Hous. Corp. v Iran*, (1984) 4 Iran-US CTR 123, 23 ILM 1090, 1115 (Holtzmann J., concurring) (observing in analogous circumstances that 'under some methods of valuation, [a] later date of expropriation might have relatively little monetary significance as compared to an earlier date').

[149] *Metalclad Corp. v United Mexican States*, ICSID Case No. ARB/96/3, Award of Aug. 30, 2000, (2001) 40 ILM 36, 52.

[150] *Compañia del Desarrollo de Santa Elena, S.A. v Costa Rica*, ICSID Case No. ARB/96/1, Award of Feb. 17, 2000, (2000) 39 ILM 1317, 1330; *cf. Borg v Int'l Silver Co.*, 11 F.2d 147, 152 (2d Cir. 1925) (Hand, J.):

> The suggestion that the book value of the shares is any measure of their actual value is clearly fallacious. It presupposes, first, that book values can be realized on liquidation, which is practically never the case; and, second, that liquidation values are a measure of present values. Every one knows that the value of shares in a commercial or manufacturing company depends chiefly on what they will earn, on which balance sheets throw little light.

That said, the crucial point is not that the proposition enunciated by the Iran-U.S. Claims Tribunal is necessarily 'wrong'. It may well provide the appropriate standard for discerning the proper moment of expropriation in many cases of *indirect* expropriations, where it makes sense to identify the act of expropriation more closely with one or two discrete events, e.g., the fixing of a price or the appointment of a governmental 'supervisor'. It should, however, be applied with caution when invoked to assess the fair market value of an investment expropriated consequentially or by a creeping accretion of measures.[151] BITs and comparable multilateral investment treaties should, as a matter of both the intent of their drafters and the policies that animate them, be construed to deter, not reward, unlawful expropriations of all kinds. If application of the Iran-U.S. Claims Tribunal's standard in practice reduces the amount of compensation due to victims of creeping or consequential expropriations, then, we suggest, the 'moment of expropriation' should be distinguished from the 'moment of valuation' for these purposes. And again, it is in this regard that the determination in the first instance of the investor is perforce the starting point for analysis. In any event, and whatever the method adopted by a tribunal to determine the proper 'moment of expropriation' in circumstances of creeping and consequential expropriations, that determination must enable the tribunal to give full effect to *Chorzów Factory*'s imperative 'that reparation must, so far as possible, wipe out all the consequences of the illegal act and reestablish the situation which would, in all probability, have existed if that act had not been committed'.[152]

While the approach we suggest has yet to be adopted expressly, several prior awards implicitly recognize the need to distinguish between the moment of expropriation, where that phrase denotes the completion of certain formalities, and the moment of valuation, the date on which the fair market value of the claimant's property should be assessed for purposes of providing 'prompt, adequate, and effective' compensation. In *Amoco International Finance Corp. v Iran*,[153] the Iran-United States Claims Tribunal found the expropriation of Amoco's contract rights to be 'complete' on December 24, 1980, when the Iranian Minister of Petroleum formally notified Amoco's management that it viewed a 1967 joint venture between Amoco and the Iranian National Petrochemical Company as null and void. But the Tribunal nonetheless awarded Amoco compensation based on the value of its interest as of July 31, 1979, the date on which the Tribunal determined the de facto taking to have occurred.[154]

[151] This is particularly true because, as the Iran-U.S. Claims Tribunal has observed, market value 'is an ambiguous concept, to say the least . . . when an open market does not exist for the expropriated asset or for goods identical or comparable to it'. *Amoco Int'l Fin. Corp. v Iran*, (1987) 15 Iran-US CTR 189, 27 ILM 1314, 1367. [152] (*Germany v Poland*) 1928 PCIJ Rep Series A No. 13, at 47 (Sept. 13).

[153] (1987) 15 Iran-US CTR 189, (1988) 27 ILM 1314.

[154] *Id.* at 1348; *see also* Aldrich, *supra* n. 18, at 595 ('[B]y making the valuation date July 31, 1979, the Tribunal implicitly accepted that as the effective date of the taking, rather than the date of the subsequent completion of the formalities.').

Moreover, as a general matter, the approach we suggest comports with customary international law, which dictates that valuation of expropriated property must exclude 'any diminution in value attributable to wrongful acts' of the expropriating government.[155] The depressing effect on values of threats or acts of nationalization must be ignored in ascertaining the market value of subsequently nationalized enterprises. Valuation in such cases is 'calculated as if the expropriation or other governmental act had not occurred and was not threatened'.[156]

IV. Conclusion

As early as 1961, Martin Domke wrote that '[a]n outright transfer of title may no longer constitute the foremost type of "taking" property in the technique of modern nationalization. There are various other means of "creeping" or "disguised" nationalization through regulations of foreign governments.'[157] The past four decades have validated that observation. With the demise of major socialist economies and the increasing acceptance of free-market economics by even those that nominally remain—of which the People's Republic of China provides perhaps the major example—states today rarely expropriate foreign investments by formal decree. But the failure of political and economic administrations in many states continues to contribute to the relatively frequent phenomenon of indirect expropriations, particularly those that, we suggest, should more precisely be denominated 'creeping' or 'consequential' expropriations. BITs and comparable multilateral investment treaties, which have become the preeminent mechanisms for preventing expropriations, compensating its victims, and thereby preserving the 'favourable

[155] *Starrett Hous. Corp.*, (1984) 4 Iran-US CTR 122, 23 ILM 1090, 1133 (Howard M. Holtzmann, concurring); *see also id.* at 1137 (expressing the view that the majority award should not have suggested a mode of valuation, but should rather have 'included an express instruction to the expert to exclude any diminution in value attributable to wrongful acts of Iran before the date of taking.').

[156] Lillich, *supra* n. 128, at 97 note 13 (quoting 8 M. Whiteman, Digest of International Law 1143 (1967)); *see, e.g., Compañia del Desarrollo de Santa Elena, S.A. v Costa Rica*, ICSID Case No. ARB/96/1, Award of Feb. 17, 2000, (2000) 39 ILM 1317, 1331 (observing, in the course of assessing the value of the claimant's property as of the moment of expropriation, the absence of 'evidence that its value at that date was adversely affected by any prior belief or knowledge that it was about to be expropriated'). Nevertheless, in cases of 'creeping' expropriations, this rule cannot, by itself, repair the damages to the investor per *Chorzów Factory*, for a creeping expropriation may be accomplished by a series of acts that, by themselves, appear innocuous or of ambiguous legality, but together plainly deprive the foreign investor of its property rights. For instance, in the ICSID arbitration of *Benvenuti et Bonfant v People's Republic of the Congo*, Award of Aug. 8, 1980, (1982) 21 ILM 740, the claimant cited, among other events cumulatively comprising the expropriation, the failure of the Congolese government to 'convene the Board of Directors as often as would have been desirable for solving the difficulties of the Company.' *Id.* at 753. While that dereliction, by itself, may have depreciated the *value* of the company jointly owned by the claimant and the government, it would be implausible to contend that this act alone constituted an expropriation. Only in the context of the entire series of events comprising the creeping expropriation could its contribution to the creeping expropriation ultimately accomplished by the Congolese government be properly appreciated. The legality of certain expropriatory events, in short, may be less than clear where it is their cumulative effect that constitutes the expropriation.

[157] Domke, *supra* n. 31, at 588–9.

conditions' for mutually beneficial reciprocal foreign investment, must respond to these changes in a manner consistent with the longstanding principles of customary international law.[158]

To calculate compensation for consequential and creeping expropriations carried out within the legal universe of a BIT, tribunals can no longer be content to evaluate the fair market value of an expropriated investment as of the date when an accretion of governmental acts and omissions has so dramatically devalued that investment as to render it 'practically useless' or its value 'irretrievably lost'. Because these principles may, in practice, threaten the stable and mutually beneficial normative framework for reciprocal foreign investment that states design BITs to create and maintain, international tribunals seeking to award compensation for investments expropriated consequentially or by a creeping series of measures 'tantamount to' expropriation may benefit from an alternative principle. Above all, any standard adopted to determine the appropriate date from which to calculate compensation should effectively deter, not reward, consequential and creeping expropriations.

In this regard tribunals seized with cases raising these issues may find it both useful and appropriate to disaggregate the moment of expropriation and the moment of valuation—to distinguish the 'moment of expropriation', which goes to the question of *liability* (i.e. whether an accretion of measures *has* ripened into a compensable expropriation), from the 'moment of valuation', which goes to the question of *damages*. Because creeping and consequential expropriations frequently demand highly fact-sensitive inquiries, it is neither possible nor prudent to suggest a monolithic or bright-line rule for calculating compensation in these circumstances. But as a general principle, the moment of valuation should be the date on which assessing the fair market value of a foreign investment for purposes of calculating compensation will enable a tribunal to give full effect to *Chorzów Factory*'s imperative. Adoption of this principle, in our view, would contribute in the long term to fortifying the stable and predictable legal regime for reciprocal foreign investment upon which both foreign investors and developing states depend in the BIT generation.

[158] Whether and to what extent BITs codify customary international law remains an open question. The nearly 2,200 BITs in existence today, *see supra* n. 4, and the increasing citation and application of general principles enunciated in arbitral awards rendered on the basis of their standards, suggests that the broader conception of expropriation embodied by BITs to some extent has become—and to some extent remains in the process of becoming—customary international law, insofar as states begin to acknowledge these standards as legally binding in contexts not governed by BITs. In *S.D. Myers Inc. v Canada*, Award of Nov. 12, 2000, (2001) 40 ILM 1408, a NAFTA tribunal affirmed that the minimum standards of treatment for investments prescribed by NAFTA, which include the requirements for a lawful expropriation, and which mirror those contained in most BITs, conform generally to customary international law. *See id.* at 1438, paras 259, 262.; *see also CME Czech Republic B.V. v The Czech Republic*, UNCITRAL Final Award of Mar. 14, 2003, para. 497 (observing that the some 2,200 BITs and similar multilateral investment treaties have become 'truly universal in their reach and essential provisions' and suggesting that their 'concordant provisions are variations on an agreed, essential theme').

THE HYBRID FOUNDATIONS OF INVESTMENT TREATY ARBITRATION

By ZACHARY DOUGLAS*

* BA, LLM (Hons) (UniMelb), BCL (Oxon). Associate, Freshfields Bruckhaus Deringer, Paris. The opinions expressed in this article are those of the author and do not necessarily reflect the views of Freshfields Bruckhaus Deringer or its clients.

The author expresses his deepest gratitude to Professor Crawford for his encouragement and support in undertaking this study and to Jan Paulsson for a privileged introduction to the practice of investment treaty arbitration. This article benefited from their comments and criticism on earlier drafts.

I. Introduction

The analytical challenge presented by the investment treaty regime for the arbitration of investment disputes is that it cannot be adequately rationalised either as a form of public international or private transnational dispute resolution.[1] Investment treaties are international instruments between states governed by the public international law of treaties. The principal beneficiary of the investment treaty regime is most often a corporate entity established under a municipal law, while the legal interests protected by the regime are a bundle of rights in an investment arising under a different municipal law. The standards of protection are fixed by an international treaty, but liability for their breach is said to give rise to a 'civil or commercial' award for enforcement purposes.[2]

Even this superficial appraisal of the different legal relationships and categories arising out of the investment treaty regime is sufficient to

[1] See, *eg* : J. Paulsson, 'Arbitration Without Privity' (1995) 10 *ICSID Rev—Foreign Investment LJ* 232, 256, '[T]his is not a sub genre of an existing discipline. It is dramatically different from anything previously know in the international sphere.'

[2] See Part V(D) below.

disclose its hybrid or *sui generis* character.[3] Nonetheless, the present tendency is for states to see elements of the international law of diplomatic protection lurking in the shadows cast by investment treaties,[4] whereas investors are often convinced of a striking resemblance to international commercial arbitration.[5] The *lex arbitri* created by the investment treaty regime, as this study will demonstrate, is a long way from both these legal institutions for the resolution of disputes.

There is nothing new in abandoning the simple dichotomy between public and private international law conceptions of dispute resolution. Modern international society and commerce are characterised by a complex and sometimes disordered web of interrelationships between sovereign states, individuals, international organisations, and multinational corporations. As this web grows in density and coverage, traversing territorial and jurisdictional frontiers, the challenges for the international or transnational legal order become more and more critical. The response to these challenges has often been in the form of innovative international treaties that introduce a bundle of substantive norms and a distinct dispute resolution mechanism. In the sphere of legal relationships between private entities and sovereign states, there are many parallels between

[3] A definition of investment treatment arbitration is offered by: G. Sacerdoti, 'Bilateral Investment Treaties and Multilateral Instruments on Investment Protection' (1997) 269 *Hague Recueil* 251, 423, 'Arbitration of a private law character, but guaranteed by an international procedure sanctioned by a treaty . . .'. Although the present writer does not adopt this definition, it does reveal a tension between the public and private international law elements of investment treaty arbitration.

[4] The US submitted in *Loewen Group, Inc. & Raymond L. Loewen v United States of America* (Award, 26 June 2003) Case No. ARB(AF)/98/3, (2003) 42 ILM 811 (hereinafter 'Loewen'): 'The reality is that investment-protection cases . . . have often been decided in the context of claims espoused by States. "Diplomatic espousal" and "investment protection" cases are not mutually exclusive categories, just as "claims in intervention" and "claims in contract" are not mutually exclusive under municipal law. There is no reason of principle why legal rules applicable to one category should not be applicable to the other'; Reply of the United States of America to the Counter-Memorial of the Loewen Group, Inc. on Matters of Jurisdiction and Competence (26 April 2002) 38, available at <http://www.state.gov/documents/organization/9947.pdf>.

Sir Robert Jennings, in his Fifth Opinion submitted on behalf of the Claimant in *Loewen*, noted the 'surprising regressive tendency of the United States' argument' which relies on cases 'stem[ming] from the period between the two world wars when solely States were the "subjects" of international law and there was no possibility for individuals or corporations to have direct rights in international law or to be parties to international litigation'; cited in Counter-Memorial of the Loewen Group, Inc. on Matters of Jurisdiction and Competence (29 March 2002) para. 65, available at <http://www.state.gov/documents/organization/9360.pdf>.

[5] Two eminent lawyers who were involved in the negotiations leading to the NAFTA and now act as counsel for investors subscribe to this view. See D. Price, 'Chapter 11—Private Party vs. Government, Investor-State Dispute Settlement: Frankenstein or Safety Valve?' (2000) 26 *Canadian US LJ* 107, 112, 'Chapter 11 of NAFTA removes investment disputes from the political realm and puts them into the realm of commercial arbitration'; H. Alvarez, 'Arbitration Under the North American Free Trade Agreement' (2000) 16 *Arbitration Int* 393, 393–4, '[NAFTA] provides guaranteed access to international commercial arbitration.'

The Claimant in *Loewen* was at pains to reject the diplomatic protection model for investment treaty arbitration: '. . . NAFTA Chapter 11 focuses not on wrongs done to States or claims of the State, but instead gives individual investors the absolute right to bring claims on their own behalf, without having to seek the intercession of their home States as a matter of diplomatic grace', Counter-Memorial of the Loewen Group, Inc. on Matters of Jurisdiction and Competence (29 March 2002) para. 66, available at <http://www.state.gov/documents/organization/9360.pdf>. This view will be endorsed below in in Part II(E).

the legal regime created by investment treaties on the one hand and those regimes established by the European Convention of Human Rights[6] and the Algiers Accords (creating the Iran/US Claims Tribunal) on the other.[7] Citizens of many European countries have the right to pursue remedies directly against a state for violations of international minimum standards of treatment, formulated as universal and inalienable human rights, before an international tribunal.[8] Citizens of Iran and the United States have the right to pursue remedies directly against the other state for violations of international minimum standards of treatment, such as the prohibition against uncompensated expropriation, before an international tribunal.[9] Recourse to the European Court of Human Rights, the Iran/US Claims Tribunal, and the international arbitral tribunals established pursuant to investment treaties has catapulted individuals and corporate entities into an international system of adjudication along-side states. In this respect also the traditional view of the international legal order that relegated individuals and corporate entities to the status of mere 'objects' of international law is no longer credible.[10]

An analysis of these different treaty regimes can be distorted if one adheres to a strict distinction between public and private international law conceptions of dispute resolution. Many of the awards of investment treaty tribunals—and the pleadings of parties to these disputes—proceed on the basis of a dogmatic distinction between 'international' or 'treaty'

[6] This link was made by G. Burdeau, 'Nouvelles perspectives pour l'arbitrage dans le contentieux économique intéressant l'Etat' (1995) *Revue de l'arbitrage* 3, 16: '[L]a 'philosophie' des deux mécanismes paraît la même: il s'agit dans l'un et l'autre cas d'ouvrir à des particuliers non identifiés à l'avance un droit de recours direct contre un Etat en vue de sanctionner le respect de l'engagement pris par ce dernier dans un traité international d'accorder un certain traitement à des personnes privées.'

[7] Investment treaty tribunals, and counsel pleading before them, cite precedents of the Iran/US Claims Tribunal with great frequency. However, the UNCITRAL Tribunal in the NAFTA case of *Pope & Talbot Inc v Government of Canada* (Interim Award, 26 June 2000), available at <http://www.dfait-maeci.gc.ca/tna-nac/documents/pubdoc7.pdf>, appeared to reject the significance of the precedents of the Iran/US Claims Tribunal in relation to the prohibition against expropriation in Art. 1110 of NAFTA. *Ibid.* paras. 94, 104. For a critique of this approach, see: M. Brunetti, 'The Iran-United States Claims Tribunal, NAFTA Chapter 11, and the Doctrine of Indirect Expropriation' (2001) *2 Chicago J of Int L* 203.

[8] See generally: J. Fawcett, *The Application of the European Convention on Human Rights* (1987); P. Van Dijk & G. Van Hoof, *Theory and Practice of the European Convention of Human Rights* (1990); D. Harris, M. O'Boyle, & A. Warbick, *Law of the European Convention on Human Rights* (1995); D. Shelton, *Remedies in International Human Rights Law* (1999) 147; M. Janis, R. Kay, & A. Bradley, *European Human Rights Law* (2000, 2nd edn).

[9] See generally: G. Aldrich, *The Jurisprudence of the Iran-United States Claims Tribunal* (1996); R. Lillich, D. Magraw, & D. Bederman, *The Iran-United States Claims Tribunal: Its Contribution to the Law of State Responsibility* (1997); C. Brower & J. Brueschke, *The Iran-United States Claims Tribunal* (1998); M. Mohebi, *The International Law Character of the Iran-United States Claims Tribunal* (1999).

[10] The 'father' of the positivist conception of the subjects of international law was arguably Bentham, who in 1789 defined international law as 'the mutual transactions between sovereigns'. See J. Bentham, *Introduction to the Principles of Morals and Legislation* (1789) 296. Janis has pointed out the irony that in the same year as Bentham propounded this thesis, the First United States Congress authorised suits by individuals to address grievances under the law of nations before the Federal District Courts pursuant to the Judiciary Act. See M. Janis, 'Subjects of International Law' (1984) 17 *Cornell Int L J* 61.

versus 'municipal' or 'contractual' spheres, as if the two can be strictly dissociated one from the other.[11] Thus, by characterising the status of an investment treaty tribunal as 'international', arbitrators have professed to occupy a position of supremacy in a 'hierarchy' of legal orders, and thereby have dismissed the relevance of any competing law or jurisdiction. The principle of international law that is used to buttress this approach, whether expressly or implicitly, is the rule of state responsibility that a state cannot invoke provisions of its own law to justify a derogation from an international obligation. Article 3 of the ILC's Articles on the Responsibility of States for International Wrongs, titled 'Characterization of the act of a State as internationally wrongful' is a codification of this rule, which provides: 'The characterization of an act of a State as internationally wrongful is governed by international law. Such characterization is not affected by the characterization of the same act as lawful by internal law.'[12] But investment disputes are only partly concerned with the compliance of acts attributable to a state with its treaty obligations; and the principle stated in Article 3 of the ILC Articles only comes into play when there is actual conflict between the two legal orders—orders which nonetheless coexist in principle (and in fact), in relation to any investment situation. In other words, investment disputes are significantly concerned with issues pertaining to the existence, nature, and scope of the private interests comprising the investment. These issues go beyond the purview of international law and the rule of state responsibility just recalled. To treat international law as a self-sufficient legal order in the sphere of foreign investment is plainly untenable. Within this domain of private or commercial interests, problems relating to overlapping adjudicative competence and the application of municipal law cannot be resolved by playing the simple 'international trump card' of Article 3.

This study will confront the problem of jurisdictional conflicts between arbitral tribunals established pursuant to investment treaties to decide investor/state disputes ('treaty tribunals') on the one hand, and municipal courts or arbitral tribunals constituted pursuant to an arbitration clause in a contract between the investor and the host state ('contractual tribunals') on the other, in some detail, together with conflicts of law problems pertaining to various aspects of the investment dispute. These problems have been particularised as the choice of law issues pertaining to different substantive aspects of the investment dispute (examined in Part IV of this study), the applicable procedural law and its significance to the arbitral procedure (Part V), the applicable regime for the challenge and enforcement of investment treaty awards (Part VI), and the jurisdictional conflicts that arise when different courts or tribunals are seized of different elements of

[11] See the cases analysed in Parts IV(C), VII(C) and VII(E) below.

[12] The ILC's Articles and official commentary thereto are reproduced in: J. Crawford, *The International Law Commission's Articles on State Responsibility. Introduction, Text and Commentaries* (2002) 61.

the investment dispute (Part VII), whether pursuant to a forum selection clause in a contract between the investor and the host state or otherwise.

None of these problems, however, can be properly addressed in a theoretical void. Hence Parts II and III will lay the conceptual foundation with a discussion of two crucial threshold questions. First, to whom are the primary investment protection obligations in an investment treaty owed? Although investors are clearly beneficiaries of those obligations, the spectre of diplomatic protection is often summoned in investment treaty awards and pleadings in support of the idea that investors are stepping into the shoes of their national states in bringing an investment treaty claim.[13] Does, then, the modern investment treaty create a procedural device for triggering the legal rights and obligations of diplomatic protection? Or are investors the true 'owners' of rights under investment treaties? If the rights invoked by investors are not ultimately their own, then this must have consequences, for example, on their ability to waive or otherwise qualify these rights.

The second threshold question, which follows directly from the first, concerns the nature of the legal consequences that follow a breach of an investment treaty obligation. Do the secondary rules of state responsibility for international wrongful acts apply in this situation? Formulated differently, is a breach of an investment treaty in relation to a particular investor actionable by the national state of the investor so that the latter has corresponding rights to a remedy for that breach? If it is, then the resulting liability has a truly international character. This has consequences, for instance, in determining the applicable regime for the challenge and enforcement of investment treaty awards.

Bilateral investment treaties ('BITs') for the reciprocal encouragement of investment, predominantly between capital importing and exporting states, numbered 2,181 at the end of 2002.[14] Multilateral investment treaties such as the North Atlantic Free Trade Agreement ('NAFTA')[15] and the Energy Charter Treaty[16] create reciprocal investment protection obligations across the same divide but are also notable for extending the regime to investment relations between developed economies as well.[17] Investment treaties usually create two distinct dispute resolution

[13] See Part II(B) below.

[14] UNCTAD, *World Investment Report 2003* (2003) 17, available at <http://www.unctad.org/en/docs//wir2003overview_en.pdf>. Interestingly, only 7% of the world's foreign direct investment is covered by the bilateral investment treaty network, although the proportion of foreign direct investment in developing and Central and Eastern European countries covered by the network is 22%. *Ibid.*

[15] Reprinted at: (1993) 32 ILM 605.

[16] Reprinted at: (1995) 35 ILM 509.

[17] See generally the following studies on the NAFTA and Energy Charter Treaty: T. Wälde (ed.) *The Energy Charter Treaty: An East-West Gateway for Investment and Trade* (1996); M. Omalu, *NAFTA and the Energy Charter Treaty: Compliance with, Implementation, and Effectiveness of International Investment Agreements* (1999); T. Wälde, 'International Investment under the 1994 Energy Charter Treaty' (1995) 29 *J of World Trade L* 5; T. Wälde, 'Investment Arbitration under the Energy Charter Treaty' (1996) *Arbitration Int* 429; T. Weiler (ed), *NAFTA Investment Law and Arbitration: Past Issues, Current Practice, Future Prospects* (2004).

mechanisms: one for disputes between a qualifying investor and the host state in relation to its investment ('investor/state disputes') and another for disputes between the contracting state parties to the treaty ('state/state disputes'). Investment treaties generally provide that the state/state mechanism covers disputes 'concerning the interpretation or application' of the treaty,[18] whereas disputes relating to a specific investment of a particular investor (which may of course give rise to interpretative questions) are encompassed by the investor/state dispute resolution procedure.[19] This study focuses almost exclusively on the resolution of investor/state disputes through recourse to international arbitration, which is by far the most utilised dispute resolution mechanism that is available under investment treaties.[20] Nevertheless it is useful to set the stage with a brief appraisal of each type of mechanism.

The judicial forums prescribed for the resolution of investor/state disputes generally include one or more of the following at the option of the investor:

—municipal courts of the host state;[21]
—ICSID arbitration pursuant to the ICSID Arbitration Rules or the Additional Facility Rules;[22]

[18] Asian-African Legal Consultative Committee Model BIT, Art. 11(i), UNCTAD, *International Investment Instruments: A Compendium* (hereinafter 'UNCTAD Compendium') (Vol. III, 1996) 122; Chile Model BIT, Art. 9(1), *ibid.* 148; China Model BIT, Art. 8(1), *ibid.* 154; Switzerland Model BIT, Art. 9(1), *ibid.* 181; UK Model BIT, Art. 9(1), *ibid.* 190; Egypt Model BIT, Art. 9(1), *ibid.* (Vol. V, 2000) 297; France Model BIT, Art. 11(1), *ibid.* 306; Jamaica Model BIT, Art. 9(1), *ibid.* 321; Malaysia Model BIT, Art. 8(1), *ibid.* 329; Netherlands Model BIT, Art. 12(1), *ibid.* 337; Sri Lanka Model BIT, Art. 9(1), *ibid.* 344; Cambodia Model BIT, Art. 9(1), *ibid.* (Vol. VI, 2002) 467; Croatia Model BIT, Art. 11(1), *ibid.* 477; Iran Model BIT, Art. 13(1), *ibid.* 483; Peru Model BIT, Art. 9(1), *ibid.* 498; US Model BIT, Art. 10(1), *ibid.* 508; Austria Model BIT, Art. 18, *ibid.* (Vol. VII) 267; Belgo-Luxemburg Economic Union Model BIT, Art. 11(1), *ibid.* 276; Denmark Model BIT, Art. 10(1), *ibid.* 284; Finland Model BIT, Art. 10(1), *ibid.* 293; Germany Model BIT, Art. 10(1), *ibid.* 300; South Africa Model BIT, Art. 8(1), *ibid.* (Vol. VIII) 277; Turkey Model BIT, Art. 8(1), *ibid.* 284; Benin Model BIT, Art. 8(1), *ibid.* (Vol. IX) 282; Burundi Model BIT, Art. 9(1), *ibid.* 292; Maurice Model BIT, Art. 9(1), *ibid.* 300; Mongolia Model BIT, Art. 9(1), *ibid.* 306; Sweden Model BIT, Art. 9(1), *ibid.* 314; Energy Charter Treaty, Art. 27(1).

[19] See the discussion of the *ratione materiae* of investment disputes at the text accompanying nn. 438–443 below.

[20] The only example of a state/state arbitration to date has arisen under the Peru/Chile BIT, where Peru invoked the state/state dispute mechanism against Chile after being served with a notice of arbitration by a Chilean investor under the same BIT (*Lucchetti SA v Peru* (ICSID Case No. ARB/03/4)). Peru appears to be seeking a favourable interpretation of the BIT in the state/state arbitration to assist its case in the investor/state arbitration.

[21] Chile Model BIT, Art. 8(2)(a), *UNCTAD Compendium* (Vol. III, 1996) 147; China Model BIT, Art. 9(2), *ibid.* 155; Egypt Model BIT, Art. 8(2)(a), *ibid.* (Vol. V, 2000) 297; Jamaica Model BIT, Art. 8(2)(a), *ibid.* 322; Sri Lanka Model BIT, Art. 8(2)(a), *ibid.* 343; Croatia Model BIT, Art. 10(2)(a), *ibid.* (Vol. VI, 2002) 476; Iran Model BIT, Art. 12(2), *ibid.* 483; Peru Model BIT, Art. 8(2)(a), *ibid.* 497; US Model BIT, Art. 9(2)(a), *ibid.* 507; Austria Model BIT, Art. 12(1)(a), *ibid.* (Vol. VII) 264; Finland Model BIT, Art. 9(2)(a), *ibid.* 292; Benin Model BIT, Art. 9(2)(a), *ibid.* (Vol. IX) 283; Energy Charter Treaty, Art. 26(2)(a).

[22] Asian-African Legal Consultative Committee Model 'A' BIT, Art. 10(v), *UNCTAD Compendium* (Vol. III, 1996) 122; Asian-African Legal Consultative Committee Model 'B' BIT, Art. 10(v), *ibid.* 133; Chile Model BIT, Art. 8(2)(b), *ibid.* 147; Switzerland Model BIT, Art. 8(2), *ibid.* 181; UK Model BIT, Art. 8, *ibid.* 189; Egypt Model BIT, Art. 8(2)(b), *ibid.* (Vol. V, 2000) 297; France Model BIT, Art. 8,

—*ad hoc* arbitration pursuant to the UNCITRAL Arbitration Rules;[23]
—International Chamber of Commerce arbitration;[24]
—Stockholm Chamber of Commerce arbitration;[25] or
—a settlement procedure previously agreed to between the investor and host state.[26]

In relation to state/state disputes, investment treaties almost without exception refer such disputes to *ad hoc* arbitration with the President of the International Court of Justice nominated as the appointing authority.[27] Also, in the vast majority of cases, investment treaties prescribe that the arbitral tribunal shall determine its own rules of procedure, but in the rare instances that a model set of rules is specified, a set of rules

ibid. 305; Indonesia Model BIT, Art. 8(3)(a), *ibid.* 313; Jamaica Model BIT, Art. 10, *ibid.* 322; Malaysia Model BIT, Art. 7(3), *ibid.* 329; Netherlands Model BIT, Art. 9, *ibid.* 336; Sri Lanka Model BIT, Art. 8(2)(b), *ibid.* 343; Cambodia Model BIT, Art. 8(3)(a), *ibid.* (Vol. VI, 2002) 467; Croatia Model BIT, Art. 10(2)(b), *ibid.* 476; Peru Model BIT, Art. 8(2)(b), *ibid.* 497; US Model BIT, Art. 9(3)(a), *ibid.* 507; Austria Model BIT, Art. 12(1)(c), *ibid.* (Vol. VII) 264; Belgo-Luxemburg Economic Union Model BIT, Art. 10(3), *ibid.* 275; Denmark Model BIT, Art. 9(2)(a), *ibid.* 283; Finland Model BIT, Art. 9(2)(b), *ibid.* 292; Germany Model BIT, Art. 11, *ibid.* 301; South Africa Model BIT, Art. 7(2), *ibid.* (Vol. VIII) 276; Turkey Model BIT, Art. 7(2)(a), *ibid.* 284; Benin Model BIT, Art. 9(3), *ibid.* (Vol. IX) 283; Burundi Model BIT, Art. 8(3), *ibid.* 292; Mongolia Model BIT, Art. 8(2)(a), *ibid.* 306; Sweden Model BIT, Art. 8(2), *ibid.* 313; Energy Charter Treaty, Art. 26(4); NAFTA, Art. 1120(1).

[23] Asian-African Legal Consultative Committee Model 'A' BIT, Art. 10(v), *UNCTAD Compendium* (Vol. III, 1996) 122; Asian-African Legal Consultative Committee Model 'B' BIT, Art. 10(v), *ibid.* 133; UK 'Alternative' Model BIT, Art. 8, *ibid.* 189; Egypt Model BIT, Art. 8(2)(c), *ibid.* (Vol. V, 2000) 297; Indonesia Model BIT, Art. 8(3)(b), *ibid.* 313; Sri Lanka Model BIT, Art. 8(2)(f), *ibid.* 343; Cambodia Model BIT, Art. 8(3)(b), *ibid.* (Vol. VI, 2002) 467; Iran Model BIT, Art. 12(6), *ibid.* 483; US Model BIT, Art. 9(3)(a)(iii), *ibid.* 507; Austria Model BIT, Art. 12(1)(c), *ibid.* (Vol. VII) 265; Belgo-Luxemburg Economic Union Model BIT, Art. 10(3), *ibid.* 275; Denmark Model BIT, Art. 9(2)(c), *ibid.* 283; Finland Model BIT, Art. 9(2)(d), *ibid.* 292; Turkey Model BIT, Art. 7(2)(b), *ibid.* 284; Benin Model BIT, Art. 9(3)(b), *ibid.* (Vol. IX) 284; Mongolia Model BIT, Art. 8(2)(b), *ibid.* 306; Sweden Model BIT, Art. 8(2), *ibid.* 313; Energy Charter Treaty, Art. 26(4); NAFTA, Art. 1120(1). In relation to the nature of a unilateral offer of ICSID arbitration, see: P. Muchlinski, *Multinational Enterprises and the Law* (1999) 558; C. Schreuer, *The ICSID Convention: A Commentary* (2001) 212–13.

[24] UK 'Alternative' Model BIT, Art. 8(2)(b), *UNCTAD Compendium* (Vol. III, 1996) 190; Austria Model BIT, Art. 12(1)(c), *ibid.* (Vol. VII) 265; Belgo-Luxemburg Economic Union Model BIT, Art. 10(3), *ibid.* 275; Denmark Model BIT, Art. 9(2)(d), *ibid.* 283; Germany Model BIT, Art. 11, *ibid.* 301.

[25] Sri Lanka Model BIT, Art. 8(2)(e), *UNCTAD Compendium* (Vol. V, 2000) 343; Belgo-Luxemburg Economic Union Model BIT, Art. 10(3), *ibid.* (Vol. VII, 2002) 275; Energy Charter Treaty, Art. 26(4).

[26] US Model BIT, Art. 9(3)(a)(iv), *UNCTAD Compendium* (Vol. VI, 2002) 507; Austria Model BIT, Art. 12(1)(b), *ibid.* (Vol. VII) 264; Energy Charter Treaty, Art. 26(2)(6).

[27] Asian-African Legal Consultative Committee Model BIT, Art. 11(iii), *UNCTAD Compendium* (Vol. III, 1996) 122; Chile Model BIT, Art. 9(4), *ibid.* 148; China Model BIT, Art. 8(4), *ibid.* 154; Switzerland Model BIT, Art. 9(4), *ibid.* 182; UK Model BIT, Art. 9(4), *ibid.* 191; Egypt Model BIT, Art. 9(4), *ibid.* (Vol. V, 2000) 298; Jamaica Model BIT, Art. 9(4), *ibid.* 321; Malaysia Model BIT, Art. 8(4), *ibid.* 330; Netherlands Model BIT, Art. 12(4), *ibid.* 337; Sri Lanka Model BIT, Art. 9(4), *ibid.* 344; Croatia Model BIT, Art. 11, *ibid.* (Vol. VI, 2002) 477; Iran Model BIT, Art. 13, *ibid.* 483–4; Peru Model BIT, Art. 9, *ibid.* 498; Austria Model BIT, Art. 20, *ibid.* (Vol. VII) 267; Belgo-Luxemburg Economic Union Model BIT, Art. 11, *ibid.* 276; Denmark Model BIT, Art. 10, *ibid.* 284–5; Finland Model BIT, Art. 10, *ibid.* 293; Germany Model BIT, Art. 10, *ibid.* 300–1; South Africa Model BIT, Art. 8, *ibid.* (Vol. VIII) 277; Turkey Model BIT, Art. 8, *ibid.* 284–5; Benin Model BIT, Art. 8, *ibid.* (Vol. IX) 282–3; Burundi Model BIT, Art. 9, *ibid.* 292–3; Maurice Model BIT, Art. 9, *ibid.* 300; Mongolia Model BIT, Art. 9, *ibid.* 306–7; Sweden Model BIT, Art. 9, *ibid.* 314. The US Model BIT nominates the Secretary-General of ICSID as the appointing authority, Art. 10, *ibid.* (Vol. VI) 508. The France Model BIT nominates the Secretary General of the UN, Art. 11, *ibid.* (Vol. V) 307. The Energy Charter Treaty nominates the Secretary-General of the Permanent Court of Arbitration, Art. 27.

designed for public international law arbitrations between states is generally preferred.[28]

The hybrid or *sui generis* nature of the legal relationship between the investor and host state that arises out of the investment treaty regime does not prejudice a different characterisation of the legal relationship between the contracting state parties. State/state disputes under investment treaties easily fit into the familiar paradigm of arbitrations between states governed by public international law. In contradistinction, it will be demonstrated in Part II that the public international law paradigm for international claims for harm to individuals or private entities, the customary law of diplomatic protection, is inadequate and inappropriate as a basis for rationalising investor/state disputes.

A final introductory point needs to be made about the use in this study of the model BITs of certain states as evidence of state practice. These model BITs are not relied upon by the present writer as an evidentiary component for the formation of customary international law,[29] but instead as a representative sample of the types of treaty provisions that feature in the approximately 2,000 BITs in existence. The volumes of model BITs collected and published by the United Nations Conference on Trade and Development ('UNCTAD') and cited extensively in this study come from a diverse range of both capital exporting and importing states. The striking feature of this collection of model BITs is that their formal layout and substantive content are very similar, often practically identical, in spite of the different economic or cultural reality prevailing in the states in question. A suggestion that the familiar substantive obligations in treaties such as the standard of fair and equitable treatment and most-favoured nation treatment, or indeed the procedural right to submit investor/state disputes to international arbitration, are somehow thrust upon capital importing or developing states by more powerful nations with developed economies is seriously undermined by the evidence presented by this collection of model BITs. A model BIT represents the set of norms that the relevant state holds out to be both reasonable and acceptable as a legal basis for the protection of foreign investment in its own economy.[30] That there appears to

[28] The Austria Model BIT selects the Permanent Court of Arbitration Optional Rules for Arbitrating Disputes, Art. 21(2), *UNCTAD Compendium* (Vol. VII, 2002) 267. The NAFTA Parties have enacted a very detailed set of 'Model Rules of Procedure for Chapter 20 of the NAFTA' (relating to state/state disputes) in accordance with Art. 2012 of the NAFTA. Conversely, the Energy Charter Treaty makes no distinction between the procedural rules for investor/state and state/state arbitrations by selecting the UNCITRAL Arbitration Rules for state/state disputes in Art. 27(3)(f).

[29] The extent to which these bilateral investment treaties do generate customary international law was an issue debated at some length in two NAFTA cases, see: *Pope & Talbot Inc v Government of Canada* (Award in Respect of Damages, 31 May 2002), (2002) 41 ILM 1347, para. 55 *et seq.*; *United Parcel Service of America Inc v Government of Canada* (Award on Jurisdiction, 22 November 2002), para. 86 *et seq.*, available at <http://www.dfait-maeci.gc.ca/tna-nac/documents/Jurisdiction%20Award.22Nov02.pdf>. See generally: B. Kishoiyian, 'The Utility of Bilateral Investment Treaties in the Formulation of Customary International Law' (1994) 14 *Northwestern Int L and Business* 327.

[30] It is certainly possible that economic globalisation is a coercive force in the sense that developing states are under pressure to subscribe to rules and standards to compete for foreign direct investment. This form of 'coercion' does not, however, constitute a legal form of duress that could be relevant to the binding force of the treaty.

be a strong consensus on this matter among the states that have submitted model BITs to UNCTAD cannot be ignored; and this insight would be relevant to a discussion of BITs and customary international law.

II. To Whom are Investment Treaty Obligations Owed?

A. INTRODUCTION: THE IRAN/US CLAIMS TRIBUNAL

Before examining the legal nature of the investor/state regime for the settlement of disputes in investment treaties, it is important to recognise that the problem of 'pigeonholing' an international treaty regime for the settlement of disputes between states and individuals and private entities has arisen before. The precise legal status of the Iran/US Claims Tribunal remains a subject of controversy even as its mandate draws to a close after more than twenty years of activity.

The literature on this subject testifies to a complete lack of consensus. A judge of the Tribunal, Judge Brower, asserts that 'there can be little doubt that the Tribunal is an international institution established by two sovereign States and subject to public international law.'[31] Similarly, Fox regards the Tribunal as an example of 'private claims taken up by the State and presented through an inter-State arbitration.'[32] The Iranian writer, Seifi, emphasizes the Tribunal's 'exclusively international character',[33] while the US writer, Caron, takes the view that, at least in relation to claims involving nationals, 'the Accords established a clear presumption that the legal system of the Netherlands would govern the Tribunal's arbitral process.'[34] Two eminent Dutch lawyers, Hardenberg and van den Berg, reach contrary conclusions on the applicability of Dutch law as the *lex loci arbitri*.[35] Other commentators have perhaps sought the middle ground in describing the procedural regime for the Iran/US Claims Tribunal as 'denationalised':

> [I]t appears truer to the Accords to recognize the Tribunal as a denationalized body subject to its organic treaty and its rules, but not to national arbitral law.[36]

[31] C. Brower & J. Brueschke, above n. 9, 16.

[32] H. Fox, 'States and the Undertaking to Arbitrate' (1988) 37 *ICLQ* 1, 3.

[33] J. Seifi, 'State Responsibility for Failure to Enforce Iran-United States Claims Tribunal Awards by the Respective National Courts: International Character and Non-Reviewability of the Awards Reconfirmed' (1999) 16 *J of Int Arbitration* 5, 17.

[34] D. Caron, 'The Nature of the Iran-United States Claims Tribunal and the Evolving Structure of International Dispute Resolution' (1990) 84 *AJIL* 104, 146.

[35] L. Hardenberg, 'The Awards of the Iran-US Claims Tribunal Seen in Connection with the Law of the Netherlands' (1984) *Int Business Lawyer* 337 (concluding that Dutch law does not apply as the *lex loci arbitri*); A. van den Berg, 'Proposed Dutch Law on the Iran-United States Claims Settlement Declaration, A Reaction to Mr. Hardenberg's Article' (1984) *Int Business Lawyer* 341 (concluding that Dutch law does apply).

[36] W. Lake & J. Dana, 'Judicial Review of Awards of the Iran-United States Claims Tribunal: Are the Tribunal's Awards Dutch?' (1984) 16 *Law & Policy in Int Business* 755, 811. Sacerdoti also avoids the public/private dichotomy simply by characterising the awards as commercial arbitral

Another Iranian writer, Avanessian, agrees with this analysis, but adds:

> [The Tribunal] somehow exists and operates on the borderline of public and private international law, sometimes falling in the domain of one and sometimes in that of the other.[37]

A complete spectrum of views can thus be distilled from the literature on the juridical status of the Iran/US Claims Tribunal. That the authors just mentioned can reach very divergent conclusions on this subject should at least put those dealing with investment treaty arbitration on notice of the complexity of the issues at hand. Any single-sentence proclamations about the true nature of the legal regime for the settlement of investor/state disputes must be viewed with scepticism.

The Iran/US Claims Tribunal, established by the Algiers Accords,[38] has jurisdiction over (i) claims by American and Iranian nationals against Iran and the United States respectively that 'arise out of debts, contracts . . . expropriations or other measures affecting property rights';[39] (ii) 'official claims of the United States and Iran against each other arising out of contractual arrangements between them for the purpose and sale of goods and services';[40] and (iii) disputes between Iran and the United States concerning the interpretation or performance of the General Declaration or the Claims Settlement Declaration.[41]

There is an important difference between the three types of jurisdiction vested in the Iran/US Claims Tribunal.[42] Investor/state disputes under investment treaties most closely resemble the first of the three heads of jurisdiction of the Iran/US Claims Tribunal because private interests are clearly at stake. Therefore it is valuable to examine how the Tribunal itself has rationalised the nature of the claimant's cause of action. Is this example of a private claimant stepping into the shoes of its national state?

The issue arose most directly in the *Dual Nationality Case*.[43] Iran challenged the admissibility of claims brought against it by persons who were both citizens of the United States and Iran by relying on a rule of customary international law prohibiting the exercise of diplomatic protection on behalf of a national who also has the nationality of the respondent state.

awards: G. Sacerdoti, above n. 3, 423, '[J]udgments issued by the Tribunal on private claims can be equated to those of international commercial arbitral tribunals and [. . .] can be enforced accordingly.'

[37] A. Avanessian, 'The New York Convention and Denationalised Arbitral Awards (With Emphasis on the Iran-United States Claims Tribunal)' (1991) *J of Int Arbitration* 5, 8.

[38] The Iran/US Claims Tribunal was established in 1981 pursuant to the Declaration of the Government of the Democratic and Popular Republic of Algeria ('General Declaration') and the Declaration of the Government of the Democratic and Popular Republic of Algeria concerning the Settlement of Claims by the Government of the United States of America and the Government of the Islamic Republic of Iran ('Claims Settlement Declaration'), collectively referred to as the 'Algiers Accords'. The Algiers Accords are reproduced at: (1981) 75 *AJIL* 418.

[39] Article II(1) of the Claims Settlement Declaration. [40] *Ibid.* Art. II(2).

[41] *Ibid.* Art. II(3).

[42] Only a few studies emphasize this distinction, including: D. Lloyd Jones, 'The Iran-United States Claims Tribunal: Private Rights and State Responsibility' (1984) 24 *Victoria J of Int L* 259, 261–2; H. Fox, above n. 32, 21.

[43] *Islamic Republic of Iran and United States (Case A/18) (Dual Nationality)* (6 April 1984) DEC 32-A18-FT, (1984) 5 Iran-US CTR 251.

Iran justified its reliance on this rule on the basis that the Algiers Accords 'intended the function of the Tribunal to be the adjudication of international claims on the basis of the exercise of diplomatic protection.'[44]

The Full Tribunal rejected Iran's argument emphatically, clearly distinguishing its jurisdiction over *inter*-state disputes from its jurisdiction extending to private claimants:

While this Tribunal is clearly an international tribunal established by treaty and while some of its cases involve the interpretation and application of public international law, most disputes (including all of those brought by dual nationals) involve a private party on one side and a Government or Government-controlled entity on the other, and many involve primarily issues of municipal law and general principles of law. In such cases it is rights of the claimant, not of his nation, that are to be determined by the Tribunal.[45]

The Full Tribunal later reiterated in Case A/21, when confronted again with Iran's submission that the claims of nationals are in reality the claims of their governments, that 'Tribunal awards uniformly recognize that no espousal of claims by the United States is involved in the cases before it.'[46]

B. THE INVESTMENT TREATY REGIME FOR INVESTOR/STATE DISPUTES

Whereas the pronouncements of the Iran/US Claims Tribunal on the threshold problem of its own juridical status are not definitive, in the investment treaty context they are virtually non-existent. One of the few tribunals to consider the problem was the ICSID Tribunal in *Loewen Group, Inc. & Raymond L. Loewen v United States of America*[47] ('Loewen'). The Tribunal first endorsed a sharp distinction between the 'municipal' and 'international' legal orders in its description of the rights and obligations existing under NAFTA:

Rights of action under private law arise from personal obligations . . . brought into existence by domestic law and enforceable through domestic tribunals and

[44] *Ibid.* 254.

[45] *Ibid.* 261. See also: Concurring Opinion of Willem Riphagen, *ibid.* 273–4; *Esphanian (Nasser) v Bank Tejarat* (29 March 1983) 31–157–2, (1983) 2 Iran-US CTR 157, 165, '[T]he agreement of the two Governments to create this Tribunal was not a typical exercise of diplomatic protection of nationals in which a State, seeking some form of international redress for its nationals, creates a tribunal to which it, rather than its nationals, is a party. In that typical case, the State espouses the claims of its nationals, and the injuries for which it claims redress are deemed to be injuries to itself; here, the Government of the United States is not a party to the arbitration of claims of United States nationals, not even in the same claims where it acts as counsel for these nationals.'

[46] *Islamic Republic of Iran and United States (State Party Responsibility for Awards Rendered Against its Nationals)* (4 May 1987) DEC 62-A21-FT, (1987) 14 Iran-US CTR 324, 330, para. 12. The position was different in relation to the small claims. See Art. III(3) of the Claims Settlement Declaration: 'Claims of nationals of the United States and Iran that are within the scope of this Agreement shall be presented to the Tribunal either by claimants themselves or, in the case of claims of less than $250,000, by the government of such national.'

[47] (Award, 26 June 2003) Case No. ARB(AF)/98/3, (2003) 42 ILM 811 (hereinafter 'Loewen Award').

courts. NAFTA claims have a quite different character, stemming from a corner of public international law in which, by treaty, the power of States under that law to take international measures for the correction of wrongs done to its nationals has been replaced by an ad hoc definition of certain kinds of wrong, coupled with specialist means of compensation.[48]

Upon this foundation, the Tribunal then articulated a 'derivative' scheme for understanding the investor's cause of action:

There is no warrant for transferring rules derived from private law into a field of international law where *claimants are permitted for convenience to enforce what are in origin the rights of Party states*.[49]

The direct consequence of this theoretical approach in *Loewen* was the application of a (controversial) rule governing the presentation of an international claim by one state to another through the mechanism of diplomatic protection.[50]

At the heart of the 'derivative' theory is the idea that investment treaties 'institutionalise and reinforce'[51] the system of diplomatic protection.[52] In accordance with this model, the obligations of minimum treatment are owed to the contracting states just as in customary international law, however, those states confer standing upon their national investors to enforce such obligations before an international tribunal. Investors therefore procedurally step into the shoes of their national state, without thereby becoming privy to their *inter*-state legal relationship. This was the procedural regime adopted by the Mixed Claims Commissions established to hear US and British claims against Latin American States including Mexico, Chile, Venezuela, and Peru as well as claims against Germany after the First World War.[53]

The 'derivative theory' is popular among respondent states to investment treaty claims. Canada recently endorsed this position in its pleadings before the courts in Ottawa challenging the NAFTA award in *S.D. Myers Inc. v Government of Canada*:[54]

The obligations listed in Section A of NAFTA Chapter Eleven are not owed directly to individual investors. Rather, the disputing investor must prove that the NAFTA Party claimed against has breached an obligation owed to another

[48] *Ibid.* para. 233.

[49] *Ibid.* para. 233 (emphasis added). Elsewhere in its award, the *Loewen* Tribunal appears to contradict this 'derivative' approach by stating that 'Chapter Eleven of NAFTA represents a progressive development in international law whereby the individual investor may make a claim on its own behalf and submit the claim to international arbitration . . .', *ibid.* para. 223.

[50] See Part III(C) below.

[51] J. Crawford, 'The ILC's Articles on Responsibility of States for International Wrongful Acts: A Retrospect' (2002) 96 AJIL 874, 888.

[52] *Mavrommatis Palestine Concessions Case* (1924) PCIJ Rep Series A No. 2. See the discussion at Section C of this Part II below.

[53] J. Simpson & H. Fox, *International Arbitration, Law and Practice* (1959) Chs. 1–4.

[54] (Partial Award, 12 November 2000), (2001) 40 ILM 1408.

NAFTA Party under Section A and that the investor had incurred loss or damage by reason of or arising out of that breach.[55]

In the NAFTA context, similar positions have been taken by the United States[56] and Mexico.[57] Writers such as Sornarajah also support this conception of the beneficiary of rights under an investment treaty.[58]

The 'derivative theory' can be contrasted with the 'direct theory', whereby investors are recognised to be in a direct legal relationship with the host state and given procedural means to enforce their own substantive rights. This juxtaposition of 'derivative' and 'direct' models for the presentation of claims against states is implicit in several investment treaty arbitration awards, most prominently in *CMS Gas Transmission Company v The Republic of Argentina*:[59]

To some extent, diplomatic protection is intervening as a residual mechanism to be resorted to in the absence of other arrangements recognising the direct right of action by individuals.[60]

Before considering the compatibility of the 'derivative' model with the distinct features of the investment treaty regime that have emerged from the cases, it is necessary to consider in more detail the *Mavrommatis* formula[61] of diplomatic protection, which underlies the derivative model.

C. THE *MAVROMMATIS* FORMULA OF DIPLOMATIC PROTECTION

The institution of diplomatic protection is conceived of as concerning rights and obligations existing exclusively between sovereign states. The injured foreign national is not privy to this legal relationship and is thus impotent to enforce the obligations of customary international law in its own right. This has been the orthodox view of diplomatic protection

[55] Amended Memorandum of Fact and Law of the Applicant, the Attorney General of Canada, *The Attorney General of Canada v S. D. Myers, Inc*, Court File No. T-225–01, para. 67, available at <http://www.dfait-maeci.gc.ca/tna-nac/documents/Myersamend.pdf>.

[56] See, in particular, the US Government's arguments to the effect that 'direct claims' are no different, and subject to the same rules, as 'espoused claims' in its Reply to the Counter-Memorial of the Loewen Group, Inc on Matters of Jurisdiction and Competence (26 April 2002) 33 *et seq.*, available at <http://www.state.gov/documents/organization/9947.pdf>.

[57] See below n. 362.

[58] M. Sornarajah, 'State Responsibility and Bilateral Investment Treaties' (1986) 20 *J of World Trade L* 79, 93: '[T]he breach of the treaty creates an international obligation between state parties to the treaty and no benefits or rights flow directly to the affected individual.'

[59] (Decision of the Tribunal on Objections to Jurisdiction, 17 July 2003) Case No. ARB/01/8, (2003) 42 ILM 788.

[60] *Ibid.* para. 45. The Tribunal cited the ICSID Convention as one such arrangement, but clearly had in mind other treaties dealing with foreign investment as well. The investor was described as the 'beneficiary' of substantive BIT rights in *American Manufacturing and Trading, Inc. v Republic of Zaire*, (Award, 21 February 1997) Case No. ARB/93/1, 5 ICSID Rep 14, para. 6.06. Writers supporting the 'direct' theory, at least in relation to the procedural right of an investor to bring arbitration proceedings against the host state, include: G. Burdeau, above n. 6, 12 *et seq.*; J. Paulsson, above n. 1, 256; T. Wälde, 'Investment Arbitration under the Energy Charter Treaty', above n. 17, 435–7.

[61] *Mavrommatis Palestine Concessions Case* (1924) PCIJ Rep Series A No. 2.

since it was first rationalised by Vattel in the middle of the eighteenth century:

> Anyone who mistreats a citizen directly offends the State. The sovereign of that State must avenge its injury, and if it can, force the aggressor to make full reparation or punish him, since otherwise the citizen would simply not obtain the main goal of civil association, namely, security.[62]

Borchard, in his influential treatise on diplomatic protection in 1913, noted a consistent line of judicial authority supporting Vattel's premise that the rights and obligations of diplomatic protection exist only between sovereign states, and on this basis articulated his own restatement of the principle:

> Diplomatic protection is in its nature an international proceeding, constituting an appeal by nation to nation for the performance of the obligations of the one to the other, growing out of their mutual rights and duties.[63]

It was some years later that the Permanent Court of International Justice made its pronouncement in the *Mavrommatis Palestine Concessions Case*[64] in line with these earlier authorities:

> It is an elementary principle of international law that a State is entitled to protect its subjects, when injured by acts contrary to international law committed by another State, from whom they have been unable to obtain satisfaction through the ordinary channels. By taking up the case of one of its subjects and by resorting to diplomatic action or international judicial proceedings on his behalf, a State is in reality asserting its own rights—its right to ensure, in the person of its subjects, respect for the rules of international law.[65]

The dispute in the *Mavrommatis Palestine Concession Case* originated in the British Government's decision, as Mandatory of Palestine, to grant concessions for the provision of public services which duplicated earlier concessions obtained by a Greek national (Mr Mavrommatis) from the previous ruler of Palestine (the Ottoman Empire). The Permanent Court found that upon the election by the Government of Greece to espouse a diplomatic protection claim to redress the wrong to its national, the dispute became a dispute between the Mandatory (United Kingdom) and a member of the League of Nations, Greece, for the purposes of the dispute resolution provision contained in the British Mandate over Palestine.[66]

The *Mavrommatis* 'formula' was applied in several other cases before the Permanent Court[67] and found its way into the judgments of the

[62] E. de Vattel, *Le droit des gens ou les principes de la loi naturelle* (Vol. I, 1758) 309. The context of Vattel's formulation of diplomatic protection, as an alternative to the private right of reprisal, is explained by R. Lillich, 'The Current Status of the Law of State Responsibility for Injuries to Aliens' in R. Lillich (ed), *International Law of State Responsibility for Injuries to Aliens* (1983) 2–3.

[63] E. Borchard, *The Diplomatic Protection of Citizens Abroad or The Law of International Claims* (1915) 354. See also: J. Brierly, 'Implied State Complicity in International Claims' (1928) 9 *BYBIL* 48.

[64] (1924) PCIJ Rep Series A No. 2. [65] *Ibid.* 12. [66] *Ibid.*

[67] *Panecezys-Saldutiskis Railway Case* (1938) PCIJ Rep Series A/B No 76; *Serbian Loans Case* (1929) PCIJ Rep Series A No. 20; *Chorzów Factory Case* (Indemnity) (Merits) (Jurisdiction), (1928) PCIJ Rep Series A No. 17.

International Court of Justice[68] and several other international tribunals[69] so that its continued validity is beyond doubt.[70] This is not to say that the modalities of diplomatic protection have not come under criticism as out of step with the modern system of international law, which elevates the rights of individuals and private entities to a more prominent place. But deviations from the orthodox position articulated in the *Mavrommatis Palestine Concessions Case* have been few and unpersuasive. García Amador argued that developments in international human rights law have rendered the device whereby a state asserts its own right when it acts on behalf of its national an 'outdated fiction' that should be discarded.[71] O'Connell likewise rejected the *Mavrommatis* formula as 'a survival of the nineteenth-century thesis of a world composed of absolute sovereignties unwilling to limit their sovereign freedom of action except in their own interests'.[72] These critiques may be fair, but far from providing an analytical rationale for rejecting the received orthodoxy in customary international law, they simply anticipate the reason that human rights conventions and investment treaties now overshadow recourse to diplomatic protection. Attempts to equate the traditional institution of diplomatic protection to the new treaty regimes that provide direct rights of recourse are counterproductive because they ultimately undermine the possibility of diplomatic protection assuming even a residual role in the resolution of international disputes.[73]

The notion of a vicarious injury caused to the state of the national is essential to the rationalisation of diplomatic protection because it transforms damage done to private interests into an international delict opposable by one sovereign state to another. This transformation is not a procedural quirk or 'fiction' as is sometimes maintained,[74] but is instead fundamental to the compatibility of diplomatic protection with

[68] *Reparations for Injuries Suffered in the Service of the United Nations Case* (Advisory Opinion), [1949] ICJ Rep 181, '. . . [T]he defendant State has broken an obligation towards the national State in respect of its nationals'; *Nottebohm Case* (Liechtenstein v Guatemala) [1955] ICJ Rep 4; *Barcelona Traction, Light and Power Co. Case* (Belgium v Spain) [1970] ICJ Rep 3.

[69] *Administrative Decision No. V* (USA v Germany), (1924) 7 UN Rep 140 *per* Umpire Parker: '[T]he nation is injured through injury to its national and it alone may demand reparation as no other nation is injured.' See also the cases cited by: C. Amerasinghe, *Local Remedies in International Law* (1990) 57 at note 15; C. Parry, 'Some considerations upon the protection of individuals in international law' (1956) *Hague Recueil* 672, 676–680.

[70] J. Dugard, 'First Report on Diplomatic Protection' (2000) UN Doc A/CN.4/506, paras. 10–32.

[71] F. García Amador, 'State Responsibility. Some New Problems' (Vol. II, 1958) 94 *Hague Recueil* 421, 437–9, 472.

[72] D. O'Connell, *International Law* (Vol. 2, 1970, 2nd edn) 1030.

[73] In her report to the Committee on Diplomatic Protection of Persons and Property of the International Law Association, Kokott raised two possible approaches to the law of diplomatic protection. The first is to 'call for a change of the rules governing diplomatic protection with the aim of meeting the demands of investors.' The second option, which the author endorsed as more 'realistic', is 'to accept that, in the context of foreign investment, the traditional law of diplomatic protection has been to a large extent replaced by a number of treaty-based dispute settlement procedures.' It is submitted that Kokott's conclusion is correct. J. Kokott, 'Interim Report on the Role of Diplomatic Protection in the Field of the Protection of Foreign Investment' in International Law Association, *Report of the Seventieth Conference, New Delhi* (2002) 31.

[74] J. Dugard, 'First Report on Diplomatic Protection', above n. 70, paras. 19–21.

the traditional principles of state responsibility for international wrongs. It would be a mistake, therefore, to postulate that the international law of diplomatic protection could somehow do without this transformation if push came to shove. A state bringing a diplomatic protection claim is not an agent of its national who has a legally protected interest at the international level; the state is rather seeking redress for the breach of an obligation owed to itself.[75]

D. THE INVESTMENT TREATY REGIME AND DIPLOMATIC PROTECTION DISTINGUISHED

In accordance with Article 31 of the Vienna Convention on the Law of Treaties:

> A treaty shall be interpreted in good faith in accordance with the ordinary meaning to be given to the terms of the treaty in their context and in the light of its object and purpose.

Investment treaties do not identify the actual beneficiary of the substantive rights expressly or address the status of treaty tribunals hearing investor/state claims. The stated object and purpose of investment treaties is inconclusive as an interpretive aid to these complex problems, for the general objective of encouraging direct foreign investment is too crude as a guide through the subtle variations on the possible solutions. Finally, given the dearth of *travaux préparatoires* signalling the contracting state parties' intentions during the drafting process,[76] the interpretive focus must necessarily shift to the common intention of the parties that can be discerned from the general architecture of the treaties and the additional evidentiary sources set out in Article 31(3) of the Vienna Convention:

> There shall be taken into account, together with the context:
>
> (a) any subsequent agreement between the parties regarding the interpretation of the treaty or the application of its provisions;
> (b) any subsequent practice in the application of the treaty which establishes the agreement of the parties regarding its interpretation;
> (c) any relevant rules of international law applicable in the relations between the parties.

Of primary importance to the question of the beneficiary of the treaty rights and the status of the treaty tribunal, along with all the other issues

[75] *Contra*: C. de Visscher, 'Cours général de principes de droit international public' (1954 II) 86 *Hague Recueil*, 507, '[Diplomatic protection is] a procedure by which States assert the right of their citizens to a treatment in accordance with international law.'

[76] Article 32 of the Vienna Convention on the Law of Treaties provides: 'Recourse may be had to supplementary means of interpretation, including the preparatory work of the treaty and the circumstances of its conclusion, in order to confirm the meaning resulting from the application of article 31, or to determine the meaning when the interpretation according to article 31: (a) leaves the meaning ambiguous or obscure; or (b) leads to a result which is manifestly absurd or unreasonable.'

to be examined in this study, is subsequent practice in the application of the treaty.[77] This practice across a network of similar investment treaties, manifest in arbitral awards, municipal court decisions, and the parties' pleadings in investor/state cases, is generating an uncodified set of rules for resolving problems such as the admissibility of claims and conflicts of jurisdiction. In this sense, the field of subsequent practice for the interpretation of a specific treaty needs to be cast wider than envisaged by Article 31 of the Vienna Convention, limited as it is to subsequent practice between the actual contracting state parties. The reality is that a treaty tribunal will be influenced significantly, sometimes decisively, by that wider practice in resolving interpretative difficulties. In relation to the two other sources mentioned in Article 31(3), applicable rules of international law must also play a major part in resolving these issues. There have been instances of subsequent agreements between the state parties concerning the interpretation of investment treaties, the notorious example being the Free Trade Commission's 'interpretation' of Article 1105 of the NAFTA,[78] however none to date deal directly with the problems under consideration.

In deciding between the competing 'derivative' and 'direct' theories, the starting point must be that international legal theory allows for both possibilities. There is no impediment to states in effect delegating their procedural right to bring a diplomatic protection type claim to enforce substantive rights of the states concerned within a special treaty framework. On the other hand, there is also no reason why an international treaty cannot create rights for individuals and private entities, whether or not such rights fall to be classified as 'human rights', as confirmed by the International Court of Justice in the *LaGrand Case*.[79]

The following analysis of the practice of investment treaty arbitration suggests that investment treaties do not give legislative effect to the 'derivative' model based on the *Mavrommatis* formula for the presentation of international claims against a sovereign state, but rather encapsulate a 'direct model'.

[77] See G. Fitzmaurice, 'The Law and Procedure of the International Court of Justice 1951–4: Treaty Interpretation and Certain Other Treaty Points' (1957) 33 *BYBIL* 203, 223–5, who recommends subsequent practice as the most reliable interpretative tool.

[78] NAFTA, Free Trade Commission, Interpretation, 31 July 2001, reprinted at: 6 ICSID Rep 567. The Netherlands and the Czech Republic also issued a joint interpretation of their BIT in accordance with Art. 9 thereof in the 'Agreed Minutes' dated 1 July 2002. See *CME Czech Republic B. V. (The Netherlands) v The Czech Republic*, (Final Award, 14 March 2003), paras. 87–93, available at <http://www.cetvnet.com/ne/articlefiles/439-Final_Award_Quantum.pdf>.

[79] (Germany v US) (judgment on Merits, 27 June 2001), (2001) 40 ILM 1069, paras. 77–8. The Court reasoned: 'At the hearings, Germany further contended that the right of the individual to be informed without delay under Article 36, paragraph 1, of the Vienna Convention was not only an individual right, but has today assumed the character of a human right. In consequence, Germany added, "the character of the right under Article 36 as a human right renders the effectiveness of this provision even more imperative". The Court having found that the United States violated the rights accorded by Article 36, paragraph 1, to the LaGrand brothers, it does not appear necessary to it to consider the additional argument developed by Germany in this regard.' *Ibid.* para. 78.

(1) Functional control of the claim

In the context of diplomatic protection, the state of the injured national has full discretion as to whether to take up the claim on behalf of its injured national at all.[80] It may waive, compromise, or discontinue the presentation of the claim irrespective of the wishes of the injured national.[81] In exercising this discretion, the state often gives paramount consideration to the wider ramifications of the espousal of a diplomatic protection claim so far as it concerns the conduct of its foreign policy vis-à-vis the host state.[82] If the state does elect to pursue such a claim then it is master of the claim in the sense that it is not obliged to consult with its national on the conduct of the proceedings. If liability is established then damages are awarded to the state and not to the national, and there is no international rule to compel any form of distribution of the monetary award to the *de cujus*.[83] Moreover, the national state is entitled to compromise the award of full compensatory damages by settling the claim for a reduced amount with the host state. It may enter into a general lump sum agreement for the partial compensation of multiple claims.[84] It may abandon the claim entirely, in effect waiving the right in question.

The International Court of Justice gave a stark appraisal of these features of a diplomatic protection claim in the *Barcelona Traction Case*:[85]

> . . . within the limits prescribed by international law, a State may exercise diplomatic protection by whatever means and to whatever extent it thinks fit, for it is its own right that the State is asserting . . .
>
> The State must be viewed as the sole judge to decide whether its protection will be granted, to what extent it is granted, and when it will cease. It retains in this respect a discretionary power the exercise of which may be determined by considerations of a political or other nature, unrelated to the particular case.[86]

The situation with an investment treaty claim is very different. In pursuing its own claim, the investor is under no obligation to inform its national state of the existence of proceedings against the host state, nor to consult with the state on the substantive and procedural issues that arise in the proceedings. The investor is guided in the prosecution of its claim solely by the dictates of self-interest without necessary regard for any consequences to the diplomatic relationship between its national

[80] See the state practice on the regulation of this discretion under municipal law: J. Dugard, 'First Report on Diplomatic Protection', above n. 70, paras. 80–7. [81] E. Borchard, above n. 63, 366.

[82] *Barcelona Traction, Light and Power Co. Case* (Belgium v Spain) [1970] ICJ Rep 44, paras. 78–79; G. Berlia, 'Contribution à l'étude de la nature de la protection diplomatique' (1957) *Annuaire français de droit international* 63; A. Lowenfeld, 'Diplomatic Intervention in Investment Disputes' (1967) 61 *American Society Int Law Proceedings* 97.

[83] *Administrative Decision No. V* (USA v Germany) (1924) 7 UN Rep 119, 152–3. See also the precedents cited by: C. Amerasinghe, above n. 69, 60 at note 24. The same rule applies in relation to lump sum agreements; see: D. Bederman, 'Interim Report on Lump Sum Agreements and Diplomatic Protection' in International Law Association, *Report of the Seventieth Conference, New Delhi* (2002) 7.

[84] M. Bennouna, 'Preliminary Report on Diplomatic Protection' (1998) UN Doc A/CN.4/484, para. 20; [85] *Barcelona Traction, Light and Power Co. Case* (Belgium v Spain) [1970] ICJ Rep 3.

[86] *Ibid.* paras. 78–79.

state and the host state. The financial burden of presenting an investment treaty claim falls exclusively on the investor. Damages recovered in the award are to the account of the investor and the national state has no legal interest in the compensation fixed by the arbitral tribunal.

Although by no means conclusive, one would expect that if the investor was merely stepping into the shoes of its national state to enforce that state's treaty rights, the national state would retain a residual interest in the investment treaty arbitration. The precedent of the American-Turkish Claims Commission is instructive on this point. Many claims were dismissed summarily by the Commission because they were presented directly by counsel retained by the injured nationals. This was found to be incompatible with the diplomatic protection model incorporated into the American-Turkish Claims Settlement of 1937:

> It would, of course, be monstrous to suggest that a government would through some subterfuge pretend to support a claim without having any knowledge of what, if anything, had in some way come before the Commission.[87]

The conclusion must be that, in the absence of some specific provision in the BIT, the national state of the investor retains no interest in an investment treaty arbitration instituted against another contracting state. It would no doubt be open to states to regulate their nationals' conduct of arbitration proceedings under investment treaties, *eg*, by imposing an obligation to keep the relevant government ministry informed of the existence and progress of such arbitrations. Such a development is not reflected in BIT practice and this is consistent with the perception that an investor is invoking its own right in instituting an investment treaty arbitration.

This conclusion is reinforced by the instances when the national state of the investor has actually *opposed* the investor's claim before a treaty tribunal. In the NAFTA case of *GAMI Inc. v United States of Mexico*,[88] the national state of the investor, the United States of America, intervened pursuant to Article 1128 to contend that the Tribunal had no jurisdiction to hear GAMI's claim.[89] Likewise, in *Mondev International Ltd v United States of America*,[90] Canada (the national state of Mondev) made submissions to the Tribunal, which, without claiming to address the specific facts, tended to the conclusion that Mondev's claims should be dismissed on the merits.[91] This practice contradicts the view that investors are bringing derivative claims on behalf of their own national state. There may be no community of interest between them in the prosecution of investment treaty arbitrations; indeed their interests may be adverse.

[87] J. Moore, *A Digest of International Law* (1906) 616.

[88] Ongoing NAFTA arbitration under the UNCITRAL Arbitration Rules.

[89] See Submission of the United States of America, 30 June 2003, available at <http://www.state.gov/documents/organization/22212.pdf>.

[90] (Award, 11 October 2002) Case No. ARB(AF)/99/2, 7 ICSID Rep 192.

[91] See Second Submission of Canada Pursuant to NAFTA Art. 1128, 6 July 2001, available at <http://www.state.gov/documents/organization/18271.pdf>.

(2) The nationality of claims rule

The nationality of claims rule in diplomatic protection prescribes that the injured national must have the nationality of the claimant state at the time of injury through to when notice of the claim is presented or the date of the award or judgment.[92]

The doctrine of continuous nationality developed in response to the frictions caused by individuals shifting allegiances to powerful states for the purposes of espousing a diplomatic protection claim.[93] This concern is obviously not applicable to investment treaty arbitration because the procedural right of recourse vests directly in the investor and remains with that investor; hence there is less to be gained by the investor in contriving to 'swap' investment treaties with a change of nationality.[94] One would not necessarily expect, therefore, identity in the tests for nationality in the context of diplomatic protection claims in customary international law and claims advanced pursuant to investment treaties.

In relation to natural persons, the International Court of Justice in the *Nottebohm Case*[95] imposed a requirement for the admissibility of diplomatic protection claims that there must be an 'effective' or 'genuine link' between the individual who has suffered the injury and the national state prosecuting the claim. The Court thereby rejected the conferral of nationality under municipal law as definitive for this purpose.[96] The Court was concerned to ensure that only one state could have standing to bring a diplomatic protection claim on the basis that the individual 'is in fact more closely connected with the population of the State conferring nationality than with that of any other State.'[97]

The International Court in the *Barcelona Traction Case*[98] did not follow the *Nottebohm Case* with respect to corporations and declined to adopt a 'genuine link' criterion for identifying the national state eligible to bring a diplomatic protection claim on behalf of the corporation.[99] Instead the

[92] One of the major controversies in *Loewen* was whether the doctrine of continuous nationality only required the relevant nationality at the time of the presentation of the claim or through to the date of the award. The authorities are divided on this issue. The 'limited' requirement is favoured by: D. O'Connell, above n. 72, 1033; J. Dugard, 'Fourth Report on Diplomatic Protection' (2003) UN Doc A/CN.4/530, para. 93 (Draft Art. 20). The majority of lump sum agreements favour the test of nationality at the date of claim accrual, see: D. Bederman, above n. 83, 10. A majority of writers nevertheless appear to support the more 'expansive requirement': E. Borchard, 'The Protection of Citizens Abroad and Change of Original Nationality' (1933–4) 43 *Yale LJ* 359, 372; Sohn & Baxter, Harvard Draft Convention, Art. 22(8) at 186–7; *Oppenheim's International Law* (Vol. I, 1992, 9th edn by R. Jennings & A. Watts) 512–3; I. Brownlie, *Principles of Public International Law* (2003, 6th edn) 460.

[93] E. Borchard, *ibid.* 377–80.

[94] This is not to deny that the substantive provisions on the minimum standards of investment protection do differ from one investment treaty to the next.

[95] [1955] ICJ Rep 4.

[96] *Ibid.* 23.

[97] *Ibid.*

[98] [1970] ICJ Rep 3.

[99] *Ibid.* 42, para. 70. The ICJ did, nevertheless, determine *in casu* that there was 'a close and permanent' link between Barcelona Traction and Canada as it had its registered office there with its accounts, share registers and listing with the Canadian tax authorities and board meetings had been held in Canada for many years. *Ibid.* para. 71. Brownlie has argued that the authority of the Court's rejection of the *Nottebohm* principle is diluted considerably by, *inter alia*, the fact that the Court did set out the 'manifold' links of the company with Canada: I. Brownlie, above n. 92, 467. See further:

Court relied on a 'place of incorporation' test[100] that achieved the same objective of channelling the interests of an aggrieved foreign entity into a single rubric of nationality for the purposes of a diplomatic protection claim. The Court therefore ruled that Canada, as the state of incorporation of Belgium Traction Co., would have had standing against Spain for the latter's alleged expropriatory acts vis-à-vis the company; however, a claim by Belgium, whose nationals owned 88 percent of the shares in Barcelona Traction Co., was held to be inadmissible.

The *Barcelona Traction Case* has been criticised because, in practice, states will not exercise diplomatic protection merely on the basis of incorporation. In deciding whether or not to take up claims based on the corporate interests of their nationals, states are naturally preoccupied with the extent to which their own economy has been affected by the alleged violation of the host state.[101] Thus it is common for states to insist that the corporate interest comprises a dominant shareholding or beneficial ownership or a connection based on the *siège social* of the company.[102] By failing to recognise this state practice, the International Court's stipulation of a 'place of incorporation' test has been described as 'unworkable'.[103]

It is notable that the majority of investment treaties concluded after the *Barcelona Traction Case* adopt the test of mere incorporation,[104] thereby refuting the national state's interest that is recognised by the requirement that the corporation in question has significant connections to that state in order to qualify as a 'national' for the purposes of the dispute resolution mechanism. Investment treaties do not usually require a 'genuine link' between the individual investor or corporate entity and the national state.[105] The ease in which the formal requirement of incorporation can

A. Watts, 'Nationality of Claims: Some Relevant Concepts' in V. Lowe & M. Fitzmaurice (eds), *Fifty Years of the International Court of Justice. Essays in Honour of Sir Robert Jennings* (1996) 424.

[100] [1970] ICJ Rep 42, para. 70.

[101] In a separate opinion to the ICJ's judgment in the *Barcelona Traction Case*, Judge Gros criticised the Court's reliance on the place of incorporation test for the very reason that it failed to take into account the economic realities behind a state's interest in pursuing a diplomatic protection claim. Judge Gross stated that: 'The company's link of bare nationality may not reflect any substantial economic bond . . . [I]t is the State whose national economy is in fact adversely affected that possesses the right to take legal action.' *Ibid.* 279.

[102] See, *eg*, the official commentary to Rule IV of the applicable rules for the United Kingdom: 'In determining whether to exercise its right of protection, Her Majesty's Government may consider whether the company has in fact a real and substantial connection with the United Kingdom.' Reproduced at: (1988) 37 *ICLQ* 1006, 1007.

[103] S. Metzger, 'Nationality of Corporate Investment under Investment Guarantee Schemes—The Relevance of Barcelona Traction' (1971) 65 *AJIL* 532, 541.

[104] Energy Charter Treaty, Art. 1(7); UK Model BIT, Art. 1(d), *UNCTAD Compendium* (Vol, III, 1998) 186; Egypt Model BIT, Art. 2(b), *ibid.* (Vol. V, 2000) 294; Indonesia Model BIT, Art. 1(2)(ii), *ibid.* 310; Malaysia Model BIT, Art. 1(b)(ii), *ibid.* 326; Netherlands Model BIT, Art. 1(b)(iii), *ibid.* 334; Cambodia Model BIT, Art. 1(2)(ii), *ibid.* (Vol. VI, 2002) 464; Peru Model BIT, Art. 1, *ibid.* 494; United States Model BIT, Art. 1, *ibid.* 501; Austria Model BIT, Art. 1, *ibid.* (Vol. VII) 259; Belgo-Luxemburg Economic Union Model BIT, Art. 1, *ibid.* 271; Denmark Model BIT, Art. 1(5)(b), *ibid.* 280; Finland Model BIT, Art. 1(3)(b), *ibid.* 288; South Africa Model BIT, Art. 1, *ibid.* (Vol. VIII) 274; Maurice Model BIT, Art. 1(1), *ibid.* (Vol. IX) 296; Sweden Model BIT, Art. 1(2), *ibid.* 310.

[105] There are examples of BITs that require incorporation in the host state *and* the presence of the company's 'siége' or 'seat' or 'headquarters' in the host state as well, inspired by French Civil Law.

be discharged has led to the growing practice of establishing investment vehicles in a jurisdiction which is 'covered' by an investment treaty with the host state of the investment. These investment vehicles may be corporate shells in a tax friendly jurisdiction that are bound to transfer any commercial returns from the investment enterprise to the parent company in a different jurisdiction. The national state of the investor does not, in such circumstances, have a strong interest in the investment treaty claim of such an entity.

State parties to investment treaties have, furthermore, left the door wide open for claims relating to a single loss by investors with multiple nationalities. For instance, investment treaties sometimes define an investment as the ownership of *either* a company incorporated in the host state or the shares in such a company.[106] This exposes states to claims by different national investors under different investment treaties with either type of legal interest in the same underlying investment.

This possibility of competing claims over the same investment was considered in *CMS Gas Transmission Company v The Republic of Argentina*.[107] The claimant, CMS, had a 29.42 percent stake in a local Argentinean company, Transportadora de Gas del Norte ('TGN'), which had obtained a licence for the transportation of gas.[108] CMS alleged that measures adopted by the Government of Argentina following the financial crisis in 1999, and in particular a law that brought an end to the parity of the Argentine peso with the US dollar, had adversely affected its investment in TGN in breach of the Argentina/US BIT.[109] Argentina contested CMS's standing to bring this claim by relying on the *Barcelona Traction Case* for the proposition that a foreign shareholder cannot bring a derivative claim for damage suffered by a local company.[110] In the words of the International Court, 'although two separate entities may have

Thus, in the France Model BIT, Art. 1(3) reads: 'Le terme de 'sociétés' désigne toute personne morale constituée sur le territoire de l'une des Parties contractantes, conformément à la législation de celle-ci et y possédant son siège social, ou contrôlée directement ou indirectement par des nationaux de l'une de Parties contractantes, ou par des personnes morales possédant leur siège social sur le territoire de l'une des Parties contractantes et constituées conformément à la législation de celle-ci.' *UNCTAD Compendium* (Vol. V, 2000) 302. See also: China Model BIT, Art. 1(2), 'domiciled', *ibid.* 152; Jamaica Model BIT, Art. 1(3)(b), *ibid.* 318; Iran Model BIT, Art. 1(2)(b), *ibid.* (Vol. VI, 2002) 280; Germany Model BIT, Art. 1(3)(a), *ibid.* (Vol. VII) 298; Turkey Model BIT, Art. 1(1), *ibid.* (Vol. VIII) 281; Benin Model BIT, Art. 1(2), *ibid.* (Vol. IX) 280; Burundi Model BIT, Art. 1(1), *ibid.* 287. There are also some exceptional cases of BITs that, in addition to these two requirements, also demand that the company performs 'real business activity' in the host state: Chile Model BIT, Art. 1(1)(b), seat and 'effective economic activities', *ibid.* (Vol. III, 1998) 144; Switzerland Model BIT, Art. 1(1)(b), seat and 'real economic activities', *ibid.* 177; Sri Lanka Model BIT, Art. 1(2)(b), seat and 'substantial business activities', *ibid.* (Vol. V, 2000) 340; Croatia Model BIT, Art. 1(2)(b), *ibid.* (Vol. VI) 472; Mongolia Model BIT, Art. 1(1)(b), *ibid.* (Vol. IX) 303.

[106] US Model BIT, Art. 1(d), *UNCTAD Compendium* (Vol. VI, 2002) 502; Austria Model BIT, Art. 1(2), *ibid.* (Vol. VII) 259; Denmark Model BIT, Art. 1(1)(b), *ibid.* 283; Sweden Model BIT, Art. 1(b), *ibid.* (Vol. IX) 309; Energy Charter Treaty, Art. 1(6)(b); NAFTA, Art. 1139. See further: UNCTAD, *Series on Issues in International Investment Agreements: Scope and Definition* (1999) 10.

[107] (Decision of the Tribunal on Objections to Jurisdiction, 17 July 2003) Case No. ARB/01/8, (2003) 42 ILM 788.

[108] *Ibid.* para. 19.

[109] *Ibid.* para. 20.

[110] *Ibid.* para. 43.

suffered from the same wrong, it is only one entity whose rights have been infringed.'[111] The ICSID Tribunal rejected this analysis and found that, in the absence of any impediment under international law[112] or the ICSID Convention, the fact that CMS's interest in TGN fell within the definition of an 'investment' for the purposes of the BIT was sufficient to confer *jus standi* upon the Claimant in relation to its cause of action.[113] Although recognising that its finding might open the door to investors of different nationalities bringing claims under different treaties in relation to damages suffered by a single company, the ICSID Tribunal stated that '[. . .] it is not possible to foreclose rights that different investors might have under different arrangements.'[114]

Another potential source of overlapping national claims over the same underlying investment is the acceptance of an 'indirect' interest in an investment as sufficient to qualify for investment protection.[115] Thus, in *CME Czech Republic B.V. (The Netherlands) v Czech Republic*[116] ('CME') and *Ronald S. Lauder v Czech Republic*[117] ('Lauder'), two UNCITRAL tribunals established pursuant to different BITs considered the conduct of the same executive organ of the Czech Republic in relation to the same investment and came to quite different results on liability. The existence of these two proceedings was possible because the *CME* Tribunal recognised CME's 99 percent shareholding in a local Czech company with rights to operate a television licence as an investment for the purposes of the Netherlands/Czech Republic BIT,[118] whereas the *Lauder* Tribunal

[111] [1970] ICJ Rep 35, para. 44.

[112] The Tribunal referred to 'contemporary' state practice, as evidenced by lump sum agreements, the Iran/US Claims Tribunal and the United Nations Compensation Commission, and stated that '[it] finds no bar in current international law to the concept of allowing claims by shareholders independently from those of the corporation concerned, not even if those shareholders are minority or non-controlling shareholders.' (Decision of the Tribunal on Objections to Jurisdiction, 17 July 2003) Case No. ARB/01/8, (2003) 42 ILM 788, paras. 47–8. This pronouncement is controversial, because it is doubtful whether one can extract general principles of customary international law from the *sui generis* arrangements cited by the Tribunal. In any event, it was unnecessary for the Tribunal to make an affirmative ruling upon the state of general international law because the cause of action was based on the BIT. Its later comment in relation to the *jus standi* of minority shareholders is thus more measured: 'To the extent that customary international law or generally the traditional law of international claims might have followed a different approach—a proposition that is open to debate—then that approach can be considered the exception.' *Ibid.* para. 48.

[113] *Ibid.* para. 65.

[114] *Ibid.* para. 86. The *CMS Gas Transmission Company v The Republic of Argentina* decision was cited with approval in *Azurix Corp. v The Argentine Republic* (Decision on Jurisdiction, 8 December 2003) Case No. ARB/01/12, (2004) ILM 262, paras. 64, 73.

[115] The most 'indirect' investment to date, in terms of corporate layers between the claimant investor and the covered investment, was perhaps that which was recognised in *Azurix Corp. v The Argentine Republic, ibid.* Here, a local investment vehicle registered in Argentina 'Z' had concessionary rights to provide sewerage services in an Argentine Province. Z was in turn owned by two other Argentine companies, 'X' and 'Y'. The Claimant (a Delaware company qualifying under the Argentina/US BIT) ultimately owned and controlled X through another Argentine company, and Y through two levels of Cayman Island companies.

[116] (Partial Award, 13 September 2001) available at <http://www.cetv-net.com/ne/articlefiles/439-cme-cr_eng.pdf>, hereinafter 'CME Partial Award'.

[117] (Final Award, 3 September 2001) available at: <http://www.cetv-net.com/ne/articlefiles/439-lauder-cr_eng.pdf>, hereinafter 'Lauder Final Award'.

[118] *CME* Partial Award, para. 376.

deemed that Mr Lauder's (a US citizen) shareholding in the parent company of CME fell within the definition of an investment under the US/Czech Republic BIT.[119] This illustrates the point that, unlike the nationality of claims rule for diplomatic protection, the investment treaty regime is not overly concerned with the task of channelling the various interests of private entities arising from unlawful conduct attributable to a state into a single rubric of nationality with a single claimant state representing the affected interests.

Contrary to these precedents evidencing a less prominent concern with the nationality of claims, the ICSID Tribunal's decision on admissibility in the NAFTA case of *Loewen* points the other way. In the absence of a specific provision of NAFTA dealing with the temporal requirements for the nationality of claims, the Tribunal imported what it took to be the rule of customary international law requiring continuous nationality from the date of the events giving rise to the claim through the date of the award, and applied it strictly.[120] The claimant company, Loewen, was incorporated in Canada at the time of the events giving rise to the claim, but had subsequently reorganised as a US corporation after notice of the claim had been filed; it assigned its NAFTA claim to a Canadian company established for the sole purpose of retaining legal title to the claim.[121] The Tribunal attached primary significance to the fact that the beneficiary of the claim (in the sense of the ultimate recipient of a damages award) would be the reorganised US company and thus the Canadian special purpose vehicle could not 'qualify as a continuing national for the purposes of this proceeding'.[122]

The Tribunal in *Loewen* recognised that other international treaties had made special provision for the 'amelioration of the strict requirement of continuous nationality',[123] such as the Algiers Accord establishing the Iran/US Claims Tribunal and several BITs. Furthermore, the ICSID Convention, which governs the procedure of many investment treaty arbitrations upon an election of this option by the investor as permitted by the relevant BIT, expressly provides that the nationality requirement is to be tested at the time the notice of claim is filed.[124] And yet, in

[119] *Lauder* Award, para. 154. For discussion on this provision, see: P. Muchlinski, above n. 23, 623.

[120] This was highly controversial. See n. 92 above.

[121] *Loewen* Award, para. 220.

[122] *Ibid.* para. 237.

[123] *Ibid.* para. 229.

[124] Article 25(2)(b) of the ICSID Convention defines a 'National of another Contracting State' as 'any juridical person which had the nationality of a Contracting State other than the State party to the dispute on the date on which the parties consented to submit such dispute to conciliation or arbitration . . .' *In Ceskoslovenska Obchodni Banka, A.S. v The Slovak Republic* (Decision on Objections to Jurisdiction, 24 May 1999) Case No. ARB/97/4, 5 ICSID Rep 300, paras. 31–2, the date-of-submission rule was upheld to dismiss the relevance of the Respondent's objection to the Claimant's standing due to the latter's assignment of the rights to the subject matter of the dispute. See also: *Société Ouest Africaine des Bétons Industriels [SOABI] v State of Senegal* (Decision on Jurisdiction, 1 August 1984) 2 ICSID Rep 175, para. 29; *Banro American Resources, Inc. and Société Aurifère du Kivu et du Maniema SARL v Democratic Republic of the Congo* (Award, 1 September 2000) Case No. ARB/98/7, 17 ICSID Rev—Foreign Investment LJ 3. See further: C. Amerasinghe, 'The International Centre for Settlement of Investment Disputes and Development Through the Multinational Corporation' (1976) 9 *Vanderbilt J of Transnational L* 793, 809–10, '[T]he relevant time for the fulfilment of the nationality requirement is that date when the consent to jurisdiction is

the absence of a specific provision in Chapter Eleven of NAFTA, the *Loewen* Tribunal saw no reason to depart from what it perceived to be a strict rule of customary international law requiring continuous nationality.[125] Most significantly, the Tribunal implicitly rejected the argument advanced by Sir Robert Jennings as expert witness testifying on behalf of Loewen that 'the rule of the nationality of claims was never a free-standing general rule of international law; it was a concomitant, and of the very essence, of diplomatic protection.'[126]

(3) *Forum selection clauses*

An exclusive jurisdiction clause in favour of the municipal courts of the host state in an investment agreement between a foreign investor and the host state cannot prejudice the standing of the national state of the investor to bring a diplomatic protection claim against the host state. The right to bring a diplomatic protection claim vests in the national state of the investor and hence no agreement concluded by the investor can encumber this right.[127] By parity of reasoning, the foreign investor's acceptance of a 'Calvo Clause' in the investment agreement that purports to effect an express waiver of any potential diplomatic protection claim is also ineffective to diminish the right of the national state of the investor to seek redress on this basis.[128] At most, the investor's consent to a Calvo Clause raises a presumption in diplomatic protection proceedings that the rule on the exhaustion of local remedies should be applied strictly.[129]

The limited effect given by international tribunals to a Calvo Clause is naturally predicated upon the national state's own interest and right in pursuing a diplomatic protection claim to enforce the minimum standards for the protection of aliens in customary international law.[130] The status of forum selection clauses in investment agreements between the investor and host state on the jurisdiction of an international treaty tribunal is a controversial subject that will be dealt with in detail in Part VII. Less controversial, however, is the possibility that an investor can waive its

effective for both parties. It also means that any change in the nationality of a juridical person after that date is immaterial for the purposes of ICSID's jurisdiction, regardless of how inappropriate such an alignment would have been initially.' *Contra*: G. Delaume, 'Le Centre International pour le Règlement des Différends Relatifs aux Investissements (CIRDI)' (1982) 109 *Journal du droit international* 797.

[125] *Loewen* Award, paras. 220–40. Referring to the specific rule in Art. 25(2)(b) of the ICSID Convention, Loewen argued that the standing requirements of NAFTA Ch. 11 should be the same regardless of whether a claimant proceeds under the ICSID Convention (currently not possible because neither Mexico or Canada are signatories), the ICSID Additional Facility Rules or the UNCITRAL Arbitration Rules. This contention was rejected by the Tribunal. *Ibid.* para. 235.

[126] Fifth Opinion of Sir Robert Jennings, cited at Counter-Memorial of the Loewen Group, Inc. on Matters of Jurisdiction and Competence (29 March 2002) para. 69, available at <http://www.state.gov/documents/organization/9360.pdf>.

[127] E. Borchard, above n. 63, 372, 799.

[128] *North American Dredging Co. Case* (USA v Mexico), (1926) 4 UN Rep 26, 29; D. Shea, *The Calvo Clause* (1955) 217; D. O'Connell, above n. 72, 1061; *Oppenheim's International Law*, above n. 92, 930–1; K. Lipstein, 'The Place of the Calvo Clause in International Law' (1945) 22 *BYBIL* 130, 139 and cases cited at note 4; E. Borchard, *ibid.* 809–10.

[129] D. O'Connell, *ibid.* 1062.

[130] C. Amerasinghe, *State Responsibility for Injuries to Aliens* (1967) 60.

procedural right to have its treaty claims heard by an international arbitral tribunal by instituting proceedings with respect to those claims before a municipal court of the host state. This is the effect of the so called 'fork in the road' provision in many BITs, which affords the investor the option of selecting between several different judicial *fora* in the presentation of its claims based on the minimum standards of protection in the treaty.[131] By choosing to litigate in a municipal court, for instance, the investor takes a positive step down one of the paths leading from this junction with no right of return. This does not exclude the possibility that a new claim for denial of justice may ripen if the investor is denied a minimum standard of procedural fairness before the municipal court. In this instance, the investor would simply return to the same fork in the road but now in a different vehicle (perhaps relying on a breach of the fair and equitable standard of treatment to ground its cause of action for a denial of justice), and this time would predictably select the path to a hearing before an international arbitral tribunal. The point is, however, that upon the initial election by the investor to institute proceedings before a municipal court, there is no residual interest in the claim as pleaded that survives on an international level for the national state.[132] If the primary obligations in the investment treaty regime were owed to the national state rather than to the investor, this would be a curious result.

(4) *The applicable procedural law*

The law applicable to questions of procedure in arbitrations between sovereign states is generally public international law.[133] This is certainly the case for a diplomatic protection claim submitted to arbitration by a special agreement or *compromis*.[134] It is possible to assert more generally that public international law always governs arbitrations or other judicial proceedings involving two states when the cause of action is based on rights under an international treaty or customary international law. As will be considered further in Part V, this principle is likely to have its roots in the immunity of foreign states from the jurisdiction of national courts insofar as an arbitration governed by public international law remains outside the legal order of the state that provides the territorial seat of the arbitration.

Investment treaty arbitrations, in contrast, are ultimately governed by the *lex loci arbitri*, *viz*. the municipal law of the seat of the arbitration.[135] This is also a principle of general application but subject to the exceptional instance of investment treaty arbitrations conducted under the ICSID Convention, where the procedural rules set out in the

[131] See Part VII(G) below.

[132] Furthermore, if the treaty obligation is owed directly to the national state of the investor, the investor should not be able to compromise its national state's corresponding right by a forum selection in the first place.

[133] J. Simpson & H. Fox, above n. 53, 128–30; F. Mann, 'State Contracts and International Arbitration' (1967) 42 *BYBIL* 1, 2.

[134] F. Mann, *ibid*.

[135] See Part V(E) below.

Convention govern the conduct of the arbitration to the exclusion of any municipal law.[136]

If an investor was in essence bringing a claim on behalf of its national state, the logical consequence would be that public international law would govern the arbitration by default as the rights of two states under an international treaty would be the *ratione materiae* of the dispute. Put differently, if the chose in action belonged to the national state of the investor, the municipal courts at the seat of the arbitration arguably could not sit in judgment in respect to a challenge to the validity of the treaty tribunal's award. Hence the general application of the municipal law of the seat of the arbitration to investment treaty arbitrations once again refutes the derivative theory for investment treaty claims.

(5) *The exhaustion of local remedies*

The defendant state has the primary interest in compliance with the rule that the injured national must exhaust local remedies available in the host state before a diplomatic protection claim is made on its behalf.[137] This interest was described by the International Court of Justice in the *Interhandel Case*[138] in the following terms:

> Before resort may be made to an international court in such a situation, it has been considered necessary that the State where the violation occurred should have an opportunity to redress it by its own means, within the framework of its own domestic legal system.[139]

The local remedies rule is thus a concession to the sovereign independence of the host state, which must be presumed in the first instance to be capable of rendering justice by its own courts.[140] It also gives effect to the principle that foreign nationals or entities going abroad are subject to the municipal law of the host state and the means of redress available under this law for any injury to their person or property.[141]

[136] The ICSID Convention creates, according to Broches, 'a complete, exclusive and closed jurisdictional system, insulated from national law'. A. Broches, 'Awards Rendered Pursuant to the ICSID Convention: Binding Force, Finality, Recognition, Enforcement, Execution' (1987) 2 ICSID Rev—*Foreign Investment LJ* 287, 288. *Concord*: I. Shihata & A. Parra, 'Applicable Substantive Law in Disputes Between States and Private Foreign Parties: The Case of Arbitration under the ICSID Convention' (1994) 9 *ICSID Rev—Foreign Investment LJ* 183, 186; A. Parra, 'Provisions on the Settlement of Investment Disputes in Modern Investment Laws, Bilateral Investment Treaties and Multilateral Instruments on Investment' (1997) 12 *ICSID Rev—Foreign Investment LJ* 287, 301. This 'insulation' from national law is achieved as follows. Article 44 of the ICSID Convention, which exhaustively prescribes the sources of procedural rules for ICSID arbitration, makes no reference to domestic law. Article 53 excludes any remedies in relation to ICSID awards save those speficied in Arts. 50–2. The exclusivity of these remedies was confirmed by the French *Cour de cassation: Guinea v Atlantic Triton Co.*, Cass Civ 1re, 11 June 1991 (1991) 118 *Journal du droit international* 1005. Article 54 obliges Contracting States to recognise and enforce ICSID awards. The execution of ICSID awards is, however, governed by national law at the place of execution pursuant to Art. 54(3).

[137] C. Amerasinghe, above n. 69, 69–72.

[138] (Switzerland v USA) [1956] ICJ Rep 6.

[139] *Ibid*. 27.

[140] C. Amerasinghe, above n. 69, 71, citing C. de Visscher, 'Denial of Justice in International Law' (1935) 52 *Hague Recueil* 422; *Ambatielos Claim* (Greece v United Kingdom), (1956) 12 UN Rep 119.

[141] E. Borchard, above n. 63, 817–8.

Several commentators have latched onto the local remedies rule as evidence that diplomatic protection obligations are owed to the individual rather than the national state. If the rights of the national state were infringed directly, then its remedy could not, as the argument goes, be conditional upon exhaustion of local remedies by the individual.[142] But this contention ignores the reality that the national state also has a strong interest in the observance of the local remedies rule itself because it acts as a 'sieve' to prevent any grievance of its national from being transformed into an international dispute with the host state.[143] States are often vigilant about insisting on the observance of the rule by their own nationals to limit the burden of international litigation as far as possible and the concomitant political ramifications on the bilateral relationship with the host state concerned.

In the absence of a specific provision in the investment treaty,[144] investment tribunals have uniformly dispensed with the local remedies rule as a procedural impediment to proceedings before an international arbitral tribunal otherwise with jurisdiction over the investor's claims.[145] This conclusion is without prejudice to the situation where the host state's conduct only attains the requisite threshold for a breach of a treaty standard upon a denial of justice in the judicial system of the host state. In this sense, the local remedies rule is a *substantive* requirement for liability rather than a *procedural* precondition for the presentation of claims to an international court or tribunal.[146] By dispensing with the local remedies rule as a procedural requirement for the investor's treaty claims, the contracting states have also abandoned their interests that are protected by the rule. If they had a legal interest at stake in an investment treaty claim then this would be a surprising concession.

(6) *The assessment of damages*

Whilst it is true that damages are most often assessed on the basis of the loss suffered by the national in a diplomatic protection claim, other considerations can play a part such as the nature of the international obligation that has been breached. The Permanent Court of International Justice stated the position succinctly in the *Chorzów Factory Case*:[147]

The reparation due by one State to another does not however change its character by reason of the fact that it takes the form of an indemnity for the calculation of

[142] D. O'Connell, above n. 72, 1031.

[143] A. McNair, *International Law Opinions* (Vol. 2, 1956) 197; C. Amerasinghe, above n. 69, 68.

[144] A provision requiring the exhaustion of local remedies in the Argentina/Spain BIT was considered in *Maffezini v Kingdom of Spain* (Decision on Objections to Jurisdiction, 25 January 2000) Case No. ARB/97/7, 5 ICSID Rep 396.

[145] See the arbitral awards cited below at n.195.

[146] The debate as to whether the rule on the exhaustion of local remedies is a procedural precondition to the admissibility of an international claim, or a substantive precondition with the result that no breach of international law is committed until local remedies have been exhausted, has been summarised with extensive citation of authorities by J. Dugard, 'Second Report on Diplomatic Protection' (2001) UN Doc A/CN.4/514, paras. 32–62.

[147] *Chorzów Factory Case* (Germany v Poland) (Indemnity) (Merits) (Jurisdiction), (1928) PCIJ Rep Series A No. 17.

which the damage suffered by a private person is taken as the measure. The rules of law governing the reparation are the rules of international law in force between the two States concerned, and not the law governing relations between the State which has committed a wrongful act and the individual who has suffered the damage. Rights or interests of an individual the violation of which rights causes damage are always in a different plane to rights belonging to a State, which rights may also be infringed by the same act. The damage suffered by an individual is never therefore identical in kind with that which will be suffered by a State; it can only afford a convenient scale for the calculation of the reparation due to the State.[148]

As far as investment treaty claims are concerned, damages awarded to an investor do not take into account any independent interest of the national state which may have been prejudiced by the breach. For instance, it would be inconceivable that an investment treaty tribunal would increase the amount of damages to account for the fact that the host state had breached its obligations under a BIT on several occasions in relation to different investors of the same nationality. Damages in an investment treaty claim are assessed purely on the basis of the harm caused to the economic interests of the investor by the host state, without regard for any factors in the relationship between the host state and the national state of the investor.[149] This supports the conclusion that the investor is not vindicating 'public' or 'international' interests by bringing an investment treaty claim.

(7) The challenge to and enforcement of awards

A truly international judgment or award, such as a judgment of the International Court of Justice, owes its existence and binding force to the international legal order and is impervious to any challenge or review before a municipal court.[150] Only an international court or tribunal is competent to hear applications pertaining to the validity of a truly international judgment or award that has settled a public controversy between states. Thus, for instance, Nicaragua challenged the validity of an award

[148] *Chorzów Factory Case* (Germany v Poland) (Indemnity) (Merits) (Jurisdiction), (1928) PCIJ Rep Series A No. 17, 28.

[149] In *S. D. Myers, Inc. v Government of Canada* (Partial Award, 12 November 2000), (2001) 40 ILM 1408, the UNCITRAL Tribunal hearing a NAFTA claim distinguished 'lawful' expropriations pursuant to Art. 1110 from 'unlawful' breaches of the NAFTA under other provisions of the NAFTA. The Tribunal found that: 'The standard of compensation than an arbitral tribunal should apply may in some cases be influenced by the distinction between compensating for a lawful, as opposed to an unlawful, act. Fixing the fair market value of an asset that is diminished in value may not fairly address the harm done to the investor.' (*Ibid.* para. 308). This distinction is problematic because the loss suffered by the investor is a private loss and compensation must be strictly determined on the basis of causation and foreseeability. So long as the host state's act gives rise to a secondary obligation to compensate the investor, the legal character of that act on the *inter*-state plane (*ie* the distinction, for instance, between lawful and unlawful expropriations) should have no bearing on the assessment of damages.

[150] *Chorzów Factory Case* (Germany v Poland) (Indemnity) (Merits) (Jurisdiction), (1928) PCIJ Rep Series A No. 17, 33. See O. Schachter 'The Enforcement of International Judicial and Arbitral Decisions' (1960) 54 *AJIL* 1, 12–5.

rendered in favour of Honduras on the demarcation of their maritime boundary before the International Court,[151] as did Guinea-Bissau in relation to an award that favoured Senegal's position in a maritime boundary dispute.[152]

Awards rendered by international arbitral tribunals in investor/state disputes are not truly international awards and as a result they are subject to challenge and review in accordance with municipal and international legislative instruments dealing with international commercial arbitral awards. Municipal courts have been seised of challenges to investment treaty awards pursuant to legislation on international commercial arbitration,[153] and the drafters of investment treaties have expressly recognised that investor/state awards fall within the purview of the New York Convention on the Recognition and Enforcement of Foreign Arbitral Awards or the Inter-American Convention on International Commercial Arbitration.[154]

If the investor was vindicating the rights of its national state in bringing an investment treaty claim, one would expect that the resulting decision of the tribunal could be properly characterised as a public international award and binding as between the national state and the host state on the *inter*-state plane. The fact that investor/state awards are capable of being classified as 'commercial' is not consistent with them having a truly public international law status because it suggests that the primary relationship between the disputing parties is private rather than public or sovereign. Furthermore, the evidence suggests that investor/state awards are not binding on the national state of the investor.[155]

E. CONCLUSIONS ON THE NATURE OF THE INVESTOR'S RIGHTS: TWO ALTERNATIVE 'DIRECT' MODELS

In what has proven to be a prescient article on investment treaty arbitration, Paulsson contrasted diplomatic protection, which 'has proved itself unworkable as a way of protecting business interests in the context of contemporary international economic life',[156] with a new mechanism established by investment treaties that he termed 'arbitration without privity':

> The possibility of direct action—international arbitration without privity—allows the true complainant to face the true defendant. This has the immense merit of clarity and realism; these virtues, and not eloquent proclamations, are the prerequisites of confidence in the legal process.[157]

[151] *Arbitral Award Made by the King of Spain on 23 December 1906* (Honduras v Nicaragua), [1960] ICJ Rep 192.

[152] *Arbitral Award of 31 July 1989* (Guinea-Bissau v Senegal), [1991] ICJ Rep 53.

[153] See Part V(D) below.

[154] *Ibid.*

[155] Article 1136(7) of NAFTA is explicit: 'An award made by a Tribunal shall have no binding force except between the disputing parties and in respect of the particular case.'

[156] J. Paulsson, above n. 1, 255.

[157] *Ibid.* 256.

The novelty of the investor's cause of action under investment treaties was recently emphasised by Justice Kelen of the Federal Court in Ottawa, on this occasion in relation to NAFTA:

NAFTA provides, unlike its predecessor, the Canada-U.S. Free Trade Agreement, a mechanism which allows individual investors to settle disputes with respect to alleged discriminatory treatment. This creates a powerful and significant new cause of action to protect investors . . .[158]

The foregoing analysis of the principal features of diplomatic protection under customary international law and investment treaty arbitration reveals their fundamental divergence. Given that the *raison d'être* of the investment treaty mechanism for the presentation of international claims may well be a response to the inadequacies of diplomatic protection,[159] this should come as no surprise. The functional assumption underlying the investment treaty regime is clearly that the investor is bringing a cause of action based upon the vindication of its own rights rather than those of its national state. In these circumstances it is untenable to superimpose the *Mavrommatis* formula of diplomatic protection over a triangular relationship between investor, its national state and the host state of the investment in order to rationalise 'arbitration without privity' under investment treaties. In this respect, the treatment by the Special Rapporteur to the ILC, Dugard, on the relationship between diplomatic protection and 'special regimes for the protection of foreign investors provided for in bilateral and multilateral investment treaties'[160] is highly relevant. The Special Rapporteur proposed a *lex specialis* exception to the application of rules of diplomatic protection for corporations or shareholders because:

There is a clear inconsistency between the rules of customary international law on the diplomatic protection of corporate investment, which envisage protection only at the discretion of the national State and only, subject to limited exceptions, in respect of the corporation itself, and the special regime for foreign investment established by bilateral and multilateral investment treaties, which confers rights on the foreign investor, either as a corporation or as a shareholder, determinable by an international arbitration tribunal.[161]

What, then, are the conceptual alternatives to the 'derivative model' based on the *Mavrommatis* formula? It was previously stated that there is no theoretical impediment in international law to the conferral of rights upon private entities by an international treaty instrument. The clearest support for this proposition is to be found in the seminal judgment of the Permanent Court of International Justice in the *Jurisdiction of the Courts of Danzig Case*.[162] A treaty between Poland and Danzig (called

[158] The context for this statement was a challenge to a NAFTA award in *Attorney General of Canada v S.D. Myers, Inc*, Decision, 13 January 2004 (2004 FC 38), para. 32, available at <http://www.dfait-maeci.gc.ca/tna-nac/documents/ReasonsforOrder.pdf>.

[159] J. Kokott, above n. 73, 27.

[160] J. Dugard, 'Fourth Report on Diplomatic Protection', above n. 92.

[161] *Ibid.* para. 112.

[162] (Advisory Opinion), (1928) PCIJ Rep Series B No. 15.

the 'Beamtenabkommen') regulated the employment conditions for employees of the Danzig railways who had passed into the service of the Polish Railways Administration and an issue arose as to whether the Danzig employees could sue the Polish Railways directly in the Danzig Courts to recover compensation based on the provisions of the treaty. Poland's submission that the treaty only created rights and obligations as between the state parties was dismissed by the Permanent Court:

> [I]t cannot be disputed that the very object of an international agreement, according to the intention of the contracting Parties, may be the adoption by the Parties of some definite rules creating individual rights and enforceable by the national courts. That there is such an intention in the present case can be established by reference to the terms of the *Beamtenabkommen*.[163]

Hersch Lauterpacht interpreted this passage as clear authority to the effect that 'there is nothing in international law to prevent individuals from acquiring directly rights under a treaty provided that this is the intention of the contracting parties.'[164] More recently, the International Court of Justice in the *LaGrand Case*[165] decided that Article 36(1)(b) of the Vienna Convention on Consular Relations 'creates individual rights', whether or not these fall to be classified as human rights.[166] This treaty provision obliged the United States to inform Germany through the proper diplomatic channels that two of its nationals were committed to prison in the United States. The United States failed to do so and the German nationals were later executed. The Court attached significance to the final sentence of Article 36(1)(b) that the prison authorities 'shall inform the person concerned without delay of *his rights* under this subparagraph.'[167]

Investment treaties also adopt terminology consistent with the vesting of rights in foreign nationals and legal entities directly. The substantive obligations relating to minimum standards of investment protection are couched in terms of a legal relationship between the host state and the foreign investor. The United States Model BIT, for instance, prescribes that '[e]ach [state] Party shall accord a national most favoured nation treatment to covered investments . . .'[168] The Austria Model BIT is even more direct: 'An investor of a Contracting Party which claims to be affected by expropriation by the other Contracting Party *shall have the right* . . .'[169]

[163] *Ibid.* 17–19.

[164] H. Lauterpacht, 'Survey of International Law in Relation to the Work of Codification of the International Law Commission' (1949) UN Doc A/CN.4/1/Rev.1, 19–20, reprinted in *Collected Papers of Hersch Lauterpacht* (Vol.1, 1970) 469. A concise and lucid critique of the 'positivist' conception of the subjects of international law is provided by: R. Higgins, *Problems & Process: International Law and How We Use It* (1994) 49 *et seq.*

[165] (Germany v US) (Judgment on Merits, 27 June 2001), (2001) 40 ILM 1069.

[166] *Ibid.* paras. 75–8. [167] *Ibid.* para. 77.

[168] United States Model BIT, Art. 4, *UNCTAD Compendium* (Vol. VI, 2002) 504.

[169] Austria Model BIT, Art. 5(3) (emphasis added). *Ibid.* (Vol. VII) 262.

A textual analysis of investment treaties thus appears to be consistent with the conclusion that the substantive investment protection obligations proclaimed by the state parties are owed to investors directly, who then have the means of enforcing their corresponding rights pursuant to the investor/state arbitral procedure stipulated in the treaty.

Another possible approach to a direct theory of rights under investment treaties is to distinguish between the substantive obligations of investment protection and the obligation to submit to investor/state arbitration upon the filing of a notice of claim by a qualified investor. The substantive obligations might be said to exist purely on the *inter*-state plane and as such opposable only by one contracting state to another. These obligations do not pertain to investments of specific investors, which often are not reasonably in the contemplation of host states,[170] but instead require states to establish a particular regime *in abstracto*. In contradistinction, the procedural obligation is owed directly to the investor. Upon the filing of a notice of arbitration by the investor, the investor perfects the host state's unilateral offer to arbitrate, and the two parties thus enter into a direct legal relationship in the form of an arbitration agreement. At the same time, the investor becomes a counterparty to the host state's obligation to submit to international arbitration for an assessment of its conduct towards that investment on the basis of the norms of investment protection set out in the treaty. This obligation encompasses the duty of the host state to pay compensation if the international tribunal adjudges its conduct to be violative of these norms. The minimum standards of investment protection could thus be characterised as the applicable adjudicative standards for the investor's cause of action rather than binding obligations owed directly to the investor.

Whichever rationalisation of the investor's direct rights under an investment treaty is to be preferred, it is manifest that a breach of a treaty obligation owed directly to an investor does not necessarily entail a liability on the *inter*-state plane governed by the secondary rules of state responsibility for international wrongs. This problem is addressed in the next Part III.

III. The Investment Treaty Regime in the System of State Responsibility

A. Introduction

The principal conclusion of Part II was that an investor does not bring a derivative claim for the enforcement of an obligation owed to its national state pursuant to the investment treaty. The investor's cause of action is grounded upon an obligation owed to it directly. It follows that the

[170] And thus perhaps distinguishable from human rights obligations.

liability created by a breach of this obligation is not necessarily a liability on the *inter*-state plane in the sense that it may be opposable by the national state of the investor to the host state. But equally, it would appear to be fallacious to suggest that this liability has the character of a simple civil wrong, insofar as the host state's obligation emanates from an undertaking in an international treaty instrument.

A close parallel is the liability arising upon a violation of a human rights obligation. It is difficult to conceptualise a judgment of the European Court of Human Rights in favour of a national of a contracting state to the European Convention of Human Rights as creating a new international obligation on the *inter*-state plane; equally, it is counter-intuitive to regard such a judgment as a remedy for the breach of a private or civil obligation owed to the individual applicant.

One solution to this conundrum is to discard the dichotomy between public and private international law and instead to investigate the different categories of state responsibility for a breach of an international treaty that directly confers rights upon non-state actors. Such treaties, it is submitted, create a 'sub-system' of state responsibility.[171] Although these sub-systems share many of the secondary rules contained in the *inter*-state system of responsibility, they nevertheless fall to be analysed independently.

B. THE NOTION OF A 'SUB-SYSTEM' OF STATE RESPONSIBILITY

There does not exist in international law a single body of secondary rules of state responsibility for all internationally wrongful acts.[172] To the contrary, a salient tendency in the contemporary evolution of international law is the fragmentation of the general law of international responsibility into various sub-systems created by treaties dealing with particular objects of international regulation. To complement what is often a

[171] 'Sub-system' is not an entirely adequate term because it imports a connotation of autonomy or independence. The alternative term in the literature on state responsibility, 'self-contained regime', is even less appropriate because it suggests complete autonomy from the *inter*-state system of international responsibility. See generally on 'sub-systems' of state responsibility: W. Riphagen, 'State Responsibility: New Theories of Obligation in Interstate Relations' in R. Macdonald & D. Johnston (eds), *The Structure and Process of International Law: Essays in Legal Philosophy, Doctrine and Theory* (1983) 581; W. Riphagen, 'Third Report on the Content, Forms and Degrees of International Responsibility (Part 2 of the Draft Articles)' (1983) 2 *Ybk Int L Commission* 22, UN Doc A/CN.4/354/Add. 1 & 2; B. Simma, 'Self-Contained Regimes' (1985) 16 *Netherlands Ybk of Int L* 111; P. Dupuy, 'The Danger of the Fragmentation of the Unification of the International Legal System and the International Court of Justice' (1999) 31 *New York University J of Int L & Politics* 791, 797; G. Abi-Saab, 'Fragmentation or Unification: Some Concluding Remarks' (1999) 31 *New York University J of Int L & Politics* 791, 796; C. Tomuschat, 'Some Reflections on the Consequences of a Breach of an Obligation under International Law' in Haller, Kölz, Müller & Thürer (eds), *Im Dienst an der Gesellschaft Festschrift für Dietrich Schindler zum 65 Geburtstag* (1989) 148.

[172] See the Introduction to the Commentary to the ILC's Articles on State Responsibility, above n. 12, 76 and the commentary to Article 55 (*lex specialis*), *ibid.* 306–8; International Law Commission (1976) 2 *Ybk Int L Commission* 117, para. 53, commentary to Art. 19 (international crimes and international delicts); W. Riphagen, 'Third Report on the Content, Forms and Degrees of International Responsibility (Part 2 of the Draft Articles)', *ibid.* para. 35; B. Simma, *ibid.*

sophisticated system of primary rights and obligations, modern treaty regimes also contain discrete secondary rules of state responsibility. The WTO Understanding on Dispute Settlement and the Treaty Establishing the European Economic Community are two leading examples, each creating a complex enforcement mechanism for the primary obligations arising under the treaty regime. But more important for the current analysis are the relatively new treaty regimes that confer rights directly upon non-state actors and create a dispute resolution procedure for the enforcement of such rights at the suit of non-state actors. In the human rights field, the European Convention on Human Rights is the outstanding example of such a treaty. The Algiers Accords establishing the Iran/US Claims Tribunal are also notable for creating a regime of international responsibility that appears to transcend the traditional public/private dichotomy.[173]

Like the European Convention on Human Rights and the Algiers Accords, investment treaties establish a distinct system of secondary rules of state responsibility in recognition of the independent legal interest conferred to investors by these treaties. The general principles of state responsibility for international wrongs cannot be presumed, in such a case, to apply without qualification to the invocation by a non-state actor of a state's liability for breach of a treaty obligation because the new legal relationship which arises upon the commission of the breach in this context is not between the contracting states to the treaty, but instead between the investor and the host state.

The sub-system created by treaties which confer rights directly upon non-state actors to be enforced at the suit of the non-state actors is without prejudice to the application of the general rules of state responsibility as between the state parties to the treaties.[174] Investment treaties have two separate dispute resolution procedures to deal with investor/state disputes on the one hand and state/state disputes on the other.[175] The general rules of state responsibility undoubtedly regulate the consequences of liability for international wrongs in the latter case.

It is useful to test these observations against the Articles on the Responsibility of States for Internationally Wrongful Acts drafted by the International Law Commission. The existence of sub-systems of international law with distinct secondary rules of state responsibility was recognised from an early stage of the ILC's codification project. Thus, with respect to the different consequences flowing from an international crime and delict, it was stated that:

> . . . The Commission must nevertheless emphasize here and now that it would be absolutely mistaken to believe that contemporary international law contains only

[173] See Part II(A) above.

[174] See generally on the consequences of a breach of treaty: S. Rosenne, *Breach of Treaty* (1985); D. Bowett, 'Treaties and State Responsibility' in D. Bowett (ed.), *Le droit international au service de la paix, de la justice et du développement: mélanges Michael Virally* (1991) 137; A. Yahi, 'La violation d'un traité: l'articulation du droit des traités et du droit de la responsabilité internationale' (1993) 26 *Revue belge de droit internationale* 437.

[175] See Part I above.

one regime of responsibility applicable universally to every type of internationally wrongful act. . .[176]

The challenge of identifying and categorising the disparate regimes of international responsibility was taken up by Riphagen, the Third Special Rapporteur to the ILC, who introduced the relevant section of his Third Report in the following terms consistent with the previous statement of the Commission:

. . . international law as it stands today is not modelled on one system only, but on a variety of interrelated sub-systems, within each of which the so-called 'primary rules' and the so-called 'secondary rules' are closely intertwined—indeed, inseparable.[177]

Eventually, Riphagen's often complicated preoccupation with the interrelationship between the 'sub-systems' of international law gave way to a greater emphasis on a common denominator of secondary rules in the latter work of the ILC on the Articles. This was evidently the result of a certain pragmatism that crept into the drafting process about the realistic coverage of the ILC's project. In the subsequent drafts there is instead an implicit presumption of international law as a unified body of law.[178] Nevertheless, the problems identified by Riphagen were not ignored by the Fourth and Fifth Rapporteurs, and thus an important *lex specialis* reservation was made in Article 55 of the Articles on the Responsibility of States for Internationally Wrongful Acts to deal with, *inter alia*, sub-systems of international law:

These articles do not apply where and to the extent that the conditions for the existence of an internationally wrongful act or the content or implementation of the international responsibility of a State are governed by special rules of international law.[179]

As stated previously, modern treaty regimes with increasing frequency establish a mechanism whereby individuals and private entities can invoke the responsibility of the state party directly for a breach of an obligation contained in the treaty. Article 55 must apply in these circumstances. The Articles are preoccupied with the consequences flowing from the breach of international obligations *inter*-state. Riphagen

[176] (1976) 2 *Ybk Int L Commission* 117, para. 53, commentary to Art. 19 (international crimes and international delicts).

[177] W. Riphagen, above n. 171, para. 35. Later in his Report, Riphagen notes that 'there are sub-systems of international law which govern a particular substratum of international situations, without necessarily creating "primary" rights and obligations in the strict sense of the word.' He cites the GATT and the International Air Transport Agreement as examples. *Ibid.* para. 102.

[178] See D. Bodansky & J. Crook, 'Symposium: The ILC's State Responsibility Articles; Introduction and Overview' (2002) 96 *AJIL* 773, 781, and the response of the Fifth Rapporteur, J. Crawford, above n. 51, 879.

[179] J. Crawford, above n. 12, 306. The ILC's commentary to Art. 55 gives the examples of the World Trade Organization Dispute Settlement Understanding and the European Convention on Human Rights as regimes which, in varying degrees, displace the rules contained in the Articles on State Responsibility, which nevertheless 'operate in a residual way'. *Ibid.* 307.

described this limitation of the Articles in the form of a rhetorical question which he answered in the negative:

The question then again arises, whether these draft articles can be applied in respect of all types of rules of international law, in particular such types as are not simply based on the separation of states, and consequently not focused on the anti-parallel exercise of sovereignty by interference of one state in the sovereignty of another state . . .[180]

The Articles themselves carve out the problem of secondary obligations owed to non-state actors in the form of a reservation in Article 33 to the scope of obligations set out in Part 2 to the Articles:

1. The obligations of the responsible State set out in this Part may be owed to another State, to several States, or to the international community as a whole, depending in particular on the character and content of the international obligation and on the circumstances of the breach.
2. This Part is without prejudice to any right, arising from the international responsibility of a State, which may accrue directly to any person or entity other than a State.[181]

Investment treaties are mentioned explicitly in the ILC's commentary to Article 33(2) as giving rise to a situation where a 'primary obligation is owed to a non-State entity' and such entity has the possibility of invoking state responsibility 'on its own account and without the intermediation of any State'.[182] Hence Parts 2 and 3 of the Articles are not applicable, by virtue of the reservation in Article 33(2), to this legal relationship. Reference should also be made to the commentary to Article 28, where it is stated that Part 2 'does not apply to obligations of reparation to the extent that these arise towards or are invoked by a person or entity other than a State'.[183]

Some writers have criticised the paucity of any direct consideration by the Articles of the possibility of non-state actors invoking the international responsibility of states.[184] However, a cursory examination of this vast topic in a codification which, by its own terms, is almost exclusively concerned with international responsibility as between states, would more likely to have hindered rather than assisted the rapid development of this area of international law. As Judge Higgins reflected some years ago with respect to an earlier stage of the ILC's work on this project, 'less can be more'.[185]

[180] W. Riphagen, above n. 171, 593. The author continues: 'As a matter of fact, the whole construction of the draft articles is based on the international obligation of a state being a sort of middle-point on the line connecting the sovereignty of one state to that of another. The breach of such an obligation by one state is then reflected by the creation of "new" rights of the other state.' (Footnote omitted.) *Ibid.* 594.

[181] J. Crawford, above n. 12, 209.

[182] *Ibid.* 210.

[183] *Ibid.* 193.

[184] See E. Weiss, 'Invoking State Responsibility in the Twenty-First Century' (2002) 96 *AJIL* 798, 799, 816; P. Allott, 'State Responsibility and the Unmaking of International Law' (1988) 29 *Harvard Int LJ* 1, 1.

[185] R. Higgins, above n. 164, 168.

In summary, investment treaties create a sub-system of international law to regulate the relationship between states and private investors that arises upon a breach of the treaty, without prejudice to the general law of state responsibility that governs the relationship between the contracting states. The ILC's Articles on State Responsibility do not detract from this conclusion; to the contrary they provide the necessary conceptual framework to distinguish between the general system of state responsibility and sub-systems of responsibility. The sub-system created by investment treaties is by definition *sui generis*. An uncritical transplantation of secondary rules that govern, *inter alia*, the consequences of a diplomatic protection claim between two state parties is inappropriate.[186]

In order to develop and elaborate upon the sub-system established by investment treaties, it will be necessary to examine carefully the principal characteristics of the legal relationship between the host state and the investor.

C. PRINCIPAL FEATURES OF THE SUB-SYSTEM CREATED BY INVESTMENT TREATIES

Investment treaties envisage two distinct spheres of rights and obligations: one applicable to the legal relationship between the contracting state parties (the 'state/state sphere') and the other applicable to the legal relationship between investors of one contracting state and the contracting state hosting the investment (the 'investor/state sphere').

In relation to the state/state sphere, an investment treaty creates certain international obligations opposable by one contracting state to another, and the general rules of state responsibility for international wrongs regulate the consequences of any breach thereof. These obligations can generally be grouped into two categories: (i) adherence to the law of treaties in the interpretation and application of the investment treaty; (ii) the obligation not to frustrate an investor's recourse to international arbitration or the enforcement of any award against the host state. Thus, by way of example, one contracting state might seek a declaration from an international tribunal on the compatibility of domestic legislation enacted by another contracting state with the minimum standards of investment treatment in the BIT. Alternatively, if a contracting state issued a decree ordering state officials to seize and destroy all evidence relating to a investor/state dispute before an international

[186] A similar conclusion may have been reached by E. Lauterpacht in an early study of the ICSID Convention: 'Even in those situations in which individuals have had a direct right of access to international tribunals, the treaties which gave them direct access to remedial machinery, did so only in respect of rights directly conferred upon the individual by the particular treaty. Consequently, these situations do not constitute precedents for saying that, if an individual is given a direct right of access to an international tribunal, the rights conferred by customary international law upon his national State are automatically enforceable by him'. E. Lauterpacht, 'The World Bank Convention on the Settlement of International Investment Disputes' in *Recueil d'Etudes de Droit International en Hommage à Paul Guggenheim* (1968) 659.

tribunal, or enjoining state courts from giving effect to any award rendered by that tribunal, the contracting state of the investor would be able to bring a direct claim against the other contracting state for a breach of the obligation to submit investment disputes to international arbitration,[187] using the dispute resolution mechanism for *inter*-state disputes prescribed in the investment treaty.[188] Article 1136(5) of NAFTA expressly recognises that the host state's refusal to enforce an award of an international treaty tribunal on its territory may be the subject of a state/state arbitration pursuant to the procedure in Chapter 20.[189]

Under the general law of state responsibility, the commission of an internationally wrongful act by a state entails three broad consequences: (i) new obligations upon the state whose act is internationally wrongful; (ii) new rights of the injured state; and, in certain cases at least (iii) new rights and duties of third states in respect of the situation created by the internationally wrongful act.[190]

The contracting states to investment treaties have legislated for a new legal regime or sub-system to define the legal consequences that follow a violation of the minimum standards of treatment towards a qualified investment. In relation to the investor/state sphere, a breach of a treaty standard by the host state certainly creates new obligations upon that state. But these new obligations do not correspond to new rights of the national state of the investor because the injury is caused exclusively to the investor. This is so because the contracting states to investment treaties have opted out of the *inter*-state secondary rules of international responsibility in relation to a limited group of wrongs causing damage to a particular sphere of private interests. The national state of the investor

[187] Which imports the duty not to frustrate the arbitral process.

[188] *Concord*: A. Broches, 'Bilateral Investment Protection Treaties and Arbitration of Investment Disputes' in J. Schultz & A. van den Berg (eds) *The Art of Arbitration, Liber Amicorum Pieter Sanders* (1982) 66. Several writers support the proposition that a state's frustration of the arbitral process or repudiation of an arbitration clause with a foreign national constitutes denial of justice under customary international law: F. Mann, above n. 133, 27; P. Weil, 'Problèmes Relatifs aux Contrats passés entre un Etat et un Particulier' (1969) 128 *Hague Recueil* 222; S. Schwebel, *International Arbitration: Three Salient Problems* (1987) 65, 71–2; R. von Mehren & P. Kourides, 'International Arbitrations between States and Foreign Private Parties: The Libyan Nationalisation Cases' (1981) 75 *AJIL* 476, 537. There would be no need for the investor to exhaust any other remedies before the resort to this form of diplomatic protection. *Concord*: S. Schwebel & J. Wetter, 'Arbitration and the Exhaustion of Local Remedies' (1966) 60 *AJIL* 484; S. Schwebel, *ibid.* 115 *et seq.*; C. Dominicé, 'La clause CIRDI dans les traités bilatéraux suisses de protection des invertissements' in Im Dienst an der Gemeinschaft, Festschrift für Dietrich Schindler zum 65 (1989) 457, 466.

[189] Article 1136(5) provides: 'If a disputing Party fails to abide by or comply with a final award, the Commission, on delivery of a request by a Party whose investor was a party to the arbitration, shall establish a panel under Article 2008 (Request for an Arbitral Panel). The requesting Party may seek in such proceedings: (a) a determination that the failure to abide by or comply with the final award is inconsistent with the obligations of this Agreement; and (b) a recommendation that the Party abide by or comply with the final award.' Model BITs often suspend the right of either Contracting State to pursue claims through diplomatic channels if an investor has instituted arbitration proceedings unless and until the host state fails to abide by the award; see, *eg*: Chile Model BIT, Art. 8(6), *UNCTAD Compendium* (Vol. III, 1996) 147; Switzerland Model BIT, Art. 4, *ibid.* 181; United Kingdom Model BIT, Art. 8, *ibid.* 190; Jamaica Model BIT, Art. 10(5), *ibid.* (Vol. V) 322; Malaysia Model BIT, Art. 7(4), *ibid.* 329; Cambodia Model BIT, Art. 8(3)(c), *ibid.* (Vol. VI) 467; Mongolia Model BIT, Art. 8(6), *ibid.* (Vol. IX) 306.

[190] W. Riphagen, above n. 171, para. 7.

thus has no immediate secondary rights within the investment treaty regime to challenge the commission of this breach of treaty; instead the new rights arising upon the breach of treaty vest directly in the investor.

The status of the investor's new right, and the corresponding liability of the host state, is not equivalent to the new rights and obligations which come into existence upon a breach of an international obligation within a bilateral relationship between states. Neither the host state's liability, nor the secondary rights accruing to the investor, arise immediately on the *inter*-state plane. This is a distinguishing feature of the sub-system of state responsibility created by the investment treaty regime.

This scheme for understanding the legal relationships that arise upon the host state's violation of an investment treaty obligation is indirectly supported by reference to the texts of more detailed investment treaties. For instance, Article 1136(1) of Chapter 11 of the NAFTA provides:

> An award made by a Tribunal shall have no binding force except between the disputing parties and in respect of the particular case.

This provision suggests that no legal relationship arises between the host state and the national state of the investor upon the host state's breach of an investment treaty. (The term 'Parties' is used in the NAFTA text to designate the contracting states, whereas 'parties' refers to the disputants in a reference to arbitration.) If such a relationship did exist, then one might expect that the tribunal's award would settle the controversy at the *inter*-state level as well and thus be directly binding upon the national state.

Another crucial distinction between the investor/state sub-system of international responsibility and the *inter*-state system of international responsibility lies in the relevant rules for the invocation of state responsibility. The preconditions for the *mise en oeuvre* of responsibility in the *inter*-state system are codified in Part Three of the ILC's Articles on the Responsibility of States for International Wrongs and include Article 44 on the 'Admissibility of Claims':

> The responsibility of a State may not be invoked if:
>
> (a) the claim is not brought in accordance with any applicable rule relating to the nationality of claims;
> (b) the claim is one to which the rule of exhaustion of local remedies applies and any available and effective local remedy has not been exhausted.[191]

The ILC's Commentary to Article 44 makes it clear that the rules on the nationality of claims and the exhaustion of local remedies are not merely relevant to the 'jurisdiction or admissibility of claims before judicial bodies'[192] but are of a 'more fundamental character'[193] insofar as '[t]hey are conditions for invoking the responsibility of a State in the first place.'[194]

[191] J. Crawford, above n. 12, 264. [192] *Ibid.* [193] *Ibid.*

[194] *Ibid.* The leading treatises on international law also consider the rules on the nationality of claims and the exhaustion of local remedies to be general preconditions to the invocation of state responsibility rather than just a part of the law on admissibility of *inter*-state claims before international courts and tribunals. See *Oppenheim's International Law*, above n. 92, 511, 522.

If a treaty creating a judicial body to hear claims between states arising out of injuries to their nationals is silent on relevant rules on the nationality of claims and the exhaustion of local remedies, it follows from the ILC's treatment of these rules as preconditions for the invocation of state responsibility that they must nevertheless apply in this instance. The rules on the nationality of claims or the exhaustion of local remedies are not, however, applicable to the investor/state sub-system of international responsibility in the absence of an express stipulation to the contrary in the treaty instrument itself. As was concluded in Part II, the investor is enforcing its own rights against the host state by resorting to the investor/state arbitral mechanism and hence there is no basis for importing rules for the invocation of state responsibility by a state on behalf of its national in this context.

Consistent with this thesis, treaty tribunals have uniformly dismissed the application of the rule on the exhaustion of local remedies in the absence of an express provision in the investment treaty.[195] This approach cannot be justified simply because a treaty is silent on the matter, as is assumed in these decisions. To the contrary, if investor/state disputes were subject to the *inter*-state rules of international responsibility, then the local remedies rule should be applied in the absence of a waiver in the treaty itself.[196] The International Court of Justice set a high threshold for any implicit waiver in a treaty text in the *Case Concerning Electronica Sicula SpA (ELSI)*.[197] The Court stated that it was 'unable to accept that an important principle of customary international law should be held to have been tacitly dispensed with, in the absence of any words making clear an intention to do so.'[198] Hence there is a clear presumption in customary international law against implying a waiver of the local remedies rule.[199]

[195] Expressly in: *CME* Partial Award, paras. 411, 417. Implicitly in: *Waste Management Inc. v United Mexican States*, (Decision on Preliminary Objection, 26 June 2002) Case No. ARB(AF)/00/3, 6 ICSID Rep 549, para. 30; *Compañia de Aguas del Aconquija, SA and Compagnie Générale des Eaux/Vivendi Universal v Argentine Republic*, (Award, 21 November 2000) Case No. ARB/97/3, 5 ICSID Rep 299, para. 81; *Compañia de Aguas del Aconquija, SA and Compagnie Générale des Eaux/Vivendi Universal v Argentine Republic*, (Decision on Annulment, 3 July 2002) Case No. ARB/97/3, 6 ICSID Rep 340, para. 52; *Société Générale de Surveillance S.A. v Islamic Republic of Pakistan* (Decision on Jurisdiction, 6 August 2003) Case No. ARB/01/13, (2003) 42 ILM 1290, para. 151. Writers also adhere to this position: J. Paulsson, above n. 1, 239–40; C. Dominicé, above n. 188, 457, 472.

[196] For instance, in *Maffezini v Kingdom of Spain* (Decision on Objections to Jurisdiction, 25 January 2000) Case No. ARB/97/7, 5 ICSID Rep 396, the Tribunal noted that 'Article 26 [of the ICSID Convention] thus reverses the traditional international law rule, which implies the exhaustion requirement unless it is expressly or implicitly waived.' (*Ibid.* para. 22.)

[197] (United States v Italy) [1989] ICJ Rep 14.

[198] *Ibid.* 42.

[199] Concord: C. Amerasinghe, above n. 69, 253: 'Where there is a bilateral or multilateral agreement between States to submit to arbitration or international judicial settlement disputes between their nationals and host States, there is generally no understanding that the rule of local remedies is waived by the very fact of such submission to arbitration or judicial settlement . . .' See further cases cited at: *ibid.* 255 at note 13. A survey of various international treaty regimes for the protection of private interests conducted by Trindade nevertheless revealed that the rule on the exhaustion of local remedies was often not applied when the treaty was silent on the matter; see: A. Trindade, 'Exhaustion of Local Remedies in International Law Experiments Granting Procedural Status to Individuals in the First Half of the Twentieth Century' (1977) 24 *Netherlands Int L Rev* 373.

Treaty tribunals have also generally dismissed the relevance of the international rules on the nationality of claims on the strength of an unarticulated presumption that such rules have no application to investor/state arbitration. Again, it is submitted that this conclusion is correct, however, the mere silence of the treaty is not sufficient to justify such an approach in light of Article 44 of the ILC's Articles on State Responsibility. If the *inter*-state regime of international responsibility applied to investor/state disputes then the decision of the *Loewen* Tribunal would be unimpeachable. It will be recalled that in *Loewen* the residual application of international law to the nationality of claims was affirmed in a sweeping statement of general principle:

> It is that silence in the Treaty that requires the application of customary international law to resolve the question of the need for continuous national identity.[200]

It is curious that the *Loewen* Tribunal did not reflect on the experience of the Iran/US Claims Tribunal in this context. In the *Dual Nationality Case*,[201] Iran had contended that arbitrations before the Tribunal were an instance of diplomatic protection so that a solution to the admissibility of claims by dual nationals 'must be found in public international law and not disputes between one State and nationals of the other, which could be resolved by the application of private international law'.[202] The Tribunal rejected this contention because the object and purpose of the Algiers Accords was not to 'extend diplomatic protection in the normal sense'.[203] The rules of customary international law did not, therefore, prevent the Tribunal from exercising jurisdiction *ratione personae* over US claimants that simultaneously held Iranian citizenship.[204]

Regardless of whether the *Loewen* Tribunal's interpretation of the requirements of continuous nationality under customary international law was correct (*ie* by insisting upon continuous nationality of the claimant up until the award is rendered), its general approach of applying customary international law to questions of admissibility in the absence of an express provision in NAFTA is unpersuasive because it fails to acknowledge the distinct and independent nature of the investment treaty regime for the resolution of investor/state disputes.[205]

200 *Ibid.* para. 226.

201 Islamic Republic of Iran and United States (Case A/18) (Dual Nationality) (6 April 1984) DEC 32-A18-FT, (1984) 5 Iran-US CTR 251.

202 Memorial of the Islamic Republic of Iran in Case A/18 (21 October 1983), 25–6, cited in D. Caron, above n. 34, 132.

203 Islamic Republic of Iran and United States (Case A/18) (Dual Nationality) (6 April 1984) DEC 32-A18-FT, (1984) 5 Iran-US CTR 251, 261.

204 In *Sedco, Inc, for itself and on behalf of Sedco International, S. A. and Sediran Drilling Company v National Iranian Oil Company and The Islamic Republic of Iran* (28 October 1985) ITL 55–129–3, (1985) 9 Iran-US CTR 245, 256, the Tribunal once again emphasized that 'at least in the jurisdictional category of claim involved in this case, [a claim] does not involve diplomatic espousal.'

205 Investment treaties that expressly address the nationality requirements for the presentation of claims do not require continuous nationality until the rendering of the award. This practice was declared *ipse dixit* by the *Loewen* Tribunal to evidence a purposeful derogation from customary international law

IV. The Law Applicable to the Substance of Investor/State Disputes

A. THE SOURCE OF THE CHOICE OF LAW RULE

Some investment treaties contain an express choice of law for the resolution of investment disputes. In this case, the origin of the choice of law rule is self-evident: the treaty itself. Otherwise, there are four possible sources for choice of law rules that may impact upon the treaty tribunal's determination of the law applicable to the investment dispute. First, where the investor and the host state have entered into direct contractual relations, their investment agreement may contain a choice of law provision. Second, the arbitral rules governing the reference to arbitration may contain a default choice of law (*eg* Article 42(1) of the ICSID Convention or Article 33(1) of the UNCITRAL Rules). Third, the *lex loci arbitri* might supply the choice of law rule if the arbitral rules are silent on this point (very unlikely) or if the choice of law rule under the *lex loci arbitri* has a mandatory quality (virtually unheard of).[206] Fourth, the choice of law rule might be derived from the legal system which gives effect to the international treaty—public international law.

B. THE LAWS APPLICABLE TO AN INVESTMENT DISPUTE

Whichever choice of law rule is ultimately applied by the arbitral tribunal, there are three sources of substantive legal rules that must figure in the resolution of any investment dispute: (i) the municipal law of the host state (including relevant international treaties that are binding upon the host state); (ii) the investment treaty itself; and (iii) general principles of international law. This is the common denominator of the majority of express choice of law provisions in investment treaties. The Belgo-Luxemburg Economic Union Model BIT, for example, provides:

> The arbitral tribunal shall decide on the basis of the national law, including the rules relating to conflicts of law, of the Contracting Party involved in the dispute in whose territory the investment has been made, as well as on the basis of the provisions of this Agreement, of the terms of the specific agreement which

(*Loewen* Award, para. 229). Nor did the Tribunal give weight to the fact that a significant number of investment treaties envisage the option of arbitration under the ICSID Convention, Art. 25(2)(b) of which unambiguously applies the nationality requirement solely at the time the investor's consent to arbitration is filed. It is difficult to imagine that the contracting states to investment treaties contemplated that there would be such fundamental differences between investment treaty arbitrations depending on the selection by the investor of ICSID Convention arbitration on the one hand, or *ad hoc* arbitration under the UNCITRAL Arbitration Rules or institutional arbitration pursuant to the ICSID Additional Facility Rules or Rules of Arbitration of the International Chamber of Commerce on the other. The *Loewen* Tribunal nevertheless dismissed the ICSID practice as irrelevant (*ibid.* para. 235).

[206] The premise of this second possibility is that the municipal law of the *situs* of the investment treaty arbitration is indeed the *lex loci arbitri*. This topic will be considered in Part V.

may have been entered into regarding the investment, and the principles of international law.[207]

It is important to emphasize that the substantive law governing investment disputes is necessarily a hybrid of international and municipal law[208] due to the private or commercial interests at the heart of this jurisdiction. This may be contrasted with state/state disputes arising out of the interpretation or application of the investment treaty which are governed purely by international law.[209]

An investment is an embodiment of property rights, whereas the minimum standards of investment protection in treaties are derived from international law.[210] These distinct aspects of an investment dispute require a different choice of law approach, as confirmed by the case law of the mixed arbitral tribunals that were established after the First World War to hear international reclamations for interference with alien property. The American-Turkish Claims Commission expressed the principle lucidly in the *Hoachoozo Palestine Land and Development Co. Case*:[211]

In a case in which complaint is made that governmental authorities have confiscated contractual property rights, the preliminary question is one of domestic

[207] Article 10(5), *UNCTAD Compendium* (Vol. VII, 2002) 276. Similar choice of law clauses can be found in the following model BITs: South Africa Model BIT, Art. 7(4), *ibid.* (Vol. VIII, 2002) 277; Benin Model BIT, Art. 9(4), *ibid.* (Vol. IX) 284; Burundi Model BIT, Art. 8(5), *ibid.* 292. Some investment treaties contain a choice of law provision that simply refers to the provisions of the treaty and 'applicable rules of international law': Energy Charter Treaty, Art. 26(6); Austria Model BIT, Art. 16, *ibid.* (Vol. VII) 256. It is, however, still incumbent upon the treaty tribunal to apply the municipal law of the host state in this situation because international law must necessarily resort to a *renvoi* to municipal law for the determination of issues relating to property rights. The general principles of international law include the *lex situs* conflicts of law rule for this purpose. *Concord*, in relation to the Energy Charter Treaty: T. Wälde, 'Investment Arbitration under the Energy Charter Treaty', above n. 17, 457–8.

[208] *Asian Agricultural Products Ltd [AAP] v Democratic Socialist Republic of Sri Lanka* (Award, 27 June 1990), 4 ICSID Rep 250, 257, '. . . [T]he Bilateral Investment Treaty is not a self-contained closed legal system limited to provide for substantive material rules of direct applicability, but it has to be envisaged within a wider juridical context in which rules from other sources are integrated through implied incorporation methods, or by direct reference to certain supplementary rules, whether of international law character or of domestic law nature . . .'

[209] Examples of the sources of law to resolve state/state disputes included: Chile Model BIT, Art. 9(6), provisions of the BIT, 'principles of international law on this subject' and 'generally recognised principles of international law', *UNCTAD Compendium* (Vol. III, 1996) 148; China Model BIT, Art. 8(5), 'in accordance with the provisions of this Agreement and the principles of international law recognised by both Contracting Parties', *ibid.* 155; Egypt Model BIT, Art. 9(5), rules contained in the BIT and other agreements between the Contracting Parties and principles of international law, *ibid.* (Vol. V, 2000) 298; Netherlands Model BIT, Art. 12(5), 'on the basis of respect for the law', *ibid.* 337; Croatia Model BIT, Art. 11(6), 'pursuant to the rules of international law', *ibid.* (Vol. VI, 2002) 478; US Model BIT, Art. 10(1), 'applicable rules of international law', *ibid.* 508; South Africa Model BIT, Art. 8(5), 'according to this Agreement and the principles of international law', *ibid.* (Vol. VIII, 2002) 277.

[210] *Concord*: C. Schreuer, 'International and Domestic Law in Investment Disputes. The Case of ICSID.' (1996) 1 *Austrian Rev of Int and Eur L* 89, 89, 'Investment relationships typically involve domestic law as well as international law. The host State's domestic law regulates a multitude of technical questions such as admission, licensing, labour relations, tax, foreign exchange and real estate. International law is relevant for such questions as the international minimum standard for the treatment of aliens, protection of foreign owned property, especially against illegal expropriations, interpretation of treaties, especially bilateral investment treaties, State responsibility and, possibly, human rights.'

[211] F. Nielsen, *American-Turkish Claims Settlement under the Agreement of 24 December 1923* (1937) 254, cited in K. Lipstein, 'Conflict of Laws Before International Tribunals (ii)' (1949) 29 *Transactions of the Grotius Society* 51, 54.

law as to the rights of the claimant under a contract in the light of the domestic proper law governing the legal effect of the contract. The next question for determination is whether, in the light of principles or rules of international law, rights under the contract have been infringed.[212]

A similar articulation of the choice of law approach may be found in the precedents of the American-Mexican Claims Commission. In *George W. Cook v United Mexican States (No. 1)*,[213] Commissioner Nielsen stated:

When questions are raised before an international tribunal . . . with respect to the application of the proper law in the determination of rights grounded on contractual obligations, it is necessary to have clearly in mind the particular law applicable to the different aspects of the case. The nature of such contractual rights or rights with respect to tangible property, real or personal, which a claimant asserts have been invaded in a given case is determined by the local law that governs the legal effects of the contract or other form of instrument creating such rights. But the responsibility of a respondent government is determined solely by international law . . .[214]

The clearest exposition of the governing law of investment treaty disputes is to be found in the ICSID *ad hoc* Committee's decision in *Compañia de Aguas del Aconquija, SA and Compagnie Générale des Eaux/Vivendi Universal v Argentine Republic*,[215] which is considered in detail in Part VII. Suffice to state here that the *ad hoc* Committee posited a clear distinction between the law applicable to the investment contract, adjudged to be municipal law, and the law applicable to an assessment of whether the *conduct* of the host state is violative of the treaty standards, which is the treaty and international law.[216] The *ad hoc* Committee's reference to the 'conduct' of the host state in this context, rather than each and every element of the investment dispute, is consistent with the approach of these earlier authorities.

Likewise, the ICSID Tribunal in *Goetz and Others v Republic of Burundi*[217] was careful to emphasize the enduring role of municipal law in investment disputes even where the choice of law clauses in investment treaties refer exclusively to international law (such as Article 1131 of the NAFTA):

Il n'est pas sans intérêt à cet égard de noter que la référence assez fréquente dans des clauses de *choice of law* insérées dans des conventions de protection des investissements, aux dispositions de la convention elle-même—et, plus largement, aux principes et règles du droit international—provoque, après un certain reflux dans la pratique et la jurisprudence, un retour remarquable du droit international dans les relations juridiques entre les Etats d'accueil et les investisseurs étrangers. Cette internationalisation des rapports d'investissement—qu'ils

[212] *Ibid.* 259–60. See further: *Nicholas Marmaras Case* and *Ina Hoffman & Dulcie Steinhardt Case*, reported in F. Nielsen, *American-Turkish Claims Settlement under the Agreement of 24 December 1923* (1937) 286, 287–8, 473, 479–80.

[213] (1927) 4 UN Rep 213.

[214] *Ibid.* 215. The other members of the Commission did not endorse these remarks.

[215] (Decision on Annulment, 3 July 2002) Case No. ARB/97/3, 6 ICSID Rep 340.

[216] *Ibid.* paras. 96, 101.

[217] (Award, 10 February 1999) Case No. ARB/95/3, 6 ICSID Rep 5.

soient contractuels ou non—ne conduit certes pas à une «dénationalisation» radicale des relations juridiques nées de l'investissement étranger, au point que le droit national de l'Etat hôte serait privé de toute pertinence ou application au profit d'un rôle exclusive du droit international. Elle signifie seulement que ces relations relèvent simultanément—en parallèle—pourrait-on dire—de la maîtrise souveraine de l'Etat d'accueil sur son droit national et des engagements internationaux auxquels il a souscrit.[218]

The choice of law rule for the assessment of the host state's acts or omissions with respect to the investment of a qualified investor has been consistently upheld by treaty tribunals. Far more controversial has been the ignorance or disregard of the choice of law rule in relation to the existence, nature or extent of the investor's interests in its purported investment. The treatment of the applicable law to these issues will be the focus of this Part IV on the law governing the merits of the dispute.

C. THE ROLE OF THE MUNICIPAL LAW OF THE HOST STATE

Investment disputes are about investments, investments are about property, and property is about specific rights over things cognisable by the municipal law of the host state.[219] Customary international law contains no substantive rules of property law. They cannot be a source of rights in property. Nor do investment treaties purport to lay down rules for acquiring rights *in rem* that are exercisable against the world at large.[220]

[218] *Ibid.* para. 69. *Concord: Asian Agricultural Products Ltd [AAP] v Democratic Socialist Republic of Sri Lanka* (Award, 27 June 1990), 4 ICSID Rep 250, 257.

[219] Many BITs refer to 'contractual rights' among the recognised categories of 'investments' covered by the minimum standards of investment protection set out in the BITs. Consistent with the stated economic objective of BITs, which is to promote foreign direct investment, it is clear that 'contractual rights' in this context should be interpreted narrowly as those contracts that regulate the investor's rights to property in the host state. The United States Model BIT, for example, lists examples of 'contractual rights' as those 'under turnkey, construction or management contracts, production or revenue-sharing contracts, concessions, or other similar contracts'. United States Model BIT, Art. 1(d), *UNCTAD Compendium* (Vol. VI, 2002) 502. The types of property encompassed by this provision are the objects of construction projects and natural resources. On the other hand, a simple sale of goods contract between the investor and the host state would not give rise to a protected investment, both for the reason just articulated and because it is not an investment in the territory of the host state (an express or implicit requirement of all BITs). Thus, Section C of Ch. 11 of NAFTA excludes from the definition of 'investment': '(i) claims to money that arise solely from (i) commercial contracts for the sale of goods or services by a national or enterprise in the territory of a Party to an enterprise in the territory of another Party, or (ii) the extension of credit in connection with a commercial transaction, such as trade financing, other than a loan covered by subparagraph (d) [concerning loans to enterprises]; or (j) any other claims to money.' This interpretation of 'contractual rights' is broadly consistent with the definition given to 'investment' for the purposes of Art. 25 of the ICSID Convention. The minimum characteristics of an 'investment' for the purposes of the ICSID Convention are analysed by C. Schreuer, above n. 23, 121–5, 138–41. UNCTAD suggests that investment 'includes not only property rights, but contractual rights as well' but then caveats this statement: 'However, it is not so clear whether even in a broad definition of investment all contracts would be included . . .' UNCTAD, above n. 106, 20.

[220] One example of an international treaty that does create and regulate rights *in rem* is the UNIDROIT Convention on International Interests in Mobile Equipment, available at <http://www.unidroit.org/english/conventions/mobile-equipment/mobile-equipment.pdf>.

It is therefore the municipal law of the host state that determines whether a particular right *in rem* exists, the scope of that right, and in whom it vests. It is the investment treaty, however, that supplies the classification of an investment and thus prescribes whether the right *in rem* recognised by the municipal law is subject to the protection afforded by the investment treaty. This classification features in the first article of most BITs in the form of a definition, such as the following taken from the United States Model BIT:

'investment' of a national or company means every kind of investment owned or controlled directly or indirectly by that national or company, and includes investment consisting or taking the form of:

(i) a company;
(ii) shares, stock, and other forms of equity participation, and bonds, debentures, and other forms of debt interests, in a company;
(iii) contractual rights, such as under turnkey, construction or management contracts, production or revenue-sharing contracts, concessions, or other similar contracts;
(iv) tangible property, including real property, and intangible property, including rights, such as leases, mortgages, liens and pledges;
(v) intellectual property, including:
copyrights and related rights,
rights in plant varieties,
industrial designs,
rights in semiconductor layout designs,
trade secrets, including know-how and confidential business information,
trade and service marks, and
trade names; and
(vi) rights conferred pursuant to law, such as licenses and permits.[221]

This enumeration of the types or categories of investments that fall within the domain of the treaty is essential to the efficacy of the international treaty regime. It could not be left to the municipal law of the contracting states to define investments. Otherwise the protection afforded by investment treaties to shares in companies, for example, could be subverted by a law or decree at the state where the company is incorporated declaring that shares do not constitute investments. 'Investments' are, therefore, given an 'objective' treaty definition. But this definition does not in some way detach the rights *in rem* that underlie those investments from the municipal law that creates and gives recognition to those rights. Investment treaties do not contain substantive rules of property law. There must be a *renvoi* to a municipal property law. Insofar as investment treaties require a territorial nexus between the investment and one of the contracting state parties, that property law is the municipal law of the state in which the investor alleges that it has an investment. Some treaties explicitly provide that investments must be duly made in

[221] United States Model BIT, Art. 1(d), *UNCTAD Compendium* (Vol. VI, 2002) 502.

accordance with the municipal law of the host state.[222] But this would be the case even in the absence of an express stipulation, because no other law could conceivably be applicable pursuant to the relevant choice of law rule.[223]

Returning to the example of an investment in shares, the protection of an investment treaty is contingent upon securing the legal rights to those shares in accordance with the relevant municipal law where the company is incorporated. If the investment in shares is made in England, legal ownership arises upon entry onto the share register.[224] Thus, in order for a Russian investor in England to perfect its investment in the shares of an English company and be covered by the UK/Russia BIT, it will not be sufficient to accept delivery of share certificates, as would be the case in other jurisdictions such as New York.[225]

Once a right *in rem* has been recognised by the municipal law of the host state, the treaty regime takes over. Subsequent changes in that municipal law, or other acts attributable to the host state that affect the bundle of rights *in rem* that constitute the investment, must be assessed against the minimum standards of protection in the investment treaty. This follows from the rule of state responsibility alluded to previously that:

> The characterization of an act of a State as internationally wrongful is governed by international law. Such characterization is not affected by the characterization of the same act as lawful by internal law.[226]

The host state cannot, therefore, escape liability to an investor under the investment treaty regime by passing a law to the effect that title to shares obtained by the acceptance of shares certificates shall no longer be

[222] This was the case for the Greece/Egypt BIT in *Middle East Cement Shipping and Handling Co. S. A. v Arab Republic of Egypt* (Award, 12 April 2002) Case No. ARB/99/6, available at <http://www.worldbank.org/icsid/cases/me_cement-award.pdf>. See further: Chile Model BIT, Art. 1(2), *UNCTAD Compendium* (Vol. III, 1998) 144; China Model BIT, Art. 1(1), *ibid.* 151; Switzerland Model BIT, Art. 2, *ibid.* 178; Egypt Model BIT, Art. 1(1), *ibid.* (Vol. V, 2000) 293; France Model BIT, Art. 1(1), *ibid.* 302; Jamaica Model BIT, Art. 1(1), *ibid.* 321; Malaysia Model BIT, Art. 1(2)(a), *ibid.* 326; Sri Lanka Model BIT, Art. 1(1), *ibid.* 339; Cambodia Model BIT, Art. 1, *ibid.* (Vol. VI, 2002) 463; Croatia Model BIT, Art. 1, *ibid.* 471; Finland Model BIT, Art. 1(1), *ibid.* (Vol. VII) 287; Turkey Model BIT, Art. 1(2), *ibid.* (Vol. VIII) 281; Benin Model BIT, Art. 1(1), *ibid.* (Vol. IX) 279; Sweden Model BIT, Art. 1(1), *ibid.* 309.

[223] See further: *Salini Costrutorri SpA and Italstrade SpA v Kingdom of Morocco* (Decision on Jurisdiction, 23 July 2001) Case No. ARB/00/4, 6 ICSID Rep 400. The ICSID Tribunal interpreted such a provision in the Italy/Morocco BIT as follows: 'En visant "les catégories de biens investis (...) conformément aux lois et règlements de la dite partie", la disposition en cause se réfère à la régularité de l'investissement et non à sa définition.' *Ibid.* para. 46.

[224] *Gower's Principles of Modern Company Law* (1997, 6th edn by P. Davies) 328. This rule is subject to two exceptions which are not important in practice. *Ibid.* 328–30.

[225] The distinction between the English and New York rules on when title to shares is perfected was the focus of a well-known English case: *Colonial Bank v Cady* (1890) 15 App Cas 267. An investor in England without legal title to shares might nevertheless claim beneficial ownership and thus an equitable title. The question would then become whether or not an equitable title falls within the definition of an investment in the relevant investment treaty.

[226] Article 3 of the ILC's Articles on State Responsibility, above n. 12, 61.

recognised if an investor had previously acquired shares on that (lawful) basis. On the other hand, if the investor's title to the shares remains static pursuant to the municipal law of the host state but various acts taken by the host state have the *de facto* effect of rendering those shares worthless, it will be open to the treaty tribunal to find that the prohibition against *indirect* expropriation or other minimum standard of treatment in the investment treaty has been violated by the host state.

These observations point to an acquired rights paradigm[227] for understanding the object of protection under investment treaties. An eloquent expression of this theory in relation to customary international law on the protection of the property of foreign nationals is to be found in the opinion of Judge Morelli in the *Barcelona Traction Case*:[228]

> [T]he international rule postulates a certain attitude in the part of the State legal order, inasmuch as it has regard solely to interests which, within that legal order, have already received some degree of protection through the attribution of rights or other advantageous personal legal situations (faculties, legal powers or expectations): an attitude on the part of the State legal order which in itself is not obligatory in international law.
>
> It is on the hypothesis that this state of affairs has arisen in the municipal legal order that the international rule lays upon the State the obligation to observe a certain line of conduct with regard to the interests in question: with regard, one might thenceforward say, to the rights whereby the interests in question stand protected in the municipal legal order . . .
>
> [T]he fact that the rules of international law in question envisage solely such interests of foreigners as already constitute rights in the municipal order is but the necessary consequence of the very content of the obligations imposed by those rules; obligations which, precisely, presuppose rights conferred on foreigners by the legal order of the State in question.[229]

Judge Morelli's statement of principle for customary international law has been criticised because it fails to take into account the host state's international obligation to respect rights to tangible property acquired in a foreign legal system when that property comes within the territorial jurisdiction of the host state.[230] If the protection of customary international law were only to extend to rights acquired under the municipal law of the host state, the host state would be at liberty to pass legislation to the effect that any property with certain characteristics entering the territory of the host state shall be vested in the host state. For this reason, customary international law requires states to respect rights to tangible property

[227] O'Connell defines the term 'acquired rights' as follows: 'Acquired rights are any rights, corporeal or incorporeal, properly vested under municipal law in a natural or juristic person and of an assessable monetary value.' D. O'Connell, above n. 72, 764. For support of the acquired rights theory in the customary international law of expropriation, see: B. Wortley, *Expropriation in International Law* (1959) 125; G. White, *Nationalisation of Foreign Property* (1961) 226.

[228] [1970] ICJ Rep 3.

[229] *Ibid.* 233–4.

[230] C. Staker, 'Public International Law and the Lex Situs Rule in Property Conflicts and Foreign Expropriations' (1987) 58 *BYBIL* 151, 159–161.

acquired at the previous *lex situs*,[231] save in cases where the acquisition contravenes international public policy or international law.

This criticism of the acquired rights approach is not, however, relevant to the investment treaty regime. The protection afforded by investment treaties is contingent upon an individual or legal entity making an investment in the host state. This is an indispensable prerequisite; the economic rationale of investment treaties is to promote and encourage direct foreign investment in the economies of the contracting states. Unlike the broader concerns of customary international law on the protection of the property rights of aliens, the objective of investment treaties is to protect rights *in rem* acquired in accordance with the municipal law of the host state that constitute an investment according to the definition in the relevant investment treaty. The statement of Judge Morelli in the *Barcelona Traction Case* is good law for the investment treaty regime.

A threshold question may arise as to whether the investor has discharged the territorial requirement by making a qualified investment in one of the state parties to the investment treaty (the host state). In relation to tangible property, the *situs* of that property is a simple question of fact: *eg* is the waste disposal site leased by the investor situated in the territory of the host state? It is not difficult to anticipate a problem in trying to identify the *situs* of intangible property. The municipal conflict of law rules of the host state may be of assistance in resolving this problem. A debt, for example, might be deemed to have a *situs* at the debtor's domicile by the conflict rules of State X. Thus, if the debtor is domiciled in State X, an investment has been made in the territory of State X if a debt is capable of falling within the relevant definition of an investment in the treaty. Similarly, if State Y's conflict rules determine the *situs* of shares as the place where the share register is maintained, and the company in question keeps its register in State Y, the acquisition of shares in that company is a qualified investment in State Y. But what if private international law does not create a fictional *situs* for other types of intangible property, such as intellectual property rights? In these circumstances one must proceed straight to the substantive property rules of the putative host state, and, applying these rules, determine whether the municipal law of the host state recognises the intangible rights in question or is compelled to do so by a relevant international convention. Investment treaties do not oblige the contracting states to protect intangible property rights that are not recognised in the legal order of the contracting state.

A review of the investment treaty arbitration precedents reveals that where the nature or existence of rights *in rem* making up the investment is a matter

[231] *Ibid.* 166–9. The *lex situs* rule has the status of a general principle of law recognised by civilised nations. See: E. Rabel, *The Conflict of Laws: A Comparative Study* (Vol. 4, 1958) 30, 'It is at present the universal principle, manifested in abundant decisions and recognised by all writers, that the creation, modification, and termination of rights in individual tangible physical things are determined by the law of the place where the thing is physically situated.' See also P. Lalive, *The Transfer of Chattels in the Conflicts of Law* (1955).

of controversy between the parties, tribunals (and the disputing parties themselves) have either tended to ignore the relevant provisions of municipal law, or have proceeded on the assumption that such issues are only relevant to affirming their jurisdiction *ratione materiae* (*ie* by the identification of an investment duly made in accordance with the municipal law of the host state). The most striking example is the award of the UNCITRAL Tribunal in *CME Czech Republic B.V. (The Netherlands) v Czech Republic*.[232]

A public broadcasting licence was granted by the Czech Media Council in 1993 to CET 21, a Czech legal entity, which, together with a German company, formed a Czech television services company called ČNTS.[233] The Memorandum of Association of ČNTS recognised CET 21 as the licence holder and ČNTS as the operator of the broadcasting station, TV Nova.[234] The claimant, CME (a Dutch legal entity), eventually obtained a 99 percent shareholding in ČNTS and thus qualified as an investor under the Netherlands/Czech Republic BIT.[235]

The Czech Media Law was amended in 1996 with the effect that the Media Council lost its primary means of monitoring and regulating television licence holders.[236] In order to maintain some control over ČNTS outside the legislative framework, and to diffuse public concern over the foreign control of Czech broadcasting, the Media Council exerted pressure over ČNTS[237] to amend the characterisation of CET 21's contribution in its Memorandum of Association from 'use of the licence' to 'use of the know-how of the licence' and to enter into a Service Agreement with CET 21.[238] The UNCITRAL Tribunal in *CME* inferred that the purpose of this new wording was to sustain an interpretation of the investment structure whereby CET 21 did not make a contribution in kind to the share capital of ČNTS.[239]

In 1999, CET 21 terminated the Service Agreement, evidently in bad faith, on the basis that ČNTS had failed to deliver a programming day-log on the previous day.[240] This termination paved the way for ČNTS's former joint venture partner to pursue more lucrative contracts with other service providers.[241] CME's interest in ČNTS became worthless for want of a licence to operate the now highly profitable TV Nova.[242] Before the termination, Dr Železný, who had senior management positions in both CET 21 and ČNTS and was the principal beneficiary of CET 21's split from ČNTS, procured a letter from the Media Council that appeared to support his position in an ongoing conflict between CET 21 and ČNTS.[243] Nevertheless, as this letter contained no binding regulatory determination of any sort, it could not have provided a *legal* cause for CET 21's termination of the Service Agreement.[244]

[232] *CME* Partial Award. [233] *Ibid.* para. 8. [234] *Ibid.* para. 12. [235] *Ibid.* para. 5.
[236] *Ibid.* para. 15. [237] *Ibid.* para. 463. [238] *Ibid.* para. 16. [239] *Ibid.* para. 470.
[240] *Ibid.* para. 18. [241] *Ibid.* para. 18. [242] *Ibid.* para. 17. [243] *Ibid.* para. 544.

[244] The UNCITRAL Tribunal in the *Lauder* Final Award found that the letter 'does not constitute a "measure" within the meaning of the Treaty, but merely expresses the general opinion of a regulatory body regarding the proper interpretation which should be given to the Media Law' and hence the letter 'was not aimed at having, and could not have, any legal effect.' *Ibid.* paras. 282, 283.

The 1999 contractual termination appears to have been instigated by Dr Železný on behalf of CET 21 for reasons associated with personal financial gain. He was at no time an officer of the Czech State and hence his conduct could not be attributable to the Czech Republic under international law. Consequently, for the Czech Republic to be liable for the alleged 'destruction' of CME's investment in ČNTS, there had to be a causal link either back to the Media Council's conduct in procuring the 1996 modification of the investment structure or to the issuance of the letter by the Media Council in 1999. The UNCITRAL Tribunal held that both acts constituted a breach of the Netherlands/Czech Republic BIT.[245] The Tribunal was, however, careful to find that the causal basis for CME's loss was directly related to the 1996 modification rather that the 1999 letter, describing the latter as only 'compound[ing] and complet[ing] the [Media] Council's part in the destruction of CME's investment'[246] rather than the proximate cause of the 'destruction'.[247]

The Tribunal thus held that the Media Council had unlawfully coerced ČNTS to change the structure of the investment in 1996 and that this had the effect of leaving ČNTS vulnerable to the loss of its right over the television licence at the instigation of CET 21.[248] Of paramount importance to the Tribunal's reasoning was its finding, repeated on several occasions in the award, that the 'use of "know-how" of a broadcasting licence is meaningless and worthless'.[249] If, to the contrary, this change in wording in ČNTS's Memorandum of Association had no effect on ČNTS's rights, then the Media Council's coercion could not be the cause of CME's loss.[250]

The only law that could determine the status of ČNTS's interest in the licence at the time of its original investment in 1993 and immediately following the 1996 modification was Czech law. But there is no reference to any provision of Czech law, or indeed to any other law, in the Tribunal's reasoning on this issue. Any criticism of this omission must be tempered by the observation that the Czech Republic, inexplicably, did not tender any expert evidence on Czech law during the liability phase of the arbitration proceedings. This certainly created a real dilemma for the

[245] *CME* Partial Award, paras. 591 *et seq.* [246] *Ibid.* para. 601.

[247] It is unclear whether the Tribunal found that the issuance of the letter in 1999 was, in and of itself, an act of expropriation. In concluding its remarks on the letter itself, the Tribunal found that '[t]his interference by the Media Council in the economic and legal basis of CME's investment carries the stigma of a Treaty violation' (*ibid.* para. 551) without specifying which provision of the Treaty was thereby violated. On the other hand, the Tribunal concludes its section on expropriation by stating: '[t]his qualifies the Media Council's actions in 1996 and actions and inactions in 1999 as expropriation under the Treaty', thus suggesting that the expropriation consisted of composite acts (*ibid.* para. 609). [248] *Ibid.* para. 469.

[249] *Ibid.* para. 470. See also: paras. 469, 535, 593, 595.

[250] The UNCITRAL Tribunal in the *Lauder* Final Award came to this precise conclusion: 'All property rights of the Claimant were actually fully maintained until the contractual relationship between CET 21 and ČNTS was terminated by the former. It is at that time, and at that time only, that Mr. Lauder's property rights, i.e. the use of the benefits of the License by ČNTS, were affected.' (*Ibid.* para. 202).

Tribunal, which was resolved by the majority in the form of several unsubstantial assertions on the 'legal' modification in 1996:

The amendment of the MOA by replacing the licence-holder's contribution of the Licence by the worthless 'use of the know-how of the Licence' is nothing else than the destruction of the legal basis . . . of the Claimant's investment.[251]

[. . .]

The contribution of the use of the Licence under the MOA is legally substantially stronger than the Service Agreement . . .[252]

[. . .]

The Media Council violated the Treaty when dismantling the legal basis of the foreign investor's investments by forcing the foreign investor's joint venture company ČNTS to give up substantial accrued legal rights.[253]

This aspect of the Tribunal's decision was reviewed by the Svea Court of Appeals in Stockholm upon a challenge to the award by the Czech Republic,[254] relying on a particular ground in Section 34 of the Swedish Arbitration Act which provides that an award rendered in Sweden can be wholly or partially set aside at the request of a party if 'through no fault of the party, an irregularity has occurred in the course of the proceedings which probably has influenced the outcome of the case.'[255]

The Svea Court of Appeals formulated the test for 'irregularity' with respect to this choice of law issue as follows:

[W]hether the arbitral tribunal applied any of the sources of law listed in the choice of law clause or whether the tribunal has not based its decision on any law at all but, rather, judged in accordance with general reasonableness.[256]

The Court found that the Tribunal complied with the choice of law clause in the Netherlands/Czech Republic BIT by applying relevant sources of law, 'primarily international law'.[257]

This ruling is unfortunate because it ignores the choice of law rule for questions pertaining to the existence, nature, and scope of the investment.

[251] The UNCITRAL Tribunal in the *Lauder* Final Award came to this precise conclusion: CME Partial Award, para. 593.

[252] *Ibid.* para. 473.

[253] *Ibid.* para. 520.

[254] *Czech Republic v CME Czech Republic B.V.* (Svea Court of Appeals, 15 May 2003), reproduced and translated in (2003) 42 ILM 919. The Czech Republic submitted that the following issues should have been determined by application of Czech law: the protection afforded the original investor pursuant to the 1993 MOA, the commencement of the administrative proceedings in 1996, and the alleged coercion in conjunction therewith, the relationship between the 1996 MOA and the 1993 MOA, the service agreement, what transpired when CME acquired the interests in ČNTS from CME Media Enterprises B.V. in 1997, the Media Council's letter of March 15, 1999 and the alleged collusion with Železný, the obligation of the Media Council to intervene, and the termination of the service agreement. *Ibid.* 931.

[255] Swedish Arbitration Act 1999 (SFS 1999:116), translation by K. Hobér, (2001) 17 *Arbitration Int* 425.

[256] *Czech Republic v CME Czech Republic B.V.* (Svea Court of Appeals, 15 May 2003), reproduced and translated in (2003) 42 ILM 919, 965.

[257] *Ibid.*

If the law of the host state is to have any role in an investment dispute, this is precisely the context in which it must do so. As previously stated, general international law cannot purport to regulate the complex problems of proprietary and contractual rights over a television licence. The Court's finding that the Tribunal discharged its mandate by applying 'primarily international law' exposes the weakness in its ruling because there simply is no international law of licence agreements and the UNCITRAL Tribunal made no effort to unearth one. Sympathize as one might with the Tribunal's plight in the absence of any expert evidence on Czech law, it is difficult to conclude that the Tribunal did anything else but adjudge according to general notions of reasonableness.

Another prominent failure to heed to the *lex situs* choice of law rule with respect to matters concerning the existence and extent of the investment occurred in the ICSID Tribunal's award in *Wena Hotels Ltd v Arab Republic of Egypt*.[258]

Wena alleged that Egypt breached several provisions of the UK/Egypt BIT when a state-owned company, the Egyptian Hotel Company ('EHC'), seized two hotels (the 'Luxor Hotel' and the 'Nile Hotel') which were the subject of separate lease agreements between Wena and EHC. In accordance with the investor/state dispute resolution provision in the BIT, Wena elected to bring its treaty claims to an international arbitral tribunal established pursuant to the ICSID Convention.

The lease agreements between Wena and EHC stipulated that disputes between the parties must be submitted to *ad hoc* arbitration in Cairo.[259]

Following the seizure, Wena had brought a contractual arbitration against EHC for breach of the Nile Hotel lease on 2 December 1993.[260] Wena was awarded EGP 1.5 million in damages as compensation for the seizure of the Nile Hotel; however, this *ad hoc* tribunal simultaneously ordered that Wena surrender the hotel to EHC due to its own breaches of the lease agreement.[261] Wena continued to operate the Nile hotel until 1995 when it was evicted pursuant to the Tribunal's decision.

Wena brought similar contractual arbitration proceedings against EHC with respect to the Luxor Hotel lease on 12 January 1994. The second *ad hoc* tribunal also found in favour of Wena and awarded EGP 9.06 million in damages and also ordered Wena to surrender the hotel to EHC.[262] The award was subsequently annulled by the Cairo Court of Appeal.[263] Wena remained in occupancy until 1999, when the Luxor Hotel was placed in judicial receivership on account of Wena's failure to pay rent.

The ICSID Tribunal ignored the findings of the contractual arbitral tribunals in its decision on the merits. This became one of the grounds for annulment alleged by Egypt in the subsequent annulment proceedings.

[258] (Award, 8 December 2000) Case No. ARB/98/4, 6 ICSID Rep 89. [259] *Ibid.* para. 17.
[260] *Ibid.* para. 60. [261] *Ibid.* para. 61. [262] *Ibid.* para. 62. [263] *Ibid.*

The *ad hoc* Committee upheld the Tribunal's award in full and also dismissed the relevance of the previous arbitral decisions for the following reasons:

> The dispute before the Tribunal involved different parties, namely the investor and the Egyptian State, and concerned a subject matter entirely different from the commercial aspects under the leases . . .[264]
> [. . .]
> The leases deal with questions that are by definition of a commercial nature. The [BIT] deals with questions that are essentially of a government nature, namely the standards of treatment accorded by the State to foreign investors.[265]

This simple dichotomy between 'commercial' and 'BIT' questions is an inaccurate over-simplification. Far from having an 'entirely different' subject matter, the contractual arbitrations and the treaty arbitration were about precisely the same thing, *viz.* Wena's investment in Egypt. That investment was in the form of leaseholds over two hotels. If Wena had breached its obligations under the lease agreements such that Egypt was entitled to terminate the leases in accordance with their governing law, then there would have been no investment to expropriate. In response to Egypt's submission to this effect, the Tribunal found opaquely that: '[i]t is sufficient for this proceeding simply to acknowledge, as both parties agree, that there were serious disagreements between Wena and EHC about their respective obligations under the leases.'[266] With respect, this was not sufficient at all. The Tribunal was bound to analyse the existence and extent of Wena's investment under the lease agreements at the time of the seizure of the hotels. In conducting this analysis the Tribunal should have considered the previous determinations made by the contractual tribunals or made its own findings on the status of Wena's investment in accordance with the governing law of the lease agreements. Both the ICSID Tribunal and the *ad hoc* Committee dismissed the relevance of the lease agreements under Egyptian law to the question of Egypt's liability under the BIT, even though the lease agreements were the sole foundation of Wena's investment.[267] The Tribunal and the *ad hoc* Committee did, however, consider that the lease agreements were relevant to positively establishing the Tribunal's jurisdiction and the question of damages flowing from Egypt's substantive violation of the BIT. On the first point, the *ad hoc* Committee stated:

> This Committee cannot ignore of course that there is a connection between the leases and the [BIT] since the former were designed to operate under the

[264] (Decision on Annulment, 5 February 2002) Case No. ARB/98/4, 6 ICSID Rep 129, para. 29.
[265] *Ibid.* para. 31. [266] *Ibid.* para. 19.
[267] The *ad hoc* Committee stated with respect to the Tribunal's consideration of this issue: '[T]he Tribunal declared irrelevant to consider the rights and obligations of the parties to the leases for the purpose of reaching a decision on the dispute submitted to it. The Award confirms that Wena has been expropriated and lost its investment, and this irrespective of the particular contractual relationship between Wena and EHC. The explanation thus given for not determining the respective obligations of Wena and EHC under the leases is sufficient to understand the premises on which the Tribunal's decision is based in this respect.' *Ibid.* para. 86.

protection of the [BIT] as materialization of the investment. But this is simply a condition precedent to the operation of the [BIT].[268]

Thus, the *ad hoc* Committee in effect declared that the factual existence of the leases established Wena's credentials as a qualified investor under the terms of the BIT, but their significance ended here, only to re-emerge later in the quantum phase of the decision after bypassing the determination of liability. In considering Wena's previous recovery of damages in the contractual arbitration concerning the Nile Hotel, the *ad hoc* Committee reversed its previous position on the significance of the leases:

It is here where the relationship between one dispute and the other becomes relevant. The ultimate purpose of the relief sought by Wena is to have its losses compensated. To the extent this relief was partially obtained in the domestic arbitration, the Tribunal in awarding damages under the [BIT] did take into account such partial indemnification so as to prevent a kind of double dipping in favour of the investor. The two disputes are still separate but the ultimate result is the compensation of the investor for the wrongdoings that have affected its business.[269]

The Tribunal and *ad hoc* Committee were therefore prepared to give effect to the damages component of the Nile Hotel award, but not the *ad hoc* Tribunal's finding that the lease had been validly terminated.

The ICSID Tribunal in *Mihaly International Corporation v Democratic Socialist Republic of Sri Lanka*[270] appears to have arrived at the correct conclusion on an objection to its jurisdiction *ratione materiae*, but its reasoning is not entirely persuasive. The problem started with the Tribunal's characterisation of the issue as whether the definition of 'investment' covered pre-investment expenditures.[271] This formulation of the issue simply begs the question as to when an investment is consummated. Expenditures in an investment project in the host state become an investment if and only if the investor acquires a legal interest that falls within the definition of an investment in the relevant BIT. That legal interest must be acquired in accordance with the *lex situs*.

Contrary to these principles, the Tribunal purported to survey the 'sources of international law'[272] to determine whether 'pre-investment and development expenditures in the circumstances of the present case could automatically be admitted as an "investment"'.[273] There is no analysis of various instruments between the putative investor and the Sri Lankan authorities to determine whether such transactions gave rise to a proprietary interest under Sri Lankan law cognisable as an investment pursuant to the definition of such in the US/Sri Lanka BIT (that key provision of the BIT is not even quoted in the Award). Nevertheless, the Tribunal did analyse the three relevant instruments (a Letter of Intent,

[268] *Ibid*. para. 35.

[269] *Ibid*. para. 49. See also: (Award, 8 December 2000) Case No. ARB/98/4, 6 ICSID Rep 89, para. 127.

[270] (Award, 15 March 2002) Case No. ARB/00/2, 6 ICSID Rep 310.

[271] See, *eg*: para. 34.

[272] *Ibid*. para. 60.

[273] *Ibid*.

a Letter of Agreement, and a Letter of Extension) and found that none of them created any contractual obligations with respect to the building, ownership and operation of the power station.[274] This conclusion appears to be correct due to the stipulations in the instruments that they were subject to a final contract. But this intuitive presumption was never tested against Sri Lankan law, or any other law. The only real question confronting the Tribunal was whether Sri Lankan law in some way recognised a right of the putative investor in the power plant project on the basis of the transactions between the parties so that the investor could be said to have 'any right conferred by law or contract' for the purposes of Article I(1)(a)(v) of the Sri Lanka/US BIT.[275] That question was never directly raised or addressed by the Tribunal.

The ICSID Tribunal in *Marvin Feldman v Mexico*,[276] also struggled with the application of the municipal law of the host state to questions pertaining to the claimant's investment. A US national, Feldman, owned a Mexican exporting business 'CEMSA'.[277] A significant part of CEMSA's business consisted of the purchase of cigarettes in Mexico from bulk suppliers for resale in third countries. Mexico imposed a tax on the production and sale of cigarettes in the domestic market, but in some circumstances a zero tax rate was applied to cigarettes that are exported.[278] In 1991, Mexico passed new legislation to ensure that only the exports of producers of cigarettes in Mexico qualified for the zero tax rate, rather than the exports of resellers such as CEMSA.[279] This legislation was challenged as contravening the principle of 'equity of taxpayers',[280] and was then amended to apply the zero tax rate to all exporters of cigarettes.[281] The amended tax legislation remained unchanged between 1992 and 1997, which was the relevant period for the claims advanced by Feldman (the 'Tax Legislation').

The zero tax rate operated as a tax rebate to be claimed by the exporters of cigarettes. The 85 percent tax on production was initially paid by the cigarette producers, and this was passed on to the purchasers in the sales price for the cigarettes.[282] The Tax Legislation provided that, in order for exporters to claim the tax rebate, the tax on production on the cigarettes must be stated 'separately and expressly on their invoices'.[283] The effect of this invoice requirement, which was a feature of the Tax Legislation from its inception,[284] was to discriminate between the exports of cigarette producers and resellers, despite the amendments to the legislation in 1992. Nevertheless, tax discrimination on this basis is consistent with international practice; the Tribunal noted that it was

[274] See, *eg*, para. 48.
[275] ICSID, *Investment Promotion and Protection Treaties* (Release 92–4, 1993).
[276] (Award, 16 December 2002) Case No. ARB(AF)/99/1, (2003) 42 ILM 625.
[277] The acronym for Corporación de Exportaciones Mexicanas, S. A. de C. V. *Ibid.* para. 1.
[278] *Ibid.* para. 7. [279] *Ibid.* para. 10. [280] *Ibid.* para. 11. [281] *Ibid.* para. 12.
[282] *Ibid.* para. 15. [283] *Ibid.*
[284] And four years before Feldman established CEMSA in Mexico, *ibid.* para. 128.

a 'rational tax policy and a reasonable legal requirement'[285] and could not constitute a violation of international law *per se*.[286]

Insofar as CEMSA purchased its cigarettes from volume retailers rather than producers, at a price that included the tax on production, the tax was not itemized separately on the invoice.[287] Therefore, in accordance with the tax regime prescribed by the Tax Legislation, CEMSA was not entitled to claim the tax rebate. Nevertheless, CEMSA was granted the tax rebates for a total of sixteen months between 1996 to 1997.[288]

Feldman claimed that Mexico's denial of tax rebates on cigarettes exported by CEMSA constituted an expropriation under Article 1110 of NAFTA. In its analysis of this claim, the ICSID Tribunal reasoned that the Tax Legislation never afforded CEMSA a right to export cigarettes and that neither customary international law or NAFTA required Mexico to do so.[289] Furthermore, according to the Tribunal, Feldman's investment, which consisted of the exporting business CEMSA, remained under the complete control of Feldman.[290] Finally, the Tribunal noted that the profitability of Feldman's 'gray market' export business (CEMSA was not an authorised reseller of cigarettes in Mexico)[291] was wholly dependent upon obtaining the tax rebate, because otherwise the combined cost to CEMSA of the Mexican tax on production and the excise taxes imposed by the importing country would price CEMSA out of the market.[292] The claim for expropriation was dismissed by the Tribunal.[293]

Feldman also invoked Article 1102 of NAFTA by pleading that certain *Mexican*-owned resellers of cigarettes had received the tax rebates from the Mexican authorities at various times when CEMSA was denied the rebate, despite the invoice requirements of the Tax Legislation, and that this constituted a failure by Mexico to accord CEMSA national treatment.[294]

The Tribunal found that: (i) there was one Mexican-owned company in like circumstances to CEMSA for the purposes of the national treatment analysis (the 'Poblano Group');[295] (ii) the Poblano Group was granted the tax rebates during a period when CEMSA was denied them;[296] (iii) CEMSA had been audited by the Mexican tax authorities and ordered to repay the tax rebates that it had received, whereas there was no clear evidence about the status of a similar audit of the Poblano Group;[297] and (iv) this discrimination was the result of Feldman's US nationality.[298] The majority of the ICSID Tribunal concluded that Mexico had violated Article 1102 of NAFTA.[299]

The main focus of the dissenting opinion rendered in *Marvin Feldman v Mexico*[300] was that the majority's finding of discrimination was unsupported by the evidence.[301] This controversy will be left aside. Instead the

[285] *Ibid*. para. 129. [286] *Ibid*. para. 118. [287] *Ibid*. para. 15. [288] *Ibid*. para. 19.
[289] *Ibid*. para. 111. [290] *Ibid*. [291] *Ibid*. para. 115. [292] *Ibid*. para. 117.
[293] *Ibid*. para. 153. [294] *Ibid*. para. 154. [295] *Ibid*. para. 172. [296] *Ibid*. para. 173.
[297] *Ibid*. para. 174. [298] *Ibid*. para. 182. [299] *Ibid*. para. 188.
[300] (Dissenting Opinion of J. Bravo, 3 December 2002), (2003) 42 ILM 673.
[301] *Ibid*. pp. 675–80.

analysis that follows concentrates on a contradiction between the Tribunal's findings on the nature of the investment in its consideration of Feldman's expropriation claim and the majority's conclusion on national treatment.

In relation to Feldman's investment, the Tribunal held:

> [T]he only significant asset of the investment, the enterprise known as CEMSA, is its alleged right to receive [. . .] tax rebates upon exportation of cigarettes, and to profit from that business.[302]

However, the Tribunal found:

> [T]he Claimant never really possessed a 'right' to obtain tax rebates upon exportation of cigarettes . . .[303]

Hence the right to obtain tax rebates upon the exportation of cigarettes did not feature among the bundle of rights that made up Feldman's investment in CEMSA in accordance with Mexican law. As Mexico could not expropriate something that never belonged to the investor, the Tribunal correctly dismissed Feldman's Article 1110 claim. The Tribunal's analysis of the nature of Feldman's investment should not, however, have been discarded by the majority when it came to deal with national treatment under Article 1102. The essence of Feldman's complaint was that its *investment*, CEMSA, had been accorded less favourable treatment than that which Mexico accorded to investments of its own investors.[304]

If Feldman's investment in CEMSA did not include the right to a tax rebate, and yet the receipt of the rebate was essential to the commercial viability of CEMSA's cigarette export activities (and indeed the sole alleged 'asset' of CEMSA), it is difficult to fathom how Mexico's sporadic conferral of tax rebates to a Mexican-owned cigarette reseller constituted discrimination with respect to Feldman's *investment*.

Another cause for concern is the majority's assessment of the damages flowing from its finding of discrimination. The majority held that Feldman through CEMSA was entitled to certain tax rebates that it had been denied.[305] If this finding were to be generalised, the resulting proposition would be that where a tax authority has improperly assessed the tax liability of X, with the effect that a benefit is conferred upon X, then Y, a competitor of X, is able to claim damages based on non-receipt of the same benefit to itself. The effect of the majority's decision is thus to compel Mexico to breach its own legislation (legislation held by the Tribunal to be unimpeachable) and confer an unlawful benefit to an investor.

If Feldman did have an investment in Mexico (*ie* a business whose viability did not rest upon the misapplication of Mexican legislation) and

302 (Award, 16 December 2002) Case No. ARB(AF)/99/1, (2003) 42 ILM 625, para. 118.
303 *Ibid.* 304 *Ibid.* para. 155. 305 *Ibid.* paras. 202–5.

Mexico were found to have systematically derogated from its own legislation in favour of Feldman's Mexican competitors in like circumstances, then damages should be assessed on the basis of the harm caused to Feldman's business by such derogation. This might, for instance, include damages representing a loss of market share due to the competitive advantage obtained by Feldman's competitors.

D. CONCLUSION

Different choice of law rules apply to the different analytical stages for adjudging an investment treaty claim. At the first stage, the treaty tribunal must decide, if it is a matter of contention, whether particular rights *in rem* constituting the alleged investment exist, the scope of those rights, and in whom they vest. In relation to an investment composed of tangible property rights in the host state, the *lex situs* choice of law rule points to the application of the municipal law of the host state. For intangible property, it follows from the requirement that the investment must be in the territory of the host state that the intangible property rights underlying the alleged investment must be recognised by the municipal law of the host state, at least at the time the investment is consummated. Hence the requirement of a territorial connection also points to the application of the municipal law of the host state to questions relating to intangible property rights. At the first stage of the analysis, the treaty tribunal must also determine whether or not the rights *in rem* that have been identified in accordance with the municipal law of the host state constitute an investment as defined by the investment treaty itself. This is a question of treaty interpretation that is ultimately governed by principles of international law.

At the second analytical stage for an investment treaty claim, the conduct of the host state (alleged to have caused damage to the investment as defined at the first stage of analysis) is examined on the basis of the minimum standards of treatment set out in the treaty. Thus the treaty, as supplemented by general principles of international law, is the applicable law at the second stage of analysis.

Issues pertaining to the rights *in rem* underlying a covered investment may be relevant to establishing the treaty tribunal's jurisdiction *ratione materiae* and to liability and quantum. If, as is often the case, the treaty tribunal elects to bifurcate its consideration of any jurisdictional controversies between the parties and the merits of the investor's claims, then certain problems of timing and coordination may arise. At the jurisdictional phase, it is sufficient that the investor is able to demonstrate a *prima facie* case that it has rights *in rem* that fall within the definition of an investment. The treaty tribunal can reserve its definitive ruling on the precise scope of such rights until the merits and it may be prudent to do so if the pleadings reveal complex and contentious issues of fact and law on this point. It is, however, expedient for the tribunal to determine finally whether the *prima facie* legal interests in property meet the definition of an investment pursuant to the investment treaty because this issue will not surface again at the merits or quantum phases of the arbitration. If, on the other hand, jurisdictional questions are joined to the merits, then it makes sense for the treaty tribunal to define questions relating to the alleged investment as preliminary issues (rather than as issues going to jurisdiction or the merits of the dispute) in a separate section of the award.

The ICSID Tribunal's award in *Technicas Medioambientales TECMED S.A. v United Mexican States*[306] illustrates the suggested approach to preliminary issues concerning the rights *in rem* that comprise the investment. The Claimant was the Spanish parent company of the Mexican company 'Tecmed', which in turn owned another Mexican company 'Cytrar'.[307] At an auction of public utilities by the Mexican municipal agency 'Promotora',[308] Tecmed purchased rights to a landfill for hazardous industrial waste.[309] These rights were later transferred from Tecmed to Cytrar with the consent of the relevant Mexican authority 'INE'.[310] When a new operating licence for the landfill was issued by INE in Cytrar's name, it was expressed to be valid only for a year and renewable thereafter on an annual basis.[311] This was in contrast with the operating licence that was originally granted to Tecmed for an unlimited duration. Cytrar's licence was renewed after the first year. INE refused to grant any further renewals thereafter.[312]

The Claimant's principal claim was that the failure to renew Cytrar's operating licence amounted to an expropriation of its investment under the Spain/Mexico BIT as it brought Cytrar's exploitation of the landfill facility to an end.[313]

If the Claimant (through Tecmed and Cytrar) had acquired its investment fully cognisant of a Mexican law to the effect that operating licences are issued for one year and may be terminated by the Mexican authorities at will thereafter, it is difficult to conceive how Mexico's exercise of its regulatory authority could amount to an expropriation. If, however, the Claimant had acquired, along with the tangible property interest in the landfill, certain intangible property rights including the right to the requisite licences to operate the landfill, the subsequent interference with the Claimant's intangible rights might also be protected.

The Claimant advanced its case on this basis and the ICSID Tribunal decided to consider the 'price and scope of the acquisition by Cytrar and Tecmed of assets relating to the Las Víboras landfill' as a 'preliminary

[306] (Award, 29 May 2003) Case No. ARB(AF)/00/2, (2004) 43 ILM 133.

[307] *Ibid.* para. 4.

[308] Promotora Inmobiliaria del Ayuntamiento de Hermosillo, a decentralized municipal agency of the Municipality of Hermosillo located in the State of Sonora, Mexico. *Ibid.* para. 35.

[309] *Ibid.* para. 35.

[310] *Ibid.* para. 38. 'INE' is an acronym for the Hazardous Materials, Waste and Activities Division of the National Ecology Institute of Mexico, an agency of the Federal Government of the United Mexican States within the Ministry of the Environment. *Ibid.* para. 36.

[311] *Ibid.* para. 38.

[312] *Ibid.* para. 39.

[313] *Ibid.* para. 41.

matter'.[314] What then followed was a meticulous examination by the Tribunal of all the transactional documents relating to the acquisition of the landfill to ascertain whether part of the consideration provided by Tecmed was for intangible property rights of the type alleged. This question was ultimately decided in the affirmative,[315] and the Tribunal went on to rule in a separate section of the award dealing with the merits that Mexico had used its regulatory power to revoke Cytrar's licence (thereby depriving Cytrar of its right thereto) in a manner inconsistent with its obligations under the investment treaty.[316]

V. The Law Applicable to the Procedure of Investor/State Disputes

A. INTRODUCTION

The municipal legal system at the seat of the arbitration has jurisdiction under international law to adjudge the validity or scope of the arbitration agreement, to regulate the arbitral procedure and determine the ultimate validity of the arbitral award, subject to any international treaty obligations that are binding on the territorial sovereign.[317] This is best conceptualised as an aspect of civil jurisdictional competence under international law on the basis of a subject-matter interest of the forum state that arises due to the agreement of the parties to a particular seat.[318] The international law of jurisdiction gives effect to the parties' agreement due to considerations of the good administration of international justice, for it is essential that a single municipal system be identified in advance as having primary control over an international arbitral procedure.[319] The most important and generally accepted international obligation that is binding on the territorial

[314] *Ibid.* para. 52. [315] *Ibid.* para. 91. [316] *Ibid.* para. 151.

[317] This is a principle evidenced by the consistent practice of states that, it is submitted, would give rise to a norm of customary international law. Municipal court decisions have confirmed their jurisdiction on the basis of this principle, see: *American Diagnostica, Inc. v Gradipore Ltd et al.* (1998) 44 NSWLR 312; *Coop International Pty Ltd v Ebel SA* [1998] 3 SLR 670; *Naviera Amazonica Peruana SA v Cia Internacional de Seguros del Peru* [1988] 1 Lloyd's Rep 116 (CA); *The Bay Hotel and Resort Ltd v Cavalier Construction Ltd* [2001] UKPC 34.

[318] (Or the agreement of the parties to allow the arbitral tribunal to fix the seat of arbitration.) This is a more persuasive justification than civil adjudicatory competence on the basis of the temporary physical presence of the arbitrators and parties at the territorial seat of the arbitration, which is one of the jurisdictional factors listed by Mann, see: F. Mann, 'Lex Facit Arbitrum' in P. Sanders (ed), *International Arbitration Liber Amicorum for Martin Domke* (1967), reprinted in (1986) 2 *Arbitration Int* 241, 236. The simple reason for rejecting this factor as controlling is that many arbitrations are successfully conducted without the arbitrators and parties ever entering the territorial jurisdiction of the country of the seat of arbitration.

[319] See F. Mann, *ibid.* 238–9. This would also be consistent with the 'fairness theory' for allocating adjudicatory jurisdiction because the parties' choice of a seat of arbitration might be assumed to have taken into account a fair distribution of the litigational burdens associated with that choice. This is obviously less persuasive when the choice is left to the arbitral tribunal. The seminal work on the fairness theory (as opposed to the power theory) of adjudicatory jurisdiction is: A. von Mehren, 'Adjudicatory Jurisdiction: General Theories Compared and Evaluated' (1983) 63 *Boston University L Rev* 279, esp. 311–7.

sovereign with jurisdiction over an international arbitral procedure is Article II of the New York Convention on the Recognition and Enforcement of Foreign Arbitral Awards, which compels the contracting state parties to recognise arbitration agreements and desist from exercising jurisdiction over the substance of disputes covered by such agreements.

Although the doctrine of jurisdiction in international law generally recognises the adjudicative competence of the state providing the seat of the arbitration, this principle is subject to an important exception in relation to arbitrations involving state parties. To the extent that an arbitration involving states is subject to public international law, those arbitration proceedings and the resulting award are grounded in, and regulated by, the international legal order and thus remain detached from the municipal legal system at the seat of the arbitration or from any other municipal legal system.[320] From the absence of jurisdiction of the territorial sovereign over an arbitration subject to public international law follows the principle that the international responsibility of the territorial sovereign cannot be engaged in relation to any aspect of that arbitration.[321]

This phenomenon of detachment of an arbitration from the municipal legal system at the seat of the arbitration is by prescription of international law and thus should be distinguished from situations where the municipal legal system voluntarily relinquishes or curtails its adjudicative or supervisory competence over international commercial arbitrations conducted within its jurisdiction. There is indeed a growing trend for municipal laws on international arbitration to curtail the scope for municipal courts at the seat of the arbitration to interpret or adjudge the validity of the arbitration agreement, to regulate the arbitral procedure or determine the ultimate validity of the arbitral award.[322] Detachment by application of public international law should also be distinguished from the incidence of 'delocalised arbitral awards', the debate over which in essence concerns the possibility that acts taken by municipal courts under the *lex loci arbitri* with respect to an arbitral procedure and award might not be recognised by a third municipal legal system for the purposes of enforcing that award.[323]

[320] *Eg, X v Germany* (Application 235/56) (1958–9) 2 Ybk of the European Convention on Human Rights 256, 294: '[T]he Supreme Restitution Court [established under the 1954 Paris Settlement Convention in the Federal Republic of Germany] must be regarded as an international tribunal in respect of which the Federal Republic had no power of legislation or control.'

[321] *X v Germany, ibid.* 294: '[I]n general a State does not have international responsibility for acts or omissions of an international tribunal merely by reason that it has its seat and exercises its functions on the territory of that State.' See further: F. Mann, above n. 133, 3–4. The same principle has been applied to the Iran/US Claims Tribunal, see *Spaans v The Netherlands* (Application 12516/86) (1988) 58 DR 119, 120.

[322] See generally: J. Lew, L. Mistelis, & S. Kröll, *Comparative International Commercial Arbitration* (2003) 356–62.

[323] See J. Paulsson, 'Arbitration Unbound: Award Detached from the Law of its Country of Origin' (1981) 30 *ICLQ* 358; W. Park, 'The *Lex Loci Arbitri* and International Commercial Arbitration: When and Why it Matters' (1983) 32 *ICLQ* 21; J. Paulsson, 'Delocalization of International Commercial Arbitration: When and Why it Matters' (1983) 32 *ICLQ* 53. For a useful update of the arguments for and against delocalisation, see: R. Goode, 'The Role of the *Lex Loci Arbitri* in International Commercial Arbitration' (2001) 17 *Arbitration Int* 19.

The exception to the adjudicative competence of states under international law over arbitrations conducted within their territory has been stated to apply *to the extent* that an arbitration involving states is subject to public international law. It is commonly assumed that arbitrations between states are always subject to public international law by force of an *a priori* rule, but this is doubtful as a general proposition.[324] States are at liberty to transact with one another on a commercial basis (say for the supply of goods for civilian consumption) and, in so doing, subject their contract to a municipal system of law or the *lex mercatoria* and refer disputes arising out of the contract to arbitration. In such a case, there is no reason in principle to assume that public international law would govern that arbitration simply because the two parties are sovereign states. It is clear, therefore, that the law applicable to arbitrations involving states may to some extent depend on the subject matter of the dispute or the status of the arbitral agreement or *compromis*.

The scope for public international law to govern arbitrations is ultimately reducible to the existence of an international obligation upon a municipal court to respect an express or implied choice of public international law and to uphold the consequences that follow from this choice (*eg* non-interference in the arbitral process). In view of the enormous latitude often granted to arbitral tribunals by municipal laws on international arbitration to settle their own procedure,[325] the parties' choice of public international law to govern their arbitration or an arbitral tribunal's determination to the same effect is likely to be of little or no consequence to the conduct of the arbitration or the rendering of an award, unless and until one of the parties invokes the jurisdiction of a municipal court with respect to that arbitration. At that moment, is the municipal court *bound* to decline jurisdiction under international law?

One source of an obligation upon a municipal court to desist from exercising jurisdiction over an arbitration involving a state party might derive from participation in a treaty on the settlement of disputes. For instance, Article 54 of the ICSID Convention requires that: 'Each Contracting State shall recognise an award rendered pursuant to this Convention as binding and enforce the pecuniary obligations imposed by that award within its territories as if it were a final judgment of a court in that State.' A municipal court of a Contracting State is therefore bound to recognise the *res judicata* effect of the award if a party to the ICSID arbitration attempts to relitigate matters decided in that award.

[324] F. Mann, above n. 133, 2.

[325] Article 182 of the Swiss Private International Law Act 1987 is representative in this sense:

> The parties, may, directly or by reference to arbitration rules, determine the arbitral procedure; they may also submit it to a procedural law of their choice.
>
> When the parties have not determined the procedure, the arbitral tribunal shall determine it to the extent necessary, either directly or by reference to a law or to arbitration rules.
>
> Whatever procedure is chosen, the arbitral tribunal shall assure equal treatment of the parties and the rights of the parties to be heard in an adversarial procedure.

On the other hand, if an investor seizes a municipal court of a state not party to the ICSID Convention, then the court would not be bound by international treaty or customary law to decline jurisdiction over the merits of its claim.[326]

This very situation arose in the context of the Iran/US Claims Tribunal in *Dallal v Bank Mellat*,[327] where the US claimant instituted proceedings in the English courts after his claims were dismissed in an award rendered by the Iran/US Claims Tribunal.[328] As the United Kingdom is not a party to the Algiers Accords, its courts are not bound by the obligations with respect to the finality of awards thereunder. Moreover, Justice Hobhouse expressed the view that the New York Convention is not applicable to the Tribunal's awards.[329] He nevertheless gave effect to the award in question by relying on principles of international comity and the inherent jurisdiction of the English court to prevent an abuse of process. Justice Hobhouse was not, however, under any international obligation to do so.

The more common source of international obligations curtailing the competence of municipal courts over arbitrations with state parties is the law of sovereign immunity from jurisdiction as found in customary international law or international treaty and municipal laws giving effect to these international rules.[330]

B. SOVEREIGN IMMUNITY FROM JURISDICTION AND ARBITRATIONS INVOLVING STATES

If the forum state adheres to the absolute doctrine of sovereign immunity, then the respondent's status as a sovereign state will suffice to oblige the municipal court to decline jurisdiction.[331] Adherence to the restrictive doctrine of sovereign immunity, however, requires the municipal court to give controlling significance to the subject matter of the dispute.[332] The inquiry shifts to whether the legal relationship underlying the dispute arises out of acts *jure imperii* (acts of sovereign authority), to which sovereign immunity applies, or acts *jure gestionis* (acts of a private or commercial character), to which it does not.[333]

Sovereign immunity must, therefore, attach to arbitrations between states concerning differences arising out of an international legal relationship that exists between sovereign states, such as disputes about diplomatic

[326] If the state of the municipal court is a signatory to the New York Convention then it may be argued that this international treaty would compel the court to give *res judicata* effect to the ICSID award.

[327] [1986] 1 All ER 239.

[328] *Ibid.* 246.

[329] *Ibid.* 250.

[330] H. Lauterpacht was one of the first writers to conceive of sovereign immunity from jurisdiction as the negation of jurisdictional competence that would otherwise exist on the basis of the subject-matter of the dispute or transaction being governed by international law. See H. Lauterpacht, 'The Problem of Jurisdictional Immunities of Foreign States' (1951) 28 *BYBIL* 220, 236–40.

[331] R. Higgins, above n. 164, 79.

[332] *Ibid.* 80.

[333] H. Fox, *The Law of State Immunity* (2002) 36–9.

immunities, diplomatic protection claims, and territorial disputes. It follows that the law governing the procedure of such arbitrations must be public international law.

It may be expected that the instances in which the *lex arbitri* of state/state arbitrations will be anything other than public international law will be rare. Hence the test to determine the applicable procedural law assumes a greater functional importance in the case of mixed arbitrations between states and private entities.

It is customary in any discussion of the procedural law applicable to mixed arbitrations to pay homage to the major *ad hoc* oil arbitrations involving Middle-Eastern States and Western oil companies, including: *Saudi Arabia v Arabian American Oil Co.*[334] ('ARAMCO'), *Sapphire International Petroleums v National Iranian Oil Co.*,[335] *British Petroleum Exploration Co. v Libyan Arab Republic*,[336] *Texaco Overseas Petroleum & California Asiatic Oil Co. v Libya*[337] ('TOPCO'), and *Libyan American Oil Co. v Libyan Arab Republic*[338] ('LIAMCO'). No purpose would be served by providing yet another comprehensive review of these awards,[339] but it will be useful to extract a number of principles from them that are important to the present discussion.

The *ARAMCO* Tribunal found that international law governed the arbitration between a private party and a sovereign state, rather than Swiss law as the *lex loci arbitri*, in deference to Saudi Arabia's jurisdictional immunity before the Swiss courts:

> The jurisdictional immunity of States . . . excludes the possibility, for the judicial authorities of the country of the seat, of exercising their right of supervision and interference in the arbitral proceedings which they have in certain cases . . .
>
> [. . .]
>
> Considering the jurisdictional immunity of foreign States, recognized by international law in a spirit of respect for the essential dignity of sovereign power, the Tribunal is unable to hold that arbitral proceedings to which a sovereign State is a Party could be subject to the law of another State.[340]

This precedent therefore clearly supports the suggested approach of giving primary weight to the availability or otherwise of sovereign immunity from jurisdiction in determining whether public international law applies to the arbitral procedure. The *ad hoc* Tribunal's decision to apply international law appears to have rested on a preference for the absolute

334 (1958) 27 ILR 117.

335 (1963) 35 ILR 136.

336 (Award on the Merits), (1973) 53 ILR 297.

337 (Award on the Merits), (1978) 17 ILM 1.

338 (1978) 20 ILM 1.

339 See R. von Mehren & P. Kourides, above n. 188; R. White, 'Expropriation of the Libyan Oil Concessions—Two Conflicting International Arbitrations' (1981) 30 *ICLQ* 1; C. Greenwood, 'State Contracts in International Law—The Libyan Oil Arbitrations' (1982) 53 *BYBIL* 27; S. Toope, *Mixed International Arbitration* (1990) Ch. II; A. Fatouros, 'International Law and the Internationalized Contract' (1980) *AJIL* 134; G. Delaume, 'State Contracts and Transnational Arbitration' (1981) *AJIL* 784.

340 (1958) 27 ILR 117, 155–6.

doctrine of sovereign immunity, despite the fact that Switzerland recognised the restrictive doctrine of sovereign immunity at that time:

It is true that the practice of the Swiss Courts has limited the jurisdictional immunity of States and does not protect that immunity, in disputes of a private nature, when legal relations between the Parties have been created, or when their obligations have to be performed in Switzerland. The Arbitration Tribunal must, however, take that immunity into account when determining the law to be applied to an arbitration which will lead to a purely declaratory award. By agreeing to fix the seat of the Tribunal in Switzerland, the foreign State which is a Party to the arbitration is not presumed to have surrendered its jurisdictional immunity in case of disputes relating to the implementation of the 'compromis' itself.[341]

Whilst the Tribunal's approach to the problem in *ARAMCO* is correct, there is cause for doubting whether a review of state practice on sovereign immunity would yield the same response today. It was 15 years later that Judge Lagergren, the sole arbitrator in *BP v Libya*, referred to the *ARAMCO* award at length but could not 'share the view that the application of municipal procedural law to an international arbitration like the present one would infringe upon such prerogatives as a State party to the proceedings may have by virtue of its sovereign status'.[342] Hence for Judge Lagergren the restrictive doctrine of sovereign immunity was a more persuasive reflection of customary international law and he had no difficulty in applying Danish law as the *lex loci arbitri* to the arbitral proceedings rather than public international law.[343]

After *BP v Libya*, the pendulum swung back to the application of the international law of procedure in *TOPCO* by sole arbitrator Dupuy, who was impressed by the discussion of sovereign immunity in *ARAMCO*. He buttressed his choice of international law to govern the procedure by reference to the fact of his appointment as arbitrator by the President of the International Court of Justice, and that the parties to the arbitration had not objected to his formulation of the rules of procedure as excluding the *lex loci arbitri*.[344] Dupuy's analysis of the procedural law does not, however, address the crucial question as to whether the courts at the seat of the arbitration are bound to refrain from exercising jurisdiction over the arbitration.

The situation in *LIAMCO* is more interesting because the award rendered by the sole arbitrator, Mahmassani, featured in multiple enforcement proceedings before the municipal courts of several jurisdictions. Mahmassani had given contrary indications about the *lex arbitri* by expressly determining the seat of the arbitration to be Geneva but at the same time stating that he would 'be guided as much as possible by the general principles contained in the Draft Convention on Arbitral

[341] (1958) 27 ILR 117, 156.

[342] (Award on the Merits), (1973) 53 ILR 297, 309.

[343] *Ibid.* In support of this finding, Judge Lagergren cited: *Sapphire International Petroleums Ltd. v The National Iranian Oil Co.* (1963) 35 ILR 136, and *Asling Trading Co. & Svenska Tändsticks Aktiebolaget v The Greek State* (1954) 23 ILR 633.

[344] (1978) 17 ILM 1, 8–9.

Procedure elaborated by the International Law Commission of the United Nations in 1958.'[345] Most commentators have interpreted his remarks as indicating a choice of a-national or international law.[346] As an excellent illustration of how futile a tribunal's abstract inquiry into its own procedural law can be, the courts of Switzerland, the United States, France, and Sweden all nevertheless assumed that the arbitration was governed by Swiss law as the *lex loci arbitri*.[347]

C. SOVEREIGN IMMUNITY AND INVESTMENT TREATY ARBITRATION

One must begin by distinguishing ICSID arbitrations, which are subject to a self-contained regime of procedural rules established by an international treaty, from other types of investment treaty arbitrations. In the case of ICSID arbitrations, the municipal courts of Contracting States are bound to refrain from exercising jurisdiction over the interpretation of the arbitration agreement, the arbitral procedure and the challenge and enforcement of the award.[348] Hence there is no scope for the application of the *lex loci arbitri* because the procedural rules contained in the ICSID Convention and the other 'basic documents' promulgated by ICSID are designed to create a self-contained system with an internal supervisory mechanism that replicates this function of the municipal courts at the seat of the arbitration and at the place of enforcement.[349]

For investment treaty arbitrations outside the auspices of the ICSID Convention, the choice of law rule for procedural questions is influenced by whether the state party to the investment treaty dispute has a right to expect immunity from the jurisdiction of the municipal courts at the seat of the arbitration in relation to the conduct of that arbitration or the validity of the resulting award. If the state party does have such a right in international law, and the municipal court—a corresponding obligation to respect it, then there would be a strong presumption that the arbitration should be subject to international law and thereby be detached from the *lex loci arbitri*.

It will be assumed, in accordance with the prevailing view of writers based on the trends in state practice,[350] that the restrictive doctrine of sovereign immunity represents the current state of customary international law. The clearest exposition of the restrictive doctrine of sovereign immunity with

[345] (1981) 20 ILM 1, 42–3. [346] W. Lake & J. Dana, above n. 36, 804.

[347] In France: Trib. Gr. Inst. Paris, 5 March 1979, *Procureur de la Republique v Société LIAMCO*, reprinted in (1979) 106 *Journal du droit international* 857. In Sweden: CA Svea, 18 June 1980, *Libyan American Oil Co. v Socialist People's Arab Republic of Libya*, translated in (1981) 20 ILM 893. In the United States: *Libyan American Oil Co. v Socialist People's Libyan Arab Jamahiriya*, 482 F. Supp. 1175 (D.D.C. 1980). [348] See above n. 136.

[349] *Ibid.*

[350] See the surveys of state practice in H. Fox, above n. 333, 124–5; I. Brownlie, above n. 92, 323–5. The writers emphasizing the trend towards adopting the restrictive doctrine of sovereign immunity are listed at *ibid.* 325 at note 40.

respect to arbitrations may be found in Article 12 of the European Convention on State Immunity:[351]

1. Where a Contracting State has agreed in writing to submit to arbitration a dispute which has arisen or may arise out of a civil or commercial matter, that State may not claim immunity from the jurisdiction of a court of another Contracting State on the territory or according to the law of which the arbitration has taken or will take place in respect of any proceedings relating to:
   a. the validity or interpretation of the arbitration agreement;
   b. the arbitration procedure;
   c. the setting aside of the award,

   unless the arbitration agreement otherwise provides.
2. Paragraph 1 shall not apply to an arbitration agreement between States.[352]

In applying the principles reflected in this test to investment treaty arbitrations, one must first anticipate and refute an argument to the effect that investment treaty arbitrations arise out of 'an arbitration agreement between States' for the purposes of Article 12(2) of the European Convention on State Immunity. The reference to the possibility of arbitrating disputes between the investor and the host state common to most investment treaties is an *offer* to arbitrate, not an *agreement* to arbitrate. The agreement to arbitrate is perfected upon the filing of a notice of arbitration by the investor, and at this juncture it is the host state and the investor that are privy to this agreement rather than the two contracting state parties to the treaty. As a further preliminary point, it should be noted that neither the investment treaties themselves, nor the arbitration agreement created upon the investor's acceptance of the state's offer to arbitrate, contain any express provisions on the issue of sovereign immunity. Hence the fundamental question to address, in accordance with Article 12(1) of the European Convention, is whether investment treaty arbitrations are capable of being described as disputes that 'arise out of a civil or commercial matter'.

D. STATE PRACTICE ON THE LEGAL NATURE OF INVESTMENT TREATY ARBITRATIONS

There is already sufficient state practice discernable from the texts of investment treaties and decisions of municipal courts to conclude that investment disputes should be considered to 'arise out of a civil or commercial matter' for the purposes of the law of sovereign immunity. From the review of this state practice that now follows, it will be clear that a

[351] The authors of a leading treatise on international law state that: 'The Convention may be regarded as reflecting with sufficient general accuracy the prevailing rules of international law and the current practice of states in the field of state immunity.' *Oppenheim's International Law*, above n. 92, 343.

[352] European Convention on State Immunity (1972) ETS No 74. A similar provision can be found in the legislation of many countries including the United States, see Foreign Sovereign Immunities Act, 1976, 28 USC § 1605(a)(6), and the United Kingdom, see State Immunity Act 1978, s. 9(1). A commentary on these provisions can be found in H. Fox, above n. 333, 166–7 (UK Act), 194–5 (US Act).

major concern of the treaty drafters has been to describe the status of investment arbitration awards for the purposes of their challenge and enforcement. It is perfectly legitimate to extrapolate from this definition a general categorisation of the investment treaty dispute as 'civil or commercial' rather than 'public international' because the status of an arbitration cannot fluctuate at different stages of the procedure. Thus, for example, an investment treaty arbitration cannot be categorised as a public international procedure detached from the *lex loci arbitri* for the purposes of a request for provisional measures, but at the same time be said to arise out of a civil or commercial matter and thereby fall within the scope of enforcement regimes for foreign arbitral awards.

Starting with the relevant provisions of investment treaties dealing with the enforcement of treaty awards, Article 1136(7) of NAFTA provides that a claim under Chapter 11 'shall be deemed to arise out of a commercial relationship or transaction for the purposes of Article I of the New York Convention and Article 1 of the Inter-American Convention'. A near identical provision is contained in Article 26(5)(b) of the Energy Charter Treaty and in several model BITs.[353] Other evidence that the New York Convention applies to investment treaty awards[354] is the common provision in BITs that consent and submission to international arbitration by the host state and the investor satisfies the requirement for 'agreement in writing' in Article II of the New York Convention,[355] or that the arbitration should be conducted in a state that is party to the New York Convention.[356]

There are four municipal court decisions to date dealing with a challenge to investment treaty awards. The first was the Supreme Court of British Columbia in *United Mexican States v Metalclad Corporation*.[357] A preliminary issue arose in relation to the statutory basis for the Court's review given the uncertainty as to whether the International Commercial Arbitration Act or the Commercial Arbitration Act should apply.[358] The pretext for the lengthy submissions by the parties on this point was the wider scope of review permissible under the Commercial Arbitration Act, which extends to the examination of points of law.[359] Justice Tysoe of the Supreme Court of British Columbia found that the NAFTA award was the product of a 'commercial arbitration' for the purposes of the

[353] *Eg*, Austria Model BIT, Art. 14, *UNCTAD Compendium* (Vol. VI, 2002) 265.

[354] UNCTAD has also recognised the applicability of the New York Convention to bilateral investment treaty awards. See UNCTAD, *Bilateral Investment Treaties in the Mid-1990s* (1998) 97–8.

[355] United States Model BIT, Art. 9(4)(b), *UNCTAD Compendium* (Vol. VI, 2002) 507; Denmark Model BIT, Art. 9(5), *ibid.* (Vol. VII) 284; Sweden Model BIT, Art. 8(5), *ibid.* (Vol. IX) 313.

[356] Denmark Model BIT, Art. 9(4), *UNCTAD Compendium* (Vol. VII, 2002) 284; Sweden Model BIT, Art. 8(4), *ibid.* (Vol. IX) 313.

[357] (Judgment, 2 May 2001) (2001 BCSC 664), 5 ICSID Rep 236. See generally: J. Cole, 'Domestic Court Control of Investment Awards: Necessary Evil or Achilles Heel within NAFTA and the Proposed FTAA' (2002) 19 *J of Int Arbitration* 185; D. Williams, 'International Commercial Arbitration and Globalization: Review and Recourse against Awards Rendered under Investment Treaties' (2003) 4 *J of World Investment* 251.

[358] (Judgment, 2 May 2001) (2001 BCSC 664), 5 ICSID Rep 236, paras. 39–49.

[359] *Ibid.* para. 39.

International Commercial Act because it met the following definition in section 1(6) therein:

An arbitration is commercial if its arises out of a relationship of a commercial nature including, but not limited to, the following:

. . .

(p) investing.[360]

No review of the NAFTA award with respect to conclusions of law was thus permitted in this instance.

Mexico had argued that the dispute with Metalclad had actually arisen out of a 'regulatory relationship'[361] insofar as the central issue in the NAFTA award related to the bureaucratic obstacles that prevented Metalclad from obtaining a municipal permit for the construction of its hazardous waste landfill and thereby developing its investment. Mexico also used the language of the 'derivative' theory for investment treaty claims by pleading that claimants were procedurally 'stepping into the shoes' of their national states and exercising rights vested in their national states.[362] Justice Tysoe rejected this submission and his appraisal of the nature of the relationship between the host state and the investor is worthy of full quotation:

It is true that the dispute between Metalclad and the Municipality arose because the Municipality was purporting to exercise a regulatory function. However, the primary relationship between Metalclad and Mexico was one of investing and the exercise of a regulatory function by the Municipality was incidental to that primary relationship. The arbitration did not arise under an agreement between Metalclad and the Municipality in connection with regulatory matters. Rather, the arbitration was between Metalclad and Mexico pursuant to an agreement dealing with the treatment of investors.[363]

In addition, it must be remembered that Metalclad qualified to make a claim against Mexico by way of arbitration under Chapter 11 because it was an investor of Mexico. If Metalclad was not considered to be an investor of Mexico, the arbitration could not have taken place.[364]

It is submitted that Justice Tysoe was correct to emphasize the commercial nature of the primary relationship between the investor and host state. If Mexico's contention were to be taken to its logical conclusion, a NAFTA award would be 'public in nature' for the purposes of a challenge, and yet 'commercial' in the context of enforcement as envisaged by Article 1136(7) of NAFTA. This analysis of the legal relationship between the investor and the host state is also consistent with the

[360] (Judgment, 2 May 2001) (2001 BCSC 664), 5 ICSID Rep 236, para. 41. [361] *Ibid.* para. 44.

[362] Transcript of Proceedings (19 February 2001) 61, available at <http://www.dfait-maeci.gc.ca/tna-nac/NAFTA-e.asp#Metalclad>. This part of Mexico's submissions was cited in: C. H. Brower, 'Investor-State Disputes under NAFTA: The Empire Strikes Back' (2001) 40 *Columbia J of Transnational L* 43, 63, 70.

[363] (2001 BCSC 664), 5 ICSID Rep 236, para. 46 (Judgment, 2 May 2001).

[364] *Ibid.* para. 47.

conclusion in Part III that the *inter*-state regime of international responsibility does not govern the consequences of the breach of the host state's obligation vis-à-vis the investor.

The second challenge of a treaty award was in *Czech Republic v CME Czech Republic B.V.*[365] before the Svea Court of Appeals in Stockholm. Without elaborate analysis, the Court assumed that the award was part of the Swedish legal order because the seat of the arbitration was in Stockholm.[366] Hence the Swedish Arbitration Act governed the challenge proceedings 'notwithstanding that the dispute has an international connection'.[367]

Similarly, in *United Mexican States v Marvin Roy Feldman Karpa*,[368] Justice Chilcolt of the Ontario Superior Court of Justice applied the Ontario International Commercial Arbitration Act by reason of the parties' designation of Ottawa as the place of arbitration in the NAFTA proceedings.[369] In *Attorney General of Canada v S.D. Myers, Inc.*,[370] Justice Kelen of the Federal Court in Ottawa simply noted that the Commercial Arbitration Act 'expressly applies to an arbitral claim under Chapter 11 of NAFTA.'[371]

Thus, on four separate occasions, a municipal court at the seat of the arbitration has exercised jurisdiction over an investment treaty award pursuant to municipal legislation dealing with commercial arbitration. This state practice is evidence that investment disputes 'arise out of a civil or commercial matter' for the purposes of Article 15 of the European Convention on Sovereign Immunity and the rule of customary international law which it is likely to accurately reflect. It follows that a state party to an investment treaty arbitration cannot plead sovereign immunity from the jurisdiction of a municipal court properly seized of an application pertaining to that arbitration, whether or not the participation of that state in the arbitration constitutes a waiver of immunity.[372] This conclusion, in turn, raises a very strong presumption that the procedural law governing investment treaty arbitrations is the *lex loci arbitri* because the municipal courts of that legal system are under no international obligation to decline jurisdiction over such arbitrations. In the absence of concrete evidence of a contrary intention of the state parties to investment treaties, public international law is not, therefore, the procedural law of investment treaty arbitrations.

365 (Judgment of 15 May 2003), reproduced and translated in (2003) 42 ILM 919.

366 *Ibid.* 960.

367 Section 46 of the Swedish Arbitration Act 1999 provides that: 'This Act shall apply to arbitral proceedings which take place in Sweden notwithstanding the fact that the dispute has an international connection.' *Ibid.*

368 Decision, 3 December 2003 (03-CV-23500), available at <http://www.economia-snci.gob.mx/sphp_pages/importa/sol_contro/consultoria/Casos_Mexico/Marvin/revision/031203_Decision_Chilcott.pdf >.

369 *Ibid.* paras. 51–2.

370 Decision, 13 January 2004 (2004 FC 38), available at <http://www.dfait-maeci.gc.ca/tna-nac/documents/ReasonsforOrder.pdf >.

371 *Ibid.* para. 21.

372 There is some controversy as to whether a state's consent to an arbitral procedure constitutes a waiver of immunity regardless of the subject matter of the arbitration, or whether the arbitration must nevertheless concern 'civil or commercial matters'. See H. Fox, above n. 333, 269–70.

There is further evidence to support this finding. Many investment treaties contain an offer to arbitrate before an *ad hoc* tribunal pursuant to the UNCITRAL Arbitration Rules, which were designed for international commercial arbitration. Article 1(2) of the Rules provides that '[t]hese Rules shall govern the arbitration except that where any of the Rules is in conflict with a provision of the law applicable to the arbitration from which the parties cannot derogate, that provision shall prevail.' It is widely accepted that Article 1(2) of the UNCITRAL Arbitration Rules contemplates the application of the mandatory rules of the *lex loci arbitri*,[373] and this would not follow from a choice of public international law to govern the arbitration.

It was open to the contracting states of investment treaties to make reference to procedural rules designed for state/state arbitration such as the UN Draft Convention on Arbitral Procedure in their offer to arbitrate with investors. Instead, most investment treaties disclose a clear preference for arbitral rules inspired by international commercial arbitration in the context of investor/state disputes, without replicating that choice for the state/state arbitral mechanism in investment treaties. The clearest example is the radical difference in the choice of procedural rules for investor/state disputes in Chapter 11 of the NAFTA and those rules adopted for state/state disputes in Chapter 20.

E. THE RELEVANCE OF THE PROCEDURAL LAW IN PRACTICE

Investor/state arbitrations under investment treaties are governed by the express provisions of the investment treaty, the relevant procedural rules chosen by the parties (such as the UNCITRAL Rules) and the municipal law of the seat of the arbitration (*lex loci arbitri*). The municipal courts at the seat of the arbitration are competent to exercise a supervisory jurisdiction over the arbitral process and hear applications by the parties for intervention in that process, such as for interim or conservatory measures or the appointment of an arbitrator. They are also competent to hear challenges to the award rendered by the treaty tribunal as demonstrated in *United Mexican States v Metalclad*,[374] *Czech Republic v CME Czech*

[373] At the ninth session of the drafting committee for the UNCITRAL Arbitration Rules it was decided 'to add to article 1 a general reference to the effect that all provisions in these Rules were subject to the national law applicable to the arbitration.' Report of Committee II, Ninth Session (1976) UN Doc A/CN.9/IX/CRP.1, para. 12. See also: K. Böckstiegel, 'The Relevance of National Arbitration Law for Arbitrators under the UNCITRAL Arbitration Rules' (1984) 1 *J of Int Arbitration* 223, 230; A. van den Berg, above n. 35, 342–3. It is interesting to note in this respect that the Permanent Court of Arbitration has issued model arbitration rules for arbitrations between two states that do not replicate Art. 1(2) of the UNCITRAL Arbitration Rules, whereas the model rules for arbitrations between states and private parties do replicate Art. 1(2). See Permanent Court of Arbitration Optional Rules for Arbitrating Disputes Between Two States, available at <http://www.pca-cpa.org/ENGLISH/BD/2stateeng.htm>; Permanent Court of Arbitration Optional Rules for Arbitrating Disputes Between Two Parties of Which Only One is a State, Art. 1(3), available at <http://pca-cpa.org/ENGLISH/BD/1stateeng.htm>.

[374] (Judgment, 2 May 2001) (2001 BCSC 664), 5 ICSID Rep 236.

Republic B.V.,[375] *United Mexican States v Martin Roy Feldman Karpa*[376] and *Attorney General of Canada v S.D. Myers, Inc.*[377] Finally, as investment treaty arbitration awards are not public international law awards, they are enforceable under the New York Convention and other international instruments for the recognition and enforcement of foreign arbitral awards.

F. ICSID ARBITRATIONS

Against this background it is necessary to briefly return to the *sui generis* nature of arbitrations conducted under the aegis of the ICSID Convention and the ICSID Arbitration Rules. It is normally assumed that the *lex arbitri* for ICSID arbitrations is international law. But what does this simple designation actually mean? Does it entail, for example, that customary international law on the admissibility of claims should supplement the ICSID Convention and Arbitration Rules?

ICSID arbitration is 'international' in the sense that it is detached from any system of municipal law. That much is uncontroversial. But there is a real danger in making blanket assertions about the *lex arbitri* of ICSID arbitrations as being 'international law'. International procedural rules for the admissibility of claims, such as the rules on the nationality of claims and the exhaustion of local remedies, have developed in the context of diplomatic protection. As was discussed at length in Part II, there is no reason to import such concepts into investment treaty arbitrations. An analysis of the *lex arbitri* of ICSID arbitrations thus requires a far more nuanced approach to reflect the complexities of this *sui generis* regime. For instance, it is clear from the *travaux préparatoires* for the ICSID Convention that the international rules on the nationality of claims were not intended to supplement the express provision of Article 25 of the ICSID Convention.[378] In contrasting the rules on nationality for the purposes of diplomatic protection and the ICSID Convention, Amerasinghe has written:

> In the case of the [ICSID] Convention the role of nationality is different. It serves as a means of bringing the private party within the jurisdictional pale of the Centre. There is no question of diplomatic protection, nor is it by virtue of a State's right to exercise diplomatic protection over a private party that he has the capacity to appear in proceedings before the Centre.[379]

[375] (Svea Court of Appeals, 15 May 2003), reproduced and translated in (2003) 42 ILM 919.

[376] Decision, 3 December 2003 (03-CV-23500), available at <http://www.economia-snci.gob.mx/sphp_pages/importa/sol_contro/consultoria/Casos_Mexico/Marvin/revision/031203_Decision_Chilcott.pdf>.

[377] Decision, 13 January 2004 (2004 FC 38), available at <http://www.dfait-maeci.gc.ca/tna-nac/documents/ReasonsforOrder.pdf>.

[378] C. Amerasinghe, 'Jurisdiction *Ratione Personae* Under the Convention on the Settlement of Investment Disputes Between States and Nationals of Other States' (1976) 48 *BYBIL* 227, 256, 259.

[379] *Ibid.* 244–5, 247, 249, 256. The author further states: '[T]he question of nationality of juridical persons for the purpose of the Centre's jurisdiction can be dealt with by a tribunal or commission in extremely flexible terms and particularly because it is not bound by the law of diplomatic protection

ICSID tribunals have often been sensitive to the *sui generis* nature of this arbitration regime. In *Ceskoslovenska Obchodni Banka, A.S. v Slovak Republic*,[380] the ICSID Tribunal was confronted with a jurisdictional challenge by the Respondent to the effect that the Claimant was no longer the real party in interest because it had assigned the beneficial interest of its claims to its national state, the Czech Republic, after the arbitral proceedings had commenced.[381] The Tribunal distanced itself from the rule of customary international law that an alien must have beneficial ownership over contractual claims that provide the factual basis of a diplomatic protection claim by its national state:

> [A]bsence of beneficial ownership by a claimant in a claim or the transfer of the economic risk in the outcome of a dispute should not and has not been deemed to affect that standing of a claimant in an ICSID proceeding, regardless whether or not the beneficial owner is a State Party or a private party.[382]

It is reasonably clear from the existing authority in diplomatic protection cases that this finding contradicts the rule in general international law[383] and can only be justified by the *sui generis* nature of the ICSID regime.

VI. Challenge and Enforcement of Awards

A. Introduction

If the ultimate counterparty to the host state's obligations under an investment treaty were the national state of the investor, and the *inter*-state regime of international responsibility were applicable to a violation of such obligations, treaty tribunals would render true international awards governed by public international law and incapable of being challenged or enforced in municipal courts. As was concluded in Part III, the sub-system of international responsibility that governs a breach of an investment treaty by the host state vis-à-vis the investor does not generate a liability that is comparable to a state's breach of a treaty that is actionable by another state. The liability created by this sub-system of international responsibility is perhaps more adequately described as having a transnational commercial nature in view of the commercial interests at the heart of the dispute, although in itself this label is in practice unlikely to be of great utility. Moreover, this responsibility is backed by an international treaty instrument, and is thus not comparable with, for instance, the

in this regard. The nationality of a juridical person under the Convention can be seen in the light of a broad definition which requires some adequate connection between the juridical person and a State.' *Ibid.* 259.

380 (Decision on Objections to Jurisdiction, 24 May 1999) Case No. ARB/97/4, 5 ICSID Rep 300.

381 *Ibid.* para. 28. 382 *Ibid.* para. 32.

383 *American Security and Trust Company Claim* (1958) 26 ILR 322: 'It is clear that the national character of the claim must be tested by the nationality of the individual holding a beneficial interest therein rather than by the nationality of the nominal or record holder of the claim', cited in I. Brownlie, above n. 92, 462. See further: *Oppenheim's International Law*, above n. 92, 514.

contractual liability that follows a breach of an international sale of goods contract by a state party. Hence the *sui generis* nature of the secondary rules of responsibility that govern a breach of an investment treaty.

Although these observations on the consequences that flow from a breach of an investment treaty might be novel, it reflects existing state practice. This state practice was reviewed in Part V and yielded the conclusion that treaty instruments and municipal court decisions give controlling weight to the 'private' or 'commercial' aspects of investment treaty awards as opposed to their public international or public regulatory elements.

Judicial consideration of this issue is limited to the four court judgements dealing with challenges to investment treaty awards, namely *United Mexican States v Metalclad Corporation*[384] in the Supreme Court of British Colombia, *Czech Republic v CME Czech Republic B.V.*[385] in the Svea Court of Appeals, *United Mexican States v Marvin Roy Feldman Karpa*[386] in the Superior Court of Justice of Ontario and *Attorney General of Canada v S.D. Myers, Inc.*[387] in the Federal Court in Ottawa. There is no precedent at the time of writing on recognition and enforcement proceedings with respect to investment treaty awards. It is instructive in this context to examine the problems that have arisen in the recognition and enforcement of awards rendered by the Iran/US Claims Tribunal, as many of the insights from this body of precedents will be invaluable in evaluating the applicable enforcement regime for investment treaty awards.

B. PRECEDENTS OF THE IRAN/US CLAIMS TRIBUNAL

The Algiers Accords envisage a strict procedure for the enforcement of awards against Iran whereby payment under such awards is made out of a security fund created from Iran's assets frozen by the United States.[388] Thus, for all practical purposes, awards against Iran are self-executing when rendered. The constituent documents of the Iran/US Claims Tribunal are, on the other hand, silent on the enforcement procedure for awards against US nationals, save for general provisions to the effect that 'all decisions and awards of the Tribunal shall be final and binding'[389] and that the state parties are obliged 'to carry out the award without delay'.[390]

[384] (2001 BCSC 664), 5 ICSID Rep 236.

[385] Reproduced and translated in (2003) 42 ILM 919.

[386] Decision, 3 December 2003 (03-CV-23500), available at <http://www.economia-snci.gob.mx/sphp_pages/importa/sol_contro/consultoria/Casos_Mexico/Marvin/revision/031203_Decision_Chilcott.pdf>.

[387] Decision, 13 January 2004 (2004 FC 38), available at <http://www.dfait-maeci.gc.ca/tna-nac/documents/ReasonsforOrder.pdf>.

[388] The Declaration of the Government of the Democratic and Popular Republic of Algeria Relating to the Commitments made by Iran and the United States, para. 7.

[389] The Declaration of the Government of Algeria Concerning the Settlement of Claims by Iran and the United States, Art. IV(1); Art. 32(2) of the Tribunal Rules of Procedure.

[390] Article 32(2) of the Tribunal Rules of Procedure. See generally: R. Lewis, 'What Goes Around Comes Around: Can Iran Enforce Awards of the Iran-U.S. Claims Tribunal in the United States?' (1988) 26 *Columbia J of Transnational L* 515.

Not long after the Iran/US Claims Tribunal came into existence, Iran requested an interpretation by the Full Tribunal of the nature of the United State's obligation to satisfy promptly any awards rendered by the Iran/US Claims Tribunal against citizens of the United States.

In Case A/21,[391] the Full Tribunal held that, consistent with other instruments relating to international arbitration, the rule that awards shall be 'final and binding' does not entail that the awards are self-executing. Rather, a failure by the award debtor to comply voluntarily with an award that is ripe for enforcement opens the door for the other party to compel compliance through municipal court procedures.[392] The Full Tribunal also rejected Iran's contention that the United States is under an obligation to step in and pay awards against its nationals when such nationals refuse to do so voluntarily due to the 'reciprocal system of commitments' created by the Algiers Accords:

> [T]he Tribunal cannot find that any obligation of the United States to satisfy Tribunal awards against its nationals flows from the 'international' character of the Tribunal, or from any principle of customary international law based on the United States having been a party to the treaty that established the Tribunal.[393]

This conclusion was supported by reference to the *dicta* of a previous interpretative decision of the Full Tribunal in Case A/18[394] to the effect that 'it is the rights of the claimant, not of his nation, that are to be determined by the Tribunal.'[395]

The Full Tribunal in Case A/21 then provided some important guidance on the content of the United States' obligation under the Algiers Accords to respect the final and binding awards of the Iran/US Claims Tribunal:

> [T]he act of entering into a treaty in good faith carries with it the obligation to fulfil the object and purpose of that treaty—in other words, to take steps to ensure its effectiveness. In this respect, the Algiers Declarations impose upon the United States a duty to implement the Algiers Declarations in good faith so as to ensure that the jurisdiction and authority of the Tribunal are respected. The Parties to the Algiers Declarations are obligated to implement them in such a way that the awards of the Tribunal will be treated as valid and enforceable in their respective national jurisdictions.
>
> This good faith obligation leaves a considerable latitude to the State Parties as to the nature of the procedures and mechanisms by which Tribunal awards rendered against their nationals may be enforced. The Tribunal has no authority under the Algiers Declarations to prescribe the means by which each of the States provides for such enforcement. Certainly, if no enforcement procedure were available in a State Party, or if recourse to such procedure were eventually to result in a refusal to implement Tribunal awards, or unduly delay their

391 Islamic Republic of Iran and United States (Case A/21) (4 May 1987) DEC 62-A21-FT, 13 Iran/US CTR 324.

392 *Ibid.* para. 10.

393 *Ibid.* para. 13.

394 Islamic Republic of Iran and United States (Case A/18) (Dual Nationality) (6 April 1984) DEC 32-A18-FT, 5 Iran-US CTR 251

395 *Ibid.* 261.

> enforcement, this would violate the State's obligations under the Algiers Declarations. It is therefore incumbent on each State Party to provide some procedure or mechanism whereby enforcement may be obtained within its national jurisdiction, and to ensure that the successful Party has access thereto. If procedures did not already exist as part of the State's legal system they would have to be established, by means of legislation or other appropriate measures. Such procedures must be available on a basis at least as favorable as that allowed to parties who seek recognition or enforcement of foreign arbitral awards.[396]

Case A/21 has been cited at length because the Full Tribunal's comments on the nature and content of the obligation upon the state parties to enforce awards of the Tribunal are apposite for the same obligation on state parties in the context of investment treaty awards. The final sentence of the above quotation indicates that the New York Convention regime is an appropriate enforcement mechanism for Iran/US Claims Tribunal awards and this is consistent with the reference to the New York Convention in many investment treaties.

It might be said that the problem of enforcement is more acute in the Iran/US Claims Tribunal context than for investment treaty arbitration because the work of the former has been more frequently concerned with arbitral awards *against* private parties. Nevertheless, as the challenges to awards in the *United Mexican States v Metalclad Inc.*,[397] *Czech Republic v CME Czech Republic B.V.*,[398] *United Mexican States v Marvin Roy Feldman Karpa*[399] and *Attorney General of Canada v S.D. Myers, Inc.*[400] demonstrate, state parties to investment disputes may be no less resilient than private parties to the enforcement of adverse awards. Moreover, it is reasonable to expect that investment treaty tribunals may have the occasion in the future to award damages against the investor in satisfaction of a counterclaim brought by the state party.[401]

Two issues emerge from the application of the New York Convention, and other international or municipal regimes for the enforcement of foreign awards, to awards rendered by investment treaty tribunals. The first is whether the courts of the enforcement state are at liberty to consider and uphold defences to enforcement such as those set out in Article V of the New York Convention. Formulated differently, is there anything

[396] Islamic Republic of Iran and United States (Case A/21) (4 May 1987) DEC 62-A21-FT, 13 Iran/US CTR 324, paras 14, 15.

[397] (Judgment, 2 May 2001) (2001 BCSC 664), 5 ICSID Rep 236, para. 46.

[398] (Svea Court of Appeals, 15 May 2003), reproduced and translated in (2003) 42 ILM 919

[399] Decision, 3 December 2003 (03-CV-23500), available at <http://www.economia-snci.gob.mx/sphp_pages/importa/sol_contro/consultoria/Casos_Mexico/Marvin/revision/031203_Decision_Chilcott.pdf>.

[400] Decision, 13 January 2004 (2004 FC 38), available at <http://www.dfait-maeci.gc.ca/tna-nac/documents/ReasonsforOrder.pdf>.

[401] The only reported investment treaty case where a counterclaim has been raised by the respondent state (and dismissed on its merits by the tribunal) is: *Genin and Others v Republic of Estonia* (Award, 25 June 2001) Case No. ARB/99/2, 6 ICSID Rep 241. Counterclaims were also advanced by the respondent state in: *Saluka Investments B.V. v Czech Republic* (UNCITRAL arbitration administered by the PCA, Netherlands/Czech Republic BIT). The Tribunal's jurisdiction over these counterclaims was contested. (This case was pending as this article was finalised.)

'special' about an investment treaty award that would lead to a different approach? The second is whether the investor might have a remedy against an improper refusal to enforce a treaty award, for instance, in the courts of the respondent state. The Iran/US Claims Tribunal has grappled with both these issues.

The first instance of non-enforcement was in *Gould Marketing Inc., v Ministry of Defence of the Islamic Republic of Iran.*[402] The US Court of Appeal, consistent with the guidance in Case A/21,[403] ruled that it had jurisdiction on the basis of the New York Convention.[404] It confirmed the award with respect to the order to pay damages of USD 3.6 million to Iran (requested by counterclaim), but refused to enforce an order for specific performance requiring Gould Marketing to surrender certain communications equipment to Iran in Gould's possession. This refusal was motivated by deference to US export regulations, which would have been violated if the communications equipment had been transported to Iran. Iran appealed this part of the District Court's decision, however, in the intervening months the parties reached a settlement.

The second instance was in relation to the award in *Avco Corp. v Iran Aircraft Industries*,[405] pursuant to which the tribunal had upheld the Iranian party's counterclaim for USD 3.5 million. Iran Aircraft Industries brought enforcement proceedings in the US District Court for the District of Connecticut, which again assumed jurisdiction pursuant to the New York Convention.[406] The enforcement petition was denied on the basis of Article V(1)(b) of the New York Convention due to an alleged impediment suffered by Avco in presenting its case caused by detrimental reliance on a procedural direction of the tribunal.[407] The essence of the direction was that Avco could dispense with submitting voluminous invoices in support of its claim by submitting an expert report *in lieu*. A differently constituted tribunal then appeared to draw an adverse inference from this omission in evidence in its final award.[408] The US Court of Appeals affirmed the District Court's judgment. It expressly rejected Iran Aircraft's submission that awards of the Iran/US Claims Tribunals are directly enforceable in the US Courts, and found that 'even a "final" and "binding" arbitral award is subject to the defenses to enforcement provided for in the New York Convention'.[409]

Iran then sought another interpretation of the United States' obligations under the Algiers Accords in light of these two instances of non-enforcement. The Full Tribunal in Case A/27[410] was faced with a dilemma that originated in the guidance previously provided in Case A/21, which

[402] (29 June 1984) 136–49/50–2, 6 Iran/US CTR 272.

[403] Islamic Republic of Iran and United States (Case A/21) (4 May 1987) DEC 62-A21-FT, 13 Iran/US CTR 324.

[404] *Ministry of Defence of the Islamic Republic of Iran v Gould Marketing, Inc.*, 887 F.2d 1357 (9th Cir. 1989).

[405] (18 July 1988) 377–261–3, 19 Iran/US CTR 200.

[406] See *Iran Aircraft Industries v Avco Corp.*, 980 F.2d 141, 142 (2d Cir. 1992).

[407] *Ibid.*

[408] *Ibid.* 143.

[409] *Ibid.* 145.

[410] Islamic Republic of Iran and United States (Case A/27) (5 June 1998) 586-A27-FT.

implicitly endorsed the New York Convention as a mechanism for the recognition and enforcement of Iran/US Claims Tribunal awards by stating that the enforcement procedure 'must be available on a basis at least as favorable as that allowed to parties who seek recognition and enforcement of foreign arbitral awards'.[411] On the other hand, the Full Tribunal in Case A/21 raised the possibility of a violation of the Algiers Accords if resort to this mechanism led to a 'refusal to implement Tribunal awards'.[412] If the US is entitled to rely on the New York Convention as the enforcement mechanism, then surely the possibility of non-enforcement cannot be ruled out if the US court seized of the matter upholds a defence to enforcement on one of the grounds of Article V? The Full Tribunal's answer to this paradox in Case A/27 is not entirely persuasive:

> Indeed, Article IV, paragraph 1, of the Claims Settlement Declaration, which provides that '[a]ll decisions and awards of the Tribunal shall be final and binding,' rules out the possibility of readjudication of the *merits* of Tribunal awards by a municipal court, either under the guise of Article V of the New York Convention or by any other means.[413]

The problem is, of course, that the New York Convention does not permit municipal courts seized with an enforcement application to readjudicate the merits of a foreign arbitral award. The US Court of Appeal had affirmed a decision to refuse enforcement in *Avco* due to a perceived procedural deficiency in the arbitral process. The Full Tribunal essentially reviewed the merits of *that* decision by expressly ruling that the US Court of Appeal was wrong in its assessment of the procedural deficiency. According to the Full Tribunal, the failure of Avco to present the invoices was not material to the Tribunal's decision to dismiss its claim,[414] and hence the US Court's decision to the contrary amounted to 'reconsidering an issue that had been already aired and decided by the Tribunal.'[415] This in turn constituted a failure to treat the award as 'final and binding' in accordance with the Claims Settlement Declaration. The Full Tribunal went on to find that this amounted to a breach of international law attributable to the US for which there was an obligation to make reparation.[416]

Even assuming that the Full Tribunal was correct in its interpretation of the Tribunal's award in *Avco*, it is clear that the US Court's decision cannot be characterised as a denial of justice under customary international law because there was no suggestion that there were serious procedural inadequacies in the administration of justice by the US Courts.[417]

[411] Islamic Republic of Iran and United States (Case A/21) (4 May 1987) DEC 62-A21-FT, 13 Iran/US CTR 324, para. 15. [412] *Ibid.*

[413] Islamic Republic of Iran and United States (Case A/27) (5 June 1998) 586-A27-FT, para. 63 (emphasis added).

[414] This decision by the Second Circuit appears to be erroneous. A careful reading of the Tribunal's award in Avco shows that it was based not on the absence of the invoices underlying Avco's claims, but on a lack of proof that those invoices were payable. *Ibid.* para. 66. [415] *Ibid.* para. 69.

[416] *Ibid.* para. 71.

[417] An authoritative definition of denial of justice is provided by Art. 9 of the Harvard Research Draft of 1929: 'A State is responsible if an injury to an alien results from a denial of justice. Denial of

The Full Tribunal nevertheless found that the United States violated the Algiers Accords.

In reaching this decision, the Full Tribunal entertained the possibility that the 'final and binding' rule of the Claims Settlement Declaration prohibited the US Courts from exercising their jurisdiction to review awards on the grounds of Article V of the New York Convention. Such a ruling would have contradicted its previous finding that the New York Convention was an appropriate mechanism for the enforcement of Iran/US Claims Tribunal awards in the United States. If the New York Convention applies, then a party resisting the enforcement of an award in the United States would be entitled to rely on Article V grounds, unless the Algiers Accords creates an exception within the meaning of Article VII(1).[418] This is unlikely because there is a stipulation in most arbitral rules that an award is 'final and binding' when rendered by an arbitral tribunal, but it has never seriously been argued that an award of an ICC tribunal,[419] for instance, cannot be refused enforcement on the basis of Article V of the New York Convention.

Another problem with this approach is that it would mandate the enforcement of an award regardless of any procedural injustice or fraud that might have infected the arbitral process. Under customary international law, an award procured by fraud or duress or rendered in proceedings violative of fundamental norms of fairness is a nullity.[420] It would be surprising if the special character of the Iran/US Claims Tribunal created a void in which such awards could be enforced. The Full Tribunal actually touched upon this point in a footnote to its decision and intimated a possible solution:

> The Tribunal recognizes that no tribunal can declare itself immune from procedural error or the possibility of fraud, forgery, or perjury that it may not detect. *In such hypothetical cases, however, revision of the award could be done only by the Tribunal, if it concluded that it had the authority to do so, not by any other court.*[421]

justice exists when there is a denial, unwarranted delay or obstruction of access to courts, gross deficiency in the administration of judicial or remedial process, failure to provide those guarantees which are generally considered indispensable to the proper administration of justice, or a manifestly unjust judgment.' (1929) 23 *AJIL* 173. For approval of this definition, see: D. O'Connell, above n. 72, 947; I. Brownlie, above n. 92, 506, and writers listed at note 51.

418 Article VII(1) of the New York Convention provides: 'The provisions of the present Convention shall not affect the validity of multilateral or bilateral agreements concerning the recognition and enforcement of arbitral awards entered into by the Contracting States nor deprive any interested party of any right he may have to avail himself of an arbitral award in the manner and to the extent allowed by the law or the treaties of the country where such award is sought to be relied upon.'

419 Article 28(6) of the ICC Rules of Arbitration provides: 'Every Award shall be binding on the parties. By submitting the dispute to arbitration under these Rules, the parties undertake to carry out any Award without delay and shall be deemed to have waived their right to any form of recourse insofar as such waiver can validly be made.'

420 See generally: W. Reisman, *Nullity and Revision: The Review and Enforcement of International judgments and Awards* (1971) 64 *et seq.*

421 Islamic Republic of Iran and United States (Case A/27) (5 June 1998) 586-A27-FT, para. 64 at note 6 (emphasis added), available at <http://www.iusct.org/awards/award-586–927-ft-eng.pdf>.

The Full Court thus appears to discourage parties from raising these fundamental grounds for the nullity of an Iran/US Claims Tribunal award before municipal courts, while at the same time reserving for itself jurisdiction over the revision of an award '*if* it had the authority to do so'.

There is no provision in the Algiers Accords dealing with the competence of the Iran/US Claims Tribunal to review its own awards and it would be extraordinary for an arbitral tribunal created by an international treaty instrument to confer upon itself an inherent jurisdiction to do so in the absence of an express stipulation in that instrument.[422] Unlike the Algiers Accords, the ICSID Convention does have an internal mechanism for the review of awards, but to suggest that the ICSID Secretariat could exercise an inherent jurisdiction and establish a control mechanism in the absence of Article 52 is less than convincing.

In the end, the Full Tribunal backed away from a definitive ruling on what it considered to be the legitimate route to the revision of an award by refusing to accede to Iran's request for an order requiring the United States to establish a suitable procedure for the enforcement of all future awards against United States nationals.[423] The Full Tribunal thereby left the *status quo* of the application of the New York Convention mechanism for enforcement intact, but reserved for itself the power to test the compatibility of US Court decisions dealing with the Article V grounds for the refusal of enforcement with the obligation of the US to respect the provision in the Claims Settlement Declaration that '[a]ll decisions and awards of the Tribunal shall be final and binding.'[424]

The problem of enforcement of awards rendered under the auspices of the Iran/US Claims Tribunals has been discussed at length because of its importance to a proper analysis of how similar issues should be resolved in the context of investment treaty awards. In particular, consideration of a more optimal approach to the situation facing the Full Tribunal in A/27 will shed light on the form of any recourse an investor or state might have in the event that an investment treaty award is annulled or not enforced by a municipal court.

In considering the problem arising in Case A/27, it is first necessary to clarify the significance of a treaty provision to the effect that awards are 'final and binding'. Such a provision, in the context of the Iran/US Claims Tribunal, ensures that decisions of tribunals on the matters in dispute is *res judicata* between the parties in international *fora* and before US and Iranian courts. That an award is 'final and binding' does not mean, however, that the award's validity is impervious to review on narrow grounds relating to procedural irregularity or international public policy. Furthermore, as previously mentioned, most arbitral rules contain

[422] The Iran/US Claims Tribunal considered whether it had an inherent or implied power to review its awards upon an allegation of fraud or perjury on several occasions but never reached any definitive conclusions. See the cases cited by G. Aldrich, above n. 9, 456–7; C. Brower & J. Brueschke, above n. 9, 245–59.

[423] *Ibid.* para. 74.

[424] *Ibid.* para. 63.

a provision to the effect that awards are 'final and binding', and yet awards rendered pursuant to the UNCITRAL or ICC Arbitration Rules are most certainly subject to review under Article V of the New York Convention by municipal courts at the place of enforcement.

The US Court of Appeal did not, therefore, violate the Algiers Accords by exercising its jurisdiction to review the *Avco* award in accordance with the grounds set out in Article V of the New York Convention, and the decision of the Full Tribunal did not rest upon such a conclusion. Instead, the Full Tribunal interpreted the Algeirs Accords to 'rule out the possibility of readjudication of the merits of Tribunal awards . . . under the New York Convention,'[425] and found that the US Court's decision strayed into such a readjudication by reopening the Tribunal's findings with respect to the relevance of the invoices.[426] This conclusion, limited to the specific instance of the US Court's application of Article V of the New York Convention, is far more defensible than the common interpretation that the Full Tribunal categorically denied the possibility of any review of its awards against the grounds in Article V. [427] It is submitted, however, that it would have been preferable for the Full Court to be less equivocal about the legitimacy of the US Court's jurisdiction to review the awards of the Iran/US Claims Tribunal pursuant to Article V of the New York Convention and test the US Court's compliance with its obligations under that international treaty rather than the Algiers Accords. The New York Convention contains more detailed and specific provisions on the scope of the review of arbitral awards and there is a considerable body of judicial precedents to provide interpretative guidance. The New York Convention is, therefore, a more stable platform for invoking the international responsibility of the United States if a breach was to be found. If, on the face of the award, it was in fact clear that Avco's failure to present the original invoices was irrelevant to the tribunal's dismissal of part of its claim, then the US Court's failure to respect the *res judicata* effect of this finding on the significance of the invoices, together with its misplaced reliance on Article V(1)(b) of the New York Convention that followed, might constitute a breach of Article III of the same Convention.[428]

C. CHALLENGES TO AND ENFORCEMENT OF INVESTMENT TREATY AWARDS

The starting point is that it is well settled that the New York Convention is applicable to awards involving states[429] and investment treaties have

[425] Islamic Republic of Iran and United States (Case A/27) (5 June 1998) 586-A27-FT, para. 63.

[426] *Ibid.* para. 66.

[427] See, *eg* : J. Seifi, above n. 33, 21: '[I]t is certain that grounds against enforcement identified in Art. V of the New York Convention cannot be applicable to Tribunal awards.'

[428] On the *res judicata* aspect of Art. III, see generally: A. van den Berg, *The New York Convention* (1981) 244.

[429] In the Netherlands: *Société Europóene d'Études et d'Entreprises v Socialist Federal Republic of Yugoslavia*, HR Oct. 26, 1973, NJ 361, translated in (1974) 5 *Netherlands Yrb of Int L* 290. In France: CA Rouen, Nov. 13, 1984, *Société Europóene d'Études et d'Entreprises v République Fédérale*

expressly confirmed that this international legal regime for the recognition and enforcement of awards extends to awards rendered by treaty tribunals.[430] Moreover, the existing practice of municipal courts relating to the challenge of investment treaty awards, which have upheld their jurisdiction over such awards on the basis of domestic legislation on international commercial arbitration, is consistent with the characterisation of investment treaty awards as 'foreign' or 'commercial' for the purposes of the New York Convention. In short, there is no evidence from the text of investment treaties or subsequent practice to refute the conclusion that the New York Convention applies to investment treaty awards not rendered under the auspices of the ICSID Convention.

Investors might be aggrieved by the unjustified annulment of awards at the seat of the arbitration or the refusal to enforce awards in the host state or in a third country. What forum would be competent to grant a remedy in such a situation? If the municipal courts of the host state have failed to enforce an award, the investor might bring a fresh claim under the relevant investment treaty to redress the unlawful frustration of its right to enforce against the award debtor. The legal sources of such a right might be several. In relation to a failure to enforce, a cause of action could be advanced on the basis of the state's violation of the New York Convention or a denial of justice in seeking enforcement under customary international law.[431] Each of these grounds would have to be advanced within the scope of one of the express treaty obligations, such as the host state's duty to accord an investment 'fair and equitable treatment'. Furthermore, it would be necessary for the investor to establish that the new dispute relates to the same investment that was the subject of the original award for the purposes of *jus standi*. Alternatively, it may be argued that the award constitutes a new investment in the form of an award debt in favour of an investor.[432]

Another avenue for redress might be the state/state arbitration procedure provided in investment treaties. Although the investor will be confronted with the functional difficulties discussed in Part II that characterise diplomatic protection claims, there would be no problem of identifying the 'investment' underlying the dispute because this is not a requirement for the jurisdiction of the tribunal. The possibility that a national state is competent to bring a diplomatic protection claim to remedy the unlawful refusal to enforce an award is expressly recognised by Article 27(1) of the ICSID Convention.[433] Finally, it should be noted that, of the two possible avenues for redress, only the state/state arbitration

de Yougoslavie, translated in (1985) 24 ILM 345; affirmed, Cass. le civ., Nov. 18, 1986, translated in (1987) 26 ILM 377; as cited in G. Delaume, 'Recognition and Enforcement of State Contract Awards in the United States: A Restatement' (1997) 91 *AJIL* 476, 477 at notes 14 & 15.

430 See Part V(D) above.

431 See J. Paulsson, *Denial of Justice in International Law* (forthcoming) Ch. 6.

432 It would be necessary to demonstrate that the award debt constitutes an investment for the purposes of the definition in the relevant investment treaty and that the *situs* of that debt is at the place of the debtor.

433 Article 27(1) provides: 'No Contracting State shall give diplomatic protection, or bring an international claim, in respect of a dispute which one of its nationals and another Contracting State shall

mechanism would allow a state to seek a remedy for a failure to enforce an award in its favour in the jurisdiction of the investor (*ie*. if the state had been successful in a counterclaim or had costs awarded in its favour).

VII. Jurisdictional Conflicts in Investment Treaty Arbitration

A. INTRODUCTION

The positivist bias of traditional conflict of laws scholarship, resting on the notion of distinct municipal and international legal orders, is really beginning to show its age. A dispute with international dimensions is ever more likely to give rise to problems of overlapping jurisdictions on both the domestic and international plane. Forum shoppers of the future will be less concerned with the remedial possibilities in proceedings before the domestic courts of different states, but will instead seek advantage from the absence of hierarchy and coordination among the various types of international tribunals[434] and from the often strained relationship between such tribunals and municipal courts. There is as yet no established body of principles to deal adequately with the new realities of vertical and horizontal clashes of adjudicative competence. At the same time, the conceivable range of remedies available to foreign investors has become remarkably broad. First, an investor whose property rights in its investment have been interfered with by an executive act of an organ of the host state would normally have the right to pursue a tortious claim for damages or an administrative procedure to have the relevant decision annulled in the municipal courts. Or, if the investor acquired the investment on the basis of a contract with the host state, the interference may be actionable as a contractual claim before the municipal courts of the host state or an arbitral tribunal with jurisdiction pursuant to an arbitration clause in the contract. The competence of such a tribunal may emanate purely from the contractual incorporation of arbitral rules (for example, an ICC tribunal or an *ad hoc* UNCITRAL tribunal) or a combination of contractual incorporation and an applicable international treaty ratified by the host state and the national state of the investor (the case of an ICSID tribunal). Thirdly, the investor may also rely upon a bilateral or multilateral investment treaty which the national state of the investor has ratified together with the host state and thereby bring a claim based upon the minimum standards of treatment prescribed by the applicable treaty.

have consented to submit or shall have submitted to arbitration under this Convention, *unless such other Contracting State shall have failed to abide by and comply with the award rendered in such dispute*.' (Emphasis added.)

[434] In the human rights context, it has been estimated that there are already forty instances where virtually the same human rights complaints have been brought before both global and regional procedures: Y. Shany, *The Competing Jurisdictions of International Courts and Tribunals* (2003) 60.

Again, depending on the nationality of the investor, it might appeal to the European Court of Human Rights with a claim founded on Protocol 1, Article 1 of the European Convention on Human Rights on the protection of property rights or to the Inter-American Court of Human Rights[435] or the African Commission on Human and Peoples' Rights[436] on a similar basis. Finally, the investor might persuade the government of its national state to bring diplomatic protection proceedings on its behalf against the host state before the International Court of Justice if jurisdiction exists or seek redress through an international agreement between the two states on the lump sum settlement of claims.

At the heart of an investment dispute lies private or commercial interests that owe their existence to municipal law. Municipal courts or contractual arbitration tribunals are often competent to rule upon issues relating to the nature and extent of these interests. The municipal courts of the host state may have jurisdiction because (i) the *situs* of the investor's property is in the territory of the host state, (ii) the investor's contract with the host state envisages performance on the territory of the host state, (iii) an executive or administrative act giving rise to a dispute affecting the investor's interests emanates from an organ of the host state, or (iv) the municipal courts are chosen pursuant to a forum selection clause in an investment contract. Alternatively, a contractual arbitral tribunal might have jurisdiction on the same basis as (iv).

As far as questions pertaining to the existence and extent of property rights constituting an investment are concerned, an investment treaty tribunal has less of a warrant to occupy a pre-eminent position vis-à-vis a municipal court or contractual arbitral tribunal than with respect to questions relating to the conformity or otherwise of state conduct with the treaty standards. In testing the state's conduct, an investment treaty tribunal applies the minimum standards of investment protection set out in an international treaty with the interpretative assistance of international law. In performing this task, the principle of the international law of state responsibility that '[t]he responsible state may not rely on the provisions of its internal law as justification for failure to comply with its obligations'[437] ensures a hierarchical relationship between the international tribunal and any municipal court which has pronounced upon aspects of the state's conduct. But in adjudicating issues relating to property interests in the investment, this hierarchical principle no longer comes into play because a treaty tribunal and a municipal court or contractual arbitral tribunal apply the same law, *viz.* the municipal law of the host state. In these circumstances, the potential overlap between the investment tribunal's jurisdiction to adjudge issues pertaining to the nature and extent of the investment and the jurisdiction of other courts and tribunals to do

[435] Inter-American Human Rights Convention, Art. 21.

[436] African Human Rights Charter, Art. 14.

[437] Article 32 of the ILC's Articles on Responsibility of States for International Wrongful Acts, reproduced in J. Crawford, above n. 12, 207.

the same gives rise to what will be termed as 'asymmetrical conflicts', in recognition of the different roles played by municipal law in these *fora*. Before the municipal court or contractual arbitral tribunal, municipal law supplies the cause of action, whereas in the context of a treaty arbitration, it governs an aspect of the investment dispute where the cause of action is detached from municipal law.

Some investment treaties also create the potential for 'symmetrical conflicts' by allowing an investor to bring contractual claims or other causes of action based on municipal law before an investment treaty tribunal. Investment treaties can be divided into four groups based on the possible scope of the treaty tribunal's *ratione materiae* jurisdiction established by the host state's offer to arbitrate in the treaty. The first group of treaties permits 'all' or 'any' disputes relating to investments to be submitted to a treaty tribunal. This is by far the most prevalent type of clause in BITs.[438] The second group, inspired by the United States Model BIT, restricts the scope of the treaty tribunal's *ratione materiae* jurisdiction to three legal sources for the investor's cause of action:

> For the purposes of this Treaty, an investment dispute is a dispute between a Party and a national or company of the other Party arising out of or relating to an investment authorization, an investment agreement or an alleged breach of any right conferred, created or recognised by this Treaty with respect to a covered investment.[439]

The third group restricts the subject matter of investor/state arbitration exclusively to alleged violations of the substantive provisions of the treaty itself.[440] This is the type of clause favoured by the two relevant multilateral investment treaties, NAFTA[441] and the Energy Charter Treaty.[442] Finally, there is a fourth group of treaties, whose membership has been in

[438] Cambodia Model BIT, Art. 8(1), *UNCTAD Compendium* (Vol. VI, 2002) 466; Iran Model BIT, Art. 12(1), *ibid.* 482; Peru Model BIT, Art. 8(1), *ibid.* 497; Denmark Model BIT, Art. 9(1), *ibid.* (Vol. VII) 283; Finland Model BIT, Art. 9(1), *ibid.* 292; Germany Model BIT, Art. 11 'divergences concerning investments', *ibid.* 301; South Africa Model BIT, Art. 7(1) 'any legal dispute . . . relating to an investment', *ibid.* (Vol. VIII) 276; Turkey Model BIT, Art. 7(1), *ibid.* 284; Maurice Model BIT, Art. 8, *ibid.* (Vol. IX) 299; Sweden Model BIT, Art. 8(1), *ibid.* 313. Several model BITs simply refer to 'investment disputes' without defining this term. This provision is likely to be interpreted in the same way as the broad formulation under consideration: Croatia Model BIT, Art. 10(1), *ibid.* (Vol. VI) 476; Belgo-Luxemburg Economic Union Model BIT, Art. 10(1), *ibid.* (Vol. VII) 275; Mongolia Model BIT, Art. 8, *ibid.* (Vol. IX) 306. Other Model BITs with a wide formulation for 'investment disputes' include: Asian-African Legal Consultative Committee Model BIT, Art. 10(i), *UNCTAD Compendium* (Vol. III, 1996) 121; Switzerland Model BIT, Art. 8, *ibid.* 180; UK 'Preferred' Model BIT, Art. 8, *ibid.* 189; Egypt Model BIT, Art. 8(1), *ibid.* (Vol. V, 2000) 296; France Model BIT, Art. 8, *ibid.* 305; Indonesia Model BIT, Art. 8(1), *ibid.* 313; Jamaica Model BIT, Art. 10(1), *ibid.* 321; Netherlands Model BIT, Art. 9, *ibid.* 336; Sri Lanka Model BIT, Art. 8(1), *ibid.* 343.

[439] US Model BIT, Art. 9(1), *UNCTAD Compendium* (Vol. VI, 2002) 506; Burundi Model BIT, Art. 8(1), *ibid.* (Vol. IX) 291; Malaysia Model BIT, Art. 7(1), obligations entered into by a Contracting Party and the Investor in relation to an investment and a breach of the rights under the BIT, *ibid.* (Vol. V, 2000) 328.

[440] UK 'Alternative' Model BIT, Art. 8(1), *UNCTAD Compendium* (Vol. III, 1998) 190; Austria Model BIT, Art. 11, *ibid.* (Vol. VII, 2002) 264.

[441] Articles 1116, 1117.

[442] Article 26(1).

steady decline, that limit the investor/state jurisdiction to disputes about the *quantum* payable in the event of a proscribed expropriation.[443]

Where a treaty tribunal established pursuant to an investment treaty that falls within the first or second of these groups exercises jurisdiction over contractual claims or other causes of action based on municipal law, it will be in *direct* conflict with a municipal court or contractual arbitral tribunal that is seized of the same cause of action between the same parties. At the very least, symmetrical conflicts are latent in any situation where the investor has consummated its investment by contracting with the host state directly and the investment is covered by an investment treaty. If disputes arising out of the contract are, by the inclusion of a forum selection clause, subject to the jurisdiction of a municipal court or contractual arbitral tribunal, then the investor may attempt to bypass this jurisdiction by initiating an investment treaty claim. The treaty tribunal will then be faced with a symmetrical conflict of jurisdiction if the essence of the treaty claim rests upon a breach of contract. This was precisely the dilemma facing the ICSID Tribunal in *SGS v Pakistan*, a case that will be considered in detail in Section C of this Part VII.

Whether a conflict of jurisdiction is to be properly classified as 'asymmetrical' or 'symmetrical' thus depends on the investor's cause of action. If it is objectively based on the minimum standards of treatment set out in the treaty, then the possibility of an asymmetrical conflict arises; whereas in the case of a cause of action founded upon municipal law, or a delocalised body of rules catering for commercial contracts such as the *lex mercatoria*, the only potential conflict will be symmetrical. As each type of conflict must inevitably be resolved differently, it becomes crucial to identify the precise nature of the investor's cause of action as a preliminary matter in all investment disputes where the respondent host state raises a jurisdictional objection based on the competence of a different court or tribunal over the subject-matter of the investment dispute. The proper approach to 'cause of action analysis' will be considered in Section D of this Part VII; it will suffice to point out here that it is a matter of some controversy at present as to whether a treaty tribunal must accept the claimant's own formulation of its claims or instead inquire further into the real 'foundation' of the cause of action to determine whether it can be properly characterised as a treaty claim or a claim based on a contractual or other private law obligation.

It is useful at this juncture to summarise the issues that will be addressed in this Part VII. First, brief consideration will be given to the genesis of the conflicts of jurisdiction problem, which is the non-applicability of the rule on the exhaustion of local remedies (Section B). Symmetrical jurisdictional conflicts will then be dealt with in the context of pre-existing

[443] China Model BIT, Art. 9(3), *UNCTAD Compendium* (Vol. III, 1998) 155. Many of the first wave of BITs that followed the friendship, commerce, and navigation treaties from the communist bloc favoured this approach. An early review of these BITs can be found in: P. Peters, 'Dispute Settlement Arrangements in Investment Treaties' (1991) 22 *Netherlands YB Int L* 91.

forum selection clauses in investment agreements between the investor and host state (Section C), followed by an enquiry into 'cause of action analysis' and the proper approach to resolving symmetrical conflicts of jurisdiction (Section D). The analysis will then shift to certain types of asymmetrical jurisdictional conflicts that arise where multiple *fora* are competent over questions relating to the existence, nature, and scope of the investment (Section E) and then certain rules, both *de lege lata* and *de lege ferenda*, that might be employed to deal with asymmetrical conflicts of jurisdiction (Section F). Finally, the 'fork in the road' provision in bilateral and multilateral investment treaties will be scrutinized in Section G.

B. THE RULE ON THE EXHAUSTION OF LOCAL REMEDIES

It was concluded in Part III that the rule on the exhaustion of local remedies, of fundamental importance to the law of international responsibility and the international procedural law of diplomatic protection, has no *prima facie* application to investment treaty arbitrations in the absence of an express treaty stipulation to the contrary.[444] In other words, the rules of customary international law on the invocation of state international responsibility are not applicable to the sub-system of responsibility established by investment treaties in relation to investor/state disputes.

The fact that investors can bypass the requirement to exhaust local remedies no doubt increases the efficacy of their rights to international recourse under investment treaties. In the diplomatic protection context, a foreign national's failure to adhere to the exacting requirements of the rule is invoked with great frequency by the national's government in motivating a refusal to take up the claim, and is of course a ubiquitous objection made by respondent states to the admissibility of diplomatic protection claims before international courts and tribunals. The rule has the intended effect of delaying an international reclamation. It is all too common for potential claims to fade away due to the time and expense their prosecution may demand at each level of the municipal court system of the host state.

Investors have thus been liberated from a considerable burden by modern investment treaties that do not mandate the exhaustion of local remedies. But this liberation has come at a cost to the investment treaty system generally, measured in terms of the complex jurisdictional problems that continue to exercise treaty tribunals.

The local remedies rule has the effect of resolving conflicts of jurisdiction over the composite elements of an investment dispute. It ensures, for example, that matters within the competence of municipal courts or contractual arbitral tribunals are properly dealt with by these *fora* before the

[444] One such stipulation was considered in the Spain/Argentina BIT in: *Maffezini v Kingdom of Spain* (Decision on Objections to Jurisdiction, 25 January 2001) Case No. ARB/97/7, 5 ICSID Rep 396.

claim is elevated to the international plane.[445] In the absence of the local remedies rule, treaty tribunals must resolve issues such as (a) the significance of pending litigation in the municipal courts of the host state which touches upon an issue central to the investment treaty claim,[446] and (b) the effect of a forum selection clause in an investment agreement between the investor and the host state where the alleged grievance could be simultaneously classified as a breach of the investment agreement and the relevant investment treaty.[447] The displacement of the local remedies rule in investment treaty arbitrations has made it critical to examine the relationship between the municipal, transnational, and international legal orders. If the local remedies rule did apply to investment disputes, a claim would only reach the treaty tribunal after the other *fora* with jurisdiction over essential elements of the investment dispute had pronounced upon the issues before them. The treaty tribunal would then be in a position to survey the entire course of the dispute and test the host state's conduct against the substantive standards of the treaty, including the procedural treatment of the investor in the other *fora* if a denial of justice is alleged.[448]

C. SYMMETRICAL JURISDICTIONAL CONFLICTS: THE SIGNIFICANCE OF A FORUM SELECTION CLAUSE IN A CONTRACT BETWEEN THE INVESTOR AND THE HOST STATE

With increasing frequency, treaty tribunals must determine the effect of the investor's prior contractual acquiescence to an alternative judicial or arbitral forum with jurisdiction over disputes arising out of an investment contract with the host state. Such a forum selection clause can create a symmetrical jurisdictional conflict in four distinct ways. First, the offer to arbitrate in the treaty might be expressed in broad terms so as to include

[445] See J. Fawcett, 'The Exhaustion of Local Remedies: Substance or Procedure?' (1954) 31 *BYBIL* 452, 454, '[The local remedies rule is] a rule for resolving conflicts of jurisdiction between international law and municipal tribunals or authorities'; Y. Shany, above n. 434, 143, '[The local remedies rule is] can be described as a "more appropriate forum" provision, limiting forum selection on behalf of the parties by directing litigation, at least initially, to the more appropriate judicial body.'

[446] See, *eg*: *CME* Partial Award; *Lauder* Final Award; *Wena Hotels Ltd v Arab Republic of Egypt* (Award, 8 December 2000) Case No. ARB/98/4, 6 ICSID Rep 89, and (Decision on Annulment, 5 February 2002) 6 ICSID Rep 129.

[447] See, *eg*: *LANCO International Inc. v Argentine Republic* (Preliminary Decision on Jurisdiction, 8 December 1998) Case No. ARB/97/6, 5 ICSID Rep 367; *Salini Construtorri SpA and Italstrade SpA v Morocco* (Decision on Jurisdiction, 23 July 2001) Case No. ARB/00/4, 6 ICSID Rep 400; *Compañia de Aguas del Aconquija, SA and Compagnie Générale des Eaux/Vivendi Universal v Argentine Republic* (Award, 21 November 2000) Case No. ARB/97/3, 5 ICSID Rep 299, and (Decision on Annulment, 3 July 2002) 6 ICSID Rep 340; *Société Générale de Surveillance S.A. v Islamic Republic of Pakistan* (Decision on Jurisdiction, 6 August 2003) Case No. ARB/01/13, (2003) 42 ILM 1290; *Azurix Corp. v The Argentine Republic* (Decision on Jurisdiction, 8 December 2003) Case No. ARB/01/12, (2004) 43 ILM 262.

[448] A similar observation was made in the context of the Iran/US Claims Tribunal: D. Lloyd Jones, above n. 42, 274, '[I]f one presupposes a waiver of the requirement of exhaustion of local remedies, as described above, and consequently the absence of any proceedings before municipal courts, it necessarily follows that the international tribunal will have to deal with both the preliminary issue of whether the claimant's private rights in municipal law have been denied, and the substantive issue of whether this constitutes a denial of justice in international law.'

the possibility that the investor can bring 'any' or 'all' disputes arising out of its investment before a treaty tribunal.[449] Secondly, the treaty may expressly provide that the investor can submit disputes arising out of an investment agreement with the host state to a treaty tribunal.[450] Thirdly, although still controversial, the argument has been made that an 'umbrella clause' in a treaty, which exhorts the contracting states to respect contractual commitments with qualified investors, might have the effect of elevating contractual claims to treaty claims.[451] In such a case, the jurisdiction of the contractually selected forum and of the treaty tribunal will overlap with respect to the same claims. Fourthly, the investor might in effect 'disguise' the contractual foundation of its claims by invoking one of the open-textured minimum standards of protection contained in the treaty and pleading its cause of action on this basis before an investment treaty tribunal.

Before the precedents of treaty tribunals are considered, it will be instructive to examine the earlier international jurisprudence dealing with a similar jurisdictional conundrum in the context of interpreting the effect of the Calvo Clause.[452]

The Calvo Clause, so named in honour of its Latin American founder,[453] has two functions: (i) to ensure that all disputes arising out of the contract between the foreign investor and the host state containing the Calvo Clause are subject to the national law of that state and submitted to its local courts or, exceptionally, to private arbitration; and (ii) to effect a waiver by the investor of its right to appeal for the diplomatic protection of its own national state.[454]

The second purported function of the Calvo Clause has been almost universally denied by international tribunals that have had occasion to consider the clause, which often featured in investment contracts with Latin American states. The simple reason for this rejection is that the right of diplomatic protection vests in the national state of the investor and not in the investor itself. Hence the investor cannot waive a right which it itself does not possess.[455] More important, however, to the immediate

[449] See the examples above at n. 438. [450] See the examples above at n. 442.

[451] This was argued by the claimant in: *Société Générale De Surveillance S.A. v Islamic Republic of Pakistan* (Decision on Jurisdiction, 6 August 2003) Case No. ARB/01/13, (2003) 42 ILM 1290. Examples of 'umbrella clauses' are to be found in: Asian-African Legal Consultative Committee Model 'A' BIT, Art. 2(iv), *UNCTAD Compendium* (Vol. III, 1996) 118; Switzerland Model BIT, Art. 10(2), *ibid.* 182; Netherlands Model BIT. Art. 3(4), *ibid.* (Vol. V, 2000) 334; Belgo-Luxemburg Economic Union Model BIT, Art. 9(2), *ibid.* (Vol. VII, 2002) 275; Denmark Model BIT, Art. 2(3), *ibid.* 280; Finland Model BIT, Art. 12(2), *ibid.* 294; South Africa Model BIT, Art. 10(2), *ibid.* (Vol. VIII, 2002) 278; Energy Charter Treaty, Art. 10(1).

[452] See generally: D. Shea, above n. 128; D. O'Connell, above n. 72, 1059–67; *Oppenheim's International Law*, above n. 92, 930–1; K. Lipstein, above n. 128; E. Borchard, above n. 63, 809 *et seq.*; J. Simpson & H. Fox, above n. 53, 117 *et seq.*; R. Lillich, 'The diplomatic protection of nationals abroad: an elementary principle of international law under attack' (1975) 69 *AJIL* 359; W. Rogers, 'Of missionaries, fanatics, and lawyers: some thoughts on investment disputes in the Americas' (1978) 72 *AJIL* 1.

[453] C. Calvo, *Le droit international théorique et pratique* (1896, 5th edn).

[454] D. O'Connell, above n. 72, 1059–60; K. Lipstein, above n. 128, 131–4.

[455] *Martini (Italy) v Venezuela*, reported in J. Ralston, *The Law and Procedure of International Tribunals* (1926) No. 85, 66, 'The right of a sovereign power to enter into an agreement [for the

inquiry is the treatment that has been given to the first part of the Calvo Clause by international tribunals.

The most fertile source of case law on this point comes from the American-Mexican and American-Venezuelan Claims Commissions. The preponderance of these decisions have given effect to the first part of the Calvo Clause and thus Commissions have refrained from accepting jurisdiction over purely contractual disputes within the scope of the Calvo Clause. The persuasive rationale for such an approach is that a contractual cause of action must be adjudged in light of the contract as a whole and thus it is impermissible for an investor to plead a breach of one term and the non-applicability of another.

Thus, for example, in *Rogerio v Bolivia*[456] the American-Mexican Claims Commission declined jurisdiction 'because it is not proper to divide the unity of a juridical act, sustaining the efficacy of some of its clauses and the inefficacy of others.'[457] The effect of this interpretation was that the investor was compelled to exhaust local remedies before appealing to the United States to bring arbitration proceedings under the aegis of the American-Mexican Claims Commission. It was held in the *North American Dredging Company Case*[458] that if the treaty was to override a contractual forum selection clause, such an intention of the state parties must be made express. The express intention of the United States and Mexico could not be divined from the treaty establishing the Commission.[459]

The precedent of the American-Venezuelan Claims Commission is also consistent with this approach. In the *Flannagan, Bradley, Clark & Co. Case*,[460] a claim was made for breach of contract relating to liability under

diplomatic settlement of claims] is entirely superior to that of the subject to contract it away.'; *Mexican Union Railway Ltd. (United Kingdom) v United Mexican States* (1930) 5 UN Rep 115, 120, '[N]o person can, by [a Calvo Clause] deprive the Government of his country of its undoubted right to apply international remedies to violations of international law committed to his hurt.'; *North American Dredging Company of Texas (United States) v United Mexican States* (1926) 4 UN Rep 26, 30, '[The Calvo Clause] did not take from him his undoubted right to apply to his own Government for protection if his resort to the Mexican tribunals or other authorities available to him resulted in a denial or delay of justice . . . The basis of his appeal would be not a construction of his contract . . . but rather an internationally illegal act.'; *North and South American Construction Co. (United States) v Chile*, reported in J. Moore, *History and Digest of the Arbitrations to which the United States has been a Party* (Vol. 3, 1898) 2318, 2320. *Contra: Nitrate Railway Co. Ltd. (United Kingdom) v Chile*, reported in J. Ralston, *ibid.* No. 85, 67, '[P]rivate individuals or associations can, for the purpose of obtaining from a foreign government, privileges and concessions of public works . . . renounce the protection of their governments, and agree by contract not to resort to diplomatic action . . .'

456 Reported in J. Ralston, *ibid.* No. 88, 69.

457 See further: *Rudloff Case* (United States v Venezuela), reported in J. Ralston, *ibid.* No. 77, 63; *Mexican Union Railway Ltd. (United Kingdom) v United Mexican States* (1930) 5 UN Rep 115, 120, 'If the Commission were to act as if [the Calvo Clause] had never been written, the consequence would be that one stipulation, now perhaps onerous to the claimant, would cease to exist and that all the other provisions of the contract, including those from which claimant has derived or may still derive profit, would remain in force.'

458 *North American Dredging Company of Texas (United States) v United Mexican States* (1926) 4 UN Rep 26.

459 *Ibid.* 32. The relevant provision in the treaty provided that 'no claim shall be disallowed or rejected by the Commission by the application of the general principle of international law that the legal remedies must be exhausted as a condition precedent to the validity or allowance of any claim'. *Ibid.*

460 Reported in J. Moore, above n. 455, (Vol. 4, 1898) 3564.

state bonds held by the claimants. The contract contained the following clause:

Doubts and controversies which at any time might occur in virtue of the present agreement shall be decided by the common laws and ordinary tribunals of Venezuela, and they shall never be, as well as neither the decision which shall be pronounced upon them, nor anything relating to the agreement, the subject of international reclamation.[461]

Commissioner Findlay, speaking for the majority of the Commission, held that the claimants were barred by this clause from referring its contractual claims to any other tribunal:

We have no right to make a contract which the parties themselves did not make, and we would surely be doing so if we undertook to make that the subject of an international claim, to be adjudicated by this commission, in spite of their own voluntary undertaking that it was never to be made such, and should be determined in the municipal tribunals of the country with respect to which the controversy arose.[462]

This clause did not, however, prejudice the national state of the claimants from bringing an international reclamation if the treatment accorded to them amounted to a breach of international law, and hence the final sentence of the clause would have no effect on this possibility.[463]

This case came before the American-Venezuelan Claims Commission once again as the *Woodruff Case*,[464] which was cited by the ICSID *ad hoc* Committee in *Vivendi v Argentina*.[465] Umpire Barge approved Commission Findlay's analysis, stating that 'by the very agreement that is the fundamental basis of the claim, it was withdrawn from the jurisdiction of this commission'.[466] Umpire Barge was prepared to accept jurisdiction

[461] *Ibid.*

[462] *Ibid.* 3565–6. See further: *Turnbull, Manoa Company Ltd. and Orinoco Company Ltd. Cases* (United States v Venezuela) 9 UN Rep 261, 304 per Umpire Barge, '[The forum selection clause] forms part of the contract just as well as any of the other articles and which article has to be regarded just as well as any of the other articles, as the declaration of the will of the contracting parties, which expressed will must be respected as the supreme law between the parties, according to the immutable law of justice and equity: pacta servanda, without which law a contract would have no more worth than a treaty, and civil law would, as international law, have no other sanction than the cunning of the most astute or the brutal force of the physically strongest'. This principle was also applied to arbitration clauses. See *Tehuantepec Ship-Canal and Mexican and Pacific R.R. Co. v Mexico* (United States v Mexico), reported in J. Moore, *ibid.* (Vol. 3, 1898) 3132; *North and South American Construction Co. (United States) v Chile, ibid.* 2318.

[463] Whilst Commissioner Findlay may have left this question open, Commissioner Little was unequivocal about this principle in his dissent: 'A citizen may, no doubt, lawfully agree to settle his controversies with a foreign state in any reasonable mode or before any specified tribunal. But the agreement must not involve the exclusion of international reclamation. That question sovereigns only can deal with.' Commissioner Little dissented from the majority because, in his view, a stipulation to the contrary infected the rest of the forum selection clause and thus rendered the whole clause a nullity. *Flannagan, Bradley, Clark & Co. Case*, reported in J. Moore, *ibid.* (Vol. 4, 1898) 3564, 3566–7.

[464] (United States v Venezuela), reported in J. Ralston, above n. 455, No. 75, 62.

[465] *Compañia de Aguas del Aconquija, SA and Compagnie Générale des Eaux/Vivendi Universal v Argentine Republic* (Decision on Annulment, 3 July 2002) Case No. ARB/97/3, 6 ICSID Rep 340, para. 98.

[466] See further: *Rudloff Case* (United States v Venezuela), reported in J. Ralston, above n. 455, No. 77, 63: '[I]n such cases it has to be investigated as to every claim, whether the fact of not fulfilling this condition and of claiming another way, without first going to the tribunals of the republic,

in the event of denial of justice or unjust delay of justice, but the claimants had never even initiated proceedings in the Venezuelan courts.[467]

The leading case on the interpretation of the Calvo Clause is *North American Dredging Company of Texas (United States) v United Mexican States*.[468] The United States brought a claim on behalf of the North American Dredging Company of Texas for losses and damages arising from breaches of a contract signed by the Government of Mexico for dredging at the port of Salina Cruz in Mexico.[469] The Commission had no hesitation in finding that such claims fell within the forum selection clause in the dredging contract, which referred all disputes 'concerning the execution of work [under the contract] and the fulfilment of this contract'.[470] The Commission then distinguished between contractual and international claims:

> If [the claimant] had a claim for denial of justice, for delay of justice or gross injustice, of for any other violation of international law, committed by Mexico to its damage, it might have presented such a claim to its government which, in turn, could have espoused it and presented it here . . . But where a claimant has expressly agreed in writing . . . that in all matters pertaining to the execution, fulfilment and interpretation of the contract he will have resort to local tribunals and then wilfully ignores them by applying to his government, he will be bound by his contract and the Commission will not take jurisdiction of such claim.[471]

The Commission's reasoning should apply with greater force to the investment treaty context, where the investor has complete functional control over the prosecution of its treaty claims and any contractual arrangement to which it is privy.

If this early experience on the treatment of the Calvo Clause is assimilated to investment treaty arbitration, it is submitted that treaty tribunals should follow the same approach in declining its jurisdiction when confronted with a symmetrical jurisdictional conflict; *ie* when the investor brings a cause of action based on a contract before a treaty tribunal

does not infect the claim with a *vitium proprium*, in consequence of which the absolute equity . . . prohibits this commission from giving the benefit of its jurisdiction (for as such it is regarded by the claimants) to a claim based on a contract by which this benefit was renounced and thus absolving claimants from their obligations, whilst the enforcing of the obligations of the other party based on the same contract is precisely the aim of their claim.'

[467] A *prima facie* instance of a denial of justice was found to circumvent the claimant's obligation to comply with a contractual choice of forum for the settlement of disputes in *North & South American Construction Co. (United States) v Chile* (Reported in J. Moore, above n. 455, (Vol. 3, 1898, 2318) a case arising under the American-Chilean Claims Commission. The contract referred disputes to arbitration and the arbitral tribunal had been duly constituted, only to then be suppressed by the Chilean Government. As a result of this act, the claimant 'recovered its entire right to invoke or accept the mediation or protection of the government of the United States'. *Ibid*. 2321.

[468] (1926) 4 UN Rep 26.

[469] *Ibid*.

[470] *Ibid*. The Commission found that the US company had thereby 'waived his right to conduct himself as if no competent authorities existed in Mexico; as if he were engaged in fulfilling a contract in an inferior country subject to a system of capitulations; and as if the only real remedies available to him in the fulfilment, construction, and enforcement of this contract were international remedies.' *Ibid*. 30.

[471] *Ibid*. 32–3.

and that contract contains a forum selection clause in favour of a different court or tribunal. This rule can only be displaced by an express provision in an investment treaty that purports to override existing dispute resolution clauses to which the investor is contractually bound. No treaty that this writer is aware of contains an express stipulation to that effect. An example of an express abrogation of existing forum selection arrangements is Article II(1) of the Claims Settlement Declaration,[472] a constituent document of the Iran/US Claims Tribunal, which has been interpreted in several cases as overriding an existing jurisdiction clause in favour of the US courts.[473]

This approach to resolving symmetrical jurisdictional conflicts is supported by other authorities.

In *SPP v Egypt*,[474] an ICSID Tribunal was required to interpret a clause in an Egyptian law registering Egypt's consent to submit to three different methods for the resolution of disputes, which includes: (i) any method of settlement previously agreed to by the parties themselves; (ii) dispute resolution pursuant to an applicable BIT; and (iii) arbitration under the ICSID Convention.[475] One of the issues before the Tribunal was whether a hierarchical relationship between these methods was discernable from the text of this clause. The Tribunal noted that these methods were listed from the most specific type of agreement on the resolution of disputes to the most general. From this it was concluded that:

> A specific agreement between the parties to a dispute would naturally take precedence with respect to a bilateral treaty between the investor's State and Egypt, while such a bilateral treaty would in turn prevail with respect to a multilateral treaty such as the Washington Convention. [The clause] thus reflects the maxim *generalia specialibus non derogant* . . . [476]

The Tribunal cited several international authorities approving of this maxim, including the *Mavrommatis Case*.[477] Here the Permanent Court had jurisdiction pursuant to the general compromissory clause in the Mandate for Palestine and the question was the effect that should be given to a dispute resolution clause in another instrument, the Treaty of Lausanne, which covered part of the dispute before the Court relating to the assessment of indemnities. The Court found that the more specific reference in the Treaty of Lausanne 'excludes as regards these matters the general jurisdiction given to the Court in disputes concerning the interpretation and application of the Mandate.'[478]

472 Reproduced at (1981) 75 *AJIL* 418.

473 C. Brower & J. Brueschke, above n. 9, 60–72.

474 *Southern Pacific Properties (Middle East) Limited [SPP(ME)] v Arab Republic of Egypt* (Jurisdiction (No. 1), 27 November 1985), 3 ICSID Rep 101.

475 *Ibid.* para. 60.

476 *Southern Pacific Properties (Middle East) Limited [SPP(ME)] v Arab Republic of Egypt* (Jurisdiction (No. 2), 14 April 1988), 3 ICSID Rep 131, para. 83.

477 *Ibid.*

478 (1924) PCIJ Rep Series A No. 2, 32. The PCIJ did ultimately exercise jurisdiction over the part of the dispute in question because it was found that the issue related to a preliminary question that could not have been referred to the specific dispute resolution procedure envisaged by the Treaty of Lausanne (*ibid.*). *Contra*: *Chorzów Factory Case* (Germany v Poland) (Indemnity) (Merits) (Jurisdiction) (1928) PCIJ Rep Series A No. 17, 30 (jurisdiction not declined due to inadequate remedies in alternative

It is important to emphasize that the ICSID Tribunal in *SPP* made no distinction between the status of each judicial forum contemplated by each method of dispute resolution. It is submitted that this approach is entirely correct. The referral of contractual disputes by a foreign investor and a host state to a municipal court or arbitral tribunal in an investment agreement and the submission of the same type of disputes to a treaty tribunal based on the investor's acceptance of the state's offer to arbitrate are both acts based on the consent of both parties. It is not legitimate to make a distinction between them, either in terms of the instrument recording the state's consent to the submission, or the ultimate status of the tribunal constituted to hear the dispute, if the subject-matter of the dispute is the same, *viz*. breach of contract. Hence the general principles of *generalia specialibus non derogant*, *prior tempore, potior jure*, and *pacta sunt servunda* must govern the resolution of the symmetrical jurisdictional conflict, rather than a vacuous appeal to the hierarchy of legal orders.

These principles implicitly formed the basis of the ICSID Tribunal's decision in *Klöckner v Cameroon*.[479] The parties had entered into a protocol of agreement and a supply agreement for a fertiliser plant in Cameroon, each of which contained an ICSID arbitration clause.[480] Klöckner seized the ICSID Tribunal on the basis of the supply agreement, whereas Cameroon invoked the jurisdiction of the Tribunal over the protocol of agreement by way of counterclaim.[481] A management contract relating to the same investment in the fertiliser plant was signed by the parties several years later and contained a reference to ICC arbitration.[482] The Tribunal ruled that the 'Claimant is right in denying the jurisdiction of the Arbitral Tribunal to rule on disputes arising from this contract.'[483] The ICSID Tribunal thus upheld the validity of the parties' contractual choice of ICC arbitration for disputes arising out of the management contract, implicitly on the basis of the *generalia specialibus non derogant* principle.

The controversial part of the ICSID Tribunal's decision in *Klöckner* was the partial circumvention of its finding on the status of the ICC arbitration clause in the management contract by pronouncing upon issues pertaining to the management of the plant on the basis of a general provision in the protocol of agreement (over which the Tribunal did have jurisdiction) that recorded Klöckner's obligation to 'be responsible for the technical and commercial management of the [plant]'.[484] This aspect of the Tribunal's decision was the subject of a rigorous dissenting

forum); *Certain German Interests in Polish Upper Silesia* (Preliminary Objections) (1925) PCIJ Rep Series A No. 6, 23 (jurisdiction not declined because alternative forum without exclusive jurisdiction over subject-matter of dispute).

479 *Klöckner Industrie-Anlagen GmbH, Klöckner Belge, SA and Klöckner Handelsmaatschappij BV v Republic of Cameroon and Société Camerounaise des Engrais SA*. (Award, 21 October 1983) Case No. ARB/81/2, 2 ICSID Rep 9; (Decision on Annulment, 3 May 1985) Case No. ARB/81/2, 2 ICSID Rep 95.

480 (Award, 21 October 1983) Case No. ARB/81/2, 2 ICSID Rep 9, 13.

481 *Ibid.*

482 *Ibid.*

483 *Ibid.* 17.

484 (Award, 21 October 1983) Case No. ARB/81/2, 2 ICSID Rep 9, 13–14, 17–18, 68–70.

opinion[485] and was then sharply criticised by the *ad hoc* Committee on annulment.[486] According to the Tribunal, the fact that the management contract was executed some two years after the plant became operational was evidence that the arbitration clause in the protocol of agreement should be construed broadly as it was the only source of obligations between the parties during this intervening period.[487]

The general conclusion thus far, based primarily on the precedents of the mixed claims commissions, is that a treaty tribunal should decline jurisdiction over contractual claims in favour of a forum that has previously been chosen by the parties to resolve contractual disputes. The principles mandating this approach are the preservation of the unity of the contractual bargain (a requirement of *pacta sunt servunda*), *generalia specialibus non derogant*, and *prior tempore, potior jure*. It is important to realise that the parties' consent to investment treaty arbitration is no more 'solemn' than their consent to the submission of their contractual disputes to a different forum. An investment treaty tribunal has no independent interest in hearing a case that transcends the consent of the parties, unlike the interest of a municipal court in enforcing the law of a particular polity.[488] Moreover, the rationale of a dispute resolution clause is to create a climate of legal certainty in the contractual relations between the parties and avoid litigation over the proper forum for the resolution of disputes and thus the potential risk of multiple proceedings.[489] By accepting jurisdiction over contractual disputes subject to a different forum, a treaty tribunal subverts this contractual certainty to the detriment of one of the parties.[490] Just as municipal courts have bowed to the interests of transnational commerce by upholding dispute resolution clauses, treaty tribunals should also give effect to the collective will of the parties and the principle of *pacta sunt servanda*.[491]

These general conclusions will now be tested against the jurisdictional decisions of treaty tribunals to date.

485 *Ibid.* 89–93. 486 (Decision on Annulment, 3 May 1985), 2 ICSID Rep 95, 95–117.

487 (Award, 21 October 1983) Case No. ARB/81/2, 2 ICSID Rep 9, 13–14. This inference was criticised because the management contract expressly stated that it was to apply retroactively to when the plant became operational and yet the majority of the ICSID Tribunal failed to consider this clause. See the Dissenting Opinion, *ibid.* 90. But the retroactivity of obligations concerning the management of the plant causes conceptual problems as well. The majority of the ICSID Tribunal would have been on safer ground to hold that the mismanagement constituted a breach of one of the express clauses of the protocol of agreement relating to the operation of the plant, rather than latching onto the amorphous general clause in that agreement specifically relating to the management of the plant.

488 See V. Lowe, 'Overlapping Jurisdiction in International Tribunals' (1999) 20 *Australian YB of Int L* 191, 198–9.

489 *Scherk v Alberto-Culver Co.* 417 US 506, 516, 519 (1974); G. Born, *International Civil Litigation in the United States Courts* (1996, 3rd edn) 372–3.

490 In *Société Générale de Surveillance S.A. v Islamic Republic of Pakistan* (Decision on Jurisdiction, 6 August 2003) Case No. ARB/01/13, (2003) 42 ILM 1290, para. 157, the contractual choice of arbitration pursuant to the arbitration law of Pakistan in the investment agreement between SGS and Pakistan was considered to be a 'deal-breaker' for Pakistan. The ICSID Tribunal was correct to highlight the potential injustice to Pakistan if SGS was effectively allowed to bypass this contractual choice at its own discretion.

491 See the discussion of the US Supreme Court in: *Breman v Zapata Off-Shore Co.* 407 US 1, 12–13 (1972).

In *LANCO International Inc. v Argentine Republic*,[492] the contract in question was a concession for the development and operation of a port terminal. The parties to the concession included the Argentine Ministry of Economy and Public Works and LANCO. Clause 12 of the concession provided that: 'For all purposes derived from the agreement and the BID CONDITIONS, the parties agree to the jurisdiction of the Federal Contentious-Administrative Tribunals of the Federal Capital of the Argentine Republic.'[493] The Argentine Republic objected to the jurisdiction of the ICSID Tribunal, established upon LANCO's petition in accordance with the Argentina/US BIT, on the basis that LANCO had already agreed to refer contractual disputes to the state courts of Argentina.[494]

In its discussion of the effect of Clause 12, the Tribunal noted that the jurisdiction of the Federal Contentious-Administrative Tribunals over disputes relating to the concession arose by operation of the law and thus would exist even in the absence of any specific contractual designation. Clause 12 was not, therefore, a selection of 'a previously agreed dispute-settlement procedure' for the purposes of the 'fork in the road' provision of the treaty, which would have had the effect of precluding the investor to resort to ICSID arbitration, at least with respect to contractual disputes.[495] The clause was further weakened by the fact that the Argentina/US BIT came into force after the concession agreement was executed and hence the parties could not have had the possibility of recourse to an investment treaty tribunal in contemplation when negotiating the clause.[496] Nevertheless, Argentina maintained that by agreeing to Clause 12 the parties 'exclude the jurisdiction of ICSID for hearing any dispute associated with the contractual relationship emanating from the Concession Agreement'.[497]

The ICSID Tribunal dismissed Argentina's argument by reference to Article 26 of the ICSID Convention, which refers to the exclusivity of ICSID arbitration vis-à-vis any other remedy and to a presumption against the requirement to exhaust local remedies. Insofar as no requirement to exhaust local remedies could be discerned from the Argentina/US BIT, 'the offer made by the Argentine Republic to covered investors under [that] Treaty cannot be diminished by the submission to Argentina's domestic courts, to which the Concession Agreement remits.'[498]

Given the Tribunal's previous finding on the nature of Clause 12, it is clear that the term 'submission' should be understood in a narrow sense, *viz.* the existence of jurisdiction in domestic courts by operation of law, which is merely confirmed in the concession agreement. On this narrow basis, the Tribunal's decision is no doubt correct. If the investor has made no previous election of an alternative jurisdiction for the resolution of disputes arising out of its contract, then there is no scope for conflict with its election of ICSID arbitration for contractual claims subsequent to the

[492] (Preliminary Decision on Jurisdiction, 8 December 1998) Case No. ARB/97/6, 5 ICSID Rep 367.
[493] *Ibid.* paras. 6–7.
[494] *Ibid.* paras. 24, 34.
[495] *Ibid.* paras. 19, 26, 38.
[496] *Ibid.* para. 27.
[497] *Ibid.* para. 34.
[498] *Ibid.* para. 40.

conclusion of that contract. It must be recognised, however, that tribunals have subsequently interpreted the *LANCO* ruling as a general statement of principle,[499] with the effect that a pre-existing contractual choice of forum for the settlement of disputes might be unilaterally avoided at the investor's option in relation to disputes falling within the proper scope of this contractual choice.

Argentina's submission in *LANCO* on the effect of Clause 12 was deliberately very broad—'any dispute *associated* with the contractual relationship'.[500] No sharp distinction was thus made between a cause of action based on the contract and a cause of action based on the treaty, undoubtedly in an attempt to cover all the claims advanced by LANCO, which were based on the standards of protection afforded by the BIT. The term 'associated' was therefore likely to have been utilised to apply to any dispute factually predicated on the contractual relationship between the parties. To the extent that each cause of action advanced by LANCO was objectively based on the BIT standards, the ICSID Tribunal was correct to disregard the submission to Argentina's domestic courts, because this submission did not extend to treaty claims.

To summarise, the *LANCO* ruling is correct but must be limited to the circumstances of that case. The principle in *LANCO*, on this premise, could therefore be articulated as affirming the right of an investor to bring treaty claims to an ICSID tribunal notwithstanding the investor has previously acknowledged the jurisdiction of local courts over contractual claims.

The next treaty tribunal to grapple with this issue was in *Salini Construtorri SpA and Italstrade SpA v Morocco*.[501] The relevant contract in this case was an agreement for the construction of a highway between two Italian companies, Salini and Italstrade, on the one hand, and the Société Nationale des Autoroutes du Maroc ('ADM'), a state company founded by the Moroccan Government.[502] Upon completion of the construction, the Italian companies requested additional compensation for their work when the final account was prepared due to, *inter alia*, exceptionally bad weather and unforeseeable fluctuations in the value of the Yen.[503] ADM rejected the claims for additional compensation and appealed to the Minister of Equipment as required by administrative regulations applicable to the construction contract.[504] No reply was forthcoming and the Italian companies instituted ICSID proceedings under the Morocco/Italy BIT, relying on alleged breaches of the construction contract and the BIT.[505]

[499] See, *eg* : *Compañia de Aguas del Aconquija, SA and Compagnie Générale des Eaux/Vivendi Universal v Argentine Republic* (Award, 21 November 2000) Case No. ARB/97/3, 5 ICSID Rep 299, at note 18. Commentators have also interpreted the *LANCO* decision too broadly, *see, eg* : S. Alexandrov, 'Introductory Note to ICSID' (2001) 40 ILM 454, 455, 'The Tribunal's finding that the dispute settlement procedures in the BIT supersede any previous agreement on dispute settlement procedures—including a contractual forum selection clause—preserves the integrity and enforceability of the BIT regime.'

[500] (Preliminary Decision on Jurisdiction, 8 December 1998) Case No. ARB/97/6, 5 ICSID Rep 367, para. 34.

[501] (Decision on Jurisdiction, 23 July 2001) Case No. ARB/00/4, 6 ICSID Rep 400.

[502] *Ibid.* paras. 2–3. [503] *Ibid.* para. 5. [504] *Ibid.* [505] *Ibid.* para. 62.

Morocco objected to the jurisdiction of the ICSID tribunal because the regulations incorporated into the construction contract vested jurisdiction in the tribunals of Rabat over claims arising from the performance of the contract.[506]

The ICSID Tribunal devoted only one paragraph to an analysis of this jurisdiction clause, contained in Article 52 of the Cahier des Clauses Administrative Générales (CCAG), and held:

> La compétence des tribunaux du contentieux administratif ne pouvant être prorogée, l'acceptation décrite ci-avant de la juridiction du CIRDI [ICSID] prévaudra sur le contenu de l'article 52 du CCAG, cet article ne pouvant constituer une véritable clause de prorogation de compétence régie par le principe de l'autonomie de la volonté.[507]

Although not free from doubt, the Tribunal appears to have ruled that the incorporation in the construction contract of a submission to the tribunals of Rabat did not constitute a true contractual choice of jurisdiction,[508] but rather was imposed by operation of law. Hence, consistent with *LANCO*, the Tribunal did not perceive a conflict between the automatic jurisdiction of domestic courts over disputes arising out of a contract, and an acceptance by the investor of the host state's offer to refer such disputes to ICSID arbitration.

The *Salini* Tribunal did not ultimately uphold its jurisdiction over Salini's contractual claims. Despite acknowledging that Salini's purely contractual claims may well fall within the scope of the 'all disputes clause' and thus within the Tribunal's jurisdiction *ratione materiae*,[509] the Tribunal nevertheless found that Morocco had not extended its offer of ICSID arbitration to disputes arising out of contracts entered into by distinct legal entities such as the AMD.[510] Hence, as the State of Morocco was not a party to the construction contract, the Tribunal had no jurisdiction *ratione personae* over AMD.[511]

In contradistinction to the LANCO and *Salini* cases, the ICSID Tribunal in *Compañia de Aguas del Aconquija, SA and Compagnie Générale des Eaux/Vivendi Universal v Argentine Republic*[512] faced a true choice of forum clause for the settlement of disputes. Article 16.4 of the Concession Contract for the operation of a water and sewage system between the claimants (a French company and its Argentine subsidiary) and the Tucumán Province of Argentina provided that '[f]or the purposes of interpretation and application of this Contract the parties submit themselves to the *exclusive* jurisdiction of the Contentious Administrative Tribunals of Tucumán.'[513] The claimants (collectively 'Vivendi') contended, in part, that actions of Tucumán officials, allegedly designed to undermine the operation of the concession, were legally attributable to

[506] *Ibid.* para. 25. [507] *Ibid.* para. 27. [508] *Ibid.* para. 27. [509] *Ibid.* para. 61.
[510] *Ibid.* para. 60–1. [511] *Ibid.* para. 61.
[512] (Award, 21 November 2000) Case No. ARB/96/1, 5 ICSID Rep 153, hereinafter 'Vivendi Award'.
[513] *Ibid.* para. 27. Emphasis added.

Argentina and served as the basis for distinct violations of the Argentina/France BIT.[514] The Tribunal noted that the specific acts complained of by Vivendi fell into four groups: (i) acts that resulted in a fall in the recovery rate under the Concession Contract; (ii) acts that unilaterally reduced the tariff rate; (iii) abuses of regulatory authority; and (iv) dealings in bad faith (in particular, the conduct of the Provincial Governor in the renegotiations of the Concession Contract).[515]

On the basis of these specific acts, the claimants alleged breaches of the prohibition against expropriation and the fair and equitable treatment standard in the Argentina/France BIT. The Tribunal found that, insofar as these claims disclosed causes of action based on the treaty rather than on the Concession Contract, they fell within the jurisdiction of the Tribunal.[516] Having thus accepted jurisdiction, however, the Tribunal held that 'all of the issues relevant to the legal basis for these claims against the Respondent arose from disputes between Claimants and Tucumán concerning their performance and non-performance under the Concession Contract.'[517] The relationship between the forum selection clause in Article 16.4 in the Concession Contact and the jurisdiction of the ICSID Tribunal arising under the BIT therefore came into sharp focus. The Tribunal made the following important ruling:

> . . . [T]he Tribunal holds that, because of the crucial connection in this case between the terms of the Concession Contract and these alleged violations of the BIT, the Argentine Republic cannot be held liable unless and until the Claimants have, as Article 16.4 of the Concession Contract requires, asserted their rights in proceedings before the contentious administrative courts of Tucumán and have been denied their rights, either procedurally or substantively.[518]

In these circumstances, according to the Tribunal, a claim against Argentina could only arise if the claimants:

> [w]ere denied access to the court of Tucumán to pursue their remedy under Article 16.4 or if the Claimants were treated unfairly in those courts (denial of procedural justice) or if the judgment of those courts were substantively unfair (denial of substantive justice) or otherwise denied rights guaranteed to French investors under the BIT by the Argentine Republic.[519]

[514] The claimants also alleged that certain omissions of the Argentine Republic violated the BIT directly. These omissions primarily concerned the failure of the Argentine Republic to respond appropriately to the actions of the Tucumán officials. This second limb of the claimants' submissions was dismissed by the ICSID Tribunal on the merits. *Ibid.* paras. 87, 92.

[515] *Ibid.* para. 63.

[516] *Ibid.* para. 54.

[517] *Ibid.* para. 77. The ICSID Tribunal listed these issues as 'the reasonableness of the rates and the timing of increases in rates that the Claimants contended were authorized by the Concession Contract, whether individual metering was required or permitted, whether CGE was entitled to charge certain local taxes to its customers in addition to its service tariff, whether CGE was permitted to terminate service to users who failed to pay their water and sewerage invoices, whether CGE failed to submit an investment plan, maintain adequate insurance, or submit an emergency plan in a timely manner and, finally, whether CGE was required to continue operating the system for 10 months after it terminated the Concession Contract.' *Ibid.*

[518] *Ibid.* para. 78.

[519] *Ibid.* para. 80.

By accepting jurisdiction over Vivendi's claims based on the BIT, and then summarily dismissing those claims on the merits, the Tribunal exposed itself to a challenge under Article 52(1)(b) of the ICSID Convention on the ground that the Tribunal exceeded its powers by failing to exercise its jurisdiction. Vivendi's inevitable challenge on this basis was upheld by the ICSID *ad hoc* Committee in *Compañía de Aguas del Aconquija, S.A. & Vivendi Universal v Argentine Republic*.[520]

The *ad hoc* Committee did not find fault with the Tribunal's analysis of its own jurisdiction[521] and endorsed the distinction between contractual and treaty claims in this context.[522] The Tribunal's error was instead its failure to heed this distinction in its consideration of the merits of the treaty claims by declining to test those claims by reference to the international standards contained in the BIT, due to a perceived overlap with issues arising under the Concession Contract that were subject to resolution in a different forum. The *ad hoc* Committee's reasoning on this point is the most interesting and persuasive part of the judgment. It was first emphasized that the substantive laws applicable to contractual and treaty claims are different so that a 'state may breach a treaty without breaching a contract, and *vice versa*.'[523] This difference has consequences in relation to the proper defendant to the claims. Treaty claims are governed by international law and thus the rules of attribution apply. In this way, Argentina could be internationally responsible for acts of the Tucumán Provincial Government held to be in breach of the BIT. By contrast, according to the *ad hoc* Committee, 'the state of Argentina is not liable for the performance of contracts entered into by Tucumán, which possesses separate legal personality under its own law and is responsible for the performance of its own contracts'.[524]

The *ad hoc* Committee then proceeded to consider the effect of a forum selection clause in an investment agreement with the host state. Insofar as the Committee had previously upheld the Tribunal's decision on jurisdiction, this part of the judgment is strictly *obiter dicta*, but has nonetheless had a marked impact on subsequent developments in this area. The *ad hoc* Committee commenced with a bold statement of principle:

> In a case where the essential basis of a claim brought before an international tribunal is a breach of contract, the tribunal will give effect to any valid choice of forum clause in the contract.[525]

Support for this proposition was found in the American-Venezuelan Mixed Commission's consideration of the effects of a Calvo Clause in the *Woodruff Case*.[526] As was submitted previously, this early body of jurisprudence is highly relevant to this inquiry and the *ad hoc* Committee

[520] (Decision on Annulment, 3 July 2002) Case No. ARB/97/3, 6 ICSID Rep 340, para. 115, hereinafter '*Vivendi* Annulment Decision'.

[521] *Ibid.* para. 80.

[522] *Ibid.* para. 76.

[523] *Ibid.* para. 95.

[524] *Ibid.* para. 96.

[525] *Ibid.* para. 98 (footnote omitted).

[526] (United States v Venezuela), reported in J. Ralston, above n. 455, No. 75, 62.

was correct to delve further into pre-investment treaty jurisprudence. In the *Woodruff Case*, it was held that the clause in the contract referring disputes to the Venezuelan courts bound Woodruff, the claimant, from bringing contractual claims before the Commission.

The *ad hoc* Committee recognised that its statement of principle was subject to a stipulation to the contrary in the relevant treaty and cited the Algiers Accord as an example where jurisdiction clauses submitting disputes to US courts were expressly overridden. Whether or not the BIT had this effect was left open.[527]

The next instalment in this evolving jurisprudence was the ICSID award in *SGS Société Générale de Surveillance S.A. v Islamic Republic of Pakistan*.[528] The Government of Pakistan had entered into a contract with SGS in 1994 whereby SGS agreed to provide 'pre-shipment inspection' services with respect to goods to be exported from certain countries to Pakistan.[529] This 'PSI Agreement' contained an arbitration clause that envisaged arbitration in Islamabad in accordance with the Arbitration Act of Pakistan.[530] A dispute arose between the parties as to the adequacy of each other's performance, and the Government of Pakistan terminated the PSI Agreement with effect from 1997.[531] SGS then commenced court proceedings against Pakistan at the place of its domicile in Switzerland, alleging unlawful termination of the PSI Agreement.[532] The Swiss Courts dismissed SGS's claim, at first instance on the basis of the parties' existing agreement to arbitrate, and on appeal due to Pakistan's entitlement to sovereign immunity from jurisdiction.[533] At the same time, Pakistan commenced arbitration proceedings in Islamabad pursuant to the arbitration clause in the PSI Agreement.[534] SGS filed preliminary procedural objections to the arbitration, and also made counterclaims against Pakistan for alleged breaches of the PSI Agreement.[535] SGS then commenced ICSID arbitration proceedings by relying on the reference to arbitration in the Switzerland/Pakistan BIT.

Pakistan objected to the jurisdiction of the ICSID Tribunal, primarily because the 'essential basis' of all SGS's claims, in accordance with the dicta of the *ad hoc* Committee in *Vivendi*, was breach of contract and therefore subject to the exclusive jurisdiction of the contractual arbitral tribunal constituted pursuant to the PSI Agreement.[536] SGS defended its invocation of the ICSID Tribunal's jurisdiction by submitting in the alternative that either (i) the effect of the 'umbrella clause' in the BIT was to elevate its contractual claims into claims grounded on an alleged breach

[527] *Vivendi* Annulment Decision, note 69. In relation to the Algiers Accords, this is the combined effect of Arts II and VII of the Claims Settlement Declaration. Writers have stated the position differently in terms of an implied waiver of the rule on the exhaustion of local remedies, see: C. Amerasinghe, 'Whither the Local Remedies Rule?' (1990) 5 *ICSID Rev—Foreign Investment LJ* 292, 297.

[528] *Société Générale de Surveillance S.A. v Islamic Republic of Pakistan* (Decision on Jurisdiction, 6 August 2003) Case No. ARB/01/13, (2003) 42 ILM 1290.

[529] *Ibid.* para. 11.

[530] *Ibid.* para. 15.

[531] *Ibid.* para. 16.

[532] *Ibid.* para. 20.

[533] *Ibid.* paras. 23–4.

[534] *Ibid.* para. 26.

[535] *Ibid.* paras. 27–9.

[536] *Ibid.* paras. 43–4.

of the BIT[537] or, (ii) the Tribunal had jurisdiction over purely contractual claims based on the general reference to 'disputes with respect to investments' in the investor/state dispute resolution clause in Article 9 of the BIT.[538] In either case, SGS contended that the jurisdiction of an ICSID tribunal, an international tribunal with adjudicative competence by virtue of an international treaty, must prevail over the jurisdiction of the contractual arbitral tribunal sitting in Islamabad.[539]

The ICSID Tribunal dismissed SGS's argument based on the 'umbrella clause'.[540] This paved the way for a classic confrontation between the two competing jurisdictions over the same contractual claims because it was no longer open to SGS to appeal to the different legal nature of contractual claims before the ICSID Tribunal due to their purported 'elevation' by the 'umbrella clause' in the BIT. But this confrontation was ultimately sidestepped by the Tribunal, which denied even the possibility of a jurisdictional conflict altogether. The Tribunal found that it had no jurisdiction over purely contractual claims by attributing a narrow meaning to the wording 'disputes with respect to investments' in Article 9 of the BIT:

> That phrase . . . while descriptive of the *factual subject matter* of the disputes, does not relate to the *legal basis* of the claims, or the *cause of action* asserted in the claims.[541]

The Tribunal then makes a deduction based on this observation that is highly controversial:

> [N]o implication necessarily arises that both BIT and purely contract claims are intended to be covered by the Contracting Parties in Article 9. Neither, accordingly, does an implication arise that the Article 9 dispute settlement mechanism would supersede and set at naught all otherwise valid non-ICSID forum selection clauses in all earlier agreements between Swiss investors and the Respondent. Thus, we do not see anything in Article 9 or in any other provision of the BIT that can be read as vesting this Tribunal with jurisdiction over claims resting *ex hypothesi* exclusively on contract.[542]

537 *Ibid.* para. 98. Article 11 of the Switzerland/Pakistan BIT provides: 'Either Contracting Party shall constantly guarantee the observance of the commitments it has entered into with respect to the investments of the investors of the other Contracting Party.'

538 *Ibid.* para. 100. Article 9 of the Switzerland/Pakistan BIT provides:

(1) For the purpose of solving disputes with respect to investments between a Contracting Party and an investor of the other Contracting Party and without prejudice to Article 10 of this Agreement (Disputes between Contracting Parties), consultations will take place between the parties concerned.

(2) If these conditions do not result in a solution within twelve months and if the investor concerned gives written consent, the dispute shall be submitted to the arbitration of the International Centre for Settlement of Investment Disputes, instituted by the Convention of Washington of March 18, 1965, for the settlement of disputes regarding investments between States and nationals of other States . . .

539 *Ibid.* para. 106. 540 *Ibid.* paras. 163–174. 541 *Ibid.* para. 161.

542 *Ibid.* The Tribunal did, however, leave upon the possibility that the parties could, by special agreement, vest a tribunal established pursuant to a BIT with jurisdiction over purely contractual claims. *Ibid.* There is, in fact, already precedent for special agreements of this nature in an ongoing UNCITRAL arbitration arising under the France/Lebanon BIT.

The Tribunal's ruling appears to rest upon an unreasoned assumption that purely contractual claims should not, as a matter of general principle, be covered by the reference to arbitration in BITs. This is problematic, for the first premise quoted above on the distinction between the factual and legal basis of the claims is entirely neutral on this question. The general language of Article 9 does not expressly carve out contractual claims from its purview; to the contrary, the natural meaning of the words 'disputes with respect to investments' is broad enough to encompass any disputes that are factually related to investments. It is curious, therefore, that the Tribunal reversed the burden of persuasion in its analysis of the scope of Article 9 by stating that 'we do not see anything in Article 9 or in any other provision of the BIT that can be read as vesting this Tribunal with jurisdiction over claims resting *ex hypothesi* exclusively on contract.'[543] Given the plain meaning of the text of Article 9, it was surely incumbent on the Tribunal to positively articulate reasons why a more narrow interpretation should be preferred.

The ICSID Tribunal's assumption that contractual disputes should, by their nature, be excluded from the scope of an open-ended reference to investment disputes is refuted by treaty practice.

First, there are numerous BITs that expressly restrict the sphere of disputes that can be referred to international arbitration by the investor to alleged breaches of the substantive provisions of the investment treaty. Article 11 of the Austria Model BIT, for example, provides:

> This Part applies to disputes between a Contracting Party and an investor of the other Contracting Party concerning an alleged breach of an obligation of the former under this Agreement which causes loss or damage to the investor or his investment.[544]

Another example of this express limitation can be found in Article 1116 of the NAFTA, which states that an investor may submit to arbitration under Chapter 11 'a claim that another Party has breached an obligation' under that chapter.

In light of these types of provisions that may be found in investment treaties, it was artificial, in the absence of any further considerations, to place a more limited construction upon the general words used in reference to arbitration in the Switzerland/Pakistan BIT. It was open to the state parties to restrict the *ratione materiae* jurisdiction of international tribunals constituted pursuant to Article 9 of the BIT. They choose not to do so.

Secondly, other BITs make an express distinction between contractual claims and treaty claims in the definition of an 'investment dispute'. The United States Model BIT is a notable example:

> For the purposes of this Treaty, an investment dispute is a dispute between a Party and a national or company of the other Party arising out of or relating to

[543] *Ibid.*

[544] Austria Model BIT, Art. 11, *UNCTAD Compendium* (Vol. VII, 2002) 264.

an investment authorization, an investment agreement or an alleged breach of any right conferred, created or recognized by this Treaty with respect to a covered investment.[545]

The only plausible way to read such a clause is to admit the possibility of the investor bringing purely contractual disputes arising out of an investment agreement before the treaty tribunal.

Thirdly, the Tribunal's interpretation of Article 9 of the Swiss/Pakistan BIT is at odds with the previous *dicta* of tribunals on the interpretation of similar clauses in other BITs. The *ad hoc* Committee in *Vivendi* had clearly contemplated that a treaty tribunal can have jurisdiction over contractual disputes:

. . . Article 8 deals generally with disputes 'relating to investments made under [the France/Argentina BIT] . . . ' Article 8 does not use a narrower formulation, requiring that the investor's claim allege a breach of the BIT itself. Read literally, the requirements for arbitral jurisdiction in Article 8 do not necessitate that the Claimant allege a breach of the BIT itself . . . [546]

The ICSID Tribunal in *Salini* adopted a similar approach.[547]

Fourthly, in the absence of any previous election by the investor of a different forum (*ie* in an investment contract with the host state), there might be compelling reasons to allow an investor to bring the whole spectrum of its complaints before one tribunal. Where the investment has been made pursuant to a contract with the host state, it is often the case that the investor will have contractual claims and treaty claims, and the questions of fact arising under both will inevitably be intertwined. To avoid the possibility of conflicting judgments and awards, and to promote efficiency and finality in the resolution of disputes relating to investments, it may be appropriate for an investor to seize a single tribunal with both types of claims.

Fifthly, the Tribunal's assertion that a plain meaning interpretation of Article 9, *prima facie* extending to contractual claims, 'would supersede and set at naught' all valid forum selection clauses in contracts between Swiss investors and Pakistan is incorrect. The very issue before the Tribunal, which had been extensively pleaded by both parties, was the circumstances in which an ICSID tribunal established pursuant to a dispute resolution clause in a BIT must defer to another forum with competence over contractual claims. There was no inevitability about Article 9 having the effect postulated by the Tribunal, and indeed the *ad-hoc* Committee in *Vivendi* had laid the foundation for a test to avoid this invidious result.

In conclusion, the award in *SGS Société Générale de Surveillance S.A. v Islamic Republic of Pakistan*[548] did not significantly advance the debate on

[545] US Model BIT, Art. 9(1), *ibid.* (Vol. VI, 2002) 506.

[546] *Vivendi* Annulment Decision, para. 55.

[547] (Decision on Jurisdiction, 23 July 2001) Case No. ARB/00/4, 6 ICSID Rep 400, para. 61.

[548] (Decision on Jurisdiction, 6 August 2003) Case No. ARB/01/13, (2003) 42 ILM 1290.

what has been labelled 'symmetrical jurisdictional conflicts' in this study due to an artificially narrow construction placed upon the scope of the Tribunal's *ratione materiae* jurisdiction.

At the time of writing, the final instalment in this line of cases dealing with symmetrical jurisdictional conflicts is *Azurix Corp. v Argentine Republic*.[549] The Claimant's Argentine investment vehicle 'ABA' was awarded a thirty year concession by the Province of Buenos Aires for the distribution of potable water and the treatment and disposal of sewerage.[550] The various pre-contractual documents, together with the Concession Agreement itself, all contained an exclusive jurisdiction clause in favour of the courts of the City of La Plata and a waiver by the parties of any other forum.[551] Clause 16.7 of the Concession Agreement, signed by ABA, the Province of Buenos Aires and a municipal authority responsible for sanitation, read as follows:

> In the event of any dispute regarding the construction and execution of the Agreement, the Grantor [the Executive Authorities of the Province of Buenos Aires] and the Concessionaire [ABA] submit to the court for contentious-administrative matters of the city of La Plata, expressly waiving any other forum or jurisdiction that may correspond due to any reason.[552]

Argentina objected to the ICSID Tribunal's jurisdiction under the US/Argentina BIT on the basis that ABA's waiver of jurisdiction bound the Claimant so that the latter was precluded from bringing a claim with respect to the investment in the water concession before another forum.[553] The waiver in clause 16.7 of the Concession Agreement was in fact inserted into the contractual documents by Argentina precisely to avoid the situation that arose in *Lanco* and *Vivendi*.[554] According to Argentina, the Claimant's claims arose out of the Concession Agreement and thus the exclusive jurisdiction clause should be upheld by the ICSID Tribunal with respect to those claims.[555]

One might expect that Argentina's objection would have mandated a careful analysis of the nature of the Claimant's claims, however, such an analysis is nowhere to be found in the ICSID Tribunal's decision. Nor are the Claimant's claims as they were actually pleaded reproduced in the text of the award. In its consideration of its jurisdiction *ratione materiae* pursuant to Article 25 of the ICSID Convention, the Tribunal concluded that '(a) Azurix indirectly owns 90 percent of the shareholding in ABA, (b) Azurix indirectly controls ABA, and (c) ABA is a party to the Concession Agreement . . .'[556] and hence 'the dispute as presented by the Claimant is a dispute arising directly from that investment'.[557] If the investment was ultimately ABA's interest in the concession agreement,[558] and the dispute arose directly from that investment agreement, then there was at least a

[549] *Azurix Corp. v The Argentine Republic* (Decision on Jurisdiction, 8 December 2003) Case No. ARB/01/12, (2004) 43 ILM 262.
[550] *Ibid.* para. 22.
[551] *Ibid.* para. 26.
[552] *Ibid.*
[553] *Ibid.*
[554] *Ibid.* para. 78.
[555] *Ibid.* para. 59.
[556] *Ibid.* para. 65.
[557] *Ibid.* para. 66.
[558] *Ibid.* para. 62.

distinct possibility that the 'essential basis' of the Claimant's claims, in the words of the *ad hoc* Committee in *Vivendi*, was the concession agreement and not the BIT. Indeed, Argentina had pointed out that ABA had brought claims before the city courts of La Plata that were 'identical as to their substance' as the Claimant's claims before the ICSID Tribunal.[559]

The ICSID Tribunal articulated the relevant test as 'whether the dispute, as it has been presented by the Claimant, is *prima facie* a dispute arising under the BIT.'[560] As previously mentioned, the precise way in which the dispute was presented by the Claimant cannot be gleaned from the Tribunal's award. The Tribunal nevertheless concluded in the next sentence:

> The investment dispute which the Claimant has put before this Tribunal invokes obligations owed by the Respondent to the Claimant under the BIT and is based on a different cause of action from a claim under the Contract Documents.[561]

Jurisdiction was thus affirmed by the Tribunal and,[562] moreover, Argentina's request for a stay pending the judgment of the Supreme Court of the Province in relation to ABA's claims[563] was rejected.[564]

In summary, it is submitted that the guidance provided by the *ad hoc* Committee in *Vivendi* provides a more persuasive platform for the resolution of symmetrical conflicts of jurisdiction than the two subsequent decisions of the ICSID Tribunals in *SGS v Pakistan* and *Azurix v Argentina*, which, for very different reasons, essentially fail to confront the problem. In *SGS* the potential for a treaty tribunal assuming jurisdiction over contractual claims was denied, whereas in *Azurix* the investor's mere invocation of BIT provisions in the formulation of its claims was sufficient to found treaty jurisdiction.[565] Nevertheless, all three cases demonstrate the importance of cause of action analysis to a meaningful consideration of this problem of overlapping jurisdictions.

D. THE RESOLUTION OF SYMMETRICAL JURISDICTIONAL CONFLICTS: CAUSE OF ACTION ANALYSIS AND STAY OF PROCEEDINGS

The dilemma that confronted the ICSID Tribunal and *ad hoc* Committee in *Vivendi* relates to the classification of contractual and treaty claims. In the foregoing Section it was argued that treaty tribunals are bound to defer to other judicial *fora* vested with jurisdiction over contractual disputes in

559 *Ibid.* para. 41. 560 *Ibid.* para. 76. 561 *Ibid.*

562 *Ibid.* para. 102. It is not entirely clear whether the Tribunal relied upon the additional ground that the exclusive jurisdiction clause in the Concession Agreement was only effective between ABA and the Province of Buenos Aires, neither of whom were parties to the ICSID proceedings (see para. 85, *ibid.*). The difficulty with this approach is that Azurix was claiming through ABA's investment in the form of its interest in the concession agreement and thus it would seem only reasonable for Azurix to be equally bound by the conditions attached to ABA's investment.

563 *Ibid.* para. 46. 564 *Ibid.* para. 102.

565 If the *Azurix* finding were to be generalised, then in practice an investor would seldom need to assert contractual claims before a treaty tribunal because the mere reliance on BIT provisions would be effective to upgrade them to treaty claims for jurisdictional purposes.

case of jurisdictional conflicts.[566] This conclusion does not, however, resolve the lingering problem of identifying the boundary between contractual and treaty causes of action. If treaty tribunals are to consider that the investor's pleadings are definitive on the issue, then it will be left to the investor to invoke the jurisdiction of the treaty tribunal in conflict with a previously agreed dispute resolution clause simply by characterising its grievance as giving rise to a breach of one of the amorphous treaty standards, such as the failure to accord fair and equitable treatment. As one can discern from the facts of the cases examined in the previous Section, there are already signs in investment treaty arbitration practice that this tactic is growing in popularity.

A sound legal test is always more concerned with substance rather than form, and hence to accord the investor's articulation of its causes of action a definitive role is unsatisfactory. To hold otherwise would in effect confer the power upon one party to a contractual bargain to override one of the key terms of that bargain at its discretion. The American/Mexican Claims Commission described such an attempt of an investor thus:

> The claimant, after having solemnly promised in writing that it would not ignore the local laws, remedies, and authorities, behaved from the very beginning as if [the choice of jurisdiction clause] of its contract had no existence in fact. It used the article to procure the contract, but this was the extent of its use.[567]

Put in a different way, a dispute resolution clause in a contract between a foreign investor and a state entity would lose much of its efficacy in jurisdictions covered by applicable investment treaties. One would expect that this would have a chilling effect on negotiations between a state party and foreign investor, and the state party might feel justified in seeking different concessions from the investor in the future because the value of an agreement to refer disputes to the local courts of the state or different forum would be greatly diminished.[568]

Such a result would inevitably have consequences for the sustainability of the investment treaty protection network as well. It would compel states, before treaty tribunals, to defend what might be essentially contractual claims to the merits stage of the proceedings to be tested against

[566] For the clearest exposition of the contrary view, see: A. Parra, above n. 136, 335, 'In most cases, the consent in the BIT of the host State to the submission of the investment disputes to arbitration can also be invoked in preference to any applicable previous agreement on the settlement of such disputes, such as might be embodied in the arbitration clause of an investment contract between the investor and the host State. The consent or "offer" of the host State to submit to arbitration in the BIT, when accepted by the covered investor, simply supersedes their previous agreement to the extent of the overlap between that agreement and the new one formed by the offer in the BIT and its acceptance by the investor.' (Footnote omitted.)

[567] *North American Dredging Company of Texas (United States) v United Mexican States* (1926) 4 UN Rep 26, 31.

[568] In *Azurix Corp. v The Argentine Republic* (Decision on Jurisdiction, 8 December 2003) Case No. ARB/01/12, (2004) 43 ILM 262, the Argentine authorities had inserted a waiver of other *fora* in the contractual documents to avoid the jurisdiction of a treaty tribunal over contractual claims (*ibid.* para. 41). The ICSID Tribunal ruled that the waiver was ineffective. One wonders what Argentina will insist upon in the next round of negotiations with a foreign investor.

the treaty standards. Those claims might well be ultimately dismissed by the tribunal as failing to disclose a breach of the treaty, but the time and expense in securing this result would be perceived by most states to be unacceptable. All these considerations point to the necessity of ensuring that purely contractual claims subject to determination by a different forum are filtered at a preliminary jurisdictional stage of the treaty arbitration which can be readily separated from the merits stage.

The *ad hoc* Committee's decision in *Vivendi* does provide some guidance on the resolution of this dilemma. As previously stated, reliance was placed on the *Woodruff Case*[569] for the principle that 'where *the essential basis of a claim* brought before an international tribunal is a breach of contract, the tribunal will give effect to any valid choice of forum clause in the contract'.[570] As the previous analysis of *Woodruff* line of cases makes clear, this is a rule of jurisdiction or admissibility, and hence one may infer that it will be incumbent upon a treaty tribunal to explore the substance of the claim advanced by the investor at a preliminary stage, rather than merely its form.

The Committee's comments must, however, be interpreted in their proper context, which was the section of the decision on the relationship between international and municipal law in *substantive* matters of international responsibility. The Committee had already decided that the ICSID Tribunal was correct in upholding its jurisdiction over the treaty claims, despite their level of connectedness with purely contractual matters that were subject to the jurisdiction of the Tucumán courts. It would seem to follow that the *ad hoc* Committee had, at least implicitly, decided that the 'fundamental basis of the claim' advanced by the investor was the BIT rather than the contract so that the *Woodruff* principle, which operates as a jurisdictional or admissibility bar to the claim, was not applicable. If the contrary were true, then the Tribunal's decision on jurisdiction might be susceptible to annulment in accordance with Article 52 of the ICSID Convention on the basis that the Tribunal exercised a jurisdiction that it did not have. But in the *ad hoc* Committee's consideration of the Tribunal's decision on jurisdiction, one finds a statement endorsing the view that the forum selection clause in the contract did not exclude 'the jurisdiction of the Tribunal *with respect to a claim based on the provisions of the BIT*'.[571] There is no attempt here to investigate the 'fundamental basis of the claim', but rather what appears to be acceptance of the investor's formal characterisation of the claim. This deduction is supported by reference to other parts of the Committee's review of the Tribunal's jurisdictional decision:

> Even if it were necessary in order to attract the Tribunal's jurisdiction that the dispute be characterised not merely as one relating to an investment but as one concerning the treatment of an investment in accordance with the standards laid

[569] (United States v Venezuela), reported in J. Ralston, above n. 455, No. 75, 62.

[570] *Vivendi* Annulment Decision, para. 98. Elsewhere, the *ad hoc* Committee referred to the 'fundamental basis of the claim', which was the expression used in the *Woodruff Case*. *Ibid.* para. 101.

[571] *Ibid.* para. 76.

down under the BIT, it is the case (as the Tribunal noted) that *Claimants invoke substantive provisions of the BIT*.[572]

It is perhaps unfair to attach too much significance to the *ad hoc* Committee's choice of words in this context, especially in light of the fact that the Committee went on to say that the dispute was capable of raising issues under the BIT.[573] Nevertheless, there does appear to be some contradiction between the dictates of the *Woodruff* principle, requiring an analysis of the 'fundamental basis of the claim', and the more formal test that the *ad hoc* Committee actually applied to the facts at the jurisdictional stage.

The dilemma of distinguishing between causes of action based on contract and treaty resurfaced at a separate jurisdictional phase in *SGS Société Générale de Surveillance S.A. v Islamic Republic of Pakistan*:[574]

At this stage of the proceedings, the Tribunal has, as a practical matter, a limited ability to scrutinize the claims as formulated by the Claimant. Some cases suggest that the Tribunal need not uncritically accept those claims at face value, but we consider that if the facts asserted by the Claimant are capable of being regarded as alleged breaches of the BIT . . . the Claimant should be able to have them considered on their merits. We conclude that, at this jurisdiction phase, it is for the Claimant to characterize the claims as it sees fit. We do not exclude the possibility that there may arise a situation where a tribunal may find it necessary at the very beginning to look behind the claimant's factual claims, but this is not such a case.[575]

There is a tension in this passage between the notion that a claimant can characterise the claims 'as it sees fit' and what appears to be the imposition of a threshold in the form of a *prima facie* test of whether 'the facts asserted by the Claimant are capable of being regarded as alleged breaches of the BIT.' Furthermore, the ICSID Tribunal cited the NAFTA case of *United Parcel Service of America Inc. v Government of Canada*[576] in a footnote to this text where the UNCITRAL Tribunal adopted the following *prima facie* test for jurisdiction:

[The Tribunal] must conduct a prima facie analysis of the NAFTA obligations, which [the claimant] seeks to invoke, and determine whether the facts alleged are *capable of constituting a violation* of these obligations.[577]

572 *Ibid.* para. 74 (emphasis added). 573 *Ibid.* paras. 106, 112, 114.

574 (Decision on Jurisdiction, 6 August 2003) Case No. ARB/01/13, (2003) 42 ILM 1290.

575 *Ibid.* para. 145 (footnotes omitted). The ICSID Tribunal cited further: *Amco Asia Corp, Pan American, Ltd and PT Amoco Indonesia v Republic of Indonesia* (Jurisdiction, 25 September 1983), 1 ICSID Rep 389, 405, 'The Tribunal is of the view that in order for it to make a judgment at this time as to the substantial nature of the dispute before it, it must look firstly and only at the claim itself as presented to ICSID and the Tribunal in the Claimant's Request for Arbitration. If on its face (that is, if there is no manifest or obvious misdescription or error in the characterization of the dispute by the Claimants) the claim is one "arising directly out of an investment", then this Tribunal would have jurisdiction to hear such claims. In other words, the Tribunal must not attempt at this stage to examine the claim itself in any detail, but the Tribunal must only be satisfied that *prima facie* the claim, as stated by the Claimants when initiating this arbitration, is within the jurisdictional mandate of ICSID arbitration, and consequently of this Tribunal.'

576 (Award on Jurisdiction, 22 November 2002), available at <http://www.dfait-maeci.gc.ca/tna-nac/documents/Jurisdiction%20Award.22Nov02.pdf>. 577 *Ibid.* para. 33.

The ICSID Tribunal in *SGS v Pakistan* was clearly troubled by the Respondent's submission that claims should be subject to scrutiny at a jurisdictional stage, as suggested by the UNCITRAL Tribunal in *UPS v Canada*. This concern emanated from the 'limited ability' of an arbitral tribunal to analyse the factual basis of claims at a preliminary stage:

> [T]he Tribunal cannot subject the Request for Arbitration to too rigorous a standard of review at this stage as the Claimant is not obliged to set out extensive allegations of fact and arguments as to how the acts complained of might give rise to a breach of the Treaty.[578]

This is certainly a formidable dilemma, but one that is attenuated if the relief claimed by the respondent state is not an outright dismissal of the claims but a stay of the proceedings before the investment treaty tribunal in favour of another forum with competence over the contractual claims. The discretion available to international treaty tribunals to grant a stay of proceedings is a vastly under-utilised resource for the effective management of symmetrical and asymmetrical jurisdictional conflicts.[579] Given the consequences of a stay of proceedings for the claimant are not nearly as draconian as an outright dismissal of its claims, it is not necessary for the investment treaty tribunal to make a definitive ruling on the classification of the claims; rather, the respondent state must demonstrate to the comfortable satisfaction of the tribunal that the 'fundamental basis of the claim[s]' is an investment contract between the claimant and the respondent, and not the minimum standards of investment protection in the investment treaty.

The granting of a stay of proceedings is not completely unknown in the investment arbitration context for the discretion was utilised with prudence by the ICSID Tribunal in *SPP v Egypt*.[580] The Tribunal was in effect confronted with a 'fork in the road' provision,[581] not in a BIT but rather in a unilateral offer to arbitrate in Egyptian legislation on foreign investment. The three *fora* open to foreign investors for the resolution of disputes were listed as: (i) any method of settlement previously agreed to by the parties themselves; (ii) resolution pursuant to an applicable BIT; and (iii) arbitration under the ICSID Convention.[582] Egypt objected to the ICSID Tribunal's jurisdiction on the grounds that SPP had previously agreed to ICC arbitration for disputes arising out of an agreement on the development of two tourist complexes with an Egyptian public sector enterprise ('EGOTH').[583] An award had already been rendered by the ICC Tribunal against EGOTH and Egypt in favour of SPP, but was

578 *Société Générale de Surveillance S.A. v Islamic Republic of Pakistan* (Decision on Jurisdiction, 6 August 2003) Case No. ARB/01/13, (2003) 42 ILM 1290 at note 125.

579 In relation to arbitration under the Energy Charter Treaty, a stay has been recommended as the proper approach to dealing with parallel municipal court proceedings or contractual arbitration: T. Wälde, 'Investment Arbitration under the Energy Charter Treaty', above n. 17, 460–1.

580 *Southern Pacific Properties (Middle East) Limited [SPP(ME)] v Arab Republic of Egypt* (Jurisdiction (No. 1), 27 November 1985), 3 ICSID Rep 101.

581 *Ibid.* para. 61.

582 *Ibid.* para. 60.

583 *Ibid.* paras. 19–22.

annulled by the Paris Court of Appeal on the basis that Egypt was not privy to the arbitration clause in the agreement with EGOTH and had not waived its sovereign immunity to the jurisdiction of the ICC Tribunal.[584] If the Court of Appeals was correct, then it must have followed that SPP and Egypt had *not* previously agreed on a method for the settlement of disputes and hence there would be no obstacle to the ICSID proceedings.[585] This very issue was pending before the French Court of Cassation on appeal at the time the ICSID Tribunal became seized of SPP's new ICSID arbitration claim.[586]

The ICSID Tribunal affirmed that it was competent to judge its own jurisdiction and thus make a ruling on the issue before the Court of Cassation.[587] The Tribunal nevertheless recognised the possibility that, depending on the ultimate validity of the ICC award, 'concurrent jurisdiction might be exercised with respect to the same Parties, the same facts and the same cause of action by two different arbitral tribunals.'[588] The Tribunal then signalled one possible solution to this potential clash of jurisdictions:

> When the jurisdiction of two unrelated and independent tribunals extends to the same dispute, there is no rule of international law which prevents either tribunal from exercising its jurisdiction. However, in the interest of international judicial order, either of the tribunals may, in its discretion and as a matter of comity, decide to stay the exercise of its jurisdiction pending a decision by the other tribunal.[589]

The ICSID Tribunal thus stayed its own proceedings pending the appeal before the Court of Cassation on the issue of the validity and the scope *ratione personae* of the ICC arbitration clause.[590]

The exercise of the discretion to stay by treaty tribunals might be informed by the approach of some common law jurisdictions to the stay of proceedings in favour of a foreign court on the ground of *forum non conveniens*.[591] In relation to the proper allocation of the burden of proof, for instance, an investment treaty tribunal should recognise that it is the applicant for the stay (the respondent) that must generally persuade the tribunal to exercise its discretion to grant a stay. In accordance with the practice of the English courts on *forum non conveniens* applications, however, this general rule is subject to the evidential burden shifting to a party who seeks to establish the existence of matters which will assist it in persuading the tribunal to exercise its discretion in that party's favour.[592]

584 *Southern Pacific Properties (Middle East) Limited [SPP(ME)] v Arab Republic of Egypt* (Jurisdiction (No. 1), 27 November 1985), 3 ICSID Rep 101, para. 41.

585 *Ibid.* paras. 78–9.

586 *Ibid.* para. 44.

587 *Ibid.* para. 81.

588 *Ibid.* para. 82.

589 *Ibid.* para. 84.

590 A recent example of coordination between an international and supra-national tribunal is provided by the *Mox Plant Case* (Ireland v United Kingdom) Order No, 3, (2003) 42 ILM 1187, where an Annex VII Tribunal constituted under the Law of the Sea Convention 1982 stayed its own proceedings to await a ruling by the European Court of Justice that was relevant to its jurisdiction.

591 See, in relation to England: *Dicey & Morris The Conflict of Laws* (Vol. 1, 2000, 13th edn by L. Collins) 395–400; *Cheshire and North's Private International Law*, (1999, 13th edn by P. North & J. Fawcett) 336–47.

592 *Dicey & Morris The Conflict of Laws, ibid.* 395.

The primary test for the granting of a stay in the investment treaty context is, as previously stated, whether the 'fundamental basis of the claim[s]' is an investment contract or the treaty. If the respondent manages to discharge its burden to persuade the tribunal that the fundamental basis of the claim is a cause of action for breach of contract and that another forum with jurisdiction over such claims has been previously chosen by the parties, then the tribunal should defer to that forum and stay the proceedings.

There are, however, circumstances when a stay might cause real injustice to the claimant, such as where the respondent state has taken measures to interfere with the dispute resolution process that was previously agreed to in the investment contract.[593] Here there is a risk that a stay of proceedings could simply result in justice delayed. Therefore, where the investment treaty tribunal itself is competent to hear purely contractual claims, the test for a stay should allow the claimant to counter the *prima facie* indication that its contractual claims should be heard by an alternative forum due to the likelihood that it would suffer a denial of justice before this alternative forum. The burden of proof in this second stage of the test would fall squarely on the claimant, and could only be discharged by demonstrating actual steps taken by the respondent state to jeopardize the alternative dispute resolution process for contractual claims. Mere speculation as to the quality of justice before that forum could never be sufficient. This in a sense resembles the second stage of the *forum non conveniens* test alluded to earlier.[594]

In *SGS Société Générale de Surveillance S.A. v Islamic Republic of Pakistan*, the ICSID Tribunal found that the arbitral tribunal constituted in accordance with the 'PSI Agreement' between the parties had jurisdiction over SGS's contractual claims. Pakistan had argued that the 'essential basis' of all of SGS's claims were contractual because: (i) they were all based on the same limited factual allegations arising out of the contractual relationship;[595] (ii) the prayers for relief submitted by SGS by way of counterclaim before the contractual arbitral tribunal in Islamabad and the investment treaty tribunal were virtually identical; and (iii) SGS had conceded that 'most or all of Pakistan's acts and omissions . . . qualify as breaches of the PSI Agreement as well as violations of the BIT.'[596] In essence, SGS was arguing that either Pakistan's alleged breaches of the PSI Agreement simultaneously constituted a breach of the BIT or that Pakistan's obligations under the PSI Agreement were 'elevated' to BIT

[593] One such measure might be the enactment of legislation in order to vitiate an arbitration clause in a contract between the state and the investor, see: *Losinger Co. Case (Discontinuance Order)* PCIJ Rep Series C No. 78.

[594] *Dicey & Morris The Conflict of Laws*, above n. 594, 398–400; *Cheshire and North's Private International Law*, above n. 594, 341–7.

[595] SGS's Request for Arbitration stated that 'this dispute arises out of Pakistan's actions and omissions with respect to the Pre-Shipment Program and the PSI Agreement.' *Société Générale de Surveillance S.A. v Islamic Republic of Pakistan* (Decision on Jurisdiction, 6 August 2003) Case No. ARB/01/13, (2003) 42 ILM 1290, para. 63.

[596] *Ibid.* para. 63.

obligations by the operation of the 'umbrella clause'. The ICSID Tribunal dismissed SGS's interpretation of the 'umbrella clause', but reserved its judgment on the relationship between contractual and treaty breaches for the merits.[597] The Tribunal thus upheld its jurisdiction over SGS's claims formulated on the basis of the BIT.[598]

It is submitted that this was the paradigm situation where the grant of a stay would have been wholly justified, and indeed this was one of the forms of relief requested by Pakistan. By refusing to accede to this request,[599] the ICSID Tribunal in effect conceded that it is sufficient for a claimant to plead that a contractual breach simultaneously amounts to a violation of the BIT for the purposes of invoking the jurisdiction of an investment treaty tribunal and proceeding to the merits. One can readily imagine the potential for mischief produced by this result.

The reasoning that lead to the ICSID Tribunal's refusal to grant a stay in *SGS v Pakistan* is difficult to identify in the award. After quoting the *ad hoc* Committee in *Vivendi* on the difference between exercising contractual jurisdiction and 'tak[ing] into account the terms of a contract in determining whether there has been a breach of a distinct standard of international law',[600] the Tribunal stated:

> This Tribunal is bound to exercise its jurisdiction and proceed to consider the BIT claims that are properly before it. Accordingly, we cannot grant the request for a stay of these proceedings.[601]

This refusal to grant a stay does not logically follow from the *ad hoc* Committee's observation in *Vivendi*, which was dealing with an entirely different issue. Moreover, the refusal is not mandated by a finding that the Tribunal was 'bound to exercise its jurisdiction' over the BIT claims. The Tribunal was not bound to exercise that jurisdiction immediately and a stay would have been the most appropriate form of relief in these circumstances. Pakistan would have been saved from the expense and inconvenience of defending claims that, at the very least, were grounded in the same facts and arising from precisely the same contractual relationship as those claims properly before the contractual arbitral tribunal. On the other hand, the door to treaty arbitration would have been left open to SGS in the event that it suffered a denial of justice before the contractual

[597] The ICSID Tribunal may have inadvertently subverted its own ruling on the effect of an 'umbrella clause' in this way. If an umbrella clause does not elevate contractual obligations into treaty obligations, then, for that ruling not to be meaningless, it surely must follow that mere breaches of contract cannot amount to breaches of a treaty (authority for this latter proposition may be found in *Azinian, Davitian and Baca v United Mexican States* (Award, 1 November 1998) Case No. ARB(AF)/97/2, 5 ICSID Rep 272, 287–8). Perhaps the ICSID Tribunal was concerned not to make a definitive finding on the precise nature of SGS's BIT claims at this preliminary stage, however, as will be submitted below, this is exactly why the Tribunal should have exercised its discretion to stay the proceedings until the contractual claims had been dealt with by the contractual arbitral tribunal sitting in Islamabad.

[598] *Société Générale de Surveillance S.A. v Islamic Republic of Pakistan* (Decision on Jurisdiction, 6 August 2003) Case No. ARB/01/13, (2003) 42 ILM 1290, para. 188.

[599] *Ibid.* para. 187.

[600] *Ibid.* para. 186.

[601] *Ibid.* para. 187.

arbitral tribunal and its submission that purely contractual breaches might amount to treaty breaches would be reserved for another day.

It will be recalled that the ICSID Tribunal's award in *Vivendi* was annulled by the *ad hoc* Committee because the Tribunal had summarily dismissed BIT claims over which it had jurisdiction for the reason that such claims were interwoven with breach of contract issues subject to resolution by a different forum. The Tribunal's error in resolving the dilemma before it was to make a definitive ruling on the merits when a stay of proceedings would have achieved the desired result. The ICSID Tribunal in *SGS v Pakistan* appears to have exercised too much caution to avoid the plight of the Tribunal's award in *Vivendi*. If this was the apprehension that lead to the refusal to grant a stay, then it was misguided—a decision to grant a stay for the reasons described would be immune from the criticism that produced the annulment in *Vivendi*.

In conclusion, a treaty tribunal is bound to consider the 'fundamental basis' of the causes of action relied upon the claimant. If the 'fundamental basis' is determined to be contractual, then the treaty tribunal must give effect to any valid choice of forum clause in that contract. Where there is significant overlap between the claimant's causes of action based on contract and the minimum standards of protection set out in the treaty, then the treaty tribunal should exercise its discretion to stay its own proceedings to await the resolution of the contractual issues by the chosen forum.

E. ASYMMETRICAL JURISDICTIONAL CONFLICTS: MULTIPLE FORA WITH JURISDICTION OVER ASPECTS OF AN INVESTMENT DISPUTE

Where an investment treaty tribunal has jurisdiction over a cause of action objectively founded upon the host state's violation of a minimum standard of investment protection, that jurisdiction is exclusive of any other forum with respect to that cause of action. Nevertheless, other *fora*, namely municipal courts and contractual arbitral tribunals, may have competence over a constituent part of the investment dispute pertaining to the existence, nature, and scope of the investor's protected interests under municipal law. This has been termed an 'asymmetrical jurisdictional conflict'.

The *CME Czech Republic B.V. (The Netherlands) v The Czech Republic* case provides a good example of this type of problem in practice. ČNTS (the investment of CME) had challenged CET 21's termination of the Service Agreement with ČNTS as unlawful before the Czech courts. At first instance, ČNTS's claim for breach of contract was upheld by the Prague Regional Commercial Court,[602] however, the Court of Appeal later overturned the decision.[603] By the time the UNCITRAL Tribunal handed

[602] *CME* Partial Award, para. 140.

[603] *CME Czech Republic B.V. (The Netherlands) v The Czech Republic*, (Final Award, 14 March 2003), para. 22, available at <http://www.cetv-net.com/ne/articlefiles/439-Final_Award_Quantum.pdf>.

down its award, the Czech Supreme Court had been seized of the final appeal. Two months later, the Czech Supreme Court quashed the Court of Appeal's decision and referred the case back to the Prague Regional Commercial Court.[604]

The UNCITRAL Tribunal's consideration of the significance of the Czech court proceedings is somewhat circular. On the one hand, in the context of upholding its jurisdiction, the Tribunal conceded that whilst 'the contractual arrangements between CET 21 and ČNTS could be decisive for the claimant's claim under these arbitration proceedings',[605] the Tribunal remained competent to hear the claimant's treaty claims. This is uncontroversial. But on the merits, the Tribunal found that '[t]he outcome of the civil court proceedings is irrelevant to the decision on the alleged breach of the Treaty by the Media Council acting in concert with the Respondent.'[606]

The Tribunal appears to have conflated the two distinct analytical stages in adjudging an investment dispute that have previously been described. It is certainly true that a judgment of a Czech court could not be dispositive of the compatibility or otherwise of the Media Council's conduct with the treaty standards. In relation to the first stage of the analysis, however, a judgment of a Czech court may well have been crucial in determining whether the 1996 amendment was the proximate cause of the destruction of CME's investment. The Prague Regional Commercial Court had in fact upheld the exclusivity in the relationship between CET 21 and ČNTS and thus ruled in favour of ČNTS.[607] From this ruling it followed that the 1996 amendment had no bearing on the legal foundation of ČNTS's investment as a matter of Czech law. If the Czech Supreme Court had reinstated this ruling, then the parties would have been put back into the position that existed prior to CET 21's termination of the Service Agreement and it is difficult to conceive how CME's treaty claim could survive. In this respect it is interesting to note that CME had initially, in its Notice of Arbitration, requested relief in the form of the restitution of 'ČNTS's exclusive rights to provide broadcasting services for TV NOVA'.[608] This was precisely the relief granted by the Czech Regional Commercial Court and the very issue pending before the Czech Supreme Court.

In light of the foregoing, it is difficult to comprehend the Tribunal's position on the significance of the Czech court proceedings:

> Even if the regional Commercial Court's judgment is reinstated by the Czech Supreme Court, this will not remedy the Claimant's investment situation. CET 21 may well, at any time, terminate again the Service Agreement for good cause,

[604] The Prague City Court then rejected ČNTS's claim in the new proceedings. ČNTS appealed. The appeal was pending when the quantum phase of the arbitral proceedings was closed on 14 November 2002.

[605] *CME* Partial Award, para. 405.

[606] *Ibid.* para. 415.

[607] *Ibid.* para. 304.

[608] *Ibid.* para. 215.

whether given or not, thereby recurrently jeopardizing the Claimant's investment.[609]

This statement is problematic because if the Czech courts had found the termination of the Service Agreement instigated by Dr Železný to be wrongful (*ie* without legal basis in Czech law) then the 1996 amendment to the investment structure could not be said to have any impact on CME's rights to its investment. As to the possibility that CET 21 might repeat its termination trick again—there is no legal system in the world that can completely shield an investor from having to defend itself against spurious litigation. The critical question is whether the Media Council's actions resulting in the 1996 amendment constituted a breach of the treaty standard in 1996. If there was a breach, then it becomes relevant to inquire whether the subsequent termination of the Service Agreement by CET 21 was causally linked thereto. It is submitted that this causal connection could be established if CET 21's termination was *lawful*, as then it would be evident that the 1996 amendment did in fact eviscerate ČNTS's exclusive rights to provide broadcasting services.

Another example of an asymmetrical jurisdictional conflict comes from *Wena Hotels Ltd v Arab Republic of Egypt*.[610] On this occasion, the other *fora* cognisant of the municipal law aspects of the investment treaty dispute were contractual arbitral tribunals that had rendered their awards well in advance of the ICSID Tribunal's determination of the investor's claims.[611]

The ICSID Tribunal did not consider any of the previous arbitral awards rendered by the *ad hoc* tribunals with jurisdiction over the lease agreements to be relevant to its decision on liability. The fallacy of this approach was considered in Part IV(C) above. It may be further noted here that one of the key findings of the ICISD Tribunal on expropriation was that Egypt breached the BIT by failing to offer Wena 'prompt, adequate and effective compensation'.[612] In truth, Egypt had left the question of compensation to the *ad hoc* tribunals that the parties had agreed would have jurisdiction over disputes arising under the lease agreements and Wena was successful in recovering damages by resorting to these fora. Thus by complying with its contractual obligation to arbitrate these disputes, Egypt was simultaneously found to breach the investment treaty with respect to its failure to offer 'prompt, adequate and effective compensation'. Furthermore, the ICSID Tribunal did, in its decision on quantum of damages, take into account the amount previously awarded to Wena in the contractual arbitrations and deducted this amount from its damages award.[613]

[609] *Ibid.* para. 475. The UNICTRAL Tribunal also stated: 'Even if ČNTS would be in the position to restore the status of the TV station as it was on August, 5 1999, CET 21 could easily jeopardize the arrangement by repeating the same procedure, terminating the Service Agreement for purported good cause and again dragging CNTS into Civil Court proceedings.' *Ibid.* para. 414.

[610] (Award, 8 December 2000) Case No. ARB/98/4, 6 ICSID Rep 89.

[611] See the account of the facts of this case at the text above accompanying n. 258 *et seq.*

[612] *Ibid.* para. 100. [613] *Ibid.* para. 127.

F. THE RESOLUTION OF ASYMMETRICAL JURISDICTIONAL CONFLICTS

The current trend for investment treaty tribunals, as was demonstrated by the *CME v Czech Republic* and *Wena v Egypt* cases, is to refute the relevance of proceedings or decisions of other judicial *fora* relating to the part of the investment dispute governed by the municipal law of the host state. The common justification for this approach is based on the simplistic notion that treaty tribunals are superior to these other *fora*, although the foundation of this superiority in relation to questions of municipal law has never been articulated. To date, treaty tribunals have considered any potential overlap in the jurisdiction of different courts and tribunals over elements of the investment dispute to be a problem relating to the quantum of damages in the sense of maintaining the prohibition against double recovery for a single loss. Thus, in *CME*, it was stated that:

> The outcome of the civil court proceedings is irrelevant to the decision on the alleged breach of the Treaty by the Media Council acting in concert with the Respondent. It may affect the quantum of a damage claim which, pursuant to agreement between the parties, is not a subject of this Partial Award.[614]

Again in *Wena v Egypt*, the ICSID Tribunal ruled that, although irrelevant to liability, the amounts recovered by Wena in the contractual arbitrations must be deducted from the Tribunal's own award of damages.[615]

The choice of law rule for determining the existence, nature, and scope of the investment mandates the application of the municipal law of the host state. Hence the crucial question is the extent to which an investment treaty tribunal must defer to (i) an existing decision of a municipal court or contractual arbitral tribunal on these issues relating to the investment or (ii) concurrent proceedings in which such *fora* are seized of the same subject matter.

It must be first recognised that there are no international rules on the conflicts of jurisdiction in existence that provide a neat solution to these problems. The general principle of *res judicata*,[616] whilst applicable to international arbitral awards,[617] requires that the 'parties, object and cause' are the same.[618] The object and cause of contractual claims or other

[614] *CME* Partial Award, para. 415. The UNICTRAL Tribunal considered the ICC arbitration proceedings in the same way: '[T]he Claimant's claim is not reduced by the Claimant's and/or ČNTS's possible claims to be pursued against Dr. Zelezn [Managing Director of CET 21] in other courts or arbitration proceedings, although the Claimant may collect from the Respondent and any other potential tortfeasor only the full amount of its damage'. *Ibid.* para. 582.

[615] See (Award, 8 December 2000) Case No. ARB/98/4, 6 ICSID Rep 89, para. 127; (Decision on Annulment, 5 February 2002) Case No. ARB/98/4, 6 ICSID Rep 129, para. 49.

[616] *Trail Smelter Case* (United States v Canada), (1941) 3 UN Rep 1905, 1951–2, 'The sanctity of *res judicata* attached to a final decision of an international tribunal is an essential and settled rule of international law.'

[617] See, *eg*: New York Convention on the Recognition and Enforcement of Arbitral Awards, Art. III; (France) New Code of Civil Procedure, Arts. 1476, 1500; (Switzerland) Private International Law Act, Art. 190; (Netherlands) Code of Civil Procedure, Art. 1059; (England) Arbitration Act 1996, s. 58.

[618] See, *eg*: *Trail Smelter Case* (United States v Canada), (1941) 3 UN Rep 1905, 1952; *China Navigation Co. Ltd. (UK) v United States (S.S. Newchang)*, (1921) 6 UN Rep 64, 65; ICC Case 6363/1991, (1992) XVII YB Commercial Arbitration 186, 198; *Waste Management, Inc. v United Mexican States* (Decision on Preliminary Objection, 26 June 2002) Case No. ARB(AF)/00/3, 6 ICSID Rep 549, para. 39.

claims or applications before municipal courts arising out of investment are different from claims based on the substantive investment protection obligations in an investment treaty. A treaty tribunal is not, therefore, formally bound by a decision of a contractual tribunal or municipal court that purports to decide these issues. Likewise, the doctrine of *lis alibi pendens* is constrained by similar requirements on the identity of the parties and the cause of action in the multiple proceedings.[619]

Consistent with a strict application of these doctrines, treaty tribunals and contractual tribunals established pursuant to the ICSID Convention have almost unanimously rejected the *res judicata* effect of existing municipal court judgments or contractual arbitral awards that deal with aspects of the dispute[620] and likewise have uniformly declined to cede their jurisdiction, whether by dismissal of the proceedings or a stay, to competing *fora* on the basis of *lis alibi pendens*.[621]

An early precedent of the France/Mexico Mixed Claims Commission provides some useful guidance on questions of litispendence between 'international' and municipal tribunals. In *Estate of Jean-Baptiste Caire (France) v United Mexican States*,[622] the widow of a French national assassinated by Mexican soldiers in Mexico had sought compensation before a national commission in France. The French legislation establishing the national commission did not provide for compensation for damage caused by conventional forces (being restricted in scope to damage by the revolutionary forces) and thus no indemnity was paid to the French national's widow in these domestic proceedings. France nonetheless brought a claim against Mexico before the France/Mexico Mixed Claims Commission seeking the same amount of compensation for the same delict. The France/Mexico Claims Commission rejected Mexico's submission that the existence of the national proceedings rendered the international claim inadmissible:

> En effect, le droit international n'oblige point un tribunal international de s'abstenir, dans des conditions telles qu'elles se présentent dans les cas des présentes réclamations, de connaître d'un litige international, par le motif que le même différend est pendant devant un autre tribunal.[623]

The Presiding Commissioner, writing for the majority, was nonetheless careful to specify certain situations when the litispendence doctrine

[619] See, *eg*: *Certain German Interests in Polish Upper Silesia* (Preliminary Objections) (1925) PCIJ Rep Series A No 6, 19–20; *Socaciu v Etat Autrichien et autres* (1927) 7 Recueil des décisions des Tribunaux arbitraux mixtes 785, 791 (different object); *Boskovitz v S. A. Haditermeny et Etat hongrois* (1928) 8 Recueil des décisions des Tribunaux arbitraux mixtes 607, 611 (different parties); *Selwyn Case* (Great Britain v Venezuela) (1904) 9 UN Rep 380, 383 (different object); B. Cheng, *General Principles of Law as Applied by International Courts and Tribunals* (1987) 339–47.

[620] See, *eg*: *Southern Pacific Properties (Middle East) Limited [SPP(ME)] v Arab Republic of Egypt* (Jurisdiction (No. 2), 14 April 1988), 3 ICSID Rep 131, 162–3; *Wena Hotels Ltd v Arab Republic of Egypt* (Decision on Annulment, 5 February 2002) Case No. ARB/98/4, 6 ICSID Rep 129, para. 86; *CME* Partial Award, paras. 415, 582.

[621] See, *eg*: *Société Générale De Surveillance S.A. v Islamic Republic of Pakistan* (Decision on Jurisdiction, 6 August 2003) Case No. ARB/01/13, (2003) 42 ILM 1290, para. 182; *CME* Partial Award, para. 415.

[622] (1929) 5 UN Rep 516.

[623] *Ibid.* 520.

might be applicable between international and municipal judicial *fora*:

Pour éviter des malentendus, je crois, toutefois, devoir réserver expressément les cas particuliers, dans lesquels, par exemple, la Commission franco-mexicaine se trouverait en présence de questions préliminaires du droit civil, pendantes devant les tribunaux ordinaires mexicains, et donc la solution serait d'importance décisive pour la réclamation en indemnité devant la Commission franco-mexicaine (question préjudicielle de savoir si un bien immeuble appartient en propriété à une personne dont les droits de propriété sont contestés devant un tribunal civil mexicain, mais qui, entre-temps, a présenté à ladite Commission une réclamation en indemnité pour cause de destruction de ce même bien immeuble, etc.).[624]

The Commission thus anticipated that questions of municipal law, such as ownership rights to property under the *lex situs*, could assume an 'importance décisive pour la réclamation en indemnité devant la Commission' and was prepared to accord to municipal courts a leading role in resolving such issues.

An practical example of the type of deference to a municipal court envisaged by the France/Mexico Mixed Claims Commission on questions of municipal law may be found in a preliminary decision rendered by the Permanent Court of International Justice a few years later in the *Prince von Pless Case*.[625] The delict concerned alleged tax abuses by the Polish authorities against a German national, Prince von Pless. The Prince had instituted municipal proceedings against the Polish authorities and, by the time Germany had taken up his case before the Permanent Court, the matter was before the Supreme Polish Administrative Tribunal. The Court dealt with the pending proceedings in a highly pragmatic fashion:

[I]t will certainly be an advantage to the Court, as regards the points which have to be established in the case, to be acquainted with the final decisions of the Supreme Polish Administrative Tribunal upon the appeals brought by the Prince von Pless and now pending before that Tribunal . . . the Court must therefore arrange its procedure so as to ensure that this will be possible.[626]

It is not within the scope of the present study to propose a code of principles to deal with the multifaceted problem of asymmetrical conflicts of

[624] (1929) 5 UN Rep. 525.

[625] (1933) (Interim Protection Order) PCIJ Rep Series A/B No. 52, cited by W. Reisman, above n. 420, 366–7.

[626] *Ibid.* 16. The PCIJ was less pragmatic several years earlier in *Certain German Interests in Polish Upper Silesia* (1925) (Decision on Jurisdiction) PCIJ Rep Series A No 6. The Court appeared to almost deny the possibility of litispendence in relation to disputes before the PCIJ and other international *fora*, in this case the German/Polish Mixed Arbitral Tribunal: *ibid.* 20. Professor Reisman's critique of this decision together with his suggestion that the PCIJ should have directed the parties to suspend the specific proceedings for the restitution of property before the Mixed Arbitral Tribunal pending the Court's decision on general issues concerning the interpretation of the relevant treaties is persuasive. See W. Reisman, above n. 423, 373–4.

jurisdiction, which, unlike symmetrical conflicts, are not susceptible to being resolved pursuant to a general formula. Nevertheless, at least the starting point should be that there is no strict hierarchical distinction between the investment treaty tribunal and other *fora* in resolving questions pertaining to the existence, nature, and extent of an investment. This is not an instance when the principle that an international tribunal only takes account of municipal law as 'facts' comes into play,[627] because the municipal court decision is not being relied upon to determine whether conduct attributable to the state is violative of an international obligation. To the contrary, these judicial pronouncements by municipal courts and contractual tribunals are invoked in a context where the applicable law relating to this part of the dispute is precisely the same as before treaty tribunals.

It is thus untenable in principle, but also irresponsible as a matter of policy, for treaty tribunals to dismiss out of hand the relevance of prior judicial decisions on the 'private' aspects of an investment dispute or concurrent proceedings in different *fora* where such issues are to be resolved. More often than not, the judges and arbitrators of such *fora* are more qualified to deal with intricate questions relating to the proprietary and contractual rights of the investor that fall to be examined under the governing municipal system of law than the arbitrators with competence over the treaty claims that have been selected for their expertise in international law. With disturbing frequency, questions of municipal law relating to aspects of the investment are brushed aside as peripheral or dealt with superficially by tribunals that are not predisposed, at least without the assistance of detailed expert evidence, to make informed rulings on these questions. The difficulties of pleading foreign law in municipal courts have been researched and exposed,[628] but little attention has been given to the same phenomena before international tribunals that, due to the nature of their subject matter jurisdiction, are sometimes bound to rule upon complex questions of municipal law.[629]

It is submitted that there should be a rebuttable presumption to the effect that a decision of a competent court or tribunal on questions of municipal law relating to the existence, nature, or extent of the investor's interests in the investment will be followed by the treaty tribunal. The presumption could be rebutted by the party resisting the findings of the competent court or tribunal by the tendering of evidence that the judgment or award is defective due to a serious procedural irregularity (such

[627] *Certain German Interests in Polish Upper Silesia* (1926) (Judgment on Merits) PCIJ Rep Series A No. 7, 19, 'From the standpoint of International Law and of the Court which is its organ, municipal laws are merely facts which express the will and constitute the activities of States, in the same manner as to legal decisions or administrative measures.'

[628] See, *eg*, in relation to the English courts: R. Fentiman, *Foreign Law in the English Courts* (1998).

[629] A timely reminder of what the application of municipal law by an international tribunal actual entails is provided by W. Reisman, 'The Regime for *Lacunae* in the ICSID Choice of Law Provision and the Question of Its Threshold' (2000) 15 *ICSID Rev—Foreign Investment LJ* 362, 368–71.

as those grounds that would normally defeat the *res judicata* effect of a judgment or award)[630] or a serious error of law. The treaty tribunal would always retain the ultimate discretion as to whether to adopt the reasoning and findings of another court or tribunal and would in any case need to properly motivate its decision to accept such reasoning and findings so as to discharge the mandate of its own jurisdiction.

Such an approach would require the treaty tribunal in some cases to assume the role of a court of appeal vis-à-vis a municipal court or arbitral tribunal. But it is more of an affront to judicial comity to completely ignore the prior decisions of competent courts and tribunals than to subject such decisions to a level of scrutiny before adopting their findings.

In relation to concurrent proceedings before other judicial *fora* relevant to aspects of the investment dispute before the treaty tribunal, the grounds for the latter exercising a stay are less compelling than was the case for symmetrical jurisdictional conflicts. As far as asymmetrical conflicts are concerned, the concurrent proceedings do not arise out of the same cause of action but instead are relevant to a composite part of the investment dispute. Nevertheless, there may be situations when a treaty tribunal would be prudent to exercise a stay to await the judicial pronouncements of other *fora* in the manner suggested by the Permanent Court in the *Prince von Pless Case*. For instance, if a treaty tribunal has determined that the fundamental basis of the investor's claim is an alleged violation of the treaty standards and yet, as in *Vivendi*, there is a very close connection with the contractual relationship between the same parties, then a stay of the proceedings before the treaty tribunal might well be appropriate. As previously mentioned, this approach would have saved the ICSID Tribunal's award in *Vivendi* from annulment. It is also relevant to distinguish between a forum seized of certain aspects of the investment dispute by the assertion of subject matter jurisdiction (*ie* before a municipal court) and a forum competent on the basis of a forum selection clause between the investor and the host state. A stay should be exercised by a treaty tribunal with less circumspection when the investor has itself chosen the forum that is competent over questions relating to the nature and scope of its investment interests.

G. 'FORK IN THE ROAD' CLAUSES IN INVESTMENT TREATIES

Many investment treaties allow the investor to choose between different judicial *fora* for the submission of the defined categories of investment disputes. In accordance with what has come to be known as a 'fork in the road' clause, once that election is made by the investor, the treaty normally prescribes that it is to be final and irrevocable. The 'fork in the road' is thus in reality a junction leading to several one-way streets.

[630] B. Cheng, above n. 619, 357–72.

The alternative judicial *fora* set out in such a provision usually include a combination of one or more of the following:[631]

- municipal courts of the host state;
- a court or tribunal previously selected by the investor and the host state in a forum selection clause;[632]
- international arbitration either in the form of an *ad hoc* arbitration pursuant to the UNCITRAL Rules or institutional arbitration under the ICSID Arbitration or Additional Facility Rules.

The rationale underpinning the 'fork in the road' provision in investment treaties is clearly the avoidance of multiple proceedings in multiple *fora* in relation to the same investment dispute. In more colloquial terms, it is designed to prevent the investor having several bites at the cherry. The UNCITRAL Tribunal in *Ronald S. Lauder v Czech Republic* described the purpose of the clause as follows:

> The purpose of [the fork in the road provision in US/Czech Republic BIT] is to avoid a situation where the same investment dispute . . . is brought by the same claimant . . . against the same respondent (a Party to the Treaty) for resolution before different arbitral tribunals and/or different state courts of the Party to the Treaty that is also a party to the dispute.[633]

The most detailed analysis of the 'fork in the road' is to be found in the *Vivendi v Argentina* decisions. The particular clause in question in this case was Article 8 of the Argentina/France BIT:

> 1. Any dispute relating to investments, within the meaning of this agreement, between one of the Contracting Parties and an investor of the other Contracting Party shall, as far as possible, be resolved through amicable consultations between both parties to the dispute.
> 2. If such dispute could not be resolved within six months from the time it was stated by any of the parties concerned, it shall be submitted, at the request of the investor:
>
>   - either to the national jurisdictions of the Contracting Party involved in the dispute;
>   - or to international arbitration in accordance with the terms of paragraph 3 below.
>
> Once an investor has submitted the dispute either to the jurisdictions of the Contracting Party involved or to international arbitration, the choice of one or the other of these procedures shall be final.[634]

[631] See below n. 634.

[632] The requirements for such a selection in an investment contract were considered in *LANCO International Inc. v Argentine Republic* (Preliminary Decision on Jurisdiction, 8 December 1998) Case No. ARB/97/6, 5 ICSID Rep 367, paras. 24–8.

[633] *Lauder* Final Award, para. 161.

[634] *Vivendi* Award, at Appendix 1. Other examples of 'fork in the road' provisions may be found in the Energy Charter Treaty, Art. 26(2)(3) and the following model BITs: Chile Model BIT, Art. 8(3), *UNCTAD Compendium* (Vol. III, 1998) 147; Iran Model BIT, Art. 12(3), *ibid.* (Vol. VI, 2002) 483; Peru Model BIT, Art. 8(3), *ibid.* 497; US Model BIT, Art. 9(3), *ibid.* 507; Austria Model BIT, Art. 13, *ibid.* (Vol. VII) 265; Benin Model BIT, Art. 9(2), *ibid.* (Vol. VIII) 283.

Paragraph 3 of Article 8 gives the investor the choice of either *ad hoc* arbitration pursuant to the UNCITRAL Rules or ICSID arbitration. In this case the claimants opted for the latter.

The interpretation given to this clause by the ICSID Tribunal and the *ad hoc* Committee is strictly obiter, because the investor was found to have made a valid choice of ICSID arbitration and the jurisdiction of the Tribunal over the investment dispute submitted by the claimants was upheld.[635] The mere existence of the dispute resolution clause in the Concession Contract between the investor and the Tucumán Province did not, therefore, constitute an election by the investor in favour of the 'national jurisdictions' of Argentina. Both the Tribunal and the *ad hoc* Committee did, nonetheless, consider the hypothetical effect of the investor bringing its contractual grievances relating to its investment before the Tucumán courts in terms of the 'fork in the road' in Article 8 of the BIT, and came to opposite conclusions. This was despite the common ground on the clear distinction between claims grounded in contract and claims based on the BIT. The Tribunal found that, had the investor brought its contractual claims to the Tucumán courts pursuant to the dispute resolution clause of the Concession Contract, this would not have constituted a waiver of any right to subsequently submit treaty claims to an international tribunal pursuant to Article 8 precisely because of the different legal foundations of these causes of action.[636] The *ad hoc* Committee, on the other hand, attached significance to the broad formulation of Article 8(1) as it refers to 'any disputes relating to investments made under this Agreement', thereby encompassing contractual *or* treaty claims arising out of the same investment.[637] Thus if the claimants had brought contractual claims against the Tucumán Province before the Tucumán courts, it would have thereby foreclosed any recourse to an investment treaty tribunal based on a different cause of action.[638]

If the *ad hoc* Committee's interpretation is correct, the 'fork in the road' provision would undoubtedly have a chilling effect on the submission of disputes by investors to domestic judicial *fora* even where the issues in contention are purely contractual, tortious or even administrative, and clearly within the domain of municipal law. One would expect, as a result, an increase in claims simply not ripe for international adjudication on

635 *Vivendi* Annulment Decision, paras. 72–80.

636 The reasoning provided by the ICSID Tribunal for this conclusion is sparse: '. . . submission of claims against Tucumán to the contentious administrative tribunals of Tucumán for breaches of the contract, as Article 16.4 required, would not . . . have been the kind of choice by Claimants of legal action in national jurisdictions (*i.e.* courts) against the Argentine Republic that constitutes the "fork in the road" under Article 8 of the BIT, thereby foreclosing future claims under the ICSID Convention.' *Vivendi* Award, para. 55.

637 *Vivendi* Annulment Decision, para. 55. The *ad hoc* Committee compared Art. 8 of the BIT with Art. 11 of the same instrument containing a narrower formulation for the submission of disputes to the state/state arbitration procedure which concerns disputes 'concerning the interpretation or application of this Agreement' and also Art. 1116 of the NAFTA which allows an investor to submit to arbitration 'a claim that another Party has breached an obligation' under Ch. 11. *Ibid.* para. 55.

638 *Ibid.*

the merits. An investor's premature recourse to a treaty tribunal, with the attendant time and cost this involves, would be difficult to condemn as a matter of policy because the investor would have a legitimate interest to avoid jeopardising its 'day in court' before an international tribunal. This would put both parties in a difficult position because the investor might be compelled to play what is often its best litigation card too early before its main grievances have ripened and thus risk having its treaty claims dismissed on the merits, whereas the host state would be deprived of the opportunity to dispense adequate remedies through its own courts and instead face more numerous and expensive international proceedings. One can detect both these consequences in the *Vivendi* and *SGS v Pakistan* cases.

Such a development is not inevitable. As previously stated, both the ICSID Tribunal and the *ad hoc* Committee in *Vivendi* emphasized the distinct nature of contractual claims and treaty claims, both of which are certainly capable of meeting the definition of 'investment disputes' pursuant to the 'fork in the road' provision. Although the ICSID Tribunal's reasoning in support of its interpretation is very sparse, it can nevertheless be defended for the following reasons. A 'fork in the road' provision cannot, by any reasonable interpretation of this type of clause, prevent an investor from bringing a treaty claim in respect of a grievance completely unrelated to a different grievance that was previously submitted to a municipal court, even if such complaints relate to the same investment. For instance, an application by the investor to an administrative court to challenge an increase in the municipal rates for the disposal of waste from the investor's factory cannot prevent the investor from bringing a claim to an international tribunal for the wholesale expropriation of the factory a week later by a presidential decree. These grievances would constitute different 'investment disputes' for the purposes of the provision. This point merely illustrates the fact that the generality of the 'fork in the road' clause must be subject to some limitations. It is more than plausible, and certainly desirable, to further distinguish 'investment disputes' by the legal foundation for the cause of action. To take the previous example, the investor's swift administrative court application might be partially successful in reducing the municipal charges. But the unforeseen burden of this additional expense might nevertheless destroy the financial viability of the factory so that it ultimately must be closed down. The investor then brings a claim for a breach of the national treatment standard in the relevant investment treaty, having discovered that no other factory in the same industry was subject to the hike in municipal rates. These two claims presented to two different judicial *fora* address the same measure attributable to the host state in relation to the same investment. But they are easily conceptualised as different 'investment disputes' under the 'fork in the road' provision. This approach is, in fact, more consistent with other parts of the *ad hoc* Committee's decision in *Vivendi* for the reasons that now follow.

First, the dispute resolution clause in the Concession Contract was found not to affect the jurisdiction of the ICSID Tribunal with respect to a claims based on the BIT provisions.[639] The *ad hoc* Committee was emphatic on this point: 'A state cannot rely on an exclusive jurisdiction clause in a contract to avoid the characterisation of its conduct as internationally unlawful under a treaty.'[640] By parity of reasoning, it must follow that the submission of contractual disputes to the Tucumán courts in compliance with this clause should also not affect the ICSID tribunal's jurisdiction over treaty claims. Each would constitute a separate 'investment dispute'.

Secondly, the very basis of the partial annulment was the ICSID Tribunal's summary dismissal of the investor's treaty claims due to the perceived 'crucial connection in this case between the terms of the Concession Contract and these alleged violations of the BIT'[641] which compelled the investor to first seek redress in the Tucumán courts pursuant to the Concession Contract.[642] To substantiate this basis for annulment, the *ad hoc* Committee emphasized the different juridical character of the claims at length[643] and found that each 'will be determined by reference to its own proper law'[644] so that a 'state may breach a treaty without breaching a contract, and *vice versa*'.[645] Given the fundamental difference between legal foundations of the different types of claim, it would be very curious if they could nevertheless be merged into a single 'investment dispute' for the purposes of the 'fork in the road' provision. Moreover, it would also be surprising if one type of claim could be *res judicata* in relation to the same factual investment dispute for another. It must be conceded, however, that the *ad hoc* Committee did so envisage. Having found that the investor had taken the 'fork in the road', the *ad hoc* Committee stated that it assumed the risk that the Tribunal would find that the acts complained of did not meet the threshold for a breach of the treaty.[646] If this were so, then, according to the *ad hoc* Committee, the investor 'would have lost both its treaty claim and its contract claim'.[647]

A similar problem came before another ICSID Tribunal in the NAFTA case *Waste Management, Inc. v United Mexican States*.[648] Instead of interpreting the type of proceedings that would constitute an election for a 'fork in the road' provision, the Tribunal had to determine the type of proceedings that the investor must waive in order to comply with the conditions precedent for bringing a NAFTA claim. The condition precedent

[639] *Ibid.* para. 76. [640] *Ibid.* para. 103. [641] *Vivendi* Award, para. 78.

[642] *Ibid.* paras. 79, 81.

[643] *Vivendi* Annulment Decision, para. 113: 'A treaty cause of action is not the same as a contractual cause of action; it requires a clear showing of conduct which is in the circumstances contrary to the relevant treaty standard.' [644] *Ibid.* para. 96.

[645] *Ibid.* para. 95. [646] *Ibid.* para. 113. [647] *Ibid.*

[648] (Award & Dissenting Opinion, 2 June 2000) Case No. ARB(AF)/98/2, 5 ICSID Rep 443. The arbitration proceeded under the ICSID Additional Facility Rules.

in question was Article 1121, which compels the investor to:

> [W]aive their right to initiate or continue before any administrative tribunal or court under the law of any Party, or other dispute settlement procedures, *any proceedings with respect to the measure of the disputing Party that it alleged to be a breach* of an obligation under the NAFTA.[649]

The differences between the problems in the *Vivendi v Argentina* and *Waste Management v United Mexican States* must be identified before any attempt is made to shed further light on the 'fork in the road' provision.[650] Most importantly, the 'fork in the road' provision clearly goes to the arbitral tribunal's jurisdiction, while the waiver requirement in Article 1121 of the NAFTA can only affect the admissibility of the claim.[651] This distinction should bear some influence on the interpretation of each clause because a jurisdictional objection, if successful, disposes of the claimant's case *in limine*, whereas a claim that is defective on admissibility grounds can be potentially resubmitted upon rectification by the claimant or severed from other parts of the case which remain untainted. One would expect, therefore, that jurisdictional restrictions should be approached with greater circumspection due to the draconian consequences they entail in light of the object and purpose of investment treaties. Further, the term 'dispute' in the 'fork in the road' provision is perhaps a narrower formulation than 'proceedings with respect to the measure' alleged to be in breach of the NAFTA. The latter wording could be interpreted to be open-ended, so that any proceedings bearing a relationship to the factual or legal measure adopted by the state party might be within the proper scope of the required waiver. On the other hand, a 'dispute' denotes a particular legal cause of action between two identifiable parties based on particular facts and has a singular or 'closed' quality to it (*ie* '*the* dispute' compared to '*any* proceedings').

The ICSID Tribunal in *Waste Management Inc. v United Mexican States* was divided on the proper scope of the waiver in Article 1121. The majority found that there was an overlap between the Mexican court and domestic arbitration proceedings brought by Waste Management[652] relating to non-compliance with the obligations of guarantor assumed under a line of credit agreement with the state-owned entity, on the one hand, and

[649] Emphasis added. Article 1121 exempts 'proceedings from injunctive, declaratory or other extraordinary relief, not involving the payment of damages, before an administrative tribunal or court under the law of the disputing Party'.

[650] The tribunal established to hear the Waste Management's resubmission of its claim described Art. 1121 as a 'middle course' between a 'fork in the road' provision and a provision allowing the reference of disputes to international arbitration irrespective of whether any local remedies have been pursued.

[651] This was the characterisation of Art. 1121 given in the Dissenting Opinion of Keith Highet in *Waste Management v United Mexican States* (Dissenting Opinion, 2 June 2000) Case No. ARB(AF)/98/2, 5 ICSID Reports 462, paras. 56–63. The majority did not expressly consider this issue, but dismissed the claimant's case on the basis of lack of jurisdiction. *Concord: Ethyl Corporation v Government of Canada*, (Award on Jurisdiction, 24 June 1998), (1999) 38 ILM 708, 729. *Contra: Mondev International Ltd v United States of America*, (Award, 11 October 2002) Case No. ARB(AF)/99/2), 6 ICSID Rep 192, para. 44.

[652] More precisely, Waste Management's Mexican subsidiary.

the submission to the ICSID Tribunal on the other because 'both legal actions have a legal basis derived from the same measures'.[653] By pursuing these proceedings simultaneously, Waste Management's conduct was found to be incompatible with the terms of Article 1121, with the result that the ICSID Tribunal was devoid of jurisdiction to hear its NAFTA claims.[654] In his dissenting opinion, Highet accentuated the difference in the causes of action in the different *fora* as being 'local commercial claims in the Mexican tribunals, and international treaty claims before this Tribunal'.[655] The investor's concurrent legal proceedings in local *fora* could not, on this basis, fall within the purview of the waiver requirement in Article 1121.

The reasoning underlying the dissenting opinion is closer to the 'common ground' in the award and annulment decision in *Vivendi* due to the emphasis on the different legal foundations underpinning the causes of action:

> There must be, and is, a distinction to be drawn in juridical terms between the legal obligations of Mexico under Mexican law and the legal obligations of Mexico under its international treaty obligations imposed by NAFTA.[656]

It will be recalled that the arbitral tribunal in *Vivendi* summarily dismissed the investor's treaty claims because there was a 'crucial connection'[657] to contractual issues that were to be resolved by a different judicial forum. The majority in *Waste Management* may have followed a similar path by declining jurisdiction on the basis of the interconnectedness between the contractual and international law obligations underlying the different causes of action.[658] Despite the common emphasis on the different legal foundations of these obligations, the dissenting opinion in *Waste Management* and the annulment decision in *Vivendi* appear to diverge on the consequences of this distinction for the characterisation of the dispute. It is submitted that the distinction should survive for the purposes of interpreting the 'fork in the road' provision, so causes of action based on municipal and international law obligations would entail two different 'disputes' for the purposes of this clause.

There is support for this approach in the ICSID Tribunal's decision in *CMS Gas Transmission Company v The Republic of Argentina*.[659] In the

[653] (Award, 2 June 2000) Case No. ARB(AF)/98/2, 5 ICSID Reports 443, para. 27.

[654] *Ibid.* para. 31.

[655] (Dissenting Opinion, 2 June 2000) Case No. ARB(AF)/98/2, 5 ICSID Rep 462, para. 28.

[656] *Ibid.* para. 8.

[657] (Award, 21 November 2000) Case No. ARB/97/3, 5 ICSID Rep 299, para. 78.

[658] (Award, 2 June 2000) Case No. ARB(AF)/98/2, 5 ICSID Rep 443, para. 28, 'It is clear that the provisions referred to in the NAFTA constitute obligations of international law for NAFTA signatory States, but violation of the content of those obligations may well constitute actions proscribed by Mexican legislation in this case, the denunciation of which before several courts or tribunals would constitute a duplication of proceedings.'

[659] (Decision of the Tribunal on Objections to Jurisdiction, 17 July 2003) Case No. ARB/01/8, (2003) 42 ILM 788.

section of the award entitled 'Jurisdictional objection on the "fork in the road" triggering', the Tribunal noted that:

> Decisions of several ICSID tribunals have held that as contractual claims are different from treaty claims, even if there had been or there currently was a recourse to the local courts for a breach of contract, this would not have prevented submission of the treaty claims to arbitration.[660]

The Tribunal was primarily concerned with domestic proceedings launched by TGN (the company in which the Claimant held its investment), which was a distinct entity that could not, according to the Tribunal, trigger the 'fork in the road' vis-à-vis the Claimant.[661] However, the Tribunal also highlighted the fact that the causes of action advanced by TGN in the Argentine courts, and those submitted by the Claimant before the ICSID Tribunal, were 'under separate instruments' and therefore 'different'.[662]

An analysis of investment treaties reveals that the 'fork in the road' provision is often embedded in treaties which allow the investor to invoke the jurisdiction of an international tribunal with respect to a broad sphere of 'investment disputes' that contemplates both municipal and international law claims.[663] This gives rise to the possibility of symmetrical jurisdictional conflicts and hence a more acute need to regulate the competing jurisdictions through the 'fork in the road' mechanism.[664] Treaties that confine the scope of any submission to international arbitration exclusively to claims based on the minimum treaty standards do not usually contain a 'fork in the road' provision. The risk of competing jurisdictions still exists because, in 'monist' jurisdictions where treaties become part of domestic law and thus enforceable before municipal courts, the investor could bring claims based explicitly on the treaty standards in multiple *fora*. This remedial possibility is unlikely to be utilised by investors often in practice, and there is no reported precedent to date. The 'fork in the road' clause is therefore less relevant to such treaties.

660 *Ibid.* para. 80. Footnote omitted. 661 *Ibid.*

662 *Ibid.* For further support for this approach to the fork in the road provision, see: *Genin and Others v Republic of Estonia*, (Award, 25 June 2001) Case No. ARB/99/2, 6 ICSID Rep 236, paras. 330–4; *Middle East Cement Shipping and Handling Co. S.A. v Arab Republic of Egypt*, (Award, 12 April 2002) Case No. ARB/99/6, para. 71, available at <http://www.worldbank.org/icsid/cases/mc_cement-award. pdf>.

663 See, *eg*: Chile Model BIT, Art. 8(3), *UNCTAD Compendium* (Vol. III, 1996) 148; Peru Model BIT, Art. 9(1), (Vol. VI, 2002) 497; US Model BIT, Art. 9(3), *ibid.* 507; Austria Model BIT, Art. 13, *ibid.* (Vol. VII) 265 (but only if the dispute has been submitted to a municipal court *and* a judgment has been rendered); Benin Model BIT, Art. 9(2), *ibid.* (Vol. IX) 283.

664 A novel solution to this problem that may not deter recourse to the local courts may be found in the Finland Model BIT: 'An investor who has submitted to a national court may nevertheless have recourse to one of the arbitral tribunals mentioned in paragraphs 2(b) to (d) of this Article [ICSID, ICSID Additional Facility and UNCITRAL] if, before a judgment has been delivered on the subject matter by a national court, the investor declares not to pursue the case any longer through national proceedings and withdraws the case.' Article 9(3), *ibid.* (Vol. VII, 2002), 292.

VIII. Conclusions

The principal conclusions of this study are now summarised:

1. The investment treaty regime for investor/state disputes cannot be rationalised either as a purely public international law or purely private international law form of dispute resolution. Rather it embodies elements of both, and can be applied as such in a coherent and effective way.
2. The investment treaty regime for state/state disputes is properly understood as a creation of public international law *stricto sensu*.
3. The practice of investment treaty arbitration does not support rationalising the investor's cause of action against the host state as derivative (*ie* the investor steps into the shoes of its national state to vindicate the rights of the national state).
4. The practice of investment treaty arbitration is instead consistent with a 'direct' theory whereby the investor vindicates its own rights (or the host state's direct obligations to the investor).
5. Investment treaties create certain international obligations opposable by one contracting state to another, and the general rules of state responsibility for international wrongs regulate the consequences of any breach thereof. These obligations can generally be grouped into two categories: (i) adherence to the law of treaties in the interpretation and application of the investment treaty; (ii) the obligation not to frustrate an investor's recourse to international arbitration or the enforcement of any award against the host state.
6. The secondary rules on the responsibility of states for internationally wrongful acts, as codified by the International Law Commission, are not transferable *en bloc* to the investment treaty regime for investor/state disputes.
7. Investment treaties create a sub-system of state responsibility for investor/state disputes. The host state's breach of an investment treaty creates new secondary rights and obligations as between the investor and the host state. The national state of the investor has no residual interest in these new rights and obligations.
8. The international rules on the nationality of claims and the exhaustion of local remedies are not applicable to the sub-system of state responsibility for investor/state disputes created by investment treaties.
9. The three sources of legal rules applicable to the substance of investor/state disputes are the municipal law of the host state, the investment treaty, and general principles of international law.
10. Three distinct choice of law rules are applicable to the substance of an investor/state dispute. First, the municipal law of the host state determines whether a particular property right exists, the scope of that right, and in whom it vests. Secondly, the investment treaty supplies the definition of investments and thereby determines whether

the legal property right recognised by the municipal law of the host state is subject to the protection afforded by the investment treaty. Thirdly, acts or measures attributable to the host state with respect to the investment are to be tested for compliance with the minimum standards of investment protection prescribed by the investment treaty as supplemented by the general principles of international law.

11. The procedure of investor/state arbitrations is governed by the relevant provisions of the investment treaty, the applicable arbitral rules and the *lex loci arbitri*. The *lex loci arbitri* does not, however, apply to investor/state arbitrations conducted under the ICSID Convention, which are ultimately governed by a self-contained procedural regime detached from any system of municipal law.
12. Arbitral awards rendered by treaty tribunals in investor/state cases are 'foreign' or 'commercial' awards for the purposes of the New York Convention. Recognition and enforcement may be refused to such awards on the grounds set out in Article V of the New York Convention. Where an application to recognise or enforce an ICSID award is made in a country that has not ratified the ICSID Convention, the award should also be considered as a 'foreign' or 'commercial' awards for the purposes of the New York Convention.
13. The failure of the municipal courts of the host state to recognise and enforce arbitral awards rendered by treaty tribunals in investor/state cases in accordance with an applicable international treaty on the recognition and enforcement of arbitral awards may constitute a separate breach of the investment treaty that is actionable pursuant to the investor/state or the state/state arbitral mechanism.
14. Conflicts of jurisdiction between treaty tribunals and other judicial *fora* generally arise because investors are not bound to exhaust local remedies in the host state (or other procedures previously agreed to) before instituting proceedings before a treaty tribunal.
15. 'Symmetrical' conflicts of jurisdiction arise when a treaty tribunal is seized of a claim based upon a private law obligation and a different judicial forum has jurisdiction over the same claim.
16. Where the fundamental basis of the investor's claim before a treaty tribunal rests upon a breach of contract, the treaty tribunal must dismiss or stay its proceedings in favour of a judicial forum that has been previously designated by the parties to resolve disputes arising out of the contract, save where the treaty expressly overrides a previous designation. The principles of *pacta sunt servunda*, *generalia specialibus non derogant*, and *prior tempore, potior jure* mandate this approach.
17. In determining the fundamental basis of the investor's claims, the treaty tribunal must conduct a *prima facie* analysis of the treaty obligations that the investor seeks to invoke and determine whether the facts alleged are reasonably capable of constituting a violation of these obligations. The investor's characterisation of its claims is not definitive for this purpose.

18. 'Asymmetrical' conflicts of jurisdiction arise when a municipal court or arbitral tribunal has pronounced upon or is seized of a dispute relating to the existence, nature, or scope of the investor's interests in its investment and such interests are contested in an investment dispute before a treaty tribunal.
19. Property rights are the basis of an investment. Insofar as the municipal law of the host state determines whether a particular legal right to property exists, the scope of that right, and in whom it vests, prior judicial pronouncements or concurrent proceedings that address such issues can be relevant to questions of liability before a treaty tribunal in addition to questions on the quantum of damages.
20. The principles of *res judicata* and *lis alibi pendens* are not appropriate for dealing with asymmetrical conflicts of jurisdiction. The general rule should be that there is a rebuttable presumption that a prior judicial decision will be upheld by the treaty tribunal absent any serious procedural irregularities or a manifest error of law. When there are concurrent proceedings in other judicial *fora* dealing with aspects of the investment dispute, the treaty tribunal has the discretion to stay its proceedings where appropriate.
21. A cause of action based on a private law obligation generates a different 'investment dispute' for the purposes of the 'fork in the road' provision to a cause of action based on an investment treaty obligation, even if these causes of action relate to the same investment.

IX. Postscript—*SGS Sociéte Générale de Surveillance S.A. v Republic of the Philippines*

The Editors have generously ceded a few more pages of this Yearbook to allow the present writer to briefly comment upon an arbitral decision of singular importance to this study that was rendered after the final text had been submitted for publication. The ICSID Tribunal's jurisdictional decision in *SGS Société Générale de Surveillance S.A. v Republic of the Philippines*[665] clarifies many of the issues that were addressed in Part VII of this study on 'Jurisdictional Conflicts and Investment Treaty Arbitration'.[666]

The facts of the case bear many similarities to those in *SGS v Pakistan*,[667] indeed the dispute arose out of the same type of investment activity by the same Swiss company SGS, *viz.*, the provision of certification services based on pre-shipment inspections on behalf of the customs authorities of the host state.[668] The commercial relationship between SGS

[665] (Decision of the Tribunal on Objections to Jurisdiction, 29 January 2004) Case No. ARB/02/6, available at <http://www.worldbank.org/icsid/cases/SGSvPhil-final.pdf>.

[666] The decision deals with other preliminary issues as well, such as the territorial requirement for investments and the interpretation of 'umbrella clauses'. This brief comment will, however, focus solely on the jurisdictional issues that arose due to the exclusive jurisdiction clause in the investment contract.

[667] *Ibid.* para. 95. See the text accompanying n. 528 *et seq.* in the main text.

[668] *Ibid.* para. 12.

and the Philippines was formalised in successive contracts over 15 years; the final contract (the 'CISS Agreement'[669]) had been extended several times by the parties before terminating in accordance with its terms on 31 March 2000.[670] Following the termination, SGS submitted certain monetary claims under the CISS Agreement amounting to approximately USD 140 million.[671] SGS instituted arbitration proceedings against the Philippines under the Switzerland/Philippines BIT, claiming that the Philippines, in refusing to pay this amount, violated several of its treaty obligations.[672] The Philippines objected to the jurisdiction of the ICSID Tribunal on the ground that, *inter alia*, SGS's claims were contractual and therefore subject to the jurisdiction of the Regional Trial Courts of Makati or Manilia in accordance with the forum selection clause in the CISS Agreement.[673] The Tribunal approached the question of jurisdiction:

> . . . on the footing that in the Request for Arbitration, SGS made credible allegations of non-payment of very large sums due under the CISS Agreement and claimed that the Philippines' failure to pay these was a breach of the BIT, but that the exact amount payable has neither been definitively agreed between the parties nor determined by a competent court or tribunal.[674]

The Tribunal's reasoning will now be examined under various headings that correspond to the taxonomy adopted in this study.

Can the Ratione Materiae *Jurisdiction of a Treaty Tribunal Extend to Purely Contractual Disputes?*

The ICSID Tribunal held that the reference to 'disputes with respect to investments between a Contracting Party and an investor of the other Contracting Party' in the BIT was 'not limited by reference to the legal classification of the claim that is made'[675] and thus was sufficiently broad to encompass contractual claims. The Tribunal thus rejected the problematic assumption of the ICSID Tribunal in *SGS v Pakistan*[676] that contractual claims by their very nature were incapable of falling within this broad definition of the *ratione materiae* competence of a treaty tribunal.[677] This is consistent with the critique of the *SGS v Pakistan* ruling on this point in this study.[678]

Does an Investment Treaty Override Existing Contractual Forum Selection Clauses?

The Tribunal resolved an issue left open by the *ad hoc* Annulment Committee in *Vivendi* as to whether the exclusive jurisdiction clause in a

669 'CISS' is an acronym for 'comprehensive import supervision service'. *Ibid.* para. 13.

670 *Ibid.* paras. 13–4.

671 *Ibid.* para. 15.

672 *Ibid.* paras. 16, 44.

673 *Ibid.* paras. 17, 22, 51.

674 *Ibid.* para. 43.

675 *Ibid.* para. 131

676 *Ibid.* para. 134.

677 The grounds favouring an interpretation inclusive of contractual claims are set out in para. 132 of the Decision.

678 See the text accompanying nn. 544–548 *et seq.* in the main text.

contract was somehow overridden by the BIT.[679] The answer given by the majority was in the negative.[680] The principle of *generalia specialibus non derogant* gave precedence to the forum selected in the contract because it was more specific in relation to the parties and the dispute.[681] Furthermore, according to the Tribunal, investment treaties are designed to 'support and supplement, not to override or replace, the actually negotiated investment arrangements made between the investor and the host State.'[682]

Cause of Action Analysis: The Fundamental Basis of the Claims

It was argued by the present writer that it is imperative for a treaty tribunal to objectively distinguish between contractual and treaty causes of action advanced by a claimant.[683] Where the fundamental basis of the claim is the contract rather than the treaty, then a treaty tribunal must decline its jurisdiction over such a claim if either (i) there is a valid forum selection clause in the contract that binds the parties and encompasses the claim, or (ii) the treaty tribunal's *ratione materiae* competence is limited to claims based on treaty violations.

The Tribunal in *SGS v The Philippines* clearly accepted the necessity and legitimacy of cause of action analysis and determined that 'the *substance* of SGS's claim, *viz.*, a claim to payment for services supplied under the Agreement'[684] constituted a 'dispute in connection with the obligations of either party to the CISS Agreement' for the purposes of the exclusive jurisdiction clause.[685] This terminology employed by the Tribunal was thus slightly different from the 'essential basis' test of the *ad hoc* Committee in *Vivendi*, but the distinction is unlikely to be important.

The Resolution of Symmetrical Conflicts of Jurisdiction

Having found that (i) the exclusive jurisdiction clause in the investment agreement covered the substance of SGS's claim for outstanding payments,[686] and (ii) the *ratione materiae* jurisdiction of the tribunal extended to purely contractual claims,[687] the ICSID Tribunal proceeded to deal with the resulting symmetrical conflict of jurisdiction. What effect should be given to the exclusive jurisdiction clause?

679 See n. 527 in the main text.

680 Mr Crivellaro dissented on this point and appended a 'Declaration' to the Decision, available at <http://www.worldbank.org/icsid/cases/SGSvPhil-declaration.pdf>.

681 (Decision of the Tribunal on Objections to Jurisdiction, 29 January 2004) Case No. ARB/02/6, para. 141, available at <http://www.worldbank.org/icsid/cases/SGSvPhil-final.pdf>.

682 *Ibid.* The Tribunal also considered whether the ICSID Convention has the effect of overriding the contractual forum selection clause. Again, the Tribunal refuted this possibility because, *inter alia*, the forum selection clause fell within the exception 'unless otherwise stated' to the exclusive remedy rule in Art. 26 of the ICSID Convention. *Ibid.* para. 147.

683 See Part VII(D) in the main text.

684 (Decision of the Tribunal on Objections to Jurisdiction, 29 January 2004) Case No. ARB/02/6, para. 137, available at <http://www.worldbank.org/icsid/cases/SGSvPhil-final.pdf>.

685 *Ibid.* 686 *Ibid.* para. 137. 687 *Ibid.* para. 135.

The present writer proposed the following solution to this problem:

> Where the fundamental basis of the investor's claim before a treaty tribunal rests upon a breach of contract, the treaty tribunal must dismiss or stay its proceedings in favour of a judicial forum that has been previously designated by the parties to resolve disputes arising out of the contract . . .[688]

The Tribunal's analysis is consistent with this proposed solution.

First, the Tribunal concluded that the exclusive jurisdiction clause in the final agreement must be given effect because it was not permissible for SGS to divide the unity of the contractual bargain by pleading the contract as the source of its right to outstanding payments and at the same time refuting the exclusive choice of forum for such claims in the same contract. The Tribunal cited many of the precedents of the mixed claims commissions that were analysed in this study to buttress this principle.[689] In the words of the Tribunal:

> SGS should not be able to approbate and reprobate in respect of the same contract: if it claims under the contract, it should comply with the contract in respect of the very matter which is the foundation of its claim.[690]

Secondly, the Tribunal noted that the exclusive jurisdiction clause raised an impediment to its own jurisdiction, rather than abrogating its jurisdiction altogether, and thus the matter was best conceived as one of admissibility.[691] On this basis, the Tribunal declared that it 'should not exercise its jurisdiction over a contractual claim where the parties have already agreed on how such a claim is to be resolved and have done so exclusively.'[692]

Residual jurisdiction over a 'BIT claim independent of the CISS Agreement'?

The point of departure from the principles advocated in this study arises upon the Tribunal's affirmation of jurisdiction over SGS's claims 'under the BIT which can be determined independently from the contractual issues referred to the Philippine courts by Article 12 of the CISS Agreement'.[693] It was submitted by the present writer that if the fundamental or essential basis of the claim is contractual, and the contract in question contains an exclusive jurisdiction clause in favour of a municipal court or arbitral tribunal, then the treaty tribunal must decline or stay its jurisdiction to give effect to that jurisdiction clause. The ICSID Tribunal appears to have determined that the fundamental basis of SGS's claims was contractual when it concluded that Article 12 of the CISS Agreement extended to it.[694] Nonetheless, the significance of this characterisation of the claims was limited to the particular context of the forum selection clause, because the Tribunal went on to apply a different

688 See Point 16 of the Conclusions in the main text.
689 See the cases cited at *ibid.* paras. 150–2. 690 *Ibid.* para. 155. 691 *Ibid.* para. 154.
692 *Ibid.* para. 155. 693 *Ibid.* para. 156. 694 *Ibid.* para. 137.

test to uphold its jurisdiction over two of SGS's treaty claims.[695] This jurisdictional test might be described as a *prima facie* examination of whether a claim has been properly stated under the relevant treaty provision. In the Tribunal's words:

Provided the facts as alleged by the Claimant and as appearing from the initial pleadings fairly raise questions of breach of one or more provisions of the BIT, the Tribunal has jurisdiction to determine the claim.[696]

According to the Tribunal, SGS had properly stated claims based on the 'umbrella clause'[697] and the fair and equitable treatment standard, despite the contractual essence of the dispute.

Having ruled that it had jurisdiction over certain of SGS's treaty claims, the Tribunal noted that there were nevertheless important issues between the parties relating to the quantum of the contractual debt under the CISS Agreement. The Tribunal therefore ventured into an asymmetrical conflict of jurisdiction, insofar as it upheld jurisdiction over causes of action based on the treaty, but at the same time recognised that there were contractual issues to be resolved by another forum that were crucial to the ultimate resolution of the dispute.[698] It was concluded in this study that, when faced with an asymmetrical conflict of jurisdiction, a treaty tribunal should exercise its discretion to stay in appropriate circumstances in the interests of comity and the good administration of justice. This was precisely the approach taken by the ICSID Tribunal, who, having found that 'SGS's claim is premature and must await the determination of the amount payable in accordance with the contractually-agreed process',[699] decided to stay the proceedings to await either a judgment of the courts of the Philippines or a definitive agreement between the parties on the amount payable under the CISS Agreement.[700] The ICSID Tribunal's solution to the asymmetrical conflict of jurisdiction thus resembled the one adopted by the Permanent Court of International Justice in the *Prince von Pless Case*,[701] where the international proceedings were stayed to await the determination of certain tax issues by the Polish courts. The Permanent Court desired to have the benefit of municipal decisions dealing with issues arising under Polish tax law before it adjudged Poland's international responsibility for the alleged abuse of its taxation powers towards a foreign national.[702]

Conclusion

The careful analysis by the ICSID Tribunal in *SGS v The Philippines* of its jurisdiction over contractual claims, the significance of an exclusive

[695] See the cases cited at *ibid.* paras. 157–9. [696] *Ibid.* para. 157.

[697] Article X(2) of the Switzerland/Philippines BIT reads: 'Each Contracting Party shall observe any obligation it has assumed with regard to specific investments in its territory by investors of the other Contracting Party.' [698] These issues are described at *ibid.* para. 41.

[699] *Ibid.* para. 163. [700] *Ibid.* para. 175.

[701] (1933) (Interim Protection Order) PCIJ Rep Series A/B No. 52.

[702] See the text accompanying nn. 625 and 626 in the main text.

forum selection clause in an investment contract and the resolution of competing jurisdictions over contractual claims (symmetrical jurisdictional conflicts) deserves full endorsement. Detractors will be quick to point out, however, that the Tribunal's discussion of these issues was *obiter dicta* because it upheld its jurisdiction over certain causes of action that invoked provisions of the treaty. Thus there was no direct conflict between two *fora* with jurisdiction over contractual claims. It may have been more consistent with this *obiter* analysis for the Tribunal to have stuck to its characterisation of SGS's claims as in substance contractual and then stay its jurisdiction on the basis of the exclusive jurisdiction clause in favour of the courts of the Philippines. The reasoning underlying the Tribunal's preference for a different *prima facie* test for its treaty jurisdiction is not entirely clear.

The Tribunal did, however, confront an additional complexity in the form of the 'umbrella clause', which was interpreted as addressing the performance of commitments made by the host state to specific investments, rather than the scope or extent of such commitments.[703] Once the Tribunal had asserted its jurisdiction over an element of the dispute relating to the Philippines' performance of its commitments in the CISS Agreement, then it was open to the Tribunal to refer questions relating to the other elements of the dispute (the scope or extent of those commitments) to a different forum in accordance with the forum selection clause in the same agreement. It is thus possible that the 'umbrella clause' in a sense created a jurisdictional 'wild card' which provided a route to upholding treaty jurisdiction even though the foundation of the claim was contractual.

[703] (Decision of the Tribunal on Objections to Jurisdiction, 29 January 2004) Case No. ARB/02/6, para. 126, available at <http://www.worldbank.org/icsid/cases/SGSvPhil-final.pdf>.

CONFERRALS BY STATES OF POWERS ON INTERNATIONAL ORGANIZATIONS: THE CASE OF AGENCY

By DAN SAROOSHI*

I. INTRODUCTION

A characteristic of the development of international organizations since 1945 has been the shift in the locus of decision-making on a whole range of governance issues from national governments to international organizations. This process was not at first a major focus of attention since organizations were initially cautious in the exercise of their limited powers, and when they did make decisions that potentially bound Member States there was primacy given to State consent in the acceptance of such obligations. However this institutional landscape is evolving. International organizations have increasingly interpreted their powers—even of binding decision—in a more expansive manner that blurs the role of State consent,[1] and States have increasingly conferred broader powers of governance on international organizations. Our present focus is on this initial conferral by States of powers on international organizations. It should be made clear that this is a wholly different enquiry from earlier work by this writer which examined the delegation (back) to States of powers previously conferred on an organization:[2] this article deals solely with the anterior concept of States conferring powers on international organizations.

The powers conferred by States on international organizations can be characterised as public powers of government or administration: they are powers that derive from the sovereignty of a State.[3] In theory they could

* Herbert Smith Reader in International Law, Faculty of Law, University of Oxford; Fellow, The Queens College, Oxford. The author would like to express his gratitude and appreciation for their insightful and valuable comments on earlier versions of this article to Judge Rosalyn Higgins; Professors Sir Franklin Berman, James Crawford, Vaughan Lowe, and Maurice Mendelson; and Dapo Akande and Richard Gardiner. This article was written in part while the author was an Emile Noël Fellow at the Jean Monnet Center, New York University School of Law, and the author is very grateful to Professor Joseph Weiler, Director of the Centre, for his support. Responsibility for opinions expressed remain solely those of the author.

[1] For an account and analysis of the expansion, for example, by the European Community of its powers in a number of areas, see Weiler, J., *The Constitution of Europe* (1999), pp.44–56.

[2] See, for example, Sarooshi, D., *The United Nations and the Development of Collective Security: the Delegation by the UN Security Council of its Chapter VII Powers* (1999).

[3] On what is a governmental power more generally, see Crawford, J., 'First Report on State Responsibility', A/CN.4/490/Add.5, p.15.

Concerning the content of sovereign powers, Brownlie has explained that '[t]he normal complement of state rights, the typical case of legal competence, is described commonly as "sovereignty" . . . . The legal competence of a state includes considerable liberties in respect of internal organization and the disposal of territory. This general power of government, administration, and disposition is *imperium*, a capacity recognized and delineated by international law.' (Brownlie, I., *Principles of Public International Law* (1998, 5th ed.), pp.106–7.)

include the full range of executive, legislative, or judicial powers. International law certainly does not prevent a State[4] from conferring certain of its powers of government—powers that derive from its sovereignty—on

When States confer powers on an international organization they are not as such conferring their sovereignty on an organization, but specific powers which States possess by virtue of their sovereignty. It is not possible to confer sovereignty *per se* on an international organization, since sovereignty, as reiterated in numerous national constitutions (see, for example, Amar, A., 'Of Sovereignty and Federalism', *Yale Law Journal*, 96 (1987), p.1425, and Finer, S., Bogdanor, V., and Rudden, B., *Comparing Constitutions* (1995), pp.102, 118, and 137) and as recognised by international law, is derived from, and belongs to, the peoples of a State, while the 'constituency' of an international organization is not peoples but States. See also for this approach the decision of the French *Conseil Constitutionnel: Re Direct Elections to European Assembly* case, 30 December 1976, 74 ILR 527, 528; Bermann, G., 'Regulatory Federalism: European Union and United States', *Recueil des cours*, 263 (1997), p.9 at pp.28–9, Martin Martinez, M., *National Sovereignty and International Organizations*, (1996), pp.68–9, and Rossa Phelan, D., *Revolt or Revolution: The Constitutional Boundaries of the European Community*, (1997), pp.200–4. Similarly, Alain Pellet explains in the following passage why States cannot be said to have conferred sovereignty on international organizations, but only the exercise of governmental powers that derive from their sovereignty: '. . . sovereignty is the very criterion of statehood; it can be neither "transferred" nor "limited". A State cannot be "half-sovereign"; if it is a State, it enjoys sovereignty; if it transfers its sovereignty, it is no more a State. As the Permanent Court explained in its first judgment [in the *Wimbledon* case, PCIJ, Series A No.1, 25], "the right of entering into international engagements is an attribute of State sovereignty" and "the conclusion of any treaty by which a State undertakes to perform or refrain from performing a particular act [cannot be seen as] an abandonment of sovereignty." In other words, sovereignty is the basis of state competencies and, by concluding a treaty, a State does not limit, or abandon, or transfer its sovereignty; it exercises the rights deriving from its sovereignty. . . . States may delegate powers, or, rather, the exercise of some of their powers, but they cannot "delegate" their sovereignty. . . . Member States of the European Union are still sovereign, if only because they retain their monopoly in the use of forced coercion; but that, in the long run, the Communities structure will move towards federalism. At this stage, which has not yet been reached, Members of the Communities will have ceased to be States in the word's international legal meaning. Member States, then, will not have "delegated" their sovereignty; they will simply and purely have transferred it to a new state entity. After years of approximate and questionable formulations, this analysis is shared by the *Conseil constitutionnel* since Maastricht I.' (Pellet, A., 'A French Constitutional Perspective on Treaty Implementation', in Franck, T., ed., *Delegating State Powers: The Effect of Treaty Regimes on Democracy and Sovereignty* (2000), p.281 at pp.283–4.)

[4] Cf. the domestic position of a number of States whose constitutions expressly provide for the conferral of their powers of government on international organizations: in the case of the US see Franck, T., 'Can the United States Delegate Aspects of Sovereignty to International Regimes?', in Franck, T., ed., *Delegating State Powers: The Effect of Treaty Regimes on Democracy and Sovereignty* (2000), p.1, Fisler Damrosch, L., ' "Sovereignty" and International Organizations', *U. C. Davis J. Int'l L. & Policy*, 3 (1997), p.159 at pp.165–6, Ku, J., 'The Delegation of Federal Power to International Organizations: New Problems with Old Solutions', *Minnesota Law Revue*, 85 (2000), p.71, Bradley, C., 'International Delegations, the Structural Constitution, and Non-Self-Execution', *Stanford Law Review*, 55 (2003), p.1557, and Golove, D., 'The New Confederalism: Treaty Delegations of Legislative, Executive, and Judicial Authority', *Stanford Law Review*, 55 (2003), p.1697; in the case of France see Pellet, A., 'A French Constitutional Perspective on Treaty Implementation', in Franck, *ibidem*, p.279, and Oliver, P., 'The French Constitution and the Treaty of Maastricht', *ICLQ*, 43 (1994), p.1 at pp.11–12; for Germany see Article 24(1) of the German Constitution (for comment, see Nolte, G., 'Constitutional Implications of German Participation in Treaty Regimes', in Franck, *ibidem*, p.261; for the Netherlands see Article 92 of the Constitution (for the antecedent provision to this Article see Van Puys, J., 'The Netherlands Constitution and International Law', *AJIL*, 58 (1964), p.88 at pp.98–9); for Italy see Article 11 of the Italian Constitution (for comment, see La Pergola, A., and Del Duca, P., 'Community Law, International Law and the Italian Constitution', *AJIL*, 79 (1985), p.598 at p.601, and Cassese, A., 'Modern Constitutions and International Law', *Recueil des cours*, 192 (1985-III), p.331 at p.415); for Belgium see Article 25 *Bis* of the Belgian Constitution of 7 February 1831 (as amended in 1988); for Spain see Article 93 of the Spanish Constitution of 29 December 1978; for Denmark see Section 20 of the Danish Constitution of 5 June 1953 (on this provision see Germer, P., 'European influences on the national administrative laws from the point of view of the Member States: Danish Report', in Schwarze, J., ed., *Administrative Law under European Influence: on the*

international organizations, and it may even be an important part of a State's sovereignty that it has the competence to give away certain[5] of its powers of government.[6]

convergence of the administrative law of the EU Member States (1996), p.377 at pp.403–4); for Greece see Article 28 of the Greek Constitution of 7 June 1975; for Austria see Articles 9 (2), 23 (a)–(f) of the Austrian Federal Constitution (on these provisions see Grabenwarter, C., 'The Austrian Federal Constitution and Peace between States', *ZöR*, 51 (1996), p.61 at pp.76–81; and Seidl-Hohenveldern, I., 'Constitutional Problems involved in Austria's Accession to the EU', *CMLR*, 32 (1995), p.727); and for a useful summary of the domestic constitutional requirements that need to be fulfilled in Bulgaria, Hungary, Czech Republic, Poland, Russia, and Romania for the lawful conferral of powers by these States on international organizations, see Salzberger, E., and Voigt, S., 'Economic Analysis of Constitutional Law: On Constitutional Processes and the Delegation of Power, with Special Emphasis on Israel and Central and Eastern Europe', *Theoretical Inq. L*, 3 (2002), p.207 at pp.253–7.

5 However, it does seem clear that if a State were to cede (i.e. confer on an irrevocable basis: on the elements of a cession, see *infra* Section II) too many of its governmental powers to an international organization then there may be a real question as to the continued independence and thus existence of the entity as a State under international law, due primarily to the substantial external control being exercised by the organization over the State. (On 'independence' as the central criterion of Statehood under international law, see Crawford, J., *The Creation of States in International Law* (1979), p.48 *et sequentia*; and on the lack of substantial external control of a State as an important part of a State's 'independence', see Crawford, *ibidem*, p.60, and Jennings, R., and Watts, A., *Oppenheim's International Law*, (1992, 9th ed.), p.382.) Such an outcome is not, however, problematic from the perspective of international law. As Paul Reuter observed in ILC debates in 1964: 'The number of States in the international community was not fixed by any rule of international law, by any new principle, or by any article of the Charter. A State was in no way prohibited from permanently surrendering its independence by merging with a larger unit of its own free will.' (*YBILC*, vol. I, 1964, 732nd mtg., p.59 (para.63)) However, this issue has not arisen to date in the context of international organizations since there has not been the purported ceding of governmental powers by States to an international organization. As *Oppenheim's International Law* states: 'Whether the transfer of such [sovereign] rights and powers is so extensive as to affect the continued existence of the state depends on the circumstances of the individual case, and perhaps in particular on the scope of the rights and powers transferred and on the revocability of the transfer. The most extensive transfer of this kind currently existing is that involved in membership of the European Communities, but the continued international statehood of its member states is not in question.' (Jennings and Watts, *ibidem*, p.126.) This possibility does, however, raise the issue of what governmental powers would need to be ceded by a State to an organization before the entity can no longer be regarded as a State.

In this enquiry the cases and literature concerning the ceding by a State of its independence to another State or group of States would be of considerable assistance. In the case of protected States, James Crawford has usefully provided factors to determine the issue of independence; factors which may be applied *mutatis mutandis* to determine the issue of the continued independence of a State that has ceded powers to an international organization: '. . . the legal independence of a State is consistent with a considerable degree of actual dependence [here on another State]. The priority of formal over actual independence in assessing whether an entity is a State means that quite extensive delegation of competences by treaty can coexist with statehood. Treaty provisions do not, in general, derogate from formal independence; the question is then how extensive the loss of actual independence must be, under protectorate arrangements, before the local entity can no longer be regarded as a State. As a general rule it may be said that the exercise of delegated powers pursuant to protectorate arrangements is not inconsistent with statehood if the derogations from independence are based on local consent, do not involve extensive powers of internal control, and do not leave the local entity without some degree of influence over the exercise of its foreign affairs. For example, metropolitan authority to conclude treaties for the protected entity and to implement them in the latter's territory is inevitably inconsistent with local statehood: since modern international relations may involve practically every aspect of governmental powers within a State, control of this sort implies a discretion to intervene internally over the whole range of governmental powers. But this is an unusually clear case: it may be helpful to consider various examples of delegation of responsibility, as it were on a continuum from virtually complete independence to loss of actual independence such that statehood is in question.' (Crawford, *ibidem*, pp.188–9.)

6 See also Jessup, P., *A Modern Law of Nations* (1968), pp.18–19. This relies on the proposition that the sovereignty of a State is a divisible concept (Jennings and Watts, *supra* n.5, p.124, and Pescatore, P.,

However, the broad range of measures being taken by international organizations in the exercise of these powers has led a variety of domestic political and judicial actors and commentators to question the constitutionality and propriety of conferring broad powers of governance on organizations. There is, however, a considerable lack of clarity in discussion of these issues. The labels used to describe particular conferrals of powers are often used uncritically to refer to different types of conferrals.[7] Failure to distinguish between different types of conferrals of power confuses analysis of the differing legal consequences of these conferrals and obfuscates the domestic policy debates that surround their conferral.[8] In order to provide clarity in this area our present objective is to begin to provide a typology of the different types of conferrals by States of powers on international organizations. A particular focus is the first category in our proposed typology, an agency relationship that may flow from the conferral by a State or States of powers on organizations.[9] In this context there is consideration of a number of important questions: To what extent and in what circumstances can an international organization act as an agent for one or more States, whether they are Members or not? In the case where an organization does act as an agent, whose legal relations are changed by the acts of the organization and who is responsible for breaches of international law that may occur as a result of these acts?

'L'apport du droit communautaire au droit international public', *Cahiers de droit européen* (1970), p.501 at pp.502–11) and thus that a State's sovereign powers need not be united in the one entity for sovereignty to be said to continue to exist (Jennings and Watts, *supra* n.5, p.124.)

There is, however, the possible contrary argument that States can never really confer their powers on an international organization, since State power is in a sense original and that once it is removed to a locus of decision-making external to the State's legal, political, and societal structures then it necessarily becomes something else, possibly a power of administration or supranational regulation. See, for an example of this type of approach, Lindseth, P., 'Democratic Legitimacy and the Administrative Character of Supranationalism: the example of the European Community', *Columbia Law Review*, 99 (1999), p.628.

7 Holland elegantly expressed the problem that lack of clarity in terminology can create when he stated more generally: 'If the expression of widely different ideas by one and the same term resulted only in the necessity for . . . clumsy periphrases, or obviously inaccurate paraphrases, no great harm would be done; but unfortunately the identity of terms seems irresistibly to suggest an identity between the ideas expressed by them.' (Holland, T., *Elements of Jurisprudence* (1906), p.83 as quoted in Hohfeld, W., 'Some Fundamental Legal Conceptions as Applied in Judicial Reasoning', *Yale Law Journal*, 23 (1913–1914), p.16 at pp.33–4.)

8 A good example of this is provided by the following statement by McBride: 'To the extent that obligations created by the WTO's dispute resolution process are legally binding—and numerous factors, such as the language and practice of the agreement, suggest that they are—Congress has arguably assigned a boundless, de facto legislative power to a supranational, extra-constitutional body, raising a bevy of constitutional concerns. While the United States concedes comparable power to other international bodies, such as the United Nations, the WTO's dispute resolution mechanism may uniquely deprive this country of its ultimate self-determination, something that other treaties and agreements do not do. Indeed, it appears as if the United States, when it loses a dispute, is left with an unpalatable choice between permitting supranational legislating of domestic law, or abandoning the WTO altogether and suffering through the disaster that would follow.' (McBride, S., 'Dispute Settlement in the WTO: Backbone of the Global Trading System or Delegation of Awesome Power', *Law & Pol'y Int'l Bus.*, 32 (2001), p.643.) See also Presley, M., 'Sovereignty and Delegation Issues Regarding U.S. Commitment to the World Trade Organization's Dispute Settlement Process', *J. Transnat'l L. & Pol'y*, 8 (1998), p.173.

9 On this category of agency, see *infra* Section IV.

Before turning to examine these issues of agency, it is first necessary to consider the elements of our typology and the processes by which States confer powers on international organizations.

II. Conferrals of Powers on International Organizations: A Typology

There is a considerable lack of clarity and consistent usage in the terms used to describe different types of conferrals by States of powers on international organizations. Such terms as 'ceding', 'alienation', 'transfer', 'delegation', and 'authorization' are used interchangeably by international and domestic courts as well as by commentators, often to refer to the same type of conferral of power[10] or the same conceptual label is used in a general way to refer to different types of conferrals.[11] However not all conferrals of power are the same, and there are important differences that flow from the type of conferral for the legal

[10] See, for example, just in the case of the conferral of powers by States onto the European Community the wide variety of concepts used (e.g. delegation, transfer, and cession) in the following: Cassese, A., 'Modern Constitutions and International Law', *Recueil des cours*, 192 (1985-III), p.331 at p.415; Martin Martinez, M., *National Sovereignty and International Organizations* (1996); Denza, E., 'Two Legal Orders: Divergent or Convergent?', *ICLQ*, 48 (1999), p.257 at pp.259–60; Ku, C., and Jacobson, H., 'Using military forces under international auspices and democratic accountability', *International Relations of the Asia-Pacific*, 1 (2001), p.21; Bradley, C., 'The Treaty Power and American Federalism', *Michigan Law Review*, 97 (1998), p.412; Schilling, T., 'The Anatomy of the Community Legal Order: An Analysis of Possible Foundations', *Harvard International Law Journal*, 37 (1996) 389; Lindseth, P., 'Democratic Legitimacy and the Administrative Character of Supranationalism: the example of the European Community', *Columbia Law Review*, 99 (1999), p.628 at pp.631, 633, 637, 639, & 645; Kingston, J., 'External Relations of the European Community—External Capacity Versus Internal Competence', *ICLQ*, 44 (1995), p.659; and Tangney, P., 'The New Internationalism: The Cession of Sovereign Competences to Supranational Organizations and Constitutional Change in the United States and Germany', *Yale Journal of International Law*, 21 (1996), p.395.

See also, more generally, the confused usage of concepts to describe the conferral of sovereign powers between States: e.g., *Customs Régime between Germany and Austria, PCIJ Reports Series A/B No 41*, 1931, p.37 at pp.46, 58–9, 77.

[11] Ku, for example, states: 'The constitutional issues implicated in these relationships [between the United States and international organizations] are most usefully understood as international delegations. An international delegation is the transfer of constitutionally-assigned federal powers—treaty-making, legislative, executive, and judicial powers—to an international organization.' (Ku, J., 'The Delegation of Federal Power to International Organizations: New Problems with Old Solutions', *Minnesota Law Review*, 85 (2000), p.71 at p.72.) See also, for example, uses of the conceptual label of 'delegation' to refer to different types of conferrals of powers: Seyersted, F., 'Is the International Personality of Intergovernmental Organizations valid *vis-à-vis* Non-members?', *Indian Journal of International Law*, 4 (1964), p.233 at p.247; Denza, E., 'Two Legal Orders: Divergent or Convergent?', *ICLQ*, 48 (1999), p.257 at pp.259–60; Trachtman, J., 'The Domain of WTO Dispute Settlement', *Harvard International Law Journal*, 40 (1999), p.333 at p.336; and Zemanek, K., 'The Legal Foundations of the International System: General Course on Public International Law', *Recueil des Cours*, 266 (1997), p.9 at pp.90–1.

Cf., however, the more careful use of terminology employed by Fisler Damrosch who states: 'The WTO illustrates the emerging trend toward enabling international organizations in spheres where our own Congress has plenary power under domestic constitutional law. The careful scrutiny which Congress gave to the WTO agreements before finally assenting shows that Congress is not yet ready to surrender its plenary power to this international institution.' (Fisler Damrosch, L., ' "Sovereignty" and International Organizations', *U.C. Davis J. Int'l L. & Policy*, 3 (1997), p.159 at p.165.)

relationship that is thereby established between a State conferring power and an organization.

In order to provide clarity it may be useful to consider these conferrals of powers as being on a spectrum that has at one end a conferral that establishes an agency relationship between the State and the organization and at the other extremity a conferral that involves the ceding of power to the organization. In between these two positions can be said to lie the category of a delegation of powers that is closer to the agency position on the spectrum, and the separate category of a transfer of powers that is closer to a ceding of power. The locus of a particular conferral of powers on this spectrum depends on the degree to which a State has given away its powers to the organization. There are three characteristics of a conferral that can be used to ascertain the degree to which a power has been given away by a State, and thus within which one of our categories a particular conferral of power can be placed.

First is the question of revocability. In the cases of agency and delegation in our typology the conferral of power is revocable; while in the case of a transfer the conferral of power is irrevocable. In the case where States cede a power to an organization they can be said to have conferred a power *in toto* on an organization on an irrevocable basis.

Our second characteristic is the degree to which States retain control over the exercise of power by the organization. The main difference in our typology here is between an agency position and the separate categories of delegation and transfer where, in the latter categories, States do not have the competence to control the way in which conferred powers are being exercised by the organization. In the case of a ceding of power the question of States retaining the right to exercise control over the exercise of power by the organization does not even arise, since they will have conferred the power *in toto* on the organization.

Finally, does the organization possess the sole right to exercise the power being conferred on it by States or have they retained the right to exercise the power concurrently with the organization? In the case of a delegation, States retain the right to exercise the power concurrent with, and independent of, the organization's exercise of power; while in the case of a transfer the organization is the sole place for the lawful exercise of conferred power. This third characteristic, which arises in our categories of delegation and transfer, will largely depend on the extent to which States that confer powers on an organization have accepted to be bound—in both their internal legal systems and on the international plane—by obligations that flow from the organization's exercise of the power.

There is, however, an important limitation to the application of our typology: it only applies to those conferrals where States give away, to varying degrees, their own powers to international organizations. This limitation has practical importance since there is a distinction between individual and collective conferrals by States of powers on international organizations.[12] In the case of the former, States confer powers on an organization that they possess in their individual capacity; while in the case of the latter States confer collectively powers on organizations that they do not possess in their individual capacity. An example of a collective conferral of power is where States empower an international judicial institution either to resolve a bilateral dispute (a judicial power which each State party to the dispute does not possess on an individual basis) or to render an authoritative interpretation of a constituent treaty (once again a power which States parties do not possess on an individual basis).[13]

Even when dealing with individual conferrals of power, the classification of all conferrals within one of our categories cannot, however, always be precise since the boundaries between these categories are not definitively fixed[14] and there may be cases that contain elements common to two

[12] I am grateful to James Crawford and Vaughan Lowe for drawing my attention to this distinction.

[13] Another possible example of collectively conferred powers are the Chapter VII powers of the UN Security Council. It is questionable whether individual UN Member States possessed the enforcement powers conferred on the Council through the Charter, and, accordingly, the conferral of powers on the Council may best be characterised as a collective conferral of powers (cf. Sarooshi, *Supra*. n.2, pp.25–29.

The competence of States to make such collective conferrals relies on the proposition that the powers which can be exercised—and hence conferred—by the collective totality of sovereign States is greater than the sum of the individual powers of these States. This proposition finds a parallel in domestic law-making procedures. Members of the US Congress, for example, cannot make law individually. However, when all the Members are constituted as Congress they can, subject of course to constitutional limitations, exercise a law-making power. Similarly, the argument runs, when the international community—the majority of States—acts then it can confer powers on an international organization which sovereign States acting individually could not. However the obvious difficulty in using the domestic law-making analogy to justify a collective conferral of power by States on an organization is that in the domestic sphere the collective decision of members of a national parliament creates law because a domestic constitution—a basic grundnorm—says that it does; while in the sphere of international law the existence of such a grundnorm is not so readily apparent. Nonetheless it may have been this type of approach that was being implicitly adopted by the International Court of Justice when discussing the international legal personality of the United Nations in the *Reparations* case. The Court stated: '. . . fifty States, representing the vast majority of the Members of the international community, had the power, in conformity with international law, to bring into being an entity possessing objective international personality, and not merely personality recognised by them alone . . . .' (*Reparations for Injuries suffered in the Service of the United Nations, ICJ* Reports, (1949), p.174 at p.185.) It seems clear that a State acting individually or in concert with a few other States could not confer such 'objective international personality' on an entity, but, according to the Court, the 'vast majority of the Members of the international community' do possess this power.

[14] Moreover, the type of conferral of power may be changed by the practice of an international organization such that it moves along our spectrum from one category into another. For example, an organization's powers may start out being a delegation but are then transformed over time by the organization into a transfer and then a cession. This process has been elegantly summarized by Ackerman who states in a discussion under the heading of 'I. Federalism: from Treaty to Constitution (and Vice Versa)' the following: 'In the standard case, a group of states delegates a set of functions to an embryonic center by means of a treaty. But this "treaty" turns out to be different from most. Member states find it increasingly difficult to evade the commands of the emergent center. By one means or another, the center seeks to establish that the "treaty" trumps subsequent inconsistent laws enacted by individual states on the periphery. If courts accept this view, the "treaty" begins to take on the status of a "constitution." When confronting an ordinary act of domestic legislation, judges begin to take it upon themselves to determine whether it is consistent with the overriding "treaty/constitution." If it is not, then it is not law, despite the efforts by

categories that are adjacent on our spectrum.[15] The categories in our typology provide, nonetheless, a useful analytical tool since the classification of a particular conferral of power as mainly being within one of the categories on our spectrum helps clarify the legal consequences that result from the conferral. These legal consequences include the following: When an international organization exercises a conferred power, does it do so on its own behalf or on behalf of the State? Whose legal relations are changed by the exercise of power: the State's or the organization's? And who is responsible for breaches of international law that may occur as a result of the organization's exercise of the conferred power: the State or the organization or both?[16] In order to illustrate these consequences, this present article will examine, by way of example, the first category in our proposed typology, an agency relationship that may flow from the conferral by a State or States of powers on an organization.[17] Before doing so, however, it is necessary to examine the processes by which States confer powers on international organizations.

III. The Processes by Which States Confer Powers on International Organizations

The main way States confer powers on an international organization is by concluding a treaty[18] that provides for such a

formerly sovereign states to free themselves from their obligations to the center. The (uncertain) transformation of a treaty into a constitution is at the center of the European Union today; it was also at the center of the American experience between the Revolution and the Civil War.' (Ackerman, B., 'The Rise of World Constitutionalism', *Virginia Law Review*, 83 (1997), p.771 at pp.775–6.)

[15] Moreover, an international organization will also have a wide variety of express powers conferred on it by States, and as such it is not possible to characterise all of the powers of any particular organization as falling within one of our categories. It is, accordingly, necessary to disaggregate the express powers of a particular organization and characterise each within our typology. This has the consequence that an organization will have a complex web of differing relationships with States that have conferred express powers of government depending on the type of conferral involved.

[16] As the ILC stated in the Report of its 54th Session: 'When States are responsible for an internationally wrongful act for which an international organization of which they are members is also responsible, it is necessary to inquire whether there is a joint or a joint and several responsibility or whether the member States' responsibility is only subsidiary.' ('Responsibility of International Organizations', ILC Report of its 54th Session (2002), Chapter VIII, para.479.)

[17] The author will consider in future research the remaining three categories in this typology of conferrals by States of powers on international organizations.

[18] Another, less utilized method, is by a State making a unilateral declaration that provides for such a conferral. It is generally accepted that a State can impose a legally binding obligation on itself to carry out a particular act by making a unilateral declaration. See *Legal Status of Eastern Greenland*, Rep Series A/B No 53, especially at pp.71–73; *Nuclear Tests* (Australia v France) [1974] ICJ Rep 253 especially at p.267, *Nuclear Tests* (New Zealand v France), [1974] ICJ Rep 457; Suy, E., *Les Actes juridiques unilatéraux en droit international public* (1962); De Visscher, P., 'Remarques sur l'évolution de la jurisprudence de la cour internationale de justice relative au fondement obligatoire de certains actes unilatéraux', in Makarczyk, J., ed., *Essays in International Law in Honour of Judge Manfred Lachs* (1984); Brownlie, *supra* n.3, pp.643–4; and the first, preliminary, report of the ILC Special Rapporteur on Unilateral Acts of States, A/CN.4/486 (1998)) And there is no reason why a State could not undertake in such a way to confer powers on an organization so long as the State itself possesses the power

conferral.[19] This obligation does not necessarily mean, however, that a State is precluded from being able to exercise the power in an individual capacity, nor that the State is necessarily bound by the organization's exercise of conferred power, nor in fact that the conferral is irrevocable by the State. These aspects of the conferral will depend on the *type* of conferral of power, a matter that has been considered in our typology of conferrals in Section II above. At this stage in our discussion, however, it is necessary to consider the two main treaty mechanisms by which one or more States can confer powers on an organization: by use of a constituent treaty or on a more *ad hoc* basis by use of a treaty that is separate from the constituent treaty.

1. The conferral of powers by constituent treaty

The International Court of Justice has affirmed that a constituent treaty can act as a mechanism for the conferral by States of express powers on an organization.[20] In the *WHO Advisory Opinion* case, the Court observed: 'The powers conferred on international organizations are normally the subject of an express statement in their constituent instruments.'[21] A constituent treaty is, however, a complex instrument and its function is not only to serve as a mechanism for the conferral by States of express powers on an organization.[22] This complexity does not prevent the constituent treaty from being characterised as a mechanism for the conferral of powers, but it does mean that international organizations and their constituent treaties cannot be analysed in a comprehensive

it is purporting to confer. (This latter requirement deriving from the general principle of law: *nemo dat quod non habet*: one cannot give what one does not possess. For application of this principle to another area of international law, the acquisition of title to territory, see, for example, the *Island of Palmas* case, 4 ILR 103, 104.)

Due, however, to the importance attached by States to the conferral of powers on international organizations, it is difficult to find examples of conferrals by means of the relatively informal and unclear process of making a unilateral declaration. Even where, however, a State does purport to confer powers on an organization by unilateral declaration, the conferral only becomes legally effective once it has been accepted by the organization in question. (On the necessity for such acceptance and on the methods of acceptance by means other than the organization concluding a treaty with the conferring State, see *infra* nn.27–34 and corresponding text.)

[19] On the competence of States to confer powers on international organizations, see *supra* nn. 5–6 and corresponding text.

[20] Often, however, the conferral of powers that takes place through a constituent treaty involves a collective, rather than an individual, conferral of powers by States: on this distinction, see *supra* nn.12–13 and corresponding text.

[21] *Legality of the Threat or Use of Nuclear Weapons, Advisory Opinion, ICJ Reports*, 1996, para.25.

[22] As the ICJ has recognized in its case-law, constituent treaties are more complex in nature than other treaties. In the *WHO Advisory Opinion* case, the Court held: 'But the constituent instruments of international organizations are also treaties of a particular type; their object is to create new subjects of law endowed with a certain autonomy, to which the parties entrust the task of realizing common goals. Such treaties can raise specific problems of interpretation owing, *inter alia*, to their character which is conventional and at the same time institutional; the very nature of the organization created, the objectives which have been assigned to it by its founders, the imperatives associated with the effective performance of its functions, as well as its own practice, are all elements which may deserve special attention when the time comes to interpret these constituent treaties.' (*Legality of the Threat or Use of Nuclear Weapons, Advisory Opinion, ICJ Reports*, 1996, para.19.)

fashion by focusing only on the conferral by States of express powers on organizations.[23]

One or more States may also purport to confer additional powers on an organization on an *ad hoc* basis by use of a treaty that is separate from the constituent treaty. In the case of such purported conferrals of power, the main issue that arises is whether the treaty actually contains a substantive conferral of power.[24] This enquiry is necessary since a treaty

[23] Two examples suffice to illustrate the point. First, the constituent treaty of an organization may exhibit certain constitutional characteristics which do not result directly from the conferral of express powers by States. See, for example, Sato, T., *Evolving Constitutions of International Organizations: A Critical Analysis of the Interpretative Framework of the Constituent Instruments of International Organizations* (1996), p.230. It is beyond the scope of our present discussion to examine this issue in any detail, but suffice to note that even in the case of the two most prominent international organizations—the UN and the EC—whose founding treaties would be leading contenders for being characterised as constitutional documents, there has been a vigorous, largely inconclusive, debate about their possible constitutional natures. On the possible characterization of the UN Charter as a constitution, see the statement by the representative of the US Government in the oral proceedings in the*Expenses* case, *Pleadings, Oral Arguments, Documents*, 1962, p.413 at p.427; Crawford, J., 'The Charter of the United Nations as a Constitution', in Fox, H., ed., *The Changing Constitution of the United Nations* (1997), p.3; Simma, B., 'From Bilateralism to Community Interest in International Law', *Recueil des cours*, 250 (1994-VI), p.209 at pp.258–62; Franck, T., 'The 'Powers of Appreciation': Who is the Ultimate Guardian of UN Legality', (Editorial Comment), *AJIL*, 86 (1992), p.519 at p.521; and Reisman, W.M., 'The Constitutional Crisis in the United Nations', *AJIL*, 87 (1993), p.83. But cf. Arangio-Ruiz, G., ''The Federal Analogy' and UN Charter Interpretation: A Crucial Issue', *EJIL*, 8 (1997), p.1. On the possible constitutional character of the EC, see, for example, the ECJ case, *Parti Ecologiste, 'Les Verts' v European Parliament*, Case 294/83, [1986] *ECR* 1339 at 1365; Weiler, *supra* n.1, p.12; Lenaerts, K., 'Constitutionalism and the Many Faces of Federalism', *American Journal of Comparative Law*, 38 (1990), p.205; Barendt, E., *An Introduction to Constitutional Law* (1998), pp.69–85; and Mancini, G., 'The Making of a Constitution for Europe', *Common Market Law Review*, 26 (1989), p.595. Cf., however, Schilling, T., 'The Anatomy of the Community Legal Order: An Analysis of Possible Foundations', *Harvard International Law Journal*, 37 (1996), p.389.

Our second example is that the powers of an international organization are not restricted to those which are expressly conferred by Member States, since the generally accepted view is that international organizations also possess implied powers. As the Court in the *WHO Advisory Opinion* stated: 'Nevertheless, the necessities of international life may point to the need for organizations, in order to achieve their objectives, to possess subsidiary powers which are not expressly provided for in the basic instruments which govern their activities. It is generally accepted that international organizations can exercise such powers, known as implied powers.' (*Legality of the Threat or Use of Nuclear Weapons, Advisory Opinion, ICJ Reports*, 1996, para.25.) On this doctrine of implied powers, see also *Reparation for Injuries Suffered in the Service of the United Nations* case, [1949] ICJ Rep 174 at pp.180, 182; and, from the voluminous literature, see Klabbers, J., *An Introduction to International Institutional Law* (2002), pp.67–75, and Schermers, H., and Blokker, N., *International Institutional Law* (1995, 3rd ed.), pp.158–63. Cf., however, the dissenting opinion of Judge Hackworth in the *Reparations* case who used a narrow theory of delegation of powers to find that the powers of the UN could only be implied from those powers expressly stipulated in the Charter and not from the functions or object and purpose of the Organization: *Reparation for Injuries Suffered in the Service of the United Nations* case, [1949] ICJ Rep 174 at p.198.

[24] In cases where a treaty does contain a substantive *ad hoc* conferral of power on an organization, there is an additional issue of *vires* that will require consideration: Does the organization possess the competence to exercise the specific conferred power under its constituent treaty? As Judge Lauterpacht stated in the *Voting Procedure* case concerning the conferral by States of powers on the UN: '. . . in the case of the United Nations, whether the action is taken in pursuance of the objects of [the] organization, or in pursuance of a function accepted under some extraneous instrument such as a treaty. Such function must in any case lie within the orbit of its competence as laid down in the Charter. For the organization cannot accept the fulfilment of a task which lies outside the scope of its functions as determined by its constitution.' (*South-West Africa-Voting Procedure* case [1955] ICJ Rep 67 at p.109.) This situation can be contrasted with the case of a conferral of power by constituent treaty in which case the organization is, from an internal (organizational) point of view, always empowered to exercise the powers in question.

purporting to confer powers on an *ad hoc* basis may in substance represent nothing more than either a request to the organization to exercise its existing power in a particular situation or the proffering of consent by the State in cases where such consent is necessary for the organization to be able to exercise an express or implied power that it already possesses.

2. *The conferral of powers on an ad hoc basis*

There have been a number of cases where a group of States have concluded a treaty between themselves providing for the conferral of power on an organization on an *ad hoc* basis.[25] When States ratify such a treaty they bind themselves to confer the stipulated powers on the organization. However, the organization is not usually a party to such treaties[26] and this raises the issue of the acceptance by an organization of conferred powers,

[25] Consider, for example, the Peace Treaty between Italy and the UK, US, France, and the Former USSR (the latter four States being known as the 'Four Powers') that conferred on the Four Powers the power to decide on the future of the Italian Colonies in Africa, but which in Annex XI(3) provided that if the Four Powers could not agree within one year of the entry into force of the Treaty then the power of decision was to be given to the UN General Assembly: *UNTS*, vol.49, p.3 at p.215. In the event the Four Powers could not agree and the conferral of power was accepted by the General Assembly when it adopted the following resolutions concerning the territories: 289 (IV) of 21 Nov. 1949; 387 (V) of 17 Nov. 1950 (Libya); 390 (V) of 2 Dec. 1950 (Eritrea); 442 (V) of 2 Dec. 1950 (Somalia); 515 (VI) of 1 Feb. 1952 (Libya); 617 (VII) of 17 Dec. 1952 (Eritrea); and 1418 (XIV) of 5 Dec. 1959 (Somalia). For a convenient summary of the discussion which took place in the UN concerning the use of the power, see: *UNYB, 1948–1949*, pp.256–79; *UNYB, 1950*, pp.345–73; and, specifically, in the cases of Libya (*UNYB, 1951*, pp.266–77) and Eritrea (*UNYB, 1951*, pp.277–85, and *UNYB, 1952*, pp.262–6). For analysis of the conferral of power see Crawford, J., *The Creation of States in International Law* (1979), pp.330–2, Vallat, F., 'The Competence of the United Nations General Assembly', *Recueil des cours*, 97 (1959-II), p.207 at pp.229–30, and Sloan, B., 'General Assembly Resolutions Revisited (Forty Years Later)', this *Year Book*, 58 (1987), p.39 at pp.61–2; and for a review and analysis of much of the State practice of *ad hoc* conferrals of a power of territorial disposition onto international organizations and the competence of, in particular, the UN to exercise these powers, see Crawford, *ibidem*, pp.323–33. For examples of cases where States conferred such a power of disposition on the League of Nations Council, see the *Treaty of Lausanne (Frontier between Turkey and Iraq)* case (1925) PCIJ Rep series B No 12 at pp. 27–8. See also the *ad hoc* conferral of governmental powers on the UN by treaty in the cases of Western Sahara and Cambodia (see *infra* nn.31, 43, respectively).

There has also been a significant practice of a State conferring powers on an *ad hoc* basis to another State or States. For an example of the conferral of sovereign powers between States, consider the case concerning *Rights of Nationals of the United States of America in Morocco*, where the International Court referred to and interpreted the treaties concerned with the establishment of the protectorate, in particular the Treaty of Fez of 1912 between the Sultan of Morocco and France and stated: 'Under this Treaty, Morocco remained a sovereign State but it made an arrangement of a contractual character whereby France undertook to exercise certain sovereign powers in the name and on behalf of Morocco, and, in principle, all of the international relations of Morocco'. (*Rights of Nationals of the United States of America in Morocco* [1952] ICJ Rep 188.) See also for further examples of inter-State delegations Sereni, A., 'Agency in International Law', *AJIL*, 34 (1940), p.638; and for a review and analysis of the practice where a State that has territorial sovereignty over a territory decides to confer on a group of other States the power to decide on the future status of the territory, see Crawford, *ibidem*, pp.308, 313–15.

[26] This does not of course preclude the conclusion of a treaty between States and an organization that provides for the conferral of powers. Such a treaty would be governed by the 1986 Vienna Convention on the Law of Treaties between States and International Organizations or between International Organizations: on this Convention see Gaja, G., 'A "New" Vienna Convention on Treaties between States and International Organizations or between International Organizations: A Critical Commentary', this *Year Book*, 58 (1987), p.253.

an issue which is part of the broader question of when can a substantive conferral of power on an *ad hoc* basis be said to have taken place.

The role of an organization's reaction to a conferral of powers

It is a requirement that an international organization must accept a purported conferral of power by States for the conferral to have legal effect. Article 34 of the 1969 Vienna Convention on the Law of Treaties provides that a 'treaty [between States] does not create either obligations or rights for a third State without its consent.' This general rule is applicable *mutatis mutandis* to the case of an international organization which is a third party to a treaty between States, since the rule exists as part of customary international law[27] and as such is applicable to international organizations.[28] Application of this general rule in our case means that a treaty between States which purports to confer powers on an organization does not have this effect without the consent of the organization.[29] The expression of this consent by the international organization may take a variety of forms depending on the type of organ of the organization which accepts the conferral.[30] For example, in the case of a deliberative organ the adoption of a resolution accepting the conferral may be appropriate;[31] while in the case of the Secretariat (usually represented

[27] On the customary nature of the principle in Article 34 see Jennings and Watts, *supra* n.5, pp.1260–1 and the citations to International Court of Justice decisions and the ILC debates contained in n.3.

[28] On the applicability of Article 34 to international organizations see Chinkin, C., *Third Parties in International Law* (1993), pp.11–12. This view is, moreover, supported by the reproduction of the rule, *mutatis mutandis*, in Article 34 of the 1986 Vienna Convention on the Law of Treaties between States and International Organizations or between International Organizations.

For the more general principle that international organizations are subject to international law (and thus, among other sources, customary international law), see *Interpretation of the Agreement of 25 March 1951 between the WHO and Egypt*, [1980], ICJ Rep 89–90; Higgins, R., *Problems and Process: International Law and How We Use It* (1994), p.46; and Thirlway, H., 'The Law and Procedure of the International Court of Justice 1960–1989, Part Eight', this *Year Book*, 67 (1996), p.1 at pp.12–19.

[29] However, this requirement of consent does not exist in the case of the constituent treaty of an international organization even though the organization is in law a third party to the constituent treaty (Chinkin, *supra* n.28, p.12) due to the nature of the special relationship of the organization to its constituent treaty (Chinkin, *ibidem*, p.12; and McNair, A., *The Law of Treaties* (1961), pp.259–71.)

The requirement of acceptance would though be necessary in the case of a unilateral declaration by a State that purports to confer powers on an organization.

[30] Cf., however, Article 36 which stipulates that in the case of a conferral by treaty of a right on a third State, the assent of the third State 'shall be presumed so long as the contrary is not indicated, unless the treaty otherwise provides'. If a conferral by States of power on an international organization can be equated, by analogy, with the conferral by States of a right on a third party—a proposition about which this author is at best uncertain—then it could alternatively be argued that there is no need for the indication of a clear intention by an organ of an organization that it has accepted a conferral of power.

[31] Consider the following three examples: First, the acceptance by the UN General Assembly in its resolutions of the delegation of power concerning the Italian colonies in Africa (see *supra* n.25). Second, the acceptance by the UN Security Council in resolution 745 of the delegation of power from the Paris Peace Accords concerning Cambodia (see *infra* n.43). Third, the acceptance by the UN Security Council of the conferral by Morocco and the Frente POLISARIO (although of course the only State involved was Morocco) of governmental powers on the UN Secretary-General and his Special Representative in order to conduct a referendum in Western Sahara. The exercise of these powers was carried out with the approval and support of the UN Security Council which adopted the

by a Secretary-General) a unilateral act or declaration[32] may be more appropriate.[33] In any case, however, it is not the form that is decisive, but rather the indication of a clear intention by the organ concerned that it has accepted the conferral of power.[34]

However, even where an organization may seem to have accepted a purported conferral of power, this does not mean that a substantive conferral will always have taken place. The reason for this is that the powers the States are purporting to confer by treaty on an *ad hoc* basis may already be those an organization possesses under its constituent treaty. Put differently, a substantive conferral of powers on an *ad hoc* basis only takes place when the powers purporting to be conferred are those which the organization does not otherwise possess under its constituent treaty. The determination as to whether this is the case will largely depend on the reaction of the organ on whom powers are purportedly being conferred. For example, an organ may make it clear in responding to a conferral that it is being given a power that it did not otherwise possess under its constituent treaty. This determination by an organ of the scope of its powers will, in the absence of review by a body which has jurisdiction to decide such a matter, certainly prevail over the interpretation of States purporting to confer powers on an organ of an organization.[35]

following resolutions: 621 (1988), 658 (1990), 690 (1991), 725 (1991), 809 (1993), 907 (1994), 973 (1995), 995 (1995), 1002 (1995), 1017 (1995), 1042 (1996), 1056 (1996), 1084 (1996), 1108 (1997), 1131 (1997), 1133 (1997), 1148 (1998), 1163 (1998), 1185 (1998), 1198 (1998), 1204 (1998), 1215 (1998), 1224 (1998), 1228 (1998), 1232 (1999), 1235 (1999), and 1238 (1999).

[32] The legally binding nature of these acts or declarations is akin to that of a unilateral act or declaration by a State under international law, which, if it was the State's intention, may impose a legally binding obligation on the State. The reason why such unilateral declarations may bind a State applies equally to the case of an international organization. In the context of a State, the International Court in the *Nuclear Tests* cases held: 'One of the basic principles governing the creation and performance of legal obligations, whatever their source, is the principle of good faith. . . . Just as the very rule of *pacta sunt servanda* in the law of treaties is based on good faith, so also is the binding character of an international obligation assumed by unilateral declaration. Thus interested States may take cognisance of unilateral declarations and place confidence in them, and are entitled to require that the obligation thus created be respected.' (*Nuclear Tests (New Zealand v France)* [1974] ICJ Rep 268.) There is no reason why an international organization—which like a State often possesses international legal personality and the competence to accept binding obligations under international law—should not similarly be bound by such unilateral declarations. This approach of treating an international organization in an analogous manner to a State when acting to accept binding obligations under international law is reflected in the 1986 Vienna Convention on the Law of Treaties between States and International Organizations or between International Organizations which 'generally assimilates international organizations to States' for the purposes of determining when an international organization has expressed its consent to be bound by an international agreement. (Gaja, *supra* n.26, p.258)

For an interesting application of this type of approach, see Lowe, V., 'Can the European Community Bind the Member States on Questions of Customary International Law?', in Koskenniemi, M., ed., *International Law Aspects of the European Union* (1998), p.149.

[33] In both cases, however, the relevant organ of the organization would need to possess the required competence under its constituent treaty in order to adopt such decisions.

[34] This is subject, however, to the form being consistent with the processes of lawful decision-making as specified in the practice and constituent treaty of the particular international organization.

[35] This locus of authoritative decision-making within an organization flows from the principle expounded by the International Court of Justice in the *Expenses* case that 'each organ must, in the first place at least, determine its own jurisdiction.' (*Expenses* case [1962] ICJ Rep 151, 168.)

The proper characterization of a purported conferral of powers is of practical importance, since where there is a substantive *ad hoc* conferral then the conferring States can arguably impose constraints on the organization's exercise of the conferred power. While in the case where there is no substantive conferral of power on an *ad hoc* basis then the States parties to the treaty in question cannot seek to control or impose any limitations on the exercise by the organization of its power, since this is a matter governed solely by the constituent treaty.

This important difference can be illustrated, for example, by reference to cases where the response of the UN Security Council to a purported *ad hoc* conferral of power was to utilize its own powers under Chapter VII of the Charter rather than taking up the purported conferral that was on offer. This occurred, for example,[36] in the case where the UN Security

[36] Another example of this is provided by the Dayton Peace Agreement that was concluded between three States of the former Yugoslavia and which appeared, at least arguably, to confer powers on the UN Security Council in order to ensure the implementation of the terms of the Agreement. Article 1(1)(a) of Annex 1-A to the Dayton Peace Agreement *invited* the Security Council, 'to adopt a resolution by which it will authorise Member States or regional organisations and arrangements to establish a multinational military Implementation Force (hereinafter 'IFOR'). The Parties understand and agree that this Implementation Force may be composed of ground, air and maritime units from NATO and non-NATO nations, deployed to Bosnia and Herzegovina to help ensure compliance with the provisions of this Agreement (hereinafter 'Annex'). . . .' The Security Council accepted the invitation of the Parties to establish a force (IFOR) to ensure implementation of the Agreement when, in resolution 1031, the Council, acting under Chapter VII of the Charter, decided to authorise 'the Member States acting through or in cooperation with the organization referred to in Annex 1-A of the Peace Agreement [NATO] to establish a multinational implementation force (IFOR) under unified command and control in order to fulfil the role specified in Annex 1-A and Annex 2 of the Peace Agreement'. The resolution then stated that the Council '[a]uthorizes the Member States acting under paragraph 14 above to take all necessary measures to effect the implementation of and to ensure compliance with Annex 1-A of the Peace Agreement, stresses that the parties shall be held equally responsible for compliance with that Annex, and shall be equally subject to such enforcement action by IFOR as may be necessary to ensure implementation of that Annex and the protection of IFOR, and takes note that the parties have consented to IFOR's taking such measures'.

Article 1 of Annex 1-A stipulates that the objectives of the Peace Agreement are to establish a durable cessation of hostilities; provide for the 'support and authorization of the IFOR and in particular to authorize the IFOR to take such actions as required, including the use of necessary force, to ensure compliance with this Annex, and to ensure its own protection'; and to establish lasting security and arms control measures as outlined in Annex 1-B to the General Framework Agreement. The objectives for which IFOR could use force against the parties to the Agreement subsequently became, however, the point of contention between Russia and other members of the Security Council. The Russian representative stated in the Council that the Member States participating in IFOR were authorized to do only what the parties had agreed to. (S/PV.3607, p.25.) This position conceives of the States parties to the Dayton Agreement as conferring on the Council—and its delegate, IFOR—the power to take military enforcement action against them when one of their number breaches the obligations specified in the Agreement. This is, however, a clear misconception of the legal position. The Security Council possesses under Article 42 of the Charter a power to order military enforcement to be taken against a State or an entity within a State; obviously without the need for the consent of those who are to be subject to such action. In the case of the Dayton Agreement, it was clear that once the Security Council had adopted, 'acting under Chapter VII of the Charter', resolution 1031, then the Council considered that it was exercising its own powers and not a power conferred by the States parties to the Agreement. As such, the Council was not constrained 'to do only what the Bosnian sides agreed to', since the authority of the Council did not derive from the Agreement but from its own powers under Chapter VII of the Charter which in the area of military enforcement action does not require the consent of a target State. Accordingly, the inclusion of the reference in resolution 1031 to the 'parties have consented to IFOR's taking such measures' was for political not legal reasons. The mention of State consent in the resolution was of no legal consequence.

Council—more specifically a UN subsidiary organ established by the Council, the UN Transitional Authority for Eastern Slavonia, Baranja and Western Sirmium—exercised governmental powers over these areas of the territory of the Republic of Croatia.

An agreement (the 'Basic Agreement') was signed between the Government of the Republic of Croatia and the local authorities of Serbian ethnic origin in Eastern Slavonia on 12 November 1995[37] with the intention of providing for the peaceful re-integration of the region comprising Eastern Slavonia, Baranja, and Western Sirmium into the Croatian legal and constitutional system following four years of armed conflict between the Croatian Government and the local Serbs.[38] The parties agreed in paragraph 2 of the Basic Agreement that during a transitional period, initially of 12 months, that a UN Transitional Authority would govern the region in the interest of persons resident in or returning to the region.[39] Moreover, the parties requested that the Transitional Authority seek to achieve the following specific objectives: to demilitarise the parties which 'shall include all military forces, weapons and police, except for the international force and for police operating under the supervision of, or with the consent of, the Transitional Administration'; to facilitate the 'return of refugees and displaced persons to their homes of origin'; to 'take the steps necessary to re-establish the normal functioning of all public services in the region without delay'; to 'establish and train temporary police forces'; and to organize 'elections for all local government bodies, including for municipalities, districts and counties'.[40]

The parties provided that the Basic Agreement would enter into force 'upon the adoption by the UN Security Council of a resolution responding affirmatively to the requests made in this agreement.' The Security Council in resolution 1037 'acting under Chapter VII of the Charter of the United Nations,' decided 'to establish for an initial period of 12 months a United Nations peace-keeping operation for the Region referred to in the Basic Agreement, with both military and civilian components, under the name "United Nations Transitional Administration for Eastern Slavonia, Baranja and Western Sirmium" (UNTAES)' and further 'Request[ed] the Secretary-General to appoint, in consultation with the parties and with the Security Council, a Transitional Administrator, who will have overall authority over the civilian and military components of UNTAES, and who will exercise the authority

[37] Contained in S/1995/951, Annex.

[38] See 'Report of the Secretary-General pursuant to Security Council resolutions 981 (1995), 982 (1995) and 983 (1995)', S/1995/987, para.29; and 'Report of the Secretary-General pursuant to Security Council resolution 1025 (1995)', S/1995/1028, para.6.

[39] See S/1995/951, Annex, p.2.

For a useful analysis of the exercise of a power of arrest by the UN Transitional Administration (UNTAES) to assist the work of the International Criminal Tribunal for the former Yugoslavia, see Lamb, S., 'The Powers of Arrest of the International Criminal Tribunal for the former Yugoslavia', this *Year Book*, 69 (1999), p.165 at pp.181–6.

[40] S/1995/951, Annex, p.2.

given to the Transitional Administration in the Basic Agreement'. The express reference by the Council to its Chapter VII powers is important, since it means that the Council is exercising governmental powers over parts of Croatian territory using its Charter powers, and not as a consequence of governmental powers being conferred on it by the Republic of Croatia—the only party to the Basic Agreement which was a State.

This characterization of the legal basis for the exercise of powers was to prove controversial but important when determining whether it was Croatia or the UN Security Council that had the power to terminate the activities being carried out by UNTAES.

Following the successful holding of elections in the region by UNTAES, the UN Transitional Administrator developed a two-phase 'exit strategy' which was described by the UN Secretary-General in the following terms: 'In the first phase, the Transitional Administrator would devolve to Croatia executive responsibility for the major part of civil administration of the region while maintaining his authority and ability to intervene and overrule decisions should the situation deteriorate and the achievements of UNTAES be threatened. The pace of devolution would be commensurate with Croatia's demonstrated ability to reassure the Serb population and successfully complete peaceful reintegration. In the second phase, and subject to satisfactory Croatian performance, remaining executive functions would be devolved, with Croatia assuming responsibility for the continued demilitarisation of the region and the gradual integration of the Transitional Police Force into the Croatian police force.'[41] This position was endorsed in express terms by the Security Council in resolution 1120. The Council, moreover, decided in resolution 1120 to extend the mandate of UNTAES for a further six months until 15 January 1998. This resolution was adopted despite the strong objections of Croatia who argued that UNTAES should at this time be immediately terminated and that powers of government be resumed immediately by Croatia. The fact of its adoption by the Security Council confirmed that the establishment and operation of UNTAES was an exercise by the Council of its own Chapter VII powers and not pursuant to the exercise of powers conferred by Croatia on an *ad hoc* basis. This control by the Council was further reiterated when it decided in resolution 1145 of 15 January 1998 to terminate UNTAES, the Council alone having decided that UNTAES had now fulfilled its mandate.[42]

To conclude, a treaty that purports to confer on an organization a power that it already possesses under its constituent treaty will not, in general terms,[43] have the intended legal effect. Such a treaty may usefully

[41] S/1997/487, 23 June 1997, para.48. See also S/1997/767, 2 October 1997, para.3.

[42] See the statement by the President of the Security Council on behalf of the Council: S/PRST/1998/3, 13 February 1998.

[43] There is, however, a possible exception to this general position that a substantive conferral of powers only takes place when the powers purporting to be conferred are those which the organization

be characterized as a request to the organization to exercise its power in a particular situation or even as the proffering of consent by the State in

does not possess under its constituent treaty. This exception is where the organ of an organization, although possessing the powers being conferred, chooses instead to take up the conferral using a general competence to do so under its constituent treaty rather than treating the purported conferral as an invitation to use its existing, specific, powers. This choice is not simply a matter of semantics. It may have the important practical consequence that the States conferring power can impose constraints on the exercise of power by the organization. A good example of this is provided by the practice of the UN Security Council where it has in certain cases chosen to accept a conferral of power that would seem to fall within the scope of its powers under Chapter VII thereby constraining itself to exercise the power subject to the terms and conditions of the particular conferral.

A specific instance of this occurred in relation to the case of Cambodia where there was an *ad hoc* conferral of broad powers of internal governance on the UN through the Paris Peace Accords (the 'Accords') (The Paris Conference concluded the following four Accords: the Final Act of the Paris Conference on Cambodia (*ILM*, 31 (1992), p.180); the Agreement on a Comprehensive Political Settlement of the Cambodia Conflict (*ILM*, 31 (1992), p.183); the Agreement Concerning the Sovereignty, Independence, Territorial Integrity and Inviolability, Neutrality and National Unity of Cambodia (*ILM*, 31 (1992), p.200); and the Declaration on the Rehabilitation and Reconstruction of Cambodia (*ILM*, 31 (1992), p.203))

The Accords created a Supreme National Council that was defined as the 'unique legitimate body and source of authority in which, throughout the transitional period, the sovereignty, independence and unity of Cambodia are enshrined'. (The Agreement on a Comprehensive Political Settlement of the Cambodia Conflict (Comprehensive Settlement Agreement), Articles 3 and 5, *ibidem*. Security Council resolution 668 (1990) confirmed this sovereign nature of the Supreme National Council.) The Accords went on to stipulate that the Supreme National Council 'delegates to the United Nations all powers necessary to ensure the implementation of this Agreement'. (Comprehensive Settlement Agreement, *ibidem*, Article 6.) Accordingly, Article 2 of the Accords invited the Security Council to create the United Nations Transitional Authority in Cambodia (UNTAC) 'with civilian and military components under the direct responsibility of the Secretary-General of the United Nations', 'to provide UNTAC with the mandate set forth in this Agreement,' and 'to keep its implementation under continuing review'. (*Ibidem*, Article 2.) The Security Council accepted this conferral of power and established UNTAC by resolution 745 in 1992. The Security Council in establishing UNTAC was, arguably, exercising powers conferred on it by the Paris Peace Accords and was not acting pursuant to its own Chapter VII powers, since there was no express reference in resolution 745 to Chapter VII. (It is the consistent practice of the Council to make such a reference in cases where it is using its Chapter VII powers.) Moreover as Ratner, in the case of Cambodia, has observed:

> If the United Nations were to administer Cambodia, under generally accepted interpretations of the Charter an entity authorized to represent Cambodia would need to delegate power to the Organization or otherwise indicate Cambodia's consent to the operation; or, alternatively, the Security Council would have to approve enforcement action under chapter VII to restore international peace and security in Southeast Asia. The latter option, however, never received serious consideration owing to the Council's unwillingness to impose a large UN presence on Cambodia without any agreement by the factions, especially in view of the Council's reluctance to invoke chapter VII before the Persian Gulf war. In the absence of a single government accepted by all states as politically legitimate and legally able to delegate power, the idea emerged of a Supreme National Council that would include representatives from all the factions and serve as a unique and legitimate source of authority. (Ratner, S., 'The Cambodia Settlement Agreements', *AJIL*, 87 (1993), p.1 at pp.9–10.)

As such, the Security Council was always careful to ensure that UNTAC did not exceed the mandate conferred on it by the Paris Peace Accords: thus, for example, in resolution 840 the Council requested UNTAC to 'continue to play its role in conjunction with the Supreme National Council during the transitional period in accordance with the Paris Agreements.' Moreover, UNTAC was required to comply with certain directions (what was inaccurately termed as 'advice') of the Supreme National Council. As Ratner has observed: 'the body of the Agreement and the annex include details on the authority of UNTAC, with respect to its relationships to the SNC [Supreme National Council] and the governments in place and to the tasks that it should perform, i.e., the depth and breadth of its power. The depth of UNTAC's authority is described in the annex by the following scheme: UNTAC must comply with any advice from the SNC on any aspect of the cases where such consent is necessary for the organization to be able to exercise its power, but it should not, in general terms, be characterized as a substantive conferral of power.[44] In the example discussed above, however, even this consent was not needed, since the UN Security Council does not require the consent of States to exercise its Chapter VII powers. As such, the Basic Agreement represented no more than a request to the Council to exercise its Chapter VII powers.

Let us now turn to examine the characteristics and consequences of the first category in our typology which is also the starting point on our spectrum: an agency relationship that may flow from the conferral by a State or States of powers on international organizations.

IV. Agency Relationships between States and International Organizations

An agency relationship is the only category in our typology that also exists as a distinct legal concept under international law.

The existence of agency relationships under international law have been recognised by the International Court of Justice,[45] the International

settlement if (1) the SNC is acting unanimously when it gives its views or, in the absence of unanimity, Prince Sihanouk, as President of the Council, provides the advice on the Council's behalf, "taking fully into account" its members' views; and (2) the advice is "consistent with the objectives of the present Agreement" as determined by the chief of UNTAC, the Secretary-General's Special Representative.' (Ratner, *ibidem*, p.12.) Moreover, Matheson has stated that the exercise of governmental authority delegated by the Supreme National Council to UNTAC was 'limited by the requirement that UNTAC follow any "advice" approved by a consensus of the factions represented in the Supreme National Council, to the extent that it did not conflict with the Agreement.' (Matheson, M., 'United Nations Governance of Postconflict Societies', *AJIL*, 95 (2001), p.76 at p.77.). On UN territorial administration more generally, see also Wilde, R., 'From Danzing to East Timor and Beyond: the Role of International Territorial Administration', *AJIL*, 95 (2001), p.583.

[44] Similar issues arise concerning the role that State consent plays in the establishment and utilization by the Security Council of UN peace-keeping forces. The establishment and utilization of such forces by the UN Security Council represents the exercise by the Council of an implied power under Chapter VII of the Charter (Sarooshi, D., 'The Role of the United Nations Secretary-General in United Nations Peace-Keeping Operations', *Australian Yearbook of International Law*, 20 (1999), p.279 at pp.280–2) and not the exercise of a power conferred on it by States. However, the ICJ in the *Expenses* case held that UN peace-keeping operations are not military enforcement 'action' within the terms of Chapter VII. The consequence of this being that the deployment and utilization of a UN peace-keeping force is conditional on the consent of both the States contributing troops to the force and the host State where the force is to be deployed. (*Expenses case* [1962] ICJ Rep 165. See also on consent the report of the SG, A/3302, contained in Higgins, R., *United Nations Peacekeeping 1946–1967* (vol.1, 1969), p.263; Garvey, J., 'United Nations Peacekeeping and Host State Consent', *AJIL*, 64 (1970), p.241; and Di Blase, A., 'The Role of the Host State's Consent with Regard to Non-Coercive Actions by the United Nations', in Cassese, A., ed., *United Nations Peace-Keeping: Legal Essays* (1978), p.55.) It is important, however, not to confuse this consent requirement of States to contribute troops to a UN peace-keeping force (as contained in a Status of Forces Agreement) and of States to have the force stationed on their territory as being a conferral of power on the UN such that the States concerned can seek to control or specify limits on the use by the Council of its implied powers once their consent has been given. Cf. those cases where States have tried to exercise such control in the case of UN peace-keeping, see Sarooshi, *ibidem*, pp.288, 290–1, 295.

[45] See *infra* n.48 and *infra* nn.61–2, 67 and corresponding text.

Law Commission,[46] and authoritative commentators[47] in a number of different cases where in general a principal has empowered an agent to act on its behalf to change certain of its rights and duties.[48] What emerges from these cases is that international law recognizes the existence of an agency relationship, our specific form of empowerment, where two conditions are fulfilled. The first is where a principal and agent are separate legal entities; while the second is a dual consent requirement, both principal and agent have consented to the conferral on an agent of a power to act on the principal's behalf.

1. *Principal and agent as separate legal entities*

An important condition for the existence of an agency relationship in both international and domestic law[49] is that the principal and agent are

[46] See *infra* nn.57–60, 65 and corresponding text.

[47] Importantly, for present purposes, a number of authoritative commentators have argued that organizations can act as 'agent' on behalf of Member States and other States. James Crawford, for example, states: 'Plainly an international organization *can* act as the agent of one or more members.' (Crawford, J., as part of the work of the Commission of the Institut de Droit International, contained in 'Report by Rosalyn Higgins', *Annuaire de l'Institut de Droit International* ('*AIDI*'), 66-I (1995), p.334 Original emphasis.) Moreover, Ian Brownlie states 'By agreement between the states and the organization concerned, the latter may become an agent for member states, and others, in regard to matter outside its ordinary competence.' (Brownlie, *supra* n.3, p.690.) Similarly, Christine Chinkin states: 'Just as a State may act on behalf of another State or other legal entity, so too an organization might be seen as acting as agent for its member States.' (Chinkin, *supra* n.28, p.115.) See also Amerasinghe, C., in 'Report by Rosalyn Higgins' *AIDI*, 66-I (1995), p.353.

[48] Consider, by way of illustration, the following three examples: First, there is the case of international agency that exists between Switzerland and Liechtenstein where, under a series of treaties concluded after World War I, Switzerland assumed responsibility for the diplomatic and consular representation of Liechtenstein, the protection of its borders, and the regulation of its customs (1923 Treaty contained in *League of Nations Treaty Series*, Vol.XXI, p.243.) As Eduardo Jimenez de Aréchaga stated in the ILC: 'The 1923 Treaty between Switzerland and Liechtenstein . . . seemed to constitute a case of agency, in which one State entrusted another with the power to represent it not only for the purpose of concluding certain treaties, but also for the purpose of claiming rights under those treaties.' (*YBILC*, vol. I, 1964, 732nd mtg., p.56 (para.37)) Cf., however, the amendment on 2 November 1994 of the Customs Treaty dated 29 March 1923 between Liechtenstein and Switzerland in order to allow the participation of Liechtenstein in the EEA. (see Decision of the EEA Council No 1/95 of 10 March 1995 on the entry into force of the Agreement on the European Economic Area for the Principality of Liechtenstein, *Official Journal L 086*, 20/04/1995 pp.0058–0084.)

Second, the International Court of Justice in the *Rights of United States Nationals in Morocco* case found the existence of international agency as a result of a conferral of powers. The Court held: 'The rights of France in Morocco are defined by the Protectorate Treaty of 1912 . . . Under this Treaty, Morocco remained a sovereign State, but it made an arrangement of a contractual character whereby France undertook to exercise certain sovereign powers in the name and on behalf of Morocco, and, in principle, all the international relations of Morocco . . .' [1952] (ICJ Rep 176 at pp.185, 188.)

Finally, there are those cases where one State exercises diplomatic protection on behalf of the interests of the citizens of another State in accordance with a mandate conferred upon it by the latter State. For examples of this type of international agency, see Sereni, *supra* n.25.

[49] For example, the Israeli Supreme Court in the case of *Attorney-General of Israel v Kamiar* stated: 'The conferring of powers, to which section 2(d) refers, merely has as its object the delimitation of the sphere in which a given Minister is empowered to work, not "on behalf" of the Government, but as the Government. This is not a question of the delegation or transfer of powers, or of the authorization of an agent by his principal; but merely of a division of the functions of the Government between its members in such a manner that even after this division the functions remain the functions of the Government and the powers remain the powers of the Government.' (*The Attorney-General of Israel v Kamiar*, Supreme Court of Israel sitting as the Court of Criminal

separate legal entities.[50] This flows from the principle of representation inherent in an agency relationship: that an agent acts on behalf of its principal to change certain of its rights and obligations. In our case of a potential relationship of agency between an international organization and one or more States, if the organization does not possess a separate legal personality then the organization constitutes nothing more than an extension of the States concerned and thus when the organization acts it is nothing more than the States themselves acting.[51] It was this type of scenario that

Appeal, 9 June 1968, 44 ILR, 197 at p.249.) Similarly, the US Foreign Sovereign Immunities Act of 1976 in Section 1603(b) defines an 'agency or instrumentality of a foreign state' as constituting any entity: '(1) which is a separate legal person, corporate or otherwise, and (2) which is an organ of a foreign state or political subdivision thereof, or a majority of whose shares or other ownership interest is owned by a foreign state or political subdivision thereof . . . .' Concerning this first criterion of independence, a US District Court in the case of *Williams v The Shipping Corporation of India* adopted the House of Congress report on the Foreign Sovereign Immunities Act when it stated: 'The first criterion, that the entity be a separate legal person, is intended to include a corporation, association, foundation, or any other entity which, under the law of the foreign state where it was created, can sue or be sued in its own name, contract in its own name or hold property in its own name.' (*Williams v The Shipping Corporation of India*, US District Court, Eastern District Virginia, 10 March 1980, 63 ILR 363 at p.369.) See also the cases of *Edlow International Co. v Nuklearna Elektrarna Krsko*, District Court of Columbia, 7 December 1977, 63 ILR.101 at p.103; and *Dayton v Czechoslovak Socialist Republic*, US District Court of Columbia, 19 December 1986, 79 ILR 590 at p.596.

Moreover, this requirement of a separate legal personality is also an important prerequisite for a finding of responsibility. As Giorgio Gaja, the ILC Special Rapporteur on the responsibility of international organizations, states: 'For an organization to be held as potentially responsible it should not only have legal personality and thus some obligations of its own under international law. What is required is also that in the exercise of the relevant functions the organization may be considered as a separate entity from its members and that thus the exercise of these functions may be attributed to the organization itself.' (A/CN.4/532, para.27.)

[50] The separate identity of principal and agent does not mean, however, that in the case of an agency relationship between one or more States and an international organization that the former can be considered as having 'loaned' organs to the States concerned. An international organization with separate legal personality will continue, at least in formal terms (cf. the case of *de facto* control: *infra* n.66 and corresponding text *et sequentia*), to use its processes of decision-making even when it acts as an agent for States and exercises conferred powers. This issue was raised by ILC Special Rapporteur Crawford in his First Report on State Responsibility when he stated: 'There is no doubt that an organ of an international organization may perform governmental functions for or in relation to States, pursuant to "delegated" powers or even on the authority of the organ itself. But this does not necessarily mean that it is "loaned" to the States concerned, or that those States are responsible for its conduct. It seems clear, for example, that the various organs of the European Commission operating on the territory of the member States retain their Community character . . . . According to the Legal Office of the United Nations Secretariat, no United Nations operation, whether in the field of technical assistance, peacekeeping, election monitoring or in any other field, would involve "loaning" an organ to a State. In every case, the United Nations body would retain its separate identity and command structure.' (First Report on State Responsibility, A/CN.4/490/Add.5, 22 July 1998, para.231.)

[51] The likelihood of this scenario occurring is not as remote as may at first appear the case for the reason that relatively few constituent treaties provide explicitly for the international legal personality of organizations, (Klabbers, *supra* n.23, p.53) and that even where they do, as Klabbers notes, '[a]t best, the provisions are ambiguous, providing quite simply that the organization concerned "shall have legal personality" or similar terms.' (Klabbers, *supra* n.23, p.53. Klabbers continues on to state: 'Thus, e.g., Art. 281 (formerly Art. 210) TEC. Also not devoid from ambiguity is Art.XVI (1) of the FAO constitution, which holds that the FAO "shall have the capacity of a legal person to perform any legal act appropriate to its purpose which is not beyond the powers granted to it by this Constitution". Clearly limited to domestic legal personality are, *inter alia*, Art. 39 ILO, Art. 66 WTO, Art. 47 ICAO and Art. 95(2) Benelux.' (*Ibidem*.)) In cases where there is no express provision for the separate legal personality of an organization then it will be necessary to employ the functional test adopted by the

existed,[52] for example, in the case of the 'Administering Authority' in relation to Nauru, as expressly recognised by the International Court of Justice in the *Case concerning Certain Phosphate Lands in Nauru* when it stated that 'this Authority did not have an international legal personality distinct from those of the States thus designated'.[53]

2. *The existence of consent*

The necessity for, and emphasis on, consent as a prerequisite for the establishment of an agency relationship exists to a much greater extent in international law than it does in domestic legal systems.[54] In domestic legal systems, the operation of the law may remove the need for

International Court in the *Reparations* case where it ascertained the existence of the UN's separate legal personality from that of its Member States. (*Reparations for Injuries Suffered in the Service of the United Nations* case, [1949] ICJ Rep 174.) This situation is complicated further in the case where the legal personality of an international organization may not be recognized under the domestic laws of a State with the consequence that on the domestic plane a Court may refuse to recognize its separate legal personality from that of its Member States. This was the approach taken by the House of Lords in the case of *Arab Monetary Fund v Hashim (No. 3)* [1991] 2 WLR 729: see further Higgins, *supra* n.28, p.48.

[52] This type of scenario was discussed, but dismissed, in the International Tin Council [ITC] litigation in the English courts: see, for example, the House of Lords in *J.H. Rayner v Department of Trade and Industry and Others and Related Appeals*, [1990] 2 AC 418 at p.503, per Lord Oliver; and *Maclaine Watson v International Tin Council, Chancery Division*, [1988] Ch.1 at pp.15–16.

[53] *Case Concerning Certain Phosphate Lands in Nauru* [1992] ICJ Rep 240 at p.258 (para.47). This has the important consequence, as explained by ILC Special Rapporteur Crawford, that the issue of responsibility did not involve the acts of an international organization, but only those acts of 'the three States (Australia, New Zealand, United Kingdom) which together constituted the Administering Authority for the Trust Territory of Nauru.' ('Second Report on State responsibility', A/CN.4/498, Add. 1, para.160.)

[54] There are similarities between the international law concept of agency and its domestic law counterpart, but agency in international law cannot solely be equated with, or constructed by analogy from, its domestic counterpart for two main reasons.

First, the domestic law of agency is in the main concerned with the conferral of private law power; while in the context of international organizations it is a public law power being conferred by a State on an organization. This limitation of the use of private law analogies has also been recognised by some domestic public law systems. For example, in the English Courts it was held in the case of *Town Investments Ltd. v Environment Secretary* that the relationship between 'the Crown' and 'Ministers of the Crown' had to be analysed in public law terms and not by using private law concepts of agency and trust. (*Town Investments Ltd. v Environment Secretary*, [1978] AC 359).

Second, the domestic law of agency is largely directed at allocating, or rather balancing, commercial risk between business actors and thus its transplantation to public international law which concerns relations between sovereign States is problematic. (I am grateful to James Crawford for this point.)

These problems do not, however, prohibit in general terms recourse to the domestic law of agency, but they do mean that the concept as it appears in public international law may differ in content. For example, the notion of an undisclosed principal in the domestic law of agency has no application in the context of public international law, since, as Chinkin states, 'any such claim should be dismissed as contrary to the principle of openness in international relations, and the right of States to select their treaty partners.' (Chinkin, *supra* n.28, p.66.) Moreover, Sereni states 'Since international agency is intended to function with relation to third parties, it is necessary that they be informed of the extent of the authority conferred upon the agent. No special form is provided as to the way in which an agency relationship is to be made known to the third parties. . . . Every international transaction is so closely connected with the special characteristics and qualities of each subject involved that each of them must necessarily know the other parties to whom rights and duties are to be assumed. There is no place in international law for the doctrine of the undisclosed principal.' (Sereni, *supra* n.25, p.649.) Cf. also the caution espoused in this context by Shabtai Rosenne: *YILC*, vol.1, (1964), p.55 at para.26.

the consent of the principal to the establishment of certain agency relationships.[55] However, international law by contrast does not presume the acceptance by States of obligations without their consent.[56]

The essential role that a State's consent plays in establishing an agency relationship was highlighted by the work of the International Law Commission (ILC) on the Law of Treaties when it considered the possibility of one State acting as agent for, and concluding a treaty on behalf of, another State. This agency approach attracted criticism from within the ILC by Grigory Tunkin who argued that the concept of agency 'had in fact been used mainly in colonial practice, in connexion with protectorates',[57] and as such should be omitted from the ILC's Draft.[58] There was, however, strong opposition voiced by a number of ILC members in response to this critique. The ILC Chairman, Roberto Ago, held an opposing view:

> 45. . . . as the agency relationship was freely established between two States, the Commission should not express a favourable or an unfavourable opinion on that practice.[59]

[55] As Sereni states: '. . . this relationship [of agency in international law] must necessarily be based on an agreement between principal and agent. The consent of both parties is indispensable: without the principal's consent the agent has no authority, without the agent's consent the principal is unrepresented. Some domestic law systems have established, besides consensual agency, several types of agency immediately derived from law, independent of the consent of the parties or at least of the principal. These types of agency *ex lege* have been provided in order to allow certain individuals without the natural or legal capacity of acting, to enter into legal relations: e.g. the father's agency for the minor child or the guardian's for the insane. In international law there is no need for these types of so-called legal agency. By the mere fact of existence, every subject of international law is privileged to participate in international transactions in person, through its own organs. The principle is assumed that every international subject has the capacity to enter directly into international intercourse.' (Sereni, *supra* n.25, p.645.)

Nonetheless, also in domestic law, however, it is generally the case that both the agent and the principal must consent to the establishment of the agency relationship. See Reuschlein, H., and Gregory, W., *The Law of Agency and Partnership* (1990, 2nd ed.), p.86; Reynolds, F., *Bowstead and Reynolds on Agency* (1996, 16th ed.), Article 1; Fridman, G., *The Law of Agency* (1996, 7th ed.), pp.14–21; and Seavey, W., 'The Rationale of Agency', *Yale Law Journal*, 29 (1919–1920), p.868.

[56] Cheng states the more general point after reviewing relevant case-law: 'There is, therefore, a general legal principle applicable between States as well as between individuals to the effect that a person is only responsible for his own acts. The application of this principle—the principle of individual responsibility—in international law is fully demonstrated by the fact that States are only responsible for those acts which are, according to international law, imputable to them. *Any exception to this principle . . . cannot be presumed but must result from an express and unequivocal treaty stipulation or a clear legal provision.* Moreover . . . juridically such exceptions are mere obligations derived either from treaty stipulations or from positive law. They are modelled upon responsibility properly so-called, and are supplementary thereto. They in no way affect the nature or the validity of the principle of individual responsibility.' (B. Cheng, *General Principles of Law as applied by International Courts and Tribunals* (1987), pp.213–14. Emphasis added.)

Brownlie, moreover, emphasises the importance of State consent in the context of establishing an agency relationship between States and an international organization when he states: 'By agreement an organization may become an agent for member states, and others, in regard to matters outside its normal competence and a state may act as agent for an organization.' (Brownlie, I., *Principles of Public International Law*, (1990, 4th ed.), p.678.)

[57] *YILC*, 1964, vol.1, 732nd mtg. p.58, para.53.

[58] A lot of the discussion that ensued on this point was strongly affected by the fact that most of the examples concerned protectorates, and decolonization was in full flow at the time.

[59] *YILC*, 1964, vol.1, 732nd mtg. p.57, para.95. (Emphasis added.) Moreover, Roberto Ago continued on in the same meeting to state: 'But he could not agree with Mr Tunkin . . . the Commission's

Moreover, Eduardo Jimenez de Arechaga also stated in the ILC debates:

The Commission should not adopt a negative attitude to the legitimate institution of agency merely because it might have been used in the past to set up protectorates. . . . It should be remembered that representation by the operation of law did not exist in international law; the only form of representation was by virtue of a treaty. Any agency relationship which might be established would therefore be subject to the rules in Parts I and II of the draft articles. Such rules as those relating to free consent, nullity on grounds of coercion, *jus cogens*, the power of denunciation in certain circumstances, and determination for change of circumstances would apply in all cases. There would thus be ample safeguards to ensure that no State would in future, as had happened in the past, use the method of agency by treaty to set up a protectorate regime against the free will of the State represented.[60]

Both these statements emphasise the necessity of a State having to consent freely to an agency relationship in international law. This is the context within which the statement by Eduardo Jimenez de Arechaga—that agency was only possible by treaty—must be read. He was emphasising that an agency relationship could only be created with State consent—he says expressed in 'a treaty' because that was the specific focus of the ILC's work—as opposed to the creation of an agency relationship 'by the operation of law'. However, the role of State consent in establishing an agency relationship can be guaranteed by means other than requiring the conclusion of a treaty, and, moreover, consent need not be expressly provided for by a State. A State's consent may be implied from its statements or actions.

The *Iran–US Hostages* case before the International Court provides an example of a case where a State's consent to an agency relationship was implied from its statements. Moreover, this case also emphasises the necessity for State consent in order to establish an agency relationship, since the International Court resisted basing its finding of Iranian responsibility for the clearly illegal and heinous acts relating to the

draft would be incomplete if the idea expressed in that paragraph was omitted. It would seem strange if the Commission decided to rule out the possibility of concluding a treaty by agency. Agency could be a stable and permanent arrangement, as in the case of the Belgium-Luxembourg Economic Union; indeed, that was an example that could well be followed as an intermediate solution between independence and federation. Agency could also be occasional, and that was the case contemplated in paragraph 1 of article 60. Agency of that kind had always existed and had always been regarded as legitimate; the Commission could not overlook it.' (*YILC*, 1964, vol.1, 732nd mtg. p.59 at para.60.)

Roberto Ago went on to conclude in the following meeting of the ILC: 'First, with regard to paragraph 1 of article 60, it was quite true that the institution of agency was not so common in international law as it was in private law. Still, it existed in international law and its use was more widespread than was generally recognized. It was not the Commission's practice to consider only matters of common occurrence. At its last session it had even adopted an article on fraud, and cases of fraud in international practice were certainly much rarer than cases of agency. The Commission should therefore deal with the case of one State acting as agent for another, taking care, of course, to draft the article and the commentary in such a way as to avoid giving the impression that it approved of obsolete institutions.' (*YILC*, 1964, vol.1, 733rd mtg. p.63 at para.33.)

[60] *YILC*, 1964, vol.1, 733rd mtg. p.60 at para.5.

occupation of the US Embassy in Iran on an agency argument without evidence of Iranian Government consent to the establishment of such a relationship. As the Court stated:

58. No suggestion has been made that the militants, when they executed their attack on the Embassy, had any form of official status as recognized 'agents' or organs of the Iranian State. Their conduct in mounting the attack, overrunning the Embassy and seizing its inmates as hostages cannot, therefore, be regarded as imputable to that State on that basis. Their conduct might be considered as itself directly imputable to the Iranian State *only if it were established that, in fact, on the occasion in question the militants acted on behalf of the State, having been charged by some competent organ of the Iranian State to carry out a specific operation.* The information before the Court does not, however, suffice to establish with the requisite certainty the existence at that time of such a link between the militants and any competent organ of the State.[61]

However, the Court did go on to find the existence of the requisite consent for the establishment of an agency relationship from the subsequent statements by the Iranian Government that adopted the unlawful acts in question. The Court held:

74. The policy thus announced by the Ayatollah Khomeni, of maintaining the occupation of the Embassy and the detention of its inmates as hostages for the purpose of exerting pressure on the United States Government was complied with by other Iranian authorities and endorsed by them repeatedly in statements made in various contexts. The result of that policy was fundamentally to transform the legal nature of the situation created by the occupation of the Embassy and the detention of its diplomatic and consular staff as hostages. The approval given to these facts by the Ayatollah Khomeni and other organs of the Iranian State, and the decision to perpetuate them, translated continuing occupation of the Embassy and detention of the hostages into acts of that State. The militants, authors of the invasion and jailers of the hostages, had now become *agents of the Iranian State for whose acts the State itself was internationally responsible.*[62]

In other words, the Court posited that the necessary consent of the Iranian State for the establishment of an agency relationship with the militants was provided by the 'approval given to these facts by the Ayatollah Khomeni and other organs of the Iranian State, and the decision to perpetuate them'.

The remaining issue that deserves consideration is whether a State's consent to an agency relationship can be implied from its exercise of control over the acts of an entity such that the latter may be considered an

[61] *United States Diplomatic and Consular Staff in Tehran* case, [1980] ICJ Rep 3 at p.29. Emphasis added.

[62] *Ibidem*, p.35. Emphasis added. As Lady Fox has observed: 'At this point, then, the acts were transformed into acts of the Iranian State, the *militants became agents of the State*, which itself became "directly" responsible for their acts. The holding of the hostages was now an act of the State for which it was directly responsible according to international law.' (Fox, H., 'The International Court of Justice's Treatment of Acts of the State and in Particular the Attribution of Acts of Individuals to the State', in Ando, N., *et al.*, eds., *Liber Amicorum Judge Shigeru Oda* (2002), p.147 at p.152. Emphasis added.)

agent of the State? Control is not being put forward here as a necessary condition for the establishment of an agency relationship, but rather as sufficient for the establishment of a State's implied consent in a particular case. Control also, of course, plays a defining role in determining whose acts are attributable to a State under international law.[63] However it is important not to conflate these separate concepts of attribution and agency. An agent can act more broadly on behalf of a principal to change the latter's rights and duties; whereas attribution is only concerned with the more limited issue of deciding whose acts can a State be held responsible for under international law.[64]

A distinction between the concept of attribution and the broader concept of agency was hinted at early on in the work of James Crawford, the final ILC Special Rapporteur on State Responsibility, when he acknowledged that agency in international law may not necessarily follow from control (the sole determinant of attribution). In his 'First Report on State Responsibility', James Crawford stated concerning Draft Article 5 of the ILC Draft Articles: '"agents" for this purpose are persons or entities in fact acting on behalf of the State by reason of some mandate or direction given by a State organ, or (*possibly*) who are to be regarded as acting on behalf of the State by reason of the control exercised over them by such an organ.'[65] In the event, the word 'agent' was not used in the final ILC Articles on State Responsibility, Article 8 of which provides:

> The conduct of a person or group of persons shall be considered an act of a State under international law if the person or group of persons is in fact acting on the instructions of, or under the direction or control of, that State in carrying out the conduct.[66]

As such, Article 8 provides that *de facto* control is the sole determinant of attribution, but the sole objective of this provision is to resolve the issue of attribution for the purposes of establishing a State's responsibility and not to resolve the broader issue of determining when an entity acts as an agent for a State. However, it is recognised that Article 8 does admit of a different interpretation, one that conflates the concepts of agency and attribution with the consequence that control appears sufficient to establish an agency relationship. Even if, however, this different interpretation is preferred, when one examines the degree of *de facto* control that is

[63] It is clear from Article 8 of the ILC Articles that control is sufficient to establish attribution for the purposes of State responsibility: see *infra* n.66 and corresponding text *et sequentia*. For the historical antecedent to this approach in international law, see the statement by Roberto Ago, *YBILC*, 1979, vol. I., p.7, and Eagleton, C., *The Responsibility of States in International Law* (1928), p.43.

[64] On attribution, Kolb provides the following useful definition: 'Attribution is in fact the legal technique by which acts performed by an individual are legally considered as acts of a moral person, be it a corporation or a State. The acts are then the acts of that entity . . . .' (Kolb, R., 'The Jurisprudence of the Yugoslav and Rwandan Criminal Tribunals on their Jurisdiction and on International Crimes', this *Year Book*, 71 (2000), p.259 at p.277.)

[65] Crawford, J., 'First Report on State Responsibility', A/CN.4/490/Add.5, 22 July 1998, para.166. Emphasis added.

[66] Crawford, J., *The International Law Commission's Articles on State Responsibility: Introduction, Text and Commentaries* (2002), pp.110–13.

required by Article 8 then it becomes clear that even in this scenario the role of consent as a condition for the establishment of an agency relationship is guaranteed.

The International Court of Justice in the *Nicaragua* case provided the test of 'effective control' in order to determine the degree of control that is required for attribution of the acts of individuals (*in casu*, the contra rebels) to a State (the USA). The Court stated in its famous passage:

> Despite the heavy subsidies and other support provided to them by the United States, there is no clear evidence of the United States having actually exercised such a degree of control in all fields as to justify treating the *contras* as acting on its behalf . . . All the forms of United States participation mentioned above, and even the general control by the respondent State over a force with a high degree of dependency on it, would not in themselves mean, without further evidence, that the United States directed or enforced the perpetration of the acts contrary to human rights and humanitarian law alleged by the applicant State. Such acts could well be committed by members of the *contras* without the control of the United States. For this conduct to give rise to legal responsibility of the United States, it would have to be proved that that State had *effective control* of the military or paramilitary operations in the course of which the alleged violations were committed.[67]

James Crawford elucidated further on the Court's 'effective control' test in his Commentary on Article 8 of the ILC Articles when he stated:

> Thus while the United States was held responsible for its own support for the *contras*, only in certain individual instances were the acts of the *contras* themselves held attributable to it, *based upon actual participation of and directions given by that State*.[68]

Accordingly, what the 'effective control' test requires for attribution to a State of a particular act is that specific instructions concerning the commission of the particular act have been issued by the State to the individual or group in question. Put differently, by requiring a specific instruction from a State, the 'effective control' test in effect requires that a State has impliedly consented to an individual or group being able to act on its behalf. As such, the condition of State consent for an agency relationship continues to be guaranteed even if the concepts of agency and attribution are conflated.

However, the 'effective control' test has been the subject of criticism by the Appeals Chamber of the International Criminal Tribunal for the former Yugoslavia (ICTY) in the *Tadic* case.[69] The test of 'effective control'

[67] *Case concerning Military and Paramilitary Activities in and against Nicaragua (Nicaragua v United States of America)* [1986] ICJ Rep 14 at pp.62, 64–5. Emphasis added.

[68] Crawford, *supra* n.66, p.111. Emphasis added.

[69] The two cases were, however, considering the issue of attribution for different purposes, *Nicaragua* for State responsibility and *Tadic* for the application of rules of international humanitarian law: see Crawford, *supra* n.66, p.112. See also Kolb who contends: 'The crux of the decision in *Tadic* (1999) seems to be the pivotal place given to the notion of imputation (or attribution) which in turn calls for control tests (effective or overall control, etc.). This merger of criteria proper to the law of State responsibility and of those necessary to the determination of the international character of an

was in fact adopted and applied by a Trial Chamber of the ICTY in the *Tadic* case,[70] but the Appeals Chamber went on to overrule the decision when it formulated a different test to determine the degree of control necessary for the acts of military or paramilitary groups to be attributed to the State. The Appeals Chamber stated:

The requirement of international law for the attribution to States of acts performed by private individuals is that the State exercises control over the individuals. *The degree of control* may, however, vary according to the factual circumstances of each case. The Appeals Chamber fails to see why in each and every circumstance international law should require a high threshold for the test of control.[71]

The Appeals Chamber continued:

that international rules do not always require the same degree of control over armed groups or private individuals for the purpose of determining whether an individual not having the status of a State official under internal legislation can be regarded as a *de facto* organ of the State. The extent of the requisite State

armed conflict does not seem warranted. Attribution and control are necessary if an entity is legally sought to be made responsible for acts performed by third persons as if they were its own. They are not required for establishing the existence of an objective state of things, i.e. the existence of an international armed conflict, where it must only be shown that there is, in fact, a substantial implication of foreign powers. Obviously, the question is not whether these foreign powers have to be responsible for the acts of the local armies as if they were their own; the question is whether their involvement is of sufficient intensity to broaden the scope of the conflict into an international armed conflict. It may be appreciated that the two tests are not at all identical. The threshold to be reached is higher for the first than for the second. These aspects were felt by Judge Shahabuddeen, who correctly points out that the question was whether the FRY was using force in Bosnia, not the distinct one whether the FRY was responsible for any breaches of humanitarian law committed by the VRS.' (Kolb, R., 'The Jurisprudence of the Yugoslav and Rwandan Criminal Tribunals on their Jurisdiction and on International Crimes', this *Year Book*, 71 (2000), p.259 at pp.277–8.)

[70] A Trial Chamber of the Tribunal stated in the *Tadic* case: '. . . the Trial Chamber must consider the essence of the test of the relationship between a *de facto* organ or agent, as a rebel force, and its controlling entity or principal, as a foreign Power, namely the more general question whether, even if there had been a relationship of great dependency on the one side, there was such a relationship of control on the other that, on the facts of the instant case, the acts of the VRS, including its occupation of opstina Prijedor [a district in Bosnia], can be imputed to the Government of the Federal Republic of Yugoslavia (Serbia and Montenegro). . . . It remains the task of the Prosecution to prove that the nature of the relationship between the VRS and the Government of the Federal Republic of Yugoslavia (Serbia and Montenegro), and between the VRS [the army of *Republika Srpska*] and VJ [the armed forces of the Federal Republic of Yugoslavia (Serbia and Montenegro)] in particular, was of such a character. In doing so it is neither necessary nor sufficient merely to show that the VRS was dependent, even completely dependent, on the VJ and the Federal Republic of Yugoslavia (Serbia and Montenegro) for the necessities of war. It must also be shown that the VJ and the Federal Republic of Yugoslavia (Serbia and Montenegro) exercised the potential for control inherent in that relationship of dependency or that the VRS had otherwise placed itself under the control of the Government of the Federal Republic of Yugoslavia (Serbia and Montenegro).' (*Prosecutor v Dusko Tadic, Judgment*, 7 May 1997, IT-94-1-T., para. 588.) A majority of the Trial Chamber found that there had not been sufficient evidence adduced in the case to allow for the determination requested by the Prosecution that the degree of control was such that the acts of the rebel forces in question could be attributed to the Federal Republic of Yugoslavia (Serbia and Montenegro). (*Prosecutor v Dusko Tadic, Judgment*, 7 May 1997, IT-94-1-T., para.605.) Cf., however, the dissenting opinion on this point by Judge McDonald: *Separate and Dissenting Opinion of Judge McDonald regarding the applicability of Article 2 of the Statute*, 7 May 1997, IT-94-1-T.

[71] *Prosecutor v Tadic*, 15 July 1999, para.117.

control varies. Where the question at issue is whether a *single* private individual or a *group that is not militarily organised* has acted as a *de facto* State organ when performing a specific act, it is necessary to ascertain whether specific instructions concerning the commission of that particular act had been issued by that State to the individual or group in question; alternatively, it must be established whether the unlawful act had been publicly endorsed or approved *ex post facto* by the State at issue. By contrast, control by a state over subordinate *armed forces or militias or paramilitary units* may be of an overall character (and must comprise more than the mere provision of financial assistance or military equipment or training). This requirement, however, does not go so far as to include the issuing of specific orders by the State, or its direction of each individual operation. . . . The control required by international law may be deemed to exist when a State (or, in the context of an armed conflict, the Party to the conflict) has *a role in organising, coordinating or planning the military actions* of the military group, in addition to financing, training and equipping or providing operational support to that group. Acts performed by the group or members thereof may be regarded as acts of *de facto* State organs regardless of any specific instruction by the controlling State concerning the commission of each of those acts.[72]

The Appeals Chamber thus replaced the 'effective control' test with an 'overall control' test for the purposes of determining the attribution of acts of armed forces or militia units to a State, since it did not see why international law should in general stipulate a high threshold for the control test. However, it is precisely at this point that the condition of consent for the establishment of an agency relationship plays an important role in this scenario where the concepts of agency and attribution are being conflated. The role of consent in establishing an agency relationship provides an answer to the question posed by the Appeals Chamber as to why should international law require a high threshold for the test of control. An answer here may be that specific instructions or directions by a State, as part of the high threshold test of 'effective control', are necessary since they provide evidence of a State's consent to an entity being able to act as its agent, and that this consent cannot be lightly presumed by the existence of a general or 'overall' degree of control—that is, in the absence of specific instructions or directions from a State.

To conclude on this point, the importance that international law places on States being able to consent to their obligations has the consequence

[72] *Ibidem*, para.137. The conclusion of the Appeals Chamber concerning the organized Bosnian Serb military force was that: 'given that the Bosnian Serb armed forces constituted a "military organization", the control of the FRY [Federal Republic of Yugoslavia] authorities over these armed forces required by international law for considering the armed conflict to be international was *overall control* going beyond the mere financing and equipping of such forces and involving also participation in the planning and supervision of military operations. By contrast, international rules do not require that such control should extend to the issuance of specific orders or instructions relating to single military actions, whether or not such actions were contrary to international humanitarian law.' (*Ibidem*, para.145). The Appeals Chamber held that the Yugoslav Army did exercise overall control over the Bosnian Serb armed forces such that their acts were attributable to the Federal Republic of Yugoslavia, (*Ibidem*, paras.156, 160) and thus that the armed conflict in Bosnia and Herzegovina between the Bosnian Serbs and the central authorities of Bosnia and Herzegovina must be classified as an *international* armed conflict. (*Ibidem*, para.162).

that consent is a prerequisite for the establishment of an agency relationship in international law. There is, however, no specific form that is required for the expression of this consent: a State's consent may be implied from its actions or statements. In the case where a State's consent is implied from the control that it exerts over an international organization, the degree of control that has to be proved is the Nicaragua case test of 'effective control' and not the *Tadic* case test of 'overall control'.

The consensual basis of an agency relationship has the important consequence that it will, in general, be revocable by the principal at any time. This element of agency in international law is the same as it appears in domestic law.[73] This similarity is not surprising since the rationale for unilateral revocability in both international and domestic law is the same. As Reuschlein and Gregory put it: 'agency is a consensual relationship and a principal, therefore, cannot be compelled to retain another as his agent.'[74] This rationale is arguably applicable with a greater degree of cogency to the case of agency under international law. The importance that international law places on States being able to express freely their consent to the acceptance of obligations means that where these obligations are being entered into on their behalf by an agent, then a State should have the right to terminate this agency relationship in order to ensure that the assumption of its obligations represents at all times the true expression of its will.

This right of termination of an agency relationship exists independent of the underlying treaty or other agreement that provided for the establishment of the agency relationship.[75] In the context of international law this means that a State has the competence to decide at any time whether an agent should be able to continue to act on its behalf regardless of the existence of any contractual agreement that may exist between the principal and agent. As Sereni states, '[a way] in which agency may be terminated is the *revocation by the principal or the renunciation by the agent*. It is correct to assume that in international law the principal has power to revoke, and the agent to renounce the authority, although doing so is a violation of an agreement between the parties expressly denying the right to revoke or to renounce. The only effect of a provision in a treaty

[73] In domestic law a principal will in general be able to revoke at any time with immediate effect its agent's authority to act on its behalf. For this position in England and the US, see, e.g., Reynolds, *supra* n.55, pp.657, 673; Fridman, *supra* n.55, p.389; Reuschlein and Gregory, *supra* n.55, pp.86–7; and in the case of France, see Guyénot, J., *The French Law of Agency and Distributorship Agreements* (1976), p.67; and in Germany, see Staubach, F., *The German Law of Agency and Distributorship Agreements*, (1977), p.24. Cf., however, the *sui generis* case of an irrevocable agency: Fridman, *supra* n.55, pp.389–91; Reynolds, *supra* n.55, pp.660–8; and Reuschlein and Gregory, *supra* n.55, pp.98–100.

This is subject to the important caveat, even in the domestic sphere, that the termination may not affect the position of a third party in her dealings with the agent who has had no notice of such termination (see Reynolds, *supra* n.55, p.656.)

[74] Reuschlein and Gregory, *supra* n.55, p.86.

[75] As Reynolds states in the context of domestic law: 'The general rule, which is perhaps not widely understood, is that the authority of an agent . . . whether or not expressed to be irrevocable, is revocable, without prejudice to the fact that such revocation may be wrongful as between principal and agent.' (Reynolds, *supra* n.55, p.673.) See also, e.g., Reuschlein and Gregory, *supra* n.55, p.86.

that the authority cannot be terminated by either party is to create liability for its wrongful termination.'[76] As such, where there is, for example, an agency relationship between a group of States and an international organization that is exercising conferred powers on their behalf, then the conferral is revocable by the States with immediate effect, even in the case where the treaty providing for the conferral of power stipulates that the conferral is irrevocable. In the case of the latter, a unilateral revocation would provide a basis for allegation of breach of treaty by the organization, but this is a separate issue from the right of termination of the agency relationship.[77]

3. *The establishment of agency relationships between States and international organizations*

The establishment of an agency relationship in international law depends, as explained above, on the principal and agent being separate entities; and the relationship between them being consensual. The germane question for our present discussion is the extent to which these conditions can be satisfied in the relationship that exists between an organization and a State or States that have conferred powers on the organization. In considering this question, it is important to distinguish, analytically, between two categories of States that may potentially have an agency relationship with an international organization: Member States and non-Member States. In both cases there is a presumption against the establishment of an agency relationship between a State and an organization for the reasons set out below, but in the case of Member States the presumption may in practice be stronger.

(a) *Member States*

There is a general presumption against the establishment of an agency relationship between an international organization and its Member States.[78] The main reason for the existence of this presumption in such

[76] Sereni, *supra* n.25, p.660. Original emphasis. On revocability being an important part of international agency, see also Bartos in the International Law Commission debates: *YBILC*, vol.I, 1964, 732nd mtg., p.57 (para.42).

[77] In any case this right of unilateral termination is arguably envisaged by Article 56(1)(b) of the 1969 Vienna Convention on the Law of Treaties which provides in effect (for present purposes) that a State can terminate a treaty that does not expressly provide for termination where the right of termination 'may be implied by the nature of the treaty.' The argument runs—in the case of a treaty establishing an agency relationship—that the consent based nature of the relationship which the treaty establishes means that the treaty should be revocable at the discretion of the State or States concerned (the principal). This right would still, however, be subject to Article 56(2) of the 1969 Vienna Convention which provides that 'A party shall give not less than twelve months' notice of its intention to denounce or withdraw from a treaty under paragraph 1.'

[78] For statements in support of this presumption, see the following: the decision of the English Court of Appeal in *Maclaine Watson v Department of Trade and Industry*, Court of Appeal, 80 ILR 39 at p.114; the opinion of Lord Oliver (with whom the other Lords agreed) in the International Tin Council case of *J.H. Rayner Ltd v Department of Trade and Industry*, [1989] 3 WLR 969 at pp.1016–17; the opinion of Justice Millet in *Maclaine Watson & Co. v the International Tin Council*, [1988] Ch Chi 1; and Crawford, J., *AIDI*, 66-I (1995), p.334, Shihata, I., in 'Report by Rosalyn Higgins', *ibidem*, p.312, and Zemanek, K., in 'Report by Rosalyn Higgins', *ibidem*, p.327.

cases is that two of the conditions for establishment of an agency relationship—consent and control—are not fulfilled on a *prima facie* basis.[79] This does not mean, for example, that an international organization can never be an agent for its Member States when exercising conferred powers under the terms of its constituent treaty.[80] It is just that there is a presumption against this being the case.

When Member States ratify a constituent treaty that confers powers on an organization they are consenting thereby to the organization exercising the power in question, but they are not usually consenting to the organization exercising the power on their behalf (as an agent) such that it can change their legal rights and obligations.[81] More specifically, an international organization with separate legal personality acts on its *own* behalf and not on behalf of its Member States when exercising powers under its constituent treaty, and as such there is a general presumption against considering Members as having consented to the establishment of an agency relationship simply by virtue of their membership in the organization. It was this approach that was adopted by the English courts in the litigation following the financial collapse of the International Tin Council (ITC), an international organization headquartered in the UK with separate international legal personality from its Member States.

In the ITC cases, one of the arguments made in favour of ITC Member States being liable for the ITC's financial liabilities was that the organization had entered into transactions with third parties as an agent acting on behalf of the Member States who were an undisclosed principal.[82]

[79] Often the very reason for setting up an international organization is precisely to act on a basis independent from Member States, a position often evidenced by the separate legal personality of an organization from its Members. As Jan Klabbers states, albeit in a different context: 'At the very least . . . explicitly to endow an organization with personality under international law indicates that the founders wish to create an entity which is somehow separate from their aggregate . . .' (Klabbers, *supra* n.23, pp.56–7.)

[80] As Ibrahim Shihata stated in response to the questions—posed by the Institut's Rapporteur Rosalyn Higgins—can an international organization act as the agent of its members and if so in what circumstances: 'The relationship between a state and an international organization of which it is a member cannot be characterised as a principal-agent relationship in the absence of a strong evidence to this effect or an explicit agreement by virtue of which the member requests the organization to act as its agent for a certain purpose (*e.g.*, under the IBRD loan agreements, for the purpose of purchasing and converting currencies on behalf of a borrower state, and under agreements with the IBRD authorizing it to administer funds provided by a member state for a special purpose).' (Shihata, I., in 'Report by Rosalyn Higgins', *AIDI*, 66-I (1995), p.312.)

[81] This position, however, relies on there being no customary international law rule that provides for a primary responsibility of Member States for the acts of an international organization: see Higgins, *supra* n.28, p.47. If such a rule did, however, exist and it was well-known, then when a State in the future ratified a constituent treaty it could be considered to have implicitly accepted that an organization was able to act as an agent on its behalf. I am grateful to Vaughan Lowe for this point.

[82] *J.H. Rayner (Mincing Lane) Ltd. v Department of Trade and Industry* [1987] BCLC, 667, *Maclaine Watson & Co. v International Tin Council* [1988] Ch 1, and *Maclaine Watson v Department of Trade and Industry*, Court of Appeal, 80 ILR 39. Chinkin usefully summarizes the conclusion of the English Courts: 'On appeal the agency argument was rejected. The Court of Appeal found that no express authority had been given to the Council by its members, thus negating any factual agency. It also held that the 6th International Tin Agreement did not establish a principal/agent relationship between the Council and its members. In the House of Lords, Lord Oliver emphasized that the law which was relied upon as creating an agency situation was the 6th International Tin Agreement, which

A useful distinction was drawn in the cases between 'constitutional' (or built-in) agency which would arguably derive directly from the ITC's constituent treaty [the 6th International Tin Agreement (ITA6), the treaty most recently constituting the International Tin Council] and 'factual' (or *ad hoc*) agency for which express authority given by the Members to the Council would have to be established.

The 'constitutional' (built-in) agency argument was dismissed by the English Courts on the basis that the ITA6 was a membership agreement, not one forming an agency relationship: the ITA6 established the rights of Members as Members of the ITC, not as principals to the transactions of the ITC. As, for example, Justice Millet in *Maclaine Watson v International Tin Council* stated: 'the treaty [ITA6] is not a contract of partnership or agency but of membership. The relationships it creates are not those of partners or of principal and agent but of an organisation and its members.'[83] This approach was upheld by the English Court of Appeal.[84] Put differently, the courts had found that Member States could not be considered as having implicitly consented to the establishment of an agency relationship when ratifying ITA6.

The English courts also considered whether participation by ITC Member States in the decision-making processes of the ITC Council, as provided for by ITA6, could be equated to control of the organ for the purposes of establishing an agency relationship. The English Court of Appeal—in the separate action brought by the ITC's creditors directly against the UK Department of Trade and Industry (*Maclaine Watson v Department of Trade and Industry*)[85]—rejected the argument that the control being exercised by Member States over the ITC through the ITC Council was sufficient to establish an agency relationship between the ITC and its Members. In so doing, the Court of Appeal in *Maclaine Watson v Department of Trade and Industry* applied the earlier House of Lords decision in *Salomon v Salomon* which had rejected the notion that the existence of control was sufficient per se to allow the piercing of the corporate veil so that a corporation could be considered as an agent for the controlling shareholders.[86] The Court of Appeal stated in *Maclaine Watson* concerning the Salomon case: 'The crucial point on which the House of Lords overruled the Court of Appeal in that landmark case was precisely the rejection of the doctrine that agency between a corporation and its members in relation to the corporation's contracts can be inferred from the control exercisable by the members over the

was not justiciable in the English courts. His Lordship indicated that even if this were not the case he would have rejected any agency argument on the same grounds as Staughton J, and the Court of Appeal.' (Chinkin, *supra* n.28, pp.116–19.)

[83] *Maclaine Watson v International Tin Council, Chancery Division*, [1988] Ch 1 at p.23.

[84] *Maclaine Watson v International Tin Council, Court of Appeal*, [1989] Ch 253 at p.257.

[85] *Maclaine Watson v Department of Trade and Industry*, Court of Appeal, 80 ILR 39.

[86] The Court of Appeal stated: 'The correct analysis of I.T.A.6 is in line with the decision of the House of Lords in *Salomon v. A. Salomon & Co. Ltd.* [1897] AC 22 and not with any contract of agency between the members as principals and the council as the members' agent.' (*Maclaine Watson v Department of Trade and Industry*, Court of Appeal, 80 ILR 39 at p.114.)

corporation or from the fact that the sole objective of the corporation's contracts was to benefit the members.'[87] This approach by the Court of Appeal was affirmed on appeal by the House of Lords which stated:

Once given the creation of a separate legal personality by the Order in Council [that established the ITC as a UK corporation], there appears to me to be no escape from the principle established by this House in *Salomon v A. Salomon and Co. Ltd.* [1897] A.C. 22, where the suggestion that Salomon and Co. Ltd. carried on business as agent for the corporators was firmly and decisively rejected. Mr Sumption has sought to distinguish the case on the ground that the I.T.C. was brought into existence to carry out the purposes of its members and not for its own purposes and that it is 'composed' of its members and operates under their immediate direction. An analysis was made of . . . the I.T.A.6 in order to support the suggestion that, unlike a board of directors, the council owes no duties to the I.T.C. but acts entirely for its own benefit. From this it was argued that the I.T.C., as a body, was simply the agent of the members. It is, perhaps, enough for me to say that . . . I can find no relevant distinction here between the governance of a limited company and the governance of the I.T.C. That they are differently constituted is irrelevant. As Kerr L.J. [1989] Ch. 72, 189, pointed out in the course of his judgment [in the Court of Appeal], whether a corporation acts directly on the instructions of its members, who constitute the directorate, or indirectly because of the members' control in general meeting, makes no difference in principle. The existence of a board of directors in Salomon's case played no part in the decision. An examination of the constitution of the I.T.C., even if permissible, does not support the suggestion of 'constitutional agency'.[88]

[87] *Ibidem*, p.113.

[88] *J.H. Rayner v Department of Trade and Industry and Others and Related Appeals*, [1990] 2 AC 418 at p.515, per Lord Oliver. Lord Oliver went on to dismiss the agency claim on the further ground that was 'accepted by Staughton J. and upheld by the Court of Appeal, that the terms of the standard form B contract of the London Metal Exchange, which governs the transactions sued upon, preclude any suggestion of agency. These terms unambiguously specified that the contract is between "ourselves and yourselves as principals" and the words which follow—"we alone being liable to you for its performance"—cannot reasonably be construed as importing that the words "as principals" refer only to the "ourselves" (the brokers) and not also to the "yourselves" (the I.T.C.).' (*J.H. Rayner v Department of Trade and Industry and Others and Related Appeals*, [1990] 2 AC 418 at p.516, per Lord Oliver.)

Moreover, Gordon Pollock in the ITC case before the House of Lords made the persuasive argument on behalf of the government of India (intervening in the case) against agency when he stated: 'In this connection two short points are made in respect of I.T.A.6. First, one is concerned with the relationship of each member vis-à-vis the ITC. "The members" are not simply one person. I.T.A.6 is not an agreement which is simply brought into existence to provide a mechanism whereby the members can harmonise their individual activities. It is to bring into being an organisation which can act against the interests of individual members or groups of members from time to time. The members, by joining it, give up their freedom of action and agree to be bound by the ITC's decisions. For these purposes the ITC is composed of the council and there has to be a certain majority [to make decisions] . . . As a result of vote [sic] decisions become decisions of the body which can be enforced on individual members, including those who voted against it. Secondly, the ITC has a number of executives. The chairman has to be of complete independence, as do all the rest of the officers of the organisation. The officers are only answerable to the council. They cannot reveal information to any of the members . . . Articles 27, 28 and 29 read together impose duties and grant powers to the buffer stock manager. That executive is under an obligation by virtue of the constitution [I.T.A.6] to exercise those powers as his rights unless and until the decision making organ of the ITC decides otherwise . . . Those are not indications of an agency.' (Submissions contained in *J.H. Rayner v Department of Trade and Industry and Others and Related Appeals*, [1990] 2 AC 418 at pp.458–9.)

The House of Lords thus dismissed the argument that the control being exercised by ITC Member States acting collectively through the decision-making processes of the ITC Council was sufficient to establish a relationship of 'constitutional agency', that is agency established by the ITC's constituent treaty (ITA6).[89] This decision has two broader implications.[90]

First, it means that the nature of the control that is necessary to establish an agency relationship between an organization—possessing its own legal personality—and its Member States must be control that is being exercised by Member States over an organization which is outside the confines of the decision-making processes of the organization.

Second, it provides further support to the approach set out above that the implication of consent to an agency relationship by virtue of control being exercised by a purported principal over a purported agent will not be lightly presumed.[91]

To summarize, there is a general presumption against Member States of an organization having established an agency relationship with the organization simply by virtue of their ratification of a constituent treaty and participation in its decision-making organs. This presumption may, however, be rebutted where a case of *ad hoc* agency can be established.[92]

Recalling our earlier discussion on the conditions for an agency relationship, the establishment of a case of *ad hoc* agency between an

[89] The existence of such a presumption against agency is further supported by the independence of international organizations (embodied usually in the secretariat of an organization) from States: see also Pollock, *supra* n.88. Moreover, as Chinkin has stated in the context of the secretariat of the International Tin Council: 'The International Tin Agreement also provided for executive staff who in the performance of their duties were prohibited from receiving instructions from any source other than the Council. Each member State was under a duty to respect the international and independent character of the responsibilities of these staff. Although the member States had created the Council, once established it became a separate entity with its own international executive. The member States were external to the Council, and were included in the prohibition against taking instructions from external governments or powers. This could be a persuasive argument against agency. An agent cannot be prohibited from taking further instructions from the principal, and a principal cannot be prevented from giving instructions to the agent. While the members may be delegates of the member States, the administrative officers were independent and exclusively international employees of the Council.' (Chinkin, *supra* n.28, pp.116–17.)

[90] The general importance for international law of these domestic court pronouncements in the ITC cases has been widely accepted: see, for example, 'Responsibility of International Organizations', ILC Report of its 54th Session (2002), Chapter VIII, para.487.

[91] See text following *supra* n.72.

[92] As Amerasinghe has stated 'The issue of factual agency could arise in any situation. It does not hinge specifically on the nature of the personality of the organization nor does it flow from the constitutional relationship between the organization and its members, since it rests entirely in the factual position which prevails between the organization and its members and on whether such position according to the law of agency warrants the inference that the organization was not acting on its own behalf but on behalf of an undisclosed principal, namely the members. Factual agency is, therefore, not intrinsic to the law of international personality which flows from the agreement creating the organization. [Nonetheless,] [i]t is entirely possible that in a given factual situation the agency relationship between the organization and its members could be established.' (Amerasinghe, C, in 'Report by Rosalyn Higgins', *AIDI*, 66-I (1995), p.353.) For possible examples of factual agency between an organization and its Member States, see Chinkin in the context of the International Tin Council (Chinkin, *supra* n.28, p.115); and Shihata who contends that in certain limited instances the International Bank for Reconstruction and Development acts as an agent for its Member States (Shihata, I., in 'Report by Rosalyn Higgins', *AIDI*, 66-I (1995), p.312.)

organization and Member States will require evidence in a particular case that an organization has accepted the *ad hoc* conferral of power to be exercised on an agency basis,[93] and that Member States have consented—either expressly or impliedly—to the organization acting on their behalf on an individual or collective basis.[94] There is an important distinction that needs to be made at this point in our analysis between the case where Member States have expressly consented to an organization acting on their behalf from the case where consent has arguably been implied. This distinction is of practical importance, since where Members have consented in express terms then there is no requirement to prove the existence of effective control over the acts of an organization in order to establish an agency relationship between the Members and the organization. Where, however, there is no such express consent by States and consent has arguably been implied from a relationship of control then the Member States in question must have exercised control over the organization in a way that is not envisaged by the organization's constituent treaty and the degree of control necessary to provide evidence of an agency relationship will need to be 'effective control'. These distinctions can be illuminated by considering the two different consent scenarios in the case, for example, of the possible establishment of an agency relationship between the North Atlantic Treaty Organization (NATO) and its Member States.

Consider if, for example, a group of NATO Member States expressly stated that NATO was acting on their behalf in a particular case and that NATO had expressly accepted this conferral of power, then notwithstanding NATO's separate legal personality[95] the dual requirement for consent would clearly be fulfilled. The express consent would operate in such a case to rebut the general presumption that an international organization with separate legal personality does not act on behalf of its Member States on an individual or collective basis.

Where, however, there is no express consent by Member States, but consent is arguably implied, then the test for the degree of control that will be necessary to establish an agency relationship is, as explained above, the International Court's more stringent 'effective control' test and not the ICTY's 'overall control' test.[96] This has the important practical consequence that in such cases it will be necessary to prove an actual instruction or direction by Member States—not envisaged by the constituent treaty—that is subsequently followed by the organization.[97]

[93] The source of this requirement is twofold. First, we recall from above that the consent requirement for an agency relationship extends to the agent (*in casu*, the organization) consenting to the establishment of an agency relationship (see *supra* nn.54–6 and corresponding text); and, second, that in order for an *ad hoc* conferral of power on an organization to have legal effect it must have been accepted by the organization (see *supra* nn.29–34 and corresponding text).

[94] See text following *supra* n.56.

[95] Cf. *infra* n.102.

[96] See text following *supra* n.72.

[97] Where this element of control can be proved there will be obvious issues of *vires* for the organization, but this does not detract from the agency relationship that would be established if the existence of such an instruction or direction was proved. This is of course subject to NATO having accepted this conferral of power: see *supra* nn.54–5 and corresponding text.

The likelihood of such an occurrence may not in practice be as remote as may at first seem the case, especially since NATO military commanders continue to serve as part of the armed forces of their Member States concurrent with their NATO command positions.[98]

The question of a possible agency relationship between NATO and its Member States was raised by the Federal Republic of Yugoslavia (FRY) before the International Court in the case brought against NATO Members. The FRY brought this case in response to the NATO bombing of its territory that was carried out in an attempt to stop the widespread human rights violations that were said to be occurring in the FRY province of Kosovo. One of the arguments made by the FRY in the provisional measures phase of the case was that '[t]he command structure of NATO constitutes an instrumentality of the respondent States, acting as their agent'[99] and thus that 'the respondent States are jointly and severally responsible for the actions of the NATO military command structure'.[100]

[98] It is precisely this type of dual function that gave rise to a possible example of an agency relationship between the UN peace-keeping operation in Somalia (UNOSOM II) and a UN Member State, Italy, that was participating in UNOSOM II. It has been explained in detail elsewhere that UNOSOM II was given by the UN Security Council a military enforcement mandate by Council resolutions 814 and 837. (Sarooshi, *supra* n.13, pp.81–2.) This was subject, however, to the condition that UNOSOM II operate under the command and control of the Secretary-General's Special Representative and the UN Force Commander. (*Ibidem.*) Despite this requirement, it seems the Italian contingent that was part of UNOSOM II obtained and followed orders from Rome which were clearly outside the UN chain-of-command. (For a description of such cases, see: S/1994/653, pp.28–9, 45; and Hirsh, J., and Oakley, R., *Somalia and Operation Restore Hope: Reflections on Peacemaking and Peacekeeping*, (1995), p.119.) In such a case—to the extent that evidence of these orders can be established—it could be argued that UNOSOM II was acting as an agent of Italy and as such that any responsibility arising from these acts are to be attributed to Italy and not the UN. This is arguably more akin to a case of agency rather than simply considering the Italian contingent as being, for the purposes of the action, part of the Italian armed forces *per se*, because the sole legal basis for the contingent being in Somalia and carrying out an enforcement mandate is the fact that it was part of UNOSOM II. The fact that the contingent may have obeyed orders issued directly from Rome—orders that were clearly outside the UN chain-of-command—does not alter the legal position that the Italian contingent was still part of UNOSOM II. What our previous analysis does illustrate though is that in order for this relationship to be characterised as one of agency, UNOSOM II would have to have consented to the agency relationship.

[99] Oral argument in the case *Yugoslavia v Canada*, CR/99/14, 10 May 1999, p.33 (from ICJ web-site: http://www.icj-cij.org).

[100] *Ibidem*, p.38. For a description of the NATO chain-of-command, see the NATO web-site: http://www.nato.int/structur/struc-mcs.htm.

See also the following Oral Pleadings made on behalf of Serbia and Montenegro in the Preliminary Objections phase of the case:

27. Mr. President, in addition to the fact that the respondent States, individually and in concert with others, took the decision to initiate and continue air strikes against Yugoslavia, their national authorities did have the power to approve or veto the targets, which power is pertinent to their international responsibility. A statement by the Dutch Defence Minister delivered in the Dutch Parliament clearly demonstrates that the ultimate control over military actions rested with each individual member State: "Dutch military in Vicenze have assessed each time again whether the targets which Saceur [Supreme Allied Commander Europe] apportioned to the Dutch F-16's, were in conformity with our views on what constitute legitimate targets. It was agreed that in case of doubt the Chief of the Defence Staff would inform the Cabinet . . . The Netherlands have the right to consider that the deployment of these weapons [cluster bombs] in some situations is not warranted. Of course, our allies are informed in these circumstances, but from a formal point of view this remains a Dutch competence. The Cabinet is responsible for the deployment of Dutch forces." . . .

This issue was not argued at length before the International Court at this interim measures phase of the case since it is a matter going more to the merits. Nonetheless, Canada did briefly respond in oral argument—although not directly addressing the issue of agency—when it stated before the Court:

Joint and several liability for acts of an international organization, or for the acts of other States acting within such an organization, cannot be established unless the relevant treaty provides for such liability. Article 5 of the 1994 NATO Convention, cited in the first round, provides no such indication of an assumption of joint and several liability, and neither do the provisions of the Handbook respecting the integrated military structure of the organization. The separate liability of Australia in *Nauru* was of course based on the specific terms of the trust instruments in issue in that case, not on general principles on international organizations. The work of the ILC on State Responsibility provides no more support for the joint and several concept. I note as well that these concepts were canvassed in the Tin Council litigation in the United Kingdom, and the outcome would not support the Applicant in the present case.[101]

28. In conclusion, it is clear that, as a matter of principle, the respondent States cannot hide behind NATO's international legal personality to escape responsibility. Further, the respondent States as sovereign States made a sovereign decision to initiate and continue the military operations against Yugoslavia and controlled the choice of targets. The fact that they did so in concert with other NATO States cannot shield them from the responsibility because the decisions were theirs, nevertheless.

(Oral Pleadings made by Mr Djeric on behalf of Serbia and Montenegro in the *Legality of Use of Force (Serbia and Montenegro v NATO Member States)* case, 21 April 2004, CR/2004/14, paras.27–8; and see also the Oral Pleadings made by Mr Djeric on behalf of Serbia and Montenegro, 23 April 2004, CR/2004/23, paras.10,12–13.)

[101] Oral argument on behalf of Canada in the case *Yugoslavia v Canada*, CR/99/27, 12 May 1999, p.7 (from ICJ web-site: http://www.icj-cij.org). Cf also the following Oral Pleadings by France in the Priliminary Objections phase of the case:

49. Monsieur le président, la France n'entend nullement minorer et encore moins nier le rôle qu'elle a tenu dans l'action collective qui a été entreprise à l'époque pour prévenir une catastrophe humanitaire au Kosovo et mettre un terme aux atrocités qui s'y sont déroulées. Mais, ainsi que l'indique la République fédérale de Yougoslavie elle-même dans son mémoire, 'The general rule on attribution of an act to a State is that a State is responsible for an act committed under guidance and control of its organ as well as for an act endorsed by its organ.'
50. En l'occurrence, la France n'a pas agi de manière individuelle et autonome. L'ensemble des actes auxquels elle a pris part à ces fins ont été accomplis sous la direction et le contrôle d'organisations internationales–et, au premier chef, de l'OTAN. C'est l'OTAN qui a conçu, décidé et réalisé l'opération militaire qui s'est déroulée sur le territoire yougoslave au printemps 1999. C'est également l'OTAN qui a créé la KFOR et en assure le commandement et le contrôle unifiés, conformément à la résolution 1244 (1999) du Conseil de securite, qui, faut-il le rappeler, a autorisé le déploiement de cette force 'sous l'égide de l'Organisation des Nations Unies'.
51. Consciente de cette difficulté, la République fédérale de Yougoslavie affirme que l'OTAN agit en réalité sous la direction et le contrôle militaires et politiques de ses Etats membres. Cette curieuse conception de la transparence de l'organisation fait évidemment fi de la persormalité juridique internationale qui doit lui être reconnue, conformément aux criteres dégagés par votre Cour dans l'avis consultatif relatif a la *Réparation des dommages subis au service des Nations Unies* . . .
52. Ce n'est done pas a la France, ni aux autres Etats membres de l'OTAN ou à ceux qui participent à la KFOR, que pourraient etre attribués les faits allégués, si tant est—ce que je ne crois aucunement—que ces fails soient constitutifs de violations d'obligations intemationales. Dès lors, il n'existe pas, dans la présente instance, de différend entre la Serbie et Monténégro et la France dont la Cour puisse connaître.

Based on our detailed analysis above, there are several propositions that emerge relating to this issue of agency in the case. First, there is a clear presumption against the establishment of an agency relationship between NATO and its Member States, assuming that NATO does indeed possess separate legal personality from its Members.[102] Second, in order to rebut this presumption the FRY must prove that both Canada and NATO consented to the establishment of an agency relationship, or, in the alternate, that Canada exercised 'effective control' over NATO forces which was outside the confines of Canada's participation in the NATO Council and that NATO consented to this arrangement. Accordingly, in the case of the alternative scenario, the FRY will need to provide evidence of an actual instruction or direction by Canada that is subsequently followed by NATO forces. These elements will likely prove difficult to establish in practice,[103] and as such the presumption against agency will in all probability be maintained if the Court does rule on the issue.

(b) Non-Member States

The establishment of an agency relationship between an organization and a State does not in theory depend on whether the State in question is a Member or not. As established above, there is no 'constitutional' (or built-in) agency that derives from the legal link established between a Member State and an organization by its constituent treaty, and as such the position of Member State and non-Member State would seem identical. However, the *ad hoc* conferral by a non-Member State of power on an organization by treaty may in practice provide much clearer evidence of express consent to an agency relationship than in the case of a Member State where such a separate treaty will be less likely to exist.[104] This has

(Oral Submission made on behalf of France in the *Legality of Use of Force (Serbia and Montenegro v NATO Member States)* case, 20 April 2004, CR/2004/12, paras.49–52.) Cf. also the Oral Submissions made on behalf of Portugal in the *Legality of Use of Force (Serbia and Montenegro v NATO Member States)* case, 19 April 2004, CR/2004/9, paras. 4.1–4.8; and *ibidem*, 22 April 2004, CR/2004/18, paras.4.3,4.5–4.6.

On this case, see also Higgins, R., 'The Responsibility of States Members for the Defaults of International Organizations: Continuing me Dialogue', in Schlemmer-Schulte, S., and Tung, K., eds., *Liber Amicorum Ibrahim F.I. Shihata: International Finance and Development Law* (2001), p.442 at p.447.

[102] This, however, may be a contentious issue that will require the International Court, if the cases reaches the merits, to determine whether NATO does in fact possess a separate legal personality from its Member States such that the presumption against agency operates. Suffice to note that a number of commentators have regarded NATO as a collective self-defence pact rather than as a regional organization with a separate legal personality. See Kelsen, H., *The Law of the United Nations*, (1951), p.327; Simma, B., ed., *The Charter of the United Nations* (1994, 1st ed.), p.731, and Gazzini, T., 'NATO Coercive Military Activities in the Yugoslav Crisis (1992–1999)', *EJIL*, 12 (2001), p.391 at p.425.

[103] For example, Gazzini, in his descriptive review of NATO military activities in the Yugoslav crisis, states that: 'Throughout the crisis, the NAC [North Atlantic Council] exercised political control—up to August 1995 jointly with the Security Council—and strategic direction over the operations, while the troops were under exclusive NATO command and control. Thus, no military activity was undertaken by NATO forces without a formal decision by the NAC.' (Gazzini, T., 'NATO Coercive Military Activities in the Yugoslav Crisis (1992–1999)', *EJIL*, 12 (2001), p.391 at p.415.) Cf., however, the view of Serbia and Montenegro, *supra* n.100.

[104] Cf., however, the Peace Treaty between Italy and the UK, US, France, and the Former USSR, which provided for the conferral of powers on the UN General Assembly: see *supra* n.25.

the important consequence that it may in practice be more difficult to establish an agency relationship—in particular to fulfil the consent requirement—in the case of the relationship between one or more Member States and an organization than in the case where one or more non-Member States have conferred powers on an organization. An example of this difficulty being provided by the NATO case set out above.[105]

(c) *Consequences of the establishment of an agency relationship*

Where an agency relationship can be established between an international organization and a State, this will have three main consequences. The first is that it makes clear whose legal relations are changed as a consequence of the exercise of conferred power. Second, it determines the issue of who is responsible for breaches of international law that may occur as a result of the organization's exercise of the conferred power. Finally, it resolves the issue in whose interest should the power be exercised: the State's or the organization's.

(i) An agent can change certain legal relations of its principal

One of the most important consequences of an agency relationship is that an agent when exercising conferred powers can change the principal's legal relations with third parties. But the acts of an agent do not *per se* change the legal relations between the agent and a third party.[106] As such, where an agency relationship can be established between an organization and one or more States that have conferred power on an organization, then the acts of the organization in the exercise of conferred power changes only the legal relations of the States in question and not those of the organization. This question of whose legal relations are changed as a consequence of the exercise by an agent of conferred power is, however, distinct from the question of responsibility for breaches of international law that may occur as a result of the agent's (*in casu*, the organization's) exercise of conferred power.

(ii) The responsibility of a principal for the acts of its agent

An important consequence of an agency relationship is that the principal is responsible for its agent's acts that are within the scope of

[105] See *supra* n.103 and corresponding text.

[106] As Chinkin, for example, has observed in relation to international agency: '[When] [a]n agent enters into a contractual relationship with a third party on behalf of a principal; the legal relationship is established between the principal and the third party, not the third party and agent.' (Chinkin, *supra* n.28, p.65.) Moreover, Sereni contends: 'The acts performed by the agent within the limits of its authority bind the principal as if they had been personally performed by the latter. When acting within its power, the agent assumes no personal responsibility towards either the principal or the third parties.' (Sereni, *supra* n.25, p.655.) This is subject in international law to the third party knowing the identity of the agent: see *supra* n.54 and corresponding text.

For the similar position in domestic law, see Reuschlein and Gregory, *supra* n.55, pp.33, 101; in German law see Staubach, *supra* n.73, p.11; and in French law see Guyénot, *supra* n.73, p.181.

conferred power.[107] Accordingly, where an organization acts[108] as an agent for certain States then the States concerned are responsible for any unlawful acts committed by the organization in the exercise of conferred powers.[109] This consequence in the case of agency flows, more specifically, from the fact that a State will have consented—either expressly or implicitly—to an organization acting on its behalf.[110]

Moreover, the requirement of consent of an international organization to the agency relationship establishes a general presumption that an organization retains a joint responsibility for any unlawful acts committed.[111] This approach is supported by the fact that in the case of an agency relationship an international organization possesses a separate legal personality, and, accordingly, in the absence of an express provision in its constituent treaty to the contrary, the international organization always possesses constitutional control over its actions—even in the case where a State is exercising *de facto* control over the organization—such that the organization could seek to prevent the commission of the unlawful act by issuing an order to override the instruction or other control to exercise its constitutional control[112] can be said to be an omission that engages a joint responsibility of the organization.

[107] As Sereni states: 'The acts performed by the agent within the limits of its authority bind the principal as if they had been personally performed by the latter. When acting within its power, the agent assumes no personal responsibility towards either the principal or the third parties.' (Sereni, *supra* n.25, p.655.) As a general matter, where acts are committed outside the scope of the agent's conferred powers then the principal is not liable for these acts. As Sereni states: 'As to the legal effects of international agency . . . the agent's acts bind the principal only in so far as they are within the authority conferred. Beyond these limits the agent's acts do not bind the principal, unless subsequently ratified by the latter.' (Sereni, *ibidem*, p.655.) For the similar position in the domestic law context, see, for example, Reynolds, *supra* n.55, p.1.

[108] On the separate issue of whose acts can be attributed to an international organization, see Klabbers, *supra* n.23, pp.307–10.

[109] As Amerasinghe states: 'It is entirely possible that in a given factual situation the agency relationship between the organization and its members could be established. In that case there would be a direct liability on the part of members for the obligations incurred. But then the organization itself would not be primarily liable, unless it has exceeded its powers under the law of agency.' (Amerasinghe, C., *AIDI*, 66-I (1995), p.353.)

[110] Klabbers suggests a different basis of liability: 'if the member-states fail to exercise proper control over the acts of the organization, then they may be held responsible for negligence.' (Klabbers, *supra* n.23, p.302.)

[111] The general principle here has been stated by Giorgio Gaja, the ILC Special Rapporteur on the responsibility of international organizations: 'It can certainly be said, as a general principle, that every internationally wrongful act on the part of an international organization entails the international responsibility of that organization.' (Gaja, G., 'First Report on Responsibility of International Organizations', A/CN.4/532, ILC 56th Session, 26 March 2003, para.35.)

[112] Where, however, an organization has in good faith sought to exercise its constitutional control to prevent the commission of an unlawful act but the control by a State over the organization has in any case caused the commission of the act, the argument that an organization possesses a joint, but secondary, responsibility gains greater cogency. This type of situation may even be considered as a type of circumstance precluding wrongfulness on the part of the international organization. On the differing circumstances precluding wrongfulness in the case of State responsibility, see Chapter V of the ILC Articles on State Responsibility and commentary thereto, contained in Crawford, *supra* n.66, pp.160–90. Cf. Lowe, V, 'Precluding Wrongfulness or Responsibility: A Plea for Excuses', *EJIL*, 10 (1999), p.405.

(iii) The fiduciary duty of the agent to act in the interests of its principal

The existence of an agency relationship imposes an obligation on the agent to act in the interests of its principal.[113] As James Crawford has stated in the context of an agency relationship between two States: '*The exercise of governmental competence on a basis of agency*. It is clear that the exercise of governmental competence by another international person or persons on behalf of and by delegation from a State is not inconsistent with formal independence. The foreign affairs and defence powers are quite often so delegated; as are certain economic or technical facilities. *The important element is always that the competence is exercised not independently but in right of the State concerned*.'[114] This fiduciary element of an agency relationship means that where an organization acts as an agent for a State then the organization must exercise conferred powers in the interests of the conferring State. Such a situation may well, however, raise an issue of *vires* for the organization, since it may have its own organizational interest specified by its constituent treaty in pursuance of which it is always bound to act. This *vires* issue may well provide a basis for a Member State to claim that the organization is not acting in conformity with an obligation under its constituent treaty to act in the organizational interest. In practice, however, the subjective—and it must be said malleable—nature of an 'organization's interest' is such that it may be difficult to establish that its content is substantially different from that of a conferring State in a particular case.

An identifiable—and practical—consequence of the fiduciary nature of an agency relationship between one or more States and an organization relates to the competence of the organization to sub-confer its powers. Sereni makes the argument cogently in the context of international law

An alternative approach may be to consider the international organization in such a case as only being responsible for its role in the commission of the unlawful act. This approach would seek to rely on the application by analogy of Article 16 of the ILC Articles on State Responsibility, which provides as follows: 'A State which aids or assists another State in the commission of an internationally wrongful act by the latter is internationally responsible for doing so if: (a) that State does so with knowledge of the circumstances of the internationally wrongful act; and (b) the act would be internationally wrongful if committed by that State.' (Contained in Crawford, *supra* n.66, p.148.) The reason why, however, this type of situation does not apply to the case of an international organization acting as an agent for States in a particular situation is that it is precisely *the act of the organization that is unlawful*; whereas Article 16 would only be applicable in the different case where it was an *act of the State* that was unlawful and the organization was merely assisting in the commission of the act. See further on Article 16: Crawford, *ibidem*, p.148; and Lowe, V, 'Responsibility for the Conduct of Other States', *Japanese Journal of International Law*, (2002), p.1 at p.4.

[113] See also in US law, Reuschlein and Gregory, *supra* n.55, p.11, and Seavey, *supra* n.55, p.863; in English law see Reynolds, *supra* n.55, p.191 *et sequentia*, and Fridman, *supra* n.55, p.157 (see also Ho, B., *Hong Kong Agency Law* (1991), p.3); in German law see Staubach, *supra* n.73, p.7; and in French law see Guyénot, *supra* n.73, p.171.

[114] Crawford, *supra* n.5, p.54. Emphasis added. Moreover, Sereni in his discussion of the way in which a State must act as an agent pursuant to an authority to exercise diplomatic protection on behalf of the citizens of another State, stipulates 'it [the State acting as agent] must perform it in the interest of the state to which the citizens belong.' (Sereni, *supra* n.25, p.644.)

when he states:

> No principle or rule of international law forbids that the agent be granted the power of appointing a sub-agent for the purpose of the agency. However, the authority of the agent does not necessarily include the power of sub-delegation. This power exists only if it has been granted by the principal . . . In international law even more than in any system of national law, the relationship of principal and agent is a fiduciary one. *Since every international transaction includes some element of discretion, the principal ordinarily relies upon the personal qualities of the agent.* It is, then, to be presumed that the subject appointed to perform some functions cannot sub-delegate another subject to fulfill them on behalf of the principal, unless expressly authorized. This presumption applies even when international agency is established in the interest of the principal.[115]

This position is certainly different from that in our next category of 'delegation' where the delegate—*in casu*, the organization—does arguably possess a limited general competence to sub-delegate conferred powers without an express authorization to do so being necessary.[116]

To conclude more generally on our discussion of agency, there are two conditions for the establishment of an agency relationship in international law: First, that the principal and agent are separate legal entities, and, second, that both the principal and agent consent to the relationship. However, in the case where one or more States confer powers on an organization there is a presumption against the establishment of an agency relationship since both of these conditions—consent and control—are not fulfilled on a *prima facie* basis. It is only a presumption against agency and not a rule since there are cases where an international organization may possibly act as an agent for a State or group of States. Where such cases of agency can be established then it has the following consequences: the organization in the exercise of conferred power can change the legal relations of the State in question but does not change its own legal relations; both the State and the organization will in general terms be jointly liable for any unlawful acts committed by the organization; and, finally, the organization is under a fiduciary duty to act in the interests of the State concerned, even though this may raise an issue of *vires* for the organization under its constituent treaty.

[115] Sereni, *supra* n.25, p.653. Emphasis added.

[116] See Sarooshi, *supra* n.12, Chapter 1.

STATE IMMUNITY IN THE EUROPEAN COURT OF HUMAN RIGHTS: REAFFIRMATIONS AND MISCONCEPTIONS

Xiaodong Yang*

Three decisions by the European Court of Human Rights (ECHR) are targets of criticism, for they involve some crucial points of confusion surrounding the important subject of State immunity.[1] In its three Grand Chamber judgments, all delivered on 21 November 2001, in the cases of *Al-Adsani v United Kingdom, Fogarty v United Kingdom*, and *McElhinney v Ireland*,[2] the ECHR, dealing for the first time with the issue of State immunity,[3] held that granting jurisdictional immunity to a foreign State in civil proceedings did not constitute an unjustified restriction on the right of access to court and was therefore not a violation of art. 6(1) of the European Convention on Human Rights, so long as such grant satisfied the criteria articulated by the ECHR in relation to art. 6(1).

* Lecturer in Law, University of Aberdeen.

[1] Some words should be said at the outset about the use of the term 'State immunity'. The word 'immunity' in both its singular and plural forms can be used interchangeably. Thus, on the one hand one finds the 1972 European Convention on State *Immunity* and the 1978 UK State *Immunity* Act; while, on the other, one finds the 1976 US Foreign Sovereign *Immunities* Act and the United Nations International Law Commission's 1991 Draft Articles on Jurisdictional *Immunities* of States and Their Property. It is quite reasonable to think that 'immunities' rather than 'immunity' should be used, so as to bring out the fact that, in a sense, there are more sorts of immunity than one (as there are different sorts of proceedings). The International Court of Justice (ICJ), for example, contrasted '*immunities* from jurisdiction in other States, both civil and criminal' with 'the *immunity* from criminal jurisdiction'. (Emphases added) (*Arrest Warrant of 11 April 2000 (Democratic Republic of the Congo v Belgium)*, ICJ, 14 February 2002, judgment, para. 51, http://www.icj-cij.org/icjwww/idocket/ iCOBE/iCOBEframe.htm). But then there are many who would find no problem with using the word 'immunity' in the singular form to cover those 'immunities' as the ICJ would see them: in the words of Lord Browne-Wilkinson, for instance, 'The foreign state is entitled to procedural *immunity* from the *processes* of the forum state. This *immunity* extends to both criminal and civil liability.' (Emphases added) (*Pinochet No. 3* [2000] 1 AC 147, 201). At any rate, the word 'immunity' in the singular form seems to have both an abstract connotation, signifying the non-amenability of a State to the jurisdiction of another State, thereby embracing all the 'immunities' collectively, and a concrete one, which refers to a particular 'immunity' from a particular proceeding. In other words, 'immunity' in the singular form is capable of covering the situations denoted by both its singular and plural forms. For this reason, the word 'immunity' is used in this article. There is also a practical consideration: if the word 'immunities' were used, then both 'immunities' and 'immunity' would have to be used, as the case might require, and this might cause some confusions.

[2] *Al-Adsani v United Kingdom*, Application No. 35763/97, (2002) 34 EHRR 11; *Fogarty v United Kingdom* Application No. 37112/97, (2002) 34 EHRR 12; *McElhinney v Ireland*, Application No. 31253/96; (2002) 34 EHRR 13.

[3] The ECHR had previously addressed the issue of immunity of international organizations, which is different from, though in many respects analogous to, that of immunity of States. See *Prince Hans-Adam II of Liechtenstein v Germany*, Application No. 42527/98, (2001) 11 BHRC 526; *Waite and Kennedy v Germany*, Application No. 26083/94, (2000) 30 EHRR 261; and *Beer and Regan v Germany*, Application No. 28934/95, (2001) 33 EHRR 3.

These three cases concerned perhaps the three most disputed areas of State immunity from jurisdiction, namely, torture committed outside the forum State, tortious conduct within the forum State, and employment relationships. The judgments share the same central holding, in identical language, regarding the relationship between the right of access to court and State immunity, which is then applied to the particular facts of each case. Thus they provide a basis for a discussion of three otherwise disparate topics of State immunity.

My criticism will be directed not so much at the central holding of the cases, which reaffirms the ECHR's consistent jurisprudence on art. 6(1) and is in line with the general international practice regarding State immunity, as at certain particular points in the Court's reasoning, which are representative of some of the most widely prevalent misconceptions about State immunity, especially with regard to human rights violations such as torture. The *Pinochet* case,[4] which concerned the immunity of a former head of State from criminal proceedings for torture committed while in office, will also be analysed in relation to the three ECHR cases.

I. The Decisions

All three applicants alleged that, as a result of the doctrine of State immunity, they had been denied access to court in the determination of their claims against foreign governments and that this denial constituted a violation of art. 6(1) of the European Convention on Human Rights, which provides: 'In the determination of his civil rights and obligations . . . everyone is entitled to a fair and public hearing . . . by an independent and impartial tribunal established by law.'

Essentially, the ECHR had to deal with two separate questions, one general and the other particular, namely: (1) whether the grant of State immunity to foreign States was compatible with the right of access to court; and (2) whether such grant of immunity by the English and Irish courts, under the special circumstances of the respective cases, exceeded the boundaries set by current international law and therefore constituted an infringement of that right.

In its three judgments, the ECHR employed identical language in explaining the right of access to court and in articulating the criteria by which possible limitations might be justified:

> The right of access to court is not . . . absolute, but may be subject to limitations; these are permitted by implication since the right of access by its very nature calls for regulation by the State. In this respect, the Contracting States enjoy a certain margin of appreciation . . . It must be satisfied that the limitations applied do not restrict or reduce the access left to the individual in such a way or to such an

[4] *R v Bow Street Metropolitan Stipendiary Magistrate and Others, Ex parte Pinochet Ugarte (No. 3) (Pinochet No. 3)* [2000] 1 AC 147(HL).

extent that the very essence of the right is impaired. Furthermore, a limitation will not be compatible with Article 6 § 1 if it does not pursue a legitimate aim and if there is no reasonable relationship of proportionality between the means employed and the aim sought to be achieved.[5]

Thus no limitation is permissible that impairs the very essence of the right of access to court, that does not pursue a legitimate aim or that is disproportionate to the aim pursued. In so holding, the ECHR was reiterating its consistent jurisprudence on art. 6(1).[6]

Applying these criteria, the ECHR noted that sovereign immunity was a concept of international law, by virtue of which one State should not be subject to the jurisdiction of another State. Thus, the grant of immunity to a foreign State in civil proceedings pursued 'the legitimate aim of complying with international law to promote comity and good relations between States through the respect of another State's sovereignty'.[7] According to the ECHR, the European Convention on Human Rights 'should so far as possible be interpreted in harmony with other rules of international law of which it forms part, including those relating to the grant of State immunity'.[8] Therefore, measures which reflected generally recognized rules of public international law on State immunity could not 'in principle be regarded as imposing a disproportionate restriction on the right of access to court as embodied in Article 6(1)' but should instead be regarded as 'inherent' in the fair trial guarantee in that article.[9]

Starting from this basic proposition, the ECHR proceeded to ascertain whether the grant of immunity in the separate cases was in conformity with international law. It reached the same conclusion for the three cases: that there had been no violation of art. 6(1). In this connection, it is interesting to note that the division of the judges in these three cases, and therefore the voting patterns, afford graphic indicia of the order of intensity of current debates on State immunity in three respective areas: torture committed outside the territory of the forum State (*Al-Adsani v United Kingdom*, 9 votes to 8), tortious conduct in the territory of the

[5] *Al-Adsani v United Kingdom*, judgment, para. 53; *McElhinney v Ireland*, judgment, para. 34; *Fogarty v United Kingdom*, judgment, para. 33.

[6] And repeating the same language as well. See, *e.g.*, *Prince Hans-Adam II of Liechtenstein v Germany*, Application No. 42527/98, (2001) 11 BHRC 526, para. 44; *Waite and Kennedy v Germany*, Application No. 26083/94, (2000) 30 EHRR 261, para. 59; *Beer and Regan v Germany*, Application No. 28934/95, (2001) 33 EHRR 3, para. 49; *Osman v United Kingdom*, Application No. 23452/94, (2000) 29 EHRR 245, para. 147; *Tinnelly & Sons Ltd and Others and McElduff and Others v United Kingdom*, Application No. 20390/92; 21322/93, (1999) 27 EHRR 249, para. 72; *Stubbings and Others v United Kingdom*, Application No. 22083/93; 22095/93, (1997) 23 EHRR 213, para. 50; and *Fayed v United Kingdom*, Application No. 17101/90, (1994) 18 EHRR 393, para. 65. See also, *e.g.*, *T.P. and K.M. v United Kingdom*, Application No. 28945/95, (2002) 34 EHRR 2, para. 98 and *Z and Others v United Kingdom*, Application No. 29392/95, (2002) 34 EHRR 3, para. 93.

[7] *Al-Adsani v United Kingdom*, judgment, para. 54; *McElhinney v Ireland*, judgment, para. 35; *Fogarty v United Kingdom*, judgment, para. 34.

[8] *Al-Adsani v United Kingdom*, judgment, para. 55; *McElhinney v Ireland*, judgment, para. 36; *Fogarty v United Kingdom*, judgment, para. 35.

[9] *Al-Adsani v United Kingdom*, judgment, para. 56; *McElhinney v Ireland*, judgment, para. 37; *Fogarty v United Kingdom*, judgment, para. 36.

forum State (*McElhinney v Ireland*, 12 votes to 5), and contracts of employment (*Fogarty v United Kingdom*, 16 votes to 1).

1. Al-Adsani v United Kingdom

Al-Adsani, a dual Kuwaiti and British national, came into possession of videotapes showing sexual activities of an influential member of the royal family of Kuwait, the contents of which later somehow became common knowledge. For this reason, he alleged, he was abducted, falsely imprisoned in a State prison and tortured by the royal family member and by prison security guards. He managed to return to England and spent six weeks in hospital being treated for serious burns. He also alleged that, once in England, he had received threats, including death threats, from agents of the Government of Kuwait, and especially from the Embassy of Kuwait in London.

Al-Adsani instituted civil proceedings in 1992 in England against the Government of Kuwait and his alleged torturers in respect of injury to his physical and mental health caused by torture in Kuwait and threats against his life made after his return to England. Kuwait claimed immunity.

In its judgment the High Court drew a distinction between the acts alleged to have taken place in Kuwait and those alleged to have occurred in England. As to the former, the Court found that the clear language of the 1978 UK State Immunity Act (UK SIA)[10] conferred immunity upon foreign sovereign States for acts committed outside the jurisdiction of English courts. As far as the latter were concerned, the Court was not satisfied on the balance of probabilities that the Kuwaiti Government was responsible for the threats made to the applicant. As a result, the tort exception provided for by s. 5 of the UK SIA did not apply and the Kuwaiti Government was immune in respect of these allegations.[11]

On appeal by Al-Adsani, the Court of Appeal held that the crucial question was whether State immunity applied in respect of the alleged events in Kuwait. The Court expressly rejected the argument that the prohibition of torture, being of a *jus cogens* nature, overrode State immunity. According to the Court, since there was no *jus cogens* exception to immunity in the UK SIA, a foreign State still enjoyed immunity in respect of torture or other acts contrary to international law, which did not fall within one of the express exceptions.[12]

Al-Adsani contended before the ECHR that the prohibition of torture had acquired the status of a peremptory norm (*jus cogens*) in international

[10] (1978) 17 ILM 1123.

[11] *Al-Adsani v Government of Kuwait* (QB) (1995) 103 ILR 420, 429–32. Section 5 provides: 'A State is not immune as respects proceedings in respect of—(a) death or personal injury; or (b) damage to or loss of tangible property, caused by an act or omission in the United Kingdom.'

[12] *Al-Adsani v Government of Kuwait* (CA) (1996), 107 ILR 536, 541–4. Byers takes the view that on the same facts immunity might not have been available at common law, which comprises rules of customary international law, including the *jus cogens* rule of prohibition of torture. Michael Byers, case note on *Al-Adsani v Government of Kuwait*, 67 *BYBIL* (1996) 537, 539–40.

law, taking precedence over treaty law and other rules of international law. But the ECHR was not persuaded:

> While the Court accepts . . . that the prohibition of torture has achieved the status of a peremptory norm in international law, it observes that the present case concerns not, as in the *Furundzija* and *Pinochet* decisions, the criminal liability of an individual for alleged acts of torture, but the immunity of a State in a civil suit for damages in respect of acts of torture within the territory of that State. Notwithstanding the special character of the prohibition of torture in international law, the Court is unable to discern . . . any firm basis for concluding that, as a matter of international law, a State no longer enjoys immunity from civil suit in the courts of another State where acts of torture are alleged.[13]

Thus, despite the growing recognition of the overriding importance of the prohibition of torture, the ECHR did not find it established in international law that States were not entitled to immunity 'in respect of civil claims for damages for alleged torture committed outside the forum State'.[14] The UK SIA, which granted immunity to States in respect of personal injury claims unless the damage was caused within the UK, was not inconsistent with those limitations generally accepted by the community of nations as part of the doctrine of State immunity. The application by the English courts of the provisions of the UK SIA to uphold Kuwait's claim to immunity could not, therefore, be said to have amounted to an unjustified restriction on the applicant's access to court.

2. *McElhinney v Ireland*

McElhinney, an Irish national, alleged that, following an incident in March 1991 at the Northern Ireland border, a British soldier assaulted him by attempting to fire a loaded gun at him in the Republic of Ireland. In that incident, McElhinney drove a truck through a British checkpoint on the border between the UK and the Republic of Ireland. The British soldier on duty at the checkpoint tried to stop him but was carried over the border into Ireland on the tow-bar of the truck. In June 1993 McElhinney started an action in Irish courts against the soldier and the British Secretary of State for Northern Ireland, claiming damages in respect of his allegation that the soldier had wrongfully assaulted him by pointing a loaded gun at him and pulling the trigger. McElhinney maintained that sovereign immunity did not apply in respect of claims for damages arising from torts committed within the jurisdiction of Ireland.

Both the Irish High Court and, on appeal, the Irish Supreme Court granted immunity on the grounds that the soldier, in carrying out his duties, was performing governmental activities when the acts complained

[13] *Al-Adsani v United Kingdom*, judgment, para. 61. For the *Furundzija* case here mentioned by the ECHR see *Prosecutor v Anto Furundzija* (*Judgment*) ICTY Trial Chamber II, Case IT-95-17/1, 10 December 1998, http://www.un.org/icty/furundzija/trialc2/judgement/index.htm, esp. para. 156.

[14] *Ibid.*, para. 66.

of occurred. These were therefore *acta jure imperii*, or sovereign acts, even if committed within the jurisdiction of Ireland, and did not fall within the commercial activity exception to sovereign immunity.[15]

In the opinion of the ECHR,

> . . . there appears to be a trend in international and comparative law towards limiting State immunity in respect of personal injury caused by an act or omission within the forum State, but . . . this practice is by no means universal. Further, it appears . . . that the trend may primarily refer to 'insurable' personal injury, that is incidents arising out of ordinary road traffic accidents, rather than matters relating to the core area of State sovereignty such as the acts of a soldier on foreign territory which, of their very nature, may involve sensitive issues affecting diplomatic relations between States and national security. Certainly, it cannot be said that Ireland is alone in holding that immunity attaches to suits in respect of such torts committed by *acta jure imperii* or that, in affording this immunity, Ireland falls outside any currently accepted international standards.[16]

The ECHR agreed with the Irish Supreme Court that it was not possible, given the present state of the development of international law, to conclude that Irish law conflicted with its general principles. The decisions of the Irish courts upholding the UK's claim to immunity could not, therefore, be said to have exceeded the margin of appreciation allowed to States in limiting an individual's right to access to court.

3. Fogarty v United Kingdom

Fogarty worked as an administrative assistant at the US Embassy in London. Following her dismissal in 1995 she instituted proceedings against the US Government in an industrial tribunal in London, claiming that her dismissal had been the result of sex discrimination. In particular she alleged that she had been the victim of persistent sexual harassment from her supervisor. The US Government appeared in court and did not claim State immunity. The industrial tribunal upheld the applicant's complaint and compensation was agreed between the parties. In June 1995, while her first claim was still pending, the applicant applied for and obtained a 12-month fixed term contract as an administrative assistant at the Embassy. Upon the expiry of the contract, she applied for two secretarial posts at the US Embassy but was unsuccessful. She then issued a second application before the industrial tribunal, claiming that the Embassy's refusal to re-employ her was a consequence of her previous successful sex discrimination claim, and accordingly constituted victimization and discrimination under the 1975 UK Sex Discrimination Act. The US Government indicated its intention to claim State immunity from the jurisdiction of the tribunal, pointing out, in particular, that each

[15] *McElhinney v Williams and Her Majesty's Secretary of State for Northern Ireland*, Ireland, High Court, 1994, [1994] 2 ILRM 115, 119–20; 103 ILR 311, 316; Supreme Court, 1995, [1996] 1 ILRM 276, 288; 104 ILR 691, 702–3.

[16] *McElhinney v Ireland*, judgment, para. 38.

of the posts for which the applicant had applied were part of the administrative and technical staff of the Embassy, and accordingly fell within the ambit of the immunity granted by s. 16(1)(a) of the UK SIA.[17]

The ECHR observed that there appeared to be a trend in international and comparative law towards limiting State immunity in respect of employment-related disputes. However, where the proceedings related to employment in a foreign mission or embassy, international practice was divided on the question whether State immunity continued to apply and, if it did, whether it covered disputes relating to the contracts of all staff or only more senior members of the mission. It could not be said that the UK was alone in holding that immunity attached to suits by employees at diplomatic missions or that, in affording such immunity the UK fell outside any currently accepted international standards. The ECHR found that

> the proceedings which the applicant wished to bring did not concern the contractual rights of a current embassy employee, but instead related to alleged discrimination in the recruitment process. Questions relating to the recruitment of staff to missions and embassies may by their very nature involve sensitive and confidential issues, related, *inter alia*, to the diplomatic and organisational policy of a foreign State. The Court is not aware of any trend in international law towards a relaxation of the rule of State immunity as regards issues of recruitment to foreign missions.[18]

The ECHR therefore considered that, in conferring immunity on the US in the present case by virtue of the provisions of the UK SIA, the UK could not be said to have exceeded the margin of appreciation allowed to States in limiting an individual's access to court.

II. State Immunity as a Principle of International Law

The ECHR's central holding in the three cases under discussion can be compared with the decision of the English House of Lords in *Holland v Lampen-Wolfe*, in which a US university professor teaching international relations at a US military base in England brought defamation proceedings against the education services officer at the base, who had written a memorandum questioning her professional competence. The plaintiff argued that a denial of jurisdiction would infringe her right of access to court afforded by art. 6(1) of the European Convention on Human Rights. Lord Millett found that art. 6(1) and State immunity were not incompatible. Obviously having in mind the stock pronouncement of the ECHR, he pointed out specifically that

[17] Section 16(1)(a) provides that 'section 4 [the employment contract exception] . . . does not apply to proceedings concerning the employment of the members of a [diplomatic] mission . . . or of the members of a consular post . . .'

[18] *Fogarty v United Kingdom*, judgment, para. 38.

> This is not because the right guaranteed by article 6 is not absolute but subject to limitations, nor is it because the doctrine of state immunity serves a legitimate aim. It is because article 6 forbids a contracting state from denying individuals the benefit of its powers of adjudication; it does not extend the scope of those powers.[19]

Unlike the ECHR, which placed the stress on the 'right' of the individual and jealously circumscribed the boundaries of any possible limitations thereon, Lord Millett focused on the 'powers' of a domestic court. Thus, art. 6 'presupposes that the contracting states have the powers of adjudication necessary to resolve the issues in dispute. But it does not confer on contracting states adjudicative powers which they do not possess.'[20] As State immunity is a limitation imposed by international law upon the sovereignty of the UK itself, the powers of the English courts are limited to the extent that immunity should be granted to a foreign State as circumstances may require. Here Lord Millett was saying that, even if the individual's right of access to court was absolute in *character*, it was not absolute in *application*, in the sense that a court might not be able to exercise the power to entertain the claim. It is then not a matter of denial of a right; it is rather a question of lack of adjudicative power. Therefore, whereas the European Court of Human Rights endeavoured to ensure that the 'margin of appreciation' allowed the Contracting States was not exceeded, Lord Millett declared pointedly that in applying the clear, applicable law of State immunity to the particular case, the domestic court had 'no discretion or margin of appreciation'.[21]

A fuller appreciation of State immunity might be achieved by combining the reasoning of both the ECHR and Lord Millett. State immunity is a limitation imposed by international law on the jurisdictional powers of national courts, so that, in certain situations, the courts are incompetent to entertain certain claims, if these claims are directed against a foreign State. In a deeper sense, words like 'competence' and 'incompetence' are only terms of convenience, for the very word 'immunity' presupposes something, i.e., jurisdiction, from which a defendant is to be immune. To be more exact, the principle of State immunity denotes the situation where the jurisdictional powers of the courts of the forum State are, in a manner of speaking, 'neutralized' by the operation of international law, in the sense that, even though the courts would have jurisdiction under normal circumstances, the fact that the defendant is a foreign State precludes the exercise of that jurisdiction. To the extent that a court is precluded from exercising an otherwise existing jurisdiction, an individual's right of access to court is inevitably qualified. As State immunity is a rule of international law, and moreover one which dictates a precise result—the non-exercise of adjudicatory jurisdiction over a foreign State—then any decision by a national court duly giving effect to this principle must be in conformity with international law. However, it must be pointed out

[19] *Holland v Lampen-Wolfe* [2000] 1 WLR 1573, 1588. [20] *Id.* [21] *Ibid.*, at 1589.

that, apart from the rule of State immunity, international law comprises many other rules, the protection of fundamental human rights being a notable example. Inevitably States would come under conflicting obligations, for instance, of granting a foreign State immunity on the one hand, and of protecting human rights, on the other. In such a situation a balancing act might well be necessary.[22] In this connection, the triple test of non-impairment of the essence of the right concerned, legitimate aim, and proportionality, as formulated by the ECHR, has much to commend it. Of course considering that State immunity is merely a procedural, forum allocation rule, there is no necessary inconsistency here—the claimant still has a right of access to court but it will be a court in the respondent State.

III. State Immunity or State Impunity?

The ECHR rightly rejected the submissions by Ireland and the UK in *McElhinney* and *Al-Adsani* that, because of the operation of State immunity, the applicant's substantive right ceased to exist under domestic law. According to the ECHR, the grant of immunity was to be seen not as qualifying a substantive right, but as only a procedural bar on the national courts' power to determine the right. Thus an applicant's substantive right still exists even though he is procedurally barred from bringing claims to vindicate it.

Stating that art. 6(1) did not itself guarantee any particular content for civil rights and obligations in the substantive law of the Contracting States but extended only to *disputes* over such rights and obligations, the ECHR said:

> Whether a person has an actionable domestic claim may depend not only on the substantive content, properly speaking, of the relevant civil right as defined under national law but also on the existence of procedural bars preventing or limiting the possibilities of bringing potential claims to court. In the latter kind of case Article 6 § 1 may be applicable.[23]

In particular, the ECHR noted that an action against a State was not barred *in limine*: if the defendant State waived immunity, the action would proceed to a hearing and judgment. Thus, the grant of immunity was to be seen 'not as qualifying a substantive right but as a procedural bar'

[22] See, *e.g.*, Lady Fox's remark in her case note on the *Holland* case: 'If domestic law is held wrongly to have extended immunity of visiting armed forces contrary to that required by international law, then, on this reasoning, Dr. Holland's right of access may prevail over the United States' claim to immunity.' Hazel Fox, Access to Justice and State Immunity (case note on *Holland*), 117 *Law Quarterly Review* (2001) 10, 14.

[23] *Al-Adsani v United Kingdom*, judgment, para. 47; *McElhinney v Ireland*, judgment, para. 24; *Fogarty v United Kingdom*, judgment, para. 25. For identical holding see *Fayed v United Kingdom*, Application No. 17101/90, ECHR 1994, para. 65.

limiting the national courts' power to determine the right or preventing the applicant from bringing a claim.[24]

This is a significant holding, not least because the Contracting States are thereby precluded from unjustifiably curtailing or negating individuals' substantive rights under the guise of procedural rules.[25] For our purposes, its significance lies in that it serves to highlight the essential, procedural nature of foreign State immunity.

The procedural character of State immunity has been ignored by many scholars advocating domestic judicial jurisdiction over foreign States with respect to violations of human rights. These scholars usually use the word 'immunity' (exemption from judicial proceedings) in the sense of 'impunity' (exemption from punishment or from liability for injurious consequences).[26] State immunity thus becomes synonymous with 'State

[24] *Al-Adsani v United Kingdom*, judgment, para. 48; *McElhinney v Ireland*, judgment, para. 25; *Fogarty v United Kingdom*, judgment, para. 26.

[25] As the ECHR put it: 'Certainly the Convention enforcement bodies may not create by way of interpretation of Article 6 § 1 a substantive civil right which has no legal basis in the State concerned. However, it would not be consistent with the rule of law in a democratic society or with the basic principle underlying Article 6 § 1—namely that civil claims must be capable of being submitted to a judge for adjudication—if, for example, a State could, without restraint or control by the Convention enforcement bodies, remove from the jurisdiction of the courts a whole range of civil claims or confer immunities from civil liability on large groups or categories of persons.' *Al-Adsani v United Kingdom*, judgment, para. 47; *McElhinney v Ireland*, judgment, para. 24; *Fogarty v United Kingdom*, judgment, para. 25. For identical holding see *Fayed v United Kingdom*, Application No. 17101/90, ECHR 1994, para. 65.

For example, in *Tinnelly & Sons Ltd and Others and McElduff and Others v United Kingdom*, Application No. 20390/92; 21322/93, (1999) 27 EHRR 249, the ECHR found that the so-called 'public interest immunity', which in English law allows the prosecution, in the public interest, not to disclose or communicate to the defence all the documents in its possession and to 'reserve' some of them, constituted in that case a violation of art. 6(1) of the European Convention on Human Rights. Similarly, in *Osman v United Kingdom*, Application No. 23452/94, (2000) 29 EHRR 245, the ECHR found that the 'blanket immunity' enjoyed by the police under domestic law of England for their acts and omissions during the investigation and suppression of crime constituted in that case a violation of art. 6(1).

[26] See, *e.g.*, Santiago Villalpando, L'Affaire Pinochet: Beaucoup de Bruit pour Rien? L'Apport au Droit International de la Décision de la Chambre des Lords du 24 Mars 1999, 104 *Revue Générale de Droit International Public* (2000) 393, 423; Sir Nigel Rodley, Introduction—The Beginning of the End of Immunity and Impunity of Officials Responsible for Torture, in Reed Brody and Michael Ratner (eds.), *The Pinochet Papers: The Case of Augusto Pinochet in Spain and Britain*, The Hague/London/Boston: Kluwer Law International, 2000, p. 3 at 5; Reed Brody, The Case of Augusto Pinochet, *ibid.* p. 7 at 13; Nigel S. Rodley, Breaking the Cycle of Impunity for Gross Violations of Human Rights: The *Pinochet* Case in Perspective, 69 *Nordic Journal of International Law* (2000) 11 (This issue of this journal is explicitly devoted to the question of 'Prevention of Impunity'); Rosanne van Alebeek, The *Pinochet* Case: International Human Rights Law on Trial, 71 *BYBIL* (2000) 29, 29; Jodi Horowitz, *Regina v. Bartle and the Commissioner of Police for the Metropolis and Others ex Parte Pinochet*: Universal Jurisdiction and Sovereign Immunity for *Jus Cogens* Violations, 23 *Fordham International Law Journal* (1999–2000) 489, 522–4; Ilias Bantekas, The Pinochet Affair in International Law, 52 *Révue hellénique de droit international* (1999) 119, 129; Nehal Bhuta, Justice without Borders? Prosecuting General Pinochet, 23 *Melbourne University Law Review* (1999) 499, 530 and 531; Jill M. Sears, Confronting the 'Culture of Impunity': Immunity of Heads of State from Nuremberg to *ex parte Pinochet*, 42 *German Yearbook of International Law* (1999) 125, 125; Andrea Bianchi, Immunity versus Human Rights: The *Pinochet* Case, 10 *European Journal of International Law* (1999) 237, 260–1; M. O. Chibundu, Making Customary International Law through Municipal Adjudication: A Structural Inquiry, 39 *Virginia Journal of International Law* (1998–99) 1069, 1130–34; Jack Alan Levy, As between *Princz* and King: Reassessing the Law of Foreign Sovereign Immunity as Applied to *Jus Cogens* Violators,

impunity', and, with the public opprobrium thus rightfully attached, is then readily dismissed as anachronistic and deserving to be abolished.[27]

But State *immunity* does not mean State *impunity*. The former is a procedural matter while the latter is a substantive one. Whether a State should be exonerated from its international responsibility for violations of human rights is one thing, whether it should be held answerable for its conduct before a foreign domestic court is quite another. A State that has acted in violation of international law cannot be exempted from State responsibility under international law even if no municipal court is in a position, under current international law, to assume jurisdiction over the wrongdoing State. State immunity means only that a domestic court is precluded, under certain circumstances, by international law from exercising jurisdiction over a foreign State, but not that some other forum, *e.g.* an international tribunal, is likewise precluded, nor that, ultimately, it will always be impossible for domestic courts to exercise such jurisdiction even if the international legal system should undergo some fundamental change. The rule of State immunity is not concerned with the substantive question whether a State is internationally responsible for its acts, but with the procedural question as to which forum is to be utilized in order to settle that responsibility; that is, whether, under current international law, that responsibility is to be dealt with in a foreign domestic court or resolved through channels normally operative on a State-to-State basis. In a word, State immunity is not about substantive responsibility; it is about the proper or appropriate forum.

This point has been unequivocally confirmed by the International Court of Justice (ICJ) (though the ICJ made the remarks in the context of immunity enjoyed by incumbent ministers for foreign affairs, itself a derivative of State immunity):

> The Court emphasizes . . . that the *immunity* from jurisdiction enjoyed by incumbent Ministers for Foreign Affairs does not mean that they enjoy *impunity* in respect of any crimes they might have committed, irrespective of their gravity. Immunity from criminal jurisdiction and individual criminal responsibility are quite separate concepts. While jurisdictional immunity is procedural in nature,

86 *Georgetown Law Journal* (1997–98) 2703, 2708; Jennifer A. Gergen, Human Rights and the Foreign Sovereign Immunities Act, 36 *Virginia Journal of International Law* (1995–96) 765, 786; Mathias Reimann, A Human Rights Exception to Sovereign Immunity: Some Thoughts on *Princz v. Federal Republic of Germany*, 16 *Michigan Journal of International Law* (1994–95) 403, 432; Joan Fitzpatrick, Reducing the FSIA Barrier to Human Rights Litigation—Is Amendment Necessary and Possible? 86 *American Society of International Law Proceedings* (1992) 338, 343 and 346; Dissenting opinion of Circuit Judge Wald in *Princz v. Federal Republic of Germany*, 26 F 3d 1166, 1182 (D.C. Cir. 1994); 103 ILR 594, 618 ('Prior to the Nuremberg trials, the positivist theory of international law governed state sovereignty, and a state's treatment of its own citizens was considered *immune from the dictates of international law*.' (Emphasis added)); and Haley D. Collums, The *Letelier* Case: Foreign Sovereign Liability for Acts of Political Assassination, 21 *Virginia Journal of International Law* (1980–81) 251, 263.

[27] The sentiments can in some measure be illustrated by discussions of an alleged 'antinomy between State immunity and international human rights', which makes State immunity appear as 'legacy of a bygone epoch'. See Andrea Bianchi, Denying State Immunity to Violators of Human Rights, 46 *Austrian Journal of Public and International Law* (1993–94) 195, 195–7 and 203–7.

criminal responsibility is a question of substantive law. Jurisdictional immunity may well bar prosecution for a certain period or for certain offences; it cannot exonerate the person to whom it applies from all criminal responsibility.[28]

However, the immunity/impunity distinction should not be taken too far. Under certain circumstances immunity would for all practical purposes constitute impunity as well, so that immunity and impunity would then become indistinguishable: witness the immunity Pinochet and his ilk enjoy under a 'Decree Law' of their own making and similar 'immunity/impunity' in other countries.[29] However, a distinction has to be drawn between three types of immunity: immunity of States from proceedings in foreign domestic courts under international law; immunity enjoyed by States (and State officials) before their own courts under domestic law,[30]

[28] *Case concerning the Arrest Warrant of 11 April 2000 (Democratic Republic of the Congo v Belgium)*, ICJ, judgment of 14 February 2002, para. 60. To make the point clearer the ICJ could have said: 'Jurisdictional immunity may well bar prosecution *by a foreign State* for a certain period or for certain offences . . .'

There are indeed a few scholars who are aware of this immunity/impunity distinction. See Jean-Yves de Cara, L'Affaire Pinochet devant la Chamre des Lords, 45 *Annuaire Français de Droit International* (1999) 72, 88 and 99; Magdalini Karagiannakis, State Immunity and Fundamental Human Rights, 11 *Leiden Journal of International Law* (1998) 9, 42; Michael Byers, case note on *Al-Adsani v Government of Kuwait*, 67 *BYBIL* (1996) 537, 538. See also *Brazilian Embassy Employee Case*, Portugal, Supreme Court (1984) 116 ILR 625, 633.

[29] Such immunity has been granted in so-called 'amnesty laws', among which the most notable are the Chilean Decree Law 2191 of 19 April 1978, which exculpates from criminal responsibility all persons who committed human rights violations between 11 September 1973 and 10 March 1978, and the Peruvian Law No. 26479 of 14 June 1995, which grants a general amnesty to all those members of the security forces and civilians for human rights violations committed between May 1980 and 15 June 1995 and which is further strengthened by Law No. 26492 of 28 June 1995 prohibiting the judiciary from ruling on the legality or applicability of the first amnesty law. Relevant documents are available from Amnesty International's website (www.amnesty.org).

The Vienna Declaration and Programme of Action adopted at the World Conference on Human Rights held in Vienna, 14–25 June 1993, demands that: 'States should abrogate legislation leading to impunity for those responsible for grave violations of human rights such as torture and prosecute such violations, thereby providing a firm basis for the rule of law.' UN Doc. A/CONF.157/23 (1993), para. 60. http://www.unhchr.ch/huridocda/huridoca.nsf/(Symbol)/A.CONF.157.23.En?Open Document.

For a recent analysis of such amnesty laws see Ben Chigara, *Amnesty in International Law: the Legality under International Law of National Amnesty Laws*, Harlow, England: Pearson Education Ltd, 2002.

[30] Pinochet's immunity in Chilean courts under his 'Decree Law' falls under this category.

Immunity can be granted pursuant to constitutional principles. In the US, the United States itself, as a sovereign, is immune from suit in US courts except to the extent that it has waived its immunity, and a waiver of its sovereign immunity must be unequivocally expressed and never implied. See, *e.g., United States v Sherwood*, 312 US 584, 586 (1941); *United States v King*, 395 US 1, 4 (1969); and *United States v Mitchell*, 445 US 535, 538 (1980). The US President is entitled to *absolute immunity* from damages liability predicated on his official acts. *Nixon v Fitzgerald*, 457 US 731, 744–58 (1982). *Cf. United States v Nixon*, 418 US 683, 706 (1974). In the UK, the concept of 'public interest immunity' (formerly known as 'Crown Privilege') allows the prosecution, in the public interest, not to disclose or communicate to the defence all the documents in its possession and to 'reserve' some of them (though the scope of this immunity was somewhat limited by the English House of Lords to the extent that a court may order the disclosure of privileged information in certain circumstances: *Conway v Rimmer* [1968] AC 910. Police officers in the UK may enjoy immunity from civil suit in respect of their acts and omissions in the investigation and suppression of crime. This immunity was affirmed by the House of Lords in *Hill v Chief Constable of West Yorkshire* [1989] AC 53. Both these immunities, however, came under attack before the ECHR. In *Tinnelly & Sons Ltd and Others and McElduff and Others v United Kingdom*, Application No. 20390/92; 21322/93, (1999) 27 EHRR 249, the ECHR found and immunity (or rather non-immunity) before international tribunals.[31] These three are different concepts[32] and rules derived from one type may not be applicable to another.[33] 'State immunity' discussed in the present article means, as it usually does, immunity enjoyed by States (and, by extension, their representatives) under international law before foreign domestic courts. Once the notion of State immunity has been clearly delimited, then, on the plane of international law at least, immunity becomes distinct from impunity, since impunity thus appears to be a possible *consequence* of immunity, rather than immunity itself.

IV. The Alleged Distinction Between Criminal and Civil Proceedings

Broadly speaking, as has been shown above, the decisions of the ECHR are in keeping with the current status of international law on State immunity.[34] Yet there are certain misconceptions, the foremost among which is a supposed distinction between criminal and civil proceedings in the international law on State immunity.

In *Al-Adsani v United Kingdom*, the majority judges in the ECHR based their reasoning upon a distinction between the criminal liability of an individual for alleged acts of torture and the immunity of a State from civil proceedings for damages for acts of torture, in an obvious attempt to

that the so-called 'public interest immunity' related to the withholding of certain documents constituted in that case a violation of art. 6(1) of the European Convention on Human Rights. Similarly, in *Osman v United Kingdom*, Application No. 23452/94, (2000) 29 EHRR 245, the ECHR found that the 'blanket immunity' enjoyed by the police under domestic law of England for their acts and omissions during the investigation and suppression of crime constituted in that case a violation of art. 6(1).

[31] See, *e.g.*, art. 27(2) of the Rome Statute of the International Criminal Court: 'Immunities or special procedural rules which may attach to the official capacity of a person, whether under national or international law, shall not bar the Court from exercising its jurisdiction over such a person.' http://www.un.org/law/icc/statute/romefra.htm.

[32] See, *e.g.*, *Sanchez-Espinoza v Reagan*, 770 F.2d 202, 207, fn. 5 (D.C. Cir. 1985) ('. . . the doctrine of foreign sovereign immunity is quite distinct from the doctrine of domestic sovereign immunity . . .'); *Amerada Hess Shipping Corporation v Argentine Republic*, 638 F. Supp. 73, 76 (S.D.N.Y. 1986) ('Contemporary legal theory recognizes that foreign sovereign immunity, based on comity, is a very different matter from the sovereign immunity accorded the state in its own courts, based on separation of powers.').

[33] In *Prosecutor v Blaskic*, the Trial Chamber of the International Criminal Tribunal for the former Yugoslavia held that the principle of sovereign immunity, being developed in regard to domestic, as opposed to international, courts, was inapplicable in that case and therefore could not serve as a basis for a State to refuse to comply with orders of the International Tribunal. *Prosecutor v Blaskic (Objection to the Issue of* Subpoenae Duces Tecum*)*, ICTY Trial Chamber II, 1997, Case IT-95-14-PT, 110 ILR 607, 648–51. In this regard it is to be noted that some courts also regard State immunity and *diplomatic immunity* as two distinct regimes. See, *e.g.*, *Former Syrian Ambassador to the German Democratic Republic*, Case No. 2 BvR 1516/96, Federal Republic of Germany, Federal Constitutional Court (BVerfG) (Second Senate) (1997) 115 ILR 595, 609 ('State immunity and diplomatic immunity represent two different institutions of international law, each with their own rules, so that no inference can be drawn from any restrictions in one sphere as to possible effects in the other.').

[34] However it has to be noted that *Al-Adsani v United Kingdom* was decided only by an extremely narrow margin: 9 votes to 8. This vividly reflects the intense debate currently raging on State immunity in respect of acts of torture.

counter the applicant's claim for damages for acts of torture committed by a foreign State.[35] But this distinction is problematic, not only because the majority judges failed to observe that an individual's non-immunity does not automatically translate into a State's non-immunity, but also because their opinion missed an important aspect of the question of State immunity.

The majority's opinion that a State *enjoys* immunity from *civil* suit in the courts of another State where acts of torture are alleged might create the impression that a State *may not enjoy* immunity from *criminal* suit for acts of torture.[36] This is erroneous, for the distinction between 'criminal' and 'civil' proceedings in the context of State immunity does not exist either in doctrine or in current State practice. In current international law, States enjoy immunity as a general rule subject to a range of exceptions; and these exceptions have been formulated not on the basis of a criminal/civil distinction but in reliance on a doctrine, evolved almost exclusively in the context of civil and commercial disputes, that upholds immunity for sovereign/governmental acts but denies immunity to commercial/private acts.[37] In other words, immunity can be denied only in certain types of civil proceedings, while in all other proceedings, be they civil or criminal, States are immune from the jurisdiction of foreign domestic courts. If a distinction between criminal and civil proceedings has to be forced here, it can be stated that States are *absolutely* immune from criminal proceedings and *relatively* immune from civil proceedings subject to a limited number of exceptional cases. This is due to the evolution of the doctrine of relative/restrictive State immunity, which developed against a primordial absolute State immunity regarding any proceedings (subject, of course, to a possible waiver of immunity by the defendant State) and out of the need to protect private interests in civil and commercial matters.

The absence of any rule restricting State immunity in criminal matters can be shown at two levels: national and international. At the national level, none of the few national statutes on State immunity contains an exception to immunity from criminal proceedings. These statutes either

[35] *Cf.* the *Pinochet* case, which involves criminal proceedings.

[36] This is most probably what they had in mind without expressly declaring it. As some of the dissenting judges pointed out: 'The majority . . . contend that a distinction must be made between criminal proceedings, where apparently they accept that a *jus cogens* rule has the overriding force to deprive the rules of sovereign immunity from their legal effects, and civil proceedings, where, in the absence of authority, they consider that the same conclusion cannot be drawn.' Dissenting opinion of Judge Rozakis and Judge Caflisch joined by Judge Wildhaber, Judge Costa, Judge Cabral Barreto and Judge Vajic in *Al-Adsani v United Kingdom*, para. 4.

[37] The governmental/commercial dichotomy only captures the prototypical case. As rightly pointed out by Professor Crawford, not all State activities can be described either as 'governmental' or 'commercial': many activities might be classified as 'neutral' or 'colourless'. Moreover, all the domestic statutes on State immunity assert jurisdiction over a range of transactions or acts which may not qualify as 'commercial'. James Crawford, International Law and Foreign Sovereigns: Distinguishing Immune Transactions, 54 *BYBIL* (1983) 75, 91 and 109–13. The word 'private' (in the sense that certain acts of a State are those that can also be performed by a private individual) is introduced in the present discussion in an attempt to solve some of the problems. At any rate courts tend to adopt a contextual approach that takes into account all the relevant circumstances of a particular case. For domestic courts' jurisdiction over non-commercial torts see discussion below.

explicitly exclude criminal proceedings from their ambit, or make this exclusion clear in the explanatory commentaries.

Thus, s. 16(4) of the UK SIA stipulates: 'This Part of this Act does not apply to criminal proceedings.' 'This Part' refers to Part I of the UK SIA, which incorporates both a general rule of State immunity[38] and a number of specific exceptions.[39] As s. 16(4) disapplies both the general rule of immunity and its exceptions,[40] criminal proceedings against foreign States, if there be any, must then fall to be decided at common law. However, the common law jurisprudence, as pointed out by Lord Wilberforce in *I Congreso del Partido*,[41] had adhered to 'a pure, absolute, doctrine of state immunity in all cases' until the landmark cases of *The Philippine Admiral*[42] and *Trendtex Trading Corporation Ltd. v Central Bank of Nigeria*,[43] which adopted a restrictive doctrine of immunity. As these two cases, together with *I Congreso*, which was decided after the 1978 Act but dealt with pre-1978 Act situations, were concerned solely with *civil* matters, one may be justified in concluding that, at common law, a foreign State still enjoys absolute immunity with regard to criminal proceedings. The 1982 Canadian State Immunity Act (Canadian SIA)[44] adopts a similar formula and may be subject to similar comments.[45]

The 1976 US Foreign Sovereign Immunities Act (US FSIA)[46] does not contain a specific exclusion of criminal proceedings. However, s. 1330(a) of the US FSIA provides that 'The district courts shall have original jurisdiction . . . of any nonjury *civil* action against a foreign state . . .'[47] The legislative report on the US FSIA states that:

> This bill . . . sets forth the *sole and exclusive standards* to be used in resolving questions of sovereign immunity raised by foreign states before Federal and State courts in the United States.[48]

And that:

> S. 1330 provides a comprehensive jurisdictional scheme in cases involving foreign states.[49]

[38] Section 1(1) provides: 'A State is immune from the jurisdiction of the courts of the United Kingdom except as provided in the following provisions of this Part of this Act.'

[39] Sections 2–11.

[40] See a relevant observation made by Lord Millett, *Holland v Lampen-Wolfe* [2000] 1 WLR 1573, 1585, on s. 16(2), which excludes 'proceedings relating to anything done by or in relation to the armed forces of a State while present in the United Kingdom' from the scope of Part I.

[41] [1983] 1 AC 244, 261. [42] [1977] AC 373. [43] [1977] QB 529.

[44] (1982) 21 ILM 798.

[45] Section 17 of the Canadian SIA provides: 'This Act does not apply to criminal proceedings or proceedings in the nature of criminal proceedings.' The section likewise operates within the framework of a general rule of immunity (s. 3(1)) qualified by exceptions (ss. 4–8). See also the Singaporean State Immunity Act (1979), s. 19(2)(b); the Pakistani State Immunity Ordinance (1981), s. 17(2)(b); and the South African Foreign Sovereign Immunity Act (1981), s. 2(3). United Nations Legislative Series, ST/LEG/SER.B/20, *Materials on Jurisdictional Immunities of States and Their Property*, New York: United Nations, 1982, p. 28 at 34, p. 20 at 26 and p. 34 at 35, respectively. [46] (1976) 15 ILM 1388.

[47] Emphasis added.

[48] US Congress, House of Representatives Report No. 94–1487, 15 ILM 1398 (1976) at 1404. Emphasis added. [49] *Id.*

The US Supreme Court, interpreting the US FSIA in the *Amerada Hess* case, drew 'the plain implication that immunity is granted in those cases involving alleged violations of international law that do not come within one of the FSIA's exceptions.'[50] In this connection, two new US statutes should also be noted. The 1991 Torture Victim Protection Act[51] stipulates in s. 2(a) that an individual who subjects another individual to torture or extrajudicial killing 'shall, *in a civil action*, be liable for damages'.[52] The 1996 Antiterrorism and Effective Death Penalty Act,[53] which denies immunity with regard to, *inter alia*, torture and extra-judicial killing, seeks to add several new provisions to the US FSIA (*e.g.*, s. 1605(a)(7)) instead of creating an entirely novel regime for State immunity.[54] All this compels the conclusion that the scheme under the US FSIA allows only civil proceedings against foreign States and that, accordingly, foreign States are immune from criminal proceedings in US courts.

The 1985 Australian Foreign States Immunities Act (Australian FSIA)[55] has no specific provision to the effect that the Act does not apply to 'criminal' proceedings or that it only applies to 'civil' proceedings. Nonetheless, the Australian Law Reform Commission, which drafted the Act, noted the exclusion of criminal matters in US, UK, and other national statutes and recommended that 'the same position be taken in the Australian legislation'.[56] Thus, s. 3(1) of the Australian FSIA defines the word 'proceeding' under the Act as 'a proceeding in a court but does not include a prosecution for an offence or an appeal or other proceeding in the nature of an appeal in relation to such a prosecution'. It then appears impossible to institute a criminal action against a foreign State under the Australian FSIA. As the Commission further commented:

> Problems arising with the application of penal or regulatory legislation to foreign states cannot be resolved through the application of any general formula, but depend on the particular legislation in question. They are also matters which do not directly affect civil rights, and which have to be resolved primarily between the relevant governments or agencies and the foreign state in question.[57]

In those States that do not have specific legislation regarding State immunity, it appears that no decision has ever been rendered by a court

[50] *Argentine Republic v Amerada Hess Shipping Corporation*, 488 US 428, 436 (1989); 81 ILR 658, 664. In the *Noriega* case, a circuit court found that the US FSIA did not address 'foreign sovereign immunity in the criminal context'. *United States v Noriega*, 117 F. 3d 1206, 1212 (11th Cir. 1997).

[51] Codified at 28 U.S.C. 1350 (ATCA) note, Pub. L. 102–256, 34 ILM 1607–08 (1995) (main provisions).

[52] Emphasis added.

[53] Codified at 28 U.S.C. 1605(a)(7), Pub. L. 104–132, s. 221, 36 ILM 759 (1997). Originally, the Act applied only if both the claimant and the victim were US nationals when the act upon which the claim was based occurred (s. 1605(a)(7)(B)(ii)); but this provision was amended in 1997 to allow suit if either the claimant or the victim was a US national when the tortious act occurred. Pub. L. 105–11, 36 ILM 760 (1997).

[54] Moreover, it only applies to a handful of States specifically designated by the US State Department as 'State sponsors of terrorism'. See discussion below.

[55] (1986) 25 ILM 715.

[56] The Australian Law Reform Commission, Report No. 24, '*Foreign State Immunity*', 1984, p. 100.

[57] *Ibid.*, pp. 100–1.

which, in the absence of a waiver, denies immunity to a foreign State (as opposed to an agent of a foreign State) in a criminal proceeding.

At the international level, the 1972 European Convention on State Immunity[58] starts with the situations in which a Contracting State cannot claim immunity from the jurisdiction of a court of another Contracting State and then provides in art. 15 that:

A Contracting State shall be entitled to immunity from the jurisdiction of the courts of another Contracting State if the proceedings do not fall within Articles 1 to 14 . . .

Since arts. 1 to 14 contain no criminal proceedings exception to immunity, immunity from criminal proceedings seems to be guaranteed under the Convention.[59] The UN International Law Commission (ILC)'s 1991 Draft Articles on Jurisdictional Immunities of States and Their Property (ILC Draft)[60] lays down a general rule of immunity before enumerating specific exceptions.[61] Similarly to the 1972 European Convention, the ILC Draft contains no reference to criminal proceedings. Since a State is in principle immune unless one of the exceptions applies, immunity from criminal proceedings is likewise secured under the ILC Draft. Draft articles by other international bodies either follow the same pattern as the ILC Draft[62] or produce a similar result.[63]

To be sure, in the commentary to its draft art. 2(1)(a) (on the definition of 'court'), the ILC does note in passing that:

Although the draft articles do not define the term 'proceeding', it should be understood that they do not cover criminal proceedings.[64]

No further explanation is given of such a pronouncement, whose objective can thus only be the subject of speculation. On the one hand,

[58] (1972) 11 ILM 470.

[59] This conclusion is also supported by the fact that the UK SIA, which excludes criminal proceedings, was enacted to give effect to the 1972 European Convention.

[60] *Yearbook of the International Law Commission*, 1991, Vol. II, Part Two, p. 12.

[61] Art 5: 'A State enjoys immunity, in respect of itself and its property, from the jurisdiction of the courts of another State subject to the provisions of the present articles.' Arts. 7–17 incorporate exceptions to this general immunity.

[62] International Law Association, Montreal Draft 1982, art. II (general immunity) and art. III (exceptions), *Report of the Sixtieth Conference (Montreal)*, 1982, p. 6; Revised Draft Articles, same, *Report of the Sixty-Sixth Conference (Buenos Aires)*, 1994, p. 22. Inter-American Juridical Committee, Inter-American Draft Convention on Jurisdictional Immunity of States, (1983), 22 ILM 292 art. 1 (general immunity) and arts. 4–7 (exceptions). There is no mention of criminal proceedings in either of these two documents.

[63] L'Institut de Droit International, Contemporary problems concerning the immunity of States in relation to questions of jurisdiction and enforcement, *Annuaire de l'Institut de Droit International*, Vol. 64-II, 1992, p. 388. art. 2 (2) sets forth the 'criteria [that] are indicative of the competence of' the courts of the forum State, while art. 2(3) lists those 'indicative of the incompetence' of the courts. One wonders what should be done in any situation that falls outside these two groups of criteria. In any case, there is no mention of criminal proceedings in art. 2(2).

[64] *Yearbook of the International Law Commission*, 1991, Vol. II, Part Two, p. 14. This now seems to be a general understanding, as confirmed in the Report of the UN Ad Hoc Committee on Jurisdictional Immunities of States and Their Property, dated 24–28 February 2003, UN General Assembly Official

in stating that 'the draft articles', taken as a whole, 'do not cover criminal proceedings', the ILC seems to be of the opinion, not dissimilar to that of the Australian Law Reform Commission, that criminal proceedings against foreign States should better be handled on a State-to-State basis,[65] that is, in a mechanism distinct and separate from the judicial process, and therefore should remain outwith the scope of the regime of State immunity, as it currently stands.

On the other hand, a caveat that, though the word 'proceeding' is not defined, the draft articles do not cover criminal proceedings will have the effect of confining the word 'proceeding' (or 'proceedings') strictly to the sphere of civil process. Thus, whenever a proceeding is instituted within this framework, it must needs be a *civil* proceeding, so that, when a State is denied immunity, it is denied immunity only with regard to a civil proceeding, without impinging in any way on the issue of criminal liability. In other words, absolute immunity from criminal proceedings can be assured. Considering that all the ILC draft articles on the exceptions to State immunity follow the basic formula that a State 'cannot invoke immunity from jurisdiction in a *proceeding* before a court of another State',[66] an undefined 'proceeding' may most likely lead to the inference that immunity from both civil and criminal proceedings can be denied. The above declaration seems to have been made precisely to avert such a scenario.

The present regime of State immunity therefore has nothing to do with criminal proceedings against foreign States. It is now trite to emphasize that the restrictive doctrine of State immunity was justified on the grounds that an exercise of judicial jurisdiction over a foreign State with regard to its private/commercial activities was no encroachment on the sovereignty of the defendant State, hence not a derogation from the fundamental principle as epitomized by the maxim *par in parem non habet imperium*. In other words, the doctrine of restrictive immunity evolved exclusively in the field of civil disputes. As it now stands, the issue of State immunity actually concerns only when and to what extent a State enjoys immunity from *civil suit* in a foreign national court.[67] When State immunity

Records, 58th Session, Supplement No. 22 (A/58/22), Annex II. In its report in March 2004, the Ad Hoc Committee reiterated this understanding and recommended that the UN General Assembly include in its resolution adopting the draft UN Convention on Jurisdictional Immunities of States and Their Property the general understanding that the Convention does not cover criminal proceedings. Report of the UN Ad Hoc Committee on Jurisdictional Immunities of States and Their Property, dated 1–5 March 2004, A/59/22, paras. 11 and 14.

[65] In the words of the Australian Law Reform Commission, such proceedings 'have to be resolved primarily between the relevant governments or agencies and the foreign state in question.' The Australian Law Reform Commission, Report No. 24, '*Foreign State Immunity*', 1984, p. 101.

[66] Emphasis added. The exact wording varies slightly to accommodate the subject matter of each article.

[67] Lewis, for example, defines the term 'State immunity' as 'the immunity from *civil suit* afforded to entities of sovereign status, including the sovereign or head of State when acting in a public capacity'. (Emphasis added). Charles J. Lewis, *State and Diplomatic Immunity*, 3rd ed., London: Lloyd's of London Press Ltd., 1990, p. 1.

was absolute, there was no need to distinguish between civil and criminal immunity. After State immunity became relative or restrictive, as all the exceptions lie in the field of civil proceedings, it is reasonable to conclude that, for the time being, States still enjoy absolute immunity in criminal proceedings.

In this connection it is worth mentioning that on the plane of international law there exists no conception of a 'State' or 'international' crime. In its Draft Articles on State Responsibility adopted in 1976, the ILC proposed a category of 'international crimes of State', which comprised various serious breaches of international obligations 'of essential importance'. These crimes would be contrasted with 'international delicts', i.e., all other cases of internationally wrongful acts;[68] but the idea was abandoned in the ILC's 2001 Draft Articles.[69] The ILC commented:

> There has been . . . no development of penal consequences for States of breaches of these fundamental norms. For example, the award of punitive damages is not recognized in international law even in relation to serious breaches of obligations arising under peremptory norms.[70]

In the opinion of the ILC, a dictum by the Nuremberg Tribunal is still valid today, namely, that:

> Crimes against international law are committed by men, not by abstract entities, and only by punishing individuals who commit such crimes can the provisions of international law be enforced.[71]

The ILC pointed out that

> In line with this approach, despite the trial and conviction by the Nuremberg and Tokyo Military Tribunals of individual government officials for criminal acts committed in their official capacity, neither Germany nor Japan were treated as 'criminal' by the instruments creating these tribunals.[72]

[68] See *Yearbook of the International Law Commission*, 1976, Vol. II, Part Two, pp. 95–122, especially paras. 6–34.

[69] ILC, Commentaries to the Draft Articles on Responsibility of States for Internationally Wrongful Acts adopted in 2001, Report of the International Law Commission on the Work of Its Fifty-third Session, *Official Records of the General Assembly*, A/56/10, chp.IV.E.2, pp. 279–81, commentary to Chapter III of Part Two.

[70] ILC, Commentaries to the Draft Articles on Responsibility of States for Internationally Wrongful Acts adopted in 2001, Report of the International Law Commission on the Work of Its Fifty-third Session, *Official Records of the General Assembly*, A/56/10, chp.IV.E.2, p. 279, commentary to Chapter III of Part Two. The ILC also said: 'As far as the origin of the obligation breached is concerned, there is a single general regime of State responsibility. Nor does any distinction exist between the 'civil' and 'criminal' responsibility as is the case in internal legal systems.' *Ibid.*, p. 127, commentary to art. 12. See also James Crawford, *The International Law Commission's Articles on State Responsibility: Introduction, Text and Commentaries*, Cambridge: Cambridge University Press, 2002, pp. 16–20 and 35–8.

[71] International Military Tribunal (Nuremberg), judgment of 1 October 1946, reprinted in 41 *American Journal of International Law* (1947) 172, 221.

[72] This despite the fact that the London Charter of 1945 specifically provided for the condemnation of a 'group or organization' as 'criminal'. Charter of the International Military Tribunal, London, 82 UNTS 279, arts. 9, 10. ILC, Commentaries to the Draft Articles on Responsibility of States for Internationally Wrongful Acts adopted in 2001, Report of the International Law Commission on the

The Statutes of the International Criminal Tribunals for the former Yugoslavia and Rwanda and the 1998 Rome Statute of the International Criminal Court stipulate that the jurisdiction of the Tribunals covers 'natural persons', not States.[73] In its decision in *Prosecutor v Blaskic*, the Appeals Chamber of the International Criminal Tribunal for the former Yugoslavia held the view that the term 'subpoena' (in the sense of an injunction accompanied by threat of penalty) could not be applied or addressed to States. The Chamber based its holding on two grounds: first, that the Tribunal did not possess any power to take enforcement measures against States; second, that, with regard to States, the 'penalty' attached to a subpoena would not be penal in nature. The Chamber stated specifically that:

> Under present international law it is clear that States, by definition, cannot be the subject of criminal sanctions akin to those provided for in national criminal systems.[74]

The absolute immunity of States from criminal proceedings in foreign domestic courts can also be inferred from the absolute immunity of incumbent high officials from criminal proceedings in foreign domestic courts. In the *Pinochet* case, Lord Phillips said:

> If Senator Pinochet were still the head of state of Chile, he and Chile would be in a position to complain that the entire extradition process was a violation of the duties owed under international law to a person of his status. A head of state on a visit to another country is inviolable. He cannot be arrested or detained, let alone removed against his will to another country, and he is not subject to the judicial processes, whether civil or criminal, of the courts of the state that he is visiting.[75]

In the case of *Arrest Warrant of 11 April 2000*, the International Court of Justice found that

> . . . in international law it is firmly established that, as also diplomatic and consular agents, certain holders of high-ranking office in a State, such as the Head of State, Head of Government and Minister for Foreign Affairs, enjoy immunities from jurisdiction in other States, *both civil and criminal*.[76]

Work of Its Fifty-third Session, *Official Records of the General Assembly*, A/56/10, chp.IV.E.2, p. 280, commentary to Chapter III of Part Two.

[73] See arts. 1 and 6 of the Statute of the International Criminal Tribunal for the former Yugoslavia, adopted on 25 May 1993 by the UN Security Council Resolution 827, amended by Resolutions 1166 (1998), 1329 (2000), 1411 (2002), 1431 (2002), and 1481 (2003); arts. 1 and 5 of the Statute of the International Criminal Tribunal for Rwanda, adopted on 8 November 1994 by the UN Security Council Resolution 955, amended by Resolutions 1165 (1998), 1329 (2000), and 1411 (2002); and art. 25(1) of the Rome Statute. http://www.un.org/icty/basic/statut/stat2000_con.htm; http:// www.ictr.org and http://www.un.org/law/icc/statute/romefra.htm. See also the Statute of the semi-international Special Court for Sierra Leone, art. 1(1). http://www.sc-sl.org/.

[74] Therefore, with regard to States, the Chamber held that only binding 'orders' or 'requests' could be addressed to them. *Prosecutor v Blaskic (Objection to the Issue of* Subpoenae Duces Tecum*)* ICTY Appeals Chamber, 1997, Case IT-95-14-AR 108*bis*, 110 ILR 688, 698.

[75] Lord Phillips of Worth Matravers, *Pinochet No. 3* [2000] 1 AC 147, 280.

[76] *Arrest Warrant of 11 April 2000 (Democratic Republic of the Congo v Belgium)*, ICJ, judgment of 14 February 2002, para. 51. http://www.icj-cij.org/icjwww/idocket/iCOBE/iCOBEframe.htm. Emphasis added.

According to the ICJ, the functions of a Minister for Foreign Affairs were such that, throughout the duration of his or her office, a Minister for Foreign Affairs when abroad enjoyed 'full immunity from criminal jurisdiction and inviolability', which protected the individual concerned against any act of authority of another State that would hinder him/her in the performance of his/her duties.[77] The ICJ pointed out that:

> In this respect, no distinction can be drawn between acts performed by a Minister for Foreign Affairs in an 'official' capacity, and those claimed to have been performed in a 'private capacity', or, for that matter, between acts performed before the person concerned assumed office as Minister for Foreign Affairs and acts committed during the period of office.[78]

As the Court emphasized, this absolute immunity from criminal proceedings in foreign domestic courts enjoyed by an incumbent Minister for Foreign Affairs is not subject to any exception whatsoever.[79]

If a serving head of State or a serving minister for foreign affairs as *an individual* enjoys absolute immunity from criminal proceedings before a foreign court, then the State of which this individual is the head or representative enjoys *a fortiori* such absolute immunity *qua State*. Since the immunity enjoyed by any individual belongs to the State, not to the individual, it is hard to imagine any absolute immunity being derived from the immunity of the State, if the State itself does not have such immunity.

In sum, under current international law, a State is absolutely immune from criminal proceedings in foreign courts and enjoys relative immunity from civil proceedings subject to certain exceptions. As these exceptions, at least for the time being, do not include one to the effect that a State is not immune from civil proceedings for damages for acts of torture committed outside the forum State, it appears correct to say that a State is immune from *both criminal and civil* proceedings in a foreign court with respect to acts of torture committed in its own territory.

However, it has to be stressed that absolute immunity from criminal proceedings enjoyed by a *State* is not necessarily translatable into an absolute immunity from criminal proceedings for *State officials*. In the *Pinochet* case, whilst holding that any immunity availing Pinochet belonged to the State of Chile, not to Pinochet as an individual,[80] their Lordships found that an action against Pinochet for his *personal criminal responsibility* could not be regarded as an action against Chile.[81] Thus, in cases involving an official's individual responsibility for crimes under international law, even if the State itself can claim immunity, the individual

[77] *Ibid.*, para. 54. [78] *Ibid.*, para. 55. [79] *Ibid.*, para. 58.

[80] Lord Browne-Wilkinson, *Pinochet No. 3* [2000] 1 AC 147, 192; Lord Saville of Newdigate, 265; Lord Millett, 268; Lord Phillips of Worth Matravers, 280–1.

[81] Lord Hutton, *Pinochet No. 3* [2000] 1 AC 147, 264 (Especially drawing a distinction between the responsibility of a State for the improper and unauthorized acts of a State official outside the scope of his functions and the individual responsibility of that official in criminal proceedings for an international crime); Lord Phillips of Worth Matravers, 281 and 286.

may not be able to benefit from that immunity. This becomes more manifest where a *former* official (like Pinochet) is sued. In the case of an action against a *serving* official, there is the possibility of that official being tried by an international tribunal or by a foreign court if the official's State waives his immunity.[82]

There is yet another way of looking at this problem. Up to now the only available inroads into the once monolithic immunity of States have been made in the form of exceptions formulated through civil proceedings. The chief rationale for such inroads has been that it would be unfair for a State to enter into the private arena of business and commercial dealings, reaping benefits therefrom while at the same time maintaining the privileged position of not having to answer for any possible wrongdoing, such as a breach of contract. The possibility of prosecuting a foreign State for a crime, especially a crime that has taken place in the territory of the defendant State, has never entered into the picture. Consequently, the current regime of restrictive or relative State immunity has developed solely with regard to civil proceedings. When we now speak of 'State immunity', we actually mean no more than 'State immunity from civil proceedings'. In other words, State immunity is, under current international law, coextensive with 'State immunity from civil proceedings'. It then follows that it is hardly necessary to make a civil/criminal distinction.

Therefore, when the ECHR said in *Al-Adsani v United Kingdom* that

> . . . the Court is unable to discern . . . any firm basis for concluding that, as a matter of international law, a State no longer enjoys immunity from civil suit in the courts of another State where acts of torture are alleged,[83]

it should have said that

> the Court is unable to discern . . . any firm basis for concluding that. . . a State no longer enjoys immunity from suit, *whether civil or criminal*, in the courts of another State where acts of torture *committed outside the territory of the forum State* are alleged.[84]

The puzzlement of the ECHR over the civil/criminal dichotomy aptly reflects the poverty of current doctrine of State immunity in the face of

[82] See, *e.g.*, *Arrest Warrant of 11 April 2000 (Democratic Republic of the Congo v Belgium)*, ICJ, 14 February 2002, judgment, para. 61, http://www.icj-cij.org/icjwww/idocket/iCOBE/iCOBEframe.htm and *R v Bow Street Metropolitan Stipendiary Magistrate and Others,* Ex parte *Pinochet Ugarte* (*Pinochet No. 1*) [2000] 1 AC 61, 98 *per* Lord Lloyd of Berwick.

[83] *Al-Adsani v United Kingdom*, judgment, para. 61.

[84] The word 'territory' should be used with caution where acts of torture are concerned. Art. 2(1) of the 1984 Convention against Torture and Other Cruel, Inhuman or Degrading Treatment or Punishment (Torture Convention) (1465 UNTS 85) requires each State party to take effective measures to 'prevent acts of torture in any *territory under its jurisdiction*'. Art. 5(1)(a) and (2) of the Torture Convention likewise obligate each State party to take necessary measures to establish its jurisdiction in cases where 'the offences are committed in any *territory under its jurisdiction*' or where 'the alleged offender is present in any *territory under its jurisdiction*'. (Emphases added). The term 'territory under its jurisdiction' seems capable of excluding part of a State's territory which is not under the jurisdiction of that State or, conversely, including a piece of territory under the jurisdiction of one State but which may technically belong to another State.

major developments in international human rights law over the past few decades. On the one hand, gross violations of human rights, such as torture and genocide, are by definition criminal acts and are prohibited by various international instruments that are framed largely in criminal terms.[85] On the other hand, currently available exceptions to State immunity have evolved in the context of civil proceedings and are formulated in civil terms. Thus, where immunity is denied, it is not because of the criminality of the conduct in question, but on the grounds that the act or transaction in dispute has been carried out in a commercial/private manner (*jure gestionis*). Under these circumstances, human rights advocates, engaging in transnational human rights litigation, have to do precisely what is missing in the present regime of State immunity, that is, to argue against immunity on the basis of the *criminality* of the conduct. Confronted with an assertion of immunity in a human rights action, the applicant has no choice but to try to 'squeeze' a claim, in respect of criminal acts and on the basis of various legal provisions prohibiting those acts, into one of those exceptions to immunity, which bear no relationship to criminal proceedings. In a word, the applicant has to bring *criminal* matters, and to rely on supporting materials couched largely in *criminal* terms, within a legal framework that by its very origin is *civil* in character.

However, criminal responsibility of *individuals* before international law, even for acts committed in pursuance of the authority of the State, has long been established.[86] As the *Pinochet* case[87] indicates, it is now possible, under certain circumstances, to persuade a domestic court to deny immunity to a foreign individual, as opposed to a foreign State, violator of human rights.

V. The Significance of the Pinochet Case

In *Pinochet*, the English House of Lords held that the former President of Chile, Senator Augusto Pinochet Ugarte, could be extradited to Spain in respect of charges of acts of torture committed in Chile while he was in office. By denying immunity to a foreign former head of State in criminal proceedings, the case marked the beginning of a new era: an action in criminal proceedings formerly unknown in the field of State

[85] For example, art. 4(1) of the Torture Convention provides that 'Each State Party shall ensure that all acts of torture are offences under its *criminal law*.' (Emphasis added). Art. 1 of the 1948 Convention on the Prevention and Punishment of the Crime of Genocide (Genocide Convention) (78 UNTS 277) likewise provides that 'The Contracting Parties confirm that genocide, whether committed in time of peace or in time of war, is a *crime* under international law which they undertake to prevent and to punish.' (Emphasis added).

[86] See, especially, International Military Tribunal (Nuremberg), judgment of 1 October 1946, reprinted in 41 *American Journal of International Law* (1947) 172 and *Attorney-General of the Government of Israel v Adolf Eichmann*, judgment of the District Court of Jerusalem, 1961 and judgment of the Supreme Court of Israel, 1962, 36 ILR 5 and 277.

[87] *Pinochet No. 3* [2000] 1 AC 147.

immunity.[88] However, one should not lose sight of the limitations of the case in serving as a precedent against State immunity.

First, the case was about the immunity of an individual, not that of a State. In fact, Chile was actively claiming immunity on Pinochet's behalf. Therefore, what the case signifies is that it is now increasingly difficult for a State to claim immunity for an individual, but this might not be the case if the State is claiming immunity for itself.

Second, the case concerned only a former, as opposed to a serving, head of State. The latter's immunity remains unaffected.[89]

Third, the case dealt with criminal, not civil, proceedings. Lord Hutton said:

> . . . I consider that under international law Chile is responsible for acts of torture carried out by Senator Pinochet, but could claim state immunity if sued for damages for such acts in a court in the United Kingdom. Senator Pinochet could also claim immunity if sued in civil proceedings for damages . . .[90]

[88] As Lord Browne-Wilkinson observed: '. . . if Senator Pinochet is not entitled to immunity in relation to the acts of torture alleged to have occurred after 29 September 1988, it will be the first time . . . when a local domestic court has refused to afford immunity to a head of state or former head of state on the grounds that there can be no immunity against prosecution for certain international crimes.' *Pinochet No. 3* [2000] 1 AC 147, 201. Pinochet came to power in Chile in 1973 by overthrowing through a military coup the democratically elected Allende government, and was head of State of Chile from 1974 to 1990.

In this respect a distinction should be made between State immunity in its proper sense, namely, immunity from the jurisdiction of foreign domestic courts, and immunity (or rather non-immunity) before international tribunals, such as the Nuremberg Tribunal, the International Criminal Tribunals for the former Yugoslavia and Rwanda, and the International Criminal Court.

In *United States v Noriega*, a US district court denied immunity to General Noriega, former head of the Panamanian armed forces and *de facto* head of State, in a criminal proceeding for alleged drug trafficking. Unlike in the *Pinochet* case, in which Pinochet was expressly held to have been Chile's head of State at the material times, the *Noriega* court rejected Noriega's claim for head of State immunity on the grounds that the US had never recognized Noriega as Panama's head of State. *United States v Noriega*, 746 F. Supp. 1506, 1519–21 (S.D. Fla. 1990); 99 ILR 143, 161–3; affirmed in *United States v Noriega*, 117 F. 3d 1206, 1212 (11th Cir. 1997).

[89] See Lord Browne-Wilkinson, *Pinochet No. 3* [2000] 1 AC 147 at 201–2; Lord Hope of Craighead, at 244; Lord Hutton, at 261; Lord Saville of Newdigate, at 265–6; Lord Millett, at 268–9 and 277; and Lord Phillips of Worth Matravers, at 280 and 285.

In the case of *Arrest Warrant of 11 April 2000*, the ICJ observed that 'in international law it is firmly established that, as also diplomatic and consular agents, certain holders of high-ranking office in a State, such as the Head of State, Head of Government and Minister for Foreign Affairs, enjoy immunities from jurisdiction in other States, both civil and criminal.' *Case concerning the Arrest Warrant of 11 April 2000 (Democratic Republic of the Congo v Belgium)*, ICJ, judgment of 14 February 2002, para. 51. http://www.icj-cij.org/icjwww/idocket/iCOBE/iCOBEframe.htm. Since no qualification is attached to the phrase 'holders of high-ranking office', one might be led to infer that the ICJ had in mind both *incumbent* and *former* officials. However, as the ICJ was quick to make clear, as far as criminal jurisdiction of foreign courts (as opposed to jurisdiction of a domestic court or an international tribunal) is concerned, a former Minister for Foreign Affairs may be tried by a foreign domestic court under certain circumstances (including waiver) while an incumbent Minister can be tried by a foreign domestic court *only* when immunity is waived by his/her own State. *Ibid.*, para. 61.

[90] *Pinochet No. 3* [2000] 1 AC 147, 264. See also Lord Phillips of Worth Matravers, *Pinochet No. 3* [2000] 1 AC 147, 281 ('Were these civil proceedings in which damages were claimed in respect of acts committed by Senator Pinochet in the government of Chile, Chile could argue that it was itself indirectly impleaded. That argument does not run where the proceedings are criminal and where the issue is Senator Pinochet's personal responsibility, not that of Chile.')

There thus arises a logical difficulty, which can almost be regarded as an anomaly.[91] A working group of the ILC, commenting on the *Pinochet* case, sanguinely states that:

there can be no doubt that this case, and the widespread publicity it received, has generated support for the view that State officials should not be entitled to plead immunity for acts of torture committed in their own territories in *both civil and criminal* actions.[92]

More clearly and forcefully, the applicant in *Al-Adsani v United Kingdom* argued that:

The House of Lords in *ex parte Pinochet (No. 3)* had accepted that the prohibition of torture had acquired the status of a *jus cogens* norm in international law and that torture had become an international crime. In these circumstances there could be no rational basis for allowing sovereign immunity in a civil action when immunity would not be a defence in criminal proceedings arising from the same facts.[93]

The fact is, however, precisely that State officials now might be denied immunity in criminal proceedings but might still enjoy immunity in civil

[91] Although Lord Hutton saw 'no inconsistency between Chile and Senator Pinochet's entitlement to claim immunity if sued in civil proceedings for damages and Senator Pinochet's lack of entitlement to claim immunity in criminal proceedings for torture brought against him personally'. *Id.*

To Bianchi, the discrepancy between civil and criminal proceedings does create 'a manifest inconsistency which ought to be remedied by denying immunity also to state and state officials in civil proceedings'. Andrea Bianchi, Immunity versus Human Rights: The *Pinochet* Case, 10 *European Journal of International Law* (1999) 237, 264.

[92] Paragraph 12 of the Appendix to the Report of the Working Group on Jurisdictional Immunities of States and Their Property, annexed to the Report of the International Law Commission on the Work of its Fifty-first Session, 3 May–23 July 1999, G.A.O.R. 54th Session, Supplement No.10 (A/54/10 and Corr.1 & 2). Emphasis added.

[93] *Al-Adsani v United Kingdom*, judgment, para. 51. This may well have been the submission that led to the ill-informed distinction by the ECHR between civil and criminal proceedings.

In the same vein, Marks asks this question in her case note on *Al-Adsani v Government of Kuwait* (English Court of Appeal): 'If criminal jurisdiction with respect to torture for which the State bears responsibility is not limited to acts in the United Kingdom, why should civil jurisdiction be so limited, at least where there is some nexus with the United Kingdom . . . ?' Susan Marks, Torture and the Jurisdictional Immunity of Foreign States (case note on *Al-Adsani*), 56 *Cambridge Law Journal* (1997) 8, 10. For similar arguments see Human Rights Committee, International Law Association (British Branch), Report on Civil Actions in the English Courts for Serious Human Rights Violations Abroad, *European Human Rights Law Review* (2001) 129, 151 and 157–8.

Commenting on Marks' question, Garnett maintains that 'there is a great difference, in terms of intrusion upon a foreign State's sovereignty, between a domestic court exercising jurisdiction (whether civil or criminal) over an individual offender from that State and a court doing so over the State itself'. Richard Garnett, The Defence of State Immunity for Acts of Torture, 18 *Australian Year Book of International Law* (1997) 97, 120, note 112. But this comment seems to miss the point. At least as far as *civil* suits are concerned, the whole purpose of restrictive immunity doctrine is to put the foreign State on an equal footing with a private individual, and the crucial point has always been whether a *territorial connection* can be established, not whether a foreign State's sovereignty will be infringed. In fact, in his whole article Garnett seems to be quite oblivious to this territorial nexus requirement and indiscriminately discusses torture (with no specified location of commission, i.e. either within or outside the territory of the forum State) together with tort (in the sense of US FSIA, UK SIA, and other national legislation, that is, personal injury or death, or damage to or loss of property, occurring within the territory of the forum State).

Marks is referring to the UK's treaty obligations under the Torture Convention to establish jurisdiction over acts of torture wherever committed. However, the jurisdiction under the Torture Convention proceedings. This indeed seems strange, unless one is aware of the fact that, as demonstrated earlier, State immunity as it stands now has been largely unshaken save in the case of a limited number of clearly defined exceptions that have evolved in the context of civil proceedings. To recapitulate, a State is now *absolutely* immune from criminal proceedings and *relatively* immune from civil proceedings. Since current exceptions to immunity are limited in number (in those States with special legislation on immunity) and clearly demarcated by guiding principles (in those States without such legislation), it will be difficult (though not altogether impossible) to fit an exception to immunity from *civil* proceedings with regard to acts of torture committed outside the territory of the forum State, into this fully developed regime, not least because there is already an accumulation of precedents to overcome. On the other hand, an absolute immunity from criminal proceedings means an absence of detailed rules governing criminal matters. Thus, ironically, it might be easier for human rights applicants to argue for, and for courts to create rules requiring, a denial of immunity from criminal proceedings, at least where officials, not States, are sued.

Fourth, the majority of the Law Lords decided the case on the basis of the fact that all the three States concerned (UK, Spain, and Chile) happened to be parties to the Torture Convention.[94] If, instead of torturing them, Pinochet had simply murdered all his victims, he would either have committed no extradition crime[95] or have emerged immune.[96] The point is that, where there exists an international convention among the States concerned, the task of the human rights lawyer will be much easier. As nearly all the current international conventions on human rights have been formulated in prohibitive or criminal law terms, a criminal proceeding stands a far better chance of success than does a civil one. In a case decided in October 2001, a US court took clear notice of recent developments in this direction:

In this formative environment, agreement may exist with regard to one general proposition: that developments in the criminal context, whether concerning

covers the criminal responsibility of *individuals*, not of *States* (see arts. 1 and 5). Thus, a criminal action against a foreign State is impossible under the Torture Convention. As far as the defendants of the *Al-Adsani* case (namely the Kuwaiti Government, the royal family member and some other individuals) are concerned, a criminal action against Kuwait would have been impossible while a civil action would, as it did, fail under s. 5 of the UK SIA. A criminal action against those individuals would however have been possible had they been found in UK territory (art. 5 of the Torture Convention).

94 Lord Browne-Wilkinson: [2000] 1 AC 147, 201, and 205; Lord Hope of Craighead, 248; Lord Hutton, 261–2; Lord Saville of Newdigate, 266–7; Lord Millett, 277–8; and Lord Phillips of Worth Matravers, 290. This despite the pronouncements of some of the Law Lords that torture was already an international crime long before the Torture Convention (Lord Browne-Wilkinson, at p. 198; Lord Millett, at pp. 275–6) or before s. 134 of the UK Criminal Justice Act 1988 giving effect to the Torture Convention came into force (Lord Hutton, at p. 261).

95 See Lord Hope of Craighead, *Pinochet No. 3* [2000] 1 AC 147, 233–5.

96 Lord Browne-Wilkinson said: 'As to the charges of murder and conspiracy to murder, no one has advanced any reason why the ordinary rules of immunity should not apply and Senator Pinochet is entitled to such immunity.' [2000] 1 AC 147, 205. Lord Hope of Craighead took the same view, at p. 248. Lord Hutton agreed on this point, at p. 249. But Lord Millett thought otherwise, at p. 277 and 279.

former or sitting government leaders, have advanced more definitively than the parameters defining permissible jurisdiction over sitting heads-of-states extending to personal conduct in civil matters.[97]

Taking all the above factors into consideration, one may arrive at a reasonably practical way out of the present quandary created by the operation of immunity in human rights litigation. This will involve an approach focussing on *individualized criminal proceedings*, that is, criminal proceedings brought against individual violators of human rights within the framework of existing multilateral conventions.[98]

Recent developments seem to point in this direction. In its decision on 20 November 2000 in the *Bouterse* case, the Amsterdam Court of Appeal ordered the prosecution of Désiré Bouterse, former military ruler of Surinam, for the torture and summary execution on 8/9 December 1982 of fifteen prominent persons in Paramaribo, Surinam, by the Surinamese military authority under his command. Somewhat confusingly, while declaring that torture *as a crime against humanity* was already a crime in 1982 under customary international law, and that the offender could be held personally liable under criminal law, the Court nonetheless reaffirmed its reliance on the Torture Convention.[99] In particular, the Court refused to consider a claim for head of State immunity for Bouterse (who claimed to have held the position of head of State at the relevant

[97] *Tachiona v Mugabe*, 169 F. Supp. 2d 259, 281 (S.D.N.Y. 2001). In this case, Robert Gabriel Mugabe, current president of Zimbabwe, and other high officials of Zimbabwe were sued in the US for, among other things, murder and torture. The Court granted immunity to Mugabe in deference to a US State Department suggestion of immunity.

[98] It is to be observed in this connection that civil proceedings are possible under the US Alien Tort Claims Act of 1789 (Codified at 28 U.S.C. 1350. Also often referred to as the Alien Tort Statute, the Alien Tort Act or simply Section 1350), which provides that 'The district courts shall have original jurisdiction of any civil action by an alien for a tort only, committed in violation of the law of nations or a treaty of the United States.' But, as decided by the US Supreme Court in *Amerada Hess*, 488 US 428, 436 (1989); 81 ILR 658, 663, whenever immunity is claimed, the case has to be decided under the US FSIA. Therefore, a claim for damages based on torture committed outside US territory brought against a serving foreign State official is unlikely to succeed, as there is no such exception to immunity under the US FSIA.

As early as 1994, Lininger suggested that human rights advocates should bring *civil* proceedings for compensation against *individual* defendants. But the best such type of suits can do, when one considers the combined jurisprudence of the US FSIA and the ATCA in US courts, is to catch those individuals who are no longer beneficiaries of State immunity. In other words, such suits cannot 'overcome immunity defences' as he contemplates, but can only work where immunity is already unavailable. Tom Lininger, Overcoming Immunity Defences to Human Rights Suits in US Courts, 7 *Harvard Human Rights Journal* (1994) 177. Such civil suits might also encounter some other difficulties stemming from particular national judicial practice. According to Whomersley, for example, English courts are traditionally concerned about ensuring that 'the special privileges enjoyed by the proper defendant (i.e. the State) [are] not rendered nugatory by the plaintiff adopting the device of bringing proceedings against someone (i.e. an individual) other than the proper defendant'. C. A. Whomersley, Some Reflections on the Immunity of Individuals for Official Acts, 41 *International and Comparative Law Quarterly* (1992) 848, 850. An expert group recently concludes that State immunity at present raises 'significant' and 'insuperable' obstacles to civil actions against foreign States in English courts. Human Rights Committee, International Law Association (British Branch), Report on Civil Actions in the English Courts for Serious Human Rights Violations Abroad, *European Human Rights Law Review* (2001) 129, 158.

[99] Notably, Surinam is not a party to the Torture Convention (as of 6 June 2004).

time). The Court found that it need not decide 'whether this insufficiently substantiated statement about Bouterse's position is correct', but remarked, casually, that 'the commission of very grave punishable offences such as those in question cannot be regarded as the official duties of a head of state.'[100] However, the Hoge Raad (or 'High Court', the Netherlands Supreme Court) dismissed the case on 18 September 2001 on the grounds that the Torture Convention entered into force for the Netherlands in 1989, seven years after the alleged atrocities had taken place, and that Netherlands could only try Bouterse if he was a Dutch citizen or if he was found on Dutch territory.[101] By strictly adhering to the Torture Convention the Dutch Supreme Court seems to have sidestepped the issue of immunity, but the implication is clear: should Bouterse be unfortunate enough to find himself in Dutch territory then no immunity can avail him.[102]

On 18 June 2001, 23 survivors of the 1982 Sabra and Shatila massacres filed complaints before a Belgian court, charging Ariel Sharon, former Israeli defence minister and current Israeli prime minister, retired Israel Defense Forces (IDF) generals Amos Yaron and Rafael (Raful) Eitan, and others, with war crimes, crimes against humanity, and genocide in connection with the massacre of between 1,000 and 2,000 unarmed Palestinian and Lebanese civilians by Lebanese Christian militiamen in the Sabra and Shatila Palestinian refugee camps in Beirut on 16–18 September 1982. Thus started a high-profile legal drama the repercussions of which can still be felt today.

The *Sharon* case was brought under the Belgian Law of 10 February 1999 concerning the Punishment of Grave Breaches of International Humanitarian Law, enacted to modify the Law of 16 June 1993 concerning the Punishment of Grave Breaches of the Geneva Conventions of 12 August 1949 and Their Additional Protocols I and II of 8 June 1977.[103] The Law defines the 'grave breaches' as including genocide (art. 1(1)), crimes against humanity (art. 1(2)), and grave breaches of the four 1949 Geneva Conventions and their two 1977 Additional Protocols

[100] Ground 4(2). The Dutch original reads: '*Het hof kan in het midden laten of die onvoldoende gemotiveerde stelling omtrent de positie van Verdachte juist is. Het plegen van zeer ernstige strafbare feiten als waarom het hier gaat, kan immers niet tot de officiële taken van een staatshoofd worden gerekend.*' Gerechtshof Amsterdam, 20 November 2000, para. 4.2, Case No. R 97/163/12 Sv en R 97/176/12 Sv, http://www.rechtspraak.nl/gerechtshof/amsterdam. The English translation quoted here is found at http://www.u-j.info/index/143713.

[101] Hoge Raad der Nederlanden, 18 September 2001, Case No. 00749/01 CW 2323, the original case report can be found from the database: http://www.rechtspraak.nl/hoge_raad/default_flash.htm.

[102] The strict adherence to the Torture Convention (see especially art. 5) seems to echo the view of Professor Dugard who, in his Opinion to the Amsterdam Court of Appeal, pointed out that: 'Bouterse is not present in the Netherlands. There is therefore no obligation on the Netherlands to exercise criminal jurisdiction over him under international law. Nor is the Netherlands under a legal obligation to request his extradition from Surinam or any country that he may visit. On the other hand, if Bouterse were to visit the Netherlands, I am of the opinion that the Netherlands would be obliged to try or extradite him under the Torture Convention.' C. J. R. Dugard, Opinion re Bouterse, 7 July 2000, para. 5.7.9, http://www.rechtspraak.nl/gerechtshof/amsterdam/.

[103] (1999) 38 ILM 918 (English translation, where the Law is referred to as 'Act'). An English translation can also be found in *Yearbook of International Humanitarian Law*, Vol. 2, 1999, p. 539. The 1993/1999 Laws are also known as 'Universal Jurisdiction Laws' or 'Anti-Atrocity Laws'.

(art. 1(3)). For these definitions the Law expressly relies on the 1948 Genocide Convention, the 1998 Statute of the International Criminal Court, and the Geneva Conventions and the Additional Protocols. It is not clear whether the Law seeks to establish jurisdiction with regard to any State or only to those States parties to those conventions. Art. 7 provides that 'The Belgian courts shall be competent to deal with breaches provided for in the present Act, irrespective of where such breaches have been committed.' One wonders why, if it attempts to assert universal jurisdiction, the Law does not contain a reference to the effect that jurisdiction may be taken '*regardless of the nationality of either the offender or the victim*'. The intent of the Law seems to have been clarified on 8 June 2001 when, in the first case applying the 1993/1999 Laws, a court in Belgium found four Rwandan nationals, including two Roman Catholic nuns, guilty of participating in the genocide in Rwanda in 1994.[104] The two nuns, Sister Maria Kisito Mukabutera and Sister Getrude Mukangango, handed over to the Hutu killers some 7,000 Tutsis who had sought refuge in their convent, and even supplied cans of petrol to the Hutu militiamen, who burned a garage sheltering about 500 people. Former Rwandan Transport Minister Alphonse Higaniro was also among the defendants convicted.[105] The issue of his immunity obviously did not surface. Neither the defendants nor the victims were Belgian nationals. It is thus obvious that a Belgian court, applying the 1993/1999 Laws, will not worry about the place of the offence or the nationality of the parties concerned.

Art. 5(3) of the 1999 Law is especially remarkable, for it stipulates that 'The immunity attributed to the official capacity of a person does not prevent the application of the present Act.'[106] It makes no distinction as to the seniority of the official capacity of the person, nor does it distinguish between former and current/serving officials. Thus, in many respects the *Sharon* case would be truly epoch-making. Not only had the incident in question taken place well before the enactment of the 1993 Law, but, more important, Sharon would be the first *serving* head of government to be denied immunity from criminal proceedings before a foreign domestic court. Furthermore, this case might well be opening the floodgates to a host of other cases.[107]

[104] It might be suggested that one should not be oblivious to the historical background to this case and the *Bouterse* case in the Netherlands: Belgium is Rwanda's former colonial power and the Netherlands Surinam's.

[105] See *e.g.*, http://news.bbc.co.uk/hi/english/world/europe/newsid_1376000/1376692.stm (related news coverage can also be found on this web page).

[106] According to the Belgian Government, the wording of art. 5(3) is borrowed from art. 27(2) of the Statute of the International Criminal Court, which provides: 'Immunities or special procedural rules which may attach to the official capacity of a person, whether under national or international law, shall not bar the Court from exercising its jurisdiction over such a person.' Counter-Memorial of the Kingdom of Belgium (28 September 2001) in the case of *Arrest Warrant of 11 April 2000 (Democratic Republic of the Congo v Belgium)* before the ICJ, para. 1.11, http://www.icj-cij.org/icjwww/idocket/iCOBE/iCOBEframe.htm.

[107] In addition to the *Sharon* case, the 1993/1999 Belgian Laws have given rise to a torrent of other cases filed with Belgian courts against foreign heads of State, heads of government and other prominent figures, including former President Hissene Habre of Chad, former Chilean President

While the *Sharon* case was still pending, Belgium together with its 1993/1999 Laws was brought before the International Court of Justice (ICJ). In the case of *Arrest Warrant of 11 April 2000*, the Democratic Republic of the Congo instituted proceedings against Belgium in opposition to an international arrest warrant *in absentia* issued on 11 April 2000 under the 1993/1999 Laws by a Belgian investigating judge against Mr. Abdulaye Yerodia Ndombasi, the then Minister for Foreign Affairs of the Congo, charging him with offences constituting grave breaches of the Geneva Conventions of 1949 and of the Additional Protocols thereto, and with crimes against humanity, on the basis of his alleged speeches inciting racial hatred in the Congo in August 1998. The ICJ found (by thirteen votes to three) that the issue of the arrest warrant and its international circulation constituted violations of a legal obligation of Belgium towards the Congo, in that they failed to respect the immunity from criminal jurisdiction and the inviolability which the incumbent Minister for Foreign Affairs of the Congo enjoyed under international law; and (by ten votes to six) that Belgium must cancel the arrest warrant.[108] The ICJ pointed out, specifically, that:

> It should further be noted that the rules governing the jurisdiction of national courts must be carefully distinguished from those governing jurisdictional immunities: jurisdiction does not imply absence of immunity, while absence of immunity does not imply jurisdiction. Thus, although various international conventions on the prevention and punishment of certain serious crimes impose on States obligations of prosecution or extradition, thereby requiring them to extend their criminal jurisdiction, such extension of jurisdiction in no way affects immunities under customary international law, including those of Ministers for Foreign Affairs. These remain opposable before the courts of a foreign State, even where those courts exercise such a jurisdiction under these conventions.[109]

The ICJ avoided taking a position on the legality of the purported exercise of universal jurisdiction by Belgium.[110] However, since the ICJ approached the issue of immunity by assuming that Belgium had universal jurisdiction under international law,[111] the case definitively shows that, in

General Augusto Pinochet, former Foreign Minister Abdoulaye Yerodia Ndombasi of the Democratic Republic of the Congo, Cuban President Fidel Castro, former Iranian President Hashemi Rafsanjani, Iraqi President Saddam Hussein (as he then was), former Moroccan Minister of Interior Driss Basri, Palestinian leader Yasser Arafat, Rwandan President Paul Kagame, former US president George Bush, Sr., and US Army General Tommy Franks.

[108] *Arrest Warrant of 11 April 2000 (Democratic Republic of the Congo v Belgium)*, ICJ, Judgment of 14 February 2002, para. 78(2) and (3). http://www.icj-cij.org/icjwww/idocket/iCOBE/iCOBEframe.htm.

[109] *Ibid.*, para. 59.

[110] In its Application instituting the proceedings, the Congo originally challenged the legality of the arrest warrant of 11 April 2000 on two separate grounds: Belgium's claim to exercise a universal jurisdiction and the alleged violation of the immunities of the Minister for Foreign Affairs of the Congo then in office. However, in its final submissions the Congo abandoned the first ground. See *ibid.*, paras. 11–12, 17, 21, 41–43, and 45.

According to Judge and President Guillaume, universal jurisdiction *in absentia* as claimed by Belgium, namely, jurisdiction over offences committed abroad by foreigners against foreigners when the perpetrator is not present in the territory of the forum State, is 'unknown to international law' and would create 'total judicial chaos'. Separate opinion of President Guillaume, paras. 9, 12, 15, and 17.

[111] *Arrest Warrant*, ICJ, para. 46.

international law, universal jurisdiction is circumscribed by certain other rules, notable among which is the rule of immunity. Thus, the establishment of universal jurisdiction does not automatically lead to a loss of immunity: a loss of immunity has to be demonstrated separately from the issue of universal jurisdiction. In seeking to exercise universal jurisdiction over a foreign State or a foreign national who may benefit from State immunity, a national court has to satisfy two conditions: first, that the court has universal jurisdiction as conferred by international law; and second, that the foreign State or the individual does not enjoy immunity under the circumstances.

The ICJ was cautious not to elaborate upon the immunity of a *former* Minister for Foreign Affairs and, by extension, that of any other person previously holding high official positions such as former Heads of State and Heads of Government. However, generally speaking, the position of a former leader appears much weaker than that of a serving one. As the *Pinochet* case shows, it would be much harder for a State to argue for immunity in favour of a *former* high official.

The ICJ handed down its judgment on 14 February 2002. Four months later, on 26 June 2002, the Court of Appeal of Brussels dismissed the claim in the *Sharon* case. The Court of Appeal did not address the issue of immunity and concerned itself solely with whether, accepting that the 1993/1999 Laws had conferred universal jurisdiction on Belgian courts for violations of international humanitarian law, rules of criminal procedure currently in force in Belgium permitted lawsuits brought against foreign nationals who were alleged to be authors or co-authors of such violations but who were not found in the territory of Belgium. The Court concluded that, even though Belgian courts *had* jurisdiction over the acts alleged by the plaintiff, the complaint against Sharon and Yaron was inadmissible because these individuals were not found in Belgian territory.

The decision of the Court of Appeal of Brussels was reversed on 12 February 2003 by the Belgian Cour de Cassation, which held that the crimes under international law as envisaged by the 1993/1999 Laws did not constitute offences for the prosecution of which the law required, when such offences had been committed outside Belgian territory, that the offender be found in Belgium. However, the Cour de Cassation drew a clear distinction between Sharon, who, as the current Prime Minister of Israel, enjoyed immunity by virtue of customary international law, and other defendants, who did not enjoy immunity.[112]

Although the decision of the Cour de Cassation obviously followed the line of the ICJ's *Arrest Warrant* judgment, two significant consequences would ensue from this ruling. First, Belgian authorities could start investigations

[112] The complaint and the court decisions are conveniently set out at http://www.u-j.info/index/101391. The French text of the decision of 12 February 2003 of the Cour de Cassation of Belgium, with an English translation, can also be found at (2003) 42 ILM 596. For an account of the developments of the case and related materials see http://indictsharon.net.

into the Sabra and Shatila massacres, even if these had taken place outside Belgian territory; second, the moment Sharon should become unprotected by an official position, he would face prosecution in Belgium. It is small wonder that it gave rise to tumultuous reactions: human rights organizations hailed it a landmark case, while enormous political pressure was brought to bear on Belgium to change its position.

The change came swiftly. On 23 April 2003, the Belgian Parliament passed a new law amending the 1993/1999 Laws.[113] Art. 5 (3) of the 1993/1999 Laws now reads: 'International immunity derived from a person's official capacity does not prevent the application of the present law except under those limits established under international law.' There is no further specification of the word 'limits', but presumably they would include immunity enjoyed by a current head of government under customary international law. More important for the *Sharon* case, art. 7 has undergone a radical transformation: it now requires a strict Belgian nexus. Under art. 7(1), even though Belgian courts still have the nominally universal jurisdiction over the targeted offences 'independently of where they have been committed and even if the alleged offender is not located within Belgium',

> The criminal action will nonetheless be subject to the request of the federal prosecutor if: 1. the violation was not committed on Belgian territory; 2. the alleged offender is not Belgian; 3 the alleged offender is not located within Belgian territory; 4. the victim is not Belgian or has not resided in Belgium for at least three years.

The *Sharon* case falls squarely within all the four exceptions. In such a case, no private individual can initiate a criminal action. The matter will be entirely at the discretion of the federal prosecutor, who may dismiss the case or decide that the case should better be brought

> before the tribunals of a State in which the offender is a national or where he may be found, and as long as this tribunal is competent, independent, impartial and fair.

This means, of course, that the *Sharon* case would be referred back to Israel. And then, further amendments were made to the 1993/1999 Laws on 5 August 2003.[114] The new amendments, among other things, further clarified the immunity provision of the 1993/1999 Laws by inserting a new article into the Belgian Code of Criminal Procedure, which states specifically that:

> In accordance with international law, there shall be no prosecution with regard to: Heads of State, heads of government, and foreign ministers of foreign affairs, during their terms of office . . .

[113] The Amendment Law of 23 April 2003, together with an English translation, can be found at (2003) 42 ILM 749.

[114] The Amendment Law of 5 August 2003, together with an English translation, can be found at (2003) 42 ILM 1258. This Amendment entered into force on 7 August 2003.

More pertinently to the *Sharon* case, 'Cases pending in the prosecution phase as of the entry into force of this Law [of 5 August 2003]' shall be transferred to the Public Prosecutor (Procureur Général), who shall request the Cour de Cassation to rule on the 'removal of the cases from Belgian jurisdiction'. Not surprisingly, on 24 September 2003, the Belgian Cour de Cassation, upon request of the Procureur Général, decided to remove the *Sharon* case from Belgian jurisdiction.[115]

Besides showing the extreme sensitivity of criminal proceedings against individuals holding high official positions, these and other similar cases do demonstrate the considerable potential of individualized criminal proceedings in countering the principle of State immunity when redress for human rights violations is sought.

VI. State Immunity from Tort Proceedings

In *McElhinney v Ireland*, the ECHR's holding was founded on two concepts that are highly questionable in the context of State immunity regarding tortious conduct within the forum State: 'insurable' personal injury and a *jure imperii/jure gestionis* dichotomy. The word 'insurable' does not appear in any of the current legal instruments on State immunity and therefore does not exist as a limitation on jurisdiction over tortious conduct. The *jure imperii/jure gestionis* distinction has been discarded altogether in some States and is followed by others only to the extent that, when injury has been caused, *causing injury* will be regarded as *jure gestionis*, regardless of whether the act in the course of which injury has been caused is *jure imperii* or *jure gestionis*. Except where foreign armed forces are involved, it is rather doubtful if, in the event of actual injury being caused in the State of the forum, a court will deny jurisdiction on the sole ground that the act in question is *jure imperii*.

1. 'Insurable' Personal Injury?

The tort exception to State immunity in current State practice, even if perhaps addressing primarily 'insurable' risks, is definitely not limited to them. The word 'insurable' seems to have originated with the International Law Commission (ILC). According to the ILC, the torts covered by art. 12 of its Draft Articles are 'confined principally to *insurable risks*',[116] namely

> . . . accidental death or physical injuries to persons or damage to tangible property involved in traffic accidents, such as moving vehicles, motor cycles, locomotives or speedboats. In other words, the article covers most areas of

[115] On the same day the Cour de Cassation also removed the case against former US president George Bush Sr., http://www.juridat.be/juris/jucf.htm.

[116] *Yearbook of the International Law Commission*, 1991, Vol. II, Part Two, p. 12 at 45. Emphasis added.

accidents involved in the transport of goods and passengers by rail, road, air or waterways.[117]

But the ILC makes it quite clear that art. 12 extends well beyond 'insurable risks', for its scope 'is wide enough to cover also intentional physical harm such as assault and battery, malicious damage to property, arson or even homicide, including political assassination'.[118]

In fact, the word 'insurable' does not appear in any of the current legal instruments on State immunity, be it national statute, international convention, or draft articles by learned bodies. According to the legislative history of the US FSIA, its s. 1605(a)(5) on tort 'is directed primarily at the problem of traffic accidents but is cast in general terms as applying to all tort actions for money damages'; the purpose of the provision is 'to permit the victim of a traffic accident or *other non-commercial tort* to maintain an action against the foreign state to the extent otherwise provided by law'.[119]

The Australian Law Reform Commission expressly disfavours the term 'insurable':

> The rationale for limitation to insurable accidents is that, by allowing a right of direct recovery against the foreign State's insurer, the plaintiff can recover without suing the foreign State, thereby in a sense allowing the foreign State to retain its immunity. Although nowhere stated, it may be that some States desire to retain immunity for at least the most controversial of 'governmental' activities. Because the reason for allowing immunity in the overall provision on torts is *not based on any governmental/commercial distinction*, it is unnecessary for it to protect a foreign State by according tort immunity for 'governmental' activities. Foreign States should have no privilege with respect to tortious personal injury or tangible property damage within the jurisdiction.[120]

2. *The Jure Imperii/Jure Gestionis Distinction?*

In the context of jurisdiction over tortious conduct in the territory of the forum State, the *jure imperii/jure gestionis* dichotomy seems rather out of place in current State practice. Ireland is certainly not the only State that adopts a *jure imperii/jure gestionis* test when dealing with torts committed within its territory; but there are some States, chief among them the UK and the US, that have abandoned this test altogether in the case of torts. All the current national statutes on State immunity provide for jurisdiction in terms of personal injury or death, or damage to or loss

[117] *Id.*

[118] *Id.* In mentioning 'political assassination' the ILC is obviously prompted by such cases as *Letelier v Republic of Chile*, see below.

[119] US Congress, House of Representatives, Report No. 94–1487, 15 ILM 1398 (1976) at 1409. Emphasis added.

[120] The Australian Law Reform Commission, Report No. 24, '*Foreign State Immunity*', 1984, pp. 68–9. Emphasis added.

of property caused by an act or omission in the territory of the forum State, quite irrespective of the nature or purpose of the act or omission in question.[121] The 1972 European Convention on State Immunity,[122] as well as draft articles prepared by international bodies, adopts the same approach.[123] All these provisions found jurisdiction on the actual injury, death, damage, or loss the cause of which can be attributable to the defendant foreign State while none contains any indication that the act or omission in question has to be committed *jure gestionis*. As the Australian Law Reform Commission put it:

> Where a foreign State wrongfully causes death or personal injury or damages property within the forum State, the forum's interest in asserting jurisdiction over the wrongful act seems clear. There is no merit in such cases in requiring the plaintiff to litigate in the defendant State's courts when the forum's courts provide the obvious and convenient local remedy. This argument applies to all torts properly within the jurisdiction irrespective of whether they originate in an act which might be described as 'sovereign', 'governmental' or *jure imperii*.[124]

[121] The US FSIA 1976, s. 1605(a)(5) (A foreign State is not immune where 'money damages are sought against a foreign state for personal injury or death, or damage to or loss of property, occurring in the United States and caused by the tortious act or omission of that foreign state or of any official or employee of that foreign state while acting within the scope of his office or employment'); the UK SIA 1978, s. 5 ('death or personal injury or damage to or loss of tangible property, caused by an act or omission in the United Kingdom'); the Canadian SIA 1982, s. 6 ('any death or personal injury, or any damage to or loss of property that occurs in Canada'); the Australian FSIA, s. 13 ('the death of, or personal injury to, a person; or loss of or damage to tangible property, caused by an act or omission done or omitted to be done in Australia'). See also the South African Act, s. 6 and the Singapore Act, s. 7. The Pakistani State Immunity Ordinance 1981 is the sole exception in that it does not contain a provision on torts.

[122] Art. 11 ('injury to the person or damage to tangible property, if the facts which occasioned the injury or damage occurred in the territory of the State of the forum, and if the author of the injury or damage was present in that territory at the time when those facts occurred').

[123] ILC Draft, art. 12 ('death or injury to the person, or damage to or loss of tangible property, caused by an act or omission which is alleged to be attributable to the State, if the act or omission occurred in whole or in part in the territory of that other State and if the author of the act or omission was present in that territory at the time of the act or omission'), *Yearbook of the International Law Commission*, 1991, Vol. II, Part Two, p. 12; ILA Montreal Draft 1982, art. III(F) ('death or personal injury or damage to or loss of property . . . [if] the act or omission which caused the death, injury or damage occurred wholly or partly in the forum State.'), *Report of the Sixtieth Conference (Montreal)*, 1982, p. 6; ILA 1994 Revised Draft, art. III(F) ('death or personal injury or damage to or loss of property and the act or omission which caused the death, injury or damage either occurred wholly or partly in the forum State or if that act or omission had a direct effect in the forum State'), *Report of the Sixty-Sixth Conference (Buenos Aires)*, 1994, 22; and L'Institut de Droit International, Contemporary problems concerning the immunity of States in relation to questions of jurisdiction and enforcement, art. 2(2)(e) ('the death of, or personal injury to, a person, or loss of or damage to tangible property, which are attributable to activities of a foreign State and its agents within the national jurisdiction of the forum State'), *Annuaire de l'Institut de Droit International*, Vol. 64, Tome II, 1992, p. 388.

[124] The Australian Law Reform Commission, Report No. 24, '*Foreign State Immunity*', 1984, p. 66. The Commission's statement can serve as a direct response to the opinion of the ECHR that 'it would have been open to the applicant to bring an action in Northern Ireland against the United Kingdom Secretary of State for Defence'. *McElhinney v Ireland*, Judgment, para. 39. Indeed Judge Loucaides took the view in his dissenting opinion that 'it is unfair as well as odd to expect the applicant to have recourse to another State as a solution to his problem of lack of access to a court in his own country, against which his complaint was directed.'

The US Third Restatement holds that the foreign State should be responsible on a basis comparable to private, nongovernmental entities. The standard of liability should be the same as if the defendant were a private entity—whether for negligence, liability without fault, or intentional wrongs; and the same principle applies to such issues as contribution among tortfeasors and indemnification.[125]

The much-cited case *Letelier v Republic of Chile* serves to bring out the potential of s. 1605(a)(5) of the US FSIA in that the effects of the provision extended beyond traffic accidents to cover political assassinations. In that case, the relatives and personal representatives of the former Chilean Ambassador and Foreign Minister Orlando Letelier and of Ronni Moffitt, who had been killed in the US by a car bomb allegedly placed by Chilean intelligence agents, sought damages for tortious injuries connected with their deaths. In particular, the court held that the *jure imperii/jure gestionis* distinction was neither necessary nor warrantable in this case:

> Nowhere is there an indication that the tortious acts . . . are to only be those formerly classified as 'private', thereby engrafting onto the statute, as the Republic of Chile would have the Court do, the requirement that the character of a given tortious act be judicially analyzed to determine whether it was of the type heretofore denoted as *jure gestionis*, or should be classified as *jure imperii*.[126]

Crawford comments:

> The basis for the assertion of jurisdiction over 'governmental torts' such as these is . . . plainly not a distinction between 'governmental' and 'non-governmental' acts, but an assertion of local control over (i.e. jurisdiction over) obvious forms of harm or damage. Deliberately to cause harm or damage on the territory of another State by an act of 'public power' is, in the absence of some special exception, a plain violation of international law, whether the harm is caused by assassination or invasion. The exercise of local jurisdiction in such cases is an assertion of the forum's right, acknowledged by international law, to deal with the consequences of unlawful acts on its territory.[127]

Sucharitkul finds that 'The distinction between *jus imperii* and *jus gestionis* . . . appears to have little or no bearing in regard to this [non-commercial tort] exception' to State immunity. Sompong Sucharitkul, Fifth Report on Jurisdictional Immunities of States and Their Property, para. 67, *Yearbook of the International Law Commission*, 1983, Vol. II, Part One, p. 25 at 39. The drafters of the 1972 European Convention would simply see tort proceedings as 'private law' disputes between individuals and States. Council of Europe, *Explanatory Reports on the European Convention on State Immunity and the Additional Protocol*, Strasbourg, 1972, p. 38. Ress is of the view that 'whether the damage causing act or omission was of a private nature is not important'. Georg Ress, Second Report on Developments in the Field of State Immunity since 1982. International Law Association, *Report of the Sixty-Fifth Conference (Cairo)*, 1992, p. 290 at 317.

[125] The American Law Institute, *Restatement (Third) of the Foreign Relations Law of the United States*, Vol. 1, American Law Institute Publishers, 1987, s. 454 ('Claims in Tort'), p. 408, Comment b.

[126] *Letelier v Republic of Chile*, 488 F. Supp. 665, 671 (D.D.C. 1980); 63 ILR 378, 386. For s. 1605(a)(5) jurisdiction over political assassinations see also *Liu v Republic of China*, 892 F. 2d 1419 (9th Cir. 1989); 101 ILR 519 (Murder of a journalist by gunmen acting on the orders of Director of the Defence Intelligence Bureau of Taiwan).

[127] James Crawford, International Law and Foreign Sovereigns: Distinguishing Immune Transactions, 54 *BYBIL* (1983) 75, 111.

Essentially, it is the tortious result, not the nature of the tortious act (omission) that gives the forum court its jurisdiction.[128] One might argue that a State that causes injury is assimilated to a private person (and therefore the act or omission is rendered 'private') since a private person can also cause injury. But that is not the decisive factor, since jurisdiction will be exercised whether or not this argument is put forward. Thus, the legislation makes the distinction between acts *jure imperii* and *jure gestionis* irrelevant.

On the other hand, it is not surprising to find that the courts in the States without immunity legislation adopt a public/private law (*acta jure imperii/acta jure gestionis*) analysis, since that is the criterion they apply to virtually any action against a foreign State. Presumably, in these States, where the *jure imperii/jure gestionis* test serves as the overall criterion, it is still possible for a foreign State to argue for immunity on the ground that the act in question has been committed *jure imperii*. One would then expect the jurisdiction of the court to be restricted to a greater extent than in the States with immunity legislation. However, from the sparse case law on State immunity in tort, one observes a great measure of flexibility in the application of this test. Much depends on which aspect of the facts (the act/omission or the injury) the court sees as the core element of the tort. Thus, even if delivering an embassy's diplomatic bags may be a sovereign act, the delivery car's causing injury is not. In a case in which damages were sought for alleged damage to a motor car by the negligent driving of a car owned by the US Government,[129] the Austrian Supreme Court held that, in determining whether an act performed by a foreign government was *jure imperii* or *jure gestionis*, the Court must consider only the act itself, and not the purpose for which it was performed. The operation of a motor vehicle and the use of public roads by a foreign State belonged to the sphere of the private activities of that State even if such operation and use had occurred in the performance of official functions. Accordingly, the US Government was subject to the jurisdiction, and the fact that the car had carried mail for the US Embassy was irrelevant.

Here one sees not so much a nature/purpose dichotomy as a different characterization of the act in question; that is, instead of viewing the act as delivery of mail for the embassy, the court projected it into the more general scenario of operation of motor vehicles and use of public roads, thereby effectively stripping the act of any colour of governmental authority, and then fitted it into the nature/purpose framework. In so

[128] The American Law Institute maintains that 'a diplomatic courier carrying confidential dispatches in an automobile may be engaged in a governmental function, but if the vehicle injures a pedestrian or another vehicle, the state will be subject to suit based on the injury', though the Institute bases its conclusion on the nature/purpose test in the context of commercial activities. The American Law Institute, *Restatement (Third) of the Foreign Relations Law of the United States*, Vol. 1, American Law Institute Publishers, 1987, s. 454 ('Claims in Tort'), p. 408, Comment a.

[129] *Collision with Foreign Government-Owned Motor Car (Austria) Case*, Austria, Supreme Court, (1961) 40 ILR 73.

doing the Court ignored the fact that both characterizations would be equally tenable. The Court went on to say that:

A traffic accident creates private legal relations between the foreign State and the private individual, on a basis of equal rights between them.[130]

Thus a distinction was drawn between the immediate act (causing injury) and the 'purported' act (the act in the course of which injury was caused, in this case carrying mail for the embassy). In other words, the jurisdiction of the court was based not so much on the nature of the act of mail delivery (whatever its characterization) as on the occurrence of a traffic accident. Where there is injury, there is jurisdiction. In this way a court without immunity legislation would reach the same result as would one with such legislation, albeit from a different starting point.

In a similar case involving an embassy car, an Italian court held that, in matters regarding road traffic and civil responsibility for related matters, foreign States—and their legitimate representatives—acted *jure privatorum*. It was impossible, according to the court, to invest the use of a means of transport with the character of a public act or the exercise of the power of supremacy.[131]

In *Morocco v De Trappenberg*, a rehabilitation centre, after finding that one of its patients, the daughter of the caretaker of the Moroccan Consulate-General at Amsterdam, who had been seriously injured in an accident, was not covered by insurance for part of the costs for her medical treatment, applied for a garnishee order to secure the debt on funds held by Morocco, alleging that Morocco was liable in tort for failure to ensure that the caretaker and his family were adequately insured. The court held that, where a State became involved in a legal situation not as a public authority but in a private capacity it could be subjected to the jurisdiction of another State. Such a situation arose not only where a State undertook an obligation by entering into a legal relationship in the sphere of private law but also where such an obligation arose out of the law itself, for instance as a result of a tort committed by the State concerned acting as an employer in the same capacity as a private person. Therefore the court had jurisdiction to decide where a tort had been committed.[132]

However, like *McElhinney*, there are cases where immunity was granted on the basis of a characterization of the conduct in question as 'sovereign' or 'governmental'. For example, jurisdiction was denied by an Italian

[130] (1961) 40 ILR 73, 78.

[131] *Ciniglio v Indonesian Embassy and Compagnia di Assicurazioni Intercontinentali*, Italy, Examining Magistrate (Pretore) of Rome (1966) 65 ILR 268. But the claim was dismissed because it had been brought against the Indonesian Embassy rather than the Indonesian State, even though the plaintiff sued the insurance company of the Embassy as well.

[132] *Kingdom of Morocco v Stichting Revalidatie Centrum 'De Trappenberg'*, Netherlands, District Court of Amsterdam (summary proceedings) (1978) 65 ILR 375 and *Stichting Revalidatiecentrum 'De Trappenberg' v Kingdom of Morocco*, the Netherlands, District Court of Amsterdam (1984 and 1986) 94 ILR 355. The final conclusion of the court was that Morocco did not owe a duty of care to the caretaker to insure him and his family against medical expenses.

court in a case for requisition of property seized by the Japanese occupying troops in Shanghai, China, during the Second World War,[133] by a Dutch court in a case against the Chief of the German Federal Police in regard to a police report that was alleged to have led to an insulting magazine article,[134] and by an Irish court in a case claiming damages for alleged torts including, *inter alia*, breach of constitutional rights and conspiracy to deny the right to free movement.[135] It should be noted that, had the last two cases been brought in a court of one of those States with immunity legislation, jurisdiction would most probably have been denied since they involved only non-physical injury torts.

The case against Japan is of some interest for the present discussion as it has one thing in common with *McElhinney*: both involved acts of foreign armed forces. Some of the current immunity instruments contain a provision that precludes their application to the immunity of a foreign State with regard to its armed forces in the territory of the forum State,[136] but it has to be specifically pointed out that these provisions predicate the preclusion, not on a *jure imperii* rationale, but on possible special arrangements between the forum and the defendant States. In *McElhinney*, Hamilton C.J. of the Irish Supreme Court opined that, even if the terms of the European Convention on State Immunity could be seen as part of the domestic law of Ireland, the appellant's claim would still fail since art. 31 of that Convention preserved immunity in respect of anything done or omitted to be done by, or in relation to, armed forces when on the territory of another contracting State.[137] However, in their explanatory report, the drafters of the European Convention on State Immunity

[133] *Ministry of Foreign Affairs v Federici and Japanese State*, Italy, Tribunal of Rome (1968) 65 ILR 275.

[134] *Church of Scientology in the Netherlands Foundation and Others v (1) Herold and (2) Heinrich Bauer Verlag*, Netherlands, District Court of Amsterdam (1980) 65 ILR 380. One singular aspect of this case has to be noted: the court separated the defendant from the disputed act. In the court's opinion, since the defendant police chief, Herold, had appeared in court without pleading nullity of the writ, he could be regarded as a litigant only in his private capacity and was therefore not entitled to jurisdictional immunity. On the other hand, the act imputed to the police chief, whether committed by him personally or under his responsibility as head of the police department, could only be regarded as an act performed in his official capacity and not as a private person, so that the claim against him was inadmissible.

[135] *Schmidt v Home Secretary of the Government of the United Kingdom, the Commissioner of the Metropolitan Police and Jones*, Ireland, High Court, 1994, [1995] ILRM 301; 103 ILR 322.

[136] The European Convention on State Immunity, art. 31 ('Nothing in this Convention shall affect any immunities or privileges enjoyed by a Contracting State in respect of anything done or omitted to be done by, or in relation to, its armed forces when on the territory of another Contracting State.'); the UK SIA 1978, s. 16(2) ('This Part of this Act does not apply to proceedings relating to anything done by or in relation to the armed forces of a State while present in the United Kingdom and, in particular, has effect subject to the Visiting Forces Act 1952.'); the Australian FSIA, s. 6 ('This Act does not affect an immunity or privilege that is conferred by or under the Consular Privileges and Immunities Act 1972, the Defence (Visiting Forces) Act 1963, the Diplomatic Privileges and Immunities Act 1967 or any other Act.'); the US FSIA has no specific provision on foreign armed forces but mentions a special agreement in the legislative history of its international agreements provision (s. 1604). US Congress, House of Representatives, Report No. 94–1487,(1976) 15 ILM 1398 at 1407 ('Thus, the bill would not alter the rights or duties of the United States under the NATO Status of Forces Agreement or similar agreements with other countries. . .').

[137] *McElhinney v Williams and Her Majesty's Secretary of State for Northern Ireland*, Ireland, Supreme Court, 1995, [1996] 1 ILRM 276, 287; 104 ILR 691, 701.

only mentioned special agreements and visits by the naval forces of a foreign State,[138] but do not seem to have envisaged a scenario in which a member of foreign armed forces enters the territory of the forum State involuntarily, without prior authorization or consent, and then in his panic attempts to shoot at the applicant, which is what the British soldier did in the case of *McElhinney*. In other words, art. 31 of the European Convention, as well as the domestic statutory provisions relating to foreign armed forces cited here, contemplates special agreements or other arrangements between two States with respect to the presence and operation of foreign armed forces and is therefore predicated upon a prior consent by the forum State to the exercise of sovereign functions by foreign armed forces in the territory of the forum State. The act of the British soldier in *McElhinney*, namely entry into the territory of the forum State without authorization or consent, is obviously not envisaged by any of these provisions and might even be regarded, in the words of Crawford, 'a plain violation of international law'.[139]

At any rate, States at present seem to prefer to treat the immunity of a foreign State with regard to its armed forces quite separately from immunity in other contexts. Some courts even display considerable readiness to grant immunity where foreign armed forces are concerned.[140]

Ireland is not a party to the Convention. The Convention has now been ratified by eight States (Austria, Belgium, Cyprus, Germany, Luxembourg, the Netherlands, Switzerland, and the United Kingdom) and signed but not ratified by one State (Portugal). For latest status of the Convention see http://conventions.coe.int/treaty/EN/cadreprincipal.htm.

[138] Council of Europe, *Explanatory Reports on the European Convention on State Immunity and the Additional Protocol*, Strasbourg, 1972, p. 39.

[139] James Crawford, International Law and Foreign Sovereigns: Distinguishing Immune Transactions, 54 *BYBIL* (1983) 75, 111.

The *Rainbow Warrior* case provides a germane example. In July 1985, the *Rainbow Warrior*, a ship belonging to Greenpeace, was sunk in Auckland harbour, New Zealand, by explosives placed surreptitiously by French agents acting under orders issuing from the French Ministry of Defence. The ship was to sail into an area in the South Pacific where France was planning to conduct nuclear weapons tests, as part of a Greenpeace demonstration against those tests. One member of the *Rainbow Warrior*'s crew, a Netherlands national, was killed. Two of the agents, both of whom were serving commissioned officers in the French Armed Forces, were arrested in New Zealand, convicted of manslaughter and causing wilful damage, and sentenced to ten years' imprisonment. The High Court of the Auckland Registry held that the offences were terrorist acts and that it was 'even more reprehensible that this operation should have been carried out in the *territory* of a friendly ally.' (Emphasis added). In the correspondence between the two governments, New Zealand alleged, and France admitted, that the attack carried out against the *Rainbow Warrior* by French agents on New Zealand territory infringed the *territorial sovereignty* of New Zealand and was therefore committed *in violation of international law*. The UN Secretary-General, to whom the two governments submitted their dispute, ruled to the same effect. *The* Rainbow Warrior *Case* (1985 and 1986) 74 ILR 241, esp. at pp. 251, 253, 258, 262, and 266. The two individual defendants before the New Zealand court did not claim immunity, nor did France claim immunity on their behalf.

In this regard *McElhinney* is to be compared with the English cases of *Holland v Lampen-Wolfe* and *Littrell v U.S.A. (No. 2)* (see discussions below), where the US armed forces were stationed in the UK as an arrangement within the North Atlantic Treaty Organisation, i.e., with the prior consent of the UK Government.

[140] But see *Prefecture of Voiotia v Federal Republic of Germany*, Case No. 137/1997, Court of First Instance of Leivadia, Greece, 1997, 92 *American Journal of International Law* (1998) 765 (case note by Ilias Bantekas) (Germany was not immune with respect to atrocities (wilful murder and destruction of private property) committed by German occupation forces in a Greek village in 1944).

In *Holland v Lampen-Wolfe*, the English House of Lords held that the provision of education and training to military personnel at a US military base in England was part of a State's sovereign function of maintaining its armed forces and so accordingly was the act of writing a memorandum in the course of the supervision of the education programme.[141] The House of Lords thus confirmed the reasoning in *Littrell v U.S.A. (No. 2)*, where the English Court of Appeal held that the operation of a military hospital, although no doubt requiring much the same skills as the operation of a civilian hospital, was a recognized military activity. The standard of medical care that the US afforded its own servicemen was thus a matter within its own sovereign authority.[142] In *McElhinney*, the assault was committed by the British soldier in the course of carrying out his duties; so it is conceivable that, had a similar act been committed by an Irish soldier in the performance of his duties in the UK, UK courts might likewise have regarded the acts as *jure imperii* and held him immune. But even if this were the case, it would not mean that an English court would be deciding the case solely in reliance on a *jure imperii/jure gestionis* distinction. To start with, s. 16 (2) of the UK SIA provides:

> This Part of this Act does not apply to proceedings relating to anything done by or in relation to the armed forces of a State while present in the United Kingdom and, in particular, has effect subject to the Visiting Forces Act 1952.

Applying this provision, an English court in a case against foreign armed forces would have to perform two tests instead of one: first, it must ascertain whether the act in question has been 'done by or in relation to' foreign armed forces; and (if that test has been satisfied and therefore the relevant part of the UK SIA does not apply), second, whether the act in dispute is to be characterized as *jure imperii* or *jure gestionis* at common law. That is to say, in such a hypothetical case, the *jure imperii/jure gestionis* distinction enters into the picture only in the limited context of foreign armed forces. Thus, where an act apparently attributable to foreign armed forces is at issue, an English court has to apply first of all a test that looks at the *status of the actor* rather than the *nature of the act*. If a *McElhinney*-type act is committed by someone unrelated to foreign armed forces, *e.g.*, by a foreign *civilian policeman* instead of a *soldier*, the case will fall squarely within the tort exception to immunity contained in s. 5 of the UK SIA and the whole issue will turn only on whether any injury has resulted from the act. The *jure imperii/jure gestionis* distinction will become totally irrelevant.

It thus might be speculated that the crux of the matter in the *McElhinney* case is that no actual injury had resulted from the alleged assault. Otherwise things might have been different. What is more, the

[141] *Holland v Lampen-Wolfe* [2000] 1 WLR. 1573, 1577 (Lord Hope of Craighead); 1579 (Lord Cooke of Thorndon); 1581 (Lord Clyde); 1587 (Lord Millett).

[142] *Littrell v U.S.A. (No. 2)* [1995] 1 WLR. 82.

assault was by a soldier in the performance of his duties. Therefore, the emphasis of the ECHR's holding is to be laid, not on a *jure imperii/jure gestionis* distinction, but on the fact that the case involved 'the acts of a soldier on foreign territory which . . . may involve sensitive issues affecting diplomatic relations between States and national security.'[143]

In fact, as far as tortious conduct committed within the forum State is concerned, the most important requirement in current State practice is not that the conduct be *jure gestionis*, but that it has some connection with the territory of the forum State.

3. Territorial Connection

The requirement that the tortious act/omission or the injury/damage be somehow connected with the territory of the forum State is common to all the statutes, though differences exist as to how and to what extent that requirement should be satisfied. As the tort exception authorizes the court to adjudicate upon certain acts of foreign States that may be governmental or sovereign in nature, the territorial connection emerges as an indispensable ground for jurisdiction. Unlike in some other areas of State immunity, such as contracts of employment,[144] the status of the plaintiff is unimportant so long as the territorial nexus can be established. This means that a foreign national can be allowed to sue his own State of nationality if the tort occurs within the territory of the forum State. The formulations of this requirement are as many as the instruments: jurisdiction can be established when either (1) the tortious act/omission (the UK SIA, the Australian FSIA, the Institut de Droit International (IDI) Draft, the ILC Draft, and the European Convention on State Immunity); (2) the injury/damage (the Canadian SIA); (3) both the tortious act/omission and the injury/damage (the US FSIA) or (4) a direct effect (the ILA Draft), occurs in the forum State.

3.1. Tortious Act/Omission Only

Section 5 of the UK SIA requires that the injurious consequences be 'caused by an act or omission in the United Kingdom'.[145] Section 13 of the Australian FSIA follows the UK SIA in providing that the injurious consequences must be 'caused by an act or omission done or omitted to

[143] *McElhinney v Ireland*, Judgment, para. 38.

[144] See below, the discussion of contracts of employment.

[145] See *Al-Adsani v Government of Kuwait*, England, High Court, Queen's Bench Division (1995) 103 ILR 420, 429, *per* Mantell J. ('In clear language the Act bestows immunity upon sovereign States for acts committed outside the jurisdiction of the English courts'); *Al-Adsani v Government of Kuwait*, England, Court of Appeal (1996) 107 ILR 536, 549–50, *per* Ward L.J. ('A foreign State enjoys no immunity for acts causing personal injury committed in the United Kingdom and if that is expressly provided for the conclusion is impossible to escape that State immunity *is* afforded in respect of acts of torture committed outside this jurisdiction.' (Emphasis in the original)) and *Jones v Saudi Arabia*, England, High Court, Queen's Bench Division, 2003 WL 22187644, para. 13.

be done in Australia.'[146] The drafters explain such a formula in very clear language:

> It is clear that where all the actions making up the tort including the resulting damage occur within the jurisdiction the local courts should have jurisdiction. Difficulties occur where some acts occur in one jurisdiction, some in another or where the acts occur in one jurisdiction and the damage in another . . . Since the primary justification for asserting jurisdiction in this case is that the foreign State has no privilege to commit local physical injury or property damage, and since determining the place where the wrongful act or omission occurred is usually simpler than determining where damage occurred or the cause of action arose, it is recommended that Australian legislation follow the United Kingdom provision to this effect.[147]

Thus, if a tortfeasor sends a letter-bomb from the territory of the forum State to a person (whether or not he is a national of the forum State) in another State and that person suffers injury or death from the bomb, or if a tortfeasor constructs a timed car bomb in the territory of the forum State which later explodes in the territory of another State, courts of the forum State will have jurisdiction.

Art. 2(2)(e) of the 1991 IDI Draft affirms jurisdiction if the damage is 'attributable to activities of a foreign State and its agents within the national jurisdiction of the forum State'. This provision expands the jurisdiction of the forum State in two ways. First, by requiring that the damage be attributable to activities of a foreign State and its agents, it shifts the emphasis from the act or omission that constitutes the immediate cause of the injury/damage (the immediate act) to any activity in relation to which some injury/damage has been caused (the 'purported' act). That is, if the injury can be in any way linked to the activities of a foreign State or its agents (be they commercial or non-commercial, sovereign, or private), the court will exercise jurisdiction. Where injury has been incurred, attribution becomes more important than the act itself. In this way the *jure imperii/jure gestionis* test is effectively discarded. Second, instead of 'territory' it speaks of 'national jurisdiction'. Under modern international law, national jurisdiction extends far beyond the proper territory to such areas as the contiguous zone and the exclusive economic zone or to such objects as ships on the high seas and aircraft while in flight over areas beyond national jurisdiction. The term 'national jurisdiction' therefore gives the forum State a much wider jurisdiction than does mere 'territory'. The problem of overlapping jurisdictions seems to be inevitable, but the drafters give no indication of how this is to be resolved.

Art. 12 of the 1991 ILC Draft adopts another flexible formula by allowing jurisdiction 'if the act or omission occurred in whole or in part in the territory' of the forum State. Only part of the tortious act occurring in the territory of the forum State will be sufficient to activate jurisdiction;

[146] See *Costa Vraca v Bell Regal Pty Ltd*, Federal Court of Australia, [2003] FCA 65 (Unreported).

[147] The Australian Law Reform Commission, Report No. 24, '*Foreign State Immunity*', 1984, p. 67.

but this is subject to a further limitation, namely 'if the author of the act or omission was present in that territory at the time of the act or omission.' Thus if the tortfeasor remains all the time outside the territory of the forum State, such as shooting across a boundary, the forum State has no jurisdiction. On the other hand, it must be noted that the material time for the restriction is when the act or omission was committed but not when the proceedings are instituted. Thus if a tortfeasor commits part of the tort within the territory of the forum State and then leaves there to carry out the other part, such as constructing a car bomb in the forum State and then enters another State and detonates the bomb by remote control or so detonates it while the car is travelling in another State, the court still has jurisdiction even if, at the time the proceedings are brought, the tortfeasor is outside the territory of the forum State, because at least part of the tortious act was committed in the territory of the forum State while he was there. Art. 11 of the European Convention on State Immunity allows jurisdiction where 'the facts which occasioned the injury or damage occurred in the territory of the State of the forum' and contains a similar limitation; i.e. 'if the author of the injury or damage was present in that territory at the time when those facts occurred'.[148]

According to the ILC, the requirement of the presence of the tortfeasor within the territory of the forum State at the time of the act or omission is designed to serve the dual purpose of demanding a closer territorial connection between the State of the forum and the author or individual whose act or omission is the cause of the damage in the State of the forum[149] and excluding from the application of art. 12 'cases of transboundary injuries or trans-frontier torts or damage, such as export of explosives, fireworks or dangerous substances which could explode or cause damage through negligence, inadvertence or accident' and 'cases of shooting or firing across a boundary or of spill-over across the border of shelling as a result of an armed conflict'.[150]

It appears very difficult to draw a uniform picture as to the extent and scope of the territorial requirement: whether it covers the whole act or omission or only part of it or whether it extends only to the 'territory' in its proper sense or to other areas within the 'jurisdiction' of the forum State such as the contiguous zone and the exclusive economic zone or even to ships on the high seas and aircraft while in flight over the high seas. One might also find it hard to make sense of a 'presence of the tortfeasor' requirement.[151]

148 According to the drafters, the 'author' does not necessarily mean the 'person' liable. 'For example, when a vehicle belonging to a State is involved in a traffic accident, then, provided the driver of the vehicle was present, the State as owner or possessor of the vehicle may be sued, even though the plaintiff does not seek to establish the personal liability of the driver.' Council of Europe, *Explanatory Reports on the European Convention on State Immunity and the Additional Protocol*, Strasbourg, 1972, p. 21.

149 *Yearbook of the International Law Commission*, 1991, Vol. II, Part Two, pp. 12–62 at 45.

150 *Id.*

151 Lewis, for one, finds such a 'presence' requirement 'difficult to understand, as it seems to envisage the possibility of damage being caused within a State's boundaries at a time when the tortfeasor has either already left the country (delayed action?) or has never entered it (damage by

3.2. *Injury/Damage Only*

The regime under s. 6 of the Canadian SIA seems to be the obverse of the tortious act/omission-only pattern. Section 6 provides: 'A foreign State is not immune from the jurisdiction of a court in any proceedings that relate to (a) any death or personal injury, or (b) any damage to or loss of property, that occurs in Canada.' That is, no matter where the tortious act or omission occurs, the court has jurisdiction so long as the injurious consequences are suffered in the territory of the forum State. Such a formulation can be very advantageous to the plaintiff in the case of a tort with what one might call 'lingering' effects, that is, a tort that spans a considerable period of time or has some lapse of time between the tortious act/omission and the injurious consequences (so-called 'split tort').[152] But as long as 'instant' torts (the tortious conduct and the injury/damage occurring at the same time) are concerned, this pattern might not prove so liberal as it appears to be, and may have approximately the same effect as the one that requires the tortious act/omission to have occurred in the territory of the forum State.

In *Jaffe v Miller*, where the plaintiff alleged that he had been kidnapped from Canada and taken to Florida, US, to face false criminal charges, the court singled out three separate tortious acts: (a) the first act of malicious prosecution and (b) the kidnapping, which had occurred before the Canadian SIA entered into force and were therefore outside its scope; and (c) the second act of malicious prosecution, which had occurred after the entry into force of the Canadian SIA but in the US and was consequently not within s. 6. The court obviously did not consider as a valid cause of action lingering mental distress that might have resulted from the malicious prosecution and might continue to be felt even after the victim's return to Canada.[153] In a later case for unlawful imprisonment, conspiracy, misrepresentation, and fraud in relation to an undercover operation in which US customs officers had used false identities to mislead the plaintiff into activities prohibited by US law, which resulted in his arrest and guilty plea in the US, the court interpreted s. 6 as encompassing mental distress, emotional upset, and restriction of liberty (false imprisonment in this case) as well as physical injury. However, as he had suffered all this not in Canada, but in the US, s. 6 did not apply.[154]

3.3. *Both Tortious Act/Omission and Injury/Damage*

At first sight, the US FSIA seems also to adopt an 'injury/damage' pattern but there is some confusion regarding the interpretation of the

long-range frequencies?).' Charles J. Lewis, *State and Diplomatic Immunity*, 3rd ed., London: Lloyd's of London Press Ltd., 1990, pp. 53–4.

[152] '... such as a claim arising out of a sale of defective products manufactured abroad.' The American Law Institute, *Restatement (Third) of the Foreign Relations Law of the United States*, Vol. 1, American Law Institute Publishers, 1987, s. 454 ('Claims in Tort'), p. 410, Reporters' note 1.

[153] *Jaffe v Miller*, Canada, Ontario Court of Appeal, 1993, (1993) 13 OR (3d) 745; 95 ILR 446.

[154] *Walker v Bank of New York Inc.*, Canada, Court of Appeal for Ontario, (1994) 111 DLR (4th) 186; 104 ILR 277. Subsequent Canadian case law restricted s. 6 only to physical injury. See *United States of America v Friedland*, Canada, Ontario Court of Appeal, (1999) 182 D.L.R. (4th) 614, 621–2;

relevant provisions and the case law favours a stricter requirement, namely, that both the tortious act or omission and the injury/damage must occur in the US. Section 1605(a)(5) of the US FSIA grants jurisdiction where an action is brought against a foreign State 'for personal injury or death, or damage to or loss of property, occurring in the United States and caused by the tortious act or omission of that foreign state or of any official or employee of that foreign state while acting within the scope of his office or employment'. Doubtless, the injury has to occur in the US; but it is not altogether clear where the act or omission should take place. The legislative report provides an important clue by stating plainly that 'the tortious act or omission must occur within the jurisdiction of the United States . . . '[155] However, it does seem odd that the drafters should have added this statement as an afterthought instead of including it in the statutory provision, for failing such a statement one might naturally reach quite the opposite conclusion that the place where the act or omission occurred is irrelevant. The American Law Institute is of the opinion that

> Under s. 1605(a)(5) of the FSIA, courts in the United States have jurisdiction over tort claims against a foreign state only if the injury took place in the United States, *regardless of where the act or omission causing the injury took place*. Indirect effects in the United States, such as loss of consortium resulting from injury to a claimant's spouse inflicted by the foreign State outside the United States, are not within the jurisdiction of courts in the United States . . .

And that

> Thus, a claim arising from an injury in the United States caused by the malfunction of a defective product manufactured abroad by a foreign State instrumentality would be subject to jurisdiction in the United States under the FSIA; under the European Convention and the British Act, the court apparently would have jurisdiction of an action in tort only if the product had been manufactured in the forum State.[156]

This seems to be a correct interpretation of the language of the provision itself but is definitely at odds with the statement given by the drafters in the legislative report. If one follows the instruction of the drafters, one will demand both the act or omission and the injury to occur in the forum State; on the other hand, if one ignores this instruction and follows the language of the provision itself, one will only require the injury to take place in the forum State.

120 ILR 417, 460; *Schreiber v Federal Republic of Germany*, Canada, Ontario Court of Appeal, (2001) 196 D.L.R. (4th) 281, 294–5 and 298 and *Schreiber v Federal Republic of Germany*, Canada, Supreme Court, (2002) 216 D.L.R. (4th) 513. See also *Bouzari v Iran*, Canada, Ontario Superior Court of Justice, 2002 Ont. Sup. C.J. LEXIS 701, pp. 15–16.

155 US Congress, House of Representatives, Report No. 94–1487, (1976) 15 ILM 1398 at 1409.

156 The American Law Institute, *Restatement (Third) of the Foreign Relations Law of the United States*, Vol. 1, American Law Institute Publishers, 1987, s. 454 ('Claims in Tort'), p. 409, Commente and Reporters' note 1. Emphasis added.

In *Letelier* the district court obviously required only the injury to occur in the US when it rejected the resort to the act of State doctrine by the Chilean government:

Although the acts allegedly undertaken directly by the Republic of Chile to obtain the death of Orlando Letelier may well have been carried out entirely within that country, that circumstance alone will not allow it to absolve itself under the act of State doctrine *if the actions of its alleged agents resulted in tortious injury in this country.*[157]

But so far this remains the only case with such reasoning, and it has been rejected by the Court of Appeals for that circuit.[158] So the case law definitely requires *both the tortious act/omission and the injury* to occur in the US. Where the acts or omissions causing the injury took place in a foreign State, courts invariably denied jurisdiction.[159]

On the other hand, courts do not require that *all* the events happen in the US. In *Olsen by Sheldon v Mexico*, for example, where the plaintiffs brought an action against the Government of Mexico in respect of the deaths of their parents who had been killed in a plane crash inside US territory when being transferred from Mexico to the US as prisoners, the court rejected the argument of Mexico that the events at issue should have occurred wholly within the territory of the US. According to the court, if plaintiffs could allege 'at least one entire tort' (in that case the negligent piloting of the aircraft) occurring in the US, they might claim under s. 1605(a)(5).[160]

[157] *Letelier v Republic of Chile*, 488 F. Supp. 665, 674 (D.D.C. 1980); 63 ILR 378 at 389. Emphasis added.

[158] *Persinger v Islamic Republic of Iran (No. 2)*, 729 F. 2d 835, 842 (D.C. Cir. 1984); 90 ILR 586, 593 and *Asociacion de Reclamantes v United Mexican States*, 735 F. 2d 1517, 1524–25 (D.C. Cir. 1984); 84 ILR 87. See below.

[159] See, *e.g.*, *Abrams v Société Nationale des Chemins de Fer Français*, 175 F. Supp. 2d 423, 431 (E.D.N.Y. 2001) (Vacated and remanded on other grounds, 332 F.3d 173 (2d Cir. 2003)) (the French national railroad company's alleged deportation of Jews and others from their homes in France to various Nazi death camps during World War II); *Cicippio v Islamic Republic of Iran*, 30 F. 3d 165, 169 (D.C. Cir. 1994); 107 ILR 296, 302 (alleged abduction and hostage-taking in Lebanon by persons hired by Iran); *Fickling v Commonwealth of Australia*, 775 F. Supp. 66, 72 (E.D.N.Y. 1991); 103 ILR 447, 453 (breach of an investment guarantee in Australia); *Argentine Republic v Amerada Hess Shipping Corporation*, 488 US 428, 441 (1989); 81 ILR 658, 666 (destruction of a ship on the high seas); *Kline v Kaneko*, 685 F. Supp. 386, 391 (S.D.N.Y. 1988); 101 ILR 497, 503 (abduction in and expulsion from Mexico); *Frolova v Union of Soviet Socialist Republics*, 761 F. 2d 370, 379 (7th Cir. 1985); 85 ILR 236, 246 (denial of exit permission by Soviet authorities to a Soviet citizen); *Berkovitz v Islamic Republic of Iran and Others*, 735 F. 2d 329, 331 (9th Cir. 1984); 81 ILR 552, 554 (murder of a US citizen in Iran); *Persinger v Islamic Republic of Iran (No. 2)*, 729 F. 2d 835, 842 (D.C. Cir. 1984); 90 ILR 586, 593 (Iranian hostage crisis) (Here the court reversed an earlier decision of its own denying immunity on the ground that the definition of 'United States' was broad enough to embrace all territory under concurrent US jurisdiction, including US embassies. *Persinger v Islamic Republic of Iran*, 72 ILR 132, 141 (D.C. Cir. 1982)); *Asociacion de Reclamantes v United Mexican States*, 735 F. 2d 1517, 1524–5 (D.C. Cir. 1984); 84 ILR 87, 94–5 (alleged taking and conversion of land in Mexico); *McKeel v Islamic Republic of Iran*, 722 F. 2d 582, 589, note 10 (9th Cir. 1983); 81 ILR 543, 549 (Iranian hostage crisis); *Matter of Sedco, Inc.*, 543 F. Supp. 561, 567 (S. D. Tex. 1982); 72 ILR 110, 115 (oil well drilling disaster in Mexico); and *Perez. v The Bahamas*, 482 F. Supp. 1208, 1210–11 (D.D.C. 1980), 63 ILR 350, 353; 652 F. 2d 186, 188–9 (D.C. Cir. 1981); 63 ILR 601, 602–3 (injury in the Bahamian territorial sea).

[160] *Olsen, by Sheldon v Government of Mexico, Sanchez, by Cernie v Republic of Mexico*, 729 F. 2d 641, 645–6 (9th Cir. 1984); 84 ILR 96, 100. See also *Burnett v Al Baraka Investment & Development Corporation*, 292 F. Supp. 2d 9, 24–6 (D.D.C. 2003).

3.4. A Direct Effect

The most radical position so far is that taken by the International Law Association (ILA). Article III (F) of the 1982 ILA Montreal Draft grants jurisdiction if 'the act or omission which caused the death, injury or damage occurred *wholly or partly* in the forum State'.[161] This follows the 'tortious act/omission-only' pattern. But the ILA modified this provision in 1994 by adding 'or if that act or omission had a direct effect in the forum State', thereby putting forward a more liberal pattern in which a direct effect in the territory of the forum State is sufficient to justify a denial of immunity, regardless of where the tortious act or omission or the injury itself has occurred. According to the drafters, the aim of such a modification is to cover transboundary torts.[162] One might be led to believe that only such a 'direct effect' pattern allows jurisdiction over transboundary torts.[163] But this is a misconception. As shown above, other patterns (including that followed by the 1982 ILA Draft) only exclude certain transbounary torts, not all of them. At any rate, in view of the strict interpretation of the territorial requirement by various national courts, it seems unlikely that a very flimsy territorial connection, such as that of a mere 'direct effect' suggested by ILA, may gain wide support.

4. Summary

In view of the long-established *acta jure imperii/acta jure gestionis* distinction, the statutory authorization to exercise jurisdiction over acts or omissions attributable to foreign States causing personal injury or death or damage to or loss of property is a new development since it negates the above distinction by rendering it irrelevant and unnecessary. Provided the territorial connection can be satisfied, jurisdiction is based on the fact that some act/omission of a foreign State has resulted in injury/damage, but not on the nature of the act or omission. This seems to be now a widely accepted rule; and it aims to defeat the commonplace argument that immunity should be granted because the act or omission in question has been committed in the course of activities of a sovereign nature, such as an embassy errand. Meanwhile, court practice has shown that this exception to immunity is potentially extendable to a wider range of activities,

[161] Emphasis added.

[162] Section-by-section analysis of the 1994 Revised ILA Draft, Final Report on Developments in the Field of State Immunity and Proposal for a Revised Draft Convention on State Immunity. ILA, *Report of the Sixty-Sixth Conference (Buenos Aires)*, 1994, pp. 452–99 at 495. For the text of the Revised Draft Articles see ILA, *Report of the Sixty-Sixth Conference (Buenos Aires)*, 1994, pp. 22–8 and pp. 488–94.

[163] For targeted acts Schreuer envisages 'State-sponsored trans-boundary terrorism by way of letter bombs, explosives placed on board aircraft and the proverbial shot across the border and also . . . instances of transfrontier pollution' or even 'torts committed against nationals of the forum States suffered while temporarily present in the offending State.' In his opinion, under a wider concept of effects jurisdiction over torts committed by foreign States abroad, 'the violation of international law including human rights may become a decisive criterion.' Christoph H. Schreuer, *State Immunity: Some Recent Developments*, Cambridge: Cambridge University Press, 1988, pp. 61–2.

including those bearing a manifest sovereign attribute, such as political assassination. The most important requirement in the context of tort is a territorial connection between either the tortious act or omission or the resultant injury, or both, and the forum State. Although criticized as 'rigid' and 'limiting',[164] the requirement of a territorial nexus both fits in with the general principle of territoriality as a basis of national jurisdiction under international law and helps advance the strong argument that the forum courts provide the most convenient local remedy.[165]

In short, when torts committed in the forum State are concerned, the overriding consideration for a court is neither a *jure imperii/jure gestionis* test nor whether 'insurable' personal injury is at issue, but whether the tortious act or omission has a connection with the territory of the forum State. Thus, when, by reference to 'insurable personal injury' and the sovereign nature of the tortious act in question, the ECHR found in *McElhinney v Ireland* that Ireland did not fall outside any 'currently accepted international standards',[166] it evidently had wrongly identified 'international standards' in mind.

5. *An Important Development: the United States Act of* 1996

In this connection, an important development should be noted. The US Antiterrorism and Effective Death Penalty Act of 1996 (AEDPA)[167] adds several new provisions to the US FSIA: s. 1605(a)(7) provides that a foreign State shall not be immune from the jurisdiction of US courts in any case

> in which money damages are sought against a foreign state for personal injury or death that was caused by an act of torture, extrajudicial killing, aircraft sabotage, hostage taking, or the provision of material support or resources . . . for such an act if such act or provision of material support is engaged in by an official, employee, or agent of such foreign state while acting within the scope of his or her office, employment, or agency.[168]

According to s. 1610(a)(7), the property in the US of a foreign State, used for a commercial activity in the US, shall not be immune from

[164] See, *e.g.*, Christoph H. Schreuer, *State Immunity: Some Recent Developments*, pp. 52 and 61.

[165] See, *e.g.*, the Australian Law Reform Commission, Report No. 24, '*Foreign State Immunity*', 1984, p. 67.

[166] *McElhinney v Ireland*, judgment, para. 38.

[167] Antiterrorism and Effective Death Penalty Act of 1996, Public Law 104–32, Section 221, April 24, 1996, codified at 28 U.S.C. s. 1605(a)(7), 36 ILM 759 (1997). Originally, the Act applied only if both the claimant and the victim were US nationals when the act upon which the claim was based occurred (s. 1605(a)(7)(B)(ii)); but this provision was amended in 1997 to allow suit if either the claimant or the victim was a US national when the tortious act occurred. Public Law 105–11, April 25, 1997, (1997) 36 ILM 760.

[168] '. . . a plaintiff need not establish that the material support or resources provided by a foreign state for a terrorist act contributed directly to the act from which his claim arises . . . Sponsorship of a terrorist group which causes the personal injury or death of a United States national alone is sufficient to invoke jurisdiction.' *Flatow v Islamic Republic of Iran*, 999 F. Supp. 1, 18 (D.C.C. 1998). However, a plaintiff does have to establish 'a legally sufficient evidentiary basis for a reasonable jury to find that the acts of the defendants were a necessary condition or "but for" cause' of the injury in question. *Ungar v Islamic Republic of Iran*, 211 F. Supp. 2d 91, 98 (D.D.C. 2002).

attachment in aid of execution or from execution 'regardless of whether the property is or was involved with the act upon which the claim is based.' The property of an agency or instrumentality of a foreign State shall be denied immunity in the same way (s. 1610(b)(2) as amended).[169]

These amendments to the US FSIA 'shall apply to any cause of action arising before, on, or after the date of the enactment of this Act.' (AEDPA, s. 221(c)) That is, they apply retroactively.[170]

In addition to the denial of immunity by the AEDPA, a statutory note entitled 'Civil Liability for Acts of State Sponsored Terrorism (1996)',[171]

[169] But the separate juridical status of an entity other than the State itself is not to be lightly disregarded: *Alejandre v Telefonica Larga Distancia de P.R., Inc.*, 183 F.3d 1277, 1282–90 (11th Cir. 1999) (following the principle articulated by the Supreme Court in *First National City Bank v Banco Para El Comercio Exterior de Cuba (Bancec)*, 462 US 611 (1983); 80 ILR 566). So, unless the particular entity in question can be shown as involved in the tortious activity and therefore not immune by itself, the property of a separate entity cannot be seized to satisfy a judgment against the State.

[170] See, *e.g.*, *Wagner v Islamic Republic of Iran*, 172 F. Supp. 2d 128, 134, note 7 (D.D.C. 2001) (death in 1984 in Lebanon); *Daliberti v Republic of Iraq*, 97 F. Supp. 2d 38, 43 (D.D.C. 2000) (detention in 1992 in Iraq); *Cicippio v Islamic Republic of Iran*, 18 F. Supp. 2d 62, 68–9 (D.D.C. 1998) (kidnapping, imprisonment, and torture between 1985 and 1991 in Beirut, Lebanon); *Flatow v Islamic Republic of Iran*, 999 F. Supp. 1, 13–14 (D.C.C. 1998) (death caused by suicide bomber in 1995) and *Alejandre v Republic of Cuba*, 996 F. Supp. 1239, 1247, note 4 (S.D. Fla. 1997) (shooting down of aircraft in 1996). Most, if not all, cases under the AEDPA involved acts occurring before its enactment. See, *e.g.*, *Dammarell v Islamic Republic of Iran*, 281 F. Supp. 2d 105 (D.D.C. 2003) (bombing of the US Embassy in Beirut in 1983); *Regier v Islamic Republic of Iran*, 281 F. Supp. 2d 87 (D.D.C. 2003) (kidnapping in Beirut in 1984); *Tracy v Islamic Republic of Iran*, (D.D.C. 2003) (abduction in Beirut in 1986); *Kilburn v Republic of Iran*, 277 F. Supp. 2d 24 (D.D.C. 2003) (hostage taking in Lebanon between 1984 and 1986); *Acree v Republic of Iraq*, 271 F. Supp. 2d 179; (D.D.C. 2003) (torture of POWs in Iraq in 1991); *Peterson v Islamic Republic of Iran*, 264 F. Supp. 2d 46 (D.D.C. 2003) (the Marine barracks bombing in Beirut in 1983); *Kerr v Islamic Republic of Iran*, 245 F. Supp. 2d 59 (D.D.C. 2003) (murder in Beirut in 1984); *Cronin v Islamic Republic of Iran*, 238 F. Supp. 2d 222 (D.D.C. 2002) (kidnapping in Beirut in 1984); *Surette v Islamic Republic of Iran*, 231 F. Supp. 2d 260 (D.D.C. 2002) (kidnapping in Beirut in 1984); *Turner v Islamic Republic of Iran*, 2002 U.S. Dist. LEXIS 26730 (D.D.C. 2002) (kidnapping and imprisonment in Beirut from 1987 to 1991); three cases decided against Iran in regard of the bombing of a passenger bus in Jerusalem on 25 February 1996, two months before the enactment of the AEDPA (*Weinstein v Islamic Republic of Iran*, 184 F. Supp. 2d 13 (D.D.C. 2002); *Eisenfeld v Islamic Republic of Iran*, 172 F. Supp. 2d 1 (D.D.C. 2000) and *Mousa v Islamic Republic of Iran*, Civ. No. 00–2096 (D.D.C. 2001)); *Hill v Republic of Iraq*, 175 F. Supp. 2d 36 (D.D.C. 2001) (detention in 1990 in Kuwait and Iraq); *Simpson v Socialist People's Libyan Arab Jamahiriya*, 180 F. Supp. 2d 78 (D.D.C. 2001) (alleged hostage taking and torture in 1987 in Libya); *Polhill v Islamic Republic of Iran*, 2001 US Dist. LEXIS 15322 (D.D.C. 2001) (detention from 1987 to 1990 in Lebanon); *Jenco v Islamic Republic of Iran*, 154 F. Supp. 2d 27 (D.D.C. 2001) (detention from 1985 to 1986 in Lebanon); and *Sutherland v Islamic Republic of Iran*, 151 F. Supp. 2d 27 (D.D.C. 2001) (detention from 1985 to 1991 in Lebanon).

But see *Roeder v Islamic Republic of Iran*, 195 F. Supp. 2d 140, 144–6 (D.D.C. 2002) (The 1980 US-Iran Algiers Accords and implementing regulations prohibited lawsuits arising out of the 1979–1980 Tehran hostage crisis).

[171] Civil Liability for Acts of State Sponsored Terrorism, Public Law No. 104–208, Section 101(c), September 30, 1996, codified at 28 U.S.C. § 1605 note. This was enacted as part of the Omnibus Consolidated Appropriations Act of 1997. Public Law 104–208, Section 589. Noted at (1997) 36 ILM 759.

The defendant foreign State can be held liable for acts of its agents: 'Since a foreign state would be liable for the tortious acts of its officials, employees and agents under the theory of *respondeat superior*; the victim of a terrorist attack may seek monetary damages from the foreign state itself, and/or from an agency or instrumentality thereof.' *Alejandre v Republic of Cuba*, 42 F. Supp. 2d 1317, 1322 (S.D. Fla. 1999) (But this judgment was vacated by the Court of Appeals for the Eleventh Circuit, which held that certain debts owed to a Cuban telecommunications company could not be garnished for judgments against Cuba: *Alejandre v Telefonica Larga Distancia de P.R.*, commonly referred to as the 'Flatow Amendment',[172] was enacted to create a cause of action for any act which would give a court jurisdiction under the newly added s. 1605(a)(7) of the US FSIA. Under this note, 'an official, employee, or agent of a foreign state designated as a state sponsor of terrorism . . . shall be liable . . . for personal injury or death caused by acts of that official, employee, or agent . . . for money damages which may include economic damages, solatium, pain, and suffering, and punitive damages . . .'[173]

Thus, a foreign State is denied immunity, from both adjudication and enforcement, for personal injury or death caused by torture or certain other acts committed *outside the US*. A territorial connection with the US territory, as contemplated in the original US FSIA, has been dispensed with.[174] This amounts to a fundamental change to the immunity regime as demarcated by the US FSIA. However, this Act is subject to an important qualification, namely, that it shall only apply if the defendant foreign State has been 'designated as a state sponsor of terrorism' (s. 1605(a)(7)(A)).[175] So far only seven States have been so designated by the US Department of State: Cuba, Iran, Iraq, Libya, North Korea,

Inc., 183 F.3d 1277, 1282–90 (11th Cir. 1999)); '. . . a foreign state sponsor of terrorism is jointly and severally liable for all damages assessed against co-defendant officials, agents, and employees.' *Flatow v Islamic Republic of Iran*, 999 F. Supp. 1, 27 (D.C.C. 1998); 'If Plaintiffs prove an agent's liability under this Act, the foreign state employing the agent would also incur liability under the theory of *respondeat superior*.' *Alejandre v Republic of Cuba*, 996 F. Supp. 1239, 1249 (S.D. Fla. 1997). See also *Jenco v Islamic Republic of Iran*, 154 F. Supp. 2d 27, 34–5 (D.D.C. 2001) and *Sutherland v Islamic Republic of Iran*, 151 F. Supp. 2d 27, 48–50 (D.D.C. 2001).

[172] *Flatow v Islamic Republic of Iran*, 999 F. Supp. 1, 12–14 (D.C.C. 1998).

[173] But note that the Flatow Amendment does not list 'foreign States'. *Price v Socialist People's Libyan Arab Jamahiriya*, 294 F. 3d 82, 87 (D.C. Cir. 2002). In 1998, s. 1610 of the US FSIA was further amended to expand the categories of property subject to attachment/execution. In particular, s. 1606 of the US FSIA was amended to permit punitive damages to be awarded against a foreign State in any action under s. 1605(a)(7). Section 117 of the Omnibus Consolidated and Emergency Supplemental Appropriations Act for 1999, Public Law 105–277, Section 117, codified at 28 U.S.C. s. 1610 (f)(1)(A)(B)(2)(A)(B)). Cited in full in *Alejandre v Republic of Cuba*, 42 F. Supp. 2d 1317, 1323–4 (S.D. Fla. 1999). Punitive damages were awarded against Iran: *Eisenfeld v Islamic Republic of Iran*, 172 F. Supp. 2d 1, 9 (D.D.C. 2000). However, the punitive damages provision was soon repealed by the Victims of Trafficking and Violence Protection Act of 2000, Public Law 106–386, Section 2002(f)(2) (October 28, 2000). Thus, as previously provided for under s. 1606 of the US FSIA, a foreign State (but not its agencies or instrumentalities) is now still exempt from punitive damages. See, *e.g.*, *Stethem v Islamic Republic of Iran*, 201 F. Supp. 2d 78, 92, note 21 (D.D.C. 2002); *Weinstein v Islamic Republic of Iran*, 184 F. Supp. 2d 13, 24, note 1 (D.D.C 2002); *Hill v Republic of Iraq*, 175 F. Supp. 2d 36, 48 (D.D.C. 2001); *Wagner v Islamic Republic of Iran*, 172 F. Supp. 2d 128, 134, note 9 (D.D.C. 2001); *Polhill v Islamic Republic of Iran*, 2001 U.S. Dist. LEXIS 15322 (D.D.C. 2001), p. 17, note 5; *Elahi v Islamic Republic of Iran*, 124 F. Supp. 2d 97, 114 (D.D.C. 2000); *Anderson v Islamic Republic of Iran*, 90 F. Supp. 2d 107, 114 (D.D.C. 2000); *Alejandre v Republic of Cuba*, 996 F. Supp. 1239, 1253 (S.D. Fla. 1997).

[174] See, *e.g.*, *Price v Socialist People's Libyan Arab Jamahiriya*, 294 F. 3d 82, 89–90 (D.C. Cir. 2002), pp. 15–18. See also Lee M. Caplan, The Constitution and Jurisdiction over Foreign States: The 1996 Amendments to the Foreign Sovereign Immunities Act in Perspective, 41 *Virginia Journal of International Law* (2001) 369, 406–8 and Joseph W. Glannon & Jeffery Atik, Politics and Personal Jurisdiction: Suing State Sponsors of Terrorism under the 1996 Amendments to the Foreign Sovereign Immunities Act, 87 *Georgia Law Journal* (1999) 675, 681–2.

[175] Such a designation can happen 'either at the time the incident complained of occurred' or 'as a result of such act'. *Elahi v Islamic Republic of Iran*, 124 F. Supp. 2d 97, 107 (D.D.C. 2000). See also *Flatow v Islamic Republic of Iran*, 999 F. Supp. 1, 16 (D.D.C. 1998).

Sudan, and Syria.[176] Up to now, cases have been decided against Cuba,[177] Iran,[178] Iraq,[179] and Libya.[180] As can be expected, in most such cases the defendants did not enter an appearance.[181] This list seems to be an open-ended one and more foreign States might be designated as a 'State sponsor of terrorism' and be subjected to the jurisdiction of US courts;[182] but,

[176] *Daliberti v Republic of Iraq*, 97 F. Supp. 2d 38, 44, note 3 (D.D.C. 2000); *Flatow v. Islamic Republic of Iran*, 999 F. Supp. 1, 12, note. 4 (D.C.C. 1998). Libya was apparently taken out of the list in 2001. *Estates of Yaron Ungar & Efrat Ungar v Palestinian Authority*, 153 F. Supp. 2d 76, 93, note 4 (D.R.I. 2001) ('Currently, Cuba, Iran, Iraq, North Korea, Sudan, and Syria are designated as sponsors of terrorism').

[177] *Alejandre v Republic of Cuba*, 996 F. Supp. 1239 (S.D. Fla. 1997); *Alejandre v Republic of Cuba*, 42 F. Supp. 2d 1317, 1322 (S.D. Fla. 1999).

[178] *Campuzano v Islamic Republic of Iran*, 281 F. Supp. 2d 258 (D.D.C. 2003); *Dammarell v Islamic Republic of Iran*, 281 F. Supp. 2d 105 (D.D.C. 2003); *Regier v. Islamic Republic of Iran*, 281 F. Supp. 2d 87 (D.D.C. 2003); *Tracy v Islamic Republic of Iran*, (D.D.C. 2003); *Kilburn v Republic of Iran*, 277 F. Supp. 2d 24 (D.D.C. 2003); *Stern v Islamic Republic of Iran*, 271 F. Supp. 2d 286 (D.D.C. 2003); *Peterson v Islamic Republic of Iran*, 264 F. Supp. 2d 46 (D.D.C. 2003); *Kerr v Islamic Republic of Iran*, 245 F. Supp. 2d 59 (D.D.C. 2003); *Cronin v Islamic Republic of Iran*, 238 F. Supp. 2d 222 (D.D.C. 2002); *Surette v Islamic Republic of Iran*, 231 F. Supp. 2d 260 (D.D.C. 2002); *Turner v Islamic Republic of Iran*, 2002 U.S. Dist. LEXIS 26730 (D.D.C. 2002); *Stethem v Islamic Republic of Iran*, 201 F. Supp. 2d 78 (D.D.C. 2002); *Weinstein v Islamic Republic of Iran*, 184 F. Supp. 2d 13 (D.D.C 2002); *Wagner v Islamic Republic of Iran*, 172 F. Supp. 2d 128 (D.D.C. 2001); *Polhill v Islamic Republic of Iran*, 2001 U.S. Dist. LEXIS 15322 (D.D.C. 2001); *Jenco v Islamic Republic of Iran*, 154 F. Supp. 2d 27 (D.D.C. 2001); *Sutherland v Islamic Republic of Iran*, 151 F. Supp. 2d 27 (D.D.C. 2001); *Eisenfeld v Islamic Republic of Iran*, 172 F. Supp. 2d 1 (D.D.C. 2000); *Elahi v Islamic Republic of Iran*, 124 F. Supp. 2d 97 (D.D.C. 2000); *Cicippio v Islamic Republic of Iran*, 18 F. Supp. 2d 62 (D.D.C. 1998); *Flatow v Islamic Republic of Iran*, 999 F. Supp. 1 (D.C.C. 1998) and *Flatow v Islamic Republic of Iran*, 76 F. Supp. 2d 16 (D.D.C. 1999).

[179] *Smith v Islamic Emirate of Afghanistan*, 262 F. Supp. 2d 217 (S.D.N.Y. 2003) (In this case, Osama bin Laden, al-Qaeda, Taliban, and Islamic Emirate of Afghanistan were regarded as 'non-sovereign defendants', while Iraq and Saddam Hussein were sued under s. 1605(a)(7)); *Acree v Republic of Iraq*, 271 F. Supp. 2d 179; (D.D.C. 2003); *Hill v Republic of Iraq*, 175 F. Supp. 2d 36 (D.D.C. 2001); *Daliberti v Republic of Iraq*, 146 F. Supp. 2d 19 (D.D.C. 2001); *Daliberti v Republic of Iraq*, 97 F. Supp. 2d 38 (D.D.C. 2000).

[180] *Simpson v Socialist People's Libyan Arab Jamahiriya*, 180 F. Supp. 2d 78 (D.D.C. 2001); *Frey v Socialist People's Libyan Arab Jamahiriya*, 110 F. Supp. 2d 10 (D.D.C. 2000); *Rein v Socialist People's Libyan Arab Jamahiriya*, 995 F. Supp. 325 (E.D.N.Y. 1998), affirmed *Rein v Socialist People's Libyan Arab Jamahiriya*, 162 F. 3d 748 (2d Cir. 1998).

[181] See, *e.g.*, *Smith v Islamic Emirate of Afghanistan*, 262 F. Supp. 2d 217 (S.D.N.Y. 2003); *Campuzano v Islamic Republic of Iran*, 281 F. Supp. 2d 258 (D.D.C. 2003); *Dammarell v Islamic Republic of Iran*, 281 F. Supp. 2d 105 (D.D.C. 2003); *Regier v Islamic Republic of Iran*, 281 F. Supp. 2d 87 (D.D.C. 2003); *Tracy v Islamic Republic of Iran*, (D.D.C. 2003); *Kilburn v Republic of Iran*, 277 F. Supp. 2d 24 (D.D.C. 2003); *Stern v Islamic Republic of Iran*, 271 F. Supp. 2d 286 (D.D.C. 2003); *Acree v Republic of Iraq*, 271 F. Supp. 2d 179; (D.D.C. 2003); *Peterson v Islamic Republic of Iran*, 264 F. Supp. 2d 46 (D.D.C. 2003); *Kerr v Islamic Republic of Iran*, 245 F. Supp. 2d 59 (D.D.C. 2003); *Cronin v Islamic Republic of Iran*, 238 F. Supp. 2d 222 (D.D.C. 2002); *Surette v Islamic Republic of Iran*, 231 F. Supp. 2d 260 (D.D.C. 2002); *Turner v Islamic Republic of Iran*, 2002 U.S. Dist. LEXIS 26730 (D.D.C. 2002); *Ungar v Islamic Republic of Iran*, 211 F. Supp. 2d 91 (D.D.C. 2002); *Stethem v Islamic Republic of Iran*, 201 F. Supp. 2d 78 (D.D.C. 2002); *Roeder v Islamic Republic of Iran*, 195 F. Supp. 2d 140 (D.D.C. 2002); *Weinstein v Islamic Republic of Iran*, 184 F. Supp. 2d 13 (D.D.C 2002); *Hill v Republic of Iraq*, 175 F. Supp. 2d 36 (D.D.C. 2001); *Wagner v Islamic Republic of Iran*, 172 F. Supp. 2d 128 (D.D.C. 2001); *Polhill v Islamic Republic of Iran*, 2001 U.S. Dist. LEXIS 15322 (D.D.C. 2001); *Jenco v Islamic Republic of Iran*, 154 F. Supp. 2d 27 (D.D.C. 2001); *Sutherland v Islamic Republic of Iran*, 151 F. Supp. 2d 27 (D.D.C. 2001); *Daliberti v Republic of Iraq*, 146 F. Supp. 2d 19 (D.D.C. 2001); *Eisenfeld v Islamic Republic of Iran*, 172 F. Supp. 2d 1 (D.D.C. 2000); *Alejandre v Republic of Cuba*, 42 F. Supp. 2d 1317 (S.D. Fla. 1999); *Alejandre v Republic of Cuba*, 996 F. Supp. 1239 (S.D. Fla. 1997); *Flatow v Islamic Republic of Iran*, 999 F. Supp. 1 (D.D.C. 1998); and *Cicippio v Islamic Republic of Iran*, 18 F. Supp. 2d 62 (D.D.C. 1998).

[182] This is manifested by a minatory remark by a US court in a case arising out of the Lokerbie Incident of 1998: 'Any foreign state would know that the United States has substantial interests in protecting its flag carriers and its nationals from terrorist activities and should reasonably expect

at least for the time being, other States still enjoy immunity.[183] Furthermore, it seems that even those designated States enjoy immunity for alleged acts occurring *prior to their designation*.[184] The fact that the AEDPA is limited to certain acts and to specifically designated States has caused dissatisfaction among a number of scholars.[185] Some are also concerned about the difficulty of enforcement either in the US or abroad of judgments rendered under this Act.[186] However, the designation by the State Department of 'State sponsors of terrorism' will remain the defining feature of the AEDPA. In short, if the AEDPA is a judicial sword, this sword has to be drawn by an executive hand in the first place. Such an executive-decided non-immunity is certainly tantamount to a reversion to the pre-US FSIA mechanism of executive suggestions of immunity or non-immunity and is therefore not free from criticism of re-politicization of the question of State immunity.[187] At present, the AEDPA remains unique to the US and, as an outgrowth of the peculiar political relations between the US and those seven States specifically designated as 'State sponsors of terrorism', seems unlikely to have many followers outside the US.

that if these interests were harmed, it would be subject to a variety of potential responses, including civil actions in United States courts.' *Rein v Socialist People's Libyan Arab Jamahiriya*, 995 F. Supp. 325, 330 (E.D.N.Y. 1998). See also *Sutherland v Islamic Republic of Iran*, 151 F. Supp. 2d 27, 53 (D.D.C. 2001) ('those who intentionally harm United States nationals will be held accountable for that harm in United States courts').

[183] See, *e.g.*, *Abrams v Societe Nationale Des Chemins De Fer Francais*, 175 F. Supp. 2d 423, 433 (E.D.N.Y. 2001).

[184] See, *e.g.*, *Kalasho v Iraqi Government*, 2001 U.S. Dist. LEXIS 7504 (W.D. Mich. 2001), pp. 5–6.

[185] See, *e.g.*, Andrea Bianchi, Immunity versus Human Rights: The *Pinochet* Case, 10 *European Journal of International Law* (1999) 237, 266, note 130; Curtis A. Bradley and Jack L. Goldsmith, *Pinochet* and International Human Rights Litigation, 97 *Michigan Law Review* (1998–99) 2129, 2157; and Jennifer A. Gergen, Human Rights and the Foreign Sovereign Immunities Act, 36 *Virginia Journal of International Law* (1995–96) 765, 766 and 797–8.

[186] See, *e.g.*, Joseph W. Glannon and Jeffery Atik, Politics and Personal Jurisdiction: Suing State Sponsors of Terrorism under the 1996 Amendments to the Foreign Sovereign Immunities Act, 87 *Georgetown Law Journal* (1998–99) 675, 699–703.

[187] 'The criticism would be that the availability of judicial remedies should not turn on a political judgment by the Executive Branch: indeed . . . an important objective of the FSIA was to remove the politicised element from sovereign immunity cases by instructing courts to decide them on a principled basis.' Lori Fisler Damrosch, Enforcing International Law through Non-Forcible Measures, 269 *Recueil des Cours* (1997) 9, 175. See also Joseph W. Glannon and Jeffery Atik, Politics and Personal Jurisdiction: Suing State Sponsors of Terrorism under the 1996 Amendments to the Foreign Sovereign Immunities Act, 87 *Georgetown Law Journal* (1998–99) 675, 701 ('The 1996 amendments place U.S. policy far beyond the generally recognised bases for exerting jurisdiction over foreign states.') and Jennifer A. Gergen, Human Rights and the Foreign Sovereign Immunities Act, 36 *Virginia Journal of International Law* (1995–96) 765, 797. In this connection attention is especially to be drawn to the comments in the legislative history of the US FSIA that 'A principal purpose of this bill is to transfer the determination of sovereign immunity from the executive branch to the judicial branch, thereby reducing foreign policy implications of immunity determinations and assuring litigants that these often crucial decisions are made on purely legal grounds' and that the US FSIA 'is also designed to bring U.S. practice into conformity with that of most other nations by leaving sovereign immunity decisions exclusively to the courts, thereby discontinuing the practice of judicial deference to "suggestions of immunity" from the executive branch.' U.S. Congress, House of Representatives Report No. 94–1487, (1976) 15 ILM 1398 at 1402 and 1404. See *Tachiona v Mugabe*, 169 F. Supp. 2d 259, 271–2 (S.D.N.Y. 2001) for an account and criticism of the pre-US FSIA US practice of the State Department's 'suggestions of immunity'. Nonetheless, in deference to a State Department's suggestion of immunity, the court granted immunity to Robert Gabriel Mugabe, current president of Zimbabwe, from a suit alleging murder and torture.

VII. CONTRACTS OF EMPLOYMENT AT DIPLOMATIC AND CONSULAR MISSIONS

In *Fogarty v United Kingdom*, the ECHR based its decision on two grounds: first, that, in according immunity to foreign States in respect of suits by employees at diplomatic missions, the UK did not fall outside any 'currently accepted international standards'; second, that the proceedings the applicant wished to bring concerned the recruitment of embassy staff, to which immunity ought to attach as the ECHR was not aware of 'any trend in international law towards a relaxation of the rule of State immunity as regards issues of recruitment to foreign missions'.[188] But these are rather dubious grounds. As will be shown, as regards State immunity with respect to contracts of employment at diplomatic and consular missions, 'currently accepted international standards' are practically non-existent, if by 'international standards' one means definitive rules that dictate reasonably uniform results. And so far no decision has been rendered in favour of the claimant as regards 'recruitment' to a diplomatic mission, not because 'Questions relating to the recruitment of staff to missions and embassies may by their very nature involve sensitive and confidential issues',[189] as the ECHR saw it, but because the current law on State immunity with regard to contracts of employment requires the actual existence of *contracts* of employment. That is, the current law is predicated on an *existing*, as opposed to a *prospective*, employment relationship. As a consequence, recruitment to *any* institution, be it a diplomatic mission or a State enterprise, is outside the range of admissible claims. In other words, a claim on the basis of recruitment to a diplomatic mission will be rejected by a court, not because the claim concerns *recruitment to a diplomatic mission*, but simply because it concerns *recruitment*.

1. Employment at Diplomatic and Consular Missions: A Special Area

All the current legal instruments on State immunity contain saving clauses to the effect that provisions on State immunity shall not affect the privileges and immunities under the two Vienna Conventions on diplomatic and consular relations.[190] However, in affirming the two Vienna Conventions, these clauses focus on the personal immunities and privileges of diplomatic and consular staff but do not relate these immunities and privileges to the issue of employment contracts, nor do they envisage the situation of diplomatic or consular personnel or similar persons suing the employer State.

There is no specific provision in the US FSIA on contracts of employment. Such cases therefore have to be brought under the commercial

[188] *Fogarty v United Kingdom*, Judgment, paras. 37–8. [189] *Ibid.*, para. 38.

[190] The European Convention on State Immunity, art. 32; the US FSIA, s. 1604 (See US Congress,

activity exception to State immunity (s. 1605 (a)(2)). According to the legislative report of the US FSIA,

> Also public or governmental and not commercial in nature, would be the employment of diplomatic, civil service, or military personnel, but not the employment of American citizens or third country nationals by the foreign state in the United States.[191]

The Canadian SIA 1982 likewise contains no specific provision on contracts of employment but gives even less guidance.[192] The UK SIA, besides stating that the Act does not affect diplomatic or consular immunities or privileges (s. 16(1)), clarifies that s. 4 (on contracts of employment)[193] does not apply to proceedings concerning the employment of the members of a diplomatic mission or of a consular post (s. 16(1)(a));[194] but such a provision adds little more.

The Australian FSIA, on the other hand, attempts to solve this problem by a two-pronged approach. Besides affirming the two Vienna Conventions (s. 6), the Australian FSIA makes detailed provisions on State immunity with respect to different categories of diplomatic or consular employees. In accordance with s. 12(5) and (6), the foreign State shall enjoy immunity in relation to the employment of (a) a member of the diplomatic staff of a mission as defined by the 1961 Vienna Convention on Diplomatic Relations or a consular officer as defined by the 1963 Vienna Convention on Consular Relations; and (b) a member of the administrative and technical staff of a mission as defined by the Vienna Convention on Diplomatic Relations or a consular employee as defined by the Vienna Convention on Consular Relations unless the member or employee was, at the time when the contract of employment was made, a permanent resident of Australia. By far the Australian FSIA is the only legal instrument that brings out the relationship between diplomatic and consular immunity and State immunity in respect of

House of Representatives (94th Congress, 2d Session, 1976), Report No. 94–1487, (1976) 15 ILM 1398 at 1407); the UK SIA, s. 16(1); the Canadian SIA, s. 15; the Australian FSIA, s. 6; the ILC Draft, art. 3(1); the IDI Draft, art. 7; and the ILA Drafts, art. IX.

[191] US Congress, House of Representatives, 94th Congress, 2d Session, Report No. 94–1487 (1976), 15 ILM 1398 (1976) at 1406. Note that this statement seems ambiguous with respect to the employment of US citizens or third country nations at foreign embassies in the US. Apparently, the US FSIA grants foreign States jurisdictional immunity in disputes with the staff of their missions where the plaintiffs are nationals of the defendant State, but not in a dispute between the sending State and locally recruited staff of the mission who are of US or third State nationality.

[192] Section 5 provides that 'A foreign state is not immune from the jurisdiction of a court in any proceedings that relate to any commercial activity of the foreign state', while s. 2 defines 'commercial activity' as 'any particular transaction, act or conduct or any regular course of conduct that by reason of its nature is of a commercial character'.

[193] Section 4(1) provides that 'A State is not immune as respects proceedings relating to a contract of employment between the State and an individual . . .' and goes on to list the situations where this exception does not apply.

[194] Section 16(1)(a) provides: 'Section 4 above does not apply to proceedings concerning the employment of the members of a mission within the meaning of the Convention scheduled to the said Act of 1964 or of the members of a consular post within the meaning of the Convention scheduled to the said Act of 1968.'

employment contracts and applies the guidance derived from the former to the latter. The drafters thus explain:

. . . in recognition of the particularly sensitive relationship between foreign states and their diplomatic and consular personnel, some formal reservation of such employment contracts is desirable. On the other hand there seems no reason why *locally recruited staff employed on routine administrative, clerical or maintenance functions* should not be able to sue their foreign state employer. The appropriate balance should be struck at two levels. . . . [Such a provision] would leave the general rule to apply to the least sensitive categories of employees ('members of the service staff' or 'members of the private staff'), who are also, perhaps, most in need of protection.[195]

The draft articles prepared by the International Law Association in 1982 and 1994 imitate this method. While affirming the diplomatic and consular immunities (Art. IX), they contain a proviso to the effect that the foreign State shall enjoy immunity 'in respect of employees appointed under the public (administrative) law of foreign State' (Art. III in 1982 draft, later clarified as: 'The employee was appointed under the public (administrative) law of the foreign State, such as, inter alia, members of the mission, diplomatic, consular or military staff.' Art. III (C)(4) in 1994 draft).[196]

The International Law Commission has also accepted this. During its fifty-first session (1999), it suggested making express provisions to the effect that a State shall enjoy immunity if the employee has been recruited to perform functions in the exercise of governmental authority, in particular: (1) diplomatic staff and consular officers, as defined in the two Vienna Conventions; (2) diplomatic staff of permanent missions to international organizations and of special missions; and (3) other persons enjoying diplomatic immunity, such as persons recruited to represent a State in international conferences.[197]

When it comes to embassy/consular employment matters, many courts tend to be very cautious. English courts have maintained an absolute immunity in cases concerning employment at a diplomatic mission. In *Sengupta v Republic of India*, which was decided at common law because

[195] The Australian Law Reform Commission, Report No. 24, '*Foreign State Immunity*', 1984, pp. 58–9. Emphasis added. Note that Fogarty in *Fogarty v United Kingdom* had worked as an 'administrative assistant' in the US Embassy in London.

[196] International Law Association, Draft Articles for a Convention on State Immunity, *Report of the Sixtieth Conference (Montreal)*, 1982, pp. 6–10. The provisions in the Revised Draft Articles are identical except for the saving clause, *Report of the Sixty-Sixth Conference (Buenos Aires)*, 1994, pp. 22–8 and pp. 488–94.

[197] *Report of the International Law Commission on the Work of its Fifty-first Session*, 3 May–23 July 1999, G.A.O.R. 54th Session, Supplement No.10 (A/54/10 and Corr.1 & 2), Annex, Report of the Working Group on Jurisdictional Immunities of States and Their Property, para. 105. Provisions to this effect have been incorporated into the draft articles. See the Report of the UN Ad Hoc Committee on Jurisdictional Immunities of States and Their Property, dated 24–28 February 2003, UN General Assembly Official Records, 58th Session, Supplement No. 22 (A/58/22), Annex I, art. 11 (2)(a) and (b). Confirmed in the Report of the UN Ad Hoc Committee on Jurisdictional Immunities of States and Their Property, dated 1–5 March 2004, A/59/22, Annex I.

the contract in question had been concluded prior to the entry into force of the UK SIA, Sengupta, an Indian national who had been employed at the Indian High Commission in London as a low-level clerk, without diplomatic rank, with duties like receipt and circulation of newspapers, and selecting and making press cuttings, and without access to any confidential information, brought a claim against India alleging unfair dismissal. The tribunal held that employment, at however lowly a level, in a diplomatic mission necessarily involved the employee in the public acts of the foreign State and the dismissal of such an employee was an act done in pursuance of the public function of running that mission. As a consequence, the fairness of any dismissal from such employment was very likely to involve an investigation by the tribunal into the internal management of the diplomatic representation of India in the UK, an investigation wholly inconsistent with the dignity of the foreign State and an interference with its sovereign functions.[198]

In particular, s. 16(1)(a) of the UK SIA has been interpreted as follows:

> Section 16(1)(a) operates to exclude jurisdiction over claims relating to the employment not only of diplomatic staff but also of lower grade administrative, technical and domestic staff irrespective of their nationality.[199]

In a number of cases, the application of s. 16(1)(a) rendered immune the employment of a bilingual secretary in the Defence Office of the Embassy of the Kingdom of Saudi Arabia,[200] of drivers at the medical office of the Egyptian Embassy and at the Saudi Embassy,[201] of a senior accounts clerk at the Bahamas High Commission,[202] of an employee of the Medical Office of the Embassy of the United Arab Emirates,[203] and of a secretary in the Cultural Affairs Office at the Kuwaiti Embassy.[204] In all these cases the plaintiffs were held to have been employed in the administrative and technical service of the diplomatic missions and were thus members of the missions.[205] In another case the plaintiff's claim failed because she had been employed as a machine operator in the

[198] *Sengupta v Republic of India*, England, Employment Appeal Tribunal (1982) 64 ILR 352.

[199] *Ibid.*, at 357.

[200] *Government of the Kingdom of Saudi Arabia v Ahmed*, England, Employment Appeal Tribunal, 1993, Transcript; Court of Appeal, Civil Division, 1995, [1996] 2 All ER 248; 104 ILR 629. Noted by Michael Byers, 67 *BYBIL* (1996) 542.

[201] *Arab Republic of Egypt v Gamal-Eldin*, England, Employment Appeal Tribunal, 1995, [1996] 2 All ER 237; 104 ILR 673. Noted by Michael Byers, 67 *BYBIL* (1996) 542. *Saudi Arabia v Nasser*, England, Employment Appeal Tribunal and affirmed by the Court of Appeal, 2000, Transcript at LexisNexis.

[202] *Jayetilleke v High Commission of the Bahamas*, England, Employment Appeal Tribunal (1994) 107 ILR 622.

[203] *United Arab Emirates v Abdelghafar and Another*, England, Employment Appeal Tribunal (1995) 107 ILR 626.

[204] *Kuwait v Fevzi*, England, Employment Appeal Tribunal, 1999, 1999 WL 1425695.

[205] But *cf.* a decision by the Dutch Supreme Court which affirmed the judgment by a lower court that a chauffeur at the Mexican Embassy was not immune from criminal jurisdiction because he belonged to the *service staff* of the mission, instead of the *administrative and technical staff*. *L.F.L.M. v The Public Prosecutions Department*, the Netherlands, Supreme Court, 1993, 25 *Netherlands Yearbook of International Law* 527 (1994).

Communications Section of the Australian High Commission and later dismissed because, for security reasons, jobs in the Communications Section should be held only by Australian citizens.[206] A consular assistant at the US Embassy failed to have his claim entertained because, according to the court, he was 'a member of the mission'.[207]

Following the same line, the Irish Supreme Court held immune the employment of a chauffeur of the ambassador's car at the Canadian Embassy in Dublin, on the ground that the element of trust and confidentiality placed in the driver of an embassy car created a bond with his employers that had the effect of involving him in the employing government's public business organization and interests, reversing the lower court's decision that driving an embassy car was an act of a commercial nature.[208] In a case decided by a Dutch court, even though the work of the plaintiff, who had been employed in the administrative service of a Belgian consulate-general, consisted in typing and filing, she was held to have been employed to render services to a public body by the defendant State acting in a public capacity.[209] The Dutch Supreme Court likewise refused to investigate into the termination of the employment of a secretary in the Foreign Commercial Service Department of the US Embassy in The Hague.[210]

Some courts even treat as immune employment *in connection with* an embassy. The South African Supreme Court held that the employment of quantity surveyors by the duly appointed representatives of a foreign government in South Africa in relation to the erection of an embassy was an act *jure imperii*.[211] A US court held that the employment related to the making of some documentary films for the Information Centre of a German consulate-general was a public act.[212]

It is also common for courts to rely on the duties and functions of the employee and the principle of *ne impediatur legatio* (the functions of a mission shall not be impeded) in granting immunity (this latter principle especially when courts are called upon to examine the circumstances

[206] *Yendall v Commonwealth of Australia*, England, Employment Appeal Tribunal (1984) 107 ILR 590.

[207] *Mills v Embassy of the United States of America*, England, Court of Appeal, 2000, Transcript. See also *Caramba-Coker v. Military Affairs Office of the Kuwait Embassy*, England, Employment Appeal Tribunal, 2003, 2003 WL 1610407 (The Embassy was immune from wrongful dismissal claim because the appellant, as a shipping clerk, was a 'member of the mission').

[208] *The Government of Canada v The Employment Appeals Tribunal and Burke*, Ireland, High Court, 1991; Ireland, Supreme Court, 1992, [1992] 2 IR 484; 95 ILR 467. See *Saudi Arabia v Nasser*, England, Court of Appeal, 2000, Transcript at LexisNexis, para. 16, where the judge held that the work of an embassy driver was 'central to the diplomatic activity of the mission'.

[209] *Gootjes v Kingdom of Belgium*, the Netherlands, Local Court of Rotterdam (1978) 65 ILR 372. But see a different judgment by the same court in a case of an employee in the administrative service of the American Consulate-General with almost identical facts. *P. A. v H. v United States of America*, the Rotterdam Local Court, 10 *Netherlands Yearbook of International Law* 443, note 10 (1979).

[210] *Van der Hulst v United States*, the Netherlands, Supreme Court (1989) 94 ILR 373.

[211] *Prentice, Shaw and Schiess Incorporated v Government of the Republic of Bolivia*, South Africa, Supreme Court, Transvaal Provincial Division, 1978, 1978 (3) S. A. 938; 64 ILR 685.

[212] *Gittler v German Information Centre*, United States, New York County Supreme Court, Special Term, Part 1, 1978, 408 N. Y. S. 2d 600; 63 ILR 170.

surrounding the dismissal of an embassy employee). In a German case, the plaintiff had been employed at a UK consulate for such activities as receiving visitors, general secretarial duties, visiting British subjects, and acting as interpreter. The court held that the performance of consular duties was an activity of a sovereign nature since the legal relationship between the State and its own subjects employed in the consulate was one of public law and the same applied where German subjects were employed.[213] By the same token, in *X. Argentina*, the court stated that, where an employment relationship with a foreign State involved the performance of consular functions, including the issue and extension of passports and the processing of visas, even though the employee had a subordinate role in the performance of those functions, the employment belonged to the core sphere of sovereign activity of the State concerned and was exempt from national jurisdiction so far as the conduct and termination of the relationship were concerned. Any examination of the circumstances of the dismissal of such an employee would conflict with the principle that consular relations should not be impeded (*ne impediatur legatio*).[214] The same holding can also be found in a case brought by a caretaker at a French consulate in Germany challenging his dismissal on the ground that the consent of the local Welfare Office, which was required under German law because he was disabled, had not been obtained,[215] and in one brought by a financial assistant responsible for analysis and budgetary preparation at a US consulate-general, after his employment had been terminated for reasons of 'organizational restructuring' and he had been offered new employment at a lower grade, where the court held that the preparation and drafting of budget plans for the financing of the work of a consulate fell within the core area of consular activity and that the manner in which a foreign State provided for the fulfilment of consular tasks from an organizational standpoint was a matter for sovereign decision and could not be subject to judicial review.[216]

It is significant to note that, in all these cases, the German courts indicated in one way or another that, had the employer not been a foreign State acting in its public capacity or carrying out sovereign activities, the employment would have been regarded as a private law activity and so rightly subject to German jurisdiction, and that, if the core area of State authority was affected, the private-law character of the relationship took on secondary importance.[217]

[213] *Conrades v United Kingdom of Great Britain and Northern Ireland*, Federal Republic of Germany, Hanover Labour Court (1981) 65 ILR 205.

[214] *X. Argentina*, Federal Republic of Germany, Federal Labour Court (BAG) (1996) 114 ILR 502.

[215] *French Consulate Disabled Employee Case*, Federal Republic of Germany, Administrative Court (VG) of Mainz (1988) 114 ILR 507 (in addition to holding that the German Law on Disabled Persons were not applicable because of its public law character).

[216] *Muller v United States of America*, Federal Republic of Germany, Regional Labour Court (LAG) of Hesse (1998) 114 ILR 512.

[217] See also similar opinions in, *e.g.*, *Luna v Socialist Republic of Romania*, Italy, Court of Cassation (Joint Session) (1974) 65 ILR 313; *Gootjes v Kingdom of Belgium*, the Netherlands, Local Court of

In *Seidenschmidt*, the Austrian Supreme Court, while denying immunity, nonetheless stated that the question as to which security requirements the US should have relied upon for dismissal was not to be examined by an Austrian court, as each State retained the right to determine for itself the standard of security for its diplomatic representatives abroad, and to impose corresponding obligations in the service contracts of the personnel which it employed.[218] Swiss courts would not examine the reasons which led the sending State to terminate its relationship with a locally recruited employee of its diplomatic mission and neither would they summons the employer State to justify itself. The decision to terminate such an employment relationship was a sovereign activity (*acte de gouvernement*) and was not therefore subject to the jurisdiction of the courts of the forum State, in accordance with the rule *ne impediatur legatio*.[219] Dutch courts would take a similar position.[220]

Italian courts have consistently maintained a test of 'institutional aims' of the foreign State as the criterion for granting immunity. Thus, in *Luna v Socialist Republic of Romania*, the Court of Cassation held that the plaintiff, who had worked for eighteen years as a secretary, telephone operator, accountant, and administrator at the Romanian Commercial Agency in Italy, which was an integral part of the Romanian Embassy, had been firmly established with the organization concerned. The employment relationship then fell within the framework of activities of a public nature of a foreign State which were correlated to the *institutional ends* of the State itself, in this case to the promotion and control of commercial activities in which the State in question had a collective interest.[221] The contract of employment of an 'assistant' at the Brazilian Embassy in Italy was held to have involved the running of the embassy offices in furtherance of *institutional aims* of a public nature, the employment being of a permanent nature (over fifteen years) within the administration of the embassy.[222] The duties performed by a commercial officer at the British Consulate in Venice, who had been in charge of promoting the sale of British goods in Italy and who had been responsible to the British Embassy and ultimately to the Foreign Office, were held to be correlated with the *institutional aims* of the Foreign Office, with the result that he had participated in the public activity of the foreign State which had employed him.

Rotterdam (1978) 65 ILR 372 and *Van der Hulst v United States*, the Netherlands, Supreme Court (1989) 94 ILR 373.

[218] *Seidenschmidt v United States of America*, Austria, Supreme Court (OGH) (1992) 116 ILR 530, 532–3.

[219] *Nicoud v United States of America*, Switzerland, Labour Court of Geneva (TPH) (1994) 116 ILR 650, 654–5; *X v United States of America*, Switzerland, Labour Court (TPH) of Geneva (1995) 116 ILR 668, 674–5.

[220] *Van der Hulst v United States*, the Netherlands, Supreme Court (1989) 94 ILR 373 (dismissal of embassy secretary following security check).

[221] *Luna v Socialist Republic of Romania*, Italy, Court of Cassation (Joint Session), (1974) 65 ILR 313.

[222] *Velloso v Borla and Others*, Italy, Court of Cassation (Joint Session) (1979) 65 ILR 328.

As a commercial officer he had furthered the public interest of the British Government in encouraging British exports rather than the private interests of British firms in exporting their products, which could be served by local commercial agents appointed by the firms themselves.[223] A typist and translator of the Consul-General of Panama in Venice, who had been responsible for drafting and translating letters and drawing up ships' licences and other documents, was regarded as having been inserted into the organizational structure of the Panamanian consular office and her work served to further the very ends for which the office had been established.[224] A chancery usher at the Embassy of Germany to the Holy See was held to have been a permanent employee with a stable and integrated position within the organization of the embassy, and was considered as taking part in activities through which that State pursued its *public purposes*. Disputes concerning the relationship were therefore not subject to Italian jurisdiction. This applied even though the duties of the employee were manual or temporary, unless the performance of those duties was extraneous to the organization of the embassy.[225]

This rigid position was somewhat modified, almost imperceptibly, in *British Consulate-General in Naples v Toglia*, in which the Court of Cassation, after stating that immunity was available when the employee had been inserted into the organizational structure of the consular office, and when the work served to further the aims for which the office had been established, added that immunity should be excluded whenever a claim, and the related judgment which upheld it, concerned purely *financial aspects* of the employment relationship which gave rise to the dispute. In this case the plaintiff, who had retired from the British Consulate-General in Naples, was already outside the organization of the Consulate-General when she lodged her claim. Besides, she did not request reinstatement in her post but instead claimed only a higher grade and payment of arrears. Therefore Italian courts were competent to exercise jurisdiction over the claim.[226]

This holding was followed in *Norwegian Embassy v Quattri*, brought by a secretary and administrative officer of the Commercial Office of the

[223] *Bulli v Foreign and Commonwealth Office of the United Kingdom*, Italy, Examining Magistrate (Pretore) of Venice (1981) 65 ILR 343.

[224] *Rubin v Consul of the Republic of Panama*, Italy, Court of Cassation (Joint Session) (1977) 77 ILR 593. Note that in this case, the plaintiff sued the consul, who would in any case be immune from local jurisdiction for acts performed in the exercise of the consular functions, under both customary international law and the Vienna Convention on Consular Relations. See a substantially identical judgment in similar proceedings brought by another former employee of the Panamanian Consulate in Venice, *Hurwitz v Consul of the Republic of Panama*, Italy, Court of Cassation (Joint Session) (1977) noted 77 ILR 598 and a similar judgment in *Consul-General of Belgium in Naples v Esposito*, Italy, Court of Cassation (Plenary Session) (1986) 101 ILR 376.

[225] *Panattoni v Federal Republic of Germany*, Italy, Court of Cassation (Plenary Session) (1987) 87 ILR 42. *Cf., e.g., Embassy Interpreter Dismissal Case*, Austria, Administrative Court (1985) 77 ILR 485; *S v India*, Switzerland, Federal Tribunal (1984) 82 ILR 13 and *Rousseau v Republic of Upper Volta*, Belgium, Labour Court of Brussels (Third Chamber) (1983) 82 ILR 118.

[226] *British Consulate-General in Naples v Toglia*, Italy, Court of Cassation (Plenary Session) (1989) 101 ILR 379.

Royal Norwegian Embassy, in which the Court of Cassation held that Italian courts lacked jurisdiction over the claim for reinstatement and damages but they were competent to exercise jurisdiction over the claim for unpaid allowances. According to the Court, a foreign State was immune from the jurisdiction of other States in respect of employment relationships created for the purposes of achieving its institutional aims, but such immunity was restricted to acts carried out in exercise of its public-law functions. While any enquiry into the lawfulness of the dismissal (entailed by a claim for reinstatement) constituted a direct interference with the public-law powers of the foreign State with regard to the manner in which it organizes its ambassadorial offices and services, the examination of the other heads of claim, such as unpaid allowances, did not involve any violation of the foreign State's immunity.[227] In a similar vein, the Court rejected claims for reinstatement brought by a clerk and telephonist at a US consulate[228] and an usher and telephonist in a French consulate,[229] on the grounds that any examination of the reasons for, or lawfulness of, the dismissal would directly interfere with the exercise of the sovereign powers of a foreign State in relation to the organization of its representative offices.

The tripartite criterion of (a) integration into the structure, (b) institutional aims, and (c) non-interference was more fully enunciated by the Italian Court of Cassation in *Canada v Cargnello*. In that case, an Italian citizen, employed as a commercial officer by the Consulate-General of Canada in Milan, instituted proceedings against his employer for a declaration that his dismissal was unlawful and for compensation in lieu of reinstatement. Upon appeal by Canada, the Court held that the activities of the respondent as a commercial officer entailed his inclusion in the institutional structure of the consulate with the result that he participated in the public functions of the foreign State which employed him. Moreover, the Court said, immunity should be limited to cases where the exercise of jurisdiction would interfere with the essential core of sovereign functions. Thus jurisdiction was certainly excluded where reinstatement in an employment position was sought. It was also consistent with the jurisprudence to exclude jurisdiction where, as here, a purely monetary claim for compensation would nonetheless require an investigation into the behaviour of the foreign State as employer and thus directly concern the exercise of public-law powers related to the organization of

[227] *Norwegian Embassy v Quattri*, Italy, Court of Cassation (Plenary Session) (1991) 114 ILR 525.

[228] *United States of America v Lo Gatto*, Italy, Court of Cassation (Plenary Session) (1995) 114 ILR 555 (The Court added that the duties of a consular or embassy telephone operator, though secondary and subordinate, were based on trust and involved integration into the organizational structure of the foreign State concerned, so that the employment relationship itself involved the exercise of sovereign functions.)

[229] *Giaffreda v French Republic*, Italy, Court of Cassation (1992) 114 ILR 558 (note) (The Court added that *British Consulate-General in Naples v Toglia* was to be distinguished since it was concerned purely with the financial aspects of an employment relationship which had been terminated without reinstatement being sought.)

the administration of the foreign State and the management of its employment relationships.[230]

2. *Diverse Approaches*

In employment disputes courts often consider far more factors than in any other type of State immunity case: characterization of the employment relationship; the duties and functions of the employee; the particular activity for which the employee was engaged; the territorial connection; whether there is a choice of law clause in the contract; and whether the remedies sought affected the sovereign or public functions of the defendant State. It is not rare for a court to consider several of these factors in the same case.

2.1. *The Employment Relationship*

In some cases jurisdiction was asserted on the ground that the employment relationship between an embassy and an individual was governed by private law. Thus, in a case for damages for wrongful dismissal brought by a Portuguese national employed as a language teacher by the consular section of the Portuguese Embassy, a Belgian court held that, in hiring an individual to teach Portuguese language and culture in Belgium, Portugal had not performed an act of sovereignty.[231] The relationship between a foreign State and its embassy driver was held to have arisen from a contract of employment which had not been concluded by that State in the exercise of its sovereign rights; thus the foreign State was subject to domestic jurisdiction in respect of claims arising from the employment relationship.[232] Even the head of the visa section of a foreign consulate had her claim allowed because the court held that the foreign State had acted as a holder of private rights and concluded a contract of employment for work to be performed on the territory of the State of the forum.[233] The employment of an embassy interpreter was also held to be a private activity.[234] Similarly, a Dutch court held that the conclusion of a contract of employment with a Dutch clerical worker (a secretary) who

[230] *Canada v Cargnello*, Italy, Court of Cassation (Plenary Session) (1998) 114 ILR 559.

[231] *De Queiroz v State of Portugal*, Belgium, Labour Court of Brussels (Fourth Chamber) (1992) 115 ILR 430. See also *François v State of Canada*, Belgium, Labour Court of Brussels (First Chamber) (1989) 115 ILR 418 (The employment of a technician at the Cultural and Information Centre of the Canadian Embassy in Brussels was held to be a private act).

[232] *British Embassy Driver Case*, Austria, Superior Provincial Court (Oberlandesgericht) of Vienna (1978) 65 ILR 20. See also *Rousseau v Republic of Upper Volta*, Belgium, Labour Court of Brussels (Third Chamber) (1983) 82 ILR 118 (The contract of employment of an embassy chauffeur was held to be a contract of manual employment governed entirely by private law without any attributes of the exercise of public power); *Emilio B. M. v. Embassy of Equatorial Guinea*, Spain, Supreme Court, (1986) 86 ILR 508 (embassy chauffeur) and *Kingdom of Morocco v DR*, Belgium, Labour Court of Brussels (Sixth Chamber) (1989) 115 ILR 421 (embassy chauffeur).

[233] *French Consular Employee Claim Case*, Austria, Supreme Court (1989) 86 ILR 583.

[234] *Embassy Interpreter Dismissal Case*, Austria, Administrative Court (1985) 77 ILR 485.

had no diplomatic or civil service status was an act which the defendant State performed on the same footing as a natural or legal person under private law and that there was therefore no question of a purely governmental act in the present case.[235] Swiss courts are ready to regard contracts of employment concluded between a sending State and locally recruited staff who are not nationals of the sending State as contracts concluded *jure gestionis*.[236] The Austrian Supreme Court held that a foreign State, when concluding a contract in respect of work to be performed on the receiving State's territory, acted as a private law entity, and could not be entitled to terminate such an employment relationship merely 'on security grounds' by having recourse to an act of sovereignty.[237]

2.2. *The Duties or Functions of the Employee*

It is normal for a court to investigate into the duties or functions of the employee in order to decide whether a particular employment relationship is commercial or not. Senior employees with responsibilities closely connected with the sovereign power of the foreign State will be precluded from suing. By contrast, employees with only secondary, auxiliary, or menial duties are permitted to sue. According to the Italian Court of Cassation, the fact that the duties carried out by the plaintiff as driver/interpreter were of a secondary, auxiliary nature in relation to the purposes and functions of the Embassy of the Zambian Republic in Rome brought the dispute within the scope of the jurisdiction of Italian courts.[238]

In *S v India*, the Swiss Federal Tribunal carried out detailed analysis of the duties of the plaintiff, an Italian national who had been employed by the Indian Embassy in Berne to work as a radio-telegraph operator and was later moved from technical tasks to office work, including translation and correspondence. In the opinion of the Tribunal, the functions of a telegraph operator would normally be subordinate according to the Swiss rules governing the analogous functions and it was clear that the claimant subsequently fulfilled for many years functions which were clearly subordinate. It was hard, the Tribunal said, to see how the submission to a foreign tribunal of a dispute relating to claims arising from the activity of

[235] *MK v Republic of Turkey*, the Netherlands, Sub-District Court of The Hague (1985) 94 ILR 350, 353.

[236] See *e.g.*, *Nicoud v United States of America*, Switzerland, Labour Court of Geneva (TPH) (1994) 116 ILR 650, 653; *Landano v United States of America*, Switzerland, Labour Court (TPH) of Geneva (1987) 116 ILR 636, 642.

[237] *Seidenschmidt v United States of America*, Austria, Supreme Court (1992) 116 ILR 530, 532 (It is not clear what functions the plaintiff had performed: he was vaguely referred to as an 'official').

[238] *Zambian Embassy v Sendanayake*, Italy, Court of Cassation (Plenary Session) (1992), 114 ILR 532, 533 (embassy driver/interpreter). See also *Carbonar v Magurno*, Italy, Court of Cassation (Plenary Session) (1993) 114 ILR 534 (Italian national employed as an assistant at the Brazilian Consulate). However, the same court in *Bari Institute v Jasbez* had contrasted the responsibilities of a simultaneous interpreter with those of an *embassy interpreter*, which the court thought were connected with *public functions*. *Bari Institute of the International Centre for Advanced Mediterranean Agronomic Studies v Jasbez*, Italy, Court of Cassation (Joint Session) (1977) 77 ILR 602, 609.

the claimant could put in jeopardy, or even compromise, the interests of the defendant State.[239]

In *Coco*, the French Court of Cassation based its decision to deny immunity on a similar analysis of the duties of the plaintiff, who had been employed by the Embassy of Argentina in Paris as an assistant in the Press Section, with the task of collecting, ordering, and transmitting information of interest to the State of Argentina. According to the Court, the protected interests of the State of Argentina justifying jurisdictional immunity were not infringed in this case of the dismissal of the plaintiff. His tasks were such that he had not been charged with any special responsibility for the exercise of a public service and his dismissal therefore constituted an ordinary act of administration (*acte de gestion*).[240]

By contrast, a New Zealand court opined that the duties of a typist/clerk in the Auckland Office of the Governor of the Pitcairn, which was within the British Consulate-General, were very important:

> Mrs. Sutton's duties did not entail any significant responsibility for decision-making, but they were close to the heart of the administrative process. She was an important cog in the administrative wheel. It cannot be right for a New Zealand court to inquire into and adjudicate on how well or how badly the British overseas administrative machine dealt with her.[241]

In the *Brazilian Embassy Employee Case*, where a Portuguese national employed in an administrative capacity by the Embassy of Brazil in Lisbon instituted proceedings against Brazil claiming damages for unfair dismissal and arrears of salary, the Portuguese Supreme Court found that

239 *S v India*, Switzerland, Federal Tribunal (1984) 82 ILR 13 at 20. See also *République X c. A*, Switzerland, Federal Tribunal, 2003, 130 *Journal du Droit International* 1125 (2003) (case note by Isabelle Pingel) (cleaner at a consulate-general); *X v United States of America*, Switzerland, Labour Court (TPH) of Geneva (1995) 116 ILR 668, 670–2 (A telephonist/receptionist at the US Permanent Mission to the United Nations in Geneva did not perform an activity closely linked to the exercise of the sovereignty of the employer State, was not a consular official and did not form part of the career consular staff (consular agents) within the meaning of the Vienna Convention on Consular Relations of 1963); *M v Arab Republic of Egypt*, Switzerland, Federal Tribunal (1994) 116 ILR 656, 662 ('In this case, the plaintiff worked as a chauffeur, which is a subordinate function. The tasks performed by a chauffeur do not in practice involve the exercise of sovereign powers. The situation of a chauffeur is equivalent to that of porters, gardeners, kitchen workers, etc.') (Chauffeur at the Permanent Mission of Egypt to the United Nations in Geneva); *R v Republic of Iraq*, Switzerland, Federal Tribunal (1994) 116 ILR 664, 667 (interpreter/translator at the Permanent Mission of Iraq to the United Nations in Geneva); *Landano v United States of America*, Switzerland, Labour Court (TPH) of Geneva (1987) 116 ILR 636, 641–2 (A telephonist at the Permanent Mission of the US to the United Nations in Geneva was held to have performed no activity closely associated with the exercise of sovereign powers by the defendant State).

240 *Coco v State of Argentina*, France, Court of Cassation (Social Chamber) (1996) 113 ILR 491. See also *Saignie v Embassy of Japan*, France, Court of Cassation (First Civil Chamber), (1997) 113 ILR 492 (The function of the plaintiff as caretaker at the Japanese Embassy in Paris did not give him any special responsibility for the performance of the public service of the Embassy, so that his dismissal constituted an ordinary act of management (*acte de gestion*)). But *cf. Robert v Procureur de la République*, France, Court of Cassation (1990) 113 ILR 450 (appeal dismissed because the plaintiff, a security officer at the US Embassy in Paris, had been hired and dismissed by the ambassador, not the embassy).

241 *Governor of Pitcairn and Associated Islands v Sutton*, New Zealand, Court of Appeal (1994) 104 ILR 508, 514 *per* Cooke, P.

the case involved employment on a permanent basis as an administrative employee of a diplomatic mission. Such employment could not be classified as a simple relationship of private law since the activities of the employee formed a necessary part of the public functions of the diplomatic mission itself. There were therefore no features to justify a change in the orientation of the Portuguese case law with regard to State immunity in cases involving employment relations, especially where the dismissal of an employee was involved. Consequently Brazil enjoyed immunity.[242]

2.3. *The Nature of the Particular Activity*

Sometimes the court would rely on the nature of the activity for which the employee was engaged. If the activity itself is deemed as commercial or private, the duties or functions of the individual become immaterial. For example, in *Tsakos v Government of the United States of America*, a Swiss court took the view that, as the plaintiff was engaged by the US Mission to the International Organizations in Geneva specifically for the purpose of organizing an exhibition and his duties were clearly specified, the US Government had not acted in its capacity as a public power but rather, through an agent, as a private person with a view to the organization of an exhibition. What was at issue was therefore a private law contract in respect of which the US could not rely on jurisdictional immunity.[243]

2.4. *The Territorial Connection*

Some courts refer to a territorial connection between the contract of employment and the forum State as a ground for asserting jurisdiction. Swiss courts are well known for insisting that, for a relationship of private law to which a foreign State is party to give rise to proceedings, the relationship should have a territorial connection with Switzerland (*Binnenbeziehung* or domestic/internal connection), that is to say that the relationship should have arisen or fall to be executed in Switzerland. Thus, in *S v India*, the Swiss Federal Tribunal held that, in the case of subordinate embassy employees who were not nationals of either the sending State or the receiving State and had been *recruited locally in the forum State*, it was perfectly acceptable to subject their employment

[242] *Brazilian Embassy Employee Case*, Portugal, Supreme Court (1984) 116 ILR 625, 632–3. However, it should be noted that, according to the Supreme Court, it recognized State immunity in the majority of lawsuits against foreign States, even where they had acted as private entities; and would make an exception only in cases of explicit or implicit waiver and lawsuits involving real property and succession. *Ibid.*, 631. This position of absolute immunity was followed by a local court in a class action by 116 locally recruited employees of the US Embassy in Lisbon for wage increases. The court held that, in the absence of a clear waiver, immunity applied irrespective of whether the acts at issue had been performed by the foreign State *jure imperii* or *jure gestionis*. *Ramos v United States of America*, Portugal, High Court of Lisbon (1994) 116 ILR 634, 635. But see *Mme X c. Etat d'Israël*, Portugal, Supreme Court, 2002, 130 *Journal du Droit International* 1127 (2003) (case note by Isabelle Pingel) (cleaner at the Ambassador's residence in Lisbon), where immunity was denied.

[243] *Tsakos v Government of the United States of America*, Switzerland, Labour Tribunal of Geneva (1972) 75 ILR 78.

relationships to the jurisdiction of local courts.[244] In *M v Arab Republic of Egypt*, the Federal Tribunal found that the plaintiff had worked as a chauffeur, which was a subordinate function. In the opinion of the Tribunal, the tasks performed by a chauffeur did not in practice involve the exercise of sovereign powers. The situation of a chauffeur was equivalent to that of porters, gardeners, kitchen workers, etc. However, the Tribunal declared that that circumstance alone was insufficient to justify Switzerland exercising jurisdiction over the dispute. Not every relationship under private law entered into by a foreign State could give rise to jurisdiction in Switzerland. It was also necessary to establish that the relationship in question had certain links with Swiss territory (*Binnenbeziehung*), that is to say that 'it arose there, must be performed there, or at least that the debtor performed certain acts such as to make it [Switzerland] a place of performance of the contract'. In this case, the plaintiff was recruited in Geneva, the city in which he had worked or lived. He had lived there since 1979 although the employment relationship in dispute only began in 1988. After four years of studies, he worked in that city for the Consulate of Saudi Arabia and then for the Consulate of Egypt. The connection with Switzerland was therefore incontestable in this case.[245]

Similarly, Dutch courts have consistently held that, where the contract of employment was concluded in the Netherlands, and the agreed work was to be performed in the Netherlands, the employment relationship shall in principle be governed by Dutch law, even if the plaintiff might be a third State national.[246] The Spanish Supreme Court reaffirmed in a case in 1986 the provisions of Spanish law which conferred jurisdiction on

[244] *S v India*, Switzerland, Federal Tribunal (1984) 82 ILR 13, 19–20. See also *X v United States of America*, Switzerland, Labour Court (TPH) of Geneva (1995) 116 ILR 668, 673; *Nicoud v United States of America*, Switzerland, Labour Court of Geneva (TPH) (1994) 116 ILR 650, 652–3 (embassy driver); *Landano v United States of America*, Switzerland, Labour Court (TPH) of Geneva (1987) 116 ILR 636, 642; and *Tsakos v Government of the United States of America*, Switzerland, Labour Tribunal of Geneva (1972) 75 ILR 78.

[245] *M v Arab Republic of Egypt*, Switzerland, Federal Tribunal (1994) 116 ILR 656, 662–3 (Egyptian national employed as a chauffeur by the Arab Republic of Egypt at its Permanent Mission to the United Nations in Geneva). See similar holding in identical language in *R v Republic of Iraq*, Switzerland, Federal Tribunal (1994) 116 ILR 664, 667–8 (Moroccan national employed as an interpreter/translator by the Permanent Mission of Iraq to the United Nations in Geneva). See also *République X c. A*, Switzerland, Federal Tribunal, 2003, 130 *Journal du Droit International* 1125, 1126 (2003) (case note by Isabelle Pingel) (cleaner at a consulate-general).

[246] *E.g.*, *De Sousa v Republic of Portugal*, Netherlands, Local Court of Amsterdam (1979) 65 ILR 378; *J.P.H. v Indonesian State*, Local Court of The Hague, 1979, 11 *Netherlands Yearbook of International Law* 290, note. 1 (1980) (*Cf. Consulate-General of Italy Case*, Local Court of Rotterdam, 1979, 11 *Netherlands Yearbook of International Law* 290, note. 2 (1980), where the court dismissed the plaintiff's claims because the contract of employment was not governed by Dutch law and the plaintiff appeared to be employed by the Italian Ministry of Foreign Affairs.); *H.'t Hooft v Republic of France*, the Netherlands, Sub-District Court of The Hague, 1986, 19 *Netherlands Yearbook of International Law* 438, note. 27 (1988); *B.V v Instituto Italiano di Cultura per I Paesi Bassi and the Republic of Italy*, the Netherlands, District Court of Amsterdam, 23 *Netherlands Yearbook of International Law* 447 (1992); *M.H.C. v Republic of Cuba*, the Netherlands, Sub-District Court of The Hague, 1992, 27 *Netherlands Yearbook of International Law* 319 (1996) and *MK v Republic of Turkey*, the Netherlands, Sub-District Court of The Hague, 1985, 19 *Netherlands Yearbook of International Law* 435 (1988); 94 ILR 350.

Spanish courts over matters of rights and obligations derived from a contract of employment where the contract provided for performance of services in Spain, or where the contract was concluded on Spanish territory.[247] The Austrian Supreme Court likewise held that, where a foreign State acted as the holder of private rights and concluded a contract of employment for work to be performed on the territory of the State of the forum, that foreign State could also be subjected to proceedings concerning the employment relationship. What must be examined was not the purpose of the work but the nature of the employment obligations.[248] A Belgian court also referred to the fact that the contract of employment was executed in Belgium.[249]

2.5. *The Choice of Law Clause*

A court will assume jurisdiction by virtue of a choice of law clause in the contract, which either designates the forum court or provides for the application of the law of the forum as the proper law of the contract. The Spanish Supreme Court held that Spanish courts had jurisdiction in a case where the employment was covered by Spanish social security provisions and subjected to applicable Spanish labour laws.[250] A Belgian court assumed jurisdiction in a case where, in terminating the contract, the defendant State had allocated an indemnity in lieu of notice, making express reference to Belgian law.[251]

Surprisingly, on the other hand, the absence of a choice of law clause has also been relied upon as a basis for exercising jurisdiction. In *M.H.C. v Republic of Cuba*, a Dutch court held that Dutch law—i.e. the law of the country where the petitioner performed her work—was applicable since there was no evidence of any other choice of law.[252] In *MK v Republic of Turkey*, the same court, having found that the parties had not made any choice regarding the system of law applicable to the agreement, nevertheless founded its jurisdiction on the following facts: that the work was performed by an employee of Dutch nationality in the Netherlands, that the plaintiff received her salary in Dutch currency and that the defendant paid the contributions owing under Dutch social security legislation. Accordingly, the court said, this was clearly a case in which the

[247] *Diana A v Republic of South Africa*, Spain, Supreme Court (1986) 86 ILR 512 (bilingual secretary at embassy).

[248] *French Consular Employee Claim Case*, Austria, Supreme Court (1989) 86 ILR 583. See also *Seidenschmidt v United States of America*, Austria, Supreme Court (1992) 116 ILR 530, 532 (A foreign State, when concluding a contract in respect of work to be performed on the receiving State's territory, acts as a private law entity).

[249] *Kingdom of Morocco v DR, Belgium*, Labour Court of Brussels (Sixth Chamber) (1989) 115 ILR 421 (embassy chauffeur).

[250] *Diana A v Republic of South Africa*, Spain, Supreme Court (1986) 86 ILR 512 (bilingual secretary at embassy).

[251] *François v State of Canada*, Belgium, Labour Court of Brussels (First Chamber) (1989), 115 ILR 418.

[252] *M. H. C. v Republic of Cuba*, the Netherlands, Sub-District Court of The Hague, 1992, 27 *Netherlands Yearbook of International Law* 319 (1996).

interests of the Dutch labour market were very closely involved and the links with Dutch law were therefore of such importance and took precedence to such an extent over those with Turkish law that Dutch law was applicable.[253] In *Seidenschmidt*, the Austrian Supreme Court found that the employment relationship in question and its termination were governed by Austrian law because the parties had not made any specific choice of the applicable law.[254] A Swiss court even took the position that a contract of employment internal to Switzerland was governed, in an obligatory manner, by Swiss employment law and the parties were not free to derogate from that rule by the choice of the law of a third State.[255]

2.6. *The Remedies Sought*

In some cases the remedies sought would also be highlighted so as to bring the case under the jurisdiction of the forum court, if those remedies do not affect the sovereign or public functions of the defendant State. Thus, in a series of cases, the Italian Court of Cassation not only noted the secondary or auxiliary nature of the plaintiff's duties,[256] but also stressed the fact that the remedies sought related solely to the *financial* aspects of the employment relationship. Such a claim, opined the Court, did not amount to interference in the public affairs of the foreign State. Therefore the Court would be competent to hear the claim even if the plaintiff had performed duties closely bound up with the institutional functions of an embassy or consulate.[257]

In a case decided by the Argentine Supreme Court, the plaintiff, who had been employed by the Press Office of the Embassy of the Soviet Union in Argentina, claimed damages, from the Russian Federation as the successor, for non-payment of social security and other contributions which his employer should have made on his behalf. The Court held that what was at issue was not a governmental act since the dispute submitted to the Court related to the performance of obligations concerning employment and welfare contributions, so that the normal activity of a diplomatic representation was in no way involved.[258]

[253] *MK v Republic of Turkey*, the Netherlands, Sub-District Court of The Hague (1985) 94 ILR 350.

[254] *Seidenschmidt v United States of America*, Austria, Supreme Court (1992) 116 ILR 530, 532.

[255] *Nicoud v United States of America*, Switzerland, Labour Court of Geneva (TPH) (1994) 116 ILR 650, 653.

[256] But see *Panattoni v Federal Republic of Germany*, Italy, Court of Cassation (Plenary Session) (1987) 87 ILR 42.

[257] *British Consulate-General in Naples v Toglia*, Italy, Court of Cassation (Plenary Session) (1989) 101 ILR 379 (former employee of the British Consulate-General in Naples claiming arrears of salary and additional national insurance contributions allegedly payable under Italian law); *Zambian Embassy v Sendanayake*, Italy, Court of Cassation (Plenary Session) (1992) 114 ILR 532 (employee of the Zambian Embassy claiming arrears of salary on the ground that his remuneration had been incorrectly calculated on the basis of a national collective agreement); and *Carbonar v Magurno*, Italy, Court of Cassation (Plenary Session) (1993) 114 ILR 534 (employee of the Brazilian Consulate in Naples and then in Milan claiming for losses arising from the non-payment of social security contributions in relation to her second post).

[258] *Manauta v Embassy of Russian Federation*, Argentina, Supreme Court (1994) 113 ILR 429.

While some courts are cautious about remedies such as reinstatement,[259] others would not hesitate to grant them,[260] when applied for by the plaintiff. In a case by a Dutch court, termination of the contract of employment together with compensation of five months' salary was ordered.[261] In *MK v Republic of Turkey*, the same court declared the disputed dismissal void because the defendant had dismissed the plaintiff without the consent of the Director of the competent Regional Employment Office, without the consent of the plaintiff and without any urgent reason having existed or even having been alleged.[262]

In *François v State of Canada*, the plaintiff, who had been employed as a technician at the Cultural and Information Centre of the Canadian Embassy in Brussels, claimed, following his dismissal, that the indemnity offered to him in lieu of notice, in accordance with the provisions of Belgian law, was inadequate. The Labour Court of Brussels, after determining the employment contract as a private act, went on to say that, taking account of the seniority of the claimant (employed for nine years and nine months), his function as a technician, his annual salary, and his age (thirty-two years), the period of notice given to him should have been ten months. Since an indemnity of only nine months was paid, an additional indemnity of one month was due. For those reasons, the court declared that the claim was admissible and partially well founded.[263] In another case, in which a chauffeur of the Embassy of Morocco brought proceedings claiming compensation for unjustifiable dismissal, the same court held that, in accordance with Belgian labour law, an employer was liable to pay special compensation if he could not prove that he had dismissed his employee for reasons inherent in his aptitude for the job, or his conduct, or service requirements. Since the defendant State had brought no

[259] *See e.g., British Consulate-General in Naples v Toglia*, Italy, Court of Cassation (Plenary Session) (1989) 101 ILR 379, 385 where the Court allowed the claim since the plaintiff did not 'request reinstatement in her post'. See also *Norwegian Embassy v Quattri*, Italy, Court of Cassation (Plenary Session) (1991) 114 ILR 525; *United States of America v Lo Gatto*, Italy, Court of Cassation (Plenary Session) (1995) 114 ILR 555 and *Giaffreda v French Republic*, Italy, Court of Cassation (1992) note at 114 ILR 558, where the claims for reinstatement were rejected.

[260] *E.g., Emilio B.M. v Embassy of Equatorial Guinea*, Spain, Supreme Court (1986) 86 ILR 508 (The court said that granting Equatorial Guinea immunity from jurisdiction would imply an extension by analogy of the rules on diplomatic immunity and the recognition of absolute immunity of States from jurisdiction as a basic principle or customary rule of international law, while this principle was presently being questioned by the doctrine) and *Diana A v Republic of South Africa*, Spain, Supreme Court, 1986 86 ILR 512 (Bilingual secretary at embassy). Following these two cases, local labour courts in Spain ordered reinstatement of the respective plaintiffs and payment of arrears of salary.

[261] *M. H. C. v Republic of Cuba*, the Netherlands, Sub-District Court of The Hague, 1992 27 *Netherlands Yearbook of International Law* 319 (1996). (C. had worked as a translator for the Cuban Embassy in The Hague, the work consisting of translating newspaper articles and incoming and outgoing correspondence. On 10 January 1992 the Ambassador informed her that on account of spending cuts her employment would be terminated. If she would agree to the termination, she would receive compensation. After C. refused to sign the termination agreement the employment relationship deteriorated to such an extent that C. ultimately petitioned to terminate the contract of employment and award her compensation of 18 months' salary plus non-pecuniary damage.)

[262] *MK v Republic of Turkey*, the Netherlands, Sub-District Court of The Hague (1985) 94 ILR 350.

[263] *François v State of Canada*, Belgium, Labour Court of Brussels (First Chamber) (1989) 115 ILR 418.

proof of its grounds for dismissal, special compensation was payable.[264] Swiss courts, while refusing to examine the reasons which led the sending State to terminate the employment relationship, stated that the courts of the forum State had full jurisdiction over disputes concerning the *financial consequences of a summary dismissal.*[265]

3. International Standards?

This odyssey through a truly chaotic case law yields a picture of a diversity of approaches and a multiplicity of often conflicting results. Employees in almost identical situations could be handed different judgments by different courts. Employees with menial duties such as embassy drivers have had their claims either allowed[266] or rejected[267] depending on which court decided the case. Conflicting holdings regarding the same facts can be given by different courts in the same country. The *Barrandon* case serves as a good example. Madame Barrandon, who had been employed as a nurse and medical secretary at the US Embassy in Paris, sued the US for damages for wrongful dismissal. At first instance her claim was allowed in part. The Court of Appeal of Paris, on an appeal lodged by Madame Barrandon, even increased the award of damages against the Embassy. The *Procureur Général* then intervened to appeal to the Court of Cassation, asserting that the US should be granted the benefit of jurisdictional immunity. The Court of Cassation allowed the appeal and remitted the case to the Court of Appeal of Versailles.[268] The Court of Appeal of Versailles held that the US was entitled to rely on jurisdictional immunity since 'Madame Barrandon performed her functions for the benefit of American and non-American civil and military personnel posted in Paris, as well as visitors to the Embassy, in the interests of the public service organized by the United States of America for

[264] *Kingdom of Morocco v DR*, Belgium, Labour Court of Brussels (Sixth Chamber) (1989) 115 ILR 421.

[265] *X v United States of America*, Switzerland, Labour Court (TPH) of Geneva (1995) 116 ILR 668, 675 (Where the employer State refused to notify possible 'just cause' it would be ordered to pay salary in lieu of notice pursuant to Swiss law); *Nicoud v United States of America*, Switzerland, Labour Court of Geneva (TPH) (1994) 116 ILR 650, 655 (A refusal by the employer State to give justifiable reasons for dismissal meant that the State should be ordered to pay salary in lieu of notice as required by Swiss law).

[266] See, *e.g.*, *M v Arab Republic of Egypt*, Switzerland, Federal Tribunal (1994) 116 ILR 656; *Zambian Embassy v Sendanayake*, Italy, Court of Cassation (Plenary Session) (1992) 114 ILR 532; *Kingdom of Morocco v DR*, Belgium, Labour Court of Brussels (Sixth Chamber) (1989) 115 ILR 421; *Emilio B. M. v Embassy of Equatorial Guinea*, Spain, Supreme Court (1986) 86 ILR 508; *Rousseau v Republic of Upper Volta*, Belgium, Labour Court of Brussels (Third Chamber) (1983) 82 ILR 118; and *British Embassy Driver Case*, Austria, Superior Provincial Court (Oberlandesgericht) of Vienna (1978) 65 ILR 20.

[267] See, *e.g.*, *Arab Republic of Egypt v Gamal-Eldin*, England, Employment Appeal Tribunal, 1995 [1996] 2 All ER 237; 104 ILR 673. Noted by Michael Byers, 67 *BYBIL* (1996) 542. *Saudi Arabia v Nasser*, England, Employment Appeal Tribunal and affirmed by the Court of Appeal, 2000 Transcript at LexisNexis. *The Government of Canada v The Employment Appeals Tribunal and Burke*, Ireland, High Court, 1991; Ireland, Supreme Court, 1992 [1992] 2 IR 484; 95 ILR 467.

[268] *Barrandon v United States of America*, France, Court of Cassation (First Civil Chamber) (1992) 113 ILR 464.

the benefit of its agents, its nationals and foreign citizens subject to its authority or for whom it was responsible'.[269] However, upon appeal by Madame Barrandon, the Court of Cassation found that 'the tasks performed by Madame Barrandon did not give her any special responsibility for the performance of the public service of the Embassy, so that her dismissal constituted an ordinary act of administration (*acte de gestion*)'.[270] It is remarkable how the same tasks should have been characterized in such diametrically opposed ways.

Thus it is impossible to make any generalizations out of the current State practice, much less to distil any uniform rules.[271] As the current State practice with regard to contracts of employment displays nothing remotely resembling uniformity, *any* decision by *any* court can be regarded as not exceeding the 'margin of appreciation' allowed to States in limiting an individual's access to court. So what places the UK practice within the boundaries of current international law on State immunity is not that the UK does not fall outside 'international standards', as seen by the ECHR, but that there are at present *no* 'international standards', if by 'international standards' one means definitive rules that dictate reasonably consistent results.

4. *Recruitment to Diplomatic Missions?*

In *Fogarty v United Kingdom*, the ECHR relied on the importance of recruitment to diplomatic missions, but the word 'recruitment' does not appear in the UK SIA. In fact, with the exception of the Draft Articles by the International Law Commission (ILC), none of the current legal instruments, whether national or international, contains the word 'recruitment'. All the relevant provisions in these documents require an *existing contract of employment*,[272] thereby precluding claims based on any

[269] *Barrandon v United States of America*, Court of Appeal of Versailles (Social Chambers in Plenary Session) (1995) 113 ILR 466, 469.

[270] *Barrandon v United States of America*, France, Court of Cassation (Social Chamber) (1998) 116 ILR 622, 624. A Dutch case went through similarly conflicting holdings. *B. V. v Instituto Italiano di Cultura per I Paesi Bassi and the Republic of Italy*, the Netherlands, District Court of Amsterdam, 1990 23 *Netherlands Yearbook of International Law* 447 (1992); *B.V v Instituto Italiano di Cultura per I Paesi Bassi and the Republic of Italy*, the Netherlands, Sub-District Court of Amsterdam, 1991, 24 *Netherlands Yearbook of International Law* 341 (1993); *Republic of Italy v B. V.*, the Netherlands, District Court of Amsterdam, 1993, 26 *Netherlands Yearbook of International Law* 338 (1995).

[271] Indeed, the few scholars who have written on this subject are unanimous on this point. See Richard Garnett, State Immunity Triumphs in the European Court of Human Rights (case note on the three ECHR cases under discussion), 118 *Law Quarterly Review* (2002) 367, 370; Richard Garnett, State Immunity in Employment Matters, 46 *International and Comparative Law Quarterly* (1997) 81, 85–6 and 124; Hazel Fox, Employment Contracts as an Exception to State Immunity: Is All Public Service Immune? 66 *BYBIL* (1995) 97, 98; D. W. Greig, Specific Exceptions to Immunity under the International Law Commission's Draft Articles, 38 *International and Comparative Law Quarterly* (1989) 560, 560. See also *Report of the International Law Commission on the Work of its Fifty-first Session*, 3 May–23 July 1999, G.A.O.R. 54th Session, Supplement No. 10 (A/54/10 and Corr.1 & 2), Annex, 'Report of the Working Group on Jurisdictional Immunities of States and Their Property', para. 96.

[272] European Convention on State Immunity, art. 5(1) ('A Contracting State cannot claim immunity from the jurisdiction of a court of another Contracting State if the proceedings relate to a

pre-contract or pre-employment act (such as recruitment) in contemplation of a possible future employment relationship. Since the present rules on State immunity with regard to contracts of employment are predicated on an already existent employment relationship (there has to be a 'contract of employment'), recruitment to whatever institution (not limited to a diplomatic or consular mission) never emerges as a valid cause of action. As far as those States without immunity legislation are concerned, the above survey of case law shows that, in the cases where jurisdiction was asserted, it was likewise done over existing, as opposed to prospective, contracts of employment. As a matter of fact, so far no case has been decided in a claimant's favour on the sole basis of recruitment.

As has been pointed out, the only place where the word 'recruitment' does appear is the ILC Draft. Art. 11 provides that a State cannot invoke immunity 'in a proceeding which relates to a contract of employment between the State and an individual for work performed or to be performed, in whole or in part, in the territory of' the forum State (art. 11(1)), but that this does not apply if 'the subject of the proceeding is the recruitment, renewal of employment or reinstatement of an individual' (art. 11(2)(b)).[273] Note that here no mention is made of diplomatic or consular missions in the context of recruitment. In the commentary to this article, the ILC does not refer to diplomatic or consular missions either; instead, it finds that

> The employer State has an interest in the application of its laws in regard to the selection, *recruitment* and appointment of an employee by *the State or one of its organs, agencies or instrumentalities* acting in the exercise of governmental authority.[274]

Evidently, when it speaks of 'recruitment', the ILC has in mind, not recruitment to a diplomatic or consular mission, as the ECHR understood it, but recruitment to *any institution.* Therefore, when ECHR reasoned that, had Fogarty taken her case to an English court, immunity could have been justifiably granted because the intended proceedings

contract of employment between the State and an individual . . . '); UK SIA, s. 4(1) ('A State is not immune as respects proceedings relating to a *contract of employment* between the State and an individual . . . '); Australian FSIA, s. 12(1) ('A foreign State, as employer, is not immune in a proceeding in so far as the proceeding concerns the employment of a person under a *contract of employment* . . . '); ILA Drafts 1982 and 1994 art. III (C) ('A foreign State shall not be immune . . . Where the foreign State enters into a *contract for employment* in the forum State, or where work under such a *contract* is to be performed wholly or partly in the forum State and the proceedings relate to the *contract*'); IDI Draft, art. 2(c)('The organs of the forum State are competent in respect of proceedings concerning *contracts of employment* . . . '). Emphases added.

273 Now art. 11 (2)(c), see the Report of the UN Ad Hoc Committee on Jurisdictional Immunities of States and Their Property, dated 24–28 February 2003, UN General Assembly Official Records, 58th Session, Supplement No. 22 (A/58/22), Annex I and the Report of the UN Ad Hoc Committee on Jurisdictional Immunities of States and Their Property, dated 1–5 March 2004, A/59/22, Annex I.

274 *Yearbook of the International Law Commission*, 1991, Vol. II, Part Two, p. 12 at 42, commentary to art. 11. Emphases added.

concerned *recruitment to a diplomatic mission*, it was asserting something totally absent from current State practice.

In its commentary to art. 11 the ILC makes it clear that the provisions of this article do not prevent an employee from bringing action against the employer State in the State of the forum to seek redress for *damage* arising from recruitment (not the recruitment itself).[275] Presumably, sex discrimination in the course of recruitment may be regarded as distinct from the recruitment itself. Here it would be interesting to speculate what the ECHR would have said if the applicant had insisted that her intention was not to bring an action based upon the employment relationship itself (since there was no contract of employment yet) or, for that matter, upon the recruitment process, but to sue for sex discrimination[276] by a potential employer. But then a simple answer would have sufficed: Ms. Fogarty could not sue either for sex discrimination or for a prospective employment relationship because the UK SIA does not contain an exception to State immunity for sex discrimination and it requires an *existing contract* in order to establish jurisdiction regarding an employment relationship.[277]

CONCLUSION

Broadly speaking, the decisions of the ECHR in these three cases are in keeping with the current status of international law on State immunity, and are therefore what can reasonably be expected under the present circumstances. These decisions reaffirm two important aspects of State immunity, namely State immunity as a principle of international law and State immunity as a procedural matter.

State immunity is a limitation imposed by international law on the jurisdictional powers of national courts, so that, in certain situations, the courts are incompetent to entertain certain claims, if these are directed against a foreign State. To the extent that a court is precluded from exercising an otherwise existing jurisdiction, an individual's right of access to court is inevitably qualified. As State immunity is a principle of

[275] According to the ILC: 'The rule of immunity applies to proceedings for recruitment, renewal of employment and reinstatement of an individual only. It is without prejudice to the possible recourse which may still be available in the State of the forum for compensation or damages for "wrongful dismissal" or for breaches of obligation to recruit or to renew employment. In other words, this subparagraph does not prevent an employee from bringing action against the employer State in the State of the forum to seek redress for damage arising from recruitment, renewal of employment or reinstatement of an individual.' The ILC gives no further illustrations of possible actions. *Yearbook of the International Law Commission*, 1991, Vol. II, Part Two, p. 12 at 43, commentary to art. 11(2)(b).

[276] Judge Luocaides would prefer to see Fogarty's case as 'a claim for damages for sex discrimination' Dissenting opinion in *Fogarty v United Kingdom*.

[277] In *Banai*, the plaintiff brought proceedings alleging acts of racial discrimination on the basis of advertisements placed by the defendants for jobs. The court held that s. 4 of the 1978 UK SIA was not applicable because no contract of employment had actually been concluded. *Banai v Canadian High Commission*, England, Employment Appeal Tribunal (1990) 107 ILR 600.

international law, then any decision by a national court duly giving effect to this principle is, logically, in conformity with international law.

State *immunity* does not mean State *impunity*. The former is a procedural matter while the latter is a substantive one. The rule of State immunity is not concerned with the substantive question whether a State should be internationally responsible for its acts, but with the procedural question as to which forum is to be utilized in order to settle that responsibility; that is, whether, under current international law, that responsibility is to be dealt with in a foreign domestic court or resolved through channels normally operative on a State-to-State basis. In a word, State immunity is not about substantive responsibility; it is about forum.

Yet the ECHR did run into difficulties when it had to pronounce on current international law on State immunity. A number of misconceptions can be identified, the foremost among which is a non-existent distinction between criminal and civil proceedings in the context of State immunity, put forward by the ECHR in *Al-Adsani v United Kingdom*. In current international law, States enjoy immunity as a general rule subject to a range of exceptions; and these exceptions have been formulated not on the basis of a criminal/civil distinction but in reliance on a doctrine, evolved exclusively in the context of civil and commercial disputes, that upholds immunity for sovereign/governmental acts but denies immunity to commercial/private acts. In other words, immunity can be denied only in certain types of civil proceedings, while in all other proceedings, be they civil or criminal, States are immune from the jurisdiction of foreign domestic courts. If a distinction between criminal and civil proceedings has to be forced here, it can be stated that States are *absolutely* immune from criminal proceedings and *relatively* immune from civil proceedings subject to a limited number of exceptional cases.

However, an absolute immunity from criminal proceedings for *individuals*, as opposed to *States*, is becoming less certain, especially in the context of *former* State officials being sued for human rights violations committed outside the territory of the forum State. As the *Pinochet* case indicates, a reasonably practical way to overcome the present predicament posed by the operation of immunity in human rights litigation might be the institution of *individualized criminal proceedings*, that is, criminal proceedings brought against individual violators of human rights within the framework of existing multilateral human rights conventions.

In *McElhinney v Ireland*, the ECHR based its holding on two concepts that are highly questionable in the context of State immunity in regard to tortious conduct within the forum State: 'insurable' personal injury and a *jure imperii/jure gestionis* dichotomy. The word 'insurable' does not appear in any of the current legal instruments on State immunity, be it national or international, and therefore does not exist as a limitation on jurisdiction over tortious conduct. The *jure imperii/jure gestionis* distinction is discarded altogether in some States and is followed by others only to the extent that, when injury has been caused, *causing injury* will be regarded as *jure gestionis*, regardless of whether the act in the course of which injury has been caused is *jure imperii* or *jure gestionis*. Except where foreign armed forces are involved, it is rather doubtful if, in the event of actual injury being inflicted in the State of the forum, a court will deny jurisdiction solely on the ground that the act in question is *jure imperii*.

In *Fogarty v United Kingdom*, the ECHR's decision was founded on two likewise dubious grounds: purported 'international standards' and 'recruitment'. As far as State immunity with regard to contracts of employment at diplomatic and consular missions is concerned, 'international standards' are practically non-existent. And so far no decision has been rendered in favour of the claimant as regards 'recruitment' to a diplomatic mission, not because recruitment to diplomatic missions is vitally important and therefore sacrosanct, but simply because recruitment to *any* institution, be it a diplomatic mission or a State enterprise, is outside the range of admissible claims. The reason is that the current law on State immunity with regard to contracts of employment, by requiring there to be a *contract* to start with, is predicated on an *existing*, as opposed to a *prospective*, employment relationship.

COMPENSATING COMPANIES FOR NON-PECUNIARY DAMAGE: *COMINGERSOLL S.A. v PORTUGAL* AND THE AMBIVALENT EXPANSION OF THE ECHR SCOPE

By Marius Emberland*

A. INTRODUCTION

This article examines a propensity of the European Court of Human Rights to expand the scope of certain provisions of the European Convention on Human Rights to protect private activity in general and not just individual human beings, as was apparently the original intention.[1] What has inspired this analysis and serves as its focal point is the Court's Grand Chamber judgment of 6 April 2000 in *Comingersoll S. A. v Portugal*,[2] in which it unanimously held that Portugal had violated the applicant's right under Article 6(1) to have a civil dispute settled by domestic courts within a 'reasonable' period of time and that the Portuguese government, in accordance with Article 41, should compensate the applicant for the inconvenience, in terms of legal uncertainty, suffered as a consequence of the violation.

The *Comingersoll* judgment seems at first glance an inconspicuous example of Strasbourg adjudication. It deals with a recurrent form of ECHR violation, namely the inability of states to ensure that civil disputes between private litigants are not drawn out unreasonably by factors ascribable more to agents and organs of the state than to the petitioner. The compensation awarded amounted only to PTE 1,500,000 (approximately EUR 7,500, at current rates), a comparatively modest sum. The decision was unanimous. Moreover, the judgment has been the subject of little attention since it was delivered more than three years ago.

* D.Phil. candidate at the University of Oxford. The article was written when the author was Emile Noël Fellow at the Jean Monnet Center for International and Regional Law & Justice, New York University School of Law 2002–2003. The author would like to thank Dinah Shelton, who graciously commented on a previous draft of the article, to Ivar Alvik for commenting on a second draft, and to Lill-Tove Voje, who advised on decisions from international arbitral tribunals and the European Court of Justice. The usual disclaimer applies as to mistakes.

[1] Convention for the Protection of Human Rights and Fundamental Freedoms, Rome 4.XI.1950, 213 U.N.T.S. 221, E.T.S. 5 ('the Convention', 'the ECHR') as amended by Protocol No. 11 to the Convention for the Protection of Human Rights and Fundamental Freedoms, restructuring the control machinery established thereby, Strasbourg 11.V.1994, ETS 155 (in force 1 November 1998).

[2] *Comingersoll SA v Portugal*, judgment 6 April 2000 [Grand Chamber], Reports 2000-IV (referred to below also as '*Comingersoll*'). The Court was composed of Judges Wildhaber (Switzerland, President), Palm (Sweden), Rozakis (Greece), Bratza (United Kingdom), Pellonpää (Finland), Ferrari Bravo (Italy), Jörundsson (Iceland), Ress (Germany), Caflisch (Liechtenstein), Loucaides (Cyprus), Zupancic (Slovenia), Vajic (Croatia), Thomassen (Netherlands), Traja (Albania) and Kovler (Russia). On the judgment, see also Georg Ress 'Schmerzengeld für juristische Personen?' in *Festschrift für Akira Ishikawa zum 70. Geburtstag am 27. November 2001* (Gerhard Lüke, Takehiko Mikami, and Hanns Prütting eds) (Berlin: de Gruyter 2001) 429.

Comingersoll is significant all the same. In it, the Court for the first time discussed on principled grounds and explicitly stated that a private entity, in this case a publicly held limited liability company, was entitled under Article 41 to compensation for non-pecuniary harm suffered by the company itself. This had previously been a contentious matter in ECHR law; indeed, the unsettled state of the law was the reason for the Court's composition as a Grand Chamber.[3] *Comingersoll* represents a novel appreciation of the institution of monetary compensation for non-material loss, and has led to a flow of new remedial claims before the Court by legal persons. It also serves as a possible source of inspiration for the general law of remedies, where the issue remains controversial. The case also represents a new approach to provisions of the ECHR traditionally reserved, or believed to be reserved, for the protection of the interests of natural persons, provisions which now tend to safeguard the interests of certain entities (including businesses) as well. It may signal a shift towards permitting the protection of private activity generally, and not just individuals. More fundamentally, the judgment may reveal a gradual shift of adjudicatory emphasis away from a focus on human dignity and towards a focus on the rule of law aspects of human rights protection. Finally, the judgment represents an application of the principle of dynamic (or evolutive) interpretation in transmuted form; and whereas this approach is usually justified by reference to social and legal change within the States Parties to the ECHR, factors extrinsic to the Court, the dynamism of *Comingersoll* was justified by exclusive reference to the internal dynamics of Strasbourg adjudication. This shift from an external to an internal justification for judicial activism is problematic especially when the Court itself was not in total agreement of the relevance of the individual component in the entities that push for a favourable interpretation of Article 41.The decision reflects differing conceptions of the nature and purpose of the protection afforded by the ECHR, a disagreement which remains unresolved.

B. ARTICLE 41, 'JUST SATISFACTION' AND CLAIMS BY COMPANIES

Whatever its general relevance, *Comingersoll* deals specifically with the question of remedies under Article 41. As such, a very brief description of the framework of Article 41, as applied in the company context (which is the main point of interests in the present article), is essential.

[3] A prerequisite for Grand Chamber composition is that the applicant's complaint 'raises serious questions affecting the interpretation of the Convention', Article 30 and Rule 72(1) of the Rules of Court of the European Court of Human Rights (in effect since 1 November 1998), available at <http://www.echr.coe.int/Eng/EDocs/RulesofCourt2002.htm>('Rules of Court'). Prior to Protocol 11, the Court was constituted in plenary session; with Protocol 11, composition as a Grand Chamber replaced composition as a Plenary Court when deciding such cases of principle. Grand Chamber and Plenary Court judgments are indicated below.

1. *Just satisfaction*

Remedies for violation of the ECHR—or 'just satisfaction' in the terminology of the Convention[4]—are awarded mainly under Article 41 (formerly Article 50),[5] which provides:

> If the Court finds that there has been a violation of the Convention or the protocols thereto, and if the internal law of the High Contracting Party concerned allows only partial reparation to be made, the Court shall, if necessary, afford just satisfaction to the injured party.[6]

The concept of 'satisfaction', within the meaning of Article 41, comprises two forms of remedy, namely monetary compensation and declaratory judgments.[7] The Court is unable formally to grant other forms of remedy known to international law, such as cessation, non-repetition, or restitution in kind.[8] Beyond the context of non-pecuniary damages, claims for satisfaction by companies and other entities are treated no differently from equivalent claims by individuals. At the same time, like claims by individuals, they are subject to the general conditions for entitlement under Article 41, and these can entail difficulties peculiar to them.

[4] Suzan L Haasdijk 'The Lack of Uniformity in the Terminology of the International Law of Remedies' (1992) 5 Leiden Journal of International Law 245 notes that there is no universally accepted terminology in the area. The terms 'remedy' and 'reparation' are both current in international law. Both have broader connotations than the term 'satisfaction' used in ECHR law, which in turn bears a different meaning from the term as used in Article 37 of the International Law Commission's Draft articles on the Responsibility of States for internationally wrongful acts, UN GAOR 56th Session Supp No 10 UN Doc A/56/10, chapter IV.E.1., as acknowledged by the UN General Assembly (see UNGA Res 56/83 (28 January 2002) UN Doc A/RES/56/83). The present article uses 'remedies' and 'satisfaction' interchangeably.

[5] The Court may decide to postpone the remedy question until a later separate judgment: see Rules of Court Rules 75(1) and (2). Article 41 is supplemented by Rules of Court Rule 60. Note that this article is not concerned with the Court's capacity to determine remedies when it supervises friendly settlements, see Articles 38 and 39 and Gerhard Dannemann *Schadenersatz bei Verletzung der Europäischen Menschenrechtskonvention. Eine rechtsvergleichende Untersuchung zur Haftung nach Art. 50 EMRK* (Cologne Heymann 1994) 59–62. Neither does it consider the ability of the now defunct European Commission of Human Rights or the former power of the Committee of Ministers of the Council of Europe ('the Committee of Ministers') to award satisfaction pursuant to former Articles 28(b) and 32(1) respectively.

[6] The changes introduced to the text by Protocol 11 have no doctrinal implications, see § 97 of the 'Explanatory Report to Protocol No. 11 to the Convention for the Protection of Human Rights and Fundamental Freedoms, restructuring the control machinery established thereby' (ETS no. 155) available at <http://conventions.coe.int/Treaty/en/Treaties/html.155.htm>.

[7] This derives from the preparatory works of the Convention: see *Collected Edition of the 'travaux prépataroires' of the European Convention on Human Rights* (vol 4, Council of Europe ed) (Hague Nijhoff 1975–1985) 44; and Jonathan Sharpe, 'Article 50' in *La Convention européenne des droits de l'homme: Commentaire article par article* (Louis-Edmond Pettiti, Emmanuel Decaux and Pierre-Henri Imbert eds) (2nd ed, Paris: Economica 1999) 809.

[8] See, eg, *Belvedere Alberghieria Srl v Italy*, judgment 30 May 2000, Reports 2000-IV § 65. Dinah Shelton *Remedies in International Human Rights Law* (Oxford: OUP 1999) 148–51 and 156–58 criticizes this narrow interpretation of the remedies available under the provision. The Court has, in recent years, adopted an approach to the remedy of restitution whereby it strongly encourages the violating state to afford restitution in kind as a primary means of redress, with pecuniary satisfaction as a secondary remedy in cases where the state fails to follow the Court's advice: see especially *Papamichalopoulos v Greece (Art. 50)*, judgment 31 October 1995, Series A 330-B § 34; and *Brumarescu v Romania (Art. 41)*, judgment 23 January 2001 [Grand Chamber], Reports 2001-I, paras 19–22.

2. *Available remedies*

Companies and other entities appearing as applicants before the Court are regarded as 'injured parties', within the meaning of Article 41, in the same manner as individual victims:[9] there is little evidence that entities' claims are treated differently in this regard. This goes for declaratory judgments, a remedy whereby the Court simply observes that a violation has occurred, the finding of a violation being sufficient satisfaction.[10] When the Court opts for declarations rather than compensation for pecuniary harm in the company context, it does so as a conciliatory means because of the applicant's inability to procure proof that the general requirements for compensation have been met.[11] Conciliatory declarations are also awarded when the Court is unsure of the doctrinal validity of offering another form of satisfaction.[12]

It also goes for compensation for pecuniary damage.[13] Companies are frequently successful in claiming compensation for pecuniary harm in terms of loss of income,[14] reduced value of goodwill,[15] loss of reputation,[16] inflation of costs with respect to outstanding sums owed to them,[17] and decline in customers and business clientele.[18] Awards can assume gigantic proportions. In *Stran Greek Refineries and Stratis Andreadis v Greece*, for instance, the applicants' claim (payment of an original arbitral award) was granted almost in its entirety by the Court. Greece was ordered to pay approximately USD 16,000,000 plus interest, the biggest award of compensation in the Court's history.[19]

[9] The provision was based on pre-War arbitration clauses, under which companies' claims for compensation were not unknown: see for details, eg, Heribert Golsong 'Quelques refléxions á propos du pouvoir de la Cour européenne de droits de l'homme d'accorder une satisfaction équitable' in *René Cassin Amicorum Discipulorumque Liber Vol 1* (Paris: Pédone 1969) 89.

[10] On declarations, see Dannemann, *supra* n. 5, 365–8. The Court may decide to award no satisfaction at all: see, eg, *Tre Traktörer AB v Sweden*, judgment 7 July 1989, Series A 159 para 66.

[11] In *Academy Trading Ltd and Others v Greece*, judgment 4 April 2000 (unreported) paras 55–6 the Court dismissed the six Liberian shipping companies' unspecified claim of compensation for pecuniary (as well as non-pecuniary) damage resulting from a violation of Article 6(1) (length of civil proceedings) in a dispute with the Citibank group. It issued nevertheless a declaratory judgment to remedy the total damage sustained.

[12] See Shelton, *supra* n. 8, 203 and 205 for both forms of conciliatory declarations. Examples include *News Verlags GmbH & Co. KG v Austria, judgment 11 January 2000, Reports 2000-I* para 66; and *Manifattura FL v Italy*, judgment 24 January 1992, Series A 230-B para 22.

[13] Rule 75(3) provides for a three month period in which the respondent must pay compensation, after which interest is added. In *Christine Goodwin v United Kingdom*, judgment 11 July 2002 [Grand Chamber] (unreported) paras 123–4, the Court decided that henceforth monetary awards are to be awarded in Euros and that the default interest is three percentage points above the marginal lending rate of the European Central Bank at the time of the judgment.

[14] *Tele 1 Privatfernsehengesellschaft mbH v Austria*, judgment 21 September 2000 (unreported) paras 45–6.

[15] *Tre Traktörer AB v Sweden*, judgment 7 July 1989, Series A 159 paras 55–6.

[16] *Tinnelly & Sons, Ltd and Others v United Kingdom*, 10 July 1998, Reports 1998-IV para 89.

[17] *Unión Alimentaria Sanders SA v Spain*, judgment 7 July 1989, Series A 157 para 44.

[18] *Stratégies et Communications and Dumoulin v France*, judgment 15 July 2002 (unreported) para 58.

[19] *Stran Greek Refineries and Stratis Andreadis v Greece*, judgment 9 December 1994, Series A 301-B paras 66–83.

Companies also regularly seek reimbursement of legal costs.[20] Costs are awarded only insofar as they were 'actually incurred, . . . necessarily incurred and . . . reasonable as to quantum.'[21] The Court has found that even costs relating to work undertaken by a company's own legal expert in exercise of his normal and salaried duties were 'actually incurred' and reimbursable under Article 41.[22] Nor has the requirement that the costs be 'necessarily incurred' barred companies from being reimbursed for litigation initiated for policy purposes rather than as a means of seeking actual redress.[23] As to the requirement that costs must be 'reasonable', it is often the case that reductions are made in respect of legal advice by highly paid lawyers and other experts.[24] But the Court does not shy away from awarding huge sums for costs. In *Stran Greek Refineries and Stratis Andreadis v Greece*, the Court, although reducing the original claim for costs incurred before the Strasbourg organs by GBP 70 000, found that the Greek state was liable to pay the applicants a total of GBP 125 000 costs.[25]

3. *General requirements and the Court's discretion*

All claims for satisfaction under Article 41 must meet certain general requirements. First, satisfaction will only be awarded where full reparation has not been awarded in the domestic proceedings (a requirement akin to the local remedies rule).[26] The Court also sees its competence as dependent upon the filing of a specific and timely request for satisfaction by the applicant.[27] This condition implies, as far as companies are

[20] See generally, eg, Nicolas Sansonetis 'Costs and Expenses' in *The European System for the Protection of Human Rights* (Ronald St J Macdonald, Franz Matscher, and Herbert Petzold eds) (Dordrecht: Nijhoff 1993) 755.

[21] *Sunday Times v United Kingdom (No. 1) (Art. 50)*, judgment 6 November 1980 [Plenary Court], Series A 38 para 23.

[22] *Sunday Times v United Kingdom (No. 1) (Art. 50)*, judgment 6 November 1980 [Plenary Court], Series A 38 paras 24–5.

[23] *Sunday Times v United Kingdom (No. 1) (Art. 50)*, judgment 6 November 1980 [Plenary Court], Series A 38 para 16(4).

[24] Claims regarding lawyers' fees were halved in *Sunday Times v United Kingdom (No. 1) (Art. 50)*, judgment 6 November 1980 [Plenary Court], Series A 38 paras 63–70; *Autronic AG v Switzerland*, judgment 22 May 1990 [Plenary Court], Series A 178 paras 64–6; and in *Tre Traktörer AB v Sweden*, judgment 7 July 1989, Series A 159 paras 67–9. The Court cut the lawyers' fees by more than two thirds in *Observer and Guardian v United Kingdom,* judgment 26 November 1991 [Plenary Court] Series A 216 paras 78–84.

[25] *Stran Greek Refineries and Stratis Andreadis v Greece*, judgment 9 December 1994, Series A 301-B paras 84–7.

[26] See Pieter van Dijk and G J H van Hoof *Theory and Practice of the European Convention on Human Rights* (2nd ed, Hague Kluwer 1998) 245–8. In *Pressos Compania Naviera S. A. and Others v Belgium (Art. 50)*, judgment 3 July 1997, Reports 1997-IV, claims for compensation by 24 of the 25 applicant companies were dismissed, as the Belgian courts had not yet finished handling their compensation claims.

[27] *Sunday Times v United Kingdom (No. 1) (Art. 50)*, judgment 6 November 1980 [Plenary Court], Series A 38 para 14. The claim shall be set out 'in the written observations on the merits or, if no such written observations are filed, in a special document filed no later than two months after the decision declaring the application admissible': Rules of Court Rule 60(1).

concerned, that the company itself, not its shareholders, must file the request.[28] Next, a claim must, to a reasonable extent, be furnished with evidence of the damage sustained and the basis on which any monetary satisfaction is asserted,[29] although the Court applies the evidence requirement flexibly,[30] taking into account the nature of the claim. This has occasionally proved beneficial to company claimants.[31] Finally, the petitioner must establish a causal connection between the violation and the injury for which satisfaction is sought. An examination of compensation claims conveys the distinct impression of a recurrent inability of business entities to procure sufficient evidence of causality. The standard of proof required to demonstrate a causal link is high regardless of who the applicant is.[32] As business involves the pursuit of future profit, companies' claims tend in particular to relate to *pro futuro* damage, hypothetical loss or other forms of damage which are not easily verifiable.[33] The Court will rarely find causality in such instances.[34] It will be disinclined to award compensation if the claim requires it to hypothesise the outcome of the dispute.[35] This is what claims for pecuniary damages often require in the cases involving violations of Article 6.

Even when all these requirements are fulfilled, it is for the Court to decide—having full discretion having regard to what it deems equitable in the particular case—whether satisfaction should be awarded and, if so, what form and amount it should take.[36] The Court may decide to dismiss a claim for monetary compensation completely, or decide that a declaration represents sufficient reparation. An applicant filing a detailed claim for compensation which might be opposed at length by the respondent government can find its two claims combined or reduced by the Court

[28] *Vebeer v Estonia*, judgment 7 November 2002 (unreported) paras 79–80. There are however judgments in which shareholders have been able to 'lift the corporate veil' in such matters. See in particular *Ruiz-Mateos v Spain*, judgment 23 June 1993 [Plenary Court], Series A 262 para 69, where the individual shareholders of a holding company owning several hundred undertakings claimed compensation of pecuniary damage sustained by their companies. The Court identified the positions of the company and the shareholders.

[29] Rule 60(2).

[30] The Court makes its own assessment of the applicant's evaluations (and their probable divergence from calculations provided by the respondent government), but it is unlikely that it will not be guided by them: see details in Shelton, *supra* n. 8, 254–61.

[31] See *Unión Alimentaria Sanders SA v Spain*, judgment 7 July 1989, Series A 157 paras 44–5, where the Court conceded that the damage was not 'susceptible of precise qualification', and awarded an equitable sum to compensate for loss brought about by inflation over the period of the protracted enforcement proceedings.

[32] Shelton, *supra* n. 8, 234–44 and 239 is generally critical to the Court's strict interpretation of causality.

[33] Wolfgang Peukert 'Artikel 50' in *Europäische MenschenRechtsKonvention. EMRK-Kommentar* (Jochen Abr Frowein and Wolfgang Peukert) (2nd ed, Kehl am Rhein: N P Engel 1996) 667, 676–87 provides a comprehensive analysis of this requirement.

[34] See, eg, *Bielectric Srl v Italy*, judgment 16 November 2000 (unreported) para 26.

[35] See, eg, *Tre Traktörer AB v Sweden*, judgment 7 July 1989, Series A 159 paras 55–6; *Editions Périscope v France*, judgment 26 March 1992, Series A 234-B paras 46–7; and *Dombo Beheer BV v Netherlands*, judgment 27 October 1993, Series A 274 para 40.

[36] The discretion flows from the word 'necessary' in Article 41: *Sunday Times v United Kingdom (No. 1) (Art. 50)*, judgment 6 November 1980 [Plenary Court], Series A 38 para 15.

without further comment.[37] It is therefore difficult to forecast the outcome of an Article 41 claim, and equally difficult to find sufficient indication of the ratio of a decision.[38]

C. *COMINGERSOLL* IN CONTEXT

As seen above, claims by companies under Article 41 are not controversial in themselves. Yet the Court's decision in *Comingersoll* to convene as a Grand Chamber presupposed that the claim for compensation for non-pecuniary loss raised a controversial issue of ECHR law. Several factors account for this sense of controversy.

1. The nature of Convention rights

Article 34 of the ECHR allows for individuals and entities alike to file complaints before the Court.[39] The Court has never seriously doubted that private entities such as limited liability companies, political parties, trade unions, and other associations, with or without legal personality under national law, are included among the applicants recognised by Article 34.[40] There is no doubt that they, in principle, are entitled to protection under the Convention in the same manner as individuals.[41] Several hundred Court judgments to date concern companies' claims for protection. Many of them have had a successful outcome.

At the same time, the case law shows that private entities do not enjoy protection under every provision of the ECHR. There are some provisions that apply *ipso facto* to entities and individuals alike.[42] Others are

[37] Peukert, *supra* n. 33, 671 identifies three elements which influence the Court's exercise of its discretionary power to award satisfaction, namely the conduct of the applicant throughout the underlying dispute, the extent of the violation and its impact on the applicant, and the extent of the injury for which the applicant claims compensation.

[38] As noted in, eg, Hans Christian Krüger 'Reflections on Some Aspects of Just Satisfaction under the European Convention on Human Rights' in *Liber Amicorum Marc-André Eissen* (Gerard Cohen-Jonathan, Jean-Francois Flauss, and Pierre Lambert eds) (Brussels: Bruylant 1995) 255, 264–9.

[39] The provision states: 'The Court may receive applications from any person, non-governmental organisation or group of individuals claiming to be the victim of a violation by one of the High Contracting Parties of the rights set forth in the Convention or the protocols thereto. The High Contracting Parties undertake not to hinder in any way the effective exercise of this right.'

[40] The right of entities to file petitions would seem to flow from the terms 'person' and 'non-governmental organisation', although it is under the latter that entities are usually included: see, eg, Peukert, *supra* n. 33, 533.

[41] Overviews are provided in Christoph Schwaighofer 'Legal Persons, Organisations, Shareholders as Applicants (Article 25 of the Convention)' in *The Birth of European Human Rights Law. Liber Amicorum Carl Aaage Nørgaard* (Michele de Salvia and Mark E Villiger eds) (Baden-Baden: NOMOS 1998) 321; Michael K Addo 'The Corporation as a Victim of Human Rights Violations' in *Human Rights Standards and the Responsibility of Transnational Corporations* (Michael K Addo ed) (Hague: Kluwer 1999) 187; and Marius Emberland 'Duality and Ambiguity. The Protection of Corporations' Interests under the European Convention on Human Rights' Norwegian Institute of Human Rights *Human Rights Reports* No. 1: 2001 (Oslo 2001).

[42] Examples include Article 6(1) (right to a fair trial), Article 10 (freedom of expression), and Article 11 (freedom of association). Protocol 1, Article 1 (right to one's possessions) is the only provision which explicitly includes legal persons within its scope.

believed to be restricted by their nature to individuals alone.[43] In between these two extremes, the Court is sometimes faced with controversial issues of interpretation.[44] Article 41 belongs to this last group.

This variation in the scope of protection afforded by different provisions can be explained in different ways. One is to distinguish individual from collective rights. Another is to draw a distinction between those rights which derive from a natural law focus on the inherent dignity of the individual human being and those rights which derive from the principle of the rule of law. It is obviously difficult to distinguish clearly between these two traditions of approaching the protection of fundamental rights. Human dignity cannot possibly be effectively protected without adherence to the rule of law principle. The rule of law builds its legitimacy at least in part on qualities of the individual being. There is also profound conceptual disagreement as to what the concepts of human dignity and the rule of law really contain. It is nonetheless submitted here that all ambiguity aside, the former tradition, with its emphasis on the individual's intrinsic qualities, tends to be doctrinally unsympathetic to non-natural persons, while the latter tradition, with its focus on freedom from partial treatment and arbitrariness, is more apt to include any private person in its conception of fundamental rights because its focus lies elsewhere than on the personal qualities of the subject-holder. The distinction can be a useful vehicle for revealing a trend in Strasbourg adjudication which at any rate still has no proper 'name'. Both explanatory approaches are analytical tools familiar to German constitutional discourse. The German *Grundgesetz*'s fundamental procedural rights have immediate universal application as they originate from the *Rechtstaat* tradition (the equivalent of the rule of law).[45] The other group of fundamental rights, the *Grundrechte* (basic rights), which are set out in Part 1 of the *Grundgesetz*, are believed to derive from the natural law tradition and its emphasis on human dignity.[46] These rights have no automatic application to legal persons; rather, it depends on a complex assessment of whether the different rights, by their nature, contain sufficient collective elements as to imply protection for legal persons.[47]

[43] Examples include Article 3 (prohibition of torture) and Article 5 (right to liberty and security).

[44] Article 8 (right to respect for one's private life, family life, home, and correspondence) is a cardinal example.

[45] See especially Articles 101 (access to court), 103(1) (due process), 103(2) (*nulla poena sine lege*), and 103(3) (*ne bis in idem*) in Grundgesetz für die Bundesrepublik Deutshcland, 23 May 1949 ('the Grundgesetz'). A recent English translation of the Grundgesetz is found in Axel Tschentscher *The Basic Law (Grundgesetz). The Constitution of the Federal Republic of Germany (May 23, 1949)* (Würzburg: Jurisprudentia 2002).

[46] Sabine Michalowski and Lorna Woods *German Constitutional Law. The Protection of Civil Liberties* (Aldershot: Ashgate Dartmouth 1999) provides an English-language introduction to fundamental rights in German constitutional law.

[47] The assessment turns on an interpretation of the different provisions in their own right and in the light of Article 19(3) of the *Grundgesetz*, which provides for the application of *Grundrechte* to the extent that their nature permits it. The debate over the protection of legal persons under the various *Grundrechte* is too complex and contentious to be restated here. The best introductions to the debate are found in the standard commentaries on the *Grundgesetz*. Two comprehensive introductions are the collectivist view of Albert von Mutius 'Artikel 19 Abs. 3' (2nd ed, 1975) in *Kommentar zum Bonner Grundgesetz* (Rudolf Dolzer, Klaus Vogel, Hans Jürgen Abraham, and Bodo Dennewitz eds)

The German constitutional discourse is useful for understanding the status of non-natural persons under the Convention. It might help explain why the Court in *Comingersoll* saw the claim as controversial, and why the judges disagreed over the ratio for the decision. The violation for which the company claimed compensation related to a fundamental procedural right deriving from the rule of law tradition. The remedy in question, however, is traditionally conceived as deriving from the dignity of the individual human being. This leads us to consider the nature of Comingersoll S.A.'s remedial claim as the possible reason for the perception of controversy.

2. *The nature of the remedial claim in* Comingersoll

Comingersoll S. A. was a publicly held limited liability company claiming compensation for non-material loss sustained by the entity itself. Referring to compensation for non-pecuniary harm in international human rights law, Dinah Shelton writes:

> Intangible injuries such as physical pain and suffering have long been recognized as legitimate elements of damages. Mental anguish independent of physical injury is also now recognized as an element of recovery, including humiliation, loss of enjoyment of life and other non-pecuniary losses. . . . In civil law systems, 'préjudice moral' includes pain and suffering, sadness and humiliation caused by disfigurement, loss of amenities, loss of recreational ability, loss of any of the five senses, enjoyment of sexual relations, harm to marriage possibilities, and generally damage to the enjoyment of life. Overall, where there has been an injury, the focus is at least in part on diminution of the injured person's expectations of life, sometimes called hedonic damages.[48]

A similar focus on loss intrinsic to the human being is seen in most domestic legal systems' consideration of compensation for non-pecuniary harm. It is also reflected in traditional public international legal discourse. Two arbitral awards frequently cited in the literature concerned a state's exercise of diplomatic protection on behalf of individuals who had suffered various forms of intangible injury,[49] although the question

(Heidelberg: Müller 1950; loose leaf update) and the individualist view of Günter Dürig 'Artikel 19' in *Grundgesetz: Kommentar Vol II* (Theodor Maunz and Günter Dürig eds) (2nd ed, Munich: Beck 1963, 1985).

[48] Shelton, *supra* n. 8, 226–7 (footnotes omitted).

[49] In the *Lusitania* case, the Umpire considered that international law provided compensation for mental suffering, injury to feelings, humiliation, shame, degradation, loss of social position, or injury to credit or reputation: see Mixed Claim Commission, *United States and Germany*, Opinion 1 November 1923, (1923) 7 UNRIAA 32 (compensation for loss of individual American passengers' lives after the German sinking of the British ocean liner *SS Lusitania* in 1915). Canada, as the injured party, was awarded USD 25 000 as compensation for, *inter alia*, the indignity suffered by that state as a result of the unlawful sinking of a Canadian registered vessel, with the loss of all hands, in *Claim of the British Ship 'I'm Alone'*, report of the Commissioners 30 June 1933, (1935) 3 RIAA 1609; (1935) 7 ILR 203 (the sinking of a ship involved in the smuggling of prohibited alcoholic beverages to the United States; compensation for the loss of the lives of the individual crew members). The case does not unambiguously state whether Canada received compensation for its own indignity or for the indignity suffered by its nationals.

of private entities' entitlement to compensation for non-pecuniary harm remains unexplored.[50] The law of remedies in the European Union also traditionally focuses on individuals' claims for non-pecuniary harm.[51] Most importantly, compensation for non-pecuniary harm under the ECHR is spoken of in ways that tend to exclude consideration of matters beyond the individual's loss and suffering.[52]

There exists, in short, a rhetorical climate that renders companies' claims presumptively incompatible with the institution of compensation for non-material loss. Such claims seem misplaced when dressed in the language of 'the human being'. In a strained exercise in anthropomorphism, companies have claimed compensation for 'stress and anguish' subsequent to protracted civil proceedings;[53] for 'anxiety' caused by the inability to obtain a court order for eviction from apartments in their possession;[54] for 'feelings of frustration, powerlessness, suffering and revolt';[55] and for 'feelings of unequal treatment'.[56] Comingersoll S. A. formulated its claim by referring more neutrally to the 'inconvenience' caused to it by uncertainty. Similar examples of objective reference to 'legal uncertainty' are seen in other cases.[57] Company petitioners have also referred to non-pecuniary injury caused to them by 'the Government's attitude' in not complying with a previous judgment of the Court,[58] and to the 'duress' of having to choose between criminal proceedings for violating an injunction and loss of future profits.[59]

Such claims also appear misplaced when they concern loss which is traditionally is regarded as pecuniary rather than non-pecuniary because of the business context from which it derives. Business entities have, for instance, filed claims before the Court asserting non-pecuniary damages for 'deterioration of . . . commercial reputation and loss of customers',[60]

[50] To the author's knowledge, the two only studies of the theme under consideration are Dannemann, *supra* n. 5, 386–9; and Jean Personnaz in his *La Réparation du prejudice en droit international public* (Paris: Sirey 1939) 203.

[51] Cases typically concern intangible injury sustained by employees who have been wrongfully discharged or mistreated: see, eg, Akos G Toth 'The Concept of Damage and Causality as Elements of Non-Contractual Liability' in *The Action for Damages in Community Law* (Ton Heukels and Alison McDonnel eds) (Hague: Kluwer 1997) 179, 190–1.

[52] Van Dijk and van Hoof, *supra* n. 26, 255; David Harris, Michael O'Boyle, and Colin Warbrick *Law of the European Convention on Human Rights* (London Butterworths 1995) 687; and Peukert, *supra* n. 33, 673–4.

[53] *Alithia Publishing Company v Cyprus*, judgment 11 July 2002 (unreported) paras 43–5.

[54] *Immobiliare Saffi v Italy*, judgment 28 July 1999 [Grand Chamber], Reports 1999-V paras 77–9.

[55] *Matos e Silva, Lda and Others v Portugal*, judgment 16 September 1996, Reports 1996-IV para 98.

[56] *Dombo Beheer BV v Netherlands*, judgment 27 October 1993, Series A 274 para 39 (implied by the Commission's views on the matter before the Court).

[57] *Matos e Silva, Lda and Others v Portugal*, judgment 16 September 1996, Reports 1996-IV para 98; *Idrocalce Srl v Italy*, judgment 24 January 1992, Series A 229-F paras 21–2; *Manifattura FL v Italy*, judgment 24 January 1992, Series A 230-B paras 21–2; *Academy Trading Ltd and Others v Greece*, judgment 4 April 2000 (unreported) para 56; *Bielectric Srl v Italy*, judgment 16 November 2000 (unreported) para 26; and *Markass Car Hire Ltd v Cyprus*, judgment 11 June 2002 (unreported) paras 45–9.

[58] *Pressos Compania Naviera S. A. and Others v Belgium (Art. 50)*, judgment 3 July 1997, Reports 1997-IV para 24.

[59] *Krone Verlag GmbH & Co. KG v Austria*, judgment 26 February 2002 (unreported) para 44.

[60] *Ruiz-Mateos v Spain*, judgment 23 June 1993 [Plenary Court], Series A 262 paras 69–70.

'loss of reputation',[61] and loss of 'credibility and effectiveness' in the running of its business.[62] In international legal practice, such claims tend to be labelled as pecuniary rather than non-pecuniary.[63]

In short, claims by companies appear irreconcilable with the institution of compensation for non-material loss. This might in part explain why the Court in *Comingersoll* found the company's claim controversial. Yet, as the cases mentioned in this section demonstrate, companies claimed compensation for non-material loss prior to *Comingersoll* without the convening of a Grand Chamber or, formerly, a Plenary Court. There must, consequently, be another way of explaining the controversy.

3. *A gradual build-up towards clarification*

An obvious reason why the Court decided to convene a Grand Chamber to hear the *Comingersoll* claim was that the parties to the dispute and the Court itself were willing and ready to make the most of the potential for discussion involved in this type of claim. This willingness helps understand why the Court in at least one case prior to *Comingersoll* had afforded this particular type of compensation to companies, but without discussing the potential controversy involved.[64] In fact, a retrospective tour will show that previous case law had gradually built up towards this 'moment of truth' where the Court finally was called upon to adopt a wholesale scope of application for the particular remedy in question.

It was in the initial *Sunday Times* case—the first claim by an entity under the ECHR—that the Court was first asked to award monetary compensation to a company for non-material loss. In the event, it was not required to deal with the merits of the claim, since the applicant had failed to fulfil one of the general requirements for satisfaction.[65] The same happened in several subsequent decisions.[66] In other cases, the Court avoided considering the merits of the claim for non-material harm by using its discretionary powers to find that the violation was sufficiently remedied by a declaratory judgment.[67]

It was not until 1999, in *Freedom and Democracy Party (ÖZDEP) v Turkey*, that the Court first awarded monetary compensation to an entity

[61] *News Verlags GmbH & Co. KG v Austria*, judgment 11 January 2000, Reports 2000-I para 64.

[62] *Alithia Publishing Company v Cyprus*, judgment 11 July 2002 (unreported) paras 43–5.

[63] In *Case concerning the Factory at Chórzow* (Germany v Poland), judgment 13 September 1928, PCIJ Rep Series A No 17 at 56, the Permanent Court of International Justice awarded compensation for loss of business reputation by construing it as loss of market share.

[64] *Matos e Silva, Lda and Others v Portugal*, judgment 27 August 1996, Reports 1996-IV paras 98–101.

[65] *Sunday Times v United Kingdom (No. 1) (Art. 50)*, 6 November 1980 [Plenary Court], Series A 38 para 14 (unspecified 'moral damage' claimed by the applicant and contested by the government; dismissed by the Court as it had not been claimed in time).

[66] *Idrocalce Srl v Italy*, judgment 24 January 1992, Series A 229-F paras 21–2; *Manifattura FL v Italy*, judgment 24 January 1992, Series A 230-B paras 21–2 and *Caffé Roversi Spa v Italy*, judgment 24 January 1992, Series A 230-G paras 21–3; *Dombo Beheer BV v Netherlands*, judgment 22 September 1993, Series A 274 paras 37, 39–40; *Ruiz-Mateos v Spain*, judgment 23 June 1993 [Plenary Court], Series A 262 paras 69–70.

[67] See, eg, *Pressos Compania Naviera S.A. and Others v Belgium (Art. 50)*, judgment 3 July 1997, Reports 1997-IV paras 7 and 21; and *Academy Trading Ltd and Others v Greece*, judgment 4 April 2000 (unreported) para 56.

for non-material loss. It did so, however, not in respect of intangible harm suffered by the entity itself but in respect of intangible harm suffered by its individual members. The Court found no reason to question the entitlement of a political party, which had been dissolved in contravention of Article 11, to claim monetary compensation for non-material harm in the form of the 'frustration felt by the party's founders and members'.[68] The case acknowledged an entity's capacity to receive damages for non-pecuniary injury, but only because the entity served as a vehicle for individual activity and the medium for distributing compensation for individual loss. Indeed, seven years earlier, the Court in *Manifattura FL v Italy* had expressed doubt as to whether the applicant in question, 'a commercial company, was capable of suffering such damage' in its own capacity.[69]

A few months before *ÖZDEP*, the Court in *Immobiliare Saffi v Italy* had found it 'unnecessary to examine whether a commercial company may allege that it has sustained non-pecuniary damage through anxiety, as, having regard to the facts of the case, it decides to make no award under this head'.[70] Finally, the following year, in *News Verlags GmbH & Co KG v Austria*, the Court responded to a limited partnership's claim for EUR 50,000 in non-pecuniary damages for a violation of Article 10 with the following statement:

> As to non-pecuniary damage for the alleged loss of reputation, the Court will leave open whether a corporate applicant can claim non-pecuniary damage of this sort (see, *mutatis mutandis*, Immobiliare Saffi v. Italy [GC], no. 22774/93, § 79, ECHR 1999-V) as, in the circumstances of the case, the finding of a violation provides sufficient just satisfaction as regards any non-pecuniary damage the applicant company might have sustained.[71]

This survey of prior decisions suggest that the Court, while acknowledging the controversy involved in this particular type of remedy, simultaneously and gradually opened up for a future determination of the contentious issue of law it represents. The *Immobiliare Saffi* judgment, and even more so the *News Verlags* judgment, contain strong hints that the Court at a future junction would not anymore avoid a principled discussion if the parties to the case so wanted. *Comingersoll* was delivered just months after *News Verlags*.

[68] *Freedom and Democracy Party (ÖZDEP) v Turkey*, judgment 8 December 1999 [Grand Chamber], Reports 1999-VIII paras 55–7. It should be added that the Court in *Vereinigung demokratischer Soldaten Österreichs and Gubi v Austria*, judgment 24 November 1994, Series A 302 paras 60–2, entered a declaratory judgment in respect of non-pecuniary injury suffered by a soldiers' association.

[69] *Manifattura FL v Italy*, judgment 24 January 1992, Series A 230-B paras 21–2. The judgment is mentioned in Dannemann, *supra* n. 5, 386.

[70] *Immobiliare Saffi v Italy*, judgment 28 July 1999 (Grand Chamber), Reports 1999-V paras 77 and 79.

[71] *News Verlags GmbH & Co. KG v Austria*, judgment 11 January 2000, Reports 2000-I, (2001) 31 EHRR 8 paras 64 and 66 (claim for non-pecuniary compensation in respect of alleged loss of reputation caused by a violation of Article 10 relating to the Austrian courts' prohibition on publishing photographs of an accused).

D. THE COURT'S REASONING IN *COMINGERSOLL*

We have seen why the claim in *Comingersoll* was considered controversial by the Court. Now it is time to examine the Court's response to the controversy. The following analysis does not purport to be exhaustive but rather seeks to pinpoint and place in context the central arguments of the judgment. It seeks to expose the mechanics at work when the Court is faced with having to extend to collective entities the protection of provisions traditionally believed to be individual entitlements. These mechanics expose in turn aspects of the Court's thinking that tend to be underappreciated in ECHR discourse.[72]

1. Subsidiary arguments

Two of the arguments relied on by the Court in *Comingersoll*, though not crucial to its conclusion, underscore the need it felt to provide as much justification as possible for what it perceived as a controversial decision.

First, the Court

> . . . takes into account the practice of the member States of the Council of Europe in such cases. Although it is difficult to identify a precise rule common to all member States, judicial practice in several of the States shows that the possibility that a juristic person may be awarded compensation for non-pecuniary damage cannot be ruled out.[73]

This statement is typical of the Court's not infrequent invocation of a relevant common European standard to justify one interpretative choice over another,[74] a device which can lead to an extensive interpretation of the treaty.[75] The Court's carefully circumscribed statement reflects a lowest-common-denominator European consensus concerning monetary compensation for non-pecuniary harm sustained by entities such as companies. Quite possibly the Court had in mind the (few and incomplete) comparative studies in the field, which suggest no more than that companies are entitled to this form of compensation in some jurisdictions. The solutions adopted in European domestic law are restricted as to

[72] Introductions to ECHR interpretation include Franz Matscher 'Methods of Interpretation of the Convention', in *The European System for the Protection of Human Rights* (Ronald St John Macdonald, Franz Matscher and Herbert Petzold eds) (Dordrecht: Nijhoff 1993) 63; Heribert Golsong 'Interpreting the European Convention on Human Rights Beyond the Confines of the Vienna Convention on the Law of Treaties,' *ibid*, 147; and Rudolf Bernhardt 'Thoughts on the Interpretation of Human-Rights Treaties' in *Protecting Human Rights: The European Dimension. Studies in Honour of Gérard J Wiarda* (Franz Matscher and Herbert Petzold eds) (Cologne: Heymanns 1988) 65.

[73] *Comingersoll S. A. v Portugal*, judgment 6 April 2000, [Grand Chamber], Reports 2000-IV para 34.

[74] Walter J. Ganshof van der Meersch 'Reliance, in the Case Law of the European Court of Human Rights, on the Domestic Law of States' (1980) 1 Human Rights Law Journal 13.

[75] Laurence Helfer 'Consensus, Coherence and the European Convention on Human Rights' (1993) 26 Cornell International Law Journal 133, 134.

scope and unsettled as to justification, and seem emerging rather than settled.[76]

The Court's reference to consensus in *Comingersoll* arguably accords with the observation that 'faced with a diversity of practice, the Court has sometimes acted positively in the interests of protecting human rights'.[77] It also bears out criticism that the Court's reliance on a purported consensus can lack sufficient evidence[78] and that it sometimes forges rather than reflects a common European standard.[79] The absence of general agreement among ECHR member states tells us, at any rate, that the Court's reliance on a common European standard regarding compensation for non-material loss by legal persons could not possibly have been a decisive argument.

The Court also refers to consent as a justification for its expansive decision in *Comingersoll*, an underappreciated factor in adjudication under the Convention but one in conformity with other international legal practice.[80] The Court observes that on at least two occasions Portugal had agreed to pay monetary compensation for non-pecuniary injury sustained by limited liability companies.[81] The cases in question were settled by the Committee of Ministers under the former ECHR regime, prior to its overhaul in 1998. The Court suggests that these instances of consent should have had a bearing on Portugal's position in the *Comingersoll* dispute.[82]

But consent could not have been decisive to the outcome in *Comingersoll.* The two cases settled by the Committee of Ministers had concerned privately held companies far more assimilable to individuals than Comingersoll S.A. Compensation may have been awarded in these cases as a consequence of non-material loss sustained not by the company itself but by its individual owners. Besides, settlement by the Committee of Ministers, whatever its legally binding character, differed as a form of dispute resolution from judgment by the

[76] Dannemann, *supra* n. 5, 388–9 (noting traces of this form of remedy in French, Belgian, Dutch, Greek and Swiss tort law). See also the country reports on Belgium, Spain, France and Germany in *Damages for Non-Pecuniary Loss in a Comparative Perspective* (W V Horton Rogers ed) (Vienna: Springer 2001), at 28, 49; 192, 221; 87, 105; and 109, 123 respectively. On England, see also *McGregor on Damages* (Harvey McGregor ed) (16th ed, London Sweet & Maxwell 1997) paras 1938–9.

[77] Harris, O'Boyle and Warbrick, *supra* n. 52, 10.

[78] Helfer, *supra* n. 75, 135; and Paul Mahoney 'Judicial Activism and Judicial Self-Restraint in the European Court of Human Rights: Two Sides of the Same Coin' (1990) 11 Human Rights Law Journal 57, 62–88.

[79] John G Merrills *The Development of International Law by the European Court of Human Rights* (Manchester: Manchester University Press 1993) 78–81.

[80] See, eg, *Lithgow and Others v United Kingdom*, judgment 8 July 1996 [Plenary Court] para 118.

[81] Resolution DH(96) 604 Human Rights, Application No. 18737/91, *Dias e Costa Lda. against Portugal*, adopted by the Committee of Ministers on 15 November 1996 at the 576th meeting of the Ministers' Deputies; and Application No. 31545/96, *Biscoiteria (Fabricio e Comercialização de Produtos Alimentarias), Lda. v Portugal*, Report of the Commission 20 May 1998 (unreported). Final resolution DH(99) 708 Human Rights, Application No. 31454/96, *Biscoiteria, Lda against Portugal*, adopted by the Committee of Ministers on 3 December 1999 at the 688th meeting of the Ministers' Deputies.

[82] *Comingersoll S. A. v Portugal*, judgment 6 April 2000, [Grand Chamber], Reports 2000-IV para 33.

Court.[83] The Committee, when exercising its former function, was not an international court with contentious jurisdiction but a political organ with only quasi-judicial authority. The reasons Portugal had for agreeing to the settlements were not necessarily the same as its reasons for complying with the jurisdiction of the Court. Again, arguments other than consent must have had a greater influence on the Court's reasoning and conclusion.

2. *The Court's pragmatism*

The Court's pragmatism is important for understanding *Comingersoll* and indeed Strasbourg adjudication as a whole.[84] The Court, it should be recalled, is a dispute-settlement body, not a legislative organ; it is naturally concerned with securing outcomes reasonable to all participants. It is, moreover, disinclined when settling disputes to have recourse to meticulous textual interpretation or to embark on a comprehensive discussion of its use of doctrinal sources.[85]

A significant pragmatist element in *Comingersoll* is the Court's reliance on the principle of effectiveness.[86] The Court observes that:

> . . . the Convention must be interpreted and applied in such a way as to guarantee rights that are practical and effective. Accordingly, since the principal form of redress which the Court may order is pecuniary compensation, it must necessarily be empowered, if the right guaranteed by Article 6 of the Convention is to be effective, to award pecuniary compensation for non-pecuniary damage to commercial companies, too.[87]

The effectiveness principle can easily facilitate expansive interpretation.[88] It has no exhaustive definition, as it is applied by the Court.[89] Sometimes its teleological component is underlined: the Court looks to the purpose of the Convention, which is often referred to as the effective protection of human rights.[90] Considering the ambivalent nature of the

[83] Peter Leuprecht 'The Protection of Human Rights by Political Bodies—the Example of the Committee of Ministers of the Council of Europe' in *Progress in the Spirit of Human Rights: Festschrift für Felix Ermacora* (Manfred Nowak, Dorothea Steurer and Hannes Tretter eds) (Kehl am Rhein: N P Engel 1988) 95.

[84] 'Pragmatism' is here used in the literal rather than philosophical sense. The possible similarity between the Court's methodology and the pragmatic school of legal philosophy seems a worthwhile subject of further research, but such an examination lies outside the scope of this article.

[85] Rudolf Bernhardt, *supra* n. 79, 65: 'The interpretation of treaties and of legal norms . . . is sometimes considered to be more an art than a procedure in which legal rules and principles are applied.'

[86] This is a well-known principle of treaty interpretation, and has always been regarded as integral to the interpretation of the ECHR, even prior to the Court's explicit reference to it: see Heinz Guradze *Die Europäische Menschenrechtskonvention. Kommentar* (Berlin/Frankfurt a.M. Vahlen 1968) 34. On the effectiveness principle as applied in the ECHR, see also Merrills, *supra* n. 79, 76.

[87] *Comingersoll S. A. v Portugal*, judgment 6 April 2000, [Grand Chamber], Reports 2000-IV para 35(2).

[88] Guradze, *supra* n. 86, 34, and van Dijk and van Hoof, *supra* n. 26, 74.

[89] *Botta v Italy*, judgment 24 February 1998, Reports 1998-I, para 33.

[90] ECHR Preamble 2nd recital, 'effective protection'. On purposive interpretation of the Convention more generally, see, eg, Harris, O'Boyle, and Warbrick, *supra* n. 52, 6–7.

'human rights' enshrined in the Convention, it seems more fruitful to recall in this regard that the Court, when seeking to support a broad interpretation of the Convention, has also emphasised the function of the effectiveness principle in securing observance of the rule of law.[91] The invocation of the principle of effectiveness may be seen more generally as corresponding to a protective need.[92] Several statements in *Comingersoll* show a Court concerned with the applicant's need for recompense. It appreciated that Comingersoll S.A. was unable to meet the requirements for pecuniary loss, yet was 'left in a state of uncertainty that justified making an award for compensation'.[93] The decision to award damages for non-pecuniary injury was, in other words, motivated by the Court's desire to fill a remedial void caused by the near impossibility of proffering sufficient evidence of pecuniary loss in cases where Article 6(1) has been violated. As seen above, this form of conciliatory application of Article 41 is not novel.

The effectiveness principle can also lead the Court to disregard reasoning based on theoretical constructs.[94] The Court has often stated that the Convention 'is intended to guarantee not rights that are theoretical and illusory but rights that are practical and effective'.[95] The Court in *Comingersoll* makes ample use of this aspect of the effectiveness principle. It pays little attention, in the event, to who the petitioner is (a legal person rather than an individual) or to how the remedy was traditionally conceived (the compensation of individuals' intangible harm).[96] Nor does it endorse the submission of the respondent government that there exists an intrinsic link between damages for non-pecuniary harm and the inherent faculties of the individual.[97] The Court states that non-pecuniary harm includes 'reparation for the anxiety, inconvenience and uncertainty caused by the violation, *and other non-pecuniary loss*'[98] and that '[n]on-pecuniary damage suffered by . . . companies may include heads of claims that are to a greater or lesser extent "objective" or "subjective" '.[99]

[91] *Golder v United Kingdom*, judgment 21 February 1975, Series A 18 para 34; and *Kjeldsen, Busk Madsen and Pedersen v Denmark*, judgment 7 December 1976, Series A 23 para 53.

[92] For details, Marius Emberland 'Corporations as "Third Parties" in ECHR Law' (2002) 13 European Business Law Review 389, 398.

[93] paras 30 and 36.

[94] Pieter van Dijk ' "Positive Obligations" Implied in the European Convention on Human Rights: Are the States Still the "Masters" of the Convention?' in *The Role of the Nation-State in the 21st Century. Human Rights, International Organisations and Foreign Policy. Essays in Honour of Peter Baehr* (Monique Castermans-Holleman, Fried van Hoof, and Jacqueline Smith eds) (Hague: Kluwer 1998) 17.

[95] *Airey v Ireland*, judgment 9 October 1979, Series A 32 para 24(2) is the first explicit use of it, but it relied on implied statements in *Belgian Linguistic case*, judgment 23 July 1968, Series A 6 paras 3–4, *Golder v United Kingdom*, judgment 21 February 1975, Series A 18 para 35 *in fine*; *Luedicke, Belkacem and Koç v Germany*, judgment 28 November 1978, Series A para 42; and *Marckx v Belgium*, judgment 13 June 1979, Series A 31 para 31.

[96] *Comingersoll S.A. v Portugal*, judgment 6 April 2000, [Grand Chamber], Reports 2000-IV para 32.

[97] *Comingersoll S.A. v Portugal*, judgment 6 April 2000, [Grand Chamber], Reports 2000-IV para 28(2).

[98] *Comingersoll S.A. v Portugal*, judgment 6 April 2000, [Grand Chamber], Reports 2000-IV para 29(3), emphasis added.

[99] *Comingersoll S.A. v Portugal*, judgment 6 April 2000, [Grand Chamber], Reports 2000-IV para 35(2).

The Court did not even see the distinction between pecuniary and non-pecuniary as necessarily a workable tool,[100] an element of pragmatism which finds reflection in other international legal discourse.[101]

The Court's pragmatism provided powerful support for an expansive reading of that provision to permit compensation for non-pecuniary injury suffered by entities. Arguably, pragmatics alone might explain the outcome of *Comingersoll*. The Court, however, relied on two other significant arguments, arguments which contribute in particular to the overall effect of *Comingersoll*—and to its inherent ambivalence.

3. *The dynamic nature of ECHR law*

One of the most powerful arguments adopted by the Court in *Comingersoll* appears almost unnoticed in the judgment. In one of its final paragraphs, the Court observes:

> *In the light of its own case-law* . . . the Court cannot . . . exclude the possibility that a commercial company may be awarded pecuniary compensation for non-pecuniary damage.[102]

The Court does not characterise this statement in *Comingersoll*. Two years later, however, the Court implied that it entailed an invocation of the principle of dynamic interpretation. In *Colas Est S. A. and Others v France*, the Court, in expanding the 'right to respect for one's . . . home' in Article 8—another provision previously thought to include only individuals within its protective scope—to encompass the business premises of limited liability companies, relied on *Comingersoll* in the following way:

> La Cour rappelle que la Convention est un instrument vivant à interpréter à la lumière des conditions de vie actuelle . . . S'agissant des droits reconnus aux sociétés par la Convention, il y a lieu de souligner que la Cour a déjà, au titre de l'article 41, reconnu le droit à réparation du préjudice moral subi par une société sous l'angle de l'article 6 § 1 de la Convention (voir arrêt *Comingersoll c. Portugal* [GC] n° 1 35382/97 §§33 à 35, CEDH 2000-IV, du 6 avril 2000). *Dans le prolongement de l'interprétation dynamique de la Convention*, la Cour considère qu'il est temps de reconnaître, dans certaines circonstances, que les droits garantis sous l'angle de l'article 8 de la Convention peuvent être interprétés comme incluant pour une société, le droit au respect de son siège social, son agence ou ses locaux professionnels . . . .[103]

[100] *Comingersoll S. A. v Portugal*, judgment 6 April 2000, [Grand Chamber], Reports 2000-IV para 29(4): 'In addition, if one or more heads of damage cannot be calculated precisely or if the distinction between pecuniary and non-pecuniary damage proves difficult, the Court may decide to make a global assessment . . .'

[101] See, eg, Malcolm N Shaw *International Law* (4th ed, Cambridge: CUP 1997) 462–3.

[102] *Comingersoll S. A. v Portugal*, judgment 6 April 2000, [Grand Chamber], Reports 2000-IV para 35(1), emphasis added.

[103] *Colas Est S. A. and Others v France*, judgment 16 April 2002 Reports 2002-III para 41, emphasis added. See John Temple Lang and Carlo Rizza 'The STE Colas Est and Others v. France case: European Court of Human Rights judgment of April 16, 2002' (2002) 23 European Competition Law Review 413.

A plausible interpretation of this passage is that the Court in 2002 saw the expansive or novel reading of Article 41 in *Comingersoll* as the result of dynamic interpretation of the Convention, and that the Court, on the basis of this particular example of dynamism, considered that the time had come to recognise that Article 8, too, should apply to corporate applicants.

The principle of dynamic (or evolutive) interpretation is one of the Court's most significant aids.[104] It is traditionally described as an interpretative tool which assumes that the ECHR is 'a living instrument, which must be interpreted in light of present-day conditions'.[105] What this primarily entails is that the extent of the Convention's provisions is not to be limited by the intentions of its framers but, rather, determined in the light of current demands.[106] The principle straddles the line between applying and changing ECHR law.[107]

The 'conditions' to which the Court refers are extraneous to its own judicial activity and correspond to a higher standard of fundamental rights awareness (and, conversely, a lower standard of tolerance for violations of such rights) in the Contracting States, as measured in their laws and in their societies more generally.[108] These external reference points are useful—especially, as in the case of Article 41's concept of 'just satisfaction', when the text is indeterminate—for legitimising the Court's use of a principle with an inherent potential for judicial activism.[109] The justifications usually invoked in support of the principle make it relatively uncontroversial, for example that it has a textual basis in the Preamble (the wording of which does give the impression of a forward-looking instrument);[110] that an up-to-date Convention cultivates public confidence

[104] See, eg, Rudolf Bernhardt 'Evolutive Treaty Interpretation, Especially of the European Convention on Human Rights' (1999) 42 German Yearbook of International Law 11; Olivier de Schutter: L'interpretation de la Convention européenne des droits de l'homme: un essai en démolition, in (1992) 70 Revue de droit international, de sciences diplomatiques, politiques, et socials 83, 85–7; and Søren Prebensen 'Evolutive Interpretation of the European Convention on Human Rights' in *Protection des Droits de l'Homme la perspective européenne: mélanges à la mémoire de Rolv Ryssdal* (Paul Mahoney ed) (Cologne: Heymann 2000) 1124. It is as explicitly relied upon as the Italian constitutional doctrine of the 'living constitution': on the latter, see, eg, Gustavo Zagrebelesky 'La doctrine du droit vivant' (1986) 2 Annuaire international de justice constitutionnelle 55.

[105] *Tyrer v United Kingdom*, judgment 25 April 1978, Series A 26, para 31.

[106] Rudolf Bernhardt speaks, *supra* n. 104, 69 of it as a method whereby 'the Convention must be interpreted and applied in accordance with present-day conditions in law and society, not with past convictions.'

[107] Mahoney, *supra* n. 78, 57.

[108] *Tyrer v United Kingdom*, judgment 25 April 1978, Series A 26 para 31. Bernhardt, *supra* n. 79, 69: 'This "dynamic" interpretation dispenses with consideration of the preparatory work and the intentions of the drafters of the treaty at least to the extent to which modern convictions and conditions have been substituted for those which existed in law and society at the time of the conclusion of the treaty'. Matthijs de Blois 'The Fundamental Freedom of the European Court of Human Rights' in *The Dynamics of the Protection of Human Rights in Europe. Essays in Honour of Henry G. Schermers, Volume III* (Rick Lawson and Matthijs de Blois eds) (Dordrecht: Nijhoff 1994) 35, 57 calls the principle the 'sociological' method of ECHR interpretation.

[109] Bernhardt, *supra* n. 111, 23. The principle is the corollary of historic interpretation, yet is not to be confused with establishing new rights, which remains the domain of the member states: see *Johnston and Others v Ireland*, judgment 18 December 1986 [Plenary Court], Series A 112 para 53.

[110] Cf. Preamble's 3rd recital ('maintenance and further realisation of human rights and fundamental freedoms') and 5th recital ('the first steps for the collective enforcement of certain of the rights stated in the Universal Declaration'). See Walter J. Ganshof van der Meersch 'Le caractère

and consequently state compliance;[111] that it injects a democratic element by reflecting social and legal currents in Europe; and that it conforms to the teleological approach taken to the Convention's interpretation, in that the protection of human rights cannot be sufficiently effective without the infusion of an element of dynamism.[112] The principle is ultimately stated to derive from the constitutional nature of the treaty. All constitutional instruments contain open-ended and vague provisions subject to a constant process of development, as only this can provide the long-term stability necessary in a constitution.[113]

Legal and social currents in Europe are not, however, the kind of dynamism to which the Court refers in *Comingersoll* when coming to the conclusion that Article 41 now includes compensation for non-material loss sustained by a limited liability company. Whatever the name attributed to the approach taken in *Comingersoll*, there is no doubt that the Court's reliance on 'its own case-law' as an argument for expanding the Convention's scope is a form of dynamism distinct from that normally seen in ECHR jurisprudence. It represents the principle of dynamic interpretation in transmuted form, a form which is largely overlooked in ECHR discourse.[114] It is dynamism, and an argument for judicial activism, which does not have as its reference point external and extraneous factors, but rather factors internal to the Court's adjudicatory business. The Court, in relying on 'its own case-law', in fact argues that the Convention should be interpreted expansively since the Court itself, in decisions prior to *Comingersoll*, had gradually favoured this conclusion without actually saying so. This mode of reasoning needs elucidation.

As discussed above, Comingersoll S.A.'s claim was considered by a Grand Chamber of the Court because it raised an issue of principle: this type of claim—for compensation for non-pecuniary harm suffered by a limited liability company—had, in other words, not been considered before. Nonetheless, the Court referred to 'its own case-law' as an argument for extending the provision's scope. The judgment, read in context, informs us that the 'case-law' in question consisted of three cases: *Vereinigung demokratischer Soldaten Österreichs and Gubi (VDSÖ) v Austria* of 1994, where the Court had seen nothing controversial about awarding compensation to a soldiers' association for non-material loss, even if, in

"autonome" des termes et la "marge d'appréciation" des gouvernements dans l'interprétation de la Convention européenne des Droits de l'Homme' in *Protecting Human Rights: The European Dimenstion. Studies in Honour of Gérard J Wiarda* (Franz Matscher and Herbert Petzold eds) (Cologne: Heymanns 1988) 201, 202.

[111] Mahoney, *supra* n. 78, 64.

[112] Constance Grewe 'Vergleich zwischen den Interpretationsmethoden europäischer Verfassungsgerichte und des Europäische Gerichtshofes für Menschenrechte' (2001) 61 Zeitschrift für ausländisches öffentliches Recht und Völkerrecht 459, 466–7.

[113] Grewe, *supra* n. 112, 466.

[114] Mahoney, *supra* n. 78, 77 makes note of the 'technique of achieving jurisprudential progress by making only minimal, incremental changes in the received body of Convention law' as a mode 'generally taken to be a manifestation of judicial restraint'.

the event, it opted for a declaration;[115] *Freedom and Democracy Party (ÖZDEP) v Turkey* of 1999,[116] where the Court had awarded monetary compensation for non-pecuniary harm to a political party on account of the suffering sustained by its individual members; and *Immobiliare Saffi v Italy*, also of 1999,[117] where the Court had decided not to explore the question further. None of these cases involved facts or legal issues directly analogous those in *Comingersoll*. Indeed, had the opposite been the case, there would have been no need for the Court to sit as a Grand Chamber in the latter. Prior case law was nonetheless applied as an independent argument in *Comingersoll* for reading the Convention extensively.

It is difficult to characterise exactly this method of progressive reasoning. All the same, it reflects accepted notions of adjudication and is not necessarily controversial. As Ronald Dworkin has explained with his 'chain-novel' metaphor, good adjudication is characterised by a progressive, case-by-case process in which every court decision that paves new ground looks ahead while being embedded in the legitimacy of past judgments.[118] The dynamism of *Comingersoll* is in part a consequence of the very nature of the international judicial process. International courts inevitably develop the law they are called upon to adjudicate.[119] The European Court of Human Rights, like any other international court, relies on past decisions of relevance to the matter at hand without adhering formally to a doctrine of precedent.[120] The unsettling aspect of the progressiveness of *Comingersoll* is, rather, that there is reason to question whether it actually represents reliance on past decisions as normally understood in ECHR discourse. As it is, the Court did not openly acknowledge this particular form of progressivism; rather, it dressed it up as the principle of dynamic interpretation. It may be that this special form of reasoning calls for justifications other than those normally marshalled in support of the principle of dynamic interpretation. These are issues which exceed the scope of the present article: they concern general methods of ECHR adjudication which call for comprehensive study. There is, however, a further problematic aspect of the progressive reasoning in *Comingersoll* which warrants special attention since it was discussed at length by the Court.

[115] *Comingersoll S. A. v Portugal*, judgment 6 April 2000, [Grand Chamber], Reports 2000-IV para 32(2) citing *Freedom and Democracy Party (ÖZDEP) v Turkey*, judgment 8 December 1999 [Grand Chamber], Reports 1999-VIII.

[116] *Comingersoll S. A. v Portugal*, judgment 6 April 2000, [Grand Chamber], Reports 2000-IV para 32 (3) citing *Vereinigung demokratischer Soldaten Österreichs and Gubi v Austria*, judgment 24 November 1994, Series A 302.

[117] *Comingersoll S. A. v Portugal*, judgment 6 April 2000, [Grand Chamber], Reports 2000-IV para 32(1) citing *Immobiliare Saffi v Italy*, judgment 28 July 1999 [Grand Chamber], Reports 1999-V.

[118] Ronald Dworkin *Law's Empire* (Cambridge, MA: Belknap Press 1986) 225–38.

[119] Grewe, *supra* n. 112, 466.

[120] On the use of precedent by the Court, see Luzius Wildhaber 'Precedent in the European Court of Human Rights' in *Protection of Human Rights: the European Dimension. Studies in Memory of Rolv Ryssdal* (Paul Mahoney ed) (Cologne: Heymanns 2000) 1529; and Merrills, *supra* n. 79, 12–16.

4. The relative significance of an individual substratum

The transmuted form of dynamism seen in *Comingersoll* was applied in a context in which it had not been relied on before: it was used as an argument for expanding an entitlement traditionally believed to cater for individual interests alone so as to include interests pertaining to entities as well. In general, when the Court applies the principle of dynamic interpretation or relies on past decisions as arguments for widening the scope of the Convention, it does so in matters that directly impinge upon individual human beings.[121] The physical person is the ECHR's primary concern. The protection of the interests of individuals *qua* individuals is its core objective. Non-physical persons have a legitimate place within the scope of the Convention, but structural factors render their place marginal when it comes to provisions aimed mainly at individual activity. In *Comingersoll*, the Court used a transmuted form of dynamism as a means for expanding the scope of Article 41 with the result that the provision now effectively encompasses all private activity.

This is not wholly uncontroversial. Indeed, this aspect of *Comingersoll* was contested by some of the judges themselves, who were divided over the relative significance of the applicant company's having an individual component or, borrowing a term occasionally used in German constitutional discourse, an individual *substratum*. The Court saw it as important that its expansive reading of Article 41 entailed, albeit implicitly, the protection of individual constituents within the company. But four judges, in a joint concurring opinion, saw an individual *substratum* as wholly irrelevant.

The Court considers the existence of an individual *substratum* to be a significant vehicle for its expansive interpretation, evidence which lies in its disapproval of the contrasting view presented in the joint concurring opinion.

In the joint concurring opinion, Judge Rozakis, who wrote the opinion, states:

> The Court . . . has . . . expanded its reasoning on awarding non-pecuniary compensation by taking into account, 'albeit to a lesser degree, the anxiety and inconvenience caused to the members of the management team'. It is obvious that in so doing the Court relies on the precedent of [*ÖZDEP*] to answer the submission of the Portuguese Government that non-pecuniary compensation in length of proceedings cases 'was to provide reparation for anxiety, the mental stress of having to wait for the outcome of the case and uncertainty . . . feelings [which] were peculiar to individuals and could under no circumstances entitle a company to compensation.

[121] Note, for instance, the gradual expansion of the extra-territorial application of Article 3, which started as a way to prevent the extradition of individuals facing the death penalty in the receiving state (see *Soering v United Kingdom*, judgment 7 July 1989, Series A 163) but which has now become—through reference to previous case law in analogous contexts—a way to keep individuals in the respondent state on account of the health risks involved in deporting them to countries with inadequate healthcare systems (see *D. v United Kingdom*, judgment 2 May 1997, Reports 1997-III).

I am not able to share the approach that by awarding compensation for non-pecuniary damages the Court intends, inter alia, to indemnify the company for the anxiety and inconvenience suffered by the members of the company's management team. I think that the application by analogy of the test in the ÖZDEP case to the present one is not correct. In that case, the legal person was a political party (which, by its nature, is a looser organisation) and the protected right in question was the freedom of association of the members of that party who established and organised it. Here the situation is different: the company is an independent living organism, protected as such by the legal order of the State concerned, and whose rights also receive autonomous protection under the . . . Convention . . . Although I accept that a number of provisions . . . may be inapplicable to companies or other juristic persons (for example, Articles 2 and 3), the great majority of them apply directly to such persons as autonomous legal entities deserving the protection of the Convention. I do not see why, in matters of compensation, the Court should be obliged to deviate, even partly, from such an approach and why it should be prevented from accepting, without any reservation, implied or otherwise, that a company may suffer non-pecuniary damage, not because of the anxiety or uncertainty felt by its human components, but because, as a legal person, in the society in which it operates, it has attributes, such as its own reputation, that may be impaired by acts or omissions of the State.[122]

This represents one of the most forceful calls for the wholesale inclusion of commercial entities within ECHR law when this is possible as a matter of interpretation. It takes the view that the company *qua* company, and not *qua* its individual constituents, is entitled to protection. The joint concurring opinion invokes the 'real entity' theory of legal personality, which sees the company as a social and organic fact of individual association but enjoying an identity distinguishable from, and constituting more than, its fluctuating membership.[123] This concept of the company could hardly have been contested by the Court: the theory has been influential for more than a hundred years. The bone of contention must instead be the nature and purpose of the ECHR. Essentially, the joint concurring opinion sees Article 41 and Article 6 as deriving primarily from the rule of law tradition, whereas the Court's judgment tends to view these provisions as deriving from the dignity inspired tradition of fundamental rights. *Comingersoll* thus reflects divergent views as to the nature and purpose of the Convention in the context of entities' entitlement to protection.

[122] *Comingersoll S.A. v Portugal*, judgment 6 April 2000, [Grand Chamber], Reports 2000-IV, Concurring opinion of Judge Rozakis joined by judges Sir Nicolas Bratza, Caflisch, and Vajić, paras 2 and 3.

[123] The theory has been attributed to Otto von Gierke's *Die Genossenschaftstheorie und die deutsche Rechtsprechung* (Berlin Weidmann 1887). It soon gained influence in Anglo-American legal thought through Otto von Gierke *Political Theories of the Middle Age* (trans Frederic W Maitland Cambridge CUP 1900) and Ernst Freund *The Legal Nature of Corporations* (Chicago: U Chicago Press 1897). A good account is given by Frederick Hallis *Corporate Personality. A Study in Jurisprudence* (Oxford: OUP 1930) 137–65.

E. BEYOND *COMINGERSOLL*: THE AMBIVALENT EXPANSION OF THE CONVENTION'S SCOPE

Comingersoll SA v Portugal is a landmark in the development of remedies under ECHR law.[124] It effectively signals an end to the almost impossible task of adducing sufficient evidence of pecuniary loss caused by violations of Article 6(1) in business settings. The loss in such cases can now be construed as non-pecuniary. This is not as such negative: it merely reflects a vision of ECHR protection as deriving from the principle of the rule of law.

The decision, however, has certain challenging implications, of which the combination of two is mentioned here.

Comingersoll has enhanced the economic incentive for entities, in particular businesses, to utilise the dispute-settlement mechanism in Strasbourg, leading to a veritable flood of remedial claims before the Court; and in many decisions rendered in reliance on *Comingersoll*, the Court has awarded companies and other private entities compensation for various forms of non-pecuniary harm.[125] The case has also influenced the Court's interpretation of other ECHR provisions sufficiently open-textured as to permit discussion of entities' status as beneficiaries. Most conspicuously in this regard, the Court in *Colas Est S.A. and Others v France* in 2002 found *Comingersoll's* dynamism to be an important argument in favour of an expansive reading of a term clearly pointing to the protection of human interests alone, namely the concept of 'home' in Article 8.[126] In the short term, all this merely serves to encourage litigation before the Court, increasing its already overburdened case-load—even if, in the long

[124] It might also prove useful for litigants before the European Court of Justice. In the only private complaint yet to have reached a discussion of the merits, the respondent party signalled the same principled doubt advanced by the Court prior to *Comingersoll*. See para 29 of Case T-52/96, *Sogecable SA v Commission*, order of the President of the Court of First Instance 12 July 1996, ECR 1996-II 797.

[125] Cases include *Grande Oriente d'Italia di Palazzo Giustinanini v Italy*, judgment 2 August 2001 paras 36–8; *Fertiladour S. A. v Portugal*, judgment 18 May 2000 (unreported) paras 27–30; *F. Spa v Italy*, judgment 9 November 2000 (unreported) paras 27–30; *M. Srl v Italy*, judgment 27 February 2001 (unreported) paras 27–30; *W.I.E. Snc v Italy*, judgment 27 February 2001 (unreported) paras 12–13; and *Tor di Valle Costruzioni Spa v Italy (nos. 1–7)*, judgments 9 November 2000 (unreported) paras 14–16; *Buffalo Srl v Italy*, judgment 27 February 2001 (unreported) paras 14–15; *LSI Information Technologies v Greece*, judgment 20 December 2001 (unreported) paras 38, 40–41; *Entreprises Meton et Etep v Greece*, judgment 21 March 2002 (unreported) paras 25–9; *Koncept-Conselho em Communicação e Sensibilizia de Públicos, Lda v Portugal*, judgment 31 October 2002 (unreported) paras 30–3; and S. A. *Sitram v Belgium*, judgment 15 November 2002 (unreported) paras 22–4 (all judgments on length of civil proceedings in violation of Article 6(1), legal uncertainty being the harm occasioned); *Markass Car Hire Ltd v Cyprus*, judgment 11 June 2002 (unreported) para 50; *Société Industrielle d'Entretien et de Services v France*, judgment 19 March 2002 para 17; *Société Comabat v France*, judgment 26 March 2002 (unreported) paras 17–19. See also *Alithia Publishing Company v Cyprus*, judgment 11 July 2002 (unreported) para 45, and *Oval Sprl v Belgium*, judgment 15 November 2002 (unreported) paras 20–2; *Colas Est SA and Others v France*, judgment 16 April 2002 (unreported) para 55.

[126] *Colas Est SA and Others v France*, judgment 16 April 2002 paras 40–2. The judgment is commented in detail in Marius Emberland 'The Protection of Corporate Privacy under ECHR Article 8: *Colas Est SA and Others v France* before the European Court of Human Rights' (2003) 25 Michigan Journal of International Law (forthcoming).

term, the ensuing volume of cases and awards under Article 41 might eventually lead states to comply with the Convention, which might in turn reduce the need for private litigants to make use of the Strasbourg system.

Secondly, while the subsequent case law demonstrates the vitality of *Comingersoll*, it does so without directly addressing the divergent views expressed in the case as to the relevance of an individual *substratum*. Some subsequent decisions can be interpreted as favouring the judgment of the Court,[127] while others tend to keep open the possibility of endorsing the joint concurring opinion.[128] The underlying rationale for the ability of companies and other entities to be awarded compensation for moral prejudice remains unresolved. The disagreement's wider implications for the interpretation of other provisions remain obscure. The law of the ECHR, and potential parties to Strasbourg proceedings, would benefit from a clarification of this issue. So would international legal practice beyond Strasbourg, where the issue of compensation for immaterial loss is only infrequently encountered.[129]

Perhaps more importantly, *Comingersoll* raises the question of whether the Court has embarked on a new form of judicial activism. The belief in the inevitable expansion of the Convention has the capacity (as it did in *Comingersoll*) to prevail over profound disagreement within the Court as to the nature and purpose of ECHR protection. The judgment and the influence it has exerted give the impression of a Court itching for the continuous evolutionary development of fundamental rights law without being in agreement as to why. This would probably be less problematic if the development were for the direct benefit of individual human beings. But the status of entities under the ECHR is more troublesome and the expansion of the Convention's scope in this regard might not be as favourably received. This is something for the Court to keep in mind. It needs constantly to maintain its legitimacy by balancing the competing demands of individuals and entities, on the one hand, and sovereign states, on the other—and all in the shadow of an ever increasing caseload. *Comingersoll* calls for vigorous and open discussion within the Court of the nature of its dynamism and the relevance of an individual *substratum*. It can only be hoped that such discussion takes place when the Court is faced in future with expanding the scope of provisions traditionally reserved, or believed to be reserved, for individuals. At its most essential, it is a question of the nature and purpose of the ECHR.

[127] See, eg, *Koncept-Conselho em Communicação e Sensibilizia de Públicos, Lda v Portugal*, judgment 31 October 2002 (unreported) paras 30–3, which merely cites § 36 of *Comingersoll*, where the Court relies on the existence of an individual component.

[128] See, eg, *Colas Est SA and Others v France*, judgment 16 April 2002 (unreported) para 55, where publicly held limited liability companies were awarded compensation for non-pecuniary harm which only they themselves had suffered.

[129] Examples of a favourable approach include ICSID Case No. ARB/77/2, *Ltd Benvenuti et Bonfati srl v People's Republic of Congo*, award 8 August 1980, paras 3.95 (1982) 21 International Legal Materials 740, 761–2; and ICSID Case No. ARB/82/1, *Société Ouest-Africaine des Bétons Industriels (SOABI) v Republic of Senegal*, award 25 February 1988, paras 6–21–6.22 (1992) 17 ICCA Yearbook 42, 61.

Jurisdiction of International Tribunals, By CHITTHARANJAN E. AMERASINGHE, The Hague/London/New York: Kluwer Law International, 2003. LXI + 881 pp. £135.00.

Recent history has witnessed serious changes in the field of international judicial jurisdiction. In particular, the proliferation of international tribunals has taken place; more tribunals are established to deal with specific types of disputes, and some tribunals assume certain powers on the basis of broad interpretation of their consensual mandate. The parallel functioning of different tribunals often provokes thoughts as to the similarities and differences between them in terms of their legal nature and jurisdictional background, as well as in terms of conflict between their jurisdictions.

The literature on international law is rich in terms of writings on this subject, but a comprehensive examination of this problem is quite rare and yet important. In this regard, the monograph by C Amerasinghe is a timely response to such doctrinal need. The monograph justifies its title by examining certain general aspects of international judicial jurisdiction, such as the principle of consent and *compétence de la compétence*, admissibility of claims, as well as the issues of jurisdiction of specific tribunals, including the International Court of Justice, the European Court of Human Rights, arbitral tribunals of the ICSID, international administrative tribunals and the European Court of Justice. The author is truly innovative in his treatment of issues like jurisdiction vis-à-vis remedies, incidental jurisdiction and jurisdiction to reopen cases (Chapters 11 to 13), as a systematic treatment of these issues is not a frequent occurrence in contemporary doctrine. Due to this originality and depth of analysis, his book is entitled to claim a leading role in the field.

Each topic included is examined by the author in a detailed way, and in his attempt to clarify some general notions such as the principle of consent or *compétence de la compétence*, the author makes a useful analysis of the practice of different tribunals, which is helpful in seeing how these concepts operate in practice. The chapters on specific tribunals are also quite detailed and thought-provoking. It is particularly welcome that the author engages in imaginative treatment of certain issues in their context, as such an approach is necessary to understand international judicial jurisdiction in terms of promoting the progressive development of the international legal order. Thus, for instance, the author examines the issue of jurisdictional reservations in terms of the general doctrine of *compétence de la compétence* and *clause contraire* (145–54). The result of such an approach is to show that the issue of reservations is not a free-standing one, and its outcome may well be dependent on some wider jurisdictional issues and concepts. Such a systemic view is always necessary to understand the nature of international judicial jurisdiction.

The monograph advances a quite original view on *jus cogens* in relation to the jurisdiction of international tribunals, suggesting that certain principles, for example those relating to the judicial nature or proper constitution of tribunals, are part of *jus cogens* and no adjudication can fail to conform to such principles (pp. 222, 230). This provokes thoughts as to the nature of *jus cogens*, which consists more probably of substantive norms, such as the prohibition of aggression, genocide, or torture, than of structural norms, such as *pacta sunt servanda* or the judicial character of international tribunals. On the other hand, the requirements as to the judicial character or proper constitution of international tribunals could also mean not that States cannot, by their agreements, establish dispute settlement bodies which lack one or another feature of tribunals, such as the power to take binding decisions or *compétence de la compétence,* but rather that an organ established in such a way would not be a court or tribunal; or that once States have established a tribunal, it would inherently possess certain powers necessary for the exercise of the judicial function. The problem thus appears to relate to interpretation, as well as to categorisation of concepts, rather than to the hierarchy of norms as a constraint on the contractual freedom of states. In fact, what a tribunal would be expected to do, for instance in case of a dispute as to its *compétence de la compétence*, if such power is not expressly provided for, is not to declare its constituent instrument void for its conflict with *jus cogens*, but to assume that it inherently possesses the power to decide on its jurisdiction. It could also be said that the rule requiring proper constitution of an international tribunal is not part of *jus cogens*, because a State affected by the judgment of an improperly constituted tribunal can later consent to such judgment or acquiesce to it. In any case, to refer to *jus cogens* in such contexts is interesting and may well attract further attention in doctrine.

On the other hand, *jus cogens* could be relevant in terms of judicial jurisdiction as a body of substantive rules, thus generating a duty of tribunals to adopt specific judicial policies or exercise their powers in a specific way, and this issue can no longer be ignored. It is an important question whether tribunals may use their powers in a way to treat *jus cogens* as *jus dispositivum*. This question would be relevant in terms of remedial jurisdiction and judicial actions *proprio motu*. Can tribunals reach an outcome contrary to *jus cogens* merely because this is warranted in terms of the parties' submissions? The author does not specifically address this question. However, the issue of the *non ultra petita* principle which is dealt with seems to be related to this issue. The author understands the principle in a blanket way, meaning that a tribunal cannot award a remedy other than, or more than, requested (pp. 422–3). But could the same hold true if the litigation in question involves a serious breach of *jus cogens* such as aggression or large-scale torture? Are tribunals entitled in such cases to follow the will of the parties blindly? Situations could be imagined where, in a case involving illegal territorial acquisition, a tribunal is asked by parties just to pronounce on the existence of wrongfulness, or award monetary compensation. It is clear that what international law peremptorily requires in such cases is *restitutio in integrum*, and it is not at all clear if a tribunal would be entitled to neglect this peremptory requirement just because parties have so asked. Similar concerns could arise in terms of human rights and humanitarian law violations, and it is relevant to ask whether there are certain norms whose effect cannot be set aside by agreements between States, including agreements to make a tribunal to award certain remedies but not others.

It would be better if the monograph had a wider coverage. In particular it does not satisfactorily examine the jurisdictional background and practice of organs like the Inter-American Commission and Inter-American Court of Human Rights. The jurisprudence of these organs is highly relevant as they have elaborated on many crucial issues of jurisdiction, admissibility, interim measures, discontinuance and remedial competence, and laid down original approaches and further developed general international law standards, particularly from the point of view of challenging some implications of the so-called traditional consensual approach to international jurisdiction. A similar view could perhaps be reiterated in terms of international criminal tribunals, and a special focus on arbitral tribunals in classical sense would also be desirable in terms of their development of jurisdictional principles. Therefore, the focus on these judicial organs should be a necessary element in any attempt to examine the nature and limits of international judicial jurisdiction.

Some structural factors must also be mentioned. The book includes no concluding chapter, which would be useful in terms of a general assessment as to where we stand now. Furthermore, it includes no bibliography. But despite these shortcomings, and some points of criticism, his book is a valuable, original, comprehensive, and timely addition to existing literature. It will be useful to those who are interested in this field, and is likely to retain its relevance for quite some time to come.

ALEXANDER ORAKHELASHVILI

The Margin of Appreciation Doctrine and the Principle of Proportionality in the Jurisprudence of the ECHR. By Yutaka Arai-Takahashi. Antwerp: Intersentia, 2002. xiii 300 pp. €70.

This interesting book is a development of the author's 1998 doctoral thesis written at the University of Cambridge. The scope of the book has been widened to encompass the principle of proportionality and the case law of the full-time European Court of Human Rights.

Dr Arai-Takahashi begins by defining the margin of appreciation doctrine as '. . . the latitude a government enjoys in evaluating factual situations and in applying the provisions enumerated in international human rights treaties.' (at p. 2) He traces its origins to the domestic public law of civil law states, including France and Germany. Under the European Convention on Human Rights the doctrine was first applied by the former European Commission of Human Rights to allow a respondent State some discretion in complying with the derogation requirements of Article 15 (in *Greece v UK (Cyprus case)*, No 176/56, (1958–9) 2 Ybk 174). This approach was endorsed by the Court in *Ireland v UK*, A.25 (1978). The author considers that the major case in the expansion of the doctrine was *Handyside v UK*, A.24 (1976), because '[b]y placing the doctrinal premise in a general exercise of "balancing", which is considered "inherent" in the adjudication of the Convention, the Strasbourg organs have justified their extension of the doctrine to all Convention rights with the exception of four non-derogable rights (Articles 2, 3, 4 and 7).' (at p. 8).

The author detects two meanings of proportionality within the case law of the Strasbourg institutions. First a general requirement of fair balance between the rights of individuals and the interests of society and secondly a proportionate balance must be achieved between the means employed by States and the aims they pursue. He does not believe that the Strasbourg jurisprudence regarding this concept is as refined as that articulated by the European Court of Justice. Nevertheless, he identifies a number of specific principles utilised by the Strasbourg organs to determine if a proportionate balance has been achieved in specific circumstances. These include 'the less restrictive alternative doctrine' (*i.e.* requiring States to adopt measures which are the least burdensome for individuals), 'the comparative method' (*i.e.* having regard to how other member States deal with the same situation) and 'the evolutive/dynamic method' (*i.e.* interpreting Convention rights in accordance with contemporary social and legal attitudes).

The bulk of the work, comprising nine chapters, is devoted to an examination of the case law created by the former Commission, original Court and the current full-time Court. The author finds evidence of a certain discretion being accorded to States in applying the enumerated grounds for deprivation of liberty permitted by Article 5 (at p. 31). Together with 'an intense standard of proportionality' governing restrictions on the equality of arms principle found in Article 6 (at p. 58). Whereas he concludes that variable standards of proportionality have been used in respect of Article 8 (at p. 91). Because of the crucial role of freedom of expression in democratic societies the author discovers that the Strasbourg organs have generally been reluctant to recognise a wide margin of appreciation for States under Article 10. The exception being in disputes concerning matters of morals, where the Strasbourg institutions have tended to defer to national standards (at p. 136). Likewise, Dr Arai-Takahashi observes that the Strasbourg organs have accorded States a broad margin of appreciation when interfering with property rights under Article 1 of Protocol No. 1 (at p. 164). Such an approach has recently been vividly demonstrated by a united Grand Chamber in the just satisfaction judgment concerning the *Case of the Former King of Greece and Others v Greece* (judgment of 28 November 2002). The Court held that full compensation for the dispossession, authorised by a democratic parliament, of the real and personal property held by a former royal family was not required. As with other forms of public interest expropriations (for example, the nationalisation of industries: see *Lithgow v UK*, A. 102 (1986)) the Court granted national authorities considerable latitude to determine what measures were appropriate when replacing a monarchy with a republican constitution.

The final section of the book is composed of three chapters in which the author explores the principle of proportionality and undertakes a study of the policy grounds favouring a wide margin of appreciation (such as issues closely associated with State sovereignty, like domestic electoral law) and those encouraging a narrower deference to national determinations (for example prohibiting gender discrimination). In his final chapter Dr Arai-Takahashi seeks to consider the justification of the margin of appreciation doctrine. He concludes that its '. . . only defensible rationale during *and after* the process of integration is to enable the Strasbourg Court to provide endorsement of the maintenance of cultural diversity, ensuring to the citizens of Europe the means to articulate and practice their preferred values within a multi-cultural democracy.' (at p. 249)

This work provides a comprehensive analysis of the relevant case law and the tensions between rigorous or restrained review by the Court. Whilst the diversity of, frequently conflicting, policy factors influencing the Court means that it is not always an easy task to predict how the Court will apply the margin of appreciation doctrine (*e.g.* the Grand Chamber's united refusal to continue to accord the British government a margin of appreciation as to whether post-operative transsexuals' new identities should be legally respected in *Christine Good-win v UK,* judgment of 11 July 2002) the author has considerably enhanced our understanding of this contentious topic.

Alastair Mowbray

Non-State Actors in International Relations. Edited by B. Arts and B. Reinalda. *Aldershot: Ashgate,* 2001. 352 pp. £47.50.

Originating from three workshops held in The Netherlands during 1999 and 2000, this edited collection is the first in a series of texts dealing with non-State actors. This particular volume seeks to examine the role and impact of non-State actors on the international plane from an inter-disciplinary perspective. It is aimed at academics, practitioners and students in the spheres of international law, politics and governance.

The book is divided into four parts with the first two parts addressing theoretical issues and the third and fourth parts focusing on empirical studies. Part I broadly describes the relevant theoretical approaches adopted by the various disciplines in relation to non-State actors and includes a useful definitional chapter. The term non-State actor is widely defined and includes, among others, the traditional NGO, Inter-Governmental Organisations, Transnational Corporations, and even International Criminal Organisations and the collection aims to examine the similarities between the various categories of non-state actors. Chapter 3 by Bas Arts reflects on the increasingly blurred public-private divide and asks to what extent non-State actors are institutionalised within international policy making. It concludes that non-State actors have played a meaningful role since the 1970s and 'policy arrangements' between public and private actors will continue to increase. The international law chapter considers the interesting subject of legal personality of non-State actors, but is somewhat arbitrary in its treatment of legal theory, drawing attention only to legal positivism, pluralism, functionalism, and feminist legal theory.

Parts III and IV of the collection provide some valuable empirical studies of non-State actors, including an interesting essay by Anton Weenik on the Russian Mafiya (*Sic*) which examines the argument that despite the obvious differences between conventional NGOs and organised crime groups they are both essentially private entities and therefore could be described as 'non-governmental'. The essay concludes that despite the private and international aspects of Russian Mafiya activities, it would be unhelpful to categorise them as NGOs particularly as there is no evidence that there is any attempt at political influence. Several assumptions are made in this essay; so for example, the author argues that if criminal organisations are classified as NGOs 'we would soon find ourselves searching for a new term for the good old politically-correct private organisation.' On this analysis, transnational corporations would be excluded from the taxonomy and it is submitted that such an over-rigid adherence to labels does nothing to address the difficult questions which arise from the widely-defined participation of non-State actors in the international arena. The purpose of the volume is to question 'whether non-State actors matter?' In this context, illegitimate behaviour can and does have 'unintended impact' on an international level as the editors note.

Other essays in this section of the book look at the political role and influence of NGOs and transnational corporations in the formation of international environmental policy and regulation. The essay on environmental NGOs rather interestingly concludes that historically NGOs have been 'more influential than the business community' albeit with the qualification: 'at least as far as *observable* . . . is influence's concerned.' This is based on the assertion that corporations have traditionally tended to focus their attentions on national environmental policy and on international economic matters. The subsequent essay by Ans Kolk describes the way that business attitudes to international environmental issues have changed in recent years as witnessed by the creation of a variety of business associations which specifically represent disparate corporate environmental interests at the international level, including the Global Climate Coalition, the International Climate Change Partnership, the International Chamber of Commerce, and the Business Council for a Sustainable Energy Future.

Does the book succeed in its stated aim of transcending 'traditional disciplinary and organisational boundaries?' To a certain extent; however, there is a clear emphasis on policy issues and much less reference to legal regulation. This may be due to the fact that the majority of the contributors are political and social scientists. Whilst the editors acknowledge that the collection in no way offers a true inter-disciplinary approach, it seems that the chapters solely reflect the specific discipline without any real attempt at integration with other fields. Nevertheless, this is an interesting and timely collection which addresses important issues.

SORCHA MACLEOD

Principles of Direct and Superior Responsibility in International Humanitarian Law. By ILIAS BANTEKAS. Manchester: Manchester University Press, 2002. 150 pp. + index. £40.

In his Foreword, Hans-Peter Gasser, then editor of the *International Review of the Red Cross*, commented that this book 'is an invaluable contribution to a better understanding of the role that criminal law can play in efforts to enhance respect for the rights of victims of violence and war.' In the Preface Dr Bantekas describes his aim in writing the book is 'to identify the criminal elements of international humanitarian law . . . without losing sight of the passionate interaction between national and international law [which is] reflected throughout this book.' By tackling both the liability of the individual actor and his superior during an armed conflict Dr Bantekas has chosen a logical approach. His work displays a thorough analysis of all the relevant authorities.

The book contains five chapters. The headings for each are respectively 'punishment in warfare and the application of law'; 'forms of direct criminal responsibility'; 'ascertainment of superior status in international humanitarian law';'the substantive law of superior responsibility', and 'individual responsibility in internal armed conflicts'. From this brief synopsis it can be seen that only chapters three and four deal directly with the nature of superior orders. These chapters are very good indeed and take the reader into the often unclear world of who is, in fact, the superior and whether a particular individual could, in reality, have prevented breaches of international humanitarian law, especially if he or she is a civilian. In forming his conclusions the author has paid careful attention to the decisions (and reasoning) of the ICTY and the ICTR (along with previous trials).

A danger in considering the liability of the superior from the basis of the decisions of war crimes trials alone is that the influence of the commander's own military structures can be overlooked. Does he have, for instance, legal advice available to him when an order is being considered? Does he follow the advice given? Does he incorporate clear limits of his subordinates' action in rules of engagement? A commander who can answer all these questions in the affirmative is less likely to attract any criminal liability to himself. Indeed, a legal adviser to a commander is likely to err on the side of safety which will, if the advice is accepted, give greater protection to those with whom the commander's troops come into contact. This, it might be argued, is one of the principal benefits to a State of implementing Article 82 of Additional Protocol II, 1977. The role of the legal adviser to the commander was not well established, for instance during World War II, and reference to decisions of war crimes trials from that conflict are likely to be atypical in modern international armed conflicts.

A further difficulty in making a commander responsible in many military structures is the unwillingness to continue with an investigation where it is foreseeable that prosecution of a middle-ranking commander could lead to an implication that higher ranking commanders have also failed (often in different ways) to prevent breaches of international humanitarian law taking place. This is not a problem where the commander concerned is within the jurisdiction of an international tribunal, but it can be where enforcement of command responsibility is being carried out within the armed forces concerned. To some extent this problem may well be ameliorated in respect of States party to the Rome Statute 1998 through the actions of the prosecutor of the International Criminal Court in deciding whether a particular case is admissible before the Court.

Whilst chapters one and two show the development of individual criminal liability and the forms of committing war crimes, topics dealt with in other works, they do have the advantage of fitting logically within the total structure of the book. Chapter five, dealing with non-international armed conflict, shows the development of individual criminal liability in this type of conflict. Dr Bantekas might have considered more fully the effect of Article 8(2)(c) and (e) of the Rome Statute 1998 on the jurisprudence developed by the ICTY and the ICTR (p. 143). This chapter might also have included an analysis of how the principles of superior responsibility developed in chapters three and four could apply to organised armed groups (as compared with the armed forces of a State).

This book will prove useful to all those who want to understand the principles (and much of the details) of criminal responsibility in international humanitarian law. Serious scholars of the subject may well find the chapters dealing with the criminal liability of the superior to be the most stimulating and will have cause to be grateful to Dr Bantekas for his thorough analysis of this topic.

PETER ROWE

For an Effective Right to Adequate Food: Proceedings of the International Seminar on 'The Right to Food: A Challenge for Peace and Development in the 21st Century' Edited by MARCO BORGHI and LETIZIA BLOMMESTEIN. Fribourg: University Press, 2002, 398 pp. No price stated.

The 'right to food' was first articulated in the Universal Declaration of Human Rights, Article 25 of which provides that '[e]very one has the right to a standard of living adequate for the health and well-being of himself and his family, including food, clothing, housing and medical care and necessary social services.' Efforts were subsequently made to make the right to food a stronger feature of international human rights law, in particular within the framework of the International Covenant on Economic, Social, and Cultural Rights of 1966 (Articles 2, 11). More recently, the World Food Summit in 1996 stimulated further international legal activity on the right to food, including the adoption of an International Code of Conduct on the Right to Food in 1997 by non-governmental organizations and General Comment No. 12 on the Right to Adequate Food by the United Nations Committee on Economic, Social, and Cultural Rights in 1999.

Despite these formulations, concern lingers that this right remains ineffective for people in many countries around the world. *For an Effective Right to Adequate Food* confronts this concern and seeks to analyze some of the ways to make the right to food an *effective* right in international and national legal systems.

The book's Introduction contains two contributions that focus attention on moving from the normative appeal of the right to food to substantive action to see the right advanced. Five parts then follow, each focused on a different aspect of advancing the agenda on the right to food. Part One addresses the impact of the World Food Summit in 1996. Part Two considers the right to food and international organizations, including the Food and Agriculture Organization (FAO) and the World Trade Organization (WTO). Part Three examines the International Code, including the Code's synergy with General comment No. 12. Part Four analyzes the contribution groups within civil society—e.g., NGOs, banks, and universities—can make to the implementation of the right to food through the International Code of Conduct and other mechanisms. Part Five probes common strategies for the future and challenges the political will of nations to make the right to food effective on a global basis.

The book ends with concluding remarks and recommendations and contains as annexes the test of the International Code and General Comment No. 12. The thirty-four contributors represent a diverse range of occupations and perspectives, including national judges, governmental officials, and staff members of international organizations (e.g., FAO, WTO, and UNESCO).

The contributions succeed in communicating the fact that hunger and malnutrition remain global concerns of the highest order. The argument that the strategy needed to fight these concerns should be based in an *effective right to adequate food* is also comprehensively and often passionately made. The emphasis on a 'right to food' confronts challenges, both substantive and in terms of its implementation, and the book contains a range of view on both fronts.

Substantively, at least three approaches to the right to food can be discerned in the contributions. In their foreword, the editors assert that the 'right to food is the most sensitive and the most ethically significant of human rights'; indeed in their view this is 'incontestable' (p. x). This approach makes the right to food the most important human right in the calendar. A second approach is more traditional, focusing on the right to food as a progressively achievable economic or social right. The contributions that touch on

General Comment No. 12 reflect this perspective. The third approach interprets the right to food as drawing its significance in international law from the right to life, traditionally viewed as a civil and political right.

The three visions of the right to food raise fundamental questions. The right to food can hardly be at once the most important human right and derivative of some other human right The right to health cannot be a 'self-executing right that the citizen possesses' (as Marco Borghi claims (p. 230)) and a right that governments can only progressively realise according to their level of economic development, as Article 2 of the International Convenant on Economic. Social and Cultural Rights seems to presuppose. Nor is the conceptual tension between 'food security' and the 'right to food' adequately explored, although both concepts are frequently used in the book.

The book suffers from the lack of one or more authors to cast at least a sceptical eye on the right to food, philosophically and legally. The closest the book comes is the contribution by Frank Wolter on 'The WTO and the Right to Food' (pp. 119–130): he presents the importance of having access to adequate food as less of a right than a means for sustainable economic development. Given the perceived ineffectiveness of talking in terms of a right to food, the very concept of such a right may be more problematic than many of the contributions suggest.

In terms of implementation, the contributions in the book also fail to ask and answer central questions that the right to food raises. Many of these questions, such as the justiciability of the right, are not new—they have plagued the development of economic, social, and cultural rights in general. Although the book's theme is the *effective* right to food, most authors attempt either to justify the right to food as a fundamental human right or to present the suffering the lack of such right causes around the world. The linkage of the right to food to the right to life is one effort to provide a way to make the right to food justiciable in national court systems, but whether this approach will prevail in international human rights law is questionable. The book highlights the obligations of States to 'respect, protect, and fulfil'—issues common to most economic, social, and cultural rights; but this perspective does not appear to offer significant prospects for transforming the right to food from rhetoric to reality.

In addition, many of the arguments in favour of an effective right to food seem to be based on the premise that States are democratic and have accepted the relevant treaties containing the right to food. Correlations between non-democratic forms of government and levels of hunger and malnutrition are not seriously explored. Most (but not all) countries that can be considered in significant violation of the right to food have non-democratic governments with judicial systems that do not enjoy independence. In political contexts in which the people have no voice in how they are governed, political leaders are not accountable to the people, and the courts do not distribute impartial justice, what space is there for the right to food to be made effective in national or international law?

In his final comments, Pierre Spitz argues that the answer to the dilemma posed by the ineffectiveness of the right to food involves 'a conscious commitment of political will by countries in formulating a positive strategy for the realisation of the right to adequate food in their territories and by binding themselves to national framework legislation' (p. 365). The contributions in this book may possibly encourage people to work to strengthen the right to food in national and international law; and to that extent the book possesses value. Its weaknesses; including its unwillingness to challenge the 'right to food' conceptually and to confront more forthrightly the difficulties of implementing such a right, suggest that much work remains to be done to make the right to food an effective instrument in the elevation of human dignity around the world.

AYE HLA PHYU

The European Union as an Actor in International Relations. Edited by ENZO CANNIZZARO. The Hague: Kluwer Law International, 2002. xiv + 345 pp.£72.50, €115.

This volume is a collection of edited essays, in both English and French, which were first presented in April 2001 as reports at a symposium organised under the auspices of the two Italian universities of Macerata and Camerino. The purpose of the volume is to provide a study 'on the foreign-relations power of the European Union and its impact on the sovereignty of the Member States'[1] While the title may give the impression that this volume approaches the issue through the prism of International Relations, as almost all of the contributors are academic or practising lawyers it comes as no surprise that all of essays are written from a legal perspective. The general topic which this volume is concerned with has already been subjected to a significant amount of academic commentary, much of it of the highest quality. Collections edited by Dashwood and Hillion,[2] Kronenberger[3] and Koskenniemi,[4] with both of the latter by the same publisher as the volume under review, have all been published relatively recently. This is not to mention the abundance of journal articles, both from the formative years of the Community legal order and the more recent re-examination of aspects of it. The volume under review is thus, in many senses, seeking to find its own niche among an already burgeoning literature. In this respect it achieves some of its objectives. Some, but not all, of the essays discuss issues which have either been relatively neglected or provide a reconsideration of practice and theory and an overview of some of the commentaries that already exist. Gaja's essay on the role of the ECJ in the interpretation of Community agreements is an example. Others deal with issues which have naturally been already extensively discussed elsewhere. Baratta's essay on the overlap in competence between the EC and CFSP, while very good in terms of quality and insights, is an example of this. As is to be expected in a work of this nature, the quality of the essays does differ. The standard of the discussion in most of them, however, is such that this collection can be considered to be a valuable and, as importantly, relatively up to date discussion of the issues involved.

The volume is divided into two quite distinct parts, each of which is then subdivided into seven components. Part One is concerned with the internal decision-making procedures of the European Union as they relate to its international or external relations and some of the legal issues that arise as a consequence. Thus it includes discussion of: the decision-making processes of the EC in external relations; the decision-making processes of the CFSP; issues of competence and the overlap in powers between the EC and EU; economic and monetary union and external relations; democratic control of international relations; the role played by the ECJ in interpreting Community powers relating to Community Agreements; and a theoretical assessment of the nature of the EU's foreign relations law.

Part Two deals with legal issues which arise from the relationship between the Union and international law. In Part Two each of the seven components is composed of a general essay, three of which are then supplemented by a number of more specific essays. Each general essay deals with an identified issue and provides analysis and an overview. The supplementary essays discuss in detail a specific issue within the ambit of the general essay. Thus Tomuschat provides, in the general essay, a very good overview discussion

[1] Introduction, p. xiii.

[2] A. Dashwood and C. Hillion (eds.), *The General Law of EC External Relations*, (London, Sweet & Maxwell, 1999).

[3] V. Kronenberger, (ed.), *The European Union and the International Legal Order: Discord or Harmony?* (The Hague, Kluwer, 2001).

[4] M. Koskenniemi (ed.), *International Law Aspects of the European Union*, (The Hague, Martinus Nijhoff, 1997).

of the responsibility in international law of the Union for its acts, with the supplementary essay by Neframi examining the responsibility of the Community and Member States under mixed agreements. Similarly, Paasivirta and Rosas aim to provide an analytic framework for discussing certain punitive Union acts, such as sanctions and countermeasures, whereas the supplementary essay by Palchetti attempts to examine the very tricky subject of EU reactions to breaches of obligations *erga omnes*, an issue which has not, as far as I know, been examined in the literature before. At times, however, the allocation of main and supplementary essays looks rather odd. Thus Marchisio's main essay on the'EU's Membership in International Organisations' is supplemented by two short but very good essays on relations between the EC and the ILO and the EU and the OSCE respectively. The following general essay, however, by Professor Treves, a judge at the International Tribunal for the Law of the Sea, is on the relationship between the EC and the Law of the Sea Convention. This essay would have sat (and this is not a reflection of its quality but a question of structure), more comfortably as a supplementary essay to Marchisio's. As the introduction notes, however, the supplementary essays have been written by younger scholars and the general reports by 'distinguished EU and International law scholars'. The overall balance of the book would not have been affected, however, by Treves' essay being supplementary to Marchisio's, or by Part Two of the book only having six general essays. In terms of structure and flow this approach would have been preferable.

The omission of certain issues is also unfortunate. In his introduction Cannizzaro discusses traditional notions of sovereignty and statehood and how the Union and its nature may constitute a formidable challenge to legal research and thinking in this field. Yet the essay, by Petersmann, that supposedly brings all the themes developed in the volume together entitled 'International Activities of the European Union and Sovereignty of Member States' deals with the issue almost exclusively from a Community/Union Law perspective, and not a Public International Law one. Yet, it is a discussion from the latter perspective that currently would be more welcome. These grumbles, however, are relatively minor. This volume of essays, alongside those collections mentioned above, provide a very useful starting point for anyone wishing to further investigate, from either a Union or International Law perspective, the relationship between the two legal orders.

URFAN KHALIQ

The International Law Commission's Articles on State Responsibility. Introduction, Text and Commentaries. By JAMES CRAWFORD. Cambridge: Cambridge University Press, 2002. xxxiii + 387 pp. £55 hb, £19.95 pb.

Who is responsible for the state of State responsibility? In the late Twentieth Century there were certainties, like the Berlin Wall, on which one (thought one) could rely. For international lawyers one of these rocks of certainty–surviving even the fall of the Wall–was the recurrent failure of the International Law Commission to adopt some kind of final instrument on State Responsibility. The topic had been on the ILC's agenda more or less since the Commission's inception, having been one of the topics selected for progressive development and codification. It had drawn on the energies and talents of several Special Rapporteurs including, finally, Professor James Crawford, whose five-year stint was to achieve the feat that had eluded all of his predecessors: the adoption in 2001 of a final instrument, in this case the Draft Articles on Responsibility of States for Internationally Wrongful Acts. As Prof. Crawford himself makes clear, the final product is not his alone but should be seen as the culmination of many years' work. Nevertheless it remains the case that the work has finally been concluded without the need to look for yet another Special Rapporteur.

This is an achievement for which there is good reason to be very grateful. Not only do we now have, for better or worse, a set of Articles to which we can refer (as opposed to yet another latest draft), thereby giving us a stationary rather than a moving target; but that instrument is itself a work of highest quality. This book makes it clear, from beginning to end, exactly how the final product was arrived at. It contains just about everything you ever wanted to know about State responsibility but were always too afraid to ask. It is not a critical outsider's look at the final product; not could it be, having been written by the person at the centre of the process in the final years. But for this reason it contains the insider's insights that might otherwise only be guessed at.

The work consists of three main parts: the first a 60-page introduction by the author that provides essential background information and explanations about the Articles. This is an excellent resource because it simply makes the Articles that much more coherent. Many questions about the format and location of particular provisions are answered by a careful reading.

The second part is a reproduction of the Articles themselves, all 59 of them. That works out at about 1.5 Articles per year over the time that the subject was under consideration by the ILC. But the bulk of the book is the 241 pages of commentary that explain the background to, and reasoning for, every Article. This section serves two substantial purposes: first, whether or not the Articles ever get converted into treaty form, an eventuality not necessarily favoured by the Special Rapporteur; and second, the commentaries demonstrate the legal foundation for each of the Articles. This should promote their use by States and other bodies such as international tribunals. Indeed, the research is so extensive and meticulous that this section will likely become the first point of reference for analyses into particular aspects of the topic.

For those whose appetite for State responsibility remains unsatiated even by that amount of detail, the book goes an extra step by providing three appendices which, respectively, outline the full drafting history of each Article (including Articles proposed but not adopted), the Draft Articles as provisionally adopted in 1996, and give a table of equivalent provisions for the First Reading draft and the final version.

This book will surely not be the last word on State responsibility. Nor is it meant to be. But it should equally surely be central to any discussions on the subject for a long time to come. It is the essential companion work to the subject.

RYSZARD PIOTROWICZ

The African Charter on Human and Peoples' Rights: The System in Practice, 1986–2000. Edited by MALCOLM EVANS and RACHEL MURRAY. Cambridge: Cambridge University Press, 2002. xx + 397 pp. £55.

The African Charter is the regional instrument for the promotion and protection of human and peoples' rights on that continent. It has many singular features. However, it remains the least well known of the three major regional systems for the protection of human rights and is regarded often as a poor relation: the European Human Rights Convention machinery has attracted an extraordinary amount of literature and the American Convention on Human Rights has generated substantial analysis, whereas the African system has not spawned a significant quantity of academic scrutiny and appreciation. Rigorous scholarly analysis is hard to find. Hence the publication of this book is most timely.

Both the editors, Malcolm Evans and Rachel Murray, have special expertise in the field of human rights. Rachel Murray is well known for her particular interest in the African system. As well as contributing themselves to no less than three chapters, the editors have assembled a collection of contributors ranging from academics with a particular interest in the African system (Professor Christof Heyns, Professor Frans Viljoen, and Dr. Gino Naldi), those who have been connected intimately with the operation of the system such as Professor Victor Dankwa and Dr. Nyamkeko Barney Pityana (past Chairman and current member of the African Commission respectively), members of non-governmental organisations operating in the human rights field (Julia Harrington, Ahmad Motala, Chidi Anselm Odinkalu) and a staff member of the UN High Commissioner for Human Rights in Geneva (Tokunbo Ige).

The work examines a number of themes in the context of the African system of protection: future trends inhuman rights in Africa: the increased role of the OAU (ch. 1); the reporting system of the African Charter (ch. 2); the admissibility rules under the African Charter (ch. 3); the issue of evidence and fact-finding by the African Commission (ch. 4); civil and political rights in the African Charter (ch.5); economic, social and cultural rights under the African Charter (ch.6); the challenge of culture for human rights in Africa (ch. 7); non-governmental organisations in the African system (ch. 8); special rapporteurs in the African system (ch. 9); the African Court on Human and Peoples' Rights (ch. 10); and the promotional role of the African Commission on Human and Peoples' Rights (ch. 11). There are also three useful appendices: the text of the African Charter itself; the text of the Protocol to the African Charter establishing the African Court; and, the 'Grand Bay'(Mauritius) Declaration and Plan of Action. Finally, there is a very extensive and helpful bibliography.

All the essays make a valuable contribution to our understanding of the African system in context. The mix of contributors, all of whom have been involved closely in the operational work of the African system, produces a unique practical insight into the operation of various features of this treaty-based human rights protection system. This book also provides considerable raw information on the African system, which until recently the African Commission had not supplied, and which did not appear to be available generally, but rather confined to those with an intimate knowledge of its workings. The book will serve the purpose of drawing the work of the African Commission to a far greater audience than achieved previously: it will be useful to students of the African system, academics, non-governmental organisations, and indeed the relevant authorities of government themselves by making it clear what obligations are being undertaken and how they are implemented.

Many of the chapters provide detailed and penetrating analysis coupled with a real appreciation of the role of the African organs in dealing with both the commonplace and egregious violations that have occurred in Africa since the inception of the Charter in 1981. They also place the mechanisms and achievements of the African system in the context of the European, Inter-American and international systems (such as the International Covenants on Civil and Political Rights and Economic, Social and Cultural Rights) as a whole, by including significant and worthwhile comparative material. One exception is in the consideration of the reporting system of the African Charter in chapter 2. The authors of this chapter explain (at p. 38 footnote 6) that: '[i]t should be noted that it is not the purpose of this chapter to explore these developments nor to offer a comparative account of the reporting procedures' and reason that: '[i]ndeed, given the calls for change within the UN system, the merits of such an exercise at the current time are open to doubt since it hardly appears a stable comparator'. Even so, the reviewer feels that some comparative material here would have provided a sharper focus to the analysis. Whatever the case for not including comparative material in the context of the reporting system, the same cannot be said of the grounds for admissibility of communications under the African Charter (ch.3), which benefits greatly from the inclusion of comparative material and some detailed references to the ICCPR, IACHR, CAT, and the ECHR rules and cases thereunder.

Overall, this study makes a substantial contribution to a detailed understanding of the African system by providing a rich vein of information, thought and analysis. Perhaps, a final chapter by way of conclusion, drawing together all the strands and providing an overview would have provided a more rounded finish. The reviewer found it a worthwhile and interesting read and will certainly find it of great value in a number of different ways.

P.R. GHANDHI

The Law of State Immunity, By HAZEL FOX. Oxford: Oxford University Press, 2002, 604 pp. £80.00.

In this timely book Lady Fox discusses the general concept of State immunity, the sources of the law of State immunity, exceptions from State immunity and immunity from execution. With a particular focus upon the 1972 European Convention on State Immunity and judicial practice of individual States in terms of the so-called restrictive approach to State immunity. A notable feature of the book is its treatment of State immunity alongside cognate concepts, such as immunity of State officials, diplomatic agents, international organisations and their agents, and visiting armed forces. The monograph demonstrates that such comparative analysis is helpful in understanding the essence of different concepts of immunity. Particularly with regard to pleas of immunity of State officials accused of commission of international crimes, Lady Fox demonstrates a link between the lack of capacity of States to commit international crimes and the possibility to prosecute former State officials for such crimes (p. 516).

The author identifies State immunity as a useful procedural plea, serving as a sorting device between competing jurisdictions and as a holding device by which confrontation, between States is avoided (p. 549). However, the most problematic contemporary issue related to immunities in contemporary international law is a question of accountability of States and their officials for violation of fundamental international norms in the field of human rights and humanitarian law. At the same time, it must be borne in mind that the author's analysis relates to a general context of State immunity rather than human rights and *jus cogens* specifically, and her general conclusions seem to be explainable accordingly. With regard to the specific context of human rights, Lady Fox seems to take a rather flexible view. While noting the reluctance of the European Court of Human Rights to deny immunity in case of torture in the *Al-Adsani* case, she nevertheless considers that 'this statement of the law is neither final nor unlikely to change'(pp. 321, 540).

Having said that, the author makes another statement, perhaps incompatible with the earlier one, while she submits that giving full effect to peremptory norms would affect or change the consent-based structure of modern international law (pp. 524, 540). This proposition seems to mirror the views advanced by Georg Schwarzenberger and Prosper Weil at different times to oppose the very notion of peremptory norms as incompatible with the basic structure of international legal order, even though the author seems to share this view only partly, with regard to the enforcement aspect of *jus cogens*. Such a strict attitude seems somehow inconsistent with the view that *Al-Adsani* may, and perhaps indeed should, be subject to a change in order to secure a more responsible stance of international law towards the need to ensure effective vindication of human rights violations, which seems to be a basic purpose of this legal system.

In addition, it seems utterly formalistic to distinguish between substantive and procedural, or enforcement, aspects of *jus cogens*. As the international community accepts *jus cogens* as superior law, it must be clear that it also accepts its overriding effects. This point has rightly been made in the Joint Dissenting Opinion of six judges in *Al-Adsani*. On the other hand, while it is established that certain aspects of *jus cogens* may bind States without their consent (such as an exception to the persistent objector rule), it remains to be answered why other aspects thereof cannot have a similar effect.

With regard to most issues dealt with Lady Fox provides an extensive analysis of historical development of relevant concepts, which is helpful for understanding how the pertinent issues have been reflected at different times and by different international fora. There are cases, however, where it would be better if more were said. For example, the author considers that Article 14 of the UN Convention against Torture (1984) imposes a duty on States to provide civil remedy for torture victims only if torture has been committed within the jurisdiction ofihe forum State (p. 525). But as the text of Article 14 does not contain such qualification, it would be better to have it explained why the scope of Article 14 should be so qualified.

A particular strength of the book is the author's examination of different attitudes towards and perspectives on State immunity. For an interested reader, this offers an excellent opportunity to become familiar with different views and arguments supporting them. Accordingly, this book is likely to become a standard work of reference on all aspects of the doctrine of State immunity.

ALEXANDER ORAKHELASHVILI

Sources of State Practice in International Law. By RALPH GAEBLER and MARIA SMOLKA-DAY. Ardsley, N.Y.: Transnational Publishers, Inc., 2002. Looseleaf. US$150.00/binder.

State practice ought to be the life-blood of international law. The responses by States to the exigencies of modern life, whether confirming established legal rules or developing new legal principles, should be the clearest indication of the ways in which the part of international law that is of the greatest practical significance is moving. Yet both tribunals and jurists routinely rely upon the slenderest of evidence of State practice in making assertions about customary international law. Indeed, the practice is often confined to a handful of States, most if not all of whom are members of the OECD. The idea of customary law as the common law forged from the practice of all States' members of the international community seldom receives more than lip service. The publication of a text that offers guidance in accessing the official records of State practice is, therefore, a welcome event.

This guide has made a modest, but promising, start. Its first issue covers fourteen States: Austria, Belgium, Canada, Denmark, Finland, France, Germany, Norway, Romania, Russia, Sweden, Switzerland, the United Kingdom, and the United States of America. All of them are in Europe or North America; all but two are OECD members. There is, plainly, much work to be done in order to produce a more truly representative picture of international practice.

Each of the States covered has a separate section, written by one of the team of contributing authors. The sections list the official treaty series and collections of diplomatic documents, together with details of Yearbooks and other digests of practice in international law. They do not list sources for legislation and for case-law; nor do they list the leading textbooks which offer expositions of international law from the perspective of the State in question. While one understands the pressures of time and space that constrain compilers of volumes such as this, a modest expansion of the scope of the surveys could have significantly increased their value. If references to legislation and case-law would be too great an undertaking, a reference to other texts giving guidance on the use of national legal materials would at least provide an indirect route to this information.

Reviewers almost inevitably test the accuracy of the surveys by turning to the jurisdiction that they know best. The United Kingdom entry, as this reviewer's home turf, is a useful, but not entirely successful, guide to British practice. The main treaty series are included, as are the treaty indexes (though that appearing annually in this *Year Book* is mentioned only under the heading of 'Yearbooks' and not under 'Treaties'). Similarly, the section on diplomatic sources lists the *British and Foreign State Papers, Documents on British Foreign Policy* and its successors, and the Foreign Office *Confidential Print* (republished in the United States as *British Documents on Foreign Affairs*). The *British Digest, UKMIL* and the section on British Practice that appeared in the *ICLQ* in the 1960s are mentioned, although the sections on Current Developments in the *ICLQ* and on case-law in this *Year Book* are not. Nor are British Parliamentary materials, which are an invaluable source of detailed material.

Apart from including judicial decisions, whether in national collections, in the *International Law Reports* or in specialist compilations, there is a case for referring to at least the most important among the unofficial sources on State practice. Chroniclers of State practice, such as those who put together the invaluable *Chronique des faits* section in the *Revue générale de droit international public*, were not afraid to draw on accounts of practice in newspapers and journals, and some guidance on the most useful among such unofficial sources would have been welcomed by many researchers.

The style of this volume is more that of the professional librarian than of the legal scholar. Most scholars would gravitate naturally to the specialist distillations of practice, such as *DUSPIL, La Prassi Italian*, the *Repertoire de la pratique française*, and other digests; but those compilations (not all of which are listed) tend to be buried at the back of each country section, ceding place to the great and comprehensive collections that tend to be used only after the main features of a topic have already been mapped out using less august but more practical lawyers' tools. Again, one appreciates the problems of organising such an enormous body of material; but this reviewer, at least, would enter a plea that in revisions of the text further thought be given to the *modus operandi* of the reluctant and time-limited researcher, who hopes to find the quickest, most reliable, and easiest route to a dependable account of the practice of a State on a particular point of international law. The section on 'Multi-Jurisdictional Sources'—collections of international instruments and bilateral and multilateral treaties on particular topics—is helpful in this respect; but an extension of this approach to States, so as to list journals and other publications that collect practice on particular topics, such as human rights and environmental matters, would also be most welcome.

An index or detailed Table of Contents to the present volume would also be very helpful to readers, as the arrangement of the entries is not always intuitively grasped.

All in all, this volume is worth buying because there is no current competition; but, brave and welcome as the enterprise is, it has considerable room for improvement.

VAUGHAN LOWE

The Reality of International Law. Essays in Honour of lan Brownlie. Edited by GUY S. GOODWIN-GILL and STEFAN TALMON. Oxford: Oxford University Press, 1999. 592 pp. £60. *State, Sovereignty and International Governance.* Edited by GERARD KREIJEN, MARCEL BRUS, JORRIS DUURSMA, ELISABETH DE VOS and JOHN DUGARD. Oxford: Oxford University Press, 2002. 643 pp. £70.

The *Festschrift*, or collection of essays in honour of a colleague, is a type of publication perhaps more frequently encountered on the continent than in the Anglo-American world. There are, to be sure, exceptions; one thinks, for instance, of the excellent volume on the theme of the International Court and dedicated to Sir Robert Jennings, which was published in 1996 (*Fifty Years of the International Court of Justice*, edited by Lowe and Fitzmaurice). The *Festschrift* in honour of Ian Brownlie is nevertheless an unusual, though well deserved, accolade. In contrast, *State, Sovereignty and International Governance*, dedicated as it is to the Netherlands scholar Pieter Kooijmans, is in a more firmly rooted tradition. In other respects, however, the two books are very much alike, and reflect both the esteem in which their respective subjects are held and the diligence of their learned contributors.

As befits a volume dedicated to a distinguished law teacher, the twenty-five essays which make up *The Reality of International Law* are all written by Brownlie's present or former pupils, most of whom indeed prepared their doctorates under his supervision. The range of subject matter is wide, some naturally on the master's special interests: human rights, State responsibility, the use of force, indigenous peoples. Thus Oraa, for example, writes on human rights in emergency situations, Elagab on non-forcible counter-measures, Chesterman on the U.S. invasion of Panama, and Kingsbury on implementing the World Bank's policy on indigenous peoples. But many other issues are also covered with several essays on the law of the sea (for example, Bangert on the enforcement of fishing regimes, Evans on maritime delimitation); on criminal law (Goodwin-Gill on the duty to prosecute; Provost on 'International Criminal, Environmental Law,); and on legal personality (Crawford on Israel and Palestine, Talmon on government's in exile).

In a short review it is not possible to mention every essay, much less to comment on individual contributions. But two points struck me when reading this collection and seem worth recording. The first is the uniformly high standard of the contributions, something, which unfortunately cannot be said of all edited volumes. The other is that all the essays focus on what may be termed 'real' issues of international law on policy, as opposed to the recondite investigations of some academic writing. If the quality of the essays and their conspicuously practical orientation are essentially a product of their authors' talents, as of course they are, in the style and approach to international law of the twenty-five contributions it is also not hard to discern the critical influence of their mentor.

Unlike the Brownlie volume, the essays in the book dedicated to Pieter Kooijmans are all concerned with a common theme, namely the relation between the concept of State sovereignty and the idea of international governance. Within this broad agenda a variety of matters are addressed, ranging from conceptual issues, such as the meaning of sovereignty and its place in contemporary international law, considered by among others Jennings, van Staden, Vollard and Schermers, to practical questions such as the role of the International Court in crisis management, discussed by Rosenne, secession and dismemberment of States, considered by Tomuschat and Duursma, and jurisdiction in air and space examined by von der Dunk and Mendes de Leon. As with the other collection, the essays are of a generally high standard.

A concluding piece by Don Greig provides an instructive overview of many of the questions touched on in these papers. Highlighting the points made by other contributors in the course of his own analysis of the concepts of sovereignty, international community and interdependence, Greig argues persuasively that we find ourselves in 'a word game in which expressions like international community and interdependence are employed to promote a particular view of the law' (p. 530). Like other contributors, Greig is also interested in exploring the role of non-State actors in international affairs and here too has some pertinent observations. The volume ends with two pieces about Kooijmans himself: a bibliographical essay by Alting von Geusau on the concept of sovereignty in his published work, and a graceful tribute from his colleagues on the International Court.

The scholars to whom the volumes reviewed here are dedicated have each made far reaching contributions to international law, exercising many important roles over their long and influential careers: Brownlie as a supervisor and law teacher at Oxford and elsewhere, as a well-known writer and leading practitioner, and, not least, as editor of this *Year Book* for a quarter of a century; Kooijmans as professor at Amsterdam and Leiden, as Foreign Minister of the Netherlands, as a United Nations Special Rapporteur, and latterly as a Judge at The Hague. It scarcely needs saying that in a turbulent and dangerous world such dedicated and versatile figures are an asset of incalculable value. These collections by their friends, former pupils and fellow professionals are a fitting tribute to their distinguished and energetic recipients.

J.G. MERRILLS

Beyond the Anarchical Society. Grotius, Colonialism and Order in World Politics. By EDWARD KEENE. Cambridge: Cambridge University Press, 2002. xiv + 165 pp. £42.50 hb./£15.95 pb.

When I picked up Keene's book, I had just finished reading Barry Unsworth's novel *Sacred Hunger* (1992). In this, the story is told of the voyage of a Liverpool slave ship in 1752–1753. As the drama on board unfolds, the reader also witnesses the 'adventures' of the son of the owner of the ship, who back in Liverpool entangles himself in a love affair and makes a fool of himself by clumsily playing partner to the girl he desires in a theatre play. The tremendous gap between the cruel world of the slave trader and surreal world of the Liverpool aristocracy, cannot but move the hardest minds. Yet, the two worlds have something in common: they are both of a European design and the one does not exist without the other.

That very same idea is central to Keene's *Beyond the Anarchical Society* . Keene argues that by and large, international relations theorists ignore the historical significance of the outer-European world of the 17th to 19th centuries for the formation of current world order. Traditionally, the late twentieth century world system and its international law are seen to be rooted in the modern European States system of the 17th to 19th century, which later on expanded itself over the world. The fact that during those three centuries, there was another international order in place in the outer-European world of the colonial empires is commonly ignored. As such, there is little interest for the contribution of this order to the now universal 'international society'.

Keene narrows the argument to a critical discussion of the IR theory of Hedley Bull and the so-called British School of International Relations. Bull's work was instrumental to the advancement of the 'Grotian conception' of world order. The Grotian tradition is situated in between the Hobbesian tradition, asserting the dominance of the sovereign State and the Kantian ideal of a society of world citizens. While accepting the preponderance of the sovereign State within the European system, the Grotian tradition affirms the existence of common values, norms and institutions. The tradition is traced back to the writings of the Dutch humanist Grotius (1583–1645) who defended the existence of a *societas humana* and the validity of a universal law within it. In traditional historiography, which according to Keene is to a large extent moulded by the German defenders of dynastic sovereignty from around the French Revolution, Grotius is moreover considered the direct precursor of the classical States system laid down in the Westphalia Treaties (1648).

For this reason, Keene returns to Grotius. According to Keene, many interpreters of Grotius have struggled with some theses of the Dutch humanist that are in contradiction to the Westphalian concept of the sovereign States system. But instead of taking these seriously, they have swept them aside by calling them remnants of the Middle Ages, or simply too idealistic. Keene recuperates two of these elements of Grotian thought: the idea that sovereignty is divisible among different rulers and the protection of private property under the law of nations, and as such the direct enforceability of a private right by a private individual. The first idea served to defend the revolt in the Netherlands against the Spanish king; the second was essential to underpin the actions of the Dutch East India Company in the Indies.

In Keene's opinion, these two elements proved to be more than remnants of medieval thought. How much these ideas were rooted in the medieval tradition, the author does hot investigate. But rather similarly to what Richard Tuck did for private property and some other Grotian concepts *(The Rights of War and Peace. Political Thought and the International Order from Grotius to Kant*, Oxford 1999), he tries to prove that these two notions lived on. According to Keene, they were central to the ordering of the imperial and colonial system of the eighteenth and nineteenth centuries. While Tuck limited himself to a discussion on doctrine, Keene—without claiming that there was a direct influence of Grotius—shows that the organization of the 'international' relations outside Europe was in fact based on the principles of the divisibility of sovereignty and the recognition of the individual and his property rights. His empirical-historical research is limited both in scope and in depth. Keene only discusses pre-and post-revolutionary North America and the Dutch and British empires in the Eastern Indies. He only refers to secondary literature—and some editions of contemporary writers—but his work does not involve the re-reading of the sources.

From the conclusion of this brief empirical analysis, Keene goes on to explain that during the nineteenth century the existence of two different international orders was recognized and legitimized. While the common value of the European sovereign State for the relations among themselves was tolerance, the ideal to bring civilization to the non-Europeans came to the fore as the basis for the imperial ordering outside Europe. After the World Wars, which were seen as the struggle of the alliance of 'civilized' and 'peace-loving' nations against the modern barbarism of German imperialism and later nazism, the distinction between a European civilized world and an outer-world that was still to be civilized, became untenable. So the merger of the two international orders was inevitable.

As such, Keene concludes, the current world order is not the result of the expansion of the European system, but of the merger of two different systems each with their own logic. All this allows for a better understanding of the contradictions, which are inherent to present international law, the opposition of sovereignty and the guaranteeing of human rights first and foremost among them. The so-called new trends in international law, such as the growing importance of the individual, have a long historical tradition in colonial and imperial practices.

Though Keene is only indirectly concerned with specific questions of international law, his work is of interest to the discipline since the traditional ideas from IR theory he attacks, have proven to be quite influential among international lawyers and international legal historians. Keene is not alone in asserting the importance of the outer-European world war for the formation of the present world order. International legal historians like Heinhard Steiger and Antony Anghie have recently, on the basis of other arguments, drawn much the same conclusion. However tempting Keene's thesis, he offers little empirical evidence. Furthermore, Keene's ideas seem more plausible because he can ride on the waves of a new historiography that challenges the dominance of the sovereign State and the Hobbesian character of the European States system from the 17th to 19th centuries. In consequence of his choice not to revaluate the history of the European States system itself—a limitation which in the context of a Ph. D. is defendable—he overlooks this and therefore overestimates the differences between the European and the non-European orders. Nevertheless, Keene's book offers a challenge to historians of international relations and international law to re-read their sources and expand their scope outside the borders of the Western world.

RANDALL LESAFFER

Diversity and Self-determination in International Law. By KAREN KNOP. Cambridge: Cambridge University Press, 2002. 434 pp. £55.

This is an excellent book. It manages to provide new insights and approaches to an area of the international legal system about which much has been written. It also offers a framework of analysis that could be usefully applied to other areas of international law.

Karen Knop establishes that her aim is to explore 'the challenge of diversity for the interpretation of self-determination and—conversely—the implications of the interpretative history of self-determination, once seen in this light for the challenge of diversity in international law and perhaps law more generally' (p. 2). She does not seek to provide a detailed application of self-determination to each particular situation. Instead, she examines self-determination only in those instances when it is exercised by independence and then she explores the extent to which issues of culture and gender and the role of 'colonised groups, ethnic nations and indigenous peoples and women' (p. 3) have an effect on the interpretation of self-determination in those instances.

Her framework of analysis and methodology in undertaking this task is set out clearly. This is to be applauded, as it is all too rare for an international lawyer to do this explicitly. She states that, in relation to diversity, 'the book distinguishes three ways in which groups affected by the right of self-determination may be included in or excluded from its interpretation: *participation, identity* and *interpretation*' (p. 4—her emphasis). She clarifies each of these elements of her framework, with 'participation' meaning whether the cultural and gender groups have a voice in the process and are able to have their perspectives included, and 'identity' meaning the construction given by international law, in its language and descriptions, to these groups, as this can shape perceptions of a group, its history and entitlements. 'Interpretation' is the key for determining the validity of an argument, as 'the choice of an interpretive theory determines how to speak; it sets limits and terms of the conversation about meaning that may be had in international law' (p. 4) and so can include and exclude different types of reasoning. While elements of this framework for analysis can be found in other writers, such as Rosalyn Higgins, Nathaniel Berman and Susan Marks, Karen Knop brings all three elements together in an original way in order to engage with self-determination on the basis of equality for all those directly affected.

She uses this framework of analysis to examine the interpretation of self-determination especially by international documents, international tribunals and jurists. In each instance her focus is on external political self-determination. While this is a disappointing limitation, it is justified by the author on the basis that what is included shows most clearly the nature and history of the key debates on this issue. Thus in Part 1 of the book, she elucidates the main post-Cold War scholarship on the external political right of self-determination. She includes writers such as Antonio Cassese, James Crawford, Thomas Franck, Rosalyn Higgins, Robert McCorquodale, Oscar Schachter, and Daniel Turp. Her aim in this is to show 'the range of legally defensible interpretations of self-determination and the relationship of *interpretation* to *identity* that they instantiate' (p. 50—her emphasis).

Parts 2 and 3 of the book look at what the author calls 'case studies'. These are much more than an examination of a particular situation where self-determination has been claimed. Instead what are included are 'moments in the progressive interpretation of self-determination when an international legal authority [which is not restricted to being a tribunal] is confronted with an issue of self-determination that relates to the current debate over meaning and tells us something about the underlying contest between different schools of interpretation and normative visions of self-determination' (p. 21). Thus the case studies in Part 2, which looks at the challenge of culture to self-determination interpretations, include the views of the International Court of Justice (ICJ) concerning Western Sahara and East Timor and the European Commission's Arbitration Commission Opinion No. 2 on Yugoslavia, as well as the documents and processes arising from the activity of the International Labour Organisation and the United Nations (UN) Working Group on Indigenous Populations. Part 3, which looks at the challenge of gender to self-determination interpretations, examines the participation and identity of women in the process of self-determination in Europe after World War I and in the UN Trust Territories, as well as a chapter on indigenous women and self-determination, particularly in the *Lovelace* case before the UN Human Rights Committee.

These case studies are illuminating, stimulating, and often sharply incisive. Many new ideas or new perspectives are offered about what seem to be accepted historical situations or documents. For example, the discussion on the *Western Sahara Opinion* is illuminating in showing how different concepts and ideologies directly impacted on various ICJ judges' interpretations and the consequences of this for identity and participation. Even the battered reputation of the EC Arbitration Commission's Opinions is restored somewhat by her analysis. In each of these case studies the detailed research is evident, particularly in the UN Trustee Council's reports, which bring to life the voices of women in self-determination and how these voices are usually excluded. There are also some clever turns of phrase, such as Max Huber's 'musty paternalism' (p. 135), which express ideas most succinctly.

As was stated at the beginning, this is an excellent book. It is challenging, thought provoking, deeply researched and persuasive. It should be read and to returned to, by everyone interested in self-determination.

ROBERT MCCORQUODALE

Rethinking Humanitarian Intervention: A Fresh Legal Approach Based on Fundamental Ethical Principles in International Law and World Religions. By BRIAN D. LEPARD. Penn State University Press, 2002. xviii + 496 pp. $55.

The controversy over recognition of the legality of humanitarian intervention has been heightened in the wake of the Kosovo crisis of 1999. If academic discourse is scrutinized there is a perception that the pendulum has swung toward the legality of humanitarian intervention. Stripped of legal justifications based on spurious interpretations of Security Council resolutions, how could the bombing of the Federal Republic of Yugoslavia (FRY) be anything other than a clear instance of humanitarian intervention? However, the absence of anything like a consensus among those States intervening, as well as the rest of the world, immediately raises the previously oft-repeated question about the presence of sufficient *opinio juris* in favour of military intervention to prevent serious human rights abuses. Kosovo highlighted the divide among academics and politicians as to the legality of humanitarian intervention it did not produce any definite conclusions.

In the aftermath of Kosovo it is not possible to categorically state that the prohibition of the use of force allows for further exceptions in addition to self-defence and UN authorized military action. The crisis did, however, put the spotlight on the United Nations, in particular the Security Council, which was certainly perceived as ineffective in the face of brutal repression by the FRY of its rebellious province. Given the UN's failures in Rwanda and Bosnia (in particular Srebrenica), there appeared to be a pressing need to force the issue—to break existing law in order to make new (and better) law by qualifying the Security Council's monopoly on the use of non-defensive force. Even those doubting the legality of humanitarian intervention saw the moral case for military action in Kosovo, which is suggestive of the need to reform the law embodied in the UN

Charter. Several new legal regimes have been proposed typically containing criteria that attempt to address the weaknesses of selectivity and hegemony inherent in a right to unilateral humanitarian invention. The likelihood of such limitations being accepted by States is questionable. Thus the danger in throwing out the Charter scheme is that selective institutional (UN) action will be replaced by selective, less regulated, regional or State action. Surely, the future lies in addressing the weaknesses of the Charter scheme, including the relationship between the UN and regional organizations. If powerful States bemoaning a veto-bound Security Council focused their energies on reforming the UN, rather than trying to breathe new life into questionable 'customary' doctrines, then some progress might be made. Veto-wielding States concerned about an inactive Security Council should express a willingness to replace the veto with the requirement of a four-fifths majority among the permanent members, and should recognize the legitimacy as well as legality of the General Assembly having exceptional competence to recommend military action (see pp. 328–9, pp. 362–3, pp. 366–7). The incredible pressure that can be exerted in the Security Council should be used to free up the Security Council from the pernicious use of the veto. Of course, each permanent member values the veto, and so is unlikely to take such an altruistic course of action, but then altruism is being posited as the basis of humanitarian intervention. It appears that altruism is, like other aspects of a State's foreign policy, only to be deployed pragmatically.

A distinctive feature of Brian Lepard's fascinating book is that he does not allow Kosovo to dominate his analysis. Furthermore, this is not a book about unilateral humanitarian intervention, which is, after all very much the exception in practice, when compared to UN mandated interventions (both peacekeeping and enforcement) to protect human rights. It is clear that Lepard, in seeking the ethical basis for humanitarian intervention, recognizes that it is through the UN that such a path lies. Lepard initially puts his emphasis on the UN down to the established pattern of the last decade of the twentieth century, whereby States and organizations have generally sought authority from the Security Council for humanitarian operations (p. 1). However, his analysis of ethical principles derived from the texts of the seven main religions and philosophies, and their relationship to legal principles drawn primarily from UN texts, shows that ethics and UN law are in a complex relationship. This enables the UN's purposes, laws and mechanisms to be developed in a dynamic, ethically driven, way. Most importantly, the lack of consensus on the legality of unilateral humanitarian intervention is for Lepard a serious legal *and* ethical deficiency (see for example pp. 68–71, pp. 353–4). The net result of such an ethical approach is the conclusion that the UN should develop a more sophisticated and reliable legal regime for humanitarian intervention under its auspices.

In effect, the book is an effective ethical critique of UN action taken under Chapters VII and VIII for the protection of human rights. It is a genuine attempt to reconcile the conflicting legal norms surrounding the debate on humanitarian intervention. To 'resolve these conflicts of norms . . . it is necessary to have a legal methodology for identifying and interpreting legal norms related to humanitarian intervention that itself identifies relevant ethical principles and takes them into account. Such a methodology would help to indicate more precisely how the competing legal norms in the U.N. Charter and contemporary international law ought to be interpreted and reconciled in the context of humanitarian intervention, and how the Security Council ought from an ethical perspective to implement its legal discretion' (p. 30). In attempting to draw out the ethical principles from the world's main beliefs, Lepard has the laudable practical aim of seeking acceptance from governments and peoples from the vast majority of UN member States. In essence he is seeking a background universal morality that can resolve disputes about the applicability of legal principles in problem areas (p. 115). In this respect, arguably reference should have been made to natural lawyers going back to the ancient Greeks, as well as the texts of the world's main religions. However, by divorcing ethical analysis from the baggage of natural law, the approach does overcome charges of ethnocentricity. This, together with a clear explanation of ethically derived principles for the development of the UN system (eg pp. 241–53), make the book a very appealing addition to the considerable amount of literature on this subject. Its conclusions will not necessarily please those advocates of unilateral humanitarian intervention who intuitively claim the moral high ground (see his conclusions on NATO's intervention in Kosovo, p. 330, pp. 353–5, pp. 369–70). However, the depth and originality of its ethical analysis should help serve to break the current stalemate that exists between international lawyers.

NIGEL D. WHITE

The Uniform Interpretation of the Brussels and Lugano Conventions. By JUSTIN NEWTON. Oxford: Hart Publishing, 2002. cxxx + 595 pp. £75.

Although the title may suggest that this work is a direct competitor to Kaye's 'European Case Law on the judgments Convention',[1] and whilst both books share a common objective, namely the promotion of uniformity of interpretation of these Conventions,[2] their approaches are very different. The Kaye book takes a jurisdiction by jurisdiction approach, and its stated purpose is to inform rather than comment. Whilst this produces a very useful reference source of English language summaries of the most important cases, it is also a curiously colourless work. Thus no sense that the Netherlands courts' approach to Article 24[3] was highly controversial can be gleaned from it. It contains *Box Doccia Megius v Wilux International*[4] which held that Article 24 creates a separate jurisdiction, so that even if a court of another contracting State has jurisdiction, the Netherlands court could claim jurisdiction so far as provisional measures are concerned, but the significance of this decision is not stated. It was controversial, not least because in reaching a decision whether or not to grant provisional measures the Dutch courts use the *Kort Geding*. The *Kort Geding* procedure is in fact a form of mini trial, and thus quite different from the approach adopted in England and Wales in deciding whether or not to grant an interlocutory injunction, which is done on the balance of convenience, though paying some attention to the strengths of the respective cases.[5] The effect of the Dutch approach was, when combined with a willingness to grant Europe-wide (and even more extensive) injunctions, that Article 24 in effect trumped the basic jurisdictional rules contained in Articles 2 and 5(3).

By contrast with Kaye, the author of the present work states boldly : '. . . it provides incredulity that the deceptively simple Article 24 leaves so much out regarding the taking of jurisdiction.'

[1] John Wiley & Sons. Chichester. 1998.

[2] And see Article 1 of Protocol No. 2 to Lugano Convention and Art. 2(1) which calls for a system for the exchange of information on judgments on the Lugano and Brussels Conventions.

[3] Article 24 provides—

'Application may be made to the courts of a Contracting State for such provisional, including protective, measures as may be available under the law of that State, even if, under this Convention, the courts of another Contracting State have jurisdiction as to the substance of the matter.'

[4] (1992) KG 189.

[5] See *American Cyanamid v Ethicon* [1975] AC 396; as explained in *Series 5 Software v Clarke* [1996] 1 All ER 853; *Getmapping plc v Ordnance Survey* [2002] EWHC 1084 (Ch). In *Guardian Media Groups plc and others v Associated Newspapers Limited* 20 January 2000 Walker LJ observed 'It is not necessary to consider today whether the court's entitlement to give effect to its provisional view of the merits goes quite so far as Laddie J sought in *Series 5 Software v Clarke*', but the statement in the text nevertheless is sufficiently accurate for present purposes.

The discussion of the clarification of the jurisdiction to order provisional[6] measures in *Van Uden Maritime BV v Kommanditgesellschaft in Firma Deco-Line*[7] *and Hans-Hermann Mietz v Intership Yachting Sneek BV*[8] is lively as well as illuminating. The conclusion of this discussion seems eminently justified:

The upshot of *Van Uden Maritime* seems to be that so long as a respondent to this type of procedure has, or will have, some assets within the jurisdiction of a particular court, an applicant may ignore any litigation on the merits in any other Contracting State . . . take advantage of exorbitant rules of jurisdiction, and obtain a provisionally enforceable order, in the granting Contracting State.

If, as appears to be the case, this is a correct assessment of the *Van Uden Maritime* decision, the result will be an alarming increase in the application for such interim measures . . . to the detriment and *détournement* of the protective edifice of Title II, Articles 2, 11, 14 and 17 so carefully erected for actions on the merits.[9]

This appears to be what indeed has happened, in spite of some tightening up on the part of the Dutch courts. The way in which these cases may affect English practice is discussed at p. 318 *et seq.*[10]

The question is raised whether the effect of the *Van Uden Maritime* 'safeguards'[11] is to curtail the English courts' power to order worldwide *Mareva*/freezing injunctions under Article 24, and whether courts in other Contracting States where assets are located will be compelled to recognise the order:

An answer to this question is contingent on whether the additional 'safeguards' mentioned in *Van Uden Maritime* and *Mietz*— for provisional judgments of contractual consideration, also bite on temporary freezing injunctions, even over overseas assets.

That there is any form of protectionism at work in Contracting State jurisdictions may (now) be hard to distinguish from that built-in to the civil procedure codes and substantive law/practice on interim relief itself—*Van Uden Maritime* will simply have brought any such protectionism to the fore. If we have to direct our gaze anywhere, it should be to France, to find out the impact of *Van Uden Maritime* on the *référé—provision* procedure.

Part of the problem in the field of intellectual property has been the curiously restrictive view of Article 16(4) that has prevailed. This provides:

In proceedings concerned with the registration or validity of patents, trade marks, designs, or other similar rights required to be deposited or registered, the courts of the Contracting State in which the deposit or registration has been applied for, has taken place or is under the terms of an international convention deemed to have taken place;

A disappointing feature of Newton's book is that there is no discussion of this, nor indeed the particular concerns that have been expressed by intellectual property lawyers about the Brussels and Lugano Conventions, and the attempt (in effect) to globalize them on the part of the Hague Conference on Private International Law. Given that these concerns were forcefully enough expressed to cause the Hague Conference to set up an expert group to look specifically at this, and given that an important object of this book is to provide a critique of the Hague Conference's draft, this omission is regrettable.

[6] And protective measures. [7] Case C-391/95 [1998] ECRI-7091.

[8] Case C-99/96 [1996] ECR 1-2277.

[9] P.311 (I have omitted the footnote reference contained in this passage).

[10] The effect on German and French practice is discussed at pp. 336 *et seq.*, and 338 *et seq.*

[11] A guarantee from the claimant/plaintiff equivalent to a cross-undertaking in English domestic procedure.

Indeed, unlike the Kaye work, this is not a comprehensive study. What it covers is well done, but after the general Introduction this is no more than Articles: 5(1) (jurisdiction in matters relating to contract); Article 17 (prorogation of jurisdiction); Article 24 (provisional and protective measures); and, Article 27 (public policy). The reason appears at page 41: '. . . certain articles of the Conventions are more contentious in certain Contracting States, and have produced a greater number of (inconsistent) case law and commentary throughout the Community than others: Article 21[12] vis-à-vis Article 17 in the UK; Article 5(1) in France; Article 24 (it appears Community-wide); Article 17 in the UK Germany and France; and Article 27(1)(2) in Germany.'

Within its limited scope, however, the book is an excellent and readable contribution to the jurisprudence on the Brussels and Lugano Conventions. It does '. . . attempt to provide, in a general fashion, and in a way that has not hitherto been attempted in any coherent fashion, a comparative commentary, bibliography and repository of information concerning (continental) case law; and using primary and secondary sources written in French and German so as to be of use—it is hoped—to future scholars of European civil procedure.'[13]

JOHN N ADAMS

International Human Rights and Humanitarian Law. By RENE PREVOST. Cambridge: Cambridge University Press, 2002. xxxix + 418 pp. £55.

Any comparison of International Human Rights and Humanitarian Law must first overcome a number of prejudices. Some of these prejudices are encountered by all comparative studies; some are specific to the subject matter at hand. All comparative studies encounter the difficulties associated with detailing two or more separate systems, this project is made all the more difficult when the subjects are considered by many to be interrelated. Provost deals with these problems well.

The approach of the book is thorough, logical, clear, and interesting. It is of course assisted by the timing of its publication. The study of Humanitarian Law has been revitalised by the workings of the ICTY and ICTR. Human Rights Law and the dialogue associated with it have also developed greatly over the past decades. Provost's greatest success is in recognising the limitations on any work of this sort. Any suggestion that this book codifies or definitively explains the relationship between the two systems is rejected. Instead, it is clearly an attempt to examine the interplay between these areas of law and to 'provide a greater comprehension of ongoing transitions'. To that extent the book will continue to be of interest as the law in both areas develops; the judgement in the trial of Milosovic will not make it redundant; it is and will remain a useful reference point for discussions in both areas.

An examination of the Table of Contents reveals how ambitious a work this is. Part I is an examination of the normative frameworks of both human rights and humanitarian law in 120 pages. Part II considers the development of both systems and devotes particular attention to the concept of reciprocity. Part III is entitled 'APPLICATION: law and facts' and ranges from the issue of international and non-international armed conflicts, via states of emergency through to the legal effect of characterisation. Despite the ambition of the work it avoids the trap of superficiality. Although other texts may deal with states of emergency, etc, in a more comprehensive fashion, this book provides a more than adequate discussion for the purposes of the comparison.

As to who will buy this book it is hard to tell. Scholars and Students in the field of International Humanitarian law will certainly find it useful. The examination of the

[12] *Lis alibi pendens.* [13] P. 42.

development of Customary International Law and the possible impact of human rights upon that system will surely arouse interest International human rights lawyers often seem to believe humanitarian law is merely a branch of their discipline and therefore a comparative study may seem alien. It is they who should read this book, though whether they will remains to be seen. Graduate students may find this text an accessible gateway to the subject; however it is almost certainly beyond all but the brightest of undergraduate students. Provost certainly grounds his theory in the real world and there is an examination of recent developments before the ICTY and ICTR, for example. The usefulness of this book to NGOs and practitioners will vary depending on their interest in the theoretical basis for the subjects under consideration.

The highest compliment I can give the author is to say that his book is thought-provoking. Different commentators may object to the conclusions on the normative framework of Human Rights, for example, it appears quite grounded in political reality which may be at odds with the opinions of a few; however at all points this text contributes to the debate surrounding these issues. Rather than nodding furiously in agreement or desperately shaking one's head, one finds oneself putting the book down and reflecting thoughtfully upon its conclusions.

FERGAL DAVIS

Indigenous Peoples and Human Rights. By PATRICK THORNBERRY. Manchester: Manchester University Press, 2002. 484 pp. £45 hb, £16.99 pb.

Over the last forty years the rights of indigenous peoples have gained international prominence, partly due to the increased number of international institutions and organisations with a mandate to promote and protect them—e.g. UN Permanent Forum for Indigenous Issues, UN Working Group on Indigenous Populations, and the Organisation of American States. Contemporary developments at the international level centre on institutional representation and standard-setting. The multiplicity of issues affecting indigenous peoples—group identity, land rights, protection of cultural heritage, repatriation of ancestral remains from scientific research bodies, pollution of environment and expropriation of land for development purposes—means it is no easy task to provide a comprehensive analysis of international legal developments. Professor Patrick Thornberry's book is a judicious review of indigenous peoples' rights under international human rights law and emerging international standards. From the outset he guides our thinking through five key questions affecting indigenous rights: (1) coherence in defining indigenous peoples, (2) existing human rights standards versus a special category of indigenous rights, (3) individual and collective modes of advancing indigenous rights, (4) the relationship between cultural practices and protection of human rights, and (5) indigenous peoples' influence on international institutions and participation in decision-making.

The book is divided into six Parts. Part I explores different theories of indigenous rights, varying interpretations of individual and group rights, and the tension between State-centric views and group-based claims, without goading the reader into accepting superficially attractive arguments. Part II examines UN treaty provisions protecting mainly individual rights of indigenous peoples. Implementation problems are explained with reference to indigenous cases and periodic State reports considered by the various treaty supervisory bodies. In contrast to his earlier work, *International Law and the Rights of Minorities*, which subsumed indigenous peoples in the category of minorities, this is a much more focused analysis grappling with the complex interplay between general human rights standards and indigenous issues—e.g. the connection between land, culture, and identity. There is also recognition of the dynamic nature of indigenous claims to land, ranging from allocation and demarcation of land to economic exploitation and development (pp. 163–7).

Whilst particular attention is paid to significant cases on indigenous land rights (*Mabo* in Australia, *Awas Tingi* in Nicaragua) it is slightly disappointing not to have a section devoted entirely to land (customary land tenure systems, the doctrine of aboriginal title, the impact of colonial acquisition of territorial sovereignty on pre-existing land tenure systems) given its complexity and importance to many indigenous groups. An opportunity is missed in Part III, which considers the potential for protection of indigenous group rights under the African, Inter-American, and European regional systems, to discuss aboriginal title in the African context with the first aboriginal title case in South Africa—the *Richtersveld Community Case* . Part IV examines the ILO conventions on indigenous peoples, and Part V the emerging standards specific to indigenous peoples under the UN draft Declaration on the Rights of Indigenous Peoples, and the Proposed American Declaration on the Rights of Indigenous Peoples.

As a respected scholar and expert in the field, Thornberry's analytical vantage point is his systematic survey of how far international and regional instruments protect both individual and group rights of indigenous peoples. Neither restrictively thematic nor polemical in tone, the book is accessible to all with an interest in the application of human rights to specific beneficiaries, and can be commended to advocates of indigenous rights.

Özlem Ülgen

Remedies against International Organizations. By K. Wellens. Cambridge: Cambridge University Press, 2002. 295 pp. £45.

This book is inspired by the work of the International Law Commission's Committee on Accountability of International Organizations, of which the author is Co-Rapporteur. This background probably explains why it reaches into areas that might at first glance seem rather removed from the subject of 'remedies' and it seems that it is the idea of 'accountability' that lies at its heart. Some might feel that the concept of a 'remedy' adopted in the work is overly inclusive, being defined for the purposes of the book as 'a form of shorthand for an acceptable outcome arrived at by a means of the choice of an aggrieved party' (p. 12) but once it is realized that this is driven by the desire to project the accountability of international organizations in remedial terms this becomes explicable, if not necessarily wholly convincing. What is certainly convincing is the author's portrayal of the complexities and current difficulties of holding international organizations to account for their behaviour. What is thoroughly disquieting is, as the author acknowledges throughout, that these problems are not new and potential solutions not difficult to find: the real problem lies in effecting change and this appears to be as problematic as ever.

The first part of the work (chapters 1–6) identifies various levels and forms of accountability. The first level involves the general manner in which an organization carries out its functions. The second level concerns responsibility for injurious consequences flowing from the conduct of its activities. The third concerns acts which are in themselves in breach of international or institutional law. Various forms of 'accountability' are then identified, including political, administrative, financial and legal routes. Finally, different forms of potential claimant are identified. These include member States, who might be seeking a 'remedy' (as understood for the purposes of this work) against the organization at all three levels—though most often at the first. It also includes non-member States and non-State actors, such as private bodies or individuals who have entered into relations with the organizations as, for example, contractors or as staff members and who might be seeking a remedy at the second or third level. It is also suggested that the availability of the various forms of accountability will vary depending upon the level of accountability and the nature of the 'claimant'. This is very true. It is also true that the argument is not always as clear as the reader might like. It requires a considerable degree of mental alertness and agility to keep up with the shifting juxtapositions of the various matrices. At the end of the day, however, the underlying points are not quite so difficult to grasp as their presentation sometimes implies: for example, that if member States feel aggrieved with the manner in which international organizations conduct themselves (the first level of accountability) they are at least in a position to take political, administrative, and financial measures (i.e. three of the forms of accountability) against the organization in a manner in which non-member States cannot. And so on.

The second part of the work (chapters 7–12) then turns to the procedural problems that various categories of claimants will face in attempting to hold an international organization to account, those considered being member States, staff members, private claimants and NGOs. Common obstacles are then considered. Woven into this helpful breakdown and exploration of the difficulties are the related problems of access to local courts and, above all, the problem posed to would-be claimants by the jurisdictional immunity enjoyed by international organizations It is difficult to avoid the conclusion that the seemingly high-handed approach to their own prerogatives projected by the organizations is increasingly difficult to reconcile with the reality of their position within an increasingly less deferentially minded world, and that time is running out for them to put their own houses in order.

The prospects and possibilities for change are canvassed in the fourth part (chapters 16–20) of the work (the third part (chapters 13–15) having looked the possible 'outcomes' of the various forms of remedial action for the staff members and private claimants). This final section is perhaps the most interesting, detailing various alternative forms of action that might be taken against international organizations, and providing examples such as the role of Ombudsmen, World Bank Inspection Panels, and the role of Commissions of Inquiry. Although these all have their part to play in ensuring accountability, it is difficult to resist the impression that these should be supplements to, rather than replacements for, the greater availability of the more familiar forms of judicial remedies. Thus chapter 19 highlights the need and prospects for an enhanced role to be played by domestic courts, thus ultimately requiring a changed approach to immunity, and chapter 20 examines the case for the jurisdiction of the International Court of Justice to be extended to embrace actions by or against international organizations. This latter argument has been well rehearsed, but coming at the conclusion of this expose of the limited remedial opportunities open to those aggrieved by the behaviour of international organizations, it has rarely had such piquancy.

There is, then, much in this book to inform and stimulate. It is not always as easy to follow as one might wish, and the multi-dimensional approach, though doubtless justified, is at times as apt to confuse as to enlighten. Also, the overly broad notion of a remedy seems to this reviewer to result in some rather strained conceptualizations: in chapter 17 for example, where the potential of member States to influence the policy decision-making capacity of organizations (e.g. by voting for resolutions, etc), is cast as a form of 'pre-remedial' action (p. 175). Nevertheless, by firmly turning the spotlight on the privileged position of international organizations and subjecting it to critical scrutiny against the desiderata of ensuring greater transparency and accountability, the author has rendered a great service.

MALCOLM D. EVANS

DECISIONS OF BRITISH COURTS DURING 2003 INVOLVING QUESTIONS OF PUBLIC OR PRIVATE INTERNATIONAL LAW

A. PUBLIC INTERNATIONAL LAW[1]

State immunity—State Immunity Act 1978—positive duty on court to give effect to state immunity—contracts of employment exception—employment of members of mission—local tort exception—personal injury—statutory tort pursuant to Race Relations Act 1976—injury to feelings—psychiatric injury—submission to jurisdiction—diplomatic immunity—Diplomatic Privileges Act 1964—relationship between Diplomatic Privileges Act and State Immunity Act—whether state immunity available in respect of race discrimination in UK

Case No 1. Military Affairs Office of the Embassy of the State of Kuwait v Caramba-Coker, 10 April 2003, EAT 1054/02/RN, 2003 WL 1610407, <http://www.employmentappeals.gov.uk/judge_fr.htm> (EAT, Keith J presiding).

Section 57 of the Race Relations Act 1976 creates a statutory tort for acts of race discrimination. Section 57(4) provides that damages awardable may include, but are not limited to, compensation in respect of injury to feelings. The respondent had been employed as a shipping clerk at the Kuwaiti Embassy for a brief period before his summary dismissal. He brought complaints of wrongful dismissal and race discrimination before an employment tribunal against the Military Affairs Office of the mission. The mission did not file a notice of appearance and elected not to attend the hearing or to make written representations to the tribunal. The tribunal found in favour of the complainant, awarding him damages under both heads of complaint. The mission appealed to the Employment Appeal Tribunal (EAT) on the grounds that the mission was immune from the employment tribunal's jurisdiction in accordance with section 1 (1) of the State Immunity Act 1978.[2]

The EAT (Keith J presiding) prefaced its discussion of the merits by observing that '[t]he failure of the tribunal to consider at all the issue of state immunity would in the normal course of events have resulted in a remission of the case to the tribunal to determine whether the mission was immune from the jurisdiction of the tribunal'.[3] It had already drawn

[2] Section 1(1) provides: 'A State is immune from the jurisdiction of the courts of the United Kingdom except as provided in the following provisions of this Part of this Act.'

[3] Judgment (Revised), para. 13.

attention to the fact—in upholding the decision of the Registrar to extend the mission's time for serving its notice of appeal—'that the court itself has a positive duty to give effect to the immunity conferred by the [State Immunity] Act, even in cases where the state does not appear in the proceedings in question',[4] as spelled out in section 1(2) of the Act. But both parties had submitted, for different reasons, that this was unnecessary.

The respondent conceded that his complaint of wrongful dismissal could not be pursued under section 4 of the State Immunity Act, which abrogates state immunity in respect of certain contracts of employment,[5] since the availability of this exception was denied by section 16(1)(a), relating to the employment of the members of the mission.[6] As a consequence, the EAT upheld the appeal against the assumption of jurisdiction over that complaint and declared that the mission was immune from the jurisdiction of the tribunal in this respect.[7]

As regards the complaint of race discrimination, however, the complainant argued that this amounted to proceedings in respect of personal injury caused by an act in the UK and was therefore, by virtue of section 5 of the Act,[8] not barred by a plea of state immunity. In the light of Court of Appeal authority,[9] the EAT noted that section 57(4) of the Race Relations Act, while providing for recovery in respect of injury to feelings, did not alter the fact that 'injury to feelings is not to be regarded as a species of personal injury'.[10] As such, if the complaint was in respect of injury to feelings, it would not fit within the exception to state immunity recognized in section 5 of the State Immunity Act.[11] If, however, the complaint related to psychiatric injury, it was well established that psychiatric injury was a species of personal injury, and the complaint therefore fell within section 5 of the Act.[12] The EAT did not have before it the evidence given by the complainant to the employment tribunal, and so was unable to determine whether the damages awarded were for injury to feelings or for psychiatric injury. It therefore remitted to the tribunal

[4] Judgment, para. 11, citing *United Arab Emirates v Abdelghafar* [1995] ICR 65 at 73–4 (Mummery J), as endorsed by the Court of Appeal in *Aziz v Bethnal Green City Challenge Co, Ltd* [2000] IRLR 111.

[5] Section 4(1) reads: 'A State is not immune as respects [*sic*] proceedings relating to a contract of employment between the State and an individual where the contract was made in the United Kingdom or the work is to be wholly or partly performed there.'

[6] Section 16(1)(a) states that s. 4 does not apply to proceedings concerning the employment of the members of the mission within the meaning of the Vienna Convention on Diplomatic Relations. The claimant did not deny that the respondent was a mission, or that he was a member of that mission, within the meaning of the Convention.

[7] Judgment, para. 25.

[8] Section 5 provides in relevant part:

A State is not immune as respects [*sic*] proceedings in respect of—

(a) death or personal injury . . .

caused by an act or omission in the United Kingdom.

[9] *Sheriff v Klyne Tugs (Lowestoft) Ltd* [1999] ICR 1170 at para. 11 (Stuart-Smith LJ).

[10] Judgment, para. 16.

[11] Judgment, para. 16.

[12] Judgment, para. 17, summarising the respondent's submission with apparent approval.

the question of whether the complaint of race discrimination amounted to proceedings in respect of personal injury within the meaning of section 5 of the State Immunity Act.[13] It added that, should the mission take part in the remitted proceedings,

> [it] would be inclined to the view that where the question of jurisdiction depends on facts which are in dispute, no submission to jurisdiction would occur if the party disputing jurisdiction took part in the proceedings solely for the purpose of securing a favourable finding on those facts.[14]

It emphasised, however, that it had not been addressed on this point, and 'should not be taken as deciding that [such a move] could not amount to a submission to the tribunal's jurisdiction'.[15]

For its part, the mission submitted an argument based on the chapeau to section 16(1) of the State Immunity Act, which provides that Part I of the Act, in which section 5 is found, does not affect any immunity or privilege conferred by the Diplomatic Privileges Act 1964 or the Consular Relations Act 1968, which in turn incorporate by way of schedule the Vienna Convention on Diplomatic Relations 1961 and the Vienna Convention on Consular Relations 1963 respectively. The mission alleged that one of the persons found to have acted towards the complainant in a racially discriminatory manner was a diplomatic agent, and as such enjoyed immunity from the civil jurisdiction of the English courts by virtue of article 31(1) of the 1961 Convention. It further alleged that the two other persons who had committed acts of race discrimination were members of the administrative and technical staff of the mission, and thus—unless proved by the complainant to be nationals or permanent residents of the UK—were entitled to diplomatic immunity, in accordance with article 37(2) of the 1961 Convention, for acts performed (like those impugned) in the course of their duties. But the EAT gave these submissions short shrift:

> This elaborate and ingenious argument falls at the first hurdle. The opening words of section 16(1) of the [State Immunity] Act are in effect a 'for the avoidance of doubt' provision. They make it clear, unless it might be thought otherwise, that if a diplomat or a consular official enjoys an immunity or privilege under the 1964 or 1968 Acts, their immunity or privilege is not affected by Part I of the 1978 Act. That is because the 1964 and 1968 Acts confer immunities and privileges on what can loosely be described as diplomats and consular officials. Thus, even if [the persons in question] enjoyed immunity from civil suit under the 1964 Act, that would not create for the mission an immunity from civil suit in respect of their acts, if the mission was liable for their acts. And the mission was liable for their acts of race discrimination because section 32(1) of the Race Relations Act 1976 provides:
>
> > 'Anything done by a person in the course of his employment shall be treated for the purposes of this Act . . . as done by his employer as well as by him, whether or not it was done with the employer's knowledge or approval.'[16]

[13] Judgment, para. 26. [14] Judgment, para. 26. [15] Judgment, para. 26.
[16] Judgment, para. 24.

It followed that section 16(1) of the State Immunity Act did not defeat the complainant's reliance on section 5.

The EAT's judgment cannot be faulted. The same goes for its inclination towards the view that a state's intervention in proceedings 'solely for the purpose of securing a favourable finding on [disputed] facts' essential to its claim of immunity would not amount to its submission to the jurisdiction. Such a move would surely constitute 'an intervention . . . for the purpose only of . . . claiming immunity', within the meaning of section 2(4)(a) of the State Immunity Act, and as such could not ground an exception to that immunity.

Relationship between treaty and Scots law—unincorporated treaties—legitimate expectation—Dublin Convention—whether Article 11(5) of Dublin Convention giving rise to legitimate expectation on part of asylum seeker that removal from UK would not be effected after expiration of time limit

Case No 2. Khairandish v Secretary of State for the Home Department, 23 April 2003, 2003 SLT 1358; 2003 GWD 14–471; 2003 WL 1935402 (OH, Lord Drummond Young).

The petitioner and his five year-old son claimed refugee status on their arrival in the UK in August 2001, having claimed such status in Austria in June of that year. On 20 February 2002, in accordance with the relevant substantive and procedural provisions of the Dublin Convention,[17] the UK requested Austria to accept the petitioner's transfer so that he and his son's application could be considered there; on 28 February, again in accordance with the Convention, Austria acceded to the request. The Home Secretary promptly informed the petitioner that he had certified the claim under section 11(2) of the Immigration and Asylum Act 1999,[18] and

[17] Convention determining the State responsible for examining applications for asylum lodged in one of the Member States of the European Communities, Dublin, 15 June 1990, OJ C 254, 19.8.1997, p. 1. Article 8 provides:

> Where no Member State responsible for examining the application for asylum can be designated on the basis of the other criteria listed in this Convention, the first Member State with which the application for asylum is lodged shall be responsible for examining it.

[18] Section 11(2) reads:

> Nothing . . . prevents a person who has made a claim for asylum ('the claimant') from being removed from the United Kingdom to a Member State if—
>
> (a) the Secretary of State has certified that—
>
> (i) the Member State has accepted that, under standing arrangements, it is the responsible State in relation to the claimant's claim for asylum; and
>
> (ii) in his opinion, the claimant is not a national or citizen of the Member State to which he is to be sent . . .

The term 'standing arrangements' is defined in section 11(4) to mean 'arrangements in force as between Member States for determining which state is responsible for considering applications for asylum', and includes arrangements provided for under the Dublin Convention.

that consequently the petitioner and his son would be removed to Austria for the determination of their claim.[19] But 'operational difficulties' meant that removal was not effected within the one-month time limit prescribed by Article 11(5) of the Convention, which—like the rest of the Convention—is not enacted into UK law. Removal orders were eventually issued on 11 May, to take effect on 17 May.

The petitioner sought declarator that the removal directions were unlawful and unreasonable in that they were contrary to a legitimate expectation, to which the UK's entry into the Dublin Convention had given rise and on which he was entitled to rely, that he would not be transferred to Austria once the time limit specified in Article 11(5) of the Convention had expired. He also sought declarator that the Home Secretary's continued reliance on the 'section 11(2) certificate' was unlawful, and sought reduction of the certificate.

The Outer House of the Court of Session (Lord Drummond Young) refused the prayer of petition. Neither the Dublin Convention in general nor Article 11(5) in particular gave rise to the legitimate expectation alleged.

Lord Drummond Young was prepared in principle to 'accept that, when the United Kingdom enters into an international treaty, that may give rise to a legitimate expectation on the part of individuals that the executive will act in accordance with the terms of the treaty', quoting the reasons set forth by Mason CJ and Deane J in the High Court of Australia in *Minister for Immigration and Ethnic Affairs v Teoh*:[20]

> [R]atification of a convention is a positive statement by the executive government of this country to the world and to the Australian people that the executive government and its agencies will act in accordance with the convention. That positive statement is an adequate foundation for a legitimate expectation, absent statutory or executive indications to the contrary, that administrative decision-makers will act in conformity with the convention . . . It is not necessary that a person seeking to set up such a legitimate expectation should be aware of the convention or should personally entertain the expectation; it is enough that the expectation is reasonable in the sense that there are adequate materials to support it . . .[21]

His Lordship also quoted Mason CJ and Deane J's rider:

> The existence of a legitimate expectation that a decision-maker will act in a particular way does not necessarily compel him or her to act in that way. That is the difference between a legitimate expectation and a binding rule of law. To regard a legitimate expectation as requiring the decision-maker to act in a particular way is tantamount to treating it as a rule of law. It incorporates the provisions of the unincorporated convention into our municipal law by the back door.[22]

[19] The Secretary of State is empowered to order removal by Immigration Act 1971, Sch. 2(I), para. 8.

[20] (1995) 183 CLR 273.

[21] 2003 SLT 1358 at 1362, para. 10, quoting (1995)183 CLR 273 at 291 (Mason CJ and Deane J).

[22] 2003 SLT 1358 at 1363, para. 10, quoting (1995)183 CLR 273 at 291 (Mason CJ and Deane J).

His Lordship noted that these statements from *Teoh* had been approved by Lord Woolf MR and Hobhouse LJ respectively in the English Court of Appeal case of *R v Secretary of State for the Home Department*, Ex parte *Ahmed and Patel*.[23] They had been adopted in Scotland by Lord Carloway in *Ibrahim v Secretary of State for the Home Department*,[24] and, in Lord Drummond Young's opinion, this correctly represented the position in Scots law.

Against this backdrop of general principle, his Lordship explained that 'the ability of an international treaty to give rise to legitimate expectations is subject to three major qualifications'.[25] He elaborated:

> The first of these [qualifications] is described in the second paragraph of the passage quoted above from *Minister for Immigration and Ethnic Affairs v Teoh*: even when a legitimate expectation exists, the decision maker is not compelled to act in accordance with it; if there are valid reasons to the contrary, he may decline to do so. That is because a legitimate expectation is not a binding rule of law. The second qualification is also mentioned in *Minister for Immigration and Ethnic Affairs v Teoh*: even if a legitimate expectation might otherwise emerge from the fact that the executive has concluded a treaty, it may be negatived either by statute or by a contrary indication issued by the executive. The notion that a legitimate expectation may be negatived by statute requires no comment. The possibility that a legitimate expectation may be negatived by a declaration by the executive arises out of the fact that it is not a rule of law. The underlying basis for the recognition of legitimate expectations is the principle that government and public administration should be carried on in a reasonable manner, and that that involves consistency of decision making. If the executive makes a public statement that it will act in a particular way in a particular category of cases, the principle of consistency requires that it should act in that way unless there are valid reasons to the contrary. That is what creates a legitimate expectation. If, however, the executive makes a statement that in future it will act in a different way, the principle of consistency is not infringed; the executive has simply exercised its right to alter the basis on which it acts, in a situation where it is not bound by legislation or the common law.[26]

To the last point his Lordship added that '[t]he treaty itself, of course, is not binding in domestic law unless it is incorporated into legislation'.[27] Lord Drummond Young then outlined his third major qualification, one not alluded to in *Teoh*:

> The third qualification on the principle that entering into an international treaty may give rise to legitimate expectations is this: not every treaty will have that effect, and the particular treaty relied upon must be examined to discover whether its nature is such that it can reasonably be supposed to give rise to legitimate expectations on the part of individuals or other legal persons.

[23] 2003 SLT 1358 at 1363, para. 10, citing [1998] INLR 570, this *Year Book*, 69 (1998), pp. 330–1 (CA), at 583 (Lord Woolf MR) and 592 (Hobhouse LJ).

[24] 2003 SLT 1358 at 1363, para. 10, citing 2002 SLT 1150 (OH, Lord Carloway).

[25] 2003 SLT 1358 at 1363, para. 11.

[26] 2003 SLT 1358 at 1363, para. 11.

[27] 2003 SLT 1358 at 1363, para. 11.

> International treaties and conventions cover a vast range of subject matter. Some are clearly intended to affect the rights or status of individuals; the Geneva Convention relating to the Status of Refugees is a good example. In such cases it will usually, although perhaps not invariably, be appropriate to draw the conclusion that the treaty gives rise to a legitimate expectation that the government, and its ministers, officials and agencies, will act according to its terms. Other treaties are clearly not intended to affect the rights of individuals, but rather to regulate the relations of states or governments among themselves; military, naval and defensive treaties are obvious examples of this category. Treaties of the latter sort will not give rise to legitimate expectations on the part of individuals, because they are concerned with acts of the state or government acting as such at an international level, and acts of that nature are beyond the scope of the domestic law. In yet other cases, a treaty may have some bearing on the rights or status of individuals, but its subject matter or objectives or terms may be such as to negative any implication that it gives rise to legitimate expectations on the part of those individuals.[28]

'In every case', his Lordship stated, 'the terms and objectives of the treaty in question must be examined, and the court must decide the category into which it falls'.[29]

Applying these considerations in the instant case, Lord Drummond Young was of the view that the Dublin Convention did not give rise to a legitimate expectation on the part of individuals. First and foremost, it was a treaty intended to regulate the relations of states *inter se*. Its rationale was the allocation among Member States of the European Union of responsibility for determining asylum applications. The fact that this was 'an allocation of responsibility for a particular public function . . . in itself indicate[d] that the Convention was intended to have an interstate or intergovernmental effect, rather than to affect the substantive rights of individuals'.[30] Moreover, the Convention did not posit substantive principles to be applied when determining claims for refugee status, but merely indicated which state was to make this determination in accordance with the Geneva Convention on the Status of Refugees.[31] The intended interstate or intergovernmental import of the Convention was borne out by its provisions, including Article 11, embodying the procedures and time limits that govern the transfer of applicants among Parties: in his Lordship's eyes, '[w]hile the individual applicant is obviously affected by [these] procedures, they are expressed in such a way that they take effect between the authorities of the states concerned'.[32] Nor did the preamble to the Convention assist the petitioner, who had submitted that one of its recitals[33] 'amounted to a clear recognition that the Convention was

[28] 2003 SLT 1358 at 1363, para. 12.

[29] 2003 SLT 1358 at 1363, para. 12.

[30] 2003 SLT 1358 at 1363, para. 13.

[31] 2003 SLT 1358 at 1363, para. 13.

[32] 2003 SLT 1358 at 1364, para. 13.

[33] See preamble, fourth recital, which reads:

> Aware of the need . . . to take measures to avoid any situations arising, with the result that applicants for asylum are left in doubt for too long as regards the likely outcome of their applications and concerned to provide all applicants for asylum with a guarantee that their applications will be

intended to confer benefits on individual applicants for asylum by identifying the state that could deal with the claim'.[34] The point, his Lordship emphasised, was that these benefits were 'indirect': the Convention as such was concerned with determining the state whose authorities are responsible for examining a given claim, and that was 'a matter between states, which [did] not confer legitimate expectations upon individuals'.[35] Nor was a more limited legitimate expectation relating solely to the time limits in Article 11 capable of being founded on the Convention.[36] For all these reasons, his Lordship concluded '[t]hat the Dublin Convention does not give rise to any legitimate expectations on the part of individual applicants for asylum', and that this was enough to refuse the prayer of petition.[37]

Lord Drummond Young noted that the same conclusion had been reached in the English cases of *R v Secretary of State for the Home Department*, Ex parte *Gashi and Gjoka*,[38] *R (on the application of Zeqiri) v Secretary of State for the Home Department*[39] and *R (on the application of Lika) v Secretary of State for the Home Department*,[40] decisions which he was of the opinion accurately represented Scots law.[41] In this regard, he rejected the petitioner's submission that these cases could be distinguished on the basis that they referred to the UK legislation in force before the Immigration and Asylum Act 1999, namely the Asylum and Immigration Act 1996. The petitioner had argued that, since the provision of the 1996 Act which corresponded to section 11 of the 1999 Act did not specifically mention the arrangements in force under the Dublin

examined by one of the Member States and to ensure that applicants for asylum are not referred successively from one Member State to another without any of these States acknowledging itself to be competent to examine the application for asylum . . .

[34] 2003 SLT 1358 at 1364, para. 15.
[35] 2003 SLT 1358 at 1364, para. 15.
[36] 2003 SLT 1358 at 1364–5, para. 16.
[37] 2003 SLT 1358 at 1365, para. 17.
[38] Unreported, 15 June 2000 (QBD, Collins J), at para. 11.
[39] [2001] EWCA Civ 342; [2002] Imm AR 42, at para. 49.
[40] [2002] EWCA Civ 1855, this *Year Book*, 73 (2002), pp. 434–9 (CA), at para. 20–6.
[41] 2003 SLT 1358 at 1365, para. 17.
[42] The relevant provision of the 1996 Act was s. 2, which stated:

(1) Nothing in section 6 of the 1993 Act (protection of claimants from deportation etc) shall prevent a person who has made a claim for asylum being removed from the United Kingdom if—
(a) the Secretary of State has certified that, in his opinion, the conditions mentioned in subsection (2) below are fulfilled;
(b) the certificate has not been set aside on an appeal under section 3 below; and
(c) except in the case of a person who is to be sent to a country or territory to which subsection (3) below applies, the time for giving notice of such an appeal has expired and no such appeal is pending.

(2) The conditions are—
(a) that the person is not a national or citizen of the country or territory to which he is to be sent;
(b) that his life and liberty would not be threatened in that country or territory by reason of his race, religion, nationality, membership of a particular social group, or political opinion; and
(c) that the government of that country or territory would not send him to another country or territory otherwise than in accordance with the Convention.

Convention,[42] section 11 had effected a change in the law, with the result that the previous case-law could not be relied on. But in his Lordship's view the finding that 'the objectives and terms of the . . . Convention are such as to indicate that it was intended to have effect among states only, and not to create legitimate expectations in individuals' was unaffected by any change in the relevant UK law brought about by the 1999 Act.[43] Section 11 of that Act '[was] designed to implement the Dublin Convention' and '[could] not have any greater effect than the Convention itself in giving rise to legitimate expectations among applicants for asylum'.[44]

Furthermore, in an example of his second qualification, Lord Drummond Young considered that even if the Dublin Convention were capable of giving rise to legitimate expectations on the part of applicants for asylum, the actual existence of such expectations had been 'negatived by an executive declaration to the contrary'[45] in the form of paragraph 345 of the Immigration Rules,[46] relating to cases under the Convention. It was clear that this provision applied in the instant case, and it had not been contended to the contrary. In this light, even if the Convention could be regarded as potentially giving rise to legitimate expectations on the part of individuals, paragraph 345 of the Immigration Rules indicated that the Home Secretary would normally refuse an asylum application and issue a certificate for the removal of the applicant from the UK in cases such as the one before the Court. This was 'sufficient to negative any expectation' that an asylum application would be dealt with under the strict terms of Article 11 of the Convention: all the applicant was entitled

[43] 2003 SLT 1358 at 1366, para. 19.

[44] 2003 SLT 1358 at 1366, para. 19.

[45] 2003 SLT 1358 at 1365, para. 18.

[46] HC 395. Paragraph 345 states:

(1) In a case where the Secretary of State is satisfied that the conditions set out in either section 11(2) or section 12(7) of the Immigration and Asylum Act 1999 are fulfilled, he will normally refuse the asylum application and issue a certificate under section 11 or section 12 of the Immigration and Asylum Act 1999 (as the case may be) without substantive consideration of the applicant's claim to refugee status. The conditions are:
   (i) that the applicant is not a national or citizen of the country or territory to which he is to be sent;
   (ii) that the applicant's life and liberty would not be threatened in that country by reason of his race, religion, nationality, membership of a particular social group, or political opinion; and
   (iii) that the government of that country or territory would not send him to another country or territory otherwise than in accordance with the Convention.

(2) The Secretary of State shall not remove an asylum applicant without substantive consideration of his claim unless:
   (i) the asylum applicant has not arrived in the United Kingdom directly from the country in which he claims to fear persecution and has had an opportunity at the border or within the third country or territory to make contact with the authorities of that third country or territory in order to seek their protection; or
   (ii) there is other clear evidence of his admissibility to a third country or territory.

Provided that he is satisfied that a case meets these criteria, the Secretary of State is under no obligation to consult the authorities of the third country or territory before the removal of an asylum applicant to that country or territory.

to expect was that paragraph 345 of the Immigration Rules would be applied.[47] His Lordship noted that a similar conclusion had been reached by the English Court of Appeal in *Lika*.[48]

Finally, Lord Drummond Young addressed a submission made by the respondent in the alternative which relied on a decision of the intergovernmental committee established under Article 18 of the Dublin Convention,[49] which enjoys powers to revise or amend the Convention. In its decision number 1/97, of 9 September 1997, the committee stated that '[w]here the transfer of the asylum applicant has to be postponed due to special circumstances such as sickness, pregnancy, criminal detention, etc, and it is therefore not possible to carry out the transfer within the normal period of one month, the Member States concerned shall duly consult and agree on a case-by-case basis on the time limit within which the transfer must take place'. His Lordship was satisfied that the requirements of this decision had been met in the petitioner's case,[50] and he continued:

> If the requirements of [decision number 1/97] are satisfied, an applicant for asylum cannot complain that his legitimate expectations are being infringed. Even if the Dublin Convention is regarded as giving rise to such expectations, the most that an applicant for asylum can expect is that the respondent will act in accordance with the Convention together with any decisions of the committee set up under art 18 of the Convention. That is because that committee was expressly given power, by arts 16 and 17 of the Convention, to adopt decisions revising or amending the Convention. In the present case, accordingly, the petitioner could not have any legitimate expectation that the time limit specified in art 11(5) of the Convention would be followed or that, if the time limit could not be followed, the petitioner would be permitted to remain in the United Kingdom. The most that the petitioner could expect is that the procedures in [decision number 1/97] would be followed if special circumstances existed. In a case such

[47] 2003 SLT 1358 at 1365, para. 18. [48] See *supra*, n. 40. [49] Article 18 provides:

1. A Committee shall be set up comprising one representative of the Government of each Member State. The Committee shall be chaired by the Member State holding the Presidency of the Council of the European Communities.
   The Commission of the European Communities may participate in the discussions of the Committee and the working parties referred to in paragraph 4.
2. The Committee shall examine, at the request of one or more Member States, any question of a general nature concerning the application or interpretation of this Convention.
   The Committee shall determine the measures referred to in Article 11(6) and Article 13(2) and shall give the authorization referred to in Article 17(2).
   The Committee shall adopt decisions revising or amending the Convention pursuant to Articles 16 and 17.
3. The Committee shall take its decisions unanimously, except where it is acting pursuant to Article 17(2), in which case it shall take its decisions by a majority of two-thirds of the votes of its members.
4. The Committee shall determine its rules of procedure and may set up working parties. The Secretariat of the Committee and of the working parties shall be provided by the General Secretariat of the Council of the European Communities.

[50] 2003 SLT 1358 at 1366–7, paras. 22–3.

> as the present, where special circumstances do exist, it is open to the United Kingdom and Austria to agree precisely when the transfer should take place, and in so doing they are not constrained by the one month limit. In those circumstances [decision number 1/97] would be satisfied.[51]

'That', in his Lordship's opinion, 'satisfie[d] any legitimate expectations that the petitioner might have had under the Convention'.[52]

The Court's decision, sound in principle and consonant with English case-law, highlights once again the increasingly sophisticated nature of the relationship between unincorporated treaties and the law of the UK, as seen in 2002 in *Lika*. Like the English case-law and *Teoh* before it in Australia,[53] it strikes a clever balance. It recognises with good reason—as, for the purposes of Scots law, did *Ibrahim v Secretary of State for the Home Department*[54] just the year before—that 'ratification by [the UK] of an international convention is not to be dismissed as a merely platitudinous or ineffectual act'.[55] At the same time, it in no way threatens to scupper *The Parlement Belge*[56] and with it the separation of powers.

Relationship between international law and English law—hijacking within meaning of Convention for the Suppression of Unlawful Seizure of Aircraft—Aviation Security Act 1982—defence of duress—whether common-law defence of duress available to charge of hijacking under Aviation Security Act

Case No 3. R v Safi (Ali Ahmed), 6 June 2003, [2003] EWCA Crim 1809, 2003 WL 21236411 (CA (Crim Div)).

The eight appellants hijacked an aircraft in February 2000 in what was then Taliban-ruled Afghanistan. They detained the cabin crew and passengers, and demanded to be flown to the West. After brief landings in Tashkent (for fuel), Aktyubinsk, Kazakhstan (for minor repairs), and

[51] 2003 SLT 1358 at 1367, para. 24. [52] 2003 SLT 1358 at 1367, para. 24.

[53] Note that the decision in *Teoh* was subsequently overridden by the Australian government: see 'International Treaties and the High Court Decision in *Teoh*', Joint Statement by the Minister for Foreign Affairs, Senator Gareth Evans, and the Attorney-General, Michael Lavarch, 10 May 1995, <http://www.dfat.gov.au/media/releases/foreign/1995/m44.html>, as replaced by 'The Effect of Treaties in Administrative Decision Making', Joint Statement by the Minister for Foreign Affairs (Alexander Downer) and the Attorney-General and Minister for Justice (Daryl Williams), 27 February 1997, <http://www.lib.monash.edu.au/law/teohjs.htm>, both explicitly constituting 'executive indication to the contrary' for the purposes and in the words of *Teoh*. *Teoh* has also recently been called into question by the High Court of Australia in *Re Minister for Immigration and Multicultural Affairs; Ex parte Lam* (2003) 195 ALR 502: see, in this regard, W Lacey, 'A Prelude to the Demise of *Teoh*: The High Court Decision in *Re Minister for Immigration and Multicultural Affairs; Ex parte Lam*' (2004) 26 *Syd LR* 131.

[54] 2003 SLT 1358 at 1363, para. 10, citing 2002 SLT 1150.

[55] 2003 SLT 1358 at 1362, para. 10, quoting *Minister for Immigration and Ethnic Affairs v Teoh* (1995) 183 CLR 273 at 291 (Mason CJ and Deane J).

[56] (1878–79) 4 PD 129.

Moscow, the plane headed for the UK, eventually landing at Stansted Airport. The incident ended without bloodshed a few days later when the appellants surrendered to the UK authorities, releasing the crew and passengers unharmed. The appellants were convicted of, *inter alia*, hijacking under section 1 of the Aviation Security Act 1982, which incorporates into English law the offences provided for in the Convention for the Suppression of Unlawful Seizure of Aircraft 1970 (the 'Hague Convention').[57]

At trial, the appellants pleaded the defence of duress, arguing that they had acted in response to an imminent threat of death or serious injury to themselves or to those for whom it was reasonable for them to accept responsibility. They claimed to be members of a dissident political organisation that had recently come to the attention of the Taliban government, which had promptly arrested and tortured some of its members in order, it was thought, to extract information. Those tortured had known the names of most of the members of the organisation, including those of the appellants; there was also evidence that a list of the names of thirty-five members of the group had fallen into the Taliban's hands. It was alleged that the appellants and their families were thereby placed at imminent risk of capture, torture, and death. Moreover, the appellants would have been forced to divulge the names of the other members of the organisation, exposing them in turn to capture, torture, and death. It was further argued that their actions in Moscow and at Stansted were also the result of duress: there was an imminent threat, if the appellants were to surrender, that the local authorities would return them to face death or serious injury in Afghanistan; there was also the risk that the heavily armed troops which surrounded the plane at both airports would storm the craft and kill them. In short, the appellants submitted 'that they had no alternative but to act as they did'.[58]

On appeal to the Court of Appeal (Criminal Division) (Longmore LJ, Hooper and Cox JJ, the first giving the leading judgment), the case turned on a point of English criminal law, namely the correct jury direction in a case of duress. The appeal was allowed, the Court holding that there had been a misdirection in law.[59] The importance of the judgment for present purposes lies not in its discussion of the test for establishing the defence of duress at English law, but rather in its following the controversial ruling by a differently constituted Court of Appeal (Criminal Division) in *R v Abdul-Hussain (Mustafa Shakir)*[60] that—absent homicide—the defence of

[57] The Hague, 16 December 1970, 860 UNTS 1971.

[58] Judgment (available on Westlaw™ UK), para. 3.

[59] The Court, applying *R v Graham* [1982] 1 WLR 294, stated that the correct test for establishing a defence of duress was made up of a subjective and an objective limb—first, whether the defendants had been compelled to act in the way they did because they reasonably believed they faced death or serious injury, and, second, whether a reasonable person in the same circumstances would have acted in the same way.

[60] 17 December 1998, unreported, noted [1999] Crim LR 570 (CA (Crim Div)).

duress is in principle available, on the usual grounds, to a charge of hijacking under section 1 of the Aviation Security Act. In the words of the Court, '[o]nce it is accepted (as it was in *Abdul-Hussain*) that duress applies to hijacking, it must apply to the same extent as analogous cases'.[61]

The present ruling, like *Abdul-Hussain* before it, brings into sharp relief an unremarked feature of the municipal implementation of international criminal law: to the extent that the contrary is not expressly provided, municipal offences deriving from international law are, like other municipal offences, to be read in the light of the general part of the relevant corpus of municipal criminal law, be it code or common law. In other words, in the absence of *lex specialis*, the general material and mental elements necessary to establish criminal responsibility under the law of the state in question, and the general defences available under that law to such responsibility, are applicable in municipal courts as much to international crimes as to common crimes. The upshot is considerable national variation in the conditions and scope of responsibility for international crimes in municipal courts, with the consequence that it is quite possible for an individual to be convicted of an international crime in one state on the basis of conduct which would not lead to a conviction for the same international crime in another.

This is not in any way wrong. If we focus on defences and on international crimes provided for by treaty, as in the present case, it seems that the availability in municipal courts of municipal-law[62] defences to treaty crimes is not internationally unlawful, as a general rule.[63] The classic conventional obligation to render the offence defined in the convention punishable under municipal law[64] is not, strictly speaking, violated when a state which does enact the offence permits defences to it. Nor does the *judicare* limb of the classic conventional obligation *aut dedere aut judicare* impose on a state party anything more than a duty to 'submit [relevant cases] to

[61] Judgment, para. 25.

[62] General international law recognises duress as a defence to war crimes not involving homicide, at the least: see *eg Erdemovic*, IT-96-22-A, Appeals Chamber, Sentencing Appeal, 7 October 1997, (1997,) 111 ILR 298. The Rome Statute of the ICC recognises it, at least in principle, as a defence to all war crimes, as well as to crimes against humanity and genocide: see Rome Statute of the International Criminal Court, UN Doc A/CONF.183/9, English text as corrected, Art. 31(1)(d). But the Hague Convention makes no provision for duress, or for any other plea, as a defence to hijacking within the meaning of the Convention.

[63] *Cf* Convention against Torture and Other Cruel, Inhuman or Degrading Treatment or Punishment, 10 December 1984, 1465 UNTS 112, Art. 2(2), which states that '[a]n order from a superior officer or a public authority may not be invoked as a justification for torture' in municipal courts.

[64] See *eg* Hague Convention, Art. 2, which provides that '[e]ach Contracting State undertakes to make the offence [defined in the Convention] punishable by severe penalties'. Note that, as formulated in the Hague Convention, the obligation of municipal criminalisation is elided with the distinct obligation to impose penalties reflecting the gravity of the offence. See also *eg* Convention for the Suppression of Unlawful Acts against the Safety of Civilian Aircraft, 23 September 1971 ('Montreal Convention'), 974 UNTS 177, Art. 3; but *cf* more recent conventions, *eg* Convention for the Suppression of Terrorist Bombings, 15 December 1997, UN Treaty Reg. No. 37517, Art. 4, which teases apart the two undertakings.

its competent authorities for the purposes of prosecution':[65] it does not oblige a state to convict persons accused of the relevant crime. Moreover, the possibility of exculpation, which is not expressly provided for in any of the various international criminal conventions, has been held by the ICTY to be a general principle of criminal law recognised by national criminal justice systems and, as such, a general principle of international criminal law.[66] It is also arguable that the tolerance of municipal-law defences to international crimes is pragmatic policy. Asking the overwhelming majority of states whose criminal law is codified to remove the availability, only in cases of international crimes, of the defences otherwise permitted by the general part of the criminal law is fiddly and inconvenient, and hardly calculated to encourage widespread municipal implementation of international criminal law. As long as any relevant international obligations are observed, it might be sensible to allow for a margin of appreciation. As it is, it is hard to see how national harmonisation could be achieved, even if it were desired.

At the same time, the specific defence of duress as pleaded in *Abdul-Hussain* and in the present case might be thought to go close to constituting an excuse to responsibility for what in popular terms is a 'terrorist' offence on the basis of, broadly speaking, the political motivation behind its commission. If rightly characterised as such, it would run counter to the current international political consensus, which 'stresse[s] that all acts of terrorism, regardless of motive or origin, [are] criminal and unjustifiable'.[67] On the other hand, if terrorism is legally defined as in the current informal text of Article 2(1) of the draft comprehensive convention on international terrorism,[68] hijacking committed (as alleged here) not for the purposes of intimidation or political coercion and involving (as here) no loss of life, limb, or property is not terrorism within the meaning of international law. If this is so, then the recognition of the common-law defence of duress in such circumstances would be a welcome judicial defence of simple humanity in a climate of hysteria.

[65] See *eg* Hague Convention, Art. 7.

[66] *Kordic & Cerkez*, IT-95-14/2, Trial Chamber, Judgment, 26 February 2001, para. 449.

[67] Report of the Ad Hoc Committee established by General Assembly resolution 51/210 of 17 December 1996, Fifth session (12–23 February 2001), UN Doc A/56/37, Annex V, para. 1; see also Measures to eliminate international terrorism. Report of the Working Group, General Assembly, Sixth Committee, Fifty-Sixth session, UN Doc A/C.6/56/L.9, 29 Oct 2001, Annex IV, para. 1; SC res 1377 (2001), 12 Nov 2001, Annex, fifth recital; and, similarly, Declaration on Measures to Eliminate International Terrorism, GA res 49/60, 9 Dec 1994, Annex, para. 1; Declaration to Supplement the 1994 Declaration on Measures to Eliminate International Terrorism, GA res 51/210, 17 Dec 1996, Annex, para. 1.

[68] The current informal text of Art. 2(1) of the draft comprehensive convention (see Report of the Ad Hoc Committee established by General Assembly resolution 51/210 of 17 December 1996, Sixth session (28 January-1 February 2002), UN Doc A/57/37, Annex II) reads:

Any person commits an offence within the meaning of this Convention if that person, by any means, unlawfully and intentionally, causes:

(a) Death or serious bodily injury to any person; or

Civil jurisdiction—extraterritoriality—whether the English courts will issue third party debt order in respect of a foreign debt

Case No 4. Société Eram Shipping Company Limited v Hong Kong and Shanghai Banking Corporation Limited, also known as *Société Eram Shipping Company Limited v Compagnie Internationale de Navigation,* 12 June 2003, [2003] UKHL 30; [2003] 3 WLR 21; [2003] 3 All ER 465; 2003 WL 21236535, <http://www.parliament.the-stationery-office.co.uk/pa/ld200203/ldjudgmt/jd030612/soci-1.htm> (HL).

The respondent, a judgment creditor, was seeking to enforce a judgment registered in the English courts[69] by using the third party debt procedure[70] in respect of a foreign debt. The judgment debtors were resident in Hong Kong. The respondent wished to execute against money held by one of the judgment debtors in an account with the appellant bank, the third party, at its principal office in Hong Kong. The credit balance was a debt payable by the bank to the debtor in Hong Kong and governed by Hong Kong law. (The English courts had jurisdiction over the bank via its registered branch in London.) The bank appealed against the final third party debt order made by the Court of Appeal.

The House of Lords granted the appeal and set aside the order of the Court of Appeal. The judgment is one primarily involving questions of private international law and is discussed in that context elsewhere in this volume.[71] Its relevance for present purposes lies in statements made by Lords Hoffman and Millett regarding exorbitant exercises of civil jurisdiction.

Lord Hoffman (with whom several of the other Lords agreed[72]) returned to a theme on which he, as Hoffman J, had expounded in 1986 in *Mackinnon v Donaldson, Lufkin and Jenrette Securities Corporation*:[73]

> 54. . . . The execution of a judgment is an exercise of sovereign authority. It is a seizure by the state of an asset of the judgment debtor to satisfy the creditor's claim. And it is a general principle of international law that one sovereign state should not trespass upon the authority of another, by attempting to seize assets situated within the jurisdiction of the foreign state or compelling its citizens to do acts within its boundaries.

(b) Serious damage to public or private property, including a place of public use, a State or government facility, a public transportation system, an infrastructure facility or the environment; or

(c) Damage to property, places, facilities, or systems referred to in paragraph 1(b) of this article, resulting or likely to result in major economic loss,

when the purpose of the conduct, by its nature or context, is to intimidate a population, or to compel a Government or an international organization to do or abstain from doing any act.

69 See Civil Jurisdiction and Judgments Act 1982.

70 See Civil Procedure Rules, Part 72.

71 See *infra*, pp. 511–20.

72 See [2003] 3 WLR 21 at 35; [2003] 3 All ER 465 at 479, para. 31 (Lord Nicholls); [2003] 3 WLR 21 at 45; [2003] 3 All ER 465 at 489, para. 70 (Lord Hobhouse); [2003] 3 WLR 21 at 57; [2003] 3 All ER 465 at 500, para. 113 (Lord Millett).

73 [1986] Ch 482 at 493–4.

55. In the modern world, banking is perhaps the strongest illustration of the importance of mutual respect for national sovereignties. There are nearly 500 foreign banks in London, to say nothing of British banks with branches overseas. Banking is a highly regulated activity and each head office or branch has to comply with the laws of the jurisdiction in which it operates. If the courts of one country in which a bank operates exercise no restraint about using their sovereign powers of compulsion in relation to accounts maintained with that bank at branches in other countries, conflict and chaos is likely to follow.[74]

Lord Millett[75] considered '[t]he near universal rule of international law' to be 'that sovereignty, both legislative and adjudicative, is territorial, that is to say it may be exercised only in relation to persons and things within the territory of the state concerned or in respect of its own nationals';[76] and he thought that the English courts 'ought not to exercise an exorbitant jurisdiction contrary to generally accepted norms of international law and expect a foreign court to sort out the consequences'.[77]

While Lord Millett's sweeping statement as to the impermissibility of extraterritorial legislative and adjudicative jurisdiction overstates the position under public international law, especially in the civil context, Lord Hoffman's counsel of restraint is surely appropriate and in the interests of comity.[78]

State immunity—State Immunity Act 1978—relationship between customary international law and English law—international prohibition on torture—public policy—Human Rights Act 1998—European Convention on Human Rights, Article 6—role of European Court of Human Rights—whether department of government of foreign state entitled to state immunity in respect of allegations of torture and false imprisonment committed abroad

Case No 5. Jones v Saudi Arabia, also known as *Jones v Ministry of the Interior Al-Mamlaka Al-Arabiya as Saudiya (Kingdom of Saudi Arabia) and Lieutenant-Colonel Abdul Aziz*, 30 July 2003, 2003 WL 22187644 (QBD, Master Whitaker).

The claimant sought damages in tort, including aggravated and exemplary damages, for assault, battery, false imprisonment, and the putative

[74] [2003] 3 WLR 21 at 41–2; [2003] 3 All ER 465 at 485–6, paras. 54–5.

[75] Lord Hobhouse, who was in 'full agreement' with Lords Bingham and Hoffman, was also in 'broad agreement' with Lord Millett: [2003] 3 WLR 21 at 45; [2003] 3 All ER 465 at 489, para. 70.

[76] [2003] 3 WLR 21 at 48; [2003] 3 All ER 465 at 492, para. 80.

[77] [2003] 3 WLR 21 at 56; [2003] 3 All ER 465 at 499, para. 109.

[78] See also, in this context, *Peer International Corporation v Termidor Music Publishers Limited, Termidor Musikverlag GmBH & Co KG and Editoria Musical de Cuba*, 30 July 2003, [2003] EWCA Civ 1156, *infra*, pp. 481–6.

tort of torture,[79] to which he alleged he had been subjected in Saudi Arabia. The first defendant sought to have the claim struck out on the grounds, *inter alia*, that it was entitled to state immunity pursuant to the State Immunity Act 1978. (Attempts to effect service on the second defendant had proved unsuccessful.)

The first defendant argued that, since it was undisputed that it was a department of the government of the Kingdom of Saudi Arabia,[80] it was entitled to state immunity in accordance with Section 1 of the Act unless any of the exceptions enumerated in Sections 2 to 7 of the Act applied; that the only relevant exception was in Section 5, relating to actions in respect of personal injury;[81] that Section 5 clearly requires that the personal injury alleged be caused by an act or omission occurring in the UK; and that the claimant's injury, including alleged psychiatric injury, was said to have been caused by an act or acts occurring in Saudi Arabia. In support of its submission, the first defendant relied on the decision in *Al-Adsani v Government of Kuwait*,[82] in which the Court of Appeal upheld the striking out, for the reasons now submitted by the first defendant, of a civil claim analogous to the present one, stating that the exceptions to immunity from suit expressly provided for in the Act were exhaustive. The compatibility of this decision with the right to access to the courts guaranteed by Article 6 of the European Convention on Human Rights, as effectively incorporated in the UK by the Human Rights Act 1998, had been upheld since by a Grand Chamber of the European Court of Human Rights in *Al-Adsani v United Kingdom*.[83]

In response, the claimant conceded that the exception to state immunity embodied in Section 5 of the Act was limited to proceedings in respect of personal injury caused by an act or omission in the UK. He submitted, however, that the claim for false imprisonment was not one in respect of personal injury, and that claims in relation to torts such as this remained governed by the common law. Furthermore, as regards the claim for the putative tort of torture, he argued that public policy in 2003 demanded that state immunity not serve as a bar to suit in the English

[79] Although the judgment does not spell this out, the tort of torture asserted by the claimant clearly derives from *Al-Adsani v Government of Kuwait*, 103 ILR 420 (QBD, Mantell J) and 107 ILR 536, this *Year Book*, 67 (1996), pp. 537–42 (CA), where the Court entertained—but did not as such recognise—the existence of an English tort of 'torture' (as distinct from the torts of assault and battery) based on the customary international prohibition on torture. See also *infra*, pp. 492–3.

[80] See State Immunity Act, s. 14(1)(c).

[81] Section 5 ('Personal injuries and damage to property') reads:

A State is not immune as respects [*sic*] proceedings in respect of—

(a) death or personal injury; or
(b) damage to or loss of tangible property,

caused by an act or omission in the United Kingdom.

[82] See *supra*, n. 79.

[83] Application No 35763/97, 21 November 2001, (2002) 34 EHRR 11.

courts in respect of torture committed in foreign states against British citizens, and that the Court should construe Section 5 as not applying to such acts, relying for support for this contention on the speech of Lord Cross in *Oppenheimer v Cattermole*[84] and on the decision of the House of Lords in *Kuwait Airways Corporation v Iraqi Airways Company (Nos 4 and 5)*.[85] Finally, the claimant submitted that state immunity in respect of torture was indeed incompatible with Article 6 of the European Convention on Human Rights: since the Court of Appeal's decision in *Al-Adsani*, not only had the international prohibition on torture been recognised by the House of Lords in *R v Bow Street Metropolitan Stipendiary Magistrate*, Ex parte *Pinochet Ugarte (No 3)*[86] as a norm of *jus cogens*, *viz* a peremptory norm of international law, but 'now in the year 2003, the court should take the view that the same principles should be applied to the civil law as to the criminal law, and that there should be no civil state immunity for acts of torture'.[87]

The Court agreed with the first defendant, striking out the claim in its entirety. The assault, battery, and 'torture' claims were all in respect of personal injury caused by acts not occurring in the UK, and thus fell outside the exception to state immunity recognised in Section 5 of the Act.[88] As for the claim for false imprisonment, even if this were to be characterised as not in respect of personal injury, it still fell outside Section 5, since the purpose of the Act—as noted by Lord Goff in *Pinochet (No 3)*, pointing to the long title[89]—was to make new provision for state immunity in relation to civil actions in the English courts, replacing the common law rules completely; as such, the exceptions provided for in the Act were the only exceptions to state immunity available in the English courts in civil proceedings.[90]

Nor did the public policy exception posited by Lord Cross in *Oppenheimer v Cattermole* help the claimant:

> [T]hat statement of principle, aimed at the question of whether the English courts should recognise a foreign law which contradicts international law, cannot be turned on its head to support a submission that the courts in this country have some public policy jurisdiction to strike down an English Act of Parliament or to read it in some restrictive way on the grounds that it is now contrary to international law.[91]

Reliance on *Kuwait Airways (Nos 4 and 5)* was 'more of the same':[92]

> [I]t is clear that this case is still dealing with the question of refusal of recognition of a foreign law and . . . of itself cannot be used as a foundation for a

[84] [1976] AC 249, this *Year Book*, 47 (1974–75), pp. 372–4 (HL).
[85] [2002] 2 AC 883, this *Year Book*, 73 (2002), pp. 400–4 (HL).
[86] [2000] 1 AC 147, this *Year Book*, 70 (1999), pp. 277–95 (HL).
[87] Judgment (available on Westlaw™ UK), para. 29.
[88] Judgment, para. 13.
[89] See [2000] 1 AC 147 at 209.
[90] Judgment, para. 14.
[91] Judgment, para. 17.
[92] Judgment, para. 18.

submission that the English courts can turn the same considerations against an Act of the United Kingdom Parliament.[93]

Indeed, it was important to recall from the *Kuwait Airways* litigation that 'the House of Lords in fact upheld the submission that [Iraqi Airways] enjoyed state immunity for its acts in taking the aircraft, and removing them from Kuwait to Iraq',[94] despite the fact that the invasion and annexation of Kuwait were 'regarded by the House as a gross breach of established rules of international law'.[95]

Pinochet (No 3) was of no direct use, since it concerned the crime of torture; moreover, 'those observations which the members of the House of Lords made in their speeches in respect of the question of state immunity, in connection with civil suits, in fact [ran] counter to [the claimant]'s argument'[96] and 'support the view that the Court of Appeal's decision in *Al-Adsani* was correct'.[97] But as to the claimant's broader argument founded on *Pinochet (No 3)*, it was 'certainly true that since the decision in the House of Lords in *Pinochet*, the Greek Supreme Court . . . in *Prefecture of Voiotia v Federal Republic of Germany* ha[d] taken the view that torts that constitute crimes against humanity involve a breach of *jus cogens* and therefore result in a tacit waiver of immunity on the part of the perpetrator state';[98] the commentary provided to the Court on that case, however, 'note[d] that the [Greek] court offered no authority in supporting this position, and no further explanation for the logical leaps involved in reasoning, and that the dissenting judges were able to assert only that no such jurisdiction exists'.[99] Turning, finally, to the fate of *Al-Adsani* before the European Court of Human Rights, the Court noted that Mr Al-Adsani had indeed lost his case in Strasbourg, but felt it useful to 'say a word about the status of such a judgment of the ECHR':[100]

31. Of course [such a judgment] has to be taken into account as part of the Strasbourg jurisprudence under Section 2 of the Human Rights Act. But one has to bear in mind that . . . the 'third instance' doctrine, [or] however one likes to describe it, means that that [Strasbourg] court has a supervisory role. It is . . . for the national courts to provide the guarantees, the minimum guarantees at least, laid down by the Convention, in particular under Article 6. The fact that the European Court of Human Rights exercising its supervisory role found that as at the date of its decision in November 2001, the English courts were, by applying the State Immunity Act 1978, within the United Kingdom's margin of appreciation, and were providing the minimum guarantee required under Article 6 of access to the court, does not mean that the United Kingdom Courts should thereafter regard that as a situation which is 'set in stone'. The minimum rights guaranteed under the Convention are a floor, not a ceiling. Once the Strasbourg Court has decided that the national court is offering the minimum guarantee the

[93] Judgment, para. 20. [94] Judgment, para. 19. [95] Judgment, para. 20.
[96] Judgment, para. 22. [97] Judgment, para. 28.
[98] Judgment, para. 29. *Prefecture of Voiotia v Federal Republic of Germany* is noted at (2001) 95 *AJIL* 198 (M Gavouneli & I Bantekas). [99] Judgment, para. 29.
[100] Judgment, para. 30.

matter is in effect returned to the national courts. They may of course provide something which is better than that minimum guarantee.

32. Clearly as international law develops the attitude of the English courts towards international law may equally develop. Further, one should bear in mind that the decision of the European Court of Human Rights in the *Al-Adsani* case that the minimum guarantee was being provided was by narrow majority and I for my part have to admit to having found the minority judgments, in particular the judgment of Judge Ferrari Bravo that the ECHR missed a golden opportunity to take a firm stand on torture, very compelling. Nevertheless the judgment of the European Court of Human Rights in *Al-Adsani* must at least have the effect at the moment of precluding a successful application to a judge of this court for a ruling that the State Immunity Act is incompatible with the European Convention.

It also precluded the Court—'regrettably, in [its] judgment'—from reading down the State Immunity Act so as not to apply to acts of torture 'by regarding those acts as not being sovereign acts coming within the Act because they are contrary to international law'.[101]

In conclusion, the Court accordingly took the view that

unless Parliament specifically amends the State Immunity Act in this respect, or another case comes before the European Court of Human Rights in which the minority view in *Al-Adsani* prevails, so that our courts can thereafter consider the making of a declaration of incompatibility in respect of the 1978 Act as it applies to civil actions for torture, the Act deprive[d it] and the English courts of jurisdiction over the first defendant in this case.[102]

As a consequence, 'with the greatest sympathy for the claimant',[103] the Court allowed the first defendant's application and dismissed the claim against it.

The Court's decision is uncontroversial, at least as a formal matter. The English courts are bound by the doctrine of parliamentary supremacy to apply the provisions of the State Immunity Act, which clearly preempt the common law and which provide no exception to immunity from civil actions in respect of either personal injury caused by acts outside the UK, or from any other actions in tort, such as false imprisonment, wherever committed. Nor does the public policy exception to the act of state doctrine recognised in *Kuwait Airways (Nos 4 and 5)*, relating to flagrant breaches of international law, grant the English courts carte blanche to set aside or read down Acts of the UK Parliament allegedly contrary to international standards. As for Article 6 of the ECHR, it is difficult to argue, in effect, that a judgment rendered by the European Court of Human Rights in 2001 has ceased by 2003 to be an adequate statement of the law. At the same time, it is useful to be reminded that the ECHR imposes only a baseline level of protection—guaranteed minima above which national legislatures are free to rise.

[101] Judgment, para. 32. [102] Judgment, para. 33. [103] Judgment, para. 33.

Public policy exception to lex situs *rule—international public policy—civil jurisdiction—extraterritoriality—legislation applying to property situated in another state—whether English courts to give effect to foreign legislation purporting to transfer title to property in UK where legislation consonant with international public policy*

Case No 6. Peer International Corporation and others v Termidor Music Publishers Limited, Termidor Musikverlag GmBH & Co KG and Editoria Musical de Cuba, 30 July 2003, [2003] EWCA Civ 1156*;* 2003 WL 21554794*;* <http://www.courtservice.gov.uk/Judgments.do> (CA).

The claimants sought a declaration that they were the owners or alternatively the exclusive licensees of the UK copyright in certain Cuban music. They based their alleged rights on assignments in writing, dating from the 1930s and 1940s, made by the composers of the works, both Cuban nationals, and on certain 'Confirmations' and 'Addenda' (collectively termed the 'Confirmation of rights' documents) signed by the composers' heirs in about 1989 or 1990. The first and second defendants also claimed to be the exclusive licensees of the UK copyright, pursuant to a licence granted by the third defendant, Editoria Musical de Cuba (EMC), a Cuban state enterprise which claimed to be the owner of the disputed copyright on the basis of Cuban Law 860, promulgated in 1960, in the wake of the Cuban Revolution. This Law—passed in order 'to re-exert Cuban control over intellectual property rights owned by Cuban nationals and prevent further exploitation of these rights by foreign companies', such as the claimant[104]—provided *inter alia* that music publishers were, within sixty days of the Law's passage, to present to the relevant Cuban government authority for approval all contracts concluded between them and Cuban composers prior to the coming into force of the Law, and that failure to do so or failure to gain approval would result in the forfeiture of all the publisher's rights. This included foreign rights: Law 860 had extraterritorial effect under Cuban law. Nor was compensation to be paid. The claimants did not present their contracts for approval and as a consequence, as a matter of Cuban law, Law 860 divested the claimants of the UK copyright in the relevant works, without compensation.

The judge at first instance (Neuberger J)[105] tried three preliminary issues, without prejudice to arguments based on facts relating to the circumstances of either the assignments or subsequent transactions. He held, first, that the assignments were effective at the time to transfer title to the UK copyright in the works to the claimants. He also held that Cuban Law 860 was ineffective to deprive the claimants of this copyright: it was an established and sound rule of English conflict of laws (as stated

[104] Judgment approved by the court for handing down (subject to editorial corrections), para. 14.
[105] 11 December 2002, [2002] EWHC 2675.

by Dicey & Morris) that '[a foreign] governmental act affecting any private proprietary right in any moveable or immovable thing will be recognised as valid and effective in England if the act was valid and effective by the law of the country where the thing was situated *(lex situs)* at the moment when the act takes effect, and not otherwise', and English law did not recognise as valid and effective foreign governmental acts affecting property situated in the UK. Nor did considerations of public policy and comity dictate, as argued for by EMC, that the *lex situs* rule be qualified and Cuban law applied. Finally, the trial judge held that the 'Confirmation of rights' documents, when read together, were effective to transfer title to the reversionary copyright in the relevant works, vested in the composers' heirs, to the claimants. EMC was alone in appealing, initially on all three points but eventually just on the last two.

The Court of Appeal (Civil Division) (Aldous, Mance and Latham LJJ, the first giving the leading judgment, with which the others agreed) dismissed the appeal. It affirmed with little fuss the trial judge's findings on the intellectual property aspects (points one and three), and focused on the question of whether Cuban Law 860 was effective to divest the claimants of the copyright assigned to them by the composers.

EMC's argument was premised on the assertion that Law 860 was not confiscatory but, rather, was 'entirely consonant with English and international concepts of public policy', passed as it was 'to ensure that the music industry did not take unfair advantage of composers who were frequently unsophisticated'—that is, to redress contractual imbalance.[106] The argument proceeded by identifying two propositions central to the application of the *lex situs* rule in the instant case: first, in a corollary to the rule, that the English courts will recognise as valid and effective foreign governmental acts relating extraterritorially to property if the law of the state where the property is found when the acts takes effect does so; and, second, that the English courts will not recognise foreign governmental acts affecting property situated in the UK. EMC submitted that both propositions were subject to exception where public policy and comity required, giving as an example of an exception to the first the decision of the House of Lords in *Kuwait Airways Corporation v Iraqi Airways Company (Nos 4 and 5)*.[107] 'It would therefore not be surprising', EMC maintained, if the second proposition were subject to exception 'where the act of the foreign state was benevolent, as was Law 860, and [where] its policy was in accordance with United Kingdom public policy considerations'.[108] Indeed, just such an exception had been given effect to by Atkinson J in *Lorentzen v Lydden*,[109] which was

[106] Judgment, para. 24.

[107] [2002] 2 AC 883, this *Year Book* 73 (2002), pp. 400–4 (HL). Although it is not made clear in the judgment, counsel's use of *Kuwait Airways (Nos 4 and 5)* was presumably directed at the intended extraterritorial effect of Revolutionary Command Council resolution 369, the foreign law at issue in that case, which purported to transfer all KAC's property worldwide to IAC.

[108] Judgment, para. 27.

[109] [1942] KB 202; see Judgment, paras. 29–30.

followed by Morris J in *O/Y Wassa SS Co Ltd v Newspaper Pulp and Wood Export Ltd*;[110] and, although the judgment of Devlin J in *Bank Voor Handel En Scheepvart NV v Slatford*[111] was to the contrary, 'the law had evolved since [then] as was evidenced by the reasoning in the *Kuwait Airways* case'.[112] Summing up its argument, EMC submitted that '[a]n English court [could] give effect to the legislation of a foreign state affecting property in the United Kingdom where that foreign state is regularising a matter of legitimate interest and the legislation accords with United Kingdom law and public policy widely accepted internationally', and that '[i]n the present case public policy was served by the Cuban law.'[113]

The Court agreed that the first proposition relevant to the application of the *lex situs* rule in this case was subject to a public policy exception.[114] It denied, however, that the second was also so subject.[115] In the Court's view, *Lorentzen v Lyddon* 'was wrongly decided', was 'contrary to the overwhelming statement of judicial opinion, supported by those that have written on the subject' and was 'also contrary to public policy'.[116] In the earlier case of *The El Condado*,[117] the Scottish Court of Session—believing that Scots and English law concurred on point—had taken the opposite view to that taken in *Lorentzen*. More compellingly, in the English case of *Bank Voor Handel*, Devlin J had refused to follow *Lorentzen*, preferring the approach taken in *The El Condado*, as supported by English dicta.[118] The Court quoted extensively from both judgments, and both had in turn approved a statement by Dicey:

> A State's authority, in the eyes of other States and the courts that represent them, is, speaking very generally, coincident with, and limited by, its power. It is territorial. It may legislate for, and give judgments affecting, things and persons within its territory. It has no authority to legislate for, or adjudicate upon, things or persons not within its territory.[119]

The Court also endorsed the following quote from Devlin J:

> In the textbooks it is said sometimes that as a matter of public international law no State ought to seek to exercise sovereignty over property outside its own territory, and therefore the principle of comity is against enforcement; and sometimes it is said that the principle of effectiveness is against enforcement, since no State can expect to make its laws effective in the territory of another State.[120]

Bank Voor Handel had been approved by Nourse LJ and Lord Templeman in *Williams and Humbert Ltd v W & H Trademarks (Jersey) Ltd*,[121] the

[110] [1949] 82 Lloyd's Rep 936; see Judgment, paras. 29–30.
[111] [1953] 1 QB 248, this *Year Book* 28 (1951), pp. 397–9.
[112] Judgment, para. 45.
[113] Judgment, para. 45.
[114] Judgment, para. 28.
[115] Judgment, para. 28.
[116] Judgment, para. 31.
[117] [1939] 63 Ll L Rep 330.
[118] Judgment, paras. 37–8.
[119] Judgment, paras. 35 and 37, quoting [1939] 63 Lloyd's Rep 330 at 341 (Lord Wark, in turn quoting A V Dicey & J H C Morris, *The Conflict of Laws* (5th), p. 20) and [1953] 1 QB 248 at 257–8 (in turn quoting A V Dicey & J H C Morris, *The Conflict of Laws* (6th), p. 13) respectively.
[120] Judgment, para. 37, quoting [1953] 1 QB 248 at 257.
[121] [1986] 1 AC 368.

latter taking the view that '[t]here is undoubtedly a domestic and international rule which prevents one sovereign state from changing title to property so long as that property is situate in another state'. Most recently, in *Société Eram Shipping Co Ltd v Compagnie Internationale de Navigation,*[122] Lord Hoffman had considered it 'a general principle of international law that one sovereign state should not trespass upon the authority of another, by attempting to seize assets situated within the jurisdiction of the foreign state';[123] and Lord Millett had thought that '[t]he near universal rule of international law is that sovereignty, both legislative and adjudicative, is territorial, that is to say it may be exercised only in relation to persons and things within the territory of the state concerned or in respect of its own nationals'.[124] F A Mann and Cheshire & North were called in aid to provide scholarly support for the proposition.[125]

As for the suggestion that English public policy, reflecting international public policy, was served by Law 860, 'the evidence [did] not establish that there [was] an internationally accepted view on public policy as to assignments of copyright'.[126] There was nothing in the present case equivalent to what happened in *Kuwait Airways (Nos 4 and 5)*.[127] 'In any case', the Court reasoned,

> the submission that there should be an exception to the *lex situs* rule based on public policy is misguided. . . . Any exception based upon public policy [would be] wrong in principle because (1) it would subordinate English property law to that of a foreign state; (2) the rule would be founded and would operate by reference to public policy which could change from time to time and could be uncertain; (3) it would require the English courts to assess the merits of the foreign legislation; (4) it would lead to intractable problems when the property was situated in a third state; (5) it would require the court to balance one public policy against the public policy that states do not interfere with property situated abroad, and (6) it would lead to great uncertainty.[128]

The Court then adopted the words of Devlin J in *Bank Voor Handel*, in dismissing the suggestion that public policy required that effect should be given by the English courts to the Dutch decree in question, which purported to effect a transfer of title to property situated in the UK:

> This reasoning at once gives rise to three comments. The first is that it amounts to the formulation of a new head of public policy, and that is not a matter to be lightly undertaken. The second is that it is using public policy, not

[122] [2003] 3 WLR 21; [2003] 3 All ER 465, *supra*, pp. 475–6, see Judgment, para. 41–2.

[123] Judgment, para. 41, quoting [2003] 3 All ER 465 at 486, para. 54.

[124] Judgment, para. 41, quoting [2003] 3 All ER 465 at 492, para. 80.

[125] Judgment, paras. 43–4. The writings cited are F A Mann, 'The Doctrine of International Jurisdiction Revisited After Twenty Years', in F A Mann, *Further Studies In International Law* (1990), pp.1 *et seq* at pp. 4–5, and P N North & J J Fawcett, *Cheshire and North's Private International Law* (13th, 1999), pp. 122–3.

[126] Judgment, para. 46.

[127] Judgment, para. 46.

[128] Judgment, para. 46.

> in accordance with precedent, as a restriction upon acts which are thought to be harmful to the community, but in a novel way as a positive force to give to an act validity which it would otherwise lack. The third is that it appears to cast on the court the duty of considering to some extent the political merits of the decree itself.[129]

The Court also endorsed Devlin J's distinction between public policy proper and what he called 'political policy'.[130] Finally, as it was, the Court took the view—rejecting the essential premise of EMC's argument—that Law 860 was confiscatory, in that it deprived the claimants of their copyright without compensation.[131] The English authorities were unanimous in refusing to give effect to foreign confiscatory laws.

The Court's decision makes good sense. The public policy argument mounted on the back of *Oppenheimer v Cattermole* and *Kuwait Airways (Nos 4 and 5)* was speculative, to say the least. In both these earlier cases, English public policy—considered, in the absence of indication to the contrary, to be consonant with international public policy—was invoked as an exception to the act of state doctrine[132] to justify not giving effect to a foreign law which was in 'flagrant'[133] or 'gross'[134] violation of public international law. To borrow from Devlin J in *Bank Voor Handel*, EMC's argument in the present case was an attempt to use public policy 'not in accordance with precedent, as a restriction upon acts which are thought to be harmful to the community'—such as the Nazi denaturalisation law in *Oppenheimer* or the Iraqi law implementing the annexation of Kuwait in *Kuwait Airways*—'but in a novel way as a positive force to give to an act validity which it would otherwise lack'.[135] Moreover, as rightly pointed out by the Court, the international public policy to be served by according validity to Cuban Law 860 was hardly as compelling as that at issue in the earlier cases: no unambiguous rule of public international law, let alone one 'of fundamental importance',[136] was at stake.

Nor can the good sense of refusing to give effect to foreign laws purporting to transfer title to property located in the UK be gainsaid. At the same, one might wish to take issue with some of the Court's justifications for this refusal, at least those avowedly based on public international law. Even leaving aside the contentious *Lotus* presumption,[137] it is plainly

[129] Judgment, para. 47, quoting [1953] 1 QB 248 at 263–4.

[130] Judgment, para. 47, quoting [1953] 1 QB 248 at 265.

[131] Judgment, para. 48.

[132] That is, both the foreign act of state doctrine proper and so-called '*Buttes*' non-justiciability.

[133] [2002] 2 AC 883 at 1079, para. 20 (Lord Nicholls); [2002] 2 AC 883 at 1099, 1101, 1102, 1103, 1103, paras. 107, 113, 114 , 115, 116 (Lord Steyn); [2002] 2 AC 883 at 1111, 1111, paras. 148, 149 (Lord Hope).

[134] [2002] 2 AC 883 at 1081, para. 29 (Lord Nicholls); [2002] 2 AC 883 at 1101, para. 113 (Lord Steyn).

[135] Judgment, para. 47, quoting [1951] 1 QB 248 at 263–4.

[136] [2002] 2 AC 883 at 1079, 1081, paras. 20, 29 (Lord Nicholls, with whom Lord Hoffman concurred); see similarly his Lordship's reference at [2002] 2 AC 883 at 1081, para. 29 to '[s]uch a fundamental breach of international law'.

[137] See *The SS Lotus* (France v Turkey), PCIJ Rep Ser A No 10, at p. 19.

wrong (*pace* Dicey) to say that a state's legislative authority under public international law is restricted to matters within its territory, or (*pace* Lord Millet) only additionally to its nationals; nor (*pace* Lord Templeman) is it clear that there exists a more limited rule to the effect that a state may not legislate in respect of title to property situated in another's territory. Especially in the civil context, the public international rules regulating legislation which purports to apply extraterritorially are surprisingly permissive,[138] even if the extent of this permissiveness is uncertain.[139] This is not to say that the English courts are, or should be, obliged to give effect to foreign laws purporting to transfer title to property located in the UK. It is merely to say that a rule of English private international law against the application of such legislation is, in the final analysis, founded on a sensible, pragmatic desire for certainty and ease, rather than on the dictates of public international law. Quite simply, a rule to the opposite effect, 'so far from being a principle which resolve[d] the conflict of laws, [would] create a conflict'[140] and, with it, considerable unpredictability for private parties. In this light, '[t]here seems . . . every reason, if the authorities permit it, for giving effect to the simple rule that generally property in England is subject to English law and to none other'.[141] Moreover, there seems every reason, in the interests of comity, to suggest (as Devlin J and Lord Hoffman suggested) that, whatever they may do, states ought not to assert the application of their laws to property situated in another. In this light, the present ruling neatly complements the decision of the House of Lords in *Société Eram*—a case of having others do unto you what you would do unto them.

Misrepresentations to the UN—UN Charter, Article 73—justiciability—relationship between customary international law and English law—human right not to be subjected to exile—UK dependent territories—UK-US defence co-operation—whether Chagos Islanders entitled to compensation for removal from British Indian Ocean Territory

Case No. 7 Chagos Islanders v Attorney General and Her Majesty's British Indian Ocean Territory Commissioner, 9 October 2003, [2003] EWHC 2222; 2003 WL 22187670; <http:/www.courtservice.gov.uk/Judgments.do>; (QBD (Admin Ct), Ouseley J).

The Chagos archipelago, including Diego Garcia, Peros Banhos, and the Salomon islands, forms part of the British Indian Ocean Territory

[138] See, notably, Akehurst, 'Jurisdiction in International Law' (1972–1973) 46 *BYBIL* 145, especially at 187.

[139] See *eg* Mann, *supra*, n. 125, disputing Akehurst.

[140] Judgment, para. 37, quoting [1951] 1 QB 248 at 260.

[141] Judgment, para. 37, quoting [1951] 1 QB 248 at 260.

(BIOT), a UK dependent territory located in the middle of the Indian Ocean. Until the mid-1960s, the Chagos, consisting exclusively at that time of privately-owned coconut plantations, were administered by the Crown as 'lesser dependencies' of the then-dependent territory of Mauritius. The declining population of the archipelago—poorly educated, mostly illiterate Creole-speaking plantation workers wholly dependent on their employers for survival—comprised, on the one hand, contract workers from Mauritius and from what was then the dependency of the Seychelles and, on the other, persons born on the islands into families who had been there for a generation or more; this latter group, the descendants of plantation slaves freed in 1833 and of Mauritian labourers who stayed on, were known as the 'Ilois'.

In the early 1960s, the UK commenced negotiations with the US over the possible establishment of a US military facility either in the Chagos archipelago or on one or other Indian Ocean islands forming part of the Seychelles. With the US not wishing to rely on the uncertain goodwill of what would soon be independent states, the UK agreed in 1964 to separate the islands under consideration from its dependencies of Mauritius and the Seychelles respectively.[142] In addition, the removal and resettlement of the population of the islands was contemplated. A joint UK-US survey of the dwindling population of the islands was promptly undertaken, which reported *inter alia* that little remained of the once distinctive community on Diego Garcia, the largest of the Chagos islands. In 1965, the UK created a new colony, the British Indian Ocean Territory, comprising the Chagos archipelago (hived off from Mauritius) and the islands of Aldabra, Farquhar, and Desroches (from the Seychelles).[143] The following year, the UK and US agreed that the islands should be available for their various defence needs for an initial period of fifty years, renewable for a further twenty.[144] In 1967, as well as acquiring the freehold to Farquhar and Desroches,[145] the Crown bought out the Chagos plantation-owners, in accordance with the Acquisition of Land for Public Purposes (Private Treaty) Ordinance 1967,[146] which empowered the BIOT Commissioner to acquire land, by agreement, for a public purpose, with explicit reference to the defence purposes of the UK, the Commonwealth or other foreign countries in agreement with the UK. To recoup some of the Crown's outlay, the Commissioner leased the plantations back to the management.

[142] See approved judgment, para. 14, referring to a UK-US joint memorandum of that year.

[143] British Indian Ocean Territory Order, SI 1965/1920, 8 November 1965.

[144] See Exchange of Notes between the Government of the United Kingdom of Great Britain and Northern Ireland and the Government of the United States of America concerning the Availability for Defence Purposes of the British Indian Ocean Territory, Cmnd 3231 (1967), 30 December 1966.

[145] The Crown already owned Aldabra.

[146] BIOT Ordinance No 2 of 1967, 22 March 1967.

In July 1968, the US government requested the UK government's permission to proceed with the construction of defence facilities on Diego Garcia. The Foreign Office and the Commonwealth Office canvassed with the Prime Minister the resettlement and re-employment of the inhabitants of Diego Garcia—34% of whom they now reckoned to be Ilois[147]—on the Chagos plantation islands of Peros Banhos or the Salomons or on the more distant BIOT island of Agalega. In September 1968, the Prime Minister approved the US request regarding Diego Garcia. The US, however, was still unable to say whether other islands in the Chagos would be required, and insisted that its proposals not be publicised, all of which scared off investment in the other BIOT plantations. Finally, the UK government took the view that '[e]ven if no defence facilities were ultimately constructed, . . . it would be useful to avoid there being any permanent inhabitants in BIOT, so as to preclude obligations arising under Article 73 of the UN Charter or any other costs if the plantations were to close for economic reasons'.[148] In 1971, the BIOT Commissioner promulgated the Immigration Ordinance 1971,[149] making it unlawful for persons to remain in the territory without a permit and providing for the Commissioner to make orders directing their removal.

[147] Judgment, para. 28. The Court draws this figure from a 1968 submission to the Prime Minister by the Foreign Office and Commonwealth Office jointly.

[148] Judgment, para. 28. The Court drew evidence for this view from two submissions by the Foreign Office and Commonwealth Office to the Prime Minister and approved by him: see Judgment, paras. 28–9. Article 73 of the UN Charter provides:

Members of the United Nations which have or assume responsibilities for the administration of territories whose peoples have not yet attained a full measure of self-government recognize the principle that the interests of the inhabitants of these territories are paramount, and accept as a sacred trust the obligation to promote to the utmost, within the system of international peace and security established by the present Charter, the well-being of the inhabitants of these territories, and, to this end:

a. to ensure, with due respect for the culture of the peoples concerned, their political, economic, social, and educational advancement, their just treatment, and their protection against abuses;
b. to develop self-government, to take due account of the political aspirations of the peoples, and to assist them in the progressive development of their free political institutions, according to the particular circumstances of each territory and its peoples and their varying stages of advancement;
c. to further international peace and security;
d. to promote constructive measures of development, to encourage research, and to co-operate with one another and, when and where appropriate, with specialized international bodies with a view to the practical achievement of the social, economic, and scientific purposes set forth in this Article; and
e. to transmit regularly to the Secretary-General for information purposes, subject to such limitation as security and constitutional considerations may require, statistical and other information of a technical nature relating to economic, social, and educational conditions in the territories for which they are respectively responsible other than those territories to which Chapters XII and XIII apply.

[149] BIOT Ordinance No 1 of 1971, 16 April 1971.

Beginning in 1971, the Ilois were evacuated from Diego Garcia, some to the plantations of Peros Banhos and the Salomons, many to Mauritius and a few to the Seychelles, the latter two of which were now both independent. On the voluntary liquidation of the plantation company in 1973, the Ilois initially evacuated to Peros Banhos and the Salomons were in turn taken to Mauritius. In September 1972, a lump sum payment to meet the cost of resettling those displaced from the Chagos was agreed between the UK and Mauritian governments. The following month, the UK and US agreed to the construction of a military base on Diego Garcia,[150] which continues in use.

On 3 November 2000, in *R (Bancoult) v Secretary of State for the Foreign and Commonwealth Office*,[151] a Divisional Court of the Administrative Court (Laws LJ, Gibbs J) held that the provision of the BIOT Immigration Ordinance 1971 which excluded the Ilois—who now preferred to be called 'Chagossians'—from the Chagos archipelago was *ultra vires* the BIOT Constitution: the power to legislate for the 'peace, order and good government' of the territory was held not to permit legislation excluding the population from the territory. The Ordinance was subsequently amended[152] to permit the Chagossians to return to Peros Banhos and the Salomons, their exclusion from which was not justified by defence considerations. None have done so to date.

The present case consisted primarily of a claim by the Chagossians for compensation for their unlawful exclusion by the defendants from the archipelago (including damages for personal injury in the form of disease and mental illness linked to poor living conditions in Mauritius and the Seychelles), and for the restoration of their asserted property rights. The claimants argued six distinct wrongs, namely misfeasance in public office (that is, the intentional and malicious use of public office to injure the claimant), a novel and continuing tort of 'unlawful exile', negligence, infringement of property rights, infringement of rights under the Mauritian constitution, and deceit. The defendants sought to strike out the Particulars of Claim and to seek summary judgment on the basis that no reasonable grounds for the action were disclosed and that the claimants had no real prospect of success: if the claims were not an abuse of process or statute-barred, they did not satisfy the requirements of the pleaded causes of action, or were unknown to English law, or insofar as they relied on Mauritian law were irrelevant to the BIOT.

The Court entered summary judgment for the defendants.

150 Judgment, para. 47, referring to a UK-US Exchange of Notes of October 1972.

151 [2001] QB 1067; [2001] 2 WLR 1219, this *Year Book*, 71 (2000), pp. 433–4.

152 See Immigration Ordinance 2000, BIOT Ordinance No 1 of 2000 (date unknown).

The case bears only occasionally upon questions of public international law. As a consequence, the long judgment does not call for detailed consideration here. Several points, however, are worth a mention.[153]

One element of the Chagossians' claims both for misfeasance in public office and for deceit was an allegation that the defendants adopted a policy of misrepresentation to the UN[154] and to other states about the existence of a permanent population in the Chagos archipelago, so as to obviate the application of Article 73 of the Charter to the BIOT and to forestall diplomatic controversy. As to the facts, the Court accepted that the UK government 'arguably sought to paint a different picture from the one it knew to be correct in its dealings with the UN over whether there was a permanent population'.[155] But the existence of such a policy, even if it were substantiated, was of no legal avail to the claimants. As regards misfeasance in public office, the Court could 'not see how it can be alleged that there is an actionable legal duty of candour and truthfulness towards the UN [or] other governments . . . , let alone one which can ground an action for misfeasance by those to whom the remarks were not made'. As it was, such a policy would be non-justiciable. In the Court's view, 'whether or not it is wise to conceal facts from the UN or to give a false impression to other Governments must depend on a political judgement which it is for Parliament to judge' [*sic*]; and in the circumstances at issue, '[t]here might have been good reasons for not giving ammunition to those who would oppose the UK's defence policy and for trying to find formulae which are partial truths and only to be used if necessary'.[156] Similarly, the assessment that 'defence policy might require UN obligations not to be fulfilled' was an unreviewable question of foreign relations and defence strategy.[157] Also non-justiciable was the claimants' first argument in deceit, the submission that but for the defendants' knowingly false representations to the UN, the latter would have at least attempted to give effect to the Chagossians' rights under Article 73 of the Charter.[158] According to the Court, 'the relationship with the UN and other states over how to deal with the proposal for an internationally controversial defence arrangement and the consequences for the people on the islands in terms of UN rights is plainly a matter of high policy, in which relationship the Court should not interfere'.[159]

[153] The following examination comes with the caveat that the international law aspects of the case were not always pleaded or dealt with by the Court particularly cogently. The account given imposes a certain coherence on some passages.

[154] Although it is never made clear, reference throughout the judgment to 'the UN' is presumably to the UN Special Committee on the Situation with regard to the Implementation of the Declaration on the Granting of Independence to Colonial Countries and Peoples.

[155] Judgment, para. 338; see also Judgment, paras. 344 and 667.

[156] Judgment, para. 338.

[157] Judgment, para. 338.

[158] More fundamentally, the particulars of this aspect of the claim did not satisfy the requirements of the tort of conceit: see Judgment, paras. 342 and especially 364.

[159] Judgment, para. 342.

A second argument in deceit related to representations allegedly made by the defendants to the Chagossians that they had no right to remain on the islands and no choice but to leave. The representations were alleged to be false on account of the fact that the Chagossians were the permanent population of a Non-Self-Governing Territory and thereby enjoyed rights under Article 73 of the UN Charter. It was an argument that was rejected in no uncertain terms, the Court 'not understand[ing] how this can be thought to be arguable':[160]

> The Article confers no individual rights and can scarcely be thought to have done so. The UK is entitled so far as any domestic law obligations go to ignore it.[161]

And it was 'fanciful to suppose' that any representations made to the Ilois were 'intended to cover international treaty obligations between states'.[162]

As for the putative tort of 'unlawful exile', which the Chagossians claimed was continuing, it was argued that this was derived from Magna Carta's prohibition on exile other than by court judgment or legislation, and from Article 13(2) of the Universal Declaration of Human Rights[163] and Article 12(4) of the International Covenant on Economic, Social and Cultural Rights,[164] which were said to 'reflect the developing law'; since the claimants, relying on *Trendtex*,[165] submitted that rules of international law were incorporated into English law without the need for legislation, they were presumably relying on the Universal Declaration and the ICCPR as evidence of custom. Pointing, then, to this putative right under English law not to be exiled, the claimants argued that where there was a right, there was a remedy in tort for its breach. But the Court denied the existence of a tort of unlawful exile. The alleged tort was 'no more and no less than a particular example of a tort for unlawful administrative acts', and the House of Lords had made it 'clear for many years that an *ultra vires* act does not of itself give rise to tortious liability'.[166] The claimants had put forward no reason why that principle should not apply in the instant case. In short, even if the Court '[a]ccept[ed] for present purposes that a citizen could not be exiled as a matter of common law, that provide[d] no reason for a tort to be created'.[167] The appropriate remedy was by way of judicial review. Anyway, as it was,

> [t]here [could] be no tort of exile in relation to the enforced move of islanders from one island to another; there is no possible right to stay on one particular island unless that particular island itself is the relevant territory of citizenship.

[160] Judgment, para. 369. [161] Judgment, para. 369. [162] Judgment, para. 369.

[163] GA res 217A (III), 10 December 1948. Article 13(2) reads: 'Everyone has the right to leave any country, including his own, *and to return to his country*.' (emphasis added).

[164] 16 December 1966, 999 UNTS 171. Article 12(4) reads: 'No one shall be arbitrarily deprived of the right to enter his own country'.

[165] *Trendtex Trading Corporation v Central Bank of Nigeria* [1977] QB 529, this *Year Book* 48 (1976–1977), pp. 353–62.

[166] Judgment, para. 378.

[167] Judgment, para. 379.

> There is no basis for arguing that there is any right, in principle, for the Chagossians who lived on Diego Garcia not to be removed from Diego Garcia to another BIOT island, let alone to another island within the Chagos Archipelago. If there is a right not to be exiled, and a right to return, it can only apply to BIOT and not to Chagos, let alone to every island within the Archipelago. None of the law relied on by [the claimants] would support such a right. It is a commonplace for people to have to leave the area in which they live because of Government proposals.[168]

With the amendment in 2000 of the BIOT Immigration Ordinance 1971 to permit the Chagossians' return to Peros Banhos and the Salomons, it was unarguable that any tort of unlawful exile as might exist was continuing.

The aspects of the judgment considered here all accord with legal principle, most interestingly the Court's ruling on the relationship between the arguable customary international human right not to be exiled and the alleged English-law tort of unlawful exile. The axiom that customary international law is part of the law of England is invoked more and more frequently in the English courts, but this was the first time that claimants had sought recovery in tort explicitly on the grounds that their customary international human rights, being rights under English law by virtue of the doctrine of incorporation, had been violated.[169] The fate of the argument highlights how, in the likely majority of cases, the mere fact that rules of customary international law are received into English law without the need for legislative intervention is only the beginning of the story: whether a rule of English law derived from public international law actually affords the claimant a domestic legal remedy depends, in the end, on the content of the international rule in question[170] and on

[168] Judgment, para. 382.

[169] The claim in *Al-Adsani v Government of Kuwait*, 103 ILR 420 (QBD, Mantell J) and 107 ILR 536, this *Year Book*, 67 (1996), pp. 537–42 (CA), although amounting to a tort action for breach of a customary international human right, was unspecific as to the character of the international rule in question; and Mantell J—after referring to the relevant provisions of the Universal Declaration, the ICCPR, the European Convention on Human Rights, the Declaration on Torture and the Torture Convention, reproducing *inter alia* the right not to be subjected to torture in Art. 3 of the ECHR—referred unhelpfully to torture as 'an offence against public international law': 103 ILR 420 at 427. See also *Jones v Saudi Arabia*, 30 July 2003 (QBD, Master Whitaker), *supra*, pp. 476–80.

[170] Public international law—which regulates the conduct of 'states', as internally undifferentiated constructs, and not of any particular organs of them—embodies relatively few rules relating specifically to the conduct of domestic courts or, for that matter, of domestic legislatures or administrative decision-makers: see, in this light, *R v Lyons* [2003] AC 976 at 995, para. 40 (Lord Hoffman), this *Year Book*, 73 (2002) pp. 428–34 (HL) at p. 432; *Marchiori v Environment Agency*, 25 January 2002 (unreported), para. 48 (Laws LJ), this *Year Book*, 73 (2002) pp. 387–9 (CA) at p. 389. (Notable exceptions are the international rules governing immunity from jurisdiction, which expressly provide that a state shall afford certain foreign natural and legal persons immunity from the processes of its courts.) It is little help to a claim in a domestic court that international law obliges 'the state', as such, to act in a given manner. Equally, public international law embodies relatively few rules explicitly for the benefit of, or owed directly to, natural and municipal legal persons: see, in this light, *R v Secretary of State for the Home Department*, ex parte *Thakrar* [1974] 1 QB 684 at 702 (Lord Denning MR), this *Year Book*, 47 (1974–1975), pp. 352–6 (CA); the same insight underpins Kerr LJ's more oblique argument in *Maclaine Watson v Department of Trade and Industry* [1988] 3 WLR 1033 at 1095, this *Year Book*, 59 (1988), pp. 267–341 (CA). (Exceptions are, again, the international rules on immunity from jurisdiction, as well as international human rights.) An

the potentially countervailing principles of domestic constitutional law.[171] In the instant case, as the Court rightly emphasised, it might well be that customary international human rights law accords individuals a right as against their own state not to be subjected to exile, but, if such a right could be said to be incorporated directly into English law, it does not necessarily follow that it could be enforced in the English courts by way of an action for damages in tort;[172] and, indeed, as the Court again correctly stated, it is simply not the case as a matter of English public law that an unlawful administrative act is *ipso facto* compensable in tort.[173] It is a point that the Court would have done well to consider in *Al-Adsani v Government of Kuwait*,[174] where the claimant's argument (defeated in the event by a plea of state immunity) boiled down to the assertion that, since customary international law was part of the law of England, the customary human right not to be subjected to torture—as reflected in the Universal Declaration, the ICCPR, the European Convention on Human Rights, the Declaration on Torture, and the Torture Convention—gave rise, when violated, to a tort of torture under English law.[175]

Relationship between customary international law and English law—international crimes—crimes against peace/crime of aggression—whether waging aggressive war a crime under English law—extraterritorial jurisdiction to prescribe criminal laws

Case No 8. R (on the application of Manson) v Bow Street Magistrates' Court, 15 October 2003, [2003] EWHC 2720 Admin (QBD (Admin Ct), Divisional Ct).

The applicant sought judicial review of the refusal of the Senior District Judge, sitting at the Bow Street Magistrates' Court, to issue summonses against the Prime Minister, the Secretary of State for Foreign Affairs and the Secretary of State for Defence for having committed 'crimes against peace under the common law and against the peace of the Realm'; a further application in respect of a similar refusal by the Carmarthen

obligation not for the benefit of, or owed to, individuals or municipal legal persons is not much use to a claim brought by the same.

171 Straightforward examples of such principles are the doctrine of parliamentary supremacy, which grounds the long-established rule that statute prevails in the English (and Scots) courts over rules incorporated from customary international law, and the doctrine of the separation of powers, which explains the accepted applicability of the doctrine of non-justiciability even when rules incorporated from custom are invoked.

172 Or, indeed, by way of an administrative-law remedy.

173 The Court at Judgment, para. 378 cited Lord Steyn in *Three Rivers DC v Bank of England (No 3)* [2003] 2 AC 1 at 190, who in turn cited *X (Minors) v Bedfordshire CC* [1995] 2 AC 633.

174 See *supra*, n. 169.

175 This argument also formed the basis of the claim in *Jones v Saudi Arabia*, *supra*, pp. 476–80. As in *Al-Adsani*, the claim in *Jones* was defeated by state immunity, and the question of the existence or otherwise of an English tort of torture did not need to be definitively determined.

Magistrates was withdrawn in the course of oral submissions. The claimant argued that the District Judge had erred in law. The present application was a renewed one, the initial application having been refused on the papers by Sullivan J. The summonses sought by the claimant related to the respective roles played by the defendants in the UK's March 2003 invasion, in coalition with the US and Australia, of Iraq. The claimant submitted that in planning, preparing for, initiating, and waging an aggressive war against Iraq, the defendants were guilty of commissioning a crime against peace, a crime under customary international law and as such—customary international law being part of the law of England—a crime under common law.

The Divisional Court (Silber J, with whom Brooke LJ agreed) dismissed the application in a six-paragraph judgment unreported and not made public by Court.

Turning first to the specific allegation of waging war, the Court held that the English courts had no jurisdiction over non-statutory offences committed abroad, in this case in Iraq:

> English criminal jurisdiction is territorial so that the function of the English courts is to maintain the Queen's peace within Her Realms. Therefore, with the exception of statutory offences, the court is not concerned with conduct abroad. Indeed, the whole body of the criminal aspects of the common law of England deals with acts committed in the United Kingdom.[176]

It therefore followed 'that in so far as the claims made in respect of waging war outside England and Wales are concerned, there [was] no basis for criticising the decision of the District Judge to refuse to issue a summons'.[177]

The Court then addressed, briskly, the more fundamental issue of whether the acts—performed in the UK—of planning, preparing, and initiating what the claimant characterised as an aggressive war 'amount[ed] to crimes recognised in English law':[178]

> Even if there was [a customary] international crime of planning, preparing and initiating a war of aggression, which is a matter on which I do not express a final opinion, I am unable to accept the proposition that such an offence has been incorporated in any way into English criminal law.[179]

It followed once more that the District Judge was correct in not issuing the summonses.

The judgment of the Court is frustratingly cursory, especially on the second question, given the important legal issues at stake and the 'detailed'[180] and 'interesting'[181] submissions of the claimant. The Court gives no reasons for being 'unable to accept the proposition' that crimes

[176] Judgment, as approved by the Court, obtained from Smith Bernal Wordwave Limited (official shorthand writers to the Court), para. 3.
[177] Judgment, para. 3.
[178] Judgment, para. 4.
[179] Judgment, para. 4.
[180] Judgment, para. 5.
[181] Judgment, para. 4.

under customary international law are 'incorporated . . . into English criminal law',[182] a conclusion which begs elaboration. One can do no more than assume that, in upholding the District Judge's decision, the Court upheld his reasoning as well, at least to the extent that it did not expressly depart from it.[183] On the incorporation into English law of the putative crime of waging aggressive war, the District Judge had justified his decision on the following grounds:

> . . . I find that I am unable to accept the proposition [that] an offence against customary international law is automatically incorporated into the English common law. In recent times, no offences have been created at common law and recent offences with an international element have all been introduced by way of statute. I am therefore not satisfied that the waging of an aggressive war is a crime known to English law and I do not propose to issue the summonses.[184]

The Court agreed with this decision.

One might have expected the Court to consider the available English authority on point, especially when that authority—albeit from a single case, *obiter* and inconclusive—comes from the House of Lords. In *R v Bow Street Metropolitan Stipendiary Magistrate*, ex parte *Pinochet Ugarte (No 3)*,[185] even though (as Lord Browne-Wilkinson pointed out[186]) none of the parties had in fact suggested that torture committed outside the United Kingdom was a crime under English law before section 134 of the Criminal Justice Act 1988 came into effect, Lord Millet nonetheless expressed a forthright view on the matter,[187] a view sharply at odds with

[182] Judgment, para. 4.

[183] One such departure was over the existence under customary international law of crimes against peace (or the crime of aggression) in the first place, a point on the Court declined to express a final opinion: see Judgment, para. 4. The District Judge was not satisfied that such a customary international crime presently existed: see Judgment in the matter of the application of Mr Robert L Manson for the issuing of summonses against the Prime Minister, The Rt Hon Mr Anthony Blair, the Secretary of State for Foreign Affairs, The Rt Hon Mr John Straw, and the Secretary of State for Defence, The Rt Hon Mr Geoffrey Hoon (Bow Street Magistrates' Court, Judge Workman, Senior District Judge), 1 May 2003 (judgment obtained from Bow Street Magistrates' Court), fourth para. (unnumbered); see also Judgment in the matter of the application of Mr Michael F Davies for the issuing of summonses against the Prime Minister, The Rt Hon Mr Anthony Blair, and the Secretary of State for Defence, The Rt Hon Mr Geoffrey Hoon (Bow Street Magistrates' Court, Judge Workman, Senior District Judge), 10 April 2003 (judgment obtained from Bow Street Magistrates' Court), fourth para. (unnumbered).

[184] Judgment in the matter of the application of Mr Robert L Manson, fourth para. (unnumbered); see also Judgment in the matter of the application of Mr Michael F Davies, fourth and fifth paras. (unnumbered).

[185] [2000] 1 AC 147, this *Year Book*, 70 (1999), pp. 277–95.

[186] [2000] 1 AC 147 at 189.

[187] His Lordship stated:

> Every state has jurisdiction under customary international law to exercise extraterritorial jurisdiction in respect of international crimes . . . Whether its courts have extraterritorial jurisdiction under its internal domestic law depends, of course, on its constitutional arrangements and the relationship between customary international law and the jurisdiction of its criminal courts. The jurisdiction of the English criminal courts is usually statutory, but it is supplemented by the common law. Customary international law is part of the common law, and accordingly I consider that the English courts have and always have had extraterritorial criminal jurisdiction in respect of crimes of universal jurisdiction under customary international law.

[2000] 1 AC 147 at 276.

the decision of the Court in the present case on both the incorporation and extraterritoriality points;[188] and the views of the other Lords on the incorporation point were by no means clear.[189] In short, the Court's conclusions in the present case are not self-evident, and the issues raised by the claimant called for more considered judicial treatment.

Extradition—European Convention on Extradition 1957—Extradition Act 1989—double criminality—alleged extradition offences committed during armed conflict—human rights guarantees in extradition—request made for purpose of prosecuting or punishing defendant on account of nationality and political opinion—likely punishment on account of nationality and political opinion—whether Chechen political figure and former military commander of separatist forces extraditable to Russian Federation

Case No 9. Government of the Russian Federation v Akhmed Zakaev, 13 November 2003, unreported (Bow Street Magistrates' Court, Judge Workman, Senior District Judge)

The Government of the Russian Federation sought the extradition of the defendant in respect of thirteen allegations of conduct which it argued would have amounted, had it occurred in the UK,[190] to the offences variously of soliciting persons to murder, murder, wounding with intent to cause grievous bodily harm, false imprisonment, and conspiring with others in a course of conduct which would necessarily involve

[188] In the event, Lord Millet half-heartedly backed down on the extraterritoriality point:

For my own part, . . . I would hold that the courts of this country already possessed extraterritorial jurisdiction in respect of torture and conspiracy to torture on the scale of the charges in the present case and did not require the authority of statute to exercise it. I understand, however, that your Lordships take a different view, and consider that statutory authority is require[d] before our courts can exercise extraterritorial criminal jurisdiction even in respect of crimes of universal jurisdiction. Such authority was conferred for the first time by section 134 of the Criminal Justice Act 1988, but the section was not retrospective. I shall accordingly proceed to consider the case on the footing that Senator Pinochet cannot be extradited for any acts of torture committed prior to the coming into force of the section.

[2000] 1 AC at 276.

[189] See the passages quoted, and the analysis of them, in R O'Keefe, 'Customary International Crimes in English Courts' (2001) 72 *BYBIL* 293 at 293–4 and 300–1.

[190] The Extradition Act 1989 provides in relevant part:

1 (1) Where extradition procedures under Part III of this Act are available as between the United Kingdom and a foreign state, a person in the United Kingdom who—

(a) is accused in that state of the commission of an extradition crime . . . may be arrested and returned to that state in accordance with those procedures.

* * *

2 (1) In this Act, . . . 'extradition crime' means—

(a) conduct in the territory of a foreign state . . . which, if it occurred in the United Kingdom, would constitute an offence punishable with imprisonment for a term of 12 months, or any greater punishment, and which, however described in the law of the foreign state . . . , is so punishable under that law . . .

Section 2(1) embodies what is known as the requirement of double criminality.

the commission of the offences of murder, wounding, and hostage-taking. In 1995 and 1996, when the offences in question were alleged to have taken place, the suspect had been a commander of irregular military units of the Chechen separatist movement engaged in hostilities within the territory of the Russian Federation against that state's armed forces. He had since become a senior Chechen politician, a member of the elected Chechen government and one-time Deputy Prime Minister of the breakaway Republic of Chechnya.

Since the proceedings fell within the scope of the European Convention on Extradition 1957,[191] the court of committal (Judge Workman, Senior District Judge, Bow Street Magistrates' Court)[192] was not required to inquire into whether there was sufficient evidence to support the charges.[193] All the formalities required under the Convention had been complied with, and the court was satisfied that the defendant was the person being sought. The defence, however, raised several substantive points.

The defence submitted that, contrary to the Russian Government's assertion, the requirement of double criminality was not in fact satisfied. The hostilities in Chechnya amounted to an internal armed conflict; and 'since the offence of murder [under UK law] can only take place during the currency of the Queen's peace', and 'there is no peace during the existence of war', '[t]he killing of combatants in war would not amount to the crime of murder' if committed in the UK.[194] For its part, the Russian Government maintained that the fighting in Chechnya amounted not to an armed conflict but to 'riot and rebellion, "banditry" and terrorism'.[195] Each side provided 'a very considerable amount of evidence and background material' to support its claim as to the proper legal characterisation of the conflict.[196]

The defence also submitted that the Russian Government's request was 'in fact made for the purpose of prosecuting or punishing [the defendant] on account of his race, religion, nationality or political opinions' and that, if returned, the defendant 'would be prejudiced at his trial or punished, detained or restricted in his personal liberty by reason of his race, religion, nationality or political opinions', both of which are grounds for the refusal of the request under section 6(1) of the Extradition Act 1989.[197] In support of the first submission, the defence

[191] ETS No 24. [192] See Extradition Act 1989, ss. 8(2) and 9(1).

[193] See Extradition Act 1989, ss. 9(4) and (8), as well as European Convention on Extradition Order 2001, SI 2001/962.

[194] Text of judgment obtained from Bow Street Magistrates' Court, second page (unnumbered).

[195] Judgment, second page (unnumbered). [196] Judgment, first page (unnumbered).

[197] Extradition Act 1989, s. 6(1) provides in relevant part:

> 6 (1) A person shall not be returned under Part III of this Act, or committed or kept in custody for the purposes of return, if it appears to an appropriate authority—
>
> * * *
>
> (c) that the request for his return (though purporting to be made on account of an extradition crime) is in fact made for the purpose of prosecuting or punishing him on account of his race, religion, nationality or political opinions; or

pointed to the defendant's 'very high profile as a Chechen separatist', alleging that 'the decision to arrest [him] was a political decision based upon the fact that the Russian Government's policy is now to win a military victory [in Chechnya] and to neutralise the moderate view': one witness offered the view 'that the Government's aim was to exclude [the defendant] from the peace process', another 'that there was a desire to discredit him as a moderate and to remove him from the negotiating process'.[198] The defence backed the second submission by alleging that the defendant, as a senior Chechen politician, would be tortured while in detention.[199]

The court of committal refused the request for extradition and discharged the defendant.

Judge Workman was satisfied that 'the events in Chechnya in 1995 and 1996 amounted in law to an internal armed conflict'.[200] He acknowledged that the line between internal armed conflict and other acts of domestic violence was a difficult one to draw. He supported his finding by reference to 'the scale of the fighting—the intense carpet bombing of Grozny within excess of 100,000 casualties, [and] the recognition of the conflict in the terms of a cease fire and peace treaty'; and he 'was unable to accept the view expressed by one witness that the actions of the Russian Government in bombing Grozny were counter-terrorist operations'.[201] Judge Workman then concluded:

> Having satisfied myself that this amounted to an internal armed conflict . . . , I reach the conclusion that those crimes which allege conspiring to seize specific areas of Chechnya by the use of armed force or resistance are not extraditable crimes because the conduct in those circumstances would not amount to a crime in this country. On that basis I propose to discharge counts 7, 8, 9 and 13.[202]

When it came, however, to the other allegations of murder and conspiracy to murder, Judge Workman took a different view:

> I am satisfied that the alleged victims in those cases should have had the protection of Article 3 of the [Fourth] Geneva Convention in so far as they were civilians. As such, any unlawful killing of them could amount to murder and therefore I do not discharge those charges on this ground.[203]

(d) that he might, if returned, be prejudiced at his trial or punished, detained or restricted in his personal liberty by reason of his race, religion, nationality or political opinions.

Sections 6 (1)(c) and (d) derive from the European Convention on Extradition, Art. 3(2). The defence also alleged abuse of process by the Russian Government, an allegation not discussed here. Finally, the defence called on the court of committal to exercise, on the basis of past case-law, the High Court's jurisdiction under s. 11 (3) of the Extradition Act 1989 to discharge the defendant, on the basis that there was an overwhelming and inevitable case that the High Court would find the requested extradition unjust or oppressive. While Judge Workman had 'some sympathy with the submission', he thought 'that in any case where there was overwhelming evidence and an inevitable conclusion, it would in almost every case (as in this case) give rise to grounds for discharging the defendant under Section 6': Judgment, eleventh page (unnumbered).

[198] Judgment, fifth page (unnumbered).
[199] Judgment, fifth and sixth pages (unnumbered).
[200] Judgment, second page (unnumbered).
[201] Judgment, second page (unnumbered).
[202] Judgment, second page (unnumbered).
[203] Judgment, third page (unnumbered).

Furthermore, as regards the alleged murders of civilians, Judge Workman was satisfied that the political offence exception provided for by section 6(1)(a) of the Extradition Act 1989[204] was not available by virtue of the Suppression of Terrorism Act 1978.[205]

As to whether the defendant was entitled to the protection afforded by section 6(1)(c) of the Extradition Act 1989, Judge Workman, having sought evidence to corroborate the testimony for the defence, declared himself 'satisfied that it [was] more likely than not that the motivation of the Government of the Russian Federation was . . . to exclude [the defendant] from continuing to take part in the peace process and to discredit him as a moderate'.[206] He 'therefore [found] as a fact that the Russian Government [was] seeking extradition for purposes of prosecuting [him] on account of his nationality and his political opinions'.[207] As regards the further submission that the defendant 'would be prejudiced at his trial or punished, detained or restricted in his personal liberty by reason of his race, religion, nationality or political opinions' within the meaning of section (6)(d) of the Act, Judge Workman was prepared to accept that the trial itself would be fair: although he noted that no right to jury trial existed in Chechnya at that point, he accepted that the defendant could be tried by jury elsewhere in the Russian Federation, and took the view that the UK acknowledged, by virtue of the European Convention on Extradition, that there was 'at the very least the presumption that any trial in Russia [would] take place fairly'.[208] But when it came to the defendant's detention, Judge Workman arrived '[w]ith some reluctance' at 'the inevitable conclusion' that there was a substantial risk that the defendant would be subject to torture while in detention, and that such punishment would be by reason of his nationality and political opinions.[209] He did not doubt the good faith of the assurance to the contrary given by the responsible Russian minister, but he considered it unlikely that the minister would be able to enforce his undertaking, 'given the nature and extent of the Russian prison estate'; indeed, he thought that 'such a guarantee would be almost impossible in any country with a significant prison population'.[210] Nor could the minister guarantee that the defendant would be detained in an institution run by the Ministry of Justice, over which he exercised oversight, and not in an

[204] Extradition Act 1989, s. 6(1)(a) provides:

> 6 (1) A person shall not be returned under Part III of this Act, or committed or kept in custody for the purposes of return, if it appears to an appropriate authority—
> (a) that the offence of which that person is accused . . . is an offence of a political character . . .

Section 6(1)(a) derives from the European Convention on Extradition, Art. 3(1).

[205] Judgment, third page (unnumbered). The Suppression of Terrorism Act enacts into UK law the relevant provisions of the European Convention on the Suppression of Terrorism 1977, ETS No 90, Arts. 1 and 2 of which provide for the abrogation of the political offence exception in relation to certain cases falling within the European Convention on Extradition.

[206] Judgment, tenth page (unnumbered).

[207] Judgment, tenth page (unnumbered).

[208] Judgment, sixth page (unnumbered).

[209] Judgment, tenth page (unnumbered).

[210] Judgment, sixth page (unnumbered).

institution run by the FSB (the Russian secret service, formerly the KGB), as this was a decision taken by the prosecutor.[211] The judge also drew attention to a statement made by the Council of Europe's Anti-Torture Committee, which reported that there was 'continued resort to torture and other forms of ill treatment [by] members of the Law Enforcement Agencies and Federal forces operating in the Chechen Republic',[212] and to the views of the UN Committee on Torture, which had expressed 'deep concern over the Russian treatment of Chechens' and had 'identified numerous and consistent allegations of widespread torture of detainees'[213]—reports backed up by the testimony to the court of former Russian officials. In the event, Judge Workman placed greatest weight on the eyewitness testimony—'clear, unequivocal and unshaken by cross-examination'—of a Chechen who had himself been detained and tortured by the Russian authorities in Chechnya.[214] As a consequence, in accordance with subparagraphs (c) and (d) of section 6(1) of the Extradition Act 1989, the court of committal held that the defendant should not be returned to face trial in the Russian Federation.

The judgment—which does not emanate from a superior court of record and, as such, has no formal precedential value in the English courts—highlights the difficult and diplomatically sensitive issues that a court of committal can be called on to determine in the contexts of the requirement of double criminality and the human rights guarantees relating to extradition laid down in the European Convention on Extradition and many other conventions. Judge Workman's legal ruling on the interplay between double criminality and armed conflict is a bold one—and one, it seems, it was perfectly open to him to make. At the same time, it might be thought that the factual existence or otherwise of an armed conflict in a foreign state is the sort of question traditionally answered on the basis of an Executive Certificate sought from and issued by the Foreign and Commonwealth Office, rather than on a weighing of evidence presented by the parties. That said, the FCO was doubtless relieved to leave this delicate matter to the court. As for the court's inquiry into whether the defendant would be subject to torture in the requesting state, which amounted to an inquiry into whether a foreign state was likely to act in violation of international law, there can be no objection that this contravenes the traditional constitutional wisdom, rooted in the separation of powers (and on which the practice of executive certification is based), that the courts should defer to the executive in matters of foreign affairs. Section 6(1)(d) of the Extradition Act 1989 'require[d the judge] to make an assessment of what might happen if Mr Zakaev were to be returned to Russia',[215] in the words of Judge Workman. As such, this assessment was a wholly proper and, more to the point, obligatory

211 Judgment, sixth page (unnumbered).
212 Judgment, sixth page (unnumbered).
213 Judgment, seventh page (unnumbered).
214 Judgment, tenth page (unnumbered).
215 Judgment, fifth page (unnumbered).

exercise of the courts' constitutional mandate to give effect to legislation, even if it did involve an implicit finding as to the likelihood of internationally unlawful conduct by a foreign state.[216] It is for the same reason that neither the foreign act of state doctrine nor *Buttes* non-justiciability posed a bar to the court's inquiry.[217] (As it is, Russia itself clearly consented to such an inquiry being undertaken in the context of extradition when it became party to the European Convention on Extradition, which embodies the protections relied on by the defendant.) In terms of comity, it may even be preferable that these sorts of assessments be made by independent judges than by ministers.

*Interpretation of treaties—ordinary meaning of words—context—object and purpose—*travaux préparatoires*—relationship between treaties and English law—double taxation agreements—non-discrimination guarantee—UK-Japan double taxation agreement, Article 25(3)—UK-US double taxation agreement, Article 24(5)—OECD Model Convention with Respect to Taxes on Income and on Capital—Income and Corporation Taxes Act 1988—Human Rights Act 1998—First Protocol to European Convention on Human Rights, Article 1—whether UK subsidiary of Japanese company entitled to common-law restitution for payment of advance corporation tax*

Case No 10. NEC Semi-Conductors Limited and other test claimants v Commissioners of Inland Revenue, 24 November 2003, [2003] EWHC 2813 (Ch); 2003 WL 22656590; <http://www.courtservice.gov.uk/Judgments.do;> (QBD (Ch), Park J).

From 1973 to 1999, in accordance with what was known as the imputation system, companies resident in the UK were obliged to pay advance corporation tax (ACT) on the payment of a dividend. An exception existed, however, in favour of subsidiaries of holding companies also resident in the UK, which could make group income elections with their parent companies so as to avoid ACT liability. But group income elections were not available to subsidiaries of companies not resident in the UK (a situation which, insofar as it related to UK subsidiaries of companies resident elsewhere in the European Community (EC), was eventually held by the European Court of Justice to be incompatible with the EC Treaty).[218] The claimants, UK subsidiaries of Japanese and US companies, applied for

[216] Other examples include *Kuwait Airways Corporation v Iraqi Airways Company (Nos 4 and 5)* [2002] AC 883, this *Year Book*, 73 (2003), pp. 400–4 (HL); *R v Secretary of State for the Home Department,* ex p *Adan* [2001] 2 AC 477, this *Year Book*, 71 (2000), pp. 422–6 (HL); and even *R v Bow Street Metropolitan Stipendiary Magistrate,* ex parte *Pinochet Ugarte (No 3)* [2000] 1 AC 147, this *Year Book*, 70 (1999), pp. 277–95.

[217] See, in this light, *R v Bow Street Metropolitan Stipendiary Magistrate,* ex parte *Pinochet Ugarte (No 1)* [2000] 1 AC 61 (this *Year Book* 70 (1999), pp. 277–95), at 106–7 (Lord Nicholls) and 117 (Lord Steyn), with both of whom Lord Hoffman concurred.

[218] *Metallgesellschaft Ltd v Inland Revenue Commissioners (C397/98)* [2001] Ch 620.

common-law restitution of ACT paid by them to the Inland Revenue, arguing *inter alia* that the application of section 247 of the Income and Corporation Taxes Act 1988, through which the UK subsidiaries of parent companies resident outside the EC were denied the opportunity to make group income elections, was in breach of non-discrimination articles in bilateral double taxation agreements in force between the UK and Japan and the UK and the US respectively, and for this reason was unlawful as a matter of English law.[219] (The agreements in question, as with most of the UK's double taxation agreements, were based, with varying modifications, on the OECD model convention.)[220] The relevant identical provision of the agreements—Article 25(3) of the UK-Japan agreement and Article 24(5) of the UK-US agreement—reads:

Enterprises of a Contracting State, the capital of which is wholly or partly owned or controlled, directly or indirectly, by one or more residents of the other Contracting State shall not be subjected in the first-mentioned Contracting State to any taxation or any requirement connected therewith which is other or more burdensome than the taxation and connected requirements to which other similar enterprises of that first-mentioned State are or may be subjected.

In turn, section 788 of the Income and Corporation Taxes Act, traceable back to the Finance Act 1945, states:

(1) If Her Majesty by Order in Council declares that arrangements specified in the Order have been made with the government of any territory outside the United Kingdom with a view to affording relief from double taxation in relation to
(a) income tax,
(b) corporation tax in respect of income or chargeable gains, and
(c) any taxes of a similar character to those taxes imposed by the laws of that territory,

and that it is expedient that those arrangements should have effect, then those arrangements shall have effect in accordance with subsection (3) below.

[(2) . . .]
(3) Subject to the provisions of this Part, the arrangements shall, notwithstanding anything in any enactment, have effect in relation to income tax and corporation tax in so far as they provide—

(a) for relief from income tax, or from corporation tax in respect of income or chargeable gains;
[(b)–(d) . . .]

[219] The claimants raised an additional, alternative argument based on European law. This argument is not considered here.

[220] Organisation for Economic Co-operation and Development (OECD), Model Convention with Respect to Taxes on Income and on Capital, available at <http://www.oecd.org/dataoecd/52/34/1914467.pdf>

In turn, the Double Taxation Relief (Taxes on Income)(Japan) Order 1970,[221] made by the Queen in Council, provides in paragraph 2:

It is hereby declared—

(a) that the arrangements set out in Part I of the Schedule to this Order have been made with the Government of Japan with a view to affording relief from double taxation in relation to income tax, corporation tax, or capital gains tax and taxes of a similar character imposed by the laws of Japan; and
(b) that it is expedient that those arrangements should have effect.

The Schedule reproduces in full the text of the UK-Japan agreement. The Order in respect of the US takes the same form, with the Schedule reproducing the UK-US agreement.

The first claimant, the UK subsidiary of a company resident in Japan, premised its argument on the assertion that the requirement imposed via section 247 of the Income and Corporation Taxes Act that it pay ACT in consequence of its payment of a dividend, without the opportunity for recourse to a group income election, amounted to 'taxation' or a 'requirement connected with' taxation within the meaning of Article 25(3) of the UK-Japan agreement which was 'other or more burdensome' than the taxation and connected requirements to which 'other similar enterprises' of the UK were subjected; the 'other similar enterprises' were UK subsidiaries of UK parent companies, which were permitted to make a group income election. In short, section 247 of the Act, as applied, was contrary to the non-discrimination guarantee in Article 25(3) of the agreement. It was argued that this guarantee had been enacted into English law by the combined operation of section 788(3)(a) of the Income and Corporation Taxes Act and the Double Taxation Relief (Taxes on Income)(Japan) Order. Section 788(3)(a) of the Act stated that the provisions of a double taxation agreement made the subject of a relevant Order in Council are to have domestic effect 'in so far as they provide for relief from . . . corporation tax in respect of income or chargeable gains'. The first claimant submitted that Article 25(3) of the agreement, insofar as it meant that the UK subsidiaries concerned could make group income elections or otherwise pay dividends without being liable to ACT, provided for 'relief from . . . corporation tax in respect of income or chargeable gains'; and that, as a consequence, it was entitled at common law to restitution in respect of ACT paid.

Park J, in the Chancery Division, began 'with the background observation that, if [Article 25(3) of the agreement] did have the effect contended for by the claimants, it was certainly not an effect which was intended' by its drafters: the OECD model convention, on which the provision was based, 'was certainly not formulated with the United Kingdom's imputation system in mind', and the UK-Japan agreement, in

[221] SI 1970/1948.

which the provision was found, was entered into four years before the imputation system commenced.[222] (The argument was more plausible, though still improbable, in relation to the UK-US agreement.)[223] Nonetheless, the fact that the interpretation argued for would result in a 'fortuitous and unintended windfall' did not in itself mean that it was wrong,[224] and his Lordship proceeded to a close examination of the wording of the relevant passage of the provision. He agreed with the first claimant's submission that the 'other similar enterprises' referred to were indeed the UK subsidiaries of UK parent companies:[225] even if the article could have been more explicit in this regard,[226] 'it [was] obvious from the whole scheme and purpose of the non-discrimination article that that [was] what the particular [paragraph was] getting at';[227] this was also the view of the US Treasury, the Dutch and Swedish courts, and the French government.[228] The other possible meanings were clearly not intended, were not argued for, did violence to the language, or were less satisfactory on other grounds, including their irreconcilability with the OECD commentary to its model convention.[229] Park J further accepted that the requirements of section 247 of the Income and Corporation Taxes Act, as applied, amounted to either 'taxation' or a 'requirement connected with' taxation for the purposes of Article 25(3) of the agreement, and that this was 'other or more burdensome' that that imposed on UK subsidiaries of UK companies.[230] His Lordship therefore accepted that the application of section 247 of the Act, to the extent (and only to the extent) that it did not allow a UK subsidiary of a Japanese company to make a group income election so as to avoid paying ACT on the payment of a dividend, violated the UK-Japan double taxation agreement.[231]

Park J then turned to consider what this finding meant for the first claimant. He had made it clear at the beginning of his judgment that double taxation agreements, being treaties, formed no part of English law without the intervention of Parliament, 'either directly by statute or by statutory delegation authorising another person or body to bring the treaty into effect domestically'.[232] He now explained the relationship in more detail:

35. . . . A taxpayer who claims that some aspect of his United Kingdom tax treatment is contrary to a provision of a double taxation agreement must first succeed in showing that the treatment complained of is indeed contrary to the agreement (as I have accepted that the claimants have shown in this case): but that only gets the taxpayer part of the way home. If a resident company wishes to be able to rely on an infringement of the agreement in direct proceedings against the Inland Revenue, it also needs to establish that the particular effect of

[222] Approved judgment (amended second version), para. 22. [223] Judgment, paras. 23–4. [224] Judgment, para. 25. [225] Judgment, paras. 25 and 30. [226] Judgment, para. 27. [227] Judgment, para. 29. [228] Judgment, para. 29. [229] Judgment, paras. 27–9. [230] Judgment, paras. 31–2. [231] Judgment, para. 33. [232] Judgment, para. 9.

the agreement has been incorporated into United Kingdom domestic law. If it has not been so incorporated, then the actions of the Inland Revenue in operating the tax system in a way which conflicts with the agreement may be a breach of international law between the United Kingdom and the other State. But that does not give to the aggrieved taxpayer rights for which it can claim protection in the national courts of this country.

36. The vital point in this connection is that s. 788(3) [of the Income and Corporation Taxes Act] provides that, once the 'arrangements' in a double taxation agreement have become the subject matter of an Order in Council declaring it expedient that they shall take effect, then they shall 'notwithstanding anything in any enactment, have effect in relation to income tax and corporation tax in **so far as they provide**' for any of the various matters spelt out in paragraphs (a) to (d) of the subsection. If the infringement of the terms of the double taxation agreement is within one of the matters spelt out in those paragraphs, the taxpayer can rely on it in domestic proceedings. Usually the domestic proceedings will take the form of a conventional tax appeal which begins before the Special or General Commissioners, but exceptionally they may take the form of a civil action in the national courts. If, however, the infringement of the double taxation agreement is not within any of the matters listed in paragraphs (a) to (d) of s. 788(3), then that aspect of the agreement is not part of the domestic law of this country. The taxpayer cannot rely on it in a conventional tax appeal or in a civil action against the Inland Revenue.[233]

Justifying his view that not every aspect of a double taxation agreement was incorporated by the combined effect of section 788(3) of the Income and Corporation Taxes Act and the requisite Order in Council, his Lordship continued:

[Counsel for the first claimant] urged that I should give a wide interpretation to the various matters listed in paragraphs (a) to (d), in order that as many provisions of double taxation agreements as possible should be covered by s. 788(3) and thereby made parts of domestic law. I do not see why I should do that. I intend to give a natural interpretation, neither wide nor narrow, to those of the matters listed in paragraphs (a) to (d) which are argued to cover the particular application of the non-discrimination article in point in this case. The matter principally relied on by the claimants is the reference in paragraph (a) to providing for 'relief from . . . corporation tax in respect of income or chargeable gains'. If, as is the case, I do not think that the natural interpretation of those words includes relief from ACT, I do not think that I should give an unnatural and extended interpretation to the words in order, through the non-discrimination article, to bring treaty relief from ACT within the scope of domestic law. I do not accept the submission that the structure of s. 788(3) (or its statutory predecessors going back to the Finance Act 1945) evinces an intention on the part of the draftsman to list everything which might realistically be expected to be covered by a double taxation agreement. If the draftsman's intention had been to bring into domestic law everything contained in a double taxation agreement he could have provided that 'the arrangements shall, notwithstanding

[233] Original emphasis.

anything in any enactment, have effect'. And he could have left it at that. To my mind the structure of the subsection shows clearly that the draftsman did not want to secure that everything in a double taxation agreement should become part of domestic law. That is why he continued with the words 'in relation to income tax and corporation tax in so far as they provide for' the listed matters.[234]

He further pointed out that whereas paragraph 5 of Article 25 of the UK-Japan agreement specified that the term 'taxation', for the purposes of that article, meant 'taxes of every kind and description', section 788(3) of the Act stated that the provisions of double taxation agreements were to have effect in domestic law in relation to income tax and corporation tax, and even then only insofar as they provided for the matters listed in subparagraphs (a) to (c).[235] 'So', his Lordship concluded,

there can be provisions in the non-discrimination article of an agreement which prohibit discrimination in relation to a wide range of taxes going beyond income tax, corporation tax and capital gains tax; but it is certain that any such provisions are not brought into domestic effect by s.788(3).[236]

This conclusion was supported by the decision of the Divisional Court of Chancery in *R v Inland Revenue Commissioners*, ex parte *Commerzbank AG*.[237]

Against this background, Park J examined whether relief from ACT, as guaranteed by Article 25(3) of the agreement, constituted 'relief . . . from corporation tax in respect of income or chargeable gains', in the precise words of section 788(3)(a) relied on by the first claimant. He took the view that it did not, since ACT was not corporation tax in respect of income or chargeable gains.[238] As a consequence, he rejected the present claim, and the claims of all the test claimants, to restitution at common law. Although section 247 of the Income and Corporation Taxes Act—to the extent that it prevented UK subsidiaries of Japanese companies from making group income elections—was in breach of Article 25(3) of the UK-Japan double taxation agreement, the claimants could only claim restitution at common law 'if they had a right in domestic law to make the group income elections'.[239] In his Lordship's view, 'they did not have that right because the particular provision of the non-discrimination article on which they rely did not become part of the domestic tax law of this country'.[240]

His Lordship then took time to dispose of several other arguments canvassed by the claimants.

First, he explained that his conclusion 'that the particular application of the non-discrimination article sought to be relied on in this case' had not been incorporated into domestic law '[did] not necessarily mean that all other possible applications of the same article [were] similarly not incorporated into English law'.[241] He took the hypothetical example of a

[234] Judgment, para. 38. [235] Judgment, para. 39. [236] Judgment, para. 39.
[237] [1991] STC 271, referred to at Judgment, para. 40. [238] Judgment, paras. 43–6.
[239] Judgment, para. 48. [240] Judgment, para. 48. [241] Judgment, para. 49.

claim in respect of a Finance Act which provided that the UK subsidiaries of parent companies resident in foreign states were to be charged corporation tax at a rate substantially higher than that at which the UK subsidiaries of UK companies were charged. In such a case, his Lordship stated, the analogous non-discrimination provision of any relevant and analogous double taxation agreement would have been incorporated into English law, since the subject-matter in question was 'relief from income tax, or from corporation tax in respect of income or chargeable gains' for the purposes of section 733(a) of the Income and Corporation Taxes Act.[242]

Park J also rejected the submission that the non-incorporation of a non-discrimination provision of a double taxation agreement denied the provision practical effect:

> It can still give rise to breaches of obligations in international law owed by one Contracting State to another. And in some circumstances that can assist particular taxpayers. Double taxation agreements contain articles headed 'Mutual agreement procedure'. They provide for a taxpayer who considers that he is being taxed inconsistently with the double taxation agreement by the Contracting State other than his own to present his case to the competent authority of his own Contracting State. They visualise that the two competent authorities may discuss the matter and try to resolve the case by mutual agreement. I accept that this is not as good for a taxpayer as being able himself to rely on the particular provision of the double taxation agreement in the domestic courts, but it is a possible recourse . . . [243]

It was therefore 'wrong to say that a provision of the agreement is useless if it is not incorporated into domestic law so that the aggrieved taxpayer can rely directly upon it'.[244]

In support of their submission that the Court 'should strive to conclude that the non-discrimination article [of the agreement] took domestic effect',[245] the claimants had urged reliance on Articles 26 and 27 of the Vienna Convention on the Law of Treaties,[246] a contention to which Park J gave short shrift:

> It is necessary to distinguish between two distinct questions: (1) How should the words of a treaty be interpreted? (2) Is the effect of the treaty, as properly interpreted, incorporated into domestic law so that private parties can rely upon it against others, including against the State? The articles of the Vienna Convention are material to question (1), not to question (2). . . . The question which is determinative [in the present case] is question (2), which resolves itself into a question of the interpretation of s.788 (3) of the United Kingdom statute. The articles of the Convention are not directed at all towards a question of that nature, and in my opinion they give no assistance upon it.[247]

[242] Judgment, para. 49.
[243] Judgment, para. 49.
[244] Judgment, para. 49.
[245] Judgment, para. 50.
[246] 1155 UNTS 331.
[247] Judgment, para. 50.

In further support of the same submission, the claimants had called on the Court 'to pay careful heed' to a passage in the judgment of Diplock LJ in *Salomon v Commissioners of Customs and Excise*,[248] in which his Lordship states that where legislation enacted to give domestic effect to a treaty can reasonably be ascribed more than one meaning, and one of them is consonant with the treaty, the meaning consonant with the treaty is to be preferred. Again the argument found no favour with Park J:

I have read the passage carefully, but in my opinion it is of no assistance for much the same reason as that which I have explained in connection with the articles of the Vienna Convention. Diplock LJ is analysing the approach to the interpretation of a United Kingdom statute which seeks to enact the effect of an international treaty, and to do so, not in the actual words of the treaty itself, but rather in terms which the Parliamentary draftsman has chosen in order to reproduce what he understands the treaty to mean. The present case is not concerned with that sort of thing. Apart from anything else, in so far as the contents of a double taxation agreement become part of United Kingdom law, they do so in the actual words of the agreement (the treaty) itself. There is no question of the United Kingdom draftsman seeking to reproduce in his own chosen wording what he conceives to be the effect of the wording of the treaty. I repeat that the crucial question in this case is not what the non-discrimination article of the double taxation agreement means, but rather whether, given what it means, s.788(3) has introduced that meaning into domestic tax law. That is a question of interpretation of s.788(3), and Diplock LJ's remarks, important though they are in their context, are not relevant to it. . . .[249]

His Lordship agreed with the respondents 'that s.788 is a general enabling provision which traces back to 1945; it contemplates no particular treaty; and it is not appropriate to attempt to construe the breadth (or narrowness) of the enabling provision by reference to the detailed contents of subsequent treaties'.[250]

Finally, the first claimant had argued that Article 25(3) of the UK-Japan agreement, and especially the application of it that was relied on, had effectively been incorporated in domestic law by the Human Rights Act 1998, in that a right under national law to a tax benefit was a 'possession' protected by article 1 of the First Protocol to the European Convention on Human Rights.[251] The contention was rejected:

[I]n my view that article cannot be prayed in aid in order to establish the existence of such a right under national law. If the right exists, then I would accept that under article 1 the taxpayer is entitled to peaceful possession of it and is not to be arbitrarily deprived of it. In this case, however, the question is whether the right which the claimants assert does or does not exist under national law (*ie* under domestic United Kingdom tax law). If, absent the Human Rights Act and the Convention, it would not exist under national law, then, present the Human Rights Act and the Convention, it still does not exist under national law. The Act

[248] See [1967] 2 QB 116 at 143, this *Year Book*, 42 (1967), pp. 291–3 (CA).
[249] Judgment, para. 51. [250] Judgment, para. 51. [251] ETS No 9.

and the Convention may create some rights which would not exist without them, but a right in United Kingdom subsidiaries of overseas parent companies to make group income elections is not one of them. . . .[252]

For this reason, recent Strasbourg case-law, which 'may show a trend towards greater involvement of the Convention jurisprudence in tax law and procedure', was irrelevant for present purposes.[253]

Park J's judgment is irreproachable. His method of interpreting the double taxation agreements is refreshingly orthodox, with priority given to the ordinary meaning of the words in context and in light of their object and purpose, along with the subsequent practice of the States Parties in their interpretation, over implications drawn from the *travaux préparatoires*. In addition, his handling of the potentially confusing statutory mechanism by which such agreements are 'enacted' into English law—the aptly characterised 'general enabling provision' that is section 733 of the Income and Corporation Taxes Act—is deft. In this latter regard, the case sheds light on a technique of municipal implementation of treaty rules not often seen by English lawyers, *viz* the standing statutory direction that given treaty provisions 'shall, notwithstanding anything in any enactment, have effect' in domestic law. It is as close as English law gets to the notion of 'self-executing' treaties backed by a hierarchy of norms in which international agreements to which the state is party trump inconsistent legislative provisions.

[252] Judgment, para. 52.

[253] Judgment, para. 53, referring to *SA Dangeville v France* [2003] STC 771.

B. PRIVATE INTERNATIONAL LAW*

1 Enforcement of judgments by seizing a judgment debtor's debts: Société Eram Shipping Co Ltd v Hong Kong and Shanghai Banking Corp Ltd;[1] Kuwait Oil Tanker Co SAK v Qabazard.[2]

Two rulings of the Court of Appeal have been reversed by the House of Lords in a pair of important decisions which together examine the theory and practice of the enforcement of judgments. The particular issue was the seizing of debts owed to judgment debtors by persons not party to the litigation. This procedure, known to lawyers since Noah was a boy as 'garnishment',[3] has now been recast as the more prosaic 'third party debt order'.[4] But whatever it is called, it allows a judgment creditor to swoop on a stranger, and obtain an order that he pay a sum, contractually owed to the judgment debtor, to the judgment creditor instead. For the claimant, the procedure has an obvious attraction. He has no need to go after the judgment debtor and seek (and then seek to enforce) an order that he collect the money from his debtor and hand it over. Instead, he cuts out the middle man and goes directly to the money. Or so he may suppose.

Garnishment is part of the general law on enforcement of judgments, and is not confined to the enforcement of foreign judgments. Indeed, a judgment creditor with a foreign judgment in his favour must first sue at common law to obtain an English judgment, or must register the foreign judgment for enforcement under one of the various statutory schemes which provide that once registered, the judgment may be enforced as though it were an English one.[5] So it was that a Romanian shipping company, Eram, registered for enforcement in England a modest judgment from a French court, obtained against O,[6] a company established under

[1] [2003] UKHL 30, [2004] 1 AC 260: Lord Bingham of Cornhill, Lord Nicholls of Birkenhead, Lord Hoffmann, Lord Hobhouse of Woodborough, and Lord Millett, reversing the decision of the Court of Appeal: [2001] EWCA Civ 1317, [2001] 2 Lloyd's Rep 627, and which was noted in this *Year Book*, 72 (2001) p. 454.

[2] [2003] UKHL 31, [2004] 1 AC 300: Lord Bingham of Cornhill, Lord Nicholls of Birkenhead, Lord Hoffmann, Lord Hobhouse of Woodborough, and Lord Millett, reversing the decision of the Court of Appeal: [2002] EWCA Civ 34, [2002] 1 All ER (Comm) 351.

[3] And governed by RSC Order 49.

[4] Now governed by CPR Part 72.

[5] Administration of Justice Act 1920 s. 9(3), Foreign judgments (Reciprocal Enforcement) Act 1933 s. 2(2); Civil Jurisdiction and judgments Act 1982 s. 4, Council Regulation (EC) 44/2001 (and SI 2000/3929, Sch. 1 para. 2).

[6] Société Oceanlink Ltd.

the law of the Special Autonomous Region of Hong Kong. On discovering that O had a credit balance in its bank account with HSBC in Hong Kong, and having established that HSBC had registered itself under Companies Act 1985 s. 691, so that it could be served in London, Eram applied for, obtained, and served a garnishee order *nisi*, requiring HSBC to show cause why it should not be ordered to pay over to Eram the sum standing to the credit of O, to the value of the judgment debt. HSBC applied to have the order set aside; and Tomlinson J acceded to the application. The Court of Appeal reversed him, and the House of Lords restored the order of the judge, with costs against Eram. This must have left the claimant feeling rather bruised.

Garnishment may be a part of the conflict of laws, because the debt claimed may be created under and governed by a foreign law; the garnishee/third party debtor may be outside the jurisdiction of the English court; and the debt may be properly payable (at least, so far as its recovery by the judgment debtor is concerned) overseas. The consequence of all of this is that questions of personal jurisdiction, of the proper law of contracts, of the procedural law on the enforcement of judgments, of the *situs* of property, and of the recognition of foreign judgments, all come together in a distinctly unstable manner. At first sight it is really difficult to see which should prevail, though the present submission will be that the issue should have been treated as a matter of procedural law, and not one of the conflict of laws at all.

Though the apparent simplicity of the judgments in these two cases is deceptive, the point of departure is clear enough. Received wisdom had been that a garnishee order could be made if the garnishee was within the territorial jurisdiction of the court; and the court did not take notice of the proper law of the debt; did not take notice of the *situs* of the debt; but did apply English law on the question whether it was proper to make the order absolute.[7] According to this point of view, the only material questions were whether the garnishee were subject to the personal jurisdiction of the court, and risked being made to pay the debt for a second time even after compliance with the English order. If there was a template for this approach, it was to treat the process as though it had its roots in equity's personal jurisdiction: that if a person were within the clutches of the court, he could be made to act as the court required unless it would be inequitable to force him to do so; and it would be inequitable if there were a risk of his being made to pay the debt twice over. Some influential support for this may have been found in the earlier opinion of Lord Goff in *Deutsche Schachtbau- und Tiefbohrgesellschaft mbH v R'As al Khaimah National Oil Co (Nos 1 and 2)*, who explained that an order *nisi* would not be made absolute if it would be 'inequitable' to do so. Talking about the remedy as though it were equitable, or as operating

[7] The leading modern authority being *Deutsche Schachtbau- und Tiefbohrgesellschaft mbH v R'As al-Khaimah National Oil Co (Nos 1 and 2)* [1990] 1 AC 295.

according to equitable principles, it was easy to concentrate on the existence of personal jurisdiction over the garnishee, and to show little overt concern for choice of law. After all, if the court has power from its equitable side to order the delineation of the state boundary between Pennsylvania and Maryland,[8] it would have no trouble in ordering a local garnishee to hand over money held offshore.

But as the House explained, this was very much the wrong way to look at it. Garnishment was not equitable but statutory; and the property in question was being appropriated (or expropriated), with the result that it was the *situs* of the property, rather than that of the garnishee, which was the crucial fact. And it denatured a garnishee order to see it as an order to pay over money: it was an order to pay over money *indissociably coupled with* a statutory discharge from the debt hitherto owed to the judgment debtor. The Court of Appeal had taken the presence of HSBC in London as sufficient to justify making the order, even though the debt was situated in Hong Kong: it was wrong to have done so. The Court of Appeal had taken the view that the bank would have a good restitutionary claim against O under the law of Hong Kong to counter any action by the judgment debtor to enforce its rights as customer of HSBC. That, said the court with magnificent understatement, fell rather short of the automatic discharge provided for by the statutory scheme for garnishment.[9] Only if the debt was situated in England was it open to the court to make an order, because only if the debt was situated in England was it realistic to suppose that payment under the order of the court would operate as a discharge of the debtor's liability to the judgment debtor.

At the outset of the analysis, it is right to acknowledge the basic soundness of the court's starting position. There is nothing equitable about enforcement by garnishment, and only trouble will result from the proposition that it is. As equity operates *in personam*, it is alluring to reason that the presence of the respondent is a sufficient basis for the existence and the exercise of jurisdiction. Upon this reasoning, the presence of the garnishee would be enough to justify his being ordered to hand over the money. But when it is realised that the payment must be coupled with a discharge of the debt, it is insufficient that the garnishee is present and subject to the jurisdiction. It is the judgment debtor who must be prevented from suing to enforce his original debt; and there is no reason to suppose that he will be regarded as having been subject to the jurisdiction of the court. Indeed, O played no part in the English proceedings at all: neither on registration of the French judgment, nor in the garnishment proceedings. It would have no obvious reason to regard itself as effectively debarred from asserting its rights under its Hong Kong banking contract with HSBC. It was in no sense[10] bound by the garnishment

[8] *Penn v Baltimore* (1750) 3 Ves Sen 444. Those were the days. . .

[9] At paras. [28], [61]–[66], [109]–[110].

[10] This appears to be true as a matter of theory, but it is manifestly true as a matter of practice.

order made by the English court; still less was there any reason for it to accept that its rights had been discharged by the order of the English court. It could not be bound by the garnishment procedure or the order to be made under it. This line of analysis quickly shows why the absence of both judgment debtor and debt made it impossible for the court to make the order absolute.

But what would have made the difference? Two answers may have been suggested, but a third was adopted. As to the two suggestions, the first would have been the presence (or submission) of the judgment debtor. If the critical fact was that the debtor was be discharged of the obligations of the debt, it may have sufficed that the judgment debtor was present, so as to be bound by an order of the court not to seek to enforce the original debt. As a means of protecting the debtor from being sued over again, this may have worked; but in the context of enforcing a foreign judgment, there will be many cases—this case was one such—where the judgment debtor is not present and even if summoned, does not enter an appearance. He cannot then be regarded as bound by the order, outside England at least; and the debtor's protection would be seriously impaired. This was not seen as the key to it.

The second would have been to ask whether the law which governed by the debt would regard the English court's order as discharging the obligations of the debtor. Superficially, this would have some attraction. For the question whether a contractual obligation is discharged is, according to the Rome Convention on the law applicable to contractual obligations, a matter for the law which governs the contract.[11] This may have prompted the thought that if English law were the law which governed the garnishee/debtor's contract with the judgment debtor, such a contract would be discharged by the order of an English court so holding; and therefore the touchstone for deciding whether to make the order would be whether the debt to be garnished were an English one. But on reflection, this could not have been correct either. The issue for the garnishee, perhaps, is not one of whether English law considers the debt to have been discharged, but whether an English court can be confident that its order, that the debtor be discharged from liability, could properly be made and could reasonably be expected to be respected by other courts. If the debt is governed by English law, there is a fair chance that the debtor will not be called on to pay again; but this does not result from the application of a rule of English law as distinct from the act of an English court. In other words, the critical question will be whether a foreign court, before which the judgment debtor may seek to sue the debtor, will accept that the order of an English court discharged the debt. A foreign court may not see this as a contractual question, governed by (what it considers to be) the law governing the contract. It may prefer to see the

[11] Contracts (Applicable Law) Act 1990 Sch. 1 Art. 10(1)(d).

issue as one of acknowledging the right of an English court to hijack the debt, or even of the recognition of a foreign judgment.[12]

And if that is what the issue really is, perhaps it belongs under the rubric of recognition of foreign laws purporting to seize property. And as to that, the general understanding of lawyers is that where the property seized is within the territorial jurisdiction of the state whose government has seized it, this will be given effect outside the territory of the seizing court;[13] but where the property lay outside the territory of the seizer, the purported act of seizing it will be ignored. This appeared to be the reasoning which persuaded the court: there was no reason to suppose that the courts of Hong Kong would recognise or give other effect to an English order, effectively purporting to seize a debt situated in Hong Kong. An English court would not recognise a Hong Kong seizure of a debt situated in England. Given that, there would be no protection for the debtor, who could reasonably apprehend being sued to judgment in Hong Kong; and therefore it would not be appropriate to make the order absolute. The territoriality principle seems to have carried the day.

One may perhaps see why. A number of recent cases[14] have drawn the attention of the English courts to the territoriality principle in the conflict of laws, and it was no surprise to see its making an appearance here. But is this really correct? The 'seizure' of the debt in *Société Eram* was not governmental but judicial; not the result of a sovereign or executive act, but by a judge in the exercise of judicial power. It requires an extension to the principle in *Cammell v Sewell*[15] to treat a judgment as though it were a governmental seizure. True, courts may in some circumstances be seen as limbs of state power, but the international recognition of a judicial order is not usually governed by the *situs* of property, but by whether the defendant to the proceedings submitted to (or was otherwise bound by) the decision of the court. On the other hand, the destruction of property, in the form of statutory cancellation and discharge of the debt, was provided for by a legislative rule which came into effect upon the occurrence of an event (payment by the garnishee) required by the court. On this view, there was an expropriation by destruction, and the claim of the *lex situs* to govern would be clearer. Even so, if the concern of the court was to see that the bank was not at risk of being made to pay again, it was preferable to ask whether a court in Hong Kong would recognise the judgment of the English court which made the garnishee order absolute and decreed discharge of the debt. But what does this mean? The order sought by Eram was directed against the bank (as respondent to the application), but as far as the bank was concerned, its vulnerability to a

[12] With the fundamental difficulty that it is a judgment against HSBC which is to be regarded as effective as against the judgment debtor, O.

[13] Unless recognition of the act of seizing is contrary to public policy: *Kuwait Airways Ltd v Iraq Airways Co* [2002] UKHL 19, [2002] 2 AC 883, noted this *Year Book* 73 (2002), p. 466.

[14] *Kuwait Airways Ltd v Iraq Airways Co* [2002] UKHL 19, [2002] 2 AC 883, noted this *Year Book* 73 (2002), p. 466; and see further Note 3 in this Survey.

[15] (1860) 5 H&N 728.

claim by O was the real issue. So the real question would have been whether O was likely to be seen as bound by judgment of the English court. As to this, it is pretty clear, as said above, that the answer would be no: O was not present in England, had not submitted to the jurisdiction of the English court; and would therefore not be bound by the preclusive effect of the judgment sought by Eram. That being so, there would be a good reason not to make the order against the bank, for Hong Kong law on the recognition of foreign judgments would have left the bank exposed.

Yet even this is open to question. The requirement that a party be present or submit to the jurisdiction of a foreign court, in order to be bound by the preclusive effect of a judgment, is a rule about judgments *in personam*. Would the judgment sought by Eram have been one *in personam*? Or would it have been one *in rem*? The language of the court actually suggests the latter, as the speeches referred to the attachment of the debt, and used the reasoning of governmental seizure of property. Now the recognition of foreign judgments *in rem* occupies a rather weakly illuminated corner of the conflict of laws; but the view proposed in the scholarly sources is that a judgment *in rem* will be recognised if the *res* were within the territory of the adjudicating court.[16] If, therefore, the judgment sought by Eram was one *in rem*, it should only have been granted—because it would only be recognised overseas—if the debt were situated in England. It was not; and therefore an English judgment *in rem* could not be expected to be recognised in Hong Kong. That being so, the the House of Lords was right to apprehend that an English judgment ordering the bank to pay Eram would be given no effect in Hong Kong; the bank was therefore exposed to a real risk of having to pay twice; and it was correct that the order not be made absolute.

If that reasoning be accepted, the House of Lords would appear to have come to the right conclusion by taking a rather questionable shortcut: treating a case on the foreign effect of English judgments as though it were about the governmental seizure of property. This is a pity, but it is symptomatic of a larger confusion which appears to underpin the suggestion that the *situs* of the debt is of decisive importance. Suppose that the debt had been situated in England: would the court then have seen fit to make the order final? The answer is not given in clear and direct terms, but to judge from the speeches, and their emphasis on the limits of territoriality, one would think that the answer was yes. Such a conclusion would be very dangerous. For one still cannot be sure that the courts of Hong Kong (never mind those in other places where HSBC may have a presence) would accept that the English judicial order, and compliance with it, had discharged the debt. It was easy enough for the House of Lords to say that the courts of Hong Kong would accord no effect to the judgment and order which Eram sought; but would it have been just as

[16] Dicey & Morris, *The Conflict of Laws*, 13th edn, Rule 40.

easy to say the opposite if the debt had been situated in England? A rational suspicion exists that it would not have been. In a telling little episode in post-war Anglo-Hellenic relations, the Greek legislature dissolved two Greek banks and vested their assets in a new bank, the National Bank of Greece and Athens. When in *Metliss v National Bank of Greece and Athens SA*[17] this new bank was sued by a bondholder creditor of one of the predecessor banks, the bank argued that it had not succeeded to the liabilities of the predecessor; and it lost. The Greek legislature thereupon passed a further law, purporting to exempt the new bank from the obligations owed to bondholders. In a second action by a bondholder, *Adams v National Bank of Greece and Athens SA*,[18] it was held that the new bank remained liable to its inherited customer. It was irrelevant that the *situs* of the debt was Greece and that there had been a Greek legislative discharge of a liability situated in Greece. The discharge of a contract was, said the House of Lords, a matter for the proper law of the contract (English, not Greek, law); and the Greek legislation was without effect on the English contract, so far as an English court was concerned. There was no sign that the intervention of the *lex situs* had any relevance to the liability of the debtor and the right of its customer. If one translates that approach to a garnishment of a debt situated in England but governed by foreign law, it must be likely that the debtor would remain liable to pay over again, whatever the English *lex situs* may have said or done. If, therefore, the debt owed by HSBC had been situated in England but governed by Hong Kong law, there must have been a very real chance that HSBC would have been exposed to pay twice, and that the garnishment could not properly have been ordered.

Indeed, the more one looks at it, the more perplexing it seems to become. Should the rule be that there can be no garnishment unless English is the proper law and England the *situs* of the debt? Maybe so; but another country's court may not share an English court's conclusion (derived from the Rome Convention, as it must now be) that English was the proper law of the contract. Should the rule be that there can be no garnishment unless England is the *situs* and the proper law as identified by some other court would accept that the debtor had been discharged? This would be several degrees worse. And the root of the problem is not hard to see. One is using the rules of the English conflict of laws to make assumptions about a foreign system's system for the conflict of laws, and to do so in a context where the rights of private individuals are at stake. The truth surely is that *any* attempt to assess the position of the garnishee bank by reference to English rules of the conflict of laws, or by reference to an internationalised, or idealised, understanding of the rules of private international law would be very deficient. It will be naught to the bank's comfort to be told that it ought to be—and as a matter of English law is—protected from further legal proceedings by the debtor, its creditor,

[17] [1958] AC 509. [18] [1961] AC 255.

if this is not how the courts of another country will see it. For that reason, it is submitted that the methodological fault in the analysis in *Société Eram* lay in using rules of the English conflict of laws to assess the position of the bank. The truth is much more mundane. The bank should be allowed to show, by credible evidence, that it would be exposed to the risk of being ordered by another court to make double payment, and if it does so as a matter of fact, there should be no question of the order being made absolute. No more needs to be said to justify the outcome sought by HSBC: it was not their fight, and it is hard to see why any of the risks arising from it should be for their account. In this respect, the approach of Lord Goff in *Deutsche Schachtbau* was much to be preferred. He asked whether the garnishee was exposed to a real risk of being made to pay again by a court in R'As al Khaimah, even though the so-called court in that statelet appeared to operate a system of private international law which was uncivilised to the point of depravity. On concluding that there was such as risk, he refused to make the order absolute, without further regard to the rules of the conflict of laws of England or elsewhere. True, his discovery of a discretion not mentioned in the statutory scheme was inventive, and use of the terminology of 'inequitable' to explain why the order would not be made absolute was unfortunate, but the focus of the enquiry lay in the right place. The entire issue should be regarded as matter of procedural law only, of whether there is a risk of double payment; and this is not something upon which the English conflict of laws has any light to shine. The pity of it all is that a hapless Romanian shipping company got tangled up in all this complexity, never mind costs, in order to try to enforce a French judgment for £60,000. They must have wondered what had hit them. The proud boast of the Brussels Convention is that it will make a judgment easy to enforce across the community of contracting states. Société Eram could be forgiven for thinking that the Convention has wings of lead and feet of clay.

The question is where all this thinking aloud actually leaves us. The answer is that whenever issues of the conflict of laws arise, the enforcement of judgments by garnishment is something whose difficulties are almost unmanageable. If the predominant concern (actual enforcement aside) is to protect the garnishee from being sued twice over, and in this sense to protect him from being not discharged from the debt even though he has complied with the order, there is no salvation in looking to the law governing the debt, nor to the law of its *situs*. Even if both of these are English, a foreign court may yet come to the conclusion that the debt was not discharged in accordance with the English order, and may allow the judgment debtor to sue the debtor to recover sums still lawfully due. The only practical means of preventing this may be to bind the judgment debtor by order of the English court to oblige him, by judicial order or by undertaking, not to sue again. That in turn will require the third party debt order, successor to garnishment, to be re-cast as a procedure to which the judgment debtor and the debtor are both party and are both bound; and if (as here) the judgment debtor ignores the proceedings, this will be difficult to bring about. To reason that because the debt was English, or the debt was situated in England, it is legitimate to make the third party debt order, is to use conflict of laws idealism (or dogmatism) to answer a question where this approach may not be capable of achieving what it seeks to accomplish. For this reason, the expression of view found in *Deutsche Schachtbau*, that the question is whether an English court should exercise an 'exclusive jurisdiction' over the debt, gets the analysis off on the wrong foot. No better was the confident assertion of the Court of Appeal in *Swiss Bank Corp v Boemische Industrial Bank*, that an English garnishee order in relation to a bank debt situated in England would be respected by a court in Czechoslovakia, when it stated that the garnishee 'need have no fear' of being sued twice, or that the discharge 'would be recognised by any foreign court which applies the ordinary principles of international law'. This is just not good enough, unless the garnishee's evidence on the point is abject. The only way to ensure that the garnishee or third party debtor is protected is to focus on the statutory provision, and its invisible discretion given to a court to not make the order absolute if cause is shown why it should not do so, and to allow the garnishee to lead the evidence which tends to this conclusion. To seek to do this by a mechanical focus on the *situs* of the debt, on the law governing the debt, on the *situs* of the garnishee, and on some assumption about the law applied by foreign courts is to be doomed to fall short.

For all that, the reasoning in *Société Eram*, with its clear acceptance that the garnishment procedure was a means of enforcing a judgment against property, which was permissible as a matter of English law only if this were situated in England, made it even clearer why an order could not be made in *Kuwait Oil Tanker Co SAK v Qabazard*. The underlying judgment was an English one; and Q was believed to have money in a Swiss bank account. The Swiss bank, UBS, was therefore served at its London office with a garnishee order *nisi;* it opposed the making of a final order. The debt was in Switzerland; and the judgment in *Société Eram* meant that it could not be garnished. But the House considered that this conclusion was reinforced by Article 16(5) of the Lugano Convention,[19] which ascribes exclusive jurisdiction, regardless of domicile, 'in proceedings concerned with the enforcement of judgments' to the courts of the contracting state in which the judgment is to be enforced. It seemed plain to the court that this is what KOTCO was attempting to do when it took proceedings against UBS in respect of funds believed to stand to the credit of Q in Switzerland: to enforce in Switzerland by means of judicial proceedings brought in England; and this was plainly ruled out by the Convention. Given that the precise question for the court was one of the proper construction of the Lugano Convention, it is not

[19] Civil Jurisdiction and judgments Act 1982 Sch. 3A (inserted by Civil Jurisdiction and judgments Act 1991).

clear that it would be helpful to try to blur the picture by taking issue with the complications caused by garnishment for the English conflict of laws.

2 *Discharge of foreign debts and the winding up of insolvent companies:* Wight v Eckhardt Marine GmbH[20]

The collapse of the Bank of Credit and Commerce International continues to pose challenges for the conflict of laws among other areas of intellectual activity. An unremarkable and short decision of the Privy Council, on appeal from the Court of Appeal of the Cayman Islands, reiterates the proposition that the validity and existence of a contractual debt is a matter for the law which governs the contract itself. Eckhardt, a German company, had agreed to sell a scrap seagoing vessel to a Bangladeshi purchaser. A letter of credit was required to be opened ten days before the sale took place, and a guarantee in respect of the 10% deposit was additionally to be given by a Bangladeshi bank, this to be payable in the event that the letter of credit was not opened. The guarantee was in fact given by the Chittagong branch of BCCI (Overseas) Ltd, a company incorporated under the law of the Cayman Islands. But no letter of credit was opened as, on the very day that this was to be done, banking regulators closed down the worldwide operations of BCCI(O). A call on the deposit guarantee went unresponded to. In July 1991 a petition was presented in the Cayman Islands for the winding up of BCCI(O); in January 1992 the winding up order was made. In May 1992 Eckhardt lodged a proof of debt in respect of the unpaid guarantee with the liquidators in Cayman, which was rejected by them in 1995. The judge sided with the liquidators; the Court of Appeal reversed him; and the Privy Council restored the decision of the judge that the liquidators were correct in refusing to admit the proof of debt.

Had there been nothing else in the story, the liquidators would surely have admitted the proof of debt. But matters had also been moving in Bangladesh. An immediate moratorium had been imposed, followed in August 1992 by a statutory reconstruction of the Bangladeshi banking business of BCCI(O). This vested all Bangladeshi assets and liabilities of BCCI(O) in a new entity, Eastern Bank; and it was the reason the liquidators refused to admit proof of the debt. As the proper law of Eckhardt's debt was admitted to be Bangladeshi, and as Bangladeshi law provided that it was no longer a debt owed by BCCI(O), so extinguishing the debt formerly owed by BCCI(O), it ceased to be admissible in the Caymanian winding up of BCCI(O). The principle that all contracts have a governing law, and that they are wholly dependent on the governing law (and not on any other law) for their creation, existence, and

[20] [2003] UKPC 37, [2004] 1 AC 147, pc: Lord Hoffmann, Lord Nolan, Lord Hobhouse of Woodborough, Lord Scott of Foscote, and Lord Walker of Gestingthorpe.

termination, is too plain to require amplification. In the Greek bondholder cases mentioned in the previous Note,[21] it was explained that only the proper law of the contract or contractual debt could alter the terms of the contract or debt, and that alterations made to or by the *lex incorporationis* of the debtor did not affect the rights and obligations created by the contract and enshrined in the debt. This case stands for the opposite proposition: that if the *lex contractus*, as the forum identifies it, alters or destroys the obligations of the contract or the debt, that is that, for what the *lex contractus* gives, the *lex contractus* can take away.

An attempt was made by Eckhardt to escape from the relentless logic of the *lex contractus*, by arguing that it was not appropriate to characterise the issue as a contractual one falling within the domain of Bangladeshi law as proper law of the contract. It argued that the issue for decision was really one of confiscation of property, because a governmental act had purported to destroy an existing contractual right against BCCI(O). The submission was that the appropriate choice of law was therefore to apply the *situs* of the debt, of the thing seised, in accordance with the principles of territoriality. Not so, said the Judicial Committee, for a variety of reasons. First, the *situs* of the debt was Bangladeshi in any event, so even if well founded the submission in fact took Eckhardt nowhere. Secondly, such authority as there was led to the application of the *lex contractus* to questions of whether a debt was discharged. Thirdly, though transfers of the benefit of a debt, as transfers of property, may have been (at least as a matter of the common law as applied in the Cayman Islands) a proprietary matter, governed by the *lex situs*, that reasoning had no application to dealings with the burden. If this makes it unattractive to make a contract governed by Bangladeshi law, the fear being that such foundations are liable to be unstable, it is open to parties to choose a different law to serve as the foundation of their rights and liabilities. Or to put it another way, the parties did not make a contract, but made a *Bangladeshi* contract. More generally, parties do not make contracts, but contracts-governed-by-a-law: a contract cannot, as Lord Diplock made plain two decades ago, have an existence which is independent of its governing law.[22] Eckhardt and BCCI(O) made a contract governed by the law of Bangladesh. That was their privilege and, as it turned out for Eckhardt, its problem. As to whether Eckhardt could rely on the validity and existence of their debt under Bangladeshi law as at the date of lodging the proof of debt, or were defeated by the subsequent discharge of the debt, the Judicial Committee answered the question of basic bankruptcy law in the only way possible: as the debt had been discharged, it ceased to be admissible. No other analysis would have been even remotely credible.

The case is one of a number this year in which the courts have been asked to depart from the orthodox characterisation of issues, where this

[21] See nn. 17 and 18, above.

[22] *Amin Rasheed Shipping Corp v Kuwait Insurance Co* [1984] AC 50.

shows a rough edge to one party's submissions, in favour of some alternative. Encouragement to do this is presumably traceable back to the far-sighted judgment of Mance LJ in *Raiffeisen Zentralbank Österreich AG v Five Star Trading LLC*.[23] There, if in a rather different context, he had suggested that characterisation was the handmaid of the conflict of laws, but not its dominatrix. He may have been a little surprised to see this thoughtful observation, which saw that nineteenth-century characterisations are not always best suited to twenty-first century commercial legal problems, abused to the point where it is prayed in aid every time the characterisation handed down by authority produces an uncongenial answer. If the conflict of laws is to be kept stable and predictable and principled and rational, new characterisation of familiar factual and legal issues needs to be a matter of last resort. This is doubtless what Mance LJ meant, and it will be well if this recent flurry of attempts to rewrite established doctrine comes to a sudden end.

3 *Conflict of copyright laws and conflicts of public policies:* Peer International Corp v Termidor Music Publishers Ltd[24]

The influence of territoriality as a limiting factor in the conflict of laws was at the root of a decision concerning Cuban law and English copyright. The Peer group of companies had come by the English copyright in certain musical works created by Cuban nationals. Copyright in the works had been granted by the musicians in the years before the Cuban revolution of 1959, in return for the payment of derisory sums; and since the American economic blockade of the Republic of Cuba, even these amounts had not been paid over. But in 1960, the Cuban legislature enacted a law (Law 860) which sought to take into the ownership of the state intellectual property rights in musical copyright, and to secure for the musician a fair reward for his labour. On a true construction of Law 860, it was intended, among other things, to divest Peer of its English copyright; and in due course the competent Cuban authority purported to grant to Termidor the right to reproduce works in which Peer claimed copyright. The question for the court was therefore whether Cuban Law 860 had any effect of the rights of the holder of the English copyright. The Court of Appeal held, on entirely orthodox grounds, that it did not. The principal interest of the decision lies in its treatment of submissions designed to counter this analysis.

Orthodoxy first. Intellectual property rights are right of property, and the law which gives them existence, and governs and defines their proprietary effect, is the *lex creationis* or *lex protectionis*. More doubtfully they may be said to be governed by the *lex situs*, but in the present context the

[23] [2001] EWCA Civ 68, [2001] QB 825, CA, noted this *Year Book* 72 (2001) p. 461.

[24] [2003] EWCA Civ 1156, [2004] 2 WLR 849, CA: Aldous, Mance and Latham LJJ.

situs denotes the territory in which the law permits exploitation, as distinct from the place where the rights can be seen, felt, and touched. On any view of the matter, these were English copyrights; and on any view of the conflict of laws it lay beyond the competence of the Cuban state to alter title to them by legislation. Only an act of the English legislator could do that, and no such law had been made. For the Cuban law to seek to alter title to copyright created under English law, or to copyright situated within England, was to purport to legislate extra-territorially. Since time out of mind, the *lex situs* rule has held sway for immovables and for tangible movables; in general, its application to intangibles may be less securely established, but in the context of intellectual property rights (said in some quarters[25] to be immovables in any event) it was plainly applicable. And that was that: though a Cuban court would consider Law 860 to be effective as drafted, whether an English court would do likewise was hardly a question which needed to trouble the Court of Appeal.

For Termidor to seek to circumvent this conclusion would appear to have been hopeless. Two arguments were apparently put forward. One, that the question should really be seen as a contractual one and not as a proprietary one, seems to have been pointless, for what did it seek to achieve? Four of the five assignments of copyright from the Cuban musicians were governed by Cuban law, but this was irrelevant to the question before the court. Presumably the submission owed something to an earlier decision of the Court of Appeal,[26] applying the *lex contractus* to an issue of priority of entitlement to the proceeds of a policy of marine insurance, and not applying the law which might have governed the question if the issue were seen as a contractual one. This decision, driven by Article 12 of the Rome Convention on the law applicable to contractual obligations,[27] had accepted that the issue of entitlement to the contractual payments was within the scope of the Rome Convention, even though the common law, left to its own devices, may have seen the issue as a proprietary one. But the Giuliano & Lagarde report made it plain that the Convention did not apply to issues of property,[28] including intellectual property. Though the original grant and acquisition of copyright was by way of contract, the right acquired by these means was an intellectual property right, good against the world and not just against the musicians. This was enough to kill off the submission that this was properly to be seen as a contractual question.

Even more unexpected was the argument that the Cuban law, though irrelevant as a matter of choice of law, ought nevertheless be applied on

[25] *Potter v Broken Hill Pty Co* (1906) 3 CLR 479. Dicey & Morris, *The Conflict of Laws* 13th edn, para 22–051 treats patents, trade marks, and copyrights as movables, but adds that 'they share some of the characteristics of immoveables in the sense that the rights which they confer are territorially limited'.

[26] *Raiffeisen Zentralbank Österreich AG v Five Star General Trading LLC* [2001] EWCA Civ 68, [2001] QB 825, CA, noted this *Year Book* 72 (2001) p. 461.

[27] Contracts (Applicable Law) Act 1990, Sch. 1.

[28] [1980] OJ C282/1 at 10.

grounds of public policy. The first step in the argument was that in *Lorentzen v Lydden & Co*,[29] the High Court had given effect to a Norwegian law purporting to vest title to ships, situated in English waters, in the Norwegian state. That the judge did so was unprecedented, but as the United Kingdom and the Kingdom of Norway were at war with the German Reich and its despicable allies, it was not surprising that the judge bent the law to accommodate the reality of the facts. The second step was to submit that the Norwegian wartime decree, requisitioning ships for compensation and to prevent their falling into German hands, and the revolutionary Cuban decree, expropriating English copyright without a peso in exchange, were *in pari materia*. It was little surprise that this submission was rejected; the only surprise was that it received as much attention as it did. What can one say? Wartime Norway and revolutionary Cuba had rather different relationships with the United Kingdom; the Norwegian decree promised compensation while the Cuban one did not; the Norwegian ships were only coincidentally or accidentally in England whereas the copyright was necessarily in England. How could anyone have seriously supposed that the Cuban decree could have overridden the English *lex situs*? It is all very well to say that the law was enacted to protect Cuba's cultural heritage, but so was the New Zealand law in *Attorney-General for New Zealand v Ortiz*[30] (and this without the whiff of class warfare), yet this did not secure its application to a question otherwise governed by the English *lex situs*. By comparison with this, the chances of applying the Cuban decree added up to the square root of zero. Whether this means that *Lorentzen* has been overruled is not worth dwelling on. It will not be followed again.

The lack of judicially manageable standards for the importation of laws—which law? and from which countries?—is the fatal flaw in any argument that there should be a public policy which allows a rule from an unchosen law to be applied to litigation before an English court? No doubt the emotional case for supporting New Zealand in its attempt to guard its cultural heritage from being ransacked to feed the avarice of foreign collectors was strong; no doubt the strength of the case for providing the Cuban state with an additional source of revenue was seen with rather less clarity. But what is the line, and where could it be drawn? What would happen when the legislatures of Austria and Hungary pass laws concerning the same historic artefact once vested in the Dual Monarchy? Or when the Greek legislature passes a law re-vesting the Elgin Marbles in the Hellenic Republic? There is no basis for rational judicial decision, and to advance this submission was to invite the court to take a hopelessly subjective decision. Stability and certainty are still virtues in the law, as Mance LJ observed;[31] nothing in the submissions advanced on behalf of Peer seemed to support those goals. The fact that the Cuban law was unashamedly expropriatory simply added to the

[29] [1942] 2 KB 202. [30] [1984] 1 AC 1. [31] At para. [64].

unattractiveness of applying it to English property rights. When English law has been invited to apply the laws of foreign countries outside the scheme for choice of law, it has peered into the cauldron and refused. Article 7(1) of the Rome Convention would have permitted an English judge hearing a contractual dispute to apply the 'mandatory law' of a country having a close connection to the contract, this law not otherwise being the *lex contractus*. Parliament declined the invitation, and enacted the convention with this provision excised[32] having concluded, no doubt, that the uncertainty which might have resulted from such legislation was unjustifiable. Many years before, in *The Torni*,[33] the Court of Appeal had picked up and applied the law of a country (Palestine) closely connected with a contractual dispute, simply because it was closely connected, and the commercial policy promoted by Palestinian law was strongly favoured by English law. As soon as it got the chance, the Privy Council repudiated this decision,[34] and that was, for all practical purposes, the last anyone ever heard of it. English law does not do this sort of thing and, many will think, a jolly good thing too.

This is not to say that public policy cannot confer a cause of action upon a claimant in circumstances when none is generated by the process of choice of law. Public policy will pick up and apply English law to a case otherwise beyond its scope, in circumstances sufficiently exceptional as to justify it; but it picks up English law, not foreign law. One reading of *Kuwait Airways Corporation v Iraq Airways Co*[35] was that the English law of conversion applied to give a cause of action to a claimant who had no cause of action under the law chosen as applicable to the claim in tort. Even though other explanations for why Iraqi law was not applied to justify what the IAC had done and defeat the claim against it may be better, there was still an application of English law to displace the repellent rule of Iraqi law otherwise applicable. No-one suggested that Kuwaiti law might have been applied to conduct taking place in Iraq, not even when this could have been seen as protecting the very existence of Kuwait, an ally of the United Kingdom. The application of English law is one thing; the application of an unchosen foreign law is quite another. If the principles of the conflict of laws count for anything, the submissions for the appellants in *Peer International* were hopeless and deserved to fail even more completely than they did.

4 *Jurisdiction and recognition of judgments over parallel trade marks:* Prudential Assurance Co Ltd v Prudential Insurance Co of America.[36]

Whereas *Peer International* was concerned with choice of law in relation to copyright, the issues in *Prudential Assurance Co Ltd v Prudential*

[32] Contracts (Applicable Law) Act 1990 s. 2(2).
[33] [1932] P 27, CA.
[34] *Vita Food Products Inc v Unus Shipping Co Ltd* [1939] AC 277, PC.
[35] [2002] 2 AC 883; see also (2002) 6 Singapore J Int & Comp Law 953.
[36] [2003] EWCA Civ 32, [2003] 1 WLR 2295, CA: Kennedy, Potter and Chadwick LJJ.

Insurance Co of America were more jurisdictional, and exposed one of the several difficulties which arise when intellectual property rights are litigated in several states. Though the right as existing under the law of each state is separate and unique, it can seem very much as though parallel litigation is being permitted. At this point the exclusivity of jurisdiction in the courts for the place where the right is granted, the obligation to recognise foreign judgments, and the need to prevent the occurrence of *lis alibi pendens* come together in a difficult knot. *Prudential* illustrates the complexity without necessarily providing a happy untangling.

The claimant (PUK) was an English insurance company which had registered the trade marks 'PRU' and 'PRUDENTIAL' in England.[37] The defendant (PUS) was an American insurer which obtained permission to register the trade mark 'PRUAMERICA' in France. PUK had opposed the French application by contending that the mark was confusingly similar to its own; the argument did not succeed, and the Paris Court of Appeal authorised the registration of the mark. PUK then brought proceedings in England, alleging that the use of PRUAMERICA infringed its English rights. PUS contended that as the French courts had held that there was no confusion between the marks, its judgment was entitled to be recognised under Article 26 of the Brussels Convention, and the reasons underpinning it were to recognised as well. Laddie J rejected the submission, and the Court of Appeal held that he was right to have done so.

Chadwick LJ started with Articles 16(4) and 19, which give exclusive jurisdiction regardless of domicile to the courts for the place where the registration has taken place. The actions which fall within the benefit of this provision are those 'in proceedings concerned with the registration or validity of . . .' trade marks. It was said that the impact of this was that where a question of validity arose, even as a defence to a claim concerning infringement, the court hearing the infringement claim must decline jurisdiction. This, though it appears to be the view of the English courts, is considerably controversial. An alternative approach is taken by the courts of Germany, the Netherlands, and[38] Switzerland: the infringement proceedings are stayed pending the determination of the validity issue (and only that issue) before the court with exclusive jurisdiction under Article 16. He then proceeded to dismiss the relevance of Article 21, on which PUS had placed reliance, on the basis that it was frequently the case that each national court was seised of a question which over which it had exclusive jurisdiction, and which did not therefore call for the second court to dismiss its proceedings. It also followed that Article 22 was irrelevant, as there was no power to consolidate such diverse proceedings in the one court, nor to accomplish anything of any use by waiting for a ruling from a foreign court, even if first seised. This was surely correct,

[37] There was also registration as a Community Trade Mark under Council Regulation (EC) 40/94. The details of this part of the dispute are not examined here.

[38] In the context of the Lugano Convention.

even though it seemed a curious point for PUS to take. The proceedings in France had been brought to an end, and there were no proceedings pending outside the English courts.

The recognition obligation, in relation to the French judgment, was plainly more relevant. Chadwick LJ correctly observed that as the French proceedings had terminated in judgment, the facts before the court fell within the scope of the recognition provisions of the Convention. His conclusion was that the French judgment did not qualify for recognition under Article 26, as to do so would violate the exclusive jurisdiction provisions of Article 16(4): that if validity was a matter falling within the exclusive jurisdiction of an English court, it would violate that provision for the English court to recognise the French judgment.

If this is an accurate summary of a rather difficult paragraph[39] of the judgment, it is a very difficult conclusion. The Convention requires a court not to trespass on the exclusive jurisdiction of another court; and it forbids recognition of a judgment which had been handed down by a court in violation of those provisions on exclusive jurisdiction. But more than that it does not do. If one then asks what the Paris Court of Appeal had done which had violated Article 16(4), the plain answer is nothing; if one asks whether the recognition of its judgment would be refused by Article 28(1), a provision not mentioned in the judgment, the answer is likewise no. What seems to have happened is that the court sought to deduce a rule on the recognition and non-recognition of judgments from the rules on jurisdiction, and did not examine the specific provisions in the Convention dealing with the very point. That being done, it was unsurprising that the conclusion of the court is rather unsatisfying. The correct answer must surely have been that the French judgment required to be recognised, as in upholding the registration of a trade mark in France, the court had done nothing to put it on the wrong side of Article 16(4).

The true question for the court, therefore, was rather concerned with the nature and extent of the obligation to recognise a foreign judgment under the terms of the Convention. There is a persistent and still unresolved sense of confusion as to whether the obligation placed on a court by Part III of the Convention, or by Chapter III of the Regulation, is to give effect to the order made by the foreign court (which in this case would not have much impact in England, as that court had simply confirmed the registration of a French trade mark), or to receive the judgment, and all its reasoning, into the local legal order, and treat it exactly as though it were a local judgment. This, if done, would have allowed issue estoppel to be founded on any final determination of an issue between the parties by the French court; and as the French court had specifically been asked to consider the risk of confusion with the registered English trade mark and to rule on it in PUK's favour, to recognise as conclusive against PUK this finding when PUK sought to ventilate

[39] Paragraph 28.

the issue again. In general terms, this raises a particularly knotty problem, but when it gets entangled with the jurisdictional rules which confer exclusive jurisdiction, it becomes even trickier. All we know from the Court of Justice is that the obligation to recognise a judgment entails according it the same effect as it has under the law of the state in which it was pronounced. One does not know, but it is probably safe to assume that French principles of *res judicata* are not a million miles distant from the English equivalent. If a French court would regard the reasoning of the Paris Court of Appeal as binding on the parties to the decision, and as estopping the loser from re-opening in any subsequent litigation between the same parties any issue there determined, an English court should presumably do likewise. Of course, if the reverse were true, the conclusion would be opposite. But the broad point is that the recognition of judgments is required by Article 26 of the Convention, and the only question is as to what that obligation entails. This much is clear, though: it is not properly open to a English court to withhold recognition from a French judgment because, though the French court has not erred in its exercise of jurisdiction, the English court has exclusive jurisdiction over a matter properly before it. It is only possible to withhold recognition if it can be shown that the French court had violated Article 16(4). As this does not seem to have been alleged—indeed, it is hard to see how it could have been—the conclusion is inescapable: there was no basis in the Convention to refuse to recognise the French judgment. True, this left the English court needing to answer the earlier question of precisely what constitutes the detail of the obligation to recognise, and being obliged to see whether anything decided by the French court could properly be seen as founded on the same issue as required to be determined by the English court. But as it was reasoned, the decision is a problematic one, probably because the court was not directed to the material which should have produced the answer. The judgment resembles a fitted carpet which has been badly laid: it is simply not possible to smooth the wrinkles out of it. It is sufficient to note that the Convention is not very happily drafted, nor happily interpreted, where it deals with intellectual property disputes. Until it is given a thorough and authoritative going over, this will continue to be an area of weakness and dissatisfaction.

5 *Restraining the breach of a non-exclusive jurisdiction clause; and responding to a foreign anti-suit injunction:* Sabah Shipyard (Pakistan) Ltd v The Islamic Republic of Pakistan;[40] General Star International Indemnity Ltd v Stirling Cooke Brown Reinsurance Brokers Ltd.[41]

A contractual term which is construed as conferring non-exclusive jurisdiction on a particular court imposes no obligation on either party to sue

[40] [2002] EWCA Civ 1643, [2003] 2 Lloyd's Rep 571, CA: Pill, Waller LJJ, and Sir Martin Nourse.

[41] [2003] EWHC 3 (Comm), [2003] ILPr 314, Langley J.

there, but obliges either party to acquiesce in proceedings being instituted there by the other.[42] Such, at any rate, was the orthodox understanding, one which lay behind all those cases in which the parties fought with some energy over whether a jurisdiction agreement was exclusive or non-exclusive.[43] If the decision of the Court of Appeal in *Sabah Shipyard (Pakistan) Ltd v The Islamic Republic of Pakistan* is correct, things are not quite that straightforward.

Sabah, a Malaysian-owned company incorporated under the law of Pakistan, engaged with KESC, another Pakistani company, to construct an electrical generating plant in Pakistan. As part of the complex of agreements, the government of Pakistan (GOP) gave certain payment guarantees to Sabah. When it all began to go wrong, Sabah referred its dispute with KESC to arbitration in Singapore, in accordance with its agreement, and obtained an award of $6.8m. When KESC refused to honour the award, Sabah demanded the money from GOP under the terms of the guarantee; and the GOP likewise refused to pay. But it went one stage further, and instituted proceedings in the court at Islamabad, seeking an injunction to restrain Sabah from making any demand on the guarantee. One month later, Sabah applied in England for an injunction to restrain the GOP from continuing with its action in Islamabad. The judge made the order without notice to the GOP, and continued it after a hearing *inter partes*. The Court of Appeal dismissed the appeal of the GOP.

All this would have been uncontroversial had there been no proceedings before the Pakistani court, and had the guarantee contained an exclusive jurisdiction agreement for the English courts. Little can be made of the effect which should have been accorded to the Pakistani proceedings, for the evidence about their precise nature and scope was obscure. But the jurisdiction provision in the guarantee simply provided that 'Each party hereby consents to the jurisdiction of the Courts of England for any action filed by the other Party under this Agreement to resolve any dispute between the Parties and maybe (sic) enforced in England. . . '. This lamentable[44] provision went on to appoint agents for the service of process, and waived the 'Defence of Inconvenient Forum'. Anyone who produces rubbish like this for a commercial client should be sued or shot. If attention is focused on the elementary question whether

[42] Sometimes the clause will be accompanied by a provision which obliges a party to refrain from contending that the nominated court is a *forum non conveniens*, though in the light of the practice of the English courts, it is difficult to see that this adds anything of substance to the obligation created by the clause; and see also *UBS AG v Omni Holding AG* [2000] 1 WLR 916.

[43] In the context of the Brussels and Lugano Conventions, it was unclear precisely what effect was to be given to a non-exclusive jurisdiction agreement. The problem has been resolved by explicit provision in Article 23 of the judgments Regulation, but in a decision on the (unreformed) text of the Lugano Convention, the Court of Appeal gave such a clause the effect it was intended to have, and did not allow the unaccommodating wording of the Convention to defeat it: *Insured Financial Services Ltd v Elektrocieplownia Tychy SA* [2003] EWCA Civ 110, [2003] QB 1260. The decision is entirely orthodox, and does not otherwise require to be noted.

[44] Any jurisdiction agreement which is capable of spawning litigation as to its meaning has failed in the purpose for which it was made.

the parties agreed that proceedings *must* be brought or *may* be brought in England, the answer is that the clause does not give an answer. Of course, an answer may be reached by a court after days of argument and mountainous fees, but what is the point of that? Waller LJ went through the sorry list of authorities in which this same question had had to be answered, which included asking whether the wording had a transitive or intransitive construction, [45] and reached the conclusion that the clause was not exclusive 'in the sense of making it a breach of contract for either party to commence proceedings in a jurisdiction other than England'. That being so, what the GOP had done in going to court in Islamabad was not of itself a breach of contract. Had it opposed the jurisdiction of the English courts, this may have been a breach of the agreement, but it did not do so. That being so, an anti-suit injunction would have appeared hard to justify, though the court considered that if it were possible to show that the behaviour of the GOP were oppressive or vexatious, this could still be justified.[46]

That may be correct; but it serves as a useful reminder that there are different ways of breaking a contractual promise. The two polar cases are well understood. An undertaking to bring legal proceedings only in country A is breached by bringing any form of legal proceedings in country B; but a promise to accept to be sued in country B is not, on the face of it, broken by bringing proceedings in country A. However, if the bringing of proceedings in country A does mean, as a matter of law, that proceedings in country B are not now possible, the bringing of proceedings in country A will involve a breach of a non-exclusive jurisdiction clause for country B. We can posit at least two instances which would fit into this pattern. For one, if countries A and B are member states of the European Union, bound by Council Regulation (EC) 44/2001, or are contracting states bound by the Brussels or Lugano Conventions, the seising of the courts of country A will make it legally impossible for the same cause of action to be brought before the courts of country B;[47] and in such circumstances to sue in country A is to breach the terms of a non-exclusive jurisdiction clause for country B. For another, if the proceedings in country A are for an anti-suit injunction, to order the respondent not to bring the applicant before the courts of country B, this also will involve a breach of the non-exclusive jurisdiction agreement.

It is this possibility which had probably eluded those who had thought about the difference between exclusive and non-exclusive jurisdiction agreements in too unreflective a way. The important question for the Court of Appeal, then, in seeking to decide whether there had been a breach of contract by the GOP, was not to ask whether it had brought

[45] At paras. [32]–[34]. Though of interest to the grammarian, it is impossible to believe that this was a distinction which animated the minds of those who drafted the agreement. See *BAe v Dee Howard Corp* [1993] 1 Lloyd's Rep 368, *Cannon Street Entertainment Ltd v Handmade Films (Distributors) Ltd*, July 11th 1989.

[46] At para. [37].

[47] If the dispute is between the same parties and is in respect of the same cause of action: Art. 27 of the judgments Regulation; Art. 21 of the Brussels and Lugano Conventions.

proceedings in Pakistan, but whether the bringing of those proceedings made it impossible for Sabah to exercise its contractual right to bring the GOP before an English court. As there was no rule of English law that *lis alibi pendens* in Pakistan prevented or removed the jurisdiction of an English court, there could have been no breach unless the Pakistani action was specifically for an anti-suit injunction. As to this point, as said above, the precise nature of the Pakistani proceedings was not clearly explained or well understood. But Waller LJ stated that the Pakistani action was for an injunction to restrain Sabah from making any demand under the guarantee; and added that it was common ground that this was designed to prevent Sabah bringing any action in London. This was not therefore a case in which the breach lay in suing in Pakistan rather than London, but in seeking relief from a court in Pakistan which was designed to make it impossible for Sabah to exercise its contractual rights in London. In short, there was a breach of contract in doing what the GOP did; and the court was right to regard the case as one in which the grant of injunctive relief was, on the present state of the authorities,[48] more or less automatic.

Where it is more difficult to agree with the court is the further point made, that it would have been a breach of contract, liable to be restrained as such by injunction, for parallel proceedings to be brought in Pakistan if proceedings had been commenced in England.[49] Perhaps, as Waller LJ said, this outcome would not have been what the parties contemplated, but the critical question is whether they agreed that it would be a breach of contract. In such a case it would have been open to the court to characterise the behaviour of the GOP as vexatious or oppressive, but more difficult to see it as amounting to a breach of contract. In this one respect the judgment goes further than it needed to, and into doubt. But where the relief sought in Pakistan is a judicial order to prevent proceedings in England from being brought there, this looks like a breach of contract and is, on that ground alone, liable to be restrained by anti-suit injunction. In short, then, if the precise relief sought from the foreign court can be seen as amounting to a breach of contract, the restraint by injunction will be pretty automatic; if seeking the particular relief cannot be seen as amounting to a breach of contract, but is still vexatious or oppressive, it may be restrained on that ground also. Care in looking at what the foreign court has been asked to do will be central to the decision whether there was a breach or not. Asking whether the clause was exclusive or non-exclusive will be a good starting point but may not be a good stopping place.

Close to the end of the judgment, when Waller LJ had concluded that an injunction was required to restrain the GOP from its vexatious or oppressive behaviour, one finds this ringing statement of orthodoxy:[50]

[48] Especially *Donohue v Armco Inc* [2002] 1 Lloyd's Rep 425, HL, noted this *Year Book* 72 (2001) p. 437.

[49] At para. [42].

[50] At para. [44].

'I stress that the injunction is in personam and against the GOP. It is being granted by the court to which both parties have agreed to give effect to the bargain they made. It is not intended in any way to be an interference with the jurisdiction of the courts of Pakistan, and above all it is not implying any criticism of those courts.'

English courts say, and apparently believe, that this is a sufficient justification to relieve them of the charge that they are interfering, directly or otherwise, with proceedings before a foreign court, and that they have no right to do so. As a matter of English law, the injunction operates *in personam*, and will be granted only where there is a proper connection to England.[51] Foreign courts therefore have no reason to fear any overreaching on the part of the English courts. There is evidence that foreign courts may not always see matters in quite the same way, [52] but this has not prevented the development of this effective personal remedy. Some have occasionally wondered what would happen if a foreign court turned the tables and did this in relation to proceedings before an English court. In a startlingly revealing decision, one Commercial Court judge has now let the cat out of the bag. And what a cross and contrary cat it turns out to be.

In *General Star International Indemnity Ltd v Stirling Cooke Brown Reinsurance Brokers Ltd*, a small part of the ongoing worldwide litigation about film financing and insurance of the losses which that activity generated, there was no trace of an agreement on jurisdiction. An English insurer, Genstar, issued proceedings in London against its London broker, SCB, claiming an indemnity in respect of damages which Genstar may be ordered to pay. After Genstar had served its claim form, and just before the time limited for SCB to serve its defence, SCB brought proceedings against Genstar in the courts of New York, the 'reality' of which was that they sought an anti-suit injunction against Genstar.[53] Fortified by this order, SCB applied for a stay of the English proceedings. Such behaviour was seen by Langley J in the Commercial Court as an attempt to prevent the issue of the English court's jurisdiction being determined by the English court. The judge thereupon refused SCB's application for a stay, and granted Genstar an (anti-)anti-suit injunction, to counter and overcome the (anti-suit) injunction which had already been obtained in New York. The express reason[54] for doing so was that New York order would have had the effect of frustrating an English court's ability to establish the existence of jurisdiction over a case properly pending

[51] That is to say, England is the contractually chosen forum, or England is the most appropriate forum for the litigation of the dispute.

[52] In particular, the Court of Justice of the European Communities, in Case C-159/02 *Turner v Grovit*, April 27th 2004, has now ruled that this justification of the injunction is unacceptable, and that the interference with the foreign court is not justified by the *in personam* character of the relief sought. It may be thought that this is at odds with its approach in Case C-294/92 *Webb v Webb* [1994] ECR I-1717, but the furious indignation which the anti-suit injunction appears to provoke in some continental lawyers is not easily deflected by reason or by law.

[53] At para. [16].

[54] All set out in para. [16] of the judgment.

before it. The judge characterised what SCB and/or the New York court had engineered court as an attempt 'to hijack the hearing of forum issues to New York rather than England' the issue of the jurisdiction of the English courts. Such interference with proceedings properly before the English court was to be regarded as oppressive, even though it could not be regarded as a breach of contract. In a judgment which was very short and very clear, he granted the injunction.

As well he might. But one has to wonder where leaves the traditional justification for granting orders which hinder or prevent a foreign court from considering whether it has jurisdiction according to its own law. After all, the objection to the foreign proceedings in *Sabah Shipyards*, as in *General Star Indemnity* itself, was that the foreign proceedings unduly interfered with a jurisdictional question which was properly one for the English court to decide: in the former it was a breach of contract to do so; in the latter it was as wrong as 'hijacking'. But in *Continental Bank NA v Aeakos SA*,[55] (where there was a jurisdiction clause) and *The Angelic Grace*[56] and *The Epsilon Rosa*[57] (where there was an arbitration agreement), and in *Turner v Grovit*[58] and *Glencore International AG v Exter Shipping Ltd*[59] (where there was not), and in a hundred other modern cases in which English courts have granted anti-suit injunctions, the English courts have by their order sought and served to prevent a foreign court deciding whether it had jurisdiction over proceedings before that foreign court. Now the manifest lack of judicial confidence in their Greek and Italian cousins which was displayed by the Court of Appeal in *Continental Bank* and *The Angelic Grace* these two cases was the undoing of the whole industry;[60] and judged in the light of the Greek stage of proceedings in *Standard Bank London Ltd v Apostolakis*[61] it now looks

[55] [1994] 1 WLR 588, CA. It is worth noting that this decision was fatally weakened by the decision of the Court of Justice of the European Communities in Case C-116/02 *Erich Gasser GmbH v MISAT Srl* [2004]1 Lloyd's Rep 222, ECJ. In refusing to allow a court (Austrian) which considered itself to have jurisdiction by virtue of a contractual agreement to proceed to hear a case when another court (Italian) had been seised first in a shameless attempt to frustrate the jurisdiction agreement, the Court has removed the foundation which was supposed to support the jurisdiction of the English court in *Continental Bank*. There being no jurisdiction in such circumstances, the grant of an anti-suit injunction in pursuance of that non-existent jurisdiction is plainly insupportable; and see also Case C-159/02 *Turner v Grovit*, April 27th 2004.

[56] [1995] 1 Lloyd's Rep 87, CA.

[57] [2003] EWCA Civ 938, [2003] 2 Lloyd's Rep 509. The case is entirely orthodox in its decision to uphold the granting of an anti-suit injunction to restrain a party who, in breach of an arbitration agreement, was prosecuting a claim before the Polish courts. The fact that Poland was a party to the Lugano Convention was not material in the decision required from the court. It was accepted that if an injunction would lead to the loss of security for a claim, such a point could be put forward as a (strong) reason why enforcement by injunction should not be ordered, but as the court rejected the submission on the facts it was unnecessary to decide it. The court also observed that related proceedings would continue in Poland, as these were not covered by any agreement on jurisdiction or arbitration. But in the light of the strong policy of giving effect to an arbitration agreement, this did not furnish a reason for withholding an anti-suit injunction.

[58] [2002] 1 WLR 107, HL, noted this *Year Book* 72 (2001) p. 437.

[59] [2002] EWCA Civ 524, [2002] 2 All ER (Comm) 1, CA, noted this *Year Book* 73 (2002) p. 443.

[60] By the reference to the Court of Justice in Case C-159/02 *Turner v Grovit*, April 27th 2004.

[61] An extended footnote cannot be avoided. In the English proceedings between an English merchant bank and a Greek investor, the Commercial Court refused to give effect to an exclusive

distinctly embarrassing. A similar lack of confidence in the German courts was regarded by a Regional Court of Appeal[62] as an infringement of German public policy and of the Basic Law; the proposition that the injunction was unobjectionable as it was aimed only at the respondent was rejected with scorn. The European dimension to the general issue is principally one for the European Court.

It did not appear to have seriously crossed the mind of Langley J that the injunction was not aimed at him but only at Genstar, the party who was claiming in the English proceedings. The judge's excited reaction seems to show that the English courts claim a degree of exclusivity over jurisdictional issues which they consider properly theirs, which is not reciprocated, formally or at all, in relation to proceedings before foreign courts: not so much doing as they would be done by, and very much disliking being done by as they did. It did not appear to have comforted the judge to think that Gammerman J in New York will have paid attention to the requirements of comity before making the order he did, and that he will not have been interfering with the English courts, or criticising the English court for allowing Genstar's action to be commenced before it. All this counted for nothing in London. To put the earlier point in a plainer vernacular, the English courts can dish it out but cannot take it.

Maybe some degree of asymmetry was inevitable. Where a jurisdiction clause is present, the sharpness of the disagreement may reflect a civilian view that jurisdiction clauses raise procedural questions governed by the *lex fori*, but which sits uncomfortably with a common lawyer's view that these are substantive matters falling within the scope of the *lex contractus*. Where there is no jurisdiction clause, there may be more to be said for the practice of granting injunctions only where there are pending proceedings which are being undermined by a foreign action. Where the competing proceedings are before the courts of another member state of the European Union, the ground rules are much altered by the decisions of the

jurisdiction clause for the English courts on the footing that the contract was a consumer contract. It dismissed the action. The bank then instituted proceedings in Greece. The multi-membered Court of First Instance, in *Standard Bank of London v Apostolakis* (Case 8032/2001, [2002] Epith Emp Dik 100), [2003] ILPr 499, came to the conclusion that the contract was not a consumer contract, that the jurisdiction clause was therefore binding, and accordingly that the English courts had exclusive jurisdiction. It therefore dismissed the action. Three points may be made. (1) The Greek court took the view that the sophistication and financial standing of customers who undertook such specialist entrepreneurial activity as these Greek investors necessarily excluded their contract from the category of consumer contracts; the investments were not made for the satisfaction of private needs. (2) The Greek court characterised the English decision to the contrary as 'manifestly incorrect', a conclusion which, even if soundly based on the merits of the argument, risks chaos in the overall scheme of the Convention or Regulation. (3) The Greek court asserted that it was not obliged to recognise a foreign court's decision on whether it had jurisdiction. This is flatly contrary to the observations of Professor Schlosser at para. 191 of his Report (1979 OJ C59/71, 128); and the effect of disregarding this sage advice is that the unfortunate bank now has to proceed in England to bring an action which has already been dismissed on jurisdictional grounds. This is not consistent with the scheme of the Convention, quite apart from being at variance with common sense.

[62] *Re the Enforcement of an English anti-suit injunction* [1997] ILPr 320.

European Court in *Turner v Grovit*[63] and *Erich Gasser GmbH v MISAT srl*.[64] But quite apart from that, Langley J has raised the uncomfortable question of whether the justification given by the courts for granting an anti-suit injunction is credible. If, as he seems to have thought, it is not, one has to wonder whether there is a future for this remedy even within the free domain in which the European Court has no power to kill it off.

Judged in the light of English authority, the decision of the Court of Appeal in *Sabah Shipyards* was quite correct, if slightly unexpected. It goes to show that the division of jurisdiction clauses into exclusive and non-exclusive may be unduly simplistic, and that the true question is whether claiming the relief sought in the foreign proceedings is or is not a breach of the contractual term which gives jurisdiction (of whichever sort) to the English court. Judged by the light of *General Star International Indemnity Ltd v Stirling Cooke Brown Reinsurance Brokers Ltd*, that English authority now looks much more threadbare than it once did.

6 *The scope and validity of jurisdiction clauses in English and European law:* Roche Products Ltd v Provimi Ltd.[65]

A difficult question has been created at the borderline of European and national law when it is argued that a jurisdiction clause, which is written or otherwise valid in point of form, is not necessarily wide enough to cover a dispute which has arisen. Traditionally such a question of construction would be referred to the law which governed the jurisdiction agreement, which as far as an English court is concerned, means the law which governs the contract of which that provision is a term.[66] But where the validity of the jurisdiction agreement is also determined by Article 23 of the Judgments Regulation, or Article 17 of the Brussels or Lugano Conventions, it is less clear that the untrammelled application of the governing law is still permitted. In a complex case concerning the distribution of branded pharmaceuticals, and causes of action arising under the competition law provisions of the European Treaty, Aikens J had to face up to the uncertainties which earlier cases had left behind. He did a masterful job in very difficult circumstances.

Two large drug companies, conveniently described as Roche (a Swiss concern) and Aventis (a French concern) had operated unlawful price-fixing cartels within the European Union. They established a network of associates and subsidiaries to partition the market to their joint advantage. The Commission of the European Union published a Decision to this effect in 2001 after an investigation lasting thirty months. Investigations and proceedings involving the two companies and/or their

[63] Case C-159/02 April 27th 2004. [64] Case C-116/02, [2004] 1 Lloyd's Rep 222.
[65] [2003] EWHC 961 (Comm), [2003] 2 All ER (Comm) 683, Aikens J.
[66] *Hoerter v Hanover Telegraph Works* (1893) 10 TLR 103.

associates also took place in the United States, Canada, and Australia. And in England, civil proceedings were instituted by companies, of which Provimi was one, who had purchased the drugs in question and who were, as they alleged, caused loss by the price-fixing. The claimants' cause of action was said to arise under Article 81 of the European Treaty; objection was taken by Roche and Aventis on the ground that jurisdiction agreements and Article 23 of Council Regulation (EC) 44/2001 and Article 17 of the Lugano Convention deprived the English courts of jurisdiction. Aikens J had to decide whether the validity and scope of the jurisdiction agreements was to be determined by their individual governing laws, or by the jurisprudence of the Court of Justice on the corresponding provision of the Brussels Convention. He held that the jurisdiction agreements did not deprive the English courts of jurisdiction, mainly because they were not worded widely enough to cover, according to the various national laws, the claims under Article 81 EC.

The principal contention arose from the fact that under some potentially applicable laws, a claim having the legal foundation of the kind advanced by Provimi may not fall within a jurisdiction agreement, or within one which is framed in general terms. As a matter of English law, a claim in respect of civil liability based on Article 81 EC is a private law tort claim.[67] But where a jurisdiction clause may be read as being restricted to contractual claims, or from claims which arise from only the contract in which it appears, there is obviously room for debate as to the material scope of the clause. In the first case, the clause provided that 'this contract shall be deemed to be made in Switzerland and governed in all respects by Swiss law. Any controversies which cannot be settled amicably between the parties shall be brought before the competent courts of Arlesheim/ Switzerland.' As it was not disputed that the clause was formally and materially valid, the scope of the jurisdiction provision was to be construed according to Swiss law, not by some autonomous construction of the law; and on the evidence of Swiss law as found by the judge this did not extend to the claims under Article 81 EC.

The German clause was more challenging: 'All disputes arising from the legal relationship between the purchaser and us shall be dealt with by the Lörrach county court and the Land court of Freiburg'. It was apparently submitted that the material validity of the clause was not to be determined by national law, but by reference to an autonomous interpretation somehow to be derived from Article 17 of the Brussels Convention or Article 23 of the Regulation. It was alleged that German law did not allow a jurisdiction clause to be relied on in relation to an intentional or fraudulent tort, that this raised a question of the (partial) validity—as distinct from the scope—of the clause, and that such a question of validity was not within the competence of national law for decision. Instead, it was argued, it had to be assessed by reference only to the

[67] *Garden Cottage Foods Ltd v Milk Marketing Board* [1984] 1 AC 130, 141.

criteria in Article 23 of the Regulation. According to the judge, however, there was a distinction between whether the clause was valid at all (a matter of validity), and one whether its scope was sufficient to encompass the particular dispute (a question of scope). The judge understood the evidence of German law to be that the parties had not (or would not be taken to have) intended an Article 81 EC dispute to fall within the framework of the jurisdiction agreement, in part because German law takes a stricter approach to issues of construction than would an English court in like circumstances. That having been decided, there was no need to assess the validity of the jurisdiction agreements by reference to Article 23 of the Regulation.

The French clause provided that 'any dispute relating to the fulfilment or interpretation of our sales agreements will fall within the competence of . . .' a number of specific French courts; and it raised a different set of arguments. The approach to construction deduced from the expert evidence of French law suggested that significance attached to whether the claims were characterised as contractual or otherwise. It being accepted by the judge, at any rate, that neither side was contending that the clause was inherently invalid, the consequent question of its scope was a matter for French law to determine. But the answer to the question of characterisation was more difficult to discern, for though the jurisdiction clause was governed by French law, characterisation is in some respects and some contexts a matter for the *lex fori*; and English domestic law, at least, saw the claim as one in tort. The judge preferred the view, however, that on a question of interpretation of a French contract, English characterisation of issues was unlikely to be helpful; but how a French court would characterise an English action was not straightforward. On the evidence he concluded that a French court would see the claim as tortious and (this much being more or less common ground) if that were so, as falling outside the scope of the jurisdiction clause. The outcome was that the various jurisdiction clauses were ineffective to prevent the jurisdiction of the English court being established on such other basis as the Lugano Convention and the judgments Regulation permitted.

The distinction drawn between the validity, or essential validity, of a jurisdiction agreement and its scope, though imposed on the judge by the jurisprudence of the European Court, is really rather difficult. The contention that a jurisdiction agreement may not as a matter of law cover negligence or fraud, for example, has to be disentangled from the submission that it is not wide enough to cover negligence or fraud. With respect to the judge, who has no choice but to accept it, there is really no distinction there: the question whether there is a valid and enforceable agreement to submit certain disputes to the jurisdiction of a court is one question, not two. It is as though a claim in the tort of negligence were seen to involve two separate questions: was there a duty of care and can damages be recovered for economic loss resulting from its breach? But we now know that there is only one, indivisible, question: did the defendant owe a duty of care not to inflict economic loss? The trouble with the approach of the judge was that it seeks to distil two separate questions out of what is really only one.

That would not matter if the areas of each overlapped, so that they operated as a test of double actionability: the clause requiring to be effective under the test laid down by the Regulation, and under its governing law. But the judge correctly interpreted the jurisprudence of the European Court as involving a clear separation, so that issues to which the Regulation applied could not be affected by national law, and vice versa. His task was not one to envy. It is not the only one of its type, though. Courts frequently have to decide whether a jurisdiction clause in contract A was carried across into contract B by particular words of incorporation. The English case law has been rather coy about whether this is governed by Article 23, or the law governing the contract alleged to contain it, or both.[68] It is in truth impossible to draw a convincing distinction within the question whether there was an agreement on choice of court which reflects (i) the autonomous definition of what an agreement is, and (ii) the national law question whether the agreement as made was broad or specific enough to cover and include the jurisdiction agreement. Even if it is not impossible, it still serves next to no rational purpose. It comes about as a result of some dogmatism on the part of the European Court, rightly concerned to ensure that jurisdiction agreements are accorded equal effect by the courts of the several member states before which they come. This would be imperilled every time a court made reference to its national law of contract, or its procedural law, or its private international law, as part of the process of deciding what effect to give to the clause in question. The trouble is that the solution—to refuse to permit any recourse to national law, save (perhaps) to measure the scope of the clause agreed to—leaves an impossible burden to be borne by Article 23. It does not explain how to decide whether the clause was essentially valid and actually agreed to, and does not provide the means to define those areas which must remain the province of some other rule of law, such as the decision what particular words actually meant. The present case is a good example of why, as it is submitted, there is nothing which can be done to avoid this and that it may be healthier to stop trying. On the evidence as found by the judge, German law takes a more restrictive and wary approach to the construction of jurisdiction agreements than does English law; and French law takes a more abstract and theoretical approach than the commercial pragmatism of English law. The result is that the same form of words will be accorded divergent meanings when the laws of the various member states are asked to interpret them, even

[68] *AIG Europe (UK) Ltd v The Ethniki* [2000] 2 All ER 566, CA; *AIG Europe SA v QBE International Insurance Ltd* [2001] 2 Lloyd's Rep 268, *Assicurazioni Generali SpA v Ege Sigorta A/S* [2002] Lloyd's Rep IR 480; *Welex AG v Rosa Maritime Ltd (The Epsilon Rosa)* [2003] EWCA Civ 938, [2003] 2 Lloyd's Rep 509, CA; *Siboti v BP France* [2003] EWHC 1278 (Comm) [2003] 2 Lloyd's Rep 364; *Prifti v Musini SA de Seguros y Reaseguros* [2003] EWHC 2796 (Comm).

though all accept that the agreement was valid and binding (according to its terms) on the parties. To the extent that the decisions in *Benincasa v Dentalkit srl*[69] and *Trasporti Castelletti Spedizioni Internazionali SpA v Hugo Trumpy SpA*[70] seek to prevent this, they are attempting the impossible. It may not be easy for a Commercial Court judge to take this view, but it seems right enough.

The proper function of Article 23 is twofold. It prescribes the formalities without which the clause is not valid, and it proscribes any rules of national law which may provide that there are legal relationships within which the power of the parties to make a binding agreement on jurisdiction is excluded. This is a matter for the Regulation and for it alone. So if national law imposes restrictions on jurisdiction agreements in relation (say) to consumer contracts, or non-mercantile contracts, or private investment contracts, or employment contracts, all such rules of exclusion are overridden by Article 23. So too if national law says that the jurisdiction of its courts may not be excluded by agreement, or that the parties' agreement may sometimes be denied legal effect. But that done, there remains a question of whether the parties *did agree* to litigate the dispute in question in the court nominated: that is a matter which lies wholly within their autonomy and competence, and over which their drafting, and their choice of law against which their agreement is to be interpreted, is final and determinative. An answer to the question of what, precisely, they did agree to do must be determined by the law by reference they made that agreement, just as (in the context of Article 5(1) of the judgments Regulation) the place where the obligation in question was to be performed is a matter falling within the autonomy of the contracting parties themselves, and not the autonomy of the Regulation.[71]

It will sometimes be necessary to decide on which side of the line to locate a potentially-applicable rule of national law that (for example) a party may not be held to a jurisdiction agreement where the claim is in respect of a cause of action in tort, or for an intentional tort, or in a claim which could not have been foreseen at the time of the agreement. The answer, which is wholly consistent with the view of the judge, is on the national law, not the Article 23, side of the line. Such rules, if they exist at all, are frequently not rules of law but principles of construction: that an agreement is not effective to produce a particular result if the words used are ambiguous (construction *contra proferentem*) or insufficiently wide, or too specific. This appears to have been true of the German rule, and probably of the Swiss and French law conclusions. That being so, the question for the judge was, as he rightly concluded, one of scope of the agreement as made, and not one concerning the application of Article 23

[69] Case C-269/95, [1997] ECR I-3767. [70] Case C-159/97, [1999] ECR I-1597.

[71] Case 12/76 *Industrie Tessili Italiana Como v Dunlop AG* [1976] ECR I-1473. Though Art. 5(1) of the Regulation no longer provides that special jurisdiction is invariably vested in the place for performance of the obligation which founds the claimant's claim, it remains the case that the location of the obligation in question is for the parties to specify, or for the *lex contractus* to supply, and not otherwise.

of the Regulation. This may be a little easier to understand and apply than a distinction between validity and scope. In the case of incorporation of terms from one document to another, the English 'rule' that general words are insufficient to introduce a jurisdiction agreement from one contract to another is one of construction of words such as 'terms as original', and no more than that.[72] It therefore applies, as a part of national law (wherever English law is the *lex contractus*) to assist the court in determining what the parties agreed to, and its operation is not affected by Article 23.

It will also mean that where it is argued that a party did not make a binding agreement on jurisdiction because (say) of misrepresentation or mistake or duress, or because there was no consideration for the promise, or that he is no longer bound because the agreement has been discharged, a court should still evaluate that plea according to the national law which, in its view, governs the alleged agreement. It is true that *Benincasa* provides that a jurisdiction agreement is severable from the contract in which it is embedded, so that the invalidity or failure of the contract does not necessarily result in the invalidity or failure of the jurisdiction agreement. Quite right too: common sense would lead one to ask whether the parties intended the nominated court to be able to proceed with a claim in respect of rescission or alleging that the contract was not binding, and common sense would expect the answer to be affirmative. The law of arbitration allows for the severance of arbitration agreements;[73] the common law of jurisdiction agreements probably does as well.[74] But just because a jurisdiction agreement does not necessarily go down with the ship, it does not follow that it is impervious to the argument that it was not agreed to. As what was agreed to is a matter for the law which defines and construes the terms of the agreement this question must, whatever the Court of Justice may sometimes appear to have said, be a question for national law, as applicable to the construction of agreements, to decide. Once it has been established that the parties did in law make the agreement, and the law by reference to which it was made has determined what the scope and meaning of that agreement is, Article 23 will deal with whether it is formally valid, and whether it may be excluded from effect in the particular context in which it is to operate. But what Article 23 cannot properly do is to breathe life into that which was stillborn: if the parties did not make an agreement, the impact of Article 23 is nil. Perhaps the judge would have done better to start with the question whether (as a matter of the law which governs their agreement) the parties have made an agreement which would cover the action in question; and only once that question has been answered affirmatively, look to

[72] See n. 66, above.

[73] Arbitration Act 1996 s. 7; *Harbour Assurance Co (UK) Ltd v Kansa General International Insurance Co Ltd* [1993] QB 701, CA for the common law.

[74] *IFR Ltd v Federal Trade SpA*, September 19th 2001. It is a great pity that this decision remains unreported.

Article 23 to ascertain its formal validity and to establish its application to the type of contract in question. After all, Article 23 does open with the words 'If the parties . . . have agreed. . .'. Article 23 should therefore apply if it is shown that they have, but not until it is shown that they have, come to such an agreement; it depends on the fact of an established agreement, and does not impinge until that condition has been satisfied. One therefore starts with the question whether the parties did agree, and to answer that (as all contracts have a governing law) one looks to the law by reference to which they made their agreement. It is legitimate for the European Court to stipulate that a jurisdiction agreement is severable from the contract in which it is contained. But it would be illegitimate for it to be applied in a case in which, as a matter of their own autonomy, the parties have not agreed that a court is to have jurisdiction to settle the dispute in question.

7 *Freezing orders in aid of proceedings in foreign courts:* Motorola Credit Corp v Uzan[75]

It is generally understood that the law on provisional and protective measures in the conflict of laws falls within the category of procedure, with the consequence that each court simply applies its own domestic law to any case over which itn national law gives it jurisdiction. As the approach of Council Regulation (EC) 44/2001 is to leave the question of whether a court has jurisdiction to the national law of the court in question,[76] the Regulation like the Convention before it imposing no jurisdictional limitation on the power of the national court, the effective controls on the availability and reach of such orders are two-fold: does the court have jurisdiction under its national law? And given such foreign elements in the case as there may be, does the court have a power to make the order applied for which it will exercise on this occasion? The decision of the Court of Appeal in *Motorola v Uzan* presents a timely opportunity to examine the manner in which English law has been developing over the last few years.

Motorola, an American manufacturer of telecommunications equipment, had taken a bold decision to enter the Turkish market. It had made agreements with Telsim, a Turkish corporation, which had left Telsim owing huge sums of money to Motorola. Motorola took the view that the strings of Telsim were pulled by members of the Uzan family, that the four individual members of the family owed personal liability for the debts, and that they should be ordered to pay damages for fraud and conspiracy. Proceedings were instituted in the United States. The American court granted an injunction and an order attaching shares in

[75] [2003] EWCA Civ 752, [2004] 1 WLR 113, CA Thorpe, Potter, and Tuckey LJJ.
[76] Article 31 of the Regulation, which corresponds to Art. 24 of the Conventions.

Telsim. In defiance of this order and in breach of undertakings given to the court, there was a contemptuous and determined non-compliance. On the same day that the American proceedings were instituted, a freezing order was made against D1 in respect of his English assets. In the light of the further shenanigans in America, D2–D4 were joined to the English action, and a worldwide freezing injunction, with ancillary disclosure obligations, was made against all four defendants, even though it was far from clear that D2–D4 had any presence or assets in England. The injunction forbade Motorola to seek a similar order from foreign courts except for those which it went on to enumerate, and which included the District Court of Zürich. Compliance with the English orders was also contemptuously inadequate and sanctions for contempt for imposed. In due course the defendants 'obtained' an order from the Turkish courts which purported to restrain the American and English proceedings: possibly the first ever Turkish anti-suit injunction spotted in the wild. The American court ordered steps to be taken to rescind the Turkish order, but a different Turkish court, warming to the task, instead made a second anti-suit order, this time at the behest of employees of Telsim. Applications were then made to the English court to have the freezing injunctions set aside, the disclosure orders revoked; and the sanctions for contempt lifted. The Court of Appeal granted some but not all of the relief sought.

A preliminary question was whether the defendants could be heard at all. They were in contempt of valid judicial orders and appeared to be playing a game with the court according to which they would take advantage of any orders which they could have made in their favour, and would ignore any which went against them. Perhaps surprisingly, the court did not refuse to hear them. Two factors contributed (and one did not) to this conclusion. First, the legal points raised by the defendants were substantial and serious, and deserved to be heard and ruled on; and secondly, the defendants had been subjected to orders which, as Rix LJ had brilliantly observed, lay 'at the creative edge of a divide between comity and exorbitancy'. Foreigners, not present within the jurisdiction, had suddenly found themselves on the receiving end of orders of great intrusive effect, and it was no surprise that they were pretty cross about it. The court was not unsympathetic to the apparent sense of outrage which the defendants exhibited; and whilst deprecating the contempt, did not visit it with the sanction of refusing to hear the defendants. It also meant that there was no need to enquire whether this outcome was in any event required by Article 6 of the European Convention on Human Rights. But as the court's obligations as a matter of domestic law required it to consider whether the sanction for contempt was proportionate to the wrong done, it was improbable that reference to the Convention would have made any measurable difference.

So the question was whether the worldwide freezing orders should be continued in effect, or set aside. This raised questions of jurisdiction;

and of discretion to exercise that jurisdiction by making the orders applied for. The question of jurisdiction was in fact elementary. Civil Jurisdiction and judgments Act 1982 section 25 gave the court the power to grant such relief in aid of proceedings in an American court. All defendants had been served with process in accordance with CPR Part 6; and the jurisdiction of the court was therefore established. Thereafter, the only question was whether the court should exercise its discretion in favour of making the orders sought. As to that, section 25(2) provided the framework for the analysis. The order may be made unless 'in the opinion of the court the fact that the court has no jurisdiction apart from this section in relation to the subject matter of the proceedings in question makes it inexpedient for the court to grant it'. The question was therefore one of expediency or inexpediency.

The current pattern of thinking on the question whether it is expedient or inexpedient to grant interim relief under section 25 has been dominated by two major concerns, usually thought to work in tandem to establish a quasi-rule of double actionability. The first is to assess the degree and nature of connection to England of the defendant or his assets. In fact, in the crucial case it is the defendant's assets outside England which are the focus of attention: if the assets are within England there is much less likelihood if its being found inexpedient to make the order. But the presence or residence of the defendant will also form a significant part of the analysis. The second concern is the desire to support, and not to undermine or contradict, measures granted by the court seised of the substantive dispute. In this regard, three instances are treated separately. (1) If the foreign court had granted a worldwide freezing order, the making of an English order in supplementation of it may not be inexpedient. (2) If the foreign court had power to make such an order but had declined to do so, it may well be inexpedient for an English court to grant an order extending beyond the point where the foreign court had refused to go. (3) But if the foreign court had not made such an order because it had no power under its law to do so, there may be no particular reason to consider it inexpedient to make the order. These may be thought of as the cases of (1) the able and willing court, (2) the unwilling court, and (3) the unable court. We need to look at each, but will start with the second.

As to (2), it seems very hard to argue that if a foreign court had power under its law to make a provisional or protective order of the sort now applied for from the English court, but was unwilling to do so, an English court should nevertheless be free to act, boldly going where the foreign court did not go before. The conclusion that this is impermissible, because it undercuts and interferes with the foreign court in its management of litigation now before it, verges on being unanswerable. We may therefore conclude that in such a case it would be inexpedient for the English court to act if the foreign court was unwilling. As to (1), if the foreign court was willing and able to act, and did make such an order, it is more difficult to assess inexpediency as an abstract idea. To supplement and reinforce an order already made may seem defensible, but the foreign court may have struck its own balance in making the order to the extent that it has, and even this would be upset by the English court adding its two pennyworth. Consider what would happen if the roles were reversed. An English court may have been asked to make a worldwide freezing order, but have granted one restricted only to property within England or have made the order but with certain exceptions for the benefit of the defendant/respondent. If a foreign court makes a superadded order, it is bound to tilt the balance already struck by the English court; and this may be unwelcome to the point of inexpediency. The point is that where the court did not go it is to be regarded as unwilling; where it did, it may be appropriate for the English court to enforce the foreign order, but it will not appropriate to make an order which strikes out into new territory. In other words, the scope and extent of the court's willingness is defined by the order actually made. To the extent that it was willing, its order should not be augmented; to the extent that it was unwilling, its order should not be contradicted.

As to (3), if the foreign court was unable to act, the suggestion from *Credit Suisse Fides Trust SA v Cuoghi*[77] was that it may be appropriate for an English court to act, to meet a need which the foreign court was precluded from meeting from its own resources. But this needs very careful thought. In *Cuoghi* itself, the Swiss court in which the trial was taking place had no power under Swiss law to make any pre-judgment protective measures in relation to unidentified property, or in relation to property located outside Switzerland. As one of the defendants was resident in England, an application was made to the English courts for a freezing order, coupled with an order that there be disclosure of assets. This could have served to widen the scope of the orders actually made against or in relation to property, and to cause the identification of property which if it were in Switzerland could then be seised by way of attachment. The general approach of the Court of Appeal was to observe that an English order would not be opposed or objected to by the Swiss courts, and may be welcomed by them. The basis for this extraordinary statement is not revealed by the judgment, but on the face of it, it contradicts the law of Switzerland on security and privacy of property. How a Swiss court could properly indicate its view that it favoured the making of an order forbidden by Swiss law was not said; how it could be said that this would support the proceedings before a Swiss court was not explained either. An unable court is not just an unwilling court: it is an instrument of the state which has legislated in such a way as to deprive the court of any such pretended power. This is not at all promising as a foundation for the proposition that an English court should improve on Swiss law, at least in the absence of a formal request for such assistance.

[77] [1998] QB 808, CA.

The view that an English court should assist and not interfere with the foreign court's procedures is plainly right, but the giving effect to it is much more difficult. The decision in *Credit Suisse Fides Trust SA v Cuoghi* gave rise to the impression that one asks, in effect, what the foreign court would make of the English court's unasked-for assistance. But the answer may be pretty plain, and may not be what *Cuoghi* suggested it was.

Parliament, however, legislated that an English court should be able to act even though the trial will take place elsewhere; and it is not exactly faithful to its intention to explain why that intention should never be acted upon. One possible instance in which it may be expedient to act is where the English order mirrors the order which a foreign court could have made, or has made. For example, the foreign court may consider that its power to make orders for provisional or protective relief is limited to orders within the territory of the court: in such a case, an English order reflecting this and confined to assets in the territory of the English court may be an expedient one. But going beyond this becomes difficult for it must, if to variable degrees, contradict the order as delineated by the foreign court. It may also be that an order for disclosure of assets, rather than any freezing order, may be justified, for the disclosure does not obviously tread on the toes of the court hearing the case. None of this suggests that the reasoning in *Cuoghi* merits approval.

Judged by reference to these criteria, it would not have been expedient to make the order applied for in *Motorola*. The American courts had no power to make a worldwide freezing injunction; and as a matter of federal law as established by the Supreme Court in *Grupo Mexicano de Desarrollo SA v Alliance Bond Fund Inc*,[78] would have had no power to make any form of pre-judgment freezing order at all, never mind one with worldwide effect. New York state law did, however, allow for a limited exception from this proscription. If the American court had no right or power to make the order sought, it is very hard to see how it could have been supportive of those proceedings, and of orders made in them for an English court, in effect, to override the Constitution of the United States. No matter how it may have seemed from England, one imagines that this would have been regarded from the United States as an extraordinary way to 'support' the American action. It was therefore to be hoped that the order would not be made; and to the extent that the order made below was set aside, the decision of the Court of Appeal was welcome. But the Court of Appeal in *Motorola*, in this sense following the reasoning from *Cuoghi*, rejected the argument that the English court should be precluded from making an order which was plainly outside anything which an American court could do. It is submitted that it was wrong to do so. To the extent that the order was upheld, or was not set aside on this basis of this argument, it in necessary to ask how an English court may grant an order 'in aid' of American proceedings when

[78] 527 US 308 (1999).

the court trying the action lacks the power to act in the most fundamental way imaginable.

An analogy may be made with the contractual law of implied terms. It is well established that a court may not imply a term which contradicts the express terms of a contract. If a contract therefore contains a number of express terms only, these may be added to if the grounds for implication are satisfied. But if a contract contains express terms and also a clause excluding any other promise which might have been, but which was not, made, no implication is possible. In *Photo Productions Ltd v Securicor Ltd*[79] the defendants undertook duties by reference to a contract which contained a limited number of express promises, and which expressly excluded any other liability. That, according to the House of Lords, meant that there was no possibility of implying terms into the contract, not to supplement the express terms, nor to lend them business efficacy, or whatever. There was no gap into which they could be implied because the parties had, by a combination of positive and negative stipulations, defined the parameters of their legal relationship.

If one applies that to the American action in *Motorola*, the Constitution of the United States, just as had the law of Switzerland in *Cuoghi*, forbade the grant of a pre-judgment freezing order save where New York law allowed pre-judgment relief. There is therefore no gap in American law: it provides what may be ordered, and it stipulates what is forbidden. It would be impossible to argue that a pre-judgment freezing order could be consistent with federal law, or that there is a gap in the law which a judge may fill by making such an order. There is no 'gap'—surely an astonishing way to regard the Constitution of the United States—and any order made would contradict clear and express American law. It follows, in the writer's submission, that as any English order must have the effect of contradicting American law, it cannot then be said to support the American proceedings. American law has left no room for support to be given. Nor, surely, did the material rules of Swiss law in *Cuoghi*.

Of course, if one starts from the prejudice that defendants accused of fraud, or of fraud on the grand scale, deserve no mercy, expediency may favour adding the coercive weight of English law to whatever the foreign court can impose. The allegations against Uzan were substantial and, if proved, would have showed that Motorola had been taken for fools. But it had not been proved, and may never be proved; and one wonders what possible justification, other than *odio furti*, might have supported the English order. The principle that a defendant is innocent until shown to be liable is a sound one, and the principle that a court is entitled to have its jurisdiction uninterfered with is also a sound one. There must be a presumption, at the very least, that unless the assistance is asked for, it is not to be taken as helpful, and its grant will therefore be inexpedient. As against that, there is the opinion of the House of Lords in *South Carolina*

[79] [1980] AC 827.

Insurance Co v Assurantie Maatschappij 'De Zeven Provincien' NV[80] that an English court does not object to a party making use of foreign procedures for the obtaining of evidence, even though an English court could not have made such orders for itself. But there is also evidence that English courts are now more jealous of their jurisdiction;[81] and for an English trial to be affected by the impact of a foreign provisional or protective measure may not now be viewed with equanimity. It is submitted that the orders were wrong, should not have been made, and should have been set aside in their totality, even in the face of contumelious conduct from the Uzan family members.

It was suggested above that there was a second aspect to inexpediency, namely the connection of the respondents or their assets, or both, to England. The court in *Cuoghi* had also looked to this factor. As in that case the respondent had been an English resident, and the order had been made against him personally, it was considered that it was not inexpedient to make it. By contrast, had he been resident outside England, or had the order attached (but as an English freezing order never could) assets outside England, it would have been different. In the case of one of the four Uzan defendants, the residence criterion was satisfied, and in the case of a second, there were other factors which supported the argument that the connections were sufficient to make it (on this ground) not inexpedient to make the order. Were this to have been the only criterion by which to assess inexpediency, there would have been little more to add: an English freezing injunction does not attach assets, and so the material focus is on the residence of the respondent to the application. But it was not. It cannot be expedient to make such an order against a respondent when the effect on the proceedings in the adjudicating court will be damaging; there needs to be a two-pronged assessment of inexpediency; and if that is done, it is most unlikely that residence will be enough by itself.

The court looked briefly at two further elements of possible inexpediency. First, it noted that if the English court acted, there was an increased likelihood of conflict with the Turkish courts, which had apparently granted an anti-suit and anti-*Mareva* injunction. Though not suggesting that the Turkish order had any direct impact on it, the court saw the potential adverse consequences of stirring the cauldron further and was plainly, and rightly, cautious. The precedent value of this will, one suspects, be low. But secondly, the submission was made that as the American judgment would not be liable to recognition in England, it was inexpedient to make an order in aid of the enforcement of that judgment. What weakened the submission was that there was little or no evidence to provide a basis for accepting it: it did not appear that the Uzan defendants had avoided submitting to the jurisdiction of the American court. Nor was it clear whether an American judgment would include an

80 [1987] AC 24.

81 *Turner v Grovit* [2002] 1 WLR 107, HL, for example.

element of damages, probably trebled, under the Racketeer Influenced and Corrupt Organisations (RICO) Act, leading as it would to the unenforceability of that element of any judgment.[82] But in principle the submission must be right: a court cannot properly make, or it cannot be expedient to make, an order in aid of a judgment which cannot be enforced in England. It may be that at so early a stage of proceedings the need would be to show a good arguable case that an American judgment would have been enforceable in England. But if the court concludes that the foreign judgment will not be entitled to enforcement in England, it is next to impossible to see how it can be expedient for it to make any order in aid of its enforcement elsewhere.

The result of *Motorola v Uzan*, and what it tells us about the present state of English law, is difficult to state concisely. The court's power, which may be its jurisdiction, to make a freezing injunction in aid of proceedings in a foreign country will probably be confined to respondents/defendants who are resident in England, or to those who have an alternative connection which may be regarded as equivalent. It will not necessarily be confined to domestic orders. So where the respondent is not resident in the United Kingdom, a submission to the jurisdiction may bring about the same outcome. But further control, namely asking whether the order would interfere with the proceedings before the foreign court, will really only bite and suggest inexpediency if the foreign court had the power to make an order of the sort now applied for in England, but refused to do so: the foreign court was able and unwilling. By contrast, if the foreign court was unable to act, or was able and willing to act, the English court is likely to 'assist'. It is respectfully suggested that the unreality of these distinctions is the very reason why they cannot be right.

As a footnote to the English proceedings, though, it is appropriate to notice the decision of the Swiss Federal Tribunal in respect of proceedings brought in Zürich for a declaration that the freezing order as granted at first instance was enforceable in Switzerland, and which were instituted after the injunction had been granted at first instance. The District Court rejected the application, but its judgment was reversed by the Zürich Cantonal Court of Appeal which made the orders applied for.[83] A further appeal by the Uzan parties against this decision was dismissed by the Swiss Federal Tribunal.[84] The decision of the highest court in Switzerland to approve, and to make orders to give effect to, the English

[82] Protection of Trading Interests Act[1980] s. 5.

[83] Decision of September 29, 1999; II Chamber of the Court of Appeal of the Canton of Zürich, Case No U/O/NL990093/II.ZK (unreported); noted by Berti, in *Translating the 'Mareva'—The Enforcement of an English Freezing Order in Zürich* in 'Nur, aber immerhin', Festgabe für Anton K Schnyder zum 50. Geburtstag (eds Berti and Girsbergerer), Zürich, 2002.

[84] Decision of July 30 2003, Case No 4P.88/2003 (unreported; in fact, there were four judgments, but those in case nos 89, 90, and 91 add nothing of importance and need not be further referred to). The fact that the English Court of Appeal varied or set aside the freezing injunctions made at first instance was neither known nor relevant to the Swiss Federal Tribunal. The respondents would have needed to apply to the cantonal courts from which the appeal had been brought for such variation as was called for by the English decision. I am indebted to Dr S V Berti for all information about the proceedings in Switzerland.

freezing injunction is very important, and confirms what had become the practice of the Cantonal Court of Appeal. Objections which lay along the lines that this was an order of a kind which a Swiss court could not make, so that it should not be recognised in the Swiss legal order, were peremptorily dismissed: the Lugano Convention made no allowance for such complaints until the recognition of the judgment was so offensive that it would conflict with public policy. Nor was it a ground of objection that the English court had relied on its common law and statutory rules of jurisdiction to justify the making of the order: the English court was to be regarded as one which had, theoretically or in principle, personal jurisdiction over the parties, who were not domiciled in any other contracting state to the Lugano Convention, and as a result there was no objection to the recognition of its order. At this point, the reasoning of the Swiss Federal Tribunal echoes an argument sometimes encountered in German law, to the effect that the jurisdiction to grant provisional or protective measures depends on the court applied to having a notional or abstract jurisdiction on the merits of the claim against the defendant to the dispute.[85] It is unclear that this is an admissible or helpful component of the scheme for the recognition of orders made within the framework of the Lugano Convention, but it presented no obstacle to the obtaining of an order that the English injunction was entitled to be recognised in Switzerland. Of course, the result may have been very different if the Swiss court had not been able to find that the English courts had a 'virtual'[86] jurisdiction over the main action; and if the injunction had been made in support of proceedings in the Swiss courts, questions of public policy may have come to the surface: there was, after all, no Swiss interest in the litigation in the United States and Turkey against defendants with no Swiss domicile. Such difficulties will need to wait for another day; but the decision of the Swiss Federal Tribunal is a welcome confirmation that an English freezing injunction can expect to be recognised and given effect under the Lugano Convention, even in a country which knows nothing of such orders in its own law.

8 *Foreign judgments for multiple damages:* Eliades v Lewis[87]

Lennox Lewis, a champion heavyweight boxer, was sued in the United States by his erstwhile manager and promoter. As in the boxing ring, so in the courtroom: he gave rather better than he got. He defeated the claim and succeeded in a counterclaim which led to an award of damages

[85] That is, that the court is the 'Gericht der Hauptsache', or 'courts on the merits'. For a detailed explanation of this, and of its compatibility with the Brussels Convention scheme of jurisdiction, see Newton, *The Uniform Interpretation of the Brussels and Lugano Conventions,* (Hart, Oxford; 2002) at 289–94, 336–8.

[86] At para. 5.3.2 of the judgment.

[87] [2003] EWCA Civ 1758, [2004] 1 WLR 692, CA: Potter, Carnwath, and Jacob LJJ. The decision largely affirms the approach of Nelson J below: [2003] 1 All ER (Comm) 850. The writer appeared for Lewis. Though it lies beyond the formal scope of this Note, readers sould be aware of the recent and extraordinary judgment of the Supreme Court of Canada in *Beals v Saldanha* [2003] SCC 72,

on a number of distinct causes of action: breach of fiduciary duty, fraud, and violation of the Racketeer Influenced and Corrupt Organisations Act.[88] Though the District Court entered a single judgment for an aggregated sum, it was clear from the jury's awards that they had awarded $6.8m for breach of fiduciary duty, $56K for fraud, and $400K under RICO. This led to a total award of $7.2m, which Lewis sought to enforce in England by suing on the liquidated debt created by the judgment, and then seeking summary judgment on the claim.[89] Before the Master and the Judge he succeeded; for reasons to be explained, the Court of Appeal reduced by $400K the sum for which Lewis was allowed to enter judgment, and otherwise dismissed the appeal.

In the proceedings below, it had been contended that, in some respects, the judgment was not final and conclusive.[90] The contention failed and the Court of Appeal was not troubled with it. But more difficult was the impact on the English proceedings of section 5 of the Protection of Trading Interests Act 1980 which provides, in material part, that:

> (1) A judgment to which this section applies shall not be registered under Part II of the Administration of Justice Act 1920 or Part I of the Foreign Judgments (Reciprocal Enforcement) Act 1933 and no court in the United Kingdom shall entertain proceedings at common law for the recovery of any sum payable under such a judgment.
> (2) This section applies to any judgment given by a court of an overseas country, being (a) a judgment for multiple damages within the meaning of subsection (3) below . . .
> (3) In subsection (2)(a) above, a judgment for multiple damages means a judgment for an amount arrived at by doubling, trebling or otherwise multiplying a sum assessed as compensation for the loss or damage sustained by the person in whose favour the judgment was given.

It was argued for Eliades below that as there was a RICO element in the overall award, this served to poison the whole of the judgment, with the result that no part of the judgment could be enforced. This hopeless submission failed to persuade the judge, not least because the RICO award of $400K was not a trebled sum. This untrebling had come about by the American judge not trebling the sum assessed, notwithstanding that RICO provided for such arithmetic. Nelson J correctly saw that there

(2004) 234 DLR (4th)1, SSC. That court (by a majority) declared that a Florida judgment for treble damages with punitive damages added on top was entitled to be enforced in Canada, on the basis that the Florida court had a real and substantial connection with the case, and none of the defences to recognition or enforcement was maintainable. The totality of reasons is complex, but many will think that the approach of the majority is naïve and that of the dissentients much to be preferred.

88 Known by the offensive shorthand intended by its promoters as RICO.

89 CPR r 24.3.

90 On the basis, rather obscurely alleged, that the adjudicating court could revisit the question it had already determined.

was no element of the judgment before him which had been trebled, and that section 5 of the Act had nothing to bite on. But months later the American judge, for reasons not clear, trebled the RICO award, set aside the earlier judgment, and entered a single judgment for an amount which now included $1.2m for breach of RICO. This breathed new hope of life into Eliades, and the argument was again advanced that section 5 prevented the enforcement of all and any part of the judgment.

The turn of events in the United States would have made it impossible for Lewis to argue that the RICO award, even as to the basic amount of $400K, should remain recoverable. The policy put into legal effect by section 5 was notably hostile to judgments for multiple damages: the recovery of *any* sum under such a judgment was proscribed. In the diplomatic correspondence which had preceded the enactment of this provision the United States, sensing that the legislation was aimed at certain of its laws and (in all probability) at very little else, objected on several grounds.[91] One ground, which seemed to have something to commend it, was to the effect that they might have been able to understand an enactment which prohibited recovery of the multiplied surplus, but that it was going just too far to tar the basic award with the same brush. The United Kingdom had been loftily dismissive, taking the view that the ordering of multiple damages was so wrong that it was right to extend the prohibition to all the judgment. In saying this it seems that there was more than a trace of disingenuousness. Multiple damages, where they are available, are sometimes a surrogate for an award of costs. In those jurisdictions in which costs are not routinely awarded to a successful party, multiple damages may be awarded to counterfeit the costs order for which no provision is made. It is far too crude to suppose that every increase over and above the basic compensatory award of damages is give for one reason only and that this reason is so offensive to the United Kingdom that no element of the damages should be recoverable. A wise, rational, and pre-1980, decision of the Court of Appeal, in *SA Consortium General de Textiles v Sun & Sand Agencies Ltd*[92] accepted that a court may sometimes order damages in a manner which suggests that these are in lieu of costs; and it saw no harm in enforcing them. The legislation seems not to have heeded the lesson of that case. It may also be true that no element of the judgment should be recoverable where the damages have been awarded on the basis of a rule of foreign law, or in proceedings, to which the Secretary of State has certified the objection.[93] But Parliament's blood was up in 1980; and the effect of the wording of section 5 is clear enough. It prohibited the enforcement of any part of the 1.2m for which judgment was given under RICO.

[91] Collected conveniently in Lowe, *Extraterritorial Jurisdiction* (1983) at pp. 176 ff.

[92] [1978] QB 279, CA, dealing with the view of the common law in relation to A French judicial award of FF10,000 for 'résistance abusive', or misconduct in the defence of proceedings, was allowed to be enforced.

[93] Protection of Trading Interests Act 1980 s.1.

But did it go further? The argument for Eliades was that the 'any sum payable' form of words in section 5 reached out to touch causes of action heard and determined at the same time as a RICO claim, and made the entire judgment unenforceable. Rather like a stray red sock in the whites wash, the whole judgment, and every part of it, would be stained and tainted by the concurrent RICO judgment for multiple damages. The Court of Appeal was having none of it, and for good reason. To accept that section 5 had this effect, there would have had to be an astonishingly strong statement of legislative hostility to those individuals who had claims under RICO, valid and entirely good as a matter of American law, and who had the temerity to advance them there. To have accepted the submission for Eliades would have been to rewrite the legislation for a purpose which it was impossible to articulate. For there is no reason to suppose that the United Kingdom has any rational objection to the RICO cause of action as a matter of internal American law. More than once it has been judicially observed[94] that this is really little more than a cause of action for fraud, crafted and drafted in a way which accommodates the constitutional structures of the United States. For a claimant with a perfectly good cause of action under RICO, which he intended to enforce in the United States, to be precluded from advancing other causes of action on the basis that he may need to enforce judgments on these in England, with the result that he has[95] to bring a separate action, would serve no rational purpose. And nor would it be any of the English court's proper business to cast so long a shadow over the US proceedings. It is right and proper for English law to deal with whether a judgment may be enforced in England, and to do so by reference to criteria which are wholly concerned with the impact the judgment would have in the English legal order. In the case of arbitral awards, this is secured by Arbitration Act 1996, section 26. In the case of foreign judgments, it is reflected in the doctrine that a foreign judgment procured by what an English court defines as and finds to be fraud cannot be enforced in England, whatever the adjudicating court might have said on the subject. But a refusal to enforce a judgment or award in England is just that. It does not pretend to have any effect outside England, and especially not in the state of origin of the judgment or award. If there is fraud, the judgment creditor, or the party in whose favour the arbitrators have made an award, may still enforce his claim in the country of origin, and anywhere and everywhere else, except in England, without any interference from the English courts. So it is right that English law respect the proper limits of its power to act. English law may regard the enforcement of judgments in England as its sole and exclusive concern; and may legislate as the 1980 Act has done, to restrict rights to enforce in England. But when the terms

[94] For example, Sedley LJ in *Donohue v Armco Inc* [2000] 1 Lloyd's Rep 579, CA.

[95] Assuming that he can: an English court, in like circumstances, may be tempted to see it as an abuse of process to being separate actions which cover the same ground.

of that restriction are said to have an adverse impact on the manner in which a claimant has to bring his claim before a foreign court, something would have gone wrong. This was the fundamental flaw in the unsuccessful submission for Eliades; and it was no surprise that it failed to persuade the court.

All that was needed to secure this result was to sever the offending RICO component of the judgment from the inoffensive remainder. The template for such an approach, which leads to the severing of a judgment which is partly good and partly bad,[96] was clearly the decision in *Raulin v Fisher*,[97] but Potter LJ appeared to think that it could be applied only by analogy. It is not obvious why this is. The principle of severance of judgments, which is only one aspect of a much broader and general common law legal policy, is established by legislation[98] and by case law;[99] and it was not apparent why this principle was less than immediately applicable.

It is unclear, and Jacob LJ in particular went out of his way[100] to say that it was not deciding, what the result would have been if the American judgment under RICO had remained unmultiplied. It is tempting to think that a judgment which is, as a matter of arithmetic, for an unmultiplied sum cannot be caught by section 5 and its sledgehammer objection. But the decision will wait for another day.

9 *Foreign judgments and the protection of human rights:* Government of the United States of America v Montgomery (No 2)[101]

We noted last year[102] how the arrival into force of the European Convention for the Protection of Human Rights and Fundamental Freedoms (ECHR) had the clear potential to strike hard on the law on the recognition of foreign judgments. A case in which the impact of the ECHR was curiously under-estimated, however, concerned a judgment confiscating shares by order of the courts of the United States. It is difficult to believe that the decision can be correct, and it is to be hoped that the House of Lords will be able to restore the position in due course.

Mr Barnette was convicted by a United States court of a very substantial fraud against the government of the United States. By way of remedy, it was ordered that, *inter alia*, he transfer the shares in a Panamanian

[96] In the enforcement sense. [97] [1911] 2 KB 93.

[98] Brussels Convention (Civil Jurisdiction and judgments Act 1982 Sch 1) Art. 42; Council Regulation (EC) 44/2001 Art. 48; Foreign judgments (Reciprocal Enforcement) Act 1933 s. 2(5).

[99] Case C-220/95 *Van den Boogaard v Laumen* [1997] ECR I-1147; *Schnabel v Lui* [2002] NSWSC 15.

[100] At para. [62].

[101] [2003] EWCA Civ 392, [2003] 1 WLR 1916, CA: Lord Woolf CJ, Kennedy and Scott-Baker LJJ. The House of Lords has allowed a petition for leave to appeal: [2003] 1 WLR 2901, HL. An earlier stage of the proceedings, in which the background detail of the case is to be found, is reported at [2001] 1 WLR 196, HL.

[102] In the Note on *Maronier v Larmer* [2002] EWCA Civ 774, [2003] QB 620, CA: This *Year Book*, 73 (2002) p. 447.

company in which he had secreted the proceeds of his fraud, but which shares had, by the time of the trial, been transferred to his wife, M. Various orders were then made against Barnette and M (now separated from him and living in England), including further confiscatory orders. M seems to have been present at some or most of the judicial proceedings, but to have declined to enter a formal appearance in them. The Government of the United States[103] applied under Criminal Justice Act 1988, section 97, to register the confiscation order in England. The legislation gave the English court a discretion to decline to register the judgment if enforcing the judgment in England would be contrary to the interests of justice.[104] The courts were pressed with the argument that the American proceedings fell short of the procedural guarantees of the ECHR, and that it was therefore contrary to the interests of justice to register the judgment. Stanley Burnton J rejected the argument[105] and registered the judgment; an appeal by M to the Court of Appeal was dismissed. It is submitted that both courts fell into error.

The basis upon which Lord Woolf CJ reached his eventual conclusion is a little difficult to summarise accurately, but in essence it was his view that the 'interests of justice' were to be assessed by reference to what went on in the foreign court. In making this assessment, the court was obliged to apply section 97 of the 1988 Act, and had neither need nor duty to apply the detail of the jurisprudence of the European Court of Human Rights. His conclusion laid some stress on the observation that the United States Court of Appeals had concluded that the confiscation was the only way to secure compliance with its order, and it was on that account not contrary to the interests of justice to register the order for enforcement in England.

The gist of the objection to registration, and the basis for reliance on Article 6, ECHR, was the manner in which the Court of Appeals had applied the 'fugitive disentitlement' principle to dismiss the appeal 'made' by the non-appearing M. To put it shortly, a person had who had fled from justice, or put her property beyond the reach of the court, was to be regarded as a fugitive, and it was open to the court to decline to hear her. Now to shut a litigant out of court would violate Article 6(3) of the ECHR. But the gist of Lord Woolf CJ's rejection of the argument was neatly encapsulated in his observation that 'it is by no means obvious as to why section 6 [of the Human Rights Act 1998] should have any role to play in relation to the jurisdiction of this court under section 97 of the 1988 Act'.[106] He immediately noted that it would be unusual for the interests of justice to favour the taking of a step which violated Article 6 ECHR,[107] or Article 1 of the First Protocol to that Convention.[108] But he

[103] A designated country for the purposes of the Act: Criminal Justice Act 1988 (Designated Countries and Territories) Order 1991, SI 1991/2873.

[104] Criminal Justice Act 1988, s. 97(1)(c).

[105] [2002] EWHC 1113 (Admin).

[106] At para. [19].

[107] The right to a fair hearing.

[108] The right to peaceful enjoyment of possessions.

seems to have reasoned that as the court with a statutory[109] obligation to observe the ECHR was the English court, and any infringing activity had taken place and had been completed in the United States, long before the English court got involved, there was a chronological flaw in the argument that the English court should assess the compliance of the American proceedings with the European Convention. And not only was the problem one of chronology, for he added that there were: 'difficulties in seeking to judge the procedures of a court in a jurisdiction to which the Convention does not apply by applying article 6'. He considered that the principle of 'fugitive disentitlement' was one whose significance to and role within American law was difficult for a non-American court to assess; and noted that English law had for many a year long past and until very recently taken a similar approach to a seriously obstructive contemnor.[110]

All of which is very well, but it flies in the face of two decisions of the European Court of Human Rights, one of which casts doubt on the acceptability of the principle of 'fugitive disentitlement', and the other of which contradicts the proposition that a violation taking place in the United States is out of sight and reach of the European Convention. Neither case appears to have been cited to the Court of Appeal, which is a matter of concern. In *Krombach v France*[111] it was held by the ECtHR that for a French court to refuse to hear a contemnor was capable of violating Article 6, ECHR, on the basis that the response was disproportionate to the wrong. No doubt this lies behind the fact that the English approach to such behaviour may now be less intolerant than it was in *Hadkinson v Hadkinson*. But this pales into insignificance alongside the decision in *Pellegrini v Italy*.[112] As we noted last year, this case involved a decision from the organs of the Vatican City, a statelet not party to the European Convention, to dissolve the marriage of an Italian citizen. The procedure by which this unfortunate victim found her marital status changed was preposterous and manifestly unfair to her. Called upon to recognise the Vatican decree, and to register her civil status as that of a single woman, the Italian courts appear to have concluded that the European Convention had nothing to do with the Vatican, and the shortcomings in the Vatican procedure were nothing to do with the decision to be taken by the Italian courts. The European Court of Human Rights pointed out the obvious error in all of that. It was not open to the Italian court come over all Pilate-like, and to say that it was nothing to do with them. The human rights of persons within the protective scope of the Convention—which means everybody—are not to be set at nought just because they have been first trodden underfoot by a tribunal in a

[109] Section 6 of the 1998 Act. [110] *Hadkinson v Hadkinson* [1952] P 285, CA.

[111] February 13, 2001 (ECtHR). The proceedings before the Court of Justice of the European Communities are at [2000] ECR I-1935, Case C-7/98.

[112] (2002) 35 EHRR 44, (ECtHR).

non-contracting state.[113] This decision should have sufficed to explain why the task in *Montgomery*, laid upon the English courts by the Convention, was to ensure that the proceedings in the United States were in conformity with the standards of the Convention. Whether they were in conformity is not a matter for this Note; but the correct identification of the basis for the court's decision is important; and it is respectfully suggested that the Court of Appeal, and the judge below, got it wrong because they were not shown how to get it right.

None of which it to say that the application of *Pellegrini* is wholly intuitive or attractive. For a start, it contradicted an earlier decision of the European Court of Human Rights[114] which had appeared to say that a violation of the standards of Article 6 by Andorra was something which the French courts were entitled to overlook. This decision was, in its turn, disregarded in *Pellegrini*, and oblivion may now be its fate. But it stands as evidence that there was once another view. Next it may be observed that the decision of an open court in a civilised democracy, pronouncing a remedy against a knowing receiver of the proceeds of fraud (*Montgomery*) is at the opposite end of the spectrum from a case in which a secretive tribunal in an authoritarian theocracy dissolves the marriage of a blameless wife (*Pellegrini*). Who would have supposed that the approach to the latter is required also to be taken to the former?

What may be more is that if *Pellegrini* is correct, it must mean that recognition must be withheld from traditional muslim divorces, in which the husband exercises a religious right to repudiate his wife without her having a right to be heard, let alone to obtain an adjudication of the question. On any view, the principle which led to the denial of recognition of the results of the uncivilised procedure visited upon Mrs Pellegrini must necessarily lead to the non-recognition of most forms of islamic divorce, and for precisely the same reasons. Such flagrant denial of the human rights of a spouse cannot be acceptable for muslim wives but not for roman catholic ones, and *Pellegrini* amply shows that to drape barbarism with the threadbare rags of religion will not deflect the law. Can we therefore expect an English judge to refuse to recognise a divorce in classic muslim form? Such as the *talaq* in *Chaudhury v Chaudhury*?[115] One hopes so, for discriminating between trampled-on spouses on grounds of religion does not look very attractive as a legal policy.

The full implications and effects of the European Convention in the field of recognition of foreign judgments, as with the conflict of laws more broadly, will take a while to sink in. The Court of Appeal is not to be blamed for making what may be held by the House of Lords to have been an error of law. But error it was, and it needs putting right.

[113] Or statelet, if one is to include the Vatican City.

[114] *Drozd & Janousek v France and Spain* (1992) 14 EHRR 745 (ECtHR).

[115] [1985] Fam 19, CA.

10 *Concurrent claims against a careless professional:* Base Metal Trading Ltd v Shamurin[116]

Last year we noted the refusal of the High Court to strike out a claim against a defendant who was sued on the basis of an allegation that he was liable for breach of a contract of employment, and in tort, and for breach of fiduciary duty, and for breach of the duty owed by an officer of a company.[117] Though there was in essence one allegation against the defendant—that he had failed to exercise a proper measure of care and skill in the service of the company—it was claimed that each of these could in principle be governed by a separate choice of law rule and, as a result, by a different substantive law. This sufficed to defeat the submission that the entirety of the claim was governed by one law, Russian law and that it should on that account be struck out as doomed to fail. The issue has now been examined by Tomlinson J after a trial lasting 18 days. The judgment is of the highest degree of importance in the way that is shows that the common law conflict of laws was and is capable of producing a sensible analysis of a case whose facts had the potential to lead to irrational results.

The dispute had its roots in the shark-infested waters which swirled around the privatisation (or rapine) of the Russian metals industry; Shamurin and the brothers Z had set themselves up in this market to export and otherwise trade in metals. The vehicle through which they chose to operate was a company established by them under the law of Guernsey, Base Metal Trading Ltd (BMTL), the evidence being that no-one had any clear idea as to the status of Guernsey in relation to the other law districts making up the British Isles.[118] The corporators were to divide up the responsibilities created by the business, with Shamurin responsible for trading on the metals and futures markets. When it all fell apart in recrimination, denunciation, violence, and death threats, litigation broke out all over the place. In England the company sued Shamurin on account of the trading record of the company which was, by all accounts, not stellar. It claimed that he owed duties under a contract of employment, in tort for negligence, and in respect of his duties as director of a Guernsey company. It was common ground that, to the extent that the claim was governed by the law of Russia it must fail.[119] Tomlinson J held that it was wholly governed by Russian law, and that the claim failed in its entirety.

[116] [2003] EWHC 2419 (Comm); [2004], 1 All ER (Comm) 159, Tomlinson J. The judge also gave permission to appeal to the Court of Appeal.

[117] *Base Metal Trading Ltd v Shamurin* [2002] CLC 322; noted this *Year Book* 73, (2002) p. 459.

[118] Guernsey not being a part of the United Kingdom. It is seriously doubtful that either of the corporators could have found Guernsey on a map.

[119] It was accepted that Russian law imposed no relevant duty on the defendant, and/or that any such claims as might have lain were barred by limitation: at para. [20].

The judge's clear point of departure was not derived from the conflict of laws, but from his commercial acumen. It struck him as inescapable that the principal parties, Russian by nationality and residence, had made an agreement which was governed by Russian law. The incorporation of BMTL was not to be seen as an act which created a new legal foundation for their relationship, but as part of the implementation of an agreement which cannot have been governed by anything other than Russian law.[120] Whether or not such a conclusion could have been reached by abstract legal reasoning (or the Rome Convention), it provided the backdrop against which the technical legal reasoning was to be played out. It was spot on. So too was the judge's instinct that where there was a contract between the parties which defined and described their relations *inter se*, it was improbable that a contradictory duty of care, or equitable duty, would be found to lie.[121] In this regard his approach revealed a fundamental truth about English law. It may be established that as a matter of common law, a claimant may formulate his claim in contract, or in tort, or in equity, or in any combination of these, but if the complaint is of a breached duty of care, the substantive duties will in essence be congruent duties. Where the parties have made a contract with all deliberate seriousness of purpose, no good is done by allowing these duties to be outflanked by a different and distinct formulation of the cause of action.

The judge's approach to choice of law was informed by this insight, as he came to the conclusion that, no matter how it was put, each pleaded cause of action led to the application of Russian law. The contract of employment[122] was held to be governed by Russian law by the straightforward application of Article 6(2)(a) of the Rome Convention, and by concluding that the proviso to Article 6(2) was inapplicable. The Article allowed a contract of employment to be found to be governed by the law of another country by reason of its more close connection with that country; but on the view which the judge had taken, the duties of the employment, the control of and by the company, were all to be undertaken in and from Russia. An optimistic attempt to denature Article 6 by restricting its application to employees who may be regarded as weak and liable to be pushed around by their employers was rejected by the judge.[123]

The claim in tort[124] was dealt with in more innovative fashion. If the breach of duty were to lie in making speculative and incompetent trades on the London Metal Exchange, it seemed arguable, at least at first sight,

[120] At para. [24]. [121] At para. [35].

[122] It is not clear why it was pleaded as such, for it would have seemed more naturally to be a contract of service.

[123] Though as the other corporator and controller of the company had, according to Mr Shamurin, threatened to kill him and been complicit in a plot to assassinate the former governor of Kemerovo, and other brutalities, it would not have been stretching things to see Mr Shamurin as in such a position of weakness.

[124] Choice of law for the pleaded torts was governed by the common law, as the acts complained of were committed before the coming into force of the Private International Law (Miscellaneous Provisions) Act 1995, Part III. The common law rules required it to be determined where in substance

that the place of the tort was England. Though the acts giving rise to the loss—the incompetent instructions, and so on—could have been performed anywhere where Shamurin had access to a computer screen or a telephone, the losses resulted in payments being due and called for in London and only in London. There existed authority for the view that where the act giving rise to it was separated from the damage, it was legitimate to look for that component of the tort which had its location as a matter of neccessity as opposed to a matter of chance.[125] The judge accepted that this was correct in principle, but denied its application to a tort which was, as a matter of fact, not committed as between two parties dealing at arm's length across the seas. That the loss was immediately occasioned in London was a matter of chance, as the instruction to a broker could equally have been directed to New York. The claimant was inevitably set on the path of loss when Shamurin picked up the telephone in Moscow and transmitted his ill-starred instructions; and the loss would result in Moscow, where the liquidity of the company was located. Though this flirts with the proposition that a tort is committed, or the significant damage is that which results, in the place of ultimate loss, and not in the place in which the loss is first incurred, it is submitted that in this context it is right. The identification of the place of the damage with the place where that damage first manifests itself is well established for the purposes of jurisdiction under the judgments Regulation,[126] and has some support in relation to what is now CPR r. 6.20(8).[127] This may make sense for jurisdiction: if the damage first occurred somewhere, that place is more likely to be where the witnesses are, and so forth; and any other view would risk allowing claimants to play at home when they are really supposed to play away. But the concerns of choice of law are quite separate and distinct; and in asking the initial question of where in substance the tort occurred, a mechanical rule which located damage in the place of its initial manifestation runs the risk of distorting the search for the law which is most appropriate for application to the substance of the claim. In the result the tort was committed in Russia, for Russia was where its centre of gravity lay. Being governed by the common law, it required to satisfy a test of double actionability, the claimant failed to establish its actionability under the *lex loci delicti commissi*. There being no basis for making an exception to the need to comply with Russian law, the claim in tort failed.

It should be noted for future reference that the judge framed the material question as whether *the legal system of any other country* had a closer connection to the claim: not a country, but the legal system of a country.

the cause of action arose. If in England, English law applied; if in a foreign country, a rule of double actionability, with exceptions, would be applied instead.

[125] *Metall & Rohstoff AG v Donaldson Lufkin & Jenrette Inc* [1990] 1 QB 391, CA (inducing breach of contract: committed in English law where the breach necessarily took place).

[126] Case C-220/88 *Dumez France SA v Hessische Landesbank* [1990] ECR I-49; Case C- 364/93 *Marinari v Lloyd's Bank plc* [1995] ECR I-2719.

[127] *Batstone & Firminger Ltd v Nasima Enterprises (Nigeria) Ltd* [1996] CLC 1902.

As one is asking whether the behaviour of a defendant ought to be governed by a particular law, it is rational to ask, as the common law does, whether there is a closer connection to another *legal system*, rather than to another *country*. By contrast, if the case had fallen to be dealt with under the statutory choice of law rule in the Private International Law (Miscellaneous Provisions) Act 1995, the search would have been for the comparative closeness of connections with a country rather than a law.[128] As torts are constructs of law, and not matters of geography, the former approach is still to be preferred. Moreover, if the choice of law rules for claims in tort are in due course restated along the lines of the Final Draft of a proposal for a Regulation,[129] it will again be true that the search will be for connection with a country rather than connection with a law: this for both the general rule and the limited general exception. This point will be returned to below; it appears to be one which has not been thought through as clearly as it should have been.

The claim for compensation for breach of equitable duty was also governed by Russian law. As said above, the judge was openly sceptical of any approach which would have led him to any other conclusion, and went out of his way to not express support for the view, encountered more in Australian than English law, that the *lex fori* has a disproportionate claim to be applied.[130] In truth, there is little more than mysticism in the proposition that in equity, just because a defendant is subject to the personal jurisdiction of the court, he can be made to act in accordance with what English law would take his conscience to require. True, there are still substantial areas of commercial law in which equitable principles apply, and where an English court applies English equity to the claim advanced. But many of these (anti-suit injunctions, freezing injunctions, search orders) are often better regarded as raising issues of procedure; and those which are not (dishonest assistance of a breach of trust, knowing receipt of trust property) English equity is not applied without any regard to the provisions of foreign law.[131] Having come to the conclusion that the substance of the obligations raised by the claim was governed by Russian law, he took the view that the proper law of any concurrent or coincident equitable obligation was Russian also.[132] It was not necessary for him to deal with the issues which will arise when there is neither[133]

[128] Section 11 and (especially) s. 12.

[129] Document dated 22 July 2003; and identified as COM(2003) 427 final; 2003/0168. In this respect its drafting echoes Art. 4 of the Rome Convention, which also identifies the applicable law by reference to connections with a country rather than a law.

[130] At para. [43]. The highpoint of the Australian jurisprudence is the decision of the Full Court of the Federal Court of Australia in *Paramasivam v Flynn* (1998) 160 ALR 203 (Aust Fed Ct).

[131] *Grupo Torras SA v Sheikh Fahad Mohammed al Sabah* [2001] CLC 221, CA; *Kuwait Oil Tanker SAK v Al Bader* [2000] 2 All ER (Comm) 271, CA (noted this *Year Book* 71 (2000) p.471.

[132] Approving on this point the general observations of Tipping J in *Attorney-General of England and Wales v R* [2002] 2 NZLR 91 (NZCA).

[133] In fact it may be more complex: there will be cases where there is no contract and no tort, and equity alone defines the claim. There will be others in which a contract existed or a tort was arguably committed, but the claimant does not rely on them for the claim he advances.

contract nor tort, but only a breach of equitable duty, and it may be wondered whether in such cases the claims of the *lex fori*, now not overshadowed by any other jural relationship, may be stronger. But even here, the judge's preference appears to have been to apply the proper law of the obligation, at least where the claim arises out of some conception of wrongdoing. This may only be support at first instance. But it lends significant weight to the opinions of those[134] who have sought to accommodate claims, which are regarded as equitable when they arise within English domestic law, within the ordinary structure of the conflict of laws when they have foreign elements within them. The claim that they are somehow distinct and distinctive, and therefore governed by the *lex fori*, is increasingly untenable in England.[135]

The judge had no need to deal with a submission[136] that once a claim has been shown to fall within the material scope of the Rome Convention, the choice of law given by that Convention must be applied to the claim, and may not be sidelined by the expedient of using the common law rules of the conflict of laws to characterise the issue as other than contractual. No more needs to be said about it at this stage, except that the broad thrust submission[137] would appear to be in rough conformity with the judge's basic instinct for a commercially sensible outcome. But it is well to observe that the current draft of the proposal for a Regulation appears to allow, in what now appears as Article 3(3), that a non-contractual obligation may be governed by the law which applied to a previously-established relationship between the parties. It does not say so in clear and precise terms, but it would open the way for an English court to hold that a claim in tort is to be governed by the *lex contractus* when there is one. Of course, if the Court of Justice gets there first, and lays down the law along the lines suggested above, none of this will be necessary; and the judge's commercial instinct, that where there is a contract little benefit accrues from looking for a tort or an equitable duty, will have been vindicated.

11 *Choice of law in cross-border torts:* Morin v Bonhams & Brooks Ltd[138]

At a car auction[139] held in Monaco, the defendants, BBL and BBM[140] offered for sale a 'mighty Ferrari 410 SuperAmerica' built in 1959. This

[134] Notably Yeo, (1999) 115 LQR 571.

[135] See further Yeo, *Choice of Law for Equitable Doctrines* (Oxford, 2004).

[136] Advanced by the writer in [2003] LMCLQ 12.

[137] Though terms of its result rather than its reasoning.

[138] [2003] EWCA Civ 1802, 18th December 2003: Butler-Sloss P, Mance and Keene LJJ, on appeal from [2003] EWHC 467 (Comm), [2003] 2 All ER (Comm) 36. Mance LJ delivered the only substantial judgment.

[139] An auction of 59 'historic' cars, according to the catalogue, but which seems to have included at least one clapped out old banger.

[140] In fact, second defendant, Bonhams & Brooks SAM (BBM) was the auctioneer, and the Monegasque subsidiary of the first defendant, Bonhams & Brooks Ltd (BBL).

formidable contraption was said to have clocked up only 16,626 km or, to put it another way, 250 miles per year. Even the most optimistic of Essex car dealers might have choked at that; but the claimant went by the catalogue and bought the car at auction in Monaco for approximately £430,000. Payment was made on receipt of an invoice in London. He had had a chance to see his intended purchase prior to the auction, but had not been permitted to start its engine, never mind test drive it. When he got the thing home and lifted the bonnet, only to discover that the engine was worn out, he complained. Not being prepared to be fobbed off by the jaw-dropping disclaimers in the auctioneer's catalogue, he instituted proceedings in the English courts. The auctioneer being a Monegasque entity, BBM, permission was required to serve it out of the jurisdiction.[141] In deciding on the application for permission, a significant question was what law would govern the tort claim against BBM. If it were the law of Monaco, it was improbable that England would be clearly the most appropriate forum, and the application would fail. The judge held that it was the law of Monaco, and declined to grant permission to serve out on BBM. The Court of Appeal held that he was right to decide as he had done and dismissed the appeal.

It would have been possible for the court to have looked at a number of further issues rather more complex than the one which was taken to be decisive. The claim against BBM was taken to lie in tort, and any suggestion that it may have been, or may as a matter of Monegasque law have been, contractual in nature was not pursued,[142] on the pragmatic basis that it would plainly have been governed by the law of Monaco as well and the application for service out would have fared no better. But the previous Note suggests that there would in principle be a complicated set of questions to ask in such cases if the laws governing contract and tort claims are not conveniently the same. Likewise, the court declined to speculate on whether or how the analysis would have differed if the claimant had participated in the auction by telephone from London rather than turning up in person in Monte Carlo. It is clear that this would have tilted the balance back towards English as the *lex delicti*, though whether it would have tipped the balance is much harder to say.

Mance LJ identified the *lex delicti* from the provisions of Private International Law (Miscellaneous Provisions) Act 1995 section 11. In doing so he declined the invitation to look at cases dealing with the interpretation different tests arising under different legal rules. It is very good news that he did so, making it very plain that a new statutory formulation which is cast in terms of a 'geographical test'[143] is not illuminated by the jurisprudence generated by the common law, and by the Civil Procedure Rules[144] provision for related but distinctly different matters. The material

[141] Monaco not being a Member state to which the Council Regulation (EC) 44/2001 applies.

[142] It is mentioned at para. [27], and only parenthetically.

[143] At para. [16].

[144] Including the predecessor Rules of the Supreme Court.

part of the statute instructed the court to identify 'the country in which the most significant element or elements of [the events constituting the tort] occurred'.[145] A common law test for choice of law which first asked where in substance the tort occurred[146] was not addressing the same question; and neither did the jurisdictional tests prescribed from time to time by the rules for service out of the jurisdiction. Even less assistance was to be gained from the provisions for special jurisdiction in matters relating to tort and delict in the Brussels Convention or Council Regulation (EC) 44/2001.[147] All reference to these could do was risk distracting the court from the matter at hand; and Mance LJ set about answering the statutory question, ignoring the noises off.

He therefore approached the application of section 11(2)(c) in a manner in which, save for one point, is exemplary. Mance LJ identified what were 'the legal elements of the tort of negligent misstatement',[148] and made a 'value judgment' about the significance of each one on the facts of the instant case. This led to the conclusion that Monaco was the place of the most significant element of the events giving rise to the tort: it was where the auction took place, where the face-to-face bidding happened and where, so far as he was concerned, the claimant entered into an irrevocable and disastrous contract to buy the old banger. Though there were other elements which could be located in England,[149] these were subordinate to and consequential upon the main elements which were clearly rooted in Monaco. It is impossible to quarrel with this assessment if one starts, as Mance LJ appeared to, with the proposition that it was 'the legal elements of the tort of negligent misstatement' which set the parameters of the enquiry.

Practical as this may appear to be, one may question whether it is altogether correct. The proclaimed purpose of the statutory reform to choice of law was to replace the common law choice of law rule with its general bias in favour of the law of the forum. To achieve this goal, the common law rule of double actionability was specifically abolished before the statutory rule was put in place.[150] But with that done, it is odd to find that 'the tort of negligent misstatement' is used to frame the analysis of choice of law. There was no indication in the judgment whether the law of Monaco shared the view (i) that the claim was based on negligent misstatement, or (ii) was based on a tort or delict at all. There is a risk of readmitting through the back door a rule which has just been kicked out of the front if the English domestic law of tort is taken as the template for choice of law. Moreover, this technique will not work very well, or at

[145] Section 11(2)(c).

[146] *Distillers Co Ltd v Thompson* [1971] AC 458, PC (a case on jurisdiction in New South Wales).

[147] Article 5(3), dealing with special jurisdiction over a defendant domiciled in another Member state.

[148] At para. [18].

[149] Where the claimant received the catalogue; from where he gave instructions to his Bahamian trustees to make payment of the price.

[150] Section 10 abolished the rule of double actionability; s. 11 and 12 stated the new rule.

all, in a case in which there is no civil liability in English tort law, but is (said to be) liability in tort or delict, or on some other legal basis, under the law of another country in which some of the events took place. Such cases cannot be resolved by asking about the elements of an English-law tort. When confronted by this—a problem for which the Act, most unhelpfully, provides no solution—it will be necessary to ask the questions in a more neutral form. The court will have to enquire after the place of the most significant element or elements of the events said to give rise to the claimant's claim. This may release the test from its close association with the domestic law of tort, and achieve more naturally the goal which Parliament seems to have wanted to accomplish. It follows that, in this submission, the judge should have laid less overt stress on 'the tort of negligent misstatement', and more on the elements, more abstractly identified, which gave rise to the cause of action which, if governed by English law, would have amounted to a tort of negligent misstatement.[151]

There was no need for the court to consider whether there was an available escape from section 11 in section 12. The claimant conceded that if the law of Monaco were identified as applicable by section 11(2)(c), there was no real basis for contending that another country was more significantly connected with the tort such that it was more appropriate to apply the law of that country to displace the section 11 choice of law. But the judge was alert to the argument that, if BBM had contended that the choice of Monaco law and jurisdiction in the auction catalogue was a factor which could be taken into account in the operation of section 12, there are some[152] who find it hard to see how a connection with a *law* can be taken as a connection with a *country*; or how the place of adjudication can be located within the opaque wording of section 12(2) of the Act. It is not at all obvious that he would have acceded to this view of what section 12 does and does not allow, but he had no need to decide, and did not decide, how the analysis would have proceeded. Little more needs to be said about it, though, but it does draw attention to the fact that there is a distinction of principle between rules which connect events to a country and those which tie those events to a law. To be sure, the significance of distinction may not always have been appreciated within the common law conflict of laws.[153] But where choice of law rules have been rendered in statutory form, the distinction has been recognised as highly significant.[154] One must assume that the wording of section 12 was chosen with care if not with wisdom; and the elision of the two concepts may need more than scholarship and judicial common sense to see it home and dry.

[151] And which, if governed by Monaco law, would probably have been something different.

[152] Including the present writer: Briggs, 'On drafting agreements on choice of law' [2003] LMCLQ 389.

[153] *Whitworth Street Estates (Manchester) Ltd v James Miller and Partners* [1970] AC 583, esp at 604.

[154] In the context of choice of law for contracts: *Crédit Lyonnais v New Hampshire Insurance Co* [1997] 2 Lloyd's Rep 1, CA.

UNITED KINGDOM MATERIALS ON INTERNATIONAL LAW 2003

Compiled by KAIYAN KAIKOBAD,[1] JACQUES HARTMANN,[2] SANGEETA SHAH,[3] COLIN WARBRICK,[4] and SARAH WILLIAMS[5]

1. This selection of UK materials on international law is made from published sources. It does not purport to include everything that could be of interest to an international lawyer but it is not wholly restricted to materials that could be called "state practice" in the strictest sense: some context is provided.

We have to make very considerable excisions of material that we know would be of interest to some international lawyers. We bear in mind first, the need to avoid the purely ephemeral, and second, to exclude materials that are concerned mainly with the UK's implementation of the international law of co-operation, particularly at the general level. We are very sparing with matters of EU law, though we report some EU positions on questions of international law with which the UK is associated.

There is only limited material on UK treaties because the texts and explanatory memoranda are readily available on the Web: **www.fco.gov.uk/treaties**.

We have inserted a small amount of editorial material in the form "[ed....]" where it appears helpful to do so. Extracts are generally reproduced in their original form, which leads to inconsistencies, eg in spelling ("judgement/"judgment") or capitalisation "UN charter" or designation ("Chapter Seven"/"Chapter VII"/"Chapter 7").

2. Hansard references are to the Web version. There may be minor discrepancies between the column references in the Web edition and the bound volumes.

References to Hansard are given in the following forms:

Commons—HC Deb 13 November 2001 Vol 374 c345 or c134W or c101WH or c1WS, where W, WH and WS stand for Written Answers, Westminster Hall and Written Statements;

Lords—HL Deb 8 October 2002 Vol 639 c222 or 16 October 2003 Vol 653 cWA125, where WA stands for Written Answer or HL Deb 29 January 2003 Vol 643 cGC170, where GC stands for Grand Committee.

[1] Law Department, University of Durham. [2] Id.
[3] Human Rights Centre, Law Department, University of Nottingham.
[4] Law Department, University of Durham. [5] Id.

3. From its start in 1978 and up to and including 1996, the materials in UKMIL were classified on the basis of the *Model Plan for the Classification of Documents concerning State Practice in the Field of Public International Law* adopted by the Committee of Ministers of the Council of Europe in its Resolution (68) 17 of 28 June 1968. The Committee of Ministers considered that developments in public international law since 1968 made it necessary to amend the Model Plan. Accordingly, by Recommendation (97) 11 of 12 June 1997, it adopted an Amended Model Plan as a contribution by the Council of Europe towards implementing General Assembly Resolution 2099 (XX) on technical assistance to promote the teaching, study, dissemination and wider understanding of international law. The present issue of UKMIL is based on the 1997 Amended Model Plan.

4. We are glad to acknowledge the assistance of Chanaka Wickremasinghe and his colleagues in the Legal Adviser's Department of the Foreign & Commonwealth Office.

5. We are grateful for financial assistance in the preparation of UKMIL to the Whittuck Trust.

Index

Part One: I. A. *International Law in General: Nature, basis, purpose*

1/1

The Foreign Secretary was asked in the FAC what measures the Government could take to ensure compliance with UN mandatory resolutions. He said:

[This is] a really important point, it was not the reason for taking the military action [ed. The Foreign Secretary did not say what was the reason for using military action.] but it is an important consequence. Events since September 11 in respect of Afghanistan, terrorism, rogue states and Iraq raise very large questions about the underlying assumptions of international relations and on which international relations have been based historically since the Peace of Westphalia in the middle of the 17th century. Essentially those assumptions were that the best guarantor of peace and security was to respect the territorial integrity of sovereign states, what the states did within their territory was a matter for them however terrible it was, however, what they did with other international states was a matter for the international community. Those principles are strongly stated in the United Nations Charter. It is my belief we have to begin a discussion about how those principles are revisited in the modern environment because of threats posed other than by normally functioning sovereign states, posed by rogue states, posed by international terrorism, posed by others who are acting in an extremely oppressive way. I do not give the answers. Any changes will have to have international consent but we have to recognise the fact that the world has changed and your point about how we prevent future Saddams is a really important one. (Qu. 283)

(FAC Tenth Report, Foreign Policy Aspects of the War against Terrorism, Oral Evidence, 29 April 2003, HC 405)

Part One: I. C. *International Law in General: Nature, basis, purpose: Soft Law*

(See **16/69**)

Part Two: I. D. *Sources and Codification of International Law—Sources of international law—Unilateral acts, including acts and decisions of international organizations and conferences*

2/1

In reply to a written question, the Secretary of State, FCO, wrote:

The UK makes daily representations to UN organisations and agencies, and to other members of the UN, on a wide range of issues. Examples of the UN's achievements in the last six months to which UK representations have contributed include:

The unanimous adoption of UN Security Council Resolution 1441 and the return of weapons inspectors to Iraq;

The successful transition of the International Police Task Force in Bosnia to the European Union Police Mission;

The adoption of UN Security Council Resolution 1445 strengthening UN action against Al-Qaida;

The adoption, by a large majority, of a new international human rights instrument to combat torture: the Optional Protocol to the Convention Against Torture;

The adoption of General Assembly Resolutions on major human rights thematic issues, including torture, rights of the child, rights of the disabled and honour crimes;

Significant agreements on international sustainable development governance at the World Summit for Sustainable Development: e.g. access to sanitation, biodiversity, chemicals management and sustainable production and consumption;

Lifting sanctions in Angola.

(HC Deb 27 January 2003 Vol. 398 c566W)

Part Three: I. B. *The law of treaties—definition, conclusion, and entry into force—conclusion, including signature, ratification, and accession*

3/1

In reply to a written question the Home Office Minister wrote:

The UK ratified Protocol 13 to the European Convention for the Protection of Human Rights and Fundamental Freedoms banning the death penalty in all circumstances on 10 October 2003.

The ratification will apply at present only to the metropolitan area of the United Kingdom. Ratification will be extended to the Crown Dependencies and Overseas Territories at a later date.

We shall in due course seek parliamentary approval pursuant to section 1(4) of the Human Rights Act 1998 to add Protocol 13 to the list of scheduled convention rights.

(HL Deb 16 October 2003 Vol. 653 cWA125)

3/2

The Under-Secretary of State, FCO, made the following written statement:

Officials in the Foreign and Commonwealth Office and the Ministry of Defence have completed all the necessary work to enable the Government to proceed to ratify the Optional Protocol to the United Nations Convention on the Rights of the Child on the involvement of children in armed conflict.

We intend to complete the ratification process with the United Nations as soon as possible. To begin the formal process, I have today laid before Parliament an Explanatory Memorandum which explains the steps taken to meet our commitment to the provisions of the Protocol.

In particular, since 1 September 2002 Army personnel under 18 are no longer routinely deployed on operations outside the United Kingdom, although they may continue to participate in purely humanitarian missions where no hostile forces are involved. Furthermore, all three Services now have procedures in place to ensure that, wherever it is feasible to do so without undermining operational effectiveness or the safety of personnel, under 18s are removed from their units when there is deemed to be a greater than low risk of direct involvement in hostilities.

(HC Deb 24 February 2003 Vol. 400 c8WS)

Part Three: I. C. *The law of treaties—definition, conclusion, and entry into force—reservations, declarations, and objections*

3/3

During a debate in the House of Commons on the Nationality, Immigration and Asylum Bill, the Minister for Citizenship was asked the following question:

Is it not time to restore to the Home Secretary the ability to deport people who may threaten this country? Case law under article 3 of the European convention on human rights makes it impossible to do that, so is it not time that the Government saw sense, opted out of the ECHR, went back in with reservations, and gave the Home Secretary the power to protect this country from people who threaten it?

In reply, the Minister for Citizenship said:

The hon. Gentleman's suggestion would require the country to withdraw from the ECHR. We would then have to legislate in a way that was incompatible with article 3 and ask the Council of Europe if it would allow us to re-enter with a reservation. That would be a tortuous and difficult process. We have not ruled it out but it is fraught with uncertainty. No other country has done it. There is no certainty that the Council of Europe would allow us to re-enter with a reservation. Reservations have to be very specific and that has not been tested. We are not going down that route at the moment. However, the Prime Minister has made it clear that, if our measures to tackle such problems are not as effective as we want them to be, we will consider whether we need to revise our obligations under various treaties.

(HC Deb 24 February 2003 Vol. 400 c11–12)

3/4

The UK informed the Secretary-General of the UN of its objection to the interpretive declaration made by Uruguay when ratifying the Rome Statute of the International Criminal Court. The UK said:

At the time of the deposit of its instrument of ratification, . . . Uruguay made two statements which are called "interpretive declarations", the first of which states that, "as a State party to the Rome Statute, . . . Uruguay shall ensure its application to the full extent of the powers of the State insofar as it is competent in that respect and in strict accordance with the Constitutional provisions of the Republic".

The Government of the United Kingdom has given careful consideration to the so-called interpretive declaration quoted above. The Government of the United Kingdom is obliged to conclude that this so-called interpretive declaration purports to exclude or modify the legal effects of the Rome Statute in its application to the Eastern Republic of Uruguay and is accordingly a reservation. However, according to Article 120 of the Rome Statute, no reservations may be made thereto.

Accordingly, the Government objects to the above-quoted reservation by the Eastern Republic of Uruguay. However, this objection does not preclude the entry into force of the Rome Statute between the United Kingdom and Uruguay.

(27 August 2003, text supplied by FCO)

Part Three: II. A. *The law of treaties—observance, application, and interpretation—observance*

(See also **16/96**)

3/5

During a House of Commons debate on Foreign Policy the Foreign Secretary said:

[I]f we sign up to international treaties, they take precedence in our domestic law, and, where necessary, we have to have domestic legislation in order to implement them, which we expect of our partners. What on earth is the point of signing up to an international treaty with another country, only to find that that other country has not incorporated the treaty's obligations into their own domestic law where that is necessary?

(HC Deb 27 November 2003 Vol. 415 c151)

3/6

During a debate in the House of Commons the Under-Secretary of State, FCO, said:

[T]reaties are international law. If we sign them, we have an obligation to honour and abide by them. Pacta sunt servanda is the old Latin term, and it is honoured and enforced by tribunals and courts. There is no other way in which we can have relationships with other countries in treaty form.

(HC Deb 10 December 2003 Vol. 415 c1162)

3/7

In reply to a written question the Under-Secretary of State, FCO, wrote:

The UK has given effect to its obligations under the EU treaties through the European Communities Act 1972. *Costa* v. *ENEL* set out the clear principle that its obligations under the treaties cannot be overridden by domestic legal provisions.

In *Thorburn* v. *Sunderland City Council*, Lord Justice Laws said as part of his judgment:

> "All the specific rights and obligations which EU law creates are by the 1972 Act incorporated into our domestic law and rank supreme ...".

The ultimate guarantee of parliamentary sovereignty lies in the power of Parliament to repeal all or any of the Acts which give effect to the EU treaties in this country. As Lord Denning made clear in the case of *Macarthys Ltd.* v. *Smith*, it is within Parliament's power to legislate contrary to the UK's treaty obligations. The result of so doing, however, would be to put the UK in breach of its treaty obligations.

(HC Deb 5 November 2003 Vol. 412 c656W–657W)

3/8

In reply to a written question, the Under-Secretary of State, FCO, wrote:

The UK has a very good record in fulfilling its NPT obligations. In furtherance of the aims of Article VI of The Treaty on the Non-Proliferation of Nuclear Weapons, the UK has, since May 1997:

withdrawn and dismantled the RAF's freefall WE 177 nuclear bomb, so that Trident is now our only nuclear weapons system;

reduced our operationally available stockpile to fewer than 200 warheads, which is a reduction of more than 70 per cent in the potential explosive power of our nuclear forces since the end of the Cold War;

dismantled the UK's last Chevaline warhead in April 2002;

reduced the readiness of our nuclear forces. Only a single Trident submarine at a time is now on deterrent patrol, carrying 48 warheads. The submarine on patrol is normally on several days 'notice to fire' and its missiles are de-targeted;

placed fissile material no longer required for defence purposes under international safeguards, and all enrichment and reprocessing facilities in the UK are now liable to international inspection;

been more transparent about our nuclear and fissile material stockpiles and begun a national historical accounting study for fissile material produced;

published an initial summary report on the verification of the reduction and elimination of nuclear weapons. The Atomic Weapons Establishment Aldermaston is undertaking work on this issue;

ratified the Comprehensive Nuclear Test Ban Treaty (CTBT) and promoted its early entry into force;

ratified the relevant protocols to the Treaty of Raratonga (South Pacific Nuclear Weapon Free Zone) and signed and ratified the relevant protocols to the Treaty of Pelindaba (African Nuclear Weapon Free Zone);

supported Nuclear Weapon Free Zones in central Asia, south east Asia, and the Middle East, and is in negotiations with the relevant states for the first two of these; and continued to press for negotiations to begin at the Conference on Disarmament in Geneva of a Fissile Material Cut-Off Treaty.

(HC Deb 21 January 2003 Vol. 398 c228W–229W)

3/9

In reply to a written question, the Secretary of State, FCO, wrote:

Exchanges of information between the United Kingdom and the United States on nuclear weapon matters take place only under the auspices of the 1958 Mutual Defence Agreement, and its amendments.

There have been no transfers of nuclear weapons between the UK and the US. The UK is a member and a Depositary state for the Treaty on the Non-Proliferation of Nuclear Weapons (1968) and our actions, including under the Mutual Defence Agreement, are in compliance with that treaty.

(HC Deb 29 January 2003 Vol. 398 c881W–882W)

3/10

A Foreign Office Minister told the First Review Meeting of the Chemical Weapons Convention on 29 April 2003:

...the fact that there are now 151 States Parties to the Chemical Weapons Convention is a major and welcome achievement, which has helped to give the Convention very broad, if not yet global, support. The United Kingdom nevertheless remains concerned that a number of countries, particularly in the Middle East and North East Asia, have yet to accede to the Convention. Universality must remain a key objective if we are to deny space and opportunity to terrorist groupings. It is that threat in particular which must now give renewed impetus to our efforts.

However, if a State Party is to fully satisfy the key aims and objectives of the Convention, membership—although a very positive step—is in itself not enough. Each State Party must take the necessary measures to implement its full obligations under the Convention, and in particular the enactment of penal legislation.

Failure to adopt such measures robs States Parties of an important means of combating proliferation and chemical terrorism. It is therefore of particular concern to the United Kingdom, as we approach the sixth year since the Convention entered into force, that only 26% of States Parties have so far implemented the necessary legislation covering all the key areas for enforcement of its provisions.

I believe that this troubling situation undermines the overall effectiveness of the Convention to the detriment of all States Parties and does little to deter the scourge of terrorism.

The UK fully recognises that most States Parties have neither chemical weapons nor a developed chemical industry. But this does not mean they need not bother with such legislation. The globalisation of the chemical industry and of trade in chemicals means that a growing number of countries are undertaking activities that are relevant to the Convention. The interest that terrorists are now showing in chemical weapons means that no State Party can allow itself to believe that the prohibitions in the Convention do not need to be enforced on its territory.

We have good cause to know. The suspected terrorist incident involving ricin in London in January this year demonstrated the value of having implementing legislation in place, which could be used to apprehend and prosecute individuals suspected of involvement in activities that violate the Convention. Such activity, which took place in a residential property and involved rudimentary equipment, could have happened in any country.

The United Kingdom recognises that many States Parties may wish for assistance in order to put in place the necessary measures to implement the Convention. We are certainly prepared to see more resources directed to this area, and would welcome proposals from the OPCW for an enhanced and targeted work programme to help States Parties which need assistance with their implementation tasks.

I hope therefore that this Conference will remind all States Parties of the urgent need to give political impetus and priority to adopting the necessary measures to implement quickly and effectively their obligations under the Convention...

(29 April 2003, available at www.fco.gov.uk/speeches)

3/11

In reply to a written question, the Minister of State, Home Office, wrote:

The Government are supporting the Dealing in Cultural Property (Offences) Bill. This Bill, which has recently been introduced, would create a new criminal offence of dishonestly importing, dealing or being in possession of any cultural object, knowing or believing that the object was stolen, or illegally excavated, or removed from any monument or wreck contrary to local law. The UK formally acceded to the 1970 UNESCO Convention on the Means of Prohibiting and Preventing the Illicit Import, Export and Transfer of Ownership of Cultural Property on 31 October 2002. The convention enables countries which are parties to the convention to claim back stolen antiquities which surface in the countries of fellow signatories. Home Office officials continue to work with colleagues in the Department for Culture, Media and Sport (DCMS) and law enforcement to consider the feasibility of implementing a national database of unlawfully obtained cultural property as recommended by the House of Commons Select Committee in July 2000. Officials from the DCMS are currently in the process of drawing up a business case for such a database.

(HL Deb 7 January 2003 Vol. 642 cWA188)

3/12

During a debate in the House of Lords, the Parliamentary Under-Secretary of State, FCO, said:

There is also the important issue of land reform. The United Kingdom Government accept, and have always accepted, that land reform is essential to Zimbabwe's development. We have contributed to it. However, we have never accepted that the solution is to hand over large sums of money to the Zimbabwe Government on an unconditional and unsustainable basis. We did not agree that at Lancaster House in 1980, and we will not do so in future. We have said that we will support a land reform process that is transparent, fair and legal, as part of a wider strategy to reduce poverty. I assure my noble friend Lord Hughes of Woodside that we hope to resume support for long-term development programmes in Zimbabwe. However, that will be possible only when the needs and concerns of all stakeholders are fully addressed. The programmes must be based on the rule of law and on sensible economics and are carried out by democratic governments. None of those conditions is in place.

(HL Deb 8 October 2002 Vol. 639 c222)

Part Three: II. B. *The law of treaties—observance, application, and interpretation—application*

3/13

In *R (on the application of Quark Fishing)* v *Secretary of State for Foreign and Commonwealth Affairs*, [2003] EWHC 1747 (Admin), appeal rejected, [2004] EWCA Civ 527, the issue arose about the application of Protocol 1, European Convention of Human Rights 1950 to South Georgia and South Sandwich Islands (SGSSI), a British Overseas Territory (BOT). A witness statement was entered by a legal adviser on behalf of the Foreign Secretary. She wrote:

4. Her Majesty's Government in the United Kingdom is internally responsible for the external affairs of the BOTs. This means, inter alia, that HMG is entitled to speak on behalf of the BOTs at international fora, British Embassies abroad are entitled to protect the interest of BOTs and their inhabitants, HMG is responsible internally for ensuring compliance by the BOTs with treaties and other international obligations which apply to them, except where a specific delegation, known as an "entrustment", has been given to a BOT, it is HMG which negotiates treaties on their behalf.

. . .

12. The United Kingdom is responsible for the external relations of the BOTs. This means that as a matter of international law the United Kingdom has the responsibility for ensuring compliance by the territory with those international obligations which apply to it. Failure by a BOT to comply with an international obligation could render the United Kingdom liable to proceedings before an international court or tribunal. This is illustrated by the case of Gibraltar, which is a territory to which the EC treaty applies (with certain exceptions) by virtue of Article 299.4 of the Treaty. A failure by Gibraltar to implement a relevant EC Directive could result in the United Kingdom being subject of infraction proceedings before the European Court of Justice. On the other hand, the responsibility for implementing and observing an international obligation which applies a BOT would, as a matter of domestic law of the territory, fall within the responsibility of the BOT government concerned. Thus it would be for the BOT government to ensure the legislation is enacted, or administrative measures taken, to implement an international obligation.

. . .

13. The system of administration of BOTs presupposes their separate legal identity. For example, although the United Kingdom would normally negotiate and conclude treaties with third States in respect of a BOT, there are a number of cases where for good reasons it is desirable that a territory be given delegated authority from the United Kingdom, in the form of an "entrustment", to negotiate and conclude agreements with third countries on its own behalf. For example, entrustments in the past have been given to Jamaica, Trinidad, Barbados (before they became independent) and to Hong Kong, which prior to its hand-over to China was given a wide-ranging entrustment to negotiate and conclude limited agreements in the economic area with the United States, and to Montserrat, which by virtue of an entrustment, is a full member of the Organisation of Eastern Caribbean States. Since an entrustment, by virtue of its nature, is based on the separate identity of the BOT, it would be difficult to continue the practice of entrustments if that separate identity was not recognised legally. There are also a number of international agreements concluded by the United Kingdom with third States which apply to the BOTs and which require the competent authorities of those States to communicate directly with the competent authorities in the BOTs, such as treaties in the field of extradition and mutual legal assistance. It would complicate the implementation of agreements of this kind if the separate identity of the BOT Government and its institutions were not recognised.

. . .

19. The United Kingdom extended the ECHR to the Falkland Islands and its Dependencies, by declaration under Article 63(1) of the ECHR on 23 October 1953. On 21 September 1967 the United Kingdom extended the right of individual petition to the Commission (by declaration under Article 63(4) of the ECHR) and to the Court to a number of territories including the Falkland Islands, until 13 January 1969. The right to individual petition was periodically renewed thereafter by further declarations. Although the declarations of 1953 and 1967 do not refer expressly to the Falkland Islands dependencies, they clearly do apply to the dependencies because the first declaration renewing the right of individual petition after the making of the South Georgia and South

Sandwich Islands order 1985 (dated 17 April 1986) expressly mentions SGSSI, as do subsequent declarations. The most recent declaration renewing the right of individual petition in relation to SGSSI renews the right from 14 January 2001 for five years. The ECHR has therefore applied to SGSSI since 1953, and the right to individual petition since 1967.

20. The United Kingdom ratified Protocol 1 to the ECHR on 3 November 1952. Article 4 of Protocol 1 provides that any State may, at the time of ratification or any time thereafter, communicate to the Secretary-General of the Council of Europe a declaration stating the extent to which it undertakes that the provisions of the Protocol shall apply to such territories for whose international relations it is responsible. As with declarations under Article 63(1) (now 56(1)) of the ECHR in respect of the territorial extent of the ECHR, it is by declaration under Article 4 of Protocol 1 that the United Kingdom has indicated to the Secretary-General of the Council of Europe those territories to which the Protocol extends.

[This position was accepted by the Administrative Court and confirmed by the Court of Appeal.]

Part Three: II. D. *The law of treaties—observance, application, and interpretation—treaties and third states*

3/14

During a House of Commons debate the Under-Secretary of State, FCO, said:

The hon. Gentleman also raised the issue of the International Criminal Court. He said that the UK Government were assisting bilateral immunity agreements in contravention of the ICC statute and that that was splitting from the EU position. That accusation is completely without foundation. We have made it clear that we believe that bilateral non-surrender agreements are allowed under the existing ICC statutes, provided that they follow the framework set out in the EU guiding principles and are consistent with the language of article 16 of the Rome Statute. We have done nothing to contradict that position and we have made it clear that we will not sign a bilateral non-surrender agreement that does not conform with those principles.

(HC Deb 11 November 2003 Vol. 314 c251)

Part Four: I. *Relationship between international law and internal law—In general*

4/1

In reply to a written question the Minister for Europe wrote:

It is an established principle of international law that a state may not plead its national law to escape its international law obligations, including its treaty obligations. As a matter of UK constitutional law, international treaties have effect in UK national law to the extent that they have been implemented in national law.

(HC Deb 16 October 2003 Vol. 411 c335W)

4/2

In *R (on the application of the Campaign for Nuclear Disarmament)* v *The Prime Minister of the United Kingdom and others* [2002] EWHC 2759 (QB), a witness statement was entered by a Foreign Office official. He wrote:

3. The Claimants have asked that the Government explain its understanding of the legal position with regard to the interpretation of Security Council Resolution 1441 (2002). In the judgment of the Secretary of State and the Foreign & Commonwealth Office, and in my own opinion, it would be prejudicial to the national interest and to the conduct of the Government's foreign policy if the Government were to be constrained to make a definitive statement of its legal position under international law in relation to issues concerning the international relations of the United Kingdom. The short point is that it is an unavoidable feature of the conduct of international relations that issues of law, politics and diplomacy are usually closely bound up together. The assertion of arguments of international law by one state is in practice regarded by other states as a political act, and they react accordingly. The UK's international alliances could be damaged by incautious assertions of arguments under international law which affect the position of those states.

4. This is especially true in a situation which (like the present situation covered by resolution 1441) is sensitive and where tension is high on all sides: the assertion of arguments of international law by one state which are unpalatable to other states may have the effect of increasing tension and diminishing the possibilities for a diplomatic (and, it is hoped, peaceful) solution. It is also especially true where the issue of international law to be considered is an issue which (like the interpretation of resolution 1441) affects not just the United Kingdom, but many other states as well, who will have their own strongly held views about the matter. It is frequently important for the successful conduct of international affairs that matters should not be reduced to simple black and white, but should be left as shades of grey and open for diplomatic negotiations. Questions of international law often remain at large and may form part of the wider debate between and within states.

5. Further, there are many and obvious examples of situations where the disclosure of a legal position on the part of the Government would be prejudicial to the national interest, as tending to indicate to other states the practical constraints affecting the Government. To disclose the Government's understanding of the legal position under international law of an international negotiation (eg of an amendment to a treaty, or of a resolution) could plainly be prejudicial to the success of the Government in that negotiation—as a practical indication of the constraints under which the Government may understand itself operating, and its legal "bottom line". Where an international issue involves the possible

use of force by the Government, the advance discussion of legal advice as to the legality or otherwise of the use of force in a variety of possible circumstances could be of immense value to the potential adversary, allowing it to plan and adopt positions contrary to the interest of this country with greater assurance than would otherwise be the case.

6. The practical experience of the Foreign & Commonwealth Office shows, therefore, that the greatest care should be exercised and sensitive diplomatic judgment be brought to bear before the Government commits itself to supporting arguments in international law which may prove controversial for friends and/or opponents and which may compromise the Government's own negotiation position as a tense international situation develops.

(5 December 2002: Text supplied by the FCO)

4/3

During a debate on the proposed EU Constitution the Foreign Secretary stated:

The fact is that all international treaties take primacy over national laws—the system of international law could not function otherwise.

. . .

If the hon. Gentleman reads the leading case of Shah and Islam [ed. *R* v *IAT* and *SSHD ex p Shah; Islam* v *IAT* [1999] 2 AC 629], which is connected with the interpretation of the UN convention on refugees of 1951, he will see the argument set out in every detail. It provides a clear exposition of the fact that, when a country signs up to an international treaty, that treaty takes precedence over national law, as long as a national Parliament decides to remain a member of the treaty organisation.

(HC Deb 16 September 2003 Vol. 410 c794)

Part Four: II. *Relationship between international law and internal law—Application and implementation of international law in internal law*

4/4

During a debate in the House of Lords on the New European Constitution, the Minister for Trade made the following statements:

My Lords, a new constitutional treaty would need to be ratified according to the individual constitutional arrangements in each of the member states. This Government are committed to the existing system in the United Kingdom of parliamentary democracy rather than public referendums. Any new treaty would have to stand up to rigorous scrutiny by Parliament before the United Kingdom would ratify it.

(HL Deb 5 March 2003 Vol. 645 c803–804)

4/5

In reply to a written question, the Minister of State, FCO, wrote:

The product of the Convention on the Future of Europe will be a draft Treaty. The draft, including any reference in it to the Charter of Fundamental Rights, will require the agreement of all Member States in the next Intergovernmental Conference. The Government has put forward its views in detail on the draft text produced by the Convention so far...

Any new restructured treaty, or amendments to the existing treaties, will need to be ratified according to the individual constitutional requirements of all Member States. In the UK, as with the Nice Treaty, and all other treaties amending the original treaty structure, any new amendments would have to stand up to vigorous scrutiny by Parliament before the UK would ratify.

(HC Deb 26 March 2003 Vol. 402 c255W–256W)

4/6

During a debate in the House of Commons, the Minister for Tourism, Film and Broadcasting said:

I can confirm that the Parthenon sculptures, as my hon. Friend refers to them, would certainly not be covered by the legislation [Dealing in Cultural Objects (Offences) Bill].

The hon. Member...stressed the importance of international co-operation. Certainly, the more co-operation and co-ordination that we can get, the easier the task will be and, hopefully, the fewer the number of prosecutions under the Bill when it comes into force.

Among the other key recommendations of the ministerial advisory panel was accession to the 1970 UNESCO convention on the means of prohibiting and preventing the illicit import, export and transfer of ownership of cultural property. The convention makes provision to secure the protection of the cultural heritage of the United Kingdom and other signatory countries. People should remember that the convention protects our cultural heritage as well as that of other countries. The convention is not retroactive; it is applicable only to cultural objects stolen or illicitly exported from one state party to another state party after the date of entry into force of the convention for both states concerned. The UNESCO convention has been adopted by 93 countries to date, including in recent months Albania and Rwanda. Such widespread adoption enhances its value as a means of protecting cultural heritage in the UK and other signatory countries.

(HC Deb 4 April 2003 Vol. 402 c1237)

4/7

In the continued debate, the same Minister said:

In completing the formalities of acceptance on 31 October 2002, the UK Government sent out a powerful signal both to those who do so much damage to the world's cultural heritage and to the international community that the UK is serious about playing its full part in the international effort to stamp out the illicit trafficking in cultural objects.

The need for a criminal offence is at the heart of the Bill. Action on the matter was considered too important to be left to the vagaries of private law, and a do-nothing option is not viable, nor is a mere amendment to the existing offences under the Theft Act 1968. Given the continued and continuing growth of the illicit traffic in cultural objects, experience shows that voluntary codes of due diligence are limited in their effect on the criminal element of the trade, which ignores them. The panel has advised, and the Government agree, that a pre-emptive measure such as the creation of a new criminal offence to counter the illicit traffic in unlawfully removed cultural objects is the best solution.

It is worth remembering that until recently, the UK was branded as an internationally renowned centre of illicit trade in antiquities. It is true that for the previous 30 years or so, the UK stood on the sidelines of decisive international action against illicit traffic in art and antiquities. However, today the British art and antiquities market is operating in a very different climate. Since publication of the recommendations of the Culture, Media and Sport Committee in 2000 and of the ministerial advisory panel in December of the same year, there has been dramatic progress on measures to combat the looting of archaeological sites and the unlawful trafficking in cultural property. The Government have recently become a state party to the UNESCO convention and are working to introduce a package of measures designed to strengthen their treaty obligations, central to which is the creation of a new criminal offence of dealing unlawfully in cultural objects.

(HC Deb 4 April 2003 Vol. 402 c1237)

4/8

In a response to a written question, the Chief Secretary to the Treasury wrote:

The UK has strictly enforced the terms of UNSCR 661 since it was passed in August 1990. This has required all Iraqi assets held in the UK, including those of Rafidain Bank, to be frozen.

Neither UNSCR 661 nor the domestic legislation that implements it allows for the confiscation of assets.

Under the Iraq sanctions order, which implements UNSCR 661, all payments to residents of Iraq are prohibited, except under licence from HM Treasury.

(HC Deb 8 April 2003 Vol. 403 c146W)

4/9

Her Majesty's Government was asked the following written question:

To ask the Secretary of State for Foreign and Commonwealth Affairs if he will list the statutory instruments issued by his Department in the last 12 months...

In reply, the Secretary of State, FCO, wrote:

2002/250 The Territorial Sea Act 1987 (Jersey) (Amendment) Order 2002.

Purpose: This Order amends the Territorial Sea Act 1987 (Jersey) Order 1997, which extended the 1987 Act to Jersey, to take account of the maritime boundary established between France and Jersey in accordance with an Agreement between the United Kingdom and the French Republic, signed at St. Helier on 4 July 2000 (Cm 5024).

(HC Deb 8 April 2003 Vol. 2003 c194W)

4/10

Her Majesty's Government was asked the following written question:

To ask the Secretary of State for Foreign and Commonwealth Affairs if he will make a statement on the circumstances in which the International Criminal Court could intervene to prosecute UK citizens in cases where the British judicial system was unwilling or unable to do so.

An FCO Minister wrote:

In accordance with the complementarity provisions of the Statute of the International Criminal Court (ICC) and the International Criminal Court Act 2001 (which gave domestic effect to the Statute), the relevant UK authorities will, where appropriate, exercise jurisdiction in respect of allegations against UK service personnel, UK Citizens or residents.

(HC Deb 28 April 2003 Vol. 404 c123W)

4/11

In reply to a written question the Under-Secretary of State, FCO, wrote:

Where the United Nations Security Council has adopted a resolution deciding that states shall prohibit the supply of military and police training to specified countries or forces, the UK will generally implement this by making statutory instruments under the United Nations Act 1946 applicable to the UK, Overseas Territories and Crown Dependencies. Where the European Union has acted swiftly to implement a UN Security Council Resolution by an EC Regulation, the EC Regulation will be directly applicable in the UK and Gibraltar, and the UK and Gibraltar will legislate only to provide penalties for the breach of the Regulation in those territories.

Where the European Union has adopted measures prohibiting the supply of military and police training (for example, in the case of Zimbabwe), those measures will include an EC Regulation which is directly applicable in the UK and Gibraltar. The UK and Gibraltar will legislate only to provide penalties for the breach of the Regulation. Bermuda and the Crown Dependencies will adopt their own legislation to implement the EU measures. The UK will legislate in respect of the Overseas Territories other than Gibraltar and Bermuda using powers in the Saint Helena Act 1833, the British Settlements Acts 1887 and 1947, and prerogative powers.

The precise powers taken in legislation will depend upon the scope of the sanctions regime against that particular state. However, legislation will generally create a criminal offence of providing assistance and training to prohibited territories or individuals without a licence from an appropriate authority, and this will apply to all individuals within the territory to which the legislation applies, and also to all categories of British citizen wherever they may be. Legislation will also generally provide ancillary powers to enforce the prohibition, for example, powers for the obtaining of evidence and information, and provisions for criminal proceedings and penalties. Penalties on summary conviction will generally be imprisonment for a term not exceeding six months or a fine not exceeding £5,000 or both, and on conviction on indictment, imprisonment for a term not exceeding seven years or an unlimited fine or both.

(HC Deb 6 October 2003 Vol. 411 c1114W–1115W)

Part Five: I. A.2. *Subjects of international law—states—status and powers—sovereignty and independence*

5/1

In a written answer, the Secretary of State for Trade and Industry wrote:

It is our position that Iraqi oil is owned by the Iraqi people. Its revenues should be used for the good of the people. We make this clear in all our contacts on the subject.

However, the current situation is not about oil, it is about weapons of mass destruction and the Iraqi regime deliberately flouting the will of the United Nations.

(HC Deb 19 March 2003 Vol. 401 c768W)

5/2

In an oral answer on the number of Turkish troops who have crossed the border into northern Iraq, and on what exactly they are doing, the Prime Minister said:

There always have been Turkish troops in that position and there are obviously large numbers of Turkish troops there now. They say—as they have said consistently—that that is to provide against the possibility of large numbers of people coming over the border from northern Iraq. We and the United States have done everything that we possibly can, however, to make it very clear to the Turkish authorities, the Turkish military and the Turkish Government that any attempt to break the territorial integrity of Iraq in any way would be utterly unacceptable. I do not believe that that is their intention, but obviously we are watching the situation carefully.

(HC Deb 26 March 2003 Vol. 402 c284–285)

5/3

In response to an oral question the Under-Secretary of State, FCO, said:

As regards what is happening in the wider Middle East, again the Government's position is clear. Lasting security can be achieved only through a negotiated settlement. We want to see a state of Israel free from terror and a viable Palestinian state. Those are the planks of our policy and shall remain so.

(HC Deb 21 January 2003 Vol. 643 c460W)

5/4

At a meeting about Colombia on 30 July 2003, a Foreign Office Minister said:

The steps taken by President Uribe to tackle the violence, including the new anti-terrorist legislation that has been brought in, demonstrates his Government's commitment to tackle the dire internal security situation. But it also illustrates the difficult balancing act the Colombian Government faces in seeking to curb the increasing levels of terrorism, whilst ensuring that the rights of all its citizens are protected.

During my visit in May, I made clear that the UK's continued support to Colombia is dependent on proper respect for human rights and international humanitarian law. The Colombian Government must comply with its obligations under international human rights and humanitarian law, and with the recommendations adopted by the UN Commission on Human Rights. In early July, the EU also made representations to the Colombian Government in Bogota, raising our concerns about the risks of granting judicial powers to the armed forces. Although the Bill has now been passed by Congress and has progressed to the Senate's First Commission, the UK will continue to urge the Colombian Government to fulfil the assurances given by the Colombian Vice President that the government will look into ways of adjusting all anti-terrorist legislation in line with Colombia's international obligations.

I do not believe that there can be a purely military solution to the problems that Colombia faces. But negotiations will not prosper unless we can break the links between political violence and drugs, and unless the Colombian Government can get on top of both.

The UK Government continues to be concerned about the current human rights situation in Colombia. The violence being perpetrated by the illegal armed groups is having a devastating impact on all sections of Colombian society, including trade unionists, human rights defenders, journalists, lawyers, elected officials, as well as the legitimate Armed Forces of Colombia.

Colombia needs a healthy and vigorous civil society to function effectively, a point I raised directly with President Uribe and his Ministers during my visit. In particular, I called for the Colombian Government to make clear their support for the work of civil society, stressing that civil society is part of the solution to Colombia's problems. I was therefore pleased to learn that as a result, in a keynote speech at Bogota's Police Academy later in May, President Uribe made clear that he wanted respect to be shown for NGOs working in Colombia.

The UK is committed to assisting the Colombian Government to tackle the challenges it faces constructively: to assert the primacy of elected democratic government so that it can move forward to an eventual negotiated settlement of the internal conflict; to improve the situation on human rights and humanitarian issues; and to end collusion and impunity for those who violate human rights.

(30 July 2003: Available at www.fco.gov.uk/speeches)

5/5

In reply to a written question the Minister for Trade wrote:

The Indonesian Government are within their territorial rights to deploy Indonesian troops and police throughout their country to counter any aggressive external and internal threats. However, we have stressed to the Indonesian Government that any action undertaken in respect to their territorial rights must respect human rights and be in accordance with international law.

(HC Deb 9 September 2003 Vol. 410 c323W)

Part Five: I. A.6. *Subjects of international law—states—status and powers—state immunity (see Part Seven: IV.A. below)*

(See also **7/1**)

5/6

During a Security Council Meeting, the Foreign Secretary said:

[T]he tribunals for the former Yugoslavia and Rwanda have broken new ground in international law. They have shown that no one—no head of Government or State—is above the law.

(UN Doc. S/PV.4833, 24 September 2003)

Part Five: I. B.1. *Subjects of international law—states—recognition of states*

5/7

During a debate in the House of Lords on Chechnya, the Minister of State for Trade made the following statement:

We have made it clear that we recognise the territorial integrity of the Russian Federation and the right of the Russian Government to defend their citizens from terrorism.

(HL Deb 13 March 2003 Vol. 645 c1476)

5/8

In response to a written question the Minister for Europe wrote:

As the international community, apart from Turkey, does not recognise the "Turkish Republic of Northern Cyprus", there is no applicable extradition agreement and therefore no legal basis for the British authorities to seek the extradition of British citizens from the north of Cyprus.

(HC Deb 10 July 2003 Vol. 408 c981W)

5/9

In a written answer, the Secretary of State, FCO, wrote:

The UK recognises States, not Governments. We do not recognise "the Puntland State of Somalia".

(HC Deb 1 April 2003 Vol. 402 c654W)

Part Five: I. B.2. *Subjects of international law—states—recognition of governments*

5/10

Her Majesty's Government was asked the following oral question:

My Lords, why does the United Kingdom have a history of recognising foreign governments which manifestly have adopted power by bypassing acceptable election processes?

A Government representative responded:

My Lords, it is a long-standing convention that we recognise states not governments.

(HL Deb 10 November 2003 Vol. 654 c1086)

5/11

In reply to a written question the Minister for Trade said:

President Karzai and the Afghan Transitional Administration (ATA) are the legitimate Government of Afghanistan, following President Karzai's election by the Emergency Loya Jirga in June 2002.

(HC Deb 4 November 2003 Vol. 412 c541W)

5/12

During a debate in the House of Commons, the Prime Minister made the following statements:

The precise nature of any Government for the whole of Iraq will have to be considered carefully at a later time. The Kurdish community in the north, because it has been protected by British and American pilots over the past 12 years, has achieved a remarkable degree of autonomy. It has achieved at least something of the beginnings of democracy. As a result of that, and as a result of the way that the area is governed free from Saddam, that community actually has a far better record on things such as the poverty of its people, the building of schools and hospitals, and the reduction of child mortality. We must ensure that we retain the gains that have been made by that community. However, as I say, the precise nature of the government of Iraq will be a matter for discussion at a later point.

...

Obviously, we have to be careful of being too specific on that—otherwise it renders somewhat nugatory the discussion that we will have in the UN about exactly what the form of government should be—but we can lay down certain principles very clearly. It should be as representative as possible; it should move Iraq along the road to democracy as much as possible, given the history and the circumstances; it should protect human rights; and it should protect Iraq's territorial integrity. At this stage, before we have discussions with the UN and other allies, I cannot be more specific than that, but I believe that most people in Iraq can see the basis of how Iraq could be governed differently, and they can do so not least because, in the northern part—protected, as I say, by British and American pilots—a different Iraq has already taken shape.

(HC Deb 24 March 2003 Vol. 402 c30–32)

5/13

In response to an oral question on when the Iraqi people would be able to have representative government, the Prime Minister said:

My hon. Friend, not for the first time, has put his finger on the real issue, which is not whether we get the UN endorsement—although I think that that is important and that there is agreement on it. What we should really be asking is, "What type of Government do we want to see?" He is right to say that the Government must be broadly representative, take account of the diversity of the country, respect human rights, and move Iraq along a path towards democracy. It is interesting that, when we look at the northern part of Iraq—which is protected, as I was saying on Monday, by British and American pilots policing the no-fly zone—we can see how the Iraqi people, given the chance, can opt for, and want, a better future. I have no doubt that a major part of our justification for military conflict is that we are now in the process of ridding Iraq of weapons of mass destruction to ensure that the Iraqi people are given better government for the future.

(HC Deb 26 March 2003 Vol. 402 c286)

5/14

During a House of Lords debate on Israel and Palestine the Minister of State, FCO, said:

[T]he fact remains that Yasser Arafat is the elected leader of his people and, while he is in that position, it is of course incumbent on all of us to deal with him as the elected leader of the Palestinian people.

(HL Deb 8 September 2003 Vol. 652 c51)

Part Five: I. B.6. *Subjects of international law—state—recognition—non-recognition and its effects*

5/15

During a debate in the House of Lords on Taiwan's application to join the World Health Organisation, Her Majesty's Government was asked:

How can it be right that entities such as the PLO, the Holy See and Liechtenstein all have access to the WHO, but Taiwan, which is a stable democracy of 23 million people and a valued trading partner of this country, is denied the same access?

The Under-Secretary of State, FCO, replied:

My Lords, my noble friend will be aware that the countries [sic.] that he mentioned have observer status to the World Health Organisation. We hope that Taiwan can submit an application that all World Health Organisation parties can accept. However, we should stress that we cannot offer a view on any possible application until it has been made and its full details are known and until we have an agreed EU common position. We have supported Taiwanese applications to international organisations in the past, such as to the WTO, which is a membership organisation not based on states. However, we could not support any application from Taiwan if statehood was a prerequisite.

The Under-Secretary of State further stated:

My Lords, the noble Lord will be aware that we do not recognise Taiwan. The majority of countries in the UN also do not recognise Taiwan. Therein lies the problem with respect to WHO membership.

(HL Deb 20 January 2003 Vol. 643 c431–432)

Part Five: I. E. *Subjects of international law—states—self-determination*

5/16

During a debate in the House of Lords, the Parliamentary Under-Secretary of State, FCO, made the following statements:

In relaunching the talks, the Government have made it absolutely clear that we will abide by the pledge given by Harold Wilson's government in 1969 that there would be no change in sovereignty without the consent of the people of Gibraltar. If we could reach agreement with Spain on a comprehensive settlement, the whole package would be put to the people of Gibraltar in a referendum and they would decide. We have made that absolutely clear. That is an assurance to the people of Gibraltar that Ministers, including my right honourable friend the Prime Minister, have made again and again. It is fully understood and accepted by the Chief Minister of Gibraltar, Peter Caruana, who confirmed in his New Year message this year that he believed,

"that this assurance is totally reliable".

...

I remind noble Lords that there were other principles too: that Gibraltar should have more internal self-government; that it should retain its British traditions, customs and way of life; that Gibraltarians should retain the right to British nationality; that Gibraltar should be free to retain its institutions; and that Gibraltar could choose to participate fully in the EU single market and other arrangements. It also set out some important "red lines" on the need for a permanent settlement and for current arrangements for the British military facilities to continue. Again, it made it clear that any agreement must be acceptable to the people of Gibraltar in a referendum. The Statement also made it clear that no agreement had actually been reached and that there would be no such agreement unless Spain met those "red lines" in full. There were therefore no proposals to put to the people of Gibraltar, and that remains the position.

(HL Deb 10 December 2002 Vol. 642 c213)

5/17

During a debate in the House of Commons, the Minister for Europe made the following statements:

Gibraltar is an overseas territory with considerable devolved powers of self-government. We do of course support the principle and the right of self-determination, but it must be exercised in accordance with the UN charter, and with other treaty obligations. In Gibraltar's case, as the hon. Gentleman knows, that includes the treaty of Utrecht.

...

The treaty of Utrecht remains valid under international law—pacta sunt servanda, to use the Latin phrase. That means that we obey international law.

(HC Deb 25 February 2003 Vol. 400 c107–109)

5/18

In reply to a written question on Western Sahara, the Parliamentary Under-Secretary of State, FCO, wrote:

The Secretary General (UNSG) reported to the United Nations Security Council on the situation concerning Western Sahara in advance of the United Nations Mission for the Referendum in Western Sahara (MINURSO) mandate renewal. His personal envoy (PE), James Baker has presented a proposal to the parties to the dispute for a political solution, as requested by Security Council Resolution 1429 of 30 July 2002. His proposals have not been published.

Our position remains that we fully support the UN process and the efforts of the UNSG and PE to find a political solution to this dispute that provides for self-determination of the people of Western Sahara (as UNSCR 1429 of 30 July 2002). We supported the extension of MINURSO's mandate until 31 March 2003 as requested by the UNSG to give the parties time to consider the latest proposals.

(HC Deb 24 February 2003 Vol. 400 c55W)

5/19

The Under-Secretary of State for Foreign Affairs made the following statement regarding the Overseas Territory Consultative Council:

The fifth annual Overseas Territories Consultative Council, held in London on 8–10 December, provided an opportunity to review, with representatives of the UK overseas territories, progress in implementing the commitments made in the 1999 White Paper, "Partnership for Progress and Prosperity: Britain and the overseas territories" (Cm 4264).

Several overseas territory representatives argued, in the context of constitutional reviews currently under way, for a greater devolution of responsibility and reduction in the powers of governors, in some cases amounting to full internal self-government and total abolition of the UK Government's reserved powers. Territory representatives also sought clarification of their rights of self-determination and free association under the terms of the United Nations General Assembly resolution 1541 of 1960.

I and my right hon. Friend the Secretary of State for Foreign and Commonwealth Affairs emphasised that the security and good governance of the overseas territories remains a key foreign policy objective for the UK Government, as indicated in the White Paper "UK International Priorities: A Strategy for the FCO" Cm 6052, published on 2 December. Territories have the right to seek independence, where this is an option, but, whilst the link with the United Kingdom remains, the UK Government will have to retain sufficient powers to protect its overall responsibility for ensuring good governance and compliance with international obligations and to minimise its contingent liabilities arising from its relationship with the territories. The UK Government consider it important to protect key values, particularly the independence of the judiciary, the political impartiality and integrity of the public service, and sound financial management in the territories. Governors have a key role to play in this.

(HC Deb 18 December 2003 Vol. 415 c151WS–152WS)

Part Five: II. A.1.(a). *Subjects of international law—international organizations—general—status and powers—personality*

5/20

During a debate in the House of Lords, the Minister of State made the following statements:

My Lords, the explicit grant of legal personality to the Union would have the advantage of clarity and simplicity. But if the European Union were to have its legal personality recognised in the European treaties, it could only be on the basis that the distinct arrangements for the common foreign and security policy and aspects of justice and home affairs were fully safeguarded, along with the existing arrangements for representation in international bodies.

. . .

The specific point under discussion is the grant of legal personality. At the moment, some legal personality is granted to the European Community under the treaties of the European Community, to which all 15 current members belong. The European Union, established under the Treaty of Maastricht, is different. We need to be clear that what we are talking about would not necessarily mean a huge extension of powers provided that the kinds of safeguard that I pinpointed in my initial Answer were negotiated. I believe that those are the areas where we ought to concentrate our negotiating strength.

...

Conferring a single personality on the Union would give it the capacity to act within the legal system distinctly from the states that are its members ... In practice that would mean that the EU would have the capacity to make treaties, to sue and be sued, and to become a member of international organisations to the extent that the rules of those international organisations allow. I hope that I have made clear the position which we would take on our own membership of some of the international organisations where we would want to preserve our position. We are currently making agreements through the European Union, certainly where there are competencies on issues such as trade, with a number of countries.

(HL Deb 20 March 2003 Vol. 646 c376–378)

5/21

During the same debate, the Minister of State was asked the following oral question:

My Lords, does the Minister agree that one of the great advantages of giving legal personality to the European Union is that it could then accede to the European Convention on Human Rights—which would mean that Eurocrats would be directly bound if they abused their powers and that there would be effective remedies for the citizens of this country before the Strasbourg court against the Eurocrats of the European Union? Is that not a great advantage referred to by the Select Committee?

In reply, the Minister said:

Yes, my Lords, I think that that is one of the points that ought to be considered. The ECJ would then extend its coverage into the EU and beyond the EC which it currently covers. I agree with the noble Lord that that would be one of the outcomes.

(HL Deb 20 March 2003 Vol. 646 c378)

5/22

During a meeting of the Sixth Committee on the 2003 Report of the International Law Commission, the United Kingdom representative made the following statement on the Responsibility of International Organizations:

The topic is at a very preliminary stage, and it might therefore be appropriate to offer some thoughts on how the Commission might best approach the subject.

The parallel articles on State Responsibility occupied the Commission for decades. Yet that was a topic dealing with the State, a clear and uniform concept in international law, and the Commission's work was able to draw on a very rich foundation of practice, case-law, learned writings (not least those of the successive Special Rapporteurs). Here we are in a very different situation. The present topic relates to a category of international persons—international organisations—which are infinitely varied in their functions and powers, in their status, rights and obligations, in their membership and in their relationships with members and with others. And above all it is an area where practice, case-law and writings in the public domain remain relatively sparse.

Given this background, I would suggest that the Commission might be well advised to stand back a little and take stock, before launching into a detailed and extensive drafting exercise. I think the Commission should make even greater efforts to gather and study such materials as exist across the whole field. In this regard, one must assume that such material as is available is largely to be found in the legal branches of the Secretariats of the United Nations, the Specialised Agencies, the IFIs and other organisations, global and regional, including for example the European Community. States too may have useful background, and academic input could be encouraged. It seems to me that only once this has been done, can the broad outline of the topic be seen, and the areas ripe for codification or further study be identified.

In saying this, I appreciate, of course, that the members of the Commission have already given thought to the matter, including in last year's Working Group. But more reflection and above all more materials are needed. It is not, in my view, going to be particularly illuminating simply to work through the articles on State responsibility and see what words need changing (though of course it is exaggerating to say that this is what the ILC would do). One exercise that might be helpful, however, by way of brain-storming, might be to run swiftly though all sections of the State responsibility articles and see the magnitude of the issues that arise for the present topic.

The Commission has asked States three specific questions (paragraph 27 of the Report), each arising out of the question of attribution of conduct. I have to be frank and say that it is not easy to respond as helpfully as one would wish, in a piecemeal fashion, to questions that are put somewhat out of context. Unlike most questions which the Commission put to us, we do not have the benefit of the Commission's initial thinking, or indeed know the real background to these questions. However, I shall do my best. Assuming that the concept of an "organ of an international organisation" is central, how does one determine what is an organ? Does it include any person or entity which has the status of organ in accordance with what are called the "rules of the organisation"? It may be that neither this term nor the definition in the 1986 Vienna Convention is appropriate in this context. There are, however, obvious differences between the internal law of the State and the rules of an organisation. For example, in the case of international organisations, there is not necessarily any body within the organisation with the ultimate power to change the rules or interpret them. What happens if there is a difference of opinion over whether an entity is an organ for the purpose of these Articles? Who will decide that question?

The Commission's third question illustrates just how difficult and sensitive such a question might be, and how difficult it may be to generalise. The term "peace-keeping forces" covers a wide range of different types of force, operating in different relationships with very different organisations. They may have widely differing mandates, powers and structures. And there is often a specific agreement between the contributing State and the organisation which sets out the basic relationships of the parties.

In conclusion, Mr Chairman, I shall turn briefly to the three draft Articles provisionally adopted so far. We see from Article 1 that the Commission intends to cover the responsibility of States for the conduct of international organisations in addition to the responsibility of organisations themselves. This was, of course, a matter left open under the Commission's work on State Responsibility. It is clearly an important topic, and its inclusion may or may not prove feasible at the same time as working on the responsibility of international organisations. It may prove to be a rather separate issue. On Article 2, we are not convinced that anything is to be gained by departing from the very simple definition of "international organisation" that was contained in previous codification exercises. Of course it was not a very illuminating definition but it has served its purpose, and we are not clear as to the benefits of the additional elements that have been proposed. Indeed, their inclusion might cast doubt on the scope of earlier Conventions and on the scope of the present draft Articles. We would encourage the Commission to consider this matter once again. Article 3, on the other hand, appears straightforward and uncontentious. But I fear that this may prove to be the last article that is so clear, straightforward and uncontentious. I trust therefore that this will not lead to a belief that the State Responsibility Articles as a whole can easily be adapted to this very different field.

(28 October 2003: www.ukun.org)

Part Five: II. A.1.(c). *Subjects of international law—international organizations—general—status and powers—powers, including treaty-making power*

5/23

During a Security Council meeting the representative of the United Kingdom, Sir Jeremy Greenstock, said:

In Chapter VI of the Charter, as in so many other parts, the founding fathers of the United Nations set out a flexible and quite far-sighted mechanism that brings together several components. The Council can act on its own initiative or on that of the Secretary-General or of others outside the Council. There are many tools at its disposal: commissions of enquiry; the Secretary-General's good offices; missions to places where conflicts are taking place or where conflicts are threatened. The Council can facilitate or moderate peace processes; it can facilitate or provide a framework for the arbitration of factual disputes or for conciliation mechanisms.

Do we use all those instruments to the full? I think our speakers have asked us that question. Ambassador Marker said it is essential that the international community give consideration to the more frequent use of the devices for the peaceful settlement of disputes, requiring not just a strengthening of those methods but a greater commitment on the part of the international community and the political will to do so. The words "political will" are coming up in our interventions.

Whatever the assessment, in fact the Council can do even more than is set out in the Charter as examples. I start with prevention. The Council needs to raise questions earlier about deteriorating situations. To do this objectively, it has to be provided with better access to early-warning information and conflict analysis. The Council needs to apply lessons learned from previous conflicts; to ensure that mandates are clear and realistic and that peacekeeping operations are sufficiently strong and robust; to address the root causes of the conflict; and to provide lasting and sustainable settlements.

(UN Doc. S/PV.4756, 13 May 2003)

Part Five: II. A.2.(a) *Subjects of international law—international organizations—general—participation of states and international organizations in international organizations and in their activities—admission*

(See also **5/15**)

5/24

During a debate in the House of Lords, the Parliamentary Under-Secretary of State, FCO, said:

In March of this year I attended the Commonwealth Heads of Government Meeting in Australia. One of its themes was continuity and renewal.... The change in the Commonwealth's membership criteria showed that it was not stuck by rigid rules but open to change that would benefit its members. The proposals for the Commonwealth Institute demonstrate that one of the association's key non-governmental organisations is reforming itself to meet the needs of the next generation of Commonwealth children. These examples serve to demonstrate the continuing vigour and relevance of the Commonwealth in this new century.

(HL Deb 11 October 2002 Vol. 639 c585–586)

Part Five: II. A.2.(c) *Subjects of international law—international organizations—general—participation of states and international organizations in international organizations and in their activities—obligations of membership*

5/25

During a debate in the House of Commons, the Parliamentary Under-Secretary of State, FCO, made the following statements:

There are ongoing discussions at the United Nations and between member states about a number of UN reform issues. Reform of the United Nations Charter requires approval by two thirds of the membership of the UN. Currently, agreement on that issue does not exist. Nevertheless, the UK supports reform of the Security Council to make it more representative of the modern world. In our view, that should include enlargement of both its permanent and non-permanent membership.

. . .

It is important to expand the permanent membership of the Security Council so that it properly represents the modern world. However, were that to be agreed and implemented, we have no plans to change the number of nations that currently have the veto.

. . .

I also agree that no one should view with glee what has happened to the UN recently. The UN is not perfect: on several occasions in the past 50 years, we have failed to reach consensus on crucial issues. Nevertheless, it is the only institution within which it is possible to create consensus among peaceful nations to enhance our security. I therefore believe that we should look forwards, not backwards.

(HC Deb 25 March 2003 Vol. 402 c149–151)

Part Five: II. A.2.(d) *Subjects of international law—international organizations—in general—participation of states and international organizations in international organizations and in their activities—representation of states and international organizations to international organizations, including privileges and immunities*

(See also **Part Five: II.A.1.(b)**, above and **II.A.4**, below)

5/26

During a House of Lords debate the Minister of State, FCO, said:

We support an enlarged Security Council, expanded to 24 seats, including an enlarged membership of both its permanent and non-permanent parts.

The United Kingdom has backed Germany, Japan and India in their bids to become permanent members of an enlarged Security Council, and we have said that countries from Latin America and Africa should choose two further permanent members.

(HL Deb 14 May 2003 Vol. 648 c288)

5/27

In reply to a written question the Minister for Europe wrote:

The European Union is not a member state of the United Nations and therefore not eligible for election to the UN Security Council.

(HC Deb 17 July 2003 Vol. 409 c587W)

5/28

In reply to a written question on the implications of the new EU treaty, the Under-Secretary of State, FCO, wrote:

The UK retains the right to speak in a national capacity as a permanent member of the Security Council. This is safeguarded in Art III-206.2, which states that

> "Member States which are members of the Security Council will, in the execution of their functions, defend the positions and the interests of the Union, without prejudice to their responsibilities under the provisions of the United Nations Charter".

The Government would not accept any proposal that meant giving up its permanent membership of the UN Security Council and the rights which go with that.

(HC Deb 20 October 2003 Vol. 412 c378W)

5/29

In reply to a written question the Minister of State, FCO, wrote:

Article III-206 of the draft Constitutional Treaty states "when the Union has defined a position on a subject which is on the United Nations Security Council agenda, those Member States which sit on the Security Council shall request that the Union Minister for Foreign Affairs be asked to present the Union's position". This allows for a continuation of the current practice, in line with the Security Council's Rules of Procedure, whereby the presidency can speak at open meetings of the Council. Under the new treaty, the European Foreign Minister, not the presidency, would represent the Union where non-members of the Council are permitted to speak and when the Union has defined a common position on the subject of the meeting. The UK, as a permanent member of the United Nations Security Council, would retain the right to speak in a national capacity.

(HL Deb 27 October 2003 Vol. 654 cWA2)

Part Five: II. A.3. *Subjects of international law—international organizations—general—legal effect of the acts of international organizations*

5/30

During a debate in the House of Lords, the Minister for Media and Heritage was asked the following oral question:

Following the decision of the European Court of Justice on 8th November that bilateral agreements on air traffic between individual member states and the United States are illegal, what action they plan to take to support the European Commission in future negotiations on behalf of the European Union to ensure equitable rights for European Union registered airlines to operate to and within the United States.

In reply, the Minister for Media and Heritage said:

My Lords, the court found the UK's agreement with the United States to be in conflict with Community law only in so far as it favours UK airlines compared with other carriers. We expect existing arrangements to remain in force until a way forward is decided between member states and the Commission. Giving the Commission a mandate for negotiations with the United States is one option for consideration. We will consider carefully where the balance of UK interest lies.

(HL Deb 25 November 2002 Vol. 641 c560)

5/31

In the same debate, the Minister for Media and Heritage said:

My Lords, the Government's position is that the United Kingdom will not agree any new bilaterals or amend existing bilaterals until the issue has been resolved between member states and the Commission.

...

My Lords, I believe that the Answer that I gave was very precise. We are not proposing to agree new bilaterals or to amend existing ones. That is not to say that the existing Bermuda II agreement is perfect in every respect; that is far from being the case. However, we will not make any further changes until the issues that are the subject of the Question have been resolved.

(HL Deb 25 November 2002 Vol. 641 c561)

Part Five: II. B.2. *Subjects of international law—international organizations—particular types of organization—regional organizations*

(See **15/27**)

Part Five: II. B.3. *Subjects of international law—international organizations—particular types of organization—organizations constituting integrated (e.g. economic) communities*

5/32

During a debate in the House of Commons on the Convention on the Future of Europe, the Secretary of State for Wales said:

As hon. Members will be aware, the first set of draft constitutional treaty articles generated quite a bit of heat. So they should, because they cover key issues that go to the heart of the Convention's work. They set out the kind of European Union that we are creating—its values and objectives—and they tell us a bit about its genesis. I welcome the clear setting out of the competences of the Union and of the member states although, like many, I do not think that we are there yet. We must make it absolutely clear that the power of the Union stems from the member states, and not the other way round. I welcome the Convention president's public acceptance that that point needs to be clearly stated. A Brussels superstate is not on—full stop, end of story. The EU is and will remain a union of sovereign states.

(HC Deb 20 March 2003 Vol. 401 c303WH)

5/33

In response to a written question, the Minister for Europe wrote:

The Government consider the proposal made by the Praesidium of the Convention on the Future of Europe that "the Union . . . shall administer certain common competences on a federal basis" to be misleading. It has therefore proposed that the words "on a federal basis" be replaced by "shall co-ordinate certain policies at a European level to achieve goals that they cannot achieve on their own". EU member states will discuss the convention's outcome in an Intergovernmental Conference (IGC) before taking final decisions on it by unanimity.

(HC Deb 6 May 2003 Vol. 404 c566W)

5/34

In response to a written question, the Minister for Europe wrote:

EU citizenship was established by the Treaty on European Union. The provisions governing Union citizenship are contained in Part Two of the Treaty establishing the European Community. It is expressly stated that the EU citizenship conferred upon persons holding the nationality of a member state shall "complement and not replace national citizenship". The draft Constitutional Treaty being debated by the Convention on the Future of Europe sets out similar provisions. The Government support this policy.

(HC Deb 6 May 2003 Vol. 404 c567W)

Part Five: IV. B. *Subjects of international law—international organizations—entities and groups other than states and international organizations—dependencies*

5/35

Her Majesty's Government was asked the following written question:

To . . . list the dates on which agreements have been reached with the United States authorities regarding the requirements for the construction of facilities on the British Indian Ocean Territories; and how many separate agreements have been made concerning *(a)* development of specific areas and *(b)* technical requirements.

In reply, the Under-Secretary of State, FCO, wrote:

The agreements that have been concluded with the US authorities relating to the construction of facilities in the British Indian Ocean Territory, including agreements concerning development of specific areas and technical requirements, are the following:

(a) The Exchange of Notes of 30 December 1966 (Cmnd. 3231);

(b) The Exchange of Notes of 24 October 1972 (Cmnd. 5160);

(c) The Exchange of Notes of 25 February 1976 (Cmnd. 6413)

In addition, at various times the UK and US Governments have recorded their understanding regarding the application of the above agreements.

In 2001, certain infrastructure upgrades to the existing US Navy Support Facility on Diego Garcia and its designation as a Bomber Forward Operating Location were agreed. Further infrastructure upgrades were also agreed in 2002.

(HC Deb 11 March 2003 Vol. 401 c165W)

5/36

In reply to a written question, the Minister of State, FCO, wrote:

The provisions of the World Trade Organisation do not apply to the British Overseas Territories, with the exception of Gibraltar, which is covered by the EC's membership to the extent that the EC Treaty applies to Gibraltar. Negotiations for the Free Trade Area of the Americas (FTAA) are at an early stage and it remains unclear what, if any, implications the FTAA might have for the Overseas Territories. We will keep this under close review.

(HL Deb 14 July 2003 Vol. 651 cWA70)

5/37

In reply to a written question the Foreign Office Minister wrote:

The British Government encourage Montserrat to play a full role in regional affairs, including through its membership of CARICOM and the Organisation of Eastern Caribbean States (OECS). The British Overseas Territories require prior British Government approval, in the form of an entrustment, before undertaking international commitments. We hope to work together with the Government of Montserrat and the CARICOM Secretariat to assess the implications of Montserrat's full participation in the CARICOM single market and economy (CSME) and the Caribbean Court of Justice (CCJ) for Montserrat and the United Kingdom. Her Majesty's Government have already issued several entrustments to the Government of Montserrat to sign various protocols pertaining to CSME, but further entrustments will be required for full participation. The Government of Montserrat have not yet requested entrustments in relation to the CCJ.

(HL Deb 14 July 2003 Vol. 651 cWA71)

Part Five: IV. C. *Subjects of international law—Other subjects of international law and other entities or groups—special regimes*

5/38

During a debate in the House of Lords on UK Sovereign Bases in Cyprus, the Minister of State made the following statements:

My Lords, it has been agreed that following Cyprus's accession the sovereign based areas will remain outside the EU, with technical adjustments to ensure the continued smooth functioning of the relationship between Cyprus and the SBAs to ensure that Cypriots who live and work in the SBAs benefit from Cyprus's EU membership.

[W]e expect the detail of the arrangements to take the form of a protocol which will be part of the terms of Cyprus's accession. The accession treaty is due to be signed on 16th April in a Bill introduced to enable its ratification by the United Kingdom.

. . .

My Lords, the UK will, as now, exercise controls at the external borders of the SBAs. There will continue to be no controls on the land boundary with the Republic of Cyprus. The situation between Gibraltar and Cyprus is not analogous. The sovereign based areas are completely different from those in Gibraltar. Through our undertaking of the 1960 Treaty of Establishment, the UK is committed not to allow economic development within the SBA.

. . .

My Lords, anyone who requires a visa to enter the Republic of Cyprus will also be required to hold a valid Republic of Cyprus visa in order to enter the SBAs through any external border. The question concerning whether any such individuals would be the responsibility of the United Kingdom or the Republic of Cyprus is a matter on which I shall have to write to the noble Lord.

(HL Deb 14 January 2003 Vol. 643 c123–124)

5/39

In reply to a written question the Under-Secretary of State, FCO, wrote:

The Basic Law of the Hong Kong Special Administrative Region (SAR) contains provisions regarding the methods of selecting the Chief Executive of the SAR and the formation of the Legislative Council. The Basic Law (Annexes I and II) provides for possible changes to these methods from 2007 with the "ultimate aim" being the election of the Chief Executive and all members of the Legislative Council by universal suffrage.

The SAR Government has recently announced that it will start consulting the public about constitutional reform in early 2004. We welcome this. We have made it clear that we hope that the SAR Government will make early progress towards the Basic Law's ultimate aims of universal suffrage, at a pace in line with the wishes of the Hong Kong people.

(HC Deb 30 October 2003 Vol. 412 c362W)

Part Six: I. *The individual (including the corporation) in international law—nationality*

6/1

In reply to a written question the Under-Secretary of State, FCO, wrote:

By virtue of the British Overseas Territories Act 2002, most Chagossians, together with most of the inhabitants of the other Overseas Territories, became British citizens (as well as Overseas Territories citizens) on the commencement of the Act on 21 May 2002. They thereby acquired the right to enter and take up residence in the UK. As regards their entitlement to state services the Chagossians who have come to the UK have the same rights, and are treated in the same way, as other British citizens coming here from overseas.

The Chagossians were advised that, on arrival in the UK, they would not automatically be eligible for the whole range of state benefits and that they should therefore have sufficient funds at their disposal to support themselves until they had fulfilled the required habitual residence test.

(HC Deb 3 November 2003 Vol. 412 c396W)

6/2

During a debate in the House of Lords on the Nationality, Immigration and Asylum Bill, the Parliamentary Under-Secretary of State, Home Office, said:

My Lords, the thinking behind Clause 12 as it stands is that the option to acquire British citizenship should be extended only to those British overseas citizens, British subjects and British protected persons who have no other nationality and have not previously given up another nationality and thus a right of abode elsewhere.

It is possible to give up another nationality either actively or passively. One can take the step of applying to renounce the other nationality, or one can passively let matters take their course, knowing that under the law of the country concerned inaction will result in automatic loss of the other nationality at some point. Clause 12 would exclude the option to acquire British citizenship for a person who had lost another nationality by either of these methods.

(HL Deb 31 October 2002 Vol. 640 c294)

6/3

Her Majesty's Government was asked the following written question:

Whether the explanation... for the Government's decision not to ratify the Fourth Protocol to the European Convention on Human Rights, namely that "Her Majesty's Government believes that Article 3(2) of the Protocol could conflict with the United Kingdom immigration and nationality legislation by giving British Dependent Territories Citizens, British Overseas Citizens, British Subjects and British Nationals Overseas a right of entry to the United Kingdom that they no longer possess", no longer applies given that the Nationality, Immigration and Asylum Act 2002 has given these categories of British citizens a right of entry into the United Kingdom.

The Minister of State, FCO, replied:

There is still conflict. The Immigration Act 1971 restricts the right of abode in the United Kingdom to British citizens and to a residual class of other Commonwealth citizens who had that right before 1983. The right to registration as a British citizen under Section 4B of the British Nationality Act 1981, as inserted by Section 12 of the Nationality, Immigration and Asylum Act 2002, is a conditional one. The individual must make an application to the Secretary of State and demonstrate that he possesses certain qualifications as specified in the Act. The requirements are that the applicant is either a British Overseas citizen, a British subject under the 1981 Act or a British protected person, and has no nationality or citizenship apart from the qualifying British status, and has not, since 4 July 2002, "renounced, voluntarily relinquished or lost through action or inaction any citizenship or nationality".

British Nationals (Overseas) are entirely outside the scope of the provision.

British overseas territories citizens—as British Dependent Territories citizens are now known—are also not covered by Section 4B. However, most of these were given British citizenship by the British Overseas Territories Act 2002.

I should also mention, for the sake of completeness, that certain other provisions of the protocol may be incompatible with our arrangements for issuing passports and with Armed Forces discipline.

(HL Deb 6 November 2003 Vol. 654 cWA135–WA136)

6/4

During a debate in the House of Lords, the Parliamentary Under-Secretary of State, Home Office, said:

My Lords, under the nationality legislation in force before 1983, British women were unable to transmit their citizenship to any children born abroad. Under the British Nationality Act 1981, they are now able to do so on equal terms with men. Anticipating this development, the then Home Secretary announced on 7th February 1979 that he would use his discretion under the British Nationality Act 1948 to confer citizenship by registration on any foreign-born children of women born in the United Kingdom, provided they were still minors on the date of application. The practice continued after the commencement of the 1981 Act in respect of the children of British women born before commencement, since the change I have described did not have retrospective effect.

However, the scope of the discretion to confer citizenship in this way continued to be limited by statute to those who were still under the age of 18 when they applied for it. Inevitably, some of those born to British women before 1983 remained ignorant of the option of registration, or learned of it too late to take advantage. Such people may now be excluded from the United Kingdom and thus from contact with their families here, because there is no specific provision in our immigration rules for their admission....

The Government's amendment would confer an entitlement to registration as a British citizen, exercisable by application, on any person born after 7th February 1961 and before 1st January 1983 who, but for gender discrimination in the previous legislation, would have acquired British citizenship automatically when the British Nationality Act 1981 came into force on the latter of those two dates. The provision would thus cover any person who, had he or she applied while still a minor, would have benefited from the policy on discretionary registration announced on 7th February 1979. By that I mean that if the person had been born on or before 7th February 1961 he would have been too old, by 7th February 1979, to be registered at the Secretary of State's discretion....

However, there must be a cut-off point. British women did not acquire the right to pass on their citizenship until 1983. One can only go so far towards righting the wrongs of history before the number of "what ifs" to be taken into account becomes unmanageable. Because of the way our amendment is drafted, the removal of the words "after 7th February 1961" would simply mean that the person would need to have been born on or after 1st January 1949 to benefit. That would no doubt appear entirely arbitrary to someone born to a British mother on 31st December 1948. As I have sought to explain, there is a certain logic behind our selection of 7th February 1961 as the cut-off point.

Our amendment also proposes—again, consistent with the Committee stage amendment of the noble Lord, Lord Avebury—that any person so registered would become a British citizen by descent. The aim would be to place the person in the same position, as regards transmissibility of his citizenship to a further generation born abroad, as he would have been in had British citizenship been acquired automatically on commencement of the 1981 Act.

(HL Deb 31 October 2002 Vol. 640 c295–296)

6/5

During a debate in the House of Lords, the Parliamentary Under-Secretary of State, Home Office, made the following statements:

My Lords, this country has a long tradition, shared with others such as France, Spain and the United States, of providing in its law for deprivation of citizenship as a sanction against acts of treason and subversion. Ever since the British Nationality and Status of Aliens Act 1914 our law has made provision for citizenship conferred by administrative grant to be withdrawn where the person concerned is found subsequently to have harmed, or posed a threat to, vital state interests.

In the current legislation, such actions are expressed in terms of disloyalty or disaffection towards the Crown, or as unlawful trade or communication with an enemy in time of war. The terminology may now seem a little dated, and the European Convention on Nationality sets out a better and more modern formulation.

The Government believe that this power should be retained. In our view, deprivation is a sanction which should be available as part of a potential raft of measures that can be taken against those who act in a way that is seriously prejudicial to our vital interests. We are not content to leave this entirely to the criminal law.

I wish to emphasise, however, that we regard deprivation of citizenship as a very serious step to be contemplated only in the most flagrant cases of deception or disloyalty. It would be reserved, as it has been in the past, for serious cases in which the individual's actions were totally incompatible with the holding of British nationality. An analysis of its use in this country throughout the period since the Second World War shows that it has been similarly regarded by both Conservative and Labour governments. Except in one respect, to which I shall return, this is not a new measure. Moreover, the powers themselves are not new—they have been in statute for some time—and, although they have been used sparingly, they have been used.

I wish to emphasise also that this action would be taken only where, as has been said, a person is a dual national and would not, therefore, be made stateless as a result of the deprivation.

The purpose—which I think is apparent to the House, in the strange times in which we find ourselves—is, first, to express public abhorrence at such treasonable conduct and to demonstrate that the disloyalty shown is incompatible with being regarded as a member of the British family. Examples might be where British citizens engage in espionage against the United Kingdom or fight for an enemy against British or allied forces.

Secondly, the purpose is to afford a higher level of protection to the public. Deprivation has, of necessity, to have practical consequences for the person concerned, such that he is made aware of the abhorrence with which his conduct is regarded and is prevented or deterred from engaging in similar conduct in the future.

Thus, removal of British citizenship will result in the inability of the person concerned to hold a British passport. Deprivation may also pave the way for removal from the UK. That is not an inevitable consequence but it is something which may flow from the removal of British citizenship and with it the right of abode in the United Kingdom. Therefore, as is clear, there are two potential sanctions that can flow from the deprivation of citizenship: loss of passport and deportation from the United Kingdom. Loss of British citizenship means that the person concerned becomes subject to immigration control and requires leave from the Secretary of State to remain in the United Kingdom.

We do not accept the argument that we should always keep the people concerned within our shores. In order to deprive a person of their British citizenship for seriously prejudicial conduct they must have another nationality. We see no reason why we should allow such persons to operate within the freedom provided by the United Kingdom when they have another citizenship or nationality to call upon. I shall come later to the points raised in debate. We are, of course, still subject to all our international obligations under the ECHR and 1951 United Nations Convention and we would respect those in reaching any decision about removal as distinct from deprivation.

We acknowledge that for most, if not all, actions that would give rise to liability to deprivation of citizenship, there is provision in the criminal law for the application of a particular sanction. However, this country has a tradition of providing in its law for deprivation of citizenship as an additional sanction against acts of treason and subversion, and has had that power for almost a century. We see no good reason for removing it. I also point out that it is not within the remit of the Secretary of State to bring criminal prosecutions for terrorist offences. We wish to retain the power of the Secretary of State to deprive regardless of what decision the Director of Public Prosecutions makes about the merits of a criminal prosecution. In some cases there will be a determination as to criminal liability before a decision to deprive is made. For example, under similar provisions in the British Nationality Act 1948 Klaus Fuchs and Nicholas Prager were both deprived of their citizenship after they had been convicted of offences under the Official Secrets Act.

...

I shall not go into the detail of extraterritoriality, which is a complex issue. It is certainly clear that in some cases we could not extradite for an act of treason committed abroad as there is no extradition agreement with some countries. Therefore, we would not be able to bring those people home and make them feel the weight of the criminal law. The law on extraterritoriality is itself complex. It is not in our view totally clear that in all cases an extraterritorial act of treason could be prosecuted in this country even were we in a position to be able to extradite.

...

For those reasons I say in conclusion that it is not a new power. It seeks to treat all British citizens equally. It will be used with considerable circumspection, as has been the case in the past. There is a very extensive right of challenge. But we do not believe in these times that it would be healthy to give a signal to British citizens of whatever type that under no circumstances in practice would there be this sanction which has been with us for nearly a century.

(HL Deb 9 October 2002 Vol. 639 c280–283)

6/6

Further in the same debate, the same Minister made the following statement:

The amendments which we now propose will provide British overseas citizens, British subjects and British protected persons having no other nationality, with an entitlement to acquire, on application, and subject to some further requirements—which I shall presently explain—British citizenship.

In doing so, they would also acquire automatically a right of abode here. In other words, they would no longer be subject to United Kingdom immigration controls, but could come and go at will subject to the usual requirements for proof of right of entry on arrival. They would additionally, as EU citizens under the Treaty of Rome, acquire the right of free movement under the treaty.

The requirements for acquisition of British citizenship under the new clause are as follows. First, the applicant must be a British overseas citizen, a British subject or a British protected person. Secondly, the applicant must have no other nationality or citizenship on the date of application. Thirdly, the applicant should not previously have given up an alternative nationality or citizenship, whether through action or inaction on his part.

The latter requirement would exclude those who had lost another nationality through failure to take the steps prescribed by the law of that country for its retention beyond a certain date, as well as those who had lost another nationality as a result of some positive act on their part—such as the making of a declaration of renunciation. Such countries are tolerant of dual nationality in minors but require that on attaining the age of majority, the person must not only renounce their citizenship but also make a declaration of intention as to future residence, and/or take an oath of allegiance.

Therefore, we do not consider it appropriate to extend an entitlement to British citizenship to those who, by their actions or inaction, have given up another nationality, and one assumes the right to reside permanently in the country of that nationality.

The Secretary of State must be satisfied that the applicant has no other nationality or citizenship and has not given up another nationality or citizenship. Our experience in implementing the British Nationality (Hong Kong) Act 1990 suggests that there is endless scope for argument about that. Therefore, the intention is that in most cases the applicant will be required to produce a statement from both the authorities of the country of his birth and those of the countries in which his parents were born, if different, confirming the lack of an alternative nationality or citizenship, and the reasons for any historical loss of such citizenship.

The amendment proposes that those registered as British citizens, under the new provision would be British citizens "by descent" for the purposes of the British Nationality Act 1981. As such, they would be subject to the restrictions imposed by that Act on the ability of British citizens "by descent" to transmit their citizenship to a further generation born outside the United Kingdom. That would be consistent with their present position whereby British overseas citizenship and the status of British subject and the British protected person are usually non-transmissible.

Any children born in the United Kingdom following their parents' registration as British citizens would, of course, acquire British citizenship automatically.

(HL Deb 9 October 2002 Vol. 639 c286–287)

6/7

In reply to a written question, the Under-Secretary of State, FCO, wrote:

British citizens have the right of abode in the United Kingdom, and there is therefore no need for them to be categorised according to their skills. British passport-holders who have other categories of British nationality may enter the UK as visitors, but would need to seek prior entry clearance before coming to the UK for any other reason.

(HC Deb 24 February 2003 Vol. 400 c56W)

6/8

In reply to an oral question, a representative of Her Majesty's Government said:

My Lords, British passports are issued to persons who hold British nationality as defined by the British Nationality Act 1981. A person born in Zimbabwe before 1st January 1983 will be a British citizen if his or her father was born in the United Kingdom.

(HL Deb 5 June 2003 Vol. 648 c1487)

Part Six: II. *The individual (including the corporation) in international law—diplomatic and consular protection*

(See also **Part Thirteen** below)

6/9

The Foreign Secretary made the following written statement with regard to nationals detained overseas:

The welfare of British nationals in foreign prisons is one of the key concerns of consular staff. Our staff seek to ensure that prisoners' rights are respected in accordance with international standards. This includes ensuring that they have access to legal representation and that their welfare needs are met during their detention.

(HC Deb 14 July 2003 Vol. 409 c9WS)

6/10

In reply to a written question, the Parliamentary Under-Secretary of State, FCO, wrote:

There are five UK nationals who have contacted the FCO because they are experiencing difficulties in getting access to their children in other EU nations, following divorce settlements in the UK which entitled them to regular access. Two of these cases are in Germany, two are in France and one case is in Finland.

. . .

All EU nations are signatories to the Hague Convention on International Child Abduction, which the Lord Chancellor's Department (LCD) leads on. If a parent contacts us for advice on a child abduction case in a Hague Convention country we refer them to LCD. We can also offer practical help and support through our Posts overseas, such as providing lists of English speaking lawyers, attending court hearings etc.

(HC Deb 23 January 2003 Vol. 698 c465W–466W)

6/11

In reply to an oral question the Under-Secretary of State, FCO, said:

The hon. Gentleman asked whether, as a diplomat, Mr. Soleimanpour should have been immune from detention. The short answer is that he is not accredited as a diplomat here. He is a student at Durham university, and as such he enjoys no immunity in this country. The extradition process is currently a matter for the judicial authorities and I am sure that he will understand that the Government cannot interfere with that. It is therefore a matter of regret that some in Iran have consistently misrepresented the nature of the case and the role of the British Government.

(HC Deb 17 September 2003 Vol. 410 c301WH)

(See also **6/31** below)

6/12

In reply to a written question, the Under-Secretary of State, FCO, wrote:

Reverend Damanik has been charged with firearms offences which need to be investigated thoroughly and fully. It is essential that the legal process take its full course and the Indonesian courts hear all the evidence. Under international law we are prohibited from intervening in individual cases before the courts in another sovereign country. However, we continue to stress to the Indonesian Government the importance of a fair and transparent judicial system, and of applying the law in an even-handed way to all who break it. We have also offered human rights training for a number of Indonesian Supreme Court Judges. The Indonesians welcomed this training, and are keen for it to go ahead.

(HC Deb 24 February 2003 Vol. 400 c249W–250W)

6/13

In response to a written question, the Parliamentary Under-Secretary of State, FCO, wrote:

British officials paid a fourth visit to Guantanamo Bay between 11 and 15 November. The purpose of the visit was to ask questions relevant to national security, to check on the welfare of the seven British detainees last seen in May and to establish the identity and nationality of two further detainees believed to have British nationality. As a result of these inquiries, one was identified as British. The other detainee did not have British nationality.

The officials were from the Foreign and Commonwealth Office and the Security Service.

The FCO official met the detainees individually, US officials were able to observe the interviews. The official saw no visible signs of mistreatment. Some detainees reported minor medical problems and the official subsequently raised a number of these with the camp authorities.

The official passed to the camp authorities some personal letters for some of the detainees and was able to give oral messages to others. We have passed on to the families oral messages which were received and have briefed them on details of the detainees' circumstances. For reasons of privacy these details are not disclosed in this Answer. Detainees continue to be able to send and receive letters through the camp authorities and through the ICRC, although there is some concern about delays.

All the detainees continue to be housed in accommodation which includes individual sleeping, washing and toilet facilities. They continue to be able to practise their religion freely, to take exercise and to have access to reading material.

The visiting officials found the US camp authorities to be open and co-operative.

(HL Deb 16 December 2002 Vol. 642 cWA63–WA64)

6/14

In reply to a written question, the Under-Secretary of State, FCO, wrote:

As Guantanamo Bay is outside a recognised consular district, the US does not consider that we are entitled to formal consular access there. However, British officials have visited on four occasions to check on the welfare of the British nationals and ask questions relating to National Security. We were the first country to visit its nationals.

We understand that the International Committee of the Red Cross no longer maintain a permanent presence at Guantanamo Bay, however, they visit there approximately every six months for an extended period of up to three months[.] [T]he committee has confidential access to the detainees there. We understand that it can raise issues of concern, if necessary, with the camp authorities.

(HC Deb 24 March 2003 Vol. 402 c70W)

6/15

In reply to a written question the Solicitor-General wrote:

The Attorney-General has been involved in discussions within Government about the position of UK nationals detained in Guantanamo Bay. He has also raised the matter with those responsible in the United States Administration, to express the Government's profound concern that if the UK detainees are to be tried they should have a fair trial with all proper safeguards, and to make plain the Government's opposition to the imposition of the death penalty.

(HC Deb 10 July 2003 Vol. 408 c959W)

6/16

In reply to an oral question the Solicitor-General said:

[T]he Attorney-General has been holding discussions with the US authorities and has been seeking undertakings that if UK citizens are put on trial in the US they will have a fair trial. We have made it clear that if the Attorney-General is not satisfied that those citizens would receive a fair trial under the United States' procedures they will be returned to the UK. The hon. Gentleman can be satisfied that either they will have a fair trial or they will be returned to the UK.

(HC Deb 30 October 2003 Vol. 412 c434)

6/17

Her Majesty's Government was asked the following written question:

To ask the Secretary of State for Foreign and Commonwealth Affairs what *(a)* explanation he has requested and *(b)* assessment he has made of Ahmed Omar Saeed Sheikh being held in custody for a week by Pakistan Security Services (ISI) before the civilian authorities were notified of his arrest; and if he will make a statement.

In reply, a Government representative wrote:

The British High Commission in Islamabad and the Deputy High Commission in Karachi asked for information on the detention of Mr. Sheikh on 13 February, but did not specifically ask about the delay in notifying the civil authorities. We are investigating the case further. If Mr. Sheikh is a dual UK/Pakistani national, Pakistani authorities are not obliged to give us consular access or information.

(HC Deb 5 March 2002 Vol. 381 c202W)

6/18

In reply to a written question on British detainees held in Saudi Arabia, the Under-Secretary of State, FCO, wrote:

My right hon. Friend, the Foreign Secretary—and Ministerial colleagues—have raised the cases of the British men [Sandy Mitchell, Les Walker, James Lee and James Cottel] detained in Saudi Arabia at the highest levels with the Saudi authorities. We remain deeply concerned about these cases. The men's welfare is our paramount concern. We continue to work hard to resolve the cases. We are in close contact with the Saudi authorities and the men's lawyers.

Saudi Arabia is a signatory to a number of international human rights conventions including the Geneva Convention on Human Rights; and the Convention Against Torture. HMG raises human rights issues regularly at all levels with the Saudi government, both bilaterally and with our EU partners.

(HC Deb 24 February 2003 Vol. 400 c250W)

6/19

In reply to a written question the Under-Secretary of State, FCO, wrote:

Kenny Richey became a dual UK/US national with effect from 30 April 2003. Under international law we have no right to make formal demands on behalf of a dual national in the country of their other nationality. However, in cases of the death penalty, as a matter of principle, we will make representations in all cases at the appropriate time.

We are in touch with Mr. Richey's lawyers both in the USA and the UK, as well as Ohio state officials. Our Acting Consul General in Chicago attended Mr. Richey's Court of Appeals hearing earlier this year. We will continue to monitor his case closely to determine what representations could be made on his behalf, and we will do all we properly can to try to prevent his execution.

(HC Deb 5 November 2003 Vol. 412 c661W–662W)

6/20

In reply to a written question the Minister of State, FCO, wrote:

The British High Commission in Harare will provide assistance to any British national requesting it. The German and Dutch Governments have ratified a bilateral investment protection agreement with the Government of Zimbabwe. This gives them an additional basis on which to discuss issues on behalf of their nationals. The UK and Zimbabwe signed such an agreement in 1995, but this was not ratified by either side.

(HL Deb 6 November 2003 Vol. 654 cWA136–WA137)

Part Six: IV. *The individual (including the corporation) in international law—members of minorities*

6/21

In reply to a written question the Secretary of State for International Development wrote:

There is no universally agreed definition of the criteria for classifying certain groups as indigenous people. The Government does not have its own hard and fast definition. We recognise that indigenous people are often particularly poor and vulnerable, and encourage governments to consult carefully with them about their needs and interests. We have discussed the situation of San communities in Botswana at ministerial level on several recent occasions.

(HC Deb 8 September 2003 Vol. 410 c81W)

Part Six: V. *The individual (including the corporation) in international law—stateless persons*

6/22

Her Majesty's Government was asked the following written question:

[W]hether the non-citizens in Estonia and Latvia who hold special passports will be allowed to travel to the UK without visas for *(a)* recreation and *(b)* work following Estonia's accession to the EU.

In a reply, the Under-Secretary of State, FCO, wrote:

The UK requires non-citizens in Estonia and Latvia who hold special passports, in common with other stateless persons, to obtain a visa before travelling to the UK for any purpose. At present there are no plans to change this requirement after Estonia and Latvia join the EU. We are continuing to support the Estonian and Latvian Governments in their moves to encourage social integration and the take-up of citizenship.

(HC Deb 28 February 2003 Vol. 400 c757W)

Part Six: VI. *The individual (including the corporation) in international law—refugees*

6/23

In reply to a written question, the Parliamentary Under-Secretary of State, FCO, wrote:

A tripartite agreement by the Government, the Transitional Islamic State of Afghanistan and the United Nations High Commissioner for Refugees (UNHCR) was signed on Saturday 12 October 2002 in Kabul following the successful conclusion of negotiations. The agreement provides for return to Afghanistan in a managed and phased manner of those who have been established to have no protection needs. The United Kingdom is fully committed to the reconstruction of Afghanistan. As part of this it is important that return to Afghanistan is sustainable, and the agreement commits the United Kingdom Government to providing support to those returning, in Afghanistan, to ensure they are able to re-establish themselves in their homeland.

(HL Deb 17 October 2002 Vol. 639 cWA70)

6/24

During a debate in the House of Lords, the Parliamentary Under-Secretary of State, Home Office, made the following statement:

[E]xisting legislation prevents immigration rules being made in breach of the refugee convention. Similarly, the Human Rights Act prevents those rules being in breach of ECHR, since Section 6 would make the setting of rules which were incompatible with the convention rights an unlawful act.

The noble Earl reflected that this was a probing amendment, particularly concerned with situations where traumatised people had, for example, suffered torture in the past and might be removed from the United Kingdom should the general conditions in their country of origin improve.

On the first case where someone has refugee status and has been granted indefinite leave to remain, there are only limited circumstances where they can be removed under immigration powers. I do not think that they particularly relate to these sets of circumstances. Therefore, as the noble Earl implied, it is a question that focuses on a situation where someone has not been given refugee status under the 1951 convention, but has been given humanitarian protection and therefore exceptional leave to remain, which is, as the Committee knows, by definition for limited periods which can be removed.

It is possible that such leave might not be renewed when it has expired, as has been referred to in general terms. Whether or not it was renewed on the specific types of examples would, in the typical words, depend on the individual merits of the case. Where a person has suffered badly in a particular country, that would not of itself mean that he continues to be a refugee, but it would be a factor that would be taken into account when deciding whether it would be appropriate to grant further leave to remain. So much is obvious and what the noble Earl, Lord Russell, would expect, but it would be a factor for consideration. However, perhaps he wants to press me further than that. I cannot give a categorical assurance that in all circumstances and all types of cases people would never be removed. On reflection, I cannot go that far—which does not mean that I will not be able to go further.

What I can say is that if people were at the end of their period of leave, it would be open to them to make the case in their application for further leave and to bring to the department's attention the history of their trauma and any relevant medical evidence that pointed to it. Without being categoric, that would automatically protect them; I suspect that that would be given most serious consideration. One would have to be aware of the convention's provisions and the protections that it implies and have good reason not to be seen to be flying in its face.

(HL Deb 17 October 2002 Vol. 639 c1050–1051)

6/25

In reply to a written question, the Minister of State, FCO, wrote:

The UK has played a prominent role in international efforts to press the Russian Government to halt the closure of internally displaced persons camps in the

North Caucasus. Bilaterally, we have informed the Russian Government that the suspension of food, water and energy supplies to the camps constituted, in our view, a forced closure and reminded Russia of her obligations under the 1951 UN Convention on Refugees. The UK has also initiated and helped draft a number of EU demarches, calling for the closure of the camps to be stopped. We were therefore encouraged by President Putin's statement last month that the closures should be halted. However, we will continue to monitor the situation closely and take further action if necessary.

(HC Deb 21 January 2003 Vol. 398 c224W)

Part Six: VII. A. *The individual (including the corporation) in international law—immigration and emigration, extradition, expulsion, asylum—immigration and emigration*

6/26

In reply to a written question the Home Office Minister wrote:

Following the European Court of Justice case of Surinder Singh [ed. *R* v *IAT ex p Home Secretary* ECJ C-370/90], which was delivered in 1992, the non-EEA family member of a British national, who has legally resided in another member state, may claim a right to enter and remain in the UK under EC law instead of the UK's Immigration Rules. In the European Court of Justice case of Akrich [ed. *Home Secretary* v *Akrich* ECJ C-109/01] the court was asked to determine whether a member state could refuse to apply the Surinder Singh judgment to a British citizen who had deliberately moved to another member state with the express intention of creating an initial right of residence in the UK for their third country national spouse.

The court found that third country national spouses of EU nationals can only benefit from EC law if they have legally resided in another EU state before they first came to the UK.

This court ruling supports the UK's view that third country nationals who are illegally in the UK, and marry British citizens, should not be able to use EC law to remain here. It will allow the UK to continue to be able to apply its national immigration legislation in such cases.

(HL Deb 16 October 2003 Vol. 653 cWA135)

6/27

In reply to a written question on Port Control, the Prime Minister wrote:

This Government introduced three formal juxtaposed frontier controls in France, to cover Eurostar services at Paris Gare du Nord, Lille Europe and Calais Frethun stations, in June 2001. These controls have had a dramatic impact on the number of inadequately documented arrivals at Waterloo and Ashford International stations. There had previously been a juxtaposed immigration control at the Eurotunnel site at Coquelles.

The establishment of juxtaposed controls in Calais and Dover is a priority and was agreed in principle by the Home Secretary and his French counterpart in July 2002. UK Immigration Officers have been working with their French counterparts in an advisory capacity at Calais since August 2002. We will sign a treaty soon to set the legal framework to provide for full immigration controls at Calais and subsequently at other channel ports. We will deploy immigration service resources on a targeted and flexible, intelligence led basis to ports other than Calais to counteract any displacement that may occur.

UK Immigration Officers operate in a similar capacity in Brussels. We are negotiating with the Belgian Government to introduce a formal juxtaposed immigration control at Gare du Midi in Brussels for Eurostar services to the UK.

(HC Deb 30 January 2003 Vol. 398 c1025W–1026W)

6/28

During a House of Lords debate on immigrants from EU acceding states the Parliamentary Under-Secretary of State, Home Office, said:

My Lords, under accession treaty terms, citizens of the new EU member states will have full free movement rights for all purposes apart from work from the date of their planned accession on 1st May 2004. The treaty allows current member states to restrict freedom to work for up to seven years from accession. On 10th December 2002, the Foreign Secretary announced that these citizens will gain the same full rights to work in the UK as existing EU citizens from accession. Denmark, Greece, Ireland, the Netherlands and Sweden have also extended free movement for workers on accession.

(HL Deb 20 January 2003 Vol. 643 c427)

6/29

During a debate in the House of Lords on immigration, the Parliamentary Under-Secretary of State, Home Office, said:

We must consider whether harmonisation, which has often tended to be the legislative goal of the European Union, gets to the heart of the problem or, in a sense, just carries on the tradition that, in some way, harmonisation is the solution...

That illustrates why in Britain we believe that there is a need for fresh thinking both on asylum and immigration policy in the European Union and globally. That is why we have not opted into Title IV of the Amsterdam treaty. We have not opted into Title IV because although it is clear that in some areas harmonisation is sensible, on looking at the elements that Title IV is concerned with they do not always fit with our national interest, our geography or our history. We have strong links with many parts of the world that are different from others. We examine on a case by case basis whether it makes sense to opt into a particular measure. If we had opted in blindly to all of them we would have encountered a whole range of consequential disadvantages.

For example, we are able to take a different approach, when appropriate, to Commonwealth visa applications. And we are able to take a different approach to legal routes for employment of students, which is beneficial. In essence, when we think that we should, and it makes sense to, co-operate with our European Union partners we should do so wholeheartedly, both in legislation and operations. When it does not make sense to co-operate, we should maintain a rational evidence-based approach to policy rather than a doctrinal one and not do so.

(HL Deb 7 March 2003 Vol. 645 c1051–1052)

6/30

In a written answer, the Secretary of State for the Home Department wrote:

As part of Her Majesty's forces, Gurkhas are exempt from immigration control while serving in the UK, and therefore, the 1971 Immigration Act does not apply to them. Accordingly, no leave can be conferred on a Gurkha soldier during their service here. The question of conferring indefinite leave to remain upon termination of service does not arise, as Gurkhas are discharged in Nepal in accordance with their terms and conditions of service.

(HC Deb 31 March 2003 Vol. 402 c579W)

Part Six: VII. B. *The individual (including the corporation) in international law—immigration and emigration, extradition, expulsion, asylum—extradition*

6/31

Her Majesty's Government was asked the following written question:

What were the reasons given to the Bow Street Magistrates' Court that led them to extend the date by which a decision must be reached as to the issue of an Order to Proceed in the matter of the Argentinean request for the extradition of Mr Hadi Soleimanpour.

The Minister of State, Home Office, replied:

The court's deadline for receipt of an Order to Proceed in Mr Soleimanpour's case was initially set as 23 October. Shortly before that date, the Home Office received a substantial amount of further material in support of the Argentinean extradition request. To enable that material to be carefully considered, the court acceded to an application under the Extradition Act 1989 for the Order to Proceed deadline to be extended to 13 November. It was decided on 11 November not to issue an order and to cancel the warrant for Mr Soleimanpour's provisional arrest.

(HL Deb 18 November 2003 Vol. 654 cWA278–WA279)

6/32

In the debate in the House of Commons on the Extradition Bill, the Parliamentary Under-Secretary of State for the Home Department said:

The first point that I want to put on record is that nobody has sought to defend the United Kingdom's present extradition system. That has not been a point of contention between us. It simply cannot be right that fugitives can frustrate the system by bringing appeal after appeal, raising the same point each time, with the result that their cases can take years to resolve. The case for reform is overwhelming.

I shall set out the safeguards in part 1. Anyone who is subject to a European arrest warrant will be arrested by a British law enforcement officer. That was always the case . . . as we have made it explicit in the Bill. They can no longer make spurious claims that foreign police officers could make such arrests.

Once a person has been arrested, he must be brought before a UK judge as soon as possible. At the initial hearing, the judge will check that the person is indeed the subject of the extradition warrant and decide whether to grant bail. For the first time in extradition cases, there will be a presumption in favour of bail.

The main extradition hearing, at which the judge will consider whether extradition should take place, will be held soon after the initial hearing. Extradition is barred if the double jeopardy rule applies and if there are no specialty arrangements in the requesting state, or if the extradition request has been made for the purpose of punishing a fugitive on the grounds of race, nationality, religion or political opinion. No country that retains the death penalty will be accepted under our part 1 arrangements.

The measures that apply to extradition will be those that apply in our justice system. If changes are made to the double jeopardy rule they will be reflected in our extradition arrangements. At present, the double jeopardy rule applies. If Parliament decides to amend it, that will have ramifications for extradition.

Extradition cannot take place if it would be unjust or oppressive by virtue of a fugitive's mental or physical condition. Most important, it cannot take place when it would breach a fugitive's rights under the European convention on human rights. The Bill provides an impressive package of measures and it seems to me that only a perverse definition of "draconian" could apply to them.

. . .

No one will be extradited for conduct that occurs in the UK that is not contrary to our law. I reiterate that, because people constantly allege that that is not true: nobody can be extradited for conduct that occurs in this country that is not contrary to British law. What is the great constitutional principle that holds that we should not extradite a person who breaks the law of another EU country just because we happen not to have an exact equivalent offence in UK law? We are talking about EU countries which are mature democracies and ECHR signatories.

If a person committed an offence in another EU country and was arrested there, we should not object to them being put on trial. . . . So why should the fact that such people manage to cross a border before being apprehended allow them to evade justice? Why should the UK be a sanctuary for those who have committed crimes in another EU member state? Of course, that cuts both ways.

[I]f people come to this country and commit one of those offences, we would expect to be able to put them on trial. We would certainly not accept the excuse that the conduct happened not to be an offence in their home country. Equally important, we would want to be able to extradite such people to stand trial if they had managed to get away and leave our country. The partial abolition of the dual criminality requirement will allow us to do exactly that.

. . .

Finally, I wish to say why the Government have decided to remove the dual criminality requirement for all list offences that attract a one-year penalty in the requesting state, rather than just for those that attract a three-year penalty—the minimum required under the framework decision.

The basic threshold for extradition has been set at 12 months imprisonment for more than 100 years, and no one has seriously suggested that we should change that. However, if it is accepted that 12 months is the threshold for extradition, it would not be sensible to set a different threshold for the application of the dual criminality rule. That would be a recipe for confusion. Moreover, if the Conservative party takes the view that dual criminality is an important and necessary safeguard to prevent injustice when dealing with requests from other EU countries, that safeguard should apply not only to those offences that attract penalties of one to three years, but to more serious offences where the person concerned could face a much longer prison sentence. It would be illogical to impose a dual criminality requirement at the lower end of the offence scale, but not at the upper end.

The plain fact is that the European arrest warrant is a worthwhile measure. It will enhance co-operation between European states. It offers very real advantages to the United Kingdom and law-abiding UK citizens. We will be able to bring back more speedily those accused of serious crimes in the UK. No longer will some of our European partners be able to avoid extraditing their own nationals. It is the only mechanism available to encourage countries such as Austria to be prepared to extradite their own nationals. They are not prepared to do so currently, which can detract from our ability to offer justice to the victims of crime in our country. No longer will those countries be able to refuse to extradite for fiscal offences. No longer will they be able to refuse to extradite where their statutes of limitation have expired. All of those real weaknesses in the current extradition arrangements have caused us real difficulties. Criminals have not been slow to exploit them. The introduction of the European arrest warrant will sweep away those loopholes.

(HC Deb 25 March 2003 Vol. 402 c243–246)

6/33

In reply to a written question the Home Office Minister wrote:

The Extradition Bill, currently before Parliament, is consistent with the assurances by guaranteeing that there will be no extradition where there is a possibility of the death penalty being carried out, and no extradition where it would breach the European Convention on Human Rights.

(HL Deb 8 September 2003 Vol. 652 cWA35)

6/34

In a written Ministerial Statement, the Secretary of State for the Home Office wrote:

I am today, together with US Attorney General John Ashcroft, signing a new bilateral extradition treaty between the United Kingdom and the United States of America.

The current UK-USA extradition treaty was agreed in 1972 and ratified in 1976 with supplementary provisions from 1986. It is outdated and can be significantly improved.

The new treaty reflects best modern practice in extradition. In particular, it provides that any crime attracting a maximum sentence of 12 months' imprisonment or more in both the requesting and the requested state is extraditable rather than containing a list of offences which are extraditable, as the present treaty does. The advantage of that is that it encompasses offences, such as computer related crime, which did not exist when the 1972 treaty was drawn up.

The new treaty brings the evidential rules for requests from the United States into line with those for European countries and simplifies the procedures for the authentication of documents. As with the existing treaty, the new treaty provides that in death penalty cases, extradition may be refused unless an assurance has been received that no death sentence will be carried out.

The new treaty also maintains the present position that political motivation cannot be used to block extradition in the case of terrorist or other violent crimes. The treaty stipulates that neither nationality nor statutes of limitations will be a bar to extradition. The treaty also provides the standard speciality protection against onward extradition or surrender, and we have confirmed our understanding that this covers surrender to the International Criminal Court.

Before the treaty can come into force it needs to be ratified by the United States Senate. It will be brought into force in the United Kingdom by Order in Council. Such an order will be made under the existing Extradition Act 1989 and will carry over when the Extradition Bill, which is currently before Parliament, comes into force. At that point the United States, like all of our extradition partners, will benefit from the new streamlined extradition procedures which the Bill seeks to put in place.

The United States is one of our key extradition partners and there is a significant volume of extradition business between the two countries. It is therefore important that our bilateral extradition treaty should be as effective as possible. I am pleased that it has been possible to reach agreement on the new treaty and that I have the opportunity in person to affirm our commitment to the closest possible co-operation in the fight against terrorism and other serious crime.

(HC Deb 31 March 2003 Vol. 402 c41WS–42WS)

6/35

In response to several written questions the Under-Secretary of State, Home Office, wrote:

The new extradition Treaty was signed by my right hon. Friend the Home Secretary, and United States Attorney General John Ashcroft in Washington on 31 March.

When it comes into force it will provide that extradition requests from the United States will, like those from Council of Europe countries, not have to be accompanied by "prima facie evidence".

In accordance with the United States constitution extradition requests to the United States will have to be accompanied by sufficient evidence to provide a reasonable basis to believe that the person sought committed the offence for which extradition is sought.

. . .

Under current arrangements, with the exception of those requests made by the UK's 43 partners under the Council of Europe's European Convention on Extradition 1957, ratified by the UK in 1991, all extradition requests to the UK have to be supported by "prima facie evidence". This must be evidence sufficient to warrant the trial of the arrested person if the extradition crime had taken place within the jurisdiction of the court of committal.

. . .

Since the United Kingdom ratified the European Convention on Extradition (ECE) in 1991, other countries which are also parties to the ECE, of whom there are now more than 40, have not had to submit "prima facie" evidence to accompany their extradition requests.

We do not believe that this has human rights implications but the Extradition Bill, which is currently before Parliament, makes it clear that we cannot extradite in any case where extradition would be incompatible with the Convention rights of the person whose extradition is sought.

. . .

The UK's extradition relations with the United States are currently governed by the 1976 bilateral treaty (amended in 1986). We cannot speak for our European Union partners, but all have bilateral treaties with the USA.

The European Union has no extradition relations with the USA at present. However, the European Union and the USA signed bilateral mutual legal assistance and extradition treaties on 25 June 2003. These will come into force in the UK, once the EU and US agree to put them into force and the UK withdraws its declaration that it will not be bound by the agreements until it has completed its constitutional procedures. This declaration means that any necessary legislation will need to be in place before the agreements can be applied to the UK. The EU decision to bring the agreements into force, like the decision to sign, is subject to unanimity.

The EU/US extradition agreement has no significant impact on UK/US extradition relations, but, for example, ensures that all other member states have extradition relations with the USA based on dual criminality and a penalty threshold, rather than a list of offences.

(HC Deb 8 July 2003 Vol. 408 c720W–721W)

6/36

Her Majesty's Government was asked the following written question:

Whether, pursuant to Articles 24(5) and 38 of the Treaty on European Union, there are any constitutional procedures required to be followed in the United Kingdom in order for the Extradition and Mutual Legal Assistance Agreements between the European Union and the United States to become binding in the United Kingdom; and, if so, what those constitutional procedures entail.

In reply the Home Office Minister wrote:

No ratification procedure is required for the agreements. The provisions in the Extradition Agreement are either contained or reflected within the Extradition Bill that is currently before Parliament, or within the UK–US bilateral extradition treaty, signed on 31 March 2003; or else they require administrative changes that will simplify and speed up the procedures before transmitting extradition documentation.

The provisions of most articles of the Mutual Legal Assistance Agreement are either already in place or reflect those in the Crime (International Co-operation) Bill that is also now before Parliament; or else can be provided for using secondary legislation under that Bill and earlier Acts of Parliament.

(HL Deb 8 September 2003 Vol. 652 cWA34)

Part Six: VII. D *The individual (including the corporation) in international law—immigration and emigration, extradition, expulsion, asylum—asylum*

6/37

During a debate in the House of Lords, the Parliamentary Under-Secretary of State, Home Office, said:

The Government's view is that a person who has a genuine reason for failing to claim asylum as soon as reasonably practicable will be able to explain what that reason was. There is clearly a duty on the Secretary of State to listen to that. Similarly, if the claimant is destitute, he will be able to show why that is the case. It is easier for an asylum seeker to tell us why he has made a late claim than for the Secretary of State to establish that. The information and the evidence is with the asylum claimant; it is not with the Secretary of State. Therefore, it is fair to expect claimants to put that evidence before the Secretary of State. They are in possession of the information of why they have not made the claim. Therefore, it is right that the burden of proof is on them.

. . .

As regards Article 11(1) of the International Covenant on Economic, Social and Cultural Rights, Article 11 does not set an absolute standard. It is perfectly consistent with Article 11(1) for a state to impose reasonable conditions on the receipt of support and to guarantee only a lower level of support where a person has failed to comply with the condition in question. It is therefore reasonable to require asylum seekers to make their asylum claims as soon as reasonably practicable and to make their receipt of full support conditional on that. If they fail to do so, support will still be available to comply with Article 3 of the European Convention on Human Rights, as well as support for families with children and those with special needs, irrespective of whether they apply late. All of that is fully consistent with Article 11(1).

. . .

If people claim to have a well-founded fear of persecution under the refugee convention, that should be one of the first things that they communicate to the authorities after they arrive in the United Kingdom. Their reason for coming here is to claim asylum, not to seek work or to visit friends. It is therefore perfectly reasonable to expect them to register a claim for asylum at the first reasonable opportunity.

(HL Deb 24 October 2002 Vol. 391 c1471–1472)

6/38

Further in the same debate, the Minister of State, Home Office, said:

There are two main issues to address. The first is the relationship between previous torture and the prospect of future torture or other forms of serious harm. The policy underpinning Clause 92 is that where an asylum or human rights claim can objectively be regarded as being clearly unfounded, it is reasonable and sensible to deny a person an in-country appeal right against the refusal of their claim. The clause does not go on to define what is a clearly unfounded claim although it does create a presumption that claims from residents of certain countries will be clearly unfounded. We think that it is better to leave the term without further definition as its general meaning is well understood by the courts. Indeed, just a week ago the House of Lords restated the position in its judgment in Thangarasa . . .

There will also be some cases where we do not consider that the torture or persecution will be repeated and, accordingly, we refuse the claim but where we do not think that the claim is clearly unfounded. In such cases certification under Clause 92 would, of course, not be appropriate. But we do not discount the possibility that in some cases a person who may have been tortured in the past would in the present day have a clearly unfounded claim. Because country situations can change substantially over a period of time, it is perfectly possible that someone who was tortured 15 years ago would today face absolutely no risk of torture or persecution in their home country.

The consideration of an asylum or human rights claim involves a forward-looking assessment of risk based on present-day country information and the experiences the applicant has faced in the past and may face in the future. One cannot underestimate that the evidence of past torture is an important part of this consideration, but the amendment would elevate it to a factor which trumps all others. That would distort the process of assessing the claim—a process which should be a rounded exercise taking account of all relevant factors.

The second issue might be expressed as the argument that the clearly unfounded process is too rapid to handle the claim of a victim of torture . . . and that even if it is objectively true that an applicant in those circumstances has a clearly unfounded claim, there is too great a risk of our coming to an inaccurate decision because there may be relevant facts which come to light only after the applicant has been removed. . . .

Secondly, the noble Lord asks what the process will involve. The possibility of past torture can be identified early on in Oakington in a number of ways. The applicant may mention it directly, although I fully accept the point made by the noble Lord, Lord Hylton, and by my noble friend Lord Clinton-Davis; namely, that people who have gone through the trauma, for example, of rape, which is plainly a form of torture, may be too traumatised to speak about their experience. However, that possibility may be picked up by the on-site medical team. As the noble Lord, Lord Avebury, knows, and as everyone else who is aware of what goes on in Oakington knows, there is an on-site medical team that is keen to investigate such cases.

There is also an on-site legal team that is available to advise applicants. That team, and the medical team, are in a position to seek to draw from applicants enough of the history of such experiences to establish whether or not there may be an issue that is worth investigating. If that is the case, then either the legal or the medical representative can contact the medical foundation—an organisation with which noble Lords are familiar. They are completely free to do so. A referral form can be sent to the medical foundation, which is expert in looking for precisely the sorts of experiences about which noble Lords are concerned. Once the representatives produce a copy of the referral form to the medical foundation, the applicant would be moved out of Oakington, or out of the Oakington-type place, to enable the medical foundation to carry out its examination. A decision on the claim would not be taken until after the medical foundation had completed its assessment.

If the medical foundation finds that there is evidence of past torture, it would normally mean that the claim was not one that merited certification as being "clearly unfounded". So the process in Oakington, or in the places analogous to Oakington, allows for medical or legal advisers to identify whether or not a claim should be referred to the medical foundation. Once that reference is made—there is absolutely no evidence to suggest that references to the medical foundation are being abused as a means of delay; indeed, it is a sensible use of the process—the applicant is taken out of the process which might lead to a clearly unfounded certificate, and the result of the medical foundation's approach is considered.

As I believe I made clear, if the medical foundation finds that there is evidence of past torture, that would normally lead to the applicant's claim being taken out of the route that could lead to a "clearly unfounded" finding. I cannot rule out some exceptions to that because circumstances may have changed so significantly in an individual's case since the torture occurred that there may clearly be no risk to the person if now returned. Plainly, those would be exceptional cases; for example, torture 15 years ago in a country that has since gone through a regime change.

I have outlined how the system works. That is my answer to the point made by the noble Lord, Lord Avebury—that the process does not allow long enough for such determination. He referred to the seven-to-10 day period. If the on-site experts consider that there might be something that could lead to the belief that there is some risk of torture, they have the power to refer the matter to the medical foundation; indeed, there is no restriction in that respect. We then await the medical foundation's conclusion.

. . .

The issue here is whether or not such claims are "clearly unfounded". If, after having investigated a particular applicant's claim, a very reputable body like the medical foundation finds that that applicant has suffered torture, whether physical, psychological, or sexual violence . . . that would normally be sufficient to create enough evidence to make it clear that the case could not be "clearly unfounded". That is the issue.

If a reputable medical expert says, "This is the position", it is like asking whether he then becomes part of the decision-making process. No, that is not the case; he becomes part of the material-gathering process that must be weighed and considered in the making of the decision. Once the medical foundation indicates that there has been torture, it is very unlikely that such a case could be determined as "clearly unfounded".

Caseworkers at Oakington and the analogous organisations have guidance available to them on dealing with potential torture cases, and training is also provided. A rolling programme of seminars from the medical foundation, the UNHCR and the Red Cross has been launched to equip caseworkers to deal fairly and sensitively with those applicants who have suffered torture or other forms of trauma. Those seminars are proving very successful.

If an applicant raises the issue of previous torture or if the trained caseworkers believe that there might be something that is worthy of investigation by the medical foundation, the procedures are in place to deal with that. Should a person not mention torture, should that not emerge during the course of the substantive interview and should the inquiries by the medical and legal experts in Oakington not produce any sign of it, the amendment would not bite because no evidence of torture would have been adduced.

(HL Deb 24 October 2002 Vol. 639 c1522–1525)

6/39

During a debate in the House of Lords, the Parliamentary Under-Secretary of State, Home Office, made the following statements:

My Lords, we expect that our current measures to tackle asylum will be effective. We are also working with UNHCR and others to make the international protection system work more effectively. Should the measures we are taking not work as expected we would not shrink from reviewing our relevant international obligations but we have no current plans to renegotiate our ECHR obligations.

. . .

We are meeting our current obligations under the Geneva Convention. We have the encouragement of a vigorous legal system were we in any doubt of that. We are also optimistic that we may be moving towards some progress in this respect.

. . .

My Lords, my noble friend, as so often, puts his finger on the point. I have signalled in the House before that the issue concerns not so much the letter of the legislation but how it is operated in practice. I have signalled that our concern about the 1951 convention is not in any sense related to its aims but rather to how it works in practice as those who probably most need refugee protection do not get it while many who clearly are using it as a route for economic migration clog up the system. Currently we are having positive discussions with UNHCR on these matters. I hope to be able to say more about that before long.

(HL Deb 17 March 2003 Vol. 646 c6–7)

6/40

During a debate in the House of Lords on the Nationality, Immigration and Asylum Bill, the Parliamentary Under-Secretary of State, Home Office, wrote:

As the noble and learned Lord remarked, the other point is that European Union citizens can live and work anywhere. They can also make an asylum application to any EU member state in which they happen to be. There is nothing to stop them doing that and there is nothing wrong in principle with doing so. The Spanish protocol to the Treaty of Amsterdam merely states that any decisions made by member states are to be based on a presumption that an asylum application is manifestly unfounded [ed. viz when an application could have been made in another EU member state]. That does not mean that it can be rejected out of hand or that it can be ignored. But it means that the burden of proof is on the applicant, and the member state still has responsibility to consider and assess the application fairly. It should be justiciable if it does not do so.

. . .

The noble and learned Lord raised the issue of a well-founded fear of persecution being conditional on an applicant's motivation—that is, the question of manufactured claims. We agree that each case must be considered on its merits.

The question is: will there be a well-founded fear of persecution or of serious harm if the person is returned? The fact that a claim of fear of persecution or of suffering serious harm was manufactured does not necessarily mean that such a fear cannot be well-founded. However, clearly it raises questions as to motivation, and those questions must be considered.

With regard to the question whether appeal rights in Dublin cases should be non-suspensive, the existing legislation in the UK, which the 2002 Bill will maintain, is that a Dublin removal is non-suspensive if the Secretary of State certifies that any human rights claim is manifestly unfounded. It is possible to seek permission for judicial review of such a certificate. The House of Lords, sitting in its judicial capacity, confirmed that judicial review of a certificate was an effective remedy.

. . .

A mechanism such as Dublin II effectively puts pressure on member states which allow entry to consider how to improve their entry procedures. They bear some of the consequences of entry in ways that perhaps otherwise they would not do. Many of the negotiations between member states in the JHA concern the attempt to recognise that we all experience each other's pressures and problems and the attempt to get a "fit" between the interests of those who allow people to enter and the consequences of that. Perhaps I am still not expressing that as clearly as I should, but that is at the heart of many of the negotiations.

To make a specific point on that issue, that is why the United Kingdom has been up-front in recognising that Dublin II potentially places great burdens on the countries that border entry points into the European Union. Therefore, we saw it as only right and fair that there should be some compensatory burden-sharing in relation to the cost and difficulties of policing those borders. We have made it clear in JHA and elsewhere that we consider it to be necessary and right to place the burden on those who enter the Union. I believe that the Commission shares our view on that, and it may be one key in trying to obtain subsequent agreement on the matter.

The other reason that Dublin II will potentially work is that, unlike Dublin I, it is justiciable. I would not want to imply that that automatically means that it will work. But, in other words, it is a legally enforceable agreement. Before it goes to the Luxembourg court there will be a mechanism between member states for considering disputes and arguments—that is what should happen at a common sense level—to see how, if someone is "mucking about" repeatedly, the process can be improved.

. . .

Article 9(i) defines the act as a persecution and includes non-state actors. As I implied earlier, we support the inclusion of that definition. I take the point about the qualification directive raised by the noble Lord, Lord Clinton-Davis. We are where we are at. We are pleased at the priority given to this issue by the current Danish presidency. A fair amount of progress has been made and we hope that soon it will be finalised.

. . .

I turn to alternatives to Dublin II put forward by the Refugee Council. In essence the worry is exactly as put. If asylum seekers could choose to which country to go to claim refugee status that would be a trafficker's choice or it might disadvantage those countries which have low unemployment, a liberalised job market, fairly strong ethnic minority populations and an English language, which in itself is certainly a pull factor.

...

I turn to the incorporation of ECHR into the agreement. All directives must be consistent with ECHR as it is bedded into EU treaties. We see no real need for individual directives to refer to it at every point in time. It sits on the table as a fundamental obligation from which we cannot or would not want to resile. I touched earlier on the scrutiny of negotiation processes. I would welcome an opportunity to discuss some of those important and complicated issues at some stage outside the Chamber.

(HL Deb 1 November 2002 Vol. 640 c446–449)

6/41

In a written answer, the Minister of State for the Home Office wrote:

The Government has been instrumental in working to agree minimum standards for asylum seekers in Europe as a first step towards a common European asylum system.

These measures include specific provision for the protection of child asylum seekers, including the allocation of responsibility to protect the interests of those asylum seeker children who arrive unaccompanied, as well as their appropriate accommodation.

There is also a duty as far as possible to help unaccompanied asylum seeker children find their families.

(HC Deb 7 March 2003 Vol. 400 c1302W)

6/42

During a debate in the House of Lords on Asylum Seekers, the Parliamentary Under-Secretary of State, Home Office, made the following statement:

My Lords, we have no current plans to withdraw from our international obligations relating to asylum or the ECHR. However, we should not be afraid to review relevant international obligations if current measures to tackle asylum are not effective. We have already introduced a power to deal with suspected terrorists. The United Kingdom has derogated from Article 5 of the ECHR, which allows us to detain foreign nationals who are suspected of international terrorism of the sort that resulted in the events of September 11th and who threaten national security but cannot be deported.

(HL Deb 12 February 2003 Vol. 644 c665)

6/43

In a written answer, the Minister of State, Home Office, wrote:

Section 55 of the Nationality, Immigration and Asylum Act 2002, which came into force on 8 January 2003, prevents the provision of support to asylum seekers unless the Secretary of State is satisfied that their asylum claim was made as soon as reasonably practicable after arrival in the United Kingdom. Exceptions include families with children and those who can show they would suffer treatment contrary to the European Convention on Human Rights (ECHR). Those with care needs continue to be supported by local authorities under the National Assistance Act 1948.

On 19 February, Mr Justice Collins gave judgment in six test cases. He found that the Section 55 decision-making process was flawed, largely on the grounds that there had initially been insufficient investigation of the circumstances in which entry to the United Kingdom was achieved, to give the claimant the opportunity to rebut a suggestion of incredibility and to set out fully the reasons for decisions. He also decided that there will normally be a real risk that to leave someone destitute will violate Articles 3 and 8.1 of the ECHR, and that inquiries should be made to try to establish whether any support is likely to exist. This effectively shifted the burden of proof to the Secretary of State, rather than the asylum applicant as Section 55 had originally intended.

The Home Secretary appealed against the decision of Mr Justice Collins and the Court of Appeal gave judgment on 18 March 2003. The Attorney General made it clear that the appeal was being made on the basis of the key legal principles, not on the basis of the six individual cases.

At the Court of Appeal, the appeal was dismissed, as expected, in relation to the six cases, [but] the judgment found in favour of the Government on several key issues of legal principle:

The court's decision makes it clear that the burden of showing an asylum claim was made as soon as reasonably practicable is on the asylum seeker, the ECHR does not require state support to be given automatically to all destitute asylum seekers who have failed to make their asylum claims when required to do so, and Section 55 is not incompatible with the ECHR in any respect.

The court found against the Government on procedural fairness and drew attention to a number of areas where they considered improvements could be made.

The Home Office has already changed the procedures for making Section 55 decisions to meet the court's main concerns.

The Government will not appeal to the House of Lords against the Court of Appeal decision.

The Court of Appeal judgment means that the Government can continue to operate Section 55 as Parliament intended. It gives renewed legal backing for the Government's policy to tackle abuse of the asylum system and send a clear message to those who are abusing the system that they will not be supported at public expense.

The key legal issues have been settled by the Court of Appeal and the Government can, therefore, uphold the robust and fair asylum support system for which Parliament legislated.

(HL Deb 28 April 2003 Vol. 647 cWA73–WA75)

6/44

In reply to a written question the Minister of State, Home Office, wrote:

The suspension of removals of failed asylum seekers to Zimbabwe announced in January 2002 was in response to concerns about the serious deterioration in the situation in Zimbabwe in the build up to the presidential election held in March that year. We did not regard it as unsafe to return failed asylum seekers to Zimbabwe, but in view of the rapidly changing conditions we considered that it would be appropriate not to enforce returns.

The Government's position is, as it has been since January 2002, that each asylum (and human rights) claim made by a Zimbabwean national will be considered on its individual merits in accordance with our obligations under the 1951 UN Refugee Convention and the European Convention on Human Rights (ECHR). Each application is considered against the background of the latest available country information including that obtained from and through the Foreign and Commonwealth Office.

[W]e do of course recognise that conditions in Zimbabwe are such that there are individuals who are able to demonstrate a need for international protection. Where they meet the definition of a refugee in the 1951 Convention, asylum is granted. There may also be individuals whose circumstances make them particularly vulnerable and who would engage our obligations under the ECHR. Where this is the case these individuals will be granted humanitarian protection or discretionary leave.

In the first six months of this year, we have granted asylum to 615 Zimbabweans and granted other forms of protection to over 20 others. These statistics show that we are giving protection to the significant number of people who are found to be in need of it.

If an application is refused, there will be a right of appeal to the independent appellate authorities against that decision. Should a claim be refused and any appeal be unsuccessful that means that, for that individual, return to Zimbabwe would be safe. That is why we consider it reasonable to expect an individual in that position to leave voluntarily.

Although it would be safe to return failed asylum seekers to Zimbabwe, our view at present is that in the wider context of the Government's position on Zimbabwe, it would be inappropriate forcibly to return them at this time.

The policy remains under continuous review.

(HL Deb 3 November 2003 Vol. 654 cWA71)

Part Six: VIII. *The individual (including the corporation) in international law—human rights and fundamental freedoms*

(See also **3/3** and **6/44**)

6/45

Her Majesty's Government was asked the following written question:

Whether they [Her Majesty's Government] have any plans to seek amendments to the United Nations Universal Declaration of Human Rights, the United Nations International Covenant on Civil and Political Rights, the United Nations Convention Against Torture and Other Cruel, Inhuman and Degrading Treatment or Punishment, the European Convention on Human Rights, or the European Convention for the Elimination of Torture and Inhuman or Degrading Treatment or Punishment so as to limit or abridge the prohibition against torture or inhuman or degrading treatment or punishment.

In reply, the Parliamentary Under-Secretary of State, FCO, wrote:

We have no current plans. However, if asylum measures introduced do not dramatically reduce the number of asylum applications, the UK Government have prepared to go further, including looking fundamentally at our obligations under the European Convention on Human Rights.

(HL Deb 17 March 2003 Vol. 646 cWA3)

6/46

During a meeting in the General Assembly the representative of the European Union said:

The Conference [ed. Fifth International Conference of New or Restored Democracies] also addressed the question of the many challenges to democracy, including poverty, international terrorism, transnational economic crime, HIV/AIDS and blatant disregard for human rights. It was agreed that while it is crucial to fight those threats effectively, that must be done without eroding human rights or resorting to repression. Democracy and the protection of human rights are inseparable. We cannot protect democracy while at the same time undermining human rights. It was also noted that building up democracy is a long and difficult process, and that it should not be allowed to compromise on issues such as human rights and fundamental freedoms. The participants recognised that even though democratic processes can benefit from external supports, a democratic system must have the support of the people concerned. Nonetheless, it was acknowledged that there is no universal recipe for democracy, as democracy can take different forms in different countries.

(UN Doc. A/58/PV.57, 5 November 2003)

6/47

During a meeting in the General Assembly the representative of the European Union said:

In that context, and in connection with today's celebration, the European Union would like to underline the role of national institutions for the promotion and protection of human rights. The European Union also reiterates the strength and continuing validity of the Paris Principles [ed. Principles relating to the status and functioning of national institutions for the protection and promotion of human rights, GA Resolution 48/34] as a framework to guide the work of those institutions while guaranteeing their independence. In particular, we note the significant increase in the number of national human rights institutions in every region of the world and their efforts to achieve full compliance with the Paris Principles. We also appreciate the fact that in recent years more and more people have come to know of the existence of those Principles. Such visibility enhances the work of national institutions and contributes to strengthening the effectiveness of all human rights.

...

Let me assure the General Assembly of the firm commitment of the European Union and its member States, acceding countries, candidate countries and potential candidates. We represent, here, a group of 33 countries and as such, a firm commitment to ensure respect for human rights. We expect other States to do likewise.

The obligation to respect human rights is unconditional. Human rights belong to each and every person, no matter what he or she may have done, no matter what crime they may have or are believed to have committed. The European Union believes that efforts to combat terrorist acts should respect human rights, fundamental freedoms and humanitarian law, and that the fight against terrorism should be carried out in accordance with international human rights law, as defined in the relevant instruments.

(UN Doc. A/58/PV.73, 10 December 2003)

6/48

In a written answer, the Parliamentary Under-Secretary of State, FCO, wrote:

The British Government opposes the death penalty in all circumstances, and makes clear its position to the US Government at every appropriate opportunity. We do this not only in terms of general policy, but also on specific cases. We have also joined EU partners on regular demarches over the last two years on specific cases at State and Federal level.

(HC Deb 14 April 2003 Vol. 403 c530W)

6/49

Her Majesty's Government was asked the following written question:

To ask the Secretary of State for Foreign and Commonwealth Affairs... what steps he is taking to secure the information necessary to determine if Mr. Atkinson's continued detention is of an arbitrary nature.

In reply, the Parliamentary Under-Secretary of State, FCO, wrote:

The UN Working Group on Arbitrary Detention concluded that Mr. Atkinson's continued detention stems from the application of Dubai law. Mr. Atkinson, his family and his lawyers have repeatedly been informed that the question of the interpretation of local law can only be addressed by his solicitors through local lawyers. Our embassy in Dubai offered Mr. Atkinson's lawyers a list of local lawyers in May last year.

(HC Deb 3 April 2003 Vol. 402 c827W)

6/50

Her Majesty's Government was asked the following written question:

To ask the Secretary of State for Foreign and Commonwealth Affairs... when the Consul-General was informed of Mr. Atkinson's injury; and if he will make a statement about the circumstances of the riot in which Mr. Atkinson sustained the injury.

In reply, the Parliamentary Under-Secretary of State, FCO, wrote:

Our consular staff visited Jumeirah Central Prison in Dubai on 12 August 2002, immediately upon learning of disturbances at the prison. During the visit, Mr. Atkinson told our consular staff that some prisoners, including himself, had been beaten during the disturbances at the prison on 30 July 2002, when, we understand, police were called to quell fighting among local prisoners.

(HC Deb 3 April 2003 Vol. 402 c828W)

6/51

During a debate in the House of Lords on the Anti-terrorism, Crime and Security Act 2001 (Continuance in force of Sections 21 to 23) Order 2003, the Parliamentary Under-Secretary of State, Home Office, said:

Before September 11th, the UK had already built up 30 years' experience of dealing with terrorism and terrorists. This meant that there were proven counter-terrorism measures and legislation in place. However, the September 11th attacks in New York, Washington and Pennsylvania were on an unprecedented scale and of a different nature to what we had so far faced. We needed to address that difference swiftly and effectively. We introduced the Anti-terrorism, Crime and Security Act 2001, including the Part 4 immigration and asylum powers.

...

The detention powers in Sections 21 to 23 of Part 4 of the Act were considered essential in the light of the particular public emergency facing the life of the nation, and proportionate to that threat. They address the very specific threat from suspected international terrorists present in the UK who are further suspected of involvement in terrorism of the sort which led to the events of September 11th. In short, it involves individuals who would not normally be permitted to remain in this country but who cannot be deported for legal or practical reasons.

...

Those measures required a derogation from Article 5 of the European Convention on Human Rights (ECHR). This was not something that was undertaken lightly, but we believed—and continue to believe—that, based on the mass of evidence available to the Government, there is a public emergency threatening the life of the nation within the meaning of Article 15 of ECHR and that the measures we have taken are strictly required by the exigencies of the situation and are proportionate.

...

The detention powers that we took under Part 4 of the ATCS Act, in response to the public emergency, closed a very specific loophole. There are present in the UK a number of foreign nationals who are suspected of being concerned in the commission, preparation or instigation of acts of international terrorism of the kind which resulted in events of 11th September 2001; being members of organisations or groups so concerned, or having links with members of such organisations or groups; and who are a threat to our national security.

...

Where it is possible to remove or deport from the UK a foreign national suspected of terrorism, we make every effort to do so. But removal is precluded for some of these foreign national suspected terrorists because of the important safeguard in Article 3 of the ECHR to prevent removal if they might face torture, inhuman or degrading treatment or punishment.

Of course if it is possible to prosecute we will do so, and that would always be the preferred course of action. But it is not always possible to prosecute.

The Government have to achieve a difficult balance between our international commitments and our duty to safeguard the security of this country. The Government have reviewed closely and regularly the need for the detention powers and ECHR Article 5(1) derogation, as well as the feasibility of other possible options. We concluded that there was no responsible or indeed effective alternative but to maintain powers to detain, and the ECHR derogation. That view was upheld in the Court of Appeal in October.

The Government have also reviewed closely the application of detention powers to foreign and not UK nationals. We believe they are entirely justified, for the following reasons. The threat comes predominantly, though not exclusively, from foreign nationals present in the UK who we are not able to remove. The preferred course of prosecution may not be possible because the evidence needed for successful prosecution may be unavailable or not usable. It would be deeply damaging if the UK was seen to be unable to take action and consequently as providing safe haven, weakening the international fight against terrorism. Finally, unlike UK nationals, who have the right to be in the UK, foreign nationals are ordinarily subject to removal if they represent a threat to national security.

The Court of Appeal upheld our position on the need for these powers in its judgment in October last year, and agreed that they were not discriminatory and comply with ECHR.

To date, 15 foreign nationals have been detained under Sections 21 to 23 of the Act. Of those, two have voluntarily left the UK. The other 13 remain in detention. The decisions to certify and detain these individuals were based on detailed and compelling intelligence and other material. That material will be examined by the SIAC, as provided under ATCS Act.

All those detained have had access to legal advice throughout the detention period and there is no limit on the number of legal visits that detainees may receive. Those detained have immediate right of appeal to the Special Immigration Appeals Commission against the certificate. All but one of the detainees have already exercised that right. The ATCS Act provides for the SIAC regularly to review certificates, and it may overturn them. Detainees also have the right to apply for bail to the commission at any time and several have done so. This is not internment. It is open to the detainees to leave the United Kingdom, and two have done so.

(HL Deb 11 March 2003 Vol. 401 c1291–1293)

6/52

In reply to a written question the Minister of State, Home Office, wrote:

Sixteen foreign nationals have so far been detained using powers in Part IV of the Anti-terrorism, Crime and Security (ATCS) Act 2001. Eight were detained in December 2001, one in February 2002, two in April 2002, one in October 2002, one in November 2002, two in January 2003 and one in October 2003. One further individual has been certified under Part IV of the ATCS Act in August 2003 but is detained under other powers.

Of the total detained, two have voluntarily left the United Kingdom. The other 14 remain in detention.

The Home Secretary's decisions to detain these individuals were made on the basis of detailed and compelling evidence. That evidence is being examined by the Special Immigration Appeals Commission as the individuals' appeals are heard, as provided for under the ATCS Act. The commission is equivalent to the High Court. It has the power to overturn his decisions.

Where terrorism is concerned, our paramount responsibility is to ensure public safety and national security. So long as the public emergency subsists, where a person is suspected of terrorism but cannot currently be removed and for whom a criminal prosecution is not an option, we believe that it is necessary and proportionate to provide for extended detention, pending removal.

(HL Deb 18 November 2003 Vol. 654 cWA279)

6/53

In a debate on the Official Report of the Grand Committee on the Crime (International Cooperation) Bill, the Under-Secretary of State for Home Affairs stated:

The Human Rights Act established within UK law our obligations as a signatory to the ECHR. The obligations in the Human Rights Act apply to public authorities. In our view, foreign officers acting under Section 76A will be public authorities under the Human Rights Act. That provision will be triggered when their presence has been duly notified.

Under the Human Rights Act, a public authority is any person who has at least some functions of a public nature. Policing in the UK is obviously the responsibility of UK police officers, but under these clauses we are effectively delegating, albeit for a fixed short period of time and subject to specific conditions, that role to foreign officers where as a matter of practicality UK officers cannot immediately take over the surveillance operation. That is why we take the view that foreign officers acting under Section 76A will be public authorities under the Human Rights Act and that the amendment is therefore unnecessary.

(HL Deb 3 February 2003 Vol. 644 cGC2)

6/54

In reply to an oral question the Minister for Europe said:

My right hon. Friend, who refers to the European Court of Human Rights . . . , is right to draw attention to the fact that there are now three ways in which such law is declared: in the European Court of Human Rights, by our incorporation of the European convention on human rights into British law and as a result of the charter of fundamental rights. It is important to realise that the charter applies to EU institutions. It will not replace the French or German constitution. It is clear that the horizontal articles—this is technical language—under articles 51 and 52 maintain the rights of countries to carry on their own business in terms of national law.

(HC Deb 14 October 2003 Vol. 411 c13)

6/55

During a debate in the House of Commons, the Parliamentary Under-Secretary of State for the Home Department said:

The Prohibition of Female Circumcision Act 1985 was an important and welcome step in the fight against FGM [ed. Female Genital Mutilation], as it made it clear that the practice would not be tolerated in this country. However, as we now know, particularly because of the work of the all-party group and others, the law needs to go further because evidence suggests that parents in some communities are evading the 1985 Act, by taking their daughters abroad for FGM.

Indeed, last year, the Agency for Culture and Change Management in Sheffield—one of the groups, as we have heard, that is working very hard to eliminate the practice—informed the Home Secretary that it had received increasing numbers of reports of families planning visits to their countries of origin, with the intention of having FGM carried out on their daughters. That is why the Bill is so important: it will assist in dealing with that by making it an offence for United Kingdom nationals and permanent UK residents to aid and abet FGM undertaken outside the UK by anyone, including foreign nationals, although the offence will be limited sometimes to cases where the victim is a UK national or permanent UK resident.

Hon. Members will want to recognise the fact that the Bill represents a significant extension of the present law because it will go a step beyond the current established international practice that dual criminality is normally needed—namely, the practice needs to be an offence in both countries to apply extra-territoriality—but I am very pleased that my hon. Friend the Member for Cynon Valley has chosen to do so because of the nature of that abhorrent practice.

(HC Deb 21 March 2003 Vol. 401 c1206)

6/56

In reply to a written question, the Under-Secretary of State, FCO, wrote:

States Parties to the International Covenant on Economic, Social and Cultural Rights recognise the right of individuals to an adequate standard of living, including adequate food. They undertake to take steps to the maximum of their resources to achieve progressively the full realisation of this right. They are obliged to report every five years on the implementation of such obligations to a UN Committee monitoring the treaty. That Committee gives a public view about a State Party's record of implementation. The Covenant does not provide for other international action where a State Party might be considered to be in breach of the Covenant. But the international community can address this in appropriate fora such as the UN Commission on Human Rights in order to defend international standards.

(HC Deb 20 January 2003 Vol. 398 c80W)

6/57

In response to a written question on Racial Discrimination, the Minister for Europe wrote:

The UK Government agree with the assessment published on 21 March 2003 by the Committee on the Elimination of Racial Discrimination of Russia's implementation of the Convention. The Committee welcomed positive steps taken by the Russian Federation to improve the legislative framework and adopt other positive measures to combat discrimination. The Committee also noted a number of concerns, including: the absence of a definition of racial discrimination in domestic legislation; reports of racially selective inspections by law-enforcement officials, particularly against those from the North Caucasus; and reports of violence by, inter alia, extremist groups against ethnic minorities.

The UK Government support this assessment. We regularly raise the issue of racial discrimination with the Russian authorities, most recently during the bilateral human rights talks in September 2002 and March 2003.

(HC Deb 28 April 2003 Vol. 404 c130W–131W)

6/58

In reply to a written question, the Minister of State, FCO, wrote:

We condemn all instances where individuals are persecuted because of their faith or belief. Ministers and officials take every opportunity, including with our EU partners, to urge states to pursue laws and practices which foster tolerance and mutual respect and to protect religious minorities against discrimination, intimidation and attacks. The UK co-sponsored a resolution at the UN General Assembly in November, 2002 in New York, to work to eliminate all forms of religious intolerance. We regularly raise specific cases of religious persecution with the Governments concerned.

(HL Deb 21 January 2003 Vol. 643 c229W)

6/59

The Quadripartite Committee asked:

Has the Government implemented the undertakings about torture equipment given by Robin Cook? If so how?

Her Majesty's Government responded:

As the then Foreign Secretary announced... there is a complete ban on the export or transhipment from the UK of leg-irons, gang chains and shackles and electric-shock belts designed for the restraint of a human being. Also included in this export ban are portable devices designed, or modified, for riot or control or self-protection purposes, to administer an electric shock. This includes electric-shock batons, electric-shock shields, stun guns and lasers, and specially designed components for such devices. The necessary amendment to the Export of Goods Control Order came into force in December 1997. The export ban has a significant economical effect on any British company manufacturing these torture items for the purpose of sale. Since the relevant amendments to the Export Control Act, HM Customs and Excise have discovered no evidence of attempts to illegally export instruments of torture from the UK.

The number of Standard Individual Export Licence (SIEL) applications and Open Individual Export Licence (OIEL) applications that have been issued and refused are published in the Government's Annual Reports on Strategic Export Controls.

Having further considered the issue of the manufacture of the specified items it has been decided that there would be little reason to ban the manufacture or sale of equipment covered by the ban. There is no market for leg-irons and shackles. British police do not use them and their export is banned. Any misuse would give rise to a separate offence such as assault. The acquisition, purchase, possession, manufacture, sale and transfer of electric-shock weapons is already regulated by the Firearms Act 1968, as amended.

(Memorandum from the FCO in follow-up to Government's response to the Committee's Report, 20 February 2003, Cm 5141)

6/60

In reply to a written question, the Under-Secretary of State, FCO, wrote:

International action against torture is a priority for the Foreign and Commonwealth Office. An anti-torture initiative to tackle torture throughout the world was launched in October 1998. Phase three of the initiative was launched on 26 June 2002. As part of this initiative, which included diplomatic activity, support for regional organisations and practical projects, the Foreign and Commonwealth Office launched two rounds of worldwide lobbying for the universal ratification of the UN Convention against Torture. Since we began lobbying 25 states have ratified. We plan to launch a third round of lobbying this year focusing on implementation of obligations as well as ratification. Last year the UK Government also undertook a widespread lobbying campaign to support the Optional Protocol to the UN Convention against Torture. We believe the Protocol offers the best means available to establish an effective international mechanism to combat torture through mandatory visits by national and international independent monitoring committees to places of detention in signatory states. The Optional Protocol was adopted at the UN General Assembly in December 2002. The UK Government are now working to secure early ratification.

The Foreign and Commonwealth Office continually updates its strategies for combating torture. This year an expert panel on torture prevention was set up to consolidate the work of the past four years and to advise on future strategy.

(HC Deb 24 March 2003 Vol. 402 c74W)

6/61

In reply to a written question the Minister of State, FCO, wrote:

I am pleased to be able to announce that the UK has taken a significant step towards ratification of the Optional Protocol to the UN Convention Against Torture and Other Cruel, Inhuman or Degrading Treatment or Punishment (OPCAT). On 8 September, my honourable friend, Mr Rammell laid before Parliament an Explanatory Memorandum, which explains how the UK meets the provisions of the protocol.

We hope that the ratification process can be completed with the United Nations by the end of this year. This will make the UK one of the very first UN member states to have ratified the Optional Protocol. We signed the protocol on 26 June, becoming one of only 6 countries worldwide to have done so.

The UK is committed to the fight against torture. The Foreign and Commonwealth Office's anti-torture initiative, launched in 1998, continues to provide a focus for us on this issue. The follow-up to our ratification of the OPCAT will be an important part of the current phase of the initiative. We will undertake a lobbying campaign urging other countries to sign, ratify and implement both the Convention Against Torture and the Optional Protocol.

(HL Deb 9 September 2003 Vol. 652 cWA114)

6/62

In response to a written question, the Parliamentary Under-Secretary for Foreign Affairs wrote:

The British Embassy in Kabul receives periodic updates from the ICRC on prisoners held in Afghanistan by the Afghans. The latest information we have is that Shiberghan currently holds around 1,200 prisoners, half of them Pakistanis. We understand a number of prisoners were released from Shiberghan in February 2002 and some 50 Afghan prisoners were released in mid-January 2003 under a presidential amnesty. The international coalition has no control over prisoners held by Afghan authorities or other Afghan elements, although Her Majesty's Government continue to underline to the Afghan authorities the importance of them fulfilling their obligations under the international human rights instruments to which Afghanistan is party.

(HL Deb 4 February 2003 Vol. 644 cWA17)

6/63

In reply to a written question, the Parliamentary Under-Secretary of State, FCO, wrote:

Our embassy in Kabul has discussed our concerns about the alleged human rights abuses at Dasht-e-Leili with the United Nations Assistance Mission in Afghanistan and the Afghan Human Rights Commission. We support the UN's two-stage approach to the investigation: forensic investigations and dignified reburials now, followed, at a later stage, when the security situation improves, by more detailed witness interviews and investigations. It is important that further investigations should only take place when it is possible to protect potential witnesses. We understand that a UN-led investigation may start in the next few months.

The site is visited weekly by staff from the UN office in Mazar-e-Sharif. Following their visit to Dasht-e-Leili in January this year, Physicians for Human Rights reported that there had been no deterioration or destruction of the site at Dasht-e-Leili. The UN view is that there is no need for static protection of the site.

(HL Deb 10 February 2003 Vol. 645 cWA143)

6/64

During a debate in the House of Lords on Burma (Myanmar), a Government representative made the following statements:

Credible reports detailing instances of rape by the armed forces, again movingly recorded by the noble Lord, . . . the use of child soldiers and violence in the ethnic minority areas have been published by NGOs such as Amnesty International, Human Rights Watch, and Christian Solidarity Worldwide. However, the regime has chosen to dismiss many of these reports as the work of insurgents or political opponents. As a Government we strongly disagree and have expressed our concerns repeatedly. We welcome the fact that the United Nations Third Committee passed a resolution on Burma earlier this month and condemned the ongoing systematic human rights violations there . . .

Of particular concern were reports of torture, extra-judicial killings, rape by members of the armed forces, forced labour, the continued use of child soldiers, forced relocation, denial of freedoms of assembly, association, expression and movement, and discrimination on the basis of religious as well as ethnic background. The EU drafted and co-sponsored the United Nations resolution and we as a Government were very proud to play our part in that process.

As the Under-Secretary of State for Foreign and Commonwealth Affairs, my honourable friend Mike O'Brien said in a public statement on 21st November, the resolution is an accurate account of the Burmese regime's record.

We have been talking about forced labour . . . the regime's record on forced labour remains stubbornly abysmal. The European Commission has suspended Burma's trading privileges in response to the use of forced labour. The UK has been a staunch supporter of the ILO's efforts to get the Burmese regime to address the problem. We have welcomed the appointment of an International Labour Organisation liaison officer in Burma.

. . .

The noble Baroness asked whether Her Majesty's Government would raise with the regime human rights accusations. We regularly raise concerns over human rights with the regime and in the UN. The Foreign Office was putting our concerns again to the Burmese embassy only two days ago. Will we urge the ILO to keep investigating forced labour? Yes we will. Most recently, we did this on 21st November at the ILO meeting in Geneva. Will we press for access to all areas of Burma for NGOs and the UN to help deliver humanitarian aid? . . . The answer is yes, we do, and yes we will.

(HL Deb 3 December 2002 Vol. 641 c1129–1131)

6/65

In a reply to a written question, the Under-Secretary of State, FCO, wrote:

The overall human rights situation in Burma remains extremely poor and a matter of grave concern.

There were some very modest improvements in limited areas of human rights in Burma between January 2002 and January 2003, such as the release of political prisoners—over 200 in this period, including Daw Aung San Suu Kyi and some cooperation between the Burmese regime, the United Nations and certain international non-governmental organisations.

However, these limited improvements do not provide any assurance that the Burmese regime is now committed to substantively improving its human rights record or ending the violence and abuses in the ethnic minority areas of Burma. And since autumn 2002 there has been increasing reports of fresh restrictions of freedom of expression and politically inspired detentions and arrests in Burma.

(HC Deb 10 February 2003 Vol. 399 c567W)

6/66

In response to a written question on Burma, the Parliamentary Under-Secretary of State, FCO, wrote:

I am in regular telephone contact with Daw Aung San Suu Kyi. She remains resolute and hopeful that democracy in Burma is achievable. Daw Aung San Suu Kyi is able to travel and operate relatively freely. On 6 April she undertook a visit to Chin State where large crowds met her. There have been some instances where local authorities have obstructed Daw Aung San Suu Kyi's visits, most notably in Northern Rakhine State in December 2002. As a result of the problems encountered in Northern Rakhine State, the UK and EU have issued statements expressing concern and calling for Daw Aung San Suu Kyi's freedom to travel and operate.

(HC Deb 28 April 2003 Vol. 404 c117W)

6/67

In response to a written question on Burma, the Parliamentary Under-Secretary of State, FCO, wrote:

The EU co-sponsored a resolution on Burma at the United Nations General Assembly in November 2002 that pressed for the peaceful end to all conflicts in Burma. We are also in regular contact with the Governments of Bangladesh and Thailand to press the case for political progress in Burma. It is in the best interests of all Burma's neighbours that national reconciliation, respect for human rights and democracy is rapidly achieved.

(HC Deb 28 April 2003 Vol. 404 c117W)

6/68

In response to a written question on Burma, the Parliamentary Under-Secretary of State, FCO, wrote:

In keeping with its attitude towards other human rights problems, the State Peace and Development Council [ed. viz the Government of Myanmar] does not accept that it has a problem concerning the denial of full citizenship rights to Burmese citizens. However, there is ample evidence that this is a serious problem, in particular given the refusal to grant full rights to many of the Muslim Rohinghyas who live in Rakhine State.

(HC Deb 28 April 2003 Vol. 404 c118W)

6/69

In response to a written question on Burma and the number of internally displaced persons, the Parliamentary Under-Secretary of State, FCO, wrote:

Definitive figures are not available because international access is restricted in large areas of Burma. However, some estimates from non-government organisations have indicated that over 600,000 may be internally displaced in Burma. Despite the lack of accurate statistics, it is clear that this is a major problem and that the Burmese authorities must take action to stop fresh displacement of people and allow the safe resettlement of those currently internally displaced.

(HC Deb 28 April 2003 Vol. 404 c118W)

6/70

In response to a written question on Burma, the Parliamentary Under-Secretary of State, FCO, wrote:

The Burmese military regime has not signed up to many of the United Nations instruments covering acceptable standards of human rights adherence and does not share our concern about the unacceptable level of human rights violations in Burma. We will continue to press bilaterally with the Burmese regime and in international fora for a rapid improvement in the situation. As part of this we will continue to press for democratic reform in Burma. It is only through the return of democracy and the rule of law that the underlying problems contributing to the human rights violations can be adequately addressed.

(HC Deb 28 April 2003 Vol. 404 c120W)

6/71

In reply to a written question the Foreign Office Minister wrote:

We are aware that appalling human rights violations have taken place against the Karen, Karenni and Shan people in Burma over many years. We take into account the views of appropriate international bodies. However, we need verification of crimes against humanity, war crimes or genocide in Burma before using such terms. The United Nations Special Rapporteur for Human Rights in Burma, Sergio Pinheiro, has regular access to Burma, most recently on 17 March 2003. I understand he takes the view that he will not use these terms to describe the situation there. The terms have likewise not been used by many major international NGOs, which monitor the human rights situation in Burma.

There is room for debate about the use of particular words in different contexts but what matters in this case is that we all agree that the behaviour of the Burmese regime has been appalling and involved widespread killing and breaches of human rights.

(HL Deb 17 July 2003 Vol. 651 cWA150)

6/72

In reply to a written question on Chechnya, the Minister of State, FCO, wrote:

The question of the accountability of military and police actions in Chechnya is one which is regularly raised with the Russian government. Most recently, during human rights talks at senior official level, with the Russian government earlier this month, we stressed that all allegations of human rights violations should be thoroughly and transparently investigated, and those responsible punished. We added that the vigorous protection of the human rights of the civil population was an essential precursor to a lasting political solution to the conflict in Chechnya.

On this occasion, senior Russian officials acknowledged that violations had been committed and that action needed to be taken to prevent further abuses. Their aim was to increase the protection of the civil population's human rights through the introduction of a new constitution for Chechnya, the phased withdrawal of Federal troops and the transfer of their security duties to the Chechen Interior Ministry.

(HC Deb 26 March 2003 Vol. 402 c256W)

6/73

In reply to a written question the Under-Secretary of State, FCO, wrote:

The objectives for our UK/China human rights dialogue are detailed in the FCO Annual Human Rights Report. They cover issues relating to the rule of law, engagement with UN mechanisms, political and religious rights, economic and social rights and the situation in Tibet.

We are disappointed by China's progress to date on the recommendations made by the Special Rapporteur on Religious Freedom in 1994. We continue to raise our concerns about religious freedom in China. We did so most recently at the UK/China human rights dialogue in November 2002.

We understand that at the US/China human rights dialogue in December 2002 China agreed to invite the Special Rapporteur on Religious Freedom.

(HL Deb 5 February 2003 Vol. 644 cWA33)

6/74

During a debate in the House of Commons, the Parliamentary Under-Secretary, FCO, said:

Managing relations with Cuba is a complex business, and I shall describe how we do it through the EU and other multilateral forums, and bilaterally. We want

Cuba to develop economically, politically and socially, and to build on the significant advances that its Government have already made in health and literacy, which have been mentioned. Cuba has the natural and human resources to become one of the region's most prosperous economies, but its political and economic system needs to develop for that to happen. The EU, the United States and the UK share the same goal for Cuba: a peaceful transition to a pluralist democracy. However, we seek to achieve that through constructive engagement, rather than through isolating Cuba.

I admit that there are times when constructive engagement can be somewhat difficult. The EU has been proposing a political dialogue with Cuba for years, yet the on-off process remains frustratingly barren. Cuba will talk, but only on Cuba's terms. The human rights situation in Cuba remains a major cause for concern, and the arrest of 80 people last month in a crackdown on dissident activity is a further setback for all, including the Government, whose aim is the progressive normalisation of relations between the EU and Cuba.

Since 1996, EU relations with Cuba have been governed by a common position that sets out the EU desire to be Cuba's partner through constructive dialogue and co-operation. However, at the same time that position affirms that the intensification of those relations depends on Cuba's making progress on human rights. The common position makes it clear that full co-operation will not be possible until Cuba commits itself to international human rights standards. The EU calls for freedom of assembly and expression, a free media and freedom for all political parties. We urge an end to arbitrary detention, intimidation and imprisonment on political grounds. The common position has proved a useful means of managing EU relations with Cuba, and it has been maintained unanimously in 12 consecutive evaluations.

The EU also deals with relations with Cuba in two United Nations forums: the Commission on Human Rights and the General Assembly. The EU has co-sponsored a resolution on Cuba at the UN Commission on Human Rights for the past 10 years. The resolution voices—in modest terms—international concern at the systematic denial of fundamental civil and political rights to the people of Cuba. It also focuses the frustrations felt at Cuba's lack of co-operation with UN human rights mechanisms and its refusal to acknowledge any domestic human rights problems. This year as last, Latin American countries tabled the resolution. We welcome the involvement of countries within Cuba's home region.

The EU acts in concert in the General Assembly and each year votes against a US embargo. The EU also rejects the US attempts to pursue its Cuba policy through the extension of its legal jurisdiction beyond US borders by means of the Helms-Burton Act.

My hon. Friend referred to the Miami five. The Government believe that that is a bilateral matter between the US and Cuba, and that any questions about the sentencing and treatment of those prisoners should be addressed to the appropriate US authorities. As my hon. Friend understands, the Government have no formal standing to intervene in the United States domestic judicial processes with people who are not UK nationals.

In January, Cuba applied to join the Cotonou agreement, which is an agreement between the EU and African, Caribbean and Pacific countries that can bring benefits to those countries in trade and development. Cuba wants Cotonou, and the EU sees Cuba as a natural signatory, but we must see some improvements in human rights first. Unconditional entry to Cotonou would reward Cuba's intransigence on human rights. We cannot have that. Cuba's application is yet to be discussed formally in the EU. However, the chances of its being accepted must have receded significantly in recent weeks, following the arrests. Cotonou can and will benefit Cuba, but Cuba must show itself ready to take on the human rights obligations that Cotonou imposes. To date, it has not demonstrated its willingness to do so. Arresting a further 80 dissidents last month seems almost to have been calculated to prevent the EU from assessing Cuba's application positively.

(HC Deb 2 April 2003 Vol. 402 c322WH–324WH)

6/75

In reply to a written question on Ethiopia (Illegal Detention), the Secretary of State for International Development wrote:

In the Memorandum of Understanding I signed with the Ethiopian Government in January 2003, the Ethiopian Government renewed its commitment to protect the full range of human rights including economic and social rights of all Ethiopians, especially the poor. We are supporting the implementation of this commitment through our support for the Sustainable Development and Poverty Reduction Programme (SDPRP) and through regular dialogue with the Ethiopian Government, at which we raise human rights and other issues of concern. At my planned meeting with Prime Minister Meles, I expect to discuss progress on implementing the SDPRP and any issues of concern that arise.

(HC Deb 24 February 2003 Vol. 400 c274W)

6/76

In reply to a written question on UK citizens detained in Cuba, the Parliamentary Under-Secretary of State, FCO, wrote:

We have received representations by the legal representatives and families of the detainees. My right hon. Friend the Foreign Secretary has spoken to the US Secretary of State several times about this issue, most recently on 5 January. Ministers and officials have raised it on numerous occasions with the US Government.

We continue to encourage the US to move forward with the process of determining the future of the British detainees. We have made our position clear that if they are charged they must have a fair trial. We understand that none have been charged. The US has given assurances that the detainees are being treated humanely and consistently with the principles of the Geneva Conventions. British officials have visited Guantanamo Bay to check on the welfare of the British nationals.

(HC Deb 20 January 2003 Vol. 698 c76W)

6/77

In reply to a written question, the Parliamentary Under-Secretary of State, FCO, wrote:

I start by making it clear that religious intolerance is deplorable in the United Kingdom, India, Bhutan or wherever it occurs. The close links of many British people of Indian origin with their families in Gujarat, Kashmir, Punjab and elsewhere in India mean that Britain has an especial interest in and responsibility to human rights issues in such areas.

The Government has put the promotion of human rights at the core of their foreign policy. The United Kingdom has a long-standing tradition of raising religious freedom issues around the world. In doing so, we take the 1948 universal declaration of human rights as our starting point. Article 18 of that declaration is clear and unambiguous on religious issues:

> "Everyone has the right to freedom of thought, conscience and religion; this right includes freedom to change his religion or belief, and freedom, either alone or in community with others and in public or private, to manifest his religion or belief in teaching, practice, worship and observation."

We take that very seriously.

[T]he Government unreservedly condemn the persecution of individuals because of their faith, wherever they are and whatever religion they practise. We certainly take every opportunity, both on our own and in conjunction with European partners, to urge states to pursue laws and practices that foster tolerance and mutual respect, and to protect religious minorities against discrimination, intimidation and attacks.

Wherever possible, we work with officials, religious leaders and non-governmental organisations at international and local level to promote mutual understanding and tolerance. Indeed, at the United Nations General Assembly in New York last year, we co-sponsored a resolution that made clear our determination and that of the international community to work towards eliminating all forms of religious intolerance.

(HC Deb 28 January 2003 Vol. 398 c219WH)

6/78

In reply to a written question, the Under-Secretary of State, FCO, wrote:

We have made no specific representations to the Government of India over the case of Professor Davinderpal Singh Bhullar. In conjunction with the EU, we have demarched India about their use of the death penalty most recently in June 2001. We continue to follow Professor Bhullar's case closely, and are in discussions with EU partners over possible courses of action to take. Foreign Office officials met Professor Bhullar's wife on 12 February to discuss the case.

(HC Deb 25 February 2003 Vol. 400 c422W)

6/79

In a written answer, the Parliamentary Under-Secretary of State, FCO, wrote:

I discussed India's position regarding the Convention Against Torture (CAT) with Mr. I. D. Swami, the Indian Minister of State for Home Affairs, on 17 October 2002 during my visit to India. We understand that India is planning to start the process of ratifying CAT, although a bill has not yet been brought before the Indian Parliament. We continue to encourage India to ratify CAT.

We have made and will continue to make official level representations to the Government of India for greater general access to India of UN Special Rapporteurs and international human rights NGOs. Save in exceptional circumstances, our general policy is not to make state-specific representations. We have in the past carried out project work under the Human Rights Project Fund in co-operation with the Punjabi State Police.

(HC Deb 3 April 2003 Vol. 402 c831)

6/80

In response to a written question, the Parliamentary Under-Secretary of State, FCO, wrote:

Since the Tamil Nadu Ordinance on Religious Conversions was passed into law on 2 December 2002, some observers in the state have noted a general fall in the number of public conversions there, but we have not been able to corroborate this. The law's effects on Tamil Nadu's Dalit population are also as yet unclear. We are not aware of any cases that have yet been brought to court under the law's provisions.

Although the impact of this law is not yet clear, we are concerned that this legislation might in practice discourage Tamil Nadu's citizens from adopting the religion of their choice. Such an effect might limit religious freedoms as outlined in the International Covenant on Civil and Political Rights, which India has ratified. We have had no discussions with the Government of India about this legislation. But our Missions in India will continue to monitor closely the implementation of the law, and we will discuss with EU Partners whether any EU action is necessary.

(HC Deb 6 May 2003 Vol. 404 c570W)

6/81

Her Majesty's Government was asked the following written question:

Whether, following the hanging of Mr Hamzeh Ghaderi, a member of the Democratic Party of Iranian Kurdistan, on 7 October, their "constructive dialogue" with Iran includes pleas for clemency towards 10 other members of the same party under sentence of death.

In reply, the Under-Secretary of State, FCO, wrote:

Her Majesty's Government oppose the death penalty in all circumstances and urge all states to abolish the death penalty. We and the EU continue to make clear our views on this subject to the Iranian Government at every opportunity. We raise with the Iranian authorities specific cases which breach the international minimum standards relating to the death penalty.

The EU agreed on 21 October to establish an EU-Iran human rights dialogue with the hope that such a dialogue will bring about concrete improvements in respect for human rights and fundamental freedoms in Iran. The dialogue has been established without preconditions, and benchmarks for assessing its progress are expected to refer, inter alia, to issues relating to the death penalty.

(HL Deb 31 October 2002 Vol. 640 cWA42)

6/82

During a debate in the House of Commons, the Minister for Europe said:

The United Kingdom and European Union believe that one way of expressing their concerns is to sponsor resolutions on human rights in Iran at the UN General Assembly and the Commission on Human Rights, as has been done for many years. We were disappointed that the Commission on Human Rights failed, by just one vote, to adopt the resolution on Iran in April last year. As my hon. Friend noted, that also meant the end of the mandate of the special representative. In practice, the special representative has not been allowed to visit Iran since 1996, but his reports on the human rights situation provided valuable detail on the human rights problems in Iran, and he was active in pursuing cases with the Iranian Government.

All EU partners are concerned about the human rights situation in Iran, and we are currently consulting on the most effective way in which to encourage positive change. A resolution is one of a number of tools currently under consideration.

Following the failure of the resolution last year, Iran made a number of gestures, including inviting the EU to engage in a dialogue on human rights. After an internal debate, the EU decided to take up the offer and the first round of the dialogue took place in mid-December. The next round will take place later this month, which will give us an opportunity to assess progress before the next Commission on Human Rights begins its work on 17 March. Discussions in December were frank, and the EU made it clear to the Iranians that they need to be able to show results to get agreement for the talks to continue. Initial impressions have been positive, although change, as ever, is likely to be slow. The EU delegation handed over a list of cases on which answers were sought, and those issues will be followed up this month. My hon. Friend quoted Commissioner Chris Patten. When Chris Patten visited Tehran in February he said that it was not enough just to talk about human rights and that we needed to see progress. Of course, he was right.

In a further development following the failure of the resolution last year, there has been an open invitation to UN Human Rights Commission inspectors to visit Iran. The UN working group on arbitrary detentions was the first to take up the invitation, and completed an inspection in February. The group has still to make a full report.

Together with our EU partners, we have repeatedly expressed concern about stonings, which is a subject on which reformers, and especially women's groups, in Iran have been campaigning for years. We welcomed the announcement at the end of last year by the head of the Supreme Administrative Court that the practice has been suspended. We have also been informed that, of the four women who were sentenced to death by stoning last year, three have been given alternative sentences and the fourth is awaiting the outcome of her appeal. We are monitoring the situation closely, because that barbaric practice is not acceptable to any decent human being anywhere in the world.

We are considering other ways of developing practical co-operation on human rights issues. We have supported a number of projects through the Foreign Office's human rights projects fund. The projects include technical assistance on specific issues relating to the rule of law and work by Penal Reform International, a highly regarded worldwide organisation, which was initially approached by the Iranian prison authorities, who are keen to reform their prisons. Other projects have included specialised training for judges working with juveniles, through UNICEF; strengthening the capacities of the Islamic Human Rights Commission; human rights training courses for young adults; and a familiarisation visit by five Iranian judges to the UK, which took place last March.

[T]here is a steady, drip-by-drip attempt to show Iranian officials that an alternative system is possible. We noted at least 111 executions last year, some of which took place in public. The Government oppose the death penalty in all circumstances, and we urge all states to abolish it.

We regularly raise with the Iranian authorities our serious concerns about the treatment of the Baha'is. Persecution of individuals on religious grounds is unacceptable. Although no Baha'is remain under sentence of death, they continue to suffer harassment and discrimination in areas such as education, employment, housing and travel.

(HC Deb 5 March 2003 Vol. 400 c316WH–318WH)

6/83

In response to a written question on the human rights situation in Iraq, the Parliamentary Under-Secretary of State, FCO, wrote:

On 2 December 2002, Her Majesty's Government published a report on human rights abuses in Iraq. It is based on intelligence material, first-hand accounts of Iraqi victims of torture and oppression, and reports amassed by NGOs over the past decade. The report examines Iraq's record on torture, the treatment of women, prison conditions, arbitrary and summary killings, the persecution of the Kurds and Shia, the harassment of opposition figures outside Iraq and the occupation of Kuwait.

The Iraqi regime's contempt for international law and its attachment to weapons of mass destruction were documented in the Government's dossier published on 24 September. Its dreadful human rights record is widely known. Her Majesty's Government consider it important that Parliament and the public should have accurate information about the awful reality of Saddam Hussein's policy of regime terror, which sustains his rule inside Iraq.

(HL Deb 3 December 2002 Vol. 641 cWA92)

6/84

In reply to a written question the Minister of State, FCO, wrote:

The United Kingdom's position on the death penalty is well known—we oppose the use of the death penalty in all circumstances. With reference to Iraq, the death penalty is currently suspended under CPA Order Number 7.

(HL Deb 20 November 2003 Vol. 654 cWA361)

6/85

In response to a written question, the Parliamentary Under-Secretary of State, FCO, wrote:

The United Nations Administration Mission in Kosovo (UNMIK) has enacted regulations in order to bring specific procedures (for example, concerning arrest and detention, and surveillance and evidence gathering) in line with human rights standards, providing grounds for raising human rights arguments before the courts. Any person alleging a breach of human rights standards in Kosovo may take up the matter with the relevant authorities or seek legal advice in Kosovo with regard to available remedies.

(HL Deb 24 September 2002 Vol. 638 cWA241)

6/86

During a debate in the House of Commons on Nigeria, the Parliamentary Under-Secretary of State, FCO, said:

The Government and our EU partners regularly raise our concerns about this case [the stoning to death of Amina Lawal for adultery] with the appropriate authorities in Nigeria. Indeed, my noble Friend the Minister for Africa, Baroness Amos, expressed to President Obasanjo our concern about the harsh sentences imposed under the sharia penal codes, and emphasised the strength of feeling against them in the UK.

...

I wholeheartedly agree with my hon. Friend. We take every opportunity to raise all cases in which this extreme interpretation of sharia law is used, and we will continue to do so. I reassure my hon. Friend that, through our high commission, we also maintain close contact with the national human rights commission in Nigeria, and the non-governmental organisations. In that way, we will get advance warning in cases such as this, and that will allow us to do everything in our power to apply the maximum pressure.

...

I take comfort from the fact that the Nigerian Attorney-General has made clear his view that the cases will ultimately be ruled unconstitutional in the federal court. We should none the less continue to apply pressure on an issue that is of serious concern across the House.

(HC Deb 6 May 2003 Vol. 404 c528)

6/87

In a written answer on Nigeria, the Under-Secretary of State, FCO, wrote:

We deplore the issuing of a fatwa against Isioma Daniel. Such action is a clear violation of the International Covenant on Civil and Political Rights, to which Nigeria acceded in 1993.

With our EU partners, we have made clear our concern privately to the relevant authorities.

The Nigerian Government immediately made clear that the fatwa is null and void. Moderate Muslim leaders distanced themselves from it. On 28 November, the Supreme Council of Islamic Affairs of Nigeria (SCIA) rejected the fatwa on the grounds that Ms Daniel was not a Muslim and had apologised.

The Nigerian federal authorities are fully aware of their obligations under the international human rights instruments to which they are a signatory and the damage this illegal fatwa could do to their international reputation.

(HL Deb 12 December 2003 Vol. 642 cWA51–WA52)

6/88

During a debate in the House of Lords, the Minister of State, FCO, made the following statements:

The need to acquire reliable information on human rights is one of the driving factors behind our policy of engagement with North Korea.... We raise this issue regularly, although noble Lords will know that the nuclear issue has inevitably taken away the focus from human rights in North Korea. That is regrettable, but it is a fact of life. It has been difficult to engage with the North Koreans on any issue other than nuclear proliferation over the past six months, important though human rights issues are. I assure your Lordships that the concerns expressed in the debate have not been forgotten by Her Majesty's Government. They are integral to any dialogue with North Korea.

[A]t last year's meeting of the United Nations Commission on Human Rights the EU presidency statement clearly reflected the European Union's deep concern about continued and serious violations of human rights in North Korea.

If the EU decides that there is no evidence of any improvement since last year we will consider further action during this year.

The noble Lord, Lord Alton, my noble friend Lord Clarke, the noble Lord, Lord Hylton, and the noble Lord, Lord Chan, urged the Government to take action in respect of the 1995 agreement between UNHCR and China. I understand the concerns expressed on this issue. As a bilateral agreement rather than a treaty it is for the parties involved to interpret their obligations. But noble Lords are right that we should exert pressure.... we will continue to encourage greater co-operation on this issue between China and UNHCR at every opportunity.

...

This is indeed a terrible regime. Some will ask why we do not act now in the same way as we are acting over Iraq. Our underlying approach to Iraq and North Korea—indeed, to all other proliferation threats—is the same. We will pursue peaceful diplomatic means for as long as it is possible to do so... The fact is that our experience over 12 years of evasion and obfuscation from Iraq tells us that full co-operation is an unlikely outcome.

We are not approaching North Korea on the basis of 12 years of frustrated effort. The North Koreans tell us that they do not want to develop nuclear weapons. However, they said that at the same time as announcing their withdrawal from the NPT, which may seem perverse and unconvincing to many noble Lords; frankly, it is pretty unconvincing to me as well. We will continue to engage with them and tell them that they are missing an opportunity to put things right with regard to their weapons of mass destruction and in respect of disarmament and the considerable concerns that noble Lords raised in relation to human rights. We may not persuade them. If we do not, we need to be ready to show that we can increase the diplomatic pressure. However, we will continue the efforts to convince North Koreans that their security lies not in nuclear weapons programmes, which further isolate them from the international community, but with deeper co-operation and integration with that community. We need to see a dramatic improvement in their record in terms of weapons of mass destruction and their appalling human rights record.

(HL Deb 13 March 2003 Vol. 645 c1565–1568)

6/89

In a written answer, the Parliamentary Under-Secretary of State, FCO, wrote:

We regularly raise the issue of North Korean refugees with the Chinese, including at the biannual UK/China Human Rights Dialogue. At the last round of the dialogue, on 21 November 2002, we urged China to allow the UNHCR access to the border areas and to observe its obligations under the 1951 Refugee Convention.

We will continue to encourage greater co-operation between China and UNHCR on this issue.

(HC Deb 28 April 2003 Vol. 404 c126W)

6/90

In reply to a written question, the Parliamentary Under-Secretary of State, FCO, wrote:

We are concerned about any human rights violations in Pakistan. We have serious concerns about the situation of Christians, particularly because of the many attacks against them in the past year and the misuse of the blasphemy laws. We remain deeply concerned that the death penalty can be imposed for blasphemy. The UK opposes the death penalty in all circumstances. On 15 July 2002 I raised our concerns directly with the Pakistani high commissioner in London. Together with our EU partners, we also regularly raise our concerns with the Pakistani authorities in Islamabad. We will continue to take every appropriate opportunity to urge Pakistan to pursue laws and practices which foster tolerance and mutual respect and to protect Christians and other religious minorities against discrimination, intimidation and attacks.

(HC Deb 22 January 2003 Vol. 398 c357W)

6/91

During a debate in the House of Lords, the Parliamentary Under-Secretary of State, FCO, said:

We continue to be concerned about the human rights of all in Sudan regardless of their ethnic or religious background. The promotion of human rights remains one of our priorities. The noble Lord, Lord Moynihan, and the noble Lord, Lord Astor of Hever, raised specifically the issue of slavery and abduction. The abduction of women and children is a serious and distressing issue to which we pay particular attention. We continue to work closely with the Committee for the Eradication of Abduction of Women and Children, which is working with UNICEF and Save the Children UK.

The Government of Sudan have made clear publicly that they are committed to the success of the committee and have said that they see abduction as totally unacceptable and contrary to both Islam and Christianity. We share the concerns of many working on this issue about the paying for the return of abductees in that it could actually encourage abduction by developing a market. It rewards the abductors financially. The civilian protection team will investigate reports of abduction.

. . .

We continue to lobby the Government of Sudan, for example, to ratify the convention against torture. We actively criticise the government on human rights issues bilaterally and through the EU/Sudan dialogue. The dialogue assesses progress against benchmarks on democracy, the rule of law, freedom of religion, human rights and the peace process. The dialogue is reviewed on an annual basis—most recently, by an EU troika mission to Khartoum on 9th and 10th December last year.

(HL Deb 13 January 2003 Vol. 643 c93–94)

6/92

In reply to a written question, the Under-Secretary of State, FCO, wrote:

We are concerned about the extensive use of the death penalty in Sudan, in particular the lack of legal representation and the use of special courts. We have made representations to the Sudanese Government, most recently to the Minister of Justice on 18 January. Following the executions of 3 men on 8 January, the EU Presidency issued a statement of condemnation on 10 January and raised the case with the Under-Secretary at the Ministry of Justice on 11 January.

(HC Deb 24 February 2003 Vol. 400 c251W)

6/93

In a written answer, the Parliamentary Under-Secretary of State, FCO, wrote:

We are monitoring developments in Darfur and are following the cases of those sentenced to death. In relation to women's rights and judicial reform our focus has not been on Darfur specifically, but we have been in contact with the Government of Sudan about the role and function of the special courts.

(HC Deb 4 April 2003 Vol. 402 c905W)

6/94

In response to a written question, the Parliamentary Under-Secretary of State, FCO, wrote:

We are concerned about torture in Sudan. We part-fund the work of the Sudanese Organisation Against Torture (SOAT) which monitors incidences. SOAT's annual report states that incidences of torture have decreased across the population as a whole but that the practice continues to be used against the people of Darfur, and in particular students.

The Sudanese government has signed the Convention Against Torture and other Cruel, Inhuman and Degrading Treatment or Punishment. Our Embassy in Khartoum regularly lobbies the Government of Sudan to ratify the Convention.

(HC Deb 7 April 2003 Vol. 403 c68W)

6/95

In a written answer, the Under-Secretary of State, FCO, was asked the following question:

[W]hat recent assessment his Department has made of the human rights situations in *(a)* Uzbekistan, *(b)* Turkmenistan, *(c)* Kyrgmenistan, *(d)* Algeria, *(e)* Jordan, *(f)* Qatar and *(g)* Pakistan.

In reply, the Under-Secretary of State, FCO, wrote:

Human rights are at the heart of foreign policy and as such are integrated into policy-making at all levels. The FCO is therefore continually considering the human rights issues in all countries alongside other political, economic and security issues. However, the human rights situations in the countries raised are as follows:

Uzbekistan:
We remain deeply concerned by reports of human rights abuses in Uzbekistan. We recognise that the Uzbek Government has made small concessions in addressing the situation, including co-operating with the UN Special Rapporteur for Torture. However, Uzbekistan needs to do much more. We would like to see reform of the criminal justice system, as well as wider recognition of independent human rights groups, religious groups and political parties. The Parliamentary Under-Secretary of State at the Foreign and Commonwealth Office, my hon. Friend the Member for North Warwickshire (Mr. O'Brien), raised human rights concerns with the Uzbek Ambassador in London on 10 February. We shall continue to press for tangible improvements in Uzbekistan's human rights record. We are also thinking together with the EU how best to handle the human rights situation in Uzbekistan at the next session of the Commission on Human Rights starting in March.

Turkmenistan:
We are greatly concerned at the recent developments in Turkmenistan following the reported assassination attempt on President Niyazov last November. We encouraged the EU to make a statement calling on the Turkmen authorities to comply with Turkmenistan's human rights obligations under international law. The EU is also considering how best to handle the human rights situation at the next session of the Commission on Human Rights.

Through the Organisation for Security and Cooperation in Europe (OSCE) we have sought to establish a fact-finding mission to Turkmenistan to investigate all matters relating to the conduct of the investigations, including detentions, arrests and allegations of torture, as well as the trials, convictions and sentencing procedures. Turkmenistan has however refused to admit any mission of this kind. The OSCE has asked the Turkmen authorities to reconsider. We will continue to monitor the situation closely.

Kyrgyzstan:
We recognise efforts made by the Kyrgyz Government to improve its human rights situation and to bring about political reform. Positive developments include a presidential decree on 8 January 2003 extending a moratorium on the use of the death penalty. We are however still concerned by cases of harassment of independent media and unofficial Muslim groups. We shall continue to help Kyrgyzstan make improvements, in line with its international obligations and commitments.

Algeria:
We regularly raise our concerns about human rights violations in Algeria with the Algerian Government. We continue to urge the Algerian Government to

fully comply with all its obligations under international human rights law, including the investigation of human rights violations, and to allow visits by the UN special rapporteurs on the question of torture and on extrajudicial, summary or arbitrary executions. The UK with EU partners has also raised its concerns about a number of cases of human rights abuses with the Algerian authorities. The Algerian Ministry of Foreign Affairs has offered information on some of these cases, but both we and our EU partners will continue to press for full answers.

Jordan:
We welcome the decision by the Jordanian Government to hold general elections in June 2003 (elections were previously postponed from autumn 2002). This decision represents the opportunity for people to exercise their democratic right to vote. We will encourage the Government to hold a free and fair electoral process. We have some concerns about the human rights situation in Jordan including the treatment of religious minorities, honour killings, and freedom of expression. Toujan al-Faisal was a former member of the Jordanian Parliament who was arrested in 2002 in connection with her public criticism of the Government's policies. We welcomed her release following a Royal Pardon in July 2002. We will continue to raise each human rights case as appropriate with the Jordanian Government or in conjunction with EU Partners.

Qatar:
Qatar has a good human rights record for a conservative Islamic society with an autocratic system of government. The social and political system is comparatively tolerant and increasingly open. The Amir has the right basic instincts towards human rights issues but recognises that change which could damage the fabric of his tribal people must be handled carefully and will take time. The Amir is encouraging women to play an active part in all walks of life; he has introduced his first steps towards democratic reform; the press exercises some self censorship; freedom of worship is tolerated provided it is discreet; there are plans to build Qatar's first churches; work continues on codifying sharia and civil law but Qataris are still to some extent associated in the Western mind with their Wahabi cousins in Saudi Arabia. Death sentences have been carried out but are extremely rare. There are, however, general issues regarding the treatment of third country nationals and minors working in Qatar.

Pakistan:
The UK Government welcomed President Musharraf's speech of 12 January 2002 in which he condemned all forms of sectarianism and religious hatred and made the case for a moderate and tolerant Islam. We hope the new government will look carefully at human rights violations in Pakistan. The UK and EU are particularly concerned by sectarian and terrorist violence that has resulted in the deaths of a number of Christians across Pakistan, most recently the vicious attack on 25 December 2002.

We have concerns about the abuse of the blasphemy laws and are seriously concerned about the imposition of the death penalty for blasphemy. The UK Government opposes the death penalty in all circumstances. Women's rights issues remain a concern. We hope the new government will keep to the pledge of the out-going government to review the Hudood ordinances on Islamic punishments. We are particularly concerned by so-called "honour" crimes against women, forced marriages, domestic violence, kidnap and rape. We believe much can be done to promote women's rights within the existing Islamic legal framework.

(HC Deb 14 March 2003 Vol. 401 c444W–446W)

6/96

In reply to an oral question the Minister of State, FCO, said:

My Lords, we receive regular reporting on human rights in Uzbekistan from our embassy in Tashkent. The embassy closely monitors the human rights situation and is in regular contact with independent human rights organisations and international non-governmental organisations. The Foreign Office's recently published human rights report details our concern about Ubzekistan's human rights record.

. . .

He asked what more we can do to promote the development of human rights in Uzbekistan. He is right: there is a sorry position there. We can do so in two principal ways: we can monitor reform and exert pressure. We can set benchmarks against which political and economic reforms will be measured, agreed by the European Bank for Reconstruction and Development strategy for Uzbekistan, which will be reviewed by the EBRD later this year. Secondly, the UN Special Rapporteur's report on torture in Uzbekistan referred to torture as "systematic". It behoves us all to continue to press the Uzbek authorities to implement the recommendations in that report.

(HL Deb 11 November 2003 Vol. 654 c1212)

6/97

In reply to a written question, the Parliamentary Secretary, Lord Chancellor's Department, wrote:

In considering the possibility of legislation, the Government indeed have in mind all their international treaty obligations. As well as the European Convention on Human Rights, these include the International Covenant on Civil and Political Rights, the International Covenant on Economic, Social and Cultural Rights and the International Labour Organisation Conventions.

(HL Deb 24 March 2003 Vol. 646 cWA59–WA60)

6/98

In reply to written questions on racial discrimination the Minister of State, Home Office, wrote:

We consider that the exclusion of "colour" from the grounds of unlawful discrimination in the Race Relations Act 1976 (Amendment) Regulations 2003 is compatible with Article 14 of the European Convention on Human Rights Act 1998 to the extent that the exclusion from the directive itself is so compatible.

. . .

We consider that the exclusion of "colour" from the grounds of unlawful racial discrimination in the Race Relations Act 1976 (Amendment) Regulations 2003 is compatible with Articles 2(2) and 26 of the United Nations International Covenant on Civil and Political Rights (which treat colour as a separate element) in so far as the subject matter of the two instruments overlaps and to the extent that the exclusion from the directive itself is so compatible.

. . .

We consider that the exclusion of "colour" from the grounds of unlawful discrimination in the Race Relations Act 1976 (Amendment) Regulations is compatible with the United Nations International Convention on the Elimination of All Forms of Racial Discrimination in that the references to race and ethnicity appear to be common to the concepts of racial discrimination contained in both the EC Article 13 Race Directive and in the convention, while colour is not common to them.

(HL Deb 24 June 2003 Vol. 650 cWA9–WA10)

6/99

In reply to a written question on Morocco's statement on the Proposal of James Baker on Western Sahara, the Parliamentary Under-Secretary of State, FCO, wrote:

We understand that at this point, responses to the proposals of James Baker have been kept private. However, I welcome the views of King Mohammed VI of Morocco in his message (read by Driss Jettou, the Moroccan Prime Minister) of 14 March, to the 5th CEN-SAD summit (the Community of Sahel and Sahara states). This renewed the Kingdom of Morocco's readiness for dialogue and negotiation with a view to finding a political solution to this dispute.

The United Kingdom supports fully the efforts of the UN Secretary General (UNSG) and his Personal Envoy, James Baker to find a just, lasting and mutually acceptable solution to the Western Sahara dispute that provides for self-determination for the people of Western Sahara.

(HC Deb 28 April 2003 Vol. 404 c133W–134W)

6/100

In reply to a written question on Human Rights abuses in Western Sahara, the Parliamentary Under-Secretary of State, FCO, wrote:

FCO officials and I call regularly upon the parties to the Western Sahara dispute to take action on human rights issues. In February this year, I called for the immediate release of the remaining 1,160 Moroccan prisoners of war held by the Polisario Front, some held for over 25 years and some are in poor physical and mental health. In April this year officials took action to bring to the attention of the Moroccan authorities concerns over the trial, sentencing and prison conditions of Ali Salem Tamek, a Saharawi activist. We will continue to monitor the situation closely, taking action with the appropriate authorities where necessary.

(HC Deb 28 April 2003 Vol. 404 c134W)

Part Six: IX. *The Position of the Individual (Including the Corporation) in International Law—Crimes under international law*

(See also **3/12**)

6/101

During a debate in the House of Lords, the Parliamentary Under-Secretary of State, Home Office, said:

I turn to the definition of "terrorism". We heard interesting contributions from several noble Lords. The Terrorism Act 2000 defines terrorism as both a serious criminal act and one that is designed to influence government or to intimidate the public, and made for the purpose of advancing a political, religious or ideological cause. In essence, it carries the point made by the noble Lord, Lord Renton: it relates not merely to a criminal act but to the intent behind such an act. In other words, the context defines whether murder, as it were, moves from being simple murder to being terrorist murder. As the House knows, under UK law in general there are no specific terrorist offences. Suspected terrorists are prosecuted under criminal legislation.

On the point about listing murder as a terrorist offence, it is not terrorist specific. We are taking extra-territorial jurisdiction for murder and new Section 63B(2) lists the offences that are acts of terrorism or for purposes of terrorism as defined by Section 1 of the Terrorism Act 2000.

(HL Deb 2 December 2002 Vol. 641 c1014–1015)

6/102

During a debate in the House of Lords, the Parliamentary Under-Secretary of State, FCO, said:

We as a government have made it absolutely clear that we shall do everything we can to fight international terrorism. We have also made it absolutely clear that we shall apply all the relevant rules of international law.

(HL Deb 8 January 2003 Vol. 642 c1020)

6/103

During a meeting of the Security Council, the European Union representative stated:

The fight against terrorism must be conducted with full respect for human rights and fundamental freedoms, the rule of law and, where applicable, international humanitarian law. In its internal antiterrorist legislation, the European Union and its member States have set high standards for the safeguarding of human rights.

(UN. Doc. S/PV.4845 Resumption, 16 October 2003)

6/104

In reply to a written question the Under-Secretary of State, FCO, wrote:

During his address to the UN General Assembly debate on 1 October 2001 our then Permanent Representative, Sir Jeremy Greenstock, remarked that "what looks, smells and kills like terrorism is terrorism". An internationally agreed definition of terrorism would be beneficial and we are working in the UN to achieve one. But so deep is the controversy surrounding certain groups, an internationally agreed definition does not seem possible in the short term. Sir Jeremy Greenstock's formulation was a means to unite UN members—at a vital time—around practical steps to counter the threat, rather than on debating the definition of terrorism.

(HC Deb 10 November 2003 Vol. 413 c42W–43W)

6/105

In reply to a written question, the Minister of State for Defence wrote:

The offences contained in the Statute of the International Criminal Court (ICC) reflect international law provisions that were already applicable to the conduct of United Kingdom forces in any theatre of engagement. The ICC Statute does not therefore impose new conditions.

The consequences for our forces of UK ratification of the ICC Statute were carefully examined in preparation for the ICC Act 2001. Under the Statute, investigation and, if necessary, prosecution of any allegations of war crimes, crimes against humanity or genocide by a UK national would be carried out by the UK. The Court would intervene only if it determined that a state was unwilling or unable to pursue a particular case, but it is inconceivable that the UK would ever be unable or unwilling to investigate or take appropriate action.

(HC Deb 28 January 2003 Vol. 398 c836)

6/106

During a debate in the House of Commons, the Parliamentary Under-Secretary of State, FCO, made the following statements:

To combat genocide, the international community has drawn up a UN convention on the prevention and punishment of the crime of genocide and included provisions for jurisdiction over the crime of genocide in the statutes of both the international criminal tribunals for Rwanda and the former Yugoslavia and in the statute of the International Criminal Court.

. . .

The situation in Zimbabwe is appalling, with 60 deaths and 1,000 cases of torture in the past year. However, the ICC statute defines genocide as being committed against a national, ethnic, racial or religious grouping. It is not clear that that applies in Zimbabwe, where the actions, however reprehensible, are targeted at a political grouping and not some of the other categories that I described. Nevertheless, we shall continue to do everything in our power to put pressure on the Government of Zimbabwe to stop the appalling actions that are taking place.

(HC Deb 21 January 2003 Vol. 698 c158–159)

6/107

In reply to a written question, the Under-Secretary of State, FCO, wrote:

Criminal law provisions that explicitly include the prohibition of racist and xenophobic behaviour are in place in all EU Member States.

The joint action of 15 July 1996, adopted by the Council on the basis of Article K.3 of the Treaty on European Union, provides a common definition of racist or xenophobic behaviour, referring to public incitement to discrimination, violence or racial hatred in respect of a group of persons or a member of such a group defined by reference to colour, race, religion or national or ethnic origin. However, the interpretation of this definition does vary amongst EU member states. A number of states, including the UK, have also entered significant reservations in regard to this joint action in order to protect freedom of speech and to reflect their legal traditions in regard to use of civil law.

In its definition of racist or xenophobic behaviour, the joint action includes public condoning, for a racist or xenophobic purpose, of crimes against humanity and human rights violations; public denial of the crimes defined in Article 6 of the Charter of the International Military Tribunal appended to the London Agreement of 8 April 1945; public dissemination or distribution of tracts, pictures or other material containing expressions of racism and xenophobia; participation in the activities of groups which involve discrimination, violence, or racial, ethnic or religious hatred.

EU member states are in the process of agreeing a framework decision on racism and xenophobia which will supersede the joint action.

(HC Deb 20 January 2003 Vol. 698 c75W)

6/108

In reply to a written question the Under-Secretary of State, FCO, wrote:

Detentions of senior Ba'ath Party officials by the Coalition continue. Where senior Ba'athists pose a security risk, or are suspected of having been involved in criminal activity, they will continue to be detained by Coalition Forces. Assessments of the role of those still at large, whether involved in resistance against Coalition forces or otherwise, are ongoing.

On 16 May, the Coalition Provisional Authority issued an Order disestablishing the Ba'ath Party. This Order removes and bars all members of the Ba'ath Party at the rank of Senior Member and above from positions of authority in the future. All Ba'ath Party members suspected of criminal conduct will be investigated and, if necessary, detained.

(HC Deb 11 July 2003 Vol. 408 c1052W)

6/109

During a debate in the House of Commons, the Secretary of State, FCO, said:

There is a question as to whether an international tribunal should be established to try the leaders of the [Iraqi] regime. We have not ruled that out, but I am sceptical because of the vast costs of the international tribunals set up to deal with Yugoslavia and, even worse, Rwanda. The right hon. and learned Gentleman did not mention the International Criminal Court, but let me say that it does not have a direct role because its jurisdiction is only for events that took place after July last year.

(HC Deb 28 April 2003 Vol. 404 c33)

Part Six: X. *The Position of the Individual (Including the Corporation) in International Law—Responsibility of the Individual*

6/110

In reply to a written question on whether Robert Mugabe and his government are guilty of genocide, the Under-Secretary of State, FCO, wrote:

It is unclear whether Mugabe could be considered to have committed genocide.

Much of the intimidation, political violence and withholding of food is directed against the opposition, the Movement for Democratic Change, and the areas where it has support.

Genocide has to be committed against a "national, ethnic, racial or religious group".

(HC Deb 22 January 2003 Vol. 398 c358W)

Part Seven: I. *The state and its organs—heads of state*

(See also **5/6**)

7/1

In reply to an oral question on the prosecution of Iraqi leaders, the Attorney-General stated:

Saddam Hussein is in any event immune from criminal jurisdiction here while serving head of state of Iraq.

...

I do not agree that other lawyers would take the view that Saddam Hussein was not immune from prosecution. The immunity of heads of state was confirmed by the judgment of the International Court of Justice in *Democratic Republic of the Congo* v *Belgium* on only 14th February last year. I understand that INDICT's advisers agree with that view.

...

However, I ought to point out that what I have said is not a government statement: it is a statement of my view as an independent Law Officer, having considered the detail of the evidence in the case.

(HL Deb 27 January 2003 Vol. 643 c910–912)

7/2

In reply to a written question the Solicitor-General wrote:

On 4 June 2003 the Special Court for Sierra Leone unsealed an indictment for President Charles Taylor of Liberia as one of those who bear the greatest responsibility for war crimes, crimes against humanity and other serious violations of international humanitarian law in Sierra Leone since 1996.

The UK has called on Charles Taylor to surrender himself to the Court and continues to encourage all states, particularly those in the region, to cooperate with the Court and facilitate his arrest.

(HC Deb 15 July 2003 Vol. 409 c259W–260W)

7/3

In response to a written question on assassination of heads of state, the Minister for Europe wrote:

Our policy is to act in accordance with UK and International law. In the case of the Israeli decision in principle to expel President Arafat, the UK has made its view clear during debates in the UN Security Council and General Assembly. The expulsion or harm of President Arafat would be wrong and counter-productive. Israel should not allow its justified anger at the continuing violence to lead to actions that would undermine both the peace process and Israel's own interests.

(HC Deb 6 October 2003 Vol. 111 c1114W)

7/4

During a debate in the House of Commons the Prime Minister said:

On Iraq, the US Secretary of State is correct: Saddam Hussein will be treated with all the rights of a prisoner of war. The trial process should be determined by the Iraqi Government and the Iraqi people. It should be left to them. Of course we must ensure that the process is proper, independent and fair, but I am sure that the Iraqis have the capability to achieve that. We and other countries will work with them to ensure that that is correct.

(HC Deb 15 December 2003 Vol. 415 c1323)

Part Seven: III. *The state and its organs—other organs of the state*

7/5

Her Majesty's Government was asked the following written question:

To ask the Secretary of State for Defence (1) under what circumstances use of deadly force will be sanctioned at RAF Fairford; (2) if he will make a statement on the notices posted on the fences around RAF Fairford stating that use of deadly force is authorised.

In reply, the Minister of State for Defence wrote:

The notices are necessary to warn individuals that unauthorised entry into the inner area of the base is not permitted. They are displayed on a temporary internal security fence enclosing a much smaller area where aircraft are parked. The notices do not purport to be a statement of the law.

The reference to the authorisation of deadly force on the notice does not amount to a blanket pre-authorisation. It is US practice, in relation to specially sensitive areas, to draw attention to what is implicit whenever armed personnel (US or British) are deployed to guard military installations in the UK, namely that they are authorised to use lethal force in circumstances where it is lawful.

It is not our practice to disclose details of Rules of Engagement for reasons of operational security. I am therefore withholding the information in accordance with Exemption 1 (Defence, Security and International Relations) of Part II of the Code of Practice on Access to Government Information.

(HC Deb 11 April 2003 Vol. 403 c423W–424W)

Part Seven: IV. *The state and its organs—diplomatic missions and their members*

7/6

In reply to a written question the Minister of State, FCO, wrote:

From a community of around 20,000 in the United Kingdom entitled to immunity, 20 serious offences, allegedly committed by such persons, were drawn to the attention of the Foreign and Commonwealth Office in 2002. "Serious Offences" are defined in accordance with the 1985 White Paper on Diplomatic Immunities and Privileges—that is as offences that would, in certain circumstances, carry a penalty of 12 months or more imprisonment.

(HL Deb 10 September 2003 Vol. 652 cWA125–WA126)

7/7

During a meeting of the Sixth Committee considering the 2003 Report of the International Law Commission on Diplomatic Protection the United Kingdom representative said:

The diplomatic protection of legal persons is an important aspect of the topic, and we concur with the Special Rapporteur's decision to base his recommendations on the Judgement of the International Court of Justice in the Barcelona Traction case [ed. *Barcelona Traction, Light and Power Co. Ltd. Case (Second Phase)* 1970 ICJ Rep 3]. The Claims Rules [ed. see (1988) 37 ICLQ 1002, 1006–1008], which the UK has adopted to guide its policy and practice in this respect, are also based on that judgement, and we are therefore pleased to note the high degree of consonance between our Rules and the recommendations of the Special Rapporteur.

Nonetheless, in relation to the determination of the nationality of companies, it has been the consistent view of the UK that the nationality of a company is determined by the place of its incorporation, and this is reflected in both our Claims Rules and our investment protection treaties. Moreover we believe that this approach has the merits of being unambiguous and relatively straightforward to apply. We are therefore concerned that the text of Article 17, which was prepared by the Working Group, and which the Commission has now submitted to the Drafting Committee, requires an additional connection between an injured corporation and the protecting State. We do not believe that there is a basis for such an additional requirement as a matter of established law. Moreover the proposed language does not offer a clear basis on which such a departure from the existing law can be justified.

As regards Articles 18 and 19, we broadly concur that these set out the exceptional circumstances under which the State of nationality of shareholders may exercise diplomatic protection on their behalf. We would note that under these rules it is conceivable that shareholders may come from different nationalities, enabling more than one State to exercise protection. In the cases where the United Kingdom might be entitled to make such claims, we would, as a matter of practice rather than law, normally seek to do so in concert with other relevant States. Similarly in cases in which the requirement of continuous nationality, as set out in Article 20, was not met, our Claims Rules hold open the possibility that we may, in an appropriate case, take up a claim in concert with the State of former or subsequent nationality.

In relation to the discussion on Article 21 we note the reasons for the deletion of this proposal. We would however favour the insertion of a suitably formulated general savings clause in respect of special regimes at the end of the draft articles, as we believe that this should be made explicit and not simply left to the commentaries. This may, incidentally, provide an appropriate answer to the question raised by the Commission in paragraph 28 of its Report on the protection of a ship's crew by the flag State. We would suggest that the judgement of the International Tribunal on the Law of the Sea in the case of The M/V Saiga (No.2) be considered in this light.

Finally, on this topic, in response to the Commission's question at paragraph 28 of its Report, we believe that the protection that an international organisation, such as the United Nations, affords to members of its staff, is a functional protection which does not form part of the present topic.

(www.ukun.org, 29 October 2003)

7/8

The FCO produced a circular:

FCO CIRCULAR 029-03
DIPLOMATIC AND CONSULAR STATUS OVERSEAS

ENTITLEMENT TO DIPLOMATIC PASSPORTS AND DIPLOMATIC STATUS AND WAIVERS OF IMMUNITY

SUMMARY

1. The purpose of the international legal rules on Diplomatic/Consular immunity is to ensure the efficient performance of the functions of diplomatic and consular Missions, and not to benefit individuals. International law requires those enjoying immunity to respect the laws and regulations of the receiving State. HMG takes this requirement very seriously indeed, and expects the highest standards of conduct from diplomats and consuls in London and from British diplomats and consuls and their families overseas. This circular should be brought to the attention of all staff and their families.

DIPLOMATIC IMMUNITY

2. Staff who are diplomatic agents (have "diplomatic status") by the receiving State are entitled to immunity from the criminal and (with certain limited exceptions) civil jurisdiction of the receiving State. This status is automatically granted to staff at B and C and above, and in most cases to B and B officers carrying out Consular, Commercial, Management, Political, Economic and Entry Clearance functions at a Mission. In some Posts all staff have immunity.

Administrative and Technical (A&T) staff members of Embassies are entitled to immunity from the criminal jurisdiction of the receiving State, and from its civil jurisdiction in respect of acts carried out in the course of their official functions (this applies to some B and B and most B and A staff).

NB: Officers who are nationals of the receiving State (including dual nationals) or permanently resident there cannot be guaranteed diplomatic or A&T status. This would be up to the receiving State.

3. Members of the families of diplomatic and A&T staff enjoy analogous immunity from the receiving State's jurisdiction to that enjoyed by the officer, unless they are nationals of or permanently resident in that State—see below. Family members will not however generally have immunity from civil liability for actions taken in the course of employment outside the Mission (see Annex A to this circular). "Members of the family" are generally defined as spouses and dependents resident at post or dependents whose fares to post have been paid from public funds, excluding children who travel to post on CCJs [ed. concessionary child journeys].

4. Declared unmarried and same-sex partners who are British Nationals and officially recognised partners are eligible for diplomatic/official passports. However, the attitude towards unmarried/same-sex partners varies from one receiving State to another and local status cannot be guaranteed. The Vienna Convention on Diplomatic Relations (VCDR) does not expressly refer to partners and even if a receiving State appears to be prepared to accept the diplomatic status of a partner a local court may decide that he or she does not enjoy diplomatic immunity.

NB: If spouses or partners are dual nationals, nationals of the receiving State, permanently resident in the receiving State or third country nationals, local diplomatic or A&T status cannot be guaranteed and is within the gift of the receiving State.

CONSULAR IMMUNITY

5. Consular status differs from diplomatic status in that it carries less extensive immunities and few privileges; consular officers (consular UK-based staff) are immune from local jurisdiction only in respect of acts carried out in the exercise of their official functions. While many privileges and immunities do extend to officers' families, immunity from civil jurisdiction does not.

6. In principle, officers in grade C4 and above (and most B3 officers) hold the status of consular officer when serving at a consular Post. Some may hold diplomatic status. There are bilateral Consular Conventions between the United Kingdom and some countries that can also affect consular status and the extent of immunities.

...

STATUS FOR MEMBERS OF OTHER GOVERNMENT DEPARTMENTS (OGDs) AT POST

8. Where members of other government departments at post need diplomatic or A&T status to enable them to carry out their functions effectively, a case should be made by the relevant diplomatic post to Personnel Policy, who will consider applications on a case by case basis. A strong argument must be put forward.

"To enable them to obtain duty-free goods" is not a good argument. The request must have the written backing of the Head of Post, who will have overall responsibility for that officer's conduct in the host country. This overall responsibility, and the authority of the Head of Post to act within that responsibility, must be acknowledged, in writing, by the OGD concerned.

9. Once PP's agreement is obtained, but not before, the OGD officer concerned may apply to Consular Division for a diplomatic or official passport, as appropriate. However, even where PP agree, the decision as to whether or not to grant status locally still rests with the receiving State. NB: If an officer is a national of the receiving State (including dual nationals), permanently resident there, or a third country national, local status may be more difficult to attain.

. . .

WAIVERS OF IMMUNITY

11. Diplomatic or consular immunity belongs to the diplomat's or consul's State, not to the individual. So it can only be waived by the sending State at the request of the receiving State. In practice this means all requests for a waiver of the immunity of a UK diplomat or consul must be made through the local MFA [Ministry of Foreign Affairs] and not directly by the local judiciary or police. Under no circumstances should a court summons or other legal requests be acknowledged without prior consultation with Personal Policy (PERS-PP).

12. Immunity is a privilege not a perk. It carries with it certain obligations. HMG's staff overseas must ensure that they do not abuse this privilege, and must maintain the UK's reputation for the high standards of behaviour of its staff overseas. The main purpose of immunity is to preserve the efficient working of Missions overseas and to protect staff from hostile action on the part of the host authorities. This can only be done if staff respect local laws and regulations, and do not abuse their immunity by seeking to avoid penalties properly applicable to them, or to evade their legal duties.

HMG's General Policy on Waivers of Immunity

13. HMG's general policy is that immunity should not be unreasonably maintained. In practice all staff are expected to answer any criminal or civil charge brought against them, including cases of domestic violence (Annex E). In some countries this may present practical problems, and so decisions about waiving or claiming immunity may only be taken after consultation with PERS-PP. In making any decision the following factors will have to be considered:

- Whether local laws are alien to British ideas of justice
- Whether there are doubts about the impartiality or efficiency of local judicial procedures
- Whether the alleged offence appears to have been contrived by the receiving State for political or other reasons
- Whether there are valid security reasons (eg if the officer was privy to sensitive information which may be put in jeopardy through imprisonment or intensive police questions)
- Whether the function of the Mission would be seriously impeded

14. The most common where waivers are sought are traffic accidents, drink-drive offences, LE staff redundancies and Industrial Tribunals, and requests to appear as witnesses. [T]he general principles which should be applied in all cases are:

I. Any request for an officer to appear in court proceedings or give evidence should be made through the MFA and addressed to the Mission, not the individual.

II. The Mission should immediately consult their local Legal Advisor and then consult the PERS-PP. No decision on whether to claim or waive immunity can be taken before agreement is given by PP.

III. The Mission should try to obtain as much information as possible about the charges or claims being made. It is useful to know:

- Whether the alleged offence/summons relates to a criminal or civil charge;
- Whether the officer's status is diplomatic, A&T or consular and they employed by the FCO or an OGD;
- Whether there is any scope for an out of court settlement and, if so, how much would have to be paid;
- Whether the charge is in substance against HMG (as the individual's employer) in respect of acts carried out in the course of the individual's duties, or against the individual concerned in his/her own right;
- How long the judicial process would take if HMG were to defend the allegation(s);
- A brief description of the judicial process would follow in the case in question.

15. One factor in determining an approach in individual cases will be the way in which the host Government handles the matters of this kind in respect of its own staff in London. In some cases it may be desirable to withdraw an officer if that is the host Government's preferred way of handling the matter.

16. Even if, for these or other reasons, it is decided not to waive immunity, internal disciplinary proceedings may still be instituted if the officer's conduct constitutes a breach of Diplomatic Service Regulations.

...

Annex A

SPOUSE EMPLOYMENT

1. Under the Vienna Convention on Diplomatic Relations (VCDR), diplomats and A&T staff and their families do not enjoy immunity from civil jurisdiction in respect of actions relating to any professional or commercial activity exercised in the receiving State outside their official functions.

2. Spouses and other partners who are employed outside the Mission therefore do not enjoy immunity from civil jurisdiction in respect of actions taken in the course of their employment. Because of the embarrassment which might arise if a spouse contravened local laws in the course of their activities, it is of

paramount importance that Heads of Mission and Management Officers, when advising spouses about outside employment, draw attention to the implications of any contravention of local law. The spouse should be made aware that any wilful breach of local laws might, depending on the circumstances, jeopardise the position of their partner.

3. HMG has reached agreements about employment of diplomatic spouses with 81 countries outside of the EU which enable spouses/partners on diplomatic and consular visas to undertake work outside the Diplomatic Mission. These agreements expressly state that members of a family enjoying immunity from the civil and administrative jurisdiction of the receiving state, under the VCDR or any other international instrument, will not be entitled to such immunity in respect of their employment. Working family members are also liable to pay income tax and national insurance contributions on their earnings.

(Text supplied by the FCO)

Part Seven: VI. *The state and its organs—special missions*

7/9

During a House of Lords debate on the Vienna Document 1999 (Privileges and Immunities) Order 2002 the Minister of State, FCO, made the following statement:

My Lords, this order was laid before the House on 3rd July 2003, together with an Explanatory Memorandum, now required for all affirmative statutory instruments.

The purpose of the order is to confer privileges and immunities on observers, inspectors, evaluators and auxiliary personnel in accordance with the United Kingdom's political commitments under the Vienna Document 1999 on the negotiations on confidence and security building measures.

The order is necessary for the United Kingdom to give effect in domestic law to these provisions and it is being made under Section 1(2) of the Arms Control and Disarmament (Privileges and Immunities) Act 1988.

Adopted on 16th November 1999, the Vienna Document, which came into effect on 1st January 2000, is the latest version of a package of measures that first took shape in the Stockholm Document 1986. Its purpose is to increase military transparency and predictability. The original competence and security building measures agreed in Stockholm were primarily concerned with the monitoring of certain military activities of the Warsaw Pact and the NATO countries. The Vienna Document 1990, which was followed by the Vienna Documents of 1992, 1994 and 1999, built up, upon those confidences, security building measures. The Vienna Documents have evolved since 1986 and keep pace with the changing political map of Europe.

The Vienna Document 1999 contains a number of revisions and enhancements, including expanding the possibilities for exchange of information between states, encouraging states to promote regional measures tailored to specific regional needs, and promoting a wide range of military contact activities and seminars between states parties.

The Vienna Document deals with conventional but, I stress, not nuclear forces, and applies to all 55 of the Organisation for Security and Co-operation in Europe states. As the House is well aware, a necessary component of any arms control regime is the ability to monitor compliance with the regime's obligations. Under the Vienna Document that is done by means of observations, evaluations and short-notice on-site challenge inspections carried out by representatives of participating states.

The document requires that certain persons are granted privileges and immunities in accordance with the Vienna Convention on Diplomatic Relations. The number of missions to the United Kingdom is not likely to be high. Since the competence and security measures began in 1987, the UK has received three inspections, hosted three observations and received 15 evaluation visits. These events were completed successfully, without any complaints or objections from participating states.

The present order gives effect to the provisions of the latest version of the Vienna Document. However, the privileges and immunities accorded to the observers, inspectors, evaluators and others are unchanged from those provided in the earlier documents. Those privileges were conferred by a 1992 Order in Council, which the present order revokes. It has regrettably taken a while to implement the privileges and immunity provisions of the 1999 document, but, as far as we are aware, the delay has not caused any practical difficulties. There have been no instances where inspections or evaluation teams have sought to invoke immunity. The present order ensures that there can be no doubt about the status of individuals involved in carrying out the inspections, evaluations and observations in the United Kingdom.

I am satisfied that the order is compatible with the rights contained in the European Convention on Human Rights.

(HL Deb 9 September 2003 Vol. 652 c277–278)

Part Seven: VIII. *The state and its organs—armed forces, including visiting forces*

7/10

During a debate in the House of Commons, the Parliamentary Under-Secretary of State for Defence made the following statements:

Many right hon. and hon. Members will be aware that Gurkhas are able to serve in the British Army today only because in 1947, at the time of Indian independence, an agreement was reached with the Governments of India and Nepal to enable four Gurkha regiments to transfer into the British Army. That is known as the tripartite agreement, or TPA. The Brigade of Gurkhas today consists of approximately 3,500 men who serve mainly in the infantry, but also in Gurkha logistics, signals and engineer units...

One of the original aims of the TPA was to ensure that the Armies of Great Britain and India could recruit and maintain formed Gurkha regiments on an equal basis. It also safeguarded the cultural, religious and national heritage of Gurkha soldiers, in accordance with the wishes of the Nepalese Government. That is because it was important then, as it is now, for Gurkhas not to be seen merely as mercenaries. The TPA linked British Gurkha terms and conditions of service to those of the Indian army, reflecting sensitivities about whether the newly formed Indian army would be able to retain or attract Gurkhas if there was a substantial differential between British Gurkha and Indian army terms and conditions of service. There was also concern about creating a differential in Nepal, where British Gurkha pensioners continued to live alongside fellow citizens who served in the Nepalese and Indian armies.

While I acknowledge that perhaps not all of the principles that underpinned the TPA in 1947 apply today, I must stress that it remains the basic instrument enabling us to recruit Gurkhas. Without it, Nepalese citizens would be classed as aliens for recruiting purposes and would in practice be unable to serve in the British Army. Leaving aside difficulties relating to nationality, if it were not for the TPA, the English language skills of most Gurkha recruits would bar their entry to non-Gurkha units. The Brigade of Gurkhas has a command system that caters for the fact that Nepali is widely spoken and that English is not the first language of its soldiers. It is partly for that reason that Gurkhas serve in formed units.

There are therefore three principles that underpin service in the Brigade of Gurkhas: Gurkhas are recruited in Nepal; they serve in formed Gurkha units; and they are discharged as Nepalese citizens in Nepal. Gurkhas return home with their pension entitlement, which is a vital source of revenue to one of the poorest countries in the world. I have to tell the right hon. Lady that, given the history of the brigade and the unique nature of Gurkha service, it would be irrational if those differences were not taken into account when considering Gurkhas' conditions of employment. Most right hon. and hon. Members are already aware that while Gurkha basic pay continues to be set in accordance with the Indian army pay code, the TPA allows for a cost of living allowance to be paid for service outside Nepal. For many years, the Ministry of Defence has used that as a tool to enhance remuneration, and since 1997 "Universal Addition" has been paid, broadly aligning Gurkha income to the take-home pay of British personnel.

...

Gurkhas are discharged in Nepal because we have a duty to ensure that they return to their home country. We also have an obligation to ensure that they do not feel that they are returning to a foreign country. It is partly for this reason that Gurkhas are entitled to special periods of five months long leave in Nepal every three years, although I take account of the right hon. Lady's assertion that these tours can sometimes be reduced. This is quite unlike any provision available to British personnel.

(HC Deb 6 March 2003 Vol. 400 c1044–1046)

7/11

In reply to a written question, the Minister of State, FCO, wrote:

On 4 January 2002 the British Commander of the International Security Assistance Force (ISAF) signed a Military Technical Agreement with the Afghan Interim Administration for the protection of ISAF personnel.

The agreement was signed on behalf of the ISAF rather than in a national capacity. Other European states contributing personnel to the ISAF both at the time and since are covered by the agreement.

The agreement provides that "ISAF and supporting personnel, including associated liaison personnel, may not be surrendered to or transferred to the custody of an international tribunal or other entity or state without the express consent of the contributing state".

This is not inconsistent with the UK's commitment to co-operate with the ICC. The ICC's jurisdiction complements that of the states parties to the Rome Statute which set up the ICC. The UK is conscientious in enforcing respect for international humanitarian law among its service personnel. It is inconceivable that the UK would be unable or unwilling (as defined in Article 17 of the Rome Statute) to make its own investigation of an alleged offence within Afghanistan by a British member of ISAF, which might otherwise fall within the jurisdiction of the ICC.

(HL Deb 2 July 2003 Vol. 650 cWA100)

7/12

In reply to oral questions the Under-Secretary of State for Defence said:

The United Kingdom's rules of engagement do not strictly in law provide UK service personnel with immunity from the UK legal process. However, they are robust and are drawn up in accordance with international and domestic law. Therefore, acting within the rules [of engagement] is very likely in practice to provide protection from prosecution.

...

My Lords, the reason it cannot be certain in law is because rules of engagement are for guidance only and do not constitute law, which is for the courts to determine. I shall try to assist by making the distinction between immunity from legal process—which is the subject of the Question—where there can be no guarantee that legal process may be instituted, and practical consequences. Where a member of the Armed Forces acts within the rules of engagement—that could, of course, be a matter for the court eventually to have to decide—the matter is unlikely to go to court and almost certainly would not result in a finding of liability or guilt.

(HL Deb 13 October 2003 Vol. 653 c599–600)

7/13

In reply to a written question the Minister of State, FCO, wrote:

My Lords, the Iraq Survey Group (ISG) is not part of the Coalition Provisional Authority. It is part of the United States-led military forces in Iraq and is therefore accountable to the United States Administration. British personnel seconded to the survey group are under the tactical control of the United States' commander. They are under the operational command of and accountable to the United Kingdom Chief of Joint Operations and thus to Her Majesty's Government. On reporting, the findings of the group are available to the coalition partners, including our own Intelligence and Security Committee, which will have access to the full text of the ISG interim report.

(HL Deb 16 October 2003 Vol. 653 c1095)

Part Eight: I. A. *Jurisdiction of the state—bases of jurisdiction—territoriality*

8/1

During a debate in the House of Commons, the Parliamentary Under-Secretary of State for Transport said:

The Government take seriously the problem of disruptive passenger behaviour on aircraft. It rightly became a matter of increased public concern after a serious incident in 1998 when a stewardess was attacked and injured on board a United Kingdom aircraft. The Government took action in two ways. First, we set up a working group on disruptive passengers, which the Department chaired. It included representatives from the Civil Aviation Authority, the Home Office, the police, airlines and unions. Its remit was to advise Ministers on measures to minimise the frequency and potential impact of disruptive behaviour on board aircraft.

Secondly, on the group's advice, we introduced a standardised reporting scheme for disruptive behaviour on board United Kingdom aircraft. At the time, little hard evidence was available and it was agreed that statistics were necessary to establish the nature and scale of the problem.

. . .

United Kingdom legislation to deal with offences on board aircraft is among the most comprehensive in the world. Several specific offences relate to behaviour on aircraft: endangering the safety of an aircraft; being drunk in an aircraft; smoking when that is prohibited; disobeying a lawful command by the commander of an aircraft; and acting in a disruptive manner.

Normal criminal law applies on board United Kingdom aircraft and powers also exist for acting against offenders on board non-UK airlines whose next destination is the UK, provided that the act is an offence under both UK law and the law of the state where the aircraft is registered.

However, it is essential that offences can be properly enforced and that penalties are appropriate. In the case of the offence of endangering the safety of an aircraft, there is consensus that the maximum two-year sentence is not proportionate to the gravity of the offence. In at least one case, a judge commented that if he had been able to pass a longer sentence, he would have done so.

(HC Deb 7 February 2003 Vol. 399 c611–612)

Part Eight: I. B. *Jurisdiction of the state—bases of jurisdiction—personality (active and passive)*

(See also **6/55**)

8/2

In reply to a written question the Solicitor-General wrote:

The courts of England and Wales may have jurisdiction in respect of an offence committed abroad if the offender, or the victim, is a British national. Once such jurisdiction is established then the procedures for investigating and prosecuting the case are the same as for any case prosecuted in the courts of England and Wales.

(HC Deb 17 November 2003 Vol. 413 c467W)

Part Eight: I. C. *Jurisdiction of the state—bases of jurisdiction—protective principle*

8/3

During the debate on the Official Report of the Grand Committee on the Crime (International Cooperation) Bill, the Parliamentary Under-Secretary of State for Home Affairs stated:

The clauses currently make it clear exactly which offences we seek to take extra-territorial jurisdiction for. United Kingdom legislation is the most practical and appropriate means of ensuring that we can prosecute those involved in terrorist activity. To list or attempt to list all crimes that could be committed by terrorists in counter-terrorism legislation is not necessary or desirable.

I turn now to specifics. When we were reflecting on the offences found in Article 1, we listed all those offences in normal criminal law which could be covered by the framework decision [ed. EU Framework Decision on Terrorism]. In general, there are no exclusively terrorist offences under United Kingdom law. Therefore, we had to interpret the offences listed in the framework decision. The Suppression of Terrorism Act concerns extra-territorial jurisdiction over offences carried out in states who are signatories to the European Convention on the Suppression of Terrorism. Those clauses cover acts outside European states by and against UK nationals or residents.

The language used is standard to that used to take extra-territorial jurisdiction. Similar language is used in the Terrorism Act 2000 and other legislation. It gives jurisdiction to England and Wales, Scotland and Northern Ireland if the act committed would have been an offence there.

Finally, is there a real difference between UK tourists being attacked and physically assaulted in order to deter their presence in a foreign state or to make a point to the local government and the same terrorists conducting a campaign against UK tourists to achieve the same end? We believe that situation is unlikely, but possible.

. . .

Article 4 of the framework decision requires member states to ensure that inciting, aiding, abetting or attempting to commit an offence is made punishable. Under UK law jurisdiction for secondary and inchoate offences, such as aiding, abetting, attempting, inciting, conspiring, counselling and procuring, is dependent on whether we have taken jurisdiction for the substantive offence in the UK. As we are taking extra-territorial jurisdiction over the substantive offences listed in Article 1.1, 1.2 and 1.3 of the framework decision in certain circumstances, we do not need to legislate specifically in order to take extra-territorial jurisdiction over aiding, abetting, attempting, inciting, conspiring, counselling or procuring to commit the offences listed in Sections 63B and 63C in the particular circumstances described in those sections.

Rather, where an extra-territorial offence is created, extra-territorial jurisdiction is also automatically taken over secondary and inchoate offences.

. . .

We already take extra-territorial jurisdiction over explosives offences under Section 62 of the Terrorism Act 2000. This also covers chemical and biological offences; nuclear offences are covered by the Nuclear Material (Offences) Act 1983.

. . .

New Section 63C(1) of the Terrorism Act gives the UK extra-territorial jurisdiction over certain domestic offences where they are committed against UK nationals or residents and "protected persons" outside the UK as an act of terrorism or for the purposes of terrorism.

Subsection (3) of this section specifies those persons who are "protected persons". This includes, inter alia, a member of a UK diplomatic mission within the meaning of Article 1(b) of the Vienna Convention on Diplomatic Relations 1961.

Therefore, the definition of a member of a diplomatic mission and consular post as contained in these provisions includes the employees of the mission and consular post, as the definition includes diplomatic, technical, administrative and service staff. So employees are already covered.

The Vienna convention defines members of a diplomatic and consular mission as including diplomatic staff, administrative and technical staff and service staff.

Service staff are persons in the domestic service of the mission. Accordingly, this definition includes all those employed by the mission whatever their nationality.

(HL Deb 29 January 2003 Vol. 643 cGC170–GC176)

Part Eight: III. A. *Jurisdiction of the state—extra-territorial exercises of jurisdiction—general*

8/4

In reply to a written question, the Under-Secretary of State, FCO, wrote:

Our Embassy in Washington and Ministers and officials in the FCO and the Department of Trade and Industry frequently discuss a range of trade issues with their US counterparts. These include, from time to time, trade with Cuba in the context of the US Helms-Burton legislation. The UK and the EU oppose this legislation because of its extraterritorial effect.

(HC Deb 28 January 2003 Vol. 398 c762W)

8/5

In reply to a written question, the Parliamentary Under-Secretary, Lord Chancellor's Department, wrote:

On 17 and 18 February senior officials of the European Commission and the United States administration met to discuss the problems for airlines operating flights to or from the US arising from the requirements imposed by US legislation for airlines to disclose detailed information about passengers to US Customs.

Following the discussions the two sides issued a joint statement explaining the outcome. They agreed to work towards a bilateral arrangement which will permit the Commission to make a formal decision under Article 25.6 of the EC Data Protection Directive that there is adequate protection for the passenger information that US Customs receives from airlines which are bound by EC law. Such a decision will be based on information and undertakings provided by US Customs.

The joint statement sets out the undertakings that US Customs has already made to protect the passenger information that it receives from airlines in the interim. They include an undertaking to respect the principles of the Data Protection Directive. The requirement for airlines to provide passenger information to US Customs is effective from 5 March.

The joint statement is not binding on airlines. It is for airlines to decide whether they disclose passenger information as required by US law. Airlines not providing the information will be liable to heavy fines and other sanctions from the US side. The content of the joint statement is a matter for the two parties in whose name it was made. It requires no formal endorsement by either Her Majesty's Government or the Council of Ministers. The Government are considering the implications of the joint statement for UK law.

(HL Deb 24 March 2003 Vol. 646 cWA58–WA59)

8/6

In reply to a written question the Foreign Office Minister wrote:

The British Government oppose all unwarranted assertions of extraterritorial jurisdiction in commercial cases. Such assertions infringe on the sovereign right of states to regulate activities within their own territory, interfere with the freedom of states to conduct their own economic policies, place an unwarranted burden on businesses, and can create a climate of uncertainty which may affect the trading and investment conditions of British companies.

A number of cases have been brought under the United States' Alien Tort Statute against British companies and others in relation to their activities in third countries. Of particular concern are cases brought in the US against British companies in relation to their activities in South Africa during the Apartheid era, alleging that their presence in South Africa at the time made them complicit in human rights abuses.

The British Government have expressed to the US Government their concerns over the extraterritorial use of the Alien Tort Statute in these commercial cases. The US Government have filed an amicus brief in a related case brought under the statute, seeking to address this issue among others.

The British Government remain committed to combating impunity for human rights violations wherever they occur. We believe that the most effective means of achieving this goal is the strengthening and developing of credible national justice mechanisms that conform to international human rights standards. We believe that, in the first instance, legal remedies in the country where the act allegedly took place should be exhausted. In the apartheid cases this does not appear to have happened.

Moreover, South Africa is engaged in an ongoing post-apartheid reconciliation process, the complexities of which should not be underestimated. We believe that the South African Government are best placed and best capable of dealing with the issue of reparations for crimes under apartheid.

(HL Deb 17 July 2003 Vol. 651 cWA153–WA154)

Part Nine: I. A.1. *State territory—territory—elements of territory—land, international waters, rivers, lakes and land-locked seas*

(See also **Parts Ten** and **Eleven**)

9/1

During a debate in the House of Lords, the Parliamentary Under-Secretary of State, FCO, was asked the following question:

My Lords, having declared an interest in the International Criminal Court Act... what human rights are accorded to terrorists and to prisoners of war on Diego Garcia and how is such distinction drawn, as the United States has declined to ratify the statute?

In reply the Parliamentary Under-Secretary of State said:

My Lords, I repeat that the stories which have appeared in the press are completely without foundation. The United States Government would need to ask our permission to bring suspects to Diego Garcia and they have not done so. No suspected terrorists are being held on Diego Garcia and, under current British Indian Ocean Territory law, there would be no authority for the detention of Al'Qaeda suspects in the territory.

(HL Deb 8 January 2003 Vol. 642 c1020)

9/2

During a debate in the House of Lords, the Parliamentary Under-Secretary of State, FCO, said:

My Lords, I am of course aware of the concerns of the Chagos islanders and their wish to go back to Diego Garcia. I have been involved in discussions on that matter. We have consulted the United States, as we have a responsibility to do so under the treaties we have signed with the US. The US has not given agreement to this but we have agreed that there could be a return. We chartered a vessel but, unfortunately, it was not made available. We are happy to reinstate any such visit but it would not include Diego Garcia because of the reluctance of the US Government.

(HL Deb 8 January 2003 Vol. 642 c1020)

9/3

In reply to the written question on how far British territory extends around Diego Garcia, the Parliamentary Under-Secretary of State, FCO, wrote:

Diego Garcia has a territorial sea of three nautical miles.

(HC Deb 17 March 2003 Vol. 401 c529W)

9/4

In reply to a written question the Minister of State, FCO, wrote:

The "Wideawake" agreement between the United Kingdom and the United States Governments, which allows for the opening of Wideawake Airfield on Ascension Island to civilian charter traffic, was signed on 1 October.

At present access to Ascension Island for civilians is by ship, or on RAF flights between Brize Norton and the Falkland Islands. The UK Government wish to improve access to Ascension Island, in order to provide an essential building block for its future economic development. The UK Government have therefore agreed with the US Government that the US "Wideawake" military airbase on Ascension Island may be used for a limited number of civilian charter flights every week.

It will be for airlines to decide on commercial grounds whether to take the opportunity to fly to Ascension Island. The UK Government will work closely with the Ascension Island Government to encourage airlines to fly there. A prospectus will be issued in early 2004.

The opening of the airfield is part of the modernisation process of Ascension Island. In 2002 a fiscal regime was introduced and the first-ever Island Council was formed. The Ascension Island Government are working to continue this process and are preparing a strategic plan providing a vision for the Island for the next five years.

(HL Deb 17 November 2003 Vol. 654 cWA244–WA245)

9/5

In reply to a written question the Defence Minister wrote:

We are fully committed to ensuring the sovereignty and security of the Falkland Islands.

(HC Deb 6 October 2003 Vol. 411 c1160W)

Part Nine: I. B. *State territory—territory—good neighbourliness*

9/6

In reply to a written question, the Parliamentary Under-Secretary of State, FCO, wrote:

The Organization of American States (OAS) concluded its two-year process to help the governments of Guatemala and Belize settle their territorial dispute on 30 September. Detailed proposals drawn up by independent facilitators appointed by both governments were presented to the governments on 16 September and provide the basis for a fair and honourable settlement to this long-standing dispute. We hope both governments will now seize this historic opportunity. The facilitators have recommended some adjustment to the land border and proposed new maritime limits giving Guatemala an economic exclusion zone and continental shelf in the Gulf of Honduras of some 2,000 square nautical miles. The governments of Belize and Honduras have each agreed to contribute 1,000 square nautical miles to this zone.

The facilitators have also recommended the establishment of a tri-national ecological park covering coastal, insular and maritime areas of Belize, Guatemala and Honduras and a substantial development trust fund.

Details can be found on the Belize Government's website www.belize.gov.bz/.

At a ceremony in Washington on 30 September marking the end of the facilitation process, Dr MacShane spoke of the UK's full support for the OAS process. He welcomed the proposals highlighting the potential for investment and economic growth that will result if the referendums that are now due to be held simultaneously in both countries are successful.

Her Majesty's Government believe that the facilitators have worked patiently and meticulously to produce proposals that are fair and honourable to the governments of Guatemala and Belize. They represent the best chance yet of settling the dispute. Settlement would also have a global significance, demonstrating that with good will and determination even the most intractable problems can be resolved by negotiation. A settlement would open a new chapter of peace and harmony between the two countries and reduce the risk of potential conflict along the border.

We urge the governments and civil society of both countries to enter into constructive debate on what a settlement would mean to their populace before putting the proposals to referendums.

(HL Deb 23 October 2002 Vol. 639 cWA102)

Part Nine: II. A. *State territory—boundaries and frontiers—delimitation*

(See **5/38**)

Part Nine: III. A. *State Territory—Acquisition and transfer of territory—Acquisition*

9/7

In a written answer, the Minister for Europe wrote:

Graham Island is the tip of a small volcano 30 miles off the coast of Sicily which emerges from the sea occasionally for short periods. In 1831 the Royal Navy claimed it but in 1832 it re-submerged. We doubt whether the 1831 claim subsists and have never sought to revive it. We understand that the Italian government claims the island.

(HC Deb 8 April 2003 Vol. 403 c190W)

Part Nine: III. B. *State Territory—Acquisition and transfer of territory—Transfer*

9/8

In reply to a written question on what action is being taken to help secure a settlement in Cyprus, the Minister of State, FCO, wrote:

During the intensive negotiations which followed the Copenhagen European Council, it became clear that the issue of territorial readjustment was a key one, needing to be resolved if there was to be a settlement. In particular, it became clear that both sides attached great importance to adjustments which represented a relatively small percentage of the area of Cyprus. The Government therefore gave urgent consideration to whether we could in some way help to bridge the remaining gap. A decision was reached to inform the UN Secretary-General that Britain would be prepared to cede part of the UK's sovereign base areas, and this offer has now been included in the UN Secretary-General's ideas of 23 February. The offer consists of 45 square miles—just under half of the total area of the SBAs. This makes up 1.2 per cent of the area of the new state of affairs in Cyprus. The areas involved would bring a number of Cypriots living near Limassol, and in the Dhekelia sovereign base area, within the administration of their respective constituent state. It will also open up areas of coastline for possible development. The areas involved do not contain military infrastructure, and this offer will not have any adverse impact on the functioning of the SBAs. The offer would only become valid if there were agreement by both sides to the UN's proposals. And, of course, legislation would be introduced to bring the transfer of territory into operation. In the event that either side in Cyprus rejects the proposals, or the proposals are rejected in a referendum by either side, the offer, along with the rest of the UN proposals, will become null and void.

We urge both sides not to let this historic opportunity to heal the division of Cyprus slip away; and to go the last mile to conclude negotiations and secure the settlement.

(HL Deb 3 March 2003 Vol. 645 cWA86–WA87)

9/9

In a written answer on how long US military forces will be stationed on British territory in the Indian Ocean, the Parliamentary Under-Secretary of State, FCO, wrote:

HMG in 1966 and subsequently has entered into a series of bilateral agreements with the United States on the use of the British Indian Ocean Territory under which the whole territory is to remain available for the defence needs of the two countries for an initial period of 50 years from 1966, and thereafter for a further period of 20 years unless either party has given prior notice to terminate it.

(HC Deb 1 May 2003 Vol. 404 c503W)

Part Eleven: I. *Seas and vessels—internal waters, including ports and harbours*

11/1

In reply to a written question on the decommissioning of US ships in the UK, the Under-Secretary of State for the Environment, Food and Rural Affairs wrote:

My Lords, the Environment Agency, as the competent authority, has now made clear to the contracting parties and to relevant United States authorities that shipment of the vessels to Hartlepool cannot be completed consistent with international rules and community law.

. . .

My Lords, as I explained the last time we discussed the matter, the Environment Agency is one of many agencies with a role in the matter. It stated right at the beginning to the American authorities that some permissions that would be required for Able UK to carry out the work were either not in place or were disputed. It wrote to the American authorities in that regard. It is now clear that without those authorisations the work could not be completed at Hartlepool consistent with national and international law.

. . . The Environment Agency is the competent authority. It took the view—and warned the American authorities—that some permissions were not in place. The Environment Agency was convinced that Able UK had the basic facilities to carry out the work, but there was waste management action that had yet to be completed.

(HL Deb 6 November 2003 Vol. 654 c960)

Part Eleven: III. *Seas and vessels—straits, including overflight*

11/2

In reply to the written question, whether Her Majesty's Government are satisfied with the present arrangements for avoiding collisions and other incidents in the English Channel, the Minister for the Cabinet wrote:

The Government are satisfied with the present arrangements for the routeing of shipping.

Shipping in the English Channel is controlled through a mandatory traffic separation scheme (TSS) jointly administered by the UK and French authorities, with France looking after the north-east lane and the UK the south-west lane. The Channel Navigation Information System (CNIS) based at Dover Maritime Rescue Co-ordination Centre (MRCC) contributes to the safety of navigation within this area by encouraging vessels to comply with the IMO adopted procedures for vessels navigating within the TSS and collating and providing the latest information to shipping on activities, conditions and navigational irregularities which may affect safe navigation.

With respect to the "Tricolor", which sank on 14 December, the French authorities have marked the wreck with five Cardinal buoys, 600 metres from the wreck, one of which is fitted with a Racon, an electronic radar echo enhancing device. The French vessel the "Glaive" is on guard duty at the wreck site in addition to the salvage tug "Alphonse Letzer" and the salvage barge "Asian Hercules". Navigational warnings are being issued hourly to ships in the area.

(HL Deb 14 January 2003 Vol. 643 cWA30)

Part Eleven: VI. *Seas and vessels—exclusive economic zone, exclusive or preferential fisheries zone*

11/3

In reply to a written question the Parliamentary Under-Secretary of State for the Environment, Food and Rural Affairs wrote:

While the United Kingdom has not declared an Exclusive Economic Zone, this does not affect the rights that the UK may assume as a coastal state in accordance with the United Nations Convention on the Law of the Sea, including an obligation to protect and preserve the marine environment.

(HL Deb 3 June 2003 Vol. 648 cWA153)

Part Eleven: VII. *Seas and vessels—continental shelf*

11/4

In response to a written question, the Parliamentary Under-Secretary of State, FCO, wrote:

Under the United Nations Convention on the Law of the Sea 1982 (UNCLOS) coastal states may declare an exclusive economic zone (EEZ) beyond and adjacent to their territorial sea up to 200 nautical miles from their baselines. Coastal states may declare instead an equivalent zone and exercise more limited jurisdiction in that zone. The Falkland Islands and St. Helena and Dependencies (which include Ascension Island) have declared a 200 nautical mile fisheries zone. South Georgia and the South Sandwich Islands have declared a 200 nautical mile maritime zone.

Under Article 76 of UNCLOS coastal states claiming a continental shelf beyond 200 nautical miles are required to make a submission to the UN Commission on the Limits of the Continental Shelf (CLCS). In respect of the Falkland Islands, South Georgia and the South Sandwich Islands, Ascension Island and St. Helena any submission should be made as soon as possible, but in any event by 13 May 2009.

The preparatory work to make submissions to the CLCS in respect of the Falkland Islands, South Georgia and the South Sandwich Islands, and Ascension Island is under way and it is expected that the submissions will be made before the deadline.

No work is being undertaken to make a submission to the CLCS under Article 76 of UNCLOS in respect of St. Helena because the geomorphology of the seabed around the island does not support a claim to a continental shelf beyond 200 nautical miles.

(HC Deb 1 March 2002 Vol. 380 c1639W)

Part Eleven: VIII. D. *Seas and vessels—high seas—piracy*

11/5

In reply to a written question the Defence Minister wrote:

The Ministry of Defence acts in concert with the Foreign and Commonwealth Office and the Department for Transport in seeking to tackle both piracy on the high seas, and maritime armed crime, which takes place in states' territorial waters. The Defence Intelligence Staff is actively engaged with national and international defence intelligence and maritime security communities, as well as commercial shipping and other organisations, to promote wider awareness, understanding, and co-operation in dealing with this growing worldwide problem. The Defence Intelligence Staff also produces reports and analyses, including the "Worldwide Threat To Shipping", published on the World Wide Web at http://www.rnreference.mod.uk.

In addition, under international law, the Royal Navy, like all other navies, is obliged to render assistance to other mariners. The RN deploys ships worldwide on a range of tasks, and in the event that a RN ship encounters a clearly defined case of piracy on the high seas, RN policy is to counter the incident and arrest those responsible in accordance with the appropriate rules of engagement. Commanding Officers on all RN ships are given guidance on the threat, and on recommended courses of action. Responses to individual incidents of maritime armed crime in territorial waters are a matter for the State which holds jurisdiction.

(HC Deb 3 November 2003 Vol. 412 c427W)

Part Eleven: VIII. E. *Seas and vessels—high seas—conservation of living resources*

11/6

In a written answer, the Under-Secretary of State for the Environment, Food and Rural Affairs wrote:

All cetaceans are fully protected in EU waters under the EU Habitats Directive. While we do not oppose the creation of an EU whale sanctuary, we believe that the current measures afford the necessary safeguards which a whale sanctuary would provide.

(HC Deb 6 February 2003 Vol. 399 c373W)

Part Eleven: XIII. *Seas and vessels—protection of the marine environment*

11/7

Her Majesty's Government was asked the following written question:

To ask the Secretary of State for Transport what progress has been made since 1997 in reducing pollution in UK waters; what proposals he has to further reduce these levels; and if he will make a statement.

In reply, the Under-Secretary of State for Transport wrote:

My Department has taken a number of proactive measures since 1997 with a view to reducing pollution in UK waters. Among these measures, the following are particularly worthy of note:

in 1997 we were the first country to introduce a statutory requirement on ports to prepare a port waste management plan to address the waste disposal needs of all types of ships calling.

in 1997, we introduced legislation which enables magistrates to impose a fine of up to £250,000 on either the master or ship owner for an oil pollution offence. This is the highest fine for any offence in a magistrates court.

we have played a leading role in launching the 1997 Quality Shipping Campaign, which tackles the problem of substandard shipping and marine pollution by addressing the role of owners and flag states in fulfilling their responsibilities under relevant international conventions.

in 1999 we introduced the role of Secretary of State's Representative for Maritime Salvage and Intervention (commonly known as SOSREP), who has the power to oversee, control and, if necessary, intervene in salvage operations within UK waters involving vessels or fixed platforms where there is a significant risk of pollution. The SOSREP role has proved very successful, as well as being an international first for the UK.

in 1999 we increased the number of government-funded Emergency Towing Vessels (ETVs) around the UK coast to four (located in the Dover Strait, the Minch, the South West approaches and in the Fair Isle), and in October 2001 we extended their period of operation so that all four operate all year round.

in 2000, we published the revised National Contingency Plan for Marine Pollution from Shipping and Offshore Installations, setting out how the relevant agencies and authorities in the UK will respond to such pollution incidents.

As regards further measures, the Government are now in the final stages of the identification of Marine Environmental High Risk Areas (MEHRAs), which will further assist in the protection of our seas and coasts. We are working on a consultation document which will announce the locations of the MEHRAs and seek comments on a range of issues associated with MEHRAs. We expect to issue the document for public consultation shortly.

My Department's Maritime and Coastguard Agency annually commissions a report to compile statistics and other information on the different types of marine pollution in the waters around the British Isles. Since 1965 this work has been completed by the Advisory Committee on Protection of the Sea (ACOPS), and in 2000 the ACOPS Report was revised and now provides data on the number of incidents, the type of incident by pollutant, the source of the pollutant and the geographical distribution of the reported incidents.

(HC Deb 4 March 2003 Vol. 400 c937W–938W)

11/8

In reply to a written question a Government representative wrote:

There is a continuing right of passage through the Minch and this has to be maintained under international law.

In August 2002, the department began undertaking a programme of vessel traffic surveys at sites around the UK that are environmentally sensitive and which may be at risk from shipping. The department proposes to undertake a comprehensive radar survey of vessels using the Minch early next year. This will allow a full assessment of existing traffic patterns and allow a review of the risks associated with shipping in the Minch.

In the longer term, amendments to the Safety of Life at Sea (SOLAS) Convention agreed by the International Maritime Organization in 2002 will make it a requirement, with effect from 31 December 2004, for ships over 500 gross tonnes to carry automated identification systems. Coastal states wishing to install shore-based equipment will be able to monitor shipping around their coasts. For example, this will enable the UK to continuously monitor and record ship movements in the Minch and elsewhere.

In partnership with the General Lighthouse Authority, the Government are participating in a test programme for transmitting navigational information for display on the electronic charts now used by many ships. The Northern Lighthouse Board has installed appropriate shore-based equipment in the Minch as part of this test programme.

(HL Deb 29 October 2003 Vol. 654 cWA51–WA52)

Part Eleven: XVI. *Seas and vessels—artificial islands, installations, and structures*

11/9

In a written answer on whether the United Kingdom exercises sovereignty as regards any lighthouses outside the United Kingdom and its territorial sea, a Government representative wrote:

The lighthouses and marine aids to navigation are operated by the general lighthouse authorities. These are Trinity House Lighthouse Service, the authority for England, Wales and the Channel Islands; the Northern Lighthouse Board, the authority for Scotland and the Isle of Man; and the Commissioners of Irish Lights, the authority for aids in Northern Ireland and the Republic of Ireland.

The GLAs are beneficial owners of the lighthouse estate. In the event of the sale of any assets, the proceeds are returned to the General Lighthouse Fund that meets the costs of provision.

Trinity House is also responsible for the lighthouse at Europa Point, Gibraltar. Trinity House acts as agent for the Department for Transport in the operation of the lighthouse at Sombrero Island. Arrangements are in hand to pass responsibility for this lighthouse to the Government of Anguilla.

(HL Deb 5 November 2002 Vol. 640 cWA92–WA93)

Part Eleven: XVIII. A.1. *Seas and vessels—vessels—legal regime—warships*

11/10

In reply to a written question, the Under-Secretary of State for Defence wrote:

All of the vessels that fall under the auspices of the Ministry of Defence comply with the provisions of the marine pollution legislation quoted and which is collectively known as MARPOL 73/78. Although MARPOL 73/78 allows, under Article 3, for the exemption of military vessels from its provisions it has long been MOD policy that these vessels will comply with or put in place systems that are as good or better than the standards required by this legislation. All military ships have a management system for environmental compliance and this is audited on a regular basis. In addition, any pollution incident is reported and the appropriate steps taken to minimise the pollution potential.

(HC Deb 22 January 2003 Vol. 398 c328W)

Part Eleven: XVIII. C.1. *Seas and vessels—vessels—jurisdiction over vessels—flag state*

11/11

In reply to a written question, the Minister of State for Defence wrote:

The definition of flag of convenience is loose and ambiguous and indeed, the Department for Transport does not officially recognise this terminology.

(HC Deb 12 February 2003 Vol. 399 c742W)

Part Eleven: XVIII. C.4. *Seas and vessels—vessels—jurisdiction over vessels—exercises of jurisdiction other than by flag, coastal, and port state*

11/12

In reply to a written question, the Minister of State for Defence wrote:

No Royal Navy assets are specifically allocated to combating piracy. International Maritime Law does, however, place an obligation on any seafarer to assist others in distress if they are in a position to do so. RN ships would offer such assistance if appropriate. In areas where there is a known risk of piracy,

RN warships would take this into consideration and adjust their own level of readiness accordingly. Again, there are no RN assets dedicated specifically to counter narcotics activities. Military Forces are, however, made available upon request, when operational commitments and resources allow, to support the counter drugs activities of the law enforcement agencies. In recent years, such assistance has been provided in the Caribbean, United Kingdom waters, Atlantic and the Arabian Sea.

(HC Deb 28 January 2003 Vol. 398 c843W)

Part Thirteen: I. *International responsibility—general conception*

Part Thirteen: II. C.1.a. *International responsibility—General issues of international responsibility—Procedure—Diplomatic protection—Nationality of claims*

Part Thirteen: II. C.2. *International responsibility—General issues of international responsibility—Procedure—Consular protection*

13/1

In a written answer, the Under-Secretary of State, FCO, wrote:

The Foreign and Commonwealth Office (FCO) changed its clemency policy towards British nationals detained overseas in May 2001. Under the new policy, HMG will now consider supporting appeals on compassionate grounds, where there is prima facie evidence of a miscarriage of justice, or where the prisoner is a minor. An appeal for clemency is a request to the detaining state to release the prisoner unconditionally, not reduce the original sentence. Since the new policy came into effect, we have supported appeals on behalf of 15 British nationals. The FCO does not hold statistics on representations made before the introduction of the new clemency policy. Nor does it record the ethnic origin of those who are offered consular assistance.

As a general rule, HMG will lobby against the death penalty imposed on any British national overseas. In this instance, HMG is not appealing for unconditional release, but for the death penalty to be commuted to imprisonment. We have supported 11 such cases since May 2001.

Other than lobbying against the death penalty, HMG would not normally appeal for a reduction in sentence. This is on the basis that states must recognise the rights of other sovereign states to sentence according to their own laws. However, HMG would consider making representations to a sentencing state if a British national appeared to have been harshly sentenced purely because of nationality. There have been no instances of this since at least May 2001.

The welfare of British nationals detained overseas is of primary concern to the FCO. We ensure that prisoners are visited regularly and we raise any concerns that we, prisoners or their relatives may have about their treatment or the conduct of their trial. As a last resort, when all other options have failed, we will consider supporting an appeal for clemency under the criteria outlined above.

(HC Deb 26 February 2003 Vol. 400 c584W)

13/2

During a debate in the House of Commons on the Middle East, the Parliamentary Under-Secretary of State, FCO, was asked the following question:

[I] want to ask . . . about . . . the fact that a number of foreign nationals were shot recently as they attempted either to report what is going on over there, or to promote peace. What representations are being made to the Israeli Government, especially about the case of Tom Hurndall, who was recently shot, and is now in a coma? Yesterday, Israeli forces fired shots over a convoy carrying Mr. Hurndall, even though the convoy bore diplomatic flags and was accompanied by British embassy staff.

In reply, the Parliamentary Under-Secretary of State, FCO, said:

My hon. Friend is right to say that we have serious concerns about the incident to which he refers. I spoke to the Israeli ambassador on Saturday and expressed our deep concerns about the matter. I also asked for a full report to be made after a proper inquiry into the incidents has been held. My right hon. Friend the Foreign Secretary has also spoken to some of the families concerned. We will pursue these matters with the utmost vigour. They are very serious, and my hon. Friend need be in no doubt that the Government will treat them seriously, as consular matters. We will give as much support as we can to the families concerned, and we will make sure also that the Israeli Government are in no doubt about a problem that seems to occur all too often—the lack of discipline among Israeli defence force soldiers. That issue of discipline needs to be dealt with by the Israeli Government.

(HC Deb 6 May 2003 Vol. 2003 c527)

13/3

In reply to a written question, the Parliamentary Under-Secretary of State, FCO, wrote:

We regularly engage with the Pakistani authorities on a wide range of human rights issues. Where appropriate, we make bilateral representations in specific cases on behalf of British nationals. Mr Zardari is not a British national. The UK may on occasion raise specific cases of non-British nationals. However, we are not entitled to provide the formal consular or diplomatic protection that we can offer to British nationals. We have not concluded that there are reasons for the UK to raise Mr Zardari's case.

(HL Deb 4 March 2003 Vol. 645 cWA94)

13/4

During a debate in the House of Lords on Pakistan, the Parliamentary Under-Secretary said:

My Lords, I think I have made it absolutely clear in replies on this matter that I have given to the noble Lord that our consular responsibilities are clear. They are set out in international law. We have a responsibility to look after the welfare of British citizens abroad. Benazir Bhutto's husband is not a British national.

(HL Deb 20 March 2003 Vol. 646 c383)

Part Thirteen: II. D. *International responsibility—General issues of international responsibility—Consequences of responsibility (restitution in integrum, damages, satisfaction, guarantees)*

13/5

Her Majesty's Government was asked the following written question:

To ask the Secretary of State for Defence how many deaths in custody there have been since the start of the Iraq conflict of Iraqis *(a)* under UK responsibility, *(b)* under US responsibility and *(c)* under the responsibility of other authorities in Iraq; and if he will make a statement.

The Defence Minister responded:

There have been six recorded deaths of Iraqis while in the custody of UK Forces all of which are being investigated. The number of deaths of Iraqis in custody of authorities other than UK Forces is a matter for those authorities.

(HC Deb 4 December 2003 Vol. 415 c127W)

13/6

In reply to a written question the Defence Minister wrote:

There are no plans to pay compensation to Iraqi civilians killed during combat operations in Iraq.

The handling of claims made by Iraqis for losses which do not arise in connection with combat operations are governed by section 6 of the Coalition Provisional Authority Order Number 17. This provides that any such claims shall be submitted to and dealt with by the parent state of the person whose activities are alleged to have caused the loss. The claims will then be dealt with in a manner consistent with the national laws of that parent state.

Where a claim against British troops arises from activity which would not give rise to a legal liability to pay compensation under English law, there may nevertheless be an ex gratia payment made to the injured person or to the family of the deceased where this would be in accordance with local custom or directed to meet a particular urgent humanitarian need.

(HC Deb 17 November 2003 Vol. 413 c499W)

13/7

Her Majesty's Government was asked in a written question:

Whether Israel will be obliged to compensate the United Nations Relief and Works Agency for damage done by military action to schools, clinics, hospitals, etc.

In reply, a Government representative wrote:

UNRWA, together with the international community more widely, has made repeated representations to the Government of Israel about damage caused during Israeli incursions. UNRWA and the international community have reserved the right to seek compensation.

(HL Deb 14 March 2003 Vol. 645 cWA216)

13/8

In reply to a written question, the Under-Secretary of State, FCO, wrote:

The UK has supported the work of the United Nations Commission for Compensation (UNCC) since its creation in 1991. 25 per cent. of Oil for Food funds continue to be paid to the UNCC. The UNCC has received about 2.6 million claims seeking compensation in excess of US $300 billion for losses arising out of the illegal invasion of Kuwait by Iraq in 1991, the majority of which have been resolved. The Commission is continuing its work on outstanding claims.

(HC Deb 26 March 2003 Vol. 402 c260W)

13/9

In response to a written question, the Parliamentary Under-Secretary of State, FCO, wrote:

We regularly raise our concerns about sectarian violence and wider human rights issues with the Pakistani authorities. On 7 February 2003 the Greek Presidency of the European Union delivered a demarche to the Minister of State (Law, Justice and Human Rights). The demarche explained our concerns about cases where religious minorities, notably those from the Christian and Ahmadi communities, have been sentenced to death under the blasphemy laws. Cases raised included those of Parvez Masih, Aslam Masih and Augustine Ashiq 'Kingri' Aslam Masih.

We will continue to take appropriate opportunities, including with our European Union partners, to raise our concerns.

(HC Deb 28 April 2003 Vol. 404 c128W)

13/10

In response to a written question, the Parliamentary Under-Secretary of State, FCO, wrote:

We regularly raise our concerns about sectarian violence and wider human rights issues with the Pakistani authorities both bilaterally and through the EU.

On 7 February 2003 the Greek Presidency of the EU delivered a comprehensive demarche to the Minister of State (Law, Justice and Human Rights). The EU underlined our concerns at the recent attacks against Christian targets and urged the authorities to bring the perpetrators of these crimes to justice. The EU also urged the Pakistani Government to provide greater protection to minority groups.

It is too early to make an assessment on the Sharia Bill. The North-West Frontier Province has yet to consider draft legislation proposing the adoption of Sharia law in the province. This law cannot be fully enacted until approved by both the federal and provincial Parliaments.

(HC Deb 28 April 2003 Vol. 404 c128W)

Part Thirteen: III.A *International responsibility—responsible entities—states*

13/11

During a debate in the House of Commons, the Secretary of State, FCO, made the following statement:

On the question of whether there is a link between Iraq and terrorism, my right hon. Friend the Prime Minister has given precise answers . . . When he said that there has been no link between Iraq and terrorism, he was explicitly referring to al-Qaeda in the run-up to 11 September. There is of course a lot of linkage between Iraq and terrorism generally. One of the international terrorist organisations that I banned—proscribed under the Terrorism Act 2000—was the MEK, an Iraqi-backed terrorist organisation operating in Iran. Moreover, the Iraqi regime actively supports several rejectionist terrorist organisations, including Hamas and Hezbollah which operate inside Israel and the occupied territories. We have to recognise the possibility of great danger if we fail to deal both with what the hon. Gentleman described as international terrorism and with the murderous regimes in rogue states. Al-Qaeda would have been a shadow of what it was had it not been able to base and feed itself in a rogue state—at that stage, Taliban-ruled Afghanistan.

(HC Deb 21 January 2003 Vol. 698 c172)

13/12

In reply to a written question, the Secretary of State for Defence wrote:

Iraq has a long record of support for terrorism: this includes support for Palestinian terrorist groups (e.g. Abu Nidhal), payments to the families of suicide bombers and the activities of the MeK against Iran. As my right hon. Friend the Prime Minister said on 29 January 2003 . . . we also know of links between al-Qaeda and Iraq, although we cannot be sure of their exact extent.

(HC Deb 5 February 2003 Vol. 399 c286W)

13/13

During a debate in the House of Commons, the Parliamentary Under-Secretary of State, FCO, made the following statement:

The Iraqi regime has supported, trained and financed the Mujaheddin-e Khalq Organisation terrorist group and encouraged terrorism in the middle east for years, including assisting the murderous Abu Nidal group, the Palestinian Liberation group and Hamas, as well as making payments to the families of suicide bombers.

(HC Deb 25 March 2003 Vol. 402 c147)

Part Thirteen: III. D. *International responsibility—responsible entities—individuals and groups of individuals (including corporations)*

(See **6/109**)

Part Fourteen: II. A. *Peaceful settlement of disputes—means of settlement—negotiations*

14/1

In reply to a written question on Burma, the Parliamentary Under-Secretary of State, FCO, wrote:

I have been encouraged by reports that some of the insurgent groups fighting the Burmese regime are prepared to consider negotiating a ceasefire. The EU has called for the peaceful end to the conflicts in Burma in resolutions at the United Nations General Assembly. We strongly support the idea in principle and stand ready to help assist the process in the most effective way.

(HC Deb 18 March 2003 Vol. 401 c724W)

14/2

In response to a written question on the Democratic Republic of Congo, the Parliamentary Under-Secretary of State, FCO, wrote:

The UK is actively engaged with our African, EU and UN partners in promoting a peaceful resolution to the conflict in the Democratic Republic of Congo. The Government have supported the implementation of both the Lusaka Peace Agreement and the Pretoria Agreement of July 2002 as providing the most viable way forward.

We warmly welcome the agreement signed in Sun City on 2 April on the establishment of a transitional government with a view to democratic elections in two years time. We will play our part as a member of the International Support Committee which is tasked with supporting the transitional process in DRC.

(HC Deb 28 April 2003 Vol. 404 c121W)

14/3

In reply to a written question on Ethiopia/Eritrea, the Parliamentary Under-Secretary of State, FCO, wrote:

The UK has followed progress with the peace process closely and is fully aware of the significance of Badme in the Ethiopia/Eritrea conflict. The Algiers Peace Agreement in December 2000 set out the mandate for a neutral Boundary Commission to delimit and demarcate the border between the two countries. The Commission made its decision public on 13 April 2002. We have called on both Ethiopia and Eritrea to implement fully the Algiers Peace Agreements and to accept the Boundary Commission's decisions as final and binding. We have done this through successive UN Security Council resolutions, EU demarches and in our bilateral contacts with both countries.

(HC Deb 28 April 2003 Vol. 404 c327W)

14/4

During a debate in the House of Commons, the Parliamentary Under-Secretary of State, FCO, made the following statements:

Any assessment of relations between the United Kingdom and Argentina must take account of progress on south Atlantic issues. I will briefly restate the Government's policy on the Falkland Islands, to which my hon. Friend referred. Sovereignty is not negotiable unless that is the wish of the islanders themselves. The Government remain committed to the right of the Falkland islanders to determine their own future. The islands will be British for as long as the islanders wish them to remain so. We make that clear in all bilateral discussions with the Argentine Government.

However, our goal is to maintain a fruitful dialogue with Argentina on issues of mutual interest in the south Atlantic. Those two approaches are not contradictory. It is to the advantage of both the islanders and the Argentines to work together on challenges such as the preservation of fish stocks and continental shelf delimitation. We also want to make further progress on implementing the 1999 joint statement. We are working with the Argentine and Falkland Islands Governments on the construction of a memorial to the Argentine fallen in the Falkland Islands.

We continue to make progress in the South Atlantic Fisheries Commission. That commission, which comprises UK, Argentine and Falkland Islands officials, will meet again soon to discuss issues of mutual concern, including the prospects for a multilateral high seas fisheries agreement. However, we are concerned that that welcome progress will be set back if the draft fisheries poaching Bill that is currently before the Argentine Congress becomes law. I have discussed that matter with my hon. Friend. The Bill would have damaging implications for the Falkland Islands fishing industry as well as for the work of the commission.

(HC Deb 11 February 2003 Vol. 399 c243WH–244WH)

14/5

Her Majesty's Government was asked the following written question:

To ask the Secretary of State for Foreign and Commonwealth Affairs what steps he is taking to promote agreement with the Government of Spain regarding *(a)* better access to Gibraltar and *(b)* improved communications for the Territory.

In reply, the Under-Secretary of State, FCO, wrote:

The Government secured through the Brussels Process talks better access from Spain to Gibraltar through the opening in March 2002 of a second customs lane at the border. It remains our view that dialogue with Spain and Gibraltar is the only way to resolve such problems.

(HC Deb 3 March 2003 Vol. 400 c845W)

14/6

During a debate in the House of Lords, the Parliamentary Under-Secretary of State, MoD, made the following statements in regard to Gibraltar:

My Lords, we do not ignore the wishes of the people of Gibraltar. We recognise that the referendum result highlighted how the people of Gibraltar feel. What we still believe—I think that the government of whom the noble Lord was a distinguished member also believed this at one time—is that we need to look at how to move forward and tackle the real problems that still exist for the people of Gibraltar. The referendum did not answer the basic question of how to secure a more stable and prosperous future for Gibraltar. That is what we need to do. Nor did it address the underlying reality of the dispute with Spain, which can be resolved only through dialogue.

(HL Deb 4 March 2003 Vol. 645 c698)

14/7

In reply to a written question the Foreign Minister wrote:

The Centre for Humanitarian Dialogue (HDC) brokered the Cessation of Hostilities Agreement (COHA) agreed on 9 December 2002 between the Indonesian Government and the Free Aceh Movement (GAM). To monitor the peace agreement in Aceh both sides agreed to international observers from Thailand and the Philippines. The observers were removed in April 2003 following attacks on their offices.

We remain convinced that a long-term solution to the Aceh problem can only be achieved through political negotiation and consultation between the Indonesian Government and the Acehenese people. We support the statements issued by the EU, US, Japan and the World Bank, as co-chairs of the Tokyo Preparatory Conference on Peace and Reconstruction in Aceh, urging both sides to resume political dialogue. The UK, and the international community, support

Indonesia's territorial integrity. We see no scope, at the moment, for a supranational body to become involved in the conflict in Aceh.

(HL Deb 14 July 2003 Vol. 651 cWA73–WA74)

Part Fourteen: II. G.2. *Peaceful settlement of disputes—means of settlement—judicial settlement—courts and tribunals other than the International Court of Justice*

14/8

In reply to a written question, the Parliamentary Under-Secretary of State, FCO, wrote:

We support a UN-supported tribunal to bring to justice those Khmer Rouge leaders most responsible for the atrocities committed during their regime (1975–79). The UK abstained in a vote on the Khmer Rouge Tribunal Resolution at the 2002 General Assembly because of our concerns that Cambodia's commitment to the process appeared in doubt when it failed to co-sponsor the Resolution; and the UN Secretary General had expressed reservations on the Resolution's implementation. These concerns were shared by a number of other states who also abstained. However, we welcome the recent resumption of talks between Cambodian and United Nations negotiators in New York and remain prepared to offer advice and financial support for a UN-supported tribunal.

(HC Deb 22 January 2003 Vol. 398 c356W)

14/9

In response to a written question, the Parliamentary Secretary, MoD, wrote:

The United Kingdom is fully committed to the International Criminal Court and has not sought immunity from the ICC's powers in Afghanistan, or indeed anywhere else in the world. Although the terms of ISAF Military Technical Agreement require the consent of the contributing nation before its personnel can be transferred to any international tribunal, this in no way affects the UK's commitment to the ICC or other international tribunals.

(HL Deb 24 September 2002 Vol. 638 cWA190–WA191)

14/10

During a debate in the House of Lords, the Minister of State, FCO, said:

My Lords, we have held preliminary discussions with the United States on the possibility of a bilateral agreement. We shall ensure that any agreement which emerges will be consistent with our obligations under the statute of the International Criminal Court and within the guiding principles agreed by the European Union Foreign Ministers on 30th September.

. . .

My Lords, there are a number of states which have indicated willingness to sign up to bilateral agreements and a number which have indicated unwillingness.... The fact is that the statute itself provides for that type of agreement under Article 98(2). Agreement, of course, has to be within specific circumstances. Under the article itself we are not moving outside the legislation in coming to that sort of bilateral agreement because that is the provision within the statute. Therefore, in making such agreements, it is important to ensure that the United States is still able to form part of the important international peacekeeping forces.

...

My Lords, as we have discussed on a number of occasions, the fact is that the United Kingdom Government often take issue with the United States Government on a whole range of matters, not just the International Criminal Court—for example, the protocols around chemical and biological warfare and the important issue of capital punishment. We have taken issue over Kyoto. It is certainly not the case that the United Kingdom always agrees with the United States. The noble Baroness, Lady Williams, says that signing an agreement would weaken the International Criminal Court. I put it to the noble Baroness that we shall be far more weakened in relation to the multilateral basis on which we are trying to operate in the United Nations if we reach a position where the United States simply will not take part in peacekeeping forces. That would be a far worse position for us to be in.

(HL Deb 19 November 2002 Vol. 641 c252–254)

14/11

In reply to a written question, the Minister of State for Defence wrote:

The offences contained in the Statute of the International Criminal Court (ICC) reflect international law provisions that were already applicable to the conduct of United Kingdom forces in any theatre of engagement. The ICC Statute does not therefore impose new conditions.

The consequences for our forces of UK ratification of the ICC Statute were carefully examined in preparation for the ICC Act 2001. Under the Statute, investigation and, if necessary, prosecution of any allegations of war crimes, crimes against humanity or genocide by a UK national would be carried out by the UK. The Court would intervene only if it determined that a state was unwilling or unable to pursue a particular case, but it is inconceivable that the UK would ever be unable or unwilling to investigate or take appropriate action.

(HC Deb 28 January 2003 Vol. 398 c836)

14/12

During a debate in the House of Commons, the Parliamentary Under-Secretary of State, FCO, made the following statements:

There have been no discussions on the International Criminal Court with US counterparts since 17 October. On that date, officials met at US request for preliminary discussions on the US request for a bilateral agreement under Article 98(2) of the Rome statute. We await a further approach from the US side.

. . .

We are strong supporters of the International Criminal Court and, of course, we will do nothing that conflicts with the statute. We understand US objections to the court, but we simply do not share them. Of course article 98.2 provides a procedure, and therefore acting within that article would comply with the statute. However, we will act on the basis of the guiding principles agreed by European Union Ministers on 30 September: no immunity for US citizens, no exemption for UK citizens and exemptions only for US citizens sent by their Government. Unfortunately, there is no common EU position on that. It appears that the French have opted for their soldiers to be excluded for seven years. The French seem to be taking a more American position on this issue.

. . .

Of course, Iraq is not currently a party to the ICC statute, so the court can exercise its jurisdiction only following the referral of an allegation by the UN Security Council under chapter VII of the UN charter. Therefore, if somebody was in a country that was adhering to the statute, I assume that the procedure would still be to use the UN charter chapter VII.

(HC Deb 25 February 2003 Vol. 400 c118–119)

14/13

In a written answer, the Under-Secretary of State, FCO, wrote:

Article 98(2) of the ICC statute provides that the court may not ask a state for surrender of a suspected person if the request would require that state to act inconsistently with its obligations under a relevant international agreement. If the prosecutor nevertheless made such a request, Article 97 would require the state concerned to consult with the court in order to resolve the matter. The statute also makes provision for a case where a state fails to comply with a request from the court, contrary to its obligations under the statute: in such a case the court may refer the matter to the Assembly of States Parties or, where the Security Council has referred the case, to the Council.

(HC Deb 26 February 2003 Vol. 400 c587W)

14/14

During a Security Council Meeting the representative of the European Union said:

The entry into force of the Rome Statute of the International Criminal Court (ICC), on 1 July 2002, and the subsequent establishment of the International Criminal Court, which became fully functional this year upon the election of the 18 Judges and the Prosecutor, constitute a major step in the progressive development of international law that will allow a long-standing dream of humanity—to put an end to impunity—to finally take shape. All States members of the European

Union have ratified the Statute. The ICC is not just a judicial institution designed to prevent and put an end to the impunity of the perpetrators of serious crimes that are of concern to all States, but is also an essential means of promoting respect for international humanitarian law and human rights law, thus contributing to freedom, security, justice and the rule of law, as well as to the preservation of peace and the strengthening of international security. The objectives of the Rome Statute are therefore in conformity with the purposes and principles of the Charter of the United Nations.

From the very outset, the European Union has been strongly supportive of the early establishment of the ICC and is, and will remain, firmly committed to its effective functioning. In our Common Position, adopted by the European Union Council of Ministers in June 2001 and reaffirmed in June 2002, we pledged to promote the widest possible participation in the Statute, to share our experiences with regard to its implementation and to provide technical assistance to the best of our ability. That Common Position is now in the process of being revised with a view to being consolidated and updated and to take into account new developments, such as the adoption of the General Affairs and External Relations Council Conclusions on the ICC of 30 September 2002 and the Guiding Principles annexed thereto.

The promotion of the widest possible participation in, and the implementation of, the Statute in negotiations or political dialogues with third States, with groups of States or with relevant regional organizations, whenever appropriate, are declared objectives of the European Union. In addition, the European Union is determined to adopt initiatives to promote the dissemination of the values, principles and provisions of the Statute and related instruments. The European Union reiterates its belief that the concerns expressed by the United States about politically motivated prosecutions are unfounded, since those concerns have been met and sufficient safeguards against such prosecutions have been built into the Statute. Indeed, the latter contains substantive safeguards and fair-trial guarantees to ensure that such a situation will never arise. In addition, the European Union can now point to the high moral character and integrity of the 18 Judges and the Prosecutor of the Court, who have been elected from among the most highly qualified candidates in the world and who have given, or are about to give, a solemn undertaking to perform their functions impartially. Furthermore, the Statute incorporates the principle of complementarity, which places the primary responsibility for investigation and prosecution with domestic jurisdictions. The Court may assume responsibility as a last resort and only when a State is unable or unwilling to do so.

Among the various responses agreed upon by the drafters of the Statute to address the concerns that I have mentioned is article 16 of the Rome Statute. That article states, "No investigation or prosecution may be commenced or proceeded with under this Statute for a period of 12 months after the Security Council, in a resolution adopted under Chapter VII of the Charter of the United Nations, has requested the Court to that effect."

In our view, the article should be invoked only in conformity with the Statute.

. . .

Security Council resolution 1422 (2002) states that the Council intends to renew the request contained in it for as long as may be necessary. It is clear that any necessity to do so should also be evaluated in the light of the positive effects that the International Criminal Court will have on peacekeeping. In stating this, the European Union would point to the significant number of personnel its member States contribute to peacekeeping operations. Our adherence to the Rome Statute should be seen as an indication of complete trust in the way peacekeepers operate under their mandate and, at the same time, in the necessity to properly investigate any allegations of criminal conduct on their part, if need be.

The European Union is of the view that the inclusion in resolution 1422 (2002) of the phrase "renew the request... under the same conditions each 1 July for further 12-month periods for as long as may be necessary" (*resolution 1422 (2002), para. 2*) cannot be interpreted as permitting the automatic renewal of that resolution without taking into account the specific conditions under which such a request is being made. The European Union firmly believes that an automatic renewal of that resolution would undermine the letter and the spirit of the Statute of the International Criminal Court and of its fundamental purpose—to put an end to impunity for the most serious crimes of concern to the international community by bringing to justice in all cases all those within the Court's jurisdiction.

(UN Doc. S/PV.4772, 12 June 2003)

14/15

During a Security Council Meeting the representative of the United Kingdom, Sir Jeremy Greenstock, stated:

We regard Security Council resolution 1422 (2002) as an exceptional measure. It is not permanent; nor is it automatically renewable. It is subject to scrutiny in the Council, at least annually. We look forward to the day when it or its successor will no longer be required. But resolution 1422 (2002), and now resolution 1487 (2003), are, in our view, consistent with article 16 of the ICC Statute. The Security Council accepted that unanimously on 12 July 2002. It does not undermine the Court; nor does it infringe upon the integrity of the Rome Statute. The same is true of the resolution we have just voted on. The rollover it envisages will sustain the ability of the United States to contribute to international peacekeeping and other missions. The provisions of the resolution remain deliberately narrow, and there is no blanket immunity. Under the circumstances, we regard the adoption of this resolution as an acceptable outcome in what is for the Council a difficult situation.

(UN Doc. S/PV.4772, 12 June 2003)

14/16

In reply to a written question, the Minister of State, FCO, wrote:

UK peacekeepers are not exempt from the jurisdiction of the ICC since the UK is a state party to the ICC Statute. Security Council Resolution 1422 allowed a 12-months exemption from ICC investigation only for UN peacekeepers who are citizens of states which are not states parties to the ICC Statute. Resolution 1422 was renewed on 12 June 2003 for a period of 12 months as Resolution 1487.

(HL Deb 30 June 2003 Vol. 650 cWA55)

14/17

In reply to a written question the Foreign Minister wrote:

There is currently no international criminal tribunal with jurisdiction over Burma; and ultimately, it will be for the people of Burma to decide how they view this period of their history. The UK is against impunity for breaches of international law. That is why it is one of the strongest supporters of the International Criminal Court (ICC) which is able to try cases of genocide, war crimes and crimes against humanity.

(HL Deb 14 July 2003 Vol. 651 cWA72)

14/18

During a Security Council Meeting the representative of the European Union stated:

The international community is sometimes called upon to intervene in order to put an end to impunity for the most heinous international crimes. In such situations, the establishment of ad hoc international criminal tribunals or the setting up of national courts with varying degrees of international assistance has made an important contribution to reconciliation in emerging, post-conflict societies.

The EU also strongly believes that the International Criminal Court provides a powerful, permanent instrument of deterrence against such crimes. The EU will remain firmly committed to its effective functioning. The Court does not aim at replacing domestic jurisdictions. It may assume responsibility as a last resort and only when a State is unable or unwilling to do so. The Court is not just a judicial institution, designed to prevent and put an end to the impunity of the perpetrators of serious crimes, it is also an essential means of promoting respect for international humanitarian law and human rights law, thus contributing to freedom, security, justice and the rule of law, as well as to the preservation of peace and strengthening of international security.

(UN Doc. S/PV.4835, 30 September 2003)

14/19

During a Security Council Meeting the representative of the UK Government said:

Secondly, the Provisional Institutions of Self-Government at all levels must also cooperate with the International Criminal Tribunal for the Former Yugoslavia and UNMIK if and when any indictments are presented. Compliance is an international commitment, and it will be important for Kosovo to show its political maturity and be seen to be acting within common European Union values.

(UN Doc. S/PV.4702, 6 February 2003)

14/20

In reply to a written question on the ICTY, the Minister of State, FCO, wrote:

The British Government strongly supports the work of the International Criminal Tribunal for Yugoslavia (ICTY) and its efforts to bring all indictees to the War Crimes Tribunal. We work closely with our international partners and in Stabilisation Force (SFOR) and Kosovo Force (KFOR) to trace and detain indicted war crime suspects in Bosnia and Kosovo. In March 2003, the Office of the High Representative, in co-operation with SFOR, froze the assets of two individuals suspected of being part of Radovan Karadzic's support network. The UK supports this action. It is entirely the responsibility of the Serbian and Montenegran (SaM) authorities to transfer any indictees on their territory to the ICTY. We urge the new SaM government to fulfil their obligations in this respect and will support them in doing so.

(HC Deb 25 March 2003 Vol. 402 c124W–125W)

14/21

During a Security Council meeting the representative of the UK said:

We welcome the condemnation of the attacks by the Provisional Institutions of Self-Government, the Kosovo Assembly and the President... Let us be clear that the attack on terrorism and extremism is without favour. The United Kingdom has always emphasised that the International Criminal Tribunal for the Former Yugoslavia (ICTY) must prosecute those responsible for serious crimes, without discrimination, and must bring to justice all those involved. I share with Mr. Covic the wish that we should all bring perpetrators of war crimes indicted by ICTY and ensure their extradition to The Hague. That applies equally to those indicted who may happen to be living in Serbia today.... The right of refugees and displaced persons to return to their homes must be accepted in theory and in practice.

(UN Doc. S/PV.4809, 18 August 2003)

14/22

During a Security Council meeting the representative for the UK said:

The obligation on us, as the international community's representatives, and on our institutions is evident. We all need to do everything we can to deliver the indictees to the Tribunals and to give every possible support to the two Prosecutors... Quite apart from the legal and moral obligations, the international community and organisations like the European Union have policies that will hold directly accountable those countries and authorities that fail to take any action which is possible and, still worse, that afford protection to those individuals.... Indictments and the conduct of cases are properly for the courts and for the prosecutors. Having said that, I think I would welcome clarification of Judge Meron's remarks that it is between the Council and the prosecutor as to whether the subject of an indictment meets the standards set by the Council. I think I have quoted his remarks more or less verbatim. But the Security Council clearly has a duty to encourage the support of nations for the work of the courts and to ensure that the means are found for the necessary work to be carried out and that indictees with the gravest charges against them are tried before the Tribunal.

(UN Doc. S/PV.4838, 9 October 2003)

14/23

In reply to a written question the Minister of State, FCO, wrote:

We consider the Boundary Commission decision to be legally binding on both parties. The UK, and other members of the UN Security Council, are working hard to encourage both sides to accept the Boundary Commission decision and to begin a political dialogue on all the issues separating the two countries.

(HL Deb 17 November 2003 Vol. 654 cWA244)

14/24

Her Majesty's Government was asked the following written question:

To ask the Secretary of State for Foreign and Commonwealth Affairs what assessment he has made of whether the UN Border Commission in The Hague was acting within its remit in granting the border town of Badme to the Eritrean Government.

In reply to a written question the Under-Secretary of State, FCO, wrote:

We are not aware of any evidence suggesting that the Boundary Commission exceeded its remit.

(HC Deb 17 December 2003 Vol. 415 c974W)

14/25

The Under-Secretary of State, FCO, made the following statement during a House of Commons debate:

On 3 July, the United States designated six detainees, including two British nationals held at Guantanamo Bay, as eligible for trial under a military commission. We have strong reservations about the military commission. We have raised, and will continue to raise them energetically with the US. The Foreign Secretary spoke to the US Secretary of State, Colin Powell, about that over the weekend and will speak to him again in the next few days.

So far, neither of the detainees has been charged. However, we have made it clear to the US that we expect the process to fulfil internationally accepted standards of a fair trial. We will follow the process carefully.

The US is aware of our fundamental opposition to the use of the death penalty in all circumstances. If there is any suggestion that the death penalty might be sought in these cases, we would raise the strongest possible objections.

...

We understand that "designation" means that the persons concerned are subject to the order that governs military commissions and can now be charged and prosecuted. However, that is not automatic and we understand that matters will proceed on a case-by-case basis.

We are still seeking information about the conduct of any trial. Indeed, we continue to express strong views about the way in which we hope that a trial will be conducted. The same applies to the right of appeal.

We understand that the Americans will nominate the defence lawyers in some way. We are seeking further information about that, too. The right hon. and learned Gentleman will forgive me if I do not go into much detail, but many aspects are a cause of concern to us and we intend to pursue them all.

...

One concern that we are pursuing with the Americans is that in our view, all the evidence concerning the case against these people must clearly be made available to them, so that they are in a position to rebut it.

We understand that the detainee does have the right to choose his own defence lawyer—if he meets the security requirements laid down by the Americans. However, it is clear that this matter will have to be checked out.

(HC Deb 7 July 2003 Vol. 408 c751–752)

14/26

During a House of Commons debate the Prime Minister stated:

As the right hon. Gentleman knows, the United States is now talking about the right method by which to try anybody against whom charges would be brought. We will make active representations to the United States—indeed, we are already doing so—to make absolutely sure that any such trial will take place in accordance with proper international law.

...

It is of course important that the commission that tries these people is conducted according to proper rules. Those rules have not yet been drawn up, and it is precisely for that reason that we are making active representations, and our opposition to the death penalty is well known.

...

What my hon. Friend says must be right. If charges are brought, they must be proved in accordance with proper rules of evidence.

(HC Deb 9 July 2003 Vol. 408 c1153)

14/27

During a House of Lords debate on the detention of UK nationals in Guantanamo Bay the Foreign Office Minister said:

If the trials as originally formulated by the United States authorities do go ahead, I think that there would be grave difficulties as regards any observers feeling that those trials would be fair on the basis that we have already discussed. There is no secret about this issue. The United Kingdom Government have very strong reservations about what is being proposed at the moment. However, to take the point that were some of those issues to be resolved and the trials to go ahead, I can agree with the noble Lord that the presence of international observers would provide something of a confidence boost to the international community. As my noble friend Lord Judd pointed out, this is a question not just for the United Kingdom but also for the international community.

However, we must recognise that some of the issues which may be brought up at those trials may have to be dealt with in camera, for very obvious security reasons.

. . .

It might be argued that a system of plea-bargaining where the alternative to admitting to charges is to face the death penalty is a coercive and difficult line of pre-trial cross-examination.

. . .

My Lords, as I understand it, the United States proposes that individuals should be given an advocate chosen from a panel of military lawyers. If an individual does not want to go along with such an arrangement, there may be an opportunity for him to go to an alternative lawyer, but that lawyer will still be drawn from a panel of lawyers who have been vetted by the United States for security purposes. I understand that those are the proposals currently under discussion.

(HL Deb 17 July 2003 Vol. 651 c966–968)

14/28

In reply to a written question the Minister of State, FCO, wrote:

"Any commission or tribunal must be conducted in accordance with the proper canons of law so that a fair trial takes place and is seen to take place".

The UK has made this view clear to the US. On 18 July the US announced that they would not commence any military commission proceedings against UK nationals, pending discussions between American and British legal experts. The Attorney-General visited Washington on 21–22 July for talks with the US Administration. He secured a number of assurances from the Administration, including that the US will not seek the death penalty against the two British detainees who have been designated as eligible for the commissions, and will be returning to the US shortly for further discussions.

(HL Deb 8 September 2003 Vol. 651 cWA17)

14/29

And in reply to a further written question the same Minister wrote:

The US announced on 18 July that they would not commence any military commission proceedings against UK nationals detained at Guantanamo Bay, pending discussions between American and British legal experts. We understand from the US authorities that medical facilities, including psychiatric care, at Guantanamo Bay available to the detainees are of a high standard and are the same as those for US military personnel. We firmly believe that a fair judicial process should take account of a person's fitness to stand trial. This is one of the specific issues we have raised with the US authorities, and continue to discuss with them.

(HL Deb 8 September 2003 Vol. 651 cWA17)

14/30

Her Majesty's Government was asked the following oral question:

Whether they consider that the current plans for judicial procedures at Guantanamo Bay will permit fair trials of those detained there.

In reply the Minister of State, FCO, said:

My Lords, no. That is why, over the past few months, my noble and learned friend the Attorney-General has vigorously expressed to the United States Administration our strong reservations about the military commission's procedures. Our objective has been to ensure that if any British nationals are detained at Guantanamo Bay and prosecuted, a fair trial takes place in accordance with generally recognised principles. Discussions continue.

(HL Deb 15 October 2003 Vol. 653 c936)

14/31

In reply to a written question the Minister of State, FCO, wrote:

The order and instructions relating to military commissions can be found on the US Department of Defense website www.defenselink.mil.

...the Attorney-General, who has represented the Government in discussions with the US Administration about the military commissions, issued a statement on 22 July, following the first round of talks. This included a reference to the question of legal representation. Part of the statement says "...the US has assured us that...Begg and Abbasi will be able to be represented by an appropriately qualified US civilian lawyer of their own choosing, subject to security clearance. A UK lawyer will be able to serve as a consultant on the defence team. Each detainee will be able to decide to what extent he wished the appointed military counsel to participate in the preparation of his case."

...

[It] included a reference to the question of communications between defendants and their lawyers. Part of the statement says "...the US has assured us that . . . exceptionally, conversations between Begg or Abbasi and his defence counsel would not be monitored or reviewed by US authorities."

. . .

[It also] included a reference to the question of capital punishment. Part of the statement says ". . . the US has assured us that . . . the prosecution will not seek the death penalty in the cases of Feroz Abbasi and Moazzem Begg."

(HL Deb 3 November 2003 Vol. 654 cWA67–WA68)

14/32

In reply to a written question the Under-Secretary of State, FCO, wrote:

The Coalition Provisional Authority (CPA) has been working with the Governing Council, the Iraqi Human Rights Ministry, and local and international organisations to put in place the necessary procedures for collecting and securing evidence. The CPA has so far investigated 128 of the 250 reported mass grave sites and seized thousands of potentially relevant documents. CPA efforts are also focused on building the capacity of Iraqis to investigate the crimes committed by the former regime for both historical and prosecution purposes.

(HC Deb 30 October 2003 Vol. 412 c318W)

14/33

In reply to a written question the Prime Minister wrote:

United Nations Security Council resolution 1483 affirmed the need for accountability for crimes and atrocities committed by the previous Iraqi regime. We fully support this, as do the US. We believe it is for the Iraqi people to decide how to bring those responsible to justice, with suitable international help. The Governing Council is developing the idea of a Special Iraqi Tribunal to prosecute those suspected of serious human rights abuses under the former regime. No final decision has yet been reached.

(HC Deb 20 November 2003 Vol. 413 c1147W)

14/34

During a House of Commons debate the Prime Minister made the following comments regarding the trial of Saddam Hussein:

I think that any trial of Saddam should be for the Iraqi Government and people and that it is for them to determine the penalties that might arise from that. It is important to recognise that it is only in circumstances where a country is incapable of mounting a proper tribunal that we have recourse to international tribunals. If Iraq has that capability, it would be wrong to mount such a tribunal. The governing council has already indicated that it wants a special tribunal to try those who are guilty of serious war crimes, so it is important to allow it to do that because it is part of Iraq's prerogative as a country. Of course, that would be done on the basis that such a special tribunal could be constituted.

. . .

The precise nature of the indictment that is made against him should, as I say, be left to the Iraqis. I emphasise that Iraq has a governing council, whose members said just a few days ago, before the capture of Saddam, that they wanted to set up a special tribunal to try people who were accused of various crimes against the Iraqi people: they should be allowed to get on with that process. We should give whatever support we can in ensuring, for example, that the judiciary is properly independent and properly staffed. The terms of the indictment and the way in which any charges are framed are for the Iraqis themselves—that is part of the whole process of saying that Iraq is run by the Iraqis.

(HL Deb 15 December 2003 Vol. 415 c1326 and c1334)

Part Fifteen: I. D. *Coercive measures short of the use of force—unilateral measures—intervention*

(See also **Part Five: I. A.4,** above)

15/1

In reply to a written question on outstanding UK contracts with countries that face restrictions on arms trading, the Parliamentary Under-Secretary of State for Trade and Industry wrote:

Where a UK, EU or UN embargo is placed on a country which is being supplied by a UK contractor, there are established mechanisms in place to ensure the embargo is fully complied with. Implementation periods have been proposed relating to the new legislation to enable applicants to consider how to comply with the new legislation.

(HC Deb 6 May 2003 Vol. 404 c482W)

15/2

During a House of Lords debate the Minister of State, FCO, said:

My Lords, we have made it clear; the Foreign Secretary has issued two statements condemning the Government of Zimbabwe's attack on the free and independent media. As your Lordships may know, after a six-week ban, the administrative court ruled in favour of Associated Newspapers of Zimbabwe on 24th October. The following day, the Daily News was published with the headline, "We Are Back". Sadly, on 26th October, 18 Daily News employees were arrested. Yes, the Foreign Secretary has made a protest.

(HL Deb 28 October 2003 Vol. 654 c127)

Part Fifteen: I. E. *Coercive measures short of the use of force—unilateral measures—other unilateral measures*

15/3

During a House of Lords debate the Minister of State, FCO, said:

My Lords, in 2001, when the Foreign Secretary reviewed our arms exports policy in respect of the terrorist risk, he concluded that the consolidated criteria on which we assess all arms exports should remain unchanged. Accordingly, the Government will continue to take account inter alia of, first, the attitude of any buyer country in relation to terrorism and international crime and, secondly, the need to avoid diversion of United Kingdom exports to terrorist organisations.

(HL Deb 27 October 2003 Vol. 654 c8)

Part Fifteen: II. A. *Coercive measures short of the use of force—collective measures—United Nations*

15/4

In reply to a written question the Under-Secretary of State, FCO, wrote:

Since 1997 the UK has implemented mandatory UN arms embargoes on Sierra Leone, Afghanistan, Ethiopia/Eritrea and Liberia, an EU embargo on Indonesia and a unilateral embargo on Zimbabwe. The latter was superseded by an EU arms embargo in February 2002. The UN arms embargo on Sierra Leone from 1998 was in response to internal armed conflict between the rebel militia group, the Revolutionary United Front (RUF), and the government. In 1999 an arms embargo was imposed on Afghanistan because of internal conflict. In 2000, a UN arms embargo was placed on Ethiopia/Eritrea due to armed conflict between the two states. It was terminated in 2001. The UN arms embargo on Liberia from 2001 was imposed (superseding the UN arms embargo UNSCR 788 (1992)) because Charles Taylor's government was supporting the RUF in Sierra Leone, and at war internally with a rebel opposition group, the Liberians United for Reconciliation and Democracy (LURD). The UN Security Council deemed that all of these conflicts represented a threat to international peace and security and therefore the Security Council acted under Chapter 7 of the Charter of the United Nations. An EU arms embargo was imposed on Indonesia in September 1999 because of conflict in East Timor; this was limited to four months and it fell away in January 2000. In February 2001, the UK imposed a unilateral arms embargo on Zimbabwe because of human rights violations involving repression by the government of the Zimbabwean public. In February 2002, the EU imposed an arms embargo against Zimbabwe for the same reason, which the UK now implements instead.

(HC Deb 6 October 2003 Vol. 411 c1068W)

15/5

In reply to a written question the Foreign Office Minister wrote:

The UK was a driving force behind the adoption of [SC] Resolution 1325 [ed. Women and Peace and Security] in October 2000 and maintains an active and positive approach towards its implementation both in London and through the UK Mission to the United Nations in New York. The UK used its presidency of the UN Security Council in July 2002 to host an open debate on UNSCR 1325, led by the UN Department for Peacekeeping Operations, with the participation of the UN Special Adviser on Gender, the United Nations Development Fund for Women (UNIFEM) and the UN Department for Political Affairs.

The UK is committed to ensuring the participation of women in conflict prevention and resolution, including peace negotiations, as well as to raising awareness of the positive role that women can play in peace building and reconciliation.

The Global Conflict Prevention Pool (GCPP) continues to work and fund projects with the UN's Department of Peace Keeping Operations (DPKO) and others on gender training for peace keepers.

The UK helped UNIFEM to put together a programme of work on women, peace building and gender justice and has pledged £3m towards that work. This ambitious programme, now in its second year, aims to increase women's participation in peace negotiations and post-conflict justice mechanisms. With our support, UNIFEM has published an independent assessment of how women are affected by armed conflict.

In Iraq the UK is committed to including women in all phases and at all levels in the reconstruction. My right honourable friend the Prime Minister's special representative and his team in Baghdad are working closely with Ambassador Bremer and officials in the Coalition Provisional Authority (CPA) to increase the representation of women in all strands of the rapidly evolving political and reconstruction process, such as the governing and economic councils. In addition we have seconded a gender expert from the government's Women and Equality Unit to the CPA's gender equality team and an FCO official in the CPA's governance team, who have been engaged in the involvement of women in the political process. The CPA has also facilitated an Iraqi-led women's conference consisting of five workshops, the recommendations from which will feed into the political process.

We will continue to seek opportunities to further the implementation of Resolution 1325 in areas of conflict.

(HL Deb 18 July 2003 Vol. 651 cWA188)

15/6

In reply to a written question the Minister of State, FCO, wrote:

The United Kingdom's support for Security Council Resolution 1325 (SCR1325), three years after its adoption in October 2000, is now focused on implementing its provisions and ensuring that the necessary mechanisms are in place for monitoring its implementation. UK support has included:

providing 150,000 dollars to the United Nations' Department of Peacekeeping Operations (DPKO) to develop and implement a training manual and integrate its use into DPKO's Best Practices Unit;

providing compulsory training to all UK military and police officers embarking on peace-keeping or similar overseas missions on gender, child protection and human rights issues;

actively searching for and subsequently deploying UK female officers to missions and other conflict prevention/resolution operations, the most recent examples being the deployment of two female police officers to Sierra Leone and a senior gender expert to Baghdad to work with the Coalition Provisional Authority (CPA);

developing a database of suitably qualified women based in the UK experienced in conflict prevention/resolution work, and willing to be deployed overseas;

continuing efforts in the UN Security Council to reflect gender perspectives in a meaningful way. The UK has argued for language in SCRs that establish or renew peace-keeping mandates as one concrete method of mainstreaming gender into the council's work. The UK is systematically looking for opportunities to ensure that gender concerns are properly addressed in resolutions, mission mandates and progress reports. Recent Security Council resolutions reflecting language taken from SCR1325 or its provisions include those on Liberia, the Democratic Republic of Congo, and Côte d'Ivoire. We also repeated, at the open debate of the Security Council on women, peace and security held on 31 October to mark the third anniversary of the resolution's adoption, the suggestion made at the same debate in 2002 that the council give thought to establishing a mechanism through which it can monitor its own progress on issues relating to women, peace and security;

welcoming the International Criminal Court's willingness to include within its remit certain crimes against women;

ensuring that those members of the various UK teams in Iraq, especially those working in or with the CPA, are fully briefed on the gender aspects of their work. The UK's Special Representative, Sir Jeremy Greenstock, on a recent round of briefing calls and meetings in London, met my right honourable friend the Secretary of State for Trade and Industry, Minister for Women and Equality, and e-Minister in Cabinet (Patricia Hewitt), a representative group of Iraqi women, and representatives of UK non-governmental organisations (NGOs), including the Women's National Commission, active in the field;

funding through the Global Conflict Prevention Pool several initiatives relating to the implementation of SCR1325, including the United Nations' Development Fund for Women's efforts to gather information on women's peace-building and gender justice initiatives, and work with the Urgent Action

Fund for Women's Human Rights, an NGO that supports grass-roots activities in countries where there are multinational peace-keeping operations. It is our experience that small well targeted funding can make a big difference—for example, encouraging women to play an active role in Afghan politics by providing childcare facilities in the main Parliament building in Kabul.

Future ideas include a series of briefing workshops, held jointly by the UK and Canadian missions to the UN in New York, for newly elected Security Council members, to build a wider body of support amongst member states for SCR1325 and the broader set of issues surrounding women, peace and security.

(HL Deb 17 November 2003 Vol. 654 cWA239–WA241)

15/7

In response to a written question, the Parliamentary Under-Secretary of State, FCO, wrote:

The size of the International Security Assistance Force (ISAF) is governed by the ISAF mission, which remains as defined in UN Security Council Resolution 1386 of 20 December 2001 and most recently reconfirmed on 27 November 2002 by UNSCR 1444. This authorises ISAF to assist the Afghan authorities in the maintenance of security in Kabul and the surrounding area. Any change to the ISAF mission would require a new UN Security Council Resolution. The size of force required might then have to be reassessed.

We share the view of the Afghan people that security remains a priority and are concerned that the Afghan Transitional Administration does not yet have adequate means to deal in an effective manner with ongoing threats to security beyond Kabul. Options are currently being discussed for addressing this problem in the short term. Ultimately, the solution to the question of security in Afghanistan must lie in building up indigenous security and law and order forces capable of addressing likely sources of instability. We welcome in this context the decree signed by President Karzai on 1 December on principles governing the establishment of the new Afghan National Army and the disarmament, demobilisation and reintegration of ex-combatants into civilian life.

(HL Deb 17 December 2002 Vol. 642 cWA89)

15/8

In a written answer on sanctions, the Parliamentary Under-Secretary of State, FCO, wrote:

With the support of Her Majesty's Government, the UN Security Council on 18 October 2002 unanimously adopted UN Security Council resolution 1439(2002). The resolution lifted the travel ban on members of UNITA and their immediate families listed in paragraphs 4a and 4b of UN Security Council resolution 1127(1997) from 14 November 2002. The travel ban has been suspended since May pursuant to UN Security Council resolutions 1412(2002) and 1432(2002).

Resolution 1439(2002) also committed the Security Council to review all remaining measures imposed on UNITA by 19 November 2002. Following the review with the support of Her Majesty's Government, the Security Council voted unanimously to adopt United Nations Resolution 1448(2002) on 9 December 2002. This resolution lifted all remaining sanctions measures on Angola (UNITA). This is in recognition of the considerable progress made in Angola since the formal cessation of hostilities on 4 April 2002, and the broad fulfilment of the tenets of the Lusaka Peace Protocol by UNITA.

Sierra Leone
With the support of Her Majesty's Government, the Security Council voted unanimously to adopt Resolution 1446(2002) on 4 December 2002. The resolution extended the embargo on the export of rough diamonds without a certificate of origin, controlled by the Government of Sierra Leone. This extension will allow the Government of Sierra Leone to extend and consolidate their authority over the diamond-mining fields in the country.

Democratic Republic of Congo
With the support of Her Majesty's Government, the General Affairs and External Relations Council of 22 October agreed Council Common Position 2002/829. The European Union introduced an embargo on the export of arms to Zaire (now the Democratic Republic of Congo) in 1993 pursuant to an EU declaration of 7 April 1993. The Common Position (2002/829) amends the scope of that arms embargo by providing that the arms embargo does not apply to temporary exports for personal use of United Nations personnel; and does not prohibit the export of non-lethal military equipment with a legitimate humanitarian use to representatives of the media and humanitarian and associated personnel, or equipment to be used for the clearance and destruction of anti-personnel landmines.

Burma
With the support of Her Majesty's Government, the General Affairs and External Relations Council of 22 October agreed Council Common Position 2002/831. The Common Position extends EU sanctions against Burma for a further six months. The Common Position and the accompanying Council Regulation also update the list of individuals subject to EU sanctions to take account of recent changes to the Burmese military regime.

(HL Deb 19 December 2002 Vol. 642 cWA142–WA143)

15/9

In response to an oral question on the Democratic Republic of Congo, the Prime Minister said:

My hon. Friend makes an entirely justified point. I assure her that we are working closely with the UN and other troop-contributing countries to ensure the deployment of what was supposed to be almost 9,000 UN peacekeepers. They were mandated by the UN last December and we are trying to insert them into the situation there. Once again, we exhort all parties to abide by UN Security Council resolution 1468, which condemns violations of human rights and international humanitarian law and calls on all parties to cease their hostilities immediately. I assure my hon. Friend that, even with public attention naturally focused on Iraq, we continue to be as active as we possibly can on this issue.

(HC Deb 9 April 2003 Vol. 403 c266)

15/10

In response to a written question, the Minister of State, FCO, wrote:

Following consultations with the Foreign and Commonwealth Office and the Ministry of Defence, the Department of Trade and Industry recently approved a licence to export general purpose machine guns to Senegal. These arms will be used by the Senegalese armed forces in the UN peacekeeping mission in the Democratic Republic of Congo (DRC).

DRC is subject to an EU arms embargo, imposed by a declaration of 7 April 1993. The embargo was put in place mainly to ensure the safety of international troops and civilian personnel deployed in the DRC. The decision to grant an exemption does not affect Her Majesty's Government's continued support for the EU arms embargo on the DRC.

The decision to permit export was made on the basis that the equipment is needed by bona fide UN peacekeepers and is proportionate to the humanitarian needs of the Senegalese peacekeepers.

Her Majesty's Government fully support the Senegalese troops deployed to the UN peacekeeping mission in the DRC. The decision underlines our continued support for the work being done by peacekeepers within the country.

(HL Deb 22 October 2002 Vol. 639 cWA94)

15/11

In reply to a written question the Minister of State, FCO, wrote:

Following consultations with the Foreign and Commonwealth Office and the Ministry of Defence, the Department of Trade and Industry issued a licence for the export to the Democratic Republic of Congo (DRC) of body armour and military helmets. This equipment will be used by the UN Office for the Co-ordination of Humanitarian Affairs, who are part of the United Nations operation in the DRC.

UN Security Council Resolution (SCR) 1493 (2003), adopted on 28 July 2003, implemented an embargo on the provision of arms and any related material to all armed groups operating in the east of the country. Operative Paragraph 21 of the SCR provides an exemption to the embargo for "supplies of non-lethal equipment intended solely for humanitarian or protective use…".

(HL Deb 15 October 2003 Vol. 655 cWA133–WA134)

15/12

In a written answer, the Parliamentary Under-Secretary of State, FCO, wrote:

The Government shares the concern of the UN Panel of Experts that the revenues from timber sales in Liberia are being used to fund arms purchases in breach of UN sanctions. United Nations Security Council Resolution 1408(2002) called on the Government of Liberia to undertake a credible audit of shipping and timber revenues and to use the revenues from the timber trade for social, development and humanitarian purposes.

We support the Africa Forest Law Enforcement and Governance (AFLEG) process, which calls on all African governments and trading partners to take actions to control illegal activities in the forestry sector and associated trade. A conference to push this process forward is planned in April 2003.

(HC Deb 26 March 2003 Vol. 402 c258W)

15/13

The Under-Secretary of State, FCO, made the following written statement:

With the support of Her Majesty's Government, the United Nations Security Council on 6 May 2003 unanimously adopted United Nations Security Council resolution 1478(2003). The resolution rolled over the measures that had been in place against Liberia (a travel ban against senior government officials and members of their immediate families, a diamond embargo and an arms embargo). The travel ban was also extended to members of Liberians United for Reconciliation and Democracy (LURD). In addition, timber sanctions were imposed against all round logs and timber products originating in Liberia. Sanctions against timber do not come into place until 7 July 2003.

(HC Deb 1 July 2003 Vol. 408 c10WS)

15/14

During a debate in the House of Lords, the Minister of State, FCO, made the following statement:

My Lords, the central issue before the House today is straightforward, solemn and serious. It is how the international community can make Iraq comply with its clear obligation to abandon its weapons of mass destruction. Saddam Hussein has those weapons. He can use them, and we believe that in time he will do so.

His obligations were set out, as my noble friend the Leader of the House has said, in UNSCR 687 of 1991. That was the resolution that suspended the military action endorsed by the United Nations after Iraq's unprovoked invasion of its neighbour Kuwait. UNSCR 687 required Iraq unconditionally to engage in, "the destruction, removal or rendering harmless, under international supervision", of its chemical and biological weapons and to abandon its nuclear programme.

The UN Special Commission (UNSCOM) was tasked with chemical and biological weapons inspection, while the International Atomic Energy Agency (IAEA) was charged with ending Iraq's nuclear weapons programme.

The briefing paper that we have placed in the Library of the House today shows that Iraq has continued to develop terrible weapons of mass destruction. It shows that Iraq has the means to deliver those weapons in armed conflict. It illustrates Saddam Hussein's record of unprovoked aggression in invading two sovereign states and his brutal suppression of internal and minority groups. All that adds up to compelling evidence that he would not hesitate to use the weapons if he saw the need.

As the Statement made by my right honourable friend the Prime Minister makes clear, our briefing paper cites example upon example of Iraqi efforts to develop weapons of mass destruction. To an unprecedented extent, the paper draws on intelligence material and leaves no doubt that Iraq's growing arsenal of such weapons can no longer be tolerated. It demonstrates that the Iraqi regime is increasing its capacity to terrorise and intimidate through the amassing of chemical and biological weapons. The regime has developed command and control systems to use those weapons, and we know that, under those systems, authority rests with Saddam Hussein and, perhaps, with his equally unsavoury son, Qusai.

The dossier goes on to show that Iraq is seeking components and uranium to take forward its already advanced nuclear programme. The dossier highlights the fact that the regime has developed mobile laboratories for military use, corroborating earlier reports about the mobile production of biological warfare agents. It shows that Iraq is developing longer-range ballistic missiles to deliver such weapons further afield. Moreover, it reveals that Iraq continues to use revenue from illicit oil sales to support those horrific programmes, in defiance of explicit UN resolutions, rather than buying food, medicine and other civilian goods for the long-suffering men, women and children of Iraq.

The dossier brings out clearly the assessment of the Joint Intelligence Committee, which brings together the heads of the three intelligence and security agencies. That assessment is that the Iraqi regime could, in certain circumstances, produce a nuclear weapon in a period of between one and two years. To the noble Baroness, Lady Williams of Crosby, I say that that is a short time in international relations. The same committee has evidence that Iraq has sought to buy the significant quantities of uranium that it needs from Africa, at a time when Iraq has no civil nuclear power programme and, therefore, no legitimate reason to acquire uranium. Appallingly, the report shows that intelligence indicates that the Iraqi military is already able to deploy chemical or biological weapons within 45 minutes of an order to do so.

The evidence from the Joint Intelligence Committee adds up to a terrible catalogue of actual and potential weaponry. We have a duty to face up to the responsibilities created by that evidence. How do we force compliance—not for its own sake, but in the knowledge that the weapons are being built for a purpose? That purpose is the domination of the Gulf, to achieve which Saddam Hussein will not hesitate to use the weapons, if he sees fit. We know that because he has already done so.

(HL Deb 24 September 2002 Vol. 638 c870–871)

15/15

During a debate in the House of Commons, the Secretary of State for Defence made the following statements:

It is not a question of identifying the number of weapons of mass destruction that would have to be found, but of upholding the clear terms of United Nations Security Council resolution 1441. That gave Saddam Hussein and his regime in Iraq the final opportunity to comply with the international community's wishes. I know that my hon. Friend strongly supports that.

The resolution also gave Saddam Hussein an opportunity to declare existing holdings of weapons of mass destruction. He purported to do that in some 11,000 pages of documentation, which were issued shortly before Christmas. It is unfortunate for the international community that the document did not disclose several significant items, some of which are now being revealed.

. . .

As the resolution itself makes clear, the question of what is or is not a material breach is a matter for the weapons inspectors, following their report to the Security Council and the discussion in the Security Council that will be required thereafter. That is all set out clearly in resolution 1441. I can therefore assure my hon. Friend, as I assure the House, that no specific decision has been taken about the use of this force, but, unless that force is prepared and made available, we would not be in a position to take military action, should it subsequently be required. As I have said to the House before, the weather is not a factor in this regard.

. . .

The hon. Gentleman is quite right about the possible length of the inspections. However, he also needs to note the provision in resolution 1441 that states that the inspectors can return to the Security Council at any stage in the process. In those circumstances, it is obviously necessary for us to have available the military force that could be required to enforce the terms of the resolution. If we did not take the decisions that I have announced today, we would not be in that position. We cannot, therefore, wait for the year that the hon. Gentleman's question implies might be necessary, if the inspectors return to the Security Council at an earlier stage to indicate their concerns.

. . .

Let me make it clear that the Government—and, I anticipate, no other Government—have any quarrel whatever with the people of Iraq. It may be that the only Government with any serious difficulty with the people of Iraq are the Iraqi regime led by Saddam Hussein, who have perpetrated unspeakable horrors on them over many years. Indeed, there is growing evidence to show that the people of Iraq are sick and tired of Saddam Hussein and are ready for a change. That is clearly anticipated by resolution 1441, but it is important that we continue to maintain the pressure on the regime and those who support them without in any way causing unnecessary difficulty for the people of Iraq.

(HC Deb 20 January 2003 Vol. 398 c40–44)

15/16

During a debate on Iraq and Terrorism, the Under-Secretary of State, FCO, made the following comments:

The noble Lord . . . asked whether we thought that Iraq was already in material breach. UN Security Council Resolution 1441 contains two elements, the first of which is failure in terms of disclosure. We already have some evidence that Iraq has failed in that regard. The second element is failure to comply with the obligations of the resolution. It remains to be seen whether Iraq has failed with respect to the second element.

. . .

On the humanitarian situation, noble Lords will know that we have given a considerable amount to Iraq in terms of humanitarian assistance. My right honourable friend the Foreign Secretary had discussions with the UN Secretary-General yesterday about humanitarian assistance; such discussions will continue. I again make it absolutely clear to the House that our policy priority is disarmament with respect to weapons of mass destruction.

The noble Lord, Lord Wallace of Saltaire, raised the importance of giving the inspectors time to do their work. We have made it absolutely clear that the report that we will receive on Monday is part of a process. That report will be made to the Security Council and the Security Council will assess it and make a decision about the next steps. I cannot agree with the noble Lord, Lord Wallace of Saltaire, that dealing with Iraq is a distraction. That country has consistently flouted UN Security Council resolutions. It must be dealt with if the will of the UN is to prevail.

. . .

Following that [UN] route remains the cornerstone of this Government's policy. But it is important that we remember that we would not have inspectors in Iraq if there had not been a visible and credible threat of force, which took us to the position of obtaining the UN resolution. It is most important that we remember that.

(HL Deb 21 January 2003 Vol. 643 c569–571)

15/17

During a debate in the House of Commons, the Prime Minister said:

The whole basis of our position is that resolution 1441 has to be upheld. That is precisely why I have said that the inspectors must have the ability to do their job. However, I return to a point that I have made before and to which President Bush alluded yesterday. We cannot go back to the situation that existed in the 1990s, when the inspectors were in Iraq for years and Saddam was effectively concealing what he was doing. Saddam's duty is to co-operate fully with the inspections regime, which is not a detective agency: it is supposed to be given the full details of what is in Iraq's programme and then be able to inspect and close the programme down. The duty to co-operate is not only about access to sites, but about being open and honest. Obviously, we will pay full attention to what the inspectors say when they report back.

(HC Deb 22 January 2003 Vol. 398 c295)

15/18

In reply to a written question, the Under-Secretary of State, FCO, wrote:

We understand from published information from UNMOVIC and the IAEA inspectors have visited all of the sites identified in the UK dossier. They have not reported uncovering any signs of weapons of mass destruction, or programmes for their production at the sites. Given that there had been considerable advance publicity about these sites, it is not entirely surprising that the inspectors failed to uncover any evidence of WMD programmes at the sites. Compliance with the terms of UN Security Council Resolution 1441 must be more than simply allowing access to UN weapons inspectors. There must be full co-operation with the inspectors and complete openness about activities at all sites visited, as the Resolution requires.

(HC Deb 22 January 2003 Vol. 398 c354W)

15/19

During a debate in the House of Commons, the Secretary of State for Defence made the following statements:

We maintain regular contact with UNMOVIC and the International Atomic Energy Agency about the progress of inspections. Dr. Blix and Dr. el-Baradei will be reporting to the United Nations Security Council later today. Dr. Blix had a meeting with my right hon. Friend the Prime Minister on 17 January at which he told the Prime Minister that, although the inspectors had encountered no direct obstruction in carrying out their tasks, the onus was on Iraq to be more proactive in its co-operation.

. . .

As I indicated to the House earlier, it is probably best that we should wait the relatively short time before Dr. Blix reports to the United Nations Security Council to see what, if any, requests he makes. I draw my hon. Friend's attention to what my right hon. Friend the Prime Minister said yesterday, namely, that the inspectors have

> "got to be given the time to do the job".

That is the British Government's position. We want to see them complete the task set out by the Security Council, but we want them also to be allowed to carry out that task by the Government in Iraq.

. . .

I would have been much happier with the hon. Gentleman's question if he had said not that the weapons inspectors require more time, but that they require to see disarmament. That is central to the United Nations Security Council resolution, around which there was a unanimous view on the part of the Security Council. We want to see the Government of Iraq accepting their responsibilities to disarm under Security Council resolution 1441. That is the position of this Government and of the other 14 members of the Security Council, as well as of the European Union, NATO and every other responsible Government in the world.

...

I do not think that it is a great surprise to the weapons inspectors that there are weapons of mass destruction in Iraq. Weapons inspectors have been in Iraq over many years since the end of the Gulf war, bearing in mind that it was a condition of the ceasefire that Iraq should abandon its programmes for the development of weapons of mass destruction. I accept that the issue is convincing the present set of inspectors that they have found proof on the ground that there are weapons of mass destruction in Iraq, but, equally, I invite hon. Members to look carefully at the terms of the UN resolution. It is a question of ensuring the co-operation of Iraq with the terms of that resolution. There is an obligation on Iraq to produce the material that it has. Although it has made a declaration, it is already clear that that declaration is insufficient, but we certainly await the further report of the weapons inspectors to take the matter further at this stage.

(HC Deb 27 January 2003 Vol. 698 c543–546)

15/20

In reply to a written question, the Under-Secretary of State, FCO, wrote:

The 10 points in the joint statement made during Dr. Blix's visit to Baghdad last week do not constitute an agreement. They are simply a statement of practical arrangements. They do not add to or alter Iraq's obligations under UN Security Council Resolution 1441.

The Government have repeatedly stated that it is essential that Iraq co-operate fully and unconditionally with the inspectors as they are required to do under UNSCR 1441.

(HC Deb 28 January 2003 Vol. 398 c765W)

15/21

Her Majesty's Government was asked the following written question:

What is their position on Iraq following the presentation of the United Nations Monitoring Verification and Inspection Committee's (UNMOVIC) and the International Atomic Energy Agency's (IAEA) updates 60 days after the resumption of weapons inspections.

The Minister of State, FCO, replied:

I have today placed in the Library copies of the statement made to the United Nations Security Council on 27 January by Dr Blix of the United

Nations Monitoring, Verification and Inspection Commission (UNMOVIC) and Dr El Baradei of the International Atomic Energy Agency (IAEA). Taken together, these statements are damning and disturbing. They show beyond doubt that the Iraqi regime is responding to Resolution 1441 not with active co-operation but with a consistent pattern of concealment and deceit.

(HL Deb 29 January 2003 Vol. 643 cWA156)

15/22

In reply to a written question, the Secretary of State, FCO, wrote:

I have had frequent discussions with my EU counterparts and other Foreign Minister colleagues on Iraq in the run-up and in the margins of the General Affairs and External Relations Council on 27–28 January; I shall continue these contacts. EU Foreign Ministers were united on Iraq at the General Affairs and External Relations Council on 27 January. We reaffirmed our view that UN Security Council resolution 1441 represents a final opportunity for Iraq to resolve the crisis peacefully. We urged Iraq to engage in full and active co-operation with the weapons inspectors and provide them, without delay, with all, additional and complete information on questions raised by the international community. The question of an EU Common Position did not arise.

The full conclusions of the Council on Iraq are as follows:

> "The Council, deeply concerned about the situation in Iraq, reaffirms that its goal remains the effective and complete disarmament of Iraq's weapons of mass destruction. The Council fully supports the efforts of the UN to ensure full and immediate compliance by Iraq with all relevant resolutions of the Security Council, in particular with UNSCR 1441 of 8 November 2002. The resolution gives an unambiguous message that the Iraqi government has a final opportunity to resolve the crisis peacefully.
>
> The Council therefore urges the Iraqi authorities to engage in full and active co-operation with UNMOVIC and IAEA. The Iraqi authorities must, as an imperative, provide the inspectors, without delay, with all additional and complete information on questions raised by the international community. The Council expresses its appreciation for the work accomplished by the inspectors so far and reiterates its confidence and full support for Dr. Blix and Dr. El Baradei to complete their mission in accordance with UNSCR 1441. It welcomes their intention to continue and intensify their operations.
>
> The Council recalls that it stands ready to engage all necessary efforts to answer the needs of UNMOVIC and IAEA in personnel and practical means.
>
> The Council underlines the fundamental importance of preventing the proliferation of weapons of mass destruction in accordance with the relevant international instruments. The Security Council has a key role to play in these endeavours.
>
> The Council reaffirms the role of the UNSC in the implementation of UNSCR 1441. The responsibility of the UNSC in maintaining international peace and security must be respected."

(HC Deb 29 January 2003 Vol. 398 c880W)

15/23

During a debate in the House of Commons, the Prime Minister said:

We are entering the final phase of a 12-year history of the disarmament of Iraq. The duty on Saddam to destroy all his weapons of mass destruction was a central part of the ceasefire agreement at the end of the Gulf war in 1991. In a series of 17 resolutions since then, the UN Security Council has put Saddam under 27 separate and categorical obligations to give full, final and complete declarations on its weapons programmes; to give inspectors unconditional and unrestricted access; to cease the concealment of Iraq's weapons of mass destruction; and to co-operate fully with the inspectors in the disarmament of all Iraq's weapons of mass destruction. Saddam has consistently flouted these obligations. That is why a sanctions regime has been in place for years against Iraq which, because of the way in which Saddam has applied it, has caused wholly unnecessary suffering for the Iraqi people.

Last November, the UN Security Council concluded unanimously that Iraq was still, and I quote, "in material breach of UN resolutions". Saddam was given "a final opportunity" to comply with his disarmament obligations. Resolution 1441 imposed on Saddam a duty to give "a currently accurate, full and complete declaration of all aspects of its programmes to develop chemical, biological and nuclear weapons, ballistic missiles, and other delivery systems"; to provide "immediate, unimpeded, unrestricted and private access" to all people the inspectors wish to interview, "in the mode or location" of the inspectors' choice; and also to co-operate actively and fully with all the inspectors' demands. Failure by Iraq at any time to comply with and co-operate fully in the implementation of the resolution was said in terms to constitute a further material breach.

Eight weeks have now passed since Saddam was given his final chance. Six hundred weeks have passed since he was given his first chance. The evidence of co-operation withheld is unmistakable. Saddam has still not answered the questions concerning thousands of missing munitions and tons of chemical and biological agents unaccounted for. Rocket warheads with chemical weapons capacity have been found by the inspectors: they should have been declared. Classified documents of relevance to Iraq's past nuclear programme have been discovered in a scientist's private house: they should have been handed over. Of the first 11 documents specifically requested by the inspectors, only three have been produced. Not a single interviewee has come to an appointment with the inspectors without their so-called official minders.

As the report we published at the weekend makes clear, and which I placed in the Library of the House, there is a huge infrastructure of deception and concealment designed to prevent the inspectors from doing their job. US Secretary of State Colin Powell will report further to the UN on this on Wednesday. As Dr. Blix, the UN Chief Inspector, reported last week:

> "Iraq appears not to have come to a genuine acceptance—not even today—of the disarmament which was demanded of it."

He said that Iraq's declaration seemed to contain no new evidence; that there are indications that Iraq has weaponised the nerve agent VX, one of the most toxic ever developed; that there are strong indications that Iraq produced more anthrax than it has declared; and that the discovery of chemical rocket warheads could be, again I quote, "the tip of an iceberg".

The situation therefore could not be clearer. There is a duty on Saddam to co-operate fully. At present, he is not co-operating fully. Failure to do so is a material breach of resolution 1441. Should Dr. Blix continue to report Iraqi non-co-operation, a second resolution should be passed confirming such a material breach. President Bush and I agreed that we should seek maximum support for such a resolution, provided, as ever, that seeking such a resolution is a way of resolving the issue, not delaying or avoiding dealing with it at all. I continue to believe that the United Nations is the right way to proceed. There is integrity in the process set out in resolution 1441 and we should follow it.

We of course discussed the fact that weapons of mass destruction are not the only threat the world faces, and Iraq is not the only country posing a risk in respect of weapons of mass destruction. Over the past few weeks, we have seen powerful evidence of the continuing terrorist threat: the suspected ricin plot in London and Manchester; al-Qaeda experiments in Afghanistan to develop chemical, biological and radiological weapons; the arrests of those linked to al-Qaeda in Spain and France; and further arrests just a few days ago in Italy. What is more, many of these arrests show the terrorist groups actively seeking to use chemical or biological means to cause as much death and injury and suffering as they can. We know too from 11 September that these terrorists have no demands that could ever be negotiated upon, no constraint in terms of finance and numbers to carry out terrorist acts, and no compunction in taking human life.

At the same time, we know that Iraq is not alone in developing weapons of mass destruction; there are unstable, fiercely repressive states either proliferating or trying to acquire WMD, like North Korea. I repeat my warning: unless we take a decisive stand now as an international community, it is only a matter of time before these threats come together. That means pursuing international terrorism across the world in all its forms. It means confronting nations defying the world over weapons of mass destruction. That is why a signal of weakness over Iraq is not only wrong in its own terms. Show weakness now and no one will ever believe us when we try to show strength in future. All our history, especially British history, points to this lesson. No one wants conflict. Even now, war could be avoided if Saddam did what he is supposed to do. But if, having made a demand backed up by a threat of force, we fail to enforce that demand, the result will not be peace or security. It will simply be returning to confront the issue again at a later time, with the world less stable, the will of the international community less certain, and those repressive states or terrorist groups that would destroy our way of life emboldened and undeterred.

Even now, I hope that conflict with Iraq can be avoided. Even now, I hope that Saddam can come to his senses, co-operate fully and disarm peacefully, as the UN has demanded. But if he does not—if he rejects the peaceful route—he must be disarmed by force. If we have to go down that route, we shall do all we can to minimise the risks to the people of Iraq, and we give an absolute undertaking to protect Iraq's territorial integrity. Our quarrel has never been with the Iraqi people, but with Saddam.

Saddam's weapons of mass destruction and the threats that they pose to the world must be confronted. In doing so, this country and our armed forces will be helping the long-term peace and security of Britain and the world.

(HC Deb 3 February 2003 Vol. 399 c21–23)

15/24

The Prime Minister further stated:

First of all, I think that the right hon. Gentleman said that we were hastening into war ahead of events. We have gone through 12 years of this process—12 years in which we have tried to get Saddam to disarm. We then came together last November and passed a resolution saying that there should be one final opportunity. That is hardly hastening into a war. If he does not comply with that UN resolution—he is not complying at the moment—we are not hastening into it ahead of events, but responding to the fact that Saddam has refused point blank, as he has done throughout 12 years, to do what the United Nations has asked him to do.

As for saying that credible evidence has not been forthcoming that Saddam is in breach of the resolution, the resolution says that he must make a full and honest declaration. I simply ask the right hon. Gentleman whether he thinks that a declaration that does not even disclose what has happened to the thousands of munitions and tonnes of nerve, chemical and biological agents that we know were left over from 1999 is full and honest. Does he really believe that a failure even to declare what has happened to that is an honest undertaking and declaration of what has happened? Does he think that the refusal to allow Iraqi experts to be interviewed—a vital part of the inspection process—unless they come with so-called Iraqi minders is acceptable? None of us can be so naive as to think that such people are present merely to offer the odd cup of coffee and comfort. If Saddam is carrying on in breach of those obligations, as Hans Blix himself says that he is, that is the credible evidence that he is not co-operating. With the greatest respect, the right hon. Gentleman seems to suggest, when he says that we are not objective, that somehow it is for us to come along and prove that Saddam is a guilty party. No; the United Nations decided that he was in breach of the UN resolutions and he has got to produce the evidence that he is now co-operating fully—and he is not doing so.

Now that is not simply our view—it is the view of Dr. Blix and the UN weapons inspectors. The right hon. Gentleman says that they should have time to complete their task. Yes, they should, but their task is not to engage in an elaborate game of hide and seek with Saddam whereby the UN inspectors go in and try to find the stuff while he tries to hide it—if they find it, they win; if he hides it, he wins. That is not how the system is supposed to operate. That was how it operated in the 1990s, however, so that a weapons inspections process that was supposed to take weeks ended up taking years. This time, therefore, the resolution—1441—said, "You've got a final opportunity; you've got to make an honest declaration; you've got to co-operate fully with the inspectors." The time that they need, and the time that we need within the United Nations, is the time to make a judgment on whether that co-operation is forthcoming. At present, it is not. All we are saying is that if that does not change, Saddam is continuing to play the game that he has been playing for 12 years, which is unacceptable. That is not a sign of our failing to be objective, but a sign of our failing to be weak in the face of a threat that is posed to us in the world community.

Finally, I simply say this to the right hon. Gentleman. I know, of course, that there is huge anxiety, and that many criticisms are made of the United States, but it would be quite wrong if we used this issue to try to polarise the United States and the international community. The United States chose to go through the UN process last November, when many people thought that it would not. It was right to do so, and we should carry on through the UN process, but that process should be a way of dealing with this issue once and for all, not of kicking it into the long grass again and avoiding it altogether.

(HC Deb 3 February 2003 Vol. 399 c26–27)

15/25

In the same debate the Prime Minister said:

I have said that there should be no artificial deadline, but the issue comes down to the question of what the task is that the inspectors are being sent in to do. If their task is to return to what happened in the 1990s, when they stayed there for long periods of time and tried to work their way around Iraqi obstruction, it could take them years to complete it. If, however, their task is to go in there on the basis that Saddam is going fully to co-operate, it will be complete when they make their judgment either that he is doing so—in which case, they can get on and close the matériel down—or that he is not, in which case they do not need to wait months or years. That would be the situation in which, in the words of resolution 1441, there would be a further material breach, because Saddam would not have taken the final opportunity to disarm.

I must point out to my hon. Friend that Saddam cannot be in any doubt as to what he has to do. It is not a great mystery. I am told that he is calling for all sorts of people to come and visit him and talk to him, but there is no mystery about what he has to do. There is a perfectly well-trodden path in relation to UN inspectors, and it involves making a full declaration. South Africa followed it when it closed down its nuclear weapons programme after the change of regime and the end of apartheid. It called in the inspectors, told them exactly what it had, and allowed them full access to all its witnesses. The whole thing was then shut down in a matter of weeks. That is what can happen. The initial stages of it happened immensely quickly, and it could happen again. If the UN inspectors were saying to us, "Yes, Iraq is doing absolutely everything it can", I would not be standing here making this statement. I am making it not because we are being led by the nose into conflict, but because we have set out a process governed by that UN resolution. That process requires full compliance by Saddam, and he is not fully complying.

(HC Deb 3 February 2003 Vol. 399 c30)

15/26

He further went on to say:

It is true that we have to approach this in a careful and measured way, which is why we went through the UN process to get the backing of the international community for the demands that we have made on Saddam. The hon. Gentleman is right to say that, approached in the wrong way, this could lead to misunderstandings—for example, that this is an attack on Iraq because it is a Muslim country, and all the rest of the propaganda that surrounds these issues. I believe that there is now a clearer understanding—I have certainly found this in my discussions with Arab Heads of State—that this is about enforcing the will of the UN. Done in the right way, and with the right guarantees to the people of Iraq, the whole process of disarmament could be seen as a victory not only for the international community, but for the people of Iraq. I must point out that the consequence of not having disarmed Saddam properly, and of allowing the will of the UN to be flouted over many years, is that we have had to put in place a very tough, punitive sanctions regime. Because of the way in which Saddam has operated it—he need not have done it in the way that he has—it has caused the most terrible misery to the people in Iraq. More than half the population is dependent on the oil-for-food programme.

I think that in the end people, not least in Iraq, will realise not just that seeing the back of Saddam is good for the peace and security of the world, but that the first beneficiaries will be the people of Iraq.

(HC Deb 3 February 2003 Vol. 399 c31)

15/27

Her Majesty's Government was asked the following written question:

To ask the Prime Minister, pursuant to his statement to the House of 25 February 2003, *Official Report*, columns 123–140W, what contingency plans he has in place relating to the honouring of current oil contracts between Iraq and France and Russia.

In reply, the Prime Minister wrote:

Contracts for the export of Iraqi oil under the Oil for Food programme continue to be honoured, with Iraq exporting 11.9 million barrels in the week beginning 15 February. Our policy is that the sanctions regime should be complied with.

(HC Deb 3 March 2003 Vol. 400 c849W)

15/28

During a debate in the House of Commons, the Secretary of State, FCO, said:

The hon. Gentleman raises a really important question, which I touched on, but only lightly, in my statement. There are two issues here: first, how one measures whether Saddam has, over a matter of days, come into compliance; then, when and if he has come into compliance, how one measures whether he has disarmed completely. One measures whether he has come into compliance on whether he is co-operating with the 29 separate clusters set out in this very detailed UNMOVIC report. As I indicated in my statement, we are discussing whether some of those can be distilled into a few possible markers or tests by which the Security Council would be able to make a judgment about whether there was compliance.

To take the issue of interviews, for example, anybody who feels that they should give the Iraqi regime the benefit of the doubt need only to look at the record in this report and in the successive reports of Dr. Blix and Dr. el-Baradei concerning the point-blank refusal of the Iraqi regime to facilitate any free interviews outside Iraq whatsoever, notwithstanding the very clear requirements of 1441. So if they were suddenly to say, "Yes, we are going to comply with that and co-operate", and the relevant people appeared, and their relatives and friends were not murdered, that would be one indicator among a number. If we got to that point, the inspectors would go in and could have the time that they needed—I made that point to my hon. Friend the Member for Barnsley, West and Penistone (Mr. Clapham). It would then be a matter of the inspectors saying, "Well, we have gone through each of these areas of the dossier and each of these clusters of issues, and they have dealt with what is required of them over a period of time." First, however, they have got to show that they are in compliance.

(HC Deb 10 March 2003 Vol. 401 c36–37)

15/29

In a written answer, the Parliamentary Under-Secretary wrote:

As a result of Iraqi concealment and deceit, UNSCOM was never able to verify the full extent of Iraq's holdings of weapons of mass destruction, so it is not possible to give an accurate estimate of what proportion of them had been destroyed.

It is clear, however, from the final report of UNSCOM's Executive Chairman Richard Butler that there were substantial numbers of chemical and biological weapons, large quantities of the materials for the manufacture of such weapons and a number of missiles with a range beyond the 150 km limit prescribed by the United Nations still unaccounted for when UNSCOM left Iraq in December 1998.

(HC Deb 12 March 2003 Vol. 401 c292W)

15/30

During a debate on Iraq in the House of Commons, the Parliamentary Under-Secretary of State, FCO, said:

The Government strongly welcome the Select Committee on International Development's fourth report, which was presented to the House a week ago. We will give a detailed response to its various recommendations in due course.

However, one of the crucial matters that it raises is the way in which the Government would move forward in the immediate post-conflict situation to try to resolve some of the humanitarian issues, and especially whether we would seek a United Nations resolution—or, indeed, more than one—to take the process forward.

I confirm that we shall seek a further resolution to deal with the humanitarian issues. We shall try to transfer the oil-for-food programme to the United Nations Secretary-General to enable him to keep the process functioning and use UN facilities to do that. We will also seek a new UN resolution to provide authority for reconstruction and development work, and a proper mandate for any interim authority that is likely to operate in the territory of Iraq when Saddam Hussein is removed. We will also try to ensure the rapid delivery of humanitarian aid, to affirm Iraq's territorial integrity and to allow UN sanctions to be lifted, thus enabling food and other necessary items to arrive. We shall also enable an international reconstruction programme to facilitate the use of oil revenues for the benefit of the Iraqi people and to endorse a post-conflict administration in Iraq, which will lead to a representative Government who would uphold human rights and rule of law for all Iraqis.

(HC Deb 19 March 2003 Vol. 401 c941–942)

15/31

During a debate in the House of Lords on Iraq, the Parliamentary Under-Secretary of State, FCO, made the following statements:

I was asked whether the oil-for-food programme is already suspended. It would be suspended when there were no Iraqi government. That is why we see as a priority the need to secure a Security Council resolution that would enable the programme to continue in the absence of a functioning Iraqi government. We envisage a temporary transfer to some kind of impartial figure, such as the UN Secretary-General, to give it authority to enter into contracts for food and essential humanitarian supplies. The purpose of that would be to use the considerable resources and existing supply networks of the oil-for-food programme in support of the immediate humanitarian needs of the people of Iraq.

...

My Lords, I entirely agree with the noble Lord, Lord Hannay, that co-ordination at an early stage is important. That is why we have held regular meetings with the NGOs within a UK context and have shared information with them. We should like to see the co-ordination handled through the UN Office for the Co-ordination of Humanitarian Affairs. But clearly we would need an agreed United Nations resolution to enable us to see that process put in place, and we shall be working towards that. I entirely agree with the noble Lord that we shall want as wide a group as possible to contribute to any humanitarian effort post any conflict. In that respect, the role of the European Union will be very important.

(HL Deb 19 March 2003 Vol. 646 c244–252)

15/32

During a debate in the House of Commons, the Prime Minister said:

The Council [European Council] agreed the need to be active in the humanitarian field, to ensure that the oil revenues are held for the Iraqi people by the United Nations and to ensure that the oil-for-food programme continues. The Council further agreed that the UN Security Council should give the UN a strong mandate for post-conflict Iraq and make sure that the new Administration is one that is representative, careful of the human rights of the Iraqi people and allows the people to live at peace inside Iraq and with their neighbours.

(HC Deb 24 March 2003 Vol. 402 c22)

15/33

In a written answer, the Secretary of State for International Development wrote:

UN resolutions currently prevent Oil for Food Programme funds being used to repay Iraqi debt, but 25 per cent. of revenues will go to the UN Compensation Commission which pays reparations claims for the 1990–91 Gulf War.

Future Iraqi debt and reparations payments will need to be addressed in due course by the future Government of Iraq and the International Financial Institutions if Iraqi reconstruction is to be sustainable.

(HC Deb 11 April 2003 Vol. 403 c455W)

15/34

During a House of Commons debate on Iraq the Foreign Secretary made the following statements:

First, on Iraq's reconstruction, the United Nations Security Council unanimously adopted resolution 1483 on 22 May. That resolution gave the UN a vital role in all aspects of Iraq's development, including the political process. Under that resolution, UN Secretary-General Kofi Annan appointed as his special representative Sergio Vieira de Mello, the highly respected United Nations high commissioner for human rights. Resolution 1483 freed Iraq from the UN sanctions regime, allowing oil revenues to be spent on humanitarian needs, economic reconstruction and other purposes benefiting the people of Iraq.

On Sunday, an important step was taken towards fulfilling the second undertaking—the establishment of a sovereign Iraqi Government. The convening of the Iraqi governing council is a significant development. The council is the principal body of the interim administration called for in resolution 1483.

. . .

The United Nations made it clear in resolutions 1441 and 1483 that it would not support anything that would undermine the current territorial integrity of Iraq. Despite that, there are opportunities for various degrees of devolution to occur.

I made the point to a group of Iraqi leaders two weeks ago that our experience shows that devolution need not occur on a symmetrical basis. Indeed, I believe the fact that we have developed asymmetrical systems is the reason why we have been better able to bind the Union. That is a lesson as the Iraqis develop their own constitution.

...

Let me satisfy my hon. Friend. Resolution 1483 lays down clearly the conditions under which all revenues, in particular oil revenues, can be used, and have to be used, for the benefit of the people of Iraq. The war was never about oil. Everyone knows that. In the initial stages, the financial responsibility rests on the coalition provisional authority, because it has to rest somewhere. As quickly as possible, it will move to the governing council. In any event, there are clear and substantial monitoring arrangements, supervised by a monitoring board established by 1483. There is also the ever-present figure of Vieira de Mello, the UN Secretary-General's special representative, who is required to make regular reports to the Security Council to ensure that 1483 is complied with.

(HC Deb 15 July 2003 Vol. 409 c151–162)

15/35

In response to a written question the Under-Secretary of State, FCO, wrote:

Since the Coalition Provisional Authority (CPA) took over the administration of Iraq, Iraqi oil has been sold by CPA through the Iraqi State Oil Marketing Organisation in accordance with the terms of paragraph 20 of United Nations Security Council Resolution 1483. Under paragraphs 20 and 21 of this resolution, all revenues from sales of Iraqi oil are deposited into the Development Fund for Iraq, less 5 per cent [ed. sic. 25 per cent] which is to be deposited into the Iraq Compensation Fund as established under UNSCR 687 of 1991. No other Iraqi assets have been sold by the CPA.

...

The Governing Council is representative of Iraq society and includes a narrow Shia majority, Sunnis and Christians and three women. The Council will work to ensure views of all Iraqis are represented. It delivers a key part of UNSCR 1483.

The Governing Council has real power and will be involved in all key decisions on Iraq's future. It will name the new Ministers in the interim administration, run the Ministries and set the budget for 2004. It will also be responsible for Iraq's representation abroad. Some of the Council's early tasks will be: launching the Constitutional process—written by Iraqis for Iraqis; rebuilding Iraq's infrastructure; restoring security and stability; revitalising the economy and provision of essential services.

In all these activities the Coalition will provide support and advice.

(HC Deb 17 July 2003 Vol. 409 c585W)

15/36

In reply to a written question a Foreign Office Minister wrote:

Under the Oil for Food programme set up by UN Security Council Resolution 986 (1995) Iraqi oil revenues were divided between the North of Iraq (13 per cent), the South and Centre of Iraq (59 per cent), the United Nations Compensation Commission (25 per cent), UNMOVIC's operating costs (0.8 per cent) and the Oil for Food Programme's operating costs (2.2 per cent). The revenues spent in North and South/Central Iraq were held in separate accounts. The funds in the Northern account were spent by the United Nations while the funds in the South and Centre account were spent by the Iraqi Government. This was done so that the oil revenue from the whole of Iraq was spent on the whole of Iraq. Had the funds not been divided in this way, Saddam Hussein would have systematically discriminated against the Kurds in the north. The need to keep the two accounts separate disappeared when Saddam Hussein fell. The two accounts were consolidated by UN Security Council Resolution 1483 so that oil revenues from the whole of Iraq could best be spent on the whole of Iraq.

(HL Deb 18 July 2003 Vol. 651 cWA191)

15/37

In reply to a written question the Minister of State, FCO, wrote:

Coalition plans for political and physical rehabilitation are as follows:

The Iraqi Governing Council formed on 13 July is the principal element of the interim administration called for in Resolution 1483 and has been welcomed by the UN. The council has significant powers that will increase over time. An early task for the council is to determine how a new constitution should be prepared. Once adopted, it will pave the way for elections and an internationally recognised representative Iraqi Government to which the coalition will hand over its powers and responsibilities.

...

The Coalition Provisional Authority (CPA) is working with the United Nations and the international community on all aspects of the reconstruction of Iraq, as called for in United Nations Security Council Resolution (UNSCR) 1483.

We are making progress. The Iraqi police force is up and running and conducting patrols with the coalition military. Prisons and courts are open to try those arrested. The new Iraqi army has started recruiting with the aim of recruiting and training a 40,000 strong force in the next two years. The CPA is working with 19 Iraqi ministries, including on the immigration and customs side, and civil servants are returning to work.

To pay for the reconstruction process, UNSCR 1483 enables the CPA to draw from the oil revenues and seized Iraqi assets transferred to the Development Fund for Iraq. The UK and other international contributors have also committed resources and specialists to help in the reconstruction process.

...

United Nations Security Council Resolution 1483 enables the Coalition Provisional Authority (CPA) to draw from the oil revenues and seized Iraqi assets transferred to the Development Fund for Iraq in order to pay for public expenditure in Iraq.

(HL Deb 8 September 2003 Vol. 652 cWA19–WA20)

15/38

During a debate on the role of the UN in Iraq, the Foreign Secretary said:

Resolution 1483, co-sponsored by the United States and the UK, talked about a vital role for the United Nations, and established a framework for the UN's involvement in all significant aspects of Iraq's reconstruction. It lifted most of the UN sanctions against Iraq. A second resolution—resolution 1500—passed on 14 August welcomed the first steps taken by Iraq towards representative government with the formation of the Iraqi Governing Council. It also created the United Nations assistance mission for Iraq, as recommended by the Secretary-General.

To pick up the point made by my hon. Friend the Member for Cambridge (Mrs. Campbell), of course there was scepticism about the question of whether the "vital role" was simply warm words or would be followed by action. I have accepted both in the House and outside that mistakes were made, not only in respect of the role of the United Nations but, more significantly, in not fully anticipating the speed with which the Saddam regime would collapse and the security vacuum that would be left. There were also mistakes in the planning for the coalition provisional authority. That said, after the passage of resolution 1483, in late May, June and July, the role of the United Nations on the ground was accelerating and, on any analysis, becoming vital.

. . .

Let me set out the key elements in the draft that is now under discussion. It reaffirms the United Nations' support for the work of the Governing Council and calls on the council—this is a very important point—to submit a timetable and programme for the drafting of a new constitution for Iraq and the holding of democratic elections. The timetable would be provided in co-operation with both the CPA and the United Nations. It would reinforce to the Iraqi people our determination to move along the path towards democratic government run by Iraqis in a sovereign Iraq. Giving that sense of progress and hope about the fact that the coalition is in the country as an occupying power only temporarily is of profound psychological importance in Iraq. It will give the international community more certainty about the direction that is being pursued in Iraq. The fact of the discussions has already tended to assist the international climate in which the Iraqi Governing Council is operating.

(HC Deb 10 September 2003 Vol. 410 c400–402)

15/39

During a House of Lords debate Her Majesty's Government was asked the following question:

My Lords, on 24th September, in a leader, the Financial Times said that the appointed interim Governing Council of Iraq does not have,

> "the political authority to sell off chunks of Iraq's national assets".

It said that that,

> "is a decision that will require the legitimacy of an elected government. Otherwise there will be no shortage of forces in Iraq...to present it as a second looting of the country".

Does the Leader of the House agree with that? If so, is it not plainly untimely to think of selling off long-term assets now?

The Minister of State for the Home Office replied:

My Lords, UN Security Council Resolution 1483 set out the terms under which the next phases in the reconstruction and rehabilitation of Iraq should take place. In that context, the Governing Council, fully supported by the CPA, made decisions with respect to the economic future of Iraq.

(HL Deb 8 October 2003 Vol. 653 c295)

15/40

The Under-Secretary of State, FCO, made the following written statement:

Following consultation with the Foreign and Commonwealth Office and the Ministry of Defence, the Department of Trade and Industry recently approved a further licence to export military list goods to Iraq. The arms embargo against Iraq remains in place under United Nations Security Council resolution 1483 (2003), with the exception of arms and other related material required by the Coalition Provisional Authority to serve the purposes of this and other related resolutions. Accordingly, Her Majesty's Government consider it appropriate to grant exemptions for the export of sub-machine guns and pistols that are to be used by private security firms contracted to provide close protection for employees of the Coalition Provisional Authority (CPA) in Iraq. The export is consistent with the consolidated EU and national arms export licensing criteria. Future applications will continue to be assessed on a case by case basis against the UN embargo and consolidated criteria, taking into account the circumstances prevailing at the time.

(HC Deb 14 October 2003 Vol. 411 c7WS)

15/41

In reply to a written question the Under-Secretary of State, FCO, wrote:

Security Council Resolution 1511, co-sponsored by the UK and unanimously adopted on 16 October, provides a further step forward in the international community's contribution to the political and economic reconstruction of Iraq. The Resolution has three main objectives:

to confirm and accelerate the transfer of power to the people of Iraq;

to send a clear signal that the international community is committed to the rapid political and economic reconstruction of a free Iraq which is secure and stable;

to ensure, as conditions permit, a strengthened vital role for the United Nations, in partnership with the Coalition and with the Iraqi people.

In particular, the Resolution invites the Governing Council of Iraq to provide by 15 December a programme and timetable for the drafting of a new constitution for Iraq and for the holding of democratic elections. It also encourages further international contributions to economic reconstruction, to the multi-national security force and to training and equipping of Iraqi police.

(HC Deb 17 October 2003 Vol. 412 c58W–59W)

15/42

In response to a written question, the Minister of State, FCO, wrote:

Following consultation with the Foreign and Commonwealth Office and the Ministry of Defence, the Department of Trade and Industry recently approved a licence to export demining equipment to the United Nations Office for Project Services in mine clearance operations in northern Iraq. The export included an electronic hand held exploder that appears on the Military List. The conclusion that this export does not represent a proliferation threat has been reached after careful assessment.

The UN Iraq Sanctions Committee approved this export to Iraq under the Oil for Food programme (OFF). Under OFF, Iraq is allowed to export unlimited quantities of oil to fund the purchase of humanitarian goods. The export is consistent with the consolidated EU and national arms export licensing criteria.

(HL Deb 22 October 2002 Vol. 639 cWA95)

15/43

In reply to a written question the Minister of State, FCO, wrote:

The political process in Iraq, including membership of the governing council, is a matter for the Council. The governing council is committed to reporting the recommendations for a future constitution by 15 December 2003 under the terms of UNSCR 1511.

(HL Deb 6 November 2003 Vol. 654 cWA134)

15/44

And in reply to a further written question the same Minister wrote:

The Iraqi Governing Council (GC) appointed a Constitutional Preparatory Committee (CPC) in August to start the process of deciding a new Iraqi constitution. Following the CPC's report to the GC in early October and the adoption of UN resolution 1511, the GC has been tasked by the United Nations Security Council to report on the way forward and set a timetable by 15 December for adoption of a new constitution and elections. The relationship between Iraq's central authorities and its governorates will be addressed during this process, which is managed entirely by Iraqis for Iraq.

(HL Deb 6 November 2003 Vol. 654 cWA134)

15/45

In reply to a written question the Under-Secretary of State, FCO, wrote:

Resolution 1483 authorises the Coalition to undertake activities to promote economic reconstruction in Iraq, in co-ordination with the Special Representative of the UN Secretary General[.] CPA Order 39 on Foreign Direct Investment permits up to 100 per cent participation in a new or existing business in Iraq, but does not allow for foreign direct and indirect ownership of the natural resources sector involving primary extraction and initial processing. In addition, this Order does not apply to banks and insurance companies. Foreign direct investment is an important means of promoting employment opportunities and improving social welfare. This Order creates the conditions for much needed capital to enter the Iraqi economy.

The Government are therefore satisfied that Security Council Resolution 1483 provides a sound legal basis for the policy goals of the CPA Foreign Investment Order. We have also satisfied ourselves through UK officials working within the CPA, and the office of the UK Special Representative for Iraq that co-ordination with the UN has taken place, in consultation with the International Financial Institutions. The Order was approved by the Governing Council and had the support of the Minister of Finance.

(HC Deb 20 November 2003 Vol. 413 c1308W)

15/46

In reply to a written question the Minister of State, FCO, wrote:

The vital role of the United Nations in Iraq has been set out in Security Council Resolutions 1483, 1500 and 1511. In particular, UNSCR 1511 requested the Secretary-General to make available, as circumstances allow, the resources of the United Nations to support Iraqi institutions in drafting a new constitution and in the holding of democratic elections.

On 15 November, the President of the Iraqi Governing Council announced the new plan outlining the timetable for the drafting of the constitution and holding of elections. He also asked the Security Council to appoint a new Special Representative to Iraq, and formally requested a UN role in support of the political process.

In his report of 10 December, Kofi Annan announced the appointment of Ross Mountain as interim UN Special Representative to Iraq and set out his views on the UN role in Iraq, outlining the UN's willingness to lend its assistance to the electoral and constitutional processes, subject to circumstances and an Iraqi request. He also set out a wide range of potential UN activities in humanitarian, development, human rights and civil society fields. We welcome the UN position, and will work with the Secretary-General to ensure the UN can play a vital role as set out in UNSCR 1511, in particular in support of the political process.

(HL Deb 16 December 2003 Vol. 655 cWA130–WA131)

15/47

During a debate in the House of Commons, the Secretary of State, FCO, made the following statements:

A settlement of the dispute between the Israelis and Palestinians would plainly enhance global security, including the security of the immediate region and of Europe and the United Kingdom. We are in active support of the Quartet of the European Union, the Russian Federation, the United States and the United Nations in working for renewed negotiations, including the publication of the road map to give effect to President Bush's vision of a two-state solution by 2005.

. . .

We have been encouraging it to be more forward in recognising the need to implement fully the very welcome statements that President Bush made last June and the very welcome United Nations Security Council resolution that was passed at the behest of the United States and that laid down for the first time that there should be a clear two-state solution. We continue in very intense dialogue with our American and other friends.

As far as conflict with Iraq is concerned, all Palestinians—including Ministers—to whom I have spoken have made it crystal clear that they are the last people in the world to have anything good to say on behalf of Saddam Hussein. The case for advancing the peace process and trying to continue to get both sides together stands on its own merits. However, I accept—given the allegation of double standards—that the case for pursuing it is all the greater when set against the possibility of military action in Iraq.

. . .

We are not discounting the use of the veto. As has every member state of the United Nations, we have had to acknowledge that there could be circumstances in which we would take action without a second resolution. However, let us be clear. As the Command Paper that has been published this morning makes clear, the authority for any military action in respect of Iraq is based very firmly on UN Security Council resolutions that have already been passed. It is of profound importance that that point is understood. I invite my hon. Friend to read, in particular, resolution 687, which agreed a conditional ceasefire, and resolution 1441, including its final operative paragraph.

. . .

I understand, as I said earlier, the argument about double standards and the fact that it has some resonance based on fact, not only in the Arab and Islamic world, but in the wider world. But what I would say to my hon. Friend is that Security Council resolutions such as 242, 338, 1397 and 1402 impose obligations not only on the Israelis, yes, to recognise a viable state, to withdraw from the settlements, to negotiate the future of East Jerusalem and to deal with the issue of refugees, but on the Palestinian Authority properly and effectively to control terrorism and on all the surrounding Arab states to recognise the state of Israel and not to support terrorism themselves. The answer to the terrible issue of the middle east is for us to continue to apply pressure to all sides to achieve an effective negotiated settlement.

(HC Deb 25 February 2003 Vol. 400 c115–117)

15/48

During a debate in the House of Commons, the Secretary of State, FCO, made the following statements:

I discussed the road map with my Israeli counterpart, the new Foreign Minister Silvan Shalom, on 21 March. The United Kingdom Government are committed to the establishment of a viable state of Palestine living in peace alongside a secure state of Israel, as provided in Security Council resolutions 242, 338 and 1397. This is achievable through full implementation of the Quartet road map, which was published, after the approval of Abu Mazen's Government, by the Palestinian Legislative Council.

In recent months, we have worked with the Palestinians on their reform effort, notably through meetings in London on 14 January and between 18 and 20 February. We have encouraged President Arafat to appoint a Prime Minister. We are grateful that he has and, by doing so, he has helped to clear the way for road map publication.

The first phase of the road map includes a requirement on Israel to take specific steps to halt settlement activity, which is illegal under international law and plainly an obstacle to peace.

...

The important thing is to get the road map published and for both sides to start work on its implementation with the facilitation provided by the Quartet. I cannot give specific time scales, but the hon. Gentleman knows that the aim of the road map is to move away from present divisions and conflict towards a situation in which there are two states in a relatively short time.

A viable and separate state of Palestine is controversial in sections of Israeli politics but also in parts of the Arab world. Some people in the Arab and Islamic world take the view that there should be a one-state solution. However, a two-state solution has been agreed, it is part of international law under resolution 1397 and it is our duty to ensure that it is implemented.

I agree entirely with the hon. Gentleman's remarks about suicide bombers and the bulldozing of people's homes in the settlements. We must end the spiral of violence and destruction. The only way the 6 million people in Israel and the 3.5 million people in the occupied territories can live together is by living in peace, which is the aim of the road map.

...

[T]he Palestinian Authority will be required to take firm security action against the terrorist organisations, but some of the Arab states that neighbour Israel and the occupied territories have an even greater responsibility to end the funding and support of terrorist organisations. Of course, one of those countries is Iraq.

...

If we are to get from where we are to where we want to be, there has to be a phasing of it. The first stage needs to be a withdrawal by the Israeli defence force and other security forces from area A, which represents the occupied territories previously and effectively controlled by the Palestinian Authority. Our policy remains that very clearly laid down in resolutions 242, 338 and 1397: a return to the 1967 borders—there may be some amendments to those, but a state based on the 1967 borders—an end to the settlements, a solution to the refugee problem and a capital for a Palestinian state in Jerusalem.

...

Let me make it clear to my hon. Friend that the publication date of the road map is a matter to be decided by the partners in the Quartet, and is not the responsibility of either the Government of Israel or the Palestinian Authority. It is, as it were, our decision, not theirs. On my hon. Friend's second point, we continue to call for the Israeli defence force to show proper restraint. In all my conversations with Israeli Foreign Ministers—with B. B. Netanyahu and now with Mr. Shalom—I have emphasised not only that that is required under international law and simple human care, but that it is not in the interests of the Government of Israel or the reputation of the Jewish people to act excessively and outside international law.

...

The US Administration are a key part of the Quartet. They are one of the four partners in the Quartet, and have signed up to the road map. It is known, of course, that Israeli politics and concern for Israeli security are a dominant theme in United States politics—that is just a fact of life. It is critical to build confidence among both the Israeli community in Israel and the Jewish community in the United States that their security is not going to be daily threatened by terrorism, particularly by suicide bombers. We have worked very hard with the Americans, the Israelis and particularly the Palestinian Authority to ensure that the maximum security action is taken against those terrorists. However, to return to the key point made by my hon. Friend, I believe that the US Administration are fully committed to the implementation of the road map, otherwise they would not have endorsed it. We shall press them, as with all the other partners in the Quartet, to press ahead with its implementation.

...

I can certainly express hope on the hon. Gentleman's first point. It is in the interests of both sides to live in peace, so they have to recognise that the only way to peace is a two-state solution. On the issue of amendment, yes, I am aware that there are those in Israel who want amendments, and I discussed that with Foreign Minister Shalom last week in a long telephone conversation. My point to him was that the road map is the property of the Quartet, not the Israeli Government or the Palestinian Authority. It is a framework: yes, some of its detail may of course be changed over time, but what we cannot see is any change to its fundamental principles.

(HC Deb 25 March 2003 Vol. 402 c142–146)

15/49

During a House of Lords debate on the Israeli security fence constructed in occupied territory, the Minister of State, FCO, said:

On 14th October the Security Council voted on a text that demanded Israel should cease the construction of the fence. We considered that that draft had insufficient references to terrorism and, therefore, that it was unbalanced and unhelpful to the implementation of the road map. We abstained in that vote, along with Germany, Bulgaria and Cameroon, and the United States used its veto. A resolution on the fence was subsequently put to an emergency special session of the UN General Assembly where the European Union proposals, which we had been pivotal in negotiating, were brought forward. We believed at that point that we had a more balanced text and voted in favour of the resolution. I hope that, on reflection, the noble Lord will recognise that the United Kingdom Government have played a constructive role in seeking a balanced way forward.

(HL Deb 28 October 2003 Vol. 654 c133)

15/50

In reply to a written question on the Ivory Coast, the Parliamentary Under-Secretary of State wrote:

Liberian involvement in Cote d'Ivoire has contributed significantly to instability in the west of the country. The nature of Liberian involvement is complex, with reports of Liberians fighting for both sides. Liberia is used as a base by rebels fighting in the West of Cote d'Ivoire, and there are large numbers of Liberian mercenaries fighting for both sides. We remain concerned at the ease with which armed groups move between the two countries. We are also concerned about the plight of over 40,000 Liberian refugees in the region.

While we do not have a full picture of the role played by the Liberian Government in Cote d'Ivoire it is clear that it continues to ignore UN Security Council demands by sponsoring armed groups in the region. Our objective remains to contain these activities by maintaining effective UN sanctions against Liberia.

(HC Deb 18 March 2003 Vol. 401 c726W)

15/51

In a written answer, the Secretary of State for Defence wrote:

Britain, along with its international partners, is working to ensure that Kosovo develops as a tolerant, multi-ethnic society. The security of churches and other religious and cultural sites in Kosovo is important to the success of this effort. British soldiers, as part of our contribution to the NATO-led Kosovo Force (KFOR), play an active role in protecting these sites. These arrangements are reviewed regularly by KFOR in the light of the security situation prevailing at the time, and in full consultation with the local and regional authorities.

(HC Deb 7 February 2003 Vol. 399 c478W)

15/52

In response to a written question, the Minister of State, FCO, wrote:

My right hon. Friend the Foreign Secretary and I are in close and regular contact with European colleagues. On 24 February 2003, Foreign Ministers issued a statement at the European Union General Affairs and External Relations Council which reiterated the importance of full respect for UNSCR 1244, and urged all parties, both in Belgrade and in Pristina, to refrain from any unilateral initiatives which were incompatible with the objective of a multi-ethnic and democratic Kosovo, and which may jeopardise stability and the normalisation process not only in Kosovo but in the entire region.

(HC Deb 4 March 2003 Vol. 400 c907W)

15/53

In a written answer, the Parliamentary Under-Secretary of State, FCO, wrote:

The UK has supported the work of the UN Compensation Commission since its creation in 1991 and four out of six categories of claims arising from the illegal invasion of Kuwait by Iraq in 1991 have been resolved. 25 per cent. of Oil for Food funds continue to be paid to the UNCC. It would be open to the Security Council to change these arrangements in the future.

(HC Deb 1 April 2003 Vol. 402 c654W)

15/54

In a written answer, the Minister of State, FCO, wrote:

We are raising the attack on Beam, in Liberia, with the UN Secretariat. The main aim of the attack seems to have been looting connected to the conflict in Cote d'Ivoire. It is unclear who orchestrated the attack but Liberian and Ivorian groups have been accused of involvement. We remain concerned about reports of Liberian involvement in the rebellion in Cote d'Ivoire and at the ease with which armed groups can pass across the border.

The Government of Liberia continues to ignore the demands of the UN Security Council by sponsoring armed groups in the region. Our aim remains to contain these activities by maintaining effective UN sanctions against Liberia.

(HC Deb 4 February 2003 Vol. 399 c203W)

15/55

In reply to a written question, the Under-Secretary of State, FCO, wrote:

Stability in Sierra Leone is threatened by conflicts in Liberia and Cote d'Ivoire. We are supporting international and regional initiatives to resolve the conflict in Liberia especially through our membership of the International Contact Group and in Cote d'Ivoire.

Liberia remains a centre of gravity for mercenaries and armed groups in the region. Liberia continues to ignore the demands of the UN Security Council by sponsoring armed groups in the region. We aim to continue to contain the activities of the Liberian regime by maintaining effective UN sanctions against Liberia. We remain concerned about reports of Liberian involvement in the rebellion in Cote d'Ivoire.

We have taken steps to limit the proliferation of small arms and light weapons in the sub-region through UN arms embargoes in Liberia and Sierra Leone, a disarmament programme in Sierra Leone and support for the ECOWAS Small Arms monitoring mechanism.

(HC Deb 5 February 2003 Vol. 399 c306W)

15/56

In reply to a written question on Liberia, the Parliamentary Under-Secretary of State wrote:

The UN imposed sanctions on Liberia as a result of the Liberian Government's complicity in fuelling the conflict in Sierra Leone. Liberia remains a serious threat to the stability of the sub-region. It has been involved in incursions into Guinea and is now being used as a base by rebels in Cote d'Ivoire. The sanctions are focused specifically on President Taylor and his ministers. We believe that they should be maintained until Liberia ends its efforts to destabilise the region.

(HC Deb 18 March 2003 Vol. 401 c727W–728W)

15/57

In response to a written question, the Parliamentary Under-Secretary of State, FCO, wrote:

The UN imposed sanctions on Liberia as a result of the Liberian Government's complicity in fuelling the conflict in Sierra Leone. Liberia remains a serious threat to the stability of the sub-region. We believe sanctions should be maintained until

Liberia stops its destabilising efforts in the region and meets in full the demands of the UN Security Council.

We share the concern of the UN Panel of Experts that the revenues from timber sales are being used to fund arms purchases in breach of UN sanctions. In resolution 1408 (2002) the UN Security Council called on the Government of Liberia to undertake the audit of shipping and timber revenues and to use the revenues from the timber trade for social, development and humanitarian purposes.

We have played a leading role in trying to restrict the Government of Liberia's sanction-busting activities. We will be calling for the Council to examine all sources of revenue, including timber sales, used to make arms purchases, and to consider ways of addressing the problem in order to prevent the Liberian regime from making illicit arms purchases.

The Government support the Africa Forest Law Enforcement and Governance (AFLEG) process, which calls on all African governments and trading partners to take action to control illegal activities in the logging sector and associated trade. The UK will be represented at an AFLEG conference in April 2003 to push this process forward.

(HC Deb 8 April 2003 Vol. 403 c192W)

15/58

In reply to a written question the Minister of State, FCO, wrote:

With the support of Her Majesty's Government, the United Nations Security Council on 6 May 2003 unanimously adopted United Nations Security Council resolution 1478 (2003). The resolution rolled over the measures that had been in place against Liberia (a travel ban against senior government officials and members of their immediate families, a diamond embargo and an arms embargo). The travel ban was also extended to members of the Liberians United for Reconciliation and Democracy (LURD). In addition, timber sanctions were imposed against all round logs and timber products originating in Liberia. Sanctions against timber do not come into place until 7 July 2003.

(HL Deb 2 July 2003 Vol. 650 cWA101)

15/59

During a meeting in the Security Council the representative for the United Kingdom said:

Since that outrage [the bombing of Pan Am 103 over Lockerbie], the authorities in the United Kingdom have worked carefully and deliberately to bring the Libyan official al-Megrahi to justice for that act. The arrangements for the trial and appeal were made in accordance with the Security Council resolution. The Council also placed sanctions on Libya until certain requirements were met, sanctions being the only means of actually delivering justice.

Libya has now met those requirements. It has accepted responsibility and has agreed to pay a substantial sum of compensation to the relatives of those who were murdered. Libya has agreed to cooperate with any further Lockerbie investigation and has renounced terrorism. Libya's renunciation of terrorism is the first time in the modern era that a State has unequivocally renounced to the United Nations the use of terror as an instrument of policy. As a demonstration of that position, Libya has signed the 12 international conventions on the fight against terrorism. The United Kingdom welcomes Libyan cooperation in the fight against international terrorism. For all the above reasons, the United Kingdom, with Bulgaria, sponsored and supported the resolution to lift the sanctions on Libya. We expect Libya to abide by the commitments and obligations it has entered into as part of the agreement.

As this case demonstrates, the United Kingdom will pursue those responsible for terrorism. The perpetrators and sponsors will have to account for their actions, however long it takes . . .

The United Kingdom condemns terrorism in all its manifestations. There can be no justification for terrorist acts. In that context we also recall the horrific bombing of the La Belle disco in Berlin in 1986. Three people died and over 200 were injured. Three Libyan officials were subsequently found guilty of attempted murder. In complying with the requirements of the Security Council, including on the renunciation of terrorism, Libya has made a continuing commitment to the international community to abide by new standards of behaviour. We urge Libya to demonstrate that commitment now by implementing the agreement with the UTA families in full and by ensuring that full comfort is given to the families of the victims of the La Belle disco. We look forward to the full re-emergence of Libya into the international community.

(UN Doc. S/PV.4820 (part II), 12 September 2003)

15/60

In reply to a written question the Minister of State, FCO, wrote:

The UK supported United Nations Security Council Resolution 1509, which gave a robust and comprehensive mandate to the UN force now deploying in Liberia. This mandate includes the creation of a disarmament, demobilisation, reintegration, and repatriation programme for all armed parties with particular attention to the special needs of child combatants and women.

We will draw on experiences learnt from Sierra Leone including the Caritas child combatant disarmament and repatriation programmes undertaken in Makeni, Sierra Leone.

(HL Deb 16 October 2003 Vol. 653 cWA132)

15/61

In reply to a written question the Under-Secretary of State, FCO, wrote:

Measured and targeted sanctions remain on Liberia, as the security situation is a threat to the stability of the sub-region. Like other members of the UN Security Council, we believe that sanctions should remain until Liberia has put in place a diamond certification scheme, and reformed the timber sector to ensure that these natural resources cannot be used to further conflict. The arms embargo and travel ban should remain until the security situation is no longer a threat to the region.

(HC Deb 17 December 2003 Vol. 415 c975W)

15/62

In a letter dated 15 August 2003 from the Permanent Representatives of the United Kingdom of Great Britain and Northern Ireland and the United States of America to the United Nations addressed to the President of the Security Council, the representatives wrote:

In view of the letter dated 15 August 2003 addressed to you by the Libyan Arab Jamahiriya related to the bombing of Pan Am 103 (S/2003/818) and in the light of the actions and commitments that form the background to the letter, the Governments of the United Kingdom and the United States are prepared to allow the lifting of the measures set forth by the Council in its resolutions 748 (1992) and 883 (1993) once the necessary sums referred to in the Libyan letter have been transferred to the agreed escrow account.

In its letter, the Libyan Arab Jamahiriya has pledged before the Council to cooperate in the international fight against terrorism and to cooperate with any further request for information in connection with the Pan Am 103 investigation. We expect Libya to adhere scrupulously to those commitments.

(UN Doc. S/2003/819, 15 August 2003)

15/63

In reply to a written question the Parliamentary Under-Secretary of State, FCO, wrote:

United Nations peacekeeping operations and their personnel are accountable, through the commander of the operation in the field, the Department of Peace-Keeping Operations at UN Headquarters and the UN Secretary-General, to the Security Council.

UN peacekeeping personnel are obliged to act in accordance with international humanitarian law and may be subject to prosecution for any breaches which they commit.

(HL Deb 10 March 2003 Vol. 645 cWA143)

15/64

In reply to a written question, the Financial Secretary wrote:

Assets seized under anti-terrorist legislation are a matter for my right hon. Friend the Home Secretary.

Following 11 September 2001, £10,230,810 was frozen under Orders applying United Nations Security Council Resolutions 1267 and 1333 which froze accounts to prevent use by, inter alia, the then Taliban Government of Afghanistan. Subsequently, the Al-Qaeda and Taliban (United Nations Measures) Order 2002 implemented United Nations Security Council Resolution 1390 and, as well as allowing for the release of funds belonging to the legitimate Afghan Government, provided for the continued freezing of accounts belonging to Al-Qaeda.

Amounts totalling £346,382 remain frozen under the Orders implementing United Nations Security Council Resolutions 1373 and 1390.

(HL Deb 24 February 2003 Vol. 400 c183W)

15/65

In a written answer, the Financial Secretary wrote:

The al-Qaeda and Taliban (United Nations Measures) Order implementing United Nations Security Council Resolution 1390 allowed for the release of Taliban funds to the legitimate Government of Afghanistan. As a result, UK financial institutions have made such funds available to the Afghan Government and no Taliban (as distinct from al-Qaeda) funds remain frozen. As I indicated in my written answer of 16 October 2001, to the hon. Member (at column 1212W), no funds belonging to Afghan National Credit and Finance have been frozen in the UK. The assets of the National Trading Company of Afghanistan were frozen on 5 October 2001 as a temporary measure but were then unfrozen since they were not covered by UN sanctions. As my written answer explained, some £63 million sterling in 33 accounts had been frozen as at 15 October 2001. Regrettably, the sterling value of the frozen account of Khalid Al Fawwaz was incorrectly printed in the *Official Report* as £23.19 million; the correct figure, as stated in my written answer and as reflected in the total figure, was £23.19.

(HC Deb 4 March 2003 Vol. 400 c911W–912W)

Part Fifteen: II. B. *Coercive measures short of the use of force—collective measures—outside the United Nations*

(See also **15/4**, **15/57**)

15/66

In response to a written question, the Minister of State, FCO, wrote:

Her Majesty's Government remain committed to the OSCE arms embargo against both Azerbaijan and Armenia, which we interpret as covering all goods and technology controlled under entries in Part III of Schedule 1 to the Export of Goods (Control) Order 1994, commonly known as the military list.

In September 2002, the Government approved an export licence application for demining vests for the Azerbaijan National Agency for Mine Actions.

In January 2002 the Government approved a similar request for protective jackets for demining operations to Azerbaijan.

The decision was made in accordance with our practice occasionally to make an exemption to our interpretation of the embargo by approving exports of non-lethal military goods to humanitarian, media or peacekeeping organisations where it is clear that the embargo was not intended to prevent those exports and there is a strong humanitarian case for them.

(HL Deb 30 June 2003 Vol. 650 cWA59)

15/67

During a debate in the House of Lords, the Parliamentary Under-Secretary of State, FCO, said:

My noble friend Lord Ponsonby asked specifically about our current policy and the noble Lord, Lord Astor, asked me to confirm our position on assistance to Belarus. Our action to deal with Belarus must necessarily be taken in concert with our EU and other partners. We are all exerting pressure for change but, in the end, the solution lies in Lukashenko's hands—we cannot run Belarus for him. He has been in power since 1994 and has four years of his current term left to run.

The UK and other EU member states have made our position clear. The measures taken by the EU in 1997 remain in place. They restrict ministerial contact with Belarus; suspend aid, except for humanitarian reasons or to support civil society; and suspend ratification of the EU-Belarus partnership and co-operation agreement. EU member states will not support Belarus's membership of the Council of Europe. The North Atlantic Treaty Organisation's "Partnership for Peace" agreement, signed in 1995, remains undeveloped. Aid to Belarus by international financial institutions is restricted—they support only small and medium-sized enterprises in the private sector, with a view to strengthening civil society.

I must make absolutely clear that we have no quarrel with the people of Belarus. We want to alleviate the problems that they face because of the misguided policies of their leader.

The situation is bleak, but we must work towards a time when Belarus will return to the path of democracy; when human rights are once again upheld; and when freedom of speech and expression is returned to its people.

(HL Deb 9 October 2003 Vol. 639 c369–370)

15/68

In a reply to a written question, the Under-Secretary of State, FCO, wrote:

The EU visa ban is targeted towards Senior Members of the Burmese State Peace and Development Council, senior members of the military and security forces who formulate, implement or benefit from policies that impede Burma's transition to democracy, senior Burmese tourism officials and the family members of all the categories listed above. People covered by the ban are not allowed to enter the EU unless they are visiting the EU for the sole purposes of attending United Nations' events. In the case of the Burmese Foreign Minister, there is also provision for a visa to be issued when, by the agreement of all member states, the visit is deemed to be in the interests of the European Union.

(HC Deb 10 February 2003 Vol. 399 c565W–566W)

15/69

In a reply to a written question, the Under-Secretary of State, FCO, wrote:

The EU Common Position contains an arms embargo, a ban on EU high-level visits to Burma, a ban on defence links, a ban on the sale of items that can be used for repression or torture, a ban on non-humanitarian assistance and a visa ban and asset freeze on senior members of the regime and armed forces. In addition the European Community suspended Burma's Generalised System of Preferences (GSP) trading privileges in response to the use of forced labour and HMG does not encourage trade, investment or tourism with Burma.

All these measures are designed to press the Burmese regime and those who support and benefit from its misrule to allow progress to be made to bring about national reconciliation, respect for human rights and democracy in Burma. UK pressure will be maintained until Burma is irreversibly committed to substantive, lasting political change.

(HC Deb 10 February 2003 Vol. 399 c566W)

15/70

In reply to oral questions on Burma the Minister of State, FCO, said:

My Lords, the military regime has put together something it describes as a "road map". It is a small but completely inadequate step. It has no time lines; it is unclear who will be allowed to join the national convention process; and as long as Aung San Suu Kyi remains under house arrest she will be unable to represent the National League for Democracy, as will others who are barred from doing so.

My noble and learned friend raised, in particular, the issue surrounding the EU. He will know that, together with EU partners, we continue to prefer selective measures targeted at the regime rather than the kind of measures introduced by the United States of America, which we believe harm many of the poorer people. However, we should like to consider ways in which we can harden up the common position, which comes up for renewal in April 2004.

. . .

The ILO and the whole question of forced labour is another pressure point on the Burmese regime. We fully support the ILO and call upon the Burmese authorities to end permanently the nasty practice of forced labour. Burma's general system of preferences was suspended by the European Union in 1997 in response to the concerns about forced labour.

I agree with the noble Lord about the use of child soldiers. These are but two of the disgraceful practices of the current regime in Burma. It is of course possible to exert pressure, not only bilaterally but through the international multilateral forums available to us.

(HL Deb 11 December 2003 Vol. 655 c867–868)

15/71

In reply to a written question the Minister of State, FCO, wrote:

Following consultations with the Foreign and Commonwealth Office and Ministry of Defence, the Department of Trade and Industry recently approved a licence to export antennae masts to Ghana. These masts will be used by the Ghanaian Armed Forces in the UN peacekeeping mission in the Democratic Republic of Congo (DRC).

The DRC is subject to an EU arms embargo, imposed by a Declaration of 7/4/1993. The embargo was put in place mainly to ensure the safety of international troops and civilian personnel deployed in the DRC. The decision to grant an exemption to the EU arms embargo on the DRC was made on the basis that the equipment is needed by bona fide UN peacekeepers and is proportionate to the needs of the Ghanaian peacekeepers. It does not affect Her Majesty's Government's continued support for the EU arms embargo on the DRC.

Her Majesty's Government fully support the Ghanaian troops deployed to the UN peacekeeping mission in the DRC. The decision underlines our continued support for the work being done by peacekeepers within the country.

(HL Deb 3 April 2003 Vol. 646 cWA147)

15/72

During a debate in the House of Lords on Iraq and Israel/Palestine, the Parliamentary Under-Secretary of State, FCO, said:

[H]ans Blix did say that Iraq had begun to take some useful steps. The point, however, is that Saddam Hussein always does. He always begins to take a few useful steps, but he always does so at the last minute. I remind the noble Lord, Lord Wallace of Saltaire, that UNSCR 1441 demands the full, active and immediate co-operation of the Iraqi regime—not a few useful steps at the last minute. In no way could anyone claim that we have had full, active co-operation, and not a single speaker at the Security Council did so last week.

So we turn to the second resolution—a resolution on which the Prime Minister is working tirelessly, as is my right honourable friend the Foreign Secretary. The noble Lord, Lord Howell, asked about the legal questions. Iraq's obligations are unambiguously set out in existing Security Council resolutions passed over the past 12 years. Iraq has consistently been in breach of them. Resolution 1441 sets out in detail the council's requirements and it makes plain to Iraq that failure to comply now will have serious consequences. The words "serious consequences" have real meaning. The United Kingdom is committed to ensuring that any military action in which we engage anywhere in the world is carried out in accordance with international law. We have made very clear our strong preference for a second resolution in the event that Saddam continues to defy the UN. But we have also made clear that we must reserve our position in the event that a second resolution proves to be unattainable. The legality of the use of force in any particular case would depend on all the circumstances at the time...

...

As regards the UN mandate on humanitarian issues, my right honourable friend's Statement mentioned that he had had discussions with Kofi Annan, the United Nations Secretary General, last week. We shall be guided by a number of considerations in the event that there is a decision to launch military action, which is not decided. I refer to considerations of maintaining the territorial integrity of Iraq and that the Iraqi people themselves, in consultation with the international community, should generate ideas for future political arrangements for Iraq. Moreover, we would expect a successor regime to be a significant improvement on the existing one in terms of good governance and respect for human rights. We also believe that the United Nations should be at the centre of any transitional administration for Iraq. I hope that those four important points are useful to the noble Lord.

(HL Deb 10 March 2003 Vol. 645 c1138–1140)

15/73

In reply to a written question, the Secretary of State for Defence wrote:

The European Security and Defence Policy (ESDP) seeks to enable the European Union to deal with the full range of conflict prevention and crisis management missions defined in the Treaty, the "Petersberg Tasks". These missions (humanitarian and rescue tasks, peacekeeping tasks and tasks of combat forces in crisis management, including peacemaking) already give ESDP considerable scope to assist in the fight against international terrorism. Further work was commissioned, building on the Declaration of the Seville European Council concerning the contribution of the European Union's Common Foreign and Security Policy, including ESDP, in the fight against terrorism. This includes strengthening arrangements for sharing intelligence, and developing common threat evaluations. We are also supporting, in the framework of the Convention on the Future of Europe and elsewhere, proposals to allow a member state to call on the resources, including military, of other EU members, for civil protection tasks, following a terrorist attack.

(HC Deb 14 March 2003 Vol. 401 c433W)

15/74

Her Majesty's Government was asked the following written question:

[W]hat assessment he has made of the effectiveness of the EU code of conduct on arms sales, with reference to sales to Iraq; and if he will make a statement.

In reply, the Parliamentary Under-Secretary of State, FCO, wrote:

The sale of military listed items and dual use items to Iraq is restricted by sanctions. Those which are not automatically prohibited require approval from the UN Iraq Sanctions Committee, of which we are a member. As a member of the Sanctions Committee our evaluation of any application for permission to export such goods, including applications from EU partners, would involve consideration against the criteria of the Code. We consider the Code to be an effective tool to apply when making such decisions.

(HC Deb 17 March 2003 Vol. 401 c548W)

15/75

In reply to a written question regarding the use of equipment manufactured in the UK being used by Israel in its offensive attacks the Under-Secretary of State, FCO, wrote:

We have not carried out specific investigations following these incidents but we routinely tour the Occupied Territories, often in difficult and dangerous conditions, to assess the situation on the ground and the activities of the Israel Defence Forces, including the equipment they use.

However, when considering licence applications for the export of controlled goods we make risk assessments at the licensing stage, including assessments about the proposed end-users and potential end-use of the proposed export. We would not issue a licence unless we were fully satisfied that the equipment would not be misused. Many UK exports have been components for pieces of technology embedded in other systems and are therefore not very visible. The UK has not sold main equipment such as tanks, aircraft, warships or artillery to Israel since May 1997.

Since the outbreak of the violence in the Occupied Territories in September 2000, we have taken account of Israeli military tactics in our licensing decisions. The Consolidated EU and National Arms Export Licensing Criteria clearly sets out our commitment to take account of the risk that exports might be used for either internal repression, prolonging an armed conflict or affecting regional stability.

(HC Deb 30 October 2003 Vol. 412 c362W)

15/76

In reply to a written question, the Under-Secretary of State, FCO, wrote:

EU Common Position 94/165/CFSP, adopted on 16 March 1994, imposed an arms embargo on Sudan in response to the ongoing civil war. We fully support the EU arms embargo and expect it to remain as long as civil war continues.

(HC Deb 11 February 2003 Vol. 399 c725W)

15/77

Her Majesty's Government was asked the following written question:

Why the deployment of Alenia Marconi radar-tracking equipment to Sudan was allowed in view of the embargo on the sale of dual-use equipment to Sudan until peace has been brokered.

The Minister of State, FCO, replied:

The air traffic control system had no military or dual-use rating and did not require an export licence. In any event, the contract has not yet gone ahead.

(HL Deb 8 July 2003 Vol. 651 cWA31)

15/78

In reply to a written question, the Parliamentary Under-Secretary of State, FCO, wrote:

To the best of our knowledge, five Zimbabweans on the EU travel ban list have travelled to the EU since the targeted sanctions were imposed on 18 February 2002. Robert Mugabe, Stan Mudenge and Joseph Made visited Rome to attend World Food Summit meetings between 10 and 13 June. Augustine Chihuri, Police Commissioner, travelled to France on three occasions to attend meetings of the Interpol Executive Committee on 14–16 May, 18–20 June and 27 August. Samuel Mumbengegwi, Trade and Industry Minister, visited Belgium from 22–29 September to attend trade talks between the EU and the Africa, Caribbean and Pacific group of countries. In all cases, the EU country concerned consulted EU partners before issuing visas.

The EU's Common Position 2002/145/CFSP imposing sanctions on Zimbabwe specifically allows member states to grant exemptions where travel is justified on grounds of attending meetings of international bodies. In all these cases, the EU country in question had a legal obligation to grant visas. In doing so, they attached maximum restrictions, ensuring that the visas were for a limited time and restricted to the host country of the meeting concerned.

(HL Deb 23 October 2002 Vol. 639 cWA101)

15/79

In reply to a written question, the Parliamentary Under-Secretary of State, FCO, wrote:

We monitor closely the situation in Zimbabwe and regularly receive detailed information on human rights violations there from a number of sources, including human rights organisations and other NGOs. The UK Government, along with other members of the international community, has consistently condemned the Government of Zimbabwe for its appalling record on human rights and have called on it to respect its obligations under international human rights conventions. Along with our EU partners, the UK Government will continue to focus international attention on human rights abuses in Zimbabwe.

The Commonwealth suspended Zimbabwe from its Councils in March 2002. The Commonwealth Troika is pressing for good governance and the rule of law to be restored in Zimbabwe. It last met in Abuja on 23 September 2002. It deferred a decision on further Commonwealth measures, but stated that it would stick to its task over the next six months "at which point further measures might need to be considered". It is due to meet again in March.

(HC Deb 27 January 2003 Vol. 398 c569W)

15/80

In reply to a written question, the Parliamentary Under-Secretary of State, FCO, wrote:

The UK Government have taken a number of measures in response to the situation in Zimbabwe including: an outright rejection of the conduct and outcome of the Presidential election in March 2002; a complete embargo on arms sales since May 2000; a suspension of non-humanitarian aid and the withdrawal of our military training team. Working with our EU partners, we have also imposed targeted sanctions, a travel ban and assets freeze, on 79 members of the Mugabe regime.

(HC Deb 27 January 2003 Vol. 398 c569W)

15/81

In reply to a written question, the Under-Secretary of State, FCO, wrote:

The EU has put in place targeted sanctions including an arms embargo, a travel ban and assets freeze, specifically targeted at 79 members of the Mugabe regime. We have also made clear our views that the British cricket team should not play in Zimbabwe at present. However, we do not believe that a general sporting boycott, power sanctions, or wider economic sanctions would be right. Such measures would only serve to harm the Zimbabwean people, who are already suffering enough under Mugabe's leadership. The latest yearly figure for imports from Zimbabwe to the UK is for 2001, when imports amounted to £91 million.

(HC Deb 28 January 2003 Vol. 398 c767W)

15/82

In reply to a question on sanctions against Zimbabwe, the Minister of State, FCO, replied:

My Lords, our position on renewing sanctions on the Mugabe regime, including the EU travel ban, remains unchanged. Our objective is to see the current EU common position on sanctions—including the travel ban on 79 members of Zanu PF—rolled-over when it expires in February. This will require a unanimous decision by all 15 EU member states. The matter was discussed at a meeting of

EU Foreign Ministers in Brussels on 27th January, but this proved inconclusive. Further discussions are due to take place tomorrow, 30th January.

. . .

[O]ur instructions to our permanent representative, Sir Nigel Sheinwald, who will be at tomorrow's meeting, will be to press for the most robust package of sanctions and the longest period of roll-over it is possible to negotiate. However, I stress that we must proceed on the basis of a unanimous agreement. The noble Lord will be aware that this matter will be pursued under the common foreign and security policy. That means that all countries will have a veto—and that can sometimes cut two ways.

. . .

There is no problem with the roll-over of most of the sanctions—the arms embargo, the assets freeze and a number of other matters—but there is an issue in regard to the travel ban. As they do every other year, the French wish to hold a summit meeting and to invite the heads of state of all the African countries to meet them in Paris. That meeting is due to take place in a period shortly after the sanctions end. The idea the French are pursuing is that there should be a window of opportunity to allow them to do that. There would therefore be a gap in the travel ban of some three to four days. Her Majesty's Government are disappointed that the French take that view.

(HL Deb 29 January 2003 Vol. 643 c1127–1129)

15/83

During a debate in the House of Commons, the Parliamentary Under-Secretary of State, FCO, said:

In the real world, Zimbabwe is a sovereign country, and the sad reality is that if a regime is determined to destroy its own country and its own people, there is a limit to what the international community can do. However, the international community is making clear to the Zimbabwean Government the effects of their policies, and we have made it very clear that the Zimbabwean Government are behaving in a way that is totally abhorrent to us. Through the Commonwealth, through the European Union and through our contacts with other countries, we have made plain our detestation of that Government, and we are continuing to apply as much pressure as we can to ensure that that message goes out throughout the whole of the international community.

(HC Deb 25 February 2003 Vol. 400 c107)

15/84

During a debate in the House of Lords, the Parliamentary Under-Secretary of State, FCO, said:

So what action have we taken? I have listened carefully to noble Lords in this and the many other debates on the issue in this House. The issues that they raised and the action that they suggested we take related to work already in hand. We clearly share the same analysis. I share the frustration that I feel around the House by noble Lords that our policies are not delivering a difference more quickly. The noble Lord, . . . , spoke of the process taking a long time to yield results. That is true. Zimbabwe is a sovereign nation. There is a limit to what we can do with a regime that is determined to ruin its own country and its own people.

We have worked with our colleagues in the European Union, the Commonwealth, the US and elsewhere to focus the attention of the world community on what is happening in Zimbabwe. That has resulted in a rollover of EU sanctions—the travel ban, the assets freeze and the arms embargo. The noble Baroness, Lady Park, asked me how much had so far been frozen. The amount now stands at just over £500,000, which is what I think I reported to the House towards the end of last year. Any future waiver of the EU travel ban will need to be agreed by a qualified majority of EU member states. That is a strengthening, not a weakening as stated by the noble Lord, Lord Astor of Hever. I agree with noble Lords that France's invitation to Zimbabwe to attend the France/Africa Summit in Paris was deeply disappointing. It is not clear to me from the readouts that I have had from the meeting that a clear message was given to Mugabe about the ruinous policies followed by ZANU-PF.

The noble Lords . . . raised the question of the Commonwealth and the work that we are doing through it. I remind noble Lords that my right honourable friend the Prime Minister was at the forefront of calls for Zimbabwe's suspension from the Commonwealth at the Commonwealth Heads of Government Meeting last year. I remind noble Lords that it was not an easy thing to achieve. The action that we have taken and the work that we have undertaken over many months to secure international agreement to what we wanted to do with respect to Zimbabwe have delivered some results. We will continue to work closely with our Commonwealth partners on Zimbabwe. The Commonwealth Secretary-General is reviewing developments since Zimbabwe's suspension from the Commonwealth's councils on 18th March last year. His report is due to be issued shortly.

. . .

I turn now to human rights. The European Union issued a declaration on Zimbabwe on 19th February. It expressed the EU's concern at the increasing incidence of arrest, inhuman treatment and torture of members of the opposition and of civil society. It called on the Government of Zimbabwe to respect human rights and to end their harassment and violence. Despite the international support for our resolution to the Commission on Human Rights last year, the commission was unable to vote on it due to a blocking campaign by some African states. We think that the deteriorating human rights situation deserves the continued attention of the Commission on Human Rights.

. . .

Perhaps I may now speak briefly about the G8 and NePAD. I believe that there is a fundamental misunderstanding in this House of the nature of the Government's policy with respect to the G8 Africa action plan. The Government have not accepted that the situation in Zimbabwe is an African issue to be settled by Africans . . . We have made absolutely clear that this is an issue for the whole international community . . . That is why the European Union, the Commonwealth, the United States and others are engaged and that is why we are talking to leaders in Africa—not just through the NePAD process, but also through our bilateral contacts and through regional institutions, such as SADC.

. . .

In conclusion, as the noble Lord, Lord Thomson, says, the situation in Zimbabwe is deeply depressing. We will continue to work for a Zimbabwe which is stable, prosperous and democratic.

(HL Deb 5 March 2003 Vol. 645 c906–910)

15/85

In reply to an oral question on travel sanctions imposed on individuals within the Mugabe regime, the Minister of State, FCO, said:

My Lords, Her Majesty's Government believe that our commitment to upholding the travel ban was demonstrated very fully by our decision not to ask for waivers for banned Zimbabweans to attend the Inter-Parliamentary Union conference which was scheduled to take place in London next year. The fact is that the IPU has now decided to move the conference from London in order to get round the travel ban in very much the way suggested by my noble friend. Her Majesty's Government regret that decision by the IPU, but we stand by our commitment, under international law, to uphold the travel ban. It is of course a matter for the IPU now to decide where it wants to hold the meeting—if, indeed, it wishes to do so—and whom it wishes to invite to such a meeting.

. . .

My Lords, we have had our—how shall I put it?—differences of opinion with some of our friends in France over the travel ban. Your Lordships may recall an interesting interlude in the operation of the travel ban earlier this year in relation to a meeting held in Paris. However, under the EU common position, there is the possibility of a country issuing a visa for Zimbabweans to travel when such travel would accommodate a meeting under a treaty obligation. I refer, of course, to the meeting in Rome from 9th to 18th October at which the EU ACP arrangements were discussed. That was an obligation under a treaty, so the travel ban did not apply.

(HL Deb 29 October 2003 Vol. 654 c260–262)

15/86

In reply to several written questions on Zimbabwe the Under-Secretary of State, FCO, wrote:

We keep our policy on sanctions against Zimbabwe under regular review. We favour multilateral sanctions wherever possible because these have a greater practical impact and send a stronger political signal.

The EU sanctions on Zimbabwe were imposed in response to serious violations of human rights and the rule of law. The present sanctions expire in February 2004. We and our EU partners will decide then, in the light of the situation in Zimbabwe, whether to maintain or amend the present arrangements.

...

When EU sanctions against Zimbabwe come up for renewal in February 2004 we and our EU partners will assess whether the Zimbabwe Government continues to engage in serious violations of human rights and of the rule of law. If the EU judges that the situation in Zimbabwe has deteriorated further it may consider extending the sanctions. It would choose to extend them in such a way as to have maximum impact on the decision makers in the Zimbabwe Government. Extending them to relatives of those on the sanctions list (within the limits of other relevant international obligations, for instance the Convention on the Rights of the Child) remains a possibility.

(HC Deb 3 November 2003 Vol. 412 c401W)

15/87

The FCO sent a memorandum to the FAC. The FAC had asked:

"What...progress has been made in cutting off sources of finance for terrorist organisations?"

The memorandum said:

70. The UK continues to raise the issue of terrorist financing in bilateral contacts with other governments and we continue to develop international co-operation at the operational level (see examples below). We continue to play a full role in the Financial Action Task Force (FATF) which is leading multilateral efforts to create best practice standards in this field. The FATF has recently agreed best practice documents on wire transfers and charity regulation and is now working on a best practice document on alternative remittance systems.

71. The international community has frozen over $120 million since 11 September 2001. The UK still has frozen £345,000 following the release of previously frozen funds to the Interim Afghan Authority. The UN has listed over 360 individuals and entities to its list of groups and individuals affiliated to Al Qa'ida, the Taliban or Usama Bin Laden.

72. In addition the UK has, under its international obligations under UNSCR 1373, taken freezing action against over 30 groups and individuals (including from the West Bank and Gaza, Colombia, and South Asia).

73. Alongside these ongoing international efforts to encourage others to raise their standards, the Chancellor of the Exchequer has issued freezing orders against the Al Aqsa Foundation, adding them to the list of groups whose assets we freeze because of their support for or involvement in terrorism. And earlier this year, two individuals were found guilty of financing terrorism.

The Committee had asked further:

"Is the Government satisfied with the current level and quality of co-operation with the police and intelligence agencies of other EU member states?"

The reply was:

74. Yes. Since the attacks of 11 September 2001, our co-operation with the relevant counter-terrorism authorities in other EU States, which was already good, has intensified and continues at a high level. It is inevitable that the quality and quantity of co-operation varies between partners, not because of lack of will but through differences in capabilities and coverage. This co-operation continues both within the framework of the EU and bilaterally.

75. The police also have in place the long established and successful Counter-Terrorism and Extremism Liaison Officer Scheme. This currently involves UK police officers with counter-terrorism expertise being based in national police headquarters in France, Belgium (covering Benelux), Germany, Austria (also covering Central Europe and Switzerland) and Italy. The main purpose of these posts is to enhance and support police co-operation in preventing, investigating and prosecuting terrorist and extremist activity. The UK also fully supports Europol's counter-terrorism remit.

(FAC Tenth Report, Foreign Policy Aspects of the War against Terrorism, Written Evidence, 22 May 2003, HC 405)

Part Sixteen: I. *Use of force—prohibition of the use of force*

16/1

In reply to a written question, the Secretary of State for International Development wrote:

We are deeply concerned about the Ugandan occupation of Bunia on 6 March and have told the Government of Uganda in the clearest terms that it should withdraw its army from Ituri immediately. We have also urged restraint on Rwanda in strong terms.

(HC Deb 8 April 2003 Vol. 403 c174W)

16/2

In reply to an oral question on Iraq, the Secretary of State for Defence said:

As the advice from the Attorney-General has set out for all right hon. and hon. Members to see, this is a perfectly lawful campaign. It will proceed resolutely to its conclusion—which is the removal of weapons of mass destruction from Iraq and the overthrow of the regime that has harboured them.

(HC Deb 26 March 2003 Vol. 402 c297)

16/3

In a written answer, the Prime Minister wrote:

The UK has never sought to use military means to enforce disarmament without first having exhausted all other avenues open to us.

(HC Deb 31 March 2003 Vol. 402 c526W)

16/4

In reply to a written question on the bombing of Syria by Israel, the Under-Secretary of State, FCO, wrote:

We deplore Israel's attack on Ayn Sahib on 5 October. As our Ambassador to the United Nations told the Security Council, this was unacceptable and represented an escalation of the situation in the region. While we understand Israel's need to protect her citizens from terrorism, we urge all sides to exercise restraint and refrain from actions that escalate tension.

(HC Deb 22 October 2003 Vol. 411 c618W)

Part Sixteen: II. A. *Use of force—legitimate use of force—self-defence*

16/5

The Defence Committee reported on the doctrine of pre-emption:

There are two dimensions to this. The first is a largely political and legal one. The Secretary of State emphasised "the importance of international law, and indeed our law, because that governs our own armed forces in the way in which they conduct their activities". We are by no means confident that Article 51 of the UN charter would provide the necessary cover for pre-emptive action. Article 51 applies, 'if an armed attack occurs against a Member of the United Nations'. The United Nations may of course provide the authority for action in a specific Resolution. There may be occasions when assembling the necessary international political support to secure such a resolution before any action is taken is possible. But we suspect that if action is being taken against what the Secretary of State called 'a sufficiently proximate threat', there may not be time. The concept of self-defence in international law, of course, runs wider than either Article 51, or the UN's specific endorsement. Nonetheless, if the new chapter of the SDR [Strategic Defence Review] is to propose a capability for pre-emptive military action it must also ensure that such action does not lead our forces to operate outside international law.

(Para. 130, Defence Committee, Second Report, 2001–2002, 18 December 2001, HC 348–I)

16/6

Her Majesty's Government was asked the following written question:

What discussion they have had on reported NATO proposals for pre-emptive military strikes against suspected terrorists without prior approval or consent from the state in question; and how such strikes can be reconciled with existing international law and the desirable global rule of law.

In reply, the Minister of State, FCO, wrote:

At the Prague Summit, NATO leaders approved a package of measures to strengthen the alliance's ability to meet the security challenges of the 21st century. They reiterated their determination to protect our populations, territory and forces from any armed attack, including terrorist attack, directed from abroad, in accordance with the Washington Treaty and the Charter of the United Nations. The Government support the right to take necessary and proportionate military action in self-defence, not only where an attack has occurred but also pre-emptively where an attack is imminent, such as in Afghanistan. The Government support the view that this right under international law applies as much to threats from terrorism and weapons of mass destruction as to the more conventional threats of the past.

(HL Deb 27 November 2002 Vol. 415 cWA46–WA47)

16/7

Her Majesty's Government was asked the following written question:

What is their view of the United States doctrine against potential aggressors as set out in The National Security Strategy of the United States of America document, published in September 2002; and whether they support it.

In reply, the Minister of State, FCO, wrote:

The Government support the right to take necessary and proportionate military action in self-defence, not only where an attack has occurred but also pre-emptively where an attack is imminent. Her Majesty's Government support the view that this right under international law applies as much to imminent threats from terrorism and weapons of mass destruction as to the more conventional threats of the past. Pre-emptive action is not just a matter of use of force. It is already at the heart of international strategy against terrorism, including police/intelligence work, cutting of financial flows, diplomatic action to address potential conflict situations, and a range of other tools. Military action is a last resort.

(HL Deb 4 November 2002 Vol. 640 cWA52–WA53)

16/8

In reply to a written question the Prime Minister wrote:

As has repeatedly been made clear, the British Government would only contemplate the use or threat of use of nuclear weapons in extreme circumstances of self-defence. We would not use our weapons, whether conventional or nuclear, contrary to international law.

(HC Deb 9 December 2003 Vol. 415 c375W)

16/9

In response to a written question, the Parliamentary Under-Secretary of State, MoD, wrote:

As set out in the discussion paper published on 9 December, the Government believe that the developing ballistic missile threat is one that we must take very seriously. We assess that at present there is no immediate significant threat to the territory of the UK from ballistic missiles. However, intentions can change quickly, and the proliferation and development of weapons of mass destruction and ballistic missiles are continuing. We could not wait until a specific threat became clear before determining how to defend against it.

(HL Deb 17 December 2002 Vol. 642 cWA101)

16/10

During a debate in the House of Commons, the Secretary of State for Defence made the following statements:

I do not accept my hon. Friend's assertion in conclusion. I assure her that no decision has been taken here, in the United States or anywhere else to use military force against Iraq, but as I indicated, it has been our experience that the credible threat of the use of military force is necessary to coerce Saddam Hussein into accepting the will of the international community.

Since the United Kingdom and other nations have accepted the need for a United Nations process, that process continues. The issue that my hon. Friend raises in relation to the United Nations charter does not arise at this stage, although I remind her that the UN charter does allow for self-defence, and pre-emptive action is no more than modern jargon to deal with the ancient right of self-defence. There are other circumstances recognised in international law—for example, the humanitarian action that was taken in Kosovo—that are justified in international law . . . I emphasise . . . that the Government are determined that there should be a process that rests on international law and carries with it the great support of the British people.

(HC Deb 20 January 2003 Vol. 398 c38–40)

16/11

In a written answer, the Secretary of State for Defence wrote:

The Government do not comment on hypothetical scenarios involving the use or threat of use of nuclear weapons.

The Government have made clear on many occasions that the use of United Kingdom nuclear weapons would only be contemplated in extreme circumstances of self-defence. We made clear in the Strategic Defence Review New Chapter that aggression against us will not secure political or military advantage, but invite a proportionately serious response. Those, at every level, responsible for any breach of international law relating to the use of weapons of mass destruction will be held personally accountable.

(HC Deb 10 February 2003 Vol. 399 c510W)

16/12

During a debate in the House of Commons, the Parliamentary Under-Secretary of State, FCO, made the following statements:

On the comments of my right hon. Friend . . . about the legal complexities of the doctrine of pre-emptive self-defence, those issues are indeed important, but they are none the less enormously complex. As a lawyer, I know that if one puts two lawyers in a room, one gets an argument. Indeed, the reason why we have so many court cases is that lawyers often cannot agree on the law. In the present context, going back to the main case of 1837—the Caroline case—it is clear that issues of legality have arisen that will need to be explored for many years to come in order to arrive at a clear and final view. No doubt, many lawyers will venture their deeply considered views in the meantime, but I suspect that final definitions will take a long time to be accepted.

In the next decade, our country faces two key threats—terrorism and the development by dangerous states of weapons of mass destruction. Problems do not come one at a time and they have to be dealt with when they come. On this occasion, two problems have presented themselves and they need to be dealt with. Obviously, we are also concerned that, at some stage, those two issues—terrorism and weapons of mass destruction—may well become linked, and we need to be prepared to deal with that as well.

. . .

In the current decade, the threat from terrorism and the proliferation of weapons of mass destruction are our two top priorities. We have helped to shape and maintain the international consensus on terrorism that is essential to change the odds in our favour so that the British public can go about their lives freely and with confidence.

Counter-terrorism operations are being maintained throughout the globe at an unprecedented level with unprecedented co-operation between countries. We shall continue to work with our traditional close partners—the EU, the United States, the G8 countries, NATO and the Commonwealth. However, we have also built on new relationships that we forged in counter-terrorism to ensure that the United Nations Counter-Terrorism Committee continues to deliver. We have developed new relationships with countries such as Syria and Libya. They, too, perceive al-Qaeda as a threat.

(HC Deb 11 March 2003 Vol. 401 c181–184)

Part Sixteen: II. B.1. *Use of force—Legitimate Use of Force—Collective Measures—United Nations*

16/13

In response to a written question, the Under-Secretary of State, FCO, wrote:

The Iraqi regime's weapons of mass destruction, and their proven willingness to use them, threatens the entire international community. We have never suggested that an Iraqi attack is imminent. But we cannot wait while Iraq seeks ever more powerful weaponry. The United Nations Security Council, through its unanimous adoption of Resolution 1441, has served notice on the Iraqi regime that it must now give up those weapons or face serious consequences.

(HL Deb 25 November 2002 Vol. 641 cWA17)

16/14

In reply to an oral question on Iraq the Attorney-General stated:

As the EU extraordinary meeting on Monday concluded, war is a last resort. But inspections cannot continue indefinitely. Iraq has a final opportunity to resolve the crisis peacefully and in the words of those conclusions:

> "The Iraqi regime alone will be responsible for the consequences if it continues to flout the will of the international community and does not take this last chance",

which, by unanimous resolution of the Security Council, it was given in November last year.

(HL Deb 19 January 2003 Vol. 644 c1140)

16/15

During a meeting of the Security Council the representative of the UK said:

Well before Security Council resolution 1441 (2002) was adopted, on 8 November last year, Saddam Hussein was already in breach, not of one or two, but of 23 mandatory obligations in nine separate Security Council resolutions stretching back over 12 years. The moment of choice for Saddam Hussein is close. He must either resolve this crisis peacefully, by active compliance with his Security Council obligations and full cooperation with inspectors, or face the serious consequences—the use of force—which the Council warned would follow when it adopted resolution 1441 (2002).

(UN Doc. S/PV.4688, 20 January 2003)

16/16

In reply to a written question, the Parliamentary Under-Secretary of State, FCO, wrote:

No decision has been taken to launch military action against Iraq and military action is not inevitable. We regularly discuss all aspects of Iraq policy with our US colleagues.

(HC Deb 20 January 2003 Vol. 398 c81W)

16/17

During a debate in the House of Commons, the Parliamentary Under-Secretary of State, FCO, made the following statements:

The whole purpose of resolution 1441 is to make sure that Saddam Hussein is not let off the hook. For all too long, he has been developing weapons of mass destruction and, indeed, abusing the rights of his people. We need to find a way of making sure that he does not develop weapons of mass destruction and does not abuse the human rights of his people. We want to pursue the matter through the United Nations and resolution 1441. That is the process that we are undertaking. We also hope that the circumstances will arise in which we will be able to deal with Saddam for the crimes that he has so obviously committed.

...

Given a choice between peace and war, I agree that we would prefer peace and Saddam to be exiled if he would agree to that. I fear that that might not be the option facing us. We will have to see. Some difficult choices are facing the international community and we will have to consider the suggestion made by Donald Rumsfeld and others that Saddam Hussein should be able to leave Iraq. I fear that given the nature of his character, it is probably unlikely that he will agree to do so. However, if the option is there, it should certainly at least be explored.

...

There is no specified time frame for the completion of the UN weapons inspectors' task laid down by UN Security Council resolution 1441. Crucially, the length of the task is dependent on the level of co-operation that Iraq provides to the inspectors. The inspectors will be making their first report on Monday.

...

We need to take the issue of the time that the inspectors have step by step. Let us see what Dr. Blix and Dr. el-Baradei say on Monday. The obligations on Iraq under resolution 1441 are very clear. This is not just about Iraq sitting back and waiting to see whether the inspectors find something. The Iraqis must stop concealing weapons of mass destruction and start complying with UN resolution 1441.

If my hon. Friend wants a path to peace, the real path to peace is compliance with resolution 1441.

...

The Iraqi opposition groups want the removal of Saddam Hussein. If there were a choice between a peaceful and democratic regime in Iraq under Saddam Hussein and a war, the issue might be different, but the fact is that Saddam Hussein has carried out the wholesale slaughter of large numbers of his people. I urge my hon. Friend to remember the 5,000 men, women and children who died at Halabja in 1988 and the 9,000 who were injured there. We need to make sure that Saddam Hussein is recognised as the tyrant that he is, and is dealt with accordingly.

...

The UN resolution [SC Res. 1441] was passed unanimously in the Security Council. Many people in this House asked for a UN resolution. Many said that it could never be done, but it was passed unanimously. Even Syria signed up to it. There are those who say that we should never have threatened force. If we had not done so, the inspectors would not be in Iraq now, UN resolutions would have been worth nothing, international law would have meant nothing and a message would have gone out to large numbers of other countries that are contemplating whether to develop weapons of mass destruction—especially nuclear weapons—saying that the UN would do nothing, that Britain would do nothing and that certain Members of this House would wish to do nothing. This is not a situation in which we can act in such an irresponsible way. This Government will act, and we will do so responsibly.

...

We want to see Iraq as one country, as is set out in resolution 1441. On the question whether that is sustainable, yes, we believe that it is. Our discussions with the opposition groups suggest that they accept that that is an international requirement set down by the UN and the view of all the countries on the Security Council. Indeed, in this case at least, all the countries around Iraq take a similar view. No one wants to see the break-up of Iraq. On weapons of mass destruction, the opposition groups understand very clearly from us—indeed, they must understand this from the UN—that there is an obligation on Iraq to remove all development of weapons of mass destruction.

On a successor Government, we want to see a Government who are not a threat to their neighbours, are not developing weapons of mass destruction and are not repressing their people, but are representative of them.

(HC Deb 21 January 2003 Vol. 398 c152–158)

16/18

During a debate in the House of Commons, the Secretary of State, FCO, was asked the following question:

Does my right hon. Friend agree that it is for the United Nations Security Council to uphold its mandatory resolutions in accordance with article 2(4), and that if the UN fails to do so it would badly let down the international community?

In reply the Secretary of State, FCO, said:

I entirely agree with my hon. Friend. We have responsibilities, but so, too, does the whole international community, within the Security Council, have a responsibility to ensure compliance with 1441 or, if not, to take effective action.

(HC Deb 21 January 2003 Vol. 398 c174)

16/19

During a debate in the House of Commons, the Secretary of State, FCO, said:

I hope as surely as my hon. Friend does that it is possible to resolve the Iraq crisis peacefully. None of us wishes military action to be taken against Iraq unless that becomes absolutely justified and the only possible course to enforce international will, but I ask him to consider that we have to face the fact that Iraq has been in the most flagrant violation not of our rule or that of the United States, but of the rule of the UN. If the international community is to mean anything at all, it has to mean that its will can be enforced. For that reason, 15 member states of the Security Council quite voluntarily signed up to the terms of resolution 1441, including the mandatory resolution and the last paragraph, which says that there had to be serious consequences if Iraq failed to comply, and we are now following through that UN resolution.

(HC Deb 21 January 2003 Vol. 398 c176)

16/20

The Parliamentary Under-Secretary of State, FCO, was asked in a written question if he would make a statement on the action of the UK Government should the UN decide not to take military action against Iraq. In reply, the Parliamentary Under-Secretary of State, FCO, wrote:

In the event that there is a material breach, the preference of the British Government is for a second resolution. So far, the UN Security Council has, as Kofi Annan has said, "faced up to its responsibilities". We believe it will continue to do so. But we must reserve our position in the event that it does not.

(HC Deb 21 January 2003 Vol. 398 c223W)

16/21

The Parliamentary Under-Secretary of State, FCO, was asked in a written question why the report from Iraq on weapons of mass destruction was not presented in its entirety to the UN. In reply, the Parliamentary Under-Secretary of State, FCO, wrote:

Under relevant non-proliferation conventions, China, France, the Russian Federation, the United Kingdom and the United States of America are obliged to prevent the dissemination of information relating to the production of biological, chemical, and nuclear weapons.

The President of the UN Security Council therefore decided that the full Iraqi declaration should only be given to these members of the Security Council, who also have the expertise to assess the risks of proliferation. His decision followed consultations with all members of the Security Council.

The other members received the main body of the declaration excluding a number of sensitive passages and words that were omitted by UNMOVIC and the IAEA who, after consulting the Security Council members with expertise to assess the risks of proliferation, judged them to contain information that might be of use to potential WMD proliferators.

(HC Deb 21 January 2003 Vol. 398 c223W–224W)

16/22

During a debate concerning the use of force against Iraq in the House of Commons, the Secretary of State for Defence made the following statements:

I am not sure that I agree that there are such different views. The only country that has specifically ruled out the use of military force is Germany. There was an agreement at the Copenhagen summit to support United Nations resolution 1441, and I anticipate that at its meeting today the General Affairs and External Relations Council will again issue a unanimous declaration supporting resolution 1441, making it clear to the Iraqi Government that they have a final opportunity to resolve the crisis peacefully. I do not detect the disunity that may be implied by the hon. Gentleman's question.

...

[I] agree to the extent that it is important that there should be unity of purpose, as demonstrated by the unanimous vote of the UN Security Council on resolution 1441 and the Copenhagen European Council. I am sure that it will also be demonstrated by the General Affairs and External Relations Council today. All those bodies have given consistent support to the agreed international position adopted by all countries.

...

We are aware that there are well-established links between the Iraqi regime and terrorist organisations. The links with al-Qaeda are much less strong, as I have made clear to the House over a period of time, and certainly the case for a connection with the events of 11 September 2001 is not at all persuasive. Nevertheless, it clearly can be argued that Saddam Hussein has consistently supported terrorist groups. Part of the concern, as set out by my right hon. Friend the Prime Minister the other day, is that at some stage his weapons of mass destruction may fall into the hands of terrorist groups willing to use them.

...

My hon. Friend proceeds on a wholly false basis. The use of force against Iraq would be in support of an agreed United Nations position once there had been a discussion in the UN Security Council on the proper course of action. I want to make it clear to my hon. Friend that efforts to bring Iraq into line are efforts of the international community—something with which I would have expected him strongly to agree.

(HC Deb 27 January 2003 Vol. 398 c548–552)

16/23

In a debate in the House of Lords the Lord Privy Seal stated:

The real case for the use of armed force against Iraq depends entirely on international law and significantly, but not entirely, on Resolution 1441 and, if there is to be a second resolution, on that. The Prime Minister and the Foreign Secretary have endlessly repeated—I too have repeated to your Lordships on many occasions—that the United Kingdom's policy is to act consistent with the rules of international law.

Therefore, essentially Iraq is liable to armed force sanctions if that is the ultimate necessity because of its disobedience to the mandatory instructions of the United Nations. I am not in a position to speculate exactly what Secretary of State Colin Powell will say on Wednesday. Perhaps we should wait to hear what he has to say. I take the point made by the noble Lord that the two should not be conflated, even when they are coincident in part. Al-Qaeda is not a state; Iraq is. Al-Qaeda operates in various states, but I agree that the state of Afghanistan does not need to be pursued and punished endlessly because al-Qaeda operates there. If al-Qaeda ceases to operate there, different circumstances will arise. The truth is that we are in a period of uncertainty that can be met only by resolution and unity, which I am glad your Lordships have shown.

(HL Deb 3 February 2003 Vol. 644 c32–33)

16/24

During a meeting of the Security Council the representative of the UK said:

Three months ago we united to send Iraq an uncompromising message: cooperate fully with weapons inspectors, or face disarmament by force. After years of Iraqi deception, when resolutions were consistently flouted, resolution 1441 (2002) was a powerful reminder of the importance of international law and of the authority of the Security Council itself.

(UN Doc. S/PV.4701, 5 February 2003)

16/25

During a debate in the House of Commons, the Secretary of State, FCO, made the following statements:

The Security Council will meet in New York tomorrow to hear the latest reports from the executive chairman of UNMOVIC, Dr. Hans Blix, and the director general of the International Atomic Energy Agency, Dr. Mohamed el-Baradei. I will be joining fellow Foreign Ministers for that meeting.

United Nations Security Council resolution 1441, which was agreed three months ago, placed the onus squarely on Iraq to co-operate fully and actively with United Nations inspectors in the disarmament of its weapons of mass destruction. It gave Iraq a final warning: comply with the UN's terms immediately or face "serious consequences". European Union Foreign Ministers expressed clear support for that goal last month when they declared unanimously that

> "the resolution gives an unambiguous message that the Iraqi Government has a final opportunity to resolve the crisis peacefully".

It is also worth recalling that at the summit in Prague, NATO Heads of Government—every one of the 19 present—explicitly endorsed resolution 1441. They said that it was a final opportunity and that serious consequences would follow.

Tomorrow's briefing will be the fourth update delivered by Dr. Blix and Dr. el-Baradei. The comprehensive reports that they delivered on 27 January, just over two weeks ago, painted a disturbing picture. Most damning of all was Dr. Blix's observation that Iraq

> "appears not to have come to a genuine acceptance... of the disarmament which was demanded of it".

Dr. Blix concluded that the Iraqi declaration submitted on 7 December, in accordance with resolution 1441, was "mostly a reprint of earlier documents", and did not "contain any new evidence that would eliminate" unresolved "questions or reduce their number".

The central premise of Iraq's so-called disclosure—that Iraq possesses no weapons of mass destruction—was, and remains, a lie. Nor was there any admission of Iraq's extensive efforts to develop weapons of mass destruction since the final UNSCOM inspections in December 1998 when it was effectively excluded from Iraq, as the inspectors made clear in their final report to the Security Council in February 1999.

In their update on 27 January, Dr. Blix and Dr. el-Baradei said that Iraq had failed to account for 6,500 bombs, which could carry up to 1,000 tonnes of chemical agent. It had also failed to account for 8,500 litres of biological warfare agent and a large amount of growth media, which could be used to produce about 5,000 litres of concentrated anthrax. They said that the 12 chemical rocket warheads unearthed by UNMOVIC inspectors were potentially, in Dr. Blix's words, "the tip of a submerged iceberg".

They said that Iraq had failed to disclose the 3,000 pages of documents discovered not in an office but in the grounds of the private home of an Iraqi scientist, relating to the nuclear weapons programme of that country. They said that despite repeated requests from UNMOVIC and the IAEA, in accordance with resolution 1441, all interviews with key Iraqi personnel were being conducted in the intimidating presence of official "minders". They also said that in contravention of United Nations resolutions, Iraq had developed missiles that had been tested at ranges in excess of the 150 km limit specified in UN resolutions.

I remind the House that the British Government drew attention to Iraqi work on such missiles in the dossier that we published last September. We look forward to hearing in detail what Dr. Blix has to say tomorrow, but if media reports are correct, the al-Samoud missile programme is clearly in serious breach of Iraq's obligations. We would expect rapid action to eliminate any such illegal programme.

In drafting resolution 1441, Security Council members took pains to set two clear tests for further material breach by Iraq. In the first operational paragraph, they declared that Iraq "has been and remains in material breach" of a score or more of obligations that date back to 1991. That is still the case. As for the two tests, a further material breach would have occurred, first, if Iraq made "false statements" or "omissions" in the declaration that it submitted on 7 December, and secondly, if it failed "at any time to comply with, and co-operate fully in the implementation" of resolution 1441. The briefings by Dr. Blix and Dr. el-Baradei, as well as Secretary Powell's presentation to the Security Council last week, leave no doubt that Iraq has failed to meet both tests. The conclusion is therefore inescapable: Iraq is in further material breach of resolution 1441. We shall take full account of the reports of the chief inspectors tomorrow.

The prospect of military action causes obvious anxiety—as it should—here in the United Kingdom, here in the House, among our allies and in the region, and of course among the people of Iraq. I still hope and pray for a peaceful outcome to the crisis, but that will be possible only if we maintain unrelenting pressure on Saddam Hussein, including the threat of force, rather than casting around for excuses to delay. It is only through the pressure we have been exercising that we have got as far as we have in exposing much more of the danger represented by Saddam Hussein's regime, and exposing his lies and deception as well. If the international community lost its nerve now, that would significantly undermine the UN's authority and make the world a much more dangerous place, as dictators got the message that international law consisted of mere words and nothing else.

The Franco-German proposals announced this week to bolster the inspection regime will not deliver the assurance that the world needs about Iraq's weapons. Those proposals, I am sorry to say, are unrealistic and impractical. They shift the burden of proof from Iraq—which is where the Security Council has said it must be—to the inspectors, and they send Saddam the signal that defiance pays. What is the point of sending three times as many inspectors simply for Saddam to deceive them? What purpose is served by that? As Dr. Blix himself said on Monday, "The principal problem is not the number of inspectors but rather the active co-operation of the Iraqi side, as we have said many times." Those are the words of the chief inspector, not my words.

If the inspectors were to say that Iraq was actively co-operating, one might see a possible case for more inspectors; but I ask my hon. Friends, as well as Opposition Members, to consider what it is like to inspect anything without the co-operation of the organisation being inspected.

Iraq was found guilty of possession of weapons of mass destruction 12 years ago. The role of inspectors has always been to verify Iraqi compliance—this being based on the premise of Iraqi compliance—and not to engage in a "game of catch as catch can", to use Dr. Blix's term.

I am glad to learn that other proposals attributed to the French and German Governments, such as the establishment of a no-fly zone over the whole of Iraq and the insertion of armed blue-helmeted UN troops, have now been officially denied. Had those proposals been implemented, they would have required an even higher degree of co-operation from the Iraqi regime than was required by resolution 1441. The creation of a no-fly zone over the whole of Iraq would have required the complete grounding of the Iraqi air force and its regular inspection to that end, and the insertion of blue-helmeted UN troops in a benign environment would have required all armed troops from Iraq to retreat to barracks. That too would have been the subject of inspection by the United Nations.

Let me now turn to the position in NATO. In mid-January, discussions began in the alliance of the need for contingency planning to cope with possible threats to the security of a NATO ally, Turkey, in the event of military action in respect of Iraq. Sixteen NATO allies, including 14 European nations, supported that entirely reasonable and responsible proposal simply to set in hand some military planning for very limited defensive mutual assistance. France, Belgium and Germany have resisted on the ground that a NATO decision on that very limited mutual assistance would somehow pre-empt any Security Council consideration of Iraq's further material breach. Faced with that deadlock, on 10 February Turkey requested consultations under article 4 of the Washington treaty. The discussions continue, with the United Kingdom fully supporting the efforts of NATO Secretary-General Lord Robertson to achieve consensus.

I remind the House again that at the Prague summit, less than three months ago, NATO leaders pledged their full support for resolution 1441.

Given the obvious risks and the possibility that military action may prove necessary, we are keeping under very close review the safety and security of both visiting and resident British nationals in the various countries of the middle east. We make assessments on a case-by-case basis for each country in the region, and will make announcements as necessary.

Even at this late stage, armed intervention is not inevitable. A peaceful resolution of the crisis remains in Saddam Hussein's hands. Full Iraqi compliance with the terms of Security Council resolution 1441 will deliver the outcome that the United Kingdom and the entire international community wish to see: an Iraq that no longer poses a threat to its neighbours or to the region. In the absence of full compliance by Saddam Hussein, however, United Nations inspectors will not be able to fulfil their mandate to verify Iraqi disarmament. Resolution 1441 warns Iraq to expect "serious consequences" in that event. By now, even Saddam Hussein must be under no illusions: that can only mean disarmament by force.

(HC Deb 13 February 2003 Vol. 399 c1056–1059)

16/26

During a debate in the House of Commons, the Secretary of State, FCO, made the following statements:

I have spelled out to my hon. Friend and to the House our great preference for a second resolution, if one proves necessary. However, there has never been the least dubiety that we must reserve our position in the event that a second resolution is not possible. I understand my hon. Friend's anxieties about so-called pre-emption, but the United Nations charter, in article 50 and several other articles in chapter 7, clearly anticipates the use of what is described as "preventative force" to enforce the will of the United Nations.

...

[I]n diplomatic speak the choice was between "all necessary means" and "serious consequences". Everybody in the diplomatic community knows that "serious consequences" means the use of force. If the hon. Gentleman is saying that it would be better if diplomatic speak was more explicit, I agree, but those words mean force.

(HC Deb 13 February 2003 Vol. 399 c1071–1072)

16/27

During a debate in the House of Commons, the Secretary of State, FCO, said:

One of the paragraphs of 1441 and one of the paragraphs of the draft resolution that we submitted for consideration to the Security Council yesterday says explicitly that the territorial integrity of Iraq, including the Kurdish area, has to be preserved, and we will make sure that that happens. As my right hon. Friend will know from his contact with Kurdish representatives, they are the first fully and actively to support the strategy of the Security Council as endorsed by this House.

(HC Deb 25 February 2003 Vol. 400 c111–112)

16/28

During a debate in the House of Commons, the Secretary of State, FCO, made the following statements:

First, why Iraq? The best answer to that question is to be found in the 42 pages of text of the 13 Security Council resolutions that form the first section of the Command Paper. There we see, paragraph by paragraph, the exceptional danger posed by Iraq, and its continued defiance of the United Nations. On 2 August 1990, resolution 660 tells Iraq to withdraw from Kuwait. On 29 November 1990, resolution 678 offers Iraq a "final opportunity"—interesting words—to comply, which it fails to take. On 3 April 1991, resolution 687 gives Iraq until 18 April 1991 to make a full declaration of the "locations, amount and types" of all chemical and biological weapons and of all medium and long-range ballistic missiles. That resolution bars Iraq from ever developing biological, chemical or nuclear weapons.

...

On and on the resolutions go. Resolution 688 is "gravely concerned" about the repression of the civilian population in many parts of Iraq. In 1994, resolution 949

> "condemns military deployments by Iraq in the direction of the border with Kuwait",

three years after the original invasion. In 1999, nine years after the invasion of Kuwait, resolution 1284 establishes a further inspection regime

> "as a result of Iraq's failure to implement the Security Council Resolutions fully".

Iraq flatly and completely refuses to comply. Last November, resolution 1441 recognised

> "the threat which Iraq's non-compliance with Council Resolutions and proliferation of Weapons of Mass Destruction and long range missiles poses to international peace and security"—and gave Iraq its "final opportunity to comply".

So, for the United Nations, the answer to the "Why Iraq?" question is very clear. Iraq is the only country in such serious and multiple breach of mandatory UN obligations. It is the only country in the world to have fired missiles at five of its neighbours, the only country in history to have used chemical weapons against its own people, and the only country in the region that has invaded two of its neighbours in recent years.

...

The next question that I raised was, "Why now?" All the resolutions of the Security Council, 12 years of them, also help us answer that question.

Saddam's aim is that "now" shall never arrive. His tactics all along have been to prevaricate in the hope that by exploiting people's natural anxieties about military action he can string out the process for ever and keep his arsenal for good.

Let us look at the recent evidence. On 10 September last year, Iraq declared ... that it would never, ever readmit weapons inspectors under any circumstances. Then President Bush made his important and most welcome speech to the General Assembly. Four days later, Iraq said that it would after all readmit weapons inspectors, but made its offer subject to 19 spurious conditions of the kind that it has often come forward with. Fortunately, those were rejected.

There were then two months of intense negotiations inside the Security Council. In response, the international community united, resolution 1441 was passed unanimously and the Security Council agreed to back its diplomacy with the credible threat of force. The inspectors finally entered Iraq on 27 November, looking, as the resolution required, for full, active and immediate co-operation from Iraq.

But since the inspectors' return the story has been all too familiar. We saw first a 12,000-page Iraqi declaration, which Dr. Blix called

> "rich in volume but poor in new information ... and practically devoid of new evidence".

There have been concerted Iraqi efforts to prevent unrestricted interviews with scientists. The issue of interviews with the scientists is not a trivial matter. It is the most important way in which we can arrive at the truth of Iraq's chemical and biological weapons programmes.

Iraq refused any interviews to begin with. Since the weapons inspectors pressed the Iraqis, there have been three private interviews, all within the closing days up to Dr. Blix's report on 14 February, and, despite what we see in some newspapers about increased co-operation by the Iraqis, not one interview has been granted since.

Time after time after time the Iraqis seek to impose conditions that make free and fair interviews almost impossible.

. . .

There have been categorical Iraqi denials that the al-Samoud missile has a range in excess of the 150km limit prescribed by the United Nations, an assertion since disproved by an independent panel of experts from the five permanent members of the Security Council and by UNMOVIC.

Crucially, there have been no answers to the outstanding disarmament issues listed in UNSCOM's final report to the Security Council in February 1999.

As a result, as Dr. Blix himself indicates, in 15 weeks, the inspectors have not been able to close a single outstanding issue. There have been no answers to what has happened to the 8,500 litres of anthrax; no answers to what has happened to the 360 tonnes of bulk chemical warfare agent; no answers to what has happened to the 3,000 tonnes of precursor chemicals; no answers to what has happened to the 1.5 tonnes of the completely deadly VX nerve agent or to the 6,500 chemical bombs identified by Dr. Blix on 27 January. The intimidation of scientists and their families so that they do not give full evidence has continued.

. . .

What my right hon. Friend the Prime Minister also made clear was that our policy is 100 per cent. support for and full implementation of resolution 1441. What the hon. Gentleman is now trying to do—having got resolution 1441 and having signed up to it, having asked for the United Nations to be brought in, having asked us to take the United Nations route—is to rewrite the terms of the resolution.

. . .

The next question that I raised was about more time and more inspections. I understand why there are calls for more time and more inspections, but Saddam has not shown that he is ready to break with the past. That is exactly what Dr. Blix said today. At present, it is not even clear whether the Iraqis really want to co-operate. In these circumstances, in the absence of active and immediate Iraqi co-operation, more time will not achieve anything of substance. Nor, without that active co-operation, can it be a question of more inspectors.

It took just nine inspectors to verify the disarmament of South Africa's nuclear weapons programme at the end of apartheid. It did not take 12 years. It did not take hundreds of inspectors. It did not take endless Security Council resolutions. It took three years, nine inspectors and no resolutions. Why? Because South Africa was complying with the inspectors.

It is critical that, in respect of Iraq, we all accept one reality above all, which is that what grudging concessions on process there have been from Saddam have been secured only because of the military build-up. What is the difference between the circumstances now and the circumstances when resolution 1284 was agreed at the end of 1999, the resolution that set up the organisation of weapons inspectors, UNMOVIC? There is some difference in terms of the powers of the weapons inspectors. But the only significant, material difference is that, back at the end of 1999, the world said, "Let us try giving them more time. Let us try by a completely peaceful route to secure the disarmament of Iraq. Let us plead with the Iraqis to do the decent thing. Let us impose some sanctions, too, and hope that they will work."

Saddam's answer was to slam the door in the face of the international community. The only reason for the difference between Saddam's refusal to co-operate with one dot or comma in resolution 1284 and his very reluctant co-operation on some process today, his statement that he will co-operate, is the build-up of the credible threat of force, something clearly recognised by the United Nations charter.

...

The next question is why do we need a second resolution now? Resolution 1441 required Iraq's full, active and immediate compliance, as indeed did resolution 687, which was passed 12 years ago. Fifteen weeks after 1441, Saddam's response has been neither full, nor active, nor immediate. He has not complied, and not a single member of the Security Council says otherwise. In place of active voluntary co-operation, we have had a string of cynically timed concessions that are calculated to divide and to delay.

We saw more token concessions last night. According to the newspapers, Iraq has now told Dr. Blix that it has—and I quote—"found" a bomb. Iraq has found a bomb containing biological agents—it simply popped up from some gooseberry bush. Some will be tempted to regard this as evidence that Saddam is being successfully contained, and that the inspectors should be given endless time...

...

The conclusion that we ought to draw from this overnight admission by Iraq is that we are right to say that it does have weapons of mass destruction, that it has lied about them, that it has tried to hide them, and that it is determined to keep them behind a charade of cynical concessions. Unless we bring this game to a halt, it will go on for as long as Saddam wants. I will not be surprised if, by the end of the week, Saddam is offering concessions on the proscribed al-Samoud missiles—having said that he will never destroy a single one—in the hope, once again, of playing for time. However, if the words "final opportunity", in operative paragraph 2 of resolution 1441, have any meaning, it is that this time we must not let Saddam lure the international community into endless indecision. Resolution 1441 called for disarmament "immediately". We have waited 110 days already, which is stretching the meaning of "immediately" to breaking point.

I ask our friends in France and Germany—who share our goal of Iraqi disarmament, and who fully support resolution 1441—why Saddam is more likely to co-operate actively, fully and immediately in the further 120 days that they now propose than he was in the past 110. What does he need 120 days for: to have a look for the weapons that he says he has not got, in case he has overlooked something; to search the homes of scientists for the incriminating papers that he ordered them to hide there; to tell those scientists to attend interviews and tell the truth that, through intimidation, he has instructed them to conceal?

. . .

There are such circumstances, as it happens, and the important point is this. We are committed to implementation of 1441. I do not like the Saddam Hussein regime—I regard it as one of the most revolting and terrible regimes in the world—but the focus of 1441 is not regime change per se, but the disarmament of Saddam's weapons of mass destruction.

In his statement yesterday, my right hon. Friend the Prime Minister spelled out that if there is full, active and immediate compliance by Saddam Hussein with the full terms of 1441 and the other resolutions referred to, Saddam would remain in government, but his power would be greatly reduced because those weapons of mass destruction would have been removed.

. . .

Time is pressing, so let me turn to the next question, which in many ways is at the heart of the amendment. Why not persist with the policy of containment, rather than contemplate military action? After all, some argue that Iraq has not invaded any of its neighbours or used chemical and biological weapons in the past 12 years, and that these weapons have either been destroyed, or do not present a sufficient threat to Iraq's neighbours or to the wider world to justify the use of force to remove them if Saddam refuses to do so peacefully.

I understand the containment argument, even if I do not agree with it. However, let no one be under any illusions: the policy of containment is not the policy of disarmament as set out in resolution 1441 or any of the preceding resolutions. There can be no stable, steady state for Iraq unless it is properly disarmed, and nor can there be stability for the region and the international community. What may appear to be containment to us is rearmament for Saddam.

We do not need to speculate on this, as we have witnessed it. A de facto policy of containment existed between 1998 and 2002 following the effective expulsion of inspectors by Iraq, and Iraq's refusal to comply with resolution 1284.

Far from keeping a lid on Saddam's ambitions, that period allowed him to rebuild his horrific arsenal, his chemical and biological weapons, and the means of delivering them against his enemies at home and abroad. UNMOVIC inspectors chart in their recent reports, which are before the House, how Iraq has refurbished prohibited equipment that had previously been destroyed by UNSCOM, the earlier inspectors. That equipment included rocket motor casting chambers and chemical processors. UNMOVIC has also found that Iraq used the four-year absence of inspectors—the so-called period of containment—to build a missile test stand capable of testing engines with over four times the thrust of the already prohibited al-Samoud 2 missile. All this happened during containment. There is no steady state—the choice is between disarmament or rearmament.

Thankfully, the so-called policy of containment ended on 8 November last year. Containment requires a degree of trust in Saddam that we cannot risk and which runs contrary to all the evidence. It means leaving Saddam as a standing example that defiance pays. We cannot allow Saddam further time and space to strengthen his capabilities and to rearm further. Only disarmament—the aim of all these UN Security Council resolutions—can deal with this issue.

...

Following the adoption of resolution 1441, Saddam has now to be under no illusions that there will be no further resolutions calling for containment, no further attempts to tinker at the margins rather than to remove his weapons. This has to be a moment of choice for Saddam and for the Iraqi regime.

(HC Deb 26 February 2003 Vol. 400 c265–274)

16/29

Her Majesty's Government was asked the following written question:

To ask the Secretary of State for Foreign and Commonwealth Affairs what evidence there is to support his statement, ... that the United Nations Security Council Resolution 1441 authorises the use of force against Iraq.

In reply, the Under-Secretary of State, FCO, wrote:

The statements to which my hon. Friend refers concern the provision in United Nations Security Council resolution 1441(2002) which recalls that the Council has warned Iraq that it will face serious consequences as a result of its continued violation of its obligations. As the Government have made clear, that means consequences up to and including the use of force.

(HC Deb 4 March 2003 Vol. 400 c907W)

16/30

The Foreign Secretary told the Foreign Affairs Committee:

On material breach, the way that 1441 is structured is that the question of material breach is at large; the facts speak for themselves, and it is for the Security Council to confirm whether there has been a material breach, but not for the inspectors. You will never find an inspectors' report, even if there had been the most flagrant violation, saying "They are now in material breach" because that is not for them to say. What they will say is "We tried to do X but we ran up against a brick wall". So they will report the facts on which the inferences and conclusions will be drawn. (Qu.178)

He was asked what was required of the Iraq Government. He said:

[W]e want full, active and complete co-operation and ... we want the inspectors to be able to freely interview, in a non-intimidating environment, all the scientists. (Qus. 182, 183)

Asked if Saddam Hussein was required to try to prove a negative, the Foreign Secretary said:

In other words, are we setting him a test he cannot fulfil? No. Did the international community find him guilty 12 years ago? Yes. That is set out with absolute clarity in earlier United Nations Security Council resolutions. Did they say he remains guilty? When we passed 1441, bear in mind that operational paragraph 1 says that Iraq has been and remains in material breach of its obligations under resolutions including 687 and it goes on to spell out why. So he remains guilty. It is for them, as it were, to purge themselves of their contempt of the international community by saying what they have done, or not done, with all this unaccounted-for, very dangerous weaponry. That is the key. We know very well that they can explain this. Bear in mind... that we are now in the same position that we were in 12 years ago when Saddam was denying that he had a biological weapons capability. It is so important people understand this. They denied and denied and denied they had a biological weapons programme. They ran the same kind of propaganda efforts they are doing at the moment. Four years later the son-in-law defected. He blew the gaffe on the whole thing and it turned out to be a bigger programme than people had anticipated. Then he was lured back to Iraq on the basis of safety and he was taken out and murdered. That tells two stories: one about the nature of their deception then but it is also a rather important reminder that if you are an Iraqi scientist today you know what torture and intimidation they are going for routinely. It concentrates the mind. (Qus.182, 183)

The Foreign Secretary was then asked:

Does that not, therefore, unfortunately lead us to the conclusion that we can never be confident, given the situation of weapons of mass destruction and the difficulty of finding them—and we recognise it is not the role of the inspectors—that weapons of mass destruction have been completely removed from Iraq unless there is a regime change?

He said:

No. I, maybe rather naively, live in hope of redemption. Not only for myself but for others as well. I do not accept that. I think if there were a decision by the Iraqi regime fully, actively and immediately to comply and they started to act as, for example, the South African Government did in respect of their atomic energy, nuclear weapons programme; you had the interviews with scientists and you had a free environment and you found out an awful lot more than the current inspectors have and you, also, would have to have a continuing presence of the inspectors, then we could be as satisfied as we could... let us be clear, do I believe that it is possible for Iraq to disarm itself of its weapons of mass destruction and its capability in a peaceful way? Yes, I do. (Qu.184)

He was asked:

How would you answer those who fear that there is a certain inevitability that the only remaining superpower has so many forces assembled with our own forces on the frontier of Iraq that, if only for saving face, they dare not withdraw without regime change?

He replied:

I do not accept that. The United States, more willingly than any other nation precisely because it is the most powerful, signed up to 1441 in terms. 1441 is about the disarmament of Saddam Hussein's weapons of mass destruction; 1441, by what it does not say rather than what it does say but very plainly, makes clear that if there is that compliance—full, active, and immediate compliance—by Saddam Hussein of all his obligations going back to 1991 then he will remain in government and President Bush accepted that reality in an important speech he made in Cincinnati in November of last year, so that is there and there is no issue of loss of face. I know for certain that nothing would please the American government more than if this could be resolved peacefully. (Qu.192)

The Foreign Secretary was asked:

...at the time of the first Gulf War I was one of those who advocated giving Saddam a 72 hour ultimatum to get out, otherwise press on to Baghdad, and that was an argument squashed at the time by those who thought they knew much better. Would the Foreign Secretary consider giving Saddam an ultimatum before beginning hostilities in earnest?

He replied:

First of all on your preliminary point... that the reason the United States did not continue on to Baghdad was because the United States and the other coalition allies felt they did not have a legal mandate for this; the legal mandate they had was to free Kuwait and then to deal with WMD, not to take over the state of Iraq. They showed very commendable respect for international law which they continue to do. On the idea of some kind of ultimatum to Saddam to leave Iraq, that is a suggestion which has come from some Arab states. I have said, and I think Secretary Rumsfeld also has said for the United States, that we consider that the provision of some exile for Saddam Hussein would be a small price to pay for a peaceful resolution to this, albeit quite bluntly that we all have to hold our noses that we were not going to have this man arraigned before an international criminal court, but that remains our view. (Qu.209)

(FAC Tenth Report, Foreign Policy Aspects of the War against Terrorism, 4 March 2003, HC 405)

16/31

During a debate in the House of Commons, the Secretary of State, FCO, said:

As for ignoring the United Nations, that is a canard—it is totally untrue. My right hon. Friend the Prime Minister has moved heaven and earth to ensure that the whole issue of Iraq is dealt with through the United Nations. It was he more than anyone else who ensured that the process of negotiation through the United Nations began in August and September and led to a satisfactory conclusion; and he, with many Foreign Ministers and Heads of Government, is seeking to ensure that there is a proper conclusion now.

Everybody in the United Nations has responsibilities under the charter—not only the United States and the United Kingdom among the permanent members, but all the other permanent and non-permanent members of the Security Council, all of whom have signed up to the charter, including chapter 7, which spells out that sometimes force is necessary where there is defiance of the clear obligations under chapter 7. In the present case, force may indeed be necessary.

(HC Deb 10 March 2003 Vol. 401 c28)

16/32

During a debate in the House of Commons, the Secretary of State, FCO, said:

There is, of course, a strong humanitarian case against Saddam Hussein. We concentrate on disarmament because of our subscription to international law. The basis for any military action in the region will be implementation of resolution 1441 and its predecessors, but of course my hon. Friend is right to imply that a consequence of that will be freeing the Iraqi people from the terrible burden and humanitarian catastrophe that is the Saddam Hussein regime.

(HC Deb 10 March 2003 Vol. 401 c34)

16/33

A Foreign Office Minister told the House of Lords about the right to use force against Iraq:

The legal basis for any military action that might be taken against Iraq would be the authorisation which the Security Council, by its Resolution 678, in 1990, gave to member states to use all necessary means to restore international peace and security in the area. That authorisation was suspended, but it was not terminated by Security Council Resolution 687 in 1991. It has been revived on previous occasions and UNSCR 1441 revived it again.

In UNSCR 1441 the Security Council determined, first, that Iraq's possession of weapons of mass destruction constitutes a threat to international peace and security; secondly, that Iraq has failed in clear violation of its legal obligation to disarm; and, thirdly, that in consequence, Iraq is in material breach of the conditions for the ceasefire laid down by the Council in UNSCR 687 at the end of the hostilities in 1991.

I shall reiterate some of the detail of the argument. [I]t is a question of the full context of what has happened since Resolution 660 which we should take into account. [C]hapter 7 of the United Nations Charter gives the Security Council the power to authorise states to take such military action as may be necessary to maintain or restore international peace and security. In the case of Iraq, the Security Council took such a step following the Iraqi invasion of Kuwait. Paragraph 2 of SCR 678 authorised,

> "Member states co-operating with the Government of Kuwait...to use all necessary means to uphold and implement Resolution 660 and all subsequent relevant resolutions and to restore international peace and security in the area".

The phrase "all necessary means" was understood then, as it is now, to include the use of force. Following the liberation of Kuwait, the Security Council adopted UNSCR 687. That resolution set out the steps that the council required Iraq to take in order to restore international peace and security in the area. Iraq's acceptance of those requirements was the condition for the declaration of a formal ceasefire. Those steps included the destruction of all WMD under international supervision and the requirement that Iraq should not attempt to acquire such weapons or the means of their manufacture. As a means to achieving the disarmament required by the Security Council, UNSCR 687 also required Iraq to submit to extensive weapons inspection by UNSCOM, now UNMOVIC, and the IAEA. The Security Council was quite clear that those steps were essential for the restoration of international peace and security in the area.

... [U]NSCR 687 did not repeal the authorisation to use force in paragraph 2 of SCR 678. On the contrary, it confirmed that SCR 678 remained in force. The authorisation was suspended for so long as Iraq complied with the conditions of the ceasefire, but the authorisation could be revived if the council determined that Iraq was acting in material breach of the requirements of SCR 687.

This is an important point. SCR 687 suspended but did not terminate the authorisation. The formality of acceptance of the terms was not sufficient. Iraq was and is required to comply with those terms.

Although almost 12 years have elapsed since SCR 687 was adopted, Iraq has never taken the steps required of it by the council. Throughout that period the council has repeatedly condemned Iraq for violations of SCR 687 and has adopted numerous resolutions on the subject. In 1993 and again in 1998 the coalition took military action under the revived authority of SCR 678 to deal with the threat to international peace and security posed by those violations.

...

In relation to the action in 1993 the Minister of State at the Foreign and Commonwealth Office, Douglas Hogg, wrote:

> "The Security Council determined in its statements of 8 and 11 January that Iraq was in material breach of resolution 687 and its related resolutions, and warned Iraq that serious consequences would ensue from continued failure to comply with its obligations. Resolution 687 lays down the terms for the formal ceasefire between the coalition states and Iraq at the end of hostilities mandated by the Security Council in resolution 678. These terms are binding in themselves but also have been specifically accepted by Iraq as a condition for the formal ceasefire to come into effect. In the light of Iraq's continued breaches of Security Council resolution 687 and thus of the ceasefire terms, and the repeated warnings given by the Security Council and members of the coalition, their forces were entitled to take necessary and proportionate action in order to ensure that Iraq complies with those terms."

Again, on 14th January 1993 in relation to UK and US military action of the previous day, the then UN Secretary-General, Dr Boutros Ghali, said:

> "The raid yesterday, and the forces which carried out the raid, have received a mandate from the Security Council, according to resolution 678, and the

> cause of the raid was the violation by Iraq of resolution 687 concerning the ceasefire. So, as the Secretary-General of the United Nations, I can say that this action was taken and conforms to the resolution of the Security Council and conforms to the Charter of the United Nations."

This is not a new point. Indeed, we reiterated it fairly recently. [I]n relation to the military action taken in 1998 I said, . . . , that any action involving UK forces would be based on international law. That is our position today.

The charter of the United Nations allows for the use of force under the authority of the Security Council. The Security Council resolution adopted before the Gulf conflict authorised the use of force in order to restore international peace and security in the region. Iraq is in clear breach of Security Council Resolution 687, which laid down the conditions for the ceasefire at the end of the conflict. Those conditions included a requirement on Iraq to eliminate its weapons of mass destruction under international supervision. These conditions have been broken. It is the same argument—it goes back to Resolutions 678 and 687, but now it is reinforced by Security Council Resolution 1441.

It is against that legal background that the United Kingdom and the United States brought to the council the draft resolution which was eventually adopted unanimously as SCR 1441 on 8th November. [T]he preamble to that resolution again expressly referred to SCR 678, confirming once more that that resolution was still in force. It also recognised the threat that Iraq's non-compliance with the council resolutions posed to international peace and security; and it recalled that SCR 687 imposed obligations on Iraq as a necessary step for the achievement of its objective of restoring international peace and security . . .

> "has been and remains in material breach"

of its obligations under SCR 687 and other relevant resolutions. On this occasion, the council decided, in paragraph 2, to offer Iraq,

> "a final opportunity to comply with its disarmament obligations".

Iraq was required to produce an accurate, full and complete declaration—all those words are important; "accurate, full and complete"—of all aspects of its prohibited programmes, and to provide immediate and unrestricted access to UNMOVIC and the IAEA. Failure by Iraq to comply with the requirements of SCR 1441 was declared to be a further material breach of Iraq's obligations, in addition to the continuing breach already identified in paragraph 1.

In the event of a further breach, or interference by Iraq with the inspectors, or failure to comply with any of the disarmament obligations under any of the relevant resolutions, the matter was to be reported to the Security Council. The Security Council was then to convene,

> "to consider the situation and the need for full compliance with all of the relevant Council resolutions in order to secure international peace and security".

That appears in paragraph 12. In paragraph 13, the council warned Iraq that,

> "it will face serious consequences as a result of its continued violations of its obligations".

UNSCR 1441 did not require a further decision by the Security Council to be taken. SCR 1441 afforded Iraq a final opportunity to comply and provided for any failure by Iraq to be "considered" by the Security Council under paragraph 12. That consideration has taken place regularly since the adoption of 1441. It is plain from UNMOVIC statements to the Security Council, its 12th quarterly report and the so-called "clusters document", that Iraq has not complied, as required, with its disarmament obligations. Whatever other differences there may be on the Security Council, no member of the council has questioned that conclusion. It follows that Iraq has not taken the final opportunity offered, and remains in material breach of the disarmament obligations which, for 12 weary years, the council has insisted are essential for the restoration of peace and security. In these circumstances, the authorisation to use force contained in SCR 678 revives.

[T]he US and the UK made it clear that there were no hidden triggers or automaticity because everyone in the council understood the consequences of a finding of material breach and everyone agreed that there would be a further council discussion before force was used. The statements by the UK and the USA at the time made that clear.

Mr Negroponte, the American Ambassador to the UN, said on 8th November that if the Security Council failed to act decisively in the event of further Iraqi violation, the resolution did not constrain any member state from acting to defend itself against the threat posed by Iraq or to enforce the relevant UN resolutions and protect world peace and security. Our own ambassador, Sir Jeremy Greenstock, said at the same meeting that there was no automaticity in the resolution. He said that if there was a further Iraqi breach of its disarmament obligations, the matter would return to the council for discussion as required by OP 12 [ed. Operative Paragraph 12]. That is the point—that is what has been happening, and it has been happening for four months.

(HL Deb 17 March 2003 Vol. 646 c118–121)

16/34

During a debate in the House of Commons on Iraq, the Secretary of State, FCO, said:

As the House will be aware, in the Azores yesterday my right hon. Friend the Prime Minister, Prime Minister Aznar of Spain, President Bush of the United States and Prime Minister Barroso of Portugal called on all members of the Security Council to adopt a resolution—which would have been its 18th on Iraq—to challenge Saddam to take a strategic decision to disarm his country of his weapons of mass destruction as required by Security Council resolution 1441. Such a resolution has never been needed legally, but we have long had a preference for it politically.

There has been intense diplomatic activity to secure that end over many months, culminating in the past 24 hours. Yesterday evening, our ambassador to the United Nations, Sir Jeremy Greenstock, consulted his fellow permanent representatives from other Security Council member states. Just this morning I spoke to my Spanish, American, Russian and Chinese counterparts.

Despite those final efforts, I regret to say that we have reluctantly concluded that a Security Council consensus on a new resolution would not be possible. On my instructions, Sir Jeremy Greenstock made a public announcement to that effect at the United Nations at about 3.15 pm UK time today.

What we know about the Iraqi regime's behaviour over many years is that there is the greatest chance of their finally responding to the United Nations obligations on them if they face a united Security Council. So, over the months since resolution 1441 was unanimously adopted by the Security Council in early November, the Prime Minister and I, and our ambassador to the United Nations, have strained every nerve in search of that consensus which could finally persuade Iraq, by peaceful means, to provide the full and immediate co-operation demanded by the Security Council.

Significantly, in all the discussions in the Security Council and outside, no one has claimed that Iraq is in full compliance with the obligations placed on it. Given that, it was my belief, up to about a week ago, that we were close to achieving the consensus that we sought on the further resolution. Sadly, one country then ensured that the Security Council could not act. President Chirac's unequivocal announcement last Monday that France would veto a second resolution containing that or any ultimatum "whatever the circumstances" inevitably created a sense of paralysis in our negotiations. I deeply regret that France has thereby put a Security Council consensus beyond reach.

I need to spell out that the alternative proposals submitted by France, Germany and Russia for more time and more inspections carry no ultimatum and no threat of force. They do not implement resolution 1441 but seek to rewrite it. To have adopted such proposals would have allowed Saddam to continue stringing out inspections indefinitely, and he would rightly have drawn the lesson that the Security Council was simply not prepared to enforce the ultimatum that lies at the heart of resolution 1441: in the event of non-compliance, Iraq, as operational paragraph 13 spells out, should expect "serious consequences".

As a result of Saddam Hussein's persistent refusal to meet the UN's demands, and the inability of the Security Council to adopt a further resolution, the Cabinet has decided to ask the House to support the United Kingdom's participation in military operations, should they be necessary, with the objective of ensuring the disarmament of Iraq's weapons of mass destruction, and thereby the maintenance of the authority of the United Nations.

From the outset of this crisis the Government have promised that, if possible, the House would have the opportunity to debate our involvement in military action prior to the start of hostilities and on a substantive motion...

In addition to dealing with military action the motion states that in the event of military operations the House requires that

> "on an urgent basis, the United Kingdom should seek a new Security Council Resolution that would affirm Iraq's territorial integrity, ensure rapid delivery of humanitarian relief, allow for the earliest possible lifting of UN sanctions, an international reconstruction programme, and the use of all oil revenues for the benefit of the Iraqi people and endorse an appropriate post-conflict administration for Iraq".

In addition, the resolution goes on to endorse the middle east peace process as encapsulated in the imminent publication of the road map . . .

To inform the debate, I have circulated several documents to all right hon. and hon. Members today. These include a copy of the response from my noble and learned Friend the Attorney-General to a written question in the House of Lords in which he sets out the legal basis for the use of force against Iraq [ed. **16/35** below], as well as a detailed briefing paper summarising the legal background which I have sent to the Chairman of the Foreign Affairs Committee [ed. **16/36** below]. I have also made available a note summarising Iraq's record of non-compliance with resolution 1441. A new Command Paper comprising key recent United Nations documents, including the 173 pages of Dr Blix's paper on "Unresolved Disarmament Issues: Iraq's Proscribed Weapons Programmes", which was published on 7 March in the Security Council, is now available in the Vote Office.

The debate tomorrow will be the most important in the House for many years. Some say that Iraq can be disarmed without an ultimatum, without the threat or the use of force, but simply by more time and more inspections. That approach is defied by all our experience over 12 weary years. It cannot produce the disarmament of Iraq; it cannot rid the world of the danger of the Iraqi regime. It can only bring comfort to tyrants and emasculate the authority of the United Nations. It is for these reasons that we shall tomorrow be asking the House to endorse and support the Government's resolution.

(HC Deb 17 March 2003 Vol. 401 c703–705)

[See also the Foreign Secretary's oral evidence to the FAC in the Tenth Report, Foreign Policy Aspects of the War Against Terrorism, HC 405, especially questions 146–164]

16/35

In reply to a written question, the Attorney-General wrote:

Authority to use force against Iraq exists from the combined effect of Resolutions 678, 687 and 1441. All of these resolutions were adopted under Chapter VII of the UN Charter which allows the use of force for the express purpose of restoring international peace and security:

1. In Resolution 678, the Security Council authorised force against Iraq, to eject it from Kuwait and to restore peace and security in the area.

2. In Resolution 687, which set out the ceasefire conditions after Operation Desert Storm, the Security Council imposed continuing obligations on Iraq to eliminate its weapons of mass destruction in order to restore international peace and security in the area. Resolution 687 suspended but did not terminate the authority to use force under Resolution 678.

3. A material breach of Resolution 687 revives the authority to use force under Resolution 678.

4. In Resolution 1441, the Security Council determined that Iraq has been and remains in material breach of Resolution 687, because it has not fully complied with its obligations to disarm under that resolution.

5. The Security Council in Resolution 1441 gave Iraq "a final opportunity to comply with its disarmament obligations" and warned Iraq of the "serious consequences" if it did not.

6. The Security Council also decided in Resolution 1441 that, if Iraq failed at any time to comply with and co-operate fully in the implementation of Resolution 1441, that would constitute a further material breach.

7. It is plain that Iraq has failed so to comply and therefore Iraq was at the time of Resolution 1441 and continues to be in material breach.

8. Thus, the authority to use force under Resolution 678 has revived and so continues today.

9. Resolution 1441 would in terms have provided that a further decision of the Security Council to sanction force was required if that had been intended. Thus, all that Resolution 1441 requires is reporting to and discussion by the Security Council of Iraq's failures, but not an express further decision to authorise force.

I have lodged a copy of this Answer, together with Resolutions 678, 687 and 1441 in the Libraries of both Houses and the Vote Office of the House of Commons.

(HL Deb 17 March 2003 Vol. 646 cWA2–3)

16/36

The Foreign Secretary wrote to the Chairman of the FAC on 17 March 2003, including, inter alia, an FCO document:

IRAQ: LEGAL BASIS FOR THE USE OF FORCE

1. The legal basis for any military action against Iraq would be the authorisation which the Security Council, by its resolution 678 (1990), gave to Member States to use all necessary means to restore international peace and security in the area. That authorisation was suspended but not terminated by Security Council resolution (SCR) 687 (1991), and revived by SCR 1441 (2002). In SCR 1441, the Security Council has determined—

(1) that Iraq's possession of weapons of mass destruction (WMD) constitutes a threat to international peace and security;

(2) that Iraq has failed—in clear violation of its legal obligations—to disarm; and

(3) that, in consequence, Iraq is in a material breach of the conditions for the ceasefire laid down by the Council in SCR 687 at the end of the hostilities in 1991, thus reviving the authorisation in SCR 678.

The extent of the authority to use force contained in SCR 678

2. Chapter VII of the United Nations Charter gives the Security Council the power to authorise States to take such military action as may be necessary to maintain or restore international peace and security.

3. In the case of Iraq, the Security Council took such a step following the Iraqi invasion of Kuwait. Paragraph 2 of SCR 678 authorised "Member States co-operating with the Government of Kuwait . . . to use all necessary means

to uphold and implement resolution 660 (1990) and all subsequent relevant resolutions and to restore international peace and security in the area." The phrase "all necessary means" was understood then (as it is now) as including the use of force.

4. Following the liberation of Kuwait, the Security Council adopted SCR 687. This resolution set out the steps which the Council required Iraq to take in order to restore international peace and security in the area. Iraq's acceptance of those requirements was the condition for the declaration of a formal ceasefire. Those steps included the destruction of all WMD under international supervision and the requirement that Iraq should not attempt to acquire such weapons or the means of their manufacture. As a means to achieving the disarmament required by the Security Council, SCR 687 also required Iraq to submit to extensive weapons inspection by UNSCOM (now UNMOVIC) and the IAEA. The Security Council was quite clear that these steps were essential to the restoration of international peace and security in the area.

5. SCR 687 did not repeal the authorisation to use force in paragraph 2 of SCR 678. On the contrary, it confirmed that SCR 678 remained in force. The authorisation was suspended for so long as Iraq complied with the conditions of the ceasefire. But the authorisation could be revived if the Council determined that Iraq was acting in material breach of the requirements of SCR 687. Although almost twelve years have elapsed since SCR 687 was adopted, Iraq has never taken the steps required of it by the Council. Throughout that period the Council has repeatedly condemned Iraq for violations of SCR 687 and has adopted numerous resolutions on the subject. In 1993 and again in 1998 the coalition took military action under the revived authority of SCR 678 to deal with the threat to international peace and security posed by those violations.

6. In relation to the action in 1993, the Minister of State at the Foreign and Commonwealth Office wrote: "The Security Council determined in its statements of 8 and 11 January that Iraq was in material breach of resolutions 687 and its related resolutions, and warned Iraq that serious consequences would ensue from continued failure to comply with its obligations. Resolution 687 lays down the terms for the formal ceasefire between the coalition states and Iraq at the end of the hostilities mandated by the Security Council in resolution 678. These terms are binding in themselves but have also been specifically accepted by Iraq as a condition for the formal ceasefire to come into effect. In the light of Iraq's continued breaches of Security Council resolution 687 and thus of the ceasefire terms, and the repeated warnings given by the Security Council and members of the coalition, their forces were entitled to take necessary and proportionate action in order to ensure that Iraq complies with those terms."

7. On 14 January 1993, in relation to the UK/US military action the previous day, the then UN Secretary-General said: "The raid yesterday, and the forces which carried out the raid, have received a mandate from the Security Council, according to resolution 678, and the cause of the raid was the violation by Iraq of resolution 687 concerning the ceasefire. So, as Secretary-General of the United Nations, I can say that this action was taken and conforms to the resolutions of the Security Council and conforms to the Charter of the United Nations."

8. In relation to the military action undertaken in 1998, the then Parliamentary Under-Secretary of State (now Minister of State) at the Foreign and Commonwealth Office, Baroness Symons of Vemham Dean stated: "In our previous discussions in this House some of your Lordships asked about the legality of our action. Any action involving UK forces would be based on international law. The Charter of the United Nations allows for the use of force under the authority of the Security Council. The Security Council resolution adopted before the Gulf conflict authorised the use of force in order to restore international peace and security in the region. Iraq is in clear breach of Security Council resolution 687 which laid down the conditions for the ceasefire at the end of the conflict. Those conditions included a requirement on Iraq to eliminate its weapons of mass destruction under international supervision. Those conditions have been broken.

Security Council Resolution 1441 (2002)

9. It is against that legal background that the United Kingdom and the United States brought to the Council the draft resolution which was eventually adopted unanimously as SCR 1441 on 8 November 2002. The preamble to that resolution again expressly referred to SCR 678, confirming once more that that resolution was still in force. It also recognised the threat that Iraq's non-compliance with Council resolutions posed to international peace and security; and it recalled that SCR 687 imposed obligations on Iraq as a necessary step for the achievement of its objective of restoring international peace and security. In paragraph 1 the Council went on to decide that Iraq "has been and remains in material breach" of its obligations under SCR 687 and other relevant resolutions. The use of the term "material breach" is of the utmost importance because the practice of the Security Council during the 1990s shows that it was just such a finding of material breach by Iraq which served to revive the authorisation in SCR 678.

10. On this occasion, however, the Council decided (in paragraph 2 of SCR 1441) to offer Iraq "a final opportunity to comply with its disarmament obligations". Iraq was required to produce an accurate, full and complete declaration of all aspects of its prohibited programmes (paragraph 3), and to provide immediate and unrestricted access to UNMOVIC and IAEA (paragraph 5). Failure by Iraq to comply with the requirements of SCR 1441 was declared to be a further material breach of Iraq's obligations (paragraph 4), in addition to the continuing breach already identified in paragraph 1. In the event of a further breach (paragraph 4), or interference by Iraq with the inspectors or failure to comply with any of the disarmament obligations under any of the relevant resolutions (paragraph 11), the matter was to be reported to the Security Council. The Security Council was then to convene "to consider the situation and the need for full compliance with all of the relevant Council resolutions in order to secure international peace and security" (paragraph 12). The Council warned Iraq (paragraph 13) that "it will face serious consequences as a result of its continued violations of its obligations'.

11. It is important to stress that SCR 1441 did not revive the 678 authorisation immediately on its adoption. There was no "automaticity". The resolution afforded Iraq a final opportunity to comply and it provided for any failure by Iraq to be "considered" by the Security Council (under paragraph 12 of the

resolution). That paragraph does not, however, mean that no further action can be taken without a new resolution of the Council. Had that been the intention, it would have provided that the Council would decide what needed to be done to restore international peace and security, not that it would consider the matter. The choice of words was deliberate; a proposal that there should be a requirement for a decision by the Council, a position maintained by several Council members, was not adopted. Instead the members of the Council opted for the formula that the Council must consider the matter before any action is taken.

12. That consideration has taken place regularly since the adoption of SCR 1441. It is plain, including from UNMOVIC's statements to the Security Council, its Twelfth Quarterly Report and the so-called "Clusters Document", that Iraq has not complied as required with its disarmament obligations. Whatever other differences there may have been in the Security Council, no member of the Council has questioned this conclusion. It therefore follows that Iraq has not taken the final opportunity offered to it and remains in material breach of the disarmament obligations which, for twelve years, the Council has insisted are essential for the restoration of peace and security. In these circumstances, the authorisation to use force contained in SCR 678 revives.

(Available at www.fco.gov.uk)

16/37

The FAC addressed the question, "Was the War Lawful?". It concluded:

83. The United Nations Security Council is the only body able to provide a legal basis for the use of force in the maintenance of peace and security, beyond the circumstances described in the UN Charter. The US government's decision to address the question of Iraq through the UN Security Council is widely considered to have been—at least in part—a consequence of pressure from the United Kingdom. The Government has stressed repeatedly throughout the Iraq crisis that it intends to work within the boundaries of international law. While stressing that agreement in the Security Council was not necessary to ensure the legality of military action against Iraq, the Government made substantial efforts to secure agreement on the international response to the threat from Iraq in the Security Council during late 2002 and early 2003.

84. At the end of 2002, after the adoption of resolution 1441, the Government's policy appeared to be bearing fruit; in our last Report on this subject, we accordingly commended the Government's decision to work closely with the United States, to produce a strong and unanimous Security Council Resolution establishing an unconstrained weapons inspections regime and demanding Iraq's full disarmament of Weapons of Mass Destruction.

85. As we note above, the United Kingdom undertook military action in March 2003 without obtaining explicit support from the Security Council. We note the Foreign Secretary's recollection that before the adoption of 1441, there had been a very intense debate . . . about whether the resolution that became 1441 should explicitly say, in terms, that military action to enforce this resolution could only be taken if there were a second resolution.

According to the Foreign Secretary, this proposition "was not acceptable to a majority of members of the Security Council [and] it was never put before the Security Council".

86. Instead, the Council agreed to "the scheme laid out in the operative paragraphs of 1441 which set very clear obligations on Iraq". These included submission of a currently accurate, full, and complete declaration of all aspects of its programmes to develop chemical, biological, and nuclear weapons, ballistic missiles, and other delivery systems, and the compliance with the inspectors set out in paragraphs 5 through to 8 and so on, and then a definition in paragraph 4 of what is a further material breach.

The Foreign Secretary told us that "In . . . circumstances where you have got a further material breach"—as defined by operative paragraph 4 of 1441—you then have the Council meeting for an assessment of the situation in accordance with paragraphs 11 and 12. But what the Council has to do under 12 is to consider the situation, not necessarily to pass a second resolution.

87. The Government stated consistently that it sought a "second resolution" for political reasons, but that such a resolution was not legally necessary. On 17 March, when it was clear that efforts to convince the Security Council to adopt such a resolution had failed, the Attorney General, Lord Goldsmith, set out his views of the legal basis for the use of force against Iraq. He stated that Authority to use force against Iraq exists from the combined effect of resolutions 678, 687 and 1441. All of these resolutions were adopted under Chapter VII of the UN Charter which allows the use of force for the express purpose of restoring international peace and security.

(Tenth Report of the FAC, Foreign Policy Aspects of the War against Terrorism, 31 July 2003, HC 405)

[ed. There are substantial papers on aspects of the war against Iraq and its aftermath at http://www.parliament.uk/useful/sp_iraq.cfm#RP. Various government documents are available at http://www.fco.gov.uk/library, including the WMD dossiers of September 2002 and February 2003.]

16/38

The following motion for debate was before the House of Commons on 18 March 2003:

That this House notes its decisions of 25th November 2002 and 26th February 2003 to endorse UN Security Council Resolution 1441; recognises that Iraq's weapons of mass destruction and long range missiles, and its continuing non-compliance with Security Council Resolutions, pose a threat to international peace and security; notes that in the 130 days since Resolution 1441 was adopted Iraq has not co-operated actively, unconditionally and immediately with the weapons inspectors, and has rejected the final opportunity to comply and is in further material breach of its obligations under successive mandatory UN Security Council Resolutions; regrets that despite sustained diplomatic effort by Her Majesty's Government it has not proved possible to secure a second Resolution in the UN because one Permanent Member of the Security Council made plain in public its intention to use its veto whatever the circumstances; notes the opinion of the Attorney General that, Iraq having failed to comply and Iraq being at the time of Resolution 1441 and continuing to be in material breach, the authority to use force under Resolution 678 has revived and so continues today; believes that the United Kingdom must uphold the authority of the United Nations as set out in Resolution 1441 and many Resolutions preceding it, and therefore supports the decision of Her Majesty's Government that the United Kingdom should use all means necessary to ensure the disarmament of Iraq's weapons of mass destruction; offers wholehearted support to the men and women of Her Majesty's Armed Forces now on duty in the Middle East; in the event of military operations requires that, on an urgent basis, the United Kingdom should seek a new Security Council Resolution that would affirm Iraq's territorial integrity, ensure rapid delivery of humanitarian relief, allow for the earliest possible lifting of UN sanctions, an international reconstruction programme, and the use of all oil revenues for the benefit of the Iraqi people and endorse an appropriate post-conflict administration for Iraq, leading to a representative government which upholds human rights and the rule of law for all Iraqis; and also welcomes the imminent publication of the Quartet's roadmap as a significant step to bringing a just and lasting peace settlement between Israelis and Palestinians and for the wider Middle East region, and endorses the role of Her Majesty's Government in actively working for peace between Israel and Palestine.

(HC Deb 18 March 2003 Vol. 401 c760)

16/39

During the debate on the motion at **16/38** above in the House of Commons on Iraq, the Prime Minister said:

The country and the Parliament reflect each other. This is a debate that, as time has gone on, has become less bitter but no less grave. So why does it matter so much? Because the outcome of this issue will now determine more than the fate of the Iraqi regime and more than the future of the Iraqi people who have been brutalised by Saddam for so long, important though those issues are. It will determine the way in which Britain and the world confront the central security threat of the 21st century, the development of the United Nations, the relationship between Europe and the United States, the relations within the European Union and the way in which the United States engages with the rest of the world. So it could hardly be more important. It will determine the pattern of international politics for the next generation.

First, let us recap the history of Iraq and weapons of mass destruction. In April 1991, after the Gulf war, Iraq was given 15 days to provide a full and final declaration of all its weapons of mass destruction. Saddam had used the weapons against Iran and against his own people, causing thousands of deaths. He had had plans to use them against allied forces. It became clear, after the Gulf war, that Iraq's WMD ambitions were far more extensive than had hitherto been thought. So the issue was identified by the United Nations at that time as one for urgent remedy. UNSCOM, the weapons inspection team, was set up. It was expected to complete its task, following the declaration, at the end of April 1991. The declaration, when it came, was false: a blanket denial of the programme, other than in a very tentative form. And so the 12-year game began.

The inspectors probed. Finally, in March 1992, Iraq admitted that it had previously undeclared weapons of mass destruction, but it said that it had destroyed them. It gave another full and final declaration. Again the inspectors probed. In October 1994, Iraq stopped co-operating with the weapons inspectors altogether. Military action was threatened. Inspections resumed. In March 1996, in an effort to rid Iraq of the inspectors, a further full and final declaration of WMD was made. By July 1996, however, Iraq was forced to admit that declaration, too, was false.

In August, it provided yet another full and final declaration. Then, a week later, Saddam's son-in-law, Hussein Kamal, defected to Jordan. He disclosed a far more extensive biological weapons programme and, for the first time, said that Iraq had weaponised the programme—something that Saddam had always strenuously denied. All this had been happening while the inspectors were in Iraq.

Kamal also revealed Iraq's crash programme to produce a nuclear weapon in the 1990s. Iraq was then forced to release documents that showed just how extensive those programmes were. In November 1996, Jordan intercepted prohibited components for missiles that could be used for weapons of mass destruction. Then a further "full and final declaration" was made. That, too, turned out to be false.

In June 1997, inspectors were barred from specific sites. In September 1997, lo and behold, yet another "full and final declaration" was made—also false. Meanwhile, the inspectors discovered VX nerve agent production equipment, the existence of which had always been denied by the Iraqis.

In October 1997, the United States and the United Kingdom threatened military action if Iraq refused to comply with the inspectors. Finally, under threat of action in February 1998, Kofi Annan went to Baghdad and negotiated a memorandum with Saddam to allow inspections to continue. They did continue, for a few months. In August, co-operation was suspended.

In December, the inspectors left. Their final report is a withering indictment of Saddam's lies, deception and obstruction, with large quantities of weapons of mass destruction unaccounted for. Then, in December 1998, the US and the UK undertook Desert Fox, a targeted bombing campaign to degrade as much of the Iraqi WMD facility as we could.

In 1999, a new inspection team, UNMOVIC, was set up. Saddam refused to allow those inspectors even to enter Iraq. So there they stayed, in limbo, until, after resolution 1441 last November, they were allowed to return.

That is the history—and what is the claim of Saddam today? Why, exactly the same as before: that he has no weapons of mass destruction. Indeed, we are asked to believe that after seven years of obstruction and non-compliance, finally resulting in the inspectors' leaving in 1998—seven years in which he hid his programme and built it up, even when the inspectors were there in Iraq—when they had left, he voluntarily decided to do what he had consistently refused to do under coercion.

When the inspectors left in 1998, they left unaccounted for 10,000 litres of anthrax; a far-reaching VX nerve agent programme; up to 6,500 chemical munitions; at least 80 tonnes of mustard gas, and possibly more than 10 times that amount; unquantifiable amounts of sarin, botulinum toxin and a host of other biological poisons; and an entire Scud missile programme. We are asked now seriously to accept that in the last few years—contrary to all history, contrary to all intelligence—Saddam decided unilaterally to destroy those weapons. I say that such a claim is palpably absurd.

Resolution 1441 is very clear. It lays down a final opportunity for Saddam to disarm. It rehearses the fact that he has for years been in material breach of 17 UN resolutions. It says that this time compliance must be full, unconditional and immediate, the first step being a full and final declaration of all weapons of mass destruction to be given on 8 December last year.

I will not go through all the events since then, as the House is familiar with them, but this much is accepted by all members of the UN Security Council: the 8 December declaration is false. That in itself, incidentally, is a material breach. Iraq has taken some steps in co-operation, but no one disputes that it is not fully co-operating. Iraq continues to deny that it has any weapons of mass destruction, although no serious intelligence service anywhere in the world believes it.

On 7 March, the inspectors published a remarkable document. It is 173 pages long, and details all the unanswered questions about Iraq's weapons of mass destruction. It lists 29 different areas in which the inspectors have been unable to obtain information. On VX, for example, it says:

> "Documentation available to UNMOVIC suggests that Iraq at least had had far reaching plans to weaponise VX."

On mustard gas, it says: "Mustard constituted an important part . . . of Iraq's CW arsenal . . . 550 mustard filled shells and up to 450 mustard filled aerial bombs unaccounted for . . . additional uncertainty" with respect to over 6,500 aerial bombs, "corresponding to approximately 1,000 tonnes of agent, predominantly mustard".

On biological weapons, the inspectors' report states: "Based on unaccounted for growth media, Iraq's potential production of anthrax could have been in the range of about 15,000 to 25,000 litres . . . Based on all the available evidence, the strong presumption is that about 10,000 litres of anthrax was not destroyed and may still exist."

On that basis, I simply say to the House that, had we meant what we said in resolution 1441, the Security Council should have convened and condemned Iraq as in material breach. What is perfectly clear is that Saddam is playing the same old games in the same old way. Yes, there are minor concessions, but there has been no fundamental change of heart or mind.

However, after 7 March, the inspectors said that there was at least some co-operation, and the world rightly hesitated over war. Let me now describe to the House what then took place.

We therefore approached a second resolution in this way. As I said, we could have asked for the second resolution then and there, because it was justified. Instead, we laid down an ultimatum calling upon Saddam to come into line with resolution 1441, or be in material breach. That is not an unreasonable proposition, given the history, but still countries hesitated. They asked, "How do we judge what is full co-operation?"

So we then worked on a further compromise. We consulted the inspectors and drew up five tests, based on the document that they published on 7 March. Those tests included allowing interviews with 30 scientists to be held outside Iraq, and releasing details of the production of the anthrax, or at least of the documentation showing what had happened to it. The inspectors added another test: that Saddam should publicly call on Iraqis to co-operate with them.

So we constructed this framework: that Saddam should be given a specified time to fulfil all six tests to show full co-operation; and that, if he did so, the inspectors could then set out a forward work programme that would extend over a period of time to make sure that disarmament happened. However, if Saddam failed to meet those tests to judge compliance, action would follow.

So there were clear benchmarks, plus a clear ultimatum. Again, I defy anyone to describe that as an unreasonable proposition. Last Monday, we were getting very close with it. We very nearly had the majority agreement. If I might, I should particularly like to thank the President of Chile for the constructive way in which he approached this issue.

Yes, there were debates about the length of the ultimatum, but the basic construct was gathering support. Then, on Monday night, France said that it would veto a second resolution, whatever the circumstances. Then France denounced the six tests. Later that day, Iraq rejected them. Still, we continued to negotiate, even at that point.

Last Friday, France said that it could not accept any resolution with an ultimatum in it. On Monday, we made final efforts to secure agreement. However, the fact is that France remains utterly opposed to anything that lays down an ultimatum authorising action in the event of non-compliance by Saddam.

(HC Deb 18 March 2003 Vol. 401 c761–764)

16/40

During the same debate (**16/39** above) in the House of Commons on Iraq, the Prime Minister said:

From December 1998 to December 2002, no UN inspector was allowed to inspect anything in Iraq. For four years, no inspection took place. What changed Saddam's mind was the threat of force. From December to January, and then from January through to February, some concessions were made. What changed his mind? It was the threat of force. What makes him now issue invitations to the inspectors, discover documents that he said he never had, produce evidence of weapons supposed to be non-existent, and destroy missiles he said he would keep? It is the imminence of force. The only persuasive power to which he responds is 250,000 allied troops on his doorstep. However, when that fact is so obvious, we are told that any resolution that authorises force in the event of non-compliance will be vetoed—not just opposed, but vetoed and blocked.

. . .

For the very reason that I have just given. If a member of the permanent five indicates to members of the Security Council who are not permanent members that whatever the circumstances it will veto, that is the way to block any progress on the Security Council. With the greatest respect to whoever shouted out that the presence of the troops is working, I agree, but it is British and American troops who are there, not French troops.

The tragedy is that had such a resolution ensued and had the UN come together and united—and if other troops had gone there, not just British and American troops—Saddam Hussein might have complied. But the moment we proposed the benchmarks and canvassed support for an ultimatum, there was an immediate recourse to the language of the veto. The choice was not action now or postponement of action; the choice was action or no action at all.

. . .

We can argue about each one of those vetoes in the past and whether they were reasonable, but I define an unreasonable veto as follows. In resolution 1441, we said that it was Saddam's final opportunity and that he had to comply. That was agreed by all members of the Security Council. What is surely unreasonable is for a country to come forward now, at the very point when we might reach agreement and when we are—not unreasonably—saying that he must comply with the UN, after all these months without full compliance, on the basis of the six tests or action will follow. For that country to say that it will veto such a resolution in all circumstances is what I would call unreasonable.

The tragedy is that the world has to learn the lesson all over again that weakness in the face of a threat from a tyrant is the surest way not to peace, but—unfortunately—to conflict. Looking back over those 12 years, the truth is that we have been victims of our own desire to placate the implacable, to persuade towards reason the utterly unreasonable, and to hope that there was some genuine intent to do good in a regime whose mind is in fact evil.

Now the very length of time counts against us. People say, "You've waited 12 years, so why not wait a little longer?" Of course we have done so, because resolution 1441 gave a final opportunity. As I have just pointed out, the first test was on 8 December. But still we waited. We waited for the inspectors' reports. We waited as each concession was tossed to us to whet our appetite for hope and further waiting. But still no one, not even today at the Security Council, says that Saddam is co-operating fully, unconditionally or immediately.

(HC Deb 18 March 2003 Vol. 401 c764–766)

16/41

During the same debate in the House of Commons on Iraq, the Prime Minister said:

First, the hon. Gentleman is absolutely wrong about the position on resolution 1441. It is correct that resolution 1441 did not say that there would be another resolution authorising the use of force, but the implication of resolution 1441—it was stated in terms—was that if Iraq continued in material breach, defined as not co-operating fully, immediately and unconditionally, serious consequences should follow. All we are asking for in the second resolution is the clear ultimatum that if Saddam continues to fail to co-operate, force should be used. The French position is that France will vote no, whatever the circumstances. Those are not my words, but those of the French President. I find it sad that at this point in time he cannot support us in the position we have set out, which is the only sure way to disarm Saddam. And what, indeed, would any tyrannical regime possessing weapons of mass destruction think when viewing the history of the world's diplomatic dance with Saddam over these 12 years? That our capacity to pass firm resolutions has only been matched by our feebleness in implementing them. That is why this indulgence has to stop—because it is dangerous: dangerous if such regimes disbelieve us; dangerous if they think they can use our weakness, our hesitation, and even the natural urges of our democracy towards peace against us; and dangerous because one day they will mistake our innate revulsion against war for permanent incapacity, when, in fact, if pushed to the limit, we will act. But when we act, after years of pretence, the action will have to be harder, bigger, more total in its impact. It is true that Iraq is not the only country with weapons of mass destruction, but I say this to the House: back away from this confrontation now, and future conflicts will be infinitely worse and more devastating in their effects.

Of course, in a sense, any fair observer does not really dispute that Iraq is in breach of resolution 1441 or that it implies action in such circumstances. The real problem is that, underneath, people dispute that Iraq is a threat, dispute the link between terrorism and weapons of mass destruction, and dispute, in other words, the whole basis of our assertion that the two together constitute a fundamental assault on our way of life.

(HC Deb 18 March 2003 Vol. 401 c767)

16/42

In a letter dated 20 March 2003 from the Permanent Representative of the United Kingdom of Great Britain and Northern Ireland to the United Nations addressed to the President of the Security Council, the representative of the United Kingdom wrote:

I have the honour to inform you on behalf of my Government that the Armed Forces of the United Kingdom—in association with those of the United States and Australia—engaged in military action in Iraq on 20 March 2003. The action is continuing.

The action follows a long history of non-cooperation by Iraq with the United Nations Special Commission (UNSCOM), the United Nations Monitoring, Verification and Inspection Commission (UNMOVIC) and the International Atomic Energy Agency (IAEA) and numerous findings by the Security Council that Iraq has failed to comply with the disarmament obligations imposed on it by the Council, including in resolutions 678 (1990), 687 (1991) and 1441 (2002). In its resolution 1441 (2002), the Council reiterated that Iraq's possession of weapons of mass destruction constitutes a threat to international peace and security; that Iraq has failed, in clear violation of its obligations, to disarm; and that in consequence Iraq is in material breach of the conditions for the ceasefire at the end of hostilities in 1991 laid down by the Council in its resolution 687 (1991). Military action was undertaken only when it became apparent that there was no other way of achieving compliance by Iraq.

The objective of the action is to secure compliance by Iraq with its disarmament obligations as laid down by the Council. All military action will be limited to the minimum measures necessary to secure this objective. Operations will be conducted in accordance with the international laws of armed conflict. Targets have been carefully chosen to avoid civilian casualties.

I would be grateful if you could circulate the text of the present letter as a document of the Security Council.

(UN Doc. S/2003/350, 30 March 2003)

16/43

During a debate on the use of force against Iraq in the House of Commons, the Secretary of State for Defence made the following statements:

[I] would like to make a statement about military operations to disarm Iraq of its weapons of mass destruction.

President Bush's ultimatum to Saddam Hussein expired at 1 o'clock this morning. Just as Saddam failed to take his final opportunity to disarm by peaceful means, so he has now failed to take his final opportunity to depart in peace and avoid the need for coalition military action. I draw the House's attention to Hans Blix's comments in New York yesterday that he was disappointed that three and a half months of inspection work had not brought clear assurances from the Iraqis of the absence of weapons of mass destruction in Iraq.

President Bush announced at 3.15 this morning on behalf of the coalition that operations had begun with attacks on selected targets of military importance. Those attacks were carried out by coalition aircraft and cruise missiles on more than one target in the vicinity of Baghdad, following information relating to the whereabouts of very senior members of the Iraqi leadership. Those leaders are at the very heart of Iraq's command and control system, responsible for directing Iraq's weapons of mass destruction.

Saddam Hussein's regime is the chief obstacle to the disarmament of Iraq. The military plan is therefore crafted around his removal from power. We will place a copy of the Government's military campaign objectives in the Library later today.

In addition to those attacks, coalition forces yesterday carried out certain preliminary operations against Iraqi artillery, surface-to-surface missiles, and air defence systems within the southern no-fly zone. Those were prudent preparatory steps, using coalition air capabilities previously used in the no-fly zones, designed to reduce the threat to coalition forces in Kuwait. The protection of our servicemen and women is a matter of paramount importance.

The House will be aware of reports of Iraqi missile attacks against Kuwait. Those incidents are being investigated by personnel with appropriate skills and the necessary protection. There are no reported casualties so far, but I am afraid that there is nothing more that I can confirm to the House at this stage.

I would like to draw the attention of the House to two particular points. First, that coalition forces will take every possible care to minimise civilian casualties or damage to civilian infrastructure. The coalition will use modern weapons, which are more accurate than ever, but we can never unfortunately exclude the possibility of civilian casualties, tragic though those always are. However, people should treat with caution Iraq's claims of civilian casualties. The Iraqi people are not our enemies, and we are determined to do all we can to help them build the better future that they deserve.

...

Consistent with what I said earlier, I do not intend to comment in detail about the considerable number of missiles that have been targeted against Kuwait. We are investigating precisely the nature of the missiles and of the warheads with which they are equipped. I understand, but only from recent news reports, that defensive systems have been used to good effect to deal with at least one such missile.

There is close co-operation between the United States and Kurdish forces in the north of Iraq and I am confident that that will continue. I give the House the assurance that prisoners of war will be dealt with in accordance with international law. There are certainly signs of a growing number of disaffected Iraqis abandoning support for Saddam Hussein. This morning I discussed with my right hon. Friends the Prime Minister and the Foreign Secretary the continuing diplomatic initiatives that will be taken...

...

I emphasise that a range of weapons will have to be used to prosecute this campaign successfully and achieve the successful result that my hon. Friend rightly advocates. I will not allow our forces to be prevented from using those lawful weapons that are most suitable for achieving those tasks. I assure her equally that those weapons are used only after the most careful consideration. Depleted uranium and cluster bombs have a particular military purpose. If that purpose is necessary, they will be used; if it is not, they will not be used.

...

On previous occasions, when I have set out to the House the details of the British force deploying to the Gulf, I have made it clear that it is a flexible force—certainly designed for war-fighting but also designed for peacekeeping. As soon as any conflict draws to an end, forces will be in place to provide security to the people of Iraq but also to attend to their obvious humanitarian needs. Iraq has been devastated by the regime of Saddam Hussein over many years. It is a much poorer country than it should be. We will assist in the process of rebuilding that country.

...

The hon. Gentleman probably understands more about the nature of Iraqi society than he is letting on. In the past, we have heard many references to the palaces that the regime has constructed. Those palaces are residential—if the hon. Gentleman chooses to describe them as such—but they are also command and control centres that are operated by leaders of the regime simply because they are afraid of any close contact with their own people. In reality, those targets are perfectly legitimate military targets because they are the places from which Saddam Hussein exercises command and control over his own people and over weapons of mass destruction. It is entirely consistent with our campaign objectives that such military command and control facilities should be targeted.

...

I will defend my hon. Friend's right to be heard—as I will also defend the right of the opposition in Iraq to be heard; and I should be much happier if he emphasised that more frequently than he has sometimes done in the recent past. I assure him, as I have assured the House on previous occasions, that the actions of our armed forces are entirely lawful and based on the clear advice of the Attorney-General, which has been set out for the benefit of Members.

...

What I said was that Hans Blix was disappointed that his inspection work had not brought clear assurances from the Iraqis about the absence of weapons of mass destruction. There is no argument about that. I am not aware that any Government, whatever their position on the need for military action, have disputed the fact that Iraq possesses weapons of mass destruction. That has not been disputed even by countries opposed to military action. It is important not to lose sight of the reason for military operations: to enforce the will of the United Nations to remove the threat of weapons of mass destruction, either, as the Prime Minister has said, when they are in the hands of the Iraqi regime itself, or when there is a risk that they might fall into the hands of unscrupulous terrorist organisations such as al-Qaeda.

I have answered the question about links before. There are clear links between the Iraqi regime and al-Qaeda. We are not sure of the precise nature of those links, but we are certainly aware that they exist. It is important that we continue to monitor that.

...

It is absolutely the case that we operate in a coalition with the same principles of international law governing the targeting. I have already set out some of those principles to the House. It is important to avoid where we can civilian casualties, while recognising the risk that there will obviously be civilian harm, but working through the details of the targeting programme to minimise those risks wherever possible.

...

My right hon. Friend is right. As I said, there is inevitably a risk to civilians in times of conflict, but equally I point out again that we seek wherever we can to minimise those risks and to ensure that our statements are wholly accurate.

(HC Deb 20 March 2003 Vol. 401 c1087–1100)

16/44

During a debate in the House of Commons, the Prime Minister was asked the following oral question:

The excellent military campaign that has got rid of Saddam Hussein's regime is, obviously, to be welcomed, but will the Prime Minister clarify something that he said in his statement? He said that the war was about ending the brutalised state under Saddam Hussein. Was that actually the war objective?

In reply, the Prime Minister said:

No. The objective is to make sure that Iraq is effectively disarmed of weapons of mass destruction, but while Saddam's regime refused to co-operate fully with the UN inspectors and refused to give up those weapons, its removal became an objective of ours, so things proceeded in that way. I think that I have said before, and I will say again, that although the reasons for our action and its legitimacy had to be contained within the issue of weapons of mass destruction, the appalling nature of the regime is a reason why we did take and should have taken that action with a strong heart and a good conscience.

(HC Deb 14 April 2003 Vol. 403 c626–627)

16/45

The Foreign Secretary was asked before the FAC:

Can I just turn to weapons of mass destruction. In the course of this conflict, there is the fact that Iraq possessed WMD and it would not comply with the United Nations' inspections team. Could I just put it mildly that it is disappointing that no such weapons appear to have been found yet. I realise it is only 20 days since the fall of Baghdad, but I think everybody would agree that it would have been far better if we could have demonstrated to our own public opinion and to world public opinion that these weapons did really exist. You told the Committee on, I think it was, 4 March that Iraq had a stockpile of such weapons. Can you tell us when we might hope to find that stockpile?

The Foreign Secretary said:

...it is to be expected that the search for these weapons and for further evidence is not going to be something which is going to happen quickly. Let's be clear about this, that the evidence of the threat and the scale of Iraq's chemical and biological weapons programmes was overwhelming and it was so strong that the world community themselves entirely voluntarily passed Resolution 1441 on the 8 November and that resolution begins with the statement that, "The Security Council recognises the threat that Iraq's non-compliance with Council resolutions and its proliferation of weapons of mass destruction and long-range missiles poses to international peace and security". There was sufficient evidence to satisfy the Security Council of that as of the 8 November of last year. It is extremely important that we do not just go into some kind of collective amnesia here. The evidence about these programmes, as I say, is overwhelming. It is charted in the 173 pages of the unanswered disarmament questions, unresolved disarmament issues, Iraq's proscribed weapons programmes which UNMOVIC laid before the Security Council late on Friday 7 March, so it is all there. Along with this evidence, there is all sorts of additional circumstantial evidence. There was in addition during the military action the discovery of the chemical protection suits and the antidote, atropine, which was found in possession of the Iraqis. They would not have had either of those if they had not been anticipating their use of chemical and biological weapons because the one thing they knew for certain was that none of the coalition was going to use them. That is the current position. A lot of effort is going into finding further evidence, but this is not about finding evidence as opposed to there not being any evidence. The evidence was and remains overwhelming and we are looking for further evidence. (Qu. 265)

The Foreign Secretary was asked about weapons inspections following the intervention in Iraq, in particular about the role of UNMOVIC. He said:

It is actually UNMOVIC, Hans Blix who has recognised that the current environment in Iraq is not one in which UNMOVIC inspectors can themselves operate. As I spelled out to the House yesterday, the head of UNMOVIC, Hans Blix, in a statement to the Security Council last week, said, "In a situation that is still insecure, civilian international inspection can hardly operate". He went on, "Some of the premises on which the Security Council established UNMOVIC and gave it far-reaching powers have changed", so for sure that was the case. On the issue of verification and a role for UNMOVIC, that is obviously one of the subjects we are discussing with all of our partners in the Security Council, including the United States. What role is established for UNMOVIC will depend on the outcome of discussions in the Security Council and that in turn depends on whether there is a constructive environment for those discussions or whether we end up by getting bogged down week after week after week in pretty unconstructive discussions without producing a resolution... It does not just depend on the sentiment of the US and the UK, but it depends on the willingness of other parties to reach a constructive agreement... on the issue of verification, I would just make these observations. First of all, in practice, regardless of where UNMOVIC are sited, the initial finds of any WMD, either direct evidence of chemical biological weapons or materials or evidence of documentation or interviews, will come from the coalition forces, and that is the environment in which they are working, so a lot of that is being made to ensure the integrity of their work and that will continue. Secondly, UNMOVIC itself, as I understand it, did not have laboratories itself to provide for verification, so whether a particular substance was a sarin or was a pesticide, they used a number of independent laboratories and it is highly probable that those independent, third-country laboratories would be used in any event. So I understand the case, of course I do, for having UNMOVIC involved. Of course I understand it, but it is as much a question of how this appears as it is a matter of the realities of the inspection and verification process. (Qu.266)

He was asked whether or not a coalition inspection team would be able to establish the independence of its findings. He said:

Discussions with the United States and other colleagues continue. I would also say that it is extremely important that it is not implied that we are in a situation where there was no evidence of the WMD Programme. The evidence is here of the intent of the Iraqi regime before this military action was taken, I put it before the House of Commons. There is also evidence there from the conduct of the Iraqi regime, why did they kick out the weapons inspectors at the end of 1988 if they had nothing to hide? Why did they refuse to cooperate with the Security Council after the passage of the Security Council resolution 1284, establishing UNMOVIC, and continue to refuse to cooperate? We got 1441 through with greater powers and backed that with the threat of military force. Even when the inspectors went in they continued to refuse to cooperate. For example, in respect of a crucial source of evidence, interviews with scientists, they locked up some of the scientists and when UNMOVIC first sought interviews with named scientists the Iraqi Government insisted that five Iraqi Government minders should come along with those scientists. In the end after negotiating, which Blix was involved in, they got that down to one, but there still should not have been anybody there. Despite the clear powers of the inspectors throughout that period, from the passage of 1444 [sic. sc. 1441] on 8 November until military action was taken on 18 March, they refused real cooperation with the interviews of the scientists and not a single scientist was interviewed in a complete, free environment outside Iraq because of the Iraqi Government's intimidation of those scientists and their families. If they had nothing to hide why on earth were they going for that kind of behaviour? The evidence against them was overwhelming. I hope we will find further evidence, but there is no need to look at the crystal because people can see it in the book. (Qu.267)

He was asked further about the lack of discovery of WMDs in Iraq, given the claims about the quantities of various materials said to be held by Iraq, and whether or not as of today do you have any anxiety that this war may have been fought essentially on a false prospectus? He said:

I do not have that anxiety at all, it was not fought on a false prospectus full stop... What the Prime Minister said on 18 March was absolutely accurate. That statement about all of the unaccounted for material and programmes derived from UNSCOM's last report made to the Security Council at the end of January 1999, it was then explained to the Security Council why they had a continuing need to remain as inspectors because of all of the unanswered questions still before the Iraqis. You know what the story was. Those inspectors' lives were made so difficult they had to leave. That is what happened. All of these issues, and many more were unaccounted for. It was that report, plus other evidence which the new inspectors built up on, what they had discovered had happened from 1999, that led to this 173 page report. (Qu.270)

And he asked further, do you have high confidence as of today that these WMD in the quantities to which the Prime Minister referred will be found? He said:

What you are asking me to make a judgment about there is what the Saddam regime has been doing in respect of this material since last summer, and particularly since the military action commenced. I hope very much that the results of the most intensive enquiries that we are making with an awful lot of expert people is to pin down what has happened to them. Has it existed? Yes, without any question. Do we know where it is at the moment? No, because otherwise we would have gone and found it... We have had very good intelligence cover of this country with a lot of agents and despite all of that we still do not know where those weapons are hidden, however, we do know that the weapons exist. (Qu. 271)

A member of the Committee said:

Finally, again I must put this question to you, do you continue to have high confidence in the quality and accuracy of the intelligence you received?

The Foreign Secretary said:

Yes.

(Tenth Report of the FAC, Foreign Policy Aspects of the War against Terrorism, Minutes of Evidence, 29 April 2003, HC 405)

16/46

The Foreign Secretary was asked in the FAC about the negotiations on Resolution 1441:

When 1441 was being negotiated did France at that time provide assurances that it would support a second resolution if Saddam Hussein refused to cooperate with the United Nations weapons inspectors? Why when there were so many public indications that the French would not support did we go ahead and circulate the draft resolution on 4 February? When in the time scale of all this, I do think it is of crucial importance, but perhaps a little bit irrelevant now after the success of the campaign, in those crucial days building up to it when did you conclude that the French Government would veto the second resolution come what may?

He said:

The discussions that took place in late September, the whole of October and early November between ourselves and other key members of the Security

Council took place in a very constructive environment and one of the issues was whether or not a second resolution would be required before military action could take place in respect of a failure by Iraq to meet its obligation. As I think is now very well known the Russians and the French proposed, although they did not move, that there should be a lock-in in what became 1441 preventing military action unless there was a second resolution. There was then negotiation between ourselves, the US, France, Russia and China. The long and the short of that negotiation was that France and Russia accepted that a second resolution was not needed and instead they settled for the procedure that was laid down by operational paragraphs 4, 11, 12 and 13. Paragraph 4 of the resolution sets out what would be a further material breach by Iraq. Paragraph 1 having already said they are in further material breach, paragraph 4 sets out what would amount to a future material breach; 11 talked about a report from the inspectors; 12 that there would then be a further consideration by the Security Council and 13 asserted that if Iraq failed to meet its obligations serious consequences would follow. You cannot read that resolution nor know its negotiating history without knowing that it was accepted on all sides that a further resolution would not necessarily be needed. It was equally accepted by us that there was no "automaticity" in 1441. In other words there had to be a process leading towards any military action in the event of non-compliance by Iraq, which process we followed through. That is the background there. You then asked why we moved a second resolution, notwithstanding the fact that it looked as though there were going to be difficulties. Mr Olner, you may think there are going to be difficulties in a forum, it must be your experience as it is ours, until you put people to the test you do not know that for certain. There were plenty of difficulties anticipated with 1441 which did not arise. That was in late February. I then moved a variation of that at the meeting of the Security Council on 7 March, a few days after I last gave evidence here, that was a Friday, and it was not until the following Monday that President Chirac gave his televised interview, in which he said whatever the circumstances France would vote no. It was not until that point we had confirmation by the Head of State of Government in France that we knew that the second resolution was not going to be possible to get passed. (Qu. 290)

(Tenth Report of the FAC, Foreign Policy Aspects of the War against Terrorism, Minutes of Evidence, 29 April 2003, HC 405)

16/47

In response to a written question, the Secretary of State for Defence wrote:

To date, the main focus for coalition forces has been the establishment of a safe and secure environment in Iraq. This is a necessary precursor to the full achievement of our campaign objectives, as set out in the document placed in the Library of the House on 20 March 2003. There is no doubt that Saddam had programmes to develop weapons of mass destruction. Evidence of these programmes could take any of several forms, for example, samples of chemical or biological agents, delivery systems, research or production facilities, documentation or interviews with relevant Iraqi personnel. No conclusive evidence of Iraqi weapons of mass destruction has yet been discovered, but investigations are at an early stage. We expect gathering and collating evidence from the various sources to be a long and complex task.

(HC Deb 29 April 2003 Vol. 404 c315W–316W)

16/48

In the first edition of what will be annual reports to Parliament, "The United Kingdom in the United Nations", the Government wrote:

...the UK has 1,267 personnel serving in Bosnia, 304 in Kosovo and 415 in Afghanistan, all UN authorised missions.

[ed. There is no reference to coalition forces in Iraq.]

(Para. 37, The United Kingdom in the United Nations, September 2003, Cm 5898)

16/49

During a debate on a draft Security Council resolution on Iraq, the Foreign Secretary said:

The multinational force needs to be authorised by the United Nations and, indeed, that is proposed in the resolution. In any event, the authority for the occupying powers—the United States and the United Kingdom—derives from Security Council resolution 1483. On managing the transition, the simple fact is that the UN has never sought an exclusive role in respect of Iraq; what it seeks is a partnership. The resolution takes account of both the wish of the UN to be more heavily involved and the reluctance of the UN secretariat under Kofi Annan to put too many more of its own officials into the field until they are satisfied about security. Meanwhile, the responsibility has to rest with the governing council and the coalition provisional authority, but working, as the resolution says, in many respects as far as is practicable—in other words, at the call of the Secretary-General of the United Nations—with the UN.

(HC Deb 14 October 2003 Vol. 411 c8)

16/50

In reply to a written question on strike-missions by the RAF in the Iraqi no-fly zone, the Minister of State for Defence wrote:

Coalition aircraft only respond in self-defence to threats from the Iraqi air defence system.

(HC Deb 5 February 2003 Vol. 399 c287W)

16/51

In reply to a written question on Iraq: No-fly Zones, the Parliamentary Under-Secretary of State, MoD, wrote:

Threats to coalition aircraft patrolling the no-fly zones in Iraq include anti-aircraft artillery and/or surface-to-air missile fire, and acquisition by radar.

We do not hold separate threat figures for individual nations' aircraft; they are recorded for the coalition as a whole.

Between 1 November 2002 and 10 February 2003 Iraqi air defence systems threatened coalition aircraft conducting patrols of the no-fly zones on 120 occasions—24 in the north and 96 in the south.

(HL Deb 20 February 2003 Vol. 644 cWA197)

16/52

In reply to a written question the Foreign Minister wrote:

Under the UN Charter, the Security Council has primary responsibility for the maintenance of international peace and security. The EU's security and defence policy can be used to support the UN. This is the case in the operation in the Democratic Republic of Congo, where the EU is operating under a UN Security Council Resolution (UNSCR) mandate. In this case, the UNSCR sets out the mandate for the force and authorises the deployment of the force under that mandate. But the political control and strategic direction of the EU operation within the mandate is a matter for the EU.

The EU can also conduct crisis management operations without requiring a specific UNSCR to authorise the mission; for example, when the EU is operating at the request of the country concerned, as is the case for the EU's mission in Macedonia.

(HL Deb 14 July 2003 Vol. 651 cWA74)

Part Sixteen: II. B.2. *Use of force—Legitimate Use of Force—Collective Measures—outside the United Nations*

16/53

In reply to a written question the Minister of State, FCO, wrote:

The operation in Bunia will be undertaken by the EU in close co-operation with the UN. The Secretary-General/High Representative assisted by the EU Special Representative for the Great Lakes will, in close co-ordination with the European Presidency, act as a primary point of contact with the UN.

The IEMF force commander will maintain contact with the UN mission in the Democratic Republic of the Congo (MONUC) and other international and regional actors in theatre.

The EU's Political and Security Committee (PSC) will exercise the political control and strategic direction of the operation under the responsibility of the Council. The PSC has been authorised by the Council to take the relevant decisions in accordance with Article 25 of the Treaty on European Union. This authorisation includes powers to amend the OPLAN, the chain of command and the rules of engagement. The powers of decision with respect to the objectives and the termination of the operation will however remain vested in the European Council, assisted by the Secretary-General/High Representative.

The EU's Military Committee (EUMC) will monitor the proper execution of the military operation conducted under the responsibility of the operation commander.

France will act as the framework nation for the operation and provide the operational headquarters (OHQ). The OHQ is located in Paris and will include officers from several participating countries as well as officials from the general secretariat of the Council.

The force headquarters is located in Entebbe (Uganda) with an advanced position in Bunia. Major General Bruno Neveux (France) has been appointed the EU operation commander and Jean-Paul Thonier appointed as the EU force commander.

(HL Deb 30 June 2003 Vol. 650 cWA56–WA57)

16/54

A Foreign Office Minister wrote a lecture delivered in London on 9 July 2003 in which he said:

Since the tragic events of 11 September 2001, British forces have twice engaged in sizeable overseas combat operations: against Al Qaida and the regime sheltering them in Afghanistan; and against Saddam Hussein in order to rid Iraq of weapons of mass destruction.

Now, Iraq no longer poses a WMD threat to other countries. And a large-scale programme to bring to light Saddam's WMD programmes and prevent the hardware and technology falling into anyone else's hands is now underway. But WMD programmes elsewhere continue to progress.

How should we tackle the challenges of WMD? Not all in the same way. Our objectives are the same in each case – to eliminate the threat or potential threat of WMD. But we will deploy the tools we judge to be most appropriate and effective in each case.

Only exceptionally will we employ military means. Iraq was exceptional in that it was in breach of 17 SCRs, and showed no sign of ever abandoning its programmes.

There are no plans to use force elsewhere. In other situations we will use other tools. These will include bilateral or multilateral diplomacy, as is the case in North Korea; international non-proliferation regimes, and the verification mechanisms associated with some of them—the IAEA is making use of its verification regime to investigate Iran at present; and national and multilateral export control regimes—few countries are self-sufficient in materials and technology.

To reduce the threat from WMD, the tools we have must be used seriously and effectively. Passing Security Council Resolutions and not following through, agreeing non-proliferation regimes and not implementing them only encourages continuing proliferation. That is what puts the US off multilateralism.

As for the war on terrorism, Afghanistan is no longer a safe haven for Al-Qaida. Their operations worldwide have suffered disruption. Many key operatives have been detained. But the recent attacks in Riyadh and Casablanca show that the danger from Al-Qaida or Al-Qaida style terrorism remains an active one.

Our long-term aim is to eliminate terrorism as a force for change in international affairs. In the next 5 years, the aim is less ambitious: to move the odds in our favour.

How do we deal with the challenge of terrorism? In broad terms, our policy is to work with states which share our concerns and, like us, are working to address them. To work for states which share our concerns but do not possess all the means to address them such as the Philippines or Kenya. To work on states which need a bit of persuasion, such as Yemen. And to work against regimes such as the Taliban which harbour or support terrorists.

We have a toolbox for tackling the challenges within this broad framework:

—Diplomacy to resolve underlying political disputes. Without solving the problems of regional hotspots, breeding grounds for terrorism will persist. The clearest example of this is the Israel/Palestine issue. Which I will return to later.

—Increasing assistance to states to help them develop Counter terrorist capabilities. We now offer assistance to 70 countries. And the FCO is increasing its Counter Terrorism Assistance Budget from some £200,000 last year to £4m this, £8m next and £12m the year after.

—Toughening up domestic legislation and improving international law enforcement and intelligence co-operation. This has included closer police and judicial co-operation in the EU.

—Cracking down on the sources of finance for terrorism. A huge effort has gone into this nationally and through the UN and OECD. And we assess that the range of measures adopted world-wide have impacted significantly on the networks.

—Developing communication strategies, to explain what we are doing and why we need to work together with international partners. Engaging opinion across the Islamic world is extremely important.

—And finally, encouraging good governance and economic development across the Arab world.

(Available at www.fco.gov.uk/speeches)

Part Sixteen: II. C. *Use of force—Legitimate use of force—Others*

16/55

During a House of Lords debate the Minister of State, FCO, said:

As to the question of the mechanism for responding to human rights abuses—or the "just intervention" . . . the United Kingdom participated very actively in the debate on humanitarian intervention which followed the Kosovo conflict. We drew up principles to guide the Security Council in deciding when to intervene but we were unable to secure the agreement of other permanent members.

. . .

I agree that the reasons for intervening in Kosovo were in many ways far more ground-breaking than the issues surrounding the more recent intervention in Iraq. The emergence of the doctrine of overwhelming humanitarian need or overwhelming humanitarian disaster now seems to be a well-accepted basis for such intervention.

(HL Deb 14 May 2003 Vol. 648 c289)

16/56

During a House of Commons debate the Foreign Secretary was asked the following question:

Can he tell the House whether . . . he is working on restoring and strengthening the legal basis on which the UN and, indeed, a coalition of nations might act?

He replied:

I am grateful to my hon. Friend for what he says and the manner in which he says it. The legal argument about whether military action was justified in respect of Iraq emphasised the fact that the legal basis for military action contained in the UN charter, which was agreed just after the last world war, is no longer fully adequate to cope with today's threats. It copes very well with the traditional threats of action being taken by one sovereign nation against another, but it no longer copes with the new set of threats from rogue and/or failing states, terrorism and weapons of mass destruction. How exactly we resolve that is difficult, but it is a matter to which we are applying ourselves, to which the United States is applying itself and to which the European Union in its important draft security strategy, to which we have contributed, is also applying itself, and I undertake to keep the House informed of developments.

(HC Deb 11 November 2003 Vol. 413 c155)

16/57

Further in the same debate the Foreign Secretary said:

We should also look again at the criteria that we use to decide when the international community should intervene. There is no guarantee that the Security

Council would be any more willing to intervene today if it was again faced with a situation like the Rwandan genocide or the Serb actions in Kosovo. No one should be in any doubt that, in some circumstances, it is right, acceptable and just for the international community to intervene in another sovereign state. What happened in Rwanda in 1994 provides the most powerful argument in support of that. It was a damning indictment of the international community of the time that action was not taken.

Starting with the speech made by the Prime Minister in Chicago in 1999, the Government have put forward to the Security Council some possible criteria for intervention, and it is time to look at that issue again. We suggested then that we needed to build a better understanding of the circumstances and conditions in which the international community could act when conflict prevention failed. Intervention can take a number of forms, and the use of force should always be a last resort. We believe that the development of a set of pragmatic understandings on action in response to humanitarian crises would help the Security Council—acting on behalf of the members of the UN as referred to in the charter—to reach consensus when such crises occur, thus ensuring effective and timely action by the international community. Action should be taken only to prevent genocide or major loss of civilian life that could destabilise other states and threaten international peace and security. In those circumstances, force should be used only as a last resort and when a Government have demonstrated their unwillingness or inability to end large-scale civilian suffering within their jurisdiction.

There also has to be a pragmatic element. The scale of actual or potential human suffering must justify the risks and dangers of military action, and there must be clear and relevant objectives and the military means to ensure a high probability of success. The use of force in such circumstances should be collective and limited in scope to actions necessary and proportionate to achieving the humanitarian objective. It must also respect humanitarian law and the Geneva conventions. That, however, is only one possible way of expressing the conditions under which intervention should take place. I believe that it is timely and important that we are having a debate on this issue.

(HC Deb 11 November 2003 Vol. 314 c206–207)

Part Sixteen: III. *Use of force—disarmament and arms control*

(See also **3/8**, **3/9**, and **3/10**)

16/58

In reply to a written question on outstanding UK contracts with countries that face restrictions on arms trading, the Parliamentary Under-Secretary of State for Trade and Industry wrote:

Where a UK, EU or US embargo is placed on a country which is being supplied by a UK contractor, there are established mechanisms in place to ensure the embargo is fully complied with. Implementation periods have been proposed relating to the new legislation to enable applicants to consider how to comply with the new legislation.

(HC Deb 6 May 2003 Vol. 404 c482W)

16/59

During a debate in the House of Lords, the Leader of the House of Commons said:

I am not entirely sure to what extent such a debate [a debate on the United States' refusal to allow international inspectors into many of its chemical plants in order to verify its compliance with the Chemical Weapons Convention] would illuminate the general question of Iraq. However, it is of course the Government's policy that all countries should comply with the chemical weapons convention; indeed, we have urged the Americans to accept an inspection regime.

(HC Deb 6 February 2003 Vol. 399 c454)

16/60

During a debate in the House of Commons, the Secretary of State, FCO, made the following statement:

There are no sanctions against Israel. There are no mandatory resolutions against Israel. A series of resolutions apply to Israel and the occupied territories—to the Palestinians and the Arabs—and we want them all to be implemented, but we are not going to resolve the conflict between Israel and the Palestinians by military action. However, we may be in a situation in which the only way to resolve Iraq's defiance is by military action.

In any event, through the action that we are currently taking and the resolve of the international community in respect of Iraq we not only deal with Iraq but we also raise the game against all other proliferators. In my judgment, if we do that we shall ensure that compliance with international law on the non-proliferation treaty and much else besides is much easier to achieve, because those other countries will see the consequences that follow flagrant violation.

(HC Deb 21 January 2003 Vol. 698 c174)

16/61

In a written answer, the Prime Minister wrote:

I met Amram Mitzna on 9 January and our discussions were on the middle east peace process. The issue of defence exports was raised and I made clear that there is no arms embargo on Israel. We continue to support Israel's right to defend itself, within international law, and to buy arms from British suppliers for this in accordance with the consolidated European Union and national arms export licensing criteria.

(HC Deb 10 February 2003 Vol. 399 c582W)

16/62

In a written answer, the Prime Minister wrote:

The reference in my statement of 3 February was intended to illustrate that the process of disarmament of Iraq's weapons of mass destruction need not be a long drawn out one, provided Iraq gives full co-operation with the UN inspection teams, as required under UNSCR 1441. It need only be a matter of weeks for the UN inspectors to be able to report that Iraq is demonstrating a firm commitment to full and active co-operation with UN inspectors.

In March 1993 the South African Government invited the International Atomic Energy Agency (IAEA) to report on the status of their former nuclear weapons programme. An IAEA technical team visited South Africa for this purpose from 22 April to 4 May and its preliminary assessment was reported to the board that month. A final assessment was made to the board in September 1993.

(HC Deb 10 February 2003 Vol. 399 c656W)

16/63

During a debate in the House of Commons, the Secretary of State, FCO, made the following statement:

As for a substantive resolution on military action, again, we have made it very clear first, that there will be a substantive resolution and, secondly, that it is our earnest intention and hope that that should take place in advance of any military action save in the one circumstance in which we judge that our troops would be put at risk. On such an occasion, the arrangement, as happened with the Conservative Government in January 1991, would take place a few days afterwards. That, too, however, would be very much second best. The overwhelmingly important issue, apart from all the other issues, is that the legitimacy of any action that we take as a British Government should be endorsed by the House, so that if our troops go into any action and place their lives on the line, they do so in the knowledge that they have the support of the British people as represented in the House.

(HC Deb 13 February 2003 Vol. 399 c1061)

16/64

During a debate in the House of Commons, the Secretary of State, FCO, made the following statements:

We are asking all members of the Security Council, when they come to assess the report of Dr. Blix and Dr. el-Baradei, to follow through the true meaning of the language to which every single member of the Security Council signed up on 8 November. We cannot be in the position where we and other members of the Security Council believe that conclusions following from the true meaning of 1441 are inescapable, but one member, for example, seeks to avoid those conclusions. In the end, the decisions that the British Government make must be a matter for the British Government endorsed by the House, not for another member state.

We want a second resolution if we deem military action to be necessary. That has always been our position, but let it also be clear that 1441 is a sufficient mandate for such military action, because 1441 spells out with complete clarity that there are obligations on Iraq that it must follow through—very straightforward obligations. If Iraq follows them through, there will be—there can be—no military action whatever. If Iraq fails to follow those obligations through, it will be in further material breach, and if it is in further material breach, serious consequences—force—will follow. There was a suggestion in the United Nations when we negotiated 1441 that there had to be written into 1441 a requirement for a second resolution if military force was to take place. That was dropped from the final draft, which is how we ended up with 1441 in its present form.

The hon. Gentleman asked me about discussions with my French and Russian counterparts. We have discussions all the time. I shall be having more discussions with Igor Ivanov and Dominique de Villepin tomorrow. I accept entirely, as I did in response to the hon. Member for Rutland and Melton, that we do not want to be involved in recriminations between friendly member states of the United Nations, so we will not get involved in that.

On further United Nations inspections, I said in a speech on Tuesday this week that if the inspectors themselves ask for more resources, of course we will consider that, but we cannot be drawn into the argument from outside the inspectors' ranks, which seeks to imply that, in the absence of co-operation, more inspectors will resolve the matter. They will not. Procrastination is not the solution to the problem; co-operation is.

(HC Deb 13 February 2003 Vol. 399 c1063)

16/65

In reply to a question on Nuclear Disarmament, the Parliamentary Under-Secretary of State, FCO, wrote:

The UK remains fully committed to the Final Document adopted at the Treaty on the Non-Proliferation of Nuclear Weapons (NPT) Review Conference in 2000.

As my right hon. Friend the Secretary of State for Defence explained in answer to my hon. Friend's question of 5 March 2003, *Official Report*, column 1041W, the Government has taken substantial steps in fulfilment of its nuclear disarmament obligations under the NPT. Since 2000 we have continued to make significant progress, including dismantling the UK's last Chevaline warhead in April 2002. We have supported Nuclear-Weapon-Free Zones in Central Asia, South East Asia, and the Middle East. We also continue to press for negotiations to begin on a Fissile Material Cut-Off Treaty.

The United Kingdom supports moves towards mutual, balanced and verifiable reductions in nuclear weapons. We have always made clear that when we were satisfied with verifiable progress towards the elimination of nuclear weapons, we would ensure that our nuclear weapons were included in any negotiations.

(HC Deb 18 March 2003 Vol. 401 c727W)

16/66

In reply to a question on Nuclear Non-proliferation, the Parliamentary Under-Secretary of State, FCO, wrote:

We have regular dialogue on non-proliferation issues with all three states. The issue of their non-signature of the Nuclear Non-Proliferation Treaty (NPT) forms an integral part of that dialogue.

The United Kingdom supports the implementation of UN Security Council Resolution 1172 which calls, among other things, for India and Pakistan to sign and ratify NPT.

We also take all opportunities to urge Israel to resolve international concerns about its nuclear status by acceding to the NPT as a non-nuclear weapons state and have consistently supported resolutions in the United Nations calling for the establishment of a zone free of weapons of mass destruction in the Middle East.

(HC Deb 18 March 2003 Vol. 401 c727W)

16/67

During a debate in the House of Lords on the Arms Control and Disarmament (Inspections) Bill, the Minister of State, FCO, made the following statements:

The Bill concerns the adapted version of the Conventional Armed Forces in Europe Treaty, commonly referred to as the "CFE Treaty", which was signed in Paris on 19th November 1990. The agreement on adaptation of the Conventional Armed Forces in Europe Treaty—more commonly known as the "Adapted CFE Treaty"—was signed by all states party to the CFE Treaty at Istanbul on 19th November 1999.

The original CFE Treaty limits the holdings of five categories of heavy weapons—tanks, armoured combat vehicles, artillery, combat aircraft and attack helicopters—by the 30 member states of NATO and the former Warsaw Pact. The treaty includes an important transparency and verification regime. It is seen as a cornerstone of European security and has resulted in the destruction of more than 50,000 heavy weapons in Europe. However, the treaty was negotiated at the end of the Cold War and it needed to be adapted in order to reflect the break-up of the Warsaw Pact and NATO enlargement.

The Adapted CFE Treaty replaces the old bloc-to-bloc system with national and territorial ceilings for heavy weapons. The Adapted CFE Treaty also provides for greater transparency than the present CFE Treaty through a substantially enhanced system of information provision. In particular, it increases the amount of military information that each of the 30 states party to the treaty must provide and it enhances the regime of inspections. The Adapted CFE Treaty also includes provisions for new European states to join.

The Adapted CFE Treaty provides for inspections of larger areas than in the original CFE Treaty. In the United Kingdom, the fact that increasingly parts of military sites are owned and operated by the private sector means that we need to legislate to allow access to these private sites. The main provisions of this short technical Bill amend the Arms Control and Disarmament (Inspections) Act 1991 to provide for the additional rights of entry to private land which are required to implement the additional inspection requirements of the Protocol on Inspections of the Agreement on Adaptation. It also confers a power to make further amendments to the 1991 Act should they be needed to implement future amendments to the CFE Treaty.

The Bill thus provides the legislation necessary for the UK to ratify the Adapted CFE Treaty quickly when the time is right. While the UK is keen for the Adapted CFE Treaty to come into force as soon as possible, our position and that of our NATO allies is that ratification can be envisaged only in the context of full compliance by all states parties with agreed treaty limits and consistent with the commitments contained in the CFE Final Act.

We and other NATO allies continue to urge Russia to resolve the outstanding issues on Georgia and Moldova. The Secretary of State will not bring the Act into force in accordance with Clause 3 until the Government are ready to ratify the agreement on adaptation. I hope that your Lordships will be able to support the Bill.

(HL Deb 25 November 2002 Vol. 641 c606–607)

16/68

In reply to a written question the Minister of State, FCO, wrote:

We had hoped that Russia would succeed in meeting the extended deadline of 31 December 2003 for removal of its arms and ammunition from Transdneistria. At the OSCE Ministerial in Maastricht on 1 to 2 December 2003, my honourable friend the Minister for Europe (Dr MacShane) expressed regret at Russia's non-fulfilment of its commitment and reiterated the Government's position that Russia must meet this commitment for the Adapted CFE Treaty to be ratified. Russia is continuing to remove its arms and ammunition from Transdneistria, albeit slowly, and we stress the need for compilation of this process without further delay.

(HL Deb 15 December 2003 Vol. 655 cWA99–WA100)

16/69

In response to a written question, the Minister of State, FCO, wrote:

The United Kingdom subscribed to the International Code of Conduct (ICOC) against Ballistic Missiles at its launch in The Hague on 25 November. Her Majesty's Government will be represented at the launch by the Member for North Warwickshire, Mike O'Brien, Parliamentary Under-Secretary of State at the Foreign and Commonwealth Office.

The ICOC is a politically binding agreement designed to tackle the proliferation of ballistic missiles capable of delivering weapons of mass destruction. It does so by promoting transparency and confidence building among states. It consists of principles, commitments and confidence-building measures. It will establish international norms for the first time in the area of ballistic missiles. The code will complement the existing range of international instruments against WMD.

The non-proliferation commitments in the code include a commitment not to contribute to, support or assist any ballistic missile programme in countries which might be developing or acquiring weapons of mass destruction in contravention of international obligations; also to exercise vigilance in assistance to space launch vehicle programmes, given that these can be used to conceal ballistic missile programmes. The code also calls for maximum possible restraint in the development, testing and deployment of ballistic missiles capable of delivering weapons of mass destruction.

The confidence-building and transparency measures are designed to promote confidence through information sharing, in the form of both pre-launch notifications and annual declarations about ballistic missile and space launch programmes. The aim is to boost confidence for instance that space launch vehicle programmes are not being used as cover for ballistic missile programmes.

The code represents a significant step forward for the international community in the area of arms control—in this case, the control of one of the delivery systems of choice for weapons of mass destruction. The UK has played a leading role in the development of the ICOC since its inception. We are calling on all states to subscribe to the code.

(HL Deb 27 November 2002 Vol. 641 cWA47–WA8)

16/70

In reply to the question whether the international code of conduct against the proliferation of ballistic missiles is likely to have sufficiently robust effect to help to deal with the various problems concerning proliferation, the Government representative said:

Yes, my Lords, we have great confidence in the code of conduct. However, it is not the only instrument to deal with arms proliferation. The noble Lord, Lord Howell of Guildford, mentioned in his question that we need to use a range of responses to reinforce our defence against ballistic missile proliferation. In that sense, this is the first multi-arms control instrument in the field of ballistic missiles. It will ensure that the countries that subscribe to it—today, 99 countries subscribe to it and the Government were instrumental in writing its first draft—exercise maximum possible restraint in the development, testing and deployment of ballistic missiles, including where possible reducing national holdings of such missiles.

(HL Deb 9 December 2002 Vol. 642 c3)

16/71

During a debate in the House of Lords on the upgrading of the Fylingdales early warning facility, the Parliamentary Under-Secretary of State, MoD, made the following statement:

Once the Government were confident that they had taken all the views and arguments into account, we were able to come to a final decision. The fundamental test was whether the upgrade would ultimately enhance the security of the United Kingdom and the NATO alliance. It does so by providing the opportunity in future to defend our country and the European continent against the increasing threat from ballistic missiles armed with weapons of mass destruction. Those missiles do not, we believe, present an immediate threat to the United Kingdom population. But it would be an irresponsible government who could claim that such a threat would never develop. RAF Fylingdales would be a crucial building block on which protection for this country could be acquired. Therefore, as I informed noble Lords on 5th February, we have now replied to the United States Government agreeing to their request.

We have debated today the policy implications of that decision. The most important point is that the upgrade of RAF Fylingdales does not imply any commitment to greater participation in the US missile defence system. The US has not requested the basing of interceptors in the UK; nor has it any plans to site an X-band radar in this country.

The United States has, however, offered to extend missile defence coverage to the UK as the evolution of the system permits and subject to appropriate political and financial arrangements. At the appropriate time, the Government will need to consider whether we wish to acquire missile defence capabilities for the United Kingdom. That would involve broad consideration of the strategic circumstances of the time, including an analysis of how the threat is developing and the technological solutions available, and an assessment of the approach that offers best value for money. The insight that the Government and industry will have of the US programme will be of great benefit in informing that analysis. But that would be a discrete decision some way downstream.

The noble Lord, Lord Wallace of Saltaire, commented on leasing arrangements for both Fylingdales and Menwith Hill. I am grateful to him for referring to my recent letter to him. I shall try to make the position as clear as possible. As he said, there is no lease for RAF Fylingdales. The base is not made available to the United States visiting forces (USVF). It is, and will continue to be, commanded and operated by the RAF. The United States visiting forces have never been granted a lease to occupy RAF Menwith Hill, which is a joint US/UK base. The presence of the USVF at RAF Menwith Hill is governed by the NATO SOFA—the Status of Forces Agreement 1951. There are additional confidential government-to-government arrangements covering administrative matters. . . . it is not peculiar or special to Menwith Hill. It exists at all USVF bases in the United Kingdom.

In 1955 and again in 1976, in order to facilitate the commitment of funding by the US Congress for investment in the base, the US authorities were assured of security of tenure at Menwith Hill for a period of 21 years. The arrangements were an administrative mechanism, were not legally binding and did not constitute any form of renewable lease for the site. In 1997, the assurance expired, and no further such security of tenure assurance was required.

. . .

We already have a wide and comprehensive strategy to deal with the proliferation of ballistic missiles and weapons of mass destruction. It includes a wide range of measures, from non-proliferation and counter-proliferation to intelligence co-operation; and from law enforcement and conflict prevention to diplomacy and deterrence. All those will remain crucial elements of the UK's response to proliferation. For example, the UK took a lead in instigating the creation of the new Hague code of conduct against ballistic missile proliferation, a politically binding code to which more than 100 countries have already subscribed.

There can be no guarantee that that wide range of measures will be 100 per cent effective. If, at some point, a ballistic missile is launched at this country, there will be nothing more that co-operation and conflict prevention can do. The only means of preventing catastrophe—defending this country and its people—is shooting that missile down. If noble Lords will forgive me for stating the obvious, I must say that that is all that missile defence can do. It is not for killing people. It is not for threatening other countries. It cannot even attack military targets. The sole purpose of missile defence is to find, intercept and destroy a missile that has already been fired at us in an act of aggression or terror and may carry a weapon of mass destruction.

We should be in no doubt about the existence of that threat.... It is a huge threat to our security. It is often said that threat is a combination of capability and intent. North Korea may be a single flight test away from confirming her ability to reach Europe and the United States with a ballistic missile. Iraq has already shown intent to use weapons of mass destruction and to fire ballistic missiles at its enemies. We must not ignore the evidence.

...

The question is: is there a real problem here—a real threat? The answer of Her Majesty's Government is that there is. It is not just the United States and the UK who face that increasing threat. All our NATO allies recognise the potential threat from weapons of mass destruction.

On a number of occasions the United States has made plain its willingness to extend protection to friends and allies. NATO heads of state and government agreed at the Prague summit, an important decision, to examine ways to address the increasing threat posed by ballistic missile proliferation—not just ballistic theatre missiles, but ballistic missiles that would attack homelands—and initiated a new missile defence feasibility study in that regard.

The Government strongly support this work within NATO. In agreeing to upgrade Fylingdales, we have opened the possibility of this radar being the foundation of a missile defence system protecting the whole of Europe.

(HL Deb 12 March 2003 Vol. 645 c1396–1399)

16/72

In reply to a written question, the Minister of State, FCO, replied:

HMG hosted a successful meeting on strengthening export controls on small arms and light weapons at Lancaster House on 14 and 15 January. Over 50 nations and representatives of international organisations and NGOs attended.

My right honourable friends the Foreign Secretary and the Secretary of State for International Development addressed the delegates.

The meeting was an initiative of the Government's Global Conflict Prevention Pool. The Government's objective was to build on and develop consensus between small arms exporting nations, whether producers or stock-holders, on the need for effective export controls and controls on arms brokers. These were sensitive issues that the Government considered would benefit from further work following the UN Conference on the Illicit Trade in Small Arms and Light Weapons in All its Aspects in 2001.

Recognising the central role for the UN, the meeting discussed ways of taking forward work on international agreement to control the activities of arms brokers. There was also general agreement on the need for effective export controls on small arms.

The UK will report the outcome of the meeting to the United Nations biennial review meeting in July 2003 and follow up on the common ground established at Lancaster House.

The meeting demonstrates the strength of the international consensus to implement more effective controls on small arms exports and brokers. All who attended saw the meeting as a useful initiative to take forward key elements in the international effort to control the spread of small arms, a major factor in instability and conflict, particularly in Africa and in human rights abuses and crime world-wide.

(HL Deb 20 January 2003 Vol. 643 cWA74)

16/73

The FCO sent a memorandum to the FAC about North Korea. It said:

NORTH KOREA

UK POSITION

13. The UK established diplomatic relations with the DPRK on 12 December 2000, and opened its Embassy in Pyongyang in July 2001 as one of the three EU member states (along with Sweden and Germany) represented there. In London, the DPRK was represented by a non-resident Chargé d'Affaires until November 2002, when three North Korean diplomats arrived to establish an Embassy. Bilateral relations have enabled us to raise issues of concern—including the nuclear issue and human rights—directly with DPRK officials in Pyongyang and London. Until the end of 2002, the UK held the local EU Presidency in Pyongyang on behalf of Denmark (a role which passed to Germany in January, on behalf of Greece).

14. As a Depositary power of the NPT and a leading supporter of the Treaty, we have a close interest in resolving the DPRK nuclear issue. We hosted a meeting of the P3 (UK, France, US) on 15 January. As a Nuclear Weapons State and a member of the P5, we have an important role to play in both IAEA and UN Security Council discussions. The US has also encouraged us to take a role in

any multilateral discussions that may take place, in our capacity as an NPT Nuclear Weapons State (NWS). In the EU, too, we have played an active role both during and following our role as local EU Presidency in Pyongyang.

15. The UK has made representations about DPRK's nuclear activities to the North Koreans on a number of occasions, both in London and Pyongyang. Specifically, representations were made by our new Ambassador to Pyongyang, David Slinn, who arrived in mid-November, during his introductory calls on the President, the Foreign Minister and Vice Foreign Minister. He also delivered a demarche on behalf of the EU at the end of December. Further representations were made, including to the DPRK Chargé d'Affaires in London, on 10 January following the announcement by the DPRK of its intention to withdraw from the NPT. In all these contacts, we have made clear our concern to the DPRK authorities, and have advised them to comply with their international obligations.

EU ACTIVITY

16. The EU has discussed the nuclear issue regularly. It has expressed support for the US, Japan and ROK, and has encouraged Russia and China to engage more closely with North Korea. North Korea claims to hold the EU in high regard, and has urged it to influence US thinking, despite regular reminders that the EU fully supports the US position.

17. EU Foreign Ministers discussed North Korea at the General Affairs and External Relations Council (GAERC) meeting on 18/19 November. Conclusions from that meeting called upon North Korea to reduce regional tension and to comply with its international obligations. The GAERC met again on 27 January, when EU Foreign Ministers agreed that preparations for a possible future high level visit to Pyongyang should begin.

(Tenth Report of the FAC, Foreign Policy Aspects of the War Against Terrorism, 31 July 2003, HC 405)

16/74

In reply to a written question, the Under-Secretary of State, FCO, wrote:

The UK supports the implementation of UN Security Council Resolution 1172, adopted on 6 June 1999, which calls upon both India and Pakistan to cease nuclear testing, to stop their programmes for the development of nuclear weapons and systems for delivery of such weapons, and to enter into dialogue to reduce (and ultimately remove) tensions between them. It also urges both states to accede to both the Nuclear Non-Proliferation Treaty and the Comprehensive Nuclear Test Ban Treaty without delay and without conditions.

We regularly press both countries to abide by all the obligations placed upon them by this resolution.

(HC Deb 31 January 2003 Vol. 398 c1081W)

16/75

In reply to a written question, the Minister of State, Trade and Industry wrote:

In the European Union, the ownership of nuclear materials is governed by the Euratom provisions that deal with the supply of nuclear materials (essentially Chapter 6 of the Euratom Treaty). These provide that exchanges of material—which are basically a commercial matter for the companies concerned—require the approval of the Euratom Supply Agency on a case-by-case basis.

External obligations, for example limiting the use of such material to peaceful, non-explosive purposes, are, however, a feature of some international nuclear co-operation agreements, such as those between Euratom and the United States, Euratom and Australia and Euratom and Canada. In some cases where there are no Euratom agreements in place, there are bilateral agreements which contain comparable provisions. The owners of nuclear material can request that external obligations attached to one batch of material can be exchanged or swapped for different obligations on another equivalent batch of material. Each such request for a swap involving material that is subject to Euratom co-operation agreements must be approved by the Services of the European Commission, whose assessment takes account of the characteristics of the nuclear material concerned (i.e. to ensure that the swap would not diminish the obligations involved) and the reasoning behind the request.

(HC Deb 31 January 2003 Vol. 398 c1062W)

16/76

In reply to a written question, the Under-Secretary of State, FCO, wrote:

We regularly urge Israel to resolve international concerns about its nuclear status by acceding to the Nuclear Non-Proliferation Treaty as a non-nuclear weapons state and to enter into a full safeguards agreement with the IAEA. We also use our bilateral contacts with them to raise the issue of Israeli accession to the Chemical Weapons Convention and the Biological and Toxin Weapons Convention.

The UK has consistently supported a number of resolutions at the UN calling for the establishment of a Middle East Zone Free of Weapons of Mass Destruction.

(HC Deb 31 January 2003 Vol. 398 c1082W)

16/77

In a written answer, the Under-Secretary of State wrote:

The term "Rogue State" was first used by the Clinton Administration in the US to describe states which were pursuing illicit programmes to develop weapons of mass destruction (WMD) and those which the US Administration considered posed a threat to the US. The term has become widely used by media and commentators to describe states of proliferation concern and those which provide succour and support for terrorism. The Government generally prefers to use the phrase "Countries of Concern" to describe such states, although "Rogue States" has also been used for this purpose.

We continue to be concerned by the proliferation of WMD and the means for their delivery in several regions including the Middle East, South Asia and the Korean Peninsula.

We are also concerned about state support for terrorist activity in a number of countries. In the light of the continuing campaign against terror, it is not possible at this time to specifically name publicly any of the countries about which we are concerned or to speculate on any action that might be taken to counter our concerns.

(HC Deb 4 February 2003 Vol. 399 c205W)

16/78

In reply to a written question, the Under-Secretary of State, FCO, wrote:

We deplore North Korea's recent actions, including the expulsion of the International Atomic Energy Agency (IAEA) monitors from Yongbyon, and the stated intention to withdraw from the Nuclear Non-Proliferation Treaty. We have repeatedly made clear that North Korea must re-admit the inspectors and comply with its international obligations in full. We are working closely with the United States and regional partners, and through the IAEA, for a peaceful solution. The IAEA Board of Governors met on 12 February to discuss the matter further.

(HC Deb 13 February 2003 Vol. 399 c942W)

16/79

In reply to a written question, the Secretary of State for Defence wrote:

The United Kingdom has an excellent record in fulfilling its NPT obligations both on non-proliferation and on nuclear disarmament.

In order to prevent the spread of nuclear weapons the Government has taken the following measures to create regional nuclear weapon free zones and help stop non-nuclear weapon states from acquiring the ability to produce and test nuclear weapons:

> Ratified the relevant protocols to the Treaty of Raratonga (South Pacific Nuclear Weapon Free Zone) and signed and ratified the relevant protocols to the Treaty of Pelindaba (African Nuclear Weapon Free Zone) as well as to the Antarctic Treaty and the Treaty of Tlatelolco (Latin American and Caribbean Nuclear Weapon Free Zone);
>
> Supported Nuclear Weapon-Free Zones in Central Asia, South East Asia, and the Middle East, and is in negotiations with the relevant states for the first two of these;

Continued to press for negotiations to begin at the Conference on Disarmament in Geneva of a Fissile Material Cut-Off Treaty;

Ratified the Comprehensive Nuclear Test Ban Treaty (CTBT) and promoted its early entry into force.

To gain implementation of further non-proliferation measures aimed at preventing the diversion of civil nuclear material to military nuclear programmes the UK has:

Supported universal application of Comprehensive Safeguards Agreements;

Urged all States that have not yet done so to conclude and bring into force Additional Protocols to strengthen the safeguards system.

The UK is an active member of the Nuclear Suppliers Group and the Zangger Committee, which work to control the export and transfer of nuclear and dual use items.

To help reduce the chances of nuclear materials falling into unauthorised hands, and to terrorists, the UK is supporting amendments to improve the Convention on the Physical Protection of Nuclear Materials. The UK has also made significant voluntary contributions to the IAEA's Nuclear Security Fund, established after September 11. We have pledged a total of 750,000 over three years.

To help address the nuclear proliferation risk posed by the nuclear legacy left by the Former Soviet Union the UK committed in July 2002 up to $750 million over 10 years towards the G8 Global Partnership Against the Spread of Weapons and Materials of Mass Destruction. This includes a programme to help dispose of surplus Russian weapons grade plutonium so that it cannot be used in weapons. In the three year period ending March 2004 the UK will spend up to $84 million for the development of other programmes to deal with nuclear security and safety risks in the Former Soviet Union.

The UK continues actively to support efforts to resolve the unanswered questions about Iraq's nuclear programmes. We have also deplored North Korea's announced intention to withdraw from the NPT and supported IAEA resolutions aimed at achieving North Korea's compliance with its safeguards obligations. The Government has strengthened its ability to take action against anyone in the UK or UK citizens abroad seeking to develop, obtain or use nuclear weapons and created new offences for those seeking to do so.

To actively move towards the elimination of UK nuclear weapons the UK has:

Withdrawn and dismantled the RAF's freefall nuclear bomb so that Trident is now our only nuclear weapons system;

Reduced our operationally available stockpile to fewer than 200 warheads, which is a reduction of more than 70 per cent in the potential explosive power of our nuclear forces since the end of the Cold War;

Dismantled the UK's last Chevaline warhead in April 2002;

Reduced the readiness of our nuclear forces. Only a single Trident submarine is now on deterrent patrol, carrying 48 warheads. The submarine on patrol is normally on several days "notice to fire" and its missiles are de-targeted;

Placed fissile material no longer required for defence purposes under international safeguards and all enrichment and reprocessing facilities in the UK are now liable to international inspection;

Been more transparent about our nuclear and fissile material stockpiles and begun a national historical accounting study for fissile material produced;

Published an initial summary report on the verification of the reduction and elimination of nuclear weapons. The Atomic Weapons Establishment Aldermaston is undertaking work on this issue.

(HC Deb 5 March 2003 Vol. 400 c1031W–1033W)

16/80

In a written answer, the Under-Secretary of State, FCO, wrote:

North Korea has not admitted to possession of any weapons of mass destruction. However, since being confronted by the US over its covert uranium enrichment programme in October 2002, a Foreign Ministry spokesman claimed on 25 October that North Korea was "entitled to possess" nuclear weapons as well as weapons "more powerful" than nuclear weapons.

North Korean possession of nuclear weapons would be a clear violation of its international obligations as a State Party to the NPT. North Korea is also a State Party to the Biological and Toxin Weapons Convention, but has neither signed nor ratified the Chemical Weapons Convention.

(HC Deb 5 March 2003 Vol. 400 c1060W)

16/81

During a debate in the House of Lords, the Minister of State, FCO, made the following statements:

While so much international attention currently focuses on Iraq, he is right to remind us that it is important that we remember that we face in North Korea another serious challenge to international security and to the international efforts to restrain and counter the proliferation of weapons of mass destruction. I thank the noble Lord very much for his well-researched and excellent contribution this evening.

. . .

On the principal issues of this debate, proliferation and human rights, North Korea's record is undoubtedly utterly abysmal. All noble Lords this evening have provided substantial evidence of that. Perhaps I may add to some of the points made on the nuclear programme. North Korea admitted in discussions with US officials in early October that it had been pursuing a clandestine uranium enrichment programme. However, we have no hard evidence that North Korea has actually produced nuclear weapons. But I say to the noble Lord, Lord Howell, that we assess that they have sufficient fissile material already to make one or two nuclear weapons and the technical capability to produce them. So it is a very grim picture indeed.

...

The noble Lord, Lord Alton, asked about the UK position on negotiations. Engagement with North Korea is enormously difficult, but it is necessary in order to encourage North Korea to become a responsible member of the international community, from which it is so isolated. We decided to establish diplomatic relations with North Korea in December 2000 and to open an embassy in Pyongyang in July 2001. We are convinced that it is better to talk to each other rather than past each other. We are still trying to do so...

(HL Deb 13 March 2003 Vol. 645 c1563–1564)

16/82

In reply to a written question, the Under-Secretary of State, FCO, wrote:

We assess that North Korea has the technical capacity to manufacture nuclear weapons, and that the volume of plutonium it has diverted from its nuclear programme would be sufficient to make one or two weapons. We also believe that North Korea could flight test a missile with the potential to reach Europe within weeks of a decision to do so. Once such a missile was flight-tested, it would take several years to deploy the missile operationally.

Assessment of threat is based on both capability and intent. We currently have no evidence of North Korean intent to target the UK.

We deplore North Korea's recent actions, including the expulsion of the International Atomic Energy Agency (IAEA) monitors from Yongbyon, and the stated intention to withdraw from the Nuclear Non-Proliferation Treaty.

(HC Deb 14 March 2003 Vol. 401 c446W–447W)

16/83

In reply to a written question, the Under-Secretary of State, FCO, wrote:

During this period, my right hon. Friend the Foreign Secretary has regularly discussed North Korea with his counterparts in the United States, the European Union and with colleagues in the UN Security Council. I have also held discussions with the President of the Republic of Korea, and with counterparts from the United States, Japan, China, Russia and Australia. We have argued for a consistent message from the international community calling on North Korea to commit itself fully to international non-proliferation agreements, and to respond to the invitation to discuss in a multilateral forum the security concerns it has raised.

(HC Deb 24 March 2003 Vol. 402 c73W)

16/84

In an oral answer, the Prime Minister said:

No, we are not contemplating military action against North Korea, but that remains my position. I would simply point out two things to the hon. Gentleman. First, it is important that we deal with the nuclear weapons programme of North Korea, because that is a threat to the outside world. There is no doubt about that, and it is interesting that some of the strongest statements of support for the coalition military action in Iraq came from Japan and South Korea, which know very well the dangers of living next door to an unstable and repressive regime with weapons of mass destruction.

(HC Deb 26 March 2003 Vol. 402 c286)

16/85

In response to a written question, the Parliamentary Under-Secretary of State, FCO, wrote:

The UK supports the establishment of nuclear weapon free zones on the basis of arrangements freely arrived at among the states of the region concerned. Together with China, France, Russia and the United States, we have participated in formal consultations with the five Central Asian States concerning the establishment of the draft Central Asian Nuclear Weapon-Free Zone and its draft Protocol. As a nuclear weapon State the UK intends giving a negative security assurance to those States forming this zone, by becoming party to the draft Protocol. This would be subject to satisfactory conclusion being reached over the language in the draft Treaty and Protocol.

(HC Deb 9 April 2003 Vol. 403 c307W)

16/86

During a debate in the House of Lords on the G8 Summit, a representative of Her Majesty's Government said:

The noble Lord asked about military force being used against Korea and the noble Baroness asked about military force being used against Iran. The answer is to be found in paragraphs 3 and 4 of the G8 declaration on non-proliferation of weapons of mass destruction. Paragraph 3 states:

"We have a range of tools available to tackle this threat",

and, right at the end of that paragraph,

"if necessary other measures in accordance with international law".

Paragraph 4 states:

"While all these instruments are necessary, none is sufficient by itself".

So I think that that gives the answer.

(HL Deb 4 June 2003 Vol. 648 c1335)

16/87

In response to a written question, the Parliamentary Under-Secretary of State, FCO, wrote:

We consistently urge Israel to accede to the Nuclear Non-Proliferation Treaty as a non-nuclear weapons state, and to sign a full-scope safeguards agreement with the International Atomic Energy Agency (IAEA). We did this most recently during official-level talks with the Israeli Government in Tel Aviv in March 2003. Under the agreement with IAEA, Israel's nuclear facilities would be subject to regular inspection to detect and eliminate any diversion of nuclear materials for weapons production.

(HC Deb 9 April 2003 Vol. 403 c308W)

16/88

In reply to a written question the Minister of State, FCO, wrote:

There is no universally-accepted definition of the term weapons of mass destruction (WMD), however, it is generally taken to mean nuclear, chemical and biological weapons.

Under the terms of the Nuclear Non-Proliferation Treaty, the United Kingdom, the United States, France, Russia and China are legally entitled to possess nuclear weapons. Additionally, India and Pakistan have tested nuclear devices. We continue to urge Israel to resolve international concerns about its nuclear status by acceding to the Nuclear Non-Proliferation Treaty as a non-nuclear weapons state.

There are four states parties to the Chemical Weapons Convention that have declared possession of chemical weapons. They are currently in the process of destroying them in accordance with their obligations under the convention.

The Government have made clear in recent months that we continue to believe that Iraq had produced and had active programmes for production of WMD. We are also aware of, and very concerned by, persistent reports that Iran, The Democratic People's Republic of Korea, Libya and Syria are pursuing programmes for the development of WMD and the means for their delivery.

(HL Deb 21 October 2003 Vol. 653 cWA159)

16/89

In reply to a written question the Minister of State, FCO, wrote:

Together with his French and German colleagues, my right honourable friend the Foreign Secretary visited Tehran on 21 October for discussions on Iran's nuclear programme. They met President Khatami, Foreign Minister Kharrazi and the Secretary of the Supreme National Security Committee Hassan Rouhani. The discussions were aimed at underlining to the Iranian authorities the concerns of the international community regarding Iran's nuclear ambitions, and the necessity for Iran to comply fully with the requirements of the International Atomic Energy Agency (IAEA) board of governors' resolution adopted on 12 September.

By the end of the visit, they were able to agree a joint statement which committed Iran to comply with the three key elements of the IAEA board resolution:

> to engage in full co-operation with the IAEA to address and resolve, through full transparency, all requirements and outstanding issues of the agency, and clarify and correct any possible failures and deficiencies within the IAEA;
>
> to sign the IAEA additional protocol, and commence ratification procedures. As a confirmation of their good intentions, the Iranian Government state that they will continue to co-operate with the agency in accordance with the protocol in advance of its ratification;
>
> to suspend all uranium enrichment and reprocessing activities, as defined by the IAEA.

...

This joint statement represents a good start to the process of resolving international concerns over Iran's nuclear programme and is welcomed as such. But it was also made clear to the Iranian interlocutors that the real test will be full and early implementation of the commitments they have offered. They know that the international community will be looking closely at the evidence in the next report of the IAEA director-general, which is due to be presented to the board of governors in early November.

The joint statement makes clear that, while implementation of the steps outlined should enable the IAEA board to resolve the immediate problem with Iran, there is also a longer-term issue. Britain, France and Germany remain ready to address that issue through dialogue with Iran on a basis for longer-term co-operation, which would provide all parties with satisfactory assurances about Iran's nuclear power generation programme. It was made clear that it is only once international concerns are fully resolved that Iran could expect easier access to modern technology and supplies.

The visit has demonstrated the value of a united approach between Britain, France and Germany, working to uphold the decisions of the IAEA and its board of governors, and consistent with the common approach to Iran agreed by several European Councils.

(HL Deb 29 October 2003 Vol. 654 cWA40)

16/90

During a House of Lords debate on Iran, the Government spokesperson for Foreign Affairs and Defence said:

We start from a simple premise. We do not question the right of any country to generate electricity by nuclear power, provided—this is an important condition—that it complies fully with its international obligations on the subject. The joint statement in Tehran last month by the Foreign Secretary and his French and German counterparts, to which the noble Lord referred, stated that clearly.

However, under the non-proliferation treaty it is unacceptable for non-nuclear weapon states to seek to acquire nuclear weapons. In the Middle East it could seriously destabilise international peace and security. Recent reports by the International Atomic Energy Agency (IAEA) have given reasons to suspect that Iran has not been fully transparent with the agency or fully compliant with its safeguards obligations under the non-proliferation treaty.

Those suspicions cannot be dismissed as part of a western scheme against the Islamic Republic. They are shared by the entire international community, as the noble Lord, Lord Howell, stated. We saw that clearly in September when the IAEA board of governors passed its resolution by consensus. That resolution is intended to exercise a constructive influence. It requires Iran to take measures that would enable it to resolve the outstanding issues of concern identified by the IAEA in its reports.

As the House is aware, the Foreign Secretary and his French and German counterparts visited Tehran last month. The aim was to bring home to Iran the seriousness and urgency of international concerns and the need to act decisively to address them. Following that visit, Iran has undertaken to sign, ratify and implement an additional protocol to its safeguards agreement. That will allow for short-notice visits by IAEA inspectors to a wider variety of nuclear sites. Iran has also undertaken to act right away as if such a protocol were already in force. It has said it will co-operate in full with the IAEA and be fully transparent with the agency about its nuclear activity. It has undertaken to suspend all uranium enrichment and reprocessing activity as defined by the agency. Those are welcome promises and reflect the main points in the IAEA board resolution. They are, indeed, a step in the right direction.

The key is Iran's willingness to turn them into reality. In our view Iran could create an atmosphere of increased trust quickly and easily. The onus is on Iran to take action. Iran has already taken some welcome steps in the past three weeks. It has supplied the agency with further details of past nuclear activity. It has sent the IAEA a formal letter signalling its intention to sign an additional protocol and announced a halt to enrichment and reprocessing activities. We recognise that those have been significant steps. We also believe that they are in Iran's interest.

The next step will be discussion at the IAEA board of governors' meeting on 20th November and although noble Lords have referred to it, I hope that they will understand that it would be imprudent of me to speculate today on the outcome of that meeting. The agency's director-general, Dr Mohammed El-Baradei, submitted his latest report on Monday. It needs careful reading and analysis.

The Government's view is that the board should work to maintain the credibility of the IAEA and of the non-proliferation regime. It would be damaging if the agency were to accept less than full co-operation and transparency from a member state or, having set out the requirements in its September resolution, were now to accept less than full compliance.

I am confident that the agency will likewise be clear in reporting Iran's past failures to disclose information or breaches of its safeguards obligations. Iran should not see this as a negative step. It is one that can be used to build trust and help address the long-running challenge, which is to establish international confidence that the intentions of Iran's nuclear programme are solely peaceful.

(HL Deb 13 November 2003 Vol. 654 c1724–1725)

16/91

In reply to a written question the Defence Minister wrote:

The scope of the Non-Proliferation Treaty (NPT) is clearly restricted to nuclear weapons or other nuclear explosive devices. However, the UK raised the issue of the possible malevolent use of high-level radioactive sources by terrorists in its Statement to the Second Session of the Preparatory Committee for the NPT 2005 Review Conference on 6 May 2003. As we indicated in that Statement, we supported the work of the IAEA in concluding its Code of Conduct on the Safety and Security of Radioactive Sources which was adopted in September this year, and we encourage the IAEA in its more security-focused work relating to radioactive sources. We welcomed the findings of the international conference on the Security of Radioactive Sources held in Vienna in March 2003. We support both the G8 Statement and its Action Plan on securing radioactive sources agreed at the Evian Summit earlier this year.

(HC Deb 8 December 2003 Vol. 415 c275W)

16/92

In reply to a written question, the Under-Secretary of State, FCO, wrote:

There is an EU arms embargo against the Democratic Republic of Congo, last revised by Common Position 2002/829/CFSP of 21 October 2002.

The EU adopted Common Position 2002/145/CFSP on 18 February 2002 introducing targeted sanctions against Zimbabwe. These measures include an arms embargo, an embargo against items that could be used for internal repression, a travel ban and an asset freeze. These last two measures are targeted against 79 members of the ruling Zanu-PF party.

It is the responsibility of each EU Member State to ensure that they enforce each of these sanctions regimes.

(HC Deb 12 February 2003 Vol. 399 c791W)

16/93

In reply to a written question, the Under-Secretary of State, FCO, wrote:

The UK regularly exchanges information with its EU partners, both bilaterally and in multilateral fora such as the EU Committee on Conventional Arms Export Policy (COARM), the Wassenaar Arrangement, the Nuclear Suppliers'

Group, the Australia Group and within the Organisation for Security and Co-operation in Europe.

Under the EU Code of Conduct on Arms Exports, which relates to conventional arms, there is a Denial Notification (DN) system. EU Code of Conduct DNs are issued for all military listed and dual-use goods which have been refused a licence for export by a member state. No member state may export essentially identical goods, without first consulting the member state that issued the denial notification. Member states also contribute information about their arms export policy and licensing activity for inclusion in an annual report.

Only a minority of EU member states have legislation which controls the trafficking of arms.

(HC Deb 13 February 2003 Vol. 399 c934W)

16/94

In a written Ministerial Statement, the Secretary of State, FCO, wrote:

In our view the Israeli assurances do not cover equipment consisting of components exported by the UK to a third country, which components were then incorporated in that country into products for onward export. The Foreign Secretary's announcement of 8 July 2002 set out how the Government will approach licence applications for goods where it is understood that the goods are to be incorporated into products for onward export.

We intend to inform the Israelis of the results of our inquiries. We shall re-emphasise our current concerns about exporting arms to Israel that might be used against Palestinian targets, and that our policy on assessing Israeli export applications has not changed: we shall continue to assess export licence applications for the proposed export of controlled goods to Israel on a case-by-case basis against the consolidated EU and national arms export licensing criteria.

Our staff will continue to monitor the deployment and the use of equipment by the IDF in the OTs during their regular tours of the West Bank, Gaza and East Jerusalem; and will report to me any sightings of British-supplied equipment.

(HC Deb 28 February 2003 Vol. 400 c63WS)

16/95

In a written answer, the Parliamentary Under-Secretary of State, FCO, wrote:

The Department of Trade and Industry's export control organisation records the type of toxic chemical precursors sold to Syria, if the items are controlled for strategic reasons and an export licence application has been submitted. As with any other specific product, information on items licensed for export is normally commercially confidential and exempt from disclosure.

Since some toxic chemical precursors have legitimate uses, officials are well aware of the special risks that exist in relation to weapons of mass destruction (WMD), and for this reason give extremely careful scrutiny to all applications that involve potential WMD concerns.

(HC Deb 29 April 2003 Vol. 404 c310W)

16/96

In response to a written question, the Under-Secretary of State, FCO, wrote:

Since entry into force of the Chemical Weapons Convention in 1997, the United States has accepted the continuous monitoring of the destruction of its chemical weapons (CW) stockpiles, as well as regular OPCW inspections of its former CW production facilities. Inspections at US industrial facilities only began in May 2000, as a result of a delay in putting in place the necessary domestic enabling legislation. During that time the United Kingdom regularly urged the US to remedy this deficiency at the earliest opportunity. To date the United States has in fact hosted more CW inspections than any other State Party, and the bulk of the inspector-person days expended by the Organisation for the Prohibition of Chemical Weapons have been in the United States.

(HC Deb 13 March 2003 Vol. 401 c409W–410W)

16/97

In a written Ministerial Statement on Export Licences (Bosnia), the Minister for Europe wrote:

The Government have approved the export of four military-listed portable explosive detectors to the NATO Stabilisation Force (SFOR) headquarters in Sarajevo. Bosnia-Herzegovina is subject to an EU arms embargo, from which only de-mining equipment and the transfer of small arms to the police are specifically exempt. The embargo was put in place to ensure the safety of international troops and civilians deployed locally. SFOR requires this equipment for the protection of its premises and personnel.

This decision was made in accordance with our practice occasionally to make an exemption to our interpretation of the embargo by approving exports of non-lethal military goods to humanitarian, media or peacekeeping organisations where it is clear that the embargo was not intended to prevent those exports and there is a strong humanitarian case for them.

HMG fully supports SFOR and recognises its legitimate need for the right equipment to carry out its job safely and effectively. The decision underlines HMG's continued support for the work being done by SFOR in maintaining security and development in Bosnia-Herzegovina.

(HC Deb 25 March 2003 Vol. 402 c6WS)

16/98

In a Ministerial Statement on Dual-Use Exports (Zimbabwe), the Parliamentary Under-Secretary of State, FCO, wrote:

The Government have approved the export to Zimbabwe of a Travelling Wave Tube (TWT) which has been repaired in the UK. A TWT is radar equipment used for air traffic control.

The export licence was initially rejected because the TWT appeared on the military list. Its export would therefore have contravened the EU Arms Embargo on Zimbabwe.

The TWT has since been modified so that it is no longer suitable for military use. As a result, DTI Technologies Unit re-rated the TWT making it now a dual-use good.

The decision to overturn the original rejection was made after discussion with Export Control section of Defence Intelligence Service. They have established that the equipment is for use at Bulawayo and Harare airports. There is no Zimbabwe air force facility at Bulawayo. There is one near the civil airport in Harare, but the military have their own radar. We are therefore satisfied that the TWT is for civilian use only.

This decision underlines our policy that targeted sanctions imposed on Zimbabwe should not affect the lives of ordinary people unconnected with the Mugabe regime.

(HC Deb 9 April 2003 Vol. 403 c24WS)

Part Seventeen: I. A. *The Law of Armed Conflict and International Humanitarian Law—International armed conflict—Definition*

17/1

In reply to an oral question on declarations of war, the Attorney-General stated:

The last time there was a declaration of war was in 1939. It is not necessary to make a declaration of war these days. Since then, we have been involved in a number of armed conflicts. The existence or not of a legal state of war is nowadays irrelevant for most purposes of international law. The application of what used to be called "the law of war" and the status of prisoners of war depends upon the existence of an armed conflict, which is a factual situation and not a question of a declaration of a state of war. Whether there is a state of war might still be relevant for certain purposes of domestic law; for example, as regards the application of certain private contracts referring to war.

(HL Deb 19 February 2003 Vol. 644 c1139)

Part Seventeen: I. B.2. *The Law of Armed Conflict and International Humanitarian Law—International armed conflict—The law of international armed conflict—The commencement of international armed conflict and its effects (for example diplomatic and consular relations, treaties, private property, nationality, trading with the enemy, locus standi personae in judicio)*

17/2

During a debate in the House of Commons, the Prime Minister made the following statements:

We obviously want to see sanctions lifted as quickly as possible, which will allow the Iraqi interim authority, once it is established, to operate far more freely. We should make as speedy progress as we can on that. The debts of countries were discussed at the International Monetary Fund and World Bank meetings at the weekend and are being looked at by the Paris Club. I hope that people are generous in recognising Iraq's needs for the future.

In respect of the Iraqi interim authority and the UN, the issues have been somewhat superseded by the fact that we have agreed a process through which we will work with the UN Secretary-General to try to ensure that the right names and people come forward. In the south of the country we have already started the idea of a joint commission to get the right people to come forward—similar to what happened in Afghanistan—but in the end it will have to be endorsed by the United Nations. That was agreed several weeks ago and remains the case. I believe that, with good will, the problem can be well managed. In a sense, the IMF and World Bank meetings at the weekend went better than they might have gone, which is important.

(HC Deb 14 April 2003 Vol. 403 c620)

17/3

During a debate in the House of Commons, the Prime Minister made the following statements:

In relation to United Nations involvement [ed. in post-invasion Iraq], we have the right framework within which that can happen. There should be a vital role for the UN at every stage, but we should not get into a competition between the coalition and the UN. If we approach the process in the right spirit—one of working together—we will find our way through. The fact that Kofi Annan has appointed a special adviser is a good omen in that regard.

. . .

On what was said about Syria and the break with previous policies, support for terrorism—terrorism that deeply, adversely affects the middle east peace process—should stop, and it should stop irrespective of what has happened in relation to Iraq. We have continually made that clear to Syria. On chemical weapons, people are simply pointing out that Syria is not a signatory to the chemical weapons convention. If Syria does have chemical weapons in its possession, it should be a signatory.

(HC Deb 14 April 2003 Vol. 403 c622)

17/4

During a debate in the House of Commons, the Prime Minister made the following statement:

I said that there are no plans whatever to invade Syria. All sorts of things may come out of the newspapers about various conspiracy theories to do with parts of the American Administration, but I have the advantage of talking regularly to the American President and I can assure my hon. Friend that there are no plans to invade Syria. What people are saying, however, is that it is important that Syria does not harbour people from Saddam's regime or allow any transfer of material from Iraq to Syria. I have spoken to President Assad and he has assured me that that is not happening. I have told him that it is important that he makes sure that that assurance is valid.

(HC Deb 14 April 2003 Vol. 403 c624–625)

17/5

During a debate in the House of Commons, the Prime Minister was asked the following oral question:

Everyone rejoices at the fall of a brutal dictatorship, but will my right hon. Friend share with the House his thinking about how any subsequent war crimes tribunal may be able to bring to justice the perpetrators of the very many human rights abuses that happened in Iraq over the years of the Saddam dictatorship?

In reply the Prime Minister said:

We are discussing it with our allies and with the United Nations. It is important that any such tribunal would have legitimacy and would obviously be based in Iraq.

(HC Deb 14 April 2003 Vol. 403 c629)

17/6

During a debate in the House of Commons, the Prime Minister was asked the following oral question:

[I]s it not true that part of the rebuilding process requires the UN to take a hard look at how it deals with states that have developed weapons of mass destruction, are brutalising their own people and are destabilising the region, therefore making the middle east, in many respects, the cockpit of violence for so many years? Part of that reassessment must be an ability to deal with—let us face it—psychopathic killers who take over nation states, destabilise the area and kill their own people. We are not dealing with that because the UN was initially set up for a different purpose. The world has changed and we now need to change the UN.

In reply the Prime Minister said:

The point that my hon. Friend makes is right in the sense that such states pose a real threat. However, there are different ways to deal with them. In some circumstances, we can enter into a dialogue with those countries and help them out of the situation that they are in. One thing is clear: the continuation of brutally repressive regimes, allied to weapons of mass destruction, is a threat. That is why we have to deal with them and why the UN has to come together to do that in a concerted way.

(HC Deb 14 April 2003 Vol. 403 c631–632)

17/7

In reply to a written question on what role is envisaged for other countries in *(a)* providing humanitarian aid and *(b)* providing peacekeeping troops in a post-war Iraq, the Secretary of State for International Development wrote:

It is premature to consider the composition of any UN peacekeeping operation for Iraq. For the immediate future the coalition forces will be responsible for security in Iraq under the terms of the Geneva Convention and Hague Regulations.

(HC Deb 14 April 2003 Vol. 403 c515W)

17/8

During a debate in the House of Commons, the Secretary of State, FCO, made the following statement:

As President Bush and my right hon. Friend the Prime Minister have made clear, the United Nations will have a vital role in Iraq's reconstruction. Last week the UN Security Council unanimously adopted resolution 1476, which will extend the new arrangements for the UN's oil-for-food programme until 3 June.

In the coming weeks, the Security Council will have to consider a range of other issues. Those will include the future of the sanctions regime and the subsequent management of Iraq's oil revenues.

There is also the question of the future arrangements for verifying Iraq's disarmament of weapons of mass destruction. In his presentation to the Security Council last week, the head of UNMOVIC, Dr. Hans Blix, recognised that

> "in a situation that is still insecure . . . civilian international inspection can hardly operate", and that "some of the premises upon which the Council established UNMOVIC and gave it far-reaching powers . . . have changed".

He also accepted that coalition authorities would be as eager as UNMOVIC to find weapons of mass destruction.

In the absence of the secure environment referred to by Dr. Blix, the task of locating this material inevitably falls to coalition forces. We are actively pursuing sites, documentation and individuals connected with Iraq's programmes. Both the UK and the US have deployed specialist personnel and will be sending more in the near future.

But the investigations are unlikely to be quick. The inspection process itself will be painstaking and detailed. The testimony from scientists and documentation about WMD development and production programmes will be the key to determining the fate of the prohibited equipment, materials and munitions. But we cannot expect witnesses to come forward until they are fully confident that they can speak freely.

Even so, I know that some hon. Members have expressed concerns about the justification for military action in the absence of discoveries of illegal Iraqi weapons. Let me make two observations in this connection. First, military action was taken on the basis set out very clearly in Security Council resolution 1441, namely that Iraq's "non-compliance with Council resolutions and proliferation of weapons of mass destruction and long-range missiles"—posed a threat "to international peace and security".

The evidence against Iraq was then—and remains—overwhelming. It was charted by UNMOVIC in damning detail in the 173 pages of its report, "Unresolved Disarmament Issues: Iraq's Proscribed Weapons Programmes", which was published in New York late on Friday 7 March, and which I published before the House in Command document 5785 the following Monday, 10 March. My second point is that Saddam had ample time to conceal his WMD programmes prior to the start of military operations. Indeed, his experience in concealment dates back to the early 1990s.

(HC Deb 28 April 2003 Vol. 404 c21)

Part Seventeen: I. B.3. *The Law of Armed Conflict and International Humanitarian Law—International armed conflict—The law of international armed conflict—Land warfare*

17/9

Her Majesty's Government was asked the following written question:

To ask the Secretary of State for International Development what estimate she has made of the number of civilian deaths which occurred *(a)* directly and *(b)* indirectly as a result of military action in Afghanistan since 11 September 2001.

In reply, the Under-Secretary of State, FCO, wrote:

It is impossible to know for certain how many casualties, either military or civilian, there have been as a result of coalition action in Afghanistan. The Taliban's claims of casualties cannot be taken at face value.

Military action inevitably carries risks, but as my right hon. Friend the Secretary of State has made clear in the House, our targeting and weapons selection processes are rigorous. Every effort is made to avoid civilian casualties.

(HC Deb 10 March 2003 Vol. 401 c37W)

17/10

Her Majesty's Government were asked to comment on reports that British-made armoured vehicles were being used by Indonesian forces. The Minister of State, FCO, wrote:

The Indonesian Government announced on 23 June the deployment of 36 British-built Scorpion vehicles to Aceh to defend roads against attack by the Free Aceh Movement (FAM).

Our embassy in Jakarta spoke to senior military contacts and reminded them of the assurances that British-built military equipment should not be used offensively or to violate human rights. We are carefully monitoring the extent of compliance with these assurances.

(HL Deb 10 July 2003 Vol. 651 cWA53)

Part Seventeen: I. B.6. *The Law of Armed Conflict and International Humanitarian Law—International armed conflict—The law of international armed conflict—Distinction between combatants and non-combatants*

(See also **6/14–6/16**)

17/11

In reply to a written question, the Parliamentary Under-Secretary of State, FCO, wrote:

The US has said that the detainees are enemy combatants captured in a continuing armed conflict and held in that capacity by the US military authorities. The question of the status of the detainees at Guantanamo Bay under international humanitarian law has to be considered in the light of the facts relating to each individual detainee.

We remain in regular contact with the United States, at both ministerial and official level, about the situation of the detainees. My right honourable friend the Foreign Secretary has raised the issue several times with US Secretary of State Colin Powell, most recently on 23 January. We have been encouraging the US to move forward with the process of determining the future of the British detainees. We shall continue to do so.

The discussions between British officials and the detainees are confidential as they contain personal information about the detainees. I am withholding further details of the visits by British officials to the detainees at Guantanamo Bay under exemption 1a of the Code of Practice on Access to Government Information (information whose disclosure would harm national security or defence).

(HL Deb 18 February 2003 Vol. 644 cWA167)

17/12

During a debate in the House of Commons, the Prime Minister said:

On the latter point, the people at Guantanamo Bay are not combat troops in the service of a country. However, I have said on many occasions before that there will have to come a point when the situation at Guantanamo Bay comes to an end, although it is also true to say that information is still being provided by people there that is of importance.

(HC Deb 24 March 2003 Vol. 402 c32)

17/13

Her Majesty's Government was asked the following written question:

To ask the Secretary of State for Foreign and Commonwealth Affairs . . . whether he has (*a*) requested formal consular access to Guantanamo Bay from the US authorities and (*b*) called for the status of the prisoners held at Guantanamo Bay to be decided by a tribunal; and if he will make a statement.

In reply, the Parliamentary Under-Secretary of State, FCO, wrote:

The information is as follows:

(*a*) Yes.

(*b*) Although the Foreign Secretary has not called for a tribunal to decide the detainees' status, he has raised the issue of the detainees with Colin Powell several times, most recently on 23 January. Officials are in frequent contact.

We have made clear that whatever their status the detainees are entitled to humane treatment and, if prosecuted, a fair trial. We have been encouraging the US to move forward with the process of determining the future of the British detainees. We shall continue to do so.

(HC Deb 2 April 2003 Vol. 402 c741W–742W)

17/14

In reply to a question regarding the Government's position on the US's view that the Geneva Conventions do not apply to the detainees in Guantanamo Bay the Under-Secretary of State, FCO, replied:

It is something that we have discussed with the United States, and frankly, we disagree with them about it.

(HC Deb 7 July 2003 Vol. 408 c754)

17/15

In reply to a written question the Solicitor-General wrote:

The US Administration confirmed to the Attorney-General that its view is that all the detainees in Guantanamo Bay, including Feroz Abbasi and Moazzam Begg, have been detained as enemy combatants under the laws of armed conflict.

(HC Deb 15 July 2003 Vol. 409 c206W)

17/16

In reply to a written question the Foreign Minister wrote:

The assessment of the status of the detainees is a matter for the US, as the detaining power. We have, however, discussed the detainees' status with the US authorities. They have told us that they do not consider any of the British detainees to be entitled to prisoner of war status. The US authorities have assured us that the detainees are being treated humanely and consistently with the principles of the Geneva Conventions.

Whatever their status, the detainees are entitled to humane treatment and if prosecuted, a fair trial.

(HL Deb 14 July 2003 Vol. 651 cWA74–WA75)

17/17

During a House of Lords debate on British detainees in Guantanamo Bay, the Minister of State, FCO, said:

The question of the legal limbo in which all these detainees have been left was pinpointed by the International Red Cross in its criticisms. The noble Lord talks of a new status. Moving towards an internationally recognised new status would be enormously helped if there were an internationally recognised fair trial that went with such status. It is rather difficult to argue for one without the other.

(HL Deb 15 October 2003 Vol. 653 c939)

17/18

Her Majesty's Government was asked the following written question:

. . . what evidence has [the Minister] received from the American Administration in support of their claim that they have the right to try Moazzam Begg and Feroz Abbasi as combatants; and if he will make a statement.

The Under-Secretary of State, FCO, replied:

The US authorities have made clear their view that the detainees at Guantanamo Bay are being held as enemy combatants. The question of the legal status of the detainees at Guantanamo Bay under international law depends on the facts relating to each individual detainee. The US, as the detaining power, has access to that information and in the first instance, the question of the status of the detainees is a matter for them.

Mr. Begg and Mr. Abbasi have been designated as eligible for Military Commissions, but have not yet been charged. Proceedings against them have been suspended pending the outcome of discussions between the British and US Governments.

(HC Deb 20 November 2003 Vol. 413 c1317W)

17/19

In reply to an oral question the Under-Secretary of State for Defence said:

Captured Iraqi forces are likely to be prisoners of war unless they conceal weapons in the conduct of operations, in which case, as the noble Lord will know, they are unlawful combatants. Although unlawful combatants do not have prisoner of war status, we would have a duty, under international humanitarian law, which we would fulfil, to treat prisoners in a reasonable and humane manner.

(HL Deb 3 April 2003 Vol. 646 c1472)

17/20

In response to a written question, the Minister of State for Defence wrote:

Any individuals captured or detained by United Kingdom forces in the Gulf will be afforded the appropriate status and enjoy the protection afforded by the Geneva Convention.

(HC Deb 7 April 2003 Vol. 403 c10W)

17/21

In reply to oral questions the Under-Secretary of State for Defence said:

My Lords, the Government have long made plain that they will act in conformity with international law. The taking of prisoners of war is a recognised and legitimate means of reducing an enemy's strength and fighting capacity. Iraqi military personnel who fall into the hands of United Kingdom forces are prisoners of war and therefore will be treated in accordance with the Geneva Conventions.

...

My Lords, if such people are taken into the custody of the United Kingdom forces, they will be treated under the terms of humanitarian law and will of course be looked after both humanely and safely. If they are passed on to another coalition partner—for example, the United States partner—for example, the

Unit arrangement is in place between the coalition forces that the following will happen. First, there will be no transfer outside the borders of Iraq without the consent of the detaining power, which will in those circumstances be the United Kingdom. Secondly, jurisdiction will be exclusive to the detaining power—at least for events that occurred before their first detention. Thirdly, as the noble Baroness suggests, where there is any doubt about their status—sometimes there may be no doubt about it either way—the United Kingdom may well have to convene tribunals.

(HL Deb 8 April 2003 Vol. 647 c132)

17/22

Her Majesty's Government was asked the following written question:

Whether all prisoners captured by British forces in Iraq are, in their view, prisoners of war.

In reply the Under-Secretary of State, Ministry of Defence, wrote:

All individuals captured or detained by United Kingdom forces in the Gulf are afforded an appropriate status in accordance with the Geneva Convention. Not every individual detained is classified as a prisoner of war.

He was further asked:

Whether any prisoners held in Iraq are considered to be "enemy combatants" rather than prisoners of war.

And replied:

The Geneva Conventions of 1949 recognise the term "combatant". Any prisoner captured during an armed conflict whose status is deemed to be that of a "combatant", would be entitled to be treated as a prisoner of war.

(HL Deb 30 June 2003 Vol. 650 cWA64)

17/23

Her Majesty's Government was asked the following written question:

[H]ow many people captured by British forces in Iraq and transferred to United States internment facilities are now classified by the United States authorities as "enemy combatants" rather than prisoners of war.

The Under-Secretary of State for Defence replied:

The United States does not classify persons detained by British forces. As the detaining power, the United Kingdom has the sole authority for determining their status. This is reflected in an arrangement that exists between the two nations. All those persons captured by British forces who had the status of enemy combatant were entitled to be, and to be treated as, prisoners of war.

(HL Deb 8 July 2003 Vol. 651 cWA31–WA32)

17/24

In reply to a written question the Defence Minister wrote:

As of 15 July 2003, the United States is holding one prisoner of war and 71 other persons captured by British forces, who are either suspected of committing criminal offences or are interned where necessary for imperative reasons of security in accordance with the Fourth Geneva Convention. All other British captured prisoners of war have been released under the supervision of British forces, and with the knowledge of the International Committee of the Red Cross. The United Kingdom does not use the designation unlawful combatant.

(HC Deb 16 July 2003 Vol. 409 c403W)

17/25

In reply to a written question the Under-Secretary of State for Defence wrote:

No prisoners captured by British forces in Iraq and transferred to the United States authorities have been transferred out of Iraq. The British Government have an agreement with the United States that prisoners of war captured by United Kingdom forces will not be transferred out of Iraq without UK consent.

(HL Deb 17 July 2003 Vol. 651 cWA155)

17/26

In reply to a written question the Defence Minister wrote:

Those persons captured by British forces who had the status of enemy combatant were entitled to prisoner of war status and to be treated as such. As of 21 July 2003, the United States is holding one prisoner of war and 36 other persons captured by British forces, who are either suspected of committing criminal offences or are interned where necessary for imperative reasons of security in accordance with the Fourth Geneva Convention. No prisoners captured by British forces in Iraq and transferred to US custody have been transferred out of Iraq. The rights of persons detained who are not classified as enemy combatants are contained within the Fourth Geneva Convention.

(HC Deb 1 September 2003 Vol. 409 c906W–907W)

17/27

In reply to a written question on the fate of Iraqi detainees in the hands of UK forces the Under-Secretary of State for Defence wrote:

Of the 71 persons held for imperative reasons of security on 15 July, 49 have already been released. The remainder will be held until it is assessed that their internment is no longer necessary for reasons of security, all cases are subject to regular review. In cases where there is evidence to suggest that a criminal offence has been committed, persons captured by United Kingdom forces are handed to the Iraqi judicial system. If internment is based on intelligence material that justifies internment, the case will not be suitable for trial, although cases will be subject to regular review.

(HL Deb 8 September 2003 Vol. 652 cWA45)

17/28

In reply to a written question on the status of internees held by the British forces in Iraq, the Armed Forces Minister wrote:

Article 78 of the IV Geneva Convention (1949) allows the UK as the Occupying Power to intern people where it considers it necessary for reasons of security. Internees will continue to be held until such time as they are no longer considered a threat to Coalition Forces. A review is conducted at the 10, 28 and 90 day points (and every 90 days thereafter) to determine whether continued internment is necessary. Internees enjoy all their rights under the Geneva Conventions.

As at 1 December, all internees held by the UK Forces in Iraq are of either Iraqi or Sudanese nationality.

(HC Deb 8 December 2003 Vol. 415 c269W)

17/29

In reply to a written question the Under-Secretary of State for Defence wrote:

The Government have carried out a detailed review of the eligibility for the ex-gratia payment scheme established in 2000 for Far East Prisoners of War. This follows the ruling in the High Court by Mr Justice McCombe in November 2002.

We are now able to announce that, in accordance with the principles set out in the judgment of the court, the scheme will be formally extended to include those Gurkha Far East Prisoners of War (FEPOW) who were held captive by the Japanese in the Second World War and who, in 1951 when the peace treaty between the United Kingdom and Japan was signed, were citizens of Nepal. Claims can be made by the FEPOW or by their surviving spouse for the payment of £10,000.

(HL Deb 7 November 2003 Vol. 654 cWA150)

17/30

During a debate in the House of Commons on Iraq and civilian casualties, the Secretary of State for Defence said:

As I told the House yesterday, inevitably there are risks to civilians, but the efforts taken by the UK, the United States and elsewhere to target the campaign accurately against regime targets continue. Although I cannot give a guarantee that civilians will not be affected, I can assure my hon. Friend that there is no ambition whatever to target civilians. Our quarrel is with the regime in Iraq and our targets are designed accordingly.

(HC Deb 21 March 2003 Vol. 401 c1219–1220)

17/31

During a debate in the House of Commons, the Secretary of State for Defence said:

Cluster bombs are unlikely to be delivered at this stage of the operation, as I already told the House. The present stage of the campaign is concerned with identifying regime targets and making it clear to the population of Iraq that it is the regime that we are attacking, not the people of that country.

(HC Deb 21 March 2003 Vol. 401 c1220)

17/32

During a debate in the House of Commons, the Secretary of State for Defence said:

We do not comment in detail on rules of engagement, and certainly not on those of the United States. I would be a lot more persuaded by my hon. Friend's observations if, at the same time as mentioning the tragic deaths of seven women and children, he had also mentioned the deaths of the four US marines who were killed in a deliberate car bomb attack, perpetrated by a fanatic. In such circumstances, it is perhaps perfectly understandable—although I am not excusing it in any sense at all—that soldiers who are having to deal with a difficult situation at a checkpoint and who know that four of their comrades have been killed in that way are perhaps reacting in a way that we might not want them to. That is not to say that the accounts that have been given, again, by particular journalists are necessarily the only version of events that we should all accept. An investigation is going on into what went on at the checkpoints, and it is important that we await the outcome of that before judging the facts quite so prejudicially.

(HC Deb 3 April 2003 Vol. 402 c1085)

Part Seventeen: I. B.7. *The Law of Armed Conflict and International Humanitarian Law—International armed conflict—The law of international armed conflict—International humanitarian law*

(See also **13/8**)

17/33

In reply to a written question, the Under-Secretary of State, FCO, wrote:

The United Kingdom takes its international humanitarian law commitments extremely seriously. As a state party to the 1949 Geneva Conventions and their two additional Protocols of 1977, we observe the requirements of these and other international legal instruments and rules of customary international law which are binding upon us. We look to other states similarly to make every effort to meet their commitments.

(HL Deb 7 January 2003 Vol. 642 cWA179)

17/34

In reply to a written question, the Prime Minister wrote:

As we have said many times, the Government are committed to acting in full conformity with International Law. Our rules of engagement will reflect this.

(HC Deb 24 February 2003 Vol. 400 c252W)

17/35

In a written answer, the Parliamentary Under-Secretary of State, FCO, wrote:

We will investigate any allegation of war crimes against UK forces in the present conflict. If we find evidence to justify prosecution, we will seek to bring those responsible to justice. As regards allegations of war crimes committed by members of the Saddam regime prior to this conflict, the Government is assessing, in conjunction with coalition partners, how these can best be investigated and those responsible brought to justice.

(HC Deb 11 April 2003 Vol. 403 c438W)

17/36

In response to a written question, the Parliamentary Under-Secretary of State for Defence wrote:

All reports of coalition action resulting in the deaths of civilians are investigated. The United Kingdom works with coalition partners to verify the facts of such reported incidents. The profession of civilian casualties is not a concern when investigating such incidents.

Very careful attention is applied to ensure that in the coalition's campaign the risk of damage to civilian populations and infrastructure is minimised. However, military action is never without risk, and lawful actions against military targets may result in harm to civilians. Any civilian casualties resulting from military action are deeply regretted.

The active battlefield is not a benign environment and coalition forces cannot be held responsible for, or guarantee the safety of, journalists who enter such a location independently. This is one of the reasons why we have embedded war correspondents whose activities can be properly co-ordinated with our own forces.

(HC Deb 14 April 2003 Vol. 403 c571W)

17/37

During a Security Council meeting the representative of the European Union stated:

Furthermore, perpetrators [of violations] of international humanitarian and human rights law must be brought to justice at the national level or, where not possible, to international justice. The primary responsibility to carry that out lies with each State. The European Union therefore urges all States to ratify and implement all relevant international agreements... procedures... States contributing personnel deployed in EU-led crisis management operations should in particular ensure monitoring and reporting of alleged violations of human rights and of international humanitarian or international criminal law. Investigation of each complaint and prosecution of those responsible should be ensured. Suitable training in these areas should be provided to personnel deployed on the ground, both at a national level and through European programmes, where appropriate, in cooperation with the United Nations and other relevant international bodies. The protection of civilians in armed conflict is one of the main issues on our agenda, given its repercussions on international peace and security and respect for human rights and international humanitarian law.

(UN Doc. S/PV.4877, 9 December 2003)

17/38

In reply to a written question on prisoners taken in Afghanistan the Under-Secretary of State, FCO, wrote:

British Embassy staff in Kabul are in frequent contact with the ICRC, which monitors closely the situation and welfare of all prisoners in Afghanistan. However, the ICRC cannot provide full reports.

A number of prisoners have been released from Shiberghan prison since February. According to our most recent information, around 1,200 men are still being held there.

We are concerned about reported conditions in prisons across Afghanistan and have made clear to the Afghan Transitional Administration, which includes former Northern Alliance members, that we expect them, as the responsible authority for prisoners in Afghanistan, to respect their international obligations. This includes treating their prisoners humanely and in accordance with the Geneva Conventions and international human rights law.

(HL Deb 14 January 2003 Vol. 643 cWA10)

17/39

In reply to a written question, the Secretary of State for International Development wrote:

International humanitarian law, as embodied in the Geneva Conventions of 1949 and their Additional Protocols, prohibits the recruitment or use of children under

15 in armed conflict and provides for the protection of children, particularly those separated from their families. The Statute of the International Criminal Court, to which the UK is a state party and which has been incorporated into national law, makes the recruitment and/or use of children under 15 a war crime.

The European Convention for the Protection of Human Rights and Fundamental Freedoms, now enshrined in the Human Rights Act 1998, forbids the use of torture, inhuman or degrading treatment which may include the forcing of children to take part in hostilities.

The UK is a Party to the UN Convention on the Rights of the Child, which makes particular provision for the protection of all children under 18 years. It prescribes that the best interests of the child should be a primary consideration, severely restricts the circumstances in which children may be removed from their parents and protects children against arbitrary interference with their privacy and liberty. This Convention, along with International Labour Organisation Convention 182 (which the UK has ratified), prohibits the use of children in the worst forms of labour; and Convention 182 specifically prohibits the forced or compulsory recruitment of children for use in armed conflict.

The UK expects to ratify the Optional Protocol to the Convention on the Rights of the Child on the Involvement of Children in Armed Conflict later this year. [ed. see above **3/3**. The UK ratified the OP on 24 June 2004, TS no.48 (2003).] This provides that states parties must take all feasible measures to ensure that members of their armed forces who have not attained the age of 18 years do not take a direct part in hostilities, and that children under 18 years are not compulsorily recruited into their armed forces. Non-state actors, such as insurgent groups, are prohibited from ever recruiting or using in hostilities children under 18. We take the Protocol seriously. That is why before we ratify, we need to be clear that the detailed procedures and administrative guidelines for the armed forces are finalised. These will give concrete form to our commitment. MOD officials, in consultation with the Foreign and Commonwealth Office, are in the final stages of drafting an Explanatory Memorandum which will explain the steps being taken to meet that commitment. As part of the ratification process, we will lay the Explanatory Memorandum (EM) before Parliament. This does not require any changes to UK legislation.

The UK has many laws that prohibit the activities usually associated with the use of child soldiers, such as assault, forcing a child to perform illegal acts, deprivation of their liberty and making children take harmful drugs and alcohol.

(HC Deb 30 January 2003 Vol. 398 c965W–966W)

17/40

In reply to a written question on the assessment of the number of child soldiers in Burma; and what steps she is taking to tackle this, the Secretary of State for International Development wrote:

An exact figure is not known. But a recent Human Rights Watch study estimated that there could be up to 70,000 child soldiers in Burma.

The UN Security Council has now passed a resolution on Children Affected by Armed Conflict, which was based on the UNSG's report on child soldiers. In our statement on this to the Security Council, UK representative Jeremy Greenstock highlighted our concerns about child soldiers in Burma.

The issue of child soldiers was also taken up in the UK Co-sponsored resolution at UNGA last November. We will be ensuring that the issue is addressed at the UN Commission on Human Rights where the EU will be tabling a resolution on the human rights situation in Burma. In addition the UK has in place a weapons embargo and a ban on all military links with the Burmese armed forces in view of their appalling human rights record.

(HC Deb 24 February 2003 Vol. 400 c271W)

17/41

In a Ministerial Statement, the Minister of State for Defence wrote:

The United Kingdom's chemical protection programme is designed to protect against the use of chemical weapons. Such a programme is permitted by the Chemical Weapons Convention, with which the UK is fully compliant. Under the terms of the Convention, we are required to provide information annually to the Organisation for the Prohibition of Chemical Weapons (OPCW). In accordance with the Government's commitment to openness, I am placing in the Library of the House a copy of the summary that has been provided to the Organisation outlining the UK's chemical protection programme for 2002. To increase transparency, the format of this year's summary has been revised and for the first time information on civil protection is included.

(HC Deb 29 April 2003 Vol. 404 c12WS)

17/42

In response to a written question, the Secretary of State for Defence wrote:

Cluster bombs are only used strictly in accordance with international law. This includes the principles of distinction and proportionality as well as precautionary measures to be taken in planning and conducting an attack, as contained in the First Additional Protocol of 1977 to the Geneva Conventions of 1949. The targeting process takes account of these principles in matching the type of weapon used to the target to be attacked. There will be circumstances when it would be considered more appropriate to use other munitions than cluster bombs. These circumstances are more likely to arise in urban or populated areas as cluster bombs engage targets that cover an area. However, a decision on which type of munition to use has to take into account all the circumstances at the time of an attack. It follows that it would be unlikely that cluster bombs would be used in an urban or populated area.

(HC Deb 14 April 2003 Vol. 403 c571W)

17/43

Her Majesty's Government was asked the following written question:

Whether they [Her Majesty's Government] will now ratify the 1954 Hague Convention for the Protection of Cultural Property in the Event of Armed Conflict, with the first and second protocols to the convention; and, if not, what are their reasons for delay.

In reply, the Minister of State, FCO, wrote:

Ratification of the convention and protocols would require primary legislation, and extensive consultation is needed on legal, operational and policy issues relating to implementation of the protocols. Once this is complete, we hope to be in a position to ratify.

(HL Deb 10 March 2003 Vol. 645 cWA150)

17/44

In reply to a written question on protection of cultural property in Iraq Her Majesty's Government wrote:

Paragraph 53 of Additional Protocol 1 of the Geneva Conventions prohibits any attack against a cultural property unless that property is used to support a military effort. In our military planning, very careful attention is applied, in accordance with our responsibilities under international law, to ensure that we minimise the risk of damage from any quarter to civilian populations and infrastructure, including sites of historic, archaeological and cultural heritage.

We are confident that our servicemen and women will respect the rich heritage of the Iraqi people. Any form of indiscipline by United Kingdom Armed Forces will be taken very seriously and will be dealt with accordingly.

Iraqi military and civilian individuals will be held personally accountable for actions taken by them in the event of military action, including criminal offences.

(HL Deb 26 March 2003 Vol. 646 cWA81)

17/45

During a debate in the House of Lords, the Parliamentary Under-Secretary of State, FCO, was asked the following question:

My Lords, can the Minister assure us that the Government are fully briefed on the conditions under which the United States is keeping prisoners from the Taliban on Diego Garcia in view of the serious allegations made in the Washington Post and the Herald Tribune on 27th December? The United States is, at the very least, steering close to the wind as regards the Geneva Convention and other aspects of international law. This is sovereign British territory and therefore, as I understand it and as the Minister has confirmed, the British Government are responsible for ensuring that international law is fully observed.

In reply the Minister stated:

My Lords, I am aware of the stories in the press. Those stories are entirely without foundation. The United States Government would need to ask for our permission to bring any suspects to Diego Garcia. They have not done so and no suspected terrorists are being held on Diego Garcia.

(HL Deb 8 January 2003 Vol. 642 c1019)

17/46

During a debate in the House of Lords, the Minister of State, FCO, made the following statements:

There is also, unfortunately, a history of destruction of humanitarian aid on the part of the Israeli defence forces. We deplore such acts. We believe the action of the Israeli defence forces must be proportionate. Together with our EU partners, we have raised concerns about those issues with the Israeli Government.

...

My Lords, settlement activity and the security fence are causes of great concern to Her Majesty's Government. Settlement activity has increased during the past year; it is important to keep that issue in the forefront of our minds. We are concerned about the 360 kilometre-long fence, to which the noble Lord referred, which takes up so much Palestinian land and separates families. Our embassy in Tel Aviv has raised with the Israeli Government our concern about the location and the impact of the security fence. We fully understand Israel's need to take steps within the law to protect itself from terrorist attack, but that must be achieved through a negotiated peace, not by measures such as the security fence.

(HL Deb 25 February 2003 Vol. 645 c119–121)

17/47

In reply to a written question the Minister of State, FCO, wrote:

While the building of a separation wall for security reasons does not necessarily contravene international law, we do consider some aspects related to the construction of the "security fence" in the West Bank to be illegal. We do not believe that the route of the fence is determined by security requirements. We therefore conclude that much of the demolition and confiscation of Palestinian property associated with its construction violates the Fourth Geneva Convention, which prohibits such measures unless absolutely necessary. We are concerned that the lack of access for Palestinian owners to land on the west of the security fence results in the de facto appropriation of this territory by Israel.

The military orders, which requisition land for the fence, allow the owners of the property to request rental fees or compensation.

(HL Deb 10 July 2003 Vol. 651 cWA52)

17/48

Her Majesty's Government was asked the following written question:

To ask the Secretary of State for Foreign and Commonwealth Affairs . . . whether Article 147 of the Fourth Geneva Convention is one of the pieces of international law with which he believes the actions of the Israeli Government to be inconsistent.

The Under-Secretary of State, FCO, replied:

The Government believe that the deportation by the state of Israel of persons against whom no charges have been laid may be inconsistent with the provisions of the Fourth Geneva Convention, including Article 147.

(HC Deb 18 November 2003 Vol. 413 c774W)

17/49

During a meeting in the Security Council the representative of the European Union said:

While recognising Israel's right to protect its citizens from terrorist attacks, the European Union once again urges the Government of Israel, in exercising that right, to fully respect international law, in particular human rights and international humanitarian law, including the Fourth Geneva Convention, to take maximum precautions to avoid civilian casualties and to take no action that aggravates the humanitarian and economic plight of the Palestinian people. It also calls on Israel to abstain from any punitive measures that are not in accordance with international law, including extrajudicial killings.

. . .

The European Union calls on Israel to stop and reverse its settlement policy and to immediately dismantle settlements built after March 2001. We also call on Israel to lift the blockade on the occupied territories and withdraw its forces from Palestinian cities to the positions held prior to September 2000. Moreover, Israel must ensure full, safe and unfettered access of humanitarian personnel and assistance to the occupied territories, in accordance with international humanitarian law.

. . .

In May 2000, Israel unilaterally withdrew its forces from south Lebanon, in line with Security Council resolution 425 (1978). Even though the situation there has been characterised by a state of relative calm, serious violations of the ceasefire continue to occur. It is essential that the Lebanese Government fulfil its responsibility under that resolution and reinstate its effective authority over all of southern Lebanon, including by deploying its forces along the Blue Line, in order to restore peace and security in the area. For its part, Israel must stop the repeated air violations of the Blue Line, which are unjustified and a cause of great concern to the civilian population. Furthermore, both parties must ensure the safety of United Nations Interim Force in Lebanon (UNIFIL) personnel, as well as their full freedom of movement in discharging UNIFIL's mandate.

(UN Doc. A/58/PV.67, 2 December 2003)

17/50

In reply to a written question the Minister of State, FCO, wrote:

The Government deplore the war crimes committed during the Balkans conflict in the early 1990s, including the rape of women and girls in Bosnia.

We are sympathetic to any proposal to improve the situation of the victims of these crimes, but it is not clear that awarding civilian war victim status would be the most effective means of ensuring support for these women. What is required is recognition of their suffering as victims of rape, conviction of the perpetrators and provision of appropriate support for these women and their children.

Through the work of the Department for International Development, and support for UNICEF and local NGOs, the Government support projects to raise awareness of rape as a war crime. We strongly support the work of the International Criminal Tribunal for former Yugoslavia, which is tasked with bringing to trial those suspected of war crimes and crimes against humanity during the Balkans conflict, including rape. It has convicted a number of individuals of this crime. With our partners in the EU, we apply concerted pressure to all governments in the region for greater co-operation with ICTY, particularly in the handover and prosecution of indictees.

The best way to secure financial support for these women and their children is through successful convictions in the Bosnian courts, which can award compensation to the victims of rape. Together with our EU partners, we are working hard to strengthen the capacity of the Bosnian judicial system, so that it can prosecute the perpetrators of these crimes more effectively and efficiently, and provide sustainable support to the victims.

(HL Deb 10 December 2003 Vol. 655 cWA64)

17/51

In a written Ministerial Statement, the Secretary of State for International Development wrote:

In the event of conflict in Iraq, my Department would have two humanitarian roles. One is to help advise the Ministry of Defence and the armed forces on how best to discharge their humanitarian responsibilities under The Hague and Geneva Conventions. The other is to use the funds, expertise and influence available to us to support the direct delivery of impartial humanitarian assistance by the international humanitarian community. I will summarise what we are doing in both capacities.

In the event of conflict and the occupation of Iraqi territory by the UK military, the occupying forces would have humanitarian responsibilities under

The Hague and Geneva Conventions. It is likely that in the first stages of any conflict, UN agencies and NGOs would not be fully operational, particularly if there is a credible threat of the use of chemical or biological weapons. Military forces thus might have primary responsibility for the initial delivery of humanitarian assistance. They are also likely to play a key role over a longer time period in providing a secure environment for other organisations to deliver humanitarian assistance. . . .

The principles we apply in delivering humanitarian assistance to Iraq are the same as anywhere else. They are not determined by the nature of the conflict, or subject to military strategy or diplomatic considerations. We will respect international humanitarian law and relevant human rights laws and conventions. We will allocate our assistance impartially based on the best possible assessment of need. We will state clearly the standards we aspire to and how we are accountable for our assistance. We will respect the neutrality and independence of our humanitarian partners. Where moral dilemmas in the delivery of humanitarian assistance arise, often requiring fast and difficult decisions, with lives at stake, we will be explicit in the analysis which guides our choices, and communicate this openly.

(HC Deb 13 March 2003 Vol. 401 c22WS–23WS)

[ed. See further, http://www.parliament.uk/commons/lib/research/rp2003/rp03–051.pdf—"Iraq: Law of Occupation"]

17/52

During a debate in the House of Commons, the Secretary of State for Defence said:

Coalition operations are clearly continuing. I made that clear in my statement, and I do not think that any Member of the House would expect me to anticipate the nature of those operations save to say that whatever targets are addressed will be targets associated with Saddam Hussein's regime. I made that clear yesterday to the House, and I repeat it again today. We will not engage in indiscriminate so-called carpet bombing. Each of the targets will be individually addressed and attacked.

(HC Deb 21 March 2003 Vol. 401 c1214–1215)

17/53

During a debate in the House of Lords, the Lord Privy Seal said:

For that reason, we did not, as some expected, mount a heavy bombing campaign first, followed by a land campaign. Instead, land forces were immediately in action, securing oil installations, gaining strategic assets and retaining them, not destroying them. The air campaign has been precisely targeted. Of course there will have been civilian casualties. But we have done all we humanly can, to keep them to a minimum. Water and electricity supplies are being spared. The targets are the infrastructure, command and control of Saddam's regime not of the civilian population. And we are making massive efforts to clear lines of supply for humanitarian aid, though the presence of mines is hindering us.

By contrast, the nature of Saddam's regime is all too plainly expressed in its actions. The oil wealth was mined, and deep-mined at that. Had we not struck quickly, Iraq's future wealth would even now be burning away. Prisoners are being paraded in defiance of all international conventions. Those who dare speak criticism of the regime are being executed.

(HL Deb 24 March 2003 Vol. 646 c478–479)

17/54

During a debate in the House of Commons, the Prime Minister said:

In relation to any military targets, we have to ensure that they have a military objective—that is the legal requirement as well as the stated political objective that we have set. There is no doubt that one of the issues is how we can best communicate with the Iraqi people. That is being urgently looked at. There are different ways in which we can communicate with them, including through people inside Iraq who can tell them exactly what is happening.

(HC Deb 26 March 2003 Vol. 402 c282)

17/55

In an oral answer, the Prime Minister said:

We will obviously ensure that any Iraqi prisoners are treated by us in accordance with the Geneva convention. If my hon. Friend is referring to Guantanamo Bay—if that is the purpose of his question—I must tell him that those people are not the combat troops of a Government. As I have said before, however, it is important for them to be treated with dignity and for their human rights to be respected.

We have visited the British nationals in Guantanamo Bay many times, and have investigated each allegation of abuse of their human rights, but let me say this to my hon. Friend. There is still information that is checked with people in Guantanamo Bay that is of vital significance to protecting people in Europe. I am afraid that that is simply the reality of the situation, although, as I have said before, it cannot continue indefinitely: I agree that, at some point, it will have to come to an end.

(HC Deb 26 March 2003 Vol. 402 c289)

17/56

In a written answer, the Secretary of State for International Development wrote:

My Department has been in close discussion with the Ministry of Defence over many months working to minimise the humanitarian impact of any conflict; both to minimise the risks to the Iraqi population and the infrastructure on which they depend, and to ensure that UK forces meet their obligations under the Hague and Geneva conventions governing armed conflict. We have seconded two humanitarian specialists to work with the armed forces (UK 1 Division) and to advise on relief activities.

(HC Deb 26 March 2003 Vol. 402 c237W)

17/57

In a written answer, the Secretary of State for International Development wrote:

Humanitarian agencies cannot operate until a permissive security environment has been established. In the interim, the military will have responsibility to deliver humanitarian assistance in the territory they occupy in accordance with the Geneva and Hague conventions.

(HC Deb 26 March 2003 Vol. 402 c238W)

17/58

In a written answer, the Secretary of State for International Development wrote:

I visited New York and Washington on 19–20 March to meet the United Nations, the International Monetary Fund, the World Bank and the US Administration to try to ensure that proper preparations are being made for reconstruction in Iraq. My officials are also in regular contact with these and other partners.

A UN mandate for the reconstruction effort is a precondition for the engagement of the World Bank, the International Monetary Fund and many countries. Their engagement is key to the reforms that are needed to move the economy forward and to secure an agreement on debt rescheduling and a reparations strategy that will enable the Iraqi economy to recover and grow. I held detailed talks last week with officials of the UN and the US Administration about how that might be achieved and I am hopeful that we will soon make progress in line with the agreements reached between the Prime Minister and President Bush in the Azores.

(HC Deb 26 March 2003 Vol. 402 c239W)

17/59

In a written answer, the Secretary of State for International Development wrote:

Humanitarian agencies cannot operate until a permissive security environment has been established. The military will discharge their humanitarian obligations under the Geneva and Hague conventions in order to provide relief in the interim. Once the situation allows, NGOs will need to undertake their own security assessments before engaging.

(HC Deb 26 March 2003 Vol. 402 c239W–240W)

17/60

In a written answer, the Secretary of State for International Development wrote:

The first step is to secure a strong UN mandate for reconstruction. The European Council on 20 and 21 March agreed that the UN Security Council should give the UN such a mandate for post-conflict Iraq and make sure that the new Iraqi administration is one that is representative, respects the human rights of the Iraqi people, and allows the people of Iraq to live in peace internally and with their neighbours.

(HC Deb 26 March 2003 Vol. 402 c240W)

17/61

During a debate in the House of Commons, the Prime Minister said, in relation to Turkish troops crossing the border to Iraq:

There always have been Turkish troops in that position and there are obviously large numbers of Turkish troops there now. They say—as they have said consistently—that that is to provide against the possibility of large numbers of people coming over the border from northern Iraq. We and the United States have done everything that we possibly can, however, to make it very clear to the Turkish authorities, the Turkish military and the Turkish Government that any attempt to break the territorial integrity of Iraq in any way would be utterly unacceptable. I do not believe that that is their intention, but obviously we are watching the situation carefully.

(HC Deb 26 March 2003 Vol. 402 c284–285)

17/62

During the debate in the House of Commons, the Secretary of State for Defence made the following statement:

Coalition commanders have expressed considerable concern about the practice—which we have seen on more than one occasion—of Iraqi soldiers apparently surrendering but then attacking the forces to whom they appeared to be surrendering. That is clearly a serious breach of the Geneva Convention and one that we will continue to highlight when appropriate.

(HC Deb 26 March 2003 Vol. 402 c298)

17/63

In a written answer, the Secretary of State for Defence wrote:

Coalition military action against Iraq is in conformity with international law. The taking of prisoners of war is a recognised and legitimate means of reducing an enemy's strength and fighting capacity. Iraqi military personnel who fall into the hands of United Kingdom forces will be treated in accordance with the Geneva Convention.

(HC Deb 1 April 2003 Vol. 402 c651W)

17/64

In a written answer, the Minister of State for Defence wrote:

The United Kingdom takes its responsibilities toward the Iraqi people extremely seriously. Coalition forces are taking the utmost care to minimise the impact of the conflict on civilians and to provide humanitarian assistance where appropriate.

(HC Deb 1 April 2003 Vol. 402 c653W)

17/65

In a written answer, the Secretary of State for International Development wrote:

The coalition military are responsible for the provision of humanitarian assistance as set down in the Hague Regulations and Geneva Conventions governing Armed Conflict. The Treasury has allocated £30 million to the Ministry of Defence for this purpose. DFID is advising the MOD on its humanitarian work.

Separately DFID is providing humanitarian assistance in Iraq on the basis of greatest need. DFID has earmarked £210 million for this, the bulk of which will be allocated through the UN, Red Cross and international NGOs.

(HC Deb 1 April 2003 Vol. 402 c657W)

17/66

The Secretary of State for International Development was asked the following written question:

. . . what the legal basis is for her statements *(a)* that UK armed forces are in Iraq as an occupying power, with humanitarian responsibilities and duties to keep order and the civil administration running; and *(b)* that they do not have the authority to reorganise institutions or establish a new Government.

In reply, the Secretary of State for International Development wrote:

These statements are based on legal advice on the applicability of the 1907 Hague Regulations and the 1949 Geneva Conventions. Article 55 of the Fourth Geneva Convention states that: "To the fullest extent of the means available to it, the Occupying Power has the duty of ensuring the food and medical supplies of the population; it should, in particular, bring in the necessary foodstuffs, medical stores and other articles if the resources of the occupied territory are inadequate". Section III of the Hague Regulations sets out the limits of military authority over the territory of an occupied state; parts of the Geneva Conventions are also relevant.

(HC Deb 1 April 2003 Vol. 402 c659W)

17/67

In reply to an oral answer, the Prime Minister said:

What the Americans said—and we back them up in saying it—was that we would not find it acceptable if equipment was transferred from Syria to Iraqi forces in the field, or if there was any suggestion of any support being given by any elements in Iran to troops who are attacking coalition forces. However, we maintain relations with both those countries to ensure that those things do not happen. It is important—particularly in relation to Iran—to recognise that we are in constant contact with them to ensure that the situation is not exacerbated in any way.

(HC Deb 2 April 2003 Vol. 402 c910)

17/68

In a written answer, the Minister of State for Defence wrote:

We have no means of ascertaining the numbers of military or civilian lives lost during the conflict in Iraq to date, although we make every effort to keep any impact upon the Iraqi civilian population to an absolute minimum. All our military planning is conducted in full accordance with our obligations under international law to employ the minimum necessary use of force to achieve military effect, and to avoid injury to non-combatants or civilian infrastructure. Practically, this is achieved through a combination of an extremely careful targeting process and highly accurate precision guided weapons.

(HC Deb 2 April 2003 Vol. 402 c738W)

17/69

During a debate in the House of Commons, the Secretary of State for Defence said:

I can give the hon. Gentleman the assurance that he asked for about the observance of the Geneva convention in respect of prisoners of war. In practice, several prisoners of war have been transferred from US to UK control, particularly when the prisoners were taken in the course of the US forces' rapid progress north. Given the UK's consolidation in the south, it is sensible for the UK to be responsible for such prisoners.

I can confirm that British forces have used cluster bombs, which, as I have told the House before, are the most suitable weapons for dealing with wide-area targets. If we did not use such weapons on appropriate occasions, we would put our own and coalition forces at greater risk.

(HC Deb 3 April 2003 Vol. 402 c1075)

17/70

During a debate in the House of Commons, the Parliamentary Secretary, Privy Seal Council Office, said:

With respect to my hon. Friend, I do not accept his use of the terminology "a conquering force". We will be a liberating force, and we already are in the parts of Iraq in which the Iraqi people are sufficiently confident to speak freely and where they feel safe from retribution from Saddam's henchmen. My hon. Friend should look at the model of Afghanistan. Of course, our input and that of the international community was important to help the Afghan people to set up their conference and institutions such as the Loya Jirga, but such things were based firmly on Afghan traditions and practices. I can assure him that the same applies in Iraq. It is not in our interests to be perceived as trying to tell the Iraqi people how they should run their country once they have been liberated. In comparison with Afghanistan, Iraq has not only good natural resources but a highly educated work force and 4 million highly educated people in exile. Many may want to return to help with the redevelopment of their country.

(HC Deb 3 April 2003 Vol. 402 c1152)

17/71

In a written answer, the Secretary of State for International Development wrote:

A UN mandate for reconstruction is a legal requirement for UK involvement in significant reform of Iraqi institutions, and a precondition for the engagement of the World Bank, the International Monetary Fund and many countries.

Without a UN mandate the UK's assistance would have to be limited to providing humanitarian assistance and ensuring the continuity of the civil administration, according to our obligations under the Geneva and Hague conventions governing armed conflict.

(HC Deb 3 April 2003 Vol. 402 c806W–807W)

17/72

In reply to a written question on what measures are in place to ensure that British broadcasters do not violate the Geneva Convention in their coverage of the war in Iraq, the Secretary of State for Culture, Media and Sport wrote:

The ITC [Independent Television Commission] establish high standards in relation to privacy and human dignity by placing, in their programme code, certain requirements on UK broadcasters. These include guidance on respect for human dignity and treatment of minorities. Broadcasters must adhere to these rules and respect them as regards prisoners of war. Equally these rules apply to the treatment of footage of dead soldiers and civilians. I expect that current ITC regulations will prevent the violation of the Geneva Convention occurring in material broadcast from a UK licensed service.

BBC producers' guidelines also recognise the principles of the Geneva Convention. The BBC believes that its editorial policies are fully consistent with the principles of the Geneva Convention. Their editorial policies (which are in the public domain) include guidelines on the coverage of casualties, death and injury and prisoners of war.

(HC Deb 3 April 2003 Vol. 402 c814W)

17/73

In reply to a question on what responsibilities under the Geneva Convention coalition forces have to deliver humanitarian relief in disputed territory in Iraq, the Minister of State for Defence wrote:

The United Kingdom is a party to the Fourth Geneva Convention relative to the Protection of Civilian Persons in Time of War and will comply fully with its obligations under that Convention. The application of the provisions of that Convention depends on the progress of the conflict and may differ across the country. The provision of humanitarian assistance by United Kingdom forces has already begun in towns in southern Iraq where the situation has stabilised enough to make this possible. That effort will continue until civilian aid agencies can deploy fully.

In other areas where United Kingdom troops are present, we are monitoring the humanitarian situation and stand ready to provide whatever assistance is required once local elements of the regime collapse and a secure environment is established.

(HC Deb 4 April 2003 Vol. 402 c880W)

17/74

During a debate in the House of Commons, the Secretary of State for Defence made the following statements:

As I have said on previous occasions when that issue has arisen, the use of all weapons involves striking a balance. All weapons are capable of damaging the civilian population as well as those against whom they are targeted. It is necessary to strike a balance between not only the risk to civilians, but equally the protection of coalition forces. In relation to the use of cluster bombs, I am confident that the right balance has been struck.

. . .

No one is suggesting that we win over the hearts and minds of Iraqi civilians by using cluster bombs other than in this sense: it is necessary to succeed in the military conflict in order to win over those hearts and minds. We will not succeed in the military conflict if we prevent our armed forces from protecting themselves when they are confronted by a determined and often ruthless opposition. I invite my hon. Friend to weigh that in the balance. Is she really prepared to put the lives of our forces at risk in order to prolong the conflict, and thereby make it more difficult, in the longer term, to win the hearts and minds necessary to rebuild Iraq?

. . .

[C]areful note has been taken of where and when cluster bombs have been used and, as I have indicated to the House before, the people who most often risk their lives in dealing with the small failure rate of those weapons are members of Britain's armed forces.

(HC Deb 7 April 2003 Vol. 403 c23–33)

17/75

In response to a written question, the Minister of State for Defence wrote:

At this stage of the conflict in Iraq it is not feasible to make an accurate assessment of the effects of the use of cluster bombs.

Unexploded cluster bombs, and indeed all unexploded ordnance, are a matter of humanitarian concern. As such, we are committed to working towards the clearance of explosive remnants of war as part of the reconstruction of Iraq.

(HC Deb 7 April 2003 Vol. 403 c11W)

17/76

Her Majesty's Government was asked the following written question:

[W]hat guidance has been given to UK forces operating in the no-fly zone in southern Iraq on the holy places of the Shi'a in Nayjab and Kerbala.

In reply, the Minister of State for Defence wrote:

We are fully aware of the significance of the holy sites in Najaf and Karbala. The coalition is taking every precaution to respect and avoid damage to them.

By contrast, we know from intelligence that Saddam Hussein has plans to damage the sites and to blame the coalition. There are precedents: in 1991, Iraq troops attacked and desecrated Imam Ali's shrine and destroyed religious libraries in Najaf; they shelled and desecrated Imam Hussein's shrine in Karbala; and the shrine of Imam Abbas was also reported damaged.

The United Kingdom is fully committed to the protection of cultural property in times of armed conflict. The Government take very seriously its obligations to act in conformity with international law, the UN Charter and international humanitarian law. In all our military planning, very careful attention is applied to ensure that we minimise the risk of damage to all civilian sites.

The targeting process during current operations is conducted in accordance with all obligations under international law, including Additional Protocol 1 of the Geneva Conventions, and the Targeting Directive to United Kingdom forces stationed in the Gulf contains explicit guidance on their obligations under international and domestic law. For reasons of force protection, I cannot comment on the specifics of our targeting policy, and I am therefore withholding that information under Exemption 1 of the Code of Practice on Access to Government Information (Defence, security and international relations).

In view of the continuing air operations against Iraq, No-Fly Zone patrols have been rendered redundant. This does not mean that we have in any way reduced our humanitarian concerns for the Iraqi people. Our Servicemen and women have daily risked their lives enhancing the security of the civilian population for over a decade, and we will continue to demonstrate that commitment.

(HC Deb 8 April 2003 Vol. 403 c140W)

17/77

In response to a written question, the Secretary of State for Defence wrote:

The military campaign is crafted around the principle of minimum use of force. We attack only military objectives and combatants subject to the constraints of proportionality. If there is any expectation that harm will be caused to civilians, this must not be excessive when set against the direct and concrete military advantage anticipated from the attack. That approach fully reflects our obligations under international law.

(HC Deb 9 April 2003 Vol. 403 c297W)

17/78

In response to a written question on what the military objective is of attacking Iraqi television offices in the invasion of Iraq, the Secretary of State for Defence wrote:

Television offices and studios have not been the object of coalition attacks. The coalition has attacked, and reserves the right to continue to attack systems (such as transmitters) which are used by the regime for conveying military command and control information. Coalition attacks are designed to minimise damage to civilian infrastructure.

(HC Deb 9 April 2003 Vol. 403 c297W)

17/79

In a written answer, the Parliamentary Under-Secretary of State for Defence wrote:

We have made no representations to the US Government about Iraqi nationals in its detention. The US is a State Party to the 1949 Geneva Conventions. The treatment of persons in its detention is primarily a matter for the US as Detaining Power.

(HC Deb 14 April 2003 Vol. 403 c527W)

17/80

In response to a written question, the Minister of State for Defence wrote:

Upon being taken prisoner, Iraqi combatants are evacuated to a safe location, away from the dangers of combat, as soon as is practicable. They are held initially at collection points by the unit taking them prisoner, where their identity is established and recorded. They are then transferred to a more permanent holding facility.

In accordance with Article 70 of the Geneva Convention relative to the treatment of prisoners of war, upon capture, and subsequently following any change in location, every prisoner of war is given the opportunity to write direct to his or her family, and through the completion of a Capture Card, to the Central Prisoners of War Agency in Geneva. Prisoner of war details are given to the International Committee for the Red Cross who have the responsibility for the distribution of letters, parcels and Capture Cards.

Prisoners of war are provided with Halal food in accordance with local practice. They are given one hot and two cold meals per day, and water and hot drinks are readily available. They are provided with shelter, in the form of carpeted, tented accommodation and, if needed, medical treatment.

(HC Deb 14 April 2003 Vol. 403 c572W–573W)

17/81

In reply to a written question the Under-Secretary of State for Defence wrote:

The United Kingdom's and United States' responsibilities in relation to captured persons are contained in an arrangement between the nations. In accordance with this arrangement, the United States agreed to treat persons in accordance with the relevant Geneva Conventions. Under the terms of the arrangement, the United Kingdom has primary right to criminal jurisdiction for offences committed prior to transfer. For offences committed after transfer, the United States has primary right to jurisdiction, and in such cases it is up to the United States to decide sentence. We are not aware of any situation where United Kingdom captured persons have committed any post transfer offences. In the absence of any post transfer offences, the decision to release rests with the United Kingdom authorities.

Persons suspected of crimes other than against coalition forces or the security of Iraq are immediately handed over to Iraqi authorities. Persons suspected of crimes against coalition forces or the security of Iraq are held pending collection of evidence and a decision as to the forum for trial. Persons held for imperative reasons of security, in accordance with the Fourth Geneva Convention, will be released as soon as their internment ceases to be necessary.

(HL Deb 8 July 2003 Vol. 651 cWA32)

17/82

In reply to a written question about possible crimes against international law by the Hussein regime, a Defence Minister wrote:

United Kingdom Forces in Basra are preserving any evidence found of legacy war crimes or crimes against humanity thought to have been carried out by the Iraqi regime for possible future investigations by an appropriate authority. UK military police are currently investigating a number of incidents that occurred during recent operations involving UK forces. It would be inappropriate to comment on on-going investigations.

(HC Deb 15 July 2003 Vol. 409 c202W)

17/83

In reply to a written question the Defence Minister wrote:

We take our obligations under International Law and the Laws of Armed Conflict to avoid collateral damage and excessive military casualties very seriously. Any loss of life, particularly civilian, is deeply regrettable, but in a military operation the size of Operation Telic it is also unavoidable. Through very strict rules of engagement, the use of precision munitions and the tactical methods employed to liberate Iraq's major cities, we are satisfied that the coalition did everything possible to avoid unnecessary casualties.

(HL Deb 1 September 2003 Vol. 409 c905W)

17/84

In reply to a written question the Under-Secretary of State for Defence wrote:

The Deployed Operating Instructions issued to all United Kingdom military units state that enemy dead are to be treated the same as UK military dead. This includes a direction that, where next of kin cannot be traced, the bodies are to be given the same funeral as would UK military personnel, subject to religious practices. Wounded enemy personnel are given care and medical attention that accord fully with our obligations under the Geneva Convention.

(HL Deb 8 September 2003 Vol. 652 cWA40)

17/85

During a debate in the House of Lords the Under-Secretary of State for Defence said:

My Lords, every effort is made to minimise the impact of military operations on the Iraqi civilian population, and we deeply regret all civilian casualties. Since 1st May 2003, we have investigated every civilian fatality allegedly caused by UK military personnel, sometimes resulting in a formal investigation by the Special Investigation Branch.

We treat claims for compensation in respect of civilians who have allegedly been killed or injured by UK forces since 1st May on their merits, in accordance with English law. We have no liability to pay compensation in respect of Iraqis killed or injured during combat operations.

(HL Deb 17 December 2003 Vol. 655 c1143)

17/86

During the debate in the House of Commons, the Secretary of State for Defence made the following statement:

I made the point about the International Committee of the Red Cross and the excellence of the work that it continues to do in Basra. We will certainly seek to support its efforts. I am aware of an agreement with the committee on visits to Iraqi prisoners of war, and I anticipate no difficulty about that being achieved. I am certainly not aware that the Iraqi authorities have extended the same opportunity to visit coalition prisoners of war.

(HC Deb 26 March 2003 Vol. 402 c304)

17/87

Her Majesty's Government was asked the following written question:

To ask the Secretary of State for Foreign and Commonwealth Affairs what representations the Government has received from *(a)* Syria and *(b)* Iran on the firing of coalition missiles into (i) a bus carrying Syrian nationals from Iraq to Syria on 23 March and (ii) Iranian territory.

In reply, the Parliamentary Under-Secretary of State, FCO, wrote:

Our embassies in Damascus and Tehran have been in contact with the Syrian and Iranian Governments about these incidents. Under no circumstances would the Coalition deliberately target a civilian bus. This is a tragic accident, for which the US have already issued an apology. The Coalition is taking the utmost care to minimise civilian casualties. There are strong indications that the munitions that landed in Iranian territory were in fact Iraqi but the matter is still being examined.

(HC Deb 3 April 2003 Vol. 402 c832W)

17/88

Her Majesty's Government was asked the following written question:

To ask the Secretary of State for Foreign and Commonwealth Affairs what reports he has received concerning incursions made by Islamist mercenaries from Chad into *(a)* Sudan and *(b)* Nigeria; and what representations he will be making to the Government of Chad concerning these incursions.

In reply, the Parliamentary Under-Secretary of State, FCO, wrote:

There are persistent reports of fighting in Darfur, Western Sudan, involving tribes and groups from Chad and Libya. Recent unconfirmed reports allege that Chadian mercenaries were involved in the attack against Al-Tinah on the Sudan/Chad border. Chad has closed the border with Sudan and deployed troops there to uphold the security agreement signed between Sudan and Chad.

The Nigerian police regularly report on the presence of substantial numbers of Chadians among those arrested in violent conflicts in Northern Nigeria.

It is for the Governments of Sudan and Nigeria, rather than the British Government, to make representations to the Government of Chad on these matters.

(HC Deb 4 April 2003 Vol. 402 c902W–903W)

Part Seventeen: I. B.8. *The Law of Armed Conflict and International Humanitarian Law—International armed conflict—The law of international armed conflict—Belligerent occupation*

(See **19/33**, section 12)

17/89

In reply to a written question the Solicitor-General wrote:

[T]he United Nations Security Council has adopted Resolution 1483 of 21 May 2003. This Resolution, together with the relevant provisions of international humanitarian law, in particular the Fourth Geneva Convention of 1949 and the Hague Regulations, now governs the conduct of the United Kingdom and the United States as occupying powers in Iraq. The Resolution calls upon the occupying powers to work towards the creation of conditions in which the Iraqi people can freely determine their own political future.

(HC Deb 15 July 2003 Vol. 409 c206W)

17/90

Her Majesty's Government was asked the following written question:

To ask the Secretary of State for Foreign and Commonwealth Affairs what assessment he has made of the compatibility of order 39 [ed. On foreign investment], issued by the Coalition Administration of Iraq, with *(a)* paragraph 43 of the 1907 Hague regulations, *(b)* the 4th Geneva Convention and *(c)* UNSCR 1483.

The Under-Secretary of State, FCO, replied:

The Government are satisfied that UNSCR 1483 (2003) provides a sound legal basis for the CPA Foreign Investment Order. Resolution 1483 authorises the Coalition to undertake activities to promote economic reform in Iraq, in coordination with the Special Representative of the UN Secretary General.

(HC Deb 12 November 2003 Vol. 413 c359W)

17/91

The Foreign Secretary made the following written statement:

On 15 November, Jalal Talabani, President of the Iraqi Governing Council, announced a programme and timetable for a new constitution and elections in Iraq. Under the plan, the Governing Council will draft a Fundamental Law by February 2004, which will be based on the respect of human rights, freedom of speech and religious tolerance. The Fundamental Law will apply for the transitional period until full national elections.

A Transitional National Assembly will be established by June 2004 through transparent and democratic caucuses at provincial and local level, facilitated by the Governing Council and the Coalition Provisional Authority (CPA). The Assembly will elect an executive and ministers as the Iraqi Transitional

Government by July 2004, by then, the progressive handover of executive and legal authority from the CPA will be complete, and the Coalition's legal occupation will come to an end. The Transitional Government will oversee elections to a Constitutional Convention by March 2005, which will promulgate a new permanent constitution for Iraq. A referendum on the new constitution will take place before full elections of a new representative Iraqi government at the end of 2005.

The programme announced by Mr. Talabani is an important and welcome step forward, and comes in response to the wishes of Iraqis themselves. It should enable the Coalition to fulfil the shared goal of ensuring a progressive transfer of executive and legislative authority to the Iraqi people as soon as possible. It responds to the Iraqi people's wish that the body tasked with writing a permanent constitution be elected. The plan will bring an earlier end to the status of the UK and US as occupying powers, and will enable the Iraqis to develop their democratic institutions leading to full direct elections for a new government.

The plan announced by Mr. Talabani will also meet the requirement under UN Resolution 1511 for the Iraqi Governing Council to report to the Security Council by 15 December with "a timetable and a programme for the drafting of a new constitution for Iraq and for the holding of democratic elections under that constitution". The Secretary-General of the UN, Kofi Annan, has said he is heartened by the announcement. I have already spoken to him and stressed that we will work with him to ensure the UN plays a vital role as set out in Resolution 1511.

(HC Deb 20 November 2003 Vol. 413 c42WS–43WS)

17/92

The FCO sent a memorandum to the FAC in response to certain questions. The first question was:

The consistency of coalition actions in Iraq with the requirements of the Fourth Geneva Convention 1949 and the Hague Regulations 1907. In particular, the Committee wishes to be in a position to judge whether the US and UK have met in full their obligations to ensure food and medical supplies for the civil population, to ensure and maintain public health and hygiene, and to ensure public order and safety; and how the occupying powers have ensured that actions taken by them to create a functioning administration and to introduce democratic characteristics into Iraqi political structures have not gone beyond what is permitted under international law.

What role is the United Kingdom playing in ORHA? How many UK personnel are serving in ORHA, and in what capacities?

The answers were:

2. Under article 43 of the Hague Regulations Respecting the Laws and Customs of War on Land, an Occupying Power is required to take all measures within its power to restore and ensure, as far as possible, public order and safety, while respecting unless absolutely prevented the laws in force in the country.

3. The Fourth Geneva Convention (1949), which is concerned with the welfare of civilians, imposes broad obligations on an Occupying Power to maintain orderly government of the territory and to ensure its own security. In addition the Convention provides for a number of further specific obligations to the civilian population.

4. The Government has at all stages made every effort to comply with its responsibilities under the Fourth Geneva Convention and the Hague Regulations . . .

Maintenance of Security

12. Since the liberation of Iraq, UK forces have been working to restore security through a number of means including patrols, vehicle checkpoints and static guarding. Sites currently being guarded by UK forces include key government buildings and public record offices. However, our overall approach is to re-establish local police and guard forces that will initially be trained and overseen by UK forces.

13. The UK and the US have been working with the international community to provide a multinational stabilisation force in Iraq. The US will be in overall command in Baghdad and the central sector and the UK will command a multinational division in the south. More than 20 nations are expected to serve in Iraq, with nine represented in the UK area (Italy, the Netherlands, Denmark, the Czech Republic, Romania, Portugal, Norway, Lithuania and New Zealand). Some states have already deployed.

14. Throughout the military campaign, Coalition forces have taken care to ensure that damage to museums and other sites of historic, archaeological or cultural importance has been minimised. Ground troops were briefed on the need to be especially careful while conducting operations in the vicinity of these sites.

15. Since 1 June, a number of Iraqi courts have been operating with the assistance of UK forces.

Civil Administration

16. The Coalition Provisional Administration (CPA) was set up at the beginning of June. It is responsible for civil administration and reconstruction work, and for facilitating the political processes outlined below. It is led by President Bush's special representative in Iraq, Ambassador Paul Bremer. The CPA is working closely with Iraqis to restore normal functioning to Iraqi ministries and regions. The CPA has around 1,000 staff working in Baghdad, and regional offices in northern, south central and south-east Iraq. The latter area is coterminous with the UK military area of responsibility. It is led by a senior Danish official with a UK deputy and UK civilian secondees. Wider international support has been provided by countries including Australia, Spain, the Czech Republic, Korea, Romania and Japan

. . .

Political Process

20. United Nations Security Council Resolution 1483 "Supports the formation, by the people of Iraq with the help of the Authority and working with the Special Representative, of an Iraqi interim administration as a transitional administration run by Iraqis, until an internationally recognised, representative

government is established by the people of Iraq and assumes the responsibilities of the Authority".

Intensive consultations are taking place in Iraq between Coalition representatives, including the United Kingdom Special Representative for Iraq, and representatives of Iraqi interest groups and political parties. The United Nations Special Representative Sergio Vieira de Mello has also recently arrived in Baghdad and we expect him also to play a central role in the political process. A group of Iraqi political leaders have constituted themselves as a "Leadership Group" to work with the Coalition to carry forward the political process. The Coalition has held two larger-scale meetings with Iraqis, in Nasiriyah on 15 April and in Baghdad on 28 April.

21. The consultations undertaken so far indicate that interim political structures and processes will need to perform a number of distinct functions:

—Iraqi involvement in the day to day civil administration of Iraq in co-operation with the CPA.

—Paving the way for the establishment of a viable Iraqi government to replace the CPA.

—Carrying out essential political functions in the interim such as reform of the Constitution.

We expect a political process to be launched in the coming days. This is expected to comprise two key elements:

—A Political Council, to assist the CPA in the immediate tasks of running the civil administration. Its responsibilities will increase over time; an early task will be to nominate new Iraqi interim ministers to help run government ministries. The Political Council to create special commissions on cross-cutting issues (eg judicial reform, human rights).

—A Constitutional Conference. This is likely to have a larger membership, and to be in place by mid-July. It will draft and debate a new Iraqi constitution. This will be approved by referendum, paving the way for eventual free elections.

22. The UK's objectives are that such processes and structures should be legitimate, viable and credible. The key interest groups in Iraq must be effectively represented, including women; they must be effectively consulted and involved in decision-making on interim arrangements. An interim authority must be established in accordance with Resolution 1483.

23. The effective representation of women in the political processes and structures of post-Saddam Iraq is an important part of the Government's vision for Iraq as the Prime Minister made clear at the Azores Summit. We are taking every opportunity to promote this agenda in our contacts with Iraqis, discussions within the coalition, and more widely. A gender expert from the Women and Equality Unit has been seconded to the Coalition Provisional Authority and, in collaboration with Iraqi women and other officials in Iraq, is working to ensure women's full and equal participation in the Iraqi political and reconstruction process.

UN Authorisation

24. On 22 May the United Nations Security Council adopted Resolution 1483. The Resolution was based closely on a draft tabled by the US, UK and Spain. In summary, the Resolution:

—recognises the rights and responsibilities of the US and UK as occupying powers;

—gives the UN a vital role through wide-ranging responsibilities for a Special Representative of the Secretary General, who is given a specific mandate in such areas as the political process, humanitarian activities, economic reconstruction and promotion of human rights;

—foresees a political process leading to an internationally recognised, representative government of Iraq;

—calls on other UN member states and international organisations to play their part in fulfilling the resolution's aims, including ensuring security and stability;

—ends all sanctions, other than the arms embargo;

—arranges for the orderly wind-up of the Oil for Food Programme;

—ensures that oil sales are made in accordance with international best practice;

—creates the Development Fund for Iraq to disburse oil revenues;

—provides that these funds can only be spent to meet the humanitarian needs of the Iraqi people, for the economic reconstruction and repair of Iraq's infrastructure, for the continued disarmament of Iraq, and for the costs of Iraqi civilian administration, and for other purposes benefiting the people of Iraq;

—creates an International Advisory and Monitoring Board to oversee oil sales and spending by the Development Fund, with representatives of the UN, IMF and World Bank, and regular reporting to the Security Council;

—places an obligation on all UN Member States to assist in bringing to justice those responsible for crimes under the former Iraqi regime; and

—obliges all Member States to take action to prevent trade in stolen Iraqi antiquities.

25. The Secretary General has since appointed the UN High Commissioner for Human Rights, Sergio Vieira de Mello, as his Special Representative. De Mello arrived in Baghdad on 2 June. We are offering him our full support. His immediate priorities include assessment of the situation on the ground, the needs of the people of Iraq and the areas where the UN and international organisations can add most value. He will also work on behalf of the Secretary General to facilitate the political processes leading to an internationally recognised, representative government of Iraq.

26. In order to ensure that actions taken by the Occupying Powers to create a functioning administration accord with the international law of occupation, ORHA/CPA has an Office of Legal Counsel to provide legal advice in this respect. Procedures have been established for pre-promulgation scrutiny of legislative and other legal acts of the Coalition Provisional Authority.

27. Whilst the introduction of democratic changes in government can not be imposed by the Occupying Powers, this does not affect the rights of the Iraqi people themselves to develop their own systems of government. It is therefore permissible for the Occupying Powers to play a facilitating role in relation to reforms genuinely undertaken by the people of Iraq themselves. During the period prior to the passage of Resolution 1483 the CPA did not seek to impose such changes in government on Iraq.

28. Since the passing of United Nations Security Council Resolution 1483, the question of the UK's responsibilities in respect of political reform is no longer governed solely by the law of occupation. The resolution makes clear that the eventual aim of the political process in Iraq should be the formation by the people of Iraq of a representative government based on the rule of law that affords equal rights and justice to all Iraqi citizens. To that end, Resolution 1483 supports the formation of an Iraqi interim administration by the people of Iraq, with the help of the CPA and working with the UN Special Representative, as a transitional administration run by Iraqis, until a representative Government is established by the people of Iraq assumes the responsibilities of the CPA. The precise modalities as to how this shall be put into effect are still developing, but they will be based upon the provisions of Resolution 1483.

The Committee's next question was:

In your letter of 22 April you set out the position of an occupying power under the Fourth Geneva Convention and the Hague Regulations. No mention was made in the letter of the requirement for United Nations authority for the occupying powers to exercise some of their functions. When did the Government conclude that UN authority would be required, and was the advice of the Attorney General sought when the FCO compiled its reply of 22 April?

The memorandum said:

29. The FCO's letter of 22 April was confined to the scope of authority of Occupying Powers under the law of occupation because this is what was requested in the Committee Assistant's letter of 8 April. The Committee asked for information on what Occupying Powers are able to do under the law of occupation. There is no legal requirement under the law of occupation for UN authorisation to enable an Occupying Power to exercise its functions. UN authority is only required to enable an Occupying Power to take actions that are not otherwise authorised by the law of occupation. It was evident from the reply given to the Committee that further authority in the form of a Security Council resolution would be required to enable the Occupying Powers to go beyond their normal scope of authority under the law of occupation.

30. The Attorney General was consulted on the terms of the FCO's reply to the Committee Assistant's letter of 8 April.

The next question was:

What legal process is envisaged for dealing with crimes against humanity by the Baathist regime, evidence for which is now being uncovered?

The memorandum said:

46. UK forces have been tasked with securing and protecting evidence of legacy crimes as they encounter it, to hand over to the relevant prosecuting authority at the appropriate time. We have sent a team of nine forensic experts from the NGO Inforce to Iraq to investigate legacy crimes and mass graves and to make recommendations for further UK and CPA assistance in this area. The team will draw up a longer term strategy for dealing with forensically important sites in Iraq. The UK has also sent an expert from the NGO Indict to advise on a strategy for investigating legacy crimes.

47. We have always believed that those who have been responsible for genocide, crimes against humanity and war crimes should be brought to justice. We believe that it should be for the Iraqi people to decide how this might be done, with suitable international help. A series of mechanisms might be required, ranging from special courts to truth and reconciliation commissions.

(FAC Tenth Report, Foreign Policy Aspects of the War Against Terrorism, Written Evidence, Memorandum from the FCO, 13 and 22 May 2003, HC 405)

17/93

Her Majesty's Government was asked the following written question:

To ask the Secretary of State for Foreign and Commonwealth Affairs what assessment he has made of the implications for *(a)* the implementation of UN Resolutions on Israel and Palestine and *(b)* for Israel's obligations as an occupying power under the Geneva Conventions, of the military order issued by Israel on 2 October 2003 declaring land in the Occupied West Bank between the security fence and Israel's pre-occupation 1967 border as a closed zone; and what action the UK Government intend to take.

In reply the Under-Secretary of State, FCO, wrote:

The implementation of this Israeli military order will have grave consequences for those Palestinians who live between the fence and the 1967 border and those who farm land in this area. It reinforces the concern that Israeli construction of the fence on occupied land amounts to de facto annexation of Palestinian land west of the fence, and prejudges the outcome of a final settlement based on UN Security Council Resolutions 242 (1967), 338 (1973) and 1397 (2002).

Under Article 49 of the Fourth Geneva Convention, the Occupying Power is only permitted to evacuate a given area of the occupied territory:

"if the security of the population or imperative military reasons so demand".

We expect Israel to comply fully with this obligation.

My noble Friend the Baroness Symons of Vernham Dean has raised with the Israeli Ambassador our concerns about this and other Israeli activities affecting the humanitarian situation of Palestinians. We are in close touch with the US and other allies to ensure that Israel understands the opposition of the wider international community to the route of the fence.

(HC Deb 29 October 2003 Vol. 412 c280W)

17/94

During a House of Commons debate on Israel the Under-Secretary of State, FCO, said:

Bethlehem has a unique and historical status, and it stands as an example of how Palestinian towns in the West Bank will be affected by the building of the structure. Although my right hon. Friend referred to the Government's position, it is worth restating it. My right hon. Friend the Foreign Secretary said in the House of Commons as recently as 14 October that we consider the building of the wall on Palestinian land to be illegal, and we need to underline that point.

We are not alone in holding that view. The United Nations General Assembly and leaders of all the European Union member states at the European Council clarified their opposition to the route of the fence. President Bush and Secretary of State Colin Powell also consider the route of the fence to be a problem and have urged the Israeli Government not to build it on Palestinian land, but along the green line between Israel and the Palestinian territories. There is a significant degree of international consensus, and cross-party consensus in the House, on the issue.

I want to make it clear that the Government understand that the Israel Government must take precautionary measures within international law to protect their citizens. That is undoubtedly the duty of all Governments. However, although the wall may give some immediate relief from the relentless series of terrorist attacks inflicted on the state and people of Israel, building the fence on Palestinian territory will inflame tensions in the region and do nothing to solve the crisis. As my hon. Friend the Member for Preston (Mr. Hendrick) said, in common with many other Members, it will give only an illusion of security to the people of Israel in the longer term.

The proponents of the wall claim that it will separate the Israeli people from the Palestinians, and my hon. and right hon. Friends attested to that from their direct experience of the situation. However, on completion of the next section, agreed by the Israeli Cabinet on 1 October, an estimated 79,000 Palestinians will be left to the west of the wall—in other words, on the Israeli side of the barrier. Those people will not be able to enter Israel freely and will have severely limited access to essential services, such as schools and hospitals, in the West Bank. A powerful point was made about the situation that will arise if young people cannot go to school and are left to their own devices and the temptations that exist.

. . .

I understand the argument, and we have to restate that the wall built on the occupied territories is illegal under international law. We must make that point forcibly to the Israeli Government, and we are taking every opportunity to do so.

(HC Deb 4 November 2003 Vol. 412 c245WH–246WH)

17/95

During a debate in the House of Lords, the Minister of State, FCO, said:

I have been perfectly clear that Her Majesty's Government are extremely unhappy about the level of settlement activity. When we last discussed it I reported that in the past year there have been some 34 settlements in the Occupied Territories which Her Majesty's Government consider to be illegal.

(HL Deb 7 January 2003 Vol. 642 c1019)

17/96

During a debate in the House of Lords on Israel: Settlement Expansion, the Minister of State, FCO, made the following statements:

My Lords, we have consistently called on the Israeli Government to freeze all settlement activity, including the "natural growth" of settlements, as recommended in the Mitchell report.

On 5th November, my honourable friend Mike O'Brien raised settlement activity with the Israeli Ambassador. On 18th November, our ambassador in Tel Aviv conveyed to Prime Minister Sharon's office the Foreign Secretary's concern at reports that the Israeli Government were considering extending settlements in Hebron, which we consider to be illegal and an obstacle to peace. Those points were reiterated at official level to the Israeli Ambassador on 20th November.

...

My Lords, I agree with the noble Lord that at a time when there is a firm international consensus on a two-state solution—comprising as it does the Arab League, the United States and the European Union—it is alarming that the practical basis for this solution is in jeopardy. The fence is indeed worrying because it involves the destruction of Palestinian farmland. We have protested about the fence through our ambassador in Tel Aviv. As I indicated, we have made representations on the settlement activity. We have talked, and we continue to talk, to the United States about these concerns. We hope that Israel will see that settlement building threatens its own vital interests in a two-state solution.

...

My Lords, while the Israeli Government continue with these illegal settlements, Her Majesty's Government's view that they are a barrier to peace will remain true.

(HL Deb 4 December 2002 Vol. 641 c1140–1144)

17/97

In reply to a written question, the Economic Secretary of the Exchequer wrote:

The European Commission published in November 2001 a notice in the Official Journal of the European Communities, alerting EC importers of the ineligibility of products originating from settlements in the Occupied Territories for preferences provided for by the EU/Israel Association Agreement. Along with customs authorities in other Community member states, Customs and Excise are selecting for verification those imports where preference has been claimed under the terms of the Agreement but where there is evidence that the goods are likely to have been produced in the Occupied Territories. Security for duty is being taken on such imports while verification enquiries are undertaken. Customs require payment of duty if they do not receive adequate confirmation that goods originated in Israel itself.

(HC Deb 4 February 2003 Vol. 399 c181W)

17/98

In a written answer, the Under-Secretary of State, FCO, wrote:

Israeli settlements in the Occupied Territories are contrary to Article 49 of the Fourth Geneva Convention. We have repeatedly called on Israel to freeze all settlement activity.

Collective punishment is also contrary to the Fourth Geneva Convention. In certain circumstances this can include the demolition of homes of suicide bombers; the closure and curfew regime, denial of access for humanitarian and medical agencies to those in need. We have raised our concerns at the highest levels of the Israeli Government and have requested they take immediate steps to address concern about the situation in the Occupied Territories. In accordance with the Declaration adopted at the Conference of High Contracting Parties in Geneva on 5 December 2001 the UK continues to meet its responsibility to encourage all parties to the conflict to ensure respect for the Geneva Conventions in all circumstances.

(HC Deb 6 February 2003 Vol. 399 c381W–382W)

17/99

In a written answer, the Secretary of State for International Development wrote:

The most likely major impact, in the event of a war in Iraq, would be a complete closure by Israel of the West Bank and Gaza Strip, severely restricting travel between and within the Occupied Territories. The international community has made it clear that Israel must allow humanitarian operations to continue without impediment, including the safe passage of humanitarian staff and supplies. Lessons learned from the 1991 Gulf War and from the intense military activity of Israel's "Operation Defensive Shield" in 2002 will help international and local organisations cope more effectively should this happen.

(HC Deb 4 March 2003 Vol. 400 c949W)

17/100

During a meeting in the House of Commons, the Secretary of State for International Development made the following statements:

So far, USAID has awarded contracts involving aid money to US companies to deal with the immediate humanitarian crises. That is bad practice. The UK [aid] is untied and we always fund the most efficient provider, which is usually better for the region. However, such provision of contracts has no implications for the future reconstruction of Iraq. That will require a UN mandate to put an interim Iraqi Government in place, followed by work carried out by the International Monetary Fund and World Bank. Reform will be transparent and any contracts will be properly awarded.

...

The Prime Minister reached an agreement with President Bush in the Azores that there would be a UN mandate for reconstruction, which is also an absolute legal requirement. It is clear from the advice of our Attorney-General on 1441 and previous resolutions that our armed forces are in Iraq as an occupying power with humanitarian responsibilities and duties to keep order and the civil administration running. They do not, however, have the authority to reorganise institutions or establish a new Government. That requires a UN mandate. The UK is clear about that and I am hopeful that, as everything settles down, the international community will unite around that so that everyone involved, including the IMF and the World Bank, in providing proper help for Iraq to construct itself.

(HC Deb 26 March 2003 Vol. 402 c277)

17/101

In a written answer, the Secretary of State for International Development wrote:

Humanitarian agencies cannot operate until a permissive security environment has been established. In the interim, the military will have responsibility to deliver humanitarian assistance in the territory they occupy in accordance with the Geneva and Hague conventions.

(HC Deb 26 March 2003 Vol. 402 cWA238)

17/102

In reply to a written question the Minister of State, FCO, wrote:

The road map does not require the Israeli Government to contribute to the cost of rebuilding Palestinian property and infrastructure. Nevertheless, the 4th Geneva Convention prohibits the destruction of property except where such destruction is rendered absolutely necessary by military operations. We continue to press Israel to end the disproportionate use of force, demolitions and destruction of infrastructure.

(HL Deb 18 July 2003 Vol. 651 cWA193)

17/103

During a meeting in the Security Council the representative of the United Kingdom said:

The United Kingdom unreservedly condemns the recent escalation of violence and terrorism in Israel and in the occupied territories. We support Israeli actions within international law to act to prevent further terrorist attacks and to protect the lives of its citizens, and we understand the domestic pressure to do so. But the British Foreign Secretary has clearly voiced our fundamental disagreement with the Israeli security cabinet's decision in principle to expel President Arafat from the occupied territories. It would be wrong in principle to force the elected leader of the Palestinians to leave the Palestinian Authority area.

(UN.Doc S/PV.4824, 15 September 2003)

17/104

During a meeting in the Security Council the representative of the United Kingdom said:

The United Kingdom Government has always defended Israel's right, acting, consistent with international law, to protect its citizens. But disproportionate use of force by the Israel Defence Forces only fuels the cycle of violence.

(UN.Doc S/PV.4841, 14 October 2003)

17/105

During a House of Lords debate on Israel, the Minister of State, FCO, said:

My Lords, I hope I have made it clear that it is not the existence of the fence that we believe to be unlawful but the route that is taken. The noble Lord is quite right to remind us that since the fence built around the Gaza Strip has been in place, almost all the suicide bombings have come from the West Bank—indeed, I believe that only one has come from the Gaza Strip. I am sure that that unites Israeli public opinion around the feeling that there is a real necessity for the fence, for the sake of their own security. We wish to urge upon the Israelis that while we acknowledge that and see the difficulties they are facing, we hope that they will be a good deal more sensitive than they are being at present about the routing, which is causing a real problem and real hardship.

(HL Deb 28 October 2003 Vol. 654 c135)

17/106

In reply to a written question the Minister of State, FCO, wrote:

The UK has long taken the view that the Israeli presence in the Occupied Territories is governed by the Fourth Geneva Convention. The UK reaffirmed its view of the applicability of the Fourth Geneva Convention in the Occupied Territories at the reconvened conference of High Contracting Parties in Geneva on 5 December 2001. In accordance with the declaration adopted at the conference, we continue to call upon all parties to the conflict to respect and to ensure respect for the Geneva conventions in all circumstances.

(HL Deb 17 November 2003 Vol. 654 cWA241)

17/107

In reply to a written question the Minister of State, FCO, wrote:

The destruction of Palestinian infrastructure for the purpose of collective punishment is contrary to international humanitarian law. Furthermore, we believe such actions are provocative, and serve only to exacerbate tension and undermine efforts to bring about an end to violence and a return to negotiations. We have called on the Government of Israel to stop these demolitions and to ensure their actions in the Occupied Territories fall within international law. I last raised my concerns about the demolition of Palestinian homes with Israel's Ambassador, Mr Zvi Shtauber, on 22 October.

(HL Deb 15 December 2003 Vol. 655 cWA99–WA100)

17/108

During a House of Lords debate the Minister of State, FCO, said:

I say to him as I have done already to your Lordships that we are keen to see the transfer of responsibility for running Iraq returned to the Iraqis as soon as possible. I believe that that is a united view of all the countries sitting round the negotiating table in the Security Council, trying to find the best means of doing that by the most helpful United Nations Security Council resolution. However, I also say to my noble friend that the CPA has very clear responsibilities. It is responsible under the Geneva and Hague Conventions for ensuring that the security and humanitarian needs in Iraq are met. So I do not want to mislead my noble friend. One cannot simply say, "Let us share it out". There are specific legal responsibilities on the CPA, and those are ours to shoulder until such time as we are able to ensure that transition of power to which I referred a moment or two ago.

(HL Deb 8 September 2003 Vol. 651 c55)

17/109

In reply to a written question the Under-Secretary of State for Defence wrote:

Law and order is a high priority for the coalition in Iraq. More than 30,000 police officers have returned to work across Iraq, and are better paid than police under Saddam's regime. Coalition programmes, such as police training and the establishment of the new Iraqi army, will assist in bringing stability and ensuring that the rule of law in Iraq is enforced. United Kingdom forces operate to the highest standards, and are governed by the Geneva Convention IV, and rules of engagement derived from UK law.

(HL Deb 11 September 2003 Vol. 652 cWA145)

17/110

In reply to an oral question about his plans for post-conflict Iraq, the Prime Minister said:

We are in discussion now with not just the United States, but other allies and the United Nations. We want to ensure that any post-conflict authority in Iraq is endorsed and authorised by a new United Nations resolution, and I think that that will be an important part of bringing the international community back together again.

We have set out a vision statement for Iraq and the Iraqi people, and it might help if I highlight one or two of its aspects. First, we will support the Iraqi people in their desire for "a unified Iraq within its current borders", and we will protect their territorial integrity. Secondly, we will protect their wealth, and I repeat again that any money from Iraqi oil will go into a UN-administered trust fund for the benefit of the Iraqi people. There should be freedom ["] in an Iraq which respects fundamental human rights, including freedom of thought, conscience and religion and the dignity of family life", and there should be freedom from the fear of arbitrary arrest. There should also be an "Iraq respecting the rule of law, whose government reflects the diversity and choice of its population", and who help to rebuild Iraq, for the Iraqi people, on the basis of unifying the Iraqi people. Those principles of peace, prosperity, freedom and good government will go some way toward showing that if there is a conflict and Saddam Hussein is removed, the future for the Iraqi people will be brighter and better as a result.

(HC Deb 19 March 2003 Vol. 401 c931–932)

17/111

The Foreign Secretary was asked about the future of Iraq. He said:

Let us be clear, there are a number of people who thought that the military action would take a very long time, there would be very large numbers of casualties and so on, some people here thought that and they are entitled to their view, but that has not happened and they will have to re-examine their own judgments and in the course of re-examining the judgments, which may just turn out to be inaccurate, they are bound to alight on the next thing that they think is going to fail and we are seeing that process take place now. In all the discussions I have had with American interlocutors I have never heard the phrase Western style democracy being used. There is sometimes an assumption...that the Americans have no sense of how the world operates outside its own shores, but that is simply not the case. They have got a very sophisticated international relations establishment, sophisticated diplomats and they fully understand that the kind of democracy you can have operating inside Iraq will not be just a replication of the kind of democracy we have in Western Europe or they have in the United States, but the principles of democracy are not western, eastern, northern or southern, they are universal and it is having those principles applied within Iraq which is crucial, but they must be applied in such a way that takes account of Iraq's own tradition, culture and, above all, religion just as in Europe our own democracy also takes account of our culture, tradition and religion. (Qu.231)

(FAC Tenth Report, Foreign Policy Aspects of the War Against Terrorism, 29 April 2003, HC 405)

17/112

During a meeting of the Security Council the representative of the United Kingdom said:

I am fully aware that Member States, perhaps without exception, find the current situation deeply disappointing and distasteful. But they cannot set aside the clear, prolonged and universally available evidence that Iraq was repeatedly defying the United Nations in refusing complete disarmament of its weapons of mass destruction under the terms of successive resolutions. The express and explicit demands of the Security Council were never carried out by Iraq, and the United Nations has not succeeded in drawing the right conclusions about the consequences of that. Resolution 1441 (2002) was adopted unanimously but not implemented with any rigour by a united Council. International peace and security cannot be maintained with responsibility by avoiding hard decisions. Iraq was clearly determined—even in the face of the threat of military action—to hang on to its prohibited weapons programmes and to develop others, with all the risks that that posed to peace and security in the region and more widely, including to the national security of the United Kingdom. Iraq has, furthermore, valued its defiance over the well-being of its own people, who have as a consequence endured a decade of sanctions.

Coalition action is therefore now under way to enforce Security Council decisions on complete Iraqi disarmament. This action is being undertaken in a manner that is directed only at the regime that is responsible for this failure to respect the United Nations. We are doing everything possible to minimise the effect on civilians, to leave infrastructure intact and to ensure that the necessary humanitarian assistance reaches the Iraqi people as quickly as possible. We accept in full our obligations under international humanitarian law. The United Kingdom has already committed $80 million to support humanitarian agencies, including the excellent efforts of the Red Cross and the Red Crescent. A further $300 million has been set aside for the United Kingdom's humanitarian response. In addition to that, the United Kingdom is contributing one fifth of the growing European Union contribution. Coalition engineers are already at work building a water pipeline from Kuwait to distribute supplies in southern Iraq, while a Royal Fleet auxiliary ship will shortly be arriving at Umm Qasr, carrying the first coalition consignment by sea of humanitarian supplies. And I should like to underline that these significant efforts in Iraq will not detract from the funding and the very high priority that we are giving to all other development activity, particularly in Africa.

The action that the United Kingdom is now taking with its coalition partners to uphold United Nations resolutions is both legitimate and multilateral. The use of force is authorised in the current circumstances under Security Council resolutions 678 (1990), 687 (1991) and 1441 (2002). A broad coalition of well over 40 States is supporting this action materially or politically. We deeply regret the differences within the Security Council that have marked the past few months of discussion on this subject. Now is the time to put those behind us and to unite to ensure that the United Nations and the international community can act quickly to meet the needs of the Iraqi people during and after military action.

. . .

Looking further ahead, we will need to consider carefully the role that the United Nations can play in building a stable and prosperous Iraq. The expertise of the United Nations and that of the international community will be needed to achieve that result. The United Kingdom is convinced that the United Nations must take a central role in the future of Iraq. The Prime Minister will meet the Secretary-General at United Nations Headquarters later today to discuss precisely that. I sincerely hope that the Council will play its part with responsibility in ensuring a well-functioning Iraq that no longer presents a threat to international peace and security, where people can enjoy their fundamental rights without fear of oppression, and where a representative Government provides effectively for its people and manages natural resources for the exclusive benefit of all the people of Iraq.

(UN Doc. S/PV.4726 (Resumption 1), 27 March 2003)

17/113

During a meeting of the Security Council the representative of the United Kingdom said:

The United Kingdom has operated in Iraq from the beginning strictly in accordance with the Fourth Geneva Convention and the Hague Regulations.

(UN Doc. S/PV.4761, 22 May 2003)

17/114

During a Security Council meeting the representative of the United Kingdom said:

The text just adopted as Security Council resolution 1500 (2003) reflects the vital role of the United Nations in Iraq and creates the United Nations Assistance Mission for Iraq (UNAMI). It also rightfully welcomes the establishment of the Governing Council of Iraq. We are all agreed that the goal is to create, as soon as possible, an internationally representative Government exercising the sovereignty of Iraq. That must be worked up with and by the Iraqi people. We want to make progress rapidly, but of course it will take some time to create the rights and opportunities which have so long been denied to the Iraqi population. The United Kingdom is working with the coalition partners for an Iraq which can assume its rightful place in the international community and where the instruments of the international community can operate normally. That will entail a growing role for the United Nations and its agencies, and UNAMI will be an important catalyst for this. Lastly, the United Kingdom welcomes the support given to this resolution, reflecting the Security Council coming together and its members increasingly converging to work for the shared objective of a stable, united and free Iraq.

(UN Doc. S/PV.4808, 14 August 2003)

17/115

During a meeting of the Security Council, the representative of the United Kingdom said:

[O]ur goals in Iraq are clear and have been set out repeatedly by the Security Council: the achievement of a free, sovereign Iraq run by the people of Iraq for the people of Iraq and achieved as quickly as possible.

(UN Doc. S/PV.4812 , 21 August 2003)

17/116

Regarding Security Council Resolution 1511 (2003) [ed. On the administration of Iraq] the representative of the United Kingdom said during a Security Council meeting:

The United Kingdom saw three main objectives for the resolution: first, to confirm and accelerate the transfer of power to the people of Iraq; secondly, to send a clear signal that the international community is committed to the rapid political and economic reconstruction of a free Iraq which is secure and stable; and thirdly, to ensure, as conditions permit, a strengthened, vital role for the United Nations, in partnership with the Coalition Provisional Authority and, most importantly, with the Iraqi people. On the transfer of power, the resolution we have adopted is quite clearly about giving control of Iraq to its people as quickly as possible. Quite rightly, however, the resolution does not prescribe to the Iraqis artificial schedules for that transfer. Instead, it puts the people of Iraq in the driving seat through the Iraqi interim administration. It reaffirms Iraq's sovereignty and territorial integrity and the temporary nature of the Coalition's powers. It adds increased impetus, structure and clarity to the political process. It sets a deadline of two months from today by which the Governing Council should provide a timeline and the programme leading to an Iraqi constitution and democratic elections, and it engages the Security Council in this process. As I argued during the negotiations, it does not rule out moving to a provisional Government if that is likely to lead more rapidly and in more stable conditions to a democratic Iraq.

(UN Doc. S/PV.4844, 16 October 2003)

17/117

Her Majesty's Government was asked the following written question:

To ask the Chancellor of the Exchequer in relation to the written ministerial statement by the Economic Secretary on 3 April on duty on goods imported into the European Union which originate from Israeli settlements in the Occupied Territories, whether the standard Israeli reply referred to, sent in response to verification requests for the origin of goods, will be taken as adequate reason to suspect that goods may have originated in Israeli settlements in the Occupied Territories and for the customs debt to be applied.

In reply, the Economic Secretary wrote:

...the standard Israeli reply is insufficient to determine the real origin of the goods, or to dispel the reasonable doubt as to their entitlement to preferential duty rates under the EU/Israel Association Agreement. Preference is therefore being refused and HM Customs and Excise have now begun issuing duty demands.

(HC Deb 10 April 2003 Vol. 403 c398W)

(See also **17/97**)

17/118

The UK and the US sent a letter to the President of the Security Council on 8 May 2003. They wrote:

The United States of America, the United Kingdom of Great Britain and Northern Ireland and Coalition partners continue to act together to ensure the complete disarmament of Iraq of weapons of mass destruction and means of delivery in accordance with United Nations Security Council resolutions. The States participating in the Coalition will strictly abide by their obligations under international law, including those relating to the essential humanitarian needs of the people of Iraq. We will act to ensure that Iraq's oil is protected and used for the benefit of the Iraqi people.

In order to meet these objectives and obligations in the post-conflict period in Iraq, the United States, the United Kingdom and Coalition partners, acting under existing command and control arrangements through the Commander of Coalition Forces, have created the Coalition Provisional Authority, which includes the Office of Reconstruction and Humanitarian Assistance, to exercise powers of government temporarily, and, as necessary, especially to provide security, to allow the delivery of humanitarian aid, and to eliminate weapons of mass destruction.

The United States, the United Kingdom and Coalition partners, working through the Coalition Provisional Authority, shall inter alia, provide for security in and for the provisional administration of Iraq, including by: deterring hostilities; maintaining the territorial integrity of Iraq and securing Iraq's borders; securing, and removing, disabling, rendering harmless, eliminating or destroying (a) all of Iraq's weapons of mass destruction, ballistic missiles, unmanned aerial vehicles and all other chemical, biological and nuclear delivery systems and (b) all elements of Iraq's programme to research, develop, design, manufacture, produce, support, assemble and employ such weapons and delivery systems and subsystems and components thereof, including but not limited to stocks of chemical and biological agents, nuclear-weapon-usable material, and other related materials, technology, equipment, facilities and intellectual property that have been used in or can materially contribute to these programmes; in consultation with relevant international organizations, facilitating the orderly and voluntary return of refugees and displaced persons; maintaining civil law and order, including through encouraging international efforts to rebuild the capacity of the Iraqi civilian police force; eliminating all terrorist infrastructure and resources within Iraq and working to ensure that terrorists and terrorist groups are denied safe haven; supporting and coordinating demining and related activities; promoting accountability for crimes and atrocities committed by the previous Iraqi regime; and assuming immediate control of Iraqi institutions responsible for military and security matters and providing, as appropriate, for the demilitarization, demobilization, control, command, reformation, disestablishment, or reorganization of those institutions so that they no longer pose a threat to the Iraqi people or international peace and security but will be capable of defending Iraq's sovereignty and territorial integrity.

The United States, the United Kingdom and Coalition partners recognize the urgent need to create an environment in which the Iraqi people may freely determine their own political future. To this end, the United States, the United Kingdom and Coalition partners are facilitating the efforts of the Iraqi people to take the first steps towards forming a representative government, based on the rule of law, that affords fundamental freedoms and equal protection and justice under law to the people of Iraq without regard to ethnicity, religion or gender. The United States, the United Kingdom and Coalition partners are facilitating the establishment of representative institutions of government, and providing for the responsible administration of the Iraqi financial sector, for humanitarian relief, for economic reconstruction, for the transparent operation and repair of Iraq's infrastructure and natural resources, and for the progressive transfer of administrative responsibilities to such representative institutions of government, as appropriate. Our goal is to transfer responsibility for administration to representative Iraqi authorities as early as possible.

The United Nations has a vital role to play in providing humanitarian relief, in supporting the reconstruction of Iraq, and in helping in the formation of an Iraqi interim authority. The United States, the United Kingdom and Coalition partners are ready to work closely with representatives of the United Nations and its specialized agencies and look forward to the appointment of a special coordinator by the Secretary-General. We also welcome the support and contributions of Member States, international and regional organizations, and other entities, under appropriate coordination arrangements with the Coalition Provisional Authority.

(UN Doc. S/2003/538, 8 May 2003)

Part Seventeen: I. B.9. *The Law of Armed Conflict and International Humanitarian Law—International armed conflict—The law of international armed conflict—Conventional, nuclear, bacteriological and chemical weapons*

(See also **3/10**)

17/119

In reply to an oral question, the Prime Minister said:

I simply say in relation to any weapons or munitions that we use that we will use only those that are in accordance with international law and with the Geneva convention. That is the responsibility of the Government and is the commitment of this Government and has been of other British Governments in the past. We will do everything that we can to minimise civilian casualties. The reason why, in respect of any military action that we take, we get legal advice not merely on the military action itself but on the targeting is to make sure that that happens. Of course, I understand that, if there is conflict, there will be civilian casualties. That, I am afraid, is in the nature of any conflict, but we will do our best to minimise them. However, I point out to my hon. Friend that civilian casualties in Iraq are occurring every day as a result of the rule of Saddam Hussein. He will be responsible for many, many more deaths even in one year than we will be in any conflict.

(HC Deb 19 March 2003 Vol. 401 c934)

17/120

During a debate, the Parliamentary Under-Secretary of State, FCO, said:

I have seen in Afghanistan some of the damage that can be done by the weapons deployed in conflict situations. It is important that we support the good work being done by various NGOs in trying to ensure that there is a proper clean-up of the results of conflict. As my hon. Friend will know, the Ottawa agreement does not make the use of cluster bombs unlawful. At this stage, I cannot say what the intentions are in respect of those weapons. However, when it comes to targeting, we are determined that the coalition forces will do everything possible to ensure that they avoid civilian casualties, and to avoid creating circumstances that will cause civilian casualties in the aftermath of a conflict.

(HC Deb 19 March 2003 Vol. 401 c945)

17/121

In an oral answer, the Prime Minister said:

Yes, that is important. We are making it clear to Iraqi commanders in the field that if they use chemical or biological weapons, they will be deservedly prosecuted with the utmost severity. There are increasing reports about the distribution of equipment to Iraqi forces. It is difficult to be sure of their accuracy, but we have obviously been prepared for such an eventuality from the outset.

(HC Deb 26 March 2003 Vol. 402 c283)

17/122

In reply to a written question the Defence Minister wrote:

All weapons procured by the Ministry of Defence are subject to legal review in accordance with Article 36 of the 1977 First Additional Protocol to the 1949

Geneva Conventions and all new weapons and means and methods of warfare are reviewed to confirm their acceptability relative to the United Kingdom's obligations under the law of armed conflict. There are no exemptions for legal review for non-lethal or less-lethal weapons.

The main ethical consideration in evaluating such weapons derives from the potential effects on personnel taking part in testing. All evaluations involving human volunteers are subject to ethical constraints, specified in the Guidelines of the Royal College of Physicians. All MOD trials need to be approved by a MOD ethics committee following these guidelines. Trials involving sub-contractors are approved by a committee formed by that sub-contractor.

(HC Deb 10 July 2003 Vol. 408 c935W)

17/123

In reply to a written question, the Minister of State for the Home Office wrote:

The Government are fully committed to meeting our obligations under the Biological and Toxin Weapons Convention, which was implemented under the Biological Weapons Act 1974. More recently, we took new powers to deal with noxious substances. Sections 54 and 55 of the Terrorism Act 2000 (as amended in Section 120 of the Anti-terrorism Crime and Security Act 2001) make it an offence to provide, receive or invite another to receive instruction or training in the making or use of chemical, biological, radiological or nuclear weapons. In addition, section 113 of the Anti-terrorism Crime and Security Act 2001 makes it an offence to use any noxious substance or thing with the intention of causing serious harm to public or property, and section 114 creates an offence of hoaxing using alleged noxious substances. My right hon. Friend the Foreign Secretary has taken forward initiatives—including the Green Paper laid before the House in April 2002—intended to strengthen international efforts, and mechanisms, to counter proliferation.

(HC Deb 5 February 2003 Vol. 399 c321W–322W)

17/124

The Foreign Secretary was asked the following written question:

... pursuant to his answer of 13 February 2003 to my hon. Friend the Member for Nottingham, South (Alan Simpson), *Official Report*, column 107W, what the bio-chemical weapons referred to by US Defence Secretary Rumsfeld on 5 February 2003 in his testimony before the House Armed Services Committee are.

In reply, the Under-Secretary of State, FCO, wrote:

I understand US Defence Secretary, Donald Rumsfeld, in his evidence on 5 February to the US House Armed Services Committee, was referring to non-lethal Riot Control Agents. He went on to acknowledge that the United States has undertaken not to use any such Agents as a method of warfare. This prohibition applies to all States Parties to the CWC. Riot Control Agents are defined under the CWC as any chemical not listed in a Schedule which can produce rapidly in humans sensory irritation or disabling physical effects which disappear within a short time following termination of exposure.

(HC Deb 3 March 2003 Vol. 400 c843W)

17/125

In a written answer, the Under-Secretary of State, MoD, wrote:

In accordance with custom and practice after World War Two, many records of sea disposals of munitions, including chemical weapons (CW), were destroyed when they were perceived to be of no further administrative use. As a result of this practice, a detailed inventory of all munitions and CW dumped at sea does not exist.

Where relevant British records on sea dumpings of munitions and CW have survived, these have been declassified and transferred to the Public Record Office in accordance with the terms of the Public Records Act, 1958 and 1967. Furthermore, as the disposals took place largely between 1945 and 1948, prior to the creation of NATO, we are not aware of any NATO papers on this issue.

(HC Deb 5 March 2002 Vol. 381 c166W)

17/126

The Foreign Secretary was asked the following question:

. . . what information the Organisation for the Prohibition of Chemical Weapons has given the UK Government about when budgetary contributions should be paid?

In reply, the Parliamentary Under-Secretary of State, FCO, wrote:

The timelines for payment are in the OPCW's Financial Regulation 5.4. This states that contributions to the budget are payable in full within 30 days of receipt of the notice of assessment or on the first day of the financial period to which they relate, whichever is later. However, at 28 February 2003, 85 states parties had not paid anything towards their 2003 assessments.

(HC Deb 31 March 2003 Vol. 402 c522W)

17/127

In reply to a written question, the Parliamentary Under-Secretary of State, FCO, wrote:

The Government's policy towards the Chemical Weapons Convention (CWC) and the Biological and Toxin Weapons Convention (BWC) is to work towards their universal adoption and universal compliance with their obligations.

The United Kingdom abandoned its offensive chemical and biological weapons programmes in the 1950s. Subsequently we have played a leading role in the negotiations both of the BWC of 1975, for which we are a depositary government, and the CWC which entered into force in 1997. We are fully compliant with our obligations under both Conventions and continue to press for their full and effective implementation. To this end, both nationally and with our EU partners, we have conducted a series of demarches world-wide, with particular attention to regions of tension such as the Middle East.

The United Kingdom was instrumental in securing a successful outcome to the BWC Review Conference in November 2002, which saw agreement on a three year work programme of practical measures to deal with the BW threat. At the forthcoming CWC Review Conference (28 April–9 May 2003) the UK will be presenting a number of important technical and scientific papers. The strength of our political support and commitment to both Conventions, as well as the technical expertise we contribute, are second to none.

(HC Deb 24 February 2003 Vol. 400 c49W)

17/128

In reply to a written question, the Under-Secretary of State, FCO, wrote:

All States Parties to the Chemical Weapons Convention (CWC) have undertaken not to use any toxic chemical or its precursor, including riot control agents (RCAs), as a method of warfare. This applies in any armed conflict. RCAs are defined in the CWC as any chemical not listed in a Schedule which can produce rapidly in humans sensory irritation or disabling physical effects which disappear within a short time following termination of exposure. (A chemical listed in a Schedule is one identified for the application of verification measures under the CWC.)

(HC Deb 25 February 2003 Vol. 400 c422W)

17/129

The Minister of Defence was asked the following written question:

... will [he] make it his policy to withdraw British troops from military action where an ally uses (a) biological and (b) chemical weapons?

In reply, the Secretary of State for Defence wrote:

Our NATO allies are State Parties to both the Chemical Weapons Convention (CWC) and the Biological and Toxin Weapons Convention (BTWC) and have renounced the use of such weapons.

(HC Deb 3 March 2003 Vol. 400 c812W)

17/130

In a written answer, the Secretary of State for Defence said:

The Chemical Weapons Convention prohibits the development, production and use of all toxic chemicals (both lethal and incapacitating) and their precursors, except where they are intended for purposes not prohibited under the Convention, as long as the type and quantities are consistent with such purposes.

(HC Deb 13 March 2003 Vol. 401 c382W)

17/131

Her Majesty's Government was asked the following written question:

[W]hat assessment of ground conditions is undertaken before deployment of cluster bombs; and what alternative weapon is deployed where ground conditions might result in an unacceptably higher failure rate?

In response, the Minister of State for Defence wrote:

Decisions on the most appropriate weapon for use in attack take into account a wide variety of factors, consistent with our obligations under international law. These factors include the nature of the target, the weapons available to engage the target, and the conditions prevailing at the time of the attack. Specific ground conditions in the location of an attack, the effect of those conditions on failure rates, and the potential impact of a particular failure rate are factors that cannot normally be known by those making the decisions. Using weapons that are not the most appropriate for a target would reduce the likelihood of achieving the military objective and increase the risk of collateral damage. There are often no alternative weapons to cluster bombs that would avoid these negative consequences.

(HC Deb 28 February 2002 Vol. 380 c1457)

17/132

During a debate in the House of Commons, the Secretary of State for Defence was asked the following oral question:

Is [he] aware that the World Service is reporting that cluster bombs are being used in the area around Basra? I am sure that he is aware, as I am, of the long-term consequences for the civilian population of post-war Iraq of unexploded bomblets. Will he make it clear to his American counterpart, when they discuss Iraq, that we strongly disapprove of the use of anti-personnel land mines?

In reply, the Secretary of State for Defence said:

I have made it clear when dealing with such questions on previous occasions that it is necessary to allow our forces to use the most effective and appropriate weapons against the threats that they perceive. My hon. Friend may or may not be aware that 17 tanks sought to attack British forces yesterday. Every one of those tanks was destroyed, fortunately without allied losses. I would not be confident in saying to our forces that they could not use a particular weapon that protected them against those kinds of attack—I should not be doing my job properly. As I have indicated to my hon. Friend and others on previous occasions, we look carefully at the use of weapons, and use particular weapons only when it is absolutely appropriate to do so.

(HC Deb 26 March 2003 Vol. 402 c300)

17/133

In the continued debate, the same Minister said:

There is another imperative in the use of weapons, which is of course to try to minimise casualties among our own troops. That is the purpose of having the range of ammunition and equipment that is available to our troops in the Gulf. I would hope that the hon. Gentleman shares that objective, including the use of cluster bombs.

We have a very good record on clear-up, and we will always seek to proceed on that basis. Wherever we have been involved in conflicts involving the use of weapons, we have sought to clear up after ourselves.

(HC Deb 31 March 2003 Vol. 402 c657)

17/134

In an oral answer, the Minister of State, Ministry of Defence, said:

On DU [ed. Depleted Uranium] weapons, my hon. Friend did not name his source. He is usually quite well researched, so the fact that he did not do so could call into question the background of the research. There is still no reliable scientific or medical evidence to connect DU with ill health. More than 3,300 UK veterans of the 1990–91 Gulf conflict have been seen under the Gulf veterans medical assessment programme. Its physicians assess all those attending for signs of ill health that could be attributed to DU exposure. To date, no such evidence has been found.

The US Government have carefully monitored the health of 33 of their soldiers who were exposed to DU in extreme circumstances when DU rounds accidentally hit their vehicles during the Gulf conflict. Seventeen of them have had DU shrapnel embedded in their bodies for the past 12 years, yet they do not show signs of health problems attributable to DU. The offspring of those highly exposed US veterans, amounting to some 60 children, are all healthy.

(HC Deb 31 March 2003 Vol. 402 c663–664)

17/135

During a debate in the House of Commons, the Secretary of State for Defence said:

No doubt right hon. and hon. Members will raise the issue of cluster bombs, but my hon. Friend really has to face up to the facts. Certainly there are risks with cluster bombs, as there are risks of all munitions failing. The percentage failure rate is small, but it leaves a continuing problem, which I accept and recognise. That is why the explosive ordnance disposal people bravely risk their lives to clear up such problems. Balanced against that, my hon. Friend must face the issue of whether he would allow coalition forces to be put at risk because we are not prepared to use that particular capability. Without cluster bombs, we would have to use far larger ordnance to deal with the same problem. We would have to use far larger weapons to deal with deployed tanks, for example, which is the sort of target against which cluster bombs are used. I do not think that there is a simple answer to this issue. As I have indicated to the House on many previous occasions, we use the weapon only when it is absolutely justified, but if it is, it is because it will make the battlefield safer for our armed forces—and I am not prepared to compromise on that.

(HC Deb 3 April 2003 Vol. 404 c1076)

17/136

In a written answer, the Minister of State for Defence wrote:

The Ministry of Defence has held discussions on non-lethal weapons with United States military representatives bilaterally, multilaterally and in NATO. The United Kingdom considers that non-lethal weapons have potential military uses, where such uses are compatible with international legal obligations. No joint developments of non-lethal weapons with the United States are currently planned. All potential new weapons are subject to stringent review at all stages of the research and procurement process to ensure compliance with the United Kingdom's obligations under international and domestic law.

(HC Deb 3 February 2003 Vol. 399 c59W)

17/137

Her Majesty's Government was asked the following written question:

...whether British troops in the Gulf are equipped with disabling nerve agents; and under what circumstances they can be used?

In reply, the Secretary of State for Defence wrote:

No. As a State Party to the 1993 Chemical Weapons Convention, the United Kingdom has undertaken never to develop, produce or use chemical weapons.

(HC Deb 28 April 2003 Vol. 404 c48W)

17/138

In a written answer, the Parliamentary Under-Secretary of State, MoD, wrote:

The United Kingdom has not employed any weapons containing depleted uranium in Afghanistan. There are no air-launched bombs containing depleted uranium in UK service.

(HL Deb 6 November 2002 Vol. 640 cWA105)

17/139

In reply to a written question, the Minister of State for Defence wrote:

United Kingdom forces have two types of depleted uranium (DU) ammunition; 120 mm anti-tank rounds (CHARM 3), fired by the Army's Challenger tanks, and 20 mm rounds used by the Royal Navy's Phalanx Close-in Weapon System (a missile defence system). DU rounds are the most effective kinetic energy penetrators against armour and the British Army will use them if the need arises.

The Royal Navy's Close-in Weapon System does not require anti-armour properties and in recent years, a new tungsten round has been developed for it. Since 1996, all replacement ammunition for the Phalanx system has been of the tungsten variety. Some ships still carry the 20 mm DU round, however, and would fire it should the need arise.

(HC Deb 23 January 2003 Vol. 698 c447W)

17/140

In reply to a written question on Depleted Uranium, the Parliamentary Under-Secretary of State for Defence wrote:

Depleted uranium munitions are not illegal under any convention to which the United Kingdom is party. They are used discriminately and proportionally in accordance with the provisions of international law.

We are prepared to use DU tank munitions where necessary because they are currently the most effective anti-armour weapons. At present, we are not reviewing this policy because we have a duty to provide our troops with the best available equipment with which to protect themselves and succeed in conflict. Should future research identify a more effective alternative, the policy would be reviewed at that time.

(HL Deb 26 March 2003 Vol. 646 cWA82)

17/141

In response to a written question, the Secretary of State for Defence wrote:

The United Kingdom, as a State Party to the Ottawa Convention, does not possess operational anti-personnel mines and will not use any in Iraq.

(HC Deb 7 April 2003 Vol. 403 c8W)

17/142

In reply to a written question on whether it is the intention of the US to bring anti-personnel mines ashore onto Diego Garcia, the Parliamentary Under-Secretary of State, FCO, wrote:

The US authorities have been informed that HMG would be unable to allow the US to bring anti-personnel land mines ashore onto Diego Garcia because that would place the United Kingdom in breach of its obligations under the Ottawa Convention.

(HC Deb 17 March 2003 Vol. 401 c528W)

17/143

In reply to a written question, the Under-Secretary of State, FCO, wrote:

We have received assurances from the US authorities that no anti-personnel landmines were stored on Diego Garcia during 2001 or 2002. In contrast to anti-personnel landmines, anti-tank mines are not banned weapons under international law and are not subject to ban under international treaties. No anti-tank mines were stored on Diego Garcia by the British authorities in 2001 or 2002. The storing of such mines by the US authorities would be a matter for them under the various international agreements regulating their defence facility on the island.

(HC Deb 24 February 2003 Vol. 400 c243W)

17/144

In reply to a written question, the Minister of State for Defence wrote:

The Landmines Act 1998 prohibits certain conduct, including using or possessing an anti-personnel mine, or participating in the acquisition or transfer of an anti-personnel mine, or assisting, encouraging or inducing such conduct. These offences apply to conduct in the United Kingdom and to conduct by United Kingdom nationals elsewhere. Any indication of illegal activity would be a matter for the law enforcement agencies.

(HC Deb 14 March 2003 Vol. 401 c435W)

17/145

In reply to a written answer on Mines, the Secretary of State for Defence wrote:

Mines retained for permitted purposes under the Ottawa Convention were kept from previous operational stocks and small numbers of different types have been procured from various sources. These have been declared in the United Kingdom's annual return to the Secretary-General of the United Nations in accordance with Article 7 of the Ottawa Convention.

Retained mines have been used for training in mine detection, mine clearance and mine destruction techniques as permitted in Article 3 of the Ottawa Convention. Specific purposes include: training explosive and mine detection dogs; training military and civilian mine clearance personnel; making relevant training films, videos, and posters; testing and trials of mine clearance devices; and testing and trials of protective clothing and equipment.

(HC Deb 19 March 2003 Vol. 401 c783W–784W)

17/146

During a debate in the House of Commons, the Secretary of State for International Development said:

There are absolute duties under the Ottawa convention to record any use of munitions that may damage civilians, and the British military fully adheres to all international treaties and humanitarian obligations. Our troops always de-mine in the first instance, as they are trying to do in the waterways of Iraq now, so that they can bring in humanitarian supplies. Thereafter, we will probably bring in UNMAS [ed. UN Mine Action Service], the UN body that looks for mines, because Iraq will have to be de-mined if it is to be reconstructed.

(HC Deb 24 March 2003 Vol. 402 c43)

17/147

In reply to a written question the Under-Secretary of State, FCO, wrote:

The Government considers universalisation of the Ottawa Convention to be the best means of combating the production, use, stockpiling or transfer of anti-personnel land mines. The United Kingdom was among the first states to ratify the Convention and continues to play a leading role in follow-up work, including encouraging the widest possible adherence to the treaty. Through our diplomatic missions overseas we have recently lobbied states not party to the Convention, urging their ratification or accession at the earliest opportunity.

(HL Deb 4 November 2003 Vol. 412 c543W)

17/148

In a note of 20 December 2002 to the Minister of Foreign Affairs, France, the UK withdrew its remaining reservations to the Protocol for the Prohibition of the Use in War of Asphyxiating, Poisonous or other Gases, and of Bacteriological Methods of Warfare.

First Supplementary List of Ratifications, Accessions, Withdrawals, etc for 2003, UKTS No.38 (2003), p.3.

17/149

In reply to a written question, the Under-Secretary of State, FCO, wrote:

There is no universally accepted definition of the phrase "weapons of mass destruction", but it is generally held to refer to nuclear, chemical and biological weapons.

(HC Deb 28 January 2003 Vol. 398 c767W)

17/150

In reply to a written question, the Minister of State, FCO, wrote:

There have been long-standing concerns about Iran's ambitions to pursue a nuclear weapons programme.

We regularly urge all states to sign and ratify all the treaties and conventions covering the development of weapons of mass destruction.

The United Kingdom has consistently supported resolutions at the United Nations calling for the creation of a Middle East zone free of weapons of mass destruction.

(HL Deb 3 March 2003 Vol. 645 cWA84)

17/151

In reply to a written question, the Minister of State, FCO, wrote:

We are concerned by persistent reports that Syria is pursuing a programme for the development of weapons of mass destruction.

We regularly urge all states to sign and ratify all the treaties and conventions covering the development of such weapons.

(HL Deb 4 March 2003 Vol. 645 cWA104)

17/152

In response to a written question, the Prime Minister wrote:

Assessments of whether Iraq has nuclear, chemical and biological weapons are constantly updated in the light of information received. We continue to believe that Iraq has chemical and biological weapons, and that it is seeking to re-establish a nuclear weapons programme. Under UN Security Council Resolution 1441, the onus was placed firmly on Iraq to prove that it did not possess such weapons. It has failed to do so.

(HC Deb 7 April 2003 Vol. 403 c25W)

17/153

During a debate in the House of Commons, the Prime Minister said:

We are in discussion with the United Nations about this. Plainly, it would be a good idea from every perspective to make sure that there is some sort of objective verification of any potential weapons of mass destruction that are seized. As we speak, there is obviously an investigation going on into certain of those weapons that were taken a few days ago, and tests are being carried out. However, it is important, I think, for the international community as a whole that, as we establish control—and, indeed, as people working on these programmes are free to come forward and speak to us—we make sure that a legitimacy is given to this, so that there can be some objective assessment of the truth of the situation. Certainly, so far as we are concerned—perhaps this allows me to say this once again—we have no doubt at all that these weapons of mass destruction exist. I say to people who sometimes say, "Why haven't you been finding them as you've gone through the country?" that the truth is that there has been a six-month campaign of concealment. It is not surprising that we have not found them. We need the evidence of the experts and scientists, but we are convinced that we will get it.

(HC Deb 9 April 2003 Vol. 403 c262–263)

17/154

In reply to a written question on Export Controls, the Parliamentary Under-Secretary of State for Trade and Industry wrote:

The scope of the control on the provision of technical assistance in relation to weapons of mass destruction (WMD) was drawn up after consultation on the draft Export Control Bill which sought views on the Bill and on the Government's proposals for the content of the secondary legislation. The scope of this control is in line with both the new WMD controls on the transfer by any means of technology and with the WMD provisions contained in the EC Dual-Use Regulation. The EC Dual-Use Regulation requires member states to control the physical export and electronic transfer of dual-use goods or technology which the exporter or transferor knows, or has been informed, is or may be intended for use in connection with WMD.

The new control on the provision of technical assistance applies to anyone in the UK or any UK person anywhere.

(HC Deb 14 April 2003 Vol. 403 c482W)

17/155

During a debate in the House of Commons, the Secretary of State, FCO, said:

The right hon. Gentleman asked about the oil-for-food resolutions. The oil-for-food programme is a United Nations programme that was rolled over by resolution 1472, and again last week by resolution 1476, until 3 June. It will continue as a United Nations programme until the Security Council makes decisions about the future of oil-for-food and of the sanctions regime.

The right hon. Gentleman also asked whether there are any democratic outcomes that are unacceptable. Well, we cannot have it both ways. If we wish to see a democracy established in Iraq as elsewhere, we have to accept that in the end, such a democracy is one in which the people of Iraq—like the people of this country—have to make up their own minds about their own future. That is the essence of democracy. Of course, there are some outcomes—outcomes that would lead to a change in the territorial integrity of Iraq—that would be unacceptable.

(HC Deb 28 April 2003 Vol. 404 c26)

17/156

In response to a written question, the Parliamentary Under-Secretary of State, FCO, wrote:

Coalition action in Iraq has not been at the expense of the campaign against international terrorism, which has continued unabated. There has never been a question of choosing between the two threats. The downfall of the regime in Iraq will reduce the threat of terrorists gaining access to weapons of mass destruction.

(HC Deb 28 April 2003 Vol. 404 c115W)

17/157

During a debate in the House of Commons, the Parliamentary Under-Secretary said:

Hans Blix himself has said that he believes that the circumstances are dangerous, and it would have been unsuitable to date for the inspectors to seek to return to Iraq and complete their task. My right hon. Friend the Secretary of State has said that it is the Government's hope that inspectors will be able to return to Iraq in due course and that they will be able to give independent oversight of the process of the finding of WMD. However, their objectives will be different. The objective will no longer be detection, more a validation of findings, and our objective is to see if we can ensure that there is some independent oversight of those findings.

The right hon. and learned Gentleman asked what the other restrictions are. Obviously, we will need to ensure that the United Nations Security Council is satisfied that that is the way to proceed, and we hope that we shall be able to obtain not only further resolutions from the Security Council, but agreement on how inspection and a range of other matters will proceed in relation to Iraq.

(HC Deb 6 May 2003 Vol. 404 c513–514)

Part Seventeen: I. B.11. *The Law of Armed Conflict and International Humanitarian Law—International armed conflict—The law of international armed conflict—Termination of international armed conflict, treaties of peace*

17/158

In reply to a question on the Lusaka Ceasefire, the Parliamentary Under-Secretary of State, FCO, wrote:

FCO officials have regular discussions with all regional Governments listed and with the UN (both in New York and in the Great Lakes region) about the conflict in the Democratic Republic of Congo and the implementation of the Lusaka and Pretoria Agreements. We warmly welcomed the agreement signed in Sun City on 2 April on the establishment of a transitional government with a view to democratic elections in two years time. This concluded the Inter-Congolese Dialogue provided for under the Lusaka Agreement. We will continue to be involved in the peace process as members of the International Committee for Support to the Transition.

We were shocked to learn of the appalling massacre of civilians by militia in the DRC's Ituri Province on 3 April. My noble Friend, the Baroness Amos, issued a statement on 7 April strongly condemning this tragedy. A copy has been placed in the Library of the House. We are concerned about the effect of the situation in Ituri on relations between Rwanda and Uganda. We have urged Rwanda and Uganda to exercise restraint and not to become engaged in direct confrontation on Congolese soil.

(HC Deb 28 April 2003 Vol. 404 c125W)

17/159

In reply to a written question on the UN Compensation Commission, the Parliamentary Under-Secretary of State, FCO, wrote:

The UK, as a Security Council member, sits on the Governing Council of the United Nations Compensation Commission and is represented by HMG officials in Geneva and London. Claims for compensation from the UNCC are dealt with by the FCO Consular Claims Section and through our diplomatic mission in Geneva.

The commission has received about 2.6 million claims seeking compensation in excess of US$300 billion. The majority of these claims have been resolved. Nearly 100 Governments have submitted claims, as well as various UN organisations. Details of which countries have submitted claims can be found on the UNCC website: www.unog.ch/uncc.

(HC Deb 20 March 2003 Vol. 401 c882W)

17/160

In a written answer, the Secretary of State for International Development wrote:

The Security Council unanimously approved a resolution authorising the UN Secretary General to manage the Oil-for-Food (OFF) programme. This is very important for the 16 million Iraqis who rely on the OFF for survival.

The UN believes that some humanitarian needs might be met from existing OFF escrow accounts. The UN will keep the international community abreast of any adjustments to the flash appeal that they issued on 28 March 2003 to cover humanitarian needs over the next six months.

(HC Deb 1 April 2003 Vol. 402 c659W)

17/161

In reply to several oral questions, the Prime Minister made the following statement:

Of course we must act within the law the entire time, but until the conflict is over the fact and the law are the same: the coalition forces are there and they have certain legal obligations that they have to administer. The moment the conflict ends, it is important to have in place a UN resolution that governs the situation, so that we provide both for humanitarian aid and, as we said in our Azores statement, for the endorsement of any post-conflict Iraq. There will be difficulties when we make the transition to the Iraqi interim authority as to precisely what the negotiations in the UN bring us, but the one point in common, whatever the differences, is that everybody understands that the situation has to be UN-endorsed. I believe that with the right will, we will get that UN resolution. This situation differs from all the discussions that we had over the so-called second resolution that we did not get, because in this case everybody in

Europe—even those who oppose our position—and ourselves and the United States know that for all sorts of reasons we must have that UN endorsement.

(HC Deb 2 April 2003 Vol. 402 c911–912)

17/162

During a debate in the House of Commons, the Prime Minister said:

In relation to who we would take a surrender from, it is extremely difficult, as we speak, to know what is left of the governing higher ranks of Saddam's regime. I think that the best way of answering that would be that we must be clear that whoever we accept a final declaration from to the effect that, so far as Saddam's regime is concerned, the war is over, whoever it is has that proper authority. I cannot at the moment make a judgment as to who that may be...

(HC Deb 9 April 2003 Vol. 403 c461)

17/163

The Minister of Defence was asked the following written question:

...if he will make a statement on how the coalition forces invading Iraq convey to Iraqi citizens how they can surrender.

In reply, he wrote:

The Coalition have dropped approximately 32 million–33 million leaflets aimed at Iraqi citizens, mainly combatants, but also civilians.

Those aimed at combatants include instructions on how to surrender, including adopting a non-offensive posture, raising a white flag, stowing weapons, and parking combat vehicles in a square formation.

Those aimed at civilians advise on how to avoid being caught up in military action, by staying away from military targets, by staying indoors, and not interfering with coalition operations.

In addition, the Coalition have used radio and loudspeaker broadcasts to convey specific surrender instructions to combatants.

(HC Deb 10 April 2003 Vol. 403 c351W)

17/164

In a written answer, the Minister of State for Defence wrote:

Under the Geneva Convention, treatment of prisoners taken during hostilities is a matter for the Detaining Power. We will adhere to our obligations under the Geneva Convention towards all prisoners we capture. We are confident that the United States will do likewise.

(HC Deb 10 April 2003 Vol. 403 c352W)

17/165

In reply to a written question on what plans are in place to ensure early access for UN agencies and international aid agencies into Basra, the Secretary of State for International Development wrote:

The International Committee for the Red Cross (ICRC) are already operating in Basra.

Most humanitarian agencies require a permissive security environment before they can operate in Iraq. The Office of the UN Security Co-ordinator (UNSECOORD) provides security advice to the UN humanitarian agencies. Security updates are also being provided through the Humanitarian Operations Centre in Kuwait. NGOs are being issued passes to cross the Kuwait/Iraq border by the Humanitarian Operations Centre in Kuwait. Once the situation allows, NGOs will need to undertake their own security assessments before engaging.

The military are discharging their humanitarian obligations under the Geneva and Hague conventions in order to provide relief in the interim in the territory they occupy. The military fully appreciates the need to hand over to humanitarian agencies as soon as the situation allows.

(HC Deb 10 April 2003 Vol. 403 c389W)

17/166

In reply to a written question on the Iraqi oil production, the Parliamentary Under-Secretary of State, FCO, wrote:

The coalition will limit itself to emergency maintenance and repairs, and other short term measures, which might allow production at or above last year's level, itself about the same as in 1990. But my right hon. Friend the Prime Minister has made it quite clear on numerous occasions that Iraqi oil belongs to the people of Iraq. All major investment decisions should be taken by the Iraqis themselves, not the coalition.

(HC Deb 28 April 2003 Vol. 404 c125W)

17/167

In a written answer, the Secretary of State, FCO, wrote:

Our Military Campaign Objectives contain a commitment to withdrawal of British military forces from Iraq as soon as is practicable. It is too early at this stage to predict when the appropriate circumstance will arise to allow a full withdrawal. We will maintain an appropriate military presence in Iraq as long as is necessary to enable the conditions within which the Iraqis can get their country running effectively, politically and economically.

We have kept the House fully informed of deployments to the middle east and of subsequent withdrawals of forces from the region. We will continue to keep deployments to the region under review and will keep the House informed of future withdrawals.

(HC Deb 1 May 2003 Vol. 404 c450W)

Part Seventeen: II. *The Law of Armed Conflict and International Humanitarian Law—Non-international armed conflict*

17/168

During a debate in the House of Lords, the Minister of State, FCO, made the following statements:

...Her Majesty's Government recognise the territorial integrity of the Russian Federation and we share the Russian Government's outrage at the recent terrorist attack in Moscow. Our sympathy goes out to the families and friends of the victims of this appalling tragedy. We have unequivocally condemned the perpetrators of that attack and their links to international terrorism. Of course, we believe that the Russian response to that incident, and their military operations in Chechnya, must respect the rule of law and their human rights obligations.

...

...the attack on the theatre in Moscow was not the only attack to be perpetrated by some in Chechnya. They have perpetrated such attacks on civilian targets before; they have also used land mines indiscriminately; and they have maltreated Russian prisoners. Of course, allegations have also been made about the conduct of Russian forces. We believe that any such operations have to be proportionate and in accordance with the rule of law. We press the Russians to investigate thoroughly any allegations of human rights abuses. We would like to see more effective co-operation between the Russian authorities and humanitarian aid agencies and we do not believe that the problem can be solved by military means alone. It must also be solved through discussion.

...

...I cannot agree with the noble Baroness that the war is fundamentally inspired by Islamic extremists. I agree with the noble Baroness that some Islamic extremists have allied themselves with international Islamic extremists. I have mentioned Shamil Basayev who was responsible for what happened in Moscow; I could equally mention Abu Walid who leads the Mujaheddin operating in Chechnya. But there are other elements who, although they are by Russian lights behaving murderously, are not necessarily so closely linked with Islamic terrorism but who are perpetrating acts of violence still against civilian objectives in Chechnya.

(HL Deb 18 November 2002 Vol. 641 c135–138)

Part Nineteen: I. A. *Legal Aspects of International Relations and Co-operation in Particular Matters—General economic and financial Matters—Trade*

19/1

In reply to a written question, the Secretary of State, International Development, wrote:

World Trade Organisation (WTO) rules need to apply to all members. But they must also be achievable by developing countries, with realistic implementation schedules and targets.

New rules require the right balance between standardisation and flexibility. For rules to be strong and binding, they need to have enough flexibility to meet the varying needs of the WTO membership and to recognise that WTO members are at different stages of development.

Without flexibility, new WTO agreements will be stuck at the lowest common denominator. This will lead to richer members making agreements amongst themselves outside the WTO and without consideration for the impacts on developing countries.

The term 'special and differential treatment' is used to describe special provisions for developing countries in existing WTO agreements.[1] Many developing countries complain that in the Uruguay Round the application of special and differential treatment and the treatment of different country circumstances were haphazard and that longer implementation deadlines for developing countries were decided arbitrarily.

There needs to be a better application of flexibility in designing future WTO rules. Appropriate flexibility should be integrated systematically into WTO agreements, rather than added on as an afterthought.

Special and differential treatment reforms will eventually link into the poverty reduction strategies. Thus the integration of trade policy reform is essential if poor people are to benefit from trade liberalisation. In addition to special and differential treatment, the UK has been supporting the Integrated Framework. The Integrated Framework has two aims: to identify trade capacity building and technical assistance needs in least developed countries to which the multilateral agencies and donors can then make a co-ordinated response; and to mainstream trade into least developed countries' poverty reduction strategies, so that pro-poor trade policies are included in a consistent manner in a country's overall development strategy. The Integrated Framework is based on the principle of country ownership and partnership. It is now being implemented in 14 least developed countries and eventually will be extended to Low Income countries.

[1] These are in the form of (1) provisions aimed at increasing trade opportunities, (2) provisions that call upon WTO members to safeguard the interest of developing countries, (3) flexibility of commitments, (4) transitional time periods, and (5) technical assistance.

Ultimately the Integrated Framework should cease to be necessary as trade becomes successfully integrated into poverty reduction strategies.

(HC Deb 28 January 2003 Vol. 398 c748W)

19/2

During a debate in the House of Commons, the Parliamentary Under-Secretary of State for International Development said:

It is not true that the IMF is denying debt relief. The heavily indebted poor countries agreement for Zambia includes conditions on economic reform that the Zambian Government have yet to meet, but we hope that they will do so soon. As he knows, terms are attached to the conditions of aid or relief in relation to a number of measures, and the current situation relates to those.

(HC Deb 6 February 2003 Vol. 399 c179W)

19/3

In reply to a written question, the Minister of State, FCO, wrote:

The UK's Export Credits Guarantee Department (ECGD) has not supported any amount of export credits to British companies trading with Burma during the years 1998 to 2002. ECGD is off cover for Burma because the risks are unacceptable and in view of the political and human rights situation in Burma, it is government policy not to encourage trade or investment that directly or indirectly benefits the current Burmese regime.

(HL Deb 4 March 2003 Vol. 654 cWA103)

19/4

In reply to a written question, the Minister of State, FCO, wrote:

Since the most recent revision of the Organisation for Economic Co-operation and Development (OECD) Guidelines for Multinational Enterprises which took place in June 2000, the United Kingdom national contact point (NCP) has been in receipt of one formal complaint, received on 27 February 2002, in respect of an alleged breach by the company Anglo-American in Zambia. The national contact point replied to this submission on 1 March 2002. Further details with regard to action taken are governed by the confidentiality provisions of the guidelines.

(HL Deb 4 March 2003 Vol. 645 cWA104–WA105)

19/5

In response to a written question, the Under-Secretary of State for Environment, Food and Rural Affairs wrote:

Comprehensive records of arrests and convictions for the illegal importation of any meat are not held centrally. Prosecutions for offences relating to bushmeat can be brought under the Convention on International Trade in Endangered Species by HM Customs, and under the Products of Animal Origin (Third Country Imports) (England) Regulations by local authorities. We are aware of three convictions for offences relating to the illegal importation of bushmeat, all in 2001.

(HC Deb 7 March 2003 Vol. 400 c1290W)

19/6

During a debate in the House of Commons, the Minister for Rural Affairs and Urban Quality of Life said:

There is also the issue of the unfair application of WTO rules. For instance, concerted pressure from a number of member states, including the UK, recently led to the amendment of the classification of frozen, salted poultry meat imports to close a loophole, which some importers were exploiting to pay less tariff on lightly salted frozen products; my hon. Friend referred to that situation. That loophole has been closed but, as I have indicated, we need evidence to go further. There has been direct representation by turkey producers, rather than the UK Government, to the EC. Given the evidence, we are happy to represent the industry.

WTO rules allow for temporary special restrictions to be imposed on imports to offset a sudden significant drop in market prices or a surge in the volume of imports. Under WTO rules, however, those additional duties can be applied only to a limited number of chicken and turkey products. In general, it is fair to say that there is little obvious prospect of reducing the level of imports. Indeed, the Government's wider policy is to open up trade and it would be inconsistent to exclude poultry. In the longer term, import volumes are likely to grow further, particularly following further tariff reductions as part of a WTO settlement. Consequently, UK producers are unlikely to be able to compete on price alone, which means that they will have to rely increasingly on producing quality assured products for which they will obtain a premium price. My hon. Friend has rightly indicated the steps that the industry has taken effectively to compete in that market. It is fair to say that local and regional marketing can also assist the industry, which is something that DEFRA and the Government seek to promote.

(HC Deb 11 March 2003 Vol. 401 c27WH)

19/7

In a Ministerial Statement, the Economic Secretary to the Treasury wrote:

Under the EU/Israel Association Agreement, goods originating in the State of Israel may be imported into the European Union at preferential rates of duty, including zero rates. Under Article 49 of the Fourth Geneva Convention and following United Nations Security Council Resolutions 242 and 338, the international community, including all EU member states, does not recognise the territories which Israel occupied in June 1967 as part of the State of Israel.

Goods originating from settlements in these occupied territories are therefore not entitled to the preferences of the EU/Israel Association Agreement.

The EU/Israel Association Agreement entered into force on 1 June 2000. Article 32 of Protocol 4 provides for the verification of proofs of origin at the request of the importing state. It further provides that preference is to be refused where there is reasonable doubt as to entitlement and there is no reply within ten months, or the reply does not contain sufficient information to determine the real origin of the goods. The Israeli authorities confirmed in July 2001 that they export to the EU goods from settlements in the occupied territories while certifying that they have been produced in the State of Israel.

Importers have been warned that importing goods produced in the occupied territories may give rise to a customs debt. The European Commission published such a warning in the Official Journal in November 2001, and HM Customs & Excise issued a Joint Customs Consultative Committee (JCCC) Information Paper to notify UK importers of this European Commission warning notice. Imports from Israeli settlements in the occupied territories can still be made to EU member states but will attract duty at the appropriate rate. Goods originating in the State of Israel can continue to be imported at preferential duty rates.

Concerted action, organised by the European Commission, is being taken by customs authorities in all EU member states to ensure that goods produced in the settlements do not obtain preferential rates of duty to which they are not entitled. Customs & Excise issued a second JCCC Information Paper in March 2002 announcing how these arrangements would apply in the UK.

Customs authorities are taking steps to identify imports of goods where there is evidence of occupied territory origin, taking security for duty and sending verification requests to the Israeli authorities, specifically asking whether the goods have been produced in an occupied territory. The standard Israeli reply, sent in response to all such requests, fails to answer the direct question, stating that the goods have been produced in an area that is under Israeli customs responsibility. This answer is insufficient to determine the real origin of the goods, and the Israeli authorities have been told so on each occasion.

In a written answer I gave...on 4 February 2003... I outlined the action Customs & Excise have been taking in the UK. In line with our obligations under the Community Customs Code [Council Regulation (EEC) No 2913/92], and as the ten month deadline is reached, Customs & Excise have now begun issuing duty demands to UK importers where there is reason to suspect that goods may have originated in Israeli settlements in the occupied territories.

(HC Deb 3 April 2003 Vol. 402 c68WS–69WS)

19/8

In response to a written question, the Secretary of State for International Development wrote:

The Government have contributed to a study on measures that the EU could take to control illegal logging and trade in illegally sourced timber products.

The study indicated that the UK's money laundering legislation under the Proceeds of Crime Act 2002 could be used as a possible measure by which the proceeds of illegal logging entering the UK financial system could be identified and persons involved convicted. However, this would require illegal logging in other countries and associated trade to be defined as criminal offences under UK law.

The study also indicated that some forms of illegal logging could be targeted under the Theft Act 1968 that applies to goods that have been stolen abroad as well as within the UK. For this to be effective, there must first be a request by a court or prosecuting authority in the country of origin for the suspected stolen goods to be seized and criminal proceedings initiated or a person arrested for the offence. Therefore, using UK legislation in this regard is dependent on the activities of enforcement agencies in the countries of origin of illegal timber. Provided these actions have been taken, sale within the UK of timber known to be illegally sourced may be considered an offence.

(HC Deb 6 May 2003 Vol. 404 c576W–577W)

19/9

In reply to a written question the Financial Secretary wrote:

UNSCR 1483 welcomes the readiness of creditors, including those of the Paris Club, to seek a solution to Iraq's sovereign debt problems, protects oil revenues from seizure until December 2007, and provides a transparent route for settlement of UN compensation claims.

We welcomed the 10 July Paris Club statement that creditors "... share the view that they don't expect Iraq to be in a position to resume payments to them before end 2004". We expect this unofficial moratorium to allow sufficient time for the establishment of an internationally recognised, representative Government of Iraq, legally empowered to negotiate and agree an IMF programme and debt treatments with creditors.

(HC Deb 6 October 2003 Vol. 411 c1094W)

19/10

During a meeting in the General Assembly the representative of the European Union said:

The European Union cannot accept that its economic and commercial relations with third countries be restricted through unilateral measures imposed by the United States on specific countries, in this case Cuba. Therefore, in November 1996, the Council of Ministers of the European Union adopted a regulation and a joint action aimed at protecting the interests of natural or legal persons from the European Union against the extraterritorial effects of the Helms-Burton Act.

...

The European Union rejects the restrictions imposed on the embassies of most European Union member States by the Cuban authorities, which constitute a de facto violation of the Vienna Convention on Diplomatic Relations.

(UN Doc. A/58/PV.54, 4 November 2003)

19/11

In a written answer, the Secretary of State for Trade and Industry wrote:

I have taken every opportunity to press our concern about the continued imposition of these unjustified tariffs and to express support for the UK product exclusion requests, including a telephone conversation with Donald Evans, US Commerce Secretary on 26 March.

On 21 March the US Administration announced the outcome of the second round of product exclusion requests which was launched in September last year. Of the 72 requests submitted by 10 companies, 62 were approved. As in the first exclusion round, the Government actively supported all UK requests liaising closely with UK companies and the US Administration.

In April, the WTO Dispute Settlement Panel is expected to rule on the challenge to the US steel safeguard action by the EU (together with Brazil, China, Japan, New Zealand, Norway, South Korea and Switzerland). We expect the panel to rule against the US measures. We will urge the US Administration to take account of its WTO obligations and the wider trade liberalisation agenda and come into full and prompt compliance with the ruling and immediately withdraw the tariffs.

(HC Deb 27 March 2003 Vol. 402 c325W)

19/12

During a House of Lords debate on the WTO, the Under-Secretary of State for Science and Innovation said:

. . . it is well known that the Government are taking a strong line on the question of the US steel tariffs, which the World Trade Organisation has now rejected, declaring them to be illegal. Of course we are keen to ensure, so far as any country is concerned, that this whole round should not degenerate into any form of bilateral deal as opposed to continuing with multilateral agreements.

. . .

The matter has gone to the WTO, which has made it clear that the subsidies for the tariffs on American steel are illegal. It is for the EU to take further action in due course . . .

(HL Deb 19 November 2003 Vol. 654 c1926 and c1938)

Part Nineteen: I. B. *Legal Aspects of International Relations and Co-operation in Particular Matters—General economic and financial matters—Loans*

19/13

In a written answer, the Economic Secretary wrote:

Of the total debt currently owed to the UK Government by developing countries over 95 per cent. is owed to the Export Credits Guarantee Department. The key reason for this high percentage of commercial credits is that Official Development Assistance provided by the UK normally takes the form of grants as compared with concessional loans so there is little debt owed to the UK other than amounts owed to ECGD. The UK is at the forefront of the debate on international debt relief and participates fully in the enhanced Heavily Indebted Poor Countries (HIPC) initiative agreed at Cologne in 1999 that makes provision for the cancellation of around US$100 billion of debt. Moreover, the UK goes beyond the terms agreed under the HIPC initiative and always provides 100 per cent. debt relief. So for the 26 countries that have reached Decision Point in the HIPC initiative the UK is providing 100 per cent. debt relief.

In addition, for those HIPCs yet to reach Decision Point the UK operates a unilateral 'Hold-in-Trust' policy. For these countries yet to secure debt relief because of conflict, civil unrest or the absence of a poverty reduction programme, any debt payments made are held in trust until they can be returned to fund poverty reduction.

(HL Deb 8 April 2003 Vol. 403 c145W–146W)

19/14

In reply to a written question about debt relief to Haiti, Cambodia, Georgia and Afghanistan, a Government representative wrote:

The list of countries eligible for debt relief under the heavily indebted poor countries (HIPC) initiative is not fixed. Any country can be added to the list if it meets the three eligibility criteria: the country must be eligible only for concessional lending from the IMF and World Bank; it must face an unsustainable debt burden after the application of traditional debt relief mechanisms; and it must have demonstrated its commitment to poverty reduction.

Those countries that are not eligible for debt relief under the HIPC initiative can still approach the Paris Club (the unofficial grouping of major bilateral creditors) for relief. In December 1994, Paris Club creditors agreed to implement a new treatment, "Naples terms", on the debt of the poorest countries. Eligibility for the Naples terms is assessed on a case-by-case basis, taking into account the track record of the debtor country with the Paris Club and the IMF, and various criteria, including having a high level of indebtedness, being only eligible for IDA financing from the World Bank, and having a GDP-per-capita of 755 dollars or less. Creditors agreed in September 1999 that all Naples terms treatments would carry a 67 per cent. debt reduction.

On the basis of current debt ratios, none of the four countries named would be eligible for the HIPC initiative, but Haiti could potentially meet the Naples criteria. Cambodia received Naples terms relief in 1995 and its debt:export ratio is currently slightly higher than the 150 per cent. threshold. Around 80 per cent. of this debt is bilateral debt owed to Russia and the US. The latest available figures for Georgia suggest that their debt:export ratio is below 150 per cent. Haiti has a level of external debt significantly above 150 per cent. of exports, but would need to make significant progress in strengthening governance and institutions before it could qualify for debt relief. Finally, World Bank country data for Afghanistan give its debt:export ratio as significantly below 150 per cent.

The UK stands ready to provide generous debt reduction should these countries meet the relevant criteria and approach the Paris Club for debt relief.

(HL Deb 16 December 2003 Vol. 655 cWA121–WA122)

Part Nineteen: I. F. *Legal Aspects of International Relations and Co-operation in Particular Matters—General economic and financial matters—Development*

19/15

In a speech to the UN Commission on Human Rights on 19 March 2003, a Foreign Office Minister said:

. . . when a regime shows contempt for human rights, abandons any semblance of democratic process at home, and arms itself with weapons of mass destruction, it becomes a threat to world stability, as well as to its own population. That is why it is essential that the international community both disarms Iraq and takes all necessary steps to secure the rule of law in that country. When we entrench human rights, we entrench democracy and the rule of law. This is not only right in itself. It is also essential for sustainable development: for attracting foreign investment, for protecting local investment; for giving individuals the means to raise themselves from poverty. . .

Too often, the debate about human rights has been presented as a choice between civil and political rights on the one hand; and economic, social and cultural rights on the other. This is a false choice. The two sets of rights are inextricably linked. How can an individual assert their right to freedom from hunger, or their right to health if they don't have a voice, or if they have no way of making their Government listen to them? What hope does someone have of realising their right to education if they live in a society with no rule of law, no freedom of expression, no freedom of association? How can an individual fully enjoy their civil and political rights if their economic and social rights are not also being realised? Civil and political rights and economic and social rights are mutually reinforcing and together provide the foundations for sustainable development. That is at the heart of what we mean by the right to development.

(Text on FCO website, www.fco.gov.uk/speeches)

Part Nineteen: III. *Legal Aspects of International Relations and Co-operation in Particular Matters—Environment*

19/16

In reply to a written question the Secretary of State for the Environment, Food and Rural Affairs wrote:

The Government regard the Cartagena Protocol on Biosafety as an important international agreement governing the handling and movement of genetically modified organisms (GMOs). Once in force, it will provide a common basis for all countries of the world to take informed decisions about imports and exports of any GMOs that may affect wildlife and natural habitats. Most of the UK's obligations under the Protocol have been, or are being, implemented at European Community level. The Community legal framework for the Protocol is expected to be completed later this month with the adoption of measures governing exports of GMOs. Adoption of these measures will demonstrate that the UK is fully able to meet its obligations under the Protocol and will enable the necessary national ratification procedures to be completed shortly thereafter.

(HC Deb 26 June 2003 Vol. 407 c914W–915W)

Part Nineteen: IV. *Legal Aspects of International Relations and Co-operation in Particular Matters—Natural resources*

19/17

During a debate on endangered species a Government representative stated:

As noble Lords have recognised, reviewing the CITES regulations is only part of the answer. In answer to a point raised by the noble Lord, Lord Rotherwick, the Government have taken three other significant steps to combat illegal wildlife trade. First, at the international level, the UK delegation, led by my honourable friend the Minister for Fisheries, Water and Nature Protection, was a key player at the conference of parties to the Convention on International Trade in Endangered Species (CITES) held in Santiago, Chile, in November. The conference took a number of decisions of great importance, both for the development of CITES and for the wildlife species it protects. For example, it agreed to the UK's proposal to move the basking shark up to Appendix II of the convention and to provide similar protection for the whale shark, sea horses, mahogany and many turtle species.

...

...CITES imposes a complete trade ban on the most endangered species. Therefore, there is no question of sustainable trade in such species.

(HL Deb 28 January 2003 Vol. 643 c1086)

Part Nineteen: V. *Legal Aspects of International Relations and Co-operation in Particular Matters—Technology*

19/18

In a UN Working Group on the International Convention Against the Reproductive Cloning of Human Beings on 29 September 2003, the United Kingdom's representative said:

The United Kingdom is committed to this initiative of the United Nations, which is seeking to achieve a worldwide ban on reproductive cloning. However, we are equally convinced that such a ban should not be extended to cover so-called "therapeutic cloning", the creation of embryos through cell nuclear replacement for the purposes of research into serious disease.

The United Kingdom was one of the first countries to introduce specific legislation banning any attempt to carry out reproductive cloning. The Human Reproductive Cloning Act 2001 provides for up to ten years imprisonment and an unlimited fine on conviction. The United Kingdom Parliament considered whether this ban should be extended to all cloning research. Members of the United Kingdom Parliament voted by almost 3 to 1 to restrict the ban to reproductive cloning alone. This was a free vote where members were allowed to vote according to their conscience rather than their political party.

United Kingdom law on embryo research has evolved over 20 years of public and parliamentary debate. The Human Fertilisation and Embryology Authority, established in 1991, subjects all embryo research in both the private and public sector to a robust system of case by case review before any licence to permit research is issued. Our legislation contains other important protections for the embryo. Research is only allowed for the limited purposes set out in the legislation and no research is allowed on embryos over 14 days old.

We strongly believe that therapeutic cloning research should be allowed to continue in countries, like the United Kingdom, which have reached a national consensus on this issue and which have a rigorous and effective system of regulation of embryo research.

We are looking to a future where cellular research will lead to new treatments for a range of serious diseases which affect many millions of people and which are currently without a cure. Treatments for Parkinson's, Alzheimer's, diabetes, heart disease, stroke, repair of spinal injury and organ damage are just some of the possibilities. At the moment it is simply too early to say which research tools will deliver these anticipated healthcare benefits. Therapeutic cloning is one of the technologies that we believe has enormous promise.

In our view, all types of cell research, including therapeutic cloning, should be encouraged to maximise the chances of medical breakthrough. We do not believe it is either necessary or wise to make a choice now that might deny millions of people and their families the chance of life saving treatments.

This view is strongly supported by eminent bodies in the United Kingdom such as the Royal Society, and all the leading medical charities as well as the general public.

It is also the view of the international scientific community. More than 60 of the world's leading science academies published a joint statement last week on 22 September calling for the United Nations to ban reproductive cloning but allow therapeutic cloning to continue. This concluded: "Cloning for research and therapeutic purposes has considerable potential from a scientific perspective and should be excluded from the ban on human cloning."

In conclusion, the United Kingdom recognises the difficulties of balancing scientific progress and ethical concerns. The United Kingdom also recognises and respects the cultural, religious and social differences that may lead other countries to arrive at different conclusions on what types of research may be appropriate in their own national setting. The United Kingdom has no wish to interfere in decisions legitimately taken by other national governments.

We believe that a complete ban on therapeutic cloning research would be a draconian approach which would be completely inappropriate for those countries with nationally agreed regulatory systems for embryo research, including therapeutic cloning, and who are working to deliver new treatments for serious and life threatening diseases.

It is for these reasons that the United Kingdom cannot support the Costa Rican proposal and why we would not be party to any convention which aimed to introduce a global ban on therapeutic cloning.

(www.ukun.org)

Part Nineteen: VI. *Legal Aspects of International Relations and Co-operation in Particular Matters—Social and health matters*

19/19

During a debate in the House of Commons on Deep Vein Thrombosis, the Parliamentary Under-Secretary of State for Transport said:

My hon. Friend explained why he thinks that the Warsaw convention is unduly protective of airlines, particularly in the light of the recent High Court ruling to which he referred. Although he rightly spoke of the convention as the international agreement that is in force, the key legal instrument is now the Montreal convention, to which he also referred. The Montreal convention, which is expected to come into force later this year, consolidates and updates all the earlier Warsaw-based rules. The adoption of the Montreal convention in 1999, within the framework of the International Civil Aviation Organisation, concluded a period of intense, and at times difficult, negotiations to forge worldwide consensus from a range of divergent views.

In many ways, the Warsaw convention had become out of date and the Montreal convention is a significant step forward in consumer protection. For example, it greatly increases the financial liability of airlines in the event of accidents to passengers. The UK is ready to ratify the new convention along with our partners in the European Community. My hon. Friend will appreciate that the UK is not in a position to make unilateral changes on matters such as those. Were any further amendments to be proposed, they would have to be considered and if appropriate agreed at a global level, probably through the ICAO.

Furthermore, I expect the European Commission to assert that the existence of Community law in this area creates exclusive Community competence, which would require us to act in concert with our European partners. In practice, I see little possibility of the international aviation community wishing to consider amending the convention so soon after its adoption and before it has come into force.

With regard to the case to which my hon. Friend referred, I understand that there may be an appeal. It therefore would not be appropriate for me to comment on that case. However, I can make some general points about the effects of the Warsaw convention. Mr. Justice Nelson held that the atypical reaction of any passenger to a normal and unremarkable flight does not, without any other factor, constitute an accident under article 17 of the Warsaw convention. The judge relied on a well-established legal interpretation of the term "accident" as an unexpected or unusual event or happening that is external to the passenger. [ed. The judgment was upheld by the Court of Appeal in *Re Deep Vein Thrombosis & Air Travel Litigation* [2003] EWCA Civ 1005.]

...

That is what I was trying to say. The way in which the courts have interpreted the Warsaw convention has prevented that particular group of passengers from claiming damages from the airline. It is a complex area of policy and law and it would be difficult to go into all the legal detail and niceties of the matter in the context of the debate today.

My hon. Friend has raised some important issues today, as he has on many other occasions. Those issues are of concern to passengers, consumers, the Government and the airlines. I welcome the debate as it gave me the opportunity to respond to some of his arguments. If there are questions to which I did not respond, I will write to him.

(HC Deb 19 March 2003 Vol. 401 c268WH–269WH)

19/20

In reply to a written question, the Financial Secretary wrote:

The European Community does not have exclusive competence for economic and social cohesion. As a result, under the rule of subsidiarity, the Community's actions in this area should be limited to what cannot sufficiently be achieved by the member states. The principle of subsidiarity is set out in Article 5 of the Treaty establishing the European Community. EU regional funding and policies under the EU Framework for Devolved Regional Policy as proposed in the Government's paper "A Modern Regional Policy for the United Kingdom" would have a legal base in Article 161 and other relevant articles of the same Treaty.

(HC Deb 25 March 2003 Vol. 402 c132W)

Part Nineteen: VIII. *Legal Aspects of International Relations and Co-operation in Particular Matters—Legal matters (for example judicial assistance, crime control, etc.)*

19/21

During a debate in the House of Lords on the Crime (International Co-operation) Bill, the Attorney-General said:

The general position in relation to mutual legal assistance—and the general position under the Bill and the 1990 Act—is, as I think I heard the noble Lord say, a matter for the discretion of the state that receives the request. I am told—something of which I was not aware when I responded previously, and which may be helpful—that on occasion, by relying on that general discretion, conditions are imposed in relation to particular requests where there is concern that a fishing expedition may be being conducted. There are examples where that has taken place.

There is therefore a general ability to impose a condition in certain cases. We would not want as a matter of policy and practicality to establish a general power to do so in relation to incoming requests. Indeed, in certain cases that would be impossible. The noble Lord rightly referred to the bilateral treaty with the United States, which contains restrictions, but there are international obligations that, in a sense, go the other way. Article 23 of MLAC [ed. Mutual Legal Assistance Convention] states that certain personal data communicated under the convention can be used for specific purposes that go beyond the proceedings to which the particular request applies.

(HL Deb 24 February 2003 Vol. 645 c165)

19/22

During a debate in the House of Lords on the Crime (International Co-operation) Bill, the Attorney-General said:

Amendment No. 45 is designed to cover the matters listed in Article 1(4) of the protocol. Its effect would be to list the requirements in the Bill. Let me explain why we are not happy with that approach. The Secretary of State's discretion on receipt of a request from an EU country will be exercised with the protocol requirements in mind. Our obligation to respond to requests for banking information extends only to those from participating countries that are made on the basis of the protocol. Requests must therefore comply with all of Article 1 of the protocol in order to be valid.

We consider that the general discretion conferred on the Secretary of State in subsection (3) is preferable to a clause that explicitly states how the Secretary of State must act when a request is received in a particular form. It enables us to apply the Article 1 conditions and to exercise a general discretion, which we think is right.

Requirement for a full explanation of reasons could be interpreted—it might well be—as going way beyond what we are entitled to demand from the requesting authority under Article 1(4). It might be considered a breach of our obligations under the protocol. Article 1(4) lists certain points, but makes no requirement for a full or total explanation. It states why it is considered that the request for information is likely to be of substantial value for the purpose of the investigation into the offence—that is very clear—and on what grounds it is presumed that banks in the requested member state hold the account and, to the extent available, which banks may be involved. I do not consider that explicitly listing Article 1(4) conditions is appropriate either. It is quite clear that the Secretary of State is operating within that ambit. I am happy to stress that the Secretary of State's discretion will be exercised with the protocol requirements in mind. In addition, one of the requirements in Article 1(4) is that the request include any information available that may facilitate the execution of the request. The Secretary of State could not tell at consideration stage whether that had been complied with—whether the additional information did facilitate execution of the request—so inclusion in the Bill would be wrong. He would not be able to tell if it had been complied with until the particular circumstances were confronted on a particular application.

(HL Deb 25 February 2003 Vol. 645 c188–189)

19/23

During a debate in the House of Lords on the Crime (International Co-operation) Bill, the Attorney-General said:

I shall respond to a number of questions raised by the noble Lord, Lord Goodhart, and explain what the term "participating country" means, why only participating countries are involved, how the Proceeds of Crime Act will assist and the relevance of the Abacha case, which was the origin of the matter.

I begin with the definition of "participating countries". A participating country is defined in Clause 51(2) of the Bill as a country other than the UK which is an EU member state on a day appointed for the commencement of that provision, and any other country designated by an order. That mechanism enables different countries to be designated as participating countries for the purposes of different provisions of the Bill.

The purpose is to restrict the application of certain provisions to those countries that are under an equal obligation to provide a particular type of assistance. In other words, the arrangements will be reciprocal. The provisions of Chapter 4, to which the amendments relate, enable us to request and provide assistance in identifying and monitoring bank accounts. Those forms of assistance are regulated for the first time in the protocol to the MLA [ed. Mutual Legal Assistance] convention. We are under an obligation only to provide those forms of assistance to countries that are party to that agreement and we have chosen as a matter of policy to restrict the application of Chapter 4 to designated countries rather than giving it general application. That restriction contrasts with our policy more generally on the provision of mutual legal assistance where we do not require the existence of an agreement as a condition for assisting. However, those types of assistance are new and specialised, and the amount of work involved in executing such requests will be fairly substantial. We do not consider it appropriate to give the provisions general application when many countries will not be in a position to reciprocate. At heart, that is the reason why we started off in this tighter fashion.

With regard to changes to the relevance of the Proceeds of Crime Act, Part 11 of the Act will streamline the UK's ability to co-operate with other countries in tracing, freezing and confiscating assets. It also provides for the investigation powers in Part 8 of the Act to be used at the request of foreign jurisdictions. The investigation powers include customer information orders and account monitoring orders, which are the types of assistance that Chapter 4 of the Bill introduces in respect of EU member states. That will be accomplished by subsidiary legislation. We expect to make the relevant Orders in Council later this year. Unlike the existing legislation, an overseas territory will no longer need to be designated before restraint and confiscation co-operation can be given. In the subordinate legislation, we intend to make restraint available from the start of an overseas investigation rather than at the point when a person is charged with an offence. That was one of the main criticisms of the UK legislation that stemmed from the Abacha case. Bringing forward the availability of restraint will help to prevent the dissipation of assets in overseas cases. I am sure many Members of the House recollect that at the time of the Abacha case, UK law did not allow assets to be restrained until the suspects were being charged, and it did not require a genius to predict what had happened to the assets very shortly after that, as was found to be the case.

A second point relevant to the Abacha case is that the Act provides that the international co-operation arrangements are made by order rather than in primary legislation. I hope the House recognises that that is a further benefit. It will allow for easy amendment to keep pace with international initiatives, such as mutual recognition in the EU and enable us to deal effectively with groundbreaking and high-profile cases, such as the Abacha case. It is highly desirable that we do so and seek to prevent a recurrence of such situations. I respect the reasons that lie behind the amendment and hope that my response gives the assurance that we will not be in quite the same position again.

(HL Deb 25 February 2003 Vol. 645 c190–191)

19/24

During a debate in the House of Lords on the Crime (International Co-operation) Bill, the Attorney-General said:

The reason for the restriction in relation to tracing accounts was explained in Committee: as the noble Lord, Lord Goodhart, signalled, such requests are likely to place significant demands on the resources of countries without central bank registers, and it was judged that there is a need for proportionality between the crime in question and the measure requested. The protocol explicitly states that the obligation to assist under Article 1 is limited to those cases which we have described, for simplicity, as involving "serious criminal conduct", as defined in Clause 46(3) of the Bill. The reasons for not having an equivalent restriction in relation to account monitoring orders are perhaps less clear and merit further explanation. We do not consider that a parallel restriction in relation to account monitoring would reflect the aims of the drafters of the protocol or make full use of the opportunities available to us as the requesting state.

Article 3 of the protocol creates an obligation for member states to be able to monitor activity in specified accounts. During negotiations, as I signalled, it was not considered necessary expressly to limit that obligation only to certain types of serious offence, in contrast to Article 1. Requests for monitoring will be targeted at an already identified account and so will not place such a burden on banks—and we can already provide historical details of activity in such accounts even without new legislation.

As the noble Lord, Lord Goodhart, signalled, that did not lie behind the amendment; if I understood it correctly, that involved more an argument about balancing the civil liberties of the person whose account, unknown to them, might be being monitored against the potential level of serious criminality—or otherwise—of the suspected person. I understand that argument but I am unsympathetic to it.

The fact that we are defining some offences as "serious" in the Bill does not imply that the other offences of which a person is suspected of being connected with or potentially guilty of but which do not meet the strict tests—if I have them right, they are a maximum period of at least four years in the requesting state and at least two years in the requested state—are not serious. They simply do not meet the test. I should be happy to give a list of examples of offences that do not meet the test of being "serious" as defined in the clause to which I referred previously but which under any common-sense meaning of the word are seen by the public as being serious.

The view that we should not use legitimate, properly tested conditional and proportional powers of the state to try to find out whether criminality is going on because it is argued that it is best to protect the civil liberties of the suspected criminals is deeply unconvincing. We will not use the powers willy-nilly; they will be used although they are burdensome to the requesting states, the officiating states and the courts. It will require effort to use them but we must use them and monitor accounts when there is a suspicion that people have committed offences.

A further point is that in some cases people will be traced through account monitoring orders who may, to use the patois, be the small fish in events but they may lead us to the bigger people. For that additional reason, I am deeply unsympathetic to the restriction.

(HL Deb 25 February 2003 Vol. 645 c215–216)

19/25

In a debate on the Grand Committee's Report on the Crime (International Co-operation) Bill, the Parliamentary Under-Secretary of State for Home Affairs stated:

The Schengen arrangements and cross-border surveillance are reciprocal and clearly the Committee recognises that only by implementing them properly can we expect our law enforcement officers to be able to benefit from them. Article 40.2 of the Schengen Convention, which the clause implements, provides for the grace period of five hours for the continuation of surveillance across a national boundary in urgent circumstances.

On a practical level, one hour, which is the nature of the probing amendment, might not be sufficient time. It is our intention that UK officers will take control of all cross-border surveillance operations entering the UK, but there may be occasions in which the five-hour grace period is needed to allow time to identify the appropriate force to take over the surveillance and for the UK team to obtain authority under RIPA and then to meet up with the foreign officers to take over the surveillance. I do not sense a major disagreement in the Committee on that. There is recognition that there will be circumstances—albeit, one hopes, rare—when a UK surveillance team might not be immediately present at the port at the time when the suspect entered it.

The key to these arrangements is reciprocity. There will be occasions when UK officers will need to apply this measure in the course of their work and follow a suspect overseas. We can hardly expect foreign colleagues to give us the benefit of the full five hours if we do not reciprocate. It must be appreciated that foreign police and Customs forces face the same issues when a surveillance operation crosses into their territory. For those reasons we would resist these amendments.

Obviously, the UK was not party to the negotiations on the Schengen Convention. They were undertaken some time ago. Our understanding is that the five hours was held in negotiation to be a sufficient time for the authority of the receiving member state to respond to the immediate notification from the incoming officers signalling that they had crossed the border and for the receiving member state to take over the surveillance, or to send one of their own officers to the scene to accompany the foreign officers, making it a joint investigation.

Our understanding is further that these measures have been in operation for some time on continental Europe and experience has shown that the five hours appears to have been a reasonable period. I am not aware, but I shall check before Report stage, of any problems that have arisen as a consequence of the five hours.

Any surveillance carried out by foreign officers will be subject to the conditions set out in Article 40 of Schengen. That clearly states that foreign officers must contact UK police to alert them as soon as they have crossed the border. At this point, communication will have been established, allowing a certain level of supervision by the UK. If they do not comply with the conditions set out in Section 76A and the subsequent order, they will not be deemed authorised. Foreign officers would gain little benefit from conducting unauthorised surveillance which would take them outside the terms of Article 40.

All cross-border surveillance operations under the Schengen Convention will be the subject of a report to the authority in whose territory they took place. As with all reports of surveillance operations in the UK, these will be retained and made available to the surveillance commissioner as required.

The noble Lord, Lord Carlisle, asked whether it would be reasonably practical to apply for authority or to take over. He was asking, in essence, whether we felt that five hours put at risk surveillance. I have already signalled that I will double check that, but we do not believe that that has been the case to date.

In practice, although the latest date by which a foreign officer would notify a UK authority was when he put his foot on UK soil, as we indicated during previous discussions on the Bill, on many occasions there would be notification earlier than that. That allows for two things: first, it increases the likelihood that a surveillance team could be in place at the port; and, secondly, it gives further lead time over and above the five hours, which begins from the moment the person puts his foot on UK soil.

I was asked why not have more flexibility. First, we do not believe that it is necessary. Secondly, it is important that there is a clear-cut end date, which gives the public the reassurance that only in tightly limited circumstances will a foreign officer be able to come in and continue a surveillance, albeit without any executive powers of arrest or entry.

The noble Baroness, Lady Anelay, asked where is the UK border. The new Section 76A gives five hours automatic authorisation from,

> "the time when the [foreign] officer enters the UK".

We believe that these words should be given their natural common-sense meaning. Accordingly, we consider that entering the UK is when the foreign officers arrive at a port or airport; or, for Eurostar, when the train leaves the tunnel and enters Kent.

I was asked when we will know when the period starts. It will be from the notification of entry and, furthermore, any notification prior to entry that they were coming. We would know approximately when the ship was docking and when people were disembarking. Could we stretch the period to more than five hours? No, for the reasons I have given. We do not believe that we would want to stretch or need to stretch the period. Can Parliament change what is in the Schengen Convention? I believe that the Committee knows the answers to that. Parliament is sovereign and therefore it can do what it wills. However, if it chose to change the provision, we would not be compliant with the Schengen Convention and therefore we would not be able to benefit from the measures in it.

The National Criminal Intelligence Service will keep the record. It will therefore know when the five hours has expired because it will be five hours after the process began. The noble Baroness, Lady Anelay, and the noble Lord, Lord Carlisle, asked what happens after the five hours. After the five hours, the foreign officer would lose the lawfulness of new Section 76A; he would lose the protection against assaults in Clause 83; and he would lose the civil liabilities provision in Clause 85. After five hours, he would have no protection under those provisions and if he continued surveillance, he would be acting without authority and in breach of the agreements.

. . .

The provision is meant essentially to enhance co-operation so that British police forces are better able to obtain evidence and apprehend those who committed crime, and whom they have under surveillance, in order to bring them to justice.

From our perspective, at heart, the measures will deal with circumstances which have occurred in the past whereby people under surveillance by the British police forces have crossed the Channel and contact with them was lost, frustrating the police's ability to collect the evidence that they thought might assist in bringing prosecutions and convictions. The same is true in reverse. There have been occasions when our neighbours on the Continent had people under surveillance whom they believed had committed an offence. They thought it necessary to continue that covert surveillance in order to collect further evidence for a prosecution. When the people crossed into this country, our neighbours were unable to pursue.

To take it more sharply, most of the cross-border operations will be brought in as a result of the Bill and implementation of Article 40.2 of the Schengen convention. Let me illustrate how the operations will work in practice. Most of the cross-border operations that come from the EU into this country will be pre-planned and authorised in advance. We expect that the vast majority will be of that nature. I am slightly labouring the point because, in pre-planned operations, the surveillance operation will be taken over by British forces—in practice, the National Crime Squad—upon the suspect's entry to the UK. We expect that that is what will happen in the vast majority of cases.

There are, however, urgent cases—the focus of this clause and this issue—where it is not always possible to get either the authorisation or the authorisation and a UK surveillance team in place at the port in time to take over the surveillance operation. It is about putting in place highly limited and circumscribed regulations which, in such tightly circumscribed circumstances, allow the surveillance to continue in the United Kingdom for a limited time, until such time as British police forces can take over the surveillance. So it applies only when it is not possible to get a British force to take over the surveillance immediately, and then only in very tightly circumscribed circumstances. I shall try to illustrate those circumstances.

Foreign officers cannot operate here until they have requested assistance—as soon as it seems probable that the suspects they are following will be crossing into the United Kingdom. So there is a duty to notify NCIS as soon as it seems probable that their suspect will be coming to the United Kingdom. They must also notify NCIS as soon as they have arrived in the United Kingdom. I stress again that that applies only when it has not been possible to arrange through advance notification a joint investigatory team or a UK force at the point of entry. NCIS will be the point of contact for all requests and will authorise or refuse the operation. They have the right of refusal. The National Crime Squad or a local force will be notified by NCIS, and will identify officers to link up with the incoming foreign officers as soon as possible.

The period for which foreign officers may operate alone is strictly limited under the Schengen convention, and under the Bill's provisions, to five hours. There is a maximum of five hours to allow time for the British police forces to take over the surveillance. If they have not done so within that period, surveillance must stop. The UK may require foreign officers to stop at any time within the five hours. So, having given authorisation, they can rescind it if they think it appropriate to do so at any time within that period.

I shall labour the next point because it is germane. Foreign officers may not carry their firearms. They will be prohibited from bringing their guns into the United Kingdom. They may not enter private property. They may not challenge or arrest a suspect. They must submit a report of every operation in which they have entered the United Kingdom at short notice. In all those circumstances, even though it will not always be possible to put in a UK force before they come in, they must notify NCIS before their feet touch UK soil. So we will know that they are coming; we will know who is coming; and we will authorise their entry. We will simply be allowing them to continue for a short period in the very limited number of circumstances where it has not been possible to get our own surveillance forces into place in time. I hope that the Committee will bear with me in setting out those issues, as we are bound to revert to them on subsequent amendments. It is the novelty of leading on these amendments rather than responding to them that has led me to behave in that way.

The purpose of the amendment is straightforward. It allows officers from other countries to carry out under tight conditions lawful surveillance of a person suspected of a serious crime. I emphasise that we are talking about only serious criminal offences, not minor offences or misdemeanours. We are making the changes as part of our wider commitment to fight international crime with our EU partners. It will allow better co-operation at every instance. The measure is supported by the Association of Chief Police Officers and the National Criminal Intelligence Service. Other EU countries have been running Schengen arrangements on cross-border surveillance for years. They have managed to make them work well despite some shared difficult histories.

(HL Deb 29 January 2003 Vol. 643 cGC198–GC208)

19/26

During the continued debate the same Minister said:

[F]oreign officers will be expected to request assistance as soon as it seems probable that the suspects they are following will cross into the UK. That will be our general expectation; as soon as the foreign officers are aware of that situation arising, they will make contact. In strict legality, they could board the ferry and continue the surveillance into the United Kingdom. As I signalled earlier, and will come to on subsequent amendments, immediately the foreign officers arrive in the United Kingdom they would have to give notification of their presence.

Those circumstances are expected to be few because, while the foreign officers are waiting for their car or whatever to be loaded on to a ferry or a hovercraft, it would be relatively simple to call NCIS on the telephone number in their Schengen handbook and notify it of their arrival.

. . .

The foreign officers will be aware that they must deposit their guns within their own country. That is for two reasons. First, it will be in the Schengen handbook—surveillance officers will be expected to carry a copy. The handbook will set out the rules of entry to the UK. Secondly, it is such—how shall I put it?—a highly apparent issue that it is hard to believe that a French or a Belgian officer would not be aware that they were prohibited from bringing their gun into this country. On the mechanism of doing so, we would expect gun-carrying foreign officers to hand over their gun to an appropriate official at the embarkation port while waiting to board the ferry.

(HL Deb 29 January 2003 Vol. 643 cGC204–206)

19/27

During the House of Lords debate on the Crime (International Co-operation) Bill, the Under-Secretary of State for Home Affairs stated:

As I said, we would seek to use the powers in Clause 82 [ed. which exceptionally would allow surveillance in the UK by foreign police officers under international agreements] only in respect of serious crimes. The noble Lady . . . may press me further by saying that serious crimes will already be offences in the UK. . . . The reason for having this sort of flexibility is, of course, that we prefer to take a generic approach in legislation to one that depends on having harmonisation of offences between countries. In other words, we do not think that having an exact identity of an offence is an appropriate way of considering these issues. . . . If one looks at the offences to which Article 40.2 of Schengen applies, it will be seen that they are widely drafted but clearly refer to very serious matters.

We expect that any future agreement would take a similar approach. I do not anticipate a situation whereby foreign officers who suspect a person of committing, for instance, an offence of xenophobia, or of holocaust denial, . . . signalled, would be allowed to conduct this sort of surveillance in the United Kingdom. Those would not be seen as serious offences as a matter of public policy in terms of the United Kingdom's approach. I should also point out that the foreign officers would not conduct investigations in this country, as they would not, of course, have any executive powers. It would simply be a question of surveillance.

An example of the type of crimes that might be considered in addition to those currently covered by Article 40 and discussed in the context of the Schengen convention are organised fraud, smuggling of illegal immigrants, laundering of the proceeds from organised crime, and illicit trafficking in nuclear and radioactive substances. All of those are self-evidently serious crimes. To expect to have an exact identity—in other words, explicit dual criminality—is . . . a flawed approach because, provided one has the generic offence, one is more certain to catch the mischief that one seeks to catch. I emphasise yet again that we are talking about serious crimes in this regard. Any future agreement containing provisions of this nature would also be subject to parliamentary oversight before it could be ratified.

(HL Deb 3 March 2003 Vol. 645 c647–648)

19/28

During a debate in the House of Commons on the Crime (International Co-operation) Bill, the Minister for Citizenship and Immigration made the following statements:

The Bill implements measures in seven separate European Union agreements. The first is the Schengen implementing convention of 1990. As the House knows, the UK applied to participate in 1999 and was accepted by the Justice and Home Affairs Council in 2000. The other agreements are the mutual legal assistance convention, which updates the provisions of the 1959 convention; the protocol to that convention, finally adopted in 2001; the framework decision on the execution in the EU of freezing assets and evidence; the framework decision on combating terrorism; the convention on driving disqualification; and the framework decision on non-cash means of payment agreed in May 2001.

. . .

The Bill marks a significant advance in co-operation against serious crime and terrorism in the European Union. It will enable us to work more closely and effectively with our EU partners, and more widely outside the EU. It will make it easier to investigate and prosecute cross-border criminal activity. By implementing key EU measures directed at terrorism and serious crime, it demonstrates firmly our commitment to greater co-operation on these matters with our EU partners. The measures on driving disqualification will promote greater road safety across the EU.

The Bill comes to this place after careful and helpful scrutiny in another place, where the Government responded to some of the concerns expressed and acted on them to provide greater clarity and reassurance. Thus some key order-making powers are now subject to affirmative rather than negative procedure, and conditions attached to cross-border surveillance by foreign officers are now written into the Bill.

We are already working effectively with our EU partners through Europol and bilateral joint operations, but we need to do more. There are often too many obstacles to international investigations that serve only to protect the criminal. As Members know, bringing multinational gangs to justice may involve several trials in different countries, each with its own criminal procedures. Ensuring success for such complex procedures means cutting down on the obstacles that block effective cross-border co-operation. That is what the Bill sets out to achieve.

The Bill will make the changes needed to enable the UK to participate in the non-border aspects of the Schengen convention. The Schengen arrangements provide a very clear framework for effective co-operation, especially for cross-border police operations.

I should like to explain in more detail what the Bill contains and will achieve. Part 1 will modernise our arrangements for providing mutual legal assistance and bring them into line with new proceedings introduced by Schengen and by the mutual legal assistance convention [ed. MLAC] agreed in May 2000. MLAC, as it was called, was part of the European Union's so-called anti-terrorism road map, which was agreed after 11 September. Mutual legal assistance is the formal process by which countries request and provide assistance in obtaining evidence located in one country to assist in criminal proceedings in another. Effective and swift mutual legal assistance arrangements are essential if we and our EU partners are to run successful cross-border investigations and prosecutions.

MLA is not new—we have done it for many years—but the new provisions will speed up the process and reduce the scope for delay in respect of international co-operation. They will do so, for instance, by allowing UK prosecutors to send requests for evidence directly to courts in other EU countries, rather than going through a central authority system because of an obligation always to do so. Some of the key modernising provisions will also apply to countries outside the EU. For instance, we expect that the ability to provide other countries with evidence by TV link in mutual legal assistance cases will be of most use in cases involving countries outside the EU, because greater distances obviously make travel less feasible.

The Bill also introduces mutual recognition of orders to freeze evidence, as provided for by the EU draft framework decision on the execution of orders freezing evidence. We see that as a considerable step forward. It will significantly speed up the process of securing valuable evidence. Mutual recognition takes mutual legal assistance one step further by recognising directly, as between EU member states, a request made by a court, thus enabling a direct response to be made with the minimum of formality. The UK has been and is a keen supporter of the principle of mutual recognition, which both speeds up co-operation and respects the standards as well as the diversity of legal systems.

(HC Deb 1 April 2003 Vol. 402 c800–802)

19/29

During a debate in the House of Commons on the Crime (International Co-operation) Bill, the Minister for Citizenship and Immigration made the following statement:

Concern was expressed in another place that the Bill did not provide sufficient safeguards to protect the position of the individual in respect of the new arrangements. We listened to those concerns and have introduced extra protection in respect of double jeopardy to ensure that orders freezing evidence are dealt with promptly and to strengthen the role of UK courts in protecting the position of people giving evidence by television link.

Criminals operating across international borders are often involved in financial crime and money laundering. It is recognised that the ability to obtain comprehensive banking information from other EU countries would significantly assist domestic law enforcement. By agreeing on the protocol to the mutual legal assistance convention, the EU has created a reciprocal obligation between member states to respond to requests for financial information. The Bill will implement the protocol, allowing us to respond to requests from other EU countries for information relating to criminal suspects' bank accounts. The requests will reflect the new investigative tools introduced by the Proceeds of Crime Act 2001.

Part 2 deals with terrorism. As criminals, terrorists do not respect national boundaries. We need effective measures with persuasive penalties that are imposed consistently across the EU. Following the events of 11 September, the EU agreed a framework decision requiring all member states to introduce extensive anti-terrorism legislation. As the UK already has wide-ranging domestic anti-terrorism legislation—it was largely the starting point for the Commission's proposal—we are broadly compliant with the body of the framework decision, so implementing the measure does not require us to create any new offences or penalties. It simply requires us to take extra-territorial jurisdiction over a wider range of terrorist offences than we do presently. The Bill therefore takes extra-territorial jurisdiction over terrorist offences committed overseas against UK nationals, diplomatic staff and diplomatic premises. It will also take such jurisdiction over terrorist offences committed overseas by UK nationals. We supported that measure during its negotiation in Brussels and welcome this opportunity promptly to implement the changes needed to bring it into force.

Schedule 4 will also help us tackle terrorism by introducing arrangements to allow us to transmit abroad orders freezing terrorist assets and instrumentalities—funds and assets used to commit terrorist offences. Likewise, we will be able to act on orders from other EU member states. Allowing mutual recognition of those orders is a significant step forward, as it will make it easier for us to freeze terrorist assets even when they have been moved out of the UK, and thereby reduce terrorists' ability to operate effectively.

Part 3 deals with driving disqualifications—an issue raised by my hon. Friend the Member for Hemsworth (Jon Trickett) in relation to a specific case. It does not seem right that a person who commits a driving offence for which they are disqualified while abroad should be able to escape disqualification when they return home to their usual state of residence. The EU driving disqualification convention is therefore intended to promote the principle that drivers should abide by the rules of the road no matter where they are driving. That will help to promote greater road safety across the UK. There are safeguards to ensure that the arrangements are not misused and do not lead to unfair decisions. The process for notifying a disqualification will apply only once any appeal has been completed, and there will be a right of appeal in the UK against recognition of foreign disqualifications.

Part 3 also allows for recognition in Great Britain of driving disqualifications imposed in Northern Ireland, the Isle of Man, the Channel Islands and Gibraltar. The fact that none of those jurisdictions recognises driving disqualifications imposed by any of the others is, as I hope hon. Members will agree, an anomaly whose remedy is long overdue. A more uniform system across the UK is obviously also essential for effective implementation of the wider EU measure.

(HC Deb 1 April 2003 Vol. 402 c802–803)

19/30

During a debate in the House of Commons, the Minister for Citizenship and Immigration made the following statement:

I want to make it clear what the measures do not include. Clause 82 does not licence foreign officers to roam at will around the country. The foreign officers will have no power of arrest, because nothing exists in UK law to give them such a power. The clause simply provides that, in circumstances in which a person suspected of serious criminal activity is heading for the UK from continental Europe, and in which, for whatever reason, our own officers are unable to take over the surveillance themselves the moment the targeted person lands in the UK, the foreign officers will be able to maintain their surveillance for up to five hours. The alternative would be to risk losing valuable intelligence on key criminal suspects. This measure covers neither hot pursuit, which has to take place over land borders, nor undercover surveillance. It simply provides for the temporary extension of an ongoing operation for up to five hours until the UK police either join the operation or, having risk-assessed it, stop it.

(HC Deb 1 April 2003 Vol. 402 c805)

(See **19/27**)

19/31

Her Majesty's Government was asked the following written question:

...what police services exist between the UK and other European police forces to combat the trafficking of women from European countries into the UK.

In reply, the Parliamentary Under-Secretary of State, Home Office, wrote:

The United Kingdom (UK) works with other law enforcement agencies in Europe with Europol to tackle people trafficking from Europe to the UK. Europol has no executive or operational powers and no capabilities to gather evidence. It is intelligence based and offers a range of products and services to operational law enforcement teams in the European Union. These include analytical support for both strategic and tactical developments and a forum to process requests for assistance in UK investigations with connections in other European Union member states and candidate countries. There is ongoing operational work which is supported by Europol.

Another link between UK law enforcement and overseas partners is through the establishment of Project Reflex, a practical multi-agency taskforce on organised immigration crime. Led by the National Crime Squad (NCS), Reflex was set up in March 2000 and brings together all the key agencies, including the Immigration Service, the National Criminal Intelligence Service (NCIS), the security and intelligence agencies and key police forces including the Metropolitan police, Kent and the British Transport police. Under Reflex, a central tasking forum has been established to plan and co-ordinate multi-agency operations. It is now well established and the NCS is currently co-operating with overseas law enforcement partners on the disruption of organised criminal groups intent on trafficking.

(HC Deb 4 March 2002 Vol. 381 c45W)

19/32

During a meeting in the Security Council the representative of the European Union said:

Since 1999, the Security Council Committee established pursuant to resolution 1267 (1999) has proved to be one of the main instruments at our disposal to fight against terrorism by imposing targeted sanctions designed to focus specifically on the individuals and entities belonging to or associated with the Taliban and Al Qaeda. After the terrorist attacks of 11 September 2001, resolutions 1390 (2002) and 1455 (2003) imposed and strengthened targeted sanctions designed to focus specifically on individuals and entities that, in connection with the Taliban or Al Qaeda, were responsible for such threats to and breaches of international peace and security. Under the authority of the Security Council and with the active support of the international community, the scope of the sanctions regime has been enlarged, its tools have been extended and improved, and its working methods have been progressively adapted to the new circumstances. The Committee established pursuant to resolution 1267 (1999) has played an important role in that process, and it will continue to do so. Likewise, we appreciate the important work of the Monitoring Group and its regular reporting to the Committee and the Security Council.

The European Union and its member States immediately responded to that effort by strengthening their cooperation with this Committee. A unique regulatory framework directly applicable in all EU member States has ensured proper and timely implementation of all the relevant Security Council resolutions in this field. The result was amplified by the voluntary alignment to that framework of all countries acceding to the EU. A wide range of legal instruments has been adopted with the aim of strengthening the restrictive measures imposed by the United Nations, notably to combat the financing of terrorism.

Furthermore, the European Union and its member States entered into close cooperation with the Committee and the Monitoring Group, which assists it in the fulfilment of its tasks. That cooperation has already produced satisfactory results, although it can be further improved, and has ensured a remarkable flow of information, which proved extremely useful in enhancing the effectiveness of our overall strategy against terrorism. The European Union firmly supports the continuing efforts of the Committee to improve its working procedures, thus increasing efficiency, transparency and scope.

Respect for human rights, fundamental freedoms and the rule of law is essential in all efforts to combat terrorism. In that respect, the European Union deeply shares the approach followed by the Security Council with the adoption of resolution 1452 (2002) of 20 December 2002, aimed at defining criteria for the granting of exemptions, in specific cases, based on humanitarian needs.

The European Union remains convinced that every effort must be made to promote due process in the proceedings of the Committee. In that respect, the Union welcomes the adoption by the Committee, on 7 November 2002, of guidelines for the conduct of its work, which were further revised and expanded on 10 April this year.

Sanctions must be implemented on the basis of transparent technical criteria in order to create maximum legal certainty in the matter. The European Union stands ready to work to further improve the Committee's guidelines, as appropriate. It also welcomes the improvement of the format and content of the consolidated list of individuals and entities belonging to or associated with the Taliban and Al Qaeda, as well as the adoption by the Committee of a guidance document to assist Member States in the preparation of their implementation reports. Terrorism must and can be defeated, in accordance with the Charter and international law, by a sustained comprehensive approach involving the participation and the collaboration of all States and international and regional organizations, and by redoubled efforts at the national level. Therefore, the European Union shares the need for improved coordination and increased exchange of information between the 1267 Committee, the Counter-Terrorism Committee, established pursuant to resolution 1373 (2001), and the Terrorism Branch of the United Nations Office on Drugs and Crime. While appreciating that that cooperation is on the right track, the European Union is fully aware that much work remains to be done, and therefore it is fully committed to contributing to such an effort with its expertise and best practices in the fight against terrorism. The European Union and its member States reiterate their determination to cooperate fully with the 1267 Committee and with the Monitoring Group both by supplying information as may be requested and by facilitating, to the extent possible, the proper identification of all listed individuals and entities targeted by restrictive measures. In that respect, the European Union encourages all States that have not yet done so to provide all possible information in response to resolution 1455 (2003).

(UN Doc. S/PV.4798, 29 July 2003)

19/33

In a memorandum the Foreign and Commonwealth Office wrote:

RESPONSE BY THE FOREIGN AND COMMONWEALTH OFFICE TO QUESTIONS PUT BY THE COMMITTEE (*Questions shown here in italics*).

1. *In its response to recommendation (b), the Government told the Committee that it is "looking to deliver a range of technical assistance programmes to help states with implementing their international obligations" regarding terrorist financing. The Government reported that "the Commonwealth Secretariat and the Charity Commission, on behalf of the FCO, intend to run seminars on legislative and administrative measures to combat the financing of terrorism (including the regulation of charities). These will be delivered to a range of regions including the Gulf". The Committee would like to receive a report of progress in this area of policy.*

The Foreign & Commonwealth Office is funding the Commonwealth Secretariat and the Charity Commission to deliver assistance programmes to a range of countries in the areas of counter-terrorism legislation and combating terrorist financing, including the regulation of charities. These are areas identified by the UN Counter-Terrorism Committee under UNSCR 1373 as priority areas for implementation.

The Commonwealth Secretariat programme will assist states in implementing the 12 existing UN counter-terrorism conventions and in drafting domestic counter-terrorism legislation. The programme takes place in two stages, the first being a series of regional seminars and the second being specific in-country follow-up by expert consultants to advise individual states on their own legislation requirements. To date, regional seminars have been held in Botswana (Nov 02), Antigua (Feb 03), Sri Lanka (Mar 03) and two more are scheduled for West Africa (May 03) and the Pacific (June 03).

The Charity Commission programme focuses on the regulation of charities to ensure that they are neither knowingly nor unknowingly misused to support terrorist activities, primarily through financing activities. This programme is also being implemented in two stages, regional seminars and then specific in-country follow-up. The first seminar took place in Colombo in March 2003 for eight countries in South and South East Asia. The seminar scheduled to take place in the Gulf has been postponed primarily because of military action in Iraq. However, the delivery of this assistance will still take place at a later date. The next seminar is due to be held in South Africa in July 2003 for the countries of South and East Africa.

In total the ECO has committed £620,000 to these two programmes over two financial years.

2. *With reference to recommendation (e), the Committee wishes to receive a report of progress towards implementation of the changes to NATO agreed at the Prague summit, including new NATO capabilities to defend against WMD attack. The Committee also requests a statement of Government objectives in the development of the NATO Response Force and new NATO command structures.*

At the Prague Summit NATO leaders agreed a comprehensive package of measures aimed at strengthening NATO's ability to meet new threats, especially those of terrorism and weapons of mass destruction. To do this, NATO must have forces able to move quickly to wherever they are needed, sustain operations over distance and time and operate in an environment where they might be faced with threats from chemical and biological weapons. The UK worked hard to ensure Prague outcomes would contribute to the continuing modernisation of the Alliance. Our objective now is to ensure implementation is completed in a timely and effective manner, avoiding dilution and compromise.

—*The NATO Response Force (NRF):* the Military Committee has endorsed the military concept of the NRF, which meets UK objectives; it will now be submitted to the NAC for approval. Work on a comprehensive concept of the NRF, including political-military issues, is making good progress. The NRF will significantly enhance the Alliance's ability to act quickly; it will improve interoperability and it will provide a further stimulus to the current work to reform the NATO Command Structure. The ability to deploy a capable NRF at very short notice will demonstrate the collective political will of Allies and will also act as a significant deterrent. This should aid resolution of developing crises early and help to prevent the deterioration in situations that leads to the need for the deployment of heavier forces. The NRF is also designed to be a catalyst for the transformation of the capabilities of Alliance nations. A report on the NRF is due at the Defence Ministers meeting in June. A significant gain is that an interim NRF capability is planned to be in place by October this year, in advance of the 2004 date HOSG agreed for the Initial Operating Capability.

—*New NATO Command Structure:* a new NATO Command Structure, designed to cope with the likely tasks, risks and potential threats across the entire range of potential NATO missions, is a key element of the transformation of the Alliance. NATO leaders endorsed an outline of the Minimum Military Requirements (MMR) for the new NATO structure. NATO's Military Committee and a group of Senior Officials are close to agreeing the operational architecture and organisation of the NCS. The structure, including geographic locations, is due to be submitted to Defence Ministers in June, with an initial capability planned for June 2005.

The new NCS, consisting of one operational and one functional strategic command, should maximise NATO's operational effectiveness and its ability to deploy quickly and flexibly in response to operational needs. The operational command, based in Europe, will be trained and fully capable of commanding the land, sea and air components of operations from either their static locations or from deployed headquarters. The Transformation command, with its headquarters in the United States, will have a presence in Europe and will be the "engine room" for the continuing transformation of military capabilities, for developing doctrine and training, and for the promotion of interoperability of Alliance forces. We have worked closely with key Allies to ensure the MMR remains the foundation of the new Command Structure. Some difficult decisions remain on the final geographic spread of HQs, but we are confident that these will be made by June.

—*Capabilities for Defence against Terrorism:* work is underway to increase NATO's ability to prevent or respond to a terrorist attack. These include capabilities pledged in the Prague Capabilities Commitment (PCC); work on the five Nuclear, Biological and Chemical (NBC) Defence Initiatives; and the preparation of both the military and comprehensive concepts for the NATO Response Force.

The PCC was launched to improve capabilities in key operational areas, including defence against WMD. The NAC is kept regularly informed of progress in achieving the goals of the PCC. National progress reports have just been submitted by Allies and we await their analysis by NATO staffs. The UK's input shows that all our commitments are on track, with the minor exception of the Stormshadow PGM, which missed its in Service date, but has been used successfully in Iraq in recent weeks.

The five NBC Defence Initiatives announced in Prague (Prototype Deployable NBC Analytical Laboratory; Prototype NBC Event Response Team; Virtual Centre of Excellence for NBC Weapons Defence; NATO Biological and

Chemical Defence Stockpile; and Disease Surveillance System) will contribute to the Alliance's overall ability to respond to possible terrorist attacks employing chemical, biological or nuclear weapons.

The development of all five initiatives is on track. An accelerated timetable has been developed for the analytical laboratory, including a programme of exercises and evaluation running throughout 2003. The aim is to enable the delivery of an operational capability by the beginning of 2004.

Additionally, the UK is leading efforts to explore the scope for improving other aspects of NBC defence (eg: thorough decontamination of assets; NBC survey and reconnaissance and BW detection) through multinational Co-operation. Cooperative mechanisms might include role specialisation, role sharing, common equipment pooling and common procurement. The results of this work will be reported to NATO in May.

3. *With reference to recommendation (g), the Committee feels that the Government's response does not amount to a clear statement of policy. The Committee therefore requests that the Government provide a full statement of its policy on targeted killings, together with its opinion on the legality of the US operation in Yemen of 3 November 2002.*

We believe that our response was an unambiguous statement of the Government's policy on targeted killings. International law establishes the right to take necessary and proportionate action for the purpose of self-defence. The Government believes the scale and unpredictable nature of the terrorist threat posed by Al Qa'ida and related groups requires a preparedness to take rigorous action in self-defence. We cannot, however, prejudge what form any such actions might take; they would vary from case to case. But we would always act in accordance with international and domestic law when deciding on the action necessary to protect the UK and its citizens.

The Government is not in a position to offer a definitive opinion on the legality of the alleged US operation in Yemen. We are not in possession of all the facts concerning the precise circumstances of the operation that would be necessary to make such a determination.

4. *With reference to recommendation (h), the Committee is concerned that the Government commits itself only to informing Parliament of all important matters affecting United Kingdom nuclear policy "as necessary". The Committee wishes to be informed of all changes to United Kingdom nuclear policy. It also wishes to receive from the Government a response to recent reports (such as that in the Guardian on 7 March 2003) that the United States is developing a new generation of sub-strategic nuclear weapons.*

We made clear in our Command Paper response to the Committee of 25 February, in response to the Committee's request that the Government inform the Committee and the House if it decides to change its nuclear posture, that we would inform Parliament as necessary of all important matters affecting United Kingdom nuclear policy. This would of course include any situation in which there might be a question of a change in the UK's nuclear deterrence policy as laid out in the 1998 Strategic Defence Review.

The Committee refers to a recent UK newspaper report that the US is developing a new generation of sub-strategic nuclear weapons. Mike O'Brien, replying to a similar question from Sir John Stanley in July last year, published as Appendix 1 to the minutes of evidence in the Committee's report, set out the key facts as we understand them: "... It is, of course, for the US not for us, to set out and explain what is, and what is not, US policy." The US has emphasised, however, that there is no such programme. US Secretary of State, Colin Powell, made this clear on 10 March [2002], when he said: "What we are looking at, and what we have tasked the Pentagon to do, is to say whether or not within our lowered inventory levels we might want to modify or update or change some of the nuclear weapons in our inventory to make them more effective. But we are not developing brand new nuclear weapons, and we are not planning to undergo any testing."

The US Administration has requested and received funding in the FY 2003 US Defence Budget for a three year, $15 million per annum, feasibility study into Robust Nuclear Earth Penetrators (RNEPs). As the name implies, this is a feasibility study looking at the potential possibilities for developing a RNEP. It is not a decision by the US Administration to research, develop or deploy such a weapon nor is it a study into a new generation of sub-strategic nuclear weapons. Senior US National Nuclear Security Administration officials underlined this point when testifying to Congress in support for the FY 2003 Defence Budget request. They stated that: "RNEP is not a new design, it is not a low-yield 'mini-nuke'... and it is not a significant departure from current stockpile weapons... the three-year RNEP feasibility study will assess the feasibility of modifying one of two candidate nuclear weapons currently in the stockpile to provide enhanced penetration capability into hard rock geologies and develop out-year costs for the subsequent production phases, if a decision is made by the Nuclear Weapons Council to proceed."

5. *With reference to recommendation (i), the Committee wishes to receive a statement from the Government setting out its assessment of the extent to which international co-operation against terrorism has been disrupted by the substantial international divisions over how to address the threat from Iraq.*

There is no evidence that international co-operation against terrorism has been disrupted by disagreement over Iraq. There is continuing widespread and close international co-operation on the security, intelligence, law enforcement, military, and diplomatic fronts which is severely disrupting terrorist operations and leading to further arrests. This includes continuing close and useful co-operation with countries that have been critical of Coalition action in Iraq. The effectiveness of counter-terrorism work in the UN and in other multilateral fora such as the EU and G8 has similarly been unaffected by disagreement over Iraq. We believe that the strength of the international community's collective interest in defeating terrorism will ensure that such efforts are not derailed by short-term political differences. In the medium and longer term, disarming Iraq of weapons of mass destruction should help to reduce the threat from international terrorism.

6. *The Committee disputes the Government's assertion, in response to recommendation (o), that "Disarming Iraq removes the very real and catastrophic threat of international terrorists getting hold of weapons of mass destruction". There are*

countries other than Iraq which possess weapons of mass destruction, and these countries might also provide such weapons to terrorists. The United States argues in its National Security Strategy that "We must be prepared to stop rogue states and their terrorist clients before they are able to threaten or use weapons of mass destruction against the United States and our allies and friends." The Committee requests a statement of the Government's medium- and long-term strategy for addressing the production and proliferation of weapons of mass destruction by states other than Iraq—including any plans to enhance existing cooperative threat reduction programmes; proposed measures to strengthen multilateral arms control regimes; and British policy towards known proliferators such as North Korea. It would also like the Government to state whether or not it believes that "regime change" is an appropriate response to WMD proliferation in states other than Iraq.

The Government's response to the Committee's recommendation (o) should have referred to the removal of "a" rather than "the" threat of terrorist access to WMD.

The Government takes the proliferation of Weapons of Mass Destruction (WMD) very seriously. Together with the spread of extreme international terrorism, it represents the most serious threat to international security of the Twenty-first century. The international non-proliferation treaty regimes have not been a failure: they have limited the spread of nuclear, chemical and biological weapons successfully for over thirty years. But the treaties are not yet universal; and experience with Iraq and North Korea has demonstrated that more is needed to prevent determined proliferators from cheating on their international obligations.

There is a range of tools available to counter proliferation. The multilateral treaty regimes raise the political cost of pursuing WMD. When underpinned by effective inspection regimes, such as those of the International Atomic Energy Agency (IAEA) and Organisation for the Prevention of Chemical Weapons (OPCW), they also raise the economic cost. National and multilateral export controls on sensitive materials, technology and expertise also have a vital role: the UK is a leading and active member of the Nuclear Suppliers' Group, the Australia Group and the Missile Technology Control Regime.

Efforts to eliminate the proliferation risk posed by stocks of WMD-sensitive materials (often referred to as "co-operative threat reduction") are also part of the counter-proliferation toolbox. In this context, the Government has announced a commitment of $750 million over the next ten years to the G8 Global Partnership. Projects planned and under way concentrate on priority areas such as chemical weapons destruction, safe disposition of weapons-usable plutonium, dismantlement of submarines and secure storage of nuclear fuel which poses both an environmental and proliferation risk in North-West Russia, and retraining and employment for former Soviet nuclear scientists.

Diplomatic and economic pressure can be effective against some countries of proliferation concern: most often when it can be brought to bear multilaterally rather than bilaterally. Where possible, interception of illegal shipments of WMD-sensitive items can hinder covert proliferation programmes. Effective nuclear, biological and chemical defence—including civil defence—also has a part to play. And as a last resort, the Government does not rule out direct action, including military action in accordance with international law.

All elements of the counter-proliferation "toolbox" are necessary; none is sufficient in itself. It would be foolish to rule out any one. On the contrary, the Government is working to reinforce them all and strengthen its ability to deploy them to maximum effect. That does not mean that all are appropriate to every case. All proliferators pose a challenge to the international community, but our response must be tailored to the circumstances of each one. The Government's objective is always the same—elimination of WMD. But in pursuing that aim it deploys the measures which it judges will be most effective in each case. In the case of North Korea, tripartite discussions between China, the USA and North Korea were in prospect, at the time of writing.

Most identified WMD programmes are justified by security concerns however misconceived these may be. In addition to raising the costs of such programmes, it is also possible to reduce the perceived benefits. In that respect, the Government's actions to revitalise the Middle East Peace Process, to encourage India and Pakistan to resolve their differences, to bring lasting stability to the Korean Peninsula and to eliminate the threats posed by Iraq to its neighbours also further non-proliferation objectives.

This is not a strategy which the UK can pursue alone. Proliferation poses a global challenge and requires a collective international response. In developing and applying the counter-proliferation toolbox, the Government is working with partners and allies bilaterally, in the EU, the G8, NATO, and through the United Nations Security Council.

7. *With reference to recommendation (q), the Committee notes that on 24 February 2003, the French government published a memorandum proposing a reinforcement of the UN inspections regime. The Committee wishes to know whether, in the Government's opinion, the proposals put forward by the French government would have increased the effectiveness of the inspections regime—and if not, why not. If these proposals would have strengthened the inspections regime, why were they not incorporated in the initial structure of UNMOVIC?*

The Government continues to believe that the French Government's memorandum presented on 24 February, while no doubt well-intentioned, was misguided. The rationale it presented for reinforcing the UN inspections regime in Iraq was based on a fundamental misunderstanding of the nature of the inspections.

The UN inspectors were never intended to be detectives; to uncover Iraq's concealed WMD programmes through a massive search effort. Any such effort in a country the size of Iraq would be doomed to fail, however large the inspection teams. Similarly, the inspectors were not intended to "compel" Iraqi compliance, as the French Government's paper proposed (and it is difficult to see how they could have been adequately reinforced so as to enable them to do so). Their mandate, under repeated United Nations Security Council Resolutions, was to monitor and verify Iraq's compliance. Saddam Hussein never made the strategic decision to comply and give up his WMD programmes, which would have allowed the inspectors to fulfil their mandate. As Dr Blix himself pointed out, the principal problem was not the number of inspectors but rather the degree of active Iraqi co-operation. The Government therefore believes that it is difficult to see how the inspectors could have been reinforced in such a way as to enable them to compel Iraq to do anything.

The Government agrees with Dr Blix: without such active co-operation the inspectors would never have been able to fulfil their mandate. UNSCR 1441 placed specific emphasis on the need for Iraq to co-operate "immediately, unconditionally and actively" with UNMOVIC and the IAEA (operative paragraph 9). Iraq wholly failed to comply with this requirement.

8. *With reference to the Government's reply to recommendation (s), the Committee notes the assessment of the United States that "We must adapt the concept of imminent threat to the capabilities and objectives of today's adversaries. Rogue states and terrorists do not seek to attack us using conventional means. They know such attacks would fail. Instead, they rely on acts of terror and, potentially, the use of weapons of mass destruction—weapons that can be easily concealed, delivered covertly, and used without warning". The Government states that it "supports the view that this right [of self-defence] applies as much to imminent threats from terrorism as to the more conventional threats of the past", and therefore "the Government has not considered it necessary to review its policy" on the issue of pre-emptive defence following the publication of the US National Security Strategy. The Committee seeks some clarification of Government policy in this area: Does the Government agree with the United States' view that terrorist attacks using WMD might be launched without warning? If so, why is it not considered necessary to re-examine the question of the pre-emptive use of force to address threats, when it may sometimes be impossible to provide proof of an imminent threat of attack?*

The Government agrees with the United States' view that terrorist attacks using WMD might be launched without warning. Attacks by al Qa'ida and the groups linked to them have come without warning. Their attacks have caused civilian casualties on a massive scale. We have no reason to believe that such groups would change their methods should they use the CBRN materials that we know they are trying to obtain.

HMG have not considered it necessary to re-examine the question of the pre-emptive use of force because the right under international law to take necessary and proportionate military action in self-defence, not only where an attack has occurred but also where an attack is imminent, would apply to terrorist attacks using WMD as it does to conventional attacks. HMG believes that in accordance with existing policy that all relevant factors should be taken into account when considering action in self-defence including the likelihood of any attack and the potential seriousness of the consequences.

9. *With reference to recommendation (y), and in light of the decision to launch military action against the Iraqi regime, the Committee requests further details of the Government's plans for post-conflict Iraq. In particular, the Committee wishes to know what role the Government believes the United Nations should play in the post-conflict governance of Iraq; which "model" (if any) is being envisaged for a transitional authority; and how an international civilian authority in Iraq should interact with a post-conflict peacekeeping force. Does the Government believe, with the United States,*

that the military and civilian administrators after a US invasion should report to General Tommy Franks, commander of US forces in the Middle East?

As the Coalition proceeds with the reconstruction of Iraq, it will work with its allies, bilateral donors, the United Nations and other international institutions. The United Nations has a vital role to play in the reconstruction of Iraq. We plan to seek the adoption of new United Nations Security Council Resolutions that would affirm Iraq's territorial integrity, ensure rapid delivery of humanitarian relief and endorse an appropriate post-conflict administration for Iraq. We want to see a phased transfer of authority leading to a new and effective representative Iraqi government as soon as possible. We will work with the UN and the international community to help the people of Iraq to achieve this aspiration. As soon as possible, we envisage responsibility for administration of Iraq being transferred to a representative group of Iraqis in the form of an Iraqi Interim Authority. The two main functions of such a body would be to take on responsibility for administration and to create a constitutional framework to facilitate the formation of a democratic government. The goal would be the emergence of a representative Iraqi government, committed to the long-term political and economic reform of the country and to peaceful relations with the region. The international community would remain engaged in Iraq's future through the IFIs, regional agreements, bilateral and multilateral aid programmes, and other political and practical support. Immediately after the conflict the first task of the coalition will be to continue to stabilise the country and, working with the UN inspectors, to find and secure Iraq's weapons of mass destruction. The Office of Reconstruction and Humanitarian Aid, ORHA, will have responsibility under the Geneva and Hague Conventions for ensuring the immediate security and humanitarian needs in Iraq are met. The UK will work closely with the US and other coalition allies within ORHA, which will be headed by retired US General Jay Garner.

10. *With reference to recommendation (z), the Committee would like the Government to send an assessment of the short term effects of military action against Iraq on recruitment for, and the threat from, al Qaeda and associated terrorist groups, both in the Islamic world and in Western Europe.*

It is clear that Al Qa'ida is trying to exploit events in Iraq for its own purposes. Bin Laden's message of 11 February urged Muslims to unite in support of the Iraqi people in what he characterised as a war against Islam. He welcomed martyrdom operations against the US and Israel. We assess that, in the short term, Al Qa'ida's stance on Iraq may encourage some misguided individuals or small groups to try to commit terrorist acts, including against coalition forces in Iraq, and elsewhere in the region or further away. In the longer term, we assess that Al Qa'ida's stance on Iraq will be undermined by the benefits of disarming Iraq of weapons of mass destruction, the removal of the current Iraqi regime and evidence that the international community is making a renewed effort to advance the Middle East Peace process.

11. *With reference to recommendation (cc), the Committee wishes to receive updated information about progress towards the implementation of the Quartet "road map" and broader efforts to revive the Middle East peace process.*

UK efforts to revive the Middle East peace process continue to focus on the roadmap. Thanks in some part to UK support to Palestinian reform initiatives and to the creation of the post of a Palestinian Prime Minister, we are now nearing publication of the roadmap, which sets out clearly the steps that need to be taken by both sides to reach a final settlement.

As a follow-up to the 14 January London meeting on Palestinian reform, the UK hosted meetings of the Ad Hoc Liaison Committee (AHLC)—the international donor co-ordination mechanism—and the Task Force on Reform in London from 17–20 February. These meetings addressed the essential requirements for a renewed peace process: publication of the roadmap, on which Quartet envoys are engaged; Palestinian reform, on which the Task Force built on progress made at the on 14 January meeting; and economic support for the Palestinian Authority and people.

We have worked closely with the Palestinians on the issue of a Palestinian Prime Minister over the last few months, and welcomed the appointment of Abu Mazen on 18 March. An empowered and credible Prime Minister is an important part of the broader context of the Palestinian reform process which, as set out in Bush's speech of 24 June and the roadmap, are positive steps towards a meaningful peace process. Likewise, we continue to encourage Prime Minister Sharon and Foreign Minister Shalom to work with the international community in restoring hopes for peace.

The Prime Minister welcomed President Bush's commitment on 8 April that the roadmap will be presented to the parties when Abu Mazen takes office as Palestinian Prime Minister. This is a significant step. All parties should respond positively and start implementation without delay.

The settlement to which the roadmap leads is consistent with all the key international statements of principle on the dispute since 1967: UN Security Council Resolutions 242, 338 and 1397; the Madrid terms of reference; the principle of land for peace; existing agreements between the parties; and the March 2002 Arab League initiative, offering Israel full normalisation of relations with its neighbours in the context of a settlement.

In Phase One of the roadmap, which will formally begin once it is presented to the parties, the Palestinians must act against terrorism; rebuild their security infrastructure; and pursue reform, including constitutional reform. Israel must facilitate reform; ease the humanitarian situation in the Occupied Territories; withdraw its forces to pre-28 September 2000 positions and freeze all settlement activity. Phase Two focuses on an independent Palestinian state with provisional borders and a new constitution, and takes up the Lebanese/Syrian track of the peace process. Phase Three will see Israeli-Palestinian negotiations on a permanent status agreement. I have put an informal copy of the roadmap in the House library.

12. *In the letter of 8 April the Committee asked to receive a note on the legal rights, duties, obligations and limitations of occupying powers, both in general and also specifically under the Geneva conventions. In particular, the Committee would like the note to refer to the likely future position of the US and the UK as occupying powers in Iraq.*

The general principle is that an Occupying Power does not become the government of the occupied territory. Rather, it exercises temporary de facto control in accordance with in particular the provisions of Geneva Convention IV of 1949 and the Hague Regulations of 1907 (relevant extracts attached in Annexes A and B). These instruments are complex, but the following points give an indication of the position of an Occupying Power:

(a) Under Article 43 of the Hague Regulations, authority having passed into the hands of the Occupying Power, the latter shall take all the measures in its power to restore and ensure, as far as possible, public order and safety, while respecting, unless absolutely prevented, the laws in force in the country. Thus, while changes to the legislative and administrative structures of Iraq are permissible if they are necessary for security or public order reasons, or in order to further humanitarian objectives, the occupant should not undertake more wide ranging reforms of governmental and administrative structures.

(b) Geneva Convention IV provides that the occupant should not alter the status of public officials or judges (although officials may be removed from their posts). If there is no functioning local administration, there is scope for an Occupying Power to introduce its own administrative system if that is necessary for maintenance of good order in the occupied territory.

(c) Geneva Convention IV also provides for the penal laws of the occupied territory to remain in force except where they constitute a threat to security or an obstacle to application of the Convention. To enforce those laws the courts of the occupied territory are to be allowed to continue to function. The Occupying Power may promulgate its own laws in order to fulfil its obligations under the Convention and to maintain security and public order.

(d) Apart from rules on the collection of taxes (which must as far as possible be in accordance with existing local law), there are no specific provisions in Geneva Convention IV or the Hague Regulations dealing with the economy of the occupied territory. However, the general principle outlined in (a) above applies equally to economic reform, so that the Occupying Power should not undertake major structural economic reforms.

In each case the application of the Hague Regulations and the Geneva Conventions to the actions of the occupying powers in Iraq will need to be considered in the light of the specific circumstances.

These provisions will not apply to the people of Iraq themselves, if through a legitimately established authority they undertake governmental and administrative reform.

(FAC Tenth Report, Foreign Policy Aspects of the War on Terrorism, Minutes of Evidence, Memorandum from the FCO, April 2003, HC 405)

Part Nineteen: IX. *Legal Aspects of International Relations and Co-operation in Particular Matters—Military and security matters*

(See also **3/9** and **16/71**)

19/34

A Foreign Office Minister spoke about Strengthening Conflict Prevention in the Modern World, in New York on 13 June 2003. He said:

There are . . . other measures, in accordance with international law, with which we can tackle the threat posed by international terrorism and the proliferation of WMD. These have to include the option of military action as a last resort. Just as we have been reviewing the principles under which we intervene in sovereign states on humanitarian grounds, so I believe we must also re-examine the principles under which we intervene to tackle global threats. As Kofi Annan has said, effective diplomacy needs to be backed up with the credible threat of force.

All states, on every continent, and at all stages of development need to make common cause against these global threats, because they affect us all.

He went on:

Strengthening international co-operation to resolve the transnational problems which fuel conflict is vital. The Kimberley Process to tackle the problem of conflict diamonds was one example demonstrating what can be done when governments and international organisations work together with civil society and the private sector. We need to look for other areas, such as the regulations guiding the extractive industries, where we can use this close co-operation as a model.

About the UN, he said:

Since its inception, the UN has been working to help prevent violent conflict. It has, however, had only mixed success, not least because of the reluctance of member states to invest or contribute funds towards a seemingly elusive goal.

The UK accepts the need to respect state sovereignty. But we also suggest that in many cases this has been used as an excuse for inaction. UN member states need to be more proactive. Measuring the success of conflict prevention is almost impossible. Observing its failure is all too easy. This does not mean that we should not seek to take preventative action, but that we should be ready to try and risk failure rather than not try at all.

(Text available at www.fco.gov.uk/speeches)

19/35

In reply to a written question the Secretary of State for Defence wrote:

The Framework Ballistic Missile Defence Memorandum of Understanding (BMD MoU) signed on 12 June 2003 sets out the overarching structure for government-to-government collaboration between the United Kingdom and the United States on missile defence. It establishes and defines a framework within which specific activities, to be set out in Annexes to this MoU, can be undertaken. This includes activities already under way under the pre-existing Strategic Defence Initiative MoU. The BMD MoU itself provides no authority for placing contracts and no assessments were undertaken of the potential value of contracts resulting from collaborative projects that are in progress now, or may be undertaken in the future.

(HC Deb 1 September 2003 Vol. 409 c914W)

19/36

In response to a written question the Under-Secretary of State for Trade and Industry wrote:

The UK fully supports the UN Programme of Action (PoA) on Small Arms and Light Weapons and actively participated in the first Conference in 2001 and the follow up Biennial Meeting of States, which was held in July 2003 to review progress on implementing the PoA. To help control the supply of SALW, the UK is leading the global effort to develop common international standards on arms exports. In December 2002 the UK was instrumental in securing "Best Practice Guidelines in the Exports of SALW" in the Wassenaar Arrangement, a group of 33 of the world's major arms exporters.

The UK signed the UN Protocol against the illicit Manufacturing of and Trafficking in firearms.

We continue to work in partnership with other Governments, NGOs and industry on policies and projects to implement the UN Programme of Action on Small Arms. This includes £20 million (2001–04) to curb small arms proliferation worldwide. The UK provides funding for research, projects such as weapon destruction, building awareness of small arms issues.

(HL Deb 6 October 2003 Vol. 411 c1066W)

19/37

During a debate in the House of Lords on the North Atlantic Council, the Parliamentary Under-Secretary of State, MoD, made the following statements:

We believe that it is important to keep what has happened so far at the North Atlantic Council in context. It may help if I remind noble Lords of the sequence of events. It is not the first time that this has occurred in NATO and I dare say it will not be the last.

First, the United States and other nations issued a proposal for NATO prudent planning, defensive in character, and which does not imply any automatic NATO action. Secondly, the Secretary-General, our colleague the noble Lord, Lord Robertson, issued a proposal under the silence provisions. Thirdly, that silence was broken on Monday by France and Belgium, supported by Germany.

They were entitled to break that silence if that is what they saw fit to do. We are disappointed that they did so. I make no bones about that at all. We believe that the proposal put forward by the Secretary-General was sensible. That silence having been broken, the North Atlantic Council meeting was adjourned. It was reconvened yesterday but there was no consensus; it agreed to meet again today at 11 o'clock but that was postponed until 11.30; and that meeting was immediately adjourned without comment and will reconvene at 16.30 Brussels time, which, if I am not mistaken, is in precisely five minutes' time.

I thought that it was worth setting out the process for the House to put the matter into context. Yesterday the Turkish representative raised article 4, as he was entitled to do. That states that NATO's members will consult together whenever, in the opinion of any of them, the territorial integrity, political independence or security of any NATO country is threatened.

What our three allies did does not constitute a veto. They did what they were entitled to do, although the Government are disappointed that they broke silence in that way. The lack of consensus appears to be over timing and not substance...

We believe that a further delay in reaching agreement... will send the wrong message to the alliance on alliance unity and particularly to Iraq. We agree... that this is a serious matter, but it is no more and no less than a serious matter. In this House we must not rush to judgment when it may be sensible to sit back coolly and see what happens later today.

On the suggestion which is not accepted by the French, German and Russian Governments in relation to more inspectors, I can do no better than to quote what Dr Blix said:

> "The principal problem is not the number of inspectors but rather the act of co-operation of the Iraqi side".

Mr El-Baradei, in his turn, said that what was needed was a drastic change of mind. It is not for the weapons inspectors to discover weapons of mass destruction; it is for Saddam Hussein to disclose them. This is not a game of adult hide and seek; under the terms of Resolution 1441 Iraq must comply actively, immediately, fully and unconditionally. It has failed to do so. Therefore it is in material breach.

(HL Deb 11 February 2003 Vol. 644 c568–569)

19/38

In a written answer, the Minister of State for Defence wrote:

Any deployment of members of the US National Guard to bases made available to the US Visiting Force in the United Kingdom falls within the arrangements laid down by the NATO Status of Forces Agreement 1951.

(HC Deb 6 March 2003 Vol. 400 c1164W)

19/39

In reply to a written question, the Under-Secretary of State, FCO, wrote:

The comprehensive agreement between NATO and the EU, reached in December 2002, ensures that the European Security and Defence Policy of the EU will be based on close co-operation with NATO. The Government welcome this strategic partnership in crisis management. The EU and NATO are now finalising the detailed arrangements to give effect to this agreement. The EU has already expressed its willingness to take over from NATO the stabilisation mission in the former Yugoslav Republic of Macedonia.

(HC Deb 25 February 2003 Vol. 400 c421W)

19/40

In reply to a written question, the Secretary of State for Defence wrote:

I have regular discussions with my NATO and European Union counterparts, both bilaterally and in the framework of each organisation.

The current scope of EU Security and Defence Policy (ESDP) is defined in the EU Treaty as "humanitarian and rescue tasks, peacekeeping tasks and tasks of combat forces in crisis management, including peacemaking", the so-called "Petersberg Tasks". In the Convention on the Future of Europe, the United Kingdom has proposed modernising and extending the list, to reflect the range of roles the EU should be aiming to play in crisis management and to broaden the ESDP's proactive role in wider conflict prevention, for example by adding stabilisation, conflict prevention, and defence outreach/diplomacy. Decisions on a new EU Treaty are for the Intergovernmental Conference, and these matters have not yet been discussed internationally at ministerial level.

The Headline Goal agreed at the Helsinki European Council in 1999 stated that member states should, within the overall target, "provide smaller rapid response elements available and deployable at very high readiness". This subject was recently discussed at the General Affairs and External Relations Council in November 2002, at informal meetings of EU Defence Ministers in October 2002 and March 2003, and at bilateral meetings such as with the French Defence Minister in Le Touquet last month where we noted the need to improve further European capabilities in planning and deploying forces at short notice, including initial deployment of land, sea and air forces within 5–10 days.

At the NATO Summit in Prague last year, Heads of State and Government agreed to create a NATO Response Force (NRF). Further work on the NRF concept is currently being undertaken by the Military Committee in NATO, aiming to achieve an initial operating capability by no later than October 2004. Each nation has a single set [of] offerees which may be used nationally, or in NATO, EU or coalition operations, and ultimately it is up to nations to decide when and where to commit their forces. We are working to ensure that the work on NRF and on rapid response elements under the EU Headline Goal is mutually reinforcing.

(HC Deb 24 March 2003 Vol. 402 c9W–10W)

19/41

In a written answer, the Secretary of State for Defence wrote:

The "Berlin Plus" arrangements for ready access by the European Union to the collective assets and capabilities of NATO are now in place.

Good progress has been made on the Council's Joint Action on the EU military operation in Macedonia. For example, the EU has agreed that the Deputy Supreme Allied Commander for Europe will be appointed as the EU Operation Commander and that the Supreme Headquarters of Allied Powers in Europe will be used as the EU Operational Headquarters. Arrangements with third states have been agreed and a Committee of Contributors has been formed. The Operation Plan has been finalised, subject to approval by the Council. As envisaged, contacts and meetings between the EU and NATO have been stepped up.

The non-EU European states that are expected to take part in the operation are Bulgaria, Estonia, Latvia, Lithuania, Romania, Slovak Republic, Slovenia, Czech Republic, Poland, Iceland, Turkey, Hungary and Norway. Canada is also expected to take part. NATO has drawn up an indicative list of those assets that will be available for the EU-led operation in Macedonia, and the EU is expected to place a formal request for the assets that it wishes to use in the very near future.

(HC Deb 18 March 2003 Vol. 401 c623W–624W)

19/42

In a written answer, the Secretary of State for Defence wrote:

At the NATO summit at Washington in 1999, the Alliance declared that it stood ready to "define and adopt the necessary arrangements for ready access by the European Union to the collective assets and capabilities of the Alliance, for operations in which the Alliance as a whole is not engaged militarily as an Alliance". The main features of the arrangements, known as "Berlin Plus", are assured EU access to NATO operational planning capabilities, and a presumption of availability to the EU of pre-identified NATO capabilities and common assets for use in EU-led operations.

The North Atlantic Council (NAC) decided on 13 December 2002 that assured EU access to NATO's operational planning capabilities was effective immediately, and undertook to put in place the rest of the Berlin Plus arrangements swiftly. This has now been done.

The NATO/EU arrangements go beyond those established for the WEU in two important respects. First, because EU access to NATO operational planning is assured (i.e. continuous and guaranteed), NATO agreement is not required for any EU requests for NATO planning support; every WEU request would have required specific NAC approval. Second, there is a presumption that those NATO assets and capabilities that have been pre-identified will indeed be available to the EU. There was no such presumption under the NATO/WEU arrangements.

The implementation of the Berlin Plus arrangements is a manifestation of the genuine strategic partnership in crisis management which NATO and EU have decided to establish together.

(HC Deb 18 March 2003 Vol. 401 c625W–626W)

19/43

In a written answer, the Parliamentary Under-Secretary of State, FCO, wrote:

The NATO position on the Adapted CFE Treaty [Conventional Armed Forces in Europe] was set out most recently in the Prague Summit Declaration in November 2002. This emphasised Allies' commitment to the early entry into force of the Adapted Treaty, welcomed the significant results of Russia's efforts to reduce forces in the Treaty's Article V areas to agreed levels, and urged swift fulfilment of the outstanding Istanbul commitments on Georgia and Moldova "which will create the conditions for Allies and other states parties to move forward on ratification".

In the statement following the NATO-Russia Council at Prague, NATO and Russia agreed to continue to work co-operatively toward ratification by all States Parties and the entry into force of the Adapted Treaty.

The aim of the UK is for the Adapted Treaty to come into force as soon as possible and, with NATO allies, we continue to urge Russia to resolve the outstanding issues on Georgia and Moldova, in line with the bilateral agreements made at the Istanbul OSCE summit.

(HC Deb 14 April 2003 Vol. 403 c520W)

19/44

During a debate in the House of Lords on an EU Common Foreign Policy, the Minister of State, FCO, made the following statements:

My Lords, the CFSP has made considerable progress since its launch in the Maastricht Treaty of 1993. The appointment of Javier Solana as high representative in 1999 has further assisted the process. The CFSP plays an important part in helping to bring about stability in the Balkans. However, recent developments in relation to Iraq have demonstrated the importance of Her Majesty's Government's policy, which found effect in the Amsterdam Treaty, that the CFSP must remain intergovernmental.

...

My Lords, that is why in my Answer I stressed that the common foreign and security policy is and should remain intergovernmental. That is why it was designed that way in the Maastricht Treaty and that is why it stayed that way in the Amsterdam Treaty and in the Nice Treaty. In that way, as is right, we all have our say. Of course, on 17th February we managed to formulate an excellent statement at the European Council in relation to Iraq, but yes, there have been differences. Nothing in the CFSP implies that there should not be differences where they are so warranted. Where we can agree, we do, and where we do not agree we are all free to act independently. The CFSP provides for exactly that.

(HL Deb 10 March 2003 Vol. 645 c1108)

19/45

In response to a written question, the Parliamentary Under-Secretary of State for Defence wrote:

The United Kingdom did not require the United States to pay for support or make any direct financial payment to the UK during the Gulf conflict. The UK's contribution to the Gulf conflict was part of an international coalition force. As part of that international coalition force, coalition partners pooled resources and equipment and were able to share capabilities and facilities. This meant that the US, along with other coalition partners, loaned to the UK a certain amount of equipment. According to records held by the Ministry of Defence, the US loaned communications equipment, a number of high mobility load carriers and logistic support to UK Armed Forces.

(HL Deb 3 February 2003 Vol. 644 cWA2)

19/46

In a written answer, the Secretary of State for Defence wrote:

The United Kingdom and France agreed a joint declaration on defence at the Le Touquet Summit on 4 February. I have placed a copy of the declaration in the Library of the House.

Two Letters of Intent were also agreed at the Summit. These were a general agreement on navy-to-navy co-operation and an agreement on exploring possibilities for closer co-ordination of aircraft carrier operations, in particular harmonising activity cycles and training. Both documents contain information received in confidence from the French Government. I am therefore withholding these documents under Exemption Ic (Defence, Security and International Relations) of the Code of Practice on Access to Government Information.

(HC Deb 5 March 2003 Vol. 400 c1027W)

19/47

In reply to a written question a Government representative wrote:

The PSI aims to expand capabilities to conduct maritime, aviation and land interdiction operations in order to help counter the threat of WMD proliferation. At the Paris meeting, PSI participants agreed a statement of interdiction principles, outlining the aims and scope of the initiative, and making clear that all action will be in accordance with international law. Following its publication, we have been drawing governments' attention to, and eliciting support for, the statement.

At the London meeting, we analysed the responses to date. So far the results have been very good: over 50 countries have already expressed support for the PSI. We hope to build on this over the coming weeks and months. WMD proliferation is a global threat: we need to encourage a global response.

The London meeting also agreed a short statement on the focus of the PSI efforts. This makes clear that the initiative does not target any particular country—there are no blacklists—but aims to impede and stop trafficking of WMD, their delivery systems and related materials by any state or non-state actor engaged in or supporting WMD proliferation programmes, at any time and in any place.

The PSI is a global initiative with an inclusive mission. It is an activity, not an organisation. Successful interdiction of trafficking in WMD, their delivery systems and related materials requires the widest possible co-operation between states. It was agreed at the London meeting that participation in the PSI should be open to any state or international body that accepts the Paris statement of interdiction principles and makes an effective contribution. Participation will vary with the activity taking place, and the contribution participants could provide. Some countries have particular experience, assets or expertise relevant to all PSI activities; other countries or organisations could be expected to contribute according to their particular capabilities. I hope that we can therefore ensure as wide participation in the initiative as practically possible, including—where appropriate—contributions from the EU and NATO.

(HL Deb 27 October 2003 Vol. 654 cWA9–WA10)

TABLE OF CASES

INDEX